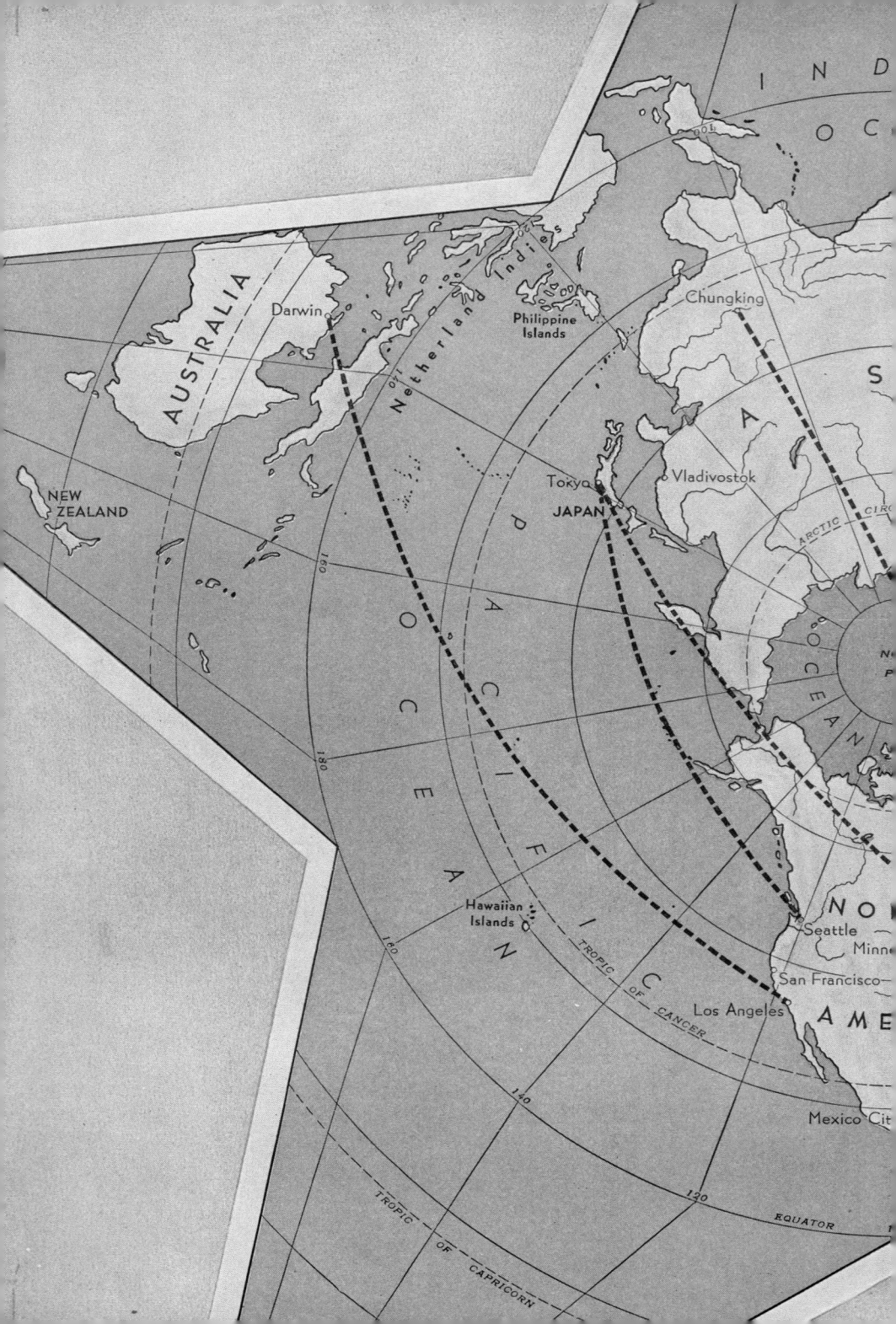

A Short History of

AMERICAN DEMOCRACY

John D. Hicks

Morrison Professor of American History
University of California, Berkeley

HOUGHTON   MIFFLIN   COMPANY
BOSTON · NEW YORK · CHICAGO · DALLAS · ATLANTA · SAN FRANCISCO
The Riverside Press Cambridge

COPYRIGHT, 1949
BY JOHN D. HICKS
COPYRIGHT, 1943, 1946, BY JOHN D. HICKS

ALL RIGHTS RESERVED INCLUDING THE RIGHT TO REPRODUCE
THIS BOOK OR PARTS THEREOF IN ANY FORM

The Riverside Press
CAMBRIDGE · MASSACHUSETTS
PRINTED IN THE U.S.A.

TO

Frederic Logan Paxson

CONTENTS

CONTENTS

PREFACE

IT IS GRATIFYING to the teacher of American history to note that the significance of his subject for American students is being recognized as never before. Not to him alone, but now to many others also, it is evident that only through a fair knowledge of their nation's past can young Americans hope to understand, not only "what we are fighting for," but also what makes the United States a nation at all. The people of our country are of many diverse races, they speak a borrowed language, they owe their literary, artistic, religious, and even their constitutional beginnings to foreign lands. But they have, nonetheless, an unmistakable unity, born of the common heritage which many generations of Americans, whatever their Old World origins, have helped to create. We are all, save only a few of Indian blood, the descendants of immigrants, of men and women who for the most part deliberately chose to transplant themselves to a strange environment in search of a richer and better life. Some of our ancestors crossed the Atlantic centuries ago; others came only recently. But the time element is less important than the fact that we are all of immigrant stock, the inheritors of a common tradition of change, closely related in spirit whether our parents were twelfth-generation Americans or first-generation Americans. We are all, too, the descendants of pioneers. Some of these pioneers were country people who conquered a continent in covered wagons, and created a civilization where there had been only wilderness before. But they are in no wise to be preferred to those other pioneers, later-comers as a rule, who built our cities, made and manned our new industries, transformed our nation from a rural to an urban republic, prepared the way for a new internationalism to replace the provincialism of earlier years.

Our much-talked-about American way of life is only the product of our immigrant-pioneer past. Here in the American mixing-bowl our forefathers retained such Old World habits and ideas as fitted the new scene, but gradually sloughed off the rest. Out of a common experience they developed their belief in the value of life, liberty, and the pursuit of happiness; their conviction that the state exists for the individual and not the individual for the state; their assurance that personal rights are to be esteemed above property rights; their insistence that equality of opportunity must not perish from the earth. There is nothing new about the

"Four Freedoms"; they are all old American ideals, never fully realized, to be sure, but a part of the rich inheritance that makes us, in spite of our diverse origins, a nation. "We hold these truths to be self-evident."

If this book can serve, even a very little, to make young Americans more conscious of their nation's past, more able to understand its present problems, more fitted to help shape its course in the future, it will have justified its existence.

A Short History of American Democracy borrows heavily from my two earlier texts, *The Federal Union* and *The American Nation*, from which many chapters, particularly on social and economic history, have been lifted bodily. But it has involved much condensation, and much rewriting. Prepared for publication in large part since the entrance of the United States into the second World War, it profits, or should profit, from the new perspective, and it includes a considerable amount of new material not found in either of the older volumes.

The well-advised teacher will call frequent attention to the footnote references, which are designed to point the way to further reading rather than to buttress the statements in the text. For history is not a subject that can long survive neglect. If it is to prove useful, it must be used. The student who acquires in college the habit of reading history, and of reading history into all he reads, is the student who really gets something out of his course.

JOHN D. HICKS

BERKELEY, CALIFORNIA

LIST OF ILLUSTRATIONS

LIST OF MAPS

A Short History of

AMERICAN DEMOCRACY

1

The Old World and the New

It is well to remember that American society is definitely European in origin. The western world before Columbus produced no great civilization of its own, and such remnants of the Indian way of life as endured were always inconsequential in comparison with the heritage that came from across the seas. But the importance of the new environment should not be discounted, for in a great variety of ways it bent and transformed the traditions that European immigrants brought with them to their new homes. The mingling in the United States of many diverse races, the persistent efforts of the original pioneers and their successors to conquer the continent, and the development from these varied traditions and experiences of an essentially new civilization constitute the main currents of American national history.

Europe in America

That portion of the American continent which was destined to become the United States was potentially well fitted to become a great nation. It was free alike from arctic cold and from tropical heat, but because it possessed every other variety of climate, every degree of rainfall, every texture and composition of soil, its agricultural possibilities were limitless. Forests and mineral resources of incalculable value awaited exploitation. The Indians themselves, incapable of serious resistance, were a rich resource, for they taught the European pioneers how to live in America, what wealth the land possessed, and how best to take it.

Easy communications with Europe were of the greatest significance. From the very beginning of American history the Atlantic Ocean was less a barrier than a highway. Colonies could thrive in the New World because in their infancy the all-essential connections with the mother country could be maintained. The innumerable sheltered bays and landlocked harbors of the Atlantic coast welcomed the newcomers, and led the British to found many colonies instead of a single colony. Indeed, the early colonists found it more natural to maintain their connections with England than to build up

The Atlantic Coast

contacts with each other, and so each tended to develop quite independently. American political institutions still reveal the influence of this early geographic environment. The thirteen colonies could not surrender their separate political life merely because they had broken with Great Britain. They became thirteen independent states, and the system of government they worked out provided for a federal union, not for a consolidated republic.

The Appalachian mountain barrier played a hardly less important part in determining the future of the American nation. While these

The Appalachians

mountains were neither high nor difficult to penetrate, they served as a restraining influence against the too rapid extension of settlement. Because of them the English tended to densify along the coast before the conquest of the interior was begun. The French, on the other hand, let through to the West too readily by the Valley of the St. Lawrence and the waters of the Great Lakes, dissipated their energies over too extensive an area. When the final test of strength came, their scattered villagers were no match for the more numerous and more concentrated English. The Appalachians served further to promote the development of a strictly American nationality. Their parallel ranges and fertile valleys bent toward the South the course of the westward movement, and promoted the mingling of pioneers from the northern colonies, immigrants from Europe, and Southerners to form a new people, not much concerned with local loyalties, and citizens of one nation rather than of individual states. From these "backwoodsmen" all future generations of western pioneers were to inherit a common legacy of blood and custom.[1]

The interior basin of the North American continent is a vast, undulating plain, bounded on the east by the Appalachians, on the west by the

The Mississippi Valley

Rockies, on the south by the Gulf of Mexico, and on the north, so far as the United States is concerned, by the Great Lakes. The one great river system which drains this region gives it remarkable unity and a name, the Mississippi Valley. Here lies nearly half the land now contained within the national borders, and far more than half the arable land. Here the process of racial amalgamation, already begun in the troughs of the Appalachians, was long continued. Here, too, Northerners met Southerners, here travelers from afar met those who had come from regions near by, and here foreigners met natives, all to be absorbed rapidly into one American race. A pronounced similarity of type and culture still exists among the people of the Mississippi Valley. They speak a common language; their institu-

[1] F. J. Turner, *The Frontier in American History* (1920), finds in the conquest of the continent the central theme of American history.

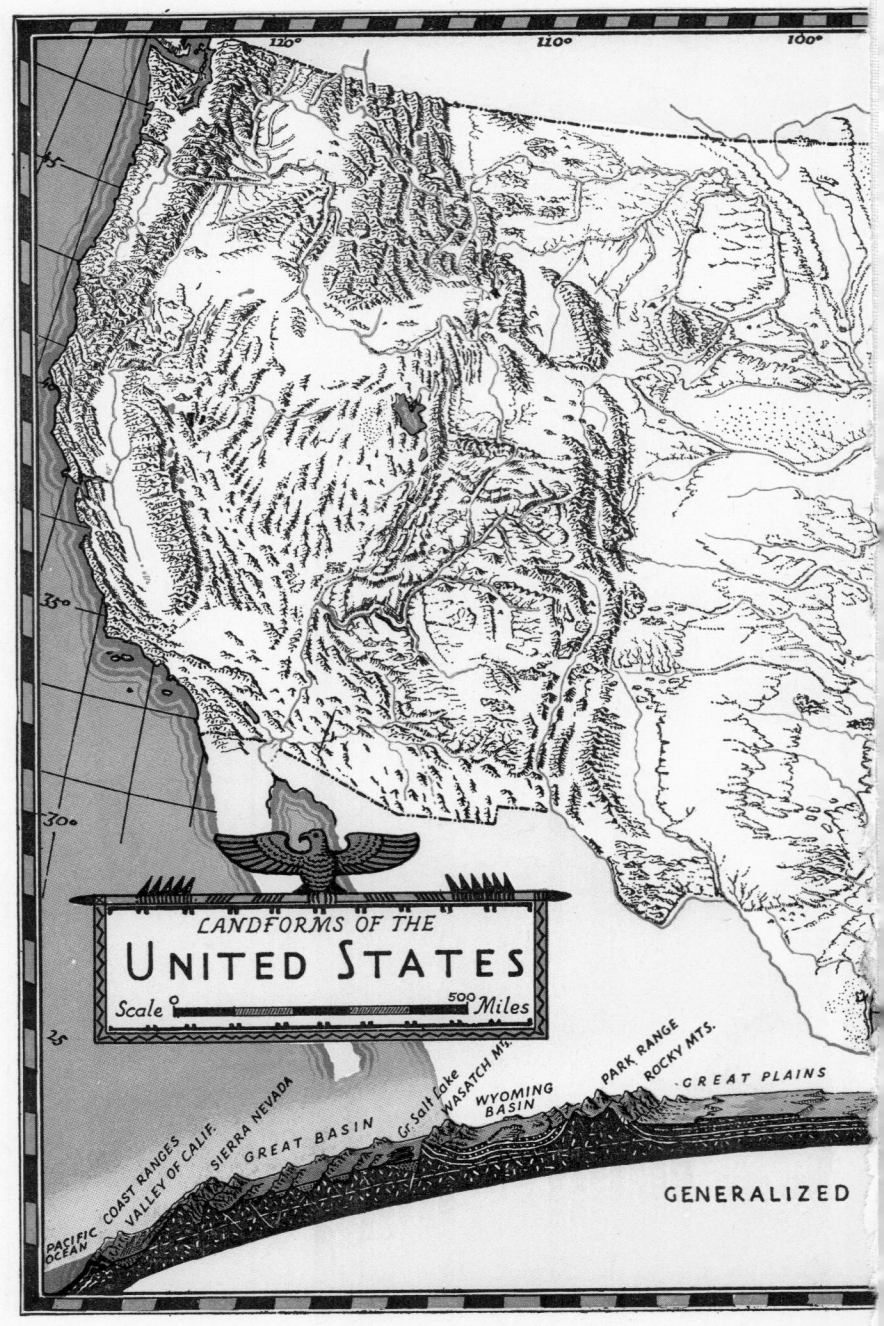

LANDFORMS OF THE
UNITED STATES
Scale 0 ——— 500 Miles

PACIFIC OCEAN · VALLEY OF CALIF. · SIERRA NEVADA · GREAT BASIN · Gr. Salt Lake · WASATCH Mts. · WYOMING BASIN · PARK RANGE · ROCKY MTS. · GREAT PLAINS

GENERALIZED

RELIEF MAP OF T

OSAGE PLAINS   OZARK PLATEAU   Mississippi R   Tennessee R   Nashville Basin   Highland Rim   APPALACHIAN PLATEAU   VALLEYS and RIDGES   GREAT VALLEY   BLUE RIDGE   PIEDMONT   COASTAL PLAIN   ATLANTIC OCEAN   E Raisz

SECTION

E UNITED STATES

tions vary but slightly from place to place; and their local loyalties, in part because of an enduring mobility, remain weak.

A striking physical feature of the North American continent is the great Cordillera or Rocky Mountain system of the West. The plateau from which the ranges of this system rise is everywhere from five to ten thousand feet above sea-level; it extends southward into Mexico and Central America and with considerable change of character northward through Canada into Alaska; it spreads out within the United States to a width of a thousand miles, and its peaks rise to magnificent heights. For all their prominence, however, these mountains lack the significance in American history that attaches to the Appalachians, or to most of the other great physical features of the continent. They possessed immense mineral wealth, they offered valuable grazing facilities, and their valleys could by means of irrigation be made agriculturally productive; but they were unfitted to shelter a large population, such as the Mississippi Valley naturally invited, and they were entered only when the formative period in the life of the nation was over.

The Rockies

As for the Pacific slope, it too had relatively little to do with the making of American civilization. The narrowness of the western coastal plain, and the scarcity of its harbors, precluded such developments as took place along the Atlantic. Spanish settlements there were, but they began only when the English colonies were ripe for revolution, and they unloosed few forces of permanent significance. In due time man conquered notably the obstacles that Nature here placed in his way, but not until the habits of the American people were already well set, and the nature of the American nation well defined.

The Pacific slope

The discovery of the American continent was an episode in the history of European commercial expansion.[1] During the later Middle Ages the Italian cities, especially Venice, Genoa, and Pisa, emerged as vigorous city-states, possessed of considerable wealth and population, and virtually independent of outside control. From ports in the eastern Mediterranean they obtained carpets, sugar, and spices, while from their own workshops came leather, fabrics of linen, silk, and wool, and such articles as glass, paper, and soap. All this produce they sold for good profits to other Europeans. Galleys a hun-

Medieval Europe

---

[1] There was an earlier, but unimportant, pre-view. Late in the tenth century Eric the Red, a Norwegian, discovered Greenland and planted a colony there. Shortly afterward a Norwegian vessel bound for Greenland lost its way, and landed at a coast nine days' sail to the south. In the year 1000 Leif the Lucky, a son of Eric, explored this region and called it Vinland. Presumably what he found was the coast of New England. Here an effort was made a few years later to found a colony, but the project was abandoned because of the hostility of the natives.

dred feet in length plied the Mediterranean with Italian wares, and Italian traders, seeking markets, found their way by sea far around the coasts of western Europe, and by land deep into its barbaric center.

Many of the articles in which the Italian traders dealt were purchased from Levantine merchants whose business it was to buy from the distant East and to sell to the West. The riches of the Orient were brought to the Mediterranean usually by one of three main routes. The southernmost of these routes was by water from India and the farther East across the Indian Ocean and through the Red Sea. Caravans completed the journey to Alexandria or Cairo, where the European traders found the goods. The northern route was a tedious relay journey by caravan from the hinterlands of China and India to the Black Sea, and thence to the Mediterranean. The central route was both by sea and by land. Chinese junks, or other native craft, brought the wares to the Persian Gulf, whence Arab traders took them by way of Bagdad to Antioch or Jaffa or occasionally to some Egyptian port. Whether at Alexandria or Constantinople or Antioch the Arab traders were met by Italian merchants. Competitors from outside Italy had little chance because of the greater proximity of the Italian cities to the eastern markets, and because of the special privileges that the Italians had obtained. As middlemen for all the rest of Europe their prosperity was prodigious, and so complete was their monopoly of the eastern trade that the various Italian cities warred for commercial advantages not with others but among themselves.

While the Italian merchants thus made sure profits, the rest of Europe found the situation far from satisfactory. Especially unfavored were the people of Spain and Portugal, of France and England, who were far from the Mediterranean trade centers and habitually bought much more than they sold. To these new Atlantic nations commercial vassalage was all the more humiliating because they were no longer feudal states, but centralized monarchies whose kings hoped for self-sufficiency and whose people knew the meaning of national pride. Small wonder that the sailors of these nations dreamed of new routes to the "Indies," routes which the Italian profiteers could not control. These dreams were encouraged by such tales as Marco Polo, the Venetian, told of his long sojourn in Asia during the thirteenth century. According to these tales the original cost of eastern wares was only a fraction of the Italian price, and in the Orient gold itself was easy to obtain. The hopes of sailors were further encouraged by important inventions, the compass and the astrolabe to aid in the navigation of ships, printing presses set with movable type to make available the maps and guide-books of other travelers, and guns and gunpowder to use in warding off the attacks of savages.

The Portuguese were the first to take up the search for a new route to the East that would end the Italian monopoly. Their theory was that by sailing around Africa they could reach the eastern markets, and from the time of Prince Henry the Navigator (1394–1460) on they pushed their way farther and farther southward along the African coast. In 1487, under the valiant Bartholomew Diaz, they rounded the Cape of Good Hope, and in 1498, with Vasco da Gama in command, they landed at Calicut, erected a monument to commemorate their discovery of the new route, and returned to Portugal with spices, jewels, silks, and tapestries, in proof of their accomplishment. The new route, which eliminated the profits of so many middlemen, was soon in use, and as a result the prices of eastern wares in western markets dropped to much lower levels. The Italian merchants suffered acutely from the new competition, while to add to their distress the Turks grew steadily more powerful and less tolerant of Christian traders. Slowly but surely the splendor of the Italian cities was dimmed, and the commercial leadership of western Europe shifted from the Mediterranean to the Atlantic.

While the Portuguese were first in the field, they were not alone in their desire to find a new route to the East. The Spanish government was convinced through the arguments of a Genoese navigator, Christopher Columbus, that the Indies might be **Columbus** found by sailing directly west. Columbus was a well-informed sailor who had lived in the Madeira Islands, had sailed to the north as far as England and perhaps as far as Iceland, and had doubtless heard the gossip of distant lands across the Atlantic, then current among sailors. The common people of the time believed that the earth was flat, but medieval scholars knew well enough that it was round, and Columbus shared their views. By underestimating the size of the earth, he argued convincingly that this directly western route would be shorter than the route around Africa that the Portuguese were then still seeking, but for a long time he had great difficulty in securing the support of anyone who had means enough to finance a voyage of discovery. At last he won over King Ferdinand of Aragon and Queen Isabella of Castile, the joint rulers of Spain, and under their patronage he set sail in August, 1492, with three small ships and fewer than a hundred men. The Spanish monarchs provided him with letters of introduction to the great Khan of Cathay, and a grant of authority to govern such unappropriated lands as he might discover.

When on the twelfth of October, 1492, Columbus reached one of the small coral islands of the Bahamas, he rejoiced in the belief that he was near the coast of Asia. Exploring farther, he visited Cuba **Discovery of** and Haiti, but he failed to reach the mainland, and he failed **America** too to find the spices and jewels and rich fabrics he had sought. But his conviction that he had reached the Indies was unshaken; he called the natives he met Indians, and he returned to Spain to announce that the new route had been found. Columbus made three other voyages of exploration to the New World, but he died in the belief that it was a new route to the Orient, not another continent, that he had discovered.[1]

Further explorations, including voyages by one Americus Vespucius, whose name was given to the New World, soon revealed how mistaken

Other explorations

Columbus had been, but trinkets of gold which the Indians displayed were sufficient to maintain Spanish interest in the new land.[2] Moreover, it seemed reasonable that there must be somewhere an opening through which the journey to the Indies could be continued. For a long time this latter idea fascinated adventurers, French and English as well as Spanish, but early in the sixteenth century it was learned that Asia was far more than a few days' journey from the new land. In 1519 a navigator named Magellan set sail from Spain, discovered and passed through the straits that bear his name, and crossed the Pacific. Magellan himself was killed by Philippine Islanders, but in 1522 one of his ships sailed on by the Portuguese route around Africa to Europe, the first ship to complete a voyage around the world.

Magellan's voyage blasted the Spanish hope of a route to the East that would rival the Portuguese route, but the discovery of America led to an even more valuable source of wealth. In 1519 Hernando Cortez defeated Montezuma, Emperor of the Aztecs, and opened the riches of Mexico for Spanish exploitation. What Cortez did to the Aztecs was repeated about 1531 by another Spaniard, Pizarro, who conquered the equally rich Incas of Peru. Thereafter for many years Spain drew a tribute from the New World that made her easily the first nation of Europe. Colonies followed conquests, and the Spanish empire in America became the marvel and envy of the whole civilized world.[3]

Thus two new trade monopolies appeared to supplant the supremacy from which the Italian cities had profited so long. Portugal, with her route around Africa to Asia, had a monopoly on the trade of the Orient, while Spain, by her conquests in the New World, had a monopoly, or

[1] Samuel E. Morison, *Admiral of the Ocean Sea* (2 vols., 1942), completely supplants the earlier biographies of Columbus.

[2] Edward Channing, *A History of the United States* (6 vols., 1905–30), gives in his first volume an excellent account of the exploration of America. In a total of six volumes he carries his history through the Civil War. Based, as it is, upon the results of recent critical scholarship, this work is indispensable to the serious student of American history.

[3] E. G. Bourne, *Spain in America* (1904), covers this subject in detail. See also H. I. Priestley, *The Coming of the White Man* (1929). This is the first of thirteen volumes, *A History of American Life*, edited by A. M. Schlesinger and D. R. Fox, which together constitute an admirable survey of the non-political activities of the American people.

almost a monopoly, on the trade of America. These two powers, by the
famous Demarcation Line of 1494, had even sought to divide the whole
world, outside of Europe, between them. To the east of a meridian
described as three hundred and seventy leagues west of the Cape Verde
Islands, all discoveries were to go to Portugal, while to the west of it all
were to go to Spain. It happened that the easternmost tip of triangular
South America lay on the Portuguese side of the Demarcation Line;
hence, when some years later a Portuguese ship was blown out of its
intended course down the coast of Africa and touched instead upon the
coast of Brazil, the Portuguese king could, and promptly did, claim that
part of the New World for his own. Otherwise the Spanish monopoly on
America was for many years practically unchallenged.

The profitable monopoly of the New World by the Spanish and of the
new route to Asia by the Portuguese aroused at length the opposition
of the English. England under the rule of Queen Elizabeth
had achieved a stable government, a satisfactory religious   English
settlement, and a state of domestic tranquillity that tempted   rivalry with
her merchants and sailors to look well beyond the national   Spain
confines for new fields to conquer. On every hand they encountered
monopolies: the Italians in the Mediterranean; the Portuguese in Africa
and Asia; the Spanish in America. One English sea-captain, the pious
John Hawkins, defied both the Portuguese and the Spanish by procuring
slaves in Africa and selling them at a great profit to the Spanish in the
West Indies (1562–68). Others, in a day which knew nothing of international law, attacked the Spanish treasure-ships and brought back rich
booty. One such, Sir Francis Drake, in 1577 sailed down the eastern and
up the western coasts of South America, plundering as he went, and after
advancing as far north as San Francisco turned westward, crossed the
Pacific to the East Indies, rounded the Cape of Good Hope, and in 1580
returned to England, the first of his race to circumnavigate the globe.
In 1586 Thomas Cavendish duplicated the exploits of Drake, taking
many prizes along the Spanish Main and in the Pacific. And then followed a veritable epidemic of piracy, the prelude of war.

The clash came finally toward the end of the sixteenth century. The
Netherlands, which by a succession of royal marriages and births had
fallen under the Spanish yoke, revolted in 1566 against the oppressive
rule of the agents that the Spanish king, Philip II, sent to govern them,
and in the later phases of the struggle received aid from Queen Elizabeth.
This interference by the English in the Netherlands, coupled with the
wholesale depredations upon Spanish commerce by English seamen, led
Philip to dispatch against England his "Invincible Armada" of one
hundred and thirty ships, manned by eight thousand sailors, and carrying

an army of invasion of nineteen thousand men. The Spanish fleet reached the English coast, but its great galleons were no match for the smaller and more skillfully managed ships of Drake and his kind. The Armada was disastrously defeated (August, 1588), many of the Spanish ships that escaped the English were destroyed by tempests in the North Sea, and less than a third of Philip's splendid fleet ever got back to Spain. Several years later England sent forth a "counter-Armada," which successfully attacked the Spanish port of Cadiz and destroyed a great quantity of enemy shipping (1596). From this time forward it was England, not Spain, who was the "mistress of the seas."

Since in 1580 Philip had successfully laid claim to the Portuguese throne, his defeat revealed to all the world that the Spanish-Portuguese commercial and colonial monopoly need no longer be respected. Among the first to take advantage of this situation were the Dutch, whose "sea-beggars" helped themselves to Portuguese holdings in Africa and the East Indies, and whose traders cast covetous eyes toward the New World. In 1609 the Dutch East India Company sent Henry Hudson, an Englishman, to search for a sea-route through North America to India. Hudson found no northwest passage, but he did discover an opportunity for fur trade with the Indians, and a Dutch trading-post was soon established on Manhattan Island. Dutch sailors also wrested from the Spanish some valuable Caribbean Islands and a strip of territory along the northern coast of South America. The French, with a claim to the valley of the St. Lawrence based upon the explorations of Jacques Cartier in 1535, established a trading-post at Quebec in 1608, and occupied Guadeloupe, Martinique, and many minor islands in the West Indies. Even the Swedes, who for the moment had attained a place of prominence in European affairs, planted a colony in 1638 at the mouth of the Delaware, a settlement which the Dutch soon absorbed.[1]

Meantime the English, whose defeat of Spain had made all this possible, had not been idle. A Venetian named John Cabot, sailing in 1497 under authority of Henry VII of England, had by his explorations marked off the north Atlantic coast of North America as British territory, and in the early seventeenth century there seemed to be many reasons why this long-claimed area should be used. The *Wanderlust* and sheer love of adventure that had braced English seamen for the defeat of the Spanish needed some further outlet. Protestant England, with the novice's enthusiasm for her creed, regarded the New World as a legitimate missionary field, also as a desirably distant

European rivalry for America

England and America

---

[1] Carl L. Becker, *Beginnings of the American People* (1915), contains an interesting account of the partition of the New World.

place toward which the minds of troublesome dissenters might well be turned. Hard times and overpopulation, long a nightmare to government officials, became worse following the peace of 1604 with Spain, which set many discharged soldiers and sailors free to roam the land in search of work. Numbers of farm laborers, with the increasing popularity of sheep-raising, also joined the ranks of the unemployed, while the care of the poor, which before Henry VIII's dissolution of the monasteries had been a major concern of the monks and nuns, completely overtaxed the resources of the civilian authorities. It seemed reasonable to suppose that if the excess of English population could only be drawn off to other lands, unemployment might be reduced, and economic conditions in general improved.[1]

All such reasons, however, were secondary to the desire of merchant and government alike to promote English trade. Owing partly to the invigorating effect of gold and silver from the New World, English commerce had taken on new life. The well-to-do required now such luxuries as spices, sugar, and tea. They built ostentatious mansions for which they must have the costliest furnishings of the East. They paid high prices cheerfully, and merchants made good profits. Capital for commercial enterprise was thus easily amassed, and with seemingly sure profits ahead it became extremely venturesome. Dozens of trading companies were chartered by the government for the purpose of establishing commercial relations with some foreign region. Perhaps the most successful of these enterprises was the English East India Company, formed in 1600 to exploit the trade of India; but many others, such as the Levant Company, which built up a prosperous trade with the eastern Mediterranean, and the Muscovy Company, which dealt with Russia, paid handsome dividends. America seemed to furnish another such business opportunity, and companies were soon organized to make profits from the American trade.

English trade and trading companies

The generous charters which trading companies received from the English crown reveal a kind of alliance between government and business that is not difficult to explain. The companies' ships left England with cargoes of English manufactures which they proposed to exchange for the raw materials of undeveloped regions. To the business man this meant merely profits; to the government, inspired as it was by the mercantilistic theory of the age, it meant security. According to the mercantilists, the chief measure of a country's strength was the amount of gold and silver it could amass. The trading companies, by exchanging expensive English manufactures for cheap raw materials, might be

[1] G. L. Beer, *The Origins of the British Colonial System, 1578–1660* (1908), is the standard authority on this subject.

counted upon to produce for England a "favorable balance of trade," because of which a steady stream of precious metals would flow into the country. By just so much the strength of the nation would be increased. The urgent necessity of promoting national self-sufficiency was another reason why the government gave special privileges to trading companies. At a time when wars were regarded as the normal state of international affairs, and peace only an interlude between wars, each nation naturally aspired to be able to care for itself without dependence on any other. Indeed, economic dependence might easily lead to the loss of political independence.

To thoughtful English officials, North America, with its rich potentialities in timber, naval stores, potash, fisheries, sugar, and even gold itself, seemed ideally fitted to become an independent source of supply for the British Isles. The Spanish had found abundant wealth in the New World, why should not also the English? Furthermore, if flourishing colonies could only be established and maintained, they would provide new and independent markets for the goods that English manufacturers were turning out in ever-increasing volume. Economic freedom for the colonies was, of course, never seriously considered. It was assumed that each colony would send its produce to the mother country, and in return would make all necessary purchases from English manufacturers. It is worth noting that the English government, although deeply interested in having colonies founded, never seriously considered founding colonies itself. Since colony founding had to do with the expansion of trade and the making of profits, it was regarded merely as a type of business, and the government, according to prevailing economic theories, while free to foster and regulate every type of private enterprise all it chose, might not itself engage in business.

Why Englishmen, most of whom expected to remain in England, favored the founding of colonies in America is one thing; why certain Englishmen chose to become colonists is quite another.

The call of free land Doubtless the love of adventure, the false hope of gold, the need of a refuge from religious persecution, and the lack of employment at home all sent their quotas to America. But probably no other motive weighed so heavily as the desire for land. In England, and indeed throughout all Europe, landholding was a test of gentility; ordinary people might not even hope to own land. In the New World land was equally open to all. The younger sons of nobles, left landless by the rule of primogeniture, turned to America for recompense; the peasants and artisans, destined if they stayed at home to remain what they were for life, saw in the colonies their only chance to become landed proprietors. Cheap land was the magnet which drew immigrants across the

Atlantic to America, just as it was later to draw their descendants, step by step, across the continent.[1]

Two early colonial ventures which failed made it evident that the exploitation of North America was not to be undertaken lightly. The first of these, under Sir Humphrey Gilbert, who shared the common illusion that there must be a northwest passage around America to the Orient, was shipwrecked in 1583 off the inhospitable shores of Newfoundland. The second, under Sir Walter Raleigh, failed twice, once in 1585 and again in 1587, to plant an enduring colony on Roanoke Island, just south of Albemarle Sound. These ill-fated experiments showed conclusively that the private resources of any one man were likely to prove inadequate for the financing of so great a venture, and left the field free for the trading company, which was able to draw upon the resources of many investors.

As early as 1606, King James I, who had succeeded Elizabeth on the English throne, was persuaded to issue a charter to some London and Plymouth merchants who had in mind the establishment of new outposts of trade in Virginia. By the terms of this charter the stockholders were subdivided into two companies, the London Company and the Plymouth Company, *The London and Plymouth Companies* each of which was promised a tract of land along the Virginia coast a hundred miles in width and extending a hundred miles into the interior. The charter stipulated further that the land of the London Company should be located somewhere between the thirty-fourth and the forty-first parallels, while the land of the Plymouth Company should lie farther north, between the thirty-eighth and the forty-fifth parallels. Neither company might establish a colony within one hundred miles of any colony established by the other.[2]

The London merchants were the first to take advantage of this grant. In December, 1606, they sent out three shiploads of colonists, who the next spring founded Jamestown at a point thirty miles inland from the mouth of the James River. Thereafter for seventeen years the Company continued to send a steady stream of colonists and supplies to Virginia. Of profits there were none, but the stockholders hopefully invested in the project a sum which today would be reckoned at not less than five million dollars. The mortality among the early colonists was frightful; as late as 1616, by which time over sixteen hundred emigrants had left England

---

[1] Among the useful one-volume works on the colonial period are the following: E. B. Greene, *The Foundations of American Nationality* (1922); O. P. Chitwood, *A History of Colonial America* (1931); C. P. Nettels, *The Roots of American Civilization* (1938).

[2] C. M. Andrews, *The Colonial Period of American History* (4 vols., 1934–38), embodies much of the research of one of the greatest of American historians. The colonial period has been the subject of many monumental works, among which John A. Doyle, *English Colonies in America* (5 vols., 1889–1907), still takes high rank.

for Virginia, the population of the colony was only about three hundred and fifty. Captain John Smith, one of the world's most picturesque characters, stands out in these early years as the man who saved the colony from extinction. But in spite of heavy odds, including an attack by the Indians in 1622, the number of Virginians grew, and by 1624 there were probably as many as twelve hundred people in the colony.

During these years the Virginia experiment was carried on as a strictly business enterprise, with local managers, or "governors," directing the work of the company's "servants" — usually paupers or convicts who had come to Virginia under indentures that bound them to work for the company from four to seven years in return for their passage across the Atlantic. Toward the end of the company's rule several innovations, designed in part to keep the colonists contented and in part to attract new settlers, were introduced. (1) The right to private ownership of land was conceded, and liberal grants were made to indentured servants whose period of service had expired, and to all freemen. (2) The harsh laws deemed necessary during the first hard years of the colony were abrogated, and (3) a representative assembly "freely elected by the inhabitants," to consist of two representatives from each "plantation," was authorized to share in the making of the laws.

Early Virginia

The original charter of 1606 was twice revised, once in 1609 and again in 1612. The new land grant gave the company a frontage along the coast of two hundred miles north and two hundred miles south of Old Point Comfort, while inland the company's rights were to extend "west and northwest" from sea to sea. Unfortunately King James I regretted the liberal powers of government he had permitted the company to exercise, and he especially disliked the concessions to popular rule that it had made. He accordingly obtained in 1624 from a subservient court an annulment of the charter. All governmental rights now devolved upon the King, and Virginia became a royal colony. By this change the Virginians lost the help they had been accustomed to receive from the London Company, but they were permitted to retain their land titles, and, after some hesitation on the part of the King, their representative assembly. As for the investments made by stockholders in the company, they were a total loss.

Charter revisions

The success of tobacco culture was what enabled the Virginia colony to survive. When the Jamestown settlement was made, the use of tobacco was already known in Europe, but the tobacco Europeans first learned to like came from the Spanish colonies in America. Virginia tobacco was regarded as inferior and undesirable until about 1616, when a new method of curing it was dis-

Tobacco culture

covered. From this time on the Jamestown colonists had a product that would yield them a profit, and the colony soon began to prosper. Land was easy to obtain under the so-called "head-right" system, by which each immigrant and each person who paid for an immigrant's passage received fifty acres. The more prosperous planters came to own many head-rights, and even in the seventeenth century the tendency toward large plantations was already marked. Beginning in 1619, Negroes were brought into the colony as slaves, although the number of such persons in early Virginia was very small. Unlike the indentured servants, the slaves could never be assimilated into the white population, and their presence ultimately produced a problem that led to the American Civil War. During the middle decades of the seventeenth century war broke out in England between the adherents of the King, or "Cavaliers," and the supporters of Parliament, or "Roundheads." When in 1649 the "Roundheads" triumphed and executed the King, many "Cavaliers" sought safety in Virginia. By 1652 the population of the colony was estimated at twenty thousand.[1]

The next successful English experiment in colony planting was at Plymouth, on the coast of what later became Massachusetts. Here the religious motive undoubtedly assumed commanding importance. The church establishment which had been worked out in England under Queen Elizabeth occupied a place   *The English dissenters* midway between extreme Catholicism and extreme Protestantism. Inevitably many Englishmen were dissatisfied with these halfway measures and wished to go further in the direction of Protestantism. Of these "dissenters," some, known as "Puritans," desired only to reform the existing English church in such a way as to bring it into closer harmony with the teachings of John Calvin; others, less numerous and influential, were called "Separatists" because they were ready to sever all connections with the Established Church. Neither group was seriously persecuted during the reign of James I, but there was enough threat of persecution to make all dissenters uneasy. A little band of Separatists from Scrooby, England, furnished the nucleus for the Plymouth settlement. They went first from England to Holland and later, in 1620, some of them, after returning to England, set sail in the *Mayflower* for America. Their venture was financed by a joint-stock company in which both the emigrants and a number of London merchants held stock. Not all who went to Holland came to America, and not all of those who came to America had been in Holland. Indeed, when the *Mayflower* set sail from

[1] The early history of Virginia has been elaborately set forth in a number of books by P. A. Bruce. Among them are *The Economic History of Virginia in the Seventeenth Century* (2 vols., 1896); *Social Life of Virginia in the Seventeenth Century* (1907); *The Institutional History of Virginia in the Seventeenth Century* (2 vols., 1910).

England, about half its passengers had never been outside their country before.[1]

On December 21, 1620, the *Mayflower* landed her hundred passengers at Plymouth harbor. Anticipating difficulty in controlling the action of some of the more turbulent members of the group, the Pilgrim "Fathers," or at least forty-one of them, affixed their signatures while still on shipboard to the famous "Mayflower Compact," by which they bound themselves together into a "civil body politic" for their "better ordering and preservation." They chose John Carver as their first governor, and as a pure democracy faced the unknown trials of the New World. The first winter took a toll in dead of over half the company, but the survivors stayed on, and with the help of a few more immigrants they were able to found an enduring settlement. Farming, fur-trading, fishing, and lumbering furnished their chief occupations.

The Pilgrims soon discovered that the site of their colony lay outside the grant of the London (or Virginia) Company, from which they had obtained settlement rights, but their second governor, William Bradford, as trustee for the colony, secured title from the New England Council (successor to the Plymouth Company) to the land about Plymouth Bay. Finally, in 1641, when the debts owing to the London merchants were fully paid, the governor formally transferred to the people the rights he had acquired. Pure democracy at Plymouth, as practiced under the Mayflower Compact, was soon succeeded by a representative system, with a "General Court" in charge of matters pertaining to the whole colony, and local affairs in the hands of town meetings. All efforts to secure royal approval of these governmental privileges failed, but the Plymouth colony was left free to govern itself as a self-constituted commonwealth until 1691, when William III joined it to Massachusetts Bay.

The founders of the Massachusetts Bay colony, unlike the Pilgrims, were Puritans rather than Separatists. Disillusioned by the arbitrary rule of King Charles I, they not only gave up hope of "purifying" the English Church, but also despaired of England as a fit home for freemen. They laid their plans carefully. They wished to establish in the New World an ideal Puritan commonwealth where a really "purified" church might thrive, and where the government would be wholly in their hands. They therefore secured complete control of a "Company for Massachusetts-Bay," with a charter

The "Mayflower Compact"

Massachusetts Bay

---

[1] C. M. Andrews, *The Fathers of New England* (1921), is an excellent short account. J. T. Adams, *The Founding of New England* (1921), is brilliant, but definitely anti-Puritan in point of view.

from the King and a grant of land from the New England Council, and in 1630, led by their elected governor, John Winthrop, took the charter with them to New England. What was originally designed to be merely the articles of incorporation of a joint-stock company became thus a kind of constitution for the government of the new colony. Before the summer was over seventeen ships had landed a thousand settlers in Massachusetts, and several villages, among them Boston, Dorchester, Watertown, and Roxbury, had been founded. Thereafter, as the troublous times continued in England, other emigrants came also, until by the year 1640 no less than twenty-five thousand refugees had found their way to Massachusetts. With that year the tide began to turn against the King in England, and the "Great Migration" came to a close.[1]

Life on the New England frontier turned out to be a bitter struggle against unyielding soils, cruel winters, ever-recurring disease, and constant privation, but in spite of almost incredible hardships the evidences of civilization could soon be observed. Livestock was imported and bred; mills to grind the grain, brick kilns and sawmills to produce better building materials, and even ironworks to turn out a few household necessities began to appear. Trade with England came about naturally, for the colonists were quick to discover that with such articles as fish, furs, lumber, and potash to exchange, they could obtain from the mother country some of the many things for which they stood in need.

As for government, all power, according to the charter, rested with the stockholders, or "freemen," who were authorized to elect as a kind of board of directors a governor, a deputy governor, and eighteen "assistants"; also to meet four times each year. Only twelve freemen had come to America, and every one of them, as governor, deputy governor, or assistant, was an officer of the company. This group, by neglecting to choose new freemen, at first kept all authority in its hands, but such arbitrary procedure did not long escape criticism. In the fall of 1630 heavy pressure from the settlers resulted in the creation of many new freemen, who were told, however, that they might vote only for new assistants, and that the assistants alone had the right to choose higher officers. Nevertheless, the freemen, two years later, not only took over for themselves the election of all officers, but voted also that each town should choose two representatives to act with the assistants in the levying of taxes. In 1634, after an examination of the charter had proved that the entire law-making power was vested in the freemen, the elected delegates began to participate in all the legislative activities of what they called the "General Court."

Puritan
government

[1] S. E. Morison, *Builders of the Bay Colony* (1930), describes the leading men of the colony with rare skill.

But the colony was still far less than a democracy. The number of freemen admitted to the corporation was cautiously restrained, only church members being deemed eligible, and not all of them being chosen. Since the deference of the common people for ministers and magistrates was so strong, the will of the leaders was rarely contested. Ultimately, following the precedent of the English Parliament, the Massachusetts General Court divided into two houses, one composed of representatives from the various towns, and the other composed of the assistants, who together with the governor were chosen annually by the votes of the freemen.

The intolerance of the Massachusetts government on all matters of belief and conduct was complete.[1] On reaching the New World the Puritans had broken away from the Church of England,

Religious intolerance

referring all theological disputes to their own ministers, sitting together in synods. They held that the Church must set up standards of conduct as well as principles of theology, and they branded anything that savored of lightness or frivolity as a sin. They believed that one of the first responsibilities of government was to punish all departures from orthodoxy in theology or from propriety in behavior. Laws were passed to make the way of the transgressor hard, and the worst offenders were punished by expulsion from the colony. Church and state worked together, each to uphold the other, the state sustaining the decisions of the church, and the church proclaiming through its ministers the supremacy of the state. Early Massachusetts was not a democracy; it was an aristocratic theocracy.

Deportations from Massachusetts for religious offenses were numerous, and two of the most famous of them resulted in the founding of a new colony, Rhode Island. Roger Williams was a godly but dis-

Rhode Island

putatious minister who came from England in 1631, and presently became the pastor at Salem. His insistence that the state had no right to punish a man for uncommon religious views or practices was regarded as dangerous, so in 1635 the General Court voted to expel him from the colony. Next spring, with the help of a few adherents, he began the settlement on Narragansett Bay that developed into the town of Providence. Anne Hutchinson, according to John Winthrop, was "a woman of a ready wit and a bold spirit." Among her heresies was the belief that some ministers were definitely superior to others because they were under a "covenant of grace" rather than merely a "covenant of works." Roger Williams had few followers, but Anne Hutchinson attracted many, and soon had the theologically-minded

[1] V. L. Parrington, *The Colonial Mind, 1620–1800* (*Main Currents in American Thought,* I, 1927), opens with a brilliant account of the Puritan heritage

colony in an uproar. Finally the General Court ruled that "two so opposite parties could not contain in the same body without hazard of ruin to the whole," and banished Mrs. Hutchinson and her disciples from the colony. In 1638 they founded a settlement at Portsmouth, near Roger Williams's town of Providence. Disagreements at Portsmouth led to the founding of a third settlement in 1639 at Newport, and in 1643 Samuel Gorton, another refugee from Massachusetts, founded Warwick.

The four Rhode Island communities wasted little love on one another, but their common fear of Massachusetts, whose leaders deeply resented such near-by nests of heretics, drew them together. In 1644 Roger Williams secured from the English Parliament a "patent" which permitted the settlers on Narragansett Bay to govern themselves so long as their laws were in harmony with the laws of England; and in 1647 representatives from the various Rhode Island towns organized a political system not unlike that of Massachusetts. Church membership was not a qualification for voting, however, and the right of religious liberty was definitely safeguarded, "notwithstanding our different consciences touching the truth as it is in Jesus." In 1663 a formal charter was secured from King Charles II in which the Rhode Island system of representative government was accorded full approval, and the Rhode Island principle of "liberty in religious concernments" was definitely accepted.[1]

Meanwhile, out in the lower Connecticut Valley, another offshoot from the Massachusetts Bay colony had appeared. Fertile lands had more to do with the founding of Connecticut than religious dissensions. The soil around Massachusetts Bay was hard to work and the harvests were not copious; hence, tales of **Beginnings of Connecticut** better lands to the southwest made a strong appeal. Thomas Hooker, minister at Newtown (later Cambridge), and John Haynes, a former governor, were the chief promoters of the Connecticut project. In the years 1635 and 1636 they led about eight hundred settlers through the forests to the Connecticut Valley. Ignoring the Dutch claims to this region and their own lack of title, they founded three towns, Hartford, Wethersfield, and Windsor. Some settlers from Plymouth had already established a trading-post not far from the site of Hartford, and some Puritans from England, acting under a grant of land from the Council of New England, had sent out a small force under John Winthrop, Jr., son of the Massachusetts governor, to found a colony at the mouth of the Connecticut River. Here Winthrop, in spite of threats from the Dutch, erected Fort Saybrook. Another settlement in the Connecticut Valley was made at Springfield by a Roxbury congrega-

[1] I. B. Richman, *Rhode Island: Its Making and its Meaning* (2 vols., 1902).

tion, but the site was discovered later to be within the jurisdiction of Massachusetts.[1]

Progress towards the establishment of an orderly government for the Connecticut River towns was rapid. In 1639 representatives from Hartford, Wethersfield, and Windsor met at Hartford to draw up a plan of union. The result was the Fundamental Orders of Connecticut, a document usually regarded as the first constitution to be written in America. The Fundamental Orders copied the governmental practices of Massachusetts, although the prerogatives of officials were somewhat more limited.

The "Fundamental Orders"

During this same period still another Puritan colony, New Haven, was in process of evolution along the shores of Long Island Sound. Its founders were John Davenport, an English Puritan minister, and Theophilus Eaton, a well-to-do English Puritan merchant. These men visited Massachusetts in 1637, but decided to found an ideal Bible commonwealth and trading center outside the confines of any existing colony. At New Haven their dreams of commercial success failed to materialize, but with this small settlement as a beginning several other towns, Guilford, Milford, and Stamford, were soon founded.

The New Haven colony

[1] G. L. Clark, *A History of Connecticut* (1914); C. M. Andrews, *Connecticut's Place in Colonial History* (1924).

THE THREE GREATEST AMERICANS

The designation of Franklin, Washington, and Lincoln as the three greatest Americans has long received almost universal approval.

BENJAMIN FRANKLIN (1706–90) *was the outstanding American of the colonial period. He was as well known in the Old World as in the New and was honored for his contributions to science and philosophy even more than for his contributions to government and politics. His well-nigh universal interests are revealed in the unmistakable imprint he left upon such varied fields as journalism, literature, education, and humanitarian reform.*

GEORGE WASHINGTON (1732–99), *in spite of the best efforts of "debunking" historians, remains the outstanding American hero. Though he may not have been a genius, his talents were equal to the difficult tasks he faced. He was a man of character, trusted by his contemporaries as no other American leader has ever been trusted.*

ABRAHAM LINCOLN (1809–65), *sixteenth President of the United States, was "the man who saved the Union." That this man — humbly born, lacking in formal education, a common man if ever there was one — rose to the highest office in the land and discharged his responsibilities effectively in time of crisis, serves as a perennial inspiration to American youth.*

WASHINGTON

FRANKLIN

LINCOLN

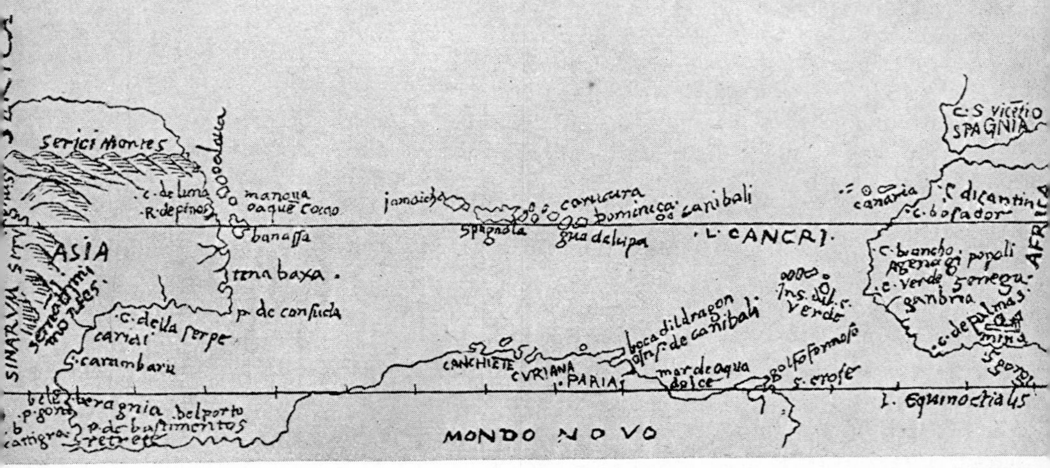

SERICI MONTES

ASIA

SINARVM SITVS

c. de luna
R. de pinos
manona
oaque coxo
banassa
tena baxa
p. de consida
c. della serpe
cariel
s. carambaru
belteragnia belporto
p. gorz p. de bastimentos
carigra retret

jamaica
spagnola
canicura
dominecca caribali
gua delupa
L. CANCRI

CANCHIETE
CVRIANA
PARIA
boca di dragon
ans. de caribali
mar de aqua dolce
golfo formoso
s. croxe

ins. del c.
verde

canaria
C. di cantini
c. boscador
c. bianco popali
agenoe
c. verde
somegu
ganabria
c. de palmas
mina
s. porgi

C. S. vicetio
SPAGNIA

AFRICA

MONDO NOVO

L. Equinoctialis

GERARDVS MERCATOR NATVS IN
RVPELMVNDA III NON. MARTII ANNO
CIƆIƆXII. VIXIT ANN. LXXXII. M. VIII. D.
XXVI. DENATVS IV. NON. DECEMBRIS
ANNO CIƆIƆXCIV.

IVDOCVS HONDIVS NATVS IN
PAGO FLANDRIÆ DICTO WACK. NE AVI
KALEND. NOVEMBRIS ANNO CIƆIƆLXII.
VIXIT ANN. XLVII. M. VII. D. XXI. DENAT
VS XIV. KAL. MARTII ANNO CIƆIƆXI.

In government and religion the New Haven colony, like Connecticut, repeated with slight variations the Massachusetts experiment; indeed, no other colony was more circumspect in its Puritanism than early New Haven. Its separate existence came to an end in 1662 when the English king, Charles II, was induced, mainly through the efforts of John Winthrop, Jr., to unite the Connecticut River towns and New Haven into the one colony of Connecticut under a liberal charter.[1]

As for the regions known as New Hampshire and Maine, their beginnings date back to 1623 when two English gentlemen, Sir Ferdinando Gorges and Captain John Mason, obtained from the New   New England Council a patent to all the land lying between the   Hampshire Kennebec and the Merrimac Rivers. They first called their   and Maine grant Laconia, but presently, on determining to divide it between them, Mason took the western half and called it New Hampshire, while Gorges took the territory along the coast and called it Maine. Both men tried to establish settlements within the confines of their grants, but success came only with the influx of settlers from Massachusetts who were reluctant to acknowledge any other authority than that of the Puritan commonwealth in which they had lived. Presently the Massachusetts govern-

[1] C. H. Levermore, *The Republic of New Haven* (1886); Isabel M. Calder, *The New Haven Colony* (1934).

THE EXPANDING WORLD

This sketch map, which labels the continent of America as "Asia," was drawn in 1503 by Bartholomew Columbus, who was with his brother Christopher Columbus on his last voyage. The map gives a good idea of the imperfect knowledge of the New World which its discoverers entertained. This is one of three sketch maps discovered by Professor Wieser as marginal drawings on the copy of a letter which Columbus wrote from Jamaica July 7, 1503. (From A. E. Nordenskvöld's "Periplus" [1897].)

GERARDUS MERCATOR (1512–94), *the figure on the left, was a Flemish geographer. He was responsible in large part for the gradual freeing of map makers from the misconceptions of Ptolemy, a second-century Egyptian, long regarded as the final authority on all matters of geographical knowledge. Among Mercator's most valued works was a planisphere for the use of navigators, the first map to be drawn on "Mercator's projection," that is, with parallels and meridians at right angles. This picture indicates many factors which made navigation easier: better geographers, globes and maps that showed new discoveries and that also were more accurate, printed books, and so forth. (From an atlas published in 1636 by Hendrick Hondius, son of Mercator's business partner who is shown on the right side of the print.) (Photo from Bettmann.)*

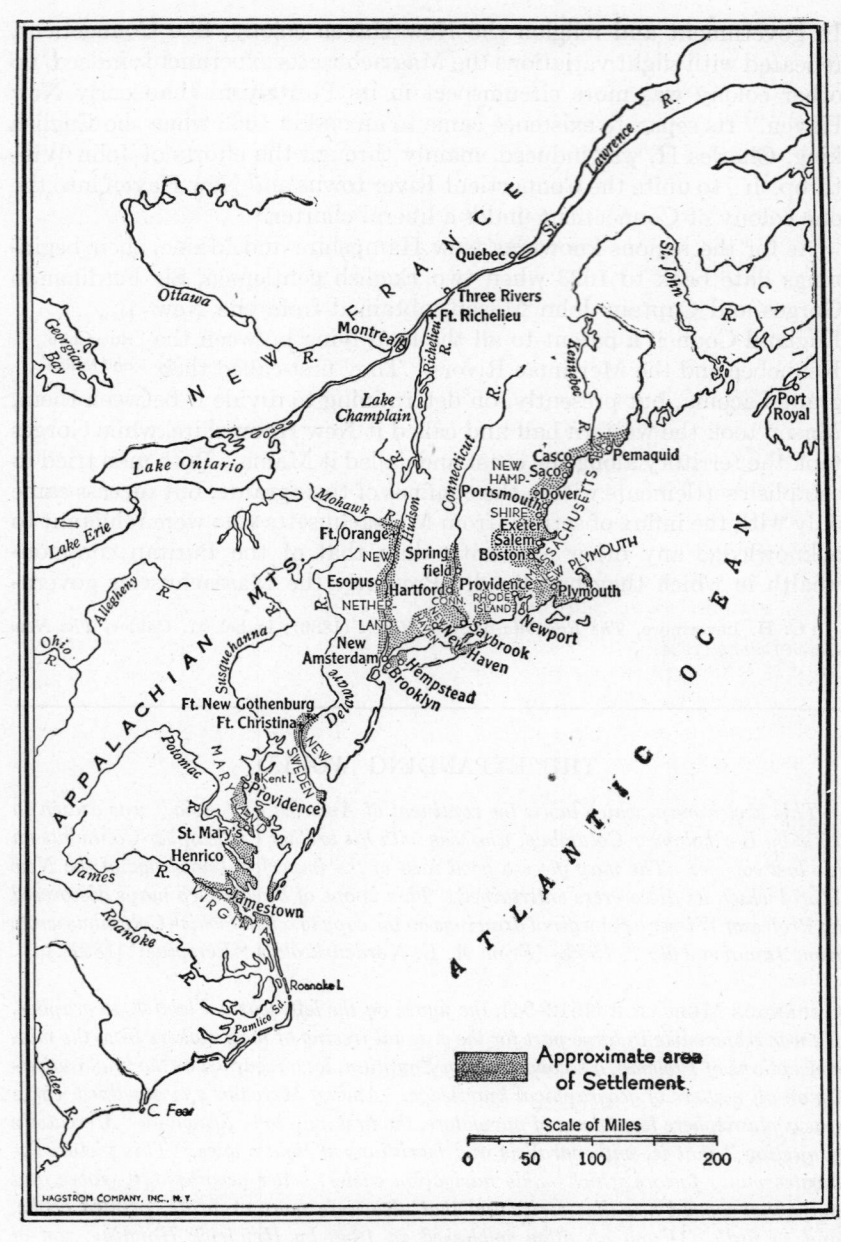

EARLY SETTLEMENTS ON
THE CONTINENT OF NORTH AMERICA, 1650

ment, on the pretext that its land grant really entitled it to do so, extended its authority first over the New Hampshire towns, and finally over those in Maine. New Hampshire remained a part of Massachusetts until 1679, when Charles II made it a separate royal colony, but Maine was not accorded a separate existence until by the well-known Compromise of 1820 it became a state in the Union.[1]

The advance of the New England frontier brought on at an early date trouble with the Indians, particularly the Pequots, whose holdings were seriously jeopardized by the founding of Connecticut. Attacks on isolated settlers resulted in a general Indian war, during which the Massachusetts colony gave valuable aid to the Connecticut pioneers. By 1637 most of the offending **The New England Confederation** Pequots were either dead or enslaved, but the memory of this conflict, coupled with the thinly veiled hostility of the Dutch in New York, aroused the New England leaders to the necessity of combining their forces. As a result the New England Confederation, consisting of Massachusetts, Plymouth, Connecticut, and New Haven, was formed in 1643. Two commissioners from each of the four colonies were entrusted with the management of the common business, which was restricted in the main to matters of military defense; but the Articles mentioned also the desirability of protecting common religious interests, presumably against such heretics as were located in Rhode Island. The Confederation lasted until 1684, and in 1675 it was of material assistance in waging another war against the Indians, generally known as King Philip's War.

Except for the futile efforts of Gilbert and Raleigh, and of Mason and Gorges, the colonial foundations so far mentioned owed their origins to the activities of trading companies rather than individuals. Investors with a strong urge for profits put up the funds which mere religious enthusiasm or love of adventure would probably have been powerless to obtain. Many other colonial ventures, however, particularly those of the later colonial period, were organized and financed by proprietors, usually royal favorites who had received from the King generous grants of land in America. Some of these lords were mere speculators who aimed chiefly at selling or letting out their American acres on advantageous terms. A few coveted political power such as nobles of the Old World were no longer permitted to possess, and others, while by no means indifferent to the prospects of financial and political rewards, sincerely desired to found havens of refuge for the oppressed.

The earliest of the successful proprietary provinces was Maryland. The launching of this colony was the work of George Calvert and his son

[1] W. H. Fry, *New Hampshire as a Royal Province* (1908); H. S. Burrage, *The Beginnings of Colonial Maine, 1602–1658* (1914).

Cecilius, more commonly known as the first and second Lords Baltimore. George Calvert was a man of means who had long been interested in colonial projects. By embracing the Catholic faith he had cut himself off from all chance of political preferment at home, but King Charles I seemingly bore him no grudge, and promised him a grant of land in America. In 1632, after the death of the first Lord Baltimore, the grant of Maryland was completed to the second Lord Baltimore, who was also a Catholic. By its terms the territory from the south bank of the Potomac northward to the fortieth parallel and inland to the source of the river was handed over to the Baltimore family as an hereditary estate. The grant also carried with it complete governmental rights, except that in the making of laws and the levying of taxes the proprietor was required to consult the freemen, or landowners, of the colony, or their representatives.

The Baltimores in Maryland

The second Lord Baltimore greatly desired to make of Maryland a place where his Catholic co-religionists might worship without fear of oppression, and, perhaps because of an unrecorded understanding with the King, the royal charter offered no opposition to such a course. But the number of prospective emigrants among English Catholics was limited, and Baltimore was too good a business man to propose the exclusion of Protestants, who were cordially welcomed and from the first seem to have outnumbered Catholics. The *Ark* and the *Dove*, two small ships which Baltimore sent to Maryland in the fall of 1633, carried about twenty gentlemen and two hundred laborers to the new colony. Most of the gentlemen were Catholics, but most of the laborers were Protestants. Two Jesuit priests accompanied the expedition and labored with great earnestness but little success to convert the Protestant settlers and the Indians to Catholicism. In February, 1634, the expedition entered the Potomac, and chose St. Mary's as the site of the first settlement. Lands were peacefully acquired from the Indians, and the economic life of Virginia was closely and successfully imitated.

A Catholic refuge

Cecilius Calvert did not himself come to America, but sent instead as lieutenant governor his brother, Leonard Calvert. Small quit-rents, charged by the proprietor against all lands granted to settlers, produced a fair revenue, but also much opposition. Furthermore, the proprietor and his lieutenant sought at first to hold popular participation in the government to a minimum. This was not long possible, and in Maryland as elsewhere a representative assembly soon developed. One of the most significant of its early acts, passed in the face of the rising power of Puritanism in England, was the Toleration Act of 1649. While this act threatened with death all non-Christians, including Jews and Unitarians, it guaranteed that no person "professing to believe in Jesus Christ, shall be in any wise molested or discountenanced for his or her religion." Persecution of Catholics, however, did break out in Maryland during the later years of the seventeenth century, and the Church of England, in spite of the Catholic origin of the colony, became the established church.[1]

The successes of the Baltimores, such as they were, inspired emulation on the part of certain courtiers of the new king, Charles II, who was restored to the English throne in 1660. This easy-going monarch readily fell in with the plans of his friends, who were **The Carolinas** helped also by the general revival of interest in colonization that set in after the period of civil war had come to an end. Eight prominent nobles, armed with an elaborate but unworkable plan drawn by John Locke for the introduction of the feudal system into America, successfully petitioned the King for the land that lay south of Virginia and north of Florida, commonly known as Carolina. In what became North Carolina, pioneers from Virginia had already settled in the Albemarle region, and they paid little attention to the unsolicited efforts of the Carolina proprietors to assert an undesired authority over them. In 1670, however, an expedition under William Sayle founded Charles-Town, or Charleston, as it was later called, and so began the settlement of South Carolina, a colony which rapidly took on a cosmopolitan tinge. French Huguenots began to arrive about 1680, and emigrants from Ireland, New England, and the West Indies, especially Barbados, were numerous. The planters used indentured servants for labor when they could, but, as in Virginia and Maryland, they bought Negro slaves when the supply of white servants was deemed inadequate. They raised foodstuffs as well as tobacco, and beginning about 1693 they introduced the culture of rice. The excellent harbor at Charleston greatly facilitated trade with the outside world. In government both South Carolina and North Carolina tended to develop along the lines already marked out in Maryland.[2]

The Carolina settlements were designed, in part, to act as buffers against the Spanish in Florida. But the Dutch colony of New Netherland, on the Hudson, was an even greater menace to the English than Spanish Florida. The beginnings of New **New Netherland** Netherland dated back to 1612, when some Dutch merchants established a post on Manhattan Island which soon became a thriving center for the fur trade. After 1621 the rule of this colony was in the hands of the Dutch West India Company, which among other things

[1] N. D. Mereness, *Maryland as a Proprietary Province* (1901).

[2] C. L. Raper, *North Carolina, A Study in English Colonial Government* (1904); Edward McCrady, *The History of South Carolina under the Proprietary Government, 1670-1719* (1897); A. H. Hirsch, *The Huguenots of Colonial South Carolina* (1928).

actively promoted the settlement of "patroons," or landlords, together with their tenants, in great estates along the Hudson. By the middle of the century a sparse Dutch population extended northward as far as the site of Albany. Many settlers from the English colonies also entered the Dutch territory. Some of them were refugees from religious persecution, others were pioneer farmers eager to accept the generous land terms offered by the Dutch, and still others were former indentured servants in full flight from the scene of their servitude. Thanks to these accessions, and to the absorption in 1655 of the small Swedish colony on the Delaware, the population of New Netherland had risen before the English conquest to about ten thousand.[1]

The presence of this Dutch colony in America was naturally distasteful to the English, whose holdings it cut squarely in two. Hence, in 1664, on the eve of one of the several wars of commercial rivalry

New York

that marked the relations of England and the Netherlands during the last half of the seventeenth century, the English king, Charles II, sent an expedition across the Atlantic to take possession of New Netherland. To his brother, the Duke of York, later King James II, he granted proprietary rights over the whole province. The British occupation took place without bloodshed, and the little colony, now renamed New York, exchanged without serious incident the autocratic rule of the Dutch merchants for an almost equally undemocratic system embodied in the "Duke's laws." Throughout the seventeenth century progress toward popular rule in New York lagged perceptibly behind that of every other English colony in America.

The Duke of York disposed of a part of his holdings to two nobles, Lord John Berkeley and Sir George Carteret, who were interested in the Carolina project also and who still hoped for riches from

New Jersey

the sale of their lands in America. These gentlemen were given proprietary rights to the territory lying between the lower Hudson and the Delaware, a region which they called New Jersey, after Carteret's home in England. Here a few Dutch settlements had already been established, and the new proprietors, by offering land to newcomers on easy terms, succeeded in attracting many emigrants from New England and from all parts of the British Isles. In 1665, the proprietors sent out Philip Carteret, a relative of Sir George, as governor. He promptly instituted a legislative assembly, but had considerable trouble with the settlers because the proprietors insisted, for the most part in vain, on the collection of quit-rents.

---

[1] John Fiske, *The Dutch and Quaker Colonies in America* (2 vols., 1899); Maud W. Goodwin, *Dutch and English on the Hudson* (1919); Amandus Johnson, *The Swedish Settlements on the Delaware, 1638–1664* (2 vols., 1911).

Down to 1674 the two proprietors held New Jersey jointly, but in that year Berkeley sold his holding to two Quakers, John Fenwick and Edward Byllinge. A division of the colony into two parts was then effected. Carteret retained as his portion the settlements in the northeast adjacent to New York, or East New Jersey, while the Quakers took the region to the south and along the Delaware, or West New Jersey. After several exchanges of titles both East New Jersey and West New Jersey emerged in Quaker hands, and with relatively democratic governmental practices.

Division of the colony

To the Jerseys came Quakers from England and Scotland, Puritans from New England, and somewhat later Scotch-Irish from the north of Ireland. The population of East New Jersey was probably twice that of West New Jersey, and in its economic character it closely resembled New England, whence so many of its settlers had come. West New Jersey, on the other hand, tended to copy the manner of life adopted by the settlers along the Chesapeake. Small holdings were the rule, but large plantations, worked in part by Negro slaves, were not unknown. By the end of the seventeenth century the two Jerseys together had a population of about fifteen thousand.

Among the most interested of the Quakers who were involved in the New Jersey project was William Penn,[1] the son of a high-ranking British naval officer. Penn's father was on friendly terms with King Charles II, with his brother the Duke of York, and with many of the nobles who had received proprietary grants of land in America. Young Penn, while still a student at Oxford, was impressed by the teachings of a Quaker preacher, and he soon became a member of the Society of Friends, as the Quakers called themselves. Penn's father was deeply distressed at his son's action, for the Quakers adhered to doctrines that were immensely at variance with the prevailing views of the time. They rejected all the sacraments, refused to pay tithes towards the support of the established church, denounced war unstintedly, declined to do military service, and in a great variety of ways put themselves entirely outside the pale of seventeenth-century respectability. Persecution under such circumstances was inevitable, and Penn, as one of the most prominent members of the sect, advanced the idea of founding as a retreat for the oppressed members of his faith a Quaker commonwealth in America.[2]

William Penn

---

[1] S. G. Fisher, *The True William Penn* (1899) and *The Quaker Colonies* (1921), furnish both good reading and good history. On the beginnings of New Jersey, see E. P. Tanner, *The Province of New Jersey, 1664–1738* (1908).

[2] George Hodges, *William Penn* (1901), is an excellent short biography. For the Quaker doctrines, see R. M. Jones, *The Faith and Practices of the Quakers* (1927); and, for the Quaker contribution to early American history, by the same author, *The Quakers in the American Colonies* (1911).

It was Penn's dream that the colony he would establish should be liberal in government as well as tolerant in religion. Believing that for this purpose he must have a charter direct from the crown, he offered, in return for full proprietary rights to the lands along the Delaware north of Maryland, to cancel a debt that King Charles had owed his father; and on March 4, 1681, his request received the sanction of the King. Penn's desire to permit the people to have democratic privileges was embodied in the various regulations he devised for the government of Pennsylvania, from the "Frame of Government" he issued in 1682 to his "Charter of Privileges" some twenty years later. Full freedom of worship was guaranteed for such persons as "acknowledged one Almighty and Eternal God," although in actual practice neither Jews nor Catholics were given quite the same political privileges that were permitted to Protestants. Not only Quakers, but members of various other oppressed sects also, looked upon the Quaker Colony as an ideal retreat.

The growth of Pennsylvania was remarkable. Penn's advertising campaigns, which featured generous land terms, religious freedom, and a liberal government, got a ready response. From Germany, in particular, where economic conditions were bad, and where minority religious groups lived under the constant shadow of persecution, came a large migration. A few Dutch and a few French Huguenots came also, and many English, Welsh, and Irish settlers, most of whom were Quakers. Some of the English settlers adhered steadfastly to the Church of England, and objected strenuously, although for the most part ineffectively, to Penn's "holy experiment" in toleration. By 1689 the population of Pennsylvania was nearly twelve thousand, and in a short time it was larger than that of any other English colony in North America. Its largest city, Philadelphia, which Penn himself laid out in squares, soon became one of the busiest in all the English overseas possessions.[1]

Delaware was at first a part of New York, then later for a long time a part of Pennsylvania. Penn was determined to have for his colony free access to the sea, and in order to effect this purpose he obtained from the Duke of York in 1682 the territory lying immediately to the west of the Delaware River. When the "Charter of Privileges" was issued in 1701, these "lower counties" were accorded the right to select an assembly of their own. This they soon did, but the Penns continued as proprietors, and the relations between Delaware and Pennsylvania remained close.[2]

Georgia was the last of the English colonies to be established on the

[1] J. T. Faris, *The Romance of Old Philadelphia* (1918).
[2] Francis Vincent, *A History of the State of Delaware* (1870).

mainland of North America. Its founder, James Oglethorpe, wished to plant a colony in the unappropriated area between the Carolinas, Florida, and Louisiana that would act as a buffer **Georgia** state against the Spanish and the French. He had also a humanitarian desire to found a haven of refuge for Englishmen who were jailed for nonpayment of debts, and for Protestants who were suffering from religious persecution on the continent of Europe. In 1732 a group of trustees, of whom Oglethorpe was the most active, secured from George II title to the land lying between the Savannah and Altamaha Rivers, and westward from their headwaters to the Pacific. This grant rigorously forbade the trustees to make any profit from their venture, and provided that at the end of twenty-one years their governmental privileges should revert to the crown.

In January, 1733, Oglethorpe brought over about a hundred settlers and founded Savannah. Other immigrants soon came, Salzburgers, Scotch Highlanders, Scotch-Irish, and Welsh, as well as English. At first the terms on which land could be obtained were unusual. Not more than five hundred acres could be taken by any one person, and all such grants were entailed to male heirs. The proprietors also prohibited slavery, on the assumption that the near-by Spaniards might incite the slaves to revolt, and forbade the importation of rum. These provisions were extremely unpopular, and they checked somewhat the growth of the colony, although they were not long retained. English debtors were not sent to Georgia in as great numbers as Oglethorpe had hoped, and by 1760 the total population of the colony was not more than nine thousand. Of this number about one-third were Negro slaves whose presence was demanded when the economic interests of Georgia began to approximate those of the other southern colonies.

Because the history of the English colonies in North America is ordinarily written as a prelude to the history of the United States, the attention of American historians has naturally centered upon the "continental colonies," and particularly upon the thirteen **The island colonies** which eventually won their independence. But Englishmen of the seventeenth and eighteenth centuries, when they thought of the English settlements in America, included also the "island colonies," which seemed in many ways even more important than those on the mainland.[1] Among these were the Bermudas, several hundred miles to the east of the Carolinas, Barbados and St. Christopher, together with a number of minor islands in the Lesser Antilles, and the large island of Jamaica directly south of Cuba. Of these the Bermudas started as a

[1] On the later history of the island colonies see L. J. Ragatz, *The Fall of the Planter Class in the British Caribbean* (1928).

company venture, and the others as proprietorships, but all emerged presently as royal colonies.   Together they probably contributed far more to
the economic prosperity of the British Empire than did the continental
colonies.   Their sugar-cane and tobacco plantations offered extraordinary
opportunities for the investment of British capital.   Their constant demand for slaves helped along the British slave trade to a pleasing prosperity.   Moreover, because they stood ready to exchange their sugar and
molasses for foodstuffs and other supplies from the continental colonies,
they played an important part in making the colonies on the mainland a
success.

Less important were the feeble British outposts in the Bahamas,
Guiana, and Honduras; but far to the north the stations of the famous
Hudson's Bay Company, chartered in 1670, tapped another
Other English outposts important source of the fur trade.   By the peace of Utrecht
in 1713 the British acquired clear titles to the Hudson's Bay
region, to Acadia, which they renamed Nova Scotia, and to the island of
Newfoundland, but the interests of English fishermen in the waters adjacent to some of these regions dated as far back as the first half of the sixteenth century.

The British possessions in America were thus at the outset of the eighteenth century a far-flung empire, stretching from the northern coast of
South America to the Arctic Circle.   Meantime the British had acquired
still other possessions in Asia, Africa, and elsewhere.   A great variety of
peoples, a wide diversity of economic interests, a hopeless expanse of
geography confronted the British statesman who turned his attention to
colonial affairs.   It is not surprising that the task of integrating such an
empire proved to be too great for eighteenth-century British statesmanship, and that the relatively homogeneous continental colonies of North
America chose presently to work out their destiny apart from the rest.[1]

[1] H. R. Muelder and D. M. Delo, *Years of this Land* (1943), is an entertaining effort to
write a geographical history of the United States.   G. R. Stewart, *Names on the Land*
(1945), draws into a fascinating narrative the origins of American place-names.   See also
Max Savelle, *The Foundations of American Civilization* (1942); Klaus E. Knorr, *British
Colonial Theories, 1570–1850* (1944).

Interesting biographies of colonial characters are: L. S. Mayo, *John Endecott: A Bi-
ography* (1936); S. H. Brockunier, *The Irrepressible Democrat, Roger Williams* (1940);
C. K. Shipton, *Roger Conant: A Founder of Massachusetts* (1944); W. W. Comfort, *William
Penn, 1644–1718* (1944).

J. T. Adams (ed.), *Dictionary of American History* (6 vols., 1940), is useful at every point.

2

Colonial America

WHILE each of the thirteen colonies had an important separate history, parallel conditions often existed in several colonies, and sometimes in all the colonies. It is possible, therefore, to ignore colonial boundaries to some extent, and to treat the development of the colonies more or less collectively. Until recent years, particularly in textbooks, this method of treatment was rare, and the reader who wished to gain a knowledge of colonial America was compelled to follow through at least thirteen separate narratives.[1]

But it is quite impossible to overlook the fact that the colonies were divided into three or four well-defined sections. The British settlements in North America extended from a region of long winters and short summers to a region of short winters and long summers. They comprehended within their boundaries extensive areas of mountains and high hills, and other extensive areas of broad valleys and fertile plains. Moreover, there were differences in the types of settlers who came to possess the various parts of English America. The plantation area, which included Maryland and Virginia and the colonies to the south of them, came early to be recognized as a section apart. The colonies of New England, also, had an identity of characteristics that drew them together, and at the same time separated them from the rest. The Middle Colonies — New York, New Jersey, Pennsylvania — had much in common with the sections to the northeast and to the south of them, but were yet different. Finally to the west of the more thickly settled areas, with boundaries less clearly defined than the other sections, lay the frontier, a region in which new settlements were constantly being made, and in which the conditions of life were apt not to vary greatly even from north to south.[2]

Sectionalism in the colonies

[1] Compare, for example, R. G. Thwaites, *The Colonies* (1891), one of the volumes of the original *Epochs of American History*, edited by A. B. Hart, with M. W. Jernegan, *The American Colonies* (1929), which the publishers of the *Epochs* series now offer.

[2] Students should have easy access to one of the following historical atlases: C. O. Paullin, *Atlas of the Historical Geography of the United States* (1932); J. T. Adams, *Atlas of American History* (1943); Clifford and Elizabeth Lord, *Historical Atlas of the United States* (1944); A. B. Hart and H. E. Bolton, *American History Atlas* (1930).

The type of civilization which developed in the plantation area was due in considerable part to the existence there of a wide coastal plain, indented frequently with spacious bays, unnumbered harbors, and wide-mouthed navigable rivers. Near the banks of the rivers a rich alluvial soil made for successful agriculture, although a little distance in from the waterline the soil was not so good. Owing to the fact that the tides swept far up the rivers, the coastal plain was frequently spoken of as the Tidewater. At varying distances into the interior waterfalls blocked navigation, and the Falls Line — that is, an imaginary line drawn from north to south through these waterfalls — marked approximately the end of the Tidewater. Between the falls and the mountains lay a rough, hilly country, known as the Piedmont.

The Plantation Area

Tobacco became the staple crop in most of the tidewater area, although in the Carolinas rice and indigo were also important products. Experience proved that the easiest road to prosperity was to raise these crops, particularly tobacco, for an outside market. In exchange for them the planter could obtain from Europe the articles he desired to make life agreeable in the New World. Of necessity the plantation owner maintained lively commercial relations with the Old World, most especially with the mother country. The Virginians and their neighbors raised all the tobacco they could raise, loaded it at their own or near-by wharves for shipment usually to England, and in return brought in all the goods they could buy.

Tobacco

As it turned out, tobacco culture led naturally to the development of large plantations. With no thought of rotation of crops, it was soon discovered that however fertile the soil might be, the constant growing of tobacco exhausted it.[1] More and more acres must therefore be acquired if the yield was to be kept up. It was observed, too, that if lands were allowed to lie fallow for a time, they could again be put in cultivation. This the large landowner could manage much more easily than the small landowner. Moreover, the fall in the price of tobacco that followed inexorably as the supply increased did its share to promote the expansion in size of the plantations. With the decline in the price of tobacco, the prosperous tobacco-raiser who had built himself a fine house and had established himself on a somewhat lavish scale of living found his income decidedly inadequate. The only way to make good this loss was to acquire more acres and raise more tobacco, and this he promptly did if he could. If he could not, he sold out to those who could afford to buy his land and possibly dropped into the small-farmer class, where his disadvantages were numerous.

Large plantations the rule

[1] A. O. Craven, *Soil Exhaustion as a Factor in the Agricultural History of Virginia and Maryland, 1606–1860* (1926).

The great planter could own his own wharf, from it ship tobacco to England, upon it receive goods in return. The small planter, on the other hand, had to use the great planter's wharf — substantially, he had to buy and sell through the great planter on whatever terms the latter chose to exact. Nor could the small planter compete with the great planter in the ownership of indentured servants and slaves. As the price of tobacco went down, the price of servants and slaves went up. Only the prosperous could afford to own them in sufficient numbers to make their possession profitable. The British rule of primogeniture in the inheritance of land, which was applied in Virginia and elsewhere, did much toward keeping together large estates, once they were created.

The successful southern planter was apt to have frontage on some winding stream such as the James, York, Rappahannock, or Potomac. If he were fortunate he might own a whole neck of land jutting out into the river. The size of the ordinary great planter's holding was about three thousand acres, but many planters — for example William Byrd of Westover, Virginia, who bequeathed to his son an estate of twenty-six thousand acres — held more. **Plantation life** The headquarters of each plantation made a little village. The planter and his family lived in a large and usually well-appointed house, near which were clustered the workhouses in which the cooking, weaving, carpenter work, blacksmithing, and other indoor activities of the plantation were done. Still other houses served as dwellings for the servants and slaves, or furnished shelter to the livestock. In so far as it was possible each plantation was a self-sufficing economic unit. Most of the food consumed on the plantation was produced upon it, and much of the wearing apparel and other necessities also. Such articles as tools, which could not easily be manufactured locally, and luxuries — fine clothes for the master and his family, expensive wines, furniture, and even building materials — were imported in return for the tobacco shipped abroad. Once a year these exchanges were made, ships bringing from England the orders sent over by the planters the year previously, and taking back with them the annual salable output of the plantation. Nearly always the planter overestimated the value of his crop, and in consequence over-ordered. Debts to British merchants began therefore to accumulate almost everywhere in the plantation area, and on the eve of the Revolution the irritation that the existence of these debts aroused helped materially to sever the ties that had bound the colonies and the mother country together.

During the eighteenth century slavery came to play a more important rôle in the life of the southern plantation than had been the case in the seventeenth century.[1] Adequate numbers of indentured servants were

[1] This subject is well treated in P. A. Bruce, *The Colonial Period, 1607–1763* (*History of Virginia*, i, 1924).

hard to get, and with an inviting wilderness to the West were harder
still to keep, whereas Negro slaves were fairly cheap and
endured the work of the plantations with fair contentment.
In the rice-growing regions of South Carolina, where the
climatic conditions were bad and white laborers quickly succumbed,
Negro laborers were able to survive and to make good profits for their
masters. By the close of the colonial period there were about four hundred thousand Negro slaves in the colonies. Three-fourths of this number
lived in the South, where they constituted two-fifths of the entire population. In South Carolina they outnumbered the white population two to
one. In the early years slaves were treated with extreme harshness, even
cruelty; but as time went on the relations between masters and slaves
greatly improved.

Slavery and servitude

The plantation system left little chance for the development of towns
and cities in the South. Annapolis, Williamsburg, and Wilmington, the
capitals respectively of Maryland, Virginia, and North Carolina, were
hardly more than villages except when a legislature met, or a court convened. Norfolk and Baltimore attained some importance as ports, and
Charleston became a thriving little city, but these were exceptional instances. The life of the South was decidedly rural rather than urban in
character.[1]

In consequence, when it came to the establishment of local political
units in the South the example offered by rural England rather than urban England was followed. In the plantation area the parish was the smallest political division. Its boundaries included the residences of all the communicants of the parish
church. A vestry, in practice consisting of the more important planters, governed the local church, cared for the poor, levied taxes
to obtain necessary funds, and looked after the affairs of the parish generally. In theory, members of the vestry were supposed to be chosen by
the parishioners, but in fact the vestrymen themselves filled vacancies in
their membership, and became thus a "close corporation." A county
usually consisted of several parishes, although sometimes the boundaries
of a county and a parish were coterminous. In each county from eight to
twenty justices of the peace were appointed by the governor from among
the planters, and these justices held county court, usually monthly, but
not less than four times a year. At such times they administered justice,
chose constables and highway surveyors for the various precincts, ordered the building of roads and bridges, and assessed taxes. Orders of

Local government in the South

---

[1] *The Pageant of America*, edited by R. H. Gabriel and others (15 vols., 1929), is a successful effort to produce a pictorial history of the United States. The first volume is
devoted to the colonial period.

the county court were executed by the sheriff and the county lieutenant, the latter being the commander of the local militia. These officers, as well as new justices of the peace, were appointed by the governor, but usually only on nomination of the county court. The county seat at which sessions of the court were held was often of hardly enough consequence to be spoken of as a village. Sometimes it was only a "courthouse" at a county crossroads.[1]

Once in two years, ordinarily, the voters of the county assembled to choose members of the colonial legislature. In Virginia each county was entitled to two representatives in the House of Burgesses. Property tests for voting were universal, but they did not exclude the small farmer from the suffrage. The elections were boisterous affairs, and by way of electioneering the opposing candidates usually treated the voters liberally to liquor. While the small farmers probably outnumbered the great planters nine or ten to one, the representatives were almost invariably chosen from the great planter class.

In religion as in government the plantation area of the South was not unlike rural England, where the strength of the Established Church was always great. In every southern colony, from Maryland to South Carolina, the Church of England was by law estab- **Religion** lished, and its ministers were held to be as much entitled to their pay as any other officers of the state. They were appointed, sometimes by the governor, sometimes by the proprietor, and sometimes, as missionaries, by an English organization known as the Society for Propagating the Gospel in Foreign Parts. These ministers were usually good men who took their duties seriously, but an occasional rake appeared among them whose conduct was injurious to the reputation of the Episcopal clergy as a whole. Unfortunately there was no bishop of the English Church resident in America, and the Bishop of London, under whose spiritual guidance the American Church was placed, never visited America. In consequence matters of discipline were extremely difficult to handle; moreover, the only way Americans could enjoy the rites of ordination and confirmation was by either themselves or the bishop making a trip across the Atlantic. The lack of an American bishop was an unending source of complaint, and contributed its share toward the general discontent with British control that lay back of the Revolution.[2] Dissenters existed in every southern colony, and well before the end of the colonial period their practices, if not always officially licensed, were at

---

[1] C. M. Andrews, *Colonial Self-Government* (1904), and E. B. Greene, *Provincial America* (1905), cover well the development of colonial institutions.

[2] A. L. Cross, *The Anglican Episcopate and the American Colonies* (1902); E. L. Goodwin, *The Colonial Church in Virginia* (1927).

least generally ignored. But the bulk of the population in the tidewater area remained loyal adherents of the Established Church.

Schools were a rarity in the South, and only the children of planters were adequately educated. Very frequently these children were taught

Education

at home by tutors, although "pay schools" were not unknown; then later, if the means were at hand, the boys were sent to England for further education. One of the leading colonial colleges, William and Mary, founded in 1693, was located in the South and was liberally supported by the ruling class. But even so important a center as Charleston lacked both colleges and public schools.

With virtually a monopoly on education, and "to the manner born," the great planters of the South, while actually a small minority in the population, played the principal rôle in southern history. They managed the affairs of their great estates with considerable ability, and they used the talents thus sharpened in discharging the political duties that fell to their lot. They were naturally averse to governmental interference in their private affairs, and were quick to resent injustices, especially when the source of trouble lay as far away as England. They fancied themselves extremely democratic because in reality the first families were very democratic among themselves, given to much visiting back and forth, and fond of showing hospitality. They possessed a charm of manner and a distinction of bearing that distinguished them clearly, even from the élite of the northern colonies. They took a paternalist interest in the affairs of the lower classes — the yeomen and the slaves — that was for the most part beneficial to all.

In New England, as in the South, physiographic conditions had much to do with shaping the course of development. The early settlers of New

New England

England found the topography exceedingly irregular, with high hills or mountains, rising in clusters rather than ranges, not far from the sea. In an earlier age the whole region had been glacier-swept, and the surface, even in the level places, was apt to be covered with boulders. The soil, where it could be found, was good, but required infinite patience and endurance to work. Rapidly flowing rivers plunged at frequent intervals into the sea, and waterfalls furnished the power that one day would turn factory wheels, but for the moment merely made penetration into the interior more difficult. Natural harbors dotted the coast-line, and foretold commerce, while heavy forests were everywhere available to furnish naval stores, masts, spars, and timbers for the builders of ships.

The inhabitants of this "stern and rock-bound coast" were a fairly homogeneous group. Probably ninety-five per cent of the emigrants to colonial New England had come from England, and furthermore, in spite of their distinguished middle-class leaders, most of them had come from little peasant villages where they had worked as artisans or from which they had gone out each day to till their land. If they were not always Puritans on coming to America, as a rule they or their children soon fell in with the dominant religious faith.

Emigration to New England proceeded usually in groups. A congregation, led by its minister and financed by some wealthy Puritan, would come to America as a unit, establish a new town, sometimes named after the town in England from which the group had come, and continue to live thereafter in much the same fashion as in old England. This procedure was closely approximated, also, in the extension of the coast settlements into the interior. Actuated perhaps by some minor religious difference, and interested at the same time in seeking out new economic opportunities, a large number of families would put out together to found another town or another site. In the formative period New-Englanders showed little disposition to settle as individuals upon separate farms. Long-established custom, aided by the great desirability of having a church easily accessible and the necessity of protecting themselves against hostile Indians, kept the settlers together in villages. The New England town thus came to be the social and economic unit around which all New England life tended to center.

Group migration

Furthermore, the town was also a natural, almost inevitable, political unit, and, as it turned out, a self-governing unit. The practice among the Puritans with respect to church government was to allow to each congregation the complete right to choose its minister, its deacons and elders, its tithing men. Even with respect to matters of doctrine the decision of the congregation was final. In the government of the town, these same ideas of democracy prevailed. All matters of importance related to local government were at first brought before the town meeting, to which usually all the church members, or perhaps even all the citizens, were entitled to come. The levying of taxes, the distribution of land, the establishment of schools, the passing of local ordinances of government, all were brought before this meeting. Between meetings "selectmen," duly elected for the purpose, carried on the government, and as time went on the unwieldy nature of the town meeting made it necessary to hand over to this smaller group many of the duties first performed by the meeting itself. The town was also the unit from which members were chosen to the lower house of the colonial legislature, and for this purpose, ordinarily once each year, the voters convened.[1]

The New England town

[1] Anne B. MacLear, *Early New England Towns* (1908); Melville Egleston, *The Land System of the New England Colonies* (1880).

Agriculture was a necessity in colonial New England, for the people had to live. Fields were cleared of timber and of stones, the latter being **Agriculture** used extensively for the construction of stone walls to serve as fences, and crops of many sorts were planted. Individual land holdings were early introduced, and generally each farmer tilled his own land. Labor was scarce, for virtually anyone might acquire land of his own, hence the holdings, in contrast to the southern plantations, tended to be no larger than one man and his family could work. Lacking money with which to buy, farmers fell back upon their own ingenuity, and fashioned for themselves the tools they used, the shoes they and their families wore, the furniture that they needed, the very houses in which they lived. The women spun wool or flax into threads, wove cloth, and made the clothes that the family wore. Habits of thrift and frugality were established which persisted down through many generations.

Agriculture was supplemented by fishing and commerce. The New England coasts were themselves rich in fish, and the banks of New-**Fishing and commerce** foundland, which had long been famed as fishing grounds, were not far away. Fishing led directly to commerce, for far more fish could be taken than could be consumed locally. According to reliable estimates not less than three hundred thousand cod were exported by New England fishermen in 1641, and by the year 1675 no less than six hundred vessels and four thousand men were engaged in the cod fisheries alone. New England fishermen found ready markets for their wares in the West Indies and in the Catholic countries of Europe.

Commerce, once opened up, diversified rapidly. Foodstuffs of various kinds were carried to the West Indies, not only from New England, but **The West Indian trade** also from ports farther down the coast where the Yankee traders stopped to complete their cargoes. In return for these commodities molasses, sugar, ginger, and other insular products were obtained, and in addition bills of exchange which could be used in the purchase of manufactured articles in England. At first the West Indian trade was confined mainly to the British islands, but by the eighteenth century trade with the Dutch, French, and Spanish islands was also common. From these sources came a good share of the money that found its way to the colonies. In 1697 the slave trade, which had for some time before been monopolized by a few English trading companies, was opened to all British subjects, and an interesting "triangular trade" developed. Molasses, brought from the West Indies to New England, was manufactured into rum, which was shipped to the African coast, where it was used in the purchase of slaves. The slaves were then brought to the West Indies and there exchanged for more molasses, which was then brought back to New England to make more rum, to acquire more slaves, to exchange for more molasses, and so on. Not all of the rum, however, was exported. The New England fishermen themselves used it liberally, and other New-Englanders, even some of the very "elect," developed a keen taste for it. Rum was useful also in the prosecution of the fur trade, which furnished yet another item for export.[1]

Shipbuilding went hand in hand with fishing and commerce. Skillful craftsmen early contrived to build fleet and sturdy ships which not only withstood well the battering of the elements, but frequently outran revenue vessels, and made an art of smuggling. Especially was this the case after the British began to collect duties under the Navigation Acts. Indeed, on the eve of the American Revolution smuggling became an industry in itself, comparable in some ways to the bootlegging industry of the Prohibition era. Timbers for shipbuilding were obtained in plenty from the easily accessible forests, and such items as barrel-staves, clapboards, and naval stores were early added to the list of exportable commodities. Yankee ships and Yankee seamen came to be seen and known all over the world, while the superiority of Yankee seamanship and the shrewdness of Yankee salesmen also received general recognition. Many New England merchants, the owners of ships and dealers in foreign wares, made comfortable fortunes; and the active business life that centered in the principal posts caused the villages so located to grow into sizable cities. Before the Revolution, Boston, with less than thirty thousand inhabitants, was the largest city in New England and the second largest in America, but many other towns, such as Salem, Newport, and New Haven, had passed well out of the village class.

Shipbuilding

Religion played a far greater part in the life of New England than in the life of the plantation South, and the theology of Calvin made a profound impression upon the New England character. The cardinal doctrine of Calvinism was predestination. As Calvin conceived it, God had created man in his own likeness and image, and had given him all the blessings of life in the Garden of Eden on condition that he must never eat of the fruit of a certain tree. But man, tempted by woman, broke the contract thus implied, and thereby lost not only all title to the joys of Eden, but also all hope of happiness in the world to come. Nor did the punishment stop here, for not only the original parents but also their children, and their descendants forever, being conceived in iniquity and born with the taint of original sin upon them, were in justice outside the pale of God's forgiveness. But God, in his infinite mercy, sent his Son into the world to suffer in the place of those who had been chosen to be saved. By the sacrifice of Christ on the Cross all those whom God had predestined and foreordained to be saved were

Calvinism

[1] S. E. Forman, *The Rise of American Commerce and Industry* (1927).

freed of the punishment that rightfully should have fallen upon them.
Only such persons as God had "elected" to be saved, however, could
benefit from the sacrifice of the Son. All the rest of mankind, including
even unborn infants, were "elected" to be damned.

This hard doctrine, morbidly dwelt upon by the long-winded Puritan
divines, was driven deeply into the marrow of the thoughtful New-
Englander. Was he of the elect whom God had chosen to be saved?
One might never know, and yet the behavior of a man should show to
some degree at least whether or not he had been deemed by God worthy
to be saved. Those who were religiously inclined watched their conduct
and searched their souls for evidences of the divine will towards them.
They displayed also a not unnatural interest in the spiritual welfare of
their neighbors. Who of those they knew were to be saved, who were to
be damned? Village life with its intimate associations gave ample opportunity for observation to those who wished to scrutinize closely the details of their neighbor's lives. The injunction to be one's brother's keeper
was cheerfully obeyed, and buttresses against temptation were erected in
the shape of "blue laws" that regulated closely the behavior of the
individual. Church attendance in some of the New England colonies
was long required by law, and on Sundays, according to one chronicle,
"no one . . . could make mince pies, dance, play cards, or play any instrument of music, except the drum, trumpet, and Jew's harp." [1]

The "New England conscience" that was born of these austere doctrines and practices endured long after some of the Calvinistic tenets
that produced it had lost their binding force. Scrupulous
observance of the moral law, rigid self-control carried even
to the length of self-denial, earnestness of purpose, and firm
belief in the righteousness of God's way with man set the
conscientious New-Englander somewhat apart from other Americans.
His conscience was apt to carry over into business and politics, both of
which he took with great seriousness. In these realms, however, the contract idea, so firmly embedded in Calvinistic theology, was not without
its helpful side. A bargain was a bargain, and a contract once signed had
to be obeyed. It behooved the maker of business contracts to watch
carefully the terms laid down, and mercy was not always vouchsafed to
the careless. Governmental charters and constitutions were likewise
held to be sacred covenants, and the principals, whether kings, lords, or

The
New England
conscience

---

[1] J. T. Adams, *Revolutionary New England* (1923), continues the anti-Puritan bias of his
Founding of New England, and should be tempered by comparison with the more orthodox
K. B. Murdock, *Increase Mather, the Foremost American Puritan* (1926). In lighter vein
is Alice Morse Earle, *The Sabbath in Puritan New England* (1891). The witchcraft delusion
that overtook Puritan New England late in the seventeenth century has been much overemphasized, although, before the frenzy was over, nearly a score of victims had lost their
lives.

commoners, might justly be held to the last letter of their plighted word. Nor was the law of the land, duly made and recorded, to be lightly ignored.

Education was taken much more seriously in New England than elsewhere in the colonies. This was due in part to the religious interest which made it seem worth while for every individual to be able to search the Scriptures on his own account, and in Education part to the existence of towns where schools and the means of education could be easily maintained. Five years after Boston was founded, it had a school, and in 1642 the General Court of Massachusetts passed a law requiring that all parents should see that their children learned how to read and how to ply some trade. Another Massachusetts law, passed in 1647, proposed the establishment of free public schools throughout the colony, an ideal that was not soon attained. But schools of one kind or another, sometimes private and sometimes public, were the rule rather than the exception throughout New England. The common schools taught reading, writing, and arithmetic; Latin or grammar schools prepared boys for college; and academies, which admitted both boys and girls, offered a somewhat wider course of study. Religion received much attention in all the schools. Pupils were taught the catechism at an early age, they read selections from the Bible as exercises in reading, and such textbooks as came into use were strongly impregnated with the Scriptures and Calvinistic theology. Discipline was extremely severe, and any wanton tendencies toward self-expression on the part of the pupils were promptly and thoroughly suppressed. Colleges, designed primarily for the purpose of training ministers, presently put in their appearance. Harvard College was founded in 1636, Yale in 1701, Brown in 1764, and Dartmouth in 1769.[1]

New-Englanders believed genuinely in their own ways, and carried them along wherever they went. Into New York, New Jersey, Maryland, and other neighboring colonies streamed New England emigrants carrying with them the New England con- New England
propagandism science and the institutions New-Englanders held dear. Indeed, in the settlement of the whole of the American West, New-Englanders were invariably present to reproduce as best they could in their new homes the civilization they had left.[2] The typical New-Englander was exceedingly intolerant of customs that diverged to any great extent from his own. Advocates of innovations were apt to be frowned upon

---

[1] Edward Eggleston, *The Transit of Civilization from England to America in the Seventeenth Century* (1901), is extremely suggestive. See also Alice Morse Earle, *Child Life in Colonial Days* (1899). On the early history of Harvard, S. E. Morison, *The Founding of Harvard College* (1935), is the definitive work.

[2] Lois Kimball Mathews [Rosenberry], *The Expansion of New England* (1909).

heavily, although in eighteenth-century New England the narrowness in religious matters that had been so characteristic of the formative period was much less in evidence. Even Episcopalians and Catholics were treated with consideration, and many such communicants were to be found, particularly Episcopalians, in all the urban centers.

The Middle Colonies rested upon a geographic foundation that combined the chief characteristics of New England and the South. Here there was a coastal plain and a piedmont, but the plain was narrower than in the plantation area, and the piedmont was wider. Toward New England, in New York, the mountains were in great glacial-ground clusters, but toward the south, in Pennsylvania, the long parallel ridges of the Alleghanies began to rise. The rivers of the central area were fewer in number, comparatively, than in the other sections, but they were longer and furnished more convenient highways into the interior than could be found elsewhere along the Atlantic seaboard. Indeed, three great river systems, the Hudson, the Delaware, and the Susquehanna, furnished the chief key to the development of the region. Each of these rivers flowed, generally speaking, from north to south, each was entered through a spacious harbor, and each was navigable even by ocean-going vessels for a considerable distance into the interior. In each river valley a distinctive civilization developed, and in due time a great city marked the point where each river reached the sea. New York commanded the trade of the Hudson Valley, Philadelphia of the Delaware, and Baltimore of the Susquehanna. Even in colonial times the spirit of rivalry between these growing towns was much in evidence.

The Dutch influence left a lasting impression upon the people of the Hudson Valley. The hopes of those who invented the patroon system were never fully realized, but the pretensions of the system did tend to mark off from the other elements of society an aristocratic caste of great landowners. One patroonship, Rensselaerswyck, which was founded near Albany by Kiliaen van Rensselaer and came to embrace many thousands of acres, worked out much as the original plans had contemplated; and a number of other estates, while by no means so closely approximating the feudal pattern, at least reached large dimensions. On some of the great estates of the lower Hudson tobacco was raised much as in Virginia. In a country where free land was so plentiful, however, and where even in the days of Dutch control emigrants were practically given all the land they could improve, it was difficult to maintain a tenant class. The great estates might exist, but many of their acres remained unworked. Nevertheless their owners came to constitute a distinguished upper class of "Vans" and "velts," who, in spite of being overwhelmingly outnumbered by small free farmers, exerted a preponderant influence in the affairs of the colony.

Dutch governmental practices also left some traces upon the subsequent English colony of New York. During the period of Dutch control very little was permitted the colonists by way of a voice in their government. New England emigrants protested vigorously against being thus deprived of rights to which they had long been accustomed, and on the eve of the British conquest Peter Stuyvesant, the Dutch governor, actually called together a representative assembly, which failed, however, to reach any important agreements. Thus, except for a limited amount of local self-government permitted in the Dutch villages, the English conquest found the colony wholly lacking in democratic political institutions. After the conquest, with the colony now under the rule of the reactionary Duke of York (later King James II), the introduction of democracy was still delayed. Richard Nicolls, the first British governor, was an astute diplomatist, and managed to keep discontent with such a system at a minimum, but his successor, Edmund Andros, had little such skill.

Absence of democracy

In 1683 the proprietor felt obliged to yield to the pressure for a representative assembly, but the Assembly adopted a charter of Liberties and Privileges which nettled him, and when he became king a year later he went back on his bargain. New-Yorkers ultimately won the right to participate in the control of their colony, although only a privileged few were granted the right to vote, and the government of the colony was distinctly less democratic than that of any other. New York politics, down to the American Revolution, tended to be little more than a series of factional fights among the important families to see whose influence would be strongest.

With respect to religion some Dutch survivals may also be noted. The Dutch adhered generally to the Dutch Reformed Church, which was as definitely Calvinistic in its teachings as even the Puritan congregations of New England could have asked. The Dutch, however, fed their souls less upon the doctrine of predestination than did the Puritans, and they were a little more content to rely upon God's abounding grace. With them religion played no such dominant rôle as in New England. Religious toleration, moreover, was a Dutch tradition, and the emigrant who came to New Netherland was rarely bothered about his faith. Peter Stuyvesant made some trouble for the Quakers, he once expelled a Baptist minister from the colony, and perhaps he discriminated unfairly against the Lutherans, but these acts were not so much an expression of Dutch policy as an expression of the personal predilections of Peter Stuyvesant. When New Netherland

Religion in New York

became New York, the Church of England supplanted the Dutch Reformed Church as the official church of the colony. But the number of Anglican communicants remained small for a long time, whereas, besides the members of the Dutch Reformed Church, there were on Long Island and elsewhere many Puritans from New England. Inasmuch as the proprietor, the Duke of York, was known to be a Catholic, it seemed expedient to carry over the Dutch spirit of toleration into the new régime, and this was done, although later some harsh anti-Catholic legislation was enacted.[1]

The Delaware Valley became the seat of a civilization quite as distinctive as was to be found along the Hudson, for it was here that the Quaker influence was preponderant. But democracy was inherent in the Quaker teaching. Quakers believed that God spoke to men directly by a voice that reached their hearts, and this "inner light" was denied to no man or woman. Since anyone might thus be in direct contact with the divine will, there was no room for ministers, or bishops, or ecclesiastical foundations. Even the Bible as a guide of faith and conduct suffered somewhat, for the "inner light" furnished quite as convincing an authority. All men were equal before God, so why should there be the distinctions in dress and manners that marked the aristocracy apart from the common run of men? Good Quakers called no man master, and used simply the word "Friend" by way of address. They objected to the use of the formal "you" when speaking to an individual, and employed instead the democratic "thee." They kept their hats on their heads even in the presence of kings, and they wore a plain, standardized garb that was designed to deny all social distinctions. Since the "inner light" came to women as well as to men, women were accorded the same privileges, at least in a religious way, that men enjoyed. Women spoke their minds freely "in meeting," notwithstanding the injunction of Saint Paul to "let the women keep silence in the church." Slavery the Quakers deeply deplored.

Quakers on the Delaware

Faith in such democratic principles as these could not but affect markedly the development of the Quaker colonies. Their tolerance of many varieties of religion, their unwillingness to propagandize in the Puritan fashion, and their generous land terms attracted great numbers of settlers. The valley of the Susquehanna, however, quite as much as the Delaware, was to profit from these inviting practices. To the Susquehanna came a mixed population, including many colonials from other regions, but in far greater numbers emigrants from Europe, in particular the so-called "Pennsylvania Dutch" and the Scotch-Irish.

Religious toleration

[1] S. H. Cobb, *The Rise of Religious Liberty in America* (1902); W. W. Sweet, *The Story of Religion in America* (1939).

The "Pennsylvania Dutch" were not Dutch at all, but Germans who had left their homes for many good reasons. For one thing, the wars that Louis XIV of France prosecuted in his attempt to attain for his country its "natural boundaries" not only drew **The "Pennsylvania Dutch"** the adjacent German states into the struggles, but made of them a periodic battlefield. For emigrants from this region, who sought relief from the brutalities of war, the Quaker doctrine of pacifism had a peculiar charm. Economic pressure furnished another motive. Petty feudal lords exacted heavy dues, required annoying services, and collected burdensome tithes for the support of state churches. Even in German Switzerland, where the ravages of war seldom touched, such exactions as these made many of the lower classes look with favor upon emigration to America. Religious persecution also played a part, for each prince of the Holy Roman Empire was left free to determine as he might choose the religious faith of his people — *cuius regio eius religio*. Catholics were in consequence subject to persecution in Lutheran states; Lutherans in Catholic states; and the minor religious sects, which came to have a great vogue in Germany, in all the states. Particularly oppressed were the sects, such as the Mennonites, who objected to military service. Penn's agents advertised persistently the advantages of America among the distressed Germans, and in 1709 the British Parliament, glad enough of the opportunity to stimulate outside immigration into the British Empire, passed a law for the naturalization of foreign Protestants.

Some German immigration reached the colonies late in the seventeenth century — Germantown, Pennsylvania, was founded in 1683 — but the great bulk of the German invasion came toward the middle of the eighteenth century. Because so many Germans **German settlements** came from the Palatinate, they were frequently called "Palatines." A few settled at Newbern, North Carolina; others settled in New York, acquiring lands as far inland as the Mohawk Valley; New Jersey, Maryland, and Virginia each were chosen by a few; but the main stream of German immigrants found their way to Pennsylvania, where they picked for themselves choice lands usually well up the valley of the Susquehanna, for the English colonists already had the Delaware. They came in such numbers that the provincials began to be alarmed, and the Pennsylvania legislature even passed laws restricting immigration. But these laws were invariably vetoed by the governors, and the Germans continued to come. It is estimated that, at the time the American Revolution broke out, about one-third of the inhabitants of Pennsylvania were German. Living together as they did, they retained their own language, established their own schools, printing

presses, and newspapers, and continued for many years to be a race
apart. Indeed, many of their descendants in central Pennsylvania still
speak and write a patois known as "Pennsylvania Dutch." [1]

The Pennsylvania Germans were not the only immigrants from Europe
to enter the Susquehanna Valley, for they were soon followed by the
The Scotch-Irish Scotch-Irish, with somewhat similar reasons for migration.
These Scotch-Irish newcomers were from the north of Ire-
land, but they were really not Irish at all. Their ancestors
had been Scotch lowlanders, some of whom had been colonized on lands
taken from the Irish during the reigns of Queen Elizabeth and King
James I, and others on the Irish lands confiscated by Oliver Cromwell
during the Protectorate. The Scotch-Irish troubles in Ireland were numerous. They could not get on well with the native Irish, to whom they
seemed to be mere trespassers. Also, being Presbyterians of the most
unbending variety, they scorned the Catholicism of their Irish neighbors,
who in turn had little pleasant to say about Scotch Presbyterianism. As
dissenters, they resented stoutly the legal requirement that they pay
tithes to the Anglican Church. They suffered also many economic grievances. The tenant system was peculiarly harsh upon them, since most
of their landlords were absentees, and were not only unconcerned about
the oppressive rentals, but were also often unaware of the still more oppressive methods of collecting them. The English government, moreover, in its efforts to protect the interests of English citizens, passed laws
against the importation of important Irish products, such as dairy cattle
and woolen goods, and placed discouraging regulations upon the production of linen. Bad harvests and frequent famines added to the Irish
discontent.

As was the case with the Pennsylvania Germans, some Scotch-Irish
colonists reached America before 1700, but the great majority did not
Scotch-Irish settlements arrive until toward the middle of the next century. Some
of the Scotch-Irish settled in New England, New York, and
New Jersey, but most of them penetrated into the back-
country of Pennsylvania by way of the Susquehanna and its tributaries.
Coming a little later than the Germans, the Scotch-Irish went a little
farther into the interior to find lands. They spoke English, and hence
were not bothered in their relations with the native Americans by the
language barrier that so often perplexed the Germans, but they were
harder to deal with than the Germans. When some of them were ac-

---

[1] A. B. Faust, *The German Element in the United States* (2 vols., 1909), is scholarly and
comprehensive. Less formidable are Lucy Bittinger, *The Germans in Colonial Times*
(1901), and J. L. Rosenberger, *The Pennsylvania Germans* (1923). Marcus Lee Hansen,
*The Atlantic Migration, A History of the Continuing Settlement of the United States, 1607–
1860* (1940), covers admirably every phase of this subject.

cused of holding lands without legal title, they replied that it was "against the laws of God and Nature, that so much land should be idle while so many Christians wanted it to labor on." There were fully as many Scotch-Irish as German emigrants to America, and probably more. At the time the American Revolution broke out, Pennsylvania was no less than one-third Scotch-Irish.[1]

Diversity of population elements was thus an important characteristic of the Middle Colonies. In addition to the Hudson Valley Dutch, the English Quakers, the Pennsylvania Germans, and the Scotch-Irish, although in no such numbers, there were here **Other nationalities** French Huguenots, Irish from the south of Ireland, Scotch from Scotland, a few Welshmen, and a few Jews. The Jews were most numerous in New York, whither they had come from South America, Holland, Germany, and Poland during the Dutch occupation.[2] Coupled with variety in population elements was a variety of religious denominations. The Middle Colonies were thus a hodgepodge of races and creeds, and a natural hotbed for factional politics. It should occasion no surprise that this region gave rise to a group of astute politicians, quick to compromise and ready to shift their ground as each new emergency appeared.

Local government in the Middle Colonies borrowed a little from the New England colonies and a little from the colonies to the south. Counties appeared after the fashion of the plantation area, but they were usually subdivided into townships that were rem- **Local government** iniscent of New England. In New York the influence of New England was more marked than elsewhere in the Middle Colonies, but well before the end of the seventeenth century a county board of supervisors, composed of representatives from the various towns, had absorbed many of the important functions of local administration. In Pennsylvania the townships were even less important than in New York. The combination of town and county government in the Middle Colonies proved to be of greater than local significance, for it was this example that most of the states of the West were to follow later on.

Public schools existed in the Middle Colonies from an early date, but the chief responsibility for educational establishments was here generally left with the various religious denominations. Colleges were relatively numerous by the time of the Revolution. The **Education** Anglicans founded Kings' College (later Columbia) in New York under

---

[1] C. A. Hanna, *The Scotch-Irish* (1902); H. J. Ford, *The Scotch-Irish in America* (1915).

[2] S. P. Orth, *Our Foreigners* (1920), covers sketchily the various immigrant elements that went into the making of the original "American stock." This is one of the fifty little volumes of *The Chronicles of America*, edited by Allen Johnson, a series which treats topically the whole course of American history.

a charter obtained in 1754; the Presbyterians established the College of
New Jersey (Princeton) as early as 1747; and Rutgers, opened in 1766,
ministered to the educational needs of the Dutch Reformed faith. Benjamin Franklin led the way for the opening at Philadelphia in 1751 of an
"Academy," free from sectarian influences, which later (1791) became
the University of Pennsylvania.

Farming furnished occupations to most of the inhabitants of the Middle Colonies, where the production and exportation of foodstuffs gave
rise to the name of "bread colonies." Indian corn, or maize,
The "bread   and other grains, livestock, particularly among the Ger-
colonies"   mans who understood the necessity of caring for domestic
animals in winter, and vegetables, most of which were native to America
and did not need to be acclimated, were produced in ever-increasing
quantities. Nuts, fruits, and berries were abundant, and required little
or no cultivation. Hemp and flax were also grown.

Manufacturing quickly sprang up, especially in Pennsylvania and New
Jersey after the coming of the Germans, among whom there were many
skilled workmen.[1] Iron, textiles, glass, and paper were
Manufacturing   among the articles commonly made in these regions. According to one observer, the inhabitants of Germantown were mostly
manufacturers who were able to "make everything in such quantity and
perfection, that, in a short time, this province will lack very little from
England, its mother country." Weavers, tanners, metal-workers, and
printers plied their respective trades with good success. Sawmills furnished excellent lumber for building purposes, but good bricks were also
made and in Philadelphia and New York brick houses abounded. Mills
were numerous, and the flour they produced was as good as could be
made anywhere in the world.

In commerce the Middle Colonies were not far behind New England,
and the merchants of Philadelphia and New York prospered no less than
those of Boston. Philadelphia, indeed, toward the close of
Commerce   the colonial period came to exceed Boston in size. Grain,
flour, and other provisions were exported in great profusion, mostly to the
West Indies. New York by the middle of the eighteenth century numbered among its items of export no less than eighty thousand barrels of
flour a year. Here the fur trade, which had been greatly fostered by the
Dutch during their control of New Amsterdam, continued under the
English as an important industry and an incentive to commerce. Shipbuilding was a natural accompaniment of overseas trade.

Interior from the seacoast, cutting across the boundaries of every other
section and of most of the colonies, lay the colonial "West" — the fron-

[1] R. M. Tryon, *Household Manufactures in the United States, 1640–1860* (1917).

tier.[1] Its limits were necessarily shifting; indeed, at some time every settled area in America had been frontier. But by the end of the colonial period the "back-country," as the western set- *The frontier* tlements were then generally called, could be marked off fairly distinctly from the rest. In the South the piedmont and mountain valleys, in the Middle Colonies the upper reaches of the Susquehanna, the Delaware, the Mohawk, and their tributaries, in New England much of what is now Vermont, and except for settlements near the coast, of New Hampshire and Maine also, belonged to the frontier. Fur-traders, who almost invariably led the English advance upon the West, cattle-growers, who especially in the South were attracted by the free grazing lands of the interior, and soldiers, who in one or another of the wars against the Indians had seen the western country, revealed the possibilities of the regions they had visited, and presently settlement followed.

Various conditions worked together to promote the rapid expansion of the frontier. Colonial families were large, and the natural increase in population provided many pioneers. The exhaustion of the eastern lands by poor methods of farming, particularly in *Why people* the tobacco-growing areas, provided others. Still others *went West* came from the ranks of the indentured servants, who, once they were free, did not often linger long near the scene of their servitude. Frequently dissenters from the locally approved or established churches of their communities sought homes in the West where they would not be looked down upon because of their religious faith. Immigrants from the Old World, who found themselves unpopular when they tried to settle in the older American communities, turned quickly to the more hospitable frontier. To all who would listen, the call of cheap western lands had an inviting sound. Speculators there were in plenty who acquired for almost nothing great holdings in the West and searched eagerly for settlers to whom they might sell them. But so abundant was the land that those who were too poor or were not too particular need pay little attention to the acquisition of land titles.

The conditions of life along the frontier were hard. Practically all the lands were heavily timbered, and the "clearings" upon which crops could be planted were made possible only through infinite labor. Luxuries were unknown. The pioneer had no money *Frontier* with which to buy them, but even if he had, the difficulty of *conditions* transporting goods from east to west held down such trade *of life* to the barest necessities. Along the "cutting edge" of the frontier, Indians were ever in evidence, and almost never wholly peaceful. Here

[1] F. L. Paxson, *A History of the American Frontier, 1763–1893* (1924), traces chronologically the successive American frontiers.

pioneer families were accustomed to select some well-located farmhouse for a "station," and to build about it a stockade, duly equipped with shelters and storehouses, to which they could flee when an Indian attack seemed imminent. All good frontiersmen were adept with the axe and the rifle. With the former they cut the trees, fashioned the logs of which they built their houses, and smoothed down the planks from which they made benches, tables, and other household necessities. With their rifles they not only fought off the Indians, but also kept the family larder filled, and provided the skins from which many of their garments were made. Each pioneer cabin was apt to be on the farm that the pioneer owned, or hoped to own, and at a considerable distance from any other dwelling. Pioneer life was therefore lonely, particularly for the pioneer housewife, and the opportunities for such privileges as churches and schools were decidedly limited.[1]

The society which was thus established in the back-country differed markedly from that to be found in the older and more settled areas along **Differences** the coast. For one thing, it was extremely cosmopolitan in **between** character. Here English emigrants from the colonial East **frontier** met Pennsylvania Germans, Scotch-Irish, and a variety of **and coast** other foreigners, and not merely met them, but mingled freely with them. The frontier thus became a great "melting-pot" out of which a new and distinctively American race was to come. Furthermore, the frontier settlements, cutting across colonial lines as they did, tended to break down local peculiarities and to lay the foundations of a truly national point of view. Geographic considerations greatly favored this process, for the mountain valleys from Pennsylvania down lay parallel to the coast, and access to them was difficult except at favored points. In North Carolina not only mountains, but eighty miles of pine barrens also, separated the frontier outposts from the settled areas. Population entered the mountains mainly from Pennsylvania, and, spreading slowly southward, presented everywhere the same characteristics, often in striking contrast with the institutions and the traditions that bound the colonists who lived closer in toward the coast.

The genuine equality of conditions that existed among the frontiersmen bred a vigorous spirit of democracy. One man could not by the very nature of pioneer life be particularly above his neigh-**Frontier** bors. He owned about the same amount of land, lived in **democracy** the same kind of house, worked with the same primitive tools, dressed in the same crude fashion as his fellows. If he possessed

[1] Archibald Henderson, *Conquest of the Old Southwest, 1740–1800* (1920); Constance Lindsay Skinner, *Pioneers of the Old Southwest* (1921).

education it was not important in the West. If he had illustrious ancestors he might as well forget them, for his neighbors surely would. If
on the other hand his ancestors were unpleasant to remember, or if he
himself had a past, those were things, too, that could easily be put out
of mind.

This emphasis upon democracy in the West was paralleled by an
equally marked emphasis upon individual freedom. Each pioneer was
practically a law unto himself, and he came to set high store
by the privilege which the wilderness gave him of managing   Individualism
his own affairs in any way he chose. The interference by government in
anything that seemed to him his own business was apt to be met by
wrathful opposition. He objected to hampering regulations with regard
to the acquisition of land, and he resented bitterly every attempt to impose upon him a religious establishment to which he did not subscribe.
The Scotch-Irish, so many of whom found their way to the West, added
a contentious note to frontier individualism. They or their ancestors
had argued as well as fought for their rights both in Scotland and in
Ireland, and the habit of mind so developed was not lost by migration to
America.

The contrasts between the people of the back-country and the people
of the coast led inevitably to some antagonisms.[1] Men of the East still
valued class distinctions and were careful to safeguard the   Antagonism
rights of property. Men of the West had foresworn aris-   between back-
tocracy, and to them the rights of the debtor were no less a   country and
matter of concern than the rights of the creditor. The   coast
strong foreign infusion in the western blood was another source of difficulty. The older elements of society feared that the institutions
they held dear would not be safe in the hands of such people. The
Westerners, on the other hand, saw little significance in racial differences, and resented the suspicions of the East. Differences of
opinion developed also on such matters as religious freedom, the right
to hold slaves, the assessment of taxes, the control of the Indians.
Skeptical of the political wisdom of the backwoodsmen, colonial legislatures under eastern control rarely accorded to the frontier counties their proportionate share of representatives. The echoes of these
conflicts could sometimes be heard as the American Revolution ran its
course.

The lives which American colonials lived seem slow and humdrum in

---

[1] An early example of antagonism between the frontier and the coast is "Bacon's Rebellion" (1676) in Virginia, which was instigated by the indifference of the eastern-con-
trolled colonial legislature to the Indian problem of the back-country. T. J. Wertenbaker,
Torchbearer of the Revolution: The Story of Bacon's Rebellion and Its Leader (1940).

comparison with the lives of Americans today.[1] Transportation was difficult. The colonies were at least six weeks from Europe,

Everyday life in the colonies

and often, with contrary winds, the passage was longer.
The coast towns communicated with one another most easily by sea; indeed, the Atlantic Ocean and the navigable
rivers which emptied into it furnished perhaps the strongest of the ties
that bound the colonies together. Even so, coastwise travel was far from
speedy and sometimes it was far from safe. Roads existed between the
principal cities, but elsewhere they were rare, and usually they were incredibly bad. Not a single hard-surfaced turnpike could be found anywhere in the colonies. By the middle of the eighteenth century horse-
drawn carriages and stage-coaches were in common use, although travel
by horseback was still very popular. At convenient distances taverns
and inns of a sort could be found where the travelers found lodging and
where local patrons found diversion. These inns were in a sense the
social clubs of the time. Here, often amidst much drinking and gambling, but unhampered by the hurry and bustle of modern life and the
noise of traffic and factories, public opinion took form.

[1] For entertaining reading on this subject the books by Alice Morse Earle are unsurpassed. See, for example, her *Colonial Dames and Goodwives* (1895); *Customs and Fashions
in Old New England* (1896); *Colonial Days in Old New York* (1896); *Stage-Coach and Tavern
Days* (1901); *Home Life in Colonial Days* (1898).

COLONIAL LIFE

*All colonial harbors, like Charleston, South Carolina, here shown, were busy
places. The American colonies, both in the seventeenth and in the eighteenth centuries, faced definitely toward the Atlantic. They were deeply conscious of their
close connection with Europe and regarded the ocean that separated the two continents less as a barrier than as a highway. Across the ocean in ships of many patterns came the products of the Old World, products that in many cases the New World
must have to live. Back across the ocean in the same ships went the commodities that
colonial producers had to sell: fish, tobacco, lumber, rum, and so forth. This trade
was basic in the economic life of the colonies and was more important to most of them
than the coastal trade between them, which also existed. (From "Scenographia
America, Or A Collection of Views in North America and the West Indies," from
Drawings Taken on the Spot by Several Officers of the British Navy and Army [Lon-
don, 1758].)*

*In early colonial houses the kitchen was usually the largest and most important
room. It served also as dining room, living room, and frequently as bedroom, all
combined. Since stoves were lacking, the fireplace, flanked by cooking utensils and
surmounted by the inevitable fowling-piece, dominated the scene. (Photo from
Culver.)*

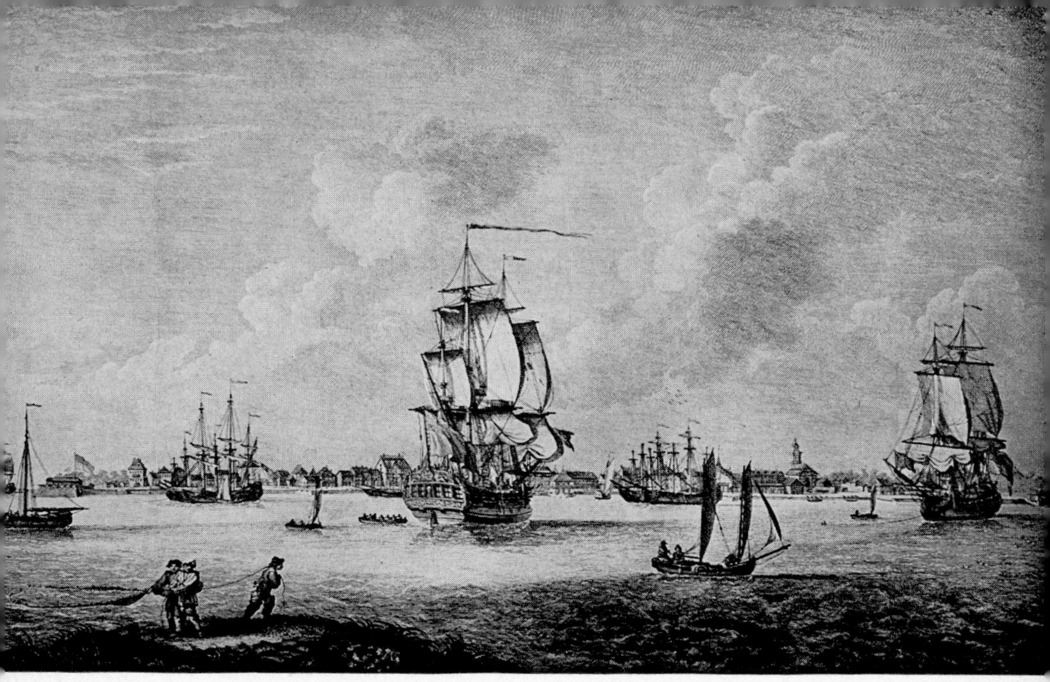

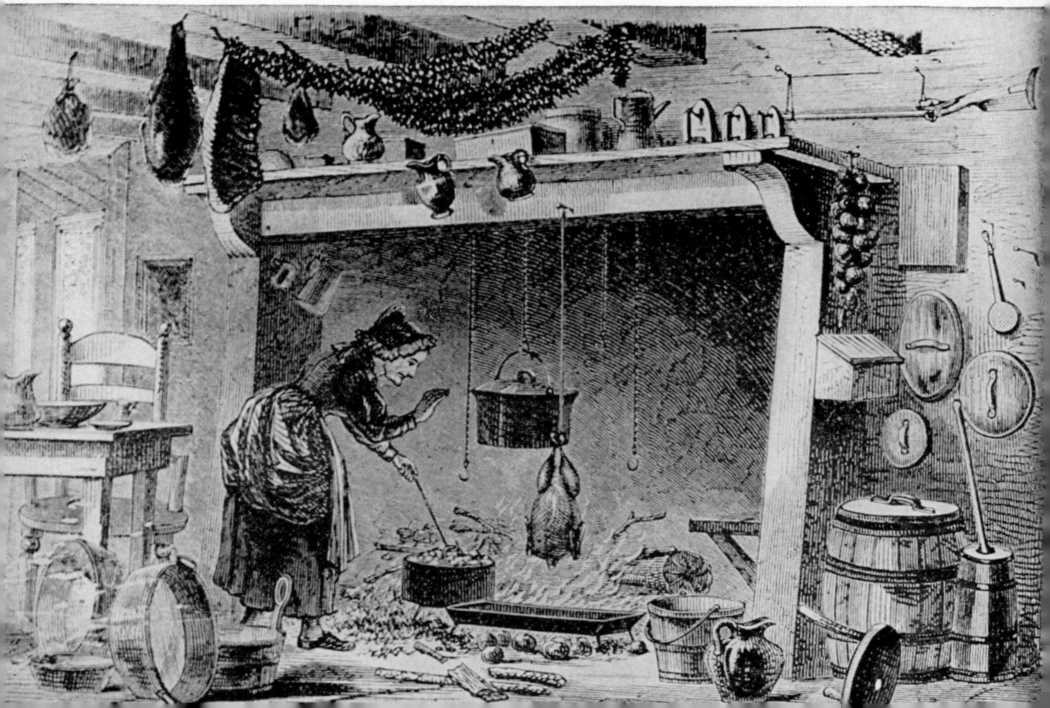

The houses in which colonial citizens lived had progressed from the crude thatch-roofed affairs of wattle or planks stood on end, used by the earliest settlers, to roomy dwellings usually of Georgian design. In the seventeenth century the imprint of Dutch, Swedish, and German as well as English architectural ideas could be discerned in various parts of America, but after about 1720 the Georgian, or as it is now generally termed "colonial," style won its way into every section, except perhaps, the frontier, where log houses were well-nigh universal. Glass windows replaced oiled paper at about the same time, and among the well-to-do merchants of the North and the great planters of the South there was much striving after good architectural effects. The houses were mostly rectangular two-storied affairs, built usually of wood, painted white, with green shutters. Sometimes, especially in New England, where the snows were deep in winter, outbuildings were attached to the main house one after another in a long procession. A little before the time of the American Revolution tall-columned porticoes, such as Washington's home at Mount Vernon possessed, became very popular. Houses of stone and brick were also common, and numerous chimneys, made necessary because of the many fireplaces, broke the roof-lines. Churches, in much the same style as the houses except for their tall spires, were everywhere abundant.

Colonial houses

COLONIAL HOUSES

Washington's residence at Mount Vernon, William Penn's brick house in Philadelphia, and the garrison house from York, Maine, illustrate the varied ways of life in the colonies.

In garrison houses, the second floor overhung the first so that defenders could pour hot pitch and grease on the enemy below. This garrison house was built about 1660 by a Scot who had come to America as an indentured servant. During King William's War, in an attack on York in 1692 in which a hundred settlers were killed and scalped and eighty others taken prisoner, this house, which was probably surrounded by a stockade, was defended successfully against the French and Indians. (Photo by Hanson and Walsh.)

Penn's house, built in the late seventeenth or early eighteenth century, was the first brick house in Philadelphia, but two-story brick houses soon abounded there. (Photo by Wallace.)

Mount Vernon on the Potomac, like many southern plantations, was a village in itself. Spinning, weaving, tailoring, shoemaking, milling, distilling, brickmaking, carpentering, blacksmithing, wagonmaking, and shipbuilding were all done on the premises. Washington, who aspired to be the first farmer of America, owned 250 slaves and 500 sheep, 200 oxen, 150 cows, and 150 horses. The tall-columned portico at Mount Vernon is typical of Georgian colonial architecture. (Photo by Brown Brothers.)

Within the most sumptuous of the houses, however, there were few conveniences, judged by present-day standards. The fireplaces rarely provided enough heat for comfort in severe winter weather,

Lack of conveniences

adequate screening against flies and insects in summer was impossible, and such items as cookstoves, refrigerators, bathtubs, and plumbing were totally unknown. Water was obtained from springs or surface wells that were easily contaminated, and this accounted for much of the disease common in colonial times. Candles usually furnished light at night, although whale-oil lamps were not uncommon in fashionable circles. Food was obtainable everywhere in great abundance and even in the cities at low prices, but often the fare was severely plain. Corn bread, hominy, and salt pork furnished the chief items of subsistence for the poorer classes, particularly in the South. Whiskey, beer, hard cider, and rum were manufactured locally and were available in great profusion, but only the upper classes could afford the finer wines and brandies that had to be imported.

The colonial cities compared fairly favorably with cities of similar size in Europe. Philadelphia was built on a plan worked out by William

Colonial cities

Penn, with wide paved streets, crossing one another at right angles. Here the houses were mostly of brick, and sometimes they were as many as three stories in height. Sidewalks were plentiful, and street lamps made the lot of the night traveler easy. Both Boston and New York were noted for their general planlessness and their narrow crooked streets, but some of the more important streets in both cities were paved, and they were usually kept clean. Charleston, as the favorite resort of the South Carolina planters, enjoyed a lively social life not found elsewhere; but its method of garbage disposal was primitive, for buzzards were here protected by law as necessary scavengers. In all the cities ashes and garbage were dumped into alleys and on vacant lots, and in most of them hogs running at large in the streets served the purpose expected of the buzzards of Charleston. Sanitary conditions were bad, and the resultant prevalence of disease was little checked by the physicians that the times afforded. Bleeding was still in common use, and the herbs and drugs prescribed were of dubious value. Shortly before the outbreak of the American Revolution medical colleges were opened, one in New York and one in Philadelphia. These were the first of their kind in the colonies. Since commerce was the chief concern of all the colonial cities, the noise attendant upon modern industrial life was wholly lacking. Creaking carts loaded with merchandise were perhaps the chief offenders against the ear.

Attendance on church, public meetings, "Thursday lectures" (mostly theological) in New England, and in the less strait-laced communities

dances and theaters furnished a large share of the amusement the people
were permitted to enjoy.   Lavish hospitality was a point
of honor with the southern planters, and the constant visit- Amusements
ing back and forth made life for the younger generation a succession
of what today might be called house-parties.   Dancing was a favorite
amusement with all classes in the South, and despite the frowns of the
godly was a common pastime nearly everywhere.   Theaters existed in
the larger cities only, but by the time of the Revolution the American
stage was definitely established.   Gambling, horse-racing, cock-fighting,
and fox-hunting were major activities with the young bloods, especially
in the South, but lotteries to raise money for churches, public works, and
even college endowments were conducted without censure in Puritan
New England, and were in especial favor with the clergy.   Out in the
rural districts, particularly along the frontier, "log-rollings," house-
raisings, husking bees, weddings, and funerals furnished relief from the
ordinary tedium of life.   Courtship was officially surrounded with many
hampering conventions that have since been wholly eliminated, but the
habit of marriage was strong with the colonials, and ways seem to have
been found.   Bachelors and widowers were under great social pressure to
marry, and sometimes laws which discriminated against the unmarried
were added to the incentive of public opinion.

There was no such thing as a colonial nobility — even among the
Cavaliers who came to America there were very few of noble birth —
but throughout the colonial period there was a well-recog-
nized aristocracy which held itself definitely above the   The colonial
aristocracy
common run of men.   To this class belonged most of the
English officials resident in America, the ministers and magistrates, the
well-to-do merchants, the owners of great estates in the central colonies,
and the great planters of the South.   Members of the aristocracy sought
to distinguish themselves from the lower classes by their manners, their
superior education, and particularly their mode of dress.   Indeed, during
early colonial times laws were actually passed in some colonies forbidding
"men and women of mean condition" to "take upon them the garb of
gentlemen."   Wealthy men wore silk stockings, breeches of velvet, silk,
or other expensive goods, and frock coats made of imported broadcloth
and richly trimmed.   Wigs were also quite generally affected during the
eighteenth century.   The colonial dames were likewise gorgeous with
dresses of costly silks, duly amplified by the use of hoopskirts.   The garb
of the lower classes more closely resembled the garments universally worn
today.   Homespun fabrics were in general use, although on the frontier
the men preferred leather jackets and breeches.   The slow breakdown of
class distinctions reflects the essential conservatism of the people who

emigrated to America. They were accustomed to caste lines in Europe, and they naturally brought to the New World what they had known in the Old. Ultimately the equality of opportunity in America, well emphasized by the existence of cheap lands along the frontier, tended to wipe out artificial class barriers. But even the aristocratic mode of dress lasted for many years after the Revolution.

Intellectual interests were for the most part confined to the upper classes. Newspapers, however, had come into vogue during the eighteenth century, and on the eve of the American Revolution they were widely read. Books were far from numerous, although among the great planters of the South it was quite the fashion to have a library. Libraries of a semi-public nature also existed, strangely enough more in the South than in the North. Benjamin Franklin was instrumental in establishing in 1731 the first public library of Philadelphia, an example that was quickly followed in other northern towns and cities. Light literature was virtually unknown, and books on theology and law such as Calvin's *Institutes*, Blackstone's *Commentaries*, Locke's *Treatises on Government*, and Montesquieu's *Spirit of the Laws* had a wider appeal than would seem reasonable today. The Bible was everywhere read with much diligence.

Intellectual interests

Although literary achievement was not yet within the reach of most Americans, the intense theological interest of New England had not failed to produce visible results. Probably the most able of the theological writers was Jonathan Edwards (1703–1758), whose expositions of Calvinistic doctrines rivaled in logic and lucidity the works of Calvin himself. Edwards was the only son of a learned Connecticut clergyman, who himself prepared his boy for college. Jonathan turned out to be unusually precocious, and at fourteen read Locke's *Essay on Human Understanding* with unfeigned delight. He was among the first to attend Yale College, where Newtonian science also made a profound impression upon him. Graduated from Yale in 1720, he was soon hard at work as a Congregational minister, proclaiming and expounding the Calvinistic doctrines that his soul had learned to love. Predestination, which once had appeared to him a "horrible doctrine," quickly won his intense admiration. As Edwards saw it, the right to bestow salvation wherever He chose was an essential attribute of divine sovereignty. No man could paint more clearly the dire vengeance that was to overtake the damned, or make less promising the prospect of being saved, yet he set greater store than the earlier theologians on the importance of the individual, and became the foremost American preacher of the "Great Awakening," a religious movement that spread from Europe to America in the middle of the eighteenth

Jonathan Edwards

century.[1] He was a successful revivalist, and counted his converts by the scores.

Edwards lived a life of great austerity. He rose at four o'clock each morning, studied and wrote thirteen hours each day, and even when he sought recreation by walks through the woods carried with him a notebook in which he jotted down his thoughts. He wrote many books, most of which had long theological titles. In 1754 he published *A Careful and Strict Enquiry into the Modern Prevailing Notions of that Freedom of Will which is Supposed to be Essential to Moral Agency, Vertue and Vice, Reward and Punishment, Praise and Blame.* On this work rests much of his fame as a philosopher. Shortly before his death he accepted the presidency of the Presbyterian College at Princeton, New Jersey, but his period of office was too short for him to make a profound impression upon that institution.

More palatable to present-day readers are the writings of Benjamin Franklin (1706–90),[2] who, in the opinion of many historians, ranks as the first American of his time. Franklin's span of life, like Edwards's, lay entirely within the eighteenth century, and **Benjamin Franklin** his keen zest for living contrasts markedly with the otherworldliness of the great Puritan theologian. Franklin was a Bostonian by birth, and for several years attended a Boston grammar school. His father was a tallow chandler, but since Benjamin had no liking for that trade he was apprenticed when twelve years of age to his half-brother James, a printer. Before long the apprentice was mainly responsible for the publication by his brother of a newspaper known as the *New England Courant*, which was so indiscreet in what it printed that in 1722 James was jailed for a month. Shortly afterward Benjamin left his brother's employ and went to Philadelphia. Here he established himself as a printer of merit, and in due time began to publish much that he himself had written. His *Poor Richard's Almanack*, which appeared from 1732 to 1757, presented in homely garb the wise sayings of all the ages, and won almost universal acclaim in America as well as wide recognition in Europe. The *Pennsylvania Gazette*, with which Franklin was long associated, furnished another outlet for his pen, and it was here that some of his earliest scientific observations were set down. He was interested in a

---

[1] George Whitefield, an English Methodist, who visited America about this time, helped spread the revival throughout the colonies. An excellent sketch of Edwards's life, by Francis A. Christie, is in the *Dictionary of American Biography*, VI. This work, edited by Allen Johnson and Dumas Malone (1928), provides in twenty volumes short biographies of practically every American of consequence. See also Ola E. Winslow, *Jonathan Edwards, 1703–1758* (1940).

[2] Benjamin Franklin has been a favorite of biographers. Among the best of the many studies of his life are the following: C. C. Van Doren, *Benjamin Franklin* (1938); Bernard Faÿ, *Franklin, the Apostle of Modern Times* (1929); W. C. Bruce, *Benjamin Franklin Self-Revealed* (2 vols., 1918).

great variety of natural phenomena, but won recognition as a scientist chiefly through his experiments with electricity.

Franklin wrote only one book, his *Autobiography*, and it was never finished, but his numerous occasional articles, written in a severely plain, yet remarkably effective style, made him easily the literary leader of America. Franklin was not merely a writer, but lived an exceedingly full life. He was interested in business, he had a remarkable flair for inaugurating or helping along such projects as appeared likely to improve the lot of his fellow-men, he was many times called upon for political service, and he spent years together on various errands abroad. He wrote only when he had some definite purpose to serve by his writing, but perhaps this is one of the reasons why he wrote so well.[1]

[1] The subject matter of this chapter has attracted much attention of recent years. An outstanding study on the roots of American culture is Carl Bridenbaugh, *Cities in the Wilderness: The First Century of Urban Life in America, 1625–1742* (1938). Carl and Jessica Bridenbaugh, *Rebels and Gentlemen: Philadelphia in the Age of Franklin* (1942), reveals the social handicaps of the common man. On the rise of colonial civilization see also T. J. Wertenbaker, *The Golden Age of Colonial Culture* (1942), and by the same author, *The Old South: The Founding of American Civilization* (1942). On religion, W. W. Sweet, *Religion in Colonial America* (1942). On the later immigrants, A. D. Graeff and others, *The Pennsylvania Germans* (1942); W. F. Dunaway, *The Scotch Irish of Colonial Pennsylvania* (1944).

3

England and her Colonies

CONTRARY to a common conception, not many of the colonists came to the New World with unique political ideas and a burning desire to set up new forms of government. They came, for the most part, from the British Isles; they were familiar, or at least their leaders were familiar, with the British type of government; and in their various attempts to solve the problems that soon confronted them they sought merely to adapt to new world conditions the institutions which they already knew.

At the time the colonies were founded the English government presented a far better example of the separation of powers than it does to-day. The King, in whom extensive executive authority was vested, claimed to rule by "divine right." With the advice of a "Privy Council" consisting of from twenty to forty high officials, he kept an eye on all the affairs of the realm, and sometimes issued orders that were almost as much legislative as executive in character. The principal law-making body, however, was Parliament, which consisted of two houses, the House of Lords and the House of Commons. Membership in the former was based on heredity or high ecclesiastical office, but the latter was supposed to represent the common people of the realm. Each shire, or county, was entitled to two members in the Commons, and some three hundred towns elected one or two members each. This distribution of seats was historic merely, and many great cities were left wholly without representation while "rotten boroughs" with practically no inhabitants whatever sometimes returned two members. Although the suffrage ruthlessly excluded also most of the non-propertied classes, Parliament represented in theory "all the men of England," and its right to a voice in the levying of taxes and the making of all important laws was generally conceded. A third department of government consisted of the national courts of justice. All judicial officers were appointed directly by the King, but they were guided in their decisions not only by statute law but also by the precedents and principles of the common law. Such rights as trial by jury and freedom from arbitrary arrest they defended stoutly, and in general they maintained their independence of both King and Parliament.

Such was the government with which the colonists were familiar when they established themselves in America; and such was the model after which their governments were patterned. The colonial governments, however, were not all alike.[1] Some of the colonies operated under charters of incorporation that were little constitutions in themselves, and were therefore often spoken of as "corporate" colonies; others had proprietors into whose hands governmental authority had been placed, and were usually called "proprietary" colonies; still others were under the direct supervision of the English government, and were called "royal" colonies. But the influence of the English pattern was strong in each case, and the types of government instituted in America did not differ so much from one another as the names used to describe them would seem to indicate.

The colonial governments

Indeed, government in the colonies, under whatever name, came everywhere to follow closely the English model. A single executive, corresponding to the King, a two-house legislature, corresponding to Parliament, and a judicial system, less pretentious and less complicated than the courts of England but roughly on the same plan, appeared in every colony. Colonial citizens, moreover, enjoyed the same personal rights as Englishmen that would have been their privilege in the mother country, rights that were not enjoyed in like measure by the colonists of any other nation.

It was natural that many Americans should come to think of the colonies as practically separate and independent units of the British Empire, but English officials generally looked upon the colonial foundations as mere dependencies of the English government which were entitled to the privileges they enjoyed only by its sufferance. It was quite in harmony with the English view, therefore, to suppose that the colonies should be subject to such regulations on the part of the mother country as the home government chose to establish. But for many reasons a definite policy of colonial control was slow to develop. The English government lacked experience in dealing with colonies; the American colonies were practically the first of the kind it had ever had. Moreover, during much of the seventeenth century English governmental machinery was itself in bad order. The attempts of the early Stuarts to expand the royal prerogative were bitterly resisted by Parliament, and for many years

British view of colonial governments

[1] The constitutional aspects of colonial development receive elaborate treatment in the volumes by H. L. Osgood, *The American Colonies in the Seventeenth Century* (3 vols. 1904–07) and *The American Colonies in the Eighteenth Century* (4 vols., 1924–25). Channing, I, II, are also excellent.

the boundaries between the rights of the King and the rights of Parliament in respect to colonial affairs were in heated dispute. The existence of civil war in England during much of this period also paralyzed such feeble efforts at control as the English authorities attempted. The colonies were thus left free during the formative period to work out their destinies in their own way with a minimum of outside interference.

With the restoration of the Stuarts to the throne of England in 1660 it was possible to give more definite attention to the colonial problem.[1] A group of administrative experts was assembled, known at first as the Council for Foreign Plantations, but later, with its membership somewhat altered, as the Lords of Trade or the Board of Trade and Plantations. This body was authorized to inquire into colonial affairs and to recommend to Parliament and to the Privy Council such legislation and such administrative policies as it saw fit. The Board took its duties seriously, for a time at least, and soon began to suggest ways by which the colonies might be used to make England independent of other nations, both in staple products and in markets. While never able to carry its theories into full effect, the Board of Trade wished to make England the hub and center of a self-sufficient empire. It recommended that the colonists should preferably sell all their products to England; they should, if they could, buy from England or through England only; they must not devote themselves to manufacturing, since that was England's interest; they must always be required to seek, not merely their own individual good, but rather the common imperial good.

Efforts to establish control

The much-discussed Navigation Acts were passed by Parliament as a part of this policy, and not for the purpose of vexing the American colonists. The first of these measures, passed in 1660, repeated in part the provisions of a similar law enacted during the Protectorate, and had as its primary purpose the encouragement of English shipping. England needed a large navy, and in time of war merchant ships could easily be converted into warships. The First Navigation Act required therefore that only English or colonial-owned ships with English captains and crews three-fourths English might engage in the colonial trade. A little later it was further stipulated that the ships must also be built in England or the colonies (not including Ireland). These provisions were not seriously damaging to the colonists. Temporarily there was some shortage of ships, and

The Navigation Acts

---

[1] On this subject see G. L. Beer, *Commercial Policy of England towards the American Colonies* (1893) and *The Old Colonial System, 1660–1754* (2 vols., 1912). For a somewhat different point of view see L. A. Harper, *The Navigation Laws* (1939).

freight rates rose, but there was compensation in the fact that the law tended to stimulate the shipping interests in the colonies quite as much as in the mother country; furthermore, Parliament remained deaf to all English pleas that this colonial competition be eliminated.

The First Navigation Act also contained a list of "enumerated articles" — sugar, tobacco, cotton-wool, indigo, ginger, dye-woods —
that might be sold only to England or to another colony.

Enumerated articles

This list was later expanded, but for the time being it contained only one item, tobacco, that seriously affected the continental colonies. Moreover, the intent of the English government to benefit the colonies as well as the mother country was indicated by the fact that the growing of tobacco in England, and the purchase of tobacco from foreign countries for use in England, were forbidden.

The Second Navigation Act, passed in 1663, affected the continental colonies decidedly more than did the earlier law. It provided that most
imports from Europe to the colonies must pass through England. This was designed to prevent the trade and the products of the colonies from passing to other countries,

Second Navigation Act

although by resort to smuggling the colonists managed to minimize the restrictions. It was supposed, too, that the profits of English merchants would be somewhat enhanced by the routing of foreign goods through England. Duties, both import and export, were charged by the English government, but an elaborate system of rebates, or drawbacks, enabled the colonists to buy foreign goods through England about as cheaply as Englishmen themselves could buy them. Some items, for example Dutch and German linens, the colonists, thanks to the rebates, could buy even more cheaply than could Englishmen.

The Third Navigation Act, otherwise known as the Plantation Duty Act, was passed in 1672 (effective 1673), and was meant to bear directly
upon the colonists. There had been much evasion of the law requiring the "enumerated articles" to be shipped only to England or to another colony. Colonial shipmasters

Third Navigation Act

carried such goods from one colony to another, perhaps across the Potomac from Virginia to Maryland, then, deeming the law fulfilled, shipped the goods where they chose. The Third Navigation Act required that a duty equal to the English basic duty should be collected *in the colonies* unless the ship captain would bind himself to carry the cargo to England. This law meant the appointment of a considerable number of colonial collectors who were directly responsible to the English commissioner of customs. These officials soon made themselves obnoxious to the colonists not only because of the energetic efforts they made to enforce the law, but also because of the constant complaints they registered with their English superiors on the unwillingness of the Americans to co-operate with them. Perhaps the most unpopular of the English collectors was Edward Randolph, who headed the imperial customs service in New England. If the law was not fully observed, it was hardly his fault.

This tendency on the part of the colonists to pay attention to the British regulations only when they chose to do so was in large part responsible for a very determined effort on the part of James II and his advisers to reform the colonial govern- **Efforts to** ments. The attitude of New England, whose elected of- **discipline** ficials made little or no effort to enforce the disagreeable **the colonies** laws, was regarded as particularly reprehensible. Finally the Board of Trade and Plantations brought suit for the annulment of the Massachusetts charter, and in 1684 won its case. The way now lay open for a series of radical reforms. In the interest of efficient imperial control royal colonies were to supplant corporate or proprietary colonies, small colonies were to be consolidated with their larger neighbors, and royal officials — governors and councillors — were to have their duties enlarged and their powers strengthened. These changes, it was supposed, would be of material assistance, also, in solving the problem of colonial defense.

Between 1684 and 1688 the policy of colonial consolidation went on so rapidly that by the last-mentioned year the eight northernmost colonies had been thrown together into one, the "Territory and Dominion of New England," with Sir Edmund Andros at **Dominion of** its head. All the New England colonies — Massachusetts, **New England** New Hampshire, Plymouth, Rhode Island, and Connecticut — were included in the combination, and in addition New York, East New Jersey, and West New Jersey. Colonial assemblies were abolished, quitrents were demanded of the owners of land, taxes were levied without the consent of any representative body, and religious worship according to the rites of the Anglican Church was given official encouragement.

These drastic changes, enforced as they were by a stubborn and tactless governor, would doubtless have led to revolt in the colonies had there been no "Glorious Revolution" in England. But the efforts of James II to free himself from the control **The Glorious** of Parliament had aroused as deep resentment in the mother **Revolution** country as the arbitrary acts of Andros had aroused in America. In 1688, without bloodshed and almost by common consent, James was deprived of his royal rights, and by act of Parliament William and Mary of the Netherlands were invited to mount the throne of England as joint sovereigns. James II fled with his family to France, and the kings of England thereafter owed their title to the throne solely to the will of the English people as expressed in Parliament. To leave no doubt in the matter this doctrine was presently recorded in the famous Bill of Rights and also in the Act of Settlement, passed in 1701. As for the pretentious "Dominion of New England," it promptly collapsed, and Andros was thrown into prison.[1]

When the English government was free to turn its attention once more to America, it abandoned the principle of consolidation, which James II had so strongly favored, but it did not hesitate to establish royal colonies in preference to any other type wherever that could conveniently be done. New Hampshire was again cut off from Massachusetts, and given a royal governor. Massachusetts was given a new charter (1691), according to which the governor was appointed by the crown instead of being elected by the people as formerly. Connecticut and Rhode Island were allowed to keep their old charters, but the Plymouth Bay Colony and the settlements in Maine were now joined to Massachusetts. In New York, where a popular leader named Leisler had seized control, the revolt was suppressed by English troops, and a royal governor reinstalled. Maryland became a royal colony with a Protestant governor, and the rights of the pro-prietor were not restored until 1715. Penn's friendship with the fallen Stuarts was held against him, and in 1692 Pennsylvania became a royal colony with the governor of New York at its head. Two years later, however, Penn got back the rights he had lost. For the time being the Jerseys, since they were regarded as of small consequence anyway, were left to their proprietors, but in 1702 they were united as the royal colony of New Jersey, although until 1738 they had the same governor as New York.

Governmental changes

These changes in America registered far less progress toward democracy than can be credited to the Glorious Revolution in England. In the mother country before many years the English King reigned, but ministers, responsible to Parliament rather than to the King, really ruled. For America, however, no such transformation was in sight. It made little difference whether royal governors were appointed on the recommendation of the English ministers or at the whim of the English monarch. In either event the source of authority lay entirely outside the colony, and the right of the people to control their executive was denied.

The following diagram will perhaps make clearer the contrast between the English and the American results of the Revolution of 1688:

[1] Viola F. Barnes, *The Dominion of New England* (1923), covers this subject admirably.

THE ENGLISH AND THE AMERICAN GOVERNMENTS

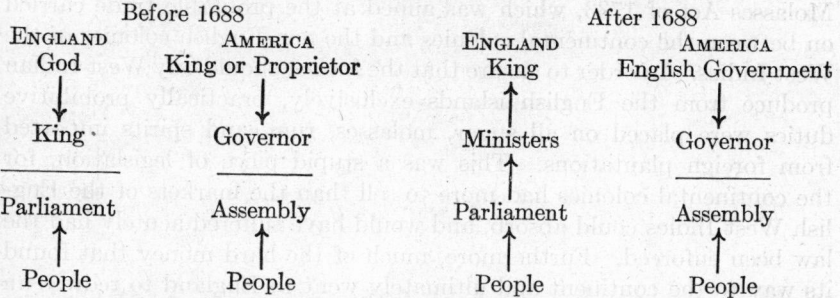

Before 1688		After 1688	
ENGLAND	AMERICA	ENGLAND	AMERICA
God	King or Proprietor	King	English Government
↓	↓	↓	↓
King	Governor	Ministers	Governor
↑	↑	↑	↑
Parliament	Assembly	Parliament	Assembly
↑	↑	↑	↑
People	People	People	People

Neither did the Glorious Revolution mean any abatement of the English determination to control the trade of the colonies in the interest of the mother country and of the Empire as a whole.[1] Indeed, the Navigation Act of 1696 was designed to make more effective than ever before the enforcement of the three Navigation Acts passed during the reign of Charles II. According to the law of 1696 all colonial governors, whether royal governors or not, must take a strong oath to enforce the English regulations, and in case they failed to do so, or failed to live up to their oaths, they were made liable to heavy fine and removal from office. Governors not directly appointed by the crown had to receive the King's approval — a difficult requirement for the self-governing colonies to meet. Provisions were also made for tightening up the colonial customs service, and colonial laws out of harmony with the acts of trade were declared null and void. Furthermore, after the passage of this act admiralty courts were established in the colonies to enforce the English regulations. Inasmuch as these courts were patterned after the Roman law, they were not embarrassed by the necessity of holding jury trials; hence colonial juries, ever a source of irritation in the enforcement of English law in America, could be avoided.

Another Navigation Act

The determination to enforce commercial regulations upon the colonies continued unabated during the early years of the eighteenth century. The list of enumerated articles was lengthened by the addition of rice, molasses, naval stores, ship timbers, copper, and beaver skins. Even non-enumerated articles might not be sent to Ireland or Scotland except after payment of the regular import duties in England. Colonists were forbidden to carry wool, or articles manufactured of wool, from one colony to an-

New regulations for colonial trade

[1] O. M. Dickerson, *American Colonial Government, 1696–1765: A Study of the Board of Trade in its Relation to the American Colonies* (1912). See also the excellent study by W. T. Root, *The Relations of Pennsylvania with the British Government, 1696–1765* (1912).

other. But the most unpalatable of all such measures, however, was the Molasses Act of 1733, which was aimed at the profitable trade carried on between the continental colonies and the non-English colonies of the West Indies. In order to ensure that the former should buy West Indian produce from the English islands exclusively, practically prohibitive duties were placed on all sugar, molasses, rum, and spirits imported from foreign plantations. This was a stupid piece of legislation, for the continental colonies had more to sell than the markets of the English West Indies could absorb, and would have suffered acutely had the law been enforced. Furthermore, much of the hard money that found its way to the continent and ultimately went to England to redress an unfavorable balance of trade came from the foreign West Indies, and thus English traders and manufacturers stood a good chance to lose should the law be enforced. But as a matter of fact the Molasses Act did little harm, for from the date of its passage it was cheerfully ignored.

In various other ways, also, the English government undertook to control the behavior of the colonies. Manufacturing, it was assumed,
Other efforts at control — could best be done in England, and colonial manufactures were therefore discouraged. A law of 1732, for example, placed a limit upon the number of apprentices that colonial hat makers might employ, and a law of 1750 undertook to restrict the right of the colonists to manufacture iron goods. Paper-money issues by colonial legislatures were severely frowned upon, and excesses along this line were prohibited either by law of Parliament or by disallowance of the colonial laws involved.[1] For the latter purpose royal governors were instructed to veto or to suspend such colonial enactments as might run counter to English policy, and the Privy Council reserved for itself a further veto, which was exercised usually only on recommendation of the Board of Trade. Appeals were also taken from colonial courts to the Privy Council, and many colonial laws as a result of this process were finally set aside. Since royal governors were more easily controlled than those chosen by proprietors or by the people there was a constant tendency to eliminate as many proprietary and self-governing colonies as possible. Misgovernment in the Carolinas gave an excuse to withdraw the privileges of the proprietors there in 1728, whereupon both colonies received royal governors. When Georgia became a royal colony in 1751, there were left of the corporate colonies only Connecticut and Rhode Island, and of the proprietorships only the holdings of the Penns in Pennsylvania and Delaware, and of the current Lord Baltimore in Maryland.

---

[1] C. P. Nettels, *The Money Supply of the American Colonies before 1720* (1934), is a work of great merit.

It must not be supposed, however, that English interference in American affairs was entirely one-sided. Sometimes, as in the case of indigo, which received a generous bounty, English legislation gave special favors to the colonies. When naval stores and ship timbers were placed on the enumerated list, bounties were made available to encourage their production.

Privileges accorded the colonies

Colonial agents, among whom the most notable was Benjamin Franklin, appeared in England to lobby against proposed Parliamentary measures that might be damaging to American interests, and to argue the American case when a dispute came before the Board of Trade. Colonial governors, even when they were appointed from England, tended to place a high valuation upon American public opinion, and to interpret unpopular obligations as narrowly as possible. The fact that in most cases they were paid out of money appropriated by a colonial assembly also kept them fairly respectful of the will of the people they governed. Even the English revenue-collectors sometimes absorbed the American point of view. Many Americans could see, too, that the protection given to colonial trade by the English navy and by English treaties far more than outweighed the damage suffered by commercial restrictions; and for this protection the Americans were taxed not a cent.

Finally, it should not be forgotten that the English will to maintain restrictions on the colonies often lagged seriously. Sir Robert Walpole, who was the virtual head of the English government for more than two decades (1721–42), believed that more was to be gained for England by encouraging colonial trade

"Salutary neglect"

than by restricting it, since trade of any sort would make the colonies prosperous and better able to buy English goods. This opinion was shared also by the Duke of Newcastle, who had much to do with colonial affairs during Walpole's supremacy, and continued powerful even after Walpole's fall. Indeed, Newcastle's frankly admitted policy of "salutary neglect" was not seriously amended until the close of the French and Indian War.

A clearly understood principle of British colonial policy was that the colonies, in return for such regulation of their trade as the home government might require, could count on the mother country for help whenever they were sorely pressed in meeting their problems of defense. This was a matter of great importance, for the English settlements in America had to deal not only with the constant menace of the Indian frontier, but also with the rival colonial establishments of the Spanish to the south, and the French to the south and west. While the threat of attack from the declining Spanish empire was slight, the danger from the French was often very real. By the middle of the eighteenth century,

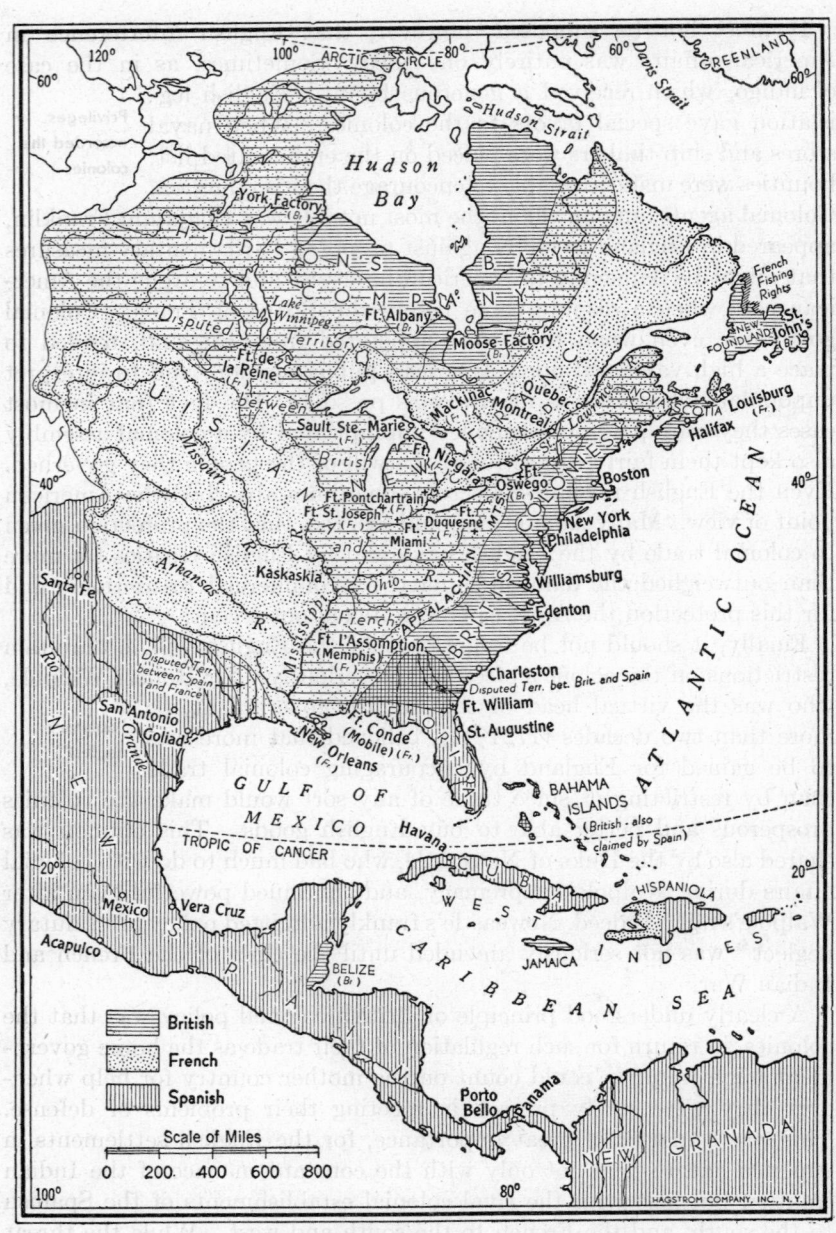

EUROPEAN CLAIMS IN NORTH AMERICA, 1754

indeed, it was clear that a struggle was impending to determine which nation, England or France, should control the interior of the continent. Should the English colonies end at the crests of the Appalachians, with France in possession of the lands beyond? Or should the great Mississippi Basin become the next swarming-place of the English?

The French settlements in North America dated back to 1608, when Samuel de Champlain founded Quebec on the St. Lawrence River.[1] In due time other French settlements appeared at Three Rivers and Montreal, and by the end of the seventeenth New France century French outposts had advanced by way of the Great Lakes and the Mississippi to the Gulf of Mexico. In numbers the French in America, most of whom were concentrated along the St. Lawrence with a few villages in the "Illinois country," were not above eighty thousand in 1750, when the English could count about a million and a half. For the most part, the French habitants came to America, not so much for reasons of their own as because the French government was determined to build up an American colony. Unlike the English Americans, who on the whole were alert and self-reliant, the French were relatively unprogressive, and still in a state of semi-dependence on the mother country. The situation might have been somewhat different had the French government permitted the Huguenots, who were driven from France after the revocation of the Edict of Nantes (1685), to come to Canada. But Roman Catholicism received as much official favor in the New World as in the Old, and many of the exiled French Protestants went instead to swell the stream of immigration into the English colonies.

In many other ways the French colonial foundation in America contrasted markedly with the English. The government of New France, like that of France in Europe, was autocratic, with all power concentrated in the hands of the governor, the intendant, and the bishop. The system of landholding imitated as closely as the proximity of the wilderness would permit the feudal practices to which the French settlers had been accustomed in the Old World. French industries compared most unfavorably with those of their English neighbors. Agriculture was sickly, and fishing was not notably successful. For the bulk of its prosperity, New France relied upon the fur-trade, in which it soon outdistanced the English traders on both sides of the Great Lakes, in the valley of the St. Lawrence, and along the upper Mississippi.

[1] New France was fortunate in having as its historian one of America's most brilliant writers, Francis Parkman, whose *Count Frontenac and New France under Louis XIV* (1877), *A Half-Century of Conflict* (2 vols., 1892), and *Montcalm and Wolfe* (2 vols., 1884) cover the period of rivalry with the English. On early French explorations see Grace Lee Nute, *Caesars of the Wilderness: Medard Chouart, Sieur des Groseilliers, and Pierre Esprit Radisson, 1618–1710* (1943).

In one other matter the French in America possessed a decided advantage over the English. When it came to the problem of defense they
Military efficiency were not embarrassed by a multiplicity of authorities; instead, there was unity of command and unity of action.
Furthermore, the French government expected little military assistance from the colonists themselves, but kept French ships and soldiers available for their protection. The English government, on the other hand, while ready at all times to guard the seas with the English navy, expected the English colonists to take care of land fighting in their own defense, except in case of great emergency. The English army was reserved for use only when the colonists had exerted themselves to the limit, and stood a chance to fail without its help. Nevertheless, events proved that the greater immediate effectiveness of the French military power was not sufficient to outweigh the other notable advantages possessed by the English.[1]

The rivalry between the French and the English, first for European hegemony and then for world empire, lasted many years and involved the two countries in numerous wars. The earlier of these struggles, "King William's War" (1689–97), "Queen Anne's War" (1701–13), and "King George's War" (1744–48), to use the American names for these conflicts, involved no very serious tests of strength, and left the status of French and English rivalry in America relatively unchanged. The final contest, however, the French and Indian War, actually began in America two years before its counterpart, the Seven Years' War, got under way, and it was fought primarily to determine whether the French or the English were to survive in North America.

The struggle for the continent was precipitated by the ambition of some Virginia gentlemen, with whom a few Englishmen were associated,
Rivalry with the English to form a settlement west of the Appalachian Mountains. For this purpose an "Ohio Land Company" was formed, and in 1749 royal consent to a grant of two hundred thousand acres of land below the "forks" of the Ohio was obtained. Next year Christopher Gist, a well-known surveyor and land prospector, was sent out to prepare the way for the coming of settlers, upon whose purchases of lands the company hoped to realize a handsome profit. This project immediately alarmed the French, who recognized at once the peril to their Ohio Valley fur-trade interests in case English settlers were allowed to come in; hence, in 1749 the governor of New France dispatched Céleron de Bienville to the contested area to plant leaden

[1] R. G. Thwaites, *France in America* (1905), is one of the twenty-eight volumes of *The American Nation* series, edited by A. B. Hart. These volumes are still unsurpassed as a general political history of the United States.

plates on which was inscribed the claim of the King of France to the region the English now sought to possess. Indians friendly to the French were induced also to attack Indians friendly to the English, and French forts made their appearance in the disputed area.

When Governor Robert Dinwiddie of Virginia received word from the British government that he was at liberty to "repel force by force," he sent George Washington, then an enterprising youth of twenty-one years, and Christopher Gist to the nearest French outpost to warn the French that they must withdraw from the Ohio Valley. Washington delivered Dinwiddie's ultimatum in the fall of 1753, but the French ignored the warning, and left the Virginians no choice but to back down or prepare for war. Next year Washington was again sent across the mountains, this time with a small detachment of troops designed to aid a British outpost lately established at the "forks of the Ohio." After some pre-

The French warned by Washington

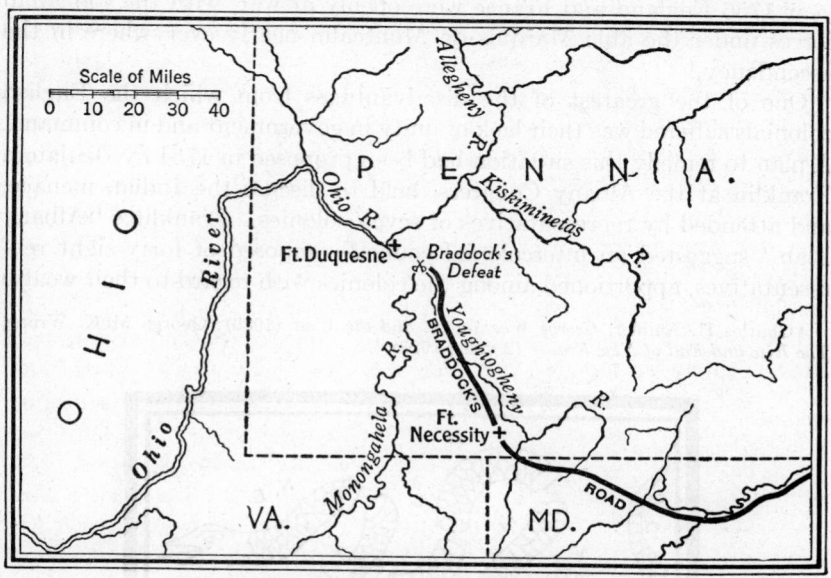

THE FORKS OF THE OHIO

liminary skirmishing, Washington was attacked and defeated at Great Meadows, July 3, 1754, and compelled to withdraw, while the British fort on the Ohio was captured and as Fort Duquesne became the headquarters for further French operations in the West.

These developments clearly marked the beginning of the French and Indian War, but the European governments concerned chose at first to

regard the frontier fighting as merely a local affair, and to postpone a
general war as long as possible. Nevertheless, the British
government soon sent General Edward Braddock with
two regiments of regulars to co-operate with the Virginians
in the capture of Fort Duquesne. With a command of more than two
thousand troops, more than half of whom were colonials, Braddock
worked his way to within about ten miles of Fort Duquesne, where on
July 9, 1755, he met an unexpected, and perhaps undeserved, defeat.
Washington, whom Braddock took along as an aide, complained bitterly
of the halting tactics the British general pursued, but one American
historian has claimed that "Braddock's defeat" might better have been
termed "Braddock's victory," for the road Braddock built became a
highway later on for the English migration that conquered the Ohio
Valley. Braddock himself was mortally wounded in the battle, and for
a long time the frontier fighting went badly with the English. By the
year 1756 England and France were openly at war, with the Canadian
forces under the able Marquis de Montcalm nearly everywhere in the
ascendancy.[1]

French and
Indian War

One of the greatest of the disadvantages from which the English
colonials suffered was their lack of unity in government and in command.
A plan to remedy this situation had been proposed in 1754 by Benjamin
Franklin at the Albany Congress, held to discuss the Indian menace,
and attended by representatives of seven colonies. Franklin's "Albany
Plan" suggested an intercolonial council composed of forty-eight representatives, apportioned among the colonies with regard to their wealth

[1] Charles H. Ambler, *George Washington and the West* (1936); George McK. Wrong,
The Rise and Fall of New France (2 vols., 1928).

FACSIMILE OF A CARTOON IN FRANKLIN'S NEWSPAPER

and population, and elected by the several colonial legislatures. Also there would have been a president-general for all the colonies, appointed and paid by the crown. Subject to veto by the president-general, the council was to have had the right to control Indian affairs, raise and pay armies, build forts, and levy the taxes necessary for these purposes. But this plan was promptly rejected by the colonial assemblies, who objected to any such curtailment of their own prerogatives, and who possibly feared also that such an intercolonial organization would transfer too much responsibility for the winning of the war from England to the colonies. A counter-proposition submitted by the English Board of Trade met a similar fate. The English plan contemplated the establishment of a council composed of one commissioner from each colony; these commissioners might then agree by majority vote upon the necessary military forces and their apportionment among the colonies. A commander-in-chief for all the colonial forces would have been appointed by the crown.

The failure of these plans left each colony free to support the war as much or as little as it chose. The colonies that were in greatest danger from the French did most; those that were far removed from the scene of conflict did least; and in general there was much waiting to see what the other planned to do. Suggestions from England that taxation of the colonies for their own defense might be undertaken by the authority of Parliament met a chilly reception in America, and were never acted upon.[1]

William Pitt, who was called to the English ministry in the fall of 1756 and next year virtually took charge of the war, worked out a requisition system which secured perhaps as much colonial assistance as was possible under existing circumstances. Pitt's plan left with the colonies the responsibility of levying, clothing, and paying provincial soldiers. The English government, however, undertook to furnish the colonial troops with arms, ammunition, and provisions, and promised further to compensate the colonies later for their outlays in accordance with the vigor of their actions. The amount of the compensation actually paid by England to the colonies was equal to about two-fifths of the expenditures the colonies made. Spurred on by this appeal, as well as by the real menace of the French and Indian attacks, the New England colonies supported the war with becoming zeal; in New York and Pennsylvania, however, quarrels between governor and legislature prevented anything like adequate support of the war; Virginia did only fairly well, considering how great she assumed her stake to be in the

[1] G. L. Beer, *British Colonial Policy, 1754–1763* (1907), is an excellent discussion of British policy towards the colonies during the French and Indian War.

outcome; and most of the other colonies scarcely participated in the war at all.

It was the vigorous direction of the war by William Pitt which in the end turned the tide of battle in favor of the English. Younger and abler officers replaced the incompetents whose blunders had at first cost the British and colonial cause so dear. With their communications cut by a British victory on the shores of Lake Ontario, the French abandoned Fort Duquesne, and the British under General Forbes quickly occupied it. The crowning event of the war came next year when Admiral Saunders and General Wolfe successfully advanced up the St. Lawrence, and forced Montcalm to fight a decisive battle (September 13, 1759) on the Plains of Abraham overlooking Quebec. Both Wolfe and Montcalm lost their lives in the struggle, but the English victory was complete. Next year Montreal surrendered to Amherst, and the conquest of Canada was at an end. Other spectacular victories for the British, in the West Indies and in the Orient, and for Frederick the Great of Prussia, their continental ally, in Europe emphasized the decisiveness of the French defeat.[1]

The British victory

By 1763 the French gave up the struggle, and at Paris, on February 10, signed a humiliating peace. Canada and all the French possessions east of the Mississippi River, most of the French stations in India, and some of the French West Indies were ceded to England. Some of the English leaders would have been willing to return Canada to France in return for a cleaner sweep of the French West Indies, but, won over perhaps by the arguments of Benjamin Franklin, the conquest of Canada was allowed to stand. From the Spanish, who had entered the war on the French side in 1761, the British demanded and received Florida. This somewhat unwarranted Spanish loss was made good by the cession of Louisiana and the Isle of Orleans from France to Spain; and thus the French possessions on the continent of North America were entirely wiped out.

In bringing about this happy solution of their difficulties with New France the colonies had played a considerable part; and yet to most Englishmen conversant with the situation it seemed that the Americans had done far less than their full duty. They had depended upon British regulars when colonial levies might well have been materially increased; they had refused to unite under the Albany Plan, or any other plan, for their common defense; and they had been guilty of almost wholesale trade with the French in utter defiance of the will of the imperial government. British officials asserted that the colonists, in spite of specific

---

[1] A book of epoch-making significance is A. T. Mahan, *The Influence of Sea Power upon History, 1660–1783* (1890).

orders to stop all commerce with the enemy, had smuggled great quantities of colonial stores, particularly foodstuffs, both to Canada and to the French West Indies, and that because of this illicit trade the war had been appreciably prolonged.

The French and Indian War, so far as the colonists were concerned, had been fought primarily to insure that the region west of the mountains should be opened to settlement, and the terms of the treaty of Paris seemed to indicate that this object had been attained. The war was hardly over, however, when grave obstacles to the expansionist program began to appear. Early in 1763 a violent outbreak against British rule by the pro-French Indians of the northwestern frontier, known as Pontiac's Conspiracy, led the British authorities to issue the famous Proclamation of 1763, which forbade colonial settlement to go beyond the sources of the rivers flowing into the Atlantic.[1] Thus the very door that the war had been fought to open seemed to have been closed. Further, the Proclamation utterly ignored the western land claims of those seaboard colonies whose original charters had contained "sea to sea" grants.

The Proclamation Line

That the British government had no intention of forever withholding the region west of the Proclamation Line from settlement was soon fairly apparent. In 1764 two strong expeditions were dispatched into the Indian country. As a result Pontiac and his allies were defeated, and finally in July, 1766, at Oswego Pontiac agreed with Sir William Johnson to a treaty of peace. Other treaties, notably Fort Stanwix with the Iroquois and Hard Labor with the Cherokees, both in 1768, gave the English title to a wide strip of land west of the mountains. Probably the government hoped to establish a neutral zone from which as a precaution against future troubles both whites and Indians should be excluded. But that some of the lands so acquired would be opened to new settlement was clear from the support given by the Board of Trade to a project which contemplated the creation of a new colony in the West to be known as Vandalia. For this purpose a British-American syndicate was formed which numbered among its membership such prominent men as Benjamin Franklin and Sir William Johnson, and much pressure was brought upon the Board of Trade to agree to the necessary land grant. After considerable dissension a patent was made out in favor of the petitioners which would have handed over to them most of what is now West Virginia and eastern Kentucky. But by the time consent to this grant had been fully won, the American Revolution was on, and the project lapsed.

---

[1] Francis Parkman, *The Conspiracy of Pontiac* (2 vols., 1851); Howard H. Peckham, *Pontiac and the Indian Uprising* (1947).

Nevertheless, the settlement of the Vandalia region had already begun. Even before the French and Indian War thousands of pioneers had found their way into the eastern part of this district,

The upper Ohio frontier

and while most of them had been compelled to get out during the war, many promptly returned as it came to an end. After the war was over, with the help of Braddock's road from Fort Cumberland to the Ohio, and the road Forbes had cut through Pennsylvania to Fort Pitt (the British name for Fort Duquesne), migration into the upper Ohio region was made relatively easy. Regardless of the Proclamation of 1763 and the absence of regular land titles, settlers pushed out along the mountain trails, and as early as 1767 permanent settlements on the upper Ohio and its tributaries were beginning to appear. Before the Revolution broke out both Pittsburgh and Wheeling were sizeable villages.[1]

During these years other irregular settlements west of the crest of the mountains were being made farther to the south. In 1769 pioneers from the back country of Virginia pushed southwestward

The Watauga settlements

across the watershed into the Watauga Valley, which they supposed to be within the limits of Virginia, although actually it was a part of North Carolina. Two years later they were joined by a number of "Regulators" from the back country of North Carolina, who were compelled to seek safety in flight because of an unsuccessful revolt they had waged against the domination of the colony by the eastern propertied class. James Robertson, who led this latter migration into the West, and John Sevier, a Virginian of French Huguenot descent who came to Watauga in 1772, furnished the little settlement with unusually effective leadership. When the Wataugans found themselves practically without a government, they adopted Articles of Association by which in the future they were to be governed, and through a convention of thirteen delegates chose a court of five members to rule the community. The Watauga Association lasted on until 1778.

In 1774 another successful war against the Indians, called Lord Dunmore's War after the last royal governor of Virginia, taught the Indians the futility of trying to stay the white man's advance across

Kentucky

the mountains, and paved the way for the settlement of Kentucky.[2] That same year Judge Richard Henderson of North Carolina, who had dreamed the not unusual dream of founding another colony to the west, formed a partnership known as the Transylvania

[1] Theodore Roosevelt, *The Winning of the West* (4 vols., 1894–96), begins with the advance of the frontier after the French and Indian War.

[2] R. G. Thwaites and L. P. Kellogg have edited from the Draper Manuscripts of the State Historical Society of Wisconsin a valuable *Documentary History of Dunmore's War, 1774* (1905).

Company, and purchased from the Cherokees their claim to the region between the Kentucky and the Cumberland Rivers. To promote settlement he sent Daniel Boone, a frontier hunter who had visited Kentucky as early as 1769, to cut a road through from the back country of North Carolina to the bluegrass region. By the first of April, 1775, Boone's party of thirty men had cleared their "Wilderness Road" from the Holston River through Cumberland Gap to the Kentucky River, and had begun the settlement of Boonesborough. Near-by at Harrodsburg other settlers, led by James Harrod of Pennsylvania, were already on hand, and the Kentucky pioneers were soon numbered by the hundreds. Henderson tried to organize a government for "Transylvania," as he proposed to call the colony, and held an open-air convention of delegates for the purpose, May 23, 1775. But his land title was defective, and he failed to obtain recognition of his claims either from the British government or from the American Continental Congress. In December, 1776, the Virginia legislature recognized Kentucky as a county of Virginia.

The impunity with which the British colonists pushed their settlements across the mountains in complete disregard of the Proclamation Line is only one of the many indications that they had come to think of themselves as almost entirely independent of the mother country. They obeyed only such British restrictions on their trade as they cared to obey. They magnified their governmental privileges at every opportunity, and did their best to minimize the rôle of British representatives in America. They helped in the war they themselves had made on the French only to such an extent as they cared to help. It should have been obvious to keen observers on both sides of the Atlantic that the time for the final break could not long be postponed.[1]

[1] H. A. Bruce, *Daniel Boone and the Wilderness Road* (1910); R. G. Thwaites, *Daniel Boone* (1902); W. S. Lester, *The Transylvania Colony* (1935); C. A. Barker, *The Background of the Revolution in Maryland* (1940); K. P. Bailey, *Thomas Cresap, Maryland Frontiersman* (1944); Max Savelle, *The Diplomatic History of the Canadian Boundary, 1749–1763* (1940); Louise P. Kellogg, *The French Regime in Wisconsin and the Northwest* (1925); Theodore C. Pease and Ernestine Jenison, *Illinois on the Eve of the Seven Years' War, 1747–1755* (1939); T. P. Abernethy, *Western Lands and the American Revolution* (1937); S. C. Williams, *Tennessee during the Revolutionary War* (1944).

4

The Revolution

THERE were those on both sides of the Atlantic who believed that the expulsion of the French from North America would draw England and her colonies into a closer unity, but all such hopes were **Prelude to Revolution** soon disappointed. British officials denounced freely the hesitancy with which many Americans supported a war fought in their defense, and noted with a sense of outrage the cheerful unconcern with which Americans disobeyed whatever trade regulations they disapproved. Americans, on the other hand, criticized freely the British conduct of the war, and denounced unsparingly the restrictions on their freedom of movement made by the Proclamation Line. Indeed, the colonies, with the French menace removed, saw little reason why they should submit further to British interference in their affairs. Whatever grudging obedience they had previously given the mother country had stemmed in considerable part from the knowledge that they might need help against the French. But with the war won and the French ousted, why should the colonials trouble further about conciliating the British? Instead of promoting unity, the French and Indian War in reality paved the way for the American Revolution.[1]

When the war ended it fell to the lot of George Grenville, Pitt's brother-in-law, but the leader of a faction in England far less friendly to America, to deal with the colonies. Grenville had long **The Grenville reforms** been a member of the Cabinet, but in April, 1763, as Chancellor of the Exchequer and First Lord of the Treasury, he became its head. He was a man of great obstinacy, but little talent, who made a fetish of efficiency. In order to tighten up the customs service, he ordered the commissioners of customs, who normally hired substitutes to do their work, to go themselves to America and collect the duties. He made relentless war on smugglers and, to avoid the partisanship of colonial juries, authorized admiralty courts, whose

[1] E. I. McCormac, *Colonial Opposition to Imperial Authority during the French and Indian War* (1911); W. S. McClellan, *Smuggling in the American Colonies at the Outbreak of the Revolution* (1912).

verdicts could be rendered without trial by jury, to try such law-breakers. He pushed through Parliament the famous Sugar Act of 1764, which substituted for the unenforceable duties of the Molasses Act of 1733 new and more reasonable duties that were meant to be collected. He also induced Parliament to place restrictions upon the use of paper money in the colonies, a particularly serious blow to debtor communities without an adequate supply of hard money.

But the most objectionable of the Grenville measures to the Americans was the Stamp Act, which was devised to make them pay a part of the cost involved in protecting their western frontier from Indian attacks. Since, according to Grenville and his ad- *The Stamp Act* visers, colonial troops had been found undependable in the French and Indian War, a permanent British garrison of ten thousand troops should be stationed in America. The British officials also thought it reasonable that the Americans themselves should pay about one-third of the three hundred and sixty thousand pounds that this service would cost. Estimating that about forty-five thousand pounds of the American contribution would come from the new duties to be collected under the Sugar Act, the ministers planned to raise the remaining seventy-five thousand pounds by a stamp tax levied upon newspapers, and upon the various official and legal documents through which colonial business was transacted. Notice that such a tax was about to be levied was given in 1764, and next year the Stamp Act passed Parliament.

It took some time for American sentiment on the Grenville acts to crystallize, but the reaction, when it came, was forthright. Grenville's program seemed admirably designed to cripple in the most effective manner the economic life of the colonies. The Proclamation of 1763, granted that it could be enforced, would stop migration to the West just as hard times in the East, following close on the heels of the French and Indian War, had made the search for new homes in the West all the more essential. The Sugar Act would not only hamper trade with the foreign West Indies, but since those colonies were better buyers than sellers, it would interfere also with the normal flow of hard money from the islands to the continental colonies, and would make increasingly difficult the payment of balances owed by New England merchants to London. As if this were not sufficiently embarrassing, colonial paper issues were outlawed by the Currency Act, and the Stamp Act demanded more money when money was harder than ever to obtain. The colonies were poor, and the debts that they had incurred, or that some of them at least had incurred, during the French and Indian War seemed heavy; yet this was the time the English government selected to restrict their trade, remodel their monetary system, and tax them for a kind of protection that they did not want and thought that they did not need.

The most vulnerable part of the Grenville program, and that which drew the heaviest fire, was the Stamp Act. This, from the colonial point of view, was a clear case of taxation without repre- **Colonial opposition** sentation. So Patrick Henry argued in the Virginia House of Burgesses when he defied the British king in well-remembered words, "If this be treason, make the most of it." So the Virginia Resolutions, which he supported and which passed, plainly stated. There was a fair consensus of opinion in the colonies that Parliament had definitely exceeded its authority. Most Americans were willing to admit that external taxes in the shape of duties on imports might be levied on the colonies by Parliament in the course of regulating imperial trade. But internal taxation without the direct sanction of popular representatives was "taxation without representation." Some of the northern merchants agreed among themselves that they would cease importations from England as long as the law held, and the General Court of Massachusetts sent out a circular letter inviting all the colonies to participate in a conference at New York on the first Tuesday in October through which an appeal for relief might be made to the English government.[1]

With nine colonies represented, the Stamp Act Congress, as it was generally called, added its weight to the argument. The only persons who might legally represent the colonies, it held, were those **The Stamp Act Congress** "chosen therein by themselves." Since not a single American sat in the British Parliament, that body was wholly without authority to enact such a measure as the Stamp Act. Further, the Congress denounced the use of admiralty courts as a mere device to circumvent trial by jury, and described restrictions on colonial commerce as unduly "burthensome and grievous." Thus ably led, the American public defiantly refused to buy the offensive stamps, and began also to discriminate against British-made goods. Non-importation agreements multiplied, and English merchants complained bitterly to Congress that the Grenville measures were costing them business.

Faced by this situation, there seemed nothing for the British government to do but back down. While some Englishmen agreed with William Pitt, who felt free to "rejoice that America has resisted," Parliament did not surrender to the American arguments, but to ex-

[1] C. H. Van Tyne, *The Causes of the War of Independence* (1922), is perhaps the best work by an American writer on the background of the Revolution. Other valuable books are C. M. Andrews, *The Colonial Background of the American Revolution* (1924); G. E. Howard, *Preliminaries of the Revolution* (1905); H. E. Egerton, *The Causes and Character of the American Revolution* (1923); J. C. Miller, *Origins of the American Revolution* (1943).

pediency. Englishmen, accustomed to a haphazard system of representation that left many large cities without seats in Parliament, could understand the argument of Chief Justice Mansfield that the colonists had "virtual representation" in Parliament, although they directly elected not a single member. Mansfield probably spoke also for majority opinion when he denounced the distinction many Americans had begun to draw between "internal" taxes, which only a colonial legislature might levy, and "external" taxes for the regulation of trade that Parliament might levy. When repeal was finally accomplished (March 17, 1766), it was accomplished by a Declaratory Act which stated that the King and Parliament had "full power and authority" to legislate for the colonies "in all cases whatsoever." [1]

The repeal of the Stamp Act was received with much enthusiasm in America, and the menacing gesture of the Declaratory Act was scarcely noted. Popular protests of loyalty to the mother country were numerous, and only a little tact would probably have avoided further dissension. But three unfortunate circumstances told heavily against the preservation of good relations. In the first place, George III, the English King, cherished the hope of acquiring great personal power, and by every means at his disposal added to the number of the "King's friends" in Parliament, who would vote the way the King directed. On the subject of America, unfortunately, the King was both ignorant and prejudiced. In the second place, the illness of William Pitt (now the Earl of Chatham) robbed the ministry of its only outstanding leader, and left each minister free to do about as he pleased within his own domain. The result so far as American affairs were concerned was one colossal blunder after another. The third unfortunate circumstance was that the Chancellor of the Exchequer, Charles Townshend, to whom fell the task of finding an adequate revenue, was distinctly hostile to the colonies, and did not hesitate to take advantage of his position to translate his feelings into deeds. He quarreled with the New York legislature over the sums to be voted for the support of British troops stationed in that colony, he continued the unpopular war that Grenville had begun against the smugglers, and he formally authorized the use of writs of assistance, or general search warrants, which did not require that the premises to be searched be specifically mentioned. Furthermore, he proposed to raise a revenue from the colonies, and soon presented in fulfillment of his

Obstacles to good relations

[1] The constitutional aspects of the Revolution have naturally attracted much attention. An excellent summary is to be found in A. M. Schlesinger, *New Viewpoints in American History* (1922), but this should be compared with C. H. McIlwain, *The American Revolution: a Constitutional Interpretation* (1923). C. E. Merriam, *History of American Political Theories* (1903), gives a good brief statement of the American contentions.

promise an act imposing duties upon all tea, paper, glass, painters' colors
and lead to enter American ports.

The Townshend Duty Act, as this measure was called, did mock
deference to the American distinction between internal and external
taxes, for it was a strictly external tax; but the preamble
definitely stated that the law was designed to raise a revenue
rather than to regulate trade, and that the revenue so obtained might be used at the discretion of the government to pay the
salaries of colonial governors and colonial judges. The law was in fact,
and was meant to be, a challenge to the Americans — a challenge to
them to defend if they could their theory of taxation and their practice
of disciplining governors and judges by withholding salaries. But probably neither Townshend nor the members of Parliament who voted to
support him realized fully the serious nature of the challenge they had
made. Townshend died soon after the acts that bore his name were
passed, but his successor, Lord North, one of the King's friends, attempted for three years to enforce them.

The Townshend Duty Act

The hated Townshend Acts, which did so much to inflame public
opinion in America against the mother country, included besides the
new duties a law suspending the New York legislature, and another
creating a Board of Commissioners of Customs to be located at Boston
with ample authority to enforce the Navigation Acts. The threat to self-
government implicit in the attack on the New York legislature was
deeply resented throughout the colonies, while the colonial merchants,
particularly those resident in Boston, believed that rigorous enforcement of the long-neglected Navigation Acts would ruin their business.[1]
The Duty Act was denounced generally as an unwarranted and unconstitutional measure. Many agreed with John Dickinson of Pennsylvania, whose *Letters from a Farmer* on the subject were widely read, that
an external tax designed primarily to raise a revenue was no less an instance of taxation without representation than an internal tax such as
the Stamp Act had been. Others held that not merely taxation without
representation was tyranny, but that all legislation by the British Parliament for America was unconstitutional. For the slogan, "No taxation
without representation," these extremists would substitute the slogan,
"No legislation without representation." Dickinson suggested that if
the English did not themselves put an end to the Townshend system,
the Americans, as a means of making their power felt, might well proceed with a boycott on British goods.

[1] A. M. Schlesinger, *The Colonial Merchants and the American Revolution, 1763–1776*
(1917), brings out clearly the motives that actuated the merchant class. See also Channing, III.

It fell to Samuel Adams (1722–1803), the astute leader of the popular party in the Massachusetts legislature, to lead the colonial assault upon the Townshend Acts. Adams's father was a good business man who was able to send his son to Harvard College, but Samuel Adams was better at politics than at business. Under his competent guidance all classes of malcontents were united in opposition to the vexatious Duty Act. Adams displayed rare skill as a writer, and not a little aptitude as a thinker. He maintained that the British constitution, like the constitutions of all free peoples, was "fixed in the law of Nature and of God," and that "neither the supreme legislature nor the supreme executive" could alter it. In various documents adopted by the Massachusetts House, Adams's views were set forth, and finally in a *Circular Letter*, which he drafted, all the colonial assemblies were invited to join with Massachusetts in resisting the policies of the British government. Soon legislative halls throughout the colonies began to ring with resolutions supporting the position of Massachusetts and deploring the behavior of the British.[1]

Samuel Adams

The weapon by which the colonies might defend their rights had already been forged during the controversy over the Stamp Act. Once more non-importation agreements were entered into by the merchants of the leading cities, a program which many southern planters also chose to adopt. British trade began to fall off; British merchants began to protest; the British government had little choice but to back down once again. Moreover, time had demonstrated that it cost more to collect the Townshend duties than the amount of revenue they brought in. Accordingly on March 5, 1770, Lord North moved the repeal of the duties except the tax on tea "to keep up the right."

Non-importation agreements

On this very same day the so-called "Boston Massacre" proved conclusively the wisdom of the British retreat. Irritated to desperation by the conduct of a mob of jeering men and boys, a few British soldiers from the two regiments then stationed in Boston had opened fire, killing five Americans. Probably the mob was quite as much to blame for the outrage as the soldiers, and John Adams, a rising young lawyer distantly related to Samuel Adams, acted as counsel for the British in the trial that followed. The British officer in command, although accused of giving the order to fire, was acquitted, but two of the men were given slight sentences for manslaughter.

The news that the Townshend duties had been repealed tended once more to restore good relations between the colonies and the mother

[1] R. V. Harlow, *Samuel Adams, Promoter of the American Revolution* (1923); J. C. Miller, *Sam Adams, Pioneer in Propaganda* (1936).

country. Non-importation agreements were generally rescinded or
were reduced in scope to oppose merely the importation
Good   from England of tea, which, it was well understood, could
relations   be smuggled in from Holland without much difficulty, and
restored
even the boycott on tea was not well observed. The fact
that the British government had not backed down on the right of Parliament to tax the colonies troubled very few, for most Americans cared
less about the theory of taxation than about the practice, and in practice
the British attempt to tax the colonies had failed.

It would not be correct to say, however, that the fires of discontent
had gone out; they were merely burning low. Evidence that they
might flame up again at any time was not difficult to find. In June,
1772, for example, a mob of colonists overpowered the crew of the
Gaspee, a British revenue cutter that had grounded on the Rhode Island
coast, and burned the vessel. That same year Samuel Adams, who had
heard that the King intended to pay Massachusetts judges out of money
collected from the colonial customs, organized "committees of correspondence" throughout the colony to inform one another of the current state of affairs. Soon, at the instigation of back-country radicals
in the Virginia House of Burgesses, intercolonial committees of correspondence were also established, and ultimately a whole network of

---

MAKERS OF AMERICA

Each of these six men contributed mightily to the making of the American nation.

THOMAS JEFFERSON (1743–1826) *summarized eloquently in the Declaration of
Independence the factual and philosophic basis for the American Revolution; and as
third President of the United States he introduced a degree of democracy into governmental affairs that deeply distressed such conservatives as* ALEXANDER HAMILTON
(1757–1804) *and* JOHN ADAMS (1735–1826). *Although Hamilton and Adams, as
Federalists, generally agreed on matters of principle, they represented opposing factions in the party and were not very good friends.*

SAMUEL ADAMS (1722–1803) *was the leading Massachusetts agitator against the
British in the years preceding the American Revolution and has as good a claim as
anyone to having brought that conflict to a head. He was distantly related to John
Adams, but was far less conservative by nature.*

JAMES MADISON (1751–1836), *fourth President of the United States, was known as
the "Father of the Constitution" for the work he did in the Federal Convention of
1787.* JOHN MARSHALL (1755–1835) *was for thirty-four years Chief Justice of the
United States Supreme Court, and more than any other jurist determined the pattern
of development that American constitutional law was to follow.*

JEFFERSON

SAMUEL ADAMS

MADISON

JOHN ADAMS

MARSHALL

HAMILTON

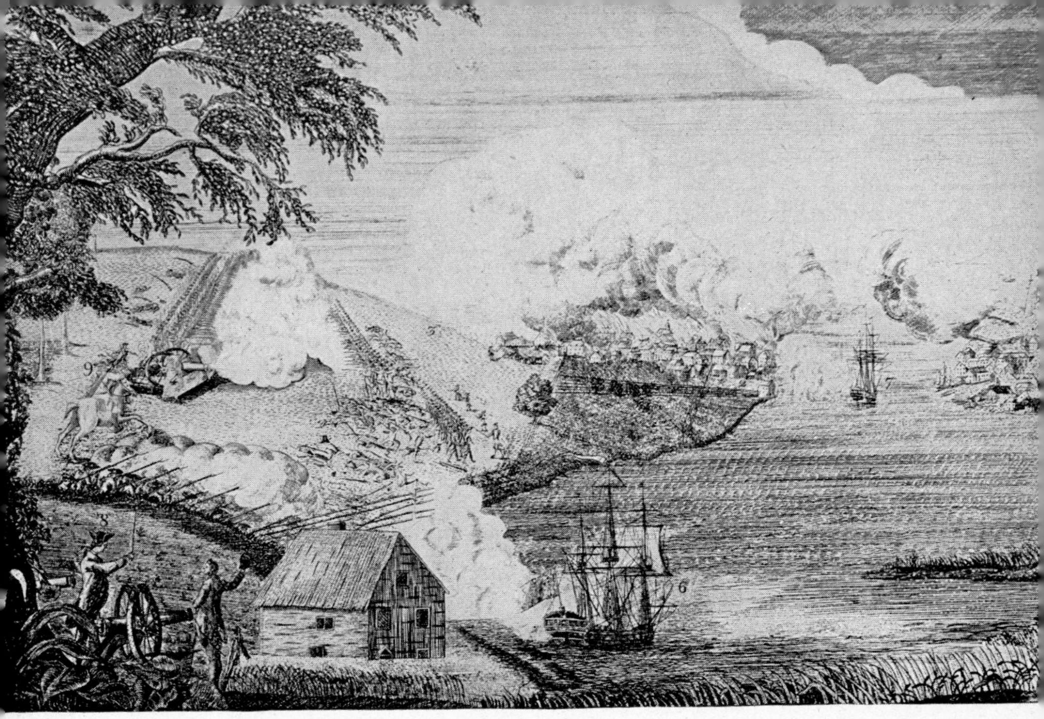

TO ALL BRAVE, HEALTHY, ABLE BODIED, AND WELL DISPOSED YOUNG MEN,

IN THIS NEIGHBOURHOOD, WHO HAVE ANY INCLINATION TO JOIN THE TROOPS,
NOW RAISING UNDER

GENERAL WASHINGTON,

FOR THE DEFENCE OF THE

LIBERTIES AND INDEPENDENCE
OF THE UNITED STATES,

Against the hostile designs of foreign enemies,

TAKE NOTICE,

THAT _____ Tuesday, Wednesday, Thursday, Friday and Saturday, at _____ in _____ county, attendance will be given by _____ with his music and recruiting party of _____ company in _____ State _____, of the 11th regiment, infantry, commanded by Lieutenant Colonel Aaron Ogden, for the purpose of receiving the enrollment of such youth of SPIRIT, as may be willing to enter into this HONOURABLE service.

The ENCOURAGEMENT at this time, to enlist, is truly liberal and generous, namely, a bounty of TWELVE dollars, an annual and fully sufficient supply of good and handsome cloathing, a daily allowance of a large and ample ration of provisions, together with SIXTY dollars a year in GOLD and SILVER money on account of pay, the whole of which the soldier may lay up for himself and friends, as all articles proper for his subsistance and comfort are provided by law, without any expense to him.

Those who may favour this recruiting party with their attendance as above, will have an opportunity of hearing and seeing in a more particular manner, the great advantages which these brave men will have, who shall embrace this opportunity of spending a few happy years in viewing the different parts of this beautiful continent, in the honourable and truly respectable character of a soldier, after which, he may, if he pleases return home to his friends, with his pockets FULL of money, and his head covered with laurels.

GOD SAVE THE UNITED STATES.

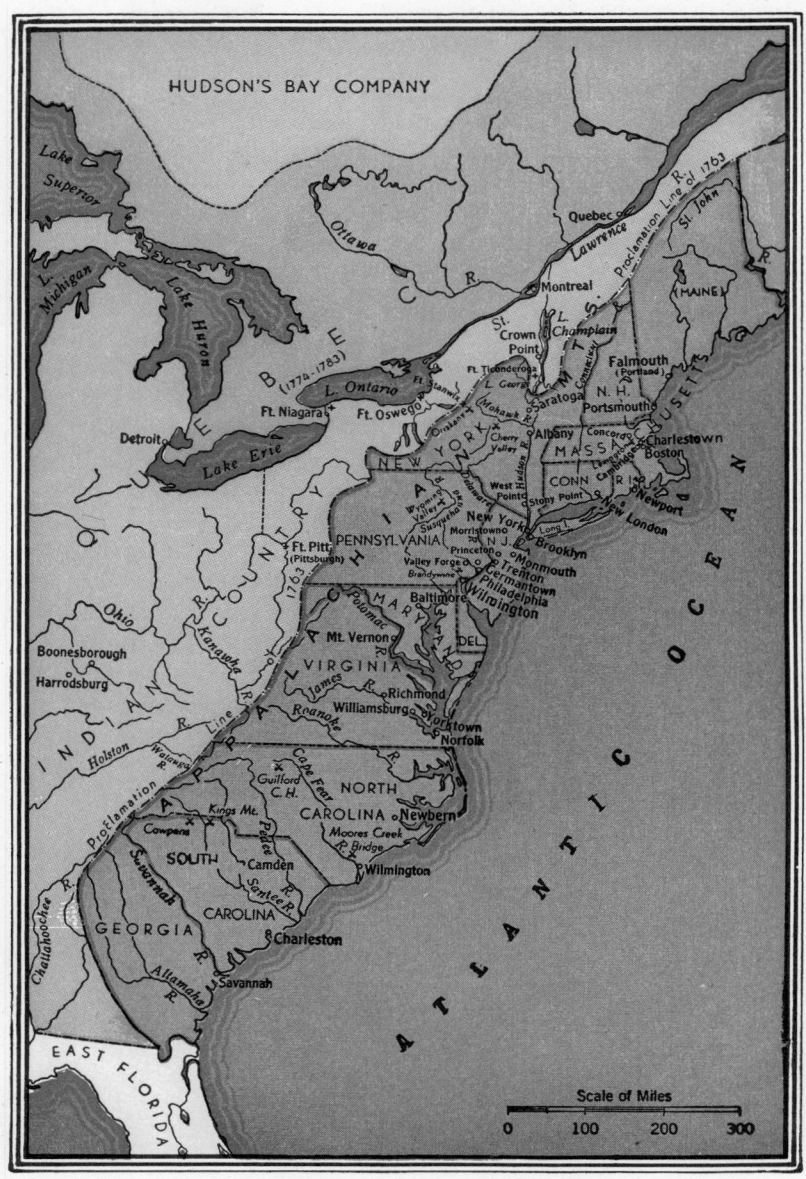

THE UNITED STATES DURING THE REVOLUTION

in Parliament, refused to yield to the clamor, and voted instead to send more troops to America.

Meantime party lines in America became more and more definite. The day of temporizing was soon over, and wavering citizens were gradually forced to decide what course they meant to support. For some time even the radicals were not precisely **Growth of** of one mind. All were agreed that no concessions should **radicalism in** be made to the British point of view, but the more moderate, **America** who hoped to avert the use of force unless in case of extreme necessity, viewed with some misgivings the military preparations under way. Similarly the conservatives disagreed among themselves. Some thought that resistance, so long as it was strictly peaceful, might well be continued in the hope of ultimate success; others were eager for conciliation and compromise. Ultimately the conservatives parted company. The extremists, preferring the British connection to anything that resistance to the mother country had to offer, became the "Tories" or "Loyalists" of the American Revolution. The moderates, on the other hand, gradually drifted over to the radicals, and ultimately joined with them as "Whigs" or "Patriots" to take up arms and to win independence. Doubtless a minority in the beginning, the radical extremists through their effective organization and aggressive tactics ultimately won over a majority to their way of thinking. But probably as many as a third of the colonists were openly or secretly loyal to the mother country throughout the Revolution.

Colonial resistance was at its worst in Massachusetts, where George III had evidently determined to stage a test of arms. Minute men drilled on village commons and collected munitions with which to defend themselves. Neither side wished to precipi- **Lexington and** tate hostilities, but finally General Gage, who had also been **Concord** made royal governor of Massahusetts, felt obliged to seize the military supplies that the radical leaders had accumulated at Concord, and to arrest two arch-conspirators, Samuel Adams and John Hancock. For this purpose a small detachment of British troops left Boston on the night of April 18, 1775. The soldiers had counted on surprise, but through the activity of Paul Revere and others the whole countryside was aroused. At Lexington the British were obliged to disperse by force of arms a small detachment of militia drawn up to oppose them. They then marched on to Concord, destroyed the American supplies, and started back toward Boston. On the return trip, however, the "redcoats" were fired upon by farmers and militiamen from the roadsides so effectively that the retreat to Boston became a humiliating rout. Greatly heartened by the good news, armed militiamen from all over New England collected around Boston to lay siege to the city.

On the tenth of May following Lexington and Concord the Second Continental Congress began its sessions at Philadelphia. It was a far more radical body than its predecessor, but enough moderates were present to induce the delegates to appeal once more to the King for a redress of grievances. But the tide of revolt could not be stemmed for long. On June 15 Congress took over the troops gathered near Boston as the Continental Army, and assumed authority to direct the course of the war. At the suggestion of John Adams, it gave the command of these troops to George Washington, the well-known Virginia aristocrat. While this selection was designed in part to flatter the South and in part to placate the upper classes of every section, probably no wiser choice could have been made.

Washington was present in uniform as a delegate to the Continental Congress from Virginia when he was chosen to head the army. He set out at once to join his command, but before he could complete his journey another battle had been fought. On June 17, 1775, General Gage, now reinforced to about ten thousand men, sent a detachment to drive the Americans from Bunker Hill (in reality Breed's Hill) overlooking Charlestown, only to suffer two humiliating reverses before the colonials, for lack of ammunition, were obliged to give way. In spite of this excellent showing, Washington found the forces under his command far less than an army, and the problem of drawing order out of chaos taxed his ability to the utmost. Nevertheless, by March, 1776, he was ready to strike. With cannon dragged overland from Ticonderoga, a captured British fort at the southern end of the Lake George–Lake Champlain approach to Canada, he occupied Dorchester Heights, to the south of Boston, and trained his artillery on the city. General Howe, who had succeeded Gage in command, recognizing that he had been outmaneuvered, quickly embarked his troops, together with about a thousand Loyalists, for Nova Scotia, and without bloodshed the Americans occupied the city.[1]

Other incidents of the first year of the war included an attack on Canada, which the capture of Ticonderoga made feasible. In November, 1775, colonial troops under Richard Montgomery took Montreal and then co-operated with Benedict Arnold, who had led another column through the Maine woods, in an attack on Quebec. But the assault, made December 31, 1775, was unsuccessful, and cost Montgomery his life. Since the French showed no desire to help the Americans, the

Bunker Hill

---

[1] Most of the books already cited in this chapter are useful also on the period of actual warfare. S. G. Fisher, *The Struggle for American Independence* (2 vols., 1908), is in many respects the most satisfactory general account of the period. Another valuable book on the war is C. H. Van Tyne, *The American Revolution, 1776–1783* (1905). On the strictly military side of the struggle F. V. Greene, *The Revolutionary War* (1911), is excellent.

winter siege that followed proved equally futile. At length Montreal
was abandoned, and the Americans retreated to Crown Point.[1] Far to
the south, at Moore's Creek Bridge in North Carolina, a band of Patriots
met and defeated a band of Loyalists, February 27, 1776, while a sea-
borne British invasion force, with Wilmington and Charleston as objectives, met such stiff resistance that the project was abandoned. Thus
the first year of the war ended in a kind of stalemate, with the Americans
repulsed in their effort to conquer Canada, and the British equally unable to secure a foothold anywhere in the colonies.

Nevertheless, American opinion during this period had by no means
remained stationary. At the outbreak of hostilities, only a few extremists were ready to go the whole length of separation
from Great Britain; the great majority thought of the con- Movement for
flict as merely a civil war within the Empire. But the events   Independence
of the year seemed to make such a settlement impossible. George III
had turned down the American petition for the redress of grievances,
apparently with the full consent of Parliament, and had even begun to
hire German troops — "Hessians" — to assist in the vigorous prosecution of the war. Revolutionary governments had replaced the old
colonial foundations. American trade with Great Britain was now
completely cut off, and new outlets were desperately needed. Military
help was needed also from the enemies of Great Britain, particularly
France, and to get it Americans clearly must avow their independence.
Under these circumstances public opinion veered sharply toward the
extremists who wished to sever all connections with the mother country,
and to transform the struggle for a redress of grievances into a real war
of revolution. Such was the opinion stated by Thomas Paine in his
widely-circulated pamphlet, *Common Sense*, which made innumerable
converts to the independence idea.

That Congress was in a mood to respond to the shift in public opinion
soon seemed evident. On the seventh of June, 1776, Richard Henry Lee
of Virginia moved "that these United Colonies are, and of
right ought to be, free and independent states," but in defer-   Declaration
ence to more conservative opinion it was voted on the tenth   of
to postpone a final decision for three weeks. When the   Independence
formal vote was taken, July 2, every state save New York, whose provincial assembly gave its assent a week later, was for independence. On
this same day a committee headed by Thomas Jefferson reported its
carefully-drawn Declaration of Independence, which, after some minor
amendments, was adopted, July 4. On August 2 such members of Con-

---

[1] This campaign is entertainingly described by Justin H. Smith, *Our Struggle for the
Fourteenth Colony — Canada and the American Revolution* (1907).

gress as were present affixed their signatures to the engrossed document, and later whenever occasion offered those who had been absent before were given an opportunity to sign their names.

The Declaration of Independence, which was written almost entirely by Jefferson, borrowed heavily from Locke's *Second Essay on Government*, and asserted in language already familiar the natural rights of men, including the right of revolution. It differed markedly from earlier American protests in that it directed its attack primarily against the King rather than against Parliament, for by this time the radicals were unwilling to concede that Parliament had the slightest authority over the American colonies. They even blamed the King for some of the offensive acts of Parliament, and held that the long list of grievances they were able to recite constituted a kind of breach of contract on the part of the monarch which gave the colonies the right, if they chose, to become free and independent states.[1]

The appearance of unanimity which accompanied the Declaration quite belied the facts, for in the course of the next few years probably as many as fifty thousand "Loyalists" proved their senti-
Loyalists vs. Patriots ments by fighting with the British forces and against the "Patriots." Inevitably the Loyalists were obliged to endure much persecution. Many of them saw their property destroyed or confiscated, they often suffered great personal violence, and they were driven by the thousands to take refuge in Canada, Florida, the West Indies, or England.[2] It is also noteworthy that the thirteen separate state governments, although in full control of the Patriots, were only imperfectly united. The new states did indeed co-operate through Congress in a way they had never done before, but Congress was an extra-legal body sadly lacking in authority, and often proved to be a debating society when what was needed was a powerful and efficient central war office.

But the mother country was hardly more united than the rebellious colonies. The King's party, which commanded a majority in Parliament and was generally supported by the upper classes, strongly
The English front favored the war, but the opposition, long schooled in the tolerant doctrines of Burke and Chatham, was far from enthusiastic at taking up arms against the Americans. Many liberals even hoped to see the King discredited by failure in America; merchants

---

[1] Naturally this document has been subjected to the closest scrutiny. The best such study is Carl L. Becker, *The Declaration of Independence; a Study in the History of Political Ideas* (1922).

[2] C. H. Van Tyne, *The Loyalists of the American Revolution* (1902), clears the "Tories" of many of the charges made against them by the "Whigs" and believed by later generations. See also *The War of Independence* (1929), by the same author.

desirous of retaining American trade were for peace at almost any price; and the common people, although practically without a voice in politics, showed their sentiments by refusing to enlist for fighting their kinsmen overseas. Furthermore, all too many of the King's friends were poor administrators, and British governmental incompetence often rivaled the worst that the inexperienced Continental Congress could do.

In the comparison of armed forces the odds told more heavily against the Americans. Washington rarely had as many as sixteen thousand men under his command at any one time, and at Valley Forge his forces had dwindled to a paltry two thousand. **Comparison of armed forces** Poor and uncertain pay together with inadequate supplies made the difficulty of obtaining enlistments, even for the short terms customary, almost insurmountable. Supplementing the Continental Army created by Congress were the state militia, who sometimes fought well in defending their own homes and firesides, but were otherwise exceedingly undependable. To oppose these troops the British had a well-trained regular army of perhaps sixty thousand men, most of whom were needed, however, on garrison duty somewhere in the far-flung British Empire. Shortages were made up by the employment of "Hessians," Loyalists or "Tories," and Indians. The British armies in America were nearly always adequate in numbers, well equipped, and well fed. They were backed also by unlimited naval power; but even so their superiority was not sufficient to enable them to win. The British soldiers operated three thousand miles away from home; their attack had to be delivered along a thousand miles of seacoast; and they were confronted, once they had penetrated into the interior, with a trackless wilderness where conquest was virtually impossible as long as the will to resist endured.

In point of military leadership, thanks mainly to the solid qualities of Washington, the Americans were superior to the British. It cannot be demonstrated that as a commanding officer Washington was a genius. He was not thoroughly versed in military **Washington the general** tactics, and he might have had great difficulty in commanding large armies. But whatever the limits of his ability, he proved equal to the existing emergency. His obvious integrity, his unflinching courage, and his dogged determination inspired his men with confidence and paved the way to ultimate victory. He was a master of the strategy of retreat, and understood thoroughly that while he had an army in the field the Patriot cause was not lost.[1] Unfortunately most of Washington's immediate subordinates were of mediocre or even inferior abilities.

[1] G. M. Wrong, *Washington and his Comrades in Arms* (1921), gives a satisfactory estimate of Washington's military achievements. More detailed are the volumes by Rupert Hughes, *George Washington, the Rebel and the Patriot, 1762–1777* (1927), and *The Savior of the States, 1777–1781* (1930).

Possibly Nathanael Greene was the best of them, although he had had virtually no military experience prior to the war. The contributions of a number of European volunteers — the two Germans, Steuben and Kalb, the two Poles, Kosciusko and Pulaski, and the young Frenchman, Lafayette — were highly creditable.

The British commanders were notably ineffective. Neither Howe, who was placed in command at the outset of the war, nor Clinton, who succeeded him, could be classified as first-rate, but even so

The British officers both men should have done better than they did. Probably Howe's lack of vigor was due in part to his hope for reconciliation between the colonies and the mother country. Clinton, too, failed to take full advantage of his opportunities, and more than once seemed to give the game away. In technical knowledge the British commanders far outmatched the Americans, but the unusual character of the fighting in America sometimes turned this seeming advantage, as for Braddock before them, into a liability.

In the matter of finances the picture was wholly one-sided. British gold was available at all times in America to purchase supplies for the

Finance British forces, while Washington usually had only paper money and promises with which to pay. Congress lacked the power of taxation, and the millions of dollars in "continental currency" that it issued fell rapidly in value — by 1780 a continental dollar was worth only two cents in gold. State issues were only a little better. Once just before the battle of Princeton, Washington, in order to keep his army from disintegrating, had to pledge the soldiers his private fortune to convince them that the money due them would be paid: and Robert Morris, upon whom Congress placed the chief burden of financing the war, was also compelled to borrow upon his own personal credit.[1]

When General Howe abandoned Boston, it was with the intention of striking a blow later on at some more strategic point. Eventually he decided to take New York, where by controlling the Hudson

Attack on New York Valley he could separate New England from the rest of the colonies, and perhaps establish connections with Canada. With a formidable army — twenty-five thousand British troops and eight thousand Hessians — he moved by sea to the attack, late in the summer of 1776. Anticipating Howe's move, Washington abandoned Boston and with perhaps eighteen thousand men under his command prepared to defend New York. Defeated at Brooklyn Heights on Long Island, August 27, 1776, Washington took advantage of the dilatory tactics of Howe and a friendly fog to ferry his troops to Manhattan

[1] E. P. Oberholtzer, *Robert Morris* (1903); W. G. Sumner, *The Financier and the Finances of the Revolution* (1891).

Island, but eventually he had to yield this also, and retreat across the Hudson to New Jersey. During the winter of 1776–77 the Patriot army dwindled to as few as three thousand men, but Howe failed to press his advantage, and twice, at Trenton (December 26, 1776) and at Princeton (January 3, 1777), permitted Washington to inflict stinging defeats upon isolated British detachments.

The year 1777 saw two major movements on the part of the British, one a shift of base on the part of Howe from New York to Philadelphia, the other an advance down the Lake Champlain–Hudson Valley route by troops under the command of General Bur- **The British** goyne. Howe chose not to proceed directly overland against **occupy** the rebel capital, but sent his troops most of the way by sea. **Philadelphia** As before New York they were met by Washington, but the Patriot army was severely defeated at Brandywine, and in September, 1777, Howe entered Philadelphia. The capture of the American capital was a serious blow to the Patriot pride, but of little military importance. Howe instead of taking Philadelphia should have sent aid to Burgoyne, whose position was rapidly becoming desperate. With the American forces under Gates and Arnold swollen to unusual size by accretions from local militia, Burgoyne was disastrously defeated at Freeman's Farm, near Saratoga, and on October 17, 1777, with his army of fifty-eight hundred men entirely surrounded, he surrendered. This was the first notable victory that the Americans — or for that matter, either side — had yet won. It gave the Patriots good reason to hope that in spite of their difficulties they might eventually win the war.

The surrender of Burgoyne made possible also the consummation of the greatly desired alliance with France. Early in 1776 Congress had sent Silas Deane to Paris with instructions to obtain what- ever aid he could get. He was presently joined by Arthur **The French** Lee and Benjamin Franklin. Deane and Lee had only **alliance** moderate success, but Franklin's personality captivated the French, and he got results. With the news of Burgoyne's defeat to support his argument, he pressed successfully for an alliance, and on February 6, 1778, two treaties were signed between France and the United States. By one of these treaties the two nations opened their ports freely to each other's commerce; by the other they united in a military alliance to effect the independence of the United States. France agreed, when peace with England should be made, not to ask for additional territory on the mainland of North America, and the United States in turn promised to guarantee to France indefinitely the French West Indies. Neither party was to make peace without the full consent of the other. There was much that was anomalous about this alliance between an absolute monarch and a people fighting for freedom, but there was also much that was natural about it. France and England were traditional enemies; furthermore, the doctrines that were to bring on the French Revolution in France were already being heard, and sympathy for American ideals was by no means lacking.[1]

The value of the alliance to the American cause can hardly be overestimated. French loans kept the American army intact and in some degree prepared to fight. French officers helped with the training of American troops. Above all, French sea-power supplied a vital need, and greatly expanded the opportunities of American sea-captains. The exploits of John Paul Jones, for example, whose *Bonhomme Richard* took the *Serapis* (September, 1779) in a naval battle justly famous, would have been impossible but for the backing of the French. Even though British superiority on the high seas was at no time fully overcome during the war, French fleets hampered the British movements of troops along the American coast, threatened an attack on England that drew attention from America at a critical time, and held the British fleet at bay during the later phases of the war.[2]

The Franco-American alliance against Great Britain was in due time heavily reinforced. The entrance of France into the war practically assured the entrance also of her ally, Spain, to whom on her own account England's possession of Gibraltar was a standing national insult. Secretly some financial aid was given the Americans before the outbreak of war between Spain and England; and after that event, which occurred in 1779, the Spanish navy co-operated constantly with the French. In 1781 the allies gained another recruit in Holland, whose defiant smugglers finally irritated the British into a declaration of war. Dutch sea-power, together with the helpful loans that the American representative to the Netherlands, John Adams, was able to negotiate, had much to do with the outcome of the war. Great Britain had also to deal with the "Armed Neutrality," a combination of neutral nations effected in 1780 by Catherine II of Russia, which included, besides Russia, such other nations as Denmark, Sweden, Portugal, and Prussia, all of which were earnest opponents of the regulations which the British navy imposed upon neutral trade, and therefore potential belligerents. Thus the British had to deal with a powerful combination of powers which might at any time become more powerful by the addition of new members.

Other aid to America

[1] E. S. Corwin, *French Policy and the American Alliance* (1916); J. B. Perkins, *France in the American Revolution* (1911); Bernard Faÿ, *The Revolutionary Spirit in France and America* (1927).

[2] C. O. Paullin, *The Navy of the American Revolution* (1906); A. T. Mahan, *The Major Operations of the Navies in the War of American Independence* (1913).

Meantime Washington, who held his army in winter quarters at Valley Forge, near Philadelphia, during the winter of 1777–78, wondered how long resistance could be maintained. During these dark days the Patriot army almost vanished, and the hand-ful of soldiers who remained true to the cause suffered incredible priva-tions. But fortunately for the Patriots, Howe took his ease in Phila-delphia, and Washington's little army, in spite of its tribulations, was allowed to come through the winter still an army. Next spring the British government, visibly shaken by the French alliance, was ready to offer the Americans almost any terms short of independence, but Congress, inspired with new hope, spurned suggestions that two years before would have been regarded as highly satisfactory.

Valley Forge

Fearful of French naval power, the British government replaced the dilatory Howe with General Clinton, and ordered him to abandon Philadelphia and concentrate his forces at New York. This movement was accomplished by a march across New Jersey, with Washington's army in close pursuit. At Mon-mouth, June 28, 1778, the Americans might have won a victory but for the disobedience of General Charles Lee, but Clinton's army made good its retreat, and once more Washington's army stood guard over New York. From this time on no major military movements took place in the North, although the British conducted many exasper-ating raids along the coast adjacent to their headquarters. Marauding bands of Tories and Indians also laid waste the northwestern frontier. In 1778 the Wyoming Valley of Pennsylvania and the Cherry Valley of New York were the scenes of terrible massacres; and well before that date constant fighting had brought the pioneer outposts in Kentucky to the very verge of extinction.

The British return to New York

It was at this point that George Rogers Clark, a young Kentucky land speculator who realized fully the gravity of the situation, obtained leave from Patrick Henry, the governor of Virginia, to organize a retaliatory expedition.[1] Clark realized that the old French towns in the Illinois country, Kaskaskia, Cahokia, and Vincennes, although seemingly indifferent to the outcome of the war, were actually havens of refuge for hostile Indians and breeding-places for conspiracies. He planned, therefore, to capture them, and if possible also the British post at Detroit. With much difficulty he suc-ceeded in organizing a few hundred frontier militia, with which in the summer of 1778 he set out down the Ohio for the Illinois towns. From the mouth of the Cumberland he marched overland, and taking the in-habitants by surprise captured Kaskaskia, then Cahokia, without a blow.

George Rogers Clark

[1] J. A. James, *The Life of George Rogers Clark* (1928), is the best Clark biography. See also, by the same author, *Oliver Pollock: The Life and Times of an Unknown Patriot* (1937).

Vincennes, also, with the connivance of the French residents in the captured towns, readily accepted Clark's control.

News of these events greatly exercised Colonel Henry Hamilton, British commander at Detroit, who determined at once to repossess Vincennes, and from that vantage-point the next year to advance against the other French towns. He succeeded without difficulty in retaking Vincennes, but he was again surprised by Clark, who marched his troops overland through midwinter cold and ice to attack and capture Vincennes once again (February, 1779). Hamilton himself was sent, none too tenderly, as a prisoner to Virginia. This exploit greatly cheered the frontiersmen, for Hamilton, it was commonly reported, had made presents to the Indians in return for scalps, and the downfall of the "hair-buying general" was no small comfort. Clark never succeeded in capturing Detroit, but his activities greatly diminished the frontier difficulties with British and Indians, and probably saved the Kentucky settlements. In order to punish the Indians for their part in the Wyoming and Cherry Valley massacres of 1778, Washington sent an expedition the following year into the Iroquois country, which succeeded fairly well. Frontier fighting did not cease, but the menace from this quarter was distinctly lessened.

The War in the West

From 1778 to the close of the war practically all other important fighting took place in the South. In this region were many Loyalists whose services the British wished to enlist. Late in 1778 Clinton dispatched an expedition by sea which captured Savannah, and with the aid of troops from Florida, the whole of Georgia. Next year an American effort to recapture Savannah was thwarted, and in May, 1780, the British took Charleston, making prisoner an entire Patriot army of five thousand men under General Lincoln. With the defeat of Gates by Cornwallis at Camden, August 16, 1780, South Carolina, like Georgia, seemed lost to the enemy, but Patriot bands under such leaders as Sumter, Marion, and Pickens kept close watch on the invaders and seriously impeded their movements. The British met their first major reverse in the South when Ferguson, whom Cornwallis had sent through the back-country to recruit Loyalists, was soundly defeated at King's Mountain in October, 1780, by Wataugans who streamed across the mountain passes to defend their homes. Next year the British advanced into North Carolina, but a defeat at Cowpens in January, and a costly victory at Guilford Court House in March persuaded them to retire to Wilmington, leaving the back-country in control of the Patriots.

Benedict Arnold

During these gloomy days, when most of the news from the South was bad, Washington's army stood guard over Clinton around New York. With American morale almost at the breaking point, word came that Benedict Arnold, the man who far more than Gates deserved the honor of bringing about Burgoyne's surrender at Saratoga, had gone over to the British. Stationed at Philadelphia after the British abandonment of that city, Arnold had married a social favorite, lived far beyond his means, and even fraternized with British sympathizers. Finally after a court-martial had sentenced him to receive a reprimand he turned informer, and from the early summer of 1779 on kept Clinton fully apprised of American plans. His plot to obtain the command of West Point in order to surrender it was foiled when Major André, through whom the negotiations were being conducted, was captured within the American lines with incriminating papers on his person. Arnold promptly fled to the British, and André was executed as a spy. Clinton found use for the traitor by sending him south to lay waste parts of Virginia, and later, of Connecticut.[1]

Nevertheless, the turn of the tide was soon to come. Early in 1781 Cornwallis had entered Virginia, giving chase to a small force of Americans under the "boy" Lafayette. But the "boy" escaped, and Cornwallis, at Clinton's suggestion, fortified himself in Yorktown the village of Yorktown on the tip of the peninsula made by the York and the James Rivers. This mistaken strategy, which left the way open for a combined sea and land attack, was not lost on Washington, who immediately laid his plans to take advantage of it. He persuaded the French naval commander, De Grasse, to bring his fleet from the West Indies to the mouth of the Chesapeake, and with his own forces strengthened by the addition of several thousand French regulars under Rochambeau started south to join Lafayette in Virginia.[2] Presently Cornwallis found himself not only cut off from retreat by sea, but hemmed in also by an allied army of sixteen thousand men, more than twice the number of British in Yorktown. He held out for several weeks, but on October 19, 1781, surrendered his entire command. Lord North's often-quoted remark when he heard of this setback, "Oh, God! it is all over," did not tell the exact truth, but Washington's victory at Yorktown did assure the ultimate independence of the United States. In March, 1782, North bowed to the inevitable and resigned, an event which marked also the end of George III's experiment in personal rule. The new ministry, headed first by Rockingham and later by Shelburne, contained many former friends of the colonies, and favored peace with all the enemies of England. The colonies would be welcomed back within the British Empire on their own terms if they would come; but if they would not come, they might have their independence.

[1] Malcolm Decker, *Benedict Arnold, Son of the Havens* (1932).

[2] Lafayette's American activities are admirably set forth in the trilogy by Louis Gottschalk, *Lafayette Comes to America* (1935), *Lafayette Joins the American Army* (1937), and *Lafayette and the Close of the American Revolution* (1942).

Congress had selected peace commissioners even before Yorktown: John Adams, Benjamin Franklin, Thomas Jefferson, John Jay, and Henry Laurens. Of these five only three, Adams, Franklin, and Jay, actually served. With needless timidity Congress instructed the commissioners to work for the Mississippi River boundary rather than to demand it, and to be governed in all matters of consequence by the advice of the French. Fortunately John Jay, who played the leading rôle for the Americans when peace negotiations were opened at Paris in 1782, refused to consider himself bound by these instructions, and on November 30, 1782, won a notable diplomatic triumph when the British and American delegations approved a separate preliminary agreement to be incorporated into the final treaty of peace. By the terms of this agreement the boundaries of the United States were to be the Great Lakes, the Mississippi River, and the thirty-first parallel in case Spain received Florida, but a line nearly a degree and a half farther north in case Great Britain retained it. The final treaty, signed September 3, 1783, and ratified by Congress, January 14, 1784, accepted the terms of the preliminary treaty, and since later on Spain received Florida, the United States regarded its southern boundary as thirty-one degrees. When the English ceded Florida to Spain without definition of boundaries, the setting was arranged for a boundary dispute that was to last for many years. Vergennes, whose plans for the United States were far less generous, was amazed at the liberality of the British terms. "The English," he wrote, "buy peace rather than make it. Their concessions . . . exceed all that I could have thought possible."

Treaty of Paris

Other provisions agreed upon at Paris included the retention of fishing rights for Americans off the coasts of Newfoundland, equal rights of navigation for the United States and Great Britain in the Mississippi River, the right of British subjects to sue for the collection of debts unpaid at the outbreak of war, and a recommendation to the several states that confiscated Loyalist property be restored to its owners. The last two provisions caused much difficulty. Ultimately, by the Jay Treaty of 1795, the central government agreed to pay off such debts still outstanding, but laws discriminating against Loyalists remained on the statute books of some states until after the War of 1812. The treaty as a whole was a magnificent victory for American diplomacy, although the lack of an adequate commercial agreement with Great Britain was long felt.[1]

[1] S. F. Bemis, *The Diplomacy of the American Revolution* (1935), is written with a sure hand. More general accounts are in S. F. Bemis, *A Diplomatic History of the United States* (1942); and Thomas A. Bailey, *A Diplomatic History of the American People* (1940; new ed., 1946). See also G. H. Guttridge, *English Whiggism and the American Revolution* (1942); F. J. Klingberg, *The Morning of America* (1941).

5

The Confederation Interlude

WHETHER the American Revolution was merely one revolution or thirteen separate revolutions will probably never be settled to the complete satisfaction of even the closest students of the period. Certain it is, however, that the outbreak of war not only brought into existence a new and revolutionary central government, but also resulted in the establishment of new and equally revolutionary governments within the several colonies — or, as they were soon more properly called, states.[1] In only two instances, Rhode Island and Connecticut, where liberal charters of self-government existed that needed only to be renamed to become constitutions, were the old forms of government retained. Elsewhere drastic changes were necessary, although in Massachusetts an effort was made for a time, in spite of the absence of a royal governor, to adhere to the terms of the colonial charter.

The colonies become states

While these transformations placed the revolutionists in actual control in all the states, they did not satisfy entirely the Anglo-American instinct for regularity, and several states applied to Congress for advice on the problem of establishing legal governments. After some hesitation Congress in May, 1776, urged the formation of permanent constitutions, a course which Virginia had adopted even before the decision of Congress had been learned. During the next few years all the other states, save only Rhode Island and Connecticut, followed the advice of Congress and the example of Virginia. Procedures varied widely, but in Massachusetts the method of forming a new constitution that was presently to become general was closely approximated. The existing legislative body postponed the calling of a constitutional convention until it had asked and received the authority of the towns for such a course, while the convention itself, although directly chosen by the people, felt obliged to submit the constitution it had drawn to the towns for approval.

State constitutions

It was natural enough that the Americans should wish to have written

---

[1] The best work on this subject is Allan Nevins, *The American States during and after the Revolution, 1775–1789* (1924).

constitutions. In the past most of the colonies had been able to point to some specific document according to which their government had been carried on, and the new states were merely following precedent when they replaced the old document with a new one. Moreover, the contract theory of government was then generally accepted, and in setting up such a relationship, between the people on the one hand and those who were to be placed in authority over them on the other, there was an obvious advantage about a plainly worded written statement. There seems to have been no disposition whatever to follow the English example and permit an accumulation of precedents to grow into an unwritten constitution.

Far from being radical, the new constitutions leaned heavily upon colonial experience, and because the colonial governments had been remarkably alike, whether classified as royal, proprietary, or corporate, it followed that the new state governments were much alike. By means of bills of rights many of them reemphasized the doctrine, already stated in the Declaration of Independence, that there were certain inalienable rights of men upon which government might not trespass. The theory that governmental powers were unlimited, or, as specifically applied in England, that the powers of Parliament were unlimited, was thoroughly distasteful to Americans, both before and after the Revolution. The framers of the first constitutions assumed also that there should be three branches of government, executive, legislative, and judicial, and that each should be kept as distinct as possible from the others. Late unpleasant relations with royal governors tended to hold the powers of that official at a minimum, while the prerogatives of the more trusted legislative branch were generally amplified. Pennsylvania and Georgia experimented for a time with single-chamber legislatures, but soon gave their adherence to the usual two-house system, common to the other states. Judicial systems were complicated and varied, but emphasized adequately the independence of the third department of government.

Conservatism of the new governments

The conservative character of the American Revolution was further emphasized by the timidity which the constitution-framers showed in entrusting full authority to the people. Property qualifications for those who were to exercise the suffrage were maintained in every state, and sometimes far higher property qualifications were prescribed for office-holders than for voters. Indirect elections, particularly for such high officials as governors and judges, were common, while the upper house of the legislature was invariably so constituted as to represent the well-to-do upper classes rather than the common people. Clearly the framers of these constitutions did not believe that the right to vote or the right to

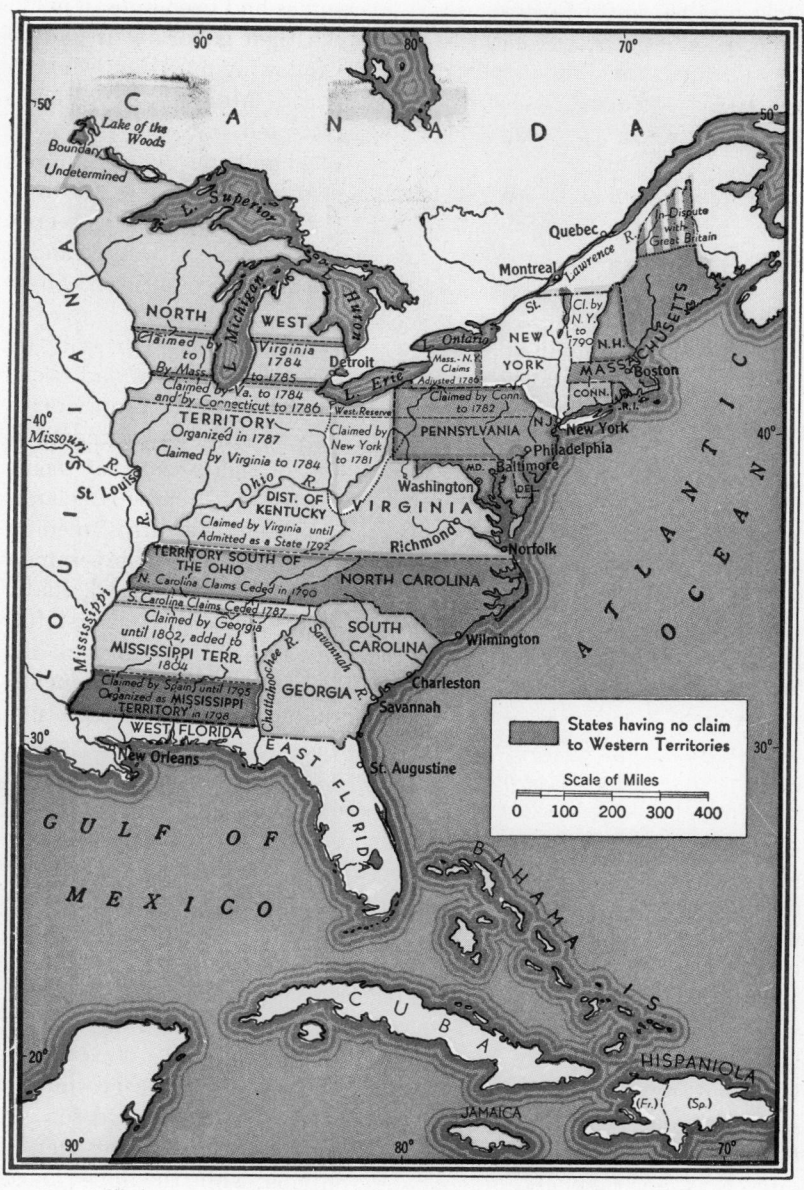

THE UNITED STATES DURING THE CONFEDERATION PERIOD

hold office should be regarded as among the natural rights of men. Only in the more or less irregular state of Vermont, formed out of territory claimed by both New Hampshire and New York, was the right of suffrage granted to all men over twenty-one years of age, but Vermont was not accorded official recognition for many years. Furthermore, the new constitutions made quite inadequate provisions for future changes. As often as not their framers overlooked the matter of amendments altogether; and when they did include a clause on this subject it was rarely workable.

The various states assumed for themselves without question all rights of sovereignty, and paid scant attention to the Continental Congress, through the work of which a central government was being evolved. Loyalty to state, indeed, was probably far stronger **State** than loyalty to nation, and it is not surprising that the idea **sovereignty** of state sovereignty died hard. Nevertheless the exigencies of war required that there be unity of action, and the problem of union, always evaded in colonial times, now had to be faced.

The Continental Congress, which in 1775 had taken over the direction of the war, was quick to recognize that it had little if any legal authority for the powers it was forced by the logic of events to exercise; and in June, 1776, with independence imminent, it ap- **Plans for** pointed a committee, headed by John Dickinson, to draft a **a national** plan of confederation. Dickinson's committee, in working **government** out this assignment, made no effort to introduce innovations. The sufficiency of the existing *de facto* central government was taken for granted; all that was deemed necessary was to describe its character, and then to obtain the necessary grant of powers from the states. Congress was to be clothed only with such authority as might be necessary to deal with problems common to all the states.

It was not until November 15, 1777, that the Articles of Confederation were recommended to the states for adoption.[1] They provided for just such a Congress as already existed. It was to be composed of delegates, not less than two nor more than seven, from **The** each of the thirteen states. These delegates were more like **Articles of** diplomatic agents than representatives, for they were paid **Confederation** by the states that sent them, and, while they were chosen annually, were subject to recall at any time. Regardless of the number of delegates it sent to Congress, each state had only one vote. A curious, and as it proved a most unfortunate, provision required that any delegate might

[1] A. C. McLaughlin, *The Confederation and the Constitution* (1905), is particularly good on the problems of union. John Fiske, *The Critical Period of American History* (1888), is generally accounted the best of Fiske's books, but for a revisionist point of view see Merrill Jensen, *The Articles of Confederation* (1940).

serve only three years out of each six. Another provision, even more unfortunate, required the consent of two-thirds of the states to pass any measure of importance. To cast the vote of a state at least two delegates must be present and in agreement. If a state delegation divided equally on any matter, then the state lost its vote. Otherwise, a majority of the delegation determined the vote of the state.

The listed powers of Congress gave it complete control over foreign affairs and some control over interstate relations. Congress might make peace or war, send and receive ambassadors, make treaties

Powers of Congress

and alliances, govern trade relations with the Indians, determine the standards of coinage (the states might still coin money) and of weights and measures, and organize a postal service. Conversely, the states might not, without the consent of Congress, make treaties with foreign powers, send or receive ambassadors, or engage in war. It was intended that within this sphere the Congress should be unhampered by state interference.

There was nevertheless no room for doubt as to where sovereignty lay under the Articles of Confederation, for they pointedly declared that each state retained its "sovereignty, freedom, and independence." Congress in a sense was merely an assembly of diplomats to whom had been entrusted the control of common problems. It could exercise only such limited powers as were assigned to it; the states had all the rest, including the all-important right of taxation. If Congress wanted money, it might requisition it from the states. The regulation of commerce was another power fully reserved to the states. Only through the incidental provisions of treaties could Congress in any way control commerce with outside nations, and it was given no authority whatever over interstate commerce. Changes in the Articles could be made only after the approval of Congress and ratification by every state legislature.

But for the objections of Maryland, the Articles of Confederation might not have been long delayed in adoption. That one state, however, speaking up in behalf of the "small" states, insisted that the

Problem of the western lands

states with claims to western lands — Massachusetts, Connecticut, Virginia, North Carolina, South Carolina, Georgia, and perhaps New York — should surrender their claims to a "common stock, to be parceled out by Congress into free, convenient, and independent Governments, as the wisdom of that body shall hereafter direct." Not until Virginia, the neighbor of whose potential greatness Maryland was most afraid, had agreed to surrender her claim to Congress was Maryland content. Her ratification, the thirteenth, came on March 1, 1781, more than two years after every other state had agreed to the Articles, and only then could they go into effect. Incidentally,

Virginia's concern over the ratification of the Articles was greatly increased by the Cornwallis invasion.

While the leaders of the American Revolution were no doubt chiefly interested in bringing about political changes, the transformation that actually took place in American life during this eventful ***The*** period was by no means confined to politics. As one dis- ***Revolution,*** tinguished historian observes, "Who shall say to the waves ***socially*** of revolution: thus far shall we go and no farther?" It is a ***considered*** fact that "many economic desires, many social aspirations were set free by the political struggle, many aspects of colonial society profoundly altered by the forces thus let loose." Nor was this social revolution ended with the conclusion of the war, for the forces making for change merely gathered momentum with each successful assault upon the older order.[1]

The downfall of the colonial aristocracy was far more than a political phenomenon. Making due allowance for exceptions — and there were many — the Patriots represented in the main the common people, and the Loyalists the upper strata of society. The victory of the former, together with their studied persecution of the latter, made it possible for men who in colonial times had been regarded as of low degree to hold high office and enjoy important privileges. Common men came naturally to hold themselves in higher esteem, and their superiors in lower. Many, indeed, read into the Declaration of Independence, with its emphasis upon the equality of men, a demand for the emancipation of the slaves, and in all the northern colonies the abolition of slavery followed fairly promptly upon the attainment of independence. Even in the South emancipation societies were common, and the gradual disappearance of slavery was generally expected.

The trend towards small independent holdings of land, which was marked even in colonial times, was greatly accelerated by the Revolution. Many of the largest estates, the property of Loyalists, ***Land-*** were confiscated and sold out in small tracts to free farmers. ***ownership*** The old feudal rules of primogeniture, which provided that property in land should descend to the eldest son, and of entail, which held such property in the family by prohibiting its owner either to sell it or to give it away, were quickly abolished. Quit-rents, always regarded as a nuisance and rarely paid without protest, became a thing of the past. Moreover, such British restrictions upon the advance of the agricultural frontier as the Proclamation of 1763 and the Quebec Act lost their mean-

[1] On non-political aspects of the Revolution the reader should consult J. F. Jameson, *The American Revolution Considered as a Social Movement* (1926). See also the entertaining essays by Dixon Ryan Fox, *Ideas in Motion* (1935), and the first volume of the monumental work by J. B. McMaster, *A History of the People of the United States from the Revolution to the Civil War* (8 vols., 1883–1913).

ing, and cheap lands to the west were available for all who wished them, particularly for those veterans of the war who had been granted land bounties as a part of the inducement to enlist. Landownership no longer served as a test of gentility, and, even as a qualification for voting, it extended the suffrage, so one conservative asserted, "to every biped of the forest."

Changes with respect to landownership were closely paralleled by changes in industry and commerce. American manufactures, always hampered to some extent by British restrictions and still more by the habit of buying manufactured articles from England, were immensely stimulated by the war. Far more attention was given than formerly to the making of such necessary articles as firearms, gunpowder, nails, salt, paper, and cloth, and the occupations of the people shifted accordingly. Commerce, on the other hand, suffered acutely from the war, although much successful privateering kept the sailors' art alive, as the speedy return of American ships to the seas at the close of the war abundantly attested. Freedom from the British restrictions on colonial trade opened up some new opportunities to American skippers, but this advantage was probably more than offset by the loss of trade privileges that the colonies had once enjoyed as a part of the British Empire.

Industry and commerce

Independence served also to force a series of readjustments with respect to the religious life of the Americans. The union of church and state that existed in nine out of thirteen of the colonies was promptly attacked, although with varying results. In the South, where the state church was the Church of England, disestablishment was naturally associated with revolution, and was early accomplished. Here the demand for religious freedom met its most vigorous resistance in Virginia, but in 1786 the legislature of the Old Dominion asserted, in words penned by Jefferson, that "no man shall be compelled to frequent or support any religious worship, place, or ministry whatsoever, nor shall be enforced, restrained, molested or burthened in his body or goods, nor shall otherwise suffer on account of his religious opinions or belief; but that all men shall be free to profess, and by argument to maintain, their opinion in matters of religion, and that the same shall in no wise diminish, enlarge, or affect their civil capacities." In New England, where, except for Rhode Island, the Congregational Church was supported by the state, patriotism could not so easily be invoked on the side of religious freedom, and the struggle lasted far into the nineteenth century. In Massachusetts, the strongest citadel of Puritanism, disestablishment was not voted until 1833.

Religious adjustments

After the Revolution most of the American denominations undertook to reorganize their systems of church government. With this in mind, the American Anglicans, when they failed to obtain the co-operation of English church officials, persuaded the non-juring bishops of Scotland to consecrate in 1784 an American bishop, Samuel Seabury. With an American episcopate thus assured, the Protestant Episcopal Church of the United States was organized. About the same time the separate status of the American Catholic Church was recognized by a decree from Rome, and in 1790 Father John Carroll was made Bishop of Baltimore. At the close of the Revolution John Wesley, the English founder of the Methodist Church (who himself never left the Church of England), sent Thomas Coke, another Englishman, to the United States as general superintendent of the American Methodists. On arriving in America, Coke promptly associated himself with Francis Asbury, the leading spirit among the American Methodists, and in December, 1784, at a conference of the church held in Baltimore, the two were designated joint superintendents. Asbury and his successors, contrary to Wesley's wishes, assumed the title of bishop, and the denomination over which they presided was officially known as the Methodist Episcopal Church. Other denominations, although freer from overseas connections than these three, generally redefined and elaborated their systems of government.

Of still greater significance was the revolution in thought and feeling that came over the American people during the period of the war. Religion, in the more formal sense, suffered disastrously, for *The* churches were destroyed, religious ties loosened, standards of *revolution in* morality lowered, and traditional beliefs swept away. On *thought and* the other hand, the revolutionary ideals of liberty and equal- *feeling* ity were deeply impressed upon the minds of the people. The inhuman penal codes of the eighteenth century were more frequently denounced, and imprisonment as a means of punishment for debt sometimes received the ridicule it deserved. A change could be noted, also, in the popular concept of education. The colonial schools, such as they were, had been virtually destroyed by the years of Revolution, and new systems had to be devised. In an age that exalted the rights of the common man, pressure upon the state to accept the obligation of popular education steadily increased. Prophetic of the future was the provision in the first constitution of the unrecognized state of Vermont that a school system, beginning with the towns and including a state university, should be established. Systems of this sort were slow to develop and seven of the original state constitutions made no mention whatever of education; but when, in the nineteenth century, the American school system did take form, it was under secular, not religious, control, and its right to public support was still defended on the grounds Jefferson had stated years before. "Above all things," he had written, "I hope the education of the common people will be attended to; convinced that on their good sense we may rely with the most security for the preservation of a due degree of liberty."

The spirit that permeated the American Revolution was well preserved in the efforts made by Congress under the Confederation to deal with the problem of the West. With little hesitation the central government prepared to follow the advice that Maryland had given so insistently by planning for the creation of new western states. All thought of establishing a western colonial empire dependent upon the East was brushed aside; the new United States was in no mood to repeat the mistakes of the British Empire. The rights of local self-government so hardly won by the Revolution were to extend across the mountains.

The cessions of western lands to Congress by the states claiming them were not completed until 1802, when Georgia at last surrendered her claim, but after the adoption of the Articles of Confederation in 1781 it was apparent that the nation rather than the states must deal with the West. Here a number of permanent settlements had already been made. Farthest in the interior lay the French villages that George Rogers Clark had conquered, which together with Detroit and other centers of fur-trade had a population numbering several thousands. On the upper Ohio around Pittsburgh, in the valleys of the Holston and Watauga Rivers, in the blue-grass region of Kentucky, and now also along the Cumberland in central Tennessee were other settlements of varying sizes, all of which were growing rapidly.[1]

That attention must be given to the needs of these western communities by the central government was soon made evident. In the region south of the Ohio River, where new settlers were entering **Western independence** more rapidly than anywhere else in the West, there was a marked tendency to disregard the authority of the present states to the east. New western states that might willingly acknowledge the supremacy of a national government, but would not forever remain content to be merely western divisions of eastern states, were in the making. When the Wataugans, who had already shown their capacity for self-government, discovered in 1784 that the state of North Carolina had ceded the region in which they lived to the central government, they promptly established the State of Franklin, and with John Sevier as governor and the laws of North Carolina as a guide to legal conduct, applied for admission to the Union. Ultimately the North Carolina legislature repented of its action, and in a few years the Wataugans returned

---

[1] F. J. Turner, *The Significance of Sections in American History* (1932), has a chapter on "Western State-Making in the Revolutionary Era."

reluctantly to their former allegiance. But they had given a clear warning that the collapse of local self-government in the West was not to be tolerated. Their earlier example, meantime, had been followed by pioneers from Watauga and from Virginia whom Judge Richard Henderson had induced to settle in the vicinity of Nashborough (or Nashville) in the valley of the Cumberland. Here in May, 1780, all the adult male settlers, two hundred and fifty-six in number, had affixed their signatures to an agreement that amounted to a constitution. For a few years this temporary government functioned smoothly, but in 1782 the Assembly of North Carolina recognized the new region by the creation of Davidson County. In Kentucky, which thousands of new pioneers had entered during the closing years of the Revolution, an insistent demand for separate statehood set in. Virginia proved generous, and three times voted to give the Kentuckians what they desired. But during the Confederation period Congress failed to take the necessary steps to make Kentucky a state.[1]

Nevertheless, the strong sentiment in the Southwest for separate statehood and the willingness of its residents to rely upon the national government for protection and support seem not to have been wholly lost upon Congress. In the territory northwest **The Northwest** of the Ohio River, where the title of the national government to the land was already clear, some provision for the future had to be made, and with this end in view Congress passed a series of "Northwest Ordinances" which showed a sympathetic appreciation of the problems of the West. Whether the attitude of Congress was directly affected by the situation in the Southwest is not entirely clear, but the Ordinances safeguarded in a most satisfactory way the right of settlers to adventure into the West and to establish states with the same privileges enjoyed by the old.

The initiative in this matter was taken by Thomas Jefferson, who was a close student of the problems of the West, and realized more fully than most men of his time that provision must be made for the development of a great country. In 1784 he introduced **Ordinance** into Congress a plan for the organization of the West into **of 1784** new states that should remain forever a part of the United States, subject to the central government only as other states were subject, and guaranteed a government republican in form. As originally drawn the Ordinance of 1784 also proposed that slavery should not exist in the West after 1800, and that the region should be gridironed into ten states with fantastic classical names. Congress eliminated both the anti-slavery clause and the pedantic names, but passed the rest of the ordinance as a kind of declaration of intention. In most of the territory under consider-

[1] R. M. McElroy, *Kentucky in the Nation's History* (1909).

ation the Indian titles had not yet been extinguished, and north of the
Ohio River, except in the French villages, white population had not yet
begun to come in.

A year later Congress went even further, and, again at Jefferson's instigation, laid out a plan for the systematic survey and sale of western
lands. Instead of permitting the location of tracts as the
whims of purchasers might direct, the Ordinance of 1785
provided for the "rectangular" or "rectilinear" system of
survey, so familiar to western Americans of later generations. Parallel
lines were to be drawn at six-mile intervals, both north and south, and
east and west, as nearly as the sphericity of the earth would permit.
Each of the squares so described was to be called a township, and each
north and south tier of townships was to be called a range. Further subdivisions of the townships were to be made by east and west as well as
north and south lines surveyed at intervals of one mile, so that each township would be marked off into thirty-six "sections." The sections, each
of which was thus a mile square and contained approximately six hundred
and forty acres, might then be divided into "halves" and "quarters,"
the "quarters" into "half-quarters" and "quarter-quarters," and so on
indefinitely.

Since two treaties with the Indians, one signed at Fort Stanwix in 1784
and the other at Fort McIntosh in 1785, had opened up for settlement the
tract of land immediately to the west of the upper Ohio, the Ordinance
of 1785 made provision for the sale as well as for the survey of the public
domain. In accordance with a New England precedent, section sixteen
of each township was to be reserved as a bounty to public schools, but the
rest of the land was to be offered for sale to the highest bidder in lots of a
section or more. The minimum price was fixed at one dollar per acre,
but it was hoped that by holding auctions in each state competitive bidding would result in a considerably higher average price being paid.
From these sales Congress hoped, in vain as events proved, to obtain a
steady and much-needed source of revenue.

With the way thus prepared, Congress authorized the survey of seven
ranges of townships west of the western boundary of Pennsylvania, and
sent out surveyors to proceed with the work. Two of them,
Generals Benjamin Tupper and Samuel Parsons, both Massachusetts veterans of the Revolutionary War, saw the
boundless possibilities for land speculation in the Northwest, and were
instrumental in creating the Ohio Company of Associates, through which
they hoped that they themselves and other war veterans of their state
might make a neat profit. Each participant was permitted to subscribe
up to five thousand dollars in the company, the subscription to be paid

Ordinance of 1785 (margin note)

The Ohio Company (margin note)

in the certificates of indebtedness — now considered worthless — which Congress had issued to soldiers in lieu of pay. Congress was then to be persuaded to sell to the company perhaps as much as a million dollars' worth of land at an extremely low price, and to take its own worthless certificates in payment. The scheme seemed reasonable, for the debt owing to the veterans was unquestionable, and the Reverend Manasseh Cutler, minister at Ipswich, Massachusetts, was sent as lobbyist to New York to push it through. Finally, when he agreed that a group of congressmen and their friends, to be known as the Scioto Company, should be let in on the deal, his efforts were crowned with success. To the Ohio Company Congress would sell a million and a half acres of land at two-thirds of a dollar an acre; to the Scioto Company it would give an option on the purchase of an additional three and a half million acres adjacent to the Ohio Company tract. When a quorum could be assembled Congress promptly chartered both companies; and Cutler, still making himself useful, succeeded in inducing the Scioto Associates to advance some $143,000 to further the work of settling up the Ohio Company's lands.[1]

Meantime Congress was at work on the famous Ordinance of 1787 for the government of the territory northwest of the Ohio River. On July 13 the Ordinance was adopted. It provided for three stages in the evolution of government. During the first stage a governor, a secretary, and three judges, all appointed by Congress, were to adopt and enforce such laws of the older states as might seem appropriate to the new territory. Whenever the district could show five thousand free male inhabitants, however, the freeholders might choose a representative assembly, which on coming together would nominate ten persons, from whom Congress would choose five to be a legislative council, or upper house. The two-house legislature thus established might then enact whatever laws it chose, subject to the governor's veto. Furthermore, a delegate to Congress might be chosen, who might speak and introduce bills, but might not vote. The Ordinance presumed that ultimately the territory northwest of the Ohio River would be divided into not less than three nor more than five states, and whenever a given district had attained a population of sixty thousand free inhabitants it should be admitted "on an equal footing with the original states in all respects whatsoever," and with full "liberty to form a permanent constitution and state government."

Ordinance of 1787

The promise of ultimate statehood and a number of other declarations

[1] Amelia C. Ford, *Colonial Precedents of Our National Land System as it Existed in 1800* (1910); P. J. Treat, *The National Land System, 1785–1820* (1910); B. H. Hibbard, *A History of the Public Land Policies (1924)*; R. M. Robbins, *Our Landed Heritage; The Public Domain, 1776–1936* (1942).

were set apart from the rest of the Ordinance as "articles of compact between the original states and the people and states in the said territory" which were to remain forever "unalterable, unless by common consent." Freedom of religious worship, freedom from arbitrary imprisonment, and the right of trial by jury were thus solemnly guaranteed; schools and the means of public education were to be forever encouraged; the utmost good faith was always to be observed toward the Indians; the settlers in the new territory were to be required to pay their share of the federal debts and the expense of federal government; the prospective territorial or state legislatures were never to interfere with the administration of the public lands by the United States; the navigable waters of the West were to remain forever free for use without tax or duty by all citizens of the United States from whatever state; and there should be "neither slavery nor involuntary servitude in the said territory, otherwise than in punishment of crimes whereof the party shall have been duly convicted." By this last clause Jefferson's plan to exclude slavery from the Northwest, which had barely failed of adoption in the Ordinance of 1784, was now revived and accepted.

In the spring of 1788, when forty-seven colonists from New England floated down the Ohio River from Pittsburgh to Marietta, the settlement of the Northwest Territory was begun. Before many months Marietta was a village of many log cabins, surrounded by numerous "clearings," and possessed of the customary "block-house" for defense against the Indians. The Ohio Company never became the money-making project that its founders had hoped, but it did stimulate colonization, and it was able to redeem a small fraction of the land to which it was entitled. The Scioto Company, except for the settlement of a few hundred forlorn French colonists at Gallipolis, down the river from Marietta and as events proved on Ohio Company land, accomplished nothing whatever of note, and was unable to take up any part of its option. Another early settlement was made at what came to be known as Cincinnati by John Cleves Symmes, a well-to-do citizen of New Jersey, who in 1788 obtained a grant of land from Congress. By 1790 the Northwest Territory had nearly forty-three hundred inhabitants as well as an acute Indian problem, which taxed to the limit the resources of Governor Arthur St. Clair, whom Congress, under the terms of the Ordinance of 1787, had sent out in 1788 to inaugurate government in the settlements.[1]

Aside from its decisions with respect to the West, the Congress of the

The Ohio settlements

---

[1] The Old Northwest has attracted many historians. Among the best general accounts are B. A. Hinsdale, *The Old Northwest* (1899); F. A. Ogg, *The Old Northwest* (1919); and B. W. Bond, Jr., *The Civilization of the Old Northwest* (1934).

Confederation had few successes to its credit. Its life span of eight years coincided closely with a period of economic depression that came in the wake of the Revolutionary War. Among the most serious of the problems that the new nation confronted was the necessity of establishing good trade relationships with Great Britain, something that the colonies as component parts of the British Empire had never really lacked. American trade had always flowed naturally to Great Britain, and once the interruption of war was at an end it tended to resume its normal channels. But American shippers soon found that they could not count on the same privileges in British ports that they had enjoyed before the war, and that in the British West Indies, where their ships had once been so free to come and go, they were confronted by the most exasperating restrictions. A good trade treaty with Great Britain thus became a kind of economic necessity.

Another problem of Anglo-American relations arose out of the fact that many of the British posts in the Northwest, despite the treaty of peace which gave the region south of the Great Lakes to the United States, were still held by British troops. The British **The Northwest** were loath to withdraw the protection they had always given **posts** the Canadian fur-trade; furthermore, it was important from the fur-traders' point of view that the settlement of the Northwest be held back, for whenever settlers came in fur-bearing animals did not long survive. Americans believed that the British posts were centers of anti-American influence among the Indians, and that because of British activities on American soil the advance of the American frontier was being opposed by the savages. From the American point of view British retention of the Northwest posts was thus both a breach of faith and an evidence of hostility.

To deal with these problems of commerce and of the frontier, John Adams was dispatched to England in 1785, but his mission failed miserably. As for the commercial treaty, it was apparent that the British could count on whatever American trade they **Adams to** wanted without it, while with reference to their retention of **England** the Northwest posts they had good excuses to offer. In spite of the terms of the treaty of 1783, British subjects found it practically impossible to collect debts owing them by Americans since before the war, and the promised restoration of Loyalist property failed also to materialize. If the Americans themselves broke the treaty, why should they expect the British to keep it?

The Confederation government was equally unsuccessful in its efforts to deal with the difficulties that existed between the United States and Spain. Since it was no longer a part of the British Empire, the United

States now had to make its own trade agreements with Spain, particularly such as were necessary to facilitate the easy exchange of commodities with the Spanish West Indies.   There
was difficulty, too, about the location of the Florida boundary, and about the right claimed by Americans to free navigation of
the Mississippi River, the mouth of which for many miles into the interior lay wholly within Spanish territory.   In 1785 Don Diego de
Gardoqui arrived in the United States with power to negotiate on these
matters as the representative of Spain.   Gardoqui proposed to John
Jay, who in 1784 had been charged by Congress with the conduct of
American foreign affairs, that the United States give up for a period
of twenty-five or thirty years its claim to the right of navigation of the
lower Mississippi, in return for a favorable trade treaty.   Jay was
tempted by this bargain, for he knew that the agreement would be of
great value to the northeastern states, while the West, as he saw it,
would grow very little in population during the next quarter-century.
But representatives from the southern states blocked the agreement.
These states had not yet surrendered their claims to western lands,
and were vitally interested in the welfare of the West.   They knew,
too, that the independent spirit of the West would never brook such
restraint as the treaty proposed, and would find a means to use the
Mississippi even at the cost of secession from the United States.[1] Without the use of the River, western settlements would have no outlet
to the sea, and little chance of growth.   The net result of this impasse was
that Confederation diplomacy failed with Spain as completely as with
Great Britain.

Jay-Gardoqui Treaty (side note)

The Confederation showed an equal lack of ability in dealing with
other foreign powers.   A few trade treaties were signed, notably those
with Sweden and Prussia, but they turned out to be relatively unimportant to American commerce.   Treaties with France and Holland, signed
during the war, were maintained and renewed, but they too failed to
attract American trade away from its normal pre-revolutionary channels, while the good relations between the United States and her former
allies in the war with England were continually imperiled by the inability
of the American government to pay its foreign debt.

The financial embarrassment of the Confederation government was
always acute.   To meet its ordinary expenditures it required
an income of about a half-million dollars a year, and this
sum made no provision for payments, either of interest or
principal, on the public debt.   Altogether the United States had incurred

Confederation finance (side note)

[1] On Spanish-American relations during this period consult A. P. Whitaker, *The Spanish American Frontier, 1783–1795* (1927); and F. A. Ogg, *The Opening of the Mississippi* (1904).

an indebtedness of well over forty million dollars during the prosecution of the war. About six million dollars had been borrowed from France, and perhaps another two millions from other foreign sources. The remainder, mostly in the shape of back pay for soldiers and certificates of indebtedness to those who had furnished supplies for the army, was owing to citizens of the United States.

The means by which the government could raise money to discharge its financial obligations was strictly limited. It might resort to paper-money issues, but during the war this source of revenue had been dried up by overuse. It might also indulge in further borrowing provided creditors could be found to lend, and some funds were actually obtained in Holland for use in paying the interest on the foreign debt. A small sum was realized from the sales of public lands, and the post-office brought in ten or fifteen thousand dollars a year. In the main, however, Congress had to rely upon requisitions levied upon the states for money it needed to meet obligations of every sort and kind. The requisition system proved to be entirely inadequate. Requests for funds were honored by the states only in so far as they chose to honor them, and probably not to exceed one-tenth of the sums asked for by Congress were ever paid in. Much of the money that was obtained, moreover, was of uncertain value, for the states also had their financial difficulties, and many of them had resorted to overissues of paper currency. Plans for the compulsory collection of the sums levied upon the states were considered, but none seemed practicable enough to warrant giving it a trial. On two occasions, once in 1781 and again in 1783, Congress sought to obtain a limited right to levy tariffs, but in each instance the proposition failed of ratification, leaving the central government still dependent upon the unsatisfactory requisition system. Thus cursed with financial impotence, the Congress of the Confederation became a butt of ridicule. Good men often refused to serve as delegates, while those who accepted so generally neglected their duties that a quorum for the transaction of business became difficult to obtain.[1]

The state governments were confronted by problems almost as difficult as those which confronted Congress. They possessed the power to levy tariffs that Congress so much coveted, but its exercise by thirteen different agencies resulted in serious complications. Imports tended to arrive at the ports of low-tariff states rather than high-tariff states, with smuggling as an inevitable concomitant. Endless confusion and much bad feeling was added by the

Confusion in the states

[1] D. R. Dewey, *Financial History of the United States* (1903), has gone through many editions, and is still the most useful general work on the subject. Somewhat broader in scope, and closer to the present in its point of view, is H. J. Carman, *Social and Economic History of the United States* (2 vols., 1930–34).

states levying duties against each other. Connecticut, for example, taxed goods from Massachusetts more than she would have taxed the same goods if imported from England. The power which the states shared with the central government was another source of trouble. During the Confederation period the lack of gold in the United States, always a chronic complaint of the continental colonies, became an acute menace. Neither gold nor silver was mined anywhere within the United States; hard money was difficult to obtain from the Spanish colonies in the West Indies because of the existing restrictions on commerce; the reward of privateering that had brought some precious metals into the country during the Revolution could no longer be reaped; and the gold left by the British army was soon drained off to meet an unfavorable balance of trade. Furthermore, the debtor classes within each state, more articulate than ever as a result of the Revolution, urged paper money because of the blessings that an inflated currency would bring to them; and in many states the more conservative propertied classes, who opposed inflation, were outvoted.

The records of Rhode Island and Massachusetts on the paper-money question give a fair understanding of the situation. In Rhode Island the paper-money faction got the upper hand in the legislature, and multiplied issues until the currency was almost valueless; then, when

---

WAR OF 1812

This cartoon was entitled "The Nation's Bulwark: A Well-Disciplined Militia." The showing of the American army during the War of 1812 was not uniformly creditable. One trouble was the heavy reliance upon state militia, which was often no better trained or disciplined than the detachment of a somewhat later date portrayed in this cartoon. On one occasion New York militia stationed on the American side of the Niagara River watched American regulars who were attacking British troops at Queenstown Heights on the Canadian side go down to defeat rather than come to their aid. (Photo from Culver.)

The burning of the Capitol and the Executive Mansion at Washington was due to another failure of ill-trained troops. The British ordered the burning of American public buildings as an act of retaliation against the Americans for their burning of the parliament buildings at York (Toronto) the preceding year. But British officers kept their troops under control. There was no general looting of the city, and little damage to private property. The "White House" got its name from the paint its sandstone walls received to cover the scars of the British burning. (Photo from Brown Bros.)

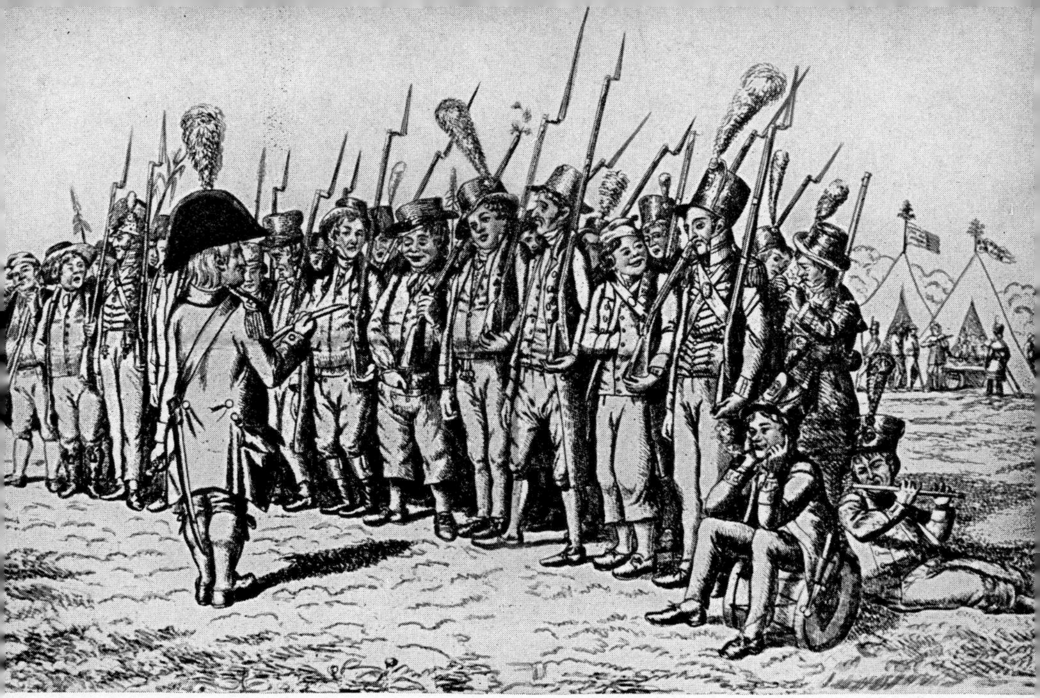

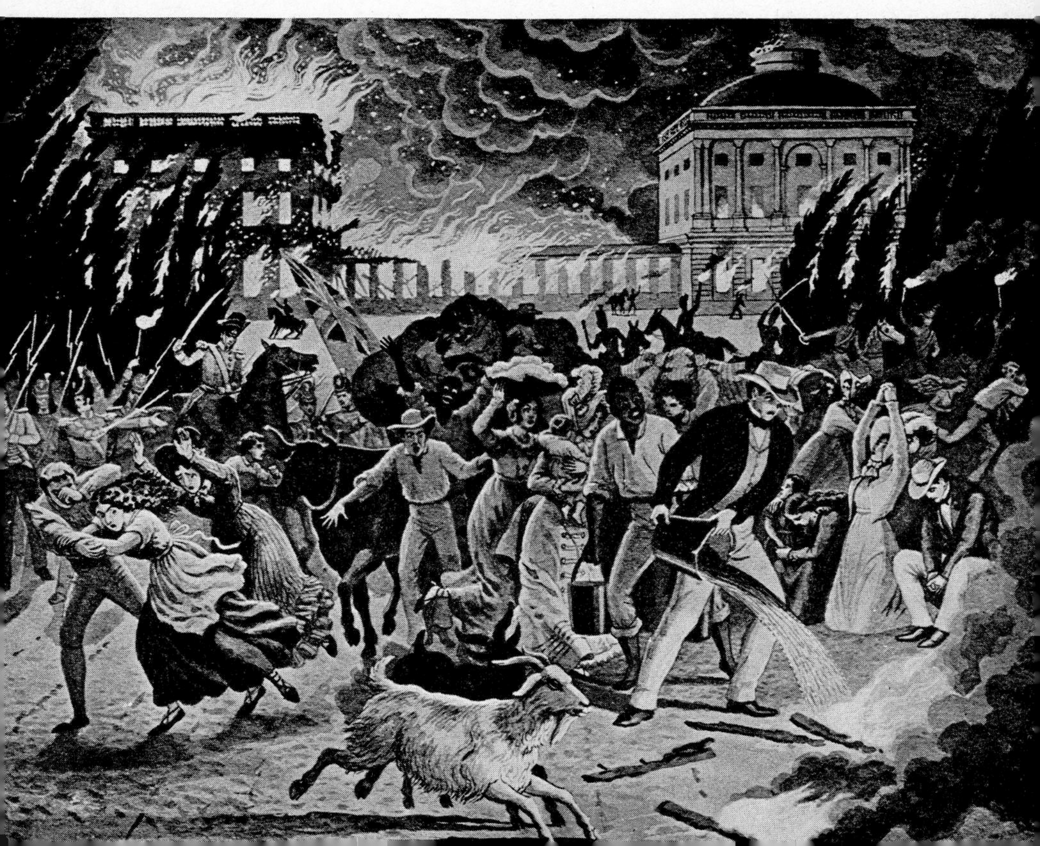

NEWBERRY & DOLE.
FORWARDING & COMMISSION
NEWBERRY & DOLE
STORAGE, FORWARD
& COMMISSION.
SALT
OSCEOLA
BUFFALO.

"legal-tender" paper money was refused, passed a law making its refusal a punishable offense without so much as requiring a trial by jury for the offender. The attempt to enforce this law led Trevett vs. Weeden to one of the most important judicial decisions in American legal history, for in the case of *Trevett vs. Weeden* (1786) the state supreme court held that the law was out of harmony with the Rhode Island charter and therefore unconstitutional. This decision was attacked by the legislature, which summoned the judges before it and voted unsatisfactory the defense of their action that they made. Furthermore, at the next election three out of the four judges concerned were retired. But the precedent set was not overthrown, and the later power of the courts over legislation which they deemed unconstitutional owed much to this decision.

In Massachusetts the contest over paper money took the form of a test of strength between the coast towns, which were relatively prosperous from what commerce still endured, and the small farmers of the interior, who found it difficult during the prevailing hard Shays's Rebellion times to pay their debts and taxes. As a measure of debt relief the rural classes demanded liberal paper-money issues, but the legislature was under the control of the coast towns and refused to comply with the farmers' demands. Instead, heavy taxes were levied to pay off

---

GOING FARTHER WEST

It was the unrecognized function of the fur-trader to "pioneer the way for civilization." Oftentimes he, rather than the official explorer, was the first white man to set foot on Indian trails and to push his canoe up uncharted streams. The fur-trade and civilization were incompatible, for settlers either drove away most of the fur-bearing animals or destroyed them. Hence, the fur-trader removed ever farther and farther into the west and north; save in the mountains and the frozen northland he had always to give way to the settler. Today most of the pelts from which fur garments are made come from "fur farms" located in such thickly settled areas as Wisconsin. (Currier & Ives, 1866. Photo from Bettmann.)

Chicago began as a fur-trading post in the seventeenth century, and by 1830 was only a village of log houses with less than a hundred people. The building of the Erie Canal and the use of sailships and steamboats on the Great Lakes increased its accessibility, and started its growth. At the time of this picture it had a population of over four thousand. Later, the coming of the railroads prepared the way for its phenomenal development. (Courtesy of the New York Public Library.)

the war debt, and sheriffs' sales were multiplied. In the summer of 1786 open rebellion broke out. Bands of insurgents, composed of farmers, artisans, and laborers, marched on the courts in several districts and prevented them from sitting. Shays's Rebellion, as this outbreak was called, after its leader, Daniel Shays, was put down by militia led by General Lincoln and paid by means of a loan to which well-to-do citizens, fearful that a wholesale attack upon property rights was imminent, subscribed generously. But the enduring power of the debtor classes was demonstrated in the next state election when Governor Bowdoin, under whom the "Rebellion" had been suppressed, was defeated for re-election by John Hancock, who was still the idol of the radicals.

Not only in Rhode Island and Massachusetts, but in practically all the states the conservative property-owners were genuinely frightened by the growing power of the agrarian and unpropertied classes. To check the democratic and inflationary tendencies so painfully in evidence, a stronger government was needed, one that could maintain order at home, and if possible also protect American rights abroad. Clearly the state governments could not be trusted to do these things, while the central government lacked the power. The Confederation was without an effective executive, and its feeble gropings in that direction had so far proved unavailing; it had no judiciary whatever; it could not regulate commerce; it had no taxing power; and it was at best a mere creature of the states utterly incapable of acting directly upon individuals. Worst of all, amendments to the Articles of Confederation required a unanimous vote, and experience seemed to prove that on this account any strictly legal change would be impossible.

The movement for a closer union was soon given added impetus by two significant interstate gatherings. The first of these was a conference of

A closer union foreshadowed

Maryland and Virginia delegates held at Alexandria, Virginia, and charged with the duty of reconciling certain conflicting regulations with regard to the navigation of Chesapeake Bay and the Potomac River. On the particular points at issue the two states reached an agreement, but the need of a general conference on all matters of commerce could not easily be overlooked. As a result the Virginia legislature invited all the states to send delegates to a convention to be held at Annapolis the first Monday in September, 1786. The Annapolis Convention was actually attended by delegates from only five states, but it adopted a report from the able pen of Alexander Hamilton which pointed out some of the conspicuous defects in the Articles of Confederation and called upon the states to send delegates to a new convention through which a remedy for these defects should be sought. The date set for the new convention was the second

Monday in May, 1787, and the place of meeting suggested was Philadelphia. This proposal was transmitted not only to the various state legislatures, but also to Congress, and on February 21, 1787, the latter body joined in the call for the Philadelphia Convention. In doing so, however, Congress stated that the purpose of the convention was merely to propose amendments to the existing Articles of Confederation. The clear inference was that only by the subsequent ratification of all the thirteen states could any such amendments be adopted.

Forces had long been at work to ensure that ultimately the hope of a stronger union would be realized. The very isolation from the rest of the world that the thirteen American states shared with one another tended to bring them together. Their inhabitants **Forces making for union** were for the most part of a common racial stock, spoke a common language, read much the same books, and had inherited practically the same traditions. Every part of the new nation had, at some time not far removed, gone through the frontier process — a process which did not differ markedly from place to place or from time to time, and tended therefore to supply a common mold for the formation of American traits. The frontier of the seventeen-eighties itself acted as a binding tie. In the mountain valleys of the Appalachians and in the new communities still farther to the west there was a continual mingling of settlers from many different states and even from the Old World. Here state boundaries were freely passed, and old loyalties were soon forgotten. Democratic frontiersmen might fear for the moment the attempt of an aristocratic group in the East to form and dominate a strong central government, but potentially at least the West was inescapably nationalistic.

Moreover, the problems that faced the American states were increasingly national in character. The conflicting interests of debtors and creditors cut across state lines. In the back-country the debtor point of view dominated; along the coast the creditors tended to maintain their control. Commerce vied with agriculture, but most of the states were neither strictly commercial nor strictly agricultural; the commercial classes everywhere tended to present a solid front against an almost equally united agricultural interest. Even in matters pertaining to religion there was a tendency to divide along national rather than along state or local lines. In the East adherents of the old settled faiths, Congregationalists in New England, Quakers in Pennsylvania, Dutch Calvinists in New York, and Episcopalians in the South, found themselves drawn together in defense of the old ways against hordes of upstart Presbyterians, Methodists, and Baptists, who challenged church establishments wherever they found them, overturned timeworn customs, and demanded complete religious freedom as the right of every man. Such common problems as these revealed lines of cleavage within the nation as a whole rather than within the individual states. Efforts to solve these problems nationally tended to draw together radicals from every state and section no less than conservatives, and to prophesy the speedy formation of a closer union.[1]

[1] Dixon Wecter, *When Johnny Comes Marching Home* (1944), explores the activities of the post-Revolutionary War veteran. E. B. Greene, *The Revolutionary Generation, 1763–1790* (1943), is of especial value on aspects of social history. Walter Havighurst, *Land of Promise: The Story of the Northwest Territory* (1946), is useful on western expansion. Louise P. Kellogg, *The British Regime in Wisconsin and the Northwest* (1936), covers the period from the French and Indian War to the War of 1812.

6

The Constitution

By the end of the Confederation Period the line of cleavage in the new nation between the possessors of considerable property and the common people was clearly drawn. The merchants and importers, the shipbuilders and shipowners, the possessors of landed estates, the speculators and money-lenders were set apart by their economic interests from the small farmers, the artisans, and the non-propertied classes generally. Among men of property the fear had grown almost to the proportions of panic that the lower classes would eventually secure control of all the state governments (as they already seemed to have done in Rhode Island), and that as a result property interests everywhere would suffer perhaps even to the point of confiscation. Out of this state of mind came the agitation in favor of a strong central government — a government which would be independent of state control, and would possess the will and the power to protect the rights of property. The movement for the Philadelphia Convention was thus primarily an upper-class affair, and when the time came for the choice of delegates it was the interested upper class that determined the selections.[1]

Classes in America

Fortunately for the well-to-do, the call for the Philadelphia Convention did not designate the method by which delegates should be chosen, and the selections were made, therefore, by the various state legislatures, in most of which the men of property still had comfortable majorities. Rhode Island refused to choose delegates, but from the other states a total of seventy-three men were elected, of whom only fifty-five ever put in their appearance at the convention. These men were typical representatives of the conservative upper class. They were almost without exception men of financial and social standing, well prepared for their labors by education and by previous governmental experience. One may fairly say that the agrarian-artisan class was not represented in the convention at all.

Conservatism of the delegates

[1] C. A. Beard, *An Economic Interpretation of the Constitution of the United States* (1913), is a work that has profoundly affected the thinking of most students of American history. Beard's flair for brilliant interpretation is also given free rein in Charles A. and Mary R. Beard, *The Rise of American Civilization* (2 vols., 1927).

When May 14, 1787, the day for opening the convention, arrived, there were too few present to organize, but on May 25 twenty-nine delegates met in Independence Hall and chose George Washington to be their presiding officer. For three and a half months the sessions continued, usually with not many more in attendance than appeared the first day. The convention at once decided that to promote freedom of discussion and to avoid outside interference, its sessions must be held behind closed doors and all proceedings carefully guarded from the public. It can hardly be denied that the delegates, while men of great ability, had little faith in democracy; indeed, one might almost say that it was their fear of democracy that had brought them together. Their problem was how to make a government democratic enough to be adopted, but not so democratic as to constitute a menace to upper-class control. As to the fundamental ends that the new government was to accomplish, they were in remarkably close agreement; they accepted with little debate many of the precedents set by the English constitution and by the constitutions of the new states; and they evinced a commendable willingness to arrange compromises on all matters of minor detail.[1]

Philadelphia Convention

It was not easy, however, to adjust the relative weight of states and nation in the new government. The extreme nationalistic point of view was embodied in the so-called Virginia Plan, which had resulted from the daily meetings of the Virginia delegation. This plan proposed a two-house legislature, the lower house to be chosen by the people of the several states in such a manner as to give small states like Delaware and Rhode Island only one representative and large states like Massachusetts and Virginia sixteen or seventeen representatives, but the upper house to be chosen by the lower house. The Virginia plan satisfied the large states fairly well, and was supported also by states in which the possibilities of growth were great. But the small states were profoundly agitated at the prospect of large-state tyranny, and feared that with such a plan they might even lose their separate identity. Their point of view finally found expression in a report by William Paterson of New Jersey, commonly called the New Jersey Plan, which proposed to retain the states as equal, and perhaps sovereign, units.[2]

The Virginia Plan

[1] There are two admirable collections of documents relating to the formation of the Constitution: Max Farrand (ed.), *Records of the Federal Convention of 1787* (4 vols., 1911–37); and C. C. Tansill (ed.), *Documents Illustrative of the Formation of the Union of the American States* (1927). The "Journal" kept by Madison summarizes the debates, and is the most important of the sources for the framing of the Constitution.

[2] From the many excellent books on the framing of the Constitution, the following are selected: Max Farrand, *The Framing of the Constitution of the United States* (1913), and *The Fathers of the Constitution* (1921); Charles Warren, *The Making of the Constitution* (1928); R. L. Schuyler, *The Constitution of the United States* (1923).

Ultimately a solution was found, sometimes called the "Great Com promise," which in a measure, at least, satisfied both parties. In accordance with the Virginia Plan the convention voted to establish a two-house legislature, with the membership of the lower house to be apportioned according to population, and an upper house in which the states should be equally represented. It was decided also that the representatives who were to sit in the lower house should be elected directly by the people, for two-year terms, while the senators, two from each state, were to be chosen for six-year terms by the various state legislatures.

There remained, however, many adjustments to be made, and one may say that almost every line of the constitution that was written came as the result of some compromise. Even on the matter of representation in the lower house a serious dispute arose. Should the slaves, so numerous in some of the southern states, be counted in apportioning the number of representatives to which the states were entitled? Or should these slaves be regarded as property rather than persons? These questions were the more perplexing in view of the fact that the convention had already agreed to assess direct taxes upon the states in accordance with the population. The northern states were unwilling to allow the South to count its slaves in determining the representation a state should have in the lower house of Congress, but desired to count them when direct taxes were to be assessed; the South, on the other hand, wished to count its slaves when the question of representation in Congress was up, but not when taxes were to be levied. A reasonable, if utterly illogical, solution was found in the decision to count five slaves as equal to three whites both in the apportionment of representatives and in the assessing of direct taxes.

During the debate that led to the "Three-Fifths" Compromise the question of the part that new western states were to be allowed to play in the new government also came to the fore. Gouverneur Morris argued earnestly that the rule of representation ought to be so fixed as to secure to the Atlantic states a prevalence for all time in the national councils. The new frontier states, he said, would know less of the public interest than the old, and in particular might involve the nation in wars with the Indians and with neighboring nations that would have to be paid for by the maritime states. Fortunately for the good of the country and the permanence of the Constitution, the narrow view expressed by Morris did not prevail. Possibly many members of the convention comforted themselves with the thought, to which Roger Sherman gave expression, that the number of future states would probably never exceed that of the existing states anyway.

The divergent views of the northern and the southern states, already apparent in the discussion of the "Three-Fifths Compromise," were revealed again in the debate on the powers to be given Congress with respect to the regulation of commerce. The northern states, in which commerce was a dominant interest, favored a generous grant of authority, but some of the southern states, whose prosperity depended mainly upon agriculture, feared that this power might be used to stimulate northern commercial prosperity at their expense. Some of the southern states, particularly Georgia and South Carolina, were also concerned lest Congress might tax heavily or even forbid the importation of slaves, and thus strike at what in their section was still believed to be an essential labor supply; consequently they insisted that there should be no tax on exports or upon "such persons" as the several states should "think proper to admit," and they demanded that navigation acts should be passed only by a two-thirds vote of both houses of Congress. To resolve these differences, the northern states yielded to the South on the prohibition of export duties, and agreed also that the importation of slaves should not be forbidden before the year 1808, although Congress might levy a tax of ten dollars per head for each person imported. The southern states, thus reassured, gave up their insistence on a two-thirds vote in Congress for the passage of navigation acts.

The convention early decided that the national government should have only "enumerated powers"; hence one of the most important sections of the Constitution was that which listed the powers of Congress. In this enumeration many provisions of the old Articles of Confederation were taken over almost intact. Such, for example, were those which authorized Congress to borrow money on the credit of the United States, to declare war, to maintain an army and navy, and to establish post-offices and post-roads. Extremely significant, however, were the new powers, especially those which gave Congress authority to lay and collect taxes, duties, imposts, and excises, to regulate commerce with foreign nations and among the several states, to pass naturalization and bankruptcy laws, and "to make all laws which shall be necessary and proper for carrying into execution the foregoing powers" — the famous "elastic clause." Congress was also authorized to provide for the calling forth of the militia to execute the laws of the Union and to suppress insurrections and repel invasions.

Hardly less important than the delegation of powers to the national government was the withdrawal of certain powers from the states. States were forbidden to coin money, to emit bills of credit, to make anything but gold and silver legal tender in payment of debts, to have direct relations with foreign coun-

Commerce

The powers of Congress

Limitations on the states

tries, to levy duties on imports or exports (without the consent of Congress), "to pass any bill of attainder, ex post facto law, or law impairing the obligation of contracts, or grant any title of nobility." Most of these provisions were designed to prevent the radical non-propertied classes, in case they should win control in any of the states, from passing legislation hostile to the interests of the propertied classes. For example, while the national government was left free to print paper money, and even to declare it legal tender, the states were expressly forbidden to exercise these powers.

While the convention had little difficulty in deciding to establish the customary three departments of government, there were many opinions as to the most desirable make-up for the executive branch.
Some wished a plural executive, but the majority stood by **The Executive** the traditional idea of an individual to head up the government. Many divergent views had to be reconciled, however, before the convention decided that the executive should be called the President, that he should be chosen for a term of four years, and that he should be eligible for indefinite re-election. In working out a plan for the election of the President, the convention sought to avoid on the one hand delegating to Congress the right to choose the executive, and on the other assigning to the people directly so important a duty. The result was the creation of an "electoral college," roughly analogous to Congress, but composed of different individuals. As many electors were to be named in each state as the state had senators and representatives, and the method of choosing the electors was to be left for each state to determine for itself. The electors were to vote for two candidates for President, and if anyone should receive the votes of a majority of the electors he was to be declared elected, while the candidate receiving the next highest number of votes, whether a majority or not, was to become Vice-President. In case no one person should receive a majority, a situation that the constitution-framers expected to recur repeatedly, then the election of the President should be the prerogative of the House, voting by states. Needless to say, the delegates failed completely to foresee the subsequent practice of presidential elections.

There was little hesitation about granting extensive powers to the President. He was made the commander-in-chief of the army and navy and also of the state militia whenever it was called into national service; he had the power to make treaties with **Powers of the President** foreign nations "by and with the advice and consent of the Senate ... provided two-thirds of the Senators present concur"; he could with the consent of the majority in the Senate name ambassadors, ministers, consuls, judges of the federal courts, and all the other officers of the United States not otherwise provided for; he might call Congress into extraordinary session when he believed such a session necessary; he must "take care that the laws be faithfully executed"; and he had the right to veto bills passed by Congress, with the qualification that a two-thirds vote of both houses might make the bill a law without the President's signature. As a safeguard against executive usurpation or other misbehavior a method of impeachment was devised, with the House bringing the indictment and the Senate sitting as a court. A two-thirds majority of the Senate was required to convict and remove from office.

The importance of a federal judiciary was not underestimated, but there was surprisingly little debate on the subject during the convention, and the section on the judiciary that was finally written was very brief. That there should be a supreme court was generally agreed, but many believed that the existence of state courts made inferior federal courts unnecessary. This difference of opinion was compromised by providing merely that Congress might establish inferior courts if it chose to do so, but nothing was put into the Constitution to require their establishment. The supreme court was given original jurisdiction over cases affecting foreign ministers and cases to which a state was party; otherwise its jurisdiction was appellate only. While the judicial power of the federal courts was so defined as to extend to all cases arising under the Constitution, the laws of Congress, and the treaties to which the United States was a party, the Constitution itself says nothing with regard to the power which the judiciary soon assumed of declaring invalid such laws as in its opinion were contrary to the Constitution. It is probable, however, that many members of the convention took this more or less for granted. Indeed, a proposition to give the supreme court a qualified veto over laws of Congress was voted down partly because the federal judges would probably exert some such authority anyway.[1]

The three-headed system of government, with its separate legislature, executive, and judiciary, provided numerous opportunities for preventing those excesses of democracy which were so much feared by the framers of the Constitution. The powerful judiciary was designed to act as a check on the President and Congress, while the executive would also check the legislature, and the legislature the executive. A number of provisions for the direct operation of this principle were written in; such, for example, as the power given the Senate to reject treaties and appointments made by the President, and the right of the President to exercise a qualified veto over the acts of Congress. Democracy was still further qualified by the insistent em-

The judiciary

Checks on democracy

[1] E. S. Corwin, *The Doctrine of Judicial Review* (1914); C. A. Beard, *The Supreme Court and the Constitution* (1912).

phasis upon the representative principle in the new government. As little as might be was left to the people themselves to do; and the powers of government were handed over instead to representatives removed once or twice from the popular will.

While from the American point of view the Constitution was, and was meant to be, an eminently conservative document, when compared with the forms of government that existed in the rest of the world it fell little short of radicalism. It continued the doctrine **Radical** of popular sovereignty that had formed the philosophic **features** background of the American Revolution, and was yet to find support from the results of the French Revolution. Thus in a day when nearly every other government adhered to the principle of monarchy, with its implied belief in the divine right of kings, the American government was strictly republican in form. Unique also was the effort to establish a dual or federal type of government, but the experiment turned out to be as successful as it was unusual. Further, although the Constitution in its original form contained no formal bill of rights, it did include such guarantees as that the privilege of the writ of habeas corpus should not ordinarily be suspended, and that bills of attainder and ex post facto laws should not be passed. The first ten amendments stated even more definitely the various "rights of man" upon which government was forbidden to transgress. The ease with which these amendments could be accomplished constituted another radical innovation. Alternative methods were provided, but ordinarily an amendment could be adopted when proposed by two-thirds of the members of Congress and ratified by the legislatures of three-fourths of the states.

The last article of the Constitution provided that as soon as the document should be ratified in nine states by conventions called for the purpose, it should go into effect among the states so ratifying. This was out of harmony with the method of amendment **Debate on the** under the Articles of Confederation, and therefore revolu- **Constitution** tionary, but the Congress of the Confederation did not even protest the procedure, and itself submitted the Constitution to the states. Ratification was not accomplished without a struggle. The men who had framed the Constitution and now favored its adoption were of the well-to-do classes, and their handiwork was regarded with much suspicion by such popular leaders as Patrick Henry, Richard Henry Lee, and Samuel Adams. They feared particularly the proposed curtailment in the rights of the states, and the absence of a bill of rights. But the Federalists, as those who favored the Constitution came to be called, made an admirable case for adoption. They did not defend every clause the Constitution contained, but asserted that it was the only alternative to the chaos of the Confederation. Among the numerous articles written in support of the Constitution, a series by Hamilton, Madison, and Jay, signed *The Federalist*, attracted much attention. These documents, collected to form a book, still constitute the best commentary on the Constitution, as its framers intended it to be interpreted.

While the opponents of the Constitution, or anti-Federalists, stated their side of the argument fully and well, the advantage from the first lay

Ratification with the Federalists.[1] In every state restrictions on the suffrage told heavily in their favor, and in some states the back-country, which was especially hostile to the Constitution, was under-represented in the ratifying conventions. By the end of the year the ratifications began to come in. Equality of representation in the Senate seemed to satisfy most of the small states, and on December 7, 1787, Delaware ratified by a unanimous vote. By June 21, 1788, when New Hampshire ratified, nine states had adopted the Constitution, enough to put it into effect. But these nine included neither Virginia nor New York, without whose support the Constitution could hardly be expected to succeed. Only three states had ratified unanimously; in each of the others there had been determined opposition. Finally, on June 25, 1788, Virginia ratified by a vote of 89 to 79, and a month and a day later New York, convinced that the Constitution would be given a trial anyway, voted its half-hearted participation. North Carolina held aloof until a bill of rights should be included in the Constitution, and Rhode Island failed so much as to hold a ratifying convention.

There was great relief that the long dispute over the government was at an end, and among the bitter opponents of ratification there were many who were ready, now that the Constitution was actually adopted, to give it a fair trial. The old Congress of the Confederation, even before the ratification of New York had been received, in acknowledgment of the fact that its authority had been supplanted, ordered the states to choose presidential electors, senators, and representatives, and set the first Wednesday in March, 1789, as the date of the new Congress to convene.

Much remained to be done, nevertheless, before the new government should really go into effect. In this crisis the talents of George Wash-

George Washington ington, whom everyone knew would be the first President, were a tremendous asset to the country. Few public leaders have captured the confidence of their contemporaries with such completeness as did Washington, and the fact that his solid judgment and rugged honesty would be at the command of the new govern-

---

[1] Some of the arguments advanced against the Constitution are given in P. L. Ford, *Pamphlets on the Constitution of the United States* (1888). For the struggle over ratification see *The Debates on the Federal Constitution*, edited by Jonathan Elliot (5 vols., 1827-45).

ment during its experimental period allayed many misgivings. In the first and second presidential elections Washington received every electoral vote, an honor that would no doubt have been accorded him for a third time also had he been willing to accept it.

Washington was born, February 22, 1732, in tidewater Virginia, the son of a moderately well-to-do planter who owned several estates. Washington's father had gone to school in England, but this privilege was denied George, whose education was somewhat limited. He took an interest in mathematics, and at an early age knew the rudiments of surveying. When he was only sixteen years old he accompanied a surveying party into the Shenandoah Valley, and after his return became surveyor-general for Fairfax County. His frequent surveying trips into the backcountry gave him a glimpse into the possibilities of the West that he was never to forget. His career as surveyor was cut short when his elder brother Lawrence died in 1752, and left to George the management of the estate at Mount Vernon. A few years later Washington married Martha Custis, the widow of a wealthy planter, and her property, added to his own, made him for the times a very rich man. For many years he lived the usual life of the prosperous southern planter, entertained lavishly, participated actively in parish affairs, and sat for his county as a member of the House of Burgesses.[1]

The fame of Washington did not escape the glamour of legend that collects so inevitably around the heroes of a nation, but when all the myths are swept aside the greatness of the man is still apparent. He was most exceptional for his many-sidedness. No doubt his knowledge of military tactics was defective, but it was sufficient to meet the needs of the situation he faced, and to win the admiration of such a master-strategist as Frederick the Great. As an administrator he was wise in his choice of advisers, made up his mind in time, acted decisively, kept abreast of his duties. As a statesman he was farsighted and sagacious. He saw clearly the important part that the West was to play in the history of the nation, he recognized the dangers involved in a growing sectionalism, he understood better than most men of his time the menace of slavery, and he realized fully the wisdom of diplomatic isolation from Europe until the nation he had helped to create could get securely upon its feet. Washington's genius was not of the spectacular sort, but his sound judgment and plain common sense saved his country many trials, and may have saved its life.

The day designated by the old Congress of the Confederation for the

[1] Good biographies of Washington are rare. H. J. Ford, *Washington and his Colleagues* (1921), is short but dependable. The best full-length study is N. W. Stephenson and W. H. Dunn, *George Washington* (2 vols., 1940).

new government to go into operation was the fourth of March, 1789, but
not until the sixth of April were majorities in both houses of
Congress present in New York, the temporary capital.
Thereupon, quorums being obtained, the electoral votes
were counted, and the election of Washington to the Presidency and John Adams to the Vice-Presidency was announced. By
April 30 the President-elect had reached New York, traveling horseback,
and the inauguration took place.

Launching the new government

But the new government was not even then fully launched. The Constitution was a relatively short document, and much legislation had to be
passed in order to make it effective. Laws had to be enacted, for example, to create departments of state, of war, and of the treasury, to establish a judiciary, and most important of all to provide for the levying and
collection of taxes. Once the essential laws were enacted the President
still had to select the officials to carry them into effect, and the Senate
had to pass on the President's appointees. In many important matters,
also, significant precedents had to be set, and new customs given time to
develop. For example, there was no provision in the Constitution for the
use of the Cabinet as an official board of advisers to meet with the President from time to time. This custom, however, grew naturally out of
the clause which provided that the President might ask for the opinions
of heads of departments *in writing* whenever he so desired.

The Confederation had failed largely because it was unable to solve the
problem of finance. If the new government was not also to go on the
rocks, clearly its financial policy must be wisely conceived.
Washington recognized this fact when he chose as his Secretary of the Treasury Alexander Hamilton,[1] a young man only
thirty-two years of age who had already displayed remarkable talent
along financial lines. Hamilton (1757–1804) was a West Indian by birth,
the son of a Scotch father and a French Huguenot mother. He was a
promising lad, no less liberally endowed with the shrewdness of his
father's race than with the charm of manner and impetuosity of his
mother's. He was sent to school in New Jersey when he was only fifteen
years of age, and later attended Kings College in New York. Here,
although New York was a Loyalist center, he absorbed the American
point of view on the quarrel with England, and when war broke out
joined the army. On financial matters, however, he was an ultra-conservative. He believed that the rights of property must be protected at

Alexander Hamilton

---

[1] Biographers of Hamilton, like those of Washington, find it difficult to write without a
bias. H. C. Lodge, *Alexander Hamilton* (1882), finds little fault in the man. Claude
Bowers, *Jefferson and Hamilton* (1925), tips the scales heavily in favor of Jefferson and
against Hamilton. See also J. S. Bassett, *The Federalist System* (1906).

all costs, and he never doubted that government, to be really effective, must be the monopoly of the upper classes. "The people," he once said in a moment of anger, "is a great beast."

As Secretary of the Treasury, Hamilton concerned himself first and foremost with the establishment of the nation's credit. To make sure that there could be no doubt about the determination of the United States to pay its just debts, he proposed that all out-standing loans be funded at their face value. The United States had borrowed from abroad about twelve million dollars, and against the meeting of this obligation in full there could be no valid complaint. But the domestic debt, which amounted to nearly forty-two million dollars, seemed to many honest men a totally different matter. Since these securities were worth on the market about twenty-five cents on the dollar, there were many who thought that for the government to purchase them back at that price, or a little above, with a new and valid issue would be an entirely respectable procedure. But Hamilton was determined to win the enthusiastic approval of the moneyed class, and insisted on the entire debt being funded at par. As a result many speculators reaped a rich harvest.

Funding the national debt

Hamilton's plan did not end merely with the funding of the debts owed by the United States. He wished also to take over such of the debts incurred by the states themselves for the cause of independence as they had not yet paid. His object, again, was to place the creditor class under deep obligation to the central government, and thus to win its hearty support. But the assumption of state debts by the central government was not accomplished without a struggle. It was all very well to argue that these debts were incurred for a common cause and should be paid out of the common treasury, but the fact remained that some states had large obligations to pass over and some did not. Virginia, for example, had financed the war to a great extent with paper-money issues that had either been redeemed in western lands or had ceased to have any value. The South in general opposed the scheme, and it was finally put through Congress only after Hamilton, working through Jefferson, the Secretary of State, had struck a notable bargain. The South was exceedingly desirous of securing the capital, and Hamilton now offered to use his influence in favor of a southern site if Jefferson would help find the votes to pass the assumption bill. The bargain worked, Congress agreed that the new capital should be located at Philadelphia for a period of ten years, and thereafter on the Potomac; and it voted also the assumption by the central government of some eighteen million dollars' worth of state war debts.

Assumption of state debts

Still further to bind the moneyed classes to the government, Hamilton

proposed, in December, 1790, that Congress should authorize the establishment of a Bank of the United States similar to the Bank
Bank of the United States of England. He could give many sound arguments in favor of such a measure, but he was unable to point to any specific grant of authority in the Constitution to warrant its passage. James Madison, who as the most active member of the Constitutional Convention knew the motives of the framers as well as any man, said that the Constitution was not meant to give Congress authority to create such a bank. But Hamilton was willing to interpret the "necessary and proper" clause broadly enough to meet the situation, and against heated opposition he induced a majority in Congress to accept his view. Thus began the perennial battle over the broad construction and the strict construction of the Constitution.

The Bank of the United States to which Congress now granted a charter was to have a capital stock of ten million dollars, for the time a very large sum. Of this amount one-fifth was to be subscribed by the United States, and the other four-fifths by private individuals. Into the bank went all the deposits of the United States, and this fact, coupled with the fact that the national government also owned a large part of the bank stock, tended to win for the institution the confidence of the public. The bank had the right to issue paper money, and these notes were made receivable for public dues. Investors were quick to take advantage of the opportunity offered them, and the bank was soon doing business. For twenty years it prospered to such an extent that those who held bank stock realized on an average about eight and one-half per cent annually on their investment.

Hamilton's plan for funding the debt cost money, and the modest tariff that Congress had levied as one of its first measures was unequal to the emergency. In consequence, the Secretary of the
The whiskey excise Treasury offered yet another suggestion. The Constitution clearly authorized Congress to levy an excise tax, and this power, Hamilton felt, should be used. Not only was money needed, but in addition the people should become accustomed to the taxing power of the central government. When it came to choosing the item upon which to place the tax, however, Hamilton took care not to offend the moneyed men whose good-will toward the government he deemed so essential to its success. Instead, he suggested a tax on whiskey which would hit the small farmers of the back-country who had opposed the adoption of the Constitution, and who were still doubtful as to whether the new government merited their support. Hamilton knew full well that such a tax might arouse the frontier farmers to wrathful action, but he was not averse to the test of strength that the conflict would bring. If necessary,

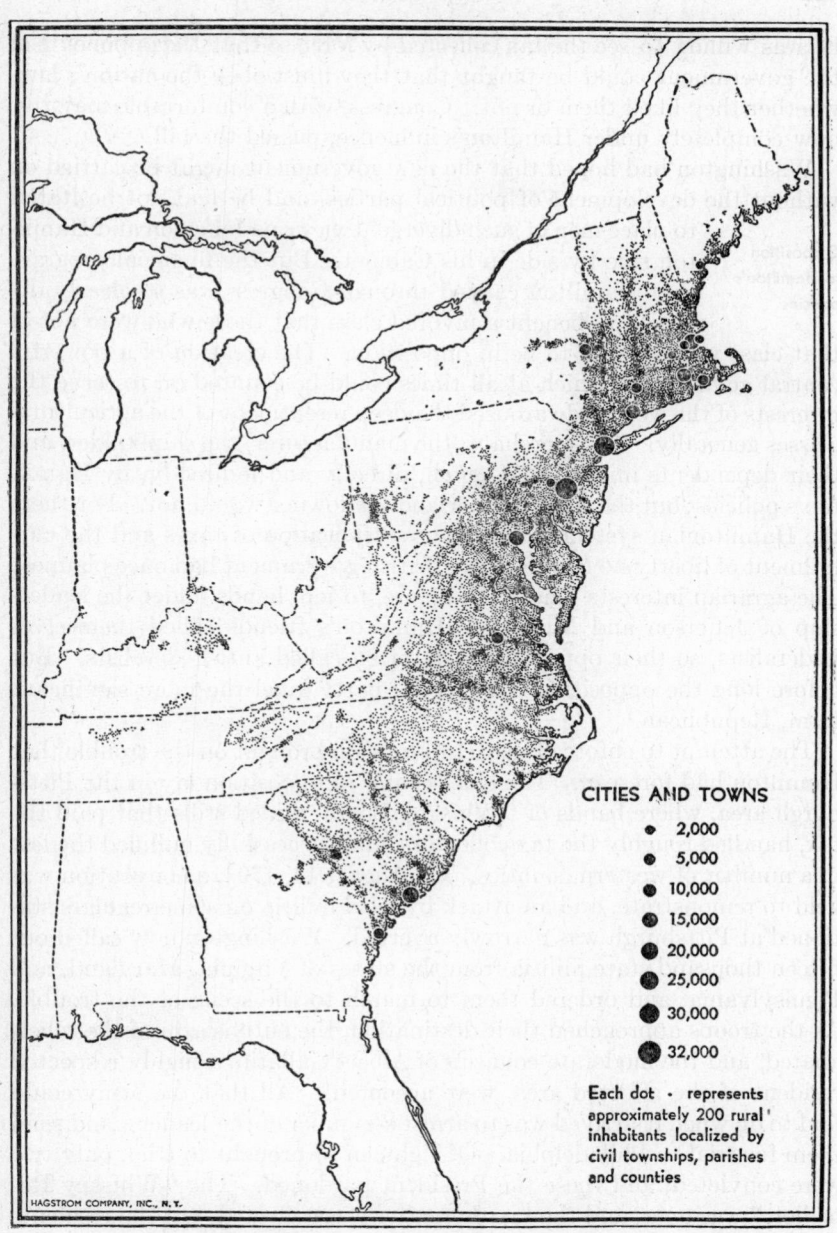

CITIES AND TOWNS

- 2,000
- 5,000
- 10,000
- 15,000
- 20,000
- 25,000
- 30,000
- 32,000

Each dot · represents
approximately 200 rural
inhabitants localized by
civil townships, parishes
and counties

HAGSTROM COMPANY, INC., N. Y.

DISTRIBUTION OF POPULATION IN 1790

he was willing to see the tax collected by force so that the opponents of
the government could be taught that they must obey the nation's laws
whether they liked them or not. Congress, with a comfortable majority
now completely under Hamilton's influence, passed the bill.

Washington had hoped that the new government might be carried on
without the development of political parties, and he had not hesitated
to place men of such divergent views as Jefferson and Hamil-
Opposition
to Hamilton's ton side by side in his Cabinet. But the financial program
policies that Hamilton carried through Congress was so clearly designed to benefit a favored class that those who were not of
that class were certain to be in opposition. The creation of a powerful
central government which at all times could be counted on to serve the
interests of the well-to-do aroused the deep resentment of the agricultural
classes generally. The merchant, the manufacturer, the shipbuilder, and
their dependents might profit much, directly and indirectly, by Hamilton's policies; but the small farmer and landowner would not. For them
the Hamiltonian system meant the multiplication of taxes and the curtailment of liberty no less than the British government had once planned.
The agrarian interests tended, therefore, to join hands under the leadership of Jefferson and Madison. Hamilton's friends called themselves
Federalists, so their opponents were often called anti-Federalists. But
before long the opposition took for its party label the more significant
term, Republican.[1]

The attempt to enforce the excise tax soon brought on the trouble that
Hamilton had foreseen. The chief center of opposition lay in the Pittsburgh area, where bands of "Whiskey Boys" raided stills that paid the
tax, handled roughly the tax collectors, and successfully nullified the law
in a number of western counties. On August 14, 1794, a convention was
held to remonstrate, and an attack by local militia on some regulars stationed at Pittsburgh was narrowly averted. Washington now called out
fifteen thousand state militia from the states of Virginia, Maryland, and
Pennsylvania, and ordered them to march to the scene of the trouble.
As the troops approached their destination, the enthusiasm of the rebels
abated, and the moderate counsels of Albert Gallatin, a highly respected
resident of the affected area, were accepted.[2] All that the army could
find to do when it arrived was to arrest a number of the leaders, and send
them for trial to Philadelphia. Of eighteen so brought to trial, only two
were convicted, and these the President pardoned. The "Whiskey Rebellion" was over, and the tax thereafter was collected, but the residents

[1] C. A. Beard, *Economic Origins of the Jeffersonian Democracy* (1915), continues the argument begun in his *Economic Interpretation of the Constitution*, already mentioned.

[2] L. D. Baldwin, *Whiskey Rebels, The Story of a Frontier Uprising* (1939).

of western Pennsylvania and many other frontier areas were aghast at the power the Federalists in control of the central government had chosen to wield, and unhesitatingly cast their lot politically with Thomas Jefferson and the Republicans.

The revolt in western Pennsylvania was not the only western problem that the new government was called upon to solve. Still farther to the west were other pioneers whose troubles with the Spanish in the Southwest, with the English in the Northwest, and with the Indians in both regions were even more perplexing than they had been in the time of the Confederation. As the West grew in population, the uncertainty of trade down the Mississippi became constantly more serious. The Spanish remained sullenly unwilling to open the river freely to trade from the United States, they continued to urge their claim to a boundary for Florida much farther north than the United States was willing to concede, and they placed no obstacles in the way of Indians under their control who moved to attack the southwestern frontier. In the Northwest the English continued to hold on to their posts south of the Great Lakes, and Canadian fur-traders gave aid and encouragement to the Indian tribes of the Northwest who had already gone on the warpath against the pioneers in Ohio. Washington realized fully that the loyalty of the West to the central government would be sorely tried if the frontier was not relieved. Moreover, the prestige of the nation was at stake.

The southwestern frontier

Unwilling to fight two wars at once, Washington tried diplomacy on the Indians of the Southwest, and through money payments to Alexander McGillivray, a half-breed Creek of great influence, obtained a somewhat undependable promise of peace. Ultimately the Tennesseans were obliged to take matters in their own hands; their extensive raids into the Indian country during 1793–94 were far more effective than Washington's diplomacy. In the Northwest the central government did not hesitate to use force. By two treaties, Fort Stanwix (1784) and Fort McIntosh (1785), the Indians had given up a large section of land west of the western boundary of Pennsylvania and north of the Ohio. But the Indian memory of treaty terms was short, and the presence of white men made game scarce. With the tacit approval of the British in the forts and fur-trading posts, the Indians had committed so many depredations by the time Washington took office that drastic retaliatory measures had to be taken.

Three separate expeditions against the Northwest Indians were required before they could be brought to terms. The first, in 1790, under General Josiah Harmar, destroyed some Indian villages, but was ambushed on the return trip and forced to make a humiliating retreat.

Next year Governor St. Clair himself took the field in command of about
two thousand militia, but on November 4, 1791, his expedition, like Harmar's, was ambushed and utterly defeated.

War in the
Northwest

Washington then turned to "Mad" Anthony Wayne, who
insisted on enlisted troops rather than militia, and after nearly two years
of preparation succeeded where his predecessors had failed. At the Battle
of Fallen Timbers, August 20, 1794, the Indians were overwhelmed, and
next year at Fort Greenville they signed a treaty which ceded vast
stretches of land in central Ohio to the whites. So stinging was the defeat they had been dealt that they gave the United States no further
trouble for many years to come.

No less gratifying to the people of the West was the willingness of the
new government to admit frontier states into the Union. Vermont had
carried on a state government since the beginning of the
Revolutionary War, but was left outside the Confederation.

Admission of
new states

In 1791, however, Congress agreed to accept Vermont as a
fourteenth state. The pleas of Kentuckians also were given favorable
consideration. In 1789 Virginia gave full consent to the separation from
the Old Dominion of the Kentucky counties, and in 1792 Congress allowed Kentucky to become a state. In Tennessee matters moved more
slowly toward the same end. The state of North Carolina finally ceded
her western lands to Congress in 1790, whereupon a territory was set up
similar to the territory established northwest of the Ohio River by the
Confederation. In 1796 this territory gave way to the state of Tennessee. The constitutions of these new western states all showed a tendency toward greater democracy than was yet the rule in the original
thirteen states. Especially were they willing to expand the right of suffrage. Vermont and Kentucky went the whole length of universal manhood suffrage, and Tennessee closely approximated it.

Meantime the new government had survived a test of strength at the
polls. It was the good fortune of the Washington administration to take
office at a time when the depression that followed the Revolution was
about at its end, and prosperity was returning. Doubtless this change
would have come in some degree regardless of the form of government,
but the public tended to believe that the adoption of the Constitution
had brought about the change. By the end of Washington's first administration there were comparatively few who regretted the establishment
of the new government. There were many, however, who felt that the
Federalists had gone too far in the direction of centralization and had
granted unreasonable favors to the propertied interests. To remedy this
defect they were already considering the wisdom of placing the government in other hands. Had Washington retired at the end of his first

term, as he had wished to do, undoubtedly there would have been a hard fight between the Hamiltonian and Jeffersonian factions over the choice of his successor. But Washington was persuaded to stand for re-election, and there was none who would oppose him. When it came to the Vice-Presidency, which John Adams held, the Republicans had fewer scruples, and gave their votes to George Clinton. In the election of 1792, Washington again received a unanimous vote, but Clinton, who carried New York, Virginia, North Carolina, and Georgia, and took one vote in Pennsylvania, received a total of 50 votes to 77 for Adams. It was clear that in the course of time a real party struggle for the control of the national government would be staged.[1]

[1] Edward Stanwood, *A History of the Presidency* (2 vols., 1898, new ed., 1916), is in reality a history of presidential elections, and as such is indispensable. Louise B. Dunbar, *A Study of "Monarchical" Tendencies in the United States from 1776 to 1801* (1923), throws light on the strength of conservative thought in the new nation. Homer C. Hockett, *The Constitutional History of the United States, 1776–1826* (1939), traces admirably the evolution of the Constitution through the formative period. Sol Bloom (ed.), *History of the Formation of the Union under the Constitution* (1941), contains an excellent study by D. M. Matteson on the formation of the new government. G. H. Hayes, *The Senate of the United States: Its History and Practice* (2 vols., 1938), is a painstaking and enlightening study. C. G. Haines, *The Role of the Supreme Court in American Government and Politics, 1789–1835* (1944), is an anti-Federalist view. On the social side, J. A. Krout and D. R. Fox, *The Completion of Independence, 1790–1830* (1944), is outstanding.

7

The Federalists and Foreign Affairs

It would be a mistake to assume that either the American colonies of
Great Britain or the new United States had ever been really isolated from
Europe. The colonies, as outlying parts of the British Empire, had been
greatly dependent on ties with the mother country for their economic
livelihood, and they had participated as a matter of course in all the wars
that involved the Empire. As a new nation, the United States was still
closely bound to Europe, and was certain to be seriously affected by any
train of events that deeply affected the Old World.[1]

The outbreak of the French Revolution was thus a matter of tremendous interest and intimate concern to the people of the new American
nation. A week after Washington's inauguration in 1789,
the French Estates-General was in session, and the evolution
of a more democratic form of government for France had
begun. Most Americans sympathized at first with the French struggle
for freedom, and saw in it a closer analogy with the American revolution
than the facts really warranted. Even European nations were not unhappy to see the French king in trouble, for most of them had suffered at
one time or another because of his ambitions. But the lengths to which
the French Revolution seemed destined to go soon made conservatives
everywhere, in America no less than in Europe, view the situation with
some alarm, especially when in April, 1792, France declared war on
Austria and it became clear that the French Revolution was no longer an
internal affair. Even so, the vast majority of Americans sympathized
with France until after the French declarations of war against Great
Britain and Spain. Then many of them began to be deeply concerned.
The United States was bound by a treaty of alliance to France. Would
another war with England have to be fought, and perhaps also a war with
Spain? Any such development might mean the death of American commerce, which ran mostly with England and Spain, and it might mean the
loss of American independence as well.

The French
Revolution

[1] *The American Secretaries of State and their Diplomacy* (10 vols., 1927–29), edited by
S. F. Bemis, is a co-operative work that covers in detail the history of American foreign
relations.

It was not long before public sentiment in the United States on the war in Europe began to divide along party lines. Hamilton, who was always the arch-conservative, made no effort to disguise his disgust with the excesses to which the French Revolution had gone, and to most of the Federalists it now seemed that England was fighting for the preservation of civilization while France had become a public enemy. But Jefferson and the Republicans took a very different view of the situation. Representing as they did mainly the agrarian interests, the safety of American commerce gave them little concern. England was the traditional enemy of American democracy, and she still unlawfully held on to the Northwest posts. Spain was an even older antagonist, and was now planted at the mouth of the Mississippi to dispute the right of western farmers to the use of that river. Republican clubs, many of which had already been formed out of sympathy for France, multiplied amazingly, particularly in the South and West. Many of the Republicans were ready to make common cause with France in a war against the English in Canada and the Spanish on the Gulf of Mexico. To Jefferson the French Revolution was still "the most sacred cause that man was ever engaged in." [1]

With public opinion thus divided, Washington received with many misgivings the news that the revolutionary government had dispatched a minister, "Citizen" Edmond Charles Genêt, to the United States. It seemed obvious that the chief purpose of the **"Citizen" Genêt** Genêt mission was to obtain the assistance of the United States in the war France was fighting against England and Spain. The President at once laid the matter before his Cabinet, and although there was sharp disagreement between Hamilton and Jefferson, particularly as to the validity of the treaties of alliance (which Jefferson upheld and Hamilton denounced), all agreed that for the time being, at least, neutrality was the only possible course. Washington decided to issue a proclamation of neutrality before Genêt should arrive at the American capital, and to live up to the treaties as well as he could without involving the United States in war. He would recognize Genêt as the rightful minister of France, but make clear to him that the United States did not intend to participate in the war.

Washington, who knew, as Genêt did not, the pro-English sentiment of the commercial sections of the nation, received the French representative coolly, and sought to make him understand that the American declaration of neutrality meant exactly what it said. But Genêt tried nevertheless to obtain funds for financing his schemes by offering to discount the debts owing by the United States to France. If only the money could be found, American ships could be outfitted as French

[1] E. P. Link, *Democratic-Republican Societies, 1790–1800* (1942).

privateers, and George Rogers Clark, whom Genêt had already commissioned an officer in the "French Revolutionary Army of America," could be sent on the expedition he had offered to lead down the Mississippi River to attack the Spanish at New Orleans. But Washington held that any other plan of payment than the one already agreed upon would constitute a breach of neutrality, so Genêt found himself without the all-essential financial resources. He managed, however, to convert a French prize, the *Little Sarah*, into an armed ship, the *Little Democrat*, and permitted it to sail without notice from an American port. Since Genêt had expressly promised not to do this, Washington asked the French government for his recall. By this time the French Revolution had progressed another step in the direction of radicalism, and Genêt was already out of favor at home. A new minister, Fauchet, was appointed, who was instructed to send his predecessor home under arrest. Genêt realized that his return to France might cost him his life, so he asked permission of Washington to stay on in the United States. Washington mercifully consented.[1]

Thus began the American doctrine of non-involvement in European affairs. For the moment it was wisely conceived. The United States was as yet a tiny nation, none too certain of survival. It was almost surrounded by two great predatory empires, the British to the north, and the Spanish to the south and west. Its ally, France, had once had American colonial possessions, and French imperialism might easily turn again toward the New World. Moreover, sentiment in the United States on the European conflict was badly divided, and, worse still, was divided along party lines. To save its life the infant nation had no alternative but to tread the precarious path of rigid neutrality.

It soon became apparent that neutrality was not altogether without its rewards. The export trade, particularly in provisions bound for the warring nations, grew by leaps and bounds. The American **The profits of neutrality** carrying trade also prospered, for neutral vessels were safer than the merchant ships of nations flying enemy flags. Particularly lucrative was the trade between the French West Indies and France, which had hitherto been a monopoly of French traders, but was now opened to vessels from the United States. Prices responded to the increased demand for American produce, sailors' wages rose, and shipbuilders as well as shipowners reaped a rich harvest. Congress under these circumstances backed the President strongly in his policy of neutrality. It established by a law of 1794 definite rules of neutrality, em-

[1] F. J. Turner, *The Significance of Sections in American History* (1932), contains two excellent essays on the diplomatic relations between the United States and France during this period.

phasizing particularly the duties of neutrals, and it appropriated seventy-five thousand dollars to be used if needed in enforcing the law.

While the public came more and more to understand and appreciate the policy of neutrality, it was not without its problems. For the most part, the diplomatic disputes in which the United States was soon involved ran with the British, whose navy controlled the high seas. There was, for example, the argument over the "rule of 1756." One of the first war measures of the French government was to open to neutral nations the trade between the French West Indies and France, trade that in normal times was permitted only to the French. Thereupon the British invoked the "rule of 1756," according to which trade not open to a nation in time of peace could not be opened to that nation in time of war. Under this rule hundreds of American ships were taken, and American seamen and passengers were subjected to the grossest indignities. Naturally, American protests rent the diplomatic air. The United States held that the British had no international sanction whatever for their "rule of 1756." The British contended that it was unfair for France to monopolize trade with her colonies in time of peace, when her ships ran no risk, and then to expect that the same trade in time of war could enjoy immunity under a neutral flag.

As time went on the disagreements multiplied. The United States maintained that neutral ships made neutral goods; hence, French goods on American ships should have been free from molestation. But the British orders flouted this doctrine. The United **Disagreements** States held that foodstuffs were not to be regarded as contra- **with England** band of war. The British argued that, inasmuch as imported provisions were essential to the French in their prosecution of the war, such cargoes might lawfully be taken over by the British and paid for. The United States adhered emphatically to the principle that a blockade to be legally binding must be effectively maintained by a blockading squadron off port, but the British did not hesitate to establish paper blockades of many French ports, or to capture neutral ships, bound for a forbidden destination, anywhere on the high seas. There were complications, too, with regard to the rules of visit and search, the United States insisting that search be confined merely to the examination of the ship's papers, and the British holding that search really meant search. Impressment presented another problem. The British insisted that every Briton owed naval service to his country whenever it might be needed, and press-gangs from British men-of-war made a practice of "impressing" sailors into the royal navy from British merchant ships. When in the course of searching American ships the British found British sailors in American crews, it seemed reasonable enough to the boarding parties that their countrymen should be taken off and made to serve under British colors; and the thing was done. Naturalization, although recognized by the United States, meant nothing to the British, who still adhered to the rule, "Once an Englishman, always an Englishman." Mistakes occurred, also, and some American-born sailors were impressed into the British navy, usually to be released as soon as proof of their identity could be made.

In general, the pro-French Republicans tended to demand drastic reprisals against the British for these alleged violations of American neutrality. They were supported in this attitude by public opinion, which strongly resented the British actions, and as a result Congress in 1794 placed a two months' embargo on all foreign trade. This embargo was meant by many who voted for it, however, only as a threat; what Hamilton and the Federalists wished to do was to come to an understanding with Great Britain whereby American trade might continue on tolerable terms. They finally persuaded Washington to send the Chief Justice, John Jay, to London with instructions to negotiate a treaty with the British. Jay's instructions explicitly required him to obtain (1) evacuation by the British of the military posts they held south of the Great Lakes, (2) compensation for their illegal seizures of American ships, (3) a satisfactory commercial treaty, which must embody, among other things, the American position on disputed points of international law. If such a treaty seemed unattainable, Jay was told to seek the co-operation of the northern nations of Europe in a joint effort to maintain neutral rights. He was then to report to his government for further instructions.

Jay paid little heed to these admonitions, but succeeded in arranging in a fairly satisfactory way the disputes that had arisen out of the settlement of the Revolutionary War. The news of the battle of Fallen Timbers had made a deep impression in England, and the British now agreed to withdraw their military posts from south of the Great Lakes. Plans were also made for a settlement of the disputes over the non-payment by Americans of their pre-Revolutionary War debts owing to British subjects, and over the boundary between Canada and Maine. Ultimately Congress was obliged to assume the debts, while a compromise boundary was drawn. On commercial matters Jay, totally ignoring his instructions, agreed to a series of halfway measures. The treaty he signed called for a commission to determine what damages should be paid for the illegal seizure of American ships, and set up a trade agreement between the two nations that was to last for a period of twelve years. One clause in the treaty, the famous Article XII, was so unfair to the United States that Senate ratification was obtained only on condition that it be expunged. On this basis the treaty ultimately went into effect, but the American public heartily condemned it, excoriated Jay at every turn, and even voiced unwonted criticism of the President himself. Nevertheless, time seemed to show that the acceptance of the treaty was no mistake. The British lived up to their agreement to abandon the northwestern posts, while on the commercial side the treaty eased somewhat the obstacles confronted by American trade, and in conjunction with the treaty of Fort Greenville opened the way for a new advance of settlement into the Northwest. Most important of all, its adoption greatly facilitated negotiations between the United States and Spain for the settlement of their long-standing difficulties over the southwestern frontier.[1]

By 1795 Spain had withdrawn from her alliance with England, and had revived her normal friendship with France. As an offset to Jay's Treaty, which was regarded on the Continent as a kind of forerunner to an alliance between Great Britain and the United States, **Pinckney's Treaty** the Spanish government suddenly determined to sign an even more generous treaty with the Americans. The result was the Treaty of San Lorenzo, or "Pinckney's Treaty," [2] as it was sometimes called, after its American negotiator. The Spanish king now consented to the thirty-first parallel as the northern boundary of Florida, conceded to Americans the navigation of the Mississippi "in its whole breadth from its source to the ocean," and agreed to allow citizens of the United States the right to deposit at New Orleans, duty-free, such merchandise as they planned to export. This "right of deposit" at New Orleans was to run for three years; thereafter the Spanish monarch promised renewal, but, if he chose, at some suitable site other than New Orleans. Thus, within a few months' time the most critical problems of the Northwest and the Southwest seemed to be solved. With trade freely opened down the Mississippi, the rapid growth of the West was assured.

Unfortunately the French reaction to Jay's Treaty was far less agreeable to the United States than the Spanish. Assuming that the American negotiations with England amounted to a virtual repudiation of the French treaties with the United States, the French government authorized French sea-captains to interfere with American trade as closely as possible after the British pattern of behavior. This order, generously interpreted, soon brought a series of French violations of American neutral rights that were about as offensive as anything ever suffered from the British. The American minister to France, James Monroe, a Republican who like most of his party sympathized with France in the war against England and was thoroughly shocked by Jay's Treaty, was no help to the United States, and possibly hinted at a change of policy in

---

[1] S. F. Bemis, *Jay's Treaty: A Study in Commerce and Diplomacy* (1923), covers the problems that led to Jay's mission, as well as the formation of the treaty. It is invaluable in this episode of American diplomacy.

[2] S. F. Bemis, *Pinckney's Treaty* (1926).

case Thomas Jefferson should win the election of 1796. At any rate, he was recalled by Washington, and the French government refused to receive the reliable Federalist, C. C. Pinckney, as his successor. In protest against Jay's Treaty, the French government also ordered its minister to the United States to give up his office, although it allowed him to stay in the United States and work for the election of Thomas Jefferson to the Presidency.

The election of 1796 thus turned to some extent upon foreign affairs. Since Washington refused a third term, the Republicans supported Jefferson, who had been out of the Cabinet since 1793, and felt free to criticize the policy of the government. For Vice-President they hoped to elect Aaron Burr of New York. The Federalists did not dare to nominate their ablest leader, Hamilton, who like Jefferson had left the Cabinet, but unlike him had retained a powerful voice in the Administration. Hamilton's ultra-conservatism, the Federalist leaders feared, would cost the party votes, so they turned instead to John Adams, who had made fewer enemies, with Thomas Pinckney as their candidate for Vice-President. By this time Jefferson had built up a strong following among the common people, who deeply resented the truckling to England characteristic of the Federalists, disliked thoroughly every item of the financial program Hamilton had forced through Congress, and were appalled at the ruthless suppression of the Whiskey Rebellion. The states'-rights element was also with Jefferson, for the Supreme Court, in one of its first important decisions, *Chisholm vs. Georgia* (1793), had held that a state might be sued by a citizen of another state. No more complete denial of the doctrine of state sovereignty could have been devised, and the decision was promptly recalled by the submission and ratification of the Eleventh Amendment. Federalists as well as Republicans favored the amendment, but Republicans blamed the Federalists for the decision, and maintained that they repudiated it only because they dared not do otherwise. By a narrow majority, 71 to 68, Adams was chosen over Jefferson, but some New England electors refused to vote for Pinckney, with the curious result that Pinckney received fewer votes than Jefferson, who thus became Vice-President in spite of the fact that he was the leader of the defeated party.

Election of 1796

Washington left office with far less popularity than when he assumed it. His dream of avoiding the formation of political parties in the United States had been shattered, and he had been forced, alike by his temperament and by his convictions, to ally himself with the Federalists. This display of partisanship exposed him to many bitter attacks. Even his Farewell Address. which later generations came to revere so much, was published on the

Washington's Farewell Address

eve of the election of 1796, and was construed by the Republicans as a campaign document. He urged loyalty to the Union, cautioned against an "irregular opposition" to government, and warned his countrymen "to steer clear of permanent alliances with any portion of the foreign world," but to trust instead "to temporary alliances for extraordinary emergencies." From the time of his retirement until his death in 1799, Washington devoted himself mainly to his Mount Vernon plantation and kept aloof from politics.

The new President, John Adams (1735–1826), while far from imposing in appearance, was one of the ablest men ever to occupy the presidential chair. He had been a lawyer of more than local fame before the Revolution, and his rôle during that eventful struggle   John Adams was always an important one. He served as minister to England during the Confederation period, and it was no fault of his that his mission did not succeed. In spite of the radicalism of his Revolutionary War utterances, Adams was a thoroughgoing aristocrat, and supported willingly the policies of Washington and Hamilton. But he was never anybody's man but his own. Vain of his own ability, and often irritable to the point of anger when crossed, he was nevertheless, in the words of Jefferson, "as disinterested as the being who made him." His decisions with regard to national policy were invariably the result of his best judgment, and were wholly disregardful of the political fortunes of John Adams. Few men have ever served their country so well.[1]

He was soon called upon to show his mettle. The result of the election of 1796 still further alienated the French, who continued their spoliation of American commerce, and even ordered the rejected American minister, Pinckney, to leave the country. Many   "X Y Z" Affair Federalists were ready by this time to sever all relations with France, even at the cost of war, but Adams knew that the United States was in no position to take such a stand, and urged instead that a mission to consist of three envoys be sent to France to treat for the restoration of good relations. As a result two Federalists, C. C. Pinckney and John Marshall, and one Republican, Elbridge Gerry, were dispatched to Paris. They arrived in the fall of 1797 during the thoroughly corrupt rule of the French Directorate. Talleyrand, the French foreign minister, quite in keeping with the times, instructed three of his subordinates, later known as X, Y, and Z, to demand a bribe of the Americans as a condition of negotiations. There followed an exchange of statements, known to history as the "X Y Z dispatches," which revealed fully the brazen cupidity of the French officials, and their insolent hostility to the Americans.

[1] J. T. Adams, *The Adams Family* (1930), contains a discriminating appraisal of the second President and his work. See also J. T. Morse, *John Adams* (1884).

Adams still hoped for peace, and did not reveal the "X Y Z dispatches" in full until called upon by Congress to do so. For a time
thereafter it looked as if an open declaration of war could not

War with France

be averted. Congress voted liberal appropriations to strengthen the national defense, and by repealing the treaties with France brought the alliance between the two countries to an end. Three powerful frigates, the *United States*, the *Constellation*, and the *Constitution*, were made ready for battle, and soon began to give a good account of themselves in action against French men-of-war. Merchantmen were permitted to carry guns for use in their own defense, and over four hundred privateers were released. The ships of the national navy were ordered to seize French privateers wherever found, and to take whatever measures were necessary for the protection of American commerce. Altogether the Americans captured eighty-four French ships, most of them privateers. American losses were also heavy. For over two years this period of "armed neutrality" continued, but the existence of a state of war went unrecognized by either nation.[1]

Meantime the creation of an army proceeded only slowly, for Adams did not much believe in it. All agreed that Washington should be first in command, but since owing to his age he must remain relatively inactive, there was much wrangling over who should be second in command. In the end Hamilton, who greatly desired the post, was chosen, although he disliked Adams cordially, and Adams knew it. The actual raising of troops was delayed again and again for lack of funds. It was the spring of 1799 before recruiting actually began, and by that time the war fever had cooled off. "The army is progressing like a wounded snake," said one observer.

The victory of the Federalists over the Republicans in 1796 was won by an extremely narrow margin, and Adams was always sensitive to the
taunt that he was "President by three votes"; but the

Pro-Federalist sentiment

threat of war with France tended both to strengthen his hands and to give courage to the diminished Federalist majority in Congress. In part to guard against the danger of anti-war activities within the United States, and in part to ensure against the calamity of a Republican victory at the polls, the Federalist leaders pushed through Congress during the summer of 1798 an extensive program of legislation known as the Alien and Sedition Acts.

Unhappily for the Federalists, most of the foreigners who came to the United States during this period joined the Republican Party. Many of them were refugee Frenchmen who had been thoroughly indoctrinated with the theories of the French Revolution. Others were Irishmen or

[1] G. W. Allen, *Our Naval War with France* (1909).

Englishmen whose radicalism had made it expedient for them to emigrate. Among the newcomers were many highly educated men who, as pamphleteers or editors of newspapers, gave no quarter to Adams and the party he represented.

Three of the Federalist measures, a naturalization law, an Alien Friends Act, and an Alien Enemies Act, dealt with the problems presented by these aliens. The period of residence before naturalization was lengthened to fourteen years; the President was authorized to order dangerous aliens out of the country; and in certain cases he might imprison aliens almost at will. *Alien and Sedition Acts* The Alien Acts were never seriously enforced. They were probably intended mainly to frighten pro-Republican Frenchmen out of the country, and undoubtedly they served their purpose well. A fourth repressive measure, the Sedition Act, was designed to subdue such scurrilous criticism of the administration as Republican editors, some of them aliens, were wont to indulge in. Under penalty of heavy fines and long imprisonment conspiracy to oppose or interfere with the legal measures of the government was forbidden, and the publication of any false or malicious writing directed against the President or Congress was made a misdemeanor. The Sedition Act, like the Alien Acts, accomplished more by the threat than by actual enforcement, but a few persons were brought to trial and convicted. Since the victims were ordinarily well-known Republicans, it seemed plausible to charge that the persecution was primarily a party affair, and that those being punished were martyrs to the cause of free speech.

To offset the Alien and Sedition Acts, which the Republicans regarded as unconstitutional, Jefferson and Madison soon put forward their famous Kentucky and Virginia Resolutions. These measures proposed that the states should assume the right to decide when Congress had exceeded its powers under the Constitution. *The Kentucky and Virginia Resolutions* Some pointed to the Supreme Court as the logical place for this authority to reside, but the case of *Marbury vs. Madison*, by which the Court first clearly declared itself on this question, was several years in the future. The resolutions of the Virginia legislature, which Madison had drafted, stopped with an assertion that the states might properly "interpose" their authority against such "palpable and alarming infractions of the constitution" as were contained in the Alien and Sedition Acts, but those which the Kentucky legislature adopted, and which had secretly come from the pen of Jefferson, went much further. They called upon the other states to join Kentucky in declaring the Alien and Sedition Acts "void and of no force, and . . . in requesting their repeal at the next session of Congress."

The Kentucky and Virginia Resolutions were not echoed by the legislatures of other states, and probably their authors had no such expectation. The chief purpose of the resolutions was to furnish Jefferson a platform on which to make his race for the Presidency in 1800. He meant to drive home to the electorate the dangers of Federalist rule. If the Federalists chose to violate the Constitution in one way, why not in another? And if a halt were not called soon, how long would it be before some Federalist administration, supported by a strong army and a strong navy, would choose to obliterate the rights of the states themselves as well as the rights of individuals? But the remedy that Jefferson had in mind was not really nullification. It was the election of Thomas Jefferson to the Presidency.

Had John Adams yielded to the demand of extremists within his party for a vigorous war policy, it seems reasonable to suppose that he would probably have been re-elected in spite of Jefferson's plans. Under stimulus of the war enthusiasm the Federalists in 1798 had increased their majorities in Congress, and with war-making rather than peace-making as a goal their period of ascendancy might easily have been lengthened. But Adams never gave up his hope of avoiding outright war, and when he learned in 1799 that the French government was ready to receive a new American minister, he sent to the Senate the nomination of William Vans Murray for the post. The more warlike Federalists were deeply shocked, but by this time the war fever had much abated and they dared not oppose the President. They urged a commission of three, however, instead of a minister, and on that the President gave in.

By the time the envoys reached Paris, Napoleon Bonaparte headed the French government, and had chosen to play the rôle of peacemaker.

Peace with France

The task of the Americans was thus an easy one. By a convention signed September 30, 1800, France agreed to the abrogation of the earlier treaties, and accepted the principle that neutral ships make neutral goods. The United States, on the other hand, waived indemnities for illegal seizures by the French of American shipping. When the treaty reached America, the country was entirely over its war mood, and however much some of the Federalists disliked the prospect of peace, the treaty could not be turned down. The Federalist Senate accorded it only a conditional ratification, but once the Federalists were out of power the new Republican Senate, on December 19, 1801, ratified it without reservation.

John Adams was much criticized by some members of his party for keeping the country out of war, but there are few now who would not concede that he was right. By his course those embarrassing entanglements with European nations that Washington had advised against were avoided, and the policy of permanent American neutrality with regard to European wars was given an added impetus. Adams was never forgiven by the extreme Federalists for his unwillingness to lead the country into war, but years later he said that as his epitaph he could ask nothing better than "Here lies John Adams, who took upon himself the responsibility of peace with France in the year 1800."

Quite as he had feared, Adams lost the election of 1800 to his brilliant rival, Thomas Jefferson. The Federalists, instead of being united in the support of a popular war, again found themselves handicapped by factional strife. Hamilton, thoroughly disgruntled by Adams's peace policy, denounced the President vigorously in a pamphlet intended for private distribution among selected Federalist leaders. The pamphlet naturally fell into the hands of the Republicans, who used it to good advantage in the campaign. When the returns were in, it appeared that seventy-three Republican electors had been chosen against sixty-five Federalists. The strength of the Republicans lay mainly to the south of the Mason and Dixon line, but they also carried New York, thanks no doubt to the activities of their candidate for Vice-President, Aaron Burr, and they won eight votes out of fifteen in Pennsylvania. It was particularly significant that the new western states, Kentucky and Tennessee, voted for Jefferson, and that nearly every state with a considerable frontier element either voted for Jefferson or gave him more votes than it gave Adams. Already the leaven of frontier democracy had begun to work.

Unfortunately, the election was not decided when the electoral college had registered its will. The provision in the Constitution which permitted each elector to vote for two candidates for the Presidency had made Jefferson Vice-President in 1796 when a majority of the electors were against him, and it now almost cost him the Presidency. A thoughtful New England Federalist threw away a vote on Jay, so that Pinckney got one less vote than Adams, but the Republican electors with greater zeal than foresight voted unanimously for Jefferson and Burr. These two having, therefore, an equal number of votes, it fell to the strongly Federalist House of Representatives, elected in 1798, to choose between them. A Federalist caucus decided to support Burr rather than Jefferson, but this decision was disobeyed by enough southern Federalists to deadlock the House. For thirty-five ballots there was no choice. At last, acting on the advice of Hamilton, who disliked Jefferson but knew Burr to be a rogue, the Federalists relented sufficiently to give the Presidency to Jefferson. Once the Republicans were in power they lost no time in amending the Constitution so that each elector should thereafter vote separately for President and for Vice-President.

The sullen unwillingness of the Federalists to bow to the popular will was shown again in the passage after the election of a new Judiciary

Judiciary Act
of 1801

Act. To make sure that the Supreme Court would not pass from Federalist control for a long time, the law provided that the next vacancy on the Court should not be filled, so that thereafter the number of Supreme Court justices would be one less than formerly. Also, the old practice whereby Supreme Court justices on circuit duty sat with district judges as courts of appeal was discontinued, and a whole new panel of circuit judges was authorized. Then, in spite of the fact that the duties of the district judges were thus reduced, their number was increased from thirteen to twenty-three. The evident and expressed intent of the law was not so much to reform the judiciary as to give the outgoing President the chance to pack it with Federalist judges who could be trusted to thwart the Republicans in the years to come. Adams, who on internal matters was as narrowly partisan as anyone, had already bequeathed to the Jefferson administration his Secretary of State, John Marshall, as Chief Justice, and he carried out the terms of the law in the spirit of its framers.[1]

It is not surprising that the Federalists went down to defeat. They failed to recognize that in a democracy the opinions of the masses must

Why the
Federalists
lost

be considered. They persisted too long in their assumption that government could be monopolized by the well-educated and the well-to-do. They proceeded too rapidly in their endeavor to build up a powerful centralized government, and they paid far too little attention to the strong state loyalties that had grown so naturally out of the separate status of the various colonies. Moreover, they were led by men who were for the most part commercially minded, and ignored the fact that the vast majority of the American people got their living from the soil.

Nevertheless, the Federalists in many important ways had served their country well. They had succeeded in making the new government work; the Constitution, and many of the precedents they had set, were destined to endure. They had successfully avoided entanglements in European affairs when a contrary policy might well have been fatal to the new nation. They had established the credit of the United States at home and abroad, and had given a praiseworthy example of honest and frugal administration.

[1] A. J. Beveridge, *The Life of John Marshall* (4 vols., 1916–19), is not only a biography of Marshall, but is also a brilliant history of the period from a conservative point of view. R. W. Van Alstyne, *American Diplomacy in Action: A Series of Case Studies* (1944), is an attempt to write diplomatic history as a guide for action today. A. Koch and W. Peden (eds.), *The Selected Writings of John and John Quincy Adams* (1946), is a useful compilation. A. E. Smith, *James Madison, Builder: A New Estimate of a Memorable Career* (1937), is of some value.

8

Jeffersonian Democracy

THOMAS JEFFERSON (1743–1826), whose election to the Presidency ushered in what he was pleased to term the "Revolution of 1800," was, like Washington, a Virginia planter, but with that the similarity ends. Jefferson's father was from Albemarle County, which at the time Thomas was born was properly regarded as "backcountry." Jefferson's mother was a Randolph, and hence from one of the first families of Virginia, but this aristocratic connection did not in the least undermine the sturdy, frontier democracy of her husband, nor prevent the development of her son into perhaps the outstanding theoretical democrat of all time. Unlike Washington, Jefferson had had the advantage of an excellent formal education. His knowledge of ancient and modern languages, mathematics, the natural sciences, music, and the arts was far more than elementary. He had studied and practiced law, but preferred the management of his estate and the fascinating game of politics.

Jefferson was an outstanding champion of liberal and democratic ideas, a convinced believer in the doctrine of the rights of man, which he wrote into the Declaration of Independence. He succeeded Patrick Henry as governor of Virginia, and made it his business then and later to promote such startling innovations as complete religious liberty and church disestablishment, the outlawry of medieval legal survivals, such as primogeniture, and even the abolition of slavery. As Secretary of State, Jefferson respected Washington, but he was alarmed at the ascendancy Hamilton was able to gain, and left the Cabinet to organize the opposition to Hamilton's policies. Even as Vice-President he kept at this work, although sometimes under the cloak of secrecy. Jefferson understood the popular whims and fancies better than most politicians, and possessed great talent as an organizer. He was not an orator, but he wrote with exceptional skill, and most of the documents he produced had an irresistibly popular appeal. If Hamilton's sympathies were with the commercial classes, Jefferson's were as definitely agrarian. A society consisting exclusively of small free farmers would, from Jefferson's point of view, have very closely approximated the ideal.

This was the man who became President on the Fourth of March, 1801.[1] He deplored the sham of pomp and ceremony, so the inauguration of Republican rule took place in a setting of extreme simplicity. The new President even walked from his boarding-house to the Capitol to deliver his inaugural address. Elaborate ceremonies might have been difficult to stage, however, if they had been desired, for Jefferson was the first President to take the oath of office in the new capital city on the Potomac, appropriately named Washington. An admirable plan for the city had been devised by a Frenchman named L'Enfant; but the streets were unpaved and most of them unopened, the public buildings were as yet unfinished, and only the distances between them were magnificent. The wisdom of laying out a new city to serve primarily as the political capital of the nation has since been amply justified, but many of those who surveyed the scene for the first time at Jefferson's inauguration undoubtedly thought otherwise.

The new capital city

And yet the capital city, in which great possibilities were only faintly realized, was not unlike the nation as a whole. The United States, with a population of only 5,308,473, according to the census of 1800, was still a small nation. Nine-tenths of these people lived to the east of the mountains; the other tenth, as far removed relatively from the rest of the population as the White House was from the Capitol, occupied the territory on both banks of the upper Ohio and of its more important tributaries in Kentucky and Tennessee. Nor had American society as yet shown many signs of sophistication.

Census of 1800

But the new nation was growing with phenomenal rapidity. In 1790 the population had been listed at 3,929,214; hence the total increase during the decade had amounted to about thirty-five per cent. This is the more important in view of the fact that the number of Europeans who had come to America during the decade was relatively insignificant — on an average probably not over four thousand a year. Indeed, not since before the Revolution, when the Scotch-Irish and the Germans came, had there been any considerable amount of foreign immigration into America. The increase in population was thus due almost exclusively to increase in the native stock. Marriages were early and families were large.

The variety of European races in America, as they mingled more and more, was beginning to develop a distinctively American type.

[1] Among the numerous lives of Jefferson the following merit citation: D. S. Muzzey, *Thomas Jefferson* (1918); A. J. Nock, *Jefferson* (1926); Gilbert Chinard, *Thomas Jefferson* (1929); J. T. Morse, *Thomas Jefferson* (1883); Bernard Mayo, *Jefferson Himself* (1942). Edward Channing, *The Jeffersonian System* (1906), is one of the best of the volumes of the *American Nation* series. Allen Johnson, *Jefferson and his Colleagues* (1921), covers the same period for the *Chronicles of America*. Claude G. Bowers, *Jefferson in Power* (1936), brilliantly defends Jefferson at every turn.

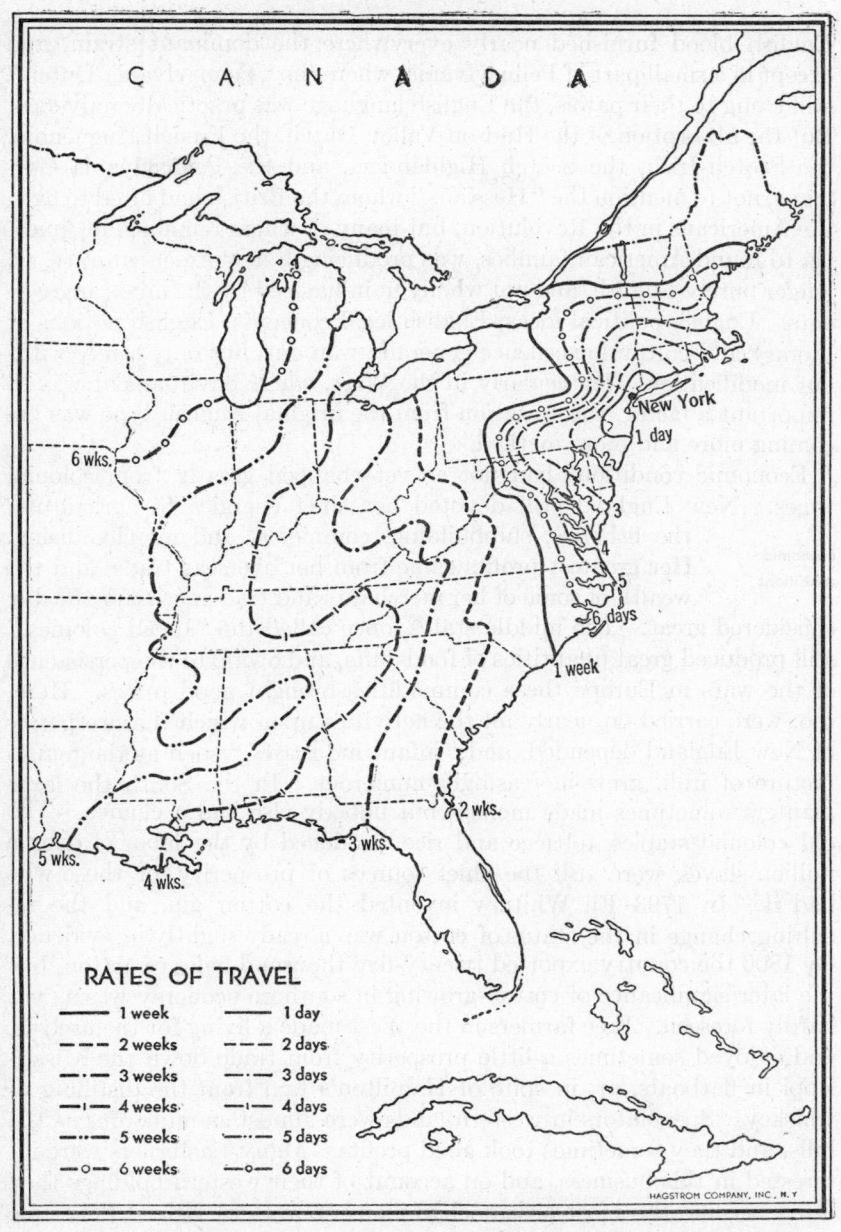

RATES OF TRAVEL

——— 1 week	——— 1 day
– – – 2 weeks	– – – 2 days
–·–·– 3 weeks	–·–·– 3 days
–ı–ı– 4 weeks	–ı–ı– 4 days
–··–··– 5 weeks	–··–··– 5 days
–o–o– 6 weeks	–o–o– 6 days

RATIO BETWEEN TIME AND DISTANCE OF TRAVEL IN THE
UNITED STATES FROM NEW YORK IN 1800

Courtesy of the Carnegie Institute of Washington and the American
Geographical Society of New York.

English blood furnished nearly everywhere the dominant strain, and except in a small part of Pennsylvania, where the "Pennsylvania Dutch" still clung to their patois, the English language was practically universal. But the absorption of the Hudson Valley Dutch, the French Huguenots, the Scotch-Irish, the Scotch Highlanders, and the Pennsylvania Germans, not to mention the "Hessians" whom the British had hired to fight the Americans in the Revolution, but many of whom remained in America to found American families, was producing a new American race, no longer purely English, and not wholly uninfluenced by the minor ingredients. English political ideas, English legal concepts, English notions of literary and cultural excellence generally won out, but only rarely without modification. Particularly in the West, where environment was so important a factor, the variation from the original English type was becoming more and more marked.

Economic conditions had not as yet changed greatly from colonial times. New England still devoted her chief energies to agriculture;
Economic
conditions the fisheries, shipbuilding, commerce, and merchandising. Her greatest profits came from her overseas trade, and the wealth of some of her merchants and traders was for the day considered great. The middle states, once called the "bread colonies," still produced great quantities of foodstuffs, and owing to the persistence of the wars in Europe these commodities brought good prices. Here, too, were carried on nearly all the activities upon which the prosperity of New England depended, and "infant industries," such as the manufacture of iron, grew increasingly numerous. In the South the large planters sometimes made money, but nobody else had a chance. The old colonial staples, tobacco and rice, produced by the labor of over a million slaves, were still the chief sources of prosperity for those who had it. In 1793 Eli Whitney invented the cotton gin, and the resulting change in the status of cotton was already slightly in evidence. By 1800 the country exported twenty-five thousand bales of cotton, but the later significance of cotton-growing in southern economy was as yet hardly foreseen. Free farmers in the West made a living for themselves, and enjoyed sometimes a little prosperity from trade down the Mississippi in flatboats, or, in spite of Hamilton's tax, from the distilling of whiskey. Speculators in western lands were almost as numerous as the hills, and they sometimes took good profits. Many Easterners were interested in this business, and on account of their western holdings they often became the most ardent champions of western rights. The rôle of the land speculator in American history has not yet been given its just due.

Americans still lived in the country rather than in the city, and the danger that Jefferson most feared, a city proletariat, seemed too far away for any but theorists to worry about. Philadelphia with 70,000 people was the most populous of American cities. New York came next with 60,000; Baltimore had 26,000; Boston, 24,000; Charleston, 20,000. These "cities" still wanted what would today be called "all modern conveniences." Sewers were conspicuously absent, and as in colonial times, hogs ran loose in the streets to dispose of the city's garbage. The country was as primitive as the city. The farmers' tools were much the same type as in the days of Ruth and Boaz, and small children had no reason to inquire what was meant by such Sunday School verses as "his yoke is easy and his burden is light."

Education and culture had as yet made no rapid strides. One might easily argue that since colonial times much ground had been lost. The war, and in its wake the hard times of the Confederation period, had undermined the foundations of the old educational systems, and had left the people with but little taste for the finer things of life. Nor did the relative prosperity of the last decade in the eighteenth century do much to improve such matters. New England still had some flourishing public academies, some short-term elementary schools, and colleges of a sort. But Harvard College in 1800 put its faith in a president, three professors, and four tutors. From New England to the South or the West educational opportunities grew progressively worse. In the whole country there was still comparatively little interest in literature; European books were read proportionately less than in colonial times; newspapers were relatively few, and in content hardly commendable; periodicals were almost non-existent. In an age when only the exceptional person could read and write, this is perhaps not surprising.

Education and culture

As in colonial times, religion still played an important part in the life of the people. Piety, or the pretense of piety, suffused New England, although the Congregational monopoly had long since been broken. In the cities the Episcopalians had a strong following, in Vermont there were many Quakers, and in Roger Williams's Rhode Island the Baptists were numerous. In the middle states there were many sects: Quakers, Presbyterians, Lutherans, Episcopalians, Dutch Reformed. In the South along the coast the Episcopalians were dominant, although in Maryland there were many Catholics and some Congregationalists. The back-country and the frontier, during and for some time after the year 1800, was experiencing one of its chronic revivals. Here the Methodists, with their intense emotionalism and their democratic doctrine that salvation was equally open to all, set the pace; but the Baptists, the Presbyterians, and numerous minor sects were not

Religion

far behind. The great revival swept like wildfire through the West, and
the pioneer people, always sorely in need of an emotional outlet, attended
the camp-meetings by the thousands and the tens of thousands.

The country stood in great need of better means of communications.
Sailboats plied slowly and without schedule from point to point along
the coast, while stage-coaches, traveling at about four miles
an hour, connected the principal cities. In the South the
Need of better communications roads were frequently unsafe for vehicles, and overland
travel was ordinarily on horseback. Inns were as primitive
as in colonial times. The rivers of the interior, even above the falls line,
were much used by all kinds of crude boats, and the "western waters"
furnished alike the easiest means of expanding the frontier and the chief
outlet of frontier trade.

The West was already "the most American part of America." Here
the melting-pot had fused racial elements more completely than elsewhere; here the difference between American ways and
The West European ways was most pronounced. Here cheap lands,
almost literally, opened opportunity equally to all. Here democracy
was practiced as well as preached, and here each citizen believed himself
to be as good as anyone else. Here people looked out for themselves,
and the ideal of individual freedom held universal sway. The society of
the West was crude and rough, and the "men of the western waters"
were mostly uncouth and illiterate, but they had begun the conquest of a
continent, and they had little time for anything else. Out of their experiences were to come many of the guiding principles of American
democracy. Jefferson understood these men, believed in them, and
thought that, as President, he fully represented them.[1]

Jefferson was at pains to introduce democratic simplicity into all the
affairs of state, but he did not surround himself with men from the lower
walks of life. For example, he chose as his Secretary of
"Revolution of 1800" State James Madison, the "father of the Constitution," and
like himself a Virginian of good position. For Secretary of
the Treasury he picked another man of consequence, Albert Gallatin of
Pennsylvania, a Genevan by birth who had excellent family connections
in Europe and had taught at Harvard. In general, the "Revolution of
1800" meant less the triumph of the lower classes, although Jefferson
believed in the solid judgment of the common people, than the transfer
of leadership in government from representatives of the commercial and
financial classes to those interested in agriculture. It was rare indeed,

---

[1] Henry Adams, *History of the United States of America during the Administrations of
Jefferson and Madison* (9 vols., 1890–91), is a work of enduring merit. The first volume
contains an admirable survey of American society in 1800.

even under Republican rule, when high office fell to a man of low estate. Jefferson really hoped to win over the rank and file of the Federalists to his party, and asserted in his inaugural address, "We are all Republicans, we are all Federalists." When it came to the removal of Federalist office-holders, he acted with extreme caution. Vacancies were filled as a rule by Republicans, but vacancies were rare. "Those by death," the President complained, "are few, by resignation, none." Nevertheless, by the end of Jefferson's first administration a majority of the office-holders were Republicans.[1]

The Republicans wasted little time in reversing many outstanding Federalist policies. The Bank of the United States, chartered in 1791 for twenty years, was performing a needed service well, and was let alone, but the excise tax, so offensive to back-country distillers of whiskey, was promptly repealed. The period of naturalization was set again at five years, and the Alien Friends and the Sedition Acts were allowed to lapse. Appropriations for public expenditures, particularly the army and navy, were mercilessly pruned down, a matter of great satisfaction to Jefferson, who believed that the functions of government should be kept at a minimum, and hoped confidently to avoid all resort to war. The Judiciary Act of 1801, under the terms of which President Adams had made many "midnight appointments" just before leaving office, was replaced by another which restored in the main the old judicial system. As for the new judges that Adams had appointed, they were left without duties and without salaries.

Repeal of Federalist laws

It was not long, however, before the Supreme Court, which was still predominantly Federalist and headed by the extremely able John Marshall, found a way to impress upon the Republicans the necessity of keeping their "revolution" within reasonable bounds. In the famous case of *Marbury vs. Madison* (1803), Marshall stated the doctrine that the Court could, if it chose, declare a law of Congress unconstitutional, and refuse to enforce it.[2] The case itself, except for the rule of law it provoked, was insignificant. A commission as justice of the peace, designed for one William Marbury, had been signed by Adams before leaving office, but was still undelivered when Jefferson became President. After inauguration, Madison, the Secretary of State, refused to deliver the commission, whereupon Marbury asked the Supreme Court to issue a mandamus requiring its surrender. This Marshall, in his momentous

[1] C. R. Fish, *The Civil Service and the Patronage* (1905); H. C. Hockett, *Western Influences on Political Parties to 1825* (1917).

[2] A. J. Beveridge, *The Life of John Marshall*, III (1919), is very complete at this point. See also E. S. Corwin, *John Marshall and the Constitution* (1919); and Charles Warren, *The Supreme Court in United States History* (2 vols., 1928).

opinion, refused to do. The law, he admitted, gave the Court abundant authority to take such action, but in granting this authority to the Supreme Court, Marshall held, Congress had exceeded its powers under the Constitution, which permitted the Court to exercise original jurisdiction only in "cases affecting ambassadors, other public ministers and consuls, and those in which a state shall be a party." With the law and the Constitution thus in direct conflict, the Chief Justice maintained that the Constitution must be followed and the law disregarded. This "doctrine of judicial review" placed a powerful weapon in the hands of the Federalist judiciary, but the Court wisely kept the weapon in reserve for many years. Not until the Dred Scott decision of 1857 was it again invoked in a case of major consequence.

Concerned lest the Federalist Court might make partisan use of its power, the Republicans were at once in search of a weapon of defense. **Impeachment proceedings** This they thought they had found in the constitutional provisions for impeachment; and in 1804 a federal district judge, John Pickering, was impeached and removed when it was clear that he had become insane. But the attempt to remove an associate justice of the Supreme Court, Samuel Chase, on the ground of gross partisanship came to naught, partly, perhaps, because the impeachment alleged also irrelevant and unprovable charges of misconduct. The precedent thus established seemed to indicate, however, that an office-holder could not be impeached for anything for which he could not also be indicted. As partisanship was no crime, the Federalist justices were free to go as far as they liked; but in the face of the growing popularity of Republican rule they conducted themselves with greater discretion.

Gallatin succeeded admirably with the reduction of the national debt, and had conditions remained normal it might have been eliminated, as he predicted, in sixteen years. Increased purchases abroad, due to the growing wealth and population of the country, led to corresponding increases in the tariff revenues. Also, except for a brief interlude, from March, 1802, to May, 1803, the European war raged on, and with British consent in the case of the *Polly* (1800), American ships were permitted to carry goods from the French West Indies to France, provided that they had first landed their cargoes at an American port and paid the duty. Before the end of Jefferson's administration Gallatin, aided by the advantages of American neutrality, had retired as much of the national debt as was due and payable. His achievement was the more remarkable in view of the unforeseen expense attendant upon the Tripolitan War and the Purchase of Louisiana.

The Tripolitan War (1801–05) probably saved the American navy from extinction. It had long been the habit of European nations to pay trib-

ute to the piratical rulers of the maritime states of northern Africa —
Morocco, Algiers, Tunis, and Tripoli — sometimes known as
the Barbary States. In this practice the new United States,   The Tripoli-
whose trade relations in the Mediterranean were of some   tan War
consequence, soon joined. To Jefferson, however, the idea of paying
tribute money to pirates was particularly offensive, and much as he
deplored the expense attached to a navy, he felt obliged to support this
arm of the national defense as a means of dealing with the corsairs.[1]
Open warfare broke out with Tripoli, whose ruler was particularly insolent in his demands. Finally, after the United States had lost one of its
best ships, the *Philadelphia*, a small overland expedition from Egypt,
headed by a pretender to the Tripolitan throne and backed by an American citizen, William Eaton, cooperated with the navy to bring the Pasha
to terms. But for many years an American squadron had to be retained
in the Mediterranean, and the practice of paying tribute did not wholly
disappear until 1815.

To Jefferson the purchase of Louisiana was as unexpected a development as the Tripolitan War. But the third President understood the
people of the Mississippi Valley far better than his predecessors, and he regarded the purchase as a necessity in order   Napoleon
to retain western loyalty to the Union. In a letter dated   acquires
April 18, 1802, Jefferson expressed to Robert R. Livingston,   Louisiana
the American minister to France, his deep concern over Bonaparte's apparent intention to acquire Louisiana from Spain:

> There is on the globe one single spot, the possessor of which is our natural
> and habitual enemy. It is New Orleans, through which the produce of $\frac{3}{8}$ of
> our territory must pass to market, and from its [the West's] fertility it will
> ere long yield more than one half of our whole produce, and contain more
> than half of our inhabitants. · France, placing herself in that door, assumes
> to us the attitude of defiance. The day that France takes possession of New
> Orleans ... we must marry ourselves to the British fleet and nation.

Jefferson's worst fears seemed confirmed when he learned a few months
later that the "right of deposit" at New Orleans had been suspended.
Actually Bonaparte had acquired title to Louisiana in 1800 by the secret
Treaty of San Ildefonso, but he had chosen not to take possession until
a long-standing revolt against French authority in the island of Santo
Domingo could be suppressed. The Spanish officials were thus left in
control at New Orleans, and the closing of the Mississippi to American
trade seems to have been the idea of the Spanish governor. But westerners, aware at last of the secret treaty, were convinced that the French
government had ordered the action, and meant to cut off their life-line to

[1] Gardner W. Allen, *Our Navy and the Barbary Corsairs* (1905); C. O. Paullin, *Commodore John Rodgers* (1910), and *Diplomatic Negotiations of American Naval Officers* (1912).

the sea. To prevent such a calamity, they were capable, as Jefferson well knew, of taking drastic action. They might seek, with or without the aid of the central government, to dislodge the French from the mouth of the Mississippi, or they might even consider leaving the Union in order to help with the formation of another New France.

Faced by this situation, Jefferson ordered Livingston to open negotiations for the purchase of the Isle of Orleans and West Florida, and in order to emphasize the seriousness of the problem he sent
Purchase of Louisiana James Monroe as special envoy to France with authority to offer as much as ten million dollars for the coveted territory. Meantime Bonaparte, discouraged by the lack of success of his forces in Santo Domingo, had decided to abandon colonial in favor of continental expansion, and as a step in that direction to sell Louisiana to the United States. He knew that his plans for attacking his neighbors would precipitate war with Great Britain, and since in time of war the British would have control of the sea, that he could not hope to protect Louisiana against British sea-power. With war in prospect, the French treasury needed money. Even before Monroe arrived, the French foreign minister, Talleyrand, had startled Livingston by asking him what he would give for the whole of Louisiana. Once Monroe arrived, the bargain was quickly struck. For about fifteen million dollars the United States acquired title to whatever territory in America Bonaparte had obtained from Spain, and incidentally to two interesting boundary disputes, one to the south, where the Spanish still held Florida, and one to the southwest between the United States and Spanish Mexico.

Jefferson was greatly astonished when he learned what his ministers had done; indeed, he seriously doubted whether the central government was authorized by the Constitution to add so much new territory to the Union. But he quickly stifled his strict-constructionist views, and submitted the treaty to the Senate, where it was ratified by a vote of 26 to 5. The sentiment in the House on the measure was shown when that body authorized the funds necessary to carry the treaty into effect by a vote of 90 to 25. Some of the Federalists were alarmed at the prospective growth of the agricultural West, which, they feared, might join with the South to tyrannize over the commercial Northeast. When they were unable to prevent ratification of the treaty, they urged that Louisiana should at least be kept in a perpetual state of dependency. It was decided, however, to adapt the Northwest Ordinance to the territory acquired from France, and to permit the formation from its area of new western states. Since the French and Spanish inhabitants of Louisiana were unaccustomed to democratic institutions, the government of the new territory was at first autocratic, with the President appointing all officials, but the process of subdivision into territories and states was soon begun. In 1812 the state of Louisiana, with its present boundaries, was admitted to the Union.[1]

Meantime the Jeffersonian régime had been at pains to seek solutions for other problems of the West. One of the most important of these was the national land policy, which originally had been designed to raise a revenue for the government. Thus the Land Law of 1796 had kept the price of land at the relatively high figure of two dollars an acre, with a minimum purchase by an individual of six hundred and forty acres. These terms were so unsatisfactory to the West that, even before Jefferson became President, William Henry Harrison, delegate from the Northwest Territory, was able to persuade Congress to liberalize them. By the Harrison Land Law of 1800, four local land offices were established in the Northwest; tracts as small as three hundred and twenty acres were offered for sale; and credit was extended to all purchasers for a period of four years, one fourth of the purchase price to be paid down, and one fourth with interest each succeeding year. As a concession to those who wished to obtain the maximum revenue from the lands, the law provided that auctions should be held for a period of three weeks whenever a new tract was opened for sale, but after the auction was over unsold lands were to be equally open to all at the minimum price, two dollars per acre. Except that it did not incorporate the right of "pre-emption," according to which the trespasser on government land claimed that he should have the first chance to purchase the land he held, this law satisfied the westerners fairly well. But the Republican Congress, in 1804, reduced the minimum unit of sale to one hundred and sixty acres, so that thereafter a man with eighty dollars in cash could make the first payment on a frontier farm.

Land policy

The Jeffersonian régime also showed its willingness to establish new governmental units in the West. The population of the Northwest Territory, greatly stimulated by the Land Law of 1800, increased so rapidly that in 1802 Congress voted to admit the new state of Ohio. A year later, under a constitution that was typically western and democratic, the seventeenth state was formally admitted. True to the promise of the Ordinance of 1785, Congress voted to grant to Ohio one section of land out of every township in aid of education, and, in return for a pledge that public land sold

Admission of Ohio

---

[1] Besides the general histories and the biographies of Jefferson, all of which devote a generous amount of space to the Louisiana Purchase, the following special works should be consulted: Charles E. Hill, *Leading American Treaties* (1922) ; E. W. Lyon, *Louisiana in French Diplomacy, 1759–1804* (1934) ; T. L. Stoddard, *The French Revolution in San Domingo* (1914) ; A. P. Whitaker, *The Mississippi Question, 1795–1803* (1934) ; J. K. Hosmer, *The History of the Louisiana Purchase* (1902).

within the state should not be taxed by the state for a five-year period, promised to apply five per cent of the proceeds of land sales within the borders of Ohio to the building of roads to and within the state.[1] A more difficult problem of territorial development appeared during these years in the Southwest, where in 1798 the new territory of Mississippi had been created out of what was left of the national domain on the admission of Tennessee. Here the land claims of the United States and of Georgia were in confusion, but in 1802 a satisfactory agreement was reached, and Georgia formally ceded her holdings to the national government.

A part of this agreement called for the indemnification of certain claimants to lands in the Yazoo district whose title had been obtained from the state of Georgia by corrupt means. This bargain was steadfastly opposed by John Randolph of Roanoke, a fiery Virginian, who over this and other differences with the Jefferson administration led a small faction of the Republican Party into open revolt.[2] The "Quids," as these insurgents were sometimes called, claimed that Jefferson had forgotten the states'-rights doctrines of 1798, and had in reality become a Federalist. In 1810 the Supreme Court in the case of *Fletcher vs. Peck* upheld the Yazoo claimants; and in 1814, with Randolph temporarily out of Congress, eight million dollars was voted for the settlement of their claims.

The Lewis and Clark Expedition, which Jefferson dispatched into the West in 1804, revealed the President's interest in the territory he had purchased, and perhaps also an interest in further expansion.

Lewis and Clark Expedition
Led by Meriwether Lewis, the President's private secretary, and William Clark, the brother of George Rogers Clark, the explorers left St. Louis in the spring of 1804, ascended the Missouri River far toward its source, crossed the Continental Divide, and reached the mouth of the Columbia. Then by approximately the same route they returned, arriving in St. Louis in September, 1806, after an absence of nearly two and one-half years. The *Journals of Lewis and Clark*, published in many editions, recorded with meticulous detail the doings and discoveries of the party, and furnished much new information for scientists and map-makers. As for the future of the country, Lewis and Clark held incorrectly that not much of it would ever be fit for white men, but their explorations nevertheless gave the United States whatever claim it wished to assert to the region beyond the Rocky Mountains.

Similar explorations by Zebulon Montgomery Pike in 1805–06 sought

---

[1] Rufus King, *Ohio: First Fruits of the Ordinance of 1787* (1888); E. O. Randall and D. J. Ryan, *History of Ohio* (4 vols., 1912); R. C. Downes, *Frontier Ohio, 1788–1803* (1935).

[2] Henry Adams, *John Randolph* (1882), is one of the best of the volumes in the *American Statesman* series, although quite unsympathetic toward Randolph.

to locate the source of the Mississippi River, and to penetrate into the Spanish-held Southwest. On the latter expedition, Pike was picked up by the Spanish, his papers taken away from him, and he and his men conducted by a circuitous route back to the United States. His verdict, like that of Lewis and Clark, showed much skepticism as to the habitability of the arid West for whites.

Expeditions of Pike

Jefferson's manifold interests, and particularly his success in purchasing Louisiana, pleased the American people immensely, and insured his re-election in 1804. Some northeastern Federalists, rather than face the prospect of continued agricultural control of the government, were ready to break up the Union. In the Vice-President, Aaron Burr, they found a willing tool for their plots. Back in 1800, when the Federalist House was attempting to choose between Jefferson and Burr for the Presidency, Burr had seemed willing to accept the office if Congress should so decide. For this breach of loyalty Jefferson never forgave him, and as Vice-President, bereft of presidential patronage, his influence with the members of the Republican Party soon faded. When, therefore, a number of Federalists suggested that he become their candidate for governor of New York in 1804, he was not averse. Their plan was to elect Burr, and then under his leadership to take New York and New England out of the Union. Fortunately Hamilton learned of the plot, and by exposing it caused it to fail. Burr, now completely discredited, challenged Hamilton to a duel, and on July 11, 1804, mortally wounded him. In the election the Federalists, compelled now to defend themselves against the charge of treason, were overwhelmed. George Clinton, Burr's chief rival in New York politics, became the Republican vice-presidential candidate and helped, as Burr had done four years before, to carry that state for Jefferson. Even New England, with the exception of Connecticut, went Republican. The electoral vote stood 162 for Jefferson to 14 for C. C. Pinckney, the Federalist candidate.

Unfortunately the last had not yet been heard of Aaron Burr. Discredited everywhere in the East, and in two states indicted for murder, he determined to carve out for himself a new career somewhere in the troubled borderland between the United States and Spain. As he well knew, the boundaries of Louisiana were only vaguely defined, and Jefferson had promptly opened a dispute with Spain over West Florida. Already hostile Indians were using Florida as a base of operations against the American frontier, and as a haven of refuge. Many Westerners were ready, by force of arms, if necessary, to push the southwest boundary of Louisiana far into Spanish territory. Moreover, the creole population of Louisiana was restive under the rule of William

Aaron Burr

C. C. Claiborne, a frontier politician whom Jefferson had sent to New Orleans as governor. An admirable foil for Burr's ambitions was available, also, in the person of General James Wilkinson, in charge of American troops in Louisiana. Wilkinson was a spy and a turncoat who was at the time and had been before in the pay of Spain.

As to what Burr really intended to do, there is no agreement among historians. He himself told one treasonous story to the British minister, and quite another to the Spanish minister. He made a trip to the West and talked freely of his plans. To some he said merely that he was going out West to make a new start in politics. To others he spoke of carving a Mississippi Valley Confederacy out of the possessions of Spain, or of the United States, or both. With consummate skill he suited the degree of treason to the taste of each listener.

Burr's "conspiracy" was well received by many Westerners. The feeling that Spain might still be a menace to the West persisted, and Burr's occasional allusions to an attack on Vera Cruz or even Mexico City won much support. Some were interested merely because of the excitement that the project promised. Wilkinson, a past master at intrigue, was easily attached to the scheme. Harmon Blennerhassett, a rich Irishman who lived in splendor on an island in the Ohio River near Parkersburg, West Virginia, furnished money, boats, and supplies. Open plans were made for an expedition to start down the Ohio River on November 15, 1806, and plans were laid for Wilkinson to be with his troops far to the west of New Orleans when Burr's boats should arrive. But everything went wrong. Burr was delayed temporarily by an unsuccessful attempt to indict him for treason in Kentucky, while Wilkinson, true to his record, turned informer, and gave the plot away. When the "expedition" finally started, it consisted of only thirteen flatboats carrying sixty men. Before it reached Natchez, Burr learned of Wilkinson's duplicity, and fled, only to be caught and sent to Richmond, Virginia, for trial.

When the case came to trial, it took on more the aspect of a test of strength between Thomas Jefferson, Republican President of the United States, and John Marshall, Federalist Chief Justice of the **Burr's trial** United States, than a trial for treason. Jefferson sent a notable array of legal talent to prosecute Burr, but the Chief Justice, before whom on circuit duty the trial was set, circumvented their best arguments by ruling that a man to be guilty of treason had to be present when the overt act was committed. Since the overt act was held to be the starting of the expedition from Blennerhasset's Island, and since Burr was not present at that time, but joined the expedition later, his acquittal followed as a matter of course. Perhaps the Chief Justice believed that

Burr was being tried less for treason to his country than for treason to his party; further, he was interested in demonstrating that the President of the United States cculd neither coerce the courts, nor use them as a means of political persecution. Nevertheless, Jefferson was not wholly bested. When the Court summoned him to appear during the proceedings, and to bring certain papers with him, he ignored the summons. The President could not be at the command of the courts. It was a drawn battle in which each department of the government stoutly and successfully maintained its independence of the other.[1]

[1] The Burr conspiracy has attracted a host of writers, many of them fictionists. W. F. McCaleb, *The Aaron Burr Conspiracy* (1903), makes an able defense of Burr. Other accounts of merit are to be found in the works of McMaster, Adams, and Beveridge. See also S. H. Wandell and Meade Minnigerode, *Aaron Burr* (2 vols., 1925).

Additional writing on Jefferson includes Dumas Malone, *Jefferson, the Virginian* (1948); Adrienne Koch, *The Philosophy of Thomas Jefferson* (1943); Marie Kimball, *Jefferson: The Road to Glory, 1743 to 1776* (1943); C. G. Bowers, *The Young Jefferson, 1743–1789* (1945). H. S. Commager, *Majority Rule and Minority Rights* (1943), is a Jeffersonian attack on judicial review; S. K. Padover, *Jefferson* (1942), is a sound popular summary of Jefferson's career; F. L. Mott, *Jefferson and the Press* (1943), is a brief exposition of Jefferson's views on a single significant subject.

Henry Adams, *The Life of Albert Gallatin* (1879; new ed., 1943), is again available.

J. R. Jacobs, *Tarnished Warrior: Major General James Wilkinson* (1938), and T. R. Hay and M. R. Werner, *The Admirable Trumpeter: A Biography of General James Wilkinson* (1941), seek with some success to evaluate Wilkinson's character and historical importance.

9

Neutrality and War

FOR all the growing interest in the West, the United States during Jefferson's administration was still bound by close commercial ties to Europe, and particularly to England. The era of American self-sufficiency had not yet arrived, and great quantities of manufactured articles still had to be imported. The United States as a producer of raw materials, particularly foodstuffs, was still heavily dependent on outside markets. During part of Jefferson's first administration, Europe was at peace, and this trade went on in normal fashion. But war between England and France was resumed in 1803, and from that time forward the twofold task of American diplomacy was to keep the United States out of the war, and at the same time to defend her rights as a neutral.[1]

The customary difficulties with England were soon in evidence. By 1805 Napoleon's best-laid plans to secure the control of the seas had come to naught at Trafalgar, and thereafter the British fleets were free to tighten their control over commerce. They now found inconvenient the decision that Sir William Scott had handed down in the case of the *Polly*, and another judge, Sir William Grant, held in the case of the *Essex* (1805) that a French-owned West Indian cargo could not be shipped by way of the United States to Europe unless the owners could show that their original intent had been to leave the goods in the United States. Thenceforth the British used their judgment as to what part of the West Indian trade in neutral ships to permit, and what part to restrain. They were freed from still further hampering regulations by the expiration in 1807 of the commercial clauses of the Jay Treaty, and by the failure of James Monroe, American minister to England, to secure a satisfactory treaty to replace them.

The struggle in Europe had now reached a degree of intensity in which

Revival of difficulties with England

---

[1] The diplomacy of this period is best set forth in the volumes of Henry Adams, *History of the United States*, already mentioned. Other works of special value are A. T. Mahan, *Sea Power in its Relation to the War of 1812* (2 vols., 1905); and F. A. Updyke, *Diplomacy of the War of 1812* (1915).

neither side cared much what happened to neutral rights. Napoleon, hopelessly foiled in his efforts to control the high seas, had resolved to bring England to terms by other means. The English, he reasoned, were a nation of shopkeepers, whose livelihood depended upon their trade with the outside world. Europe was England's chief customer, and Napoleon could, or at least thought that he could, control most of Europe. His Continental System was devised to stop as nearly as might be all imports into European ports from England. He would rob England of her markets and by an unfavorable balance of trade drain her of her gold supply. He would also, in so far as he could accomplish it by threats or violence, prevent trade between England and her customers outside of Europe, particularly the United States.

Napoleon's Continental System

Indulging his taste for the dramatic, Napoleon issued from foreign capitals the decrees by which this policy was set forth. The Berlin and Milan Decrees, issued respectively in 1806 and 1807, laid a paper blockade around Great Britain, forbade all trade in British merchandise, and ordered the confiscation of all neutral ships bound to or from a British port. Napoleon knew that he could not enforce his decrees fully, but he believed that he could stop much trade to the continent of Europe, and, even with the limited sea-power he possessed, he thought that he might interfere somewhat with trade between England and the neutral nations.

The English replied to Napoleon's decrees with a series of Orders in Council that were quite as careless of neutral rights as the decrees themselves. All trade between ports in the possession of France or her allies was forbidden, and these ports placed under a further blockade against trade with the outside world. This meant that all neutral trade with Europe, from Trieste to Copenhagen, was forbidden, although the British blockade, like Napoleon's, was a "paper" blockade which could at best only hamper the movement of goods to and from continental ports. The British hoped that a shortage of foodstuffs would develop, which would induce Napoleon to withdraw his obnoxious decrees. The plight of American shipping was now a sorry one indeed. Ships destined to France or to any of the nations controlled by France, which meant most of Europe, were subject to seizure by the English, while ships sailing for any English port were subject to seizure by the French.

British Orders in Council

Both the French and the British enforced their illegal blockades by captures on the American side of the Atlantic, where privateers and warships took what prizes they could. The French naturally took fewer, for their ships were less numerous and were themselves in danger of capture by the British. Admiralty courts in the West Indies, both French and

British, decided against the captured American ship. British impressments of sailors from American ships occurred more and more frequently, and were sometimes carried out with unbecoming brutality. American resentment against this practice, particularly among the people along the coast whose friends and relatives had been victimized, grew steadily more intense.

The supreme outrage occurred in June, 1807, when a British man-of-war, the *Leopard*, attacked an American frigate, the *Chesapeake*, and took off four members of her crew.[1] This untoward incident followed shortly after the escape of a boatload of sailors from the sloop *Halifax*, which, together with several other British warships, had put in at Lynnhaven Bay, near the mouth of the Chesapeake. The commander of the British squadron had noted that an American warship, the *Chesapeake*, was preparing to leave the harbor for a cruise in the Mediterranean, and he hastily concluded that the deserting British sailors must be upon it, and gave orders that the *Chesapeake* should be searched. When the American man-of-war finally put to sea, she was followed by the *Leopard*, which insisted on exercising the right of search, quite as if the American ship had been a merchant vessel instead of a warship. When Captain Barron of the *Chesapeake* refused to submit to the proposed indignity, the *Leopard* promptly opened fire, and forced the unready *Chesapeake* to strike its colors. The British then boarded the *Chesapeake* and took off four deserters, only one of whom, it transpired, was an Englishman.

The Chesapeake affair

The news of this outrage put the country in a belligerent mood, and had Jefferson wanted war, undoubtedly he could have had it. But the President chose to keep the peace if he could. After forbidding British warships the use of American ports and harbors, and demanding reparations from the British government, he laid before Congress as his chief weapon of retaliation an Embargo Act, which ultimately, on December 21, 1807, became law. This measure prohibited all ships, except foreign ships in ballast, to depart from the United States for any foreign port. Ships engaged in the coasting trade were required to give heavy bond that they would land their cargoes in the United States.[2]

The Embargo

Jefferson had hoped that the warring nations of Europe, rather than suffer the loss of American trade, would withdraw their obnoxious regulations, but in this he was disappointed. In the first place, the embargo could not be perfectly enforced, and many American ships continued to

[1] R. D. Paine, *The Fight for a Free Sea* (1920); J. F. Zimmerman, *Impressment of American Seamen* (1925).

[2] L. M. Sears, *Jefferson and the Embargo* (1927).

sail the seas. In the second place, the law hurt the United States at least as much as, probably more than, it hurt the European belligerents. Shippers, ship-owners, and ship-builders took terrific losses; sailors, sail-makers, and other artisans were thrown out of work; articles of trade that were normally imported became scarce and cost high prices; farm prices dropped as the crops of 1808 found their normal gateways to market closed.

The election of 1808 showed clearly that the temper of the country had changed. Jefferson was importuned to stand for re-election again, but he declined with such emphasis as to set a precedent that long remained unbroken. He did not hesitate, however, to throw the "succession" to his Secretary of State, James Madison. The Federalists supported C. C. Pinckney, and by emphasiz-ing the unpleasant features of the embargo, they won back many voters who had deserted them for Jefferson four years before. In the electoral college Madison received 122 electoral votes to 47 for Pinckney. Six electors cast their ballots for George Clinton, the Vice-President, whose claims to the succession Jefferson had overlooked. Congress remained Republican, although by a much-reduced majority.

Election of 1808

The results of the election made it abundantly apparent that the Re-publicans must repeal their embargo or witness an even more embarrass-ing revival of Federalist strength. The endurance of the country was at an end. Undoubtedly the English were also greatly distressed by the embargo, but they were willing to put up with it as a necessary accompaniment of the war with Napoleon. But the United States lacked any such effective motive, and was unwill-ing to continue its self-inflicted punishment. After the election, Jefferson left the determination of future policy to his successor, and with Madi-son's approval, a few days before he left office, he signed a bill to repeal the embargo. It was with some humiliation that he was thus compelled to confess his favorite project a failure.

Repeal of the Embargo Act

James Madison (1751–1836),[1] the fourth President, was another rep-resentative of the Virginia planter class, although from his youth he was more the politician than the planter. Only a few years out of Princeton and still undecided as to his life work, the out-break of the American Revolution determined his course for him. Suc-cessively he served as a member of the local committee on public safety, of the convention that drew up the first Virginia constitution, of the Continental Congress, of the Virginia House of Delegates, of the Con-vention that framed the Constitution of the United States, and of the national House of Representatives. For eight years he was Jefferson's

James Madison

[1] S. H. Gay, *James Madison* (1884); Gaillard Hunt, *The Life of Madison* (1902).

Secretary of State and close adviser. Certainly his political apprentice-ship had been ample.

As a substitute for the embargo, Madison gave his approval to what was called the Non-Intercourse Act, a measure which closed American ports to the ships of England and France and forbade the importation of goods into the United States from either of those nations, or from their colonies or dependencies. Amer-ican ships were permitted to leave American ports, provided only that their destinations were not French or British. The act also carried with it an offer to the offending belligerents. In case England would withdraw her Orders in Council, the President was authorized to suspend non-intercourse with England; and in case Napoleon would withdraw his decrees, to suspend non-intercourse with France.

Non-Intercourse

It would be quite inaccurate to assume that the Embargo and Non-Intercourse Acts had no effect whatever upon British policy. Shortly after the *Chesapeake* affair, a British envoy, George Rose, was sent to the United States to seek a satisfactory settlement of that unhappy episode, but neither side would yield anything, and the mission failed. Another effort to restore good relations was made by David M. Erskine, the regu-lar British minister to the United States, who was instructed by the Brit-ish government to prepare the way for a general treaty of amity between the two nations that would end all outstanding disputes. It appeared that Canning, the British foreign minister, was even ready to consider the withdrawal of the British Orders in Council in return for the opening of American trade and some other favors. Madison easily reached an agreement with Erskine, who strove hard to please, and thinking that the troubles with the British were now over, issued a proclamation restoring intercourse with Great Britain, and permitting American ships to sail for British ports. Unfortunately, however, Canning held that Erskine had exceeded his instructions, and repudiated his agreement at sight, leaving Madison no alternative but to issue another proclamation, this time restoring non-intercourse with Great Britain. The amiable Erskine was recalled, and in his place a notoriously ill-tempered diplomat, Francis James Jackson, was sent to America with the promise that he might retain his post for at least a full year. The diplomatic impasse was thus complete.

Non-intercourse was of course a transparent fraud. It was impossible to tell, once a ship had cleared from an American port, what its destina-tion might be. At the end of a year's trial, even the most ardent Republicans were willing to admit that the policy, although responsible for a great revival of American trade, was well-nigh worthless as a weapon of economic coercion. Accordingly,

Macon's Bill Number 2

non-intercourse was succeeded by a new measure, sometimes called Macon's Bill Number 2, which repealed the Non-Intercourse Act outright, and tried to bargain with the contending European powers for their favor. If England would repeal her obnoxious Orders in Council, the United States would revive non-intercourse with France; if France would withdraw her offensive decrees, the United States would revive non-intercourse with England. On May 1, 1810, this bill became a law.

The embargo had fitted in well with Napoleon's policy of crippling British trade, and non-intercourse, while far less satisfactory to the Emperor, was still better than nothing. But the abandonment of commercial coercion by the United States, as embodied in Macon's Bill Number 2, suited Napoleon not at all. He therefore proposed to take advantage of the offer that the United States would resume non-intercourse with England in case France withdrew her decrees. Accordingly, his foreign minister, the Duke of Cadore, wrote a letter to the American minister to France stating that the Berlin and Milan Decrees would be withdrawn beginning November 1, 1810, provided that the United States "shall cause their rights to be respected by the English." Thereupon Madison, who could not possibly have overlooked the conditions Napoleon specified, unwisely reinstituted non-intercourse with England. Perhaps the President, whose foreign policy to date had been so full of failures, could not resist the temptation to display one slight success. But Madison's triumph was short-lived, for Napoleon, having accomplished his purpose, laid down new regulations against American shipping in French ports that were quite as distressing as the decrees he had repealed.

But if the relations between the United States and France were bad, those between the United States and Great Britain were worse. At the end of his year, Jackson, the British minister to the United States, returned to England, and was not replaced. In re-taliation, the American minister to Great Britain was called home. When on May 16, 1811, an American frigate, the *President*, charged with the duty of protecting American commerce, attacked and defeated the British *Little Belt*, the American public rejoiced that the *Chesapeake* had at last been avenged. Convinced at last that failure to withdraw the offensive Orders in Council might mean war, the British sent a new minister, Augustus J. Foster, to the United States, and finally, on June 16, 1812, announced that the Orders in Council had been withdrawn. Obviously the British people had no stomach for an American war at a time when their nation was engaged in a life-and-death struggle with Napoleon. Furthermore, British manufacturers had suffered about all they could stand from the loss of American markets, and the British people stood in desperate need of American food.

The President and the Little Belt

Unfortunately, the British concession came too late. On the very day that the British foreign minister told Parliament that the Orders in Coun-

War declared cil were being withdrawn, the American government was pushing a declaration of war through Congress. On June 1, 1812, Madison sent in his war message; on June 4, the House by a vote of 79 to 49 declared for war; and on June 18, just two days after Castlereagh's announcement, the Senate, by a vote of 19 to 13, concurred.

To understand fully the change in American sentiment that made war possible it is essential to take note of a series of developments in the American West. There an Indian war was in the making. For many years the tribes, both in the Northwest and in the Southwest, had been obliged to retreat before the ever-advancing frontier of white settlement. The time for another stand against the aggressors had come, and for good or ill the Indians had found a leader. This was Tecumseh, in whose person, according to tradition, the blood of northern and southern tribes had been united, for his father, this tradition held, was a Shawnee and his mother was a Creek. Tecumseh did not wish for war against the whites, but he did hope to unite the Indians into a confederacy strong enough to stop the unending cessions of Indian land that the American government demanded. In 1808 he joined with his brother, a medicine man generally spoken of as the "Prophet," to found near the mouth of Tippecanoe Creek on the banks of the Wabash a headquarters soon known as "Prophet's Town." To and from this center came many young warriors whose great hope was the realization of Tecumseh's dream. From the time Prophet's Town was founded, the northwestern frontier lived under the shadow of impending war.

When in 1811 Tecumseh made a visit to the South to secure greater support from the tribes in that section, William Henry Harrison, gov-

Indian War in the Northwest ernor of Indiana, could wait no longer. With a strong force of militia he set out for Prophet's Town with the avowed intention of destroying it. But on November 6, 1811, he stopped to treat with the Indians, and next morning, before day broke, he was ambushed. Finally the Indians were driven off, but Harrison had lost sixty-one killed and one hundred and twenty-seven seriously injured. The battle of Tippecanoe, as this engagement was called, was hailed nevertheless as a great victory for the whites. The Indians did not return to the attack, and Prophet's Town, which they had abandoned, was destroyed. Even after this incident Tecumseh still counseled peace, but Indian depredations along the northwestern frontier occurred after Tippecanoe with ever-increasing frequency. The war had in truth begun.

When Harrison reported the battle of Tippecanoe, he complained bitterly that the Indians were well supplied with powder and guns obtained from the British in Canada. Possibly these supplies did not come from the King's stores as Harrison thought, but the fact that Tecumseh was in close touch with the British authorities was a matter of common knowledge. Almost the same situation existed in the Northwest that had confronted Washington when he entered the Presidency. To be sure, the British had removed their military posts to the Canadian side of the boundary, but these posts still existed, and their garrisons were as much concerned as ever with the protection of the fur-trade south of the Great Lakes. Tecumseh's plan for organized Indian resistance to the advance of the farmers' frontier fitted in well with Canadian needs. Should the Indians make good their efforts, the northward flow of pelts from the unsettled western lands of the United States might still continue. To the Westerner it appeared that the Canadian fur-trader and the Indian, with identical interests, were merely preparing once more to join forces for the protection of those interests.

It was only natural under these circumstances that the people of the West should applaud vigorously each step taken by the national government in the direction of war with England. They knew, Western certainly as early as 1811, that a war with the Indians was desire sure to come, and they believed implicitly that to make war for war against the Indians without fighting an accompanying war against the allies of the Indians in Canada was to leave the task half-done. Strong in their devotion to the doctrine of the rights of men, the Westerners resented undoubtedly such violations of this principle as the impressment of American sailors by the British, but there is room to question whether western resentment against these outrages would have been so great had there not been other and more local grievances against the British. The congenital appetite of the West for expansion was also easily whetted. If war with the British was to come, why not make it a war for the conquest and annexation of Canada? Upper Canada was as logically athwart the path of the American westward movement as the Michigan peninsula, and the need of the West for more lands was perpetual. With the English held at bay in Europe by Napoleon, what was more reasonable than that the United States should seize the opportunity to eliminate the British from North America and thus end for all time the menace of the English-Indian alliance? [1]

In the Southwest there was less certainty of immediate war than in the Northwest, but the preaching of Tecumseh had aroused the latent forebodings of the southern tribes and had bolstered up their will to resist. In this region, despite the cession of Louisiana to the United States, the

---

[1] J. W. Pratt, *Expansionists of 1812* (1925), presents with great effectiveness the reasons why the West and the South desired war with Great Britain.

Spanish were still the traditional enemies of the Americans and the
natural allies of the Indians, for Florida remained in Spanish

The southwestern frontier

hands, and the boundary dispute was still alive. As the
southwestern frontier expanded, its residents saw with increasing clarity the necessity of ousting the Spanish from the adjacent seacoast. Through the Florida panhandle ran many of the rivers by
which the produce of the new Southwest could most easily find access to
the sea. Along the coast of Florida were nests of dangerous pirates that
the now enfeebled rule of Spain was powerless to destroy. Hostile Indians
took refuge within the borders of Florida, and mingled with the runaway
Negroes and renegade whites to produce bands of ruffians as unsavory as
were to be found anywhere on the American continent. In 1810 Madison,
carrying out Jefferson's policy of acquiring West Florida, ordered the governor of Louisiana to extend his territory peacefully over that portion of
the Spanish province adjacent to the Mississippi River, but the southern
expansionists wanted more. They were ready, if it were necessary, to
fight another Indian war; they saw in a war against England the prospect
of the greatly-to-be-desired war against Spain, now the ally of England;
and they were willing to help the Northwest acquire Canada on the assumption that the Northwest in return would help the Southwest acquire
Florida.

Thus from the interior, whether to the north or to the south, every
strongly anti-British stand of the administration in Washington was received with unbounded enthusiasm, while every sign of weak-

The "War Hawks"

ening was unsparingly denounced. In the elections of 1810
and 1811 the weak-kneed policy embodied in Macon's Bill
Number 2 received a thoroughgoing rebuke. Nearly half the congressmen
who had voted for that measure were left at home, and a new generation
of politicians seized the reigns of power. Among them were John Sevier
and Felix Grundy from Tennessee, John C. Calhoun from the back-country of South Carolina, and young Henry Clay from Kentucky, whom the
newcomers banded together to make Speaker of the House. These young
patriots and their followers were eager for war, and quickly won for themselves, from the erratic John Randolph of Roanoke, the designation,
"War Hawks." They defended more stoutly than any Easterner the
rights of American sailors and American commerce on the high seas; they
denounced in unmeasured terms the assistance that the British in Canada were giving to marauding bands of Indians on the frontier; and they
pointed out as the chief prize to be won from the war the easy acquisition
of Canada.

Finally Madison, alive to the meaning of recent elections, capitulated
to the War Hawks and called for war, but the vote that he obtained from

Congress was far from unanimous. The commercial interests of the Northeast were desperately opposed to the measure, and their sentiments were reflected by a majority of the congress- *The vote for war* nen from that section. Nor were the opponents of the war ill Federalists, for a large section of the Republican Party either voted against the declaration or refused to vote at all. The vote for war was delivered mainly by representatives of the West and the South. From the four frontier states, Vermont, Ohio, Kentucky, and Tennessee, every vote but one was cast for war. Most of the rest of the majority came from the South.[1]

The election of 1812, which was held before much fighting had occurred, constituted a kind of popular referendum on the decision that the President and Congress had made. The British were known to be far from eager to fight the war, and it was generally *Election of 1812* believed that the American government could make peace on reasonable terms any time it wished. Should the war be fought, or should it be called off? As a candidate to oppose Madison, peace men among the Republicans advanced DeWitt Clinton of New York, whom the Federalists were also induced to support. The issue was clean-cut: a vote for Madison meant a vote for war, and a vote for Clinton meant a vote for peace. The results of the election made further manifest the responsibility of the West for the war. New England, with the exception of Vermont, cast 43 electoral votes for Clinton and peace, while the middle states (including Maryland and Delaware) preferred Clinton over Madison by a vote of 46 to 31. The South voted solidly, 59 to 0, for Madison and war. Thus the seaboard states — the original thirteen — were as nearly equally divided as possible, with a vote of 90 for Madison to 89 for Clinton, certainly too narrow a margin upon which to wage a war. But the five states that had been admitted to the Union by act of Congress — Vermont, Kentucky, Tennessee, Ohio, and Louisiana (admitted in 1812) — broke the balance by casting their entire vote for Madison, who was thus elected, 128 to 89. It was another victory of the West, aided by the dominantly agricultural South, over the commercial Northeast.

Financially speaking, the country could hardly have been less prepared for war. The passing of the Bank of the United States, which old-school Jeffersonian Republicans and western partisans of state *Unprepared-* banks had refused a re-charter in 1811, deprived the country *ness for war* of both a stable currency and the machinery needed for floating loans. The doubling of tariff rates hardly compensated for

[1] K. C. Babcock, *The Rise of American Nationality* (1906), covers adequately the period of the War of 1812. For the Canadian point of view see William Wood, *War with the United States* (1915).

the losses in revenue sustained as a result of the restrictions on trade that were laid down before the war, and tightened by its advent. Internal taxes, although finally accepted as a necessity, were at first spurned as "unrepublican." A direct levy on the states in 1813 brought only the most meager results. Most of the cost of the war had, therefore, to be met by loans, but in order to attract investors government securities had to be sold at a serious discount, with interest rates sometimes as high as seven and one-half per cent. New England capital practically refused to support the war. It was small wonder that by the time peace was restored the government was virtually bankrupt.

In the all-important matter of military preparedness, the country was not much better off. The regular army consisted of about seven thousand men, all of whom were needed on garrison duty. Presumably the states could muster some seven hundred thousand enrolled militia, but requisitions by the federal government on the states were half-heartedly filled, and sometimes flatly refused. At no time during the war did the government have in service more than thirty-five thousand men, and on occasion whole detachments of militia refused to fight outside the boundaries of their state. Commanding officers, some of whom had fought well in the Revolution, were now overage and often "utterly unfit for any military purpose whatever." Even the Canadians were better off than the Americans. They were far more ably commanded, they had a small nucleus of British regulars to start with, and they had better luck enlisting an army to resist invasion than the Americans had to make one. On the high seas the odds against the Americans were spectacular. The American navy numbered sixteen frigates, together with a fair number of smaller craft, but against these the British could count about one thousand ships of the line, of which nearly a hundred were assigned to duty on the western side of the Atlantic. Apparently the War Hawks were counting more heavily on the victories that Napoleon was expected to win than upon anything that the Americans could hope to do.

And yet, the American attack on Canada, to which all other considerations were subordinated, was planned with complete confidence, and undertaken with full expectation of success. Three separate, but more or less simultaneous, blows were to be delivered. Henry Dearborn, the senior major-general, was to advance northward by the Lake Champlain route toward Montreal; Stephen Van Rensselaer, relying mainly upon New York militia, was to attack the British at Niagara; and William Hull, the governor of Michigan Territory, was to launch from Detroit an invasion of Upper Canada. Unfortunately not one of the three officers mentioned was in the least fitted to cope with the situation that confronted him.

Attack on Canada

Throughout the year 1812 the news from the northern front was uniformly bad. On July 12, 1812, Hull crossed the Detroit River and marched timidly toward the British post at Malden. His doubts and fears multiplied as he observed the hostility of the inhabitants, the poverty of their country, and the evidence that a strong force was concentrating at Malden to oppose him. When finally the news came that Tecumseh and a band of Indian warriors had joined the British, Hull's courage completely evaporated, and he fell back to Detroit. There he was surrounded by British and Indians under General Isaac Brock, and on August 16 was induced to surrender. For his conduct he was later courtmartialed and sentenced to be shot, but because of his creditable record in the Revolution the President pardoned him. A month before Hull's surrender, the American garrison at Michilimackinac had been forced to capitulate and only the day before the loss of Detroit the little American garrison at Fort Dearborn (Chicago) had been massacred by the Indians. Meantime the attacks on Niagara and Montreal had failed to get under way. At Niagara some fighting occurred in October, but the unwillingness of the New York militia to cross the border destroyed all hope of invasion. The senior major-general, Dearborn, delayed his advance on Montreal until November, but when still twenty miles from the Canadian border he turned back to his headquarters at Plattsburg.

Fortunately for American morale, the fighting on the high seas was going far better. The men who manned the American ships were well-paid and competent volunteers, and the captains who com- **The high seas** manded them were veterans of the Tripolitan War. American ships, moreover, were carefully constructed to carry more guns and sail than the corresponding units of European navies. Thus in ship-for-ship engagements the Americans scored a series of spectacular victories. On July 11 the *Essex* captured the *Minerva* and two days later forced the *Alert* to surrender. On August 19, the *Constitution*, Captain Isaac Hull commanding, outfought the *Guerrière* in what was probably the most brilliant American sea-victory of the war. On October 18, the *Wasp* took the *Frolic*. On October 25, the *United States* defeated the *Macedonian*, and brought her as a prize into an American port. On December 29, the *Constitution*, under a new captain, William Bainbridge, destroyed the *Java*, and won for herself the name "Old Ironsides." On February 24, 1813, the *Hornet* sank the *Peacock* after a combat that lasted only fifteen minutes. Meantime American warships and privateers were also taking a frightful toll of British commerce.

The uninterrupted series of naval victories tremendously lightened the gloom that the military blunders along the northern frontier had cast over the American people, but the effect on the British public was even more marked. For centuries British sea-captains had been accustomed to win against whatever odds confronted them, and the defeats by Americans seemed beyond comprehension. Unfortunately the American luck was not to last. With the spring of 1813 the British established a tight blockade of the American coast, and from that time forward American ships of war scarcely dared to leave port. Four or five American warships, including the *Constitution*, managed to continue intermittently on the high seas until the war was over, and some of the American privateers took good prizes to the very end; but as a fighting weapon for either offensive or defensive purposes, the American navy had ceased to function.[1] New England, which from New London northward was exempted by the British from the blockade because of its notorious opposition to the war and its readiness to sell to the enemy, could still carry on a fair export trade, but elsewhere shipments from American ports were held down to nearly nothing. In 1814 not more than $200,000 worth of goods left the ports of New York, and hardly $17,500 worth left the ports of Virginia.

Before attempting another invasion of Canada, American war-makers wisely decided that the control of the Great Lakes must be wrested from the British. With this end in view a small fleet was con-

Battle of Lake Erie

structed on Lake Erie, and on September 10, 1813, with Commodore Oliver Hazard Perry in command, it won a significant victory. Perry's terse report, "We have met the enemy and they are ours," lives deservedly. When, shortly afterward, the British felt obliged to retreat from Detroit and Malden, they were followed by William Henry Harrison with a far larger army than Hull had commanded. In the ensuing battle of the Thames, fought on October 5, 1813, Tecumseh was slain, and the British command put to flight. The American invasion did not proceed much further, but the war ended with the Indians completely humbled, and the northwestern border in American hands. Meantime, other fighting on the Canadian frontier had produced nothing more startling than the burning of the parliament buildings at York (Toronto) by the Americans, and the capture of Fort Niagara by the British.

Efforts on the part of the British during the year 1814 to invade the United States were similarly inconclusive. In the Niagara area, where most of the fighting took place, the Americans scored a considerable victory at Lundy's Lane (July 25), but were compelled to fall back when the

---

[1] The exploits of the American navy during the War of 1812 have not been overlooked by historians. Theodore Roosevelt, *The Naval War of 1812* (1882), is most detailed. Other useful accounts are to be found in E. S. Maclay, *History of the United States Navy from 1775 to 1901* (3 vols., 1901–02); and J. R. Spears, *The History of Our Navy from its Origin to the Present Day* (4 vols., 1897).

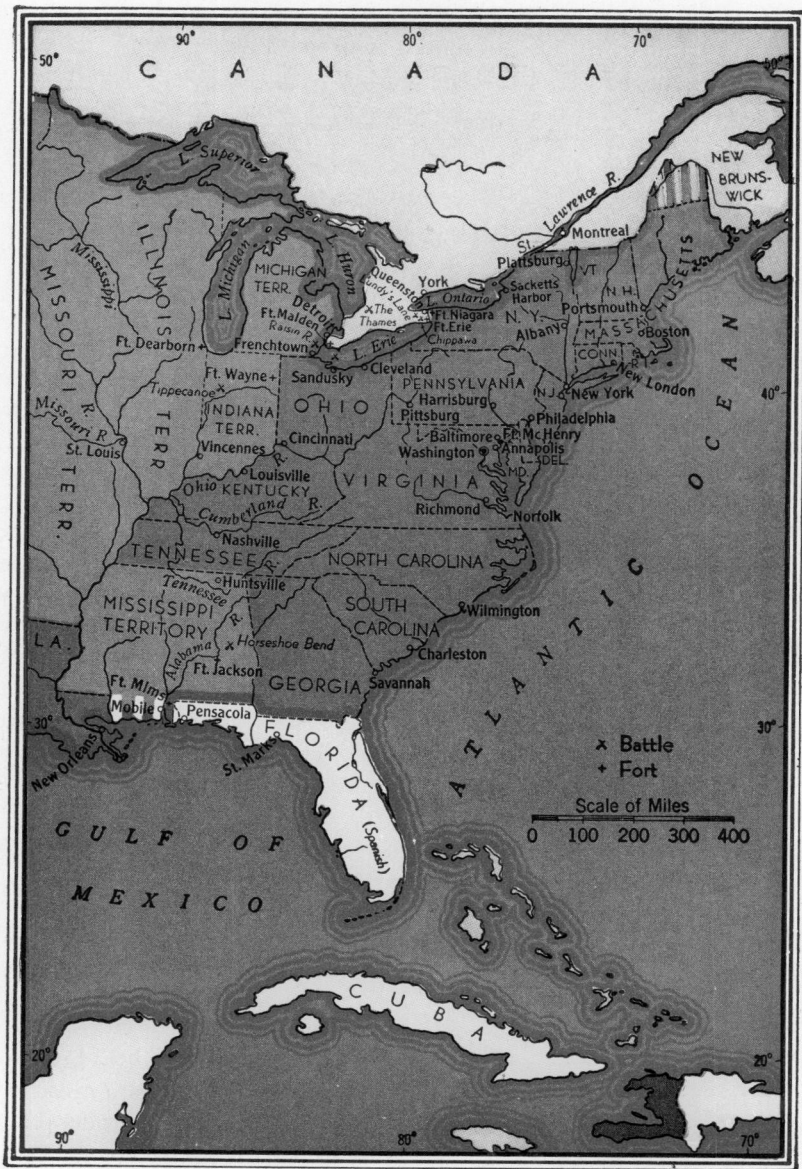

THE WAR OF 1812

news came that the British had received reinforcements. The Lake Champlain invasion route was rendered useless to the British when a small flotilla of American ships, Captain Thomas McDonough commanding, defeated a British squadron off Plattsburg Bay (September 11). This victory somewhat softened the blow that American pride had just received, when a landing party of British marines and sailors had marched into Washington (August 24), had burned the Capitol and the White House, and had returned to their ships without serious loss. A similar raid on Baltimore, however, was beaten off.

The final phase of the war was fought in the Southwest, where on August 13, 1813, an Indian massacre at Fort Mims had precipitated hostilities. At Horseshoe Bend (March 27) General Andrew Jackson in command of Tennessee troops thoroughly **The war in** avenged the white disaster, and a few months later at Fort **the Southwest** Jackson (August 9) he forced the chastened tribes to hand over to the United States thousands of acres of the choicest Indian lands. Jackson was now placed in command of all the American forces in the Southwest, and given the task of beating off the great British offensive being aimed at New Orleans. Balked along the northern border because of American superiority in the lake fighting, the British had decided to send an overwhelming force, some ten thousand veterans of the Napoleonic wars, to capture New Orleans. The invaders were met by Jackson and his frontier militia, and on January 8, 1815, from improvised defenses, consisting partly of cotton bales, were cut to pieces in the most astounding victory of the war. But the battle of New Orleans should really never have been fought, for on December 24, 1814, a treaty of peace had been signed by British and American plenipotentiaries at Ghent.

During the dark days of 1814 the loyalty to the Union of commercial New England had been put to a severe test. To the inevitable losses suffered in trade were added British raids along the coast, raids which seemingly aroused more resentment against **The Hartford** the government at Washington than against the British **Convention** themselves. Finally the legislature of Massachusetts voted to call a convention to meet at Hartford, Connecticut, for the purpose of giving voice to New England opinion. The Convention met on December 15, and after rejecting a plan of action that savored of secession condemned the "multiplied abuses of bad administrations," and "acts of Congress in violation of the Constitution." In language definitely reminiscent of the Kentucky and Virginia Resolutions, the Convention maintained "the right and duty of a state to interpose its authority" in cases of "deliberate, dangerous, and palpable infractions of the Constitution," but insisted also that it would be unwise "to fly to open resistance" upon every offense.[1] The Convention then went on to list for the consideration of the states it represented seven amendments to the national Constitution which, had they been adopted, would have limited the power of Congress to make war, to admit new states, to lay embargoes, and to restrict commerce. Other provisions were aimed at the "Virginia dynasty" and the "three-fifths" compromise. Successive Presidents might not come from the same state and a President would be ineligible for election, while in the apportionment of representatives to Congress only whites might be counted. The speedy termination of the war and the subsequent prosperity of New England made the proponents of the Hartford measures eager to forget what they had done, but since the Convention had been primarily the work of Federalists, the Republicans were able to charge the party of Washington and Adams with treason, and virtually to force it from the political scene.

Peace negotiations had meantime begun through the good offices of the Czar of Russia, and since August, 1814, commissioners representing the two warring governments had been in session at Ghent. The American delegation consisted of five exceptionally able men: James A. Bayard,

[1] On the Hartford Convention the following works will be found useful: S. E. Morison, *Life and Letters of Harrison Gray Otis* (2 vols., 1913); H. C. Lodge, *Life and Letters of George Cabot* (1877); Theodore Dwight, *History of the Hartford Convention* (1833).

EARLY AMERICAN ART (I)

The first interior here shown is a living room from West Boxford, Massachusetts, and is what one might have found in the late seventeenth century anywhere in settled New England. In looking at the picture, note the wide pine boards in the floor and the seventeenth-century silver, and remember that in this period stools were still more common than chairs.

The second interior, a dining room from Peabody, Massachusetts, is late eighteenth century and shows the characteristic differences that developed in a hundred years. Furniture in the earlier period was sombre and heavy. But cabinetmakers soon began to use lustrous woods, such as mahogany, and to make their creations light and graceful, with curved lines and highly polished surfaces. This furniture is Sheraton-type. (Photos from the Museum of Fine Arts, Boston.)

Monticello, Italian for "little mountain," was the name which Thomas Jefferson gave to his beloved estate near Charlottesville, Virginia, and to the residence there that he himself designed and built. Jefferson began construction of his "mansion" in 1769, and it shows the classical influence. From his European trips Jefferson brought back new ideas which he incorporated in his plans. Monticello thus came to have an Italian, rather than a typically colonial appearance, and a Greek portico and dome. (Photo from Bettmann.)

Albert Gallatin, John Quincy Adams, Henry Clay, and Jonathan Russell. The British government, with its best talent engaged in a European settlement at Vienna, was less effectively repre- **Peace of Ghent** sented, and partly for this reason the Americans were able to score a notable diplomatic triumph. The British, had they so desired, could have carried on the war indefinitely, although British public opinion leaned strongly in the direction of calling the war off, and favored a speedy resumption of normal trade relations with America. As finally signed, the Treaty of Ghent reflected well the existing military situation, and ignored totally the potentialities of British might. It provided, according to Adams, for "a truce rather than a peace. Neither party gave up anything; all the points of collision which had subsisted between them before the war were left open. . . . Nothing was adjusted, nothing was settled — nothing in substance but an indefinite suspension of hostilities was agreed to."

While the Peace of Ghent merely restored for the time being the *status quo ante bellum*, it did make provision for the future settlement of some of the outstanding differences between England and Amer- ica. Stimulated in part by these clauses in the treaty and **Subsequent agreements** in part by the mutual desire to clear up misunderstandings, there thus came about several important agreements between the two

---

EARLY AMERICAN ART (II)

JOHN SINGLETON COPLEY (1738–1815), *although practically self-taught, was the favorite painter of Boston society in the years preceding the American Revolution. His wife was the daughter of a rich Boston merchant, and he owned a handsome house on Beacon Hill. Copley went to London in 1774, where he did numerous portraits, including Lord and Lady North and the King and Queen. The portrait of Mrs. John Amory, here shown, was painted by Copley about 1775, and has been described as "one of Copley's most charming portraits among his ladies of eighteenth-century Boston." Mrs. Amory was one of the many Americans who, like Copley, left for London at the outbreak of the Revolution.*

This handsome double chest of drawers, "the masterpiece of Salem," was probably designed by SAMUEL MCINTIRE (1757–1811), *whose contributions not only to furniture-carving but also to architecture left a lasting impression on his native town, Salem, Massachusetts. The carved figure on the chest is Nike, the Greek goddess of victory.*

This teapot is by PAUL REVERE (1735–1818). *Revere became known to posterity mainly through Longfellow's poem about his "midnight ride," but his contemporaries knew him as a talented gold- and silver-smith and copper engraver. (Photos from the Museum of Fine Arts, Boston.)*

nations. On July 3, 1815, a commercial convention was signed by which
trade discriminations, except for the exclusion of American trade from the
British West Indies, were mutually withdrawn. Not until Jackson's
administration did the United States obtain the West Indian trade privileges it so long had sought. On April 28, 1817, the justly famous Rush-
Bagot Agreement provided for complete disarmament by both nations
on the Great Lakes. A few gunboats were permitted for police purposes
only. The agreement could be denounced by either party on six months'
notice, but it still endures. The difficult question of the northeastern
fisheries was treated in a convention signed October 20, 1818, which
acknowledged the right of American citizens to fish along the coasts of
Newfoundland and Labrador, and to dry and cure their fish on unsettled
shores. This same convention also determined the boundary line between the possessions of the United States and Great Britain in the
Northwest. The Treaty of 1783 had described a line "on a due west
course" from the Lake of the Woods to the Mississippi River. Such a
line could not be drawn. The Convention of 1818 worked out a new line
and sensibly adopted the forty-ninth parallel as the dividing line between
the United States and Canada as far west as the "Stony" mountains.
Beyond the mountains neither side was willing to acknowledge the
other's pretensions, and the dispute was left open by an agreement that
the subjects of both nations might occupy the region jointly.

A precedent in favor of arbitration was set by reference to the Czar of
Russia in 1818 of an American claim for the restitution of slaves captured
by the British during the war. The Czar decided that the
slaves need not be restored, but that they should be paid for,
and by an agreement reached in 1826 the amount of compensation to be paid by Great Britain was set at well over a
million dollars. It was this spirit of accommodation that made possible
an era of uninterrupted peace between the United States and Great Brit
ain. Indeed, the various agreements that followed the Treaty of Ghent
may be regarded as a kind of renunciation by the two nations concerned
of resort to war as a means of settling their diplomatic differences.

Anglo-American friendship

It is not surprising that the War of 1812, which was at best a drawn
battle, settled into the American consciousness as a telling victory. The
news of Jackson's magnificent triumph at New Orleans was
quickly followed by the news of peace, and the unthinking
public naturally, though wholly mistakenly, assumed that
between these two impressive events there was the relation
of cause and effect. Furthermore, the defeat of the Indians, both in
the Northwest and in the Southwest, together with the death of Tecumseh, opened the way for an unprecedented advance of the frontier. No

American im- pression of victory

real need had ever been felt for the lands of Canada, and the failure of the War Hawk program of conquest and annexation was quickly forgotten. With peace in Europe restored, American commerce on the high seas was no longer molested, and American patriots were not above imputing to the battle of New Orleans a happy situation that was in reality the result of Leipzig and Waterloo. Pride in the achievements of the American frigates during the early part of the war soon obscured their helplessness in the face of British superiority at its close. American manufacturers, moreover, had benefited greatly by the trade restrictions that preceded and accompanied the war, and their successes had promoted a degree of economic independence from England that the United States had never known before. From the political point of view it is absurd to speak of the War of 1812 as the "Second War for Independence," for political independence had been won in fact no less than in theory by the American Revolution; but from the economic point of view it is abundantly clear that the second war with England markedly accentuated the divorcement of the two countries. Possibly this situation served also to heighten materially the ill-feeling that the war had engendered between the English and the American peoples, and that was to last for so many years to come.[1]

[1] "War Hawk" activities are recounted in J. H. Parks, *Felix Grundy, Champion of Democracy* (1940); and H. J. Eckenrode, *The Randolphs: The Story of a Virginia Family* (1946). Henry Adams, *The War of 1812* (1944), consists of chapters drawn from Adams's nine-volume history. J. R. Jacobs, *The Beginning of the United States Army, 1783–1812* (1947), reveals the military unpreparedness that preceded the war. On the navy in the war, see Harold and Margaret Sprout, *The Rise of American Naval Power, 1776–1918* (1939); Fletcher Pratt, *The Navy: A History* (1938); C. S. Alden and A. Westcott, *The United States Navy: A History* (1943); C. L. Lewis, *The Romantic Decatur* (1937). E. W. McInnis, *The Unguarded Frontier: A History of American-Canadian Relations* (1942), is a useful synthesis.

10

The New Nationalism

THE War of 1812 marks a definite turning-point in the history of the United States. Prior to that conflict the American people, for all their political independence, were in their economic life still tributary to Europe, and most especially to England. The factory system was slow to take root in America, for it was cheaper to import goods from England, where manufacturing on a large scale was already well established, than to make them in America. Moreover, the commercial connections of colonial times had been promptly resumed at the close of the Revolution, and at the beginning of the nineteenth century there were no stronger vested interests in the country than those concerned with the importation and distribution of foreign goods. Planters and farmers, likewise, were accustomed to depend heavily upon foreign trade. Their excess produce was sent to Europe quite as consistently as during colonial times, while the continual wars of the French Revolution and the Napoleonic period forced the prices of American raw materials and foodstuffs to high figures. With a steady trade flowing both ways, there was little difficulty in making exports balance imports in value.

The embargo, non-intercourse, and the War of 1812 upset completely this scheme of things. American commerce was for the time being almost destroyed, and the opportunity to import foreign goods was reduced to a minimum. Naturally enough, much of the capital that had formerly been invested in commerce turned now to manufactures, for which the existing situation was equivalent to a heavy protective tariff. Manufacturing, moreover, became a patriotic duty which states, counties, municipalities, and societies sought to encourage by offering attractive bounties. As early as 1810 Gallatin reported to the House of Representatives a surprisingly long list of items in which American manufacturers were already able to supply the American demand. Throughout the period textile mills for the production of cotton, linen, and woolen cloth increased rapidly in number, and even more rapidly in the volume of their output. Facilities for the manufacture of such significant articles as paper, leather goods, woodenware, iron, and iron goods multiplied until the most urgent needs of the American market were fully met. By the end of the war American manufacturing was definitely established, and the shortage of European imports was no longer keenly felt.[1]

New England promptly took the lead among the sections in the shift toward manufacturing. Not only was there occasion here to offset with some other interest the decline in commerce; in a variety of ways New England was ideally fitted to assume the manufacturing rôle. Power to turn the wheels of the new machinery was abundantly supplied by the swift-flowing streams and their numerous waterfalls, shippers and shipping were available to send the products of the loom and factory down the coast to the other American states, and an abundant and intelligent labor supply was at hand. Workers in the New England factories consisted mainly of farmers and their families, who were only too willing to give up the unequal struggle with the hard climate and the unyielding soil to accept the more certain financial rewards of the mills. They brought with them a degree of dexterity and ingenuity, acquired through years of self-dependence on the farm, that placed them among the most capable, although possibly not among the most tractable, factory employees anywhere in the world.

New England factories

But the interest in manufacturing was by no means confined to New England. As far south as the Chesapeake the new opportunity for American manufacturers was producing results. If New England led in the production of textiles, Pennsylvania, New York, and New Jersey excelled in the production of iron ore and the manufacture of iron goods. In this region coal could be obtained cheaply to supplement water-power, and by the end of the War of 1812 bituminous, and even anthracite, coal was being used by occasional manufacturers with good success. In the South there was talk of establishing factories and putting the slaves to work in them, but practically nothing of the sort was actually accomplished. Instead the South turned to cotton-growing, and became a heavy purchaser of northern goods. In 1814, according to one estimate, New England bankers received on an average a half-million dollars a month from the banks of the South, practically all of which was drawn northward in payment for factory products.

[1] H. J. Carman, *Social and Economic History of the United States*, II (1934), covers admirably the rise of industrialism in the United States following the War of 1812. Other useful economic histories are H. U. Faulkner, *American Economic History* (1924); E. L. Bogart, *The Economic History of the United States* (1907); Katherine Coman, *The Industrial History of the United States* (1905); C. D. Wright, *Industrial Evolution of the United States* (1895); F. A. Shannon, *America's Economic Growth* (1940); R. C. McGrane, *The Economic Development of the American Nation* (1942).

EARLY AMERICAN TEXTILE MILLS

The period of enforced divorcement from Europe had witnessed many changes also in American agriculture. The growth of the woolen industry made sheep-raising profitable as never before. In the back-country of New England and in the middle states, where with the decline of the export trade foodstuffs had become a drug on the market, there was a noticeable trend in the direction of wool-growing. In the South the production of cotton took on ever-increasing significance. Before Eli Whitney's invention of the cotton gin in 1793, only the long-staple cotton grown in the lowlands could be profitably raised. But the cotton gin, by reducing immensely the cost of separating the seed from the cotton, made practicable the growing also of the short-staple cotton which throve well in the uplands. The results were revolutionary. The output of southern cotton, which in 1791 had amounted only to about two million pounds, had grown by 1801 to forty million, and by 1811 to eighty million pounds. Until the period of commercial restriction began, the bulk of this cotton had found its way to foreign markets, and only the establishment of the northern textile mills saved the southern cotton planters from deep disaster. Once the war was ended, both foreign and domestic manufacturers clamored for cotton, and the spread of cotton culture was more rapid than ever before. The increasing cultivation of sugar-cane in Louisiana, and to some extent elsewhere in the South, added another

American agriculture (margin note)

commodity to the list of articles that could be supplied within the borders of the United States.

Much was therefore achieved toward that national self-sufficiency which economists of the eighteenth century had regarded as so vital to the life of a nation. Accompanying this development the discerning observer might have noted also the rapid emergence of an American national type. When the Revolution ended, the typical American was still essentially an English colonial whose tastes and aptitudes were definitely reminiscent of the Old World. By the end of the eighteenth century some notable changes were already in evidence, but in the years following the War of 1812 a new nationality, with new and different characteristics, was clearly in the making. The decline of commerce, and the consequent lessening of contacts between Americans and Europeans, undoubtedly stimulated the divergence of American from European ways, but probably the unique opportunities of the New World, now better realized than ever before, account for most of the changes. America had become pre-eminently a land of "opportunity." To the resident of the Northeast the newly introduced factory system brought to employers and employees alike undreamed-of avenues to prosperity. To the southern planter, and to the southern small farmer who hoped to become a planter, the revolutionary possibilities of cotton culture seemed to point the way to sure success. To the restless of every section came with renewed vigor the call of the West. Almost for the first time the boundless possibilities of the new nation were fully realized. Now anyone could see that future generations of Americans had before them a task no less inviting than the conquest and exploitation of half a continent. The lure of rich rewards, whether in industry, in cotton culture, or in the development of the West, captured the imaginations of Americans and determined their characteristics. Small wonder that they saw little reason to imitate or esteem the ways of an Old World where opportunity was limited, but paid deference instead to whatever qualities in themselves seemed best calculated to ensure success in the new undertakings.

Fortunately for the historian, there came to America during the years following the War of 1812 a procession of foreign travelers who wrote down freely what they saw — or what they thought they saw. Some of these visitors, as the official or un- Foreign official agents of European governments, were in search of travelers in an outlet for European emigration. The Napoleonic wars America had left a train of economic distress in their wake, and most European nations were faced by an acute unemployment problem. Why not send their excess population to America? Those who visited the United

States in search of a land of opportunity for emigrants found what they wanted to find, and wrote glowing reports. But there were many other travelers who came to America in a purely private capacity, not so much to chronicle the opportunities they saw as to criticize a nation that flaunted its "democracy." These travelers were drawn mostly from the classes of the well-to-do and the socially élite, who found much to confirm their long-established prejudices, but were nevertheless able to see clearly many things that an American observer would have overlooked. It is chiefly upon this travel literature that the historian must rely when he seeks to set forth the traits that were peculiar to Americans of this age.[1]

All accounts agree that the typical American was very "provincial." To some extent this was only another way of saying that he differed from the typical Englishman, or Frenchman, or other European. But it was also a fact that most Americans knew little or nothing about the world outside America, and oftentimes they cared even less. Somewhat on the defensive because of this ignorance, Americans were inclined to be boastful, both about themselves and about their country. They were particularly proud of the American experiment in democratic government, and they would neither admit that mistakes had been made, nor that any other form of government was half so good. Patriotism became almost a national obsession.

American traits

In one respect, at least, foreigners were quick to consent that American boastfulness was justified. The ordinary American was truly remarkable for his ingenuity. He could turn his hand with considerable skill to almost any problem that confronted him. He was not precisely inventive, but he was a natural-born jack-of-all-trades whose adaptability rarely left him baffled by a new situation or defeated because of an unanticipated need. The American practice of moving houses, for example, struck foreigners with peculiar force. Houses in Europe usually stayed where they were built; in America one might meet them coming down the street.

American ideas as to good manners did not always conform to European standards. Such crudities as normally accompanied the unrestrained use of chewing-tobacco excited the amazement of travelers, and sometimes for good reason their anxiety as well. The American's habit of bolting his meals in record time also induced comment, and to gouty Europeans who set much store by the leisurely disposal of food the popularity of the American "quick lunch" quite passed be-

[1] *Early Western Travels, 1748–1846*, edited by R. G. Thwaites (32 vols., 1904–07), reprints nearly all of the important books of this nature. A handy compilation is *American Social History as Recorded by British Travelers*, edited by Allan Nevins (1923). See also Jane L. Mesick, *The English Traveller in America, 1785–1835* (1922).

lief. The restlessness and nervousness of the Americans also annoyed the foreigners. Americans resented delay, and were forever in a hurry. This quality, incidentally, marks a pronounced change from the habits of colonial Americans — habits for which their descendants could have found no more appropriate adjective than "lazy." Some observers blamed this restlessness on the American climate, which, they avowed, exhibited a greater variety of conditions in a given space of time than could be found in any other country on earth. Others thought that the American diet was enough to account for it, and for the sallowness of the American complexion as well. But probably the real reason why Americans were such "hustlers" was that they were so keenly aware of the challenging opportunities that confronted them. With riches seemingly a sure reward for enterprise, the typical American felt that he had no time to waste.

Optimism was another by-product of opportunity. In America there was room for all to prosper. Unemployment for the physically fit was a matter of disposition, not of necessity, for the supply of labor was rarely up to the demand. America had neither slums nor poor in the European sense of those terms, and the most worthless sort of person could at least make a living. Faith in the future sometimes overshot the mark and tempted to speculation. "Stock-watering" was often not so much a matter of fraud as of great expectations — the profits of the company were sure to grow. The misrepresentations of land speculators were more frequently than not a fair statement of what they genuinely believed, that land values would assuredly go up. Overissues of bank currency were not all made with dishonest intent — more money was needed to care for the natural demands of a growing country.

Equality of opportunity had much to do with the turn that democracy was taking in America. The equalitarian doctrine of the Declaration of Independence was in its day merely the statement of an ideal; fifty years later it was not far from a correct description of American society. To be sure, an aristocracy still existed in every part of the country, except possibly in the West, but the new aristocracy, whether of industrial New England or of the cotton-planting South, was an aristocracy to which now even the lowliest might aspire. Caste lines were ever more loosely drawn, and family trees counted for less and less. Not by birth, but by material success, was one marked as a member of the upper class, and the road to success was equally open to all. As if in deference to this new definition of aristocracy, the old distinction between the dress of the aristocrat and of the common man disappeared, but it was the aristocrat who gave up

Optimism

Equality of opportunity

his furbelows, not the common man who put them on. The status of
women in the new democracy seemed also to be rising toward a frank
admission of equality with men. In the place of the obsequious and con-
descending chivalry which Europeans of the better class were accustomed
to exhibit toward their own class only, all Americans, to the consterna-
tion of some foreign observers, tended to treat women of whatever class
with marked respect and courtesy.

For a people that set great store by its government, this democratic
trend was sure to be reflected in politics. The new western states on
Democracy   admission to the Union unhesitatingly established universal
                    manhood suffrage, and the older states of the East soon fol-
lowed their example. In the latter it did not follow at once that the
common people held the offices, for the old colonial tradition that candidates should be chosen from the better classes only died hard. In the
West, however, there was no authentic aristocracy from which to choose,
and the common people themselves held the offices. It was not to be
long before this excess of democracy should be in evidence throughout
the land. Travelers could observe even then a growing intolerance of
superiority which in time would turn into a kind of worship of mediocrity. To elect one's betters to office was to admit that one had betters.
To throw one's betters out of office was to rebuke for their pretensions
those who thought themselves superior, and to prove that the people
really ruled.

The abundance of opportunity in America opened the way to an
almost unrestrained individualism. With the chances for success every-
Individualism   where so great, anyone with an ambition to fulfill rushed
                    forward to achieve his goal by whatever means seemed good
to him. He asked only to be let alone. Fortunately there was room
enough for all. The New England manufacturer who expanded his mills
need not necessarily destroy his competitor; with abundant markets the
two might expand and prosper side by side. If new machinery threw
employees out of work, more likely than not other jobs, equally good,
soon appeared. As for the increasing number of farmers and farm laborers, cheap lands and a fertile soil beckoned them to the West, where as
pioneers they might achieve a greater success and a greater degree of
independence than they could ever have known anywhere else. Throughout the West individual freedom was a frontier heritage much prized by
all. Pioneers made their way in the world by their own efforts, and they
took pride in the work they had done. They made a fetish of their freedom, and would brook few restraints, whether of government or of society. All this was possible, however, only because of the abundance of
opportunity in America. Three quarters of a century later, when lands

and markets had become more limited, individual freedom ceased to be an unmixed blessing.

Ever since colonial times religious freedom, as a natural corollary of individual freedom, had made steady gains. During the American Revolution the number of church establishments in the United States had been greatly reduced; in 1786 Thomas **Religious** Jefferson had won his notable victory for the complete di- **freedom** vorcement of church and state in Virginia; and in the first amendment to the Constitution of the United States Congress had been forbidden to pass a law "respecting the establishment of religion or prohibiting the free exercise thereof." Nevertheless, the feeling that religion must somehow be supported by the state was slow to die. The new western states would have nothing to do with church establishments, but in New England, where the Congregationalists were strongly intrenched, the last citadels of conservatism were not broken down until after the War of 1812. In New Hampshire the reform was delayed until 1817, in Connecticut until 1818, and in Massachusetts until 1833. But by this time the complete separation of church and state in the United States had become a fixed principle. This was one of the evidences of American superiority that the typical American could point out to travelers from abroad with confidence and pride.

With the great multiplicity of religious sects, mutual toleration for all and special privileges for none were well-nigh inevitable developments. To the Congregationalist, Dutch Reformed, Quaker, Catholic, and Episcopalian denominations of the seaboard were added the Presbyterian, Lutheran, Baptist, and Methodist churches of the back-country, not to mention literally scores of minor religious units. Each denomination was now organized on a national basis, usually with a type of church government strongly reflecting the political institutions of the United States, and with as complete separation from Old World churches as was consistent with its theology. The western denominations, such as the Methodists and the Baptists, were growing with far greater rapidity than those of the East. This was due in large part to the democratic appeal that the frontier churches were willing to make. They did not insist upon an educated ministry, but were generally willing to accept as preachers all those who felt that they had received the divine "call." They were democratic in church government, they rekindled at every opportunity the revival fervor that had swept the country in the early years of the century, and in their camp-meetings they preached a gospel of salvation for the many rather than merely for the few. Even in conservative New England, where the Unitarian revolt was still in full swing, the leaven of democracy was taking hold. Calvinistic theology, with its emphasis upon the unworthiness of man, a creature "conceived in sin and born in iniquity," was losing steadily before the attacks of the Unitarians, who held that after all man was the noblest work of God, born in his Maker's image, and endowed with no less spiritual possibilities than were given to the man Jesus himself. From the religious point of view there could be no greater exaltation of democracy than was implicit in the commonly made assertion that in every man there was a spark of the divine.

Afraid as they were to confess a shortcoming, Americans generally made light of their cultural deficiencies, and featured instead their great success in dealing with the practical problems that confronted a rapidly growing nation. But there is much reason to believe that they had a secret regard for the sophistication they associated with older civilizations, that they would have rejoiced to be less completely outdone in this respect. As a matter of fact, in such realms as education, art and architecture, and even literature the new nation already had something to its credit.

One reason for the lack of popular interest in education was the slowness of the schools to adapt themselves to the needs of a democracy.

Education For the most part they still operated on the theory that it was their business to educate the leaders of society only, and to ignore the needs of the masses. This concept of education, however, was breaking down, and the popular prejudice against education was being correspondingly undermined. Free elementary schools were sometimes starved for lack of financial support, but the people were quick to acknowledge, especially in their new state constitutions, the duty of the state to provide such instruction at public expense. Private academies designed to meet the educational needs of children whose parents could afford to pay flourished in the East, and were available in surprisingly large numbers even in the West. Higher education was still left mainly to the churches, but between 1810 and 1820, while the number of American colleges was being doubled, evidence also accumulated that the strictly classical and theological training of an earlier age would not endure. Thanks mainly to the work of Jefferson, the curriculum of the College of William and Mary now included such subjects as law, history, political economy, and modern languages, while the University of Virginia, founded in 1825, not only adopted an unusually liberal course of study, but also made the entrance requirements easier, and allowed students great freedom in their choice of subjects. The democratic ideal of education for citizenship was clearly supplanting the older ideal of religious education.[1]

[1] Among the numerous manuals that recount the history of early American education

Americans cared relatively little for art, yet in an age which knew nothing of photography they could at least see point to the painting of portraits. Gilbert Stuart (1755–1828), whose skill would have won him recognition in any age, is best remembered for the great number of Washington canvases he left. He painted portraits of many other well-known Americans also, among them most of the early Presidents. Charles Willson Peale (1741–1827) portrayed famous Americans of the same generation with less technical excellence, perhaps, than Stuart, but with greater simplicity and fidelity to truth.[1] Peale was also interested in cultivating an American interest in art, and furnished much of the inspiration which led to the founding of the Pennsylvania Academy of Fine Arts (1805) and the National Academy of Design (1826). John Trumbull (1756–1843) discovered that historical paintings had an appeal for Americans that was almost as hard to resist as that of portraits. He discreetly admitted that the occupation of painting as a rule was "frivolous, little useful to society, and unworthy of a man who has talents for more serious pursuits. But to preserve and diffuse the memory of the noblest series of actions which have ever presented themselves in the history of man, is sufficient warrant for it." And so, along with his portraits, he left many colorful representations of scenes in the American Revolution — paintings deeply esteemed by many subsequent generations of patriots. It is proper to point out, however, that all the early American artists owed most of their proficiency to European training. Some of them, like John Singleton Copley (1738–1815), lived as much of the time in Europe as in the United States.[2]

Portrait Painters

In architecture, too, there were some worthy American beginnings. The practicality and good taste of the old colonial and Georgian designs were not forgotten, but shortly after the Revolution a classical revival set in which had pronounced results. Thomas Jefferson, whose variety of interests had not failed to take in architecture, was the leading exponent of this new trend. He used classical traditions in designing a house for himself at Monticello, houses for his neighbors and friends, a new capitol for his state, and a building plan for the University of Virginia that has since been called "the finest example of classical architecture in America." Throughout the country,

The classical revival

are E. P. Cubberley, *Public Education in the United States* (1919); E. G. Dexter, *A History of Education in the United States* (1904); E. E. Slosson, *The American Spirit in Education* (1921). E. M. Coulter, *College Life in the Old South* (1928), is an entertaining history of the University of Georgia before the Civil War.

[1] Stuart painted the portrait of Washington opposite page 18. Peale did the picture of Jefferson opposite page 82. The portrait of John Adams opposite page 82 is by Copley, as is that of Mrs. Amory opposite page 179.

[2] J. T. Flexner, *America's Old Masters: First Artists of the New World* (1939).

but especially in the South, the more pretentious private dwellings with their high column-supported porticos reflected clearly the classical influence, and many public buildings also, such as the White House, the Bank of the United States, and the Philadelphia Library, were similarly designed. New churches still adhered closely to colonial tradition.[1]

American writers who were interested in the exploitation of American themes found a ready outlet for their efforts in the rapidly increasing **Magazines** numbers of newspapers and magazines that were appearing. **and** By 1810 there were no less than three hundred and fifty **newspapers** newspapers in the United States, as against only forty at the close of the American Revolution. The increasing popularity of magazines is shown by the fact that in 1800 there were not more than a dozen such publications in the whole country, whereas in 1825 there were nearly a hundred. Newspapers still emphasized political news and political arguments, but the magazines, although by no means unconcerned with politics and actually at great pains to defend the new republic against foreign critics, presented more varied offerings. Both newspapers and magazines had as a rule only small and local circulations, but the *North American Review*, which was founded in 1815, soon gained a well-deserved notice even outside the United States.[2]

Although the first real flowering of American literature is usually associated with a somewhat later period, the names of at least two notable American writers, Washington Irving and William Cullen **Literary** Bryant, were known even before the War of 1812. Curi- **lights** ously, both men opened their literary careers with attacks on Thomas Jefferson. Irving's *Knickerbocker's History of New York* was less a satire on the Dutch in early New Netherland than on the policies of Jefferson's administration, while the *Embargo*, from the pen of the thirteen-year-old Bryant, disdained subtleties:

> Go, wretch, resign the Presidential chair,
> Disclose thy secret measures, foul or fair;
> Go, search with curious eye for hornéd frogs
> 'Mid the wild wastes of Louisiana bogs,
> Or, where Ohio rolls his turbid stream,
> Dig for huge bones, thy glory and thy theme.

A little later the still youthful Bryant was penning his striking lines *To a Waterfowl*, and his immortal *Thanatopsis*. Another great name in American literature won prominence when James Fenimore Cooper published *The Spy* (1821), a story of American life during the Revolution.[3]

[1] Howard Major, *The Domestic Architecture of the Early American Republic* (1926).

[2] F. L. Mott, *A History of American Magazines, 1741–1850* (1930).

[3] V. L. Parrington, *The Romantic Revolution in America* (*Main Currents in American Thought*, ii, 1927), covers the years 1800 to 1860.

The multiplication of books and libraries during these years testifies eloquently to the growing literary interests of Americans. They might pretend that there was for such a race of practical men as they professed themselves to be no charm whatever in learning and culture, but six thousand tons of paper, according to estimates made for 1816, were required annually to make the books they bought. Many Americans took great pride in assembling libraries. The largest private libraries in the country were probably those of John Quincy Adams and Thomas Jefferson, each of which ran to over five thousand volumes, but practically every prominent citizen aspired to own a library and busied himself with the collection of books. Public libraries were also becoming increasingly common, and the manufacture of books in America had reached the point where works on nearly every known subject were printed on this side of the Atlantic.

The ultra-nationalism of the American people after the War of 1812 was revealed in a great variety of ways. During the next few years Congress enacted a program of legislation that laid emphatic stress upon the importance of the nation as a whole, while the Supreme Court, still under the guidance of the nationalistic Marshall, wrote his legal concepts into final and definitive law. Then, too, the nation was expanding with astonishing rapidity. When Maine and Missouri entered the Union, only six years after the war was over, the number of states created by the nation was only two less than the number of those that had created the nation. Further, the Missouri Compromise tended to allay somewhat the fears of the South, and to pave the way for still greater expansion, while the Monroe Doctrine, a product of the same period, served notice on the rest of the world that all the American republic asked was to be let alone while it grew.

Nationalistic sentiment

President Madison in his annual message to Congress of December 5, 1815, divined clearly the nationalistic trend of the times. In a memorable statement he urged that steps be taken to provide for a stronger military establishment, a uniform national currency, a tariff to protect the new American industries, and a national system of roads and canals. Speedy action was taken on each of these items. A standing army of ten thousand men was authorized, and an appropriation of eight million dollars was voted for the construction of fifteen new naval units. The Military Academy at West Point, which had been established in 1802, was reorganized with a view to greater efficiency, and was given increased support. A second Bank of the United States, patterned after the model of the first Bank, was created to provide the national currency Madison had requested, and to end the inflationary activities of the numerous state-chartered banks that had taken over the entire banking business of the country in 1811. The new bank was stronger than Hamilton's bank, with a capital stock of $35,000,000 instead of $10,000,000, but it was almost identical in character and privileges. A full-scale tariff revision, passed in 1816, maintained or increased the special wartime duties and made every effort to protect the "infant industries," built up during and just prior to the war. Finally, Congress showed clearly that it was ready to go ahead with internal improvements when it appropriated the funds necessary to continue construction of the Cumberland Road by means of which East and West were to be joined along the route of the old Braddock Road. By 1818 the new highway was completed.

These momentous exaggerations of the nation's powers were not accomplished without opposition. The strongest protests came from New England, where the commercial interests still feared the growing strength of the representatives of agriculture. Many New-Englanders, led by Daniel Webster, objected to a protective tariff on the ground that it would interfere, as indeed it would, with their foreign trade. Webster also opposed the recharter of the Bank. The banks of his section were safe and sound, and he reflected their fear that a national bank under western and southern management might become a source of danger rather than of strength. Opposition to internal improvements, on the ground that the states which would profit most from the building of roads should pay for them, came also from New England. But the chief obstacle to a program of road-building at national expense was furnished by President Madison himself, who doubted the constitutionality of all such measures except when a specific national interest was involved. A so-called Bonus Bill, which pledged to the promotion of internal improvements the "bonus" of $1,500,000 that Congress had required of the second Bank of the United States as a condition of its charter, was killed by a presidential veto. Many southern disciples of the states'-rights dogma, ably led by John Randolph of Roanoke, joined the New-Englanders in protest against the eclipse of the states by the nation, but others were quite content. "The Constitution," said John C. Calhoun as he defended the Bonus Bill, "was not intended as a thesis for the logician to exercise his ingenuity on, [and] ought to be construed with plain good sense."

Sectionalism in New England

The election of 1816 seemed to put the stamp of popular approval upon the nationalistic program that Congress had adopted. The Federalists, whose leaders had furnished the principal opposition to the new measures, were hopelessly defeated; their candidate for President, Rufus King of New York, carried only three states. The Republicans, amidst considerable grumbling, accepted President Madison's suggestion that the "succession" should go to

Election of 1816

James Monroe. The custom had developed of making party nominations by a "congressional caucus," composed of all the members in Congress of the party concerned, and the Republican caucus chose Monroe
over W. H. Crawford of Georgia by the narrow vote of 64 to 44. In the
election the electoral vote stood 183 for Monroe to 34 for King. Undoubtedly the bad war record of the Federalists also contributed to their
defeat.

Like three out of four of his predecessors, James Monroe (1758–1831)
was a Virginia planter.[1] His family, however, was by no means of the
first families of Virginia; it was rather of the western, small-
planter class, and included in its family tree many Scotch   James Monroe
and Welsh ancestors. Monroe's political experience was more than
ample. By the time he reached the Presidency he had served in the
Virginia Assembly, in the Congress of the Confederation, and in the
United States Senate; he had represented his country on important
missions to France, Spain, and England; he had been governor of Virginia for several terms; and he had been at one time both Secretary of
State and Secretary of War. Unfortunately, Monroe found it somewhat
difficult to keep abreast of the nationalistic trend his party had taken.
Like Madison, he found little justification in the Constitution for a program of internal improvements. He allowed the Cumberland Road to
be finished, but in 1822, when a bill passed Congress to provide funds for
its repair by establishing toll gates and collecting tolls, he interposed a
veto. The exercise of such power by Congress, he claimed, implied a
"power to adopt and execute a complete system of internal improvements," and for this he found no constitutional warrant. He believed,
however, that a change in the Constitution to permit the United States
to build "great national works" would be desirable, provided that "all
minor improvements" should be left to the states.

While Madison and Monroe were struggling to adjust their consciences
to the new nationalism, the Supreme Court was doing all it could to help
them. The Chief Justice, John Marshall (1755–1835), was
another Virginian, born far out on the frontier in what be-   Marshall
came a few years later Fauquier County. He fought in the   and the
                                                                               Supreme Court
Revolution as a member of his father's regiment, but toward
the end of the war, when the fighting had died down, he attended lectures on law at William and Mary College, and in 1781 began to practice. He was soon recognized as the leader of the Virginia bar; also, as a
shrewd and successful politician. He served as one of the three com-

[1] D. C. Gilman, *James Monroe* (1883), is still useful, but W. P. Cresson, *James Monroe*
(1946), does better justice to an individual somewhat neglected by writers of American
history. See also the excellent account by Julius W. Pratt in *American Secretaries of State
and Their Diplomacy*, III, edited by S. F. Bemis.

missioners sent to make peace with France in 1797, represented his state in Congress for one term, and became Secretary of State during the last year of the Adams administration. On January 20, 1801, Marshall's name was sent to the Senate as Adams's nominee for Chief Justice, and a few days later it was confirmed. On February 4, just a month before the Federalists lost control of Congress and the Presidency for all time, the new Chief Justice took office. Curiously, he continued also as Secretary of State until the end of the Adams administration, although he accepted a salary only as Chief Justice. For thirty-four years he guided the Supreme Court in a thoroughly Federalist interpretation of the Constitution. So great was the power of his personality and so convincing his logic that, to the despair of Republican Presidents, the new judges they appointed were soon following Marshall's lead. The growth of the national spirit during and after the War of 1812, however, served to bring the Court and the dominant political party more closely together than they had ever been before. The nationalistic decisions of Marshall and his colleagues now aroused respect and approval, particularly among the young Republicans, rather than condemnation.[1]

Marshall's decision in the case of *Marbury vs. Madison*, already noted, and the utter failure of the Republicans to undo it, added greatly to the prestige of the Court. Its power to declare null and void an act of Congress out of harmony with the Constitution was repeatedly reasserted, and, in spite of the fact that the actual exercise of such authority was not again attempted in an important case until the Dred Scott decision, the doctrine of judicial review soon won general acceptance.

Marshall's opinions

Gradually, as occasion offered, the Court built up its own, and the nation's, prerogatives. In the case of *United States vs. Judge Peters* (1809), it found opportunity to show that its power, in case of conflict, transcended that of a state legislature. Neither was a legislature to be left free to void a contract it had made with individuals. In the case of *Fletcher vs. Peck* (1810), already noted, the Court held that even so dishonest an act as that by which the state of Georgia had granted lands to the Yazoo companies could not be repealed without "impairing the obligation of contract." Nor with corporations. In the case of *Dartmouth College vs. Woodward* (1819), the Court maintained that a charter of incorporation was also a contract within the meaning of the Constitution. Two notable decisions, *Martin vs. Hunter's Lessee* (1816) and *Cohens vs. Virginia* (1821), completed the picture by asserting that the

[1] A. C. McLaughlin, *A Constitutional History of the United States* (1935), covers the work of the Court under Marshall in great detail. Excellent short accounts are contained in J. W. Burgess, *The Middle Period* (1897); and Allen Johnson, *Union and Democracy* (1915). See also Albert J. Beveridge, *Life of John Marshall*, III, IV.

Supreme Court was superior to the state courts whenever federal rights were involved. As a result of these two decisions, the federal courts obtained much new business. Litigants preferred them over the state courts whenever they would accept jurisdiction because the finality of the state decision was so frequently open to question.

In the two Virginia decisions and in others also the Court was at pains to defend not only its own prerogatives as a court, but also the supremacy of the national government over the states. The classic expression of this point of view came in the case of *McCul-* *loch vs. Maryland* (1819). The state of Maryland had at- tempted to tax out of existence the Baltimore branch of the Bank of the United States, and the bank had refused to pay the tax. The state courts naturally found against the bank and ordered it to pay, but an appeal was taken to the Supreme Court of the United States. Here was a clear-cut issue between state and nation, and Marshall made the most of it. He upheld the constitutionality of the act of Congress by which the bank was created, and in so doing gave the approval of the Court to Hamilton's doctrine of implied powers. "Let the end be legiti- mate, let it be within the scope of the Constitution, and all means which are appropriate, which are plainly adapted to that end, which are not prohibited, but consist with the letter and spirit of the Constitution, are constitutional." He held also that the state of Maryland had exceeded its authority in attempting to tax the notes of the Baltimore branch. "The power to tax," he reasoned, involved the "power to destroy," which, if conceded in this case, would leave the states free to undo such strictly constitutional laws of Congress as they disliked. In the course of his argument Marshall took occasion to speak out plainly against the theory that the Constitution emanated from the states, and that the government established by it was therefore merely a creature of the states. "The government of the Union," he maintained, "is emphati- cally, and truly, a government of the people. In form and in substance it emanates from them. Its powers are granted by them, and are to be exercised on them, and for their benefit.... If any one proposition could command the universal consent of mankind, we might expect it would be this — that the government of the Union, though limited in its pow- ers, is supreme within its sphere of action...." No better statement of the supremacy of the nation over the states has ever been made.

The Chief Justice, and the majority of the Court with him, made no secret of their desire to exalt the power of the nation whenever warrant could be found for such action in the Constitution. They attempted, however, to draw a reasonable line between powers granted exclusively to the national government and powers reserved wholly or in part to the

(margin note: National supremacy approved)

states. In the case of *Gibbon vs. Ogden* (1824) the Court held unconstitutional a monopoly of the state waters of New York that the state legislature had granted, an obvious trespass upon the interstate-commerce powers of Congress; but in the case of *Ogden vs. Saunders* (1827) the Court upheld a state bankruptcy statute in spite of the fact that Congress had similar authority. It has been many times charged that Marshall's decisions were designed not merely to exalt the power of the nation, but also to prevent the states from restricting in any serious way the rights of property-holders. This in a measure is true. It should be remembered, however, that opportunities for the acquisition of property in Marshall's time were not limited to the few, but could be enjoyed by the many. Marshall's decisions fitted in well with the temper of the American people in the years immediately following the War of 1812. The country was young and growing, conscious of its strength, confident of the future. And the individuals who composed the American nation were property-minded men, as full of optimism for themselves as for their country.[1]

[1] Merle Curti, *The Roots of American Loyalty* (1946), studies the development of American patriotism. J. Q. Adams, *Parties in the United States* (1941), by the sixth President, discusses the rise and fall of the Federalist party. E. T. Mudge, *The Social Philosophy of John Taylor of Caroline: A Study in Jeffersonian Democracy* (1939), makes Taylor's ideas easily available. J. T. Horton, *James Kent: A Study in Conservatism, 1763–1847* (1939), examines the reasoning of a prominent state jurist.

Dixon Wecter, *The Saga of American Society: A Record of Social Aspirations, 1607–1937* (1937), is an entertaining study of the American quest for social prestige. Van Wyck Brooks, *The World of Washington Irving* (1944), portrays "American arts, letters and life from 1800 to 1840." James Thomas Flexner, *John Singleton Copley* (1948), throws new light on early American art.

11

The Rise of the New West

"The rise of the new west," according to Frederick Jackson Turner, "was the most significant fact in American history in the years immediately following the War of 1812."[1] Applied to a period in which so many important developments were taking place, this is a broad statement, yet only a few critics appear to have questioned it. Certainly the rapidity with which the frontier was advanced during these years set a new record. During the thirty-six years that elapsed between the signing of the Declaration of Independence and the outbreak of the War of 1812, only five new states were added to the original thirteen: Vermont, Kentucky, Tennessee, Ohio, and Louisiana. But during the half-dozen years following the War of 1812, six new states, all of them frontier and five of them definitely western, were added to the Union: Indiana (1816), Mississippi (1817), Illinois (1818), Alabama (1819), Maine (1820), and Missouri (1821).

The opening up of new western states was undoubtedly promoted by the war itself, which served greatly to advertise the region, and made an end to the Indian menace. The business dislocations produced by the conflict also stimulated westward migra- **The New West** tion, while the completion of the Cumberland Road and the speedy adaptation of Fulton's steamboat to the "western waters" made the trip to the West an easy possibility, even for residents of the Atlantic seaboard. Tall tales of the West, told with especial delight by European travelers in America, with plenty of emphasis on such unsavory stories as the frequency of steamboat disasters and the damage done by the Mississippi Valley earthquake of 1811, tended to promote rather than to discourage the westward movement. Even the journals of Lewis and Clark, and of Zebulon Pike, provided good publicity for the West, and stimulated many readers to leave their old homes for lands that the great explorers never saw.

[1] F. J. Turner, *Rise of the New West* (1906), p. 67. This book, covering the decade 1819 to 1829, treats not only of the West, but of the various other sections also, and of the nation as a whole. It takes high rank in the literature of American history.

The phenomenal growth of cotton culture in the years following the War of 1812 added a strong southern element to the stream of westward migration. The lands of the new Southwest were in large part ideally fitted for the production of cotton, whereas the cotton lands of the Southeast soon showed signs of wearing out. Sometimes well-established planters sold their eastern lands in order to purchase and move to more fertile lands in the West, but more often planters preferred to enlarge their holdings at home as the yield per acre declined. Both groups helped populate the West, for the planter who bought out his neighbors left them little alternative but to migrate. Members of the non-slaveholding class often displayed great eagerness to flee from a region where only the great planters made money, and where manual labor was esteemed by the well-to-do as beneath the dignity of free men. Most of the poorer southern whites went directly west and laid the foundations of such states as Alabama and Mississippi, but many of them, like the father of Abraham Lincoln, crossed the Ohio River to swell the population of such free states as Illinois and Indiana. Still others crossed over into Missouri, where slavery was legalized, but for climatic reasons could never flourish.[1]

GROWTH OF THE WEST, 1810–1830

	1810	1820	1830
Kentucky	406,511	564,317	687,917
Tennessee	261,727	422,823	681,904
Ohio	230,760	581,434	937,903
Louisiana	76,556	153,407	215,739
Indiana	24,520	147,178	343,031
Illinois	12,282	55,211	157,445
Mississippi	40,352	75,448	136,621
Alabama		127,901	157,445
Missouri	20,845	66,586	140,455

This rapid assault upon the West was not without its unfortunate aspects. Pioneers were usually short of funds, and they developed the habit of borrowing a large part of the funds they needed from banks. After the disappearance of the first Bank of the United States in 1811, all such business for the next six years fell to the state banks. In the West these institutions were so careless in their banking habits that they came to be known, appropriately, as "wildcatters." Because money was easily obtainable from them, western farmers and speculators made purchases of land far in excess of the needs

---

[1] Seymour Dunbar, *A History of Travel in America* (4 vols., 1915), is particularly valuable because of its excellent illustrations. Channing, v, which begins with the close of the War of 1812, gives much attention to transportation. J. T. Flexner, *Steamboats Come True: American Inventors in Action* (1944), records the early experiments.

of the actual settlers. This unhealthy situation was ended abruptly by the second Bank of the United States, chartered in 1816. At first the "B. U. S." was itself inclined to do a "wildcat" type of business, and as a result some of its branches were soon in serious financial straits. But by 1819 it had sobered up, and was requiring a similarly conservative course of the state banks. Notes of a given state bank would be accumulated by the "B. U. S." and then suddenly presented for payment in specie. Thereupon the bank so attacked would be compelled to call in its loans, while individuals who had borrowed from it would be forced in turn to raise what they owed by selling their property for whatever it would bring. With such a policy generally pursued, speculation was effectively although perhaps unintentionally, arrested, and the general liquidation which followed precipitated the panic of 1819. For more than two years the people of the United States were caught in the throes of a serious economic depression.

The political power of the New West was made manifest during these years by the success which attended its efforts to secure a change in the land policy of the United States. The Harrison Land Law of 1800 had permitted the purchaser of government land to pay only one-fourth of the purchase price in cash, and the remainder in three annual installments. In practice the collection of these debts owing to the government had proved exceedingly difficult. With that over-optimism so characteristic of the frontier, land purchasers had used up all their resources in making their first payment, and had trusted to the future for the funds with which to meet later payments. Quick to realize that evictions would cost votes, politicians induced Congress to pass "relief bills," almost annually, postponing the date of payments due, while the westerners, as their arrears accumulated, easily convinced themselves that they ought not to have been charged for the land at all. During the panic of 1819 Congress put an end to the unworkable credit system. A law passed in 1820 reduced the size of the tract that an individual might buy to eighty acres, and fixed the price per acre at $1.25 cash. Next year a final Relief Act was passed which permitted purchasers who were behind with their payments to return a proportionate part of their land to the government in lieu of cash. Purchasers who wished to keep all their land, however, were allowed to do so, with one of two alternatives, either a cash payment with a discount of thirty-seven and one-half per cent, or eight annual installments instead of four, with all interest remitted. The Land Law of 1820 and the Relief Act of 1821 gave much satisfaction to the people of the West, and facilitated materially the transition of that region from depression to normal conditions.

The rapid expansion of the West soon made the country acutely aware of an impending conflict, hitherto hardly suspected, between the North and the South. Fundamentally the issue upon which these sections came to divide was whether slavery in the United States was to be a temporary or a permanent institution, but for the moment the difference of opinion was restricted to the question of what limits, if any, should be set for the expansion of slavery in the territory west of the Mississippi River. Under French and Spanish rule slavery had been legal in the whole of Louisiana, a situation which the American occupation did not at first disturb. Most of the pioneers who crossed the Mississippi came from the southern states, and while the newcomers, particularly in the St. Louis area, were rarely slaveholders, they were accustomed to slavery and showed no disposition whatever to interfere with it. Once Northerners fully realized, however, that the entire trans-Mississippi West was in danger of being pre-empted for slavery, they were ready to call a halt.

When Jefferson purchased Louisiana from France, he acquired for the United States not only a vast area of land but about fifteen thousand new citizens as well, most of whom were of French or Spanish descent. The chief center of Louisiana settlement was along the lower Mississippi in the vicinity of New Orleans, but a somewhat smaller population was located near the confluence of the Missouri and the Mississippi, with St. Louis as its principal city. Soon after the purchase had taken place, American settlers began to enter the lower Mississippi region in numbers, and by the time of the War of 1812 thousands of them each year were crossing also in the vicinity of St. Louis to thrust a firm wedge of settlement up the valley of the Missouri. With the admission of the lower region as the state of Louisiana in 1812, the upper region received the name of Missouri, and by 1817 was an applicant for statehood. Arkansas territory was severed from it in 1819. Since there were many slaves in Missouri, the Missourians had no thought except to become a slave state, but Representative James Tallmadge of New York expressed a sentiment strongly held by many of his section when he proposed to set limits to the expansion of slavery. As an amendment to the bill before Congress to make possible statehood for Missouri, he advocated that the further introduction of slavery into Missouri should be forbidden, and that all children born of slave parents after the admission of the state should be free on reaching the age of twenty-five years.

Until the introduction of the Tallmadge amendment, the slavery question had played little part in national politics. The three-fifths compromise of the Constitution had received general acceptance, and the law contemplated by the Constitution to forbid the importation of slaves after 1808 had been duly passed. In most of the country slavery was for many years far from profitable, and by 1804 all the states that lay to the north of the Mason and Dixon line had made provision for emancipation. Active emancipation societies existed in the South as well as in the North. But the discovery that cotton could be grown profitably by means of slave labor served to revive the institution just at a time when it had seemed destined to disappear. Cotton-growing was a simple process that could easily be taught to the illiterate slaves; it was a long-continued activity that kept the slaves busy almost the whole year around; it could make use of women and children as well as men; and it could be easily supervised. Suddenly the South discovered that it could not readily give up slavery.[1]

When the question of admitting Missouri came up, it happened that, more or less by accident, the number of free states and of slave states was the same. Of the original thirteen states, seven had abolished slavery and six had retained it, while of the nine new states four had been admitted without slavery and five with it. Thus there were in the Union eleven free states and eleven slave states. Also, thanks to the fact that each state, regardless of the size of its population, was entitled to two members in the United States Senate, there were twenty-two free state senators and twenty-two slave state senators.

Balance of the sections

SLAVE STATES AND FREE STATES, 1820

ORIGINAL THIRTEEN		NEW STATES	
Slave	Free	Slave	Free
Delaware	New Hampshire	Kentucky (1792)	Vermont (1791)
Maryland	Massachusetts	Tennessee (1796)	Ohio (1803)
Virginia	Rhode Island	Louisiana (1812)	Indiana (1816)
North Carolina	Connecticut	Mississippi (1817)	Illinois (1818)
South Carolina	New York	Alabama (1819)	
Georgia	New Jersey		
	Pennsylvania		

But here the equality between the sections stopped. In population the South had grown more slowly than the North; in fact, the Northwest had been peopled in large part by emigrants from the South. Whereas in 1790 the two sections had been almost equal in population (1,968,000 for the North to 1,925,000 for the South), by 1820 the North had forged far ahead (5,144,000 to 4,372,000). This difference was reflected in the number of representatives which the free and the slave states sent to the lower house of Congress, a difference made even more marked by the fact that five slaves counted only as three free men in making the appor-

[1] Mary S. Locke, *Anti-Slavery in America, 1619–1808* (1901); Alice D. Adams, *The Neglected Period of Anti-Slavery in America, 1808–1831* (1908); W. E. B. Du Bois, *Suppression of the African Slave Trade to the United States of America. 1638–1870* (1896).

tionment of seats. Thus in 1790 there had been fifty-seven representatives from the states north of the Mason and Dixon line to forty-eight south of it, but by 1820 there were one hundred and twenty-three representatives from the free states to only eighty-nine from the slave states. It was because of this situation that the South became so excited over the Tallmadge amendment. Should Missouri and all other states admitted from the Louisiana Purchase become free states, then the balance of the sections in the Senate would be lost, and future Congresses might act, not only to exclude the slave-owner from the West in favor of the free farmer, but even to interfere with the now profitable institution of slavery where it had long existed. Not for years had there been so heated a debate in Congress. In general both sides resorted mainly to elaborate constitutional arguments, but the real issue at stake, as everyone knew, was the control of the Union.

The Tallmadge amendment passed the House on February 19, 1819, but it failed to reach a vote in the Senate. When during the next session of Congress Maine, with the consent of Massachusetts, sought admission to the Union, the chance of maintaining the historic equality of representation for slave and free states became at once apparent, and presently bills for the admission of Missouri as a slave state, and Maine as a free state, became law. This, of course, was in itself a kind of compromise, but the Missouri Compromise proper concerned the disposition of the slavery question in the Louisiana Purchase outside Missouri. A resolution introduced by Senator J. B. Thomas of Illinois proposed that in this region the line of 36°30′ should serve to divide free territory from slave territory. This measure seemed to favor the South over the North, for in 1820 much of the territory north of the dividing line was deemed uninhabitable, but it won enough northern votes to obtain the requisite majorities in both houses, and became a law on March 6, 1820.

The Missouri Compromise

The Missouri Compromise offered a natural solution to the problem of slavery expansion. East of the Mississippi River, the Mason and Dixon line and the Ohio River had long been accepted as the proper dividing line between slave and free states, and the idea of continuing such a line west of the Mississippi could readily be accepted. The Missourians, however, were somewhat irritated that Congress had even considered limiting their rights to control slavery within their borders, and in defiance included in their state constitution two aggressively pro-slavery clauses. One forbade the state legislature ever to pass a law emancipating slaves without the consent of their masters, and another forbade the entrance of free Negroes into the state on any pretense whatever. For a time it seemed

The second Missouri Compromise

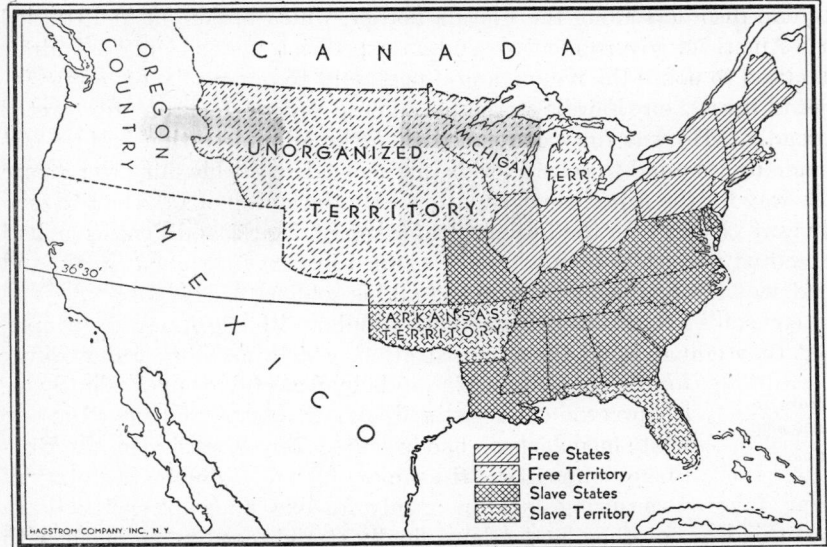

FREE AND SLAVE AREAS AFTER THE MISSOURI COMPROMISE

that the debate would break out anew in Congress, and the admission of
Missouri would have to be postponed. Finally through the efforts of
Henry Clay a second Missouri Compromise was arranged. By its terms
the state was admitted under the constitution it had written, but the Missouri legislature was required to pledge itself never to deny any citizen of
any state the privileges which he enjoyed under the Constitution of the
United States. This meant, of course, that free Negroes, if citizens of
another state, might migrate to Missouri. With Missouri at last a state,
the dispute again died down, but far-seeing men were deeply disturbed.
They knew that some day the nation must face squarely the issue it had
just evaded.[1]

Meantime the advance of population in the Southwest had brought
forcibly to the attention of the government the long-standing menace
of Spanish impotence in Florida, and the great desirability
of acquiring this territory from Spain for the use of Ameri-   Florida
can settlers. Spanish occupation had dwindled down to little more than
the maintenance of garrisons at St. Marks, Pensacola, and St. Augustine,
while the greater part of Florida was a kind of "no man's land" in which
Indians, runaway Negroes, and ruffians of every description held sway.

[1] All the general histories treat the Missouri Compromise elaborately. An excellent
special study is F. C. Shoemaker, *Missouri's Struggle for Statehood, 1804–1821* (1916).

Indian disorders along the Florida border, which broke out in 1816, led the American government to send an expedition under General Andrew Jackson to police the region, and if necessary to pursue the offending Indians into their Florida retreats. These orders Jackson interpreted broadly. He was fully convinced that the administration had at last made up its mind to seize Florida, and considered it his duty to prepare the way for the American occupation. By the spring of 1818 he had won an easy victory over the Indians, had taken St. Marks and Pensacola, had executed two white men whom he blamed in part for the outbreak, and had sent the Spanish governor and all his soldiers to Havana.

Jackson's exploits were immensely popular with the American people, but they embarrassed the administration, which in reality was working for the acquisition of Florida by peaceful means.[1] The Spanish government registered angry protests, and since the two white men Jackson had executed were Englishmen, the British government did the same. John C. Calhoun, Secretary of War, favored censuring Jackson openly for exceeding his instructions, but this was not done, and Adams finally straightened matters out with the foreign powers by offering to restore St. Marks and Pensacola to Spain whenever the Spanish government stood ready to occupy the posts with adequate garrisons, and by convincing the British government that the two subjects in question were unworthy of British protection. Adams also insisted that Spain must either police Florida adequately or turn it over to the United States, and drove home his point so successfully that in 1819 the Spanish agreed to the cession on condition that the United States should meet the claims for damages against Spain made by American citizens, a sum of about five million dollars. The treaty also described the southwestern boundary between the United States and New Spain in such a way as to place Texas on the Spanish side; hence it is not unfair to say that the Spanish exchanged their tenuous hold on Florida for a clear title to Texas. The southwestern boundary ran up the Sabine River "along the western bank to the thirty-second parallel, thence due north to the Red River, up that river to the one-hundredth meridian, thence due north to the Arkansas, up that river along its southern bank to its source, thence due north to the forty-second parallel, and then along that parallel to the 'South Sea.'" Thus the United States obtained whatever claim Spain had previously held to the Oregon country.

Treaty of 1819 with Spain

Curiosity with respect to the unsettled portions of the trans-Mississippi West led to another great exploring expedition, this time under the command of Major Stephen H. Long, who had gained some experience on a similar trip up the Mississippi River in 1817. With a Pittsburgh-built

[1] Hubert B. Fuller, *The Purchase of Florida* (1906).

steamboat, the *Western Engineer*, Long left St. Louis in June, 1819, and arrived at the mouth of the Platte the following September. Here the expedition halted until the next spring, when, reinforced by a detachment which had marched overland from St. Louis, it advanced westward along the Platte River and its southern branch to the Rockies. After sighting and naming Long's Peak, the expedition skirted the mountains to the Arkansas, and a small party pushed on to the Canadian. The return trip was attended by great hardship, and Long's report was full of pessimism. Most of the country he had visited he regarded as wholly unfit for white habitation. Probably his report did more than any other single document to fix in the American mind the legend of the "Great American Desert." *Long's expedition*

Meantime the region north and west of the route taken by Long was being penetrated with singular completeness by fur-traders rather than by official explorers. As early as 1808 agents of the Missouri Fur Company, operating from St. Louis, planned to exploit the fur-trade of the upper Missouri and its tributaries. They gained more by way of experience than by way of profits, but their knowledge was inherited by the Rocky Mountain Fur Company, which in 1823 began a series of brilliant explorations by sending Jedediah S. Smith to the Green River Valley and the Great Salt Lake. Other fur-trade activities of the period centered about the name of a New Yorker, John Jacob Astor, whose Pacific Fur Company, a subsidiary of the American Fur Company, sent out two expeditions in 1810 to the Oregon country, one by sea, the other by land, and founded Astoria. Unfortunately this outpost was sold to the British fur-trade interests at the outbreak of the War of 1812, to be known thereafter first as Fort George, and later as Fort Vancouver. When the war was over, Astor induced Congress to prohibit aliens from carrying on the fur-trade within the United States. This law did not permit him to recover Astoria, but it did give him a chance to purchase at his own price many British trading-posts south of the international border. Astor's traders made good profits, but they were less responsible for the exploration of the West than the adventurous employees of the Rocky Mountain Fur Company.[1] *The northwestern fur-trade*

The rapid settlement of the Mississippi Valley and the penetration of the farther West emphasized the feeling of aloofness from Europe that had come to characterize the United States during the period of the War of 1812. The American people were now content to concern themselves chiefly with the development of their own country, and they viewed with increasing pride their native *American isolation*

[1] Cardinal L. Goodwin, *The Trans-Mississippi West, 1803–1853* (1922), furnishes a convenient summary of western explorations and expansion during this period. See also Leroy R. Hafen and Carl Coke Rister, *Western America* (1941).

manufactures, their expanding agriculture, and particularly the west-ward advance of their population. They were aware, almost for the first time, of the physical basis of greatness with which, thanks to the size of the West, their nation was endowed; and, reasonably enough, they wished to exploit as their interests might direct the magnificent opportunities that confronted them. Thus absorbed in their own affairs, they were less concerned than formerly with what was going on in Europe, but they were willing to challenge instantly any tendency on the part of European nations to limit the natural course of development of the United States. Out of this attitude of mind came a significant statement of American foreign policy, the Monroe Doctrine.[1]

The diplomatic background of the Monroe Doctrine lay both in the New World and the Old. During the years 1807–1808, when the armies of Napoleon had overrun Spain and Portugal, the American colonies of these now satellite nations began to revolt. In this endeavor they were greatly aided by the English, who were also at war with Napoleon's Europe, and were eager at the same time to take advantage of the freer trade relationships that must surely follow independence for the Spanish and Portuguese colonies. While the Spanish-American revolutionists at first professed allegiance to Ferdinand VII, whom Napoleon had dethroned, his restoration after the fall of Napoleon left them totally unprepared to resume the Spanish yoke, and the movement for independence continued. By 1822 the Spanish Empire in the New World had dwindled down to little more than the Caribbean islands of Cuba and Puerto Rico, although Ferdinand VII consistently refused to acknowledge his defeat. In Brazil the separatist movement was equally clearly manifest. There the Portuguese royal house had taken refuge from Napoleon, but at the insistence of the Brazilians an independent empire was proclaimed in 1822, with Dom Pedro I, of the House of Braganza, as ruler.

Background of the Monroe Doctrine

The successful revolt of the Spanish-American colonies was viewed with undisguised approval by the people of the United States, who saw in the actions of their neighbors to the south full vindication of the principles enunciated in their own Declaration of Independence. Moreover, the Spanish-American republics, while unable to combine into a single union, copied in other respects the form of government which had been developed in the United States. Duly flattered by this further evidence of esteem, public opinion

Recognition by the United States

---

[1] The literature of this subject is extensive. A brief but excellent account is given in J. H. Latané, *From Isolation to Leadership* (1918). Serviceable special works are W. F. Reddaway, *The Monroe Doctrine* (1898); Dexter Perkins, *The Monroe Doctrine, 1823–1826* (1927); and by the same author, *The Monroe Doctrine, 1826–1867* (1933); *The Monroe Doctrine, 1867–1907* (1937); *Hands Off; The History of the Monroe Doctrine* (1941).

in the United States called so strongly for recognition of the Spanish-American governments that John Quincy Adams, the Secretary of State, was able only with great difficulty to postpone such action until after his negotiations with Spain for the purchase of Florida were completed. By March, 1822, with Florida safely in hand, President Monroe was able to announce that the time for recognition had come.

European nations also were interested in the course of events in Spanish America, although with the exception of England they were far from pleased with what had happened. Following the defeat of Napoleon, the great powers of Europe — England, Austria, Russia, Prussia, and, after 1818, France — were closely associated in what came to be called the European Concert. *The European system*

Disregarding totally the rights of smaller nations, representatives of these powers met from time to time to discuss international relations and the best means of preserving peace. The leading European statesman of the period was Metternich, prime minister of Austria, whose hostility to democracy was extreme. In his opinion democracy was a kind of communicable disease that must be stamped out, wherever found, if the peace of the world was to be maintained. When, therefore, the revolutionary outbreaks of 1820 occurred in Spain, and in the two Italian kingdoms of Naples and Piedmont, Metternich persuaded Russia and Prussia to agree to the principle that revolution in any European state might properly be suppressed by the great powers. England strongly dissented from this view, and France at first held aloof, but at Laibach in 1821 Austria was commissioned in the name of Austria, Russia, and Prussia (the three allies were sometimes called incorrectly the "Holy Alliance") to suppress the revolutions in Italy; and a year later at Verona France was authorized to do the same for Spain. England's opinion of this high-handed "doctrine of intervention" was plainly stated. It was the privilege of all nations, her foreign secretary insisted, "to be left free to manage their own affairs, so long as they left other nations to manage theirs." But this protest was unavailing. Austrian troops in Italy, and French troops in Spain, stamped out the revolutions, and revived in each offending state the old system of autocracy.

While the doctrine of intervention stated at Laibach was confined specifically to European countries, the possibility of European intervention to suppress the revolts in Spanish America was a subject of much speculation. It was an open secret that Ferdinand VII would be deeply grateful for any such aid, and it was supposed that he might even be generous to any nation or nations from which aid might come. France at Verona actually proposed intervention in Spanish America as well as in Spain, and while *Will the "Holy Alliance" invade America?*

the conference confined itself to the problem of suppressing European revolts, there was reasonable ground for fear that some future congress might not show such restraint. To England the possibility that the Spanish-American republics might be restored to Spain was alarming, for such a development would mean in all probability the revival of the old colonial trade-barriers and the consequent restriction of English trade. Moreover, if France should help subdue Spanish America, she could hardly be expected to do it for nothing. What pay could Ferdinand give other than an American colony for France? Could England stand idly by while France prepared to revive her empire in the New World?

All this diplomatic gossip in due time reached the United States, where it produced a reaction somewhat similar to that of England. Dare the United States permit Spain, presumably with the help of France, blot out the liberty of one American republic after another? Dare the United States risk the revival of a French empire in America, perhaps at her very doors? Moreover, if European rivalries were once more let loose in America, could the United States hope to hold aloof from them? Would she not be drawn into the whirlpool of European diplomacy and war, and away from her strictly domestic program of internal development condi-

---

SECTIONAL LEADERS

The United States has always been, and no doubt always will continue to be, a nation of diverse sections. This is inevitable in so large a country. Sectional differences furnish the background for many disputes in party conventions and in Congress, but Americans should be grateful that, with one notable exception, these sectional conflicts have not led to internal war. Were each of the American sections a separate nation, as in South America or Europe, our wars might have been many instead of only one.

Of the six men whose portraits appear opposite, JOHN QUINCY ADAMS (1767–1848), son of the second President and himself sixth President of the United States, together with DANIEL WEBSTER (1782–1852), able constitutional lawyer and senator from Massachusetts, represented New England in particular, and the Northeast in general. MARTIN VAN BUREN (1782–1862) was a New Yorker rather than a New Englander, but he, too, spoke and voted for northeastern interests. ANDREW JACKSON (1767–1845), seventh President of the United States, and HENRY CLAY (1777–1852), perennial candidate for the Presidency, represented the trans-Appalachian West, but both came from slaveholding states, and understood well the southern point of view. JOHN C. CALHOUN (1782–1850), "Statesman of the Old South," was first and foremost a southerner.

Of these men Henry Clay stands out deservedly as the "Great Compromiser," but all of them realized in some degree, at least, the necessity of "give and take" when one government had to satisfy so many divergent interests. Not they, but their successors, were the makers of the Civil War.

JACKSON

CLAY

CALHOUN

WEBSTER

VAN BUREN

JOHN QUINCY ADAMS

tioned upon westward expansion? Seeking to take advantage of the similarity between British and American views, George Canning, the British foreign minister, suggested to Richard Rush, American minister to England, that the two nations issue a joint statement disclaiming on their part any intention of acquiring Spanish-American territory, and insisting firmly that other nations, with the possible exception of Spain, also keep their hands off America.

Rush promptly referred this communication to President Monroe, who recognized its importance and gave it immediate attention. At the outset he felt inclined to accept the British proposal, although the departure involved from the policy set by Washington and Jefferson against entangling the United States in European affairs gave him much concern. On this matter, however, the counsel he received was divided. The two living Republican ex-Presidents, Jefferson and Madison, both urged him strongly to join forces with the British; with England "on our side," said Jefferson, "we need not fear the whole world." But Monroe's Secretary of State, John Quincy Adams, voiced a contrary opinion. He maintained that the United States should issue a wholly independent statement. He had no desire to see the United States appear merely as a "cock-boat in the wake of a British man-of-war"; he had caught, perhaps from Henry Clay, the vision of a

The Monroe Doctrine

TRANSPORTATION IMPROVES

The whole history of the United States, and for that matter of the world, could be written around the theme of transportation. Americans first traveled by foot and on horseback, or by canoe and sailboat. During these years American civilization was as primitive as the means of conveyance upon which it depended.

Early in the nineteenth century, improved highways greatly facilitated transportation by land; and river steamboats converted the "western waters" into a magnificent transportation system. The canal age, which began with the successful completion of the Erie Canal in 1825, was even more revolutionary; but the railroads were most revolutionary of all.

"Bound Down the River," a Currier & Ives print, shows steamboats on the Mississippi with a river boat in the foreground.

The train in the "Trial Trip of the DeWitt Clinton" might today serve as a toy but little more. This very engine was the first one ever to run in New York state, and the trial trip in 1831 marked the beginning of the New York Central Railroad. Notice that the first railroad coaches were made in the shape of stagecoaches. (Photos from Bettmann.)

The last picture shows horses pulling a canal boat on the Erie Canal about 1830.

Pan-American system in which the United States would play a leading part; he was by no means certain that the United States should bind itself not to add more American territory to its boundaries; and he knew that Great Britain would do as much to prevent European intervention in Spanish America without an alliance with the United States as with it.

Monroe at length came around to the Adams point of view. In reaching this decision he was perhaps influenced by the fact that, although several months had elapsed, he had received no further word from Canning on the subject. Had Canning's ardor cooled? As a matter of fact, although Monroe could probably have had no definite information to this effect, Canning's interest in American co-operation had declined. He had hoped originally that Rush might join him, without referring the matter to President Monroe, in an immediate declaration, and when Rush refused had turned to other expedients. From the French ambassador to England Canning now sought and obtained assurance that the French government had no idea of using force against the revolting Spanish colonies, and this statement, privately communicated to the other European powers, completely eased his mind on the subject.

It must have occasioned the British foreign secretary, and many another European statesman, much surprise when the message which President Monroe sent Congress in December, 1823, reached Europe. In two widely separated statements this document set forth clearly the position the United States had taken. With particular respect to Russia whose apparent desire to expand in the Pacific Northwest had already drawn protests from Adams, the principle was laid down that the era of colonization in the New World was over; henceforth boundaries were to be found, not made. As for the European "doctrine of intervention," Monroe asserted that the political systems of the Old World and the New — monarchy in the one, and democracy in the other — were essentially incompatible. Our policy with regard to Europe had been, and would continue to be, "not to interfere in the internal concerns of any of its powers." Likewise, any attempt on the part of the European powers "to extend their political system to any portion" of the American hemisphere would be regarded as dangerous to the peace and safety of the United States.

The implied trust in the good-will of Great Britain toward the Americas, and in the ability of the British navy to enforce this good-will, was little emphasized in the United States, then or later, but this, after all, was perhaps the most significant thing about the stand Monroe had taken. The era of enmity between the United States and Great Britain was over. Outstanding differences were being settled by conciliation and compromise. With

British good-
will toward
America

Great Britain on guard against predatory nations across the Atlantic, the United States could safely turn its eyes to the West and watch itself grow. Canning's subsequent claim to authorship of the Monroe Doctrine — "I called the New World into existence to redress the balance of the Old" — was an obvious exaggeration, in view of his private negotiations with France and his failure to achieve the joint declaration he had sought. It revealed, indeed, a certain annoyance with the American claim that the United States rather than Great Britain was pre-eminent in the western hemisphere. Furthermore, Monroe's argument that Europe had one political system and America another was hardly fair to the British, who had already come far along the road of constitutional government, and it overlooked entirely the fact that Brazil, the largest country in South America, was a monarchy. But no doubt Canning and Adams understood each other perfectly. They both knew that there was no American navy adequate to implement Monroe's pronouncements, and need not be. They both knew that Great Britain would have no choice but to back up the American assertions, however bombastic they might sound. In short, the United States had declared a doctrine that the British must enforce.[1]

[1] For the Latin-American situation in relation to the Monroe Doctrine, see F. L. Paxson, *The Independence of the South American Republics* (1903); and A. P. Whitaker, *The United States and the Independence of Latin-America, 1800–1830* (1941). On the European background, see W. P. Cresson, *The Holy Alliance* (1922). On Florida, see H. B. Fuller, *The Purchase of Florida* (1906); S. W. Martin, *Florida during the Territorial Days* (1944). On Rush's contribution, see J. H. Powell, *Richard Rush, Republican Diplomat, 1780–1859* (1942).

12

The Revolution of 1828

IN SPITE of the strongly nationalistic spirit that still pervaded the United States in the eighteen-twenties, the beginning of a three-cornered sectional struggle between Northeast, South, and West was plainly in evidence. Boundary lines between these three sections could not always be clearly drawn, but their points of view, determined respectively by the needs of the northern manufacturer, the southern cotton-planter, and the western free farmer, were fairly obvious. The election of 1824 served to throw the divergent interests of the sections into bold relief. By that time the Federalist Party had virtually ceased to exist, and because of the lack of party strife the preceding period had won for itself the designation "the Era of Good Feelings." It was in fact, however, an era of sectional strife. There was only one party that counted, the Republican Party, but the election of 1824 witnessed four different candidates, each claiming to be a good Republican, contesting for the Presidency. Two of these candidates represented the rising West, one came from the Northeast, and one from the South. Each candidate was a kind of incarnation of the prejudices and special interests of the section he represented.[1]

Sectionalism in the United States

In keeping with the already well-established tradition, Monroe was not a candidate for a third term in 1824, but he was known to favor William H. Crawford of Georgia, his Secretary of the Treasury, a typical representative of the plantation aristocracy of the South. The other leading candidates were John Quincy Adams of Massachusetts, Secretary of State; Henry Clay of Kentucky, several times Speaker of the House; and Andrew Jackson of Tennessee, the hero of New Orleans and the conqueror of Florida. John C. Calhoun of South Carolina was also interested, but he decided ultimately to bide his time, and in return for his withdrawal was very generally acclaimed as the proper person for the Vice-Presidency.

Campaign of 1824

Ordinarily the number of candidates would have been reduced to one

[1] F. J. Turner, *The Significance of Sections in American History* (1932), strongly emphasizes this point of view.

by a congressional caucus, participated in by practically all the members of the party in Congress. But this means of making nominations had fallen into ill repute, and only sixty-nine members attended the caucus. Its endorsement of Crawford, therefore, was held to be of no consequence, and state legislatures took it upon themselves to name candidates. Crawford's name was also presented by the legislature of Virginia; Adams's by the legislatures of Massachusetts and other New England states; Clay's by the Kentucky legislature and many others; Jackson's by the lower house of the Tennessee legislature, and by mass conventions in various parts of the country. Prophetic of the future were some resolutions passed by a meeting of Republicans in Lancaster County, Pennsylvania, which asserted that "the best and most unexceptionable method" of nominating a candidate would be by "a convention of delegates from all the States of the Union," a system, however, that was admittedly "impracticable, from the immense extent of the country, and from the great expense..." Of the four candidates mentioned, Crawford was soon at a hopeless disadvantage because of a paralytic stroke. The other three not only remained in the race to the end; they were also the outstanding leaders in American politics for a generation.

John Quincy Adams (1767–1848)[1] was the son of the second President, and in many respects an even abler man. In addition to his rare inheritance, no less from his mother, Abigail Adams, than from his father, he had received a rigorous training for public life. At eleven he was taken by his father to Europe, where under private tutors and in a variety of countries his education was carried on assiduously. At twenty he was graduated from Harvard, and soon after began the practice of law; at twenty-seven he began a diplomatic career that took him on important missions to England, Holland, Russia, and Sweden. On returning to the United States after the election of Jefferson to the Presidency, Adams served in the Massachusetts legislature, and was elected in 1803 to the United States Senate. This seat he resigned in 1808 because his conscience bade him approve the embargo, while the legislature of Massachusetts opposed it; and thereafter he became a member of the Republican Party, to which his diplomatic experience proved a valuable asset. He was almost painfully eager to crown his career by becoming President, but his demeanor was cold and forbidding, and the number of friends upon whom he could count was few. Moreover, he was belligerently incorruptible in all his dealings, and yet inclined to ascribe the worst motives to all who disagreed with him.

John Quincy Adams

[1] John T. Morse, *John Quincy Adams* (1882), is an appreciative biography. The chapter on the sixth President in J. T. Adams, *The Adams Family* (1930), is an excellent attempt at character analysis. See also B. C. Clark, *John Quincy Adams: "Old Man Eloquent"* (1932).

Henry Clay (1777–1852)[1] never attained the Presidency, but his name is far better known than that of many of the men who did. He was of no such distinguished lineage as Adams, for his father was only a Baptist preacher of back-country Virginia; and his education was as limited as Adams's was extensive. But Clay had a warm, magnetic personality, and won friends as easily as Adams lost them. He made the most of his meager opportunities, read law under a distinguished jurist, Chancellor Wythe, and when he was twenty years old opened a law office in Lexington, Kentucky. His legal career was successful from the start, not because he was learned in the law, but because of a native shrewdness that proved to be of greater value in the frontier courts than any amount of book learning. Within a few years he was a member of the state legislature, then for a short time, beginning even before he had attained the constitutional age of thirty years, of the United States Senate. On the eve of the War of 1812 he entered the House, where he was repeatedly chosen Speaker. He served on the commission that made peace with England after the war, and acquired from the experience an acquaintance with Europe that he sorely needed. Likable, and desiring to be liked, Clay could usually be counted on to reflect his surroundings. In his youth he was a man of the West, tempersome and aggressive — a leading "War Hawk" when the West wanted war. As he grew older, contacts with the East and with Europe had a sobering influence upon him, and a discreet moderation took the place of his former recklessness. He saw intuitively the need of a political program that would satisfy all sections — a national program — and early set himself the task of finding one. He saw, too, the necessity of compromise when conflicting interests were involved, and his willingness to strike bargains that would satisfy all concerned won him the title, not undeservedly, of the "Great Compromiser." His persuasive oratory, once it was enlisted in any cause, was a potent influence in shaping public opinion. Few American statesmen have ever maintained, through victory and defeat, a larger or more devoted personal following.

Andrew Jackson (1767–1845),[2] like Henry Clay, was a product of the upland South, a North Carolinian whose parents had emigrated from the north of Ireland to the American frontier. In spite of his extreme youth he saw service during the later years of the American Revolution,

Henry Clay

---

[1] Carl Schurz, _Henry Clay_ (2 vols., 1883); G. G. Van Deusen, _The Life of Henry Clay_ (1937); Bernard Mayo, _Henry Clay, Spokesman of the New West_ (1937).

[2] Of fascinating interest are the two books on Jackson by Marquis James, _Andrew Jackson: The Border Captain_ (1933), and _Andrew Jackson: Portrait of a President_ (1937). Less readable, but of substantial merit, are W. G. Sumner, _Andrew Jackson_ (1924); and J. S. Bassett, _Life of Andrew Jackson_ (2 vols., 1911; new ed., 1916). Of importance in estimating the effect of environment on Jackson's character is T. P. Abernethy, _From Frontier to Plantation in Tennessee_ (1932).

and out of his wartime experiences emerged with a bitter hatred of England. With the faintest of qualifications he began the practice of law in western North Carolina when he was only **Andrew Jackson** twenty years of age, but within a year he followed the course of migration into Tennessee and settled at Nashville. Here he was soon public prosecutor, then for a brief time a member of the United States Senate, then a judge of the Tennessee Supreme Court. But it was as a warrior that he won his chief renown. His successful campaign against the Creeks in 1814, his triumph next year over the British at New Orleans, and his subsequent exploits against the Indians and the Spanish in Florida made him the outstanding military hero of the time. As a fitting reward he was chosen in 1823 to represent the state of Tennessee once more in the United States Senate. The pride of the West at having produced so great a man was unbounded, particularly when the great man had attained his eminence because he possessed in marked degree those qualities that the West most highly esteemed. Jackson was a veritable personification of the western democratic ideal which held that common men were as good as aristocrats and deserved to play quite as important a part in the affairs of the nation. He exhibited, too, the contentious individualism of the frontier, its unreasoning hatreds, its rashness, and its resourcefulness. He was an ardent patriot, and identified with patriotism the Westerner's desire to obtain expanded boundaries for the nation and unlimited opportunities for its citizens. He was not at first politically ambitious, but designing politicians saw the powerful appeal his candidacy would make to the masses, and pushed him into the race.

The campaign and election of 1824 revealed clearly that the American nation, in spite of its essential unity, had strongly sectional lines of cleavage. Adams won the electoral votes of New England and most of the votes of New York. Crawford, handicapped **Election by the House** by his physical condition, led only in Virginia and Georgia. Clay carried Kentucky, Ohio, and Missouri. Jackson alone had a large enough following to win electoral votes outside the section he directly represented. He divided the West with Clay, the South with Crawford, and made an excellent showing in the middle Atlantic states. The electoral vote stood: Jackson 99, Adams 84, Crawford 41, Clay 37. No candidate having received a majority, the choice went to the House of Representatives, where Adams, with Clay's support, won an easy victory. Thereupon Adams chose Clay as his Secretary of State — a matter of "bargain and corruption," the Jacksonians charged, but never proved.

Out of the election there emerged a new political division. The supporters of Jackson had appealed, and now continued to appeal, to the more democratic elements of American society. The government of the

United States, they maintained, had been ever since its inception in the
hands of a relatively small group of aristocrats, and the
The Democratic Party foreshadowed time had come for the introduction of new blood. Jackson
was made out to be, and to a considerable extent he became,
the candidate of the masses, while those who opposed him
were the candidates of the classes. Westerners imbued with frontier
ideals of democracy, Easterners of the farmer and laborer classes who
were just beginning to be conscious of their political power, and back-
country Southerners who had long struggled within their respective
states against the domination of an eastern planter aristocracy, all rallied
enthusiastically to the Jackson standard. Ably led by such shrewd politicians as William B. Lewis of Tennessee, Martin Van Buren of New
York, and Thomas Hart Benton of Missouri, they made of the Adams
administration one prolonged campaign for the election of Jackson to the
Presidency in 1828. The *United States Telegraph*, edited by a Missourian
named Duff Green, furnished spicily written political news and views for
the use of Jacksonian supporters throughout the nation.

The forces opposed to Jackson, now united under the leadership of
Adams and Clay, were held together by bonds much stronger than
The National Republicans "bargain and corruption" could create. In the campaign of
1824 Clay alone of all the candidates had had what today
would be called a platform — his "American System."
The War of 1812 had made him deeply conscious of the need of economic
self-sufficiency for the United States, an end which he believed could best
be promoted by two policies, a protective tariff and internal improvements. The tariff could be used to build up American manufactures,
while internal improvements, paid for out of tariff receipts, would provide
the roads and canals over which the products of eastern factories could
reach the West and South, and western and southern agricultural commodities could reach the East. This program suited Adams — and New
England — as well as it suited Clay and such of the West as would follow
him. It laid firm foundations for a new intersectional party, dependent
upon voters from the Northwest no less than from the Northeast, and
soon to be known as the National Republican Party. The Jacksonian
adherents, disdaining subtleties, were presently pleased to be called
Democrats.

Sectional differences on the tariff question had become acutely apparent well before Adams entered the White House.[1] The tariff
The tariff of 1816 had received support from every section, although
the commercial elements in the Northeast and a majority of the southern

[1] F. W. Taussig, *Tariff History of the United States* (8th ed., 1931), is the standard work
on this subject. See also Edward Stanwood, *American Tariff Controversies in the Nineteenth Century* (2 vols., 1903–04).

planters had opposed it. The depression of 1819–20 led to a movement, emanating chiefly from the middle Atlantic states, for increased duties as an aid to languishing manufacturing interests, and a bill drawn along these lines failed in 1820 for the lack of a single vote in the Senate, only to pass in 1824. Still unsatisfied, the protectionists pressed on for higher duties, and in 1827 saw another bill they had sponsored defeated by the casting vote of the Vice-President, John C. Calhoun. At this juncture the Jacksonian leaders, whose party had won a majority in the House of Representatives by the mid-term election of 1826, took a hand. They knew that Jackson, in order to be elected in 1828, must win support from the South, which opposed a protective tariff, and from the Northeast and the Northwest, where a strong majority favored it. Their plan, afterward fully revealed by John C. Calhoun himself, was to present a bill which placed such excessively high rates on raw materials that some of the manufacturers of the Northeast would join with the seaboard commercial interests and the South to defeat the measure. Amendments which would make the bill more satisfactory to the manufacturers were to be voted down, and thus the Jackson men could claim credit in the North for having introduced a high-tariff measure, and in the South for having defeated it. The bill, according to the sharp-tongued John Randolph, related "to manufactures of no sort or kind but the manufacture of a President of the United States." As it turned out, the ruse failed to work, for enough northern support for the bill was obtained to enact the "Tariff of Abominations," as it was generally called, into law.

Among those who unexpectedly favored the Tariff of Abominations was Daniel Webster of Massachusetts. In preceding tariff debates Webster had always defended the point of view of the commercial interests, who feared the losses to trans-Atlantic trade that would result from high duties. His change of front in 1828 is clear indication that by that date the importance of manufacturing in New England had begun to challenge that of commerce. A similar about-face had already been registered by John C. Calhoun of South Carolina, who in 1816 had been a strong protagonist of protection, but within a few years had accepted the cotton-growers' arguments against it. To the southern planters, the ideal situation seemed to be full freedom to exchange their cotton for low-priced English manufactures without tariff barriers. The divergent views of the sections on the tariff can be easily discerned from the table on page 220.

Adams was an enthusiastic believer in internal improvements at national expense, and was unhandicapped by the constitutional scruples that had restrained Madison, and to a great extent Monroe also, in their dealings with this subject. In 1824 Monroe had given his approval to

TARIFF VOTES IN THE HOUSE OF REPRESENTATIVES

	1816		1820		1824		1828	
	For	Against	For	Against	For	Against	For	Against
New England	17	10	18	17	15	23	16	23
Middle Atlantic*	42	5	55	1	57	9	56	6
South Atlantic	16	35	5	49	4	56	4	47
Southwest	3	3	0	7	2	14	0	16
Northwest †	10	1	12	3	29	0	29	1

* Includes Delaware.
† Includes Kentucky and Missouri.

a General Survey Act which authorized the President to conduct such

Internal improvements

surveys of canal and turnpike routes as would serve an important national interest. Undoubtedly Adams hoped to use this power to lay out a great national system of transportation, and his efforts along this line were not entirely unavailing. During his term of office army engineers were detailed freely to survey prospective transportation routes, and the sums actually expended in aid of internal improvements grew by leaps and bounds. As long as Adams was President, Congress voted frequent subsidies, usually in the form of generous subscriptions of stock, to numerous state and local works of internal improvement. But almost the only strictly national project that the administration was able to carry on was the continuation westward of the Cumberland Road. Beginning in 1825 liberal appropriations were made for this purpose, and with Jefferson City, Missouri, as its intended western terminal the National Road, as it came to be called, progressed slowly across central Ohio, and then on through Indiana and Illinois. By 1838 construction reached Vandalia, Illinois, but was discontinued because of the hard times that followed the panic of 1837, and was not resumed because of the increasing evidence that railroads, not turnpikes, would soon carry the commerce of the country.

Undoubtedly the most spectacular development in transportation during this period was the building of the Erie Canal, a project which

The Erie Canal

DeWitt Clinton, governor of New York, persuaded his state to undertake in 1817. By 1825 this waterway was open for business. A lock canal, costing $7,602,000, it extended from Troy on the Hudson to Buffalo on Lake Erie, a distance of three hundred and sixty-three miles. Thanks to a lucrative local traffic that soon made cities of such points along the route as Syracuse, Rochester, and Utica, the canal was a financial success even before it was finished, and a branch canal to Lake Champlain was similarly successful.

The through traffic that began at once to make use of the Erie Canal was of immense significance in linking the East to the West. Before it was built the cost of transporting a ton of freight from New York City to Buffalo had been about one hundred dollars, and the time required, about twenty days. The canal at once reduced the cost to ten dollars and the time to eight days, and as the volume of business increased the cost of transportation went steadily down.[1] Steamboats on the Great Lakes made possible a cheap all-water route to the shores of Lake Huron and Lake Michigan as well as Lake Erie, and with the problem of transportation no longer a serious barrier to settlement, pioneers by the tens of thousands took up vacant lands in the northern parts of Ohio, Indiana, and Illinois. Michigan Territory grew so rapidly in population that by 1836 the eastern half was ready for statehood, while the western half, known later as Wisconsin, seemed likewise destined to an early maturity. Moreover, as Clinton had foreseen, the tremendous volume of trade that flowed through the Erie Canal–Great Lakes route to and from the West paid a generous tribute to New York City. In population New York grew from less than one hundred and twenty-five thousand in 1820 to over two hundred thousand by 1830; during the same time the value of its real and personal property rose sixty per cent; and the increasing volume of its import and export trade soon made it the leading American city.

The success of New York in making connections with the West led to quick emulation by her chief rivals, Philadelphia and Baltimore. The legislature of Pennsylvania in 1825 authorized the construction of an elaborate system of canals to unite the various sections of the state. By 1834 the "Pennsylvania System" stretched all the way to Pittsburgh, but a portage railway was necessary to carry the canal traffic across the mountains. This new route to the West did a flourishing local business, but it never became a serious rival to the Erie Canal, and Philadelphia never seriously challenged the lead of New York in the race for the western markets. Baltimore, meantime, began in 1828, with state backing, the Chesapeake and Ohio Canal, which was ultimately built as far west as Fort Cumberland, but for engineering reasons could never reach its goal. But the Baltimore and Ohio Railroad, projected at the same time by a few far-seeing men, finally reached its destination in 1853.

The Pennsylvania System

[1] N. E. Whitford, *History of the Canal System of the State of New York* (2 vols., 1906). See also for this and other canals of the time A. F. Harlow, *Old Towpaths, The Story of the American Canal Era* (1926).

The craze for canals that began while Adams was President went to unreasonable lengths. In the East feeders to the main canals, and connecting links between arms of the Atlantic, were built with little regard to costs involved and possible earning power.

The canal age

In the new western states the task of connecting the Ohio–Mississippi River system with the Great Lakes was eagerly embraced. Ohio led the way in 1825 by authorizing the building of two such canals, the Ohio and Erie from Portsmouth to Cleveland, and the Miami and Erie from Cincinnati to Toledo. The former was completed in 1832, and for a little while did a thriving business; the latter was finished in considerable part by 1835, but by 1845, when it was opened the whole way through, railroads were rapidly making canals obsolete. Not to be outdone by Ohio, Indiana began in 1832 and completed in 1843 the Wabash and Erie Canal, while Illinois between 1832 and 1848 built the Illinois and Michigan Canal. In the fifties Wisconsin succeeded in opening a waterway from Green Bay to the Mississippi by way of the Fox and Wisconsin Rivers, and Michigan, by building a canal around St. Mary's Falls, greatly facilitated through traffic on the Great Lakes. Except for Maryland, there was little canal construction in the South, where the mountain barriers were obstinate and the highways of the rivers and the ocean still furnished fairly adequate means of transportation. Charleston, South Carolina, was eager for connections with the West that would give her a better chance to compete with her new western rival, New Orleans, but for topographical reasons she was compelled to turn to a railroad rather than to a canal. By 1850 the total canal mileage in the United States had reached thirty-two hundred.

Because of his long experience with diplomacy, Adams expected to make a fine record as President in dealing with foreign affairs. Such, however, could hardly have been the case, for the problems

Adams and Clay

that the country faced during this period were primarily of a domestic nature. Clay, as Secretary of State, had visions of supplementing the Monroe Doctrine by actively promoting Pan-American co-operation, and in this he carried Adams with him. But the Senate blocked the principal effort of the administration in this direction when it refused, purely for reasons of party advantage, to confirm until too late the appointment of two delegates from the United States to attend the Panama Congress called by Bolivar in 1826.

The Adams administration was unfortunate also in its dealings with the South. Clay's linking of the obnoxious protective tariff with the program of internal improvements tended to make the two equally unpalatable to a section that was coming more and more to see in the high duties on manufactured articles a body blow at its prosperity. Adams

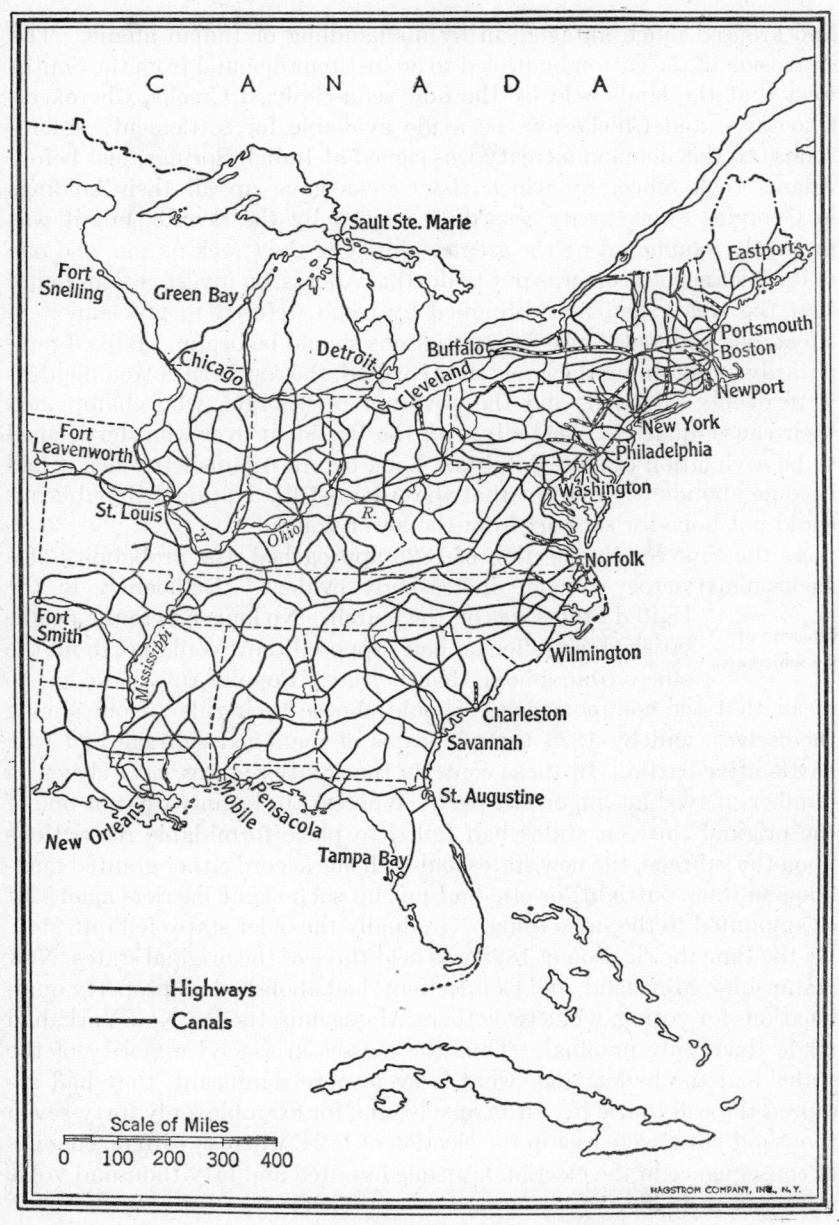

PRINCIPAL CANALS AND HIGHWAYS IN THE
UNITED STATES, 1834

also aroused much antagonism by his handling of Indian affairs. The expansion of the cotton South led to an insistent demand from the Southwest that the lands held by the now semi-civilized Creeks, Cherokees, Choctaws, and Chickasaws be made available for settlement. In response to this demand a treaty was signed at Indian Springs, just before Adams took office, by which the Creeks gave up all their holdings in Georgia. This treaty was duly ratified by the Senate, but it was promptly repudiated by the great majority of the Creek nation, and one of its chief negotiators was put to death. Adams, on investigation, found that the treaty had been obtained by fraud, refused to proclaim it in effect, and ordered that new negotiations should be begun. Balked temporarily in obtaining the lands they coveted, the southern cotton planters were deeply offended, and the governor of Georgia, who championed their cause, quarreled heatedly with the President over what he deemed to be a violation of states' rights. Long before Adams left office it had become abundantly evident that the Adams-Clay National Republicans could not hope for support from the lower South.

As the time for the election of 1828 approached, the probability of a Jacksonian victory became increasingly evident. Democracy in the United States was on the march. No longer were the people satisfied, as Jefferson had supposed they would be, to fill the offices from among their betters. Popular rule had come to mean that the common people should choose their rulers from among themselves, and by 1828 the advocates of manhood suffrage had won battle after battle. In these contests the frontier states, now eleven in number, played an important part. Whereas, to begin with, not one of the original thirteen states had failed to place formidable restrictions upon the suffrage, the new states had with one accord either granted manhood suffrage outright, or else had put up such slight barriers against it as amounted to the same thing. Gradually the older states fell into step. By the time the election of 1828 was held three of the original states, New Hampshire, Maryland, and Connecticut, had abolished all property qualifications for voting, while two others, Massachusetts and New York, had made them only nominal. Thus the masses in a good majority of the states had the ballot, and, what is even more significant, they had acquired the will to use it. In Pennsylvania, for example, only forty-seven thousand votes were cast in the election of 1824, whereas with no changes of consequence in the election laws one hundred and fifty thousand votes were cast in 1828.[1]

Extension of the suffrage

---

[1] K. H. Porter, *A History of Suffrage in the United States* (1918), gives a good account of the movement for suffrage extension. See also D. R. Fox, *The Decline of Aristocracy in the Politics of New York* (1918). The classic portrait of American democracy during this period is Alexis de Tocqueville, *Democracy in America* (new ed., 1945).

The agitation against property qualifications for voting, and other undemocratic practices, continued during the next two decades until the last citadel of aristocracy had fallen. Constitutional conventions, held in most of the states during this period, tended generally to extend the suffrage to all white males over twenty-one years of age, and in keeping with the growing spirit of democracy they also increased the number of popularly elected officials, often including even judges among those so chosen. Guided by experience, the conventions gave greater powers to the governors, and limited more closely the prerogatives of the legislatures, for which they ordinarily stipulated biennial rather than annual sessions. An extremely important step in the direction of popular rule, taken during this period, was the substitution of popular for legislative election of presidential electors. By 1828 the old system of permitting the legislatures to choose the electors had disappeared in all but two states, Delaware and South Carolina.

When at last the impatiently-awaited election year of 1828 appeared, "King Numbers" seemed safely enthroned. An aristocratic Adams in a contest with a democratic Jackson had not the remotest chance to win. Issues were lost sight of, and the personal idiosyncrasies of the candidates were mercilessly exposed. To the democratic West the arguments in favor of Clay's American System had far less appeal than the primitive prejudices to which the Jacksonian orators catered. Their whole creed might almost have been boiled down to the sentiment: "The East is bad, the West is good; turn the rascals out!"

Jackson's election was not accomplished, however, without the assistance of many voters to whom an excess of democracy did not appeal. Calhoun, as the Jacksonian candidate for the Vice-Presidency, hoped to wield a great influence in the new administration and to succeed the General after four years. This consideration weighed heavily with the aristocratic element in the South, who could hardly have supported Adams anyway because of his well-known attitude on the tariff. An alliance of the West, the South, and the lower classes of the Northeast won the election for Jackson. Every western state supported him, and every southern state except Maryland, which divided its vote. The total electoral vote stood 178 to 83, and the popular vote, as nearly as it could be ascertained, 647,276 to 508,064.

The day of Jackson's inauguration brought to Washington a "noisy and disorderly rabble" bent on celebrating the rescue of the government from the hands of the aristocrats. The capital city, which still had far to go before it could grow up to the ambitious pattern L'Enfant had cut for it, was taxed to the limit to care for the huge crowd of celebrants that overflowed the boarding-houses, lined the streets to cheer the President-elect uproariously as he walked to the capital, followed him in frenzied droves as he rode down the Avenue after taking the oath of office, surged through the White House like the Paris mob at the Tuileries, upset the presidential punch, trampled under muddy feet the presidential carpets, and in a thousand other ways gave free vent to their joy that the people had at last taken possession of their government.[1]

Jackson's Cabinet, headed by Martin Van Buren of New York as Secretary of State, was divided about evenly between his own henchmen and the supporters of Calhoun, but the new President leaned for advice principally upon a "kitchen cabinet" of intimate friends. Ablest among these men was Amos Kendall of Kentucky, whose facile pen phrased many Jacksonian state papers. William B. Lewis of Tennessee was probably the President's closest friend, and lived at the White House to offer sagacious counsel on the petty ways of politics. Others connected with the "kitchen cabinet" at one time or another included Isaac Hill, Senator from New Hampshire, Andrew Jackson Donelson of Tennessee, the President's nephew and secretary, Duff Green of the *Telegraph*, and Francis P. Blair, who after 1830 edited a new administration organ, the *Globe*. Undoubtedly this little coterie had great influence with the President, but he was himself the dominating figure of his administration, and was quite as capable of ignoring their advice as of taking it.

Jackson's Cabinet

More has been made of Jackson's introduction of the "spoils system" — "to the victor belongs the spoils" — than the facts warrant. It is true that removals of appointive officers for purely party reasons were rare before his time, but replacements after death or resignation had ordinarily been made from members of the dominant political party. Owing to the long tenure of the Republican Party it was probably a fact, as Jackson charged, that the efficiency of the public service was crippled by the presence within it of many aged and incompetent relics of an earlier day. The novelty of Jackson's action lay in the speed with which he got results. Immediately after his inauguration he began a proscription of office-holders that soon weeded out of the service hundreds of men who had supposed that they were to retain their positions indefinitely. Naturally the outcries from those who had been dispossessed and from their friends rent the

The spoils system

---

[1] Claude G. Bowers, *The Party Battles of the Jackson Period* (1922), gives an unrestrained account of the inauguration, and of the events that succeeded it. The book is intensely pro-Jackson. More dependable accounts are contained in F. J. Turner, *The United States, 1830–1850* (1935); William MacDonald, *Jacksonian Democracy* (1906); and F. A. Ogg, *The Reign of Andrew Jackson* (1919). McMaster, v, vi; and Channing, v, deal in whole or in part with this period.

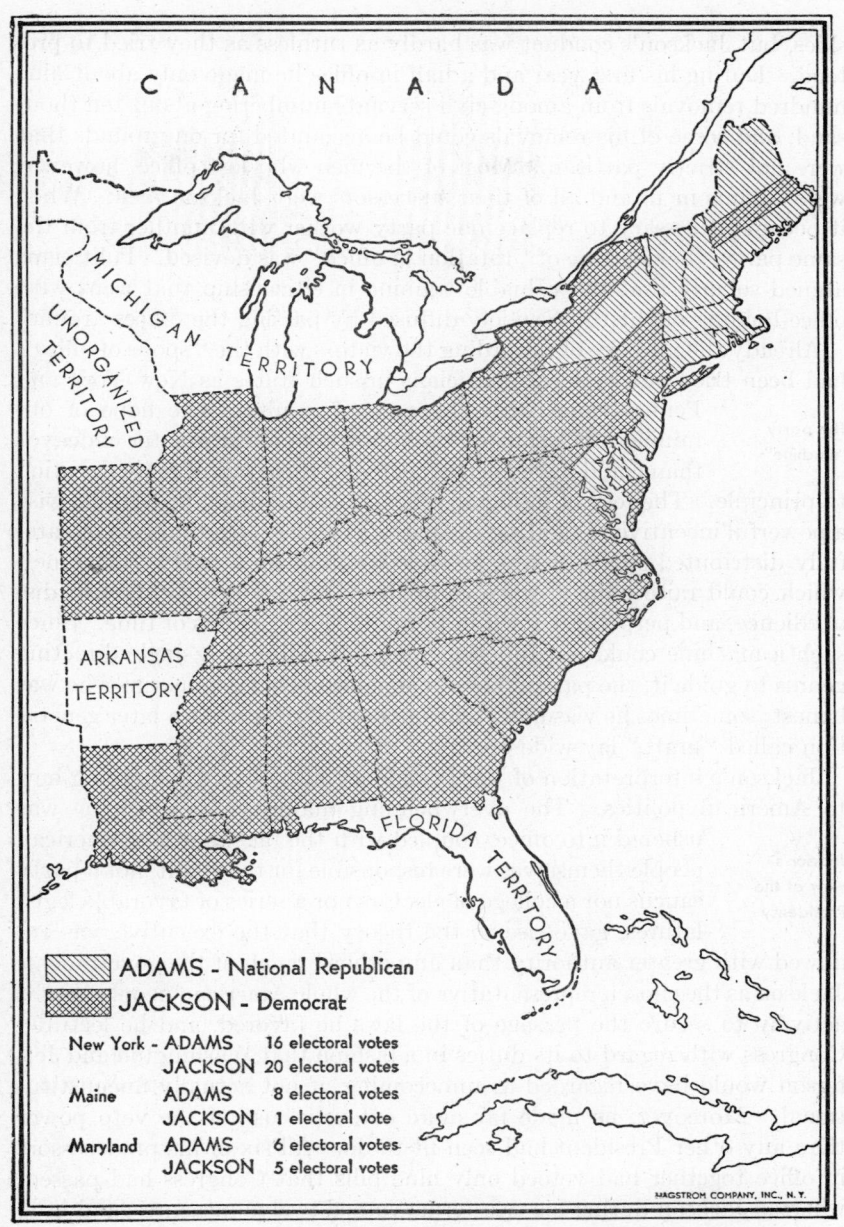

ADAMS - National Republican
JACKSON - Democrat

New York -	ADAMS	16 electoral votes
	JACKSON	20 electoral votes
Maine	ADAMS	8 electoral votes
	JACKSON	1 electoral vote
Maryland	ADAMS	6 electoral votes
	JACKSON	5 electoral votes

MAGSTROM COMPANY, INC., N. Y.

THE ELECTION OF 1828, BY STATES

skies, but Jackson's conduct was hardly as ruthless as they tried to pretend. During his first year and a half in office he made only about nine hundred removals from among civil servants numbering about ten thousand, and some of his removals could be accounted for on grounds that were not strictly partisan. Most of the men who lost office, however, were Adams men, and all of their successors were Jackson men. When it became necessary to replace one party worker with another from the same party, the doctrine of "rotation in office" was devised. Politicians argued soberly that the valuable training in citizenship that went with office-holding ought to be widely diffused by passing the offices around.

Already the practice of rewarding the victors with the "spoils of office" had been tried out by local politicians in such states as New York and Pennsylvania with phenomenal results. The hope of obtaining office spurred party workers to far greater endeavor than could have been expected of them out of mere devotion to principle. The fear of losing an office, once obtained, proved likewise a powerful incentive to fighting the party's battles. On the basis of carefully distributed spoils, it was possible to build up a party "machine" which could raise money, wage campaigns, reward loyalty, punish disobedience, and perpetuate itself in power for long periods of time. Since such a machine could not function smoothly without a single directing genius to guide it, the party "boss" came into being. Sometimes he was honest; sometimes he was not. The opportunity for what a later generation called "graft" lay wide open.[1]

The party "machine"

Jackson's interpretation of the Presidency also offered something new to American politics. The overwhelming majority by which he was ushered into office, coupled with the fact that the American people themselves were responsible for the result, not a party caucus nor a college of electors nor a series of favorable legislatures, gave rise to the theory that the executive was endowed with greater authority than any other branch of the government. Jackson as the chosen representative of the whole American people sought actively to secure the passage of the laws he favored, and he lectured Congress with regard to its duties in a fashion that Washington and Jefferson would have regarded as unbecoming, if not actually unconstitutional. Moreover, he made far more extensive use of the veto power than any other President had seen fit to do. All six of his predecessors in office together had vetoed only nine bills that Congress had passed, whereas Jackson during his two terms vetoed twelve measures, and used freely also the "pocket veto," a device which no previous President had dared to invoke. The pocket veto was made possible by a provision in

Jackson's view of the Presidency

[1] M. Ostrogorski, *Democracy and the Organization of Political Parties* (2 vols., 1902).

the Constitution that unless the President vetoed a bill within ten days after it reached him, the bill would become a law anyway, "unless Congress by their adjournment prevent its return, in which case it shall not be a law." Since many important measures were passed in the closing days of a session, the President might, if he chose, defeat legislation by a mere failure to act, or in popular parlance "pocketing" the bill. Jackson's feeling of superiority extended even to his relations with the Supreme Court, and on one occasion he is reported to have said: "John Marshall has made his decision; now let him enforce it."

This clash with the Supreme Court arose out of Jackson's attitude on the Indian question. A quarrel between the state of Georgia and the Cherokee Nation had arisen as to which had legal authority over Cherokee Indians living within the borders of the state. The matter was finally brought to the Supreme Court in the case of the *Cherokee Nation vs. the State of Georgia*, but the Court, although complimenting the Indians on their successful efforts at self-government, refused to take jurisdiction on the ground that the Cherokees were a "domestic dependent nation" rather than a "foreign state," as the suit contended. Later, however, in the case of *Worcester vs. Georgia*, the Court held that the laws of Georgia were of no effect within the Cherokee borders. This decision was openly flouted by the Georgians, and the President, whatever the precise phrases that may have sprung to his lips, made no effort to enforce it.[1]

As a matter of fact the Indian question had passed the bounds of a simple dispute between some Indians and a state. Who first caught the vision it would be hard to determine, but for a long time the idea had been afloat that a kind Providence had arranged for this vexing problem an easy solution. Explorers had reported with great unanimity that the western half of the continent would never be useful to white men; on the other hand, because of its abundance of game, it was an ideal home for Indians. Why not accept this divinely ordained plan, and colonize the Indians in the West where they need never fear the encroachments of the whites? As early as 1825, John C. Calhoun, then Secretary of War, had outlined this plan in an able state paper, and had urged it upon President Monroe, who in turn had urged it upon Congress. Few objections could be raised to so natural a solution, and from that time forward the removal of the Indians to the region west of the western borders of Missouri and Arkansas was regarded as settled policy. Thus Jackson did not inaugurate this policy, but he fell in line with it cheerfully, and under his administration it was successfully carried through. His irritation that the Supreme Court

The policy of Indian removal

[1] U. B. Phillips, *Georgia and State Rights* (1902), is the best work on this subject.

should dare to interfere with so benign a project is understandable, if not wholly defensible.

During Jackson's administration ninety-four Indian treaties were signed, most of which were treaties of cession; and under the steady pressure of the United States government even the Cherokees left sullenly for the West. Two disciplinary wars had to be fought in order to subject the Indians wholly to the white man's will. The Black Hawk War with the Sauk and Foxes, whose departure from northern Illinois was too slow to satisfy the frontiersmen, was fought in 1832; the Seminole War, which became necessary when most of that tribe refused to leave their homes, even after they had agreed to go, was an unhappy legacy that Jackson left to his successor, Van Buren, and that ended in the forties only when most of the Seminoles had been hunted down and killed.[1]

What Jackson's attitude as President would be toward "internal improvements" could hardly have been gathered from any of his previous pronouncements, but a shrewd observer might easily have foreseen that it would be as much at variance as possible with the views of Adams and Clay. While Adams was President, Congress with much encouragement from the executive, granted federal aid liberally for the building of roads and canals, the improvement of ports and harbors, and the clearing of obstructions from the channels of navigable streams. But Jackson, who in this matter seems to have leaned heavily upon the advice of Van Buren, was not long in concluding that many such expenditures were neither constitutional nor expedient. An opportunity to state his position came in May, 1830, when Congress sent him a bill which authorized federal assistance for the building of a road from Maysville, Kentucky, to Lexington, in the same state. Although this road was in reality only a link in the once famous Natchez Trace, during the eighteenth century the main overland route from Kentucky to the lower Mississippi, the measure as it stood provided merely for a strictly intra-state road. Half the stock in the turnpike company that was to do the work was to be subscribed by the United States government, and the other half in equal parts by the state of Kentucky and by private individuals.

The Maysville Road Bill

Much to the disgust of its proponents, Jackson refused his signature to the Maysville Road Bill, and in an able veto message defended the position he had taken. He doubted its constitutionality and, like Madison and Monroe, believed that a constitutional amendment should be adopted if federal aid to roads and

Jackson's veto

---

[1] Annie H. Abel, *The History of Events Resulting in Indian Consolidation West of the Mississippi* (1908), deals with this subject in great detail. See also F. L. Paxson, *The Last American Frontier* (1910); and Angie Debo, *The Road to Disappearance* (1941).

canals was to be continued; but his chief objection to the measure was the local character of the internal improvement it proposed to aid. The Maysville road, he declared, had "no connection with any established system of improvements; it is exclusively within the limits of a State, starting at a point on the Ohio river and running out sixty miles to an interior town, and even as far as the State is interested conferring partial instead of general advantages." He pointed also to the drain on the treasury entailed by lavish expenditures for internal improvements, and suggested that Congress might better reduce the revenue if it could spare the funds, or use its surplus to pay off the national debt.

The Maysville veto was the subject of acrimonious debate in Congress and in the country at large, but the veto was sustained, and Jackson clung tenaciously to the position he had taken. Other vetoes and pocket vetoes of similar measures soon followed. It should not be assumed, however, that Jackson's vetoes rang the death-knell for all national aid to improvements in transportation. The President showed no disposition to interrupt work on the National Road, he signed many bills for federal assistance to road-building in the territories, and he offered no very effective opposition to federal grants in aid of river and harbor improvement. But the cessation of appropriations for the construction of roads and canals within and among the several states was actually of even greater significance than Jackson knew. Before his administration ended canals and turnpikes were giving place to railroads, and the enormous capacity of this new variety of internal improvements for absorbing federal funds was not hard to see. Jackson's policy, however, set a strong precedent against such expenditures, and for many years the railroads were unable to induce Congress to aid them, even by grants of land.

Scarcely less important than the problem of internal improvements was the enduring problem of the public lands.[1] Flushed with the victories they had won by the Land Law of 1820, western representatives were soon demanding an even further liberalization of the public-land policy. Many of them felt particularly aggrieved that the government insisted on collecting a minimum of $1.25 for each acre of the land it sold, regardless of quality. The best lands in a newly opened plot were quickly sold, although sometimes to speculators who held them for a rise in value, rather than to actual settlers. But the poorer lands were apt to remain vacant for many years. Why not reduce the price of these left-over lands by some such sum as

The public lands

[1] R. G. Wellington, *The Political and Sectional Influence of the Public Lands, 1828–1842* (1914), shows the great extent to which sectional interests and jealousies affected the course of events. Thomas Hart Benton, *Thirty Years' View; or, A History of the Working of the American Government, 1820–1850* (2 vols., 1854–56), presents the western view on the land question, and nearly every other.

twenty-five cents a year? Any lands still untaken after four or five years might then be donated outright, either to actual settlers, or to the states in which they were located. Some extremists went even further, and urged that all the public lands be turned over to the states in which they lay, for then, as they well knew, the terms available to settlers would lack nothing in liberality.

Another western demand was for a generous right of pre-emption. With increasing frequency pioneers, either because they lacked the means

Pre-emption to pay for lands or because they were unwilling to await the slow process of extinguishing Indian titles and completing surveys, rushed far out into the West and selected for themselves the best lands they could find. Such foresight and energy the West was eager to reward, and it resented the attempts of speculators and others to acquire for little or nothing the improvements that a "squatter" had made on his "claim." The long-continued failure of Congress to recognize the right of pre-emption, or as it was more frequently called in the West, "squatters' rights," led to the formation in many frontier communities of "claims clubs," or "claims associations." Groups of settlers in a given community banded themselves together, elected a secretary or other official with whom they listed their claim, and, when land sales began, prevented by force the purchase of a member's land by anyone other than the squatter who lived upon it.

The continued growth of manufactures in the Northeast made the representatives of that section extremely wary about granting to the

The Foot Resolution West the easy land terms it desired. Ever more favorable terms for western lands tended unmistakably to drain off the surplus population of the East into the West. Also, laborers could, and did, demand higher wages than they could ever have hoped to receive had they not had the alternative of a move to the West with which to threaten their employers. Some Easterners were ready even to see the sales of public lands in the West discontinued entirely. One such was Senator Samuel Augustus Foot of Connecticut, who proposed in a famous resolution "That the Committee on Public Lands be instructed to inquire into the expediency of limiting for a certain period the sales of the public lands to such lands only as have heretofore been offered for sale, and are subject to entry at the minimum price. And also, whether the office of Surveyor General may not be abolished without detriment to the public interest." In other words, had the time not come when the growth of the West must be checked, "for who would remove to a new country if it were not to get new lands?"

Inevitably politicians made an effort to reconcile the opposing interests of the Northeast and the West on the land question. Henry Clay,

the "Great Compromiser," urged what he called "distribution" as the
ideal solution, and fitted the idea into his now somewhat
complicated American system. Let one-tenth of the proceeds   "Distribu-
from the sales of public lands be given to the states in which   tion"
the lands lay, and let the other nine-tenths be distributed among all the
states in accordance with the congressional ratio. This scheme, however,
did not please the President, who for the moment preferred, in common
with many other Westerners, that the public lands should "cease as soon
as practicable to be a source of revenue," and should be sold to actual
settlers at a price barely sufficient to reimburse the United States for the
cost of acquiring them from the Indians and conducting the necessary
surveys. Nor did it please the South, for the distribution of land revenue
might conceivably create a "vacuum in the treasury," which could be
filled only by an increased revenue from the tariff. Southerners would
have preferred to leave the land revenues intact, while cutting down on
tariff receipts.

Tariff reductions, however, were anathema to the Northeast, which
found in the easy land terms still another justification for protective
duties. For cheap lands, the manufacturers claimed, drew off their labor
supply to the West, and forced employers to pay far higher wages than
would otherwise have been necessary. A protective tariff was essential,
not only to protect American manufacturers from European competition,
but also to protect eastern industry against the lure of the West. Since
most of the Northwest, still impressed by Clay's arguments, voted consistently for high duties on imports, the South found itself, whenever the
tariff question was broached, in a hopeless minority. However much it
might suffer from the tariff, it saw little prospect of relief as long as the
Northeast and Northwest stood solidly together. There was, of course,
one long chance. The West feared northeastern views on the public-
lands question scarcely less than the South feared them on the tariff. If
the South stood by the West on the land question, might not the West be
persuaded to let the South have its way on the tariff?

South Carolina of all the southern states felt most violently on the
tariff question. The prosperity of the state, and of Charleston, its principal city, had steadily declined. The real reasons for this
were that the lands of the older South could not compete in   South
richness with the newly opened lands of the Southwest, and   Carolina's
that New Orleans rather than Charleston was the natural   grievances
center for western trade. But it was difficult to face these unpleasant
facts, and South Carolinians very generally blamed the tariff for all their
troubles. That they were hurt by the tariff, there could be small doubt,
but that one section had deliberately bought prosperity for itself at the

price of adversity for another, as they contended, would be difficult to prove.

Smarting under the injustices they suffered, whether real or fancied, southern extremists flirted dangerously with the doctrine of secession, which, in spite of Marshall's decisions, had been kept alive. The Constitution, they contended, provided merely for a partnership of sovereign and independent states, joined together merely to accomplish certain specified ends; and therefore if any state chose for any reason to withdraw at any time from the partnership, it had full power to do so. There was nothing necessarily sectional about the doctrine of secession, for many New England Federalists had once regarded it as their last defense against the tyranny of Jeffersonian democracy. The Hartford Convention, held during the War of 1812, had been restrained with difficulty from asserting secessionist views. Now the southern leaders, because their states were destined apparently to remain forever an oppressed minority section, boldly reasserted the right of a state to secede. Some of them, South Carolinians in particular, held that the time had about come when arguments should give way to deeds, and the oppressed states should leave the Union.

To the most distinguished statesman of the Old South, John C. Calhoun (1782–1850),[1] himself a South Carolinian, the disruption of the

John C. Calhoun

Union which secessionists had in mind was a disaster that must somehow be avoided. Calhoun had always been an ardent nationalist; more than that, his political career had been staged primarily in the national arena. Almost at the top of the ladder, he was now Vice-President with a strong title to the "succession." If South Carolina should leave the Union, not only the nation but also the career of John C. Calhoun would be ruined. Thus, while Calhoun felt obliged to agree with his constituents that a state had the constitutional right to secede, he was eager above all else to prevent any state, particularly his own state, from exercising that right.

Calhoun's answer to the advocates of secession was the doctrine of nullification.[2] To get what they wanted, he said, the southern states had

The doctrine of nullification

no need to secede from the Union. Just as they had originally, acting individually and separately through conventions especially called to ratify or reject the Constitution, conferred certain powers on the federal government, so in the same fashion each state might at any later time through conventions

---

[1] C. M. Wiltse, *John C. Calhoun, Nationalist, 1782–1828* (1944); Gaillard Hunt, *John C. Calhoun* (1908); W. M. Meigs, *The Life of John Caldwell Calhoun* (2 vols., 1917).

[2] Among the many illuminating studies of nullification the following merit special citation: E. P. Powell, *Nullification and Secession in the United States* (1897); D. F. Houston, *Critical Study of Nullification in South Carolina* (1896); and C. S. Boucher, *The Nullification Controversy in South Carolina* (1916).

of the same type decide whether and to what extent the federal government had exceeded the authority conferred upon it. Should such a convention find the federal government guilty of an unconstitutional act "so deliberate, palpable, and dangerous, as to justify the interposition of the State to protect its rights," it might declare the act "null and void within the limits of the State."

Calhoun's doctrine was stated as early as 1828 in an anonymous document known as the "South Carolina Exposition," and later more elaborately in an essay entitled *A Disquisition on Government.* It was readily accepted throughout the South, but the support, or at least the tolerance, of a majority of the states must be obtained if nullification was to be anything more than an empty gesture or a prelude to secession. Nothing, certainly, was to be hoped from the industrial Northeast, to which the advantages of a strong central government were increasingly obvious. But the West, although it in part favored a protective tariff, had a well-developed grievance against the Northeast because some Northeasterners were trying to choke off the growth of the West by limiting, or even abolishing, the sales of public lands. Could not the West be won over to a toleration of the nullification idea? Possibly, even, the West might find in nullification a useful weapon in case the Northeast went too far in its efforts to restrain western growth. During the debate on the Foot resolution, which suggested that no further surveys of public lands be undertaken, Senator Robert Y. Hayne of South Carolina seized the opportunity to set forth to the irritated Westerners what advantages the doctrine of nullification might hold for them. He was promptly answered by Daniel Webster of Massachusetts, who upheld brilliantly the supremacy of the Union. The doctrine of nullification was on trial, and the West was to be the jury.

Southern overtures to the West

Daniel Webster (1782–1852),[1] the son of a New Hampshire pioneer farmer, had surmounted many obstacles to obtain an education, and had won distinction as a lawyer no less because of the superb rhetoric in which his arguments were couched and the impassioned oratory with which they were presented than because of his able reasoning. For two terms, 1813–17, he served as a New Hampshire representative in the lower house of Congress, and devoted himself to the defense of the commercial interests with which his home city, Portsmouth, was then closely identified. In 1817 he changed his residence to Boston, and did not reappear in Congress until 1823. By this time the particularistic sentiments that had satisfied commercial

Daniel Webster

[1] H. C. Lodge, *Daniel Webster* (1883); John B. McMaster, *Daniel Webster* (1902); F. A. Ogg, *Daniel Webster* (1914).

New England began to be supplanted by sentiments of extreme nationalism that pleased the manufacturing classes. First in the House, then
after 1827 in the Senate, Webster led the friends of the nationalistic
Adams administration, and when Calhoun's doctrine of nullification was
proclaimed in the Senate, it was to Webster that all eyes turned for an
answer.

The Webster-Hayne debate was not an affair of an afternoon or an
evening, but of nearly two weeks' duration. The debate on the Foot
resolution began on January 13, with Benton of Missouri

**The Webster-
Hayne debate** doing most of the talking. On January 19 Hayne made his
first address, and from that time until the end of the month
either Hayne or Webster had the floor the greater share of the time.
Calhoun, as Vice-President and presiding officer of the Senate, could
take no part in the debate, but he heard his views adequately, even admirably, set forth by Hayne. Webster's oratory rose to new heights;
indeed, his orations on this occasion are generally conceded to be the
greatest ever delivered in an American forum. He attacked point blank
the theory that the states were sovereign under the Constitution, or were
ever meant to be. The Constitution, he maintained, was created primarily to impose certain restrictions on state sovereignty, and the states
were left sovereign only "so far as their sovereignty is not affected by the
supreme law." The Supreme Court, he held, was the only proper arbiter
as to what was, and what was not, constitutional. Further, he warned
the South that the nation could never admit that its laws might constitutionally be defied by a state, and that nullification, if attempted,
could lead only to a fratricidal war or the disruption of the Union. Finally, in a magnificent peroration, he appealed to the patriotism of the
whole American people in support of "Liberty *and* Union, now and forever, one and inseparable."

The South had spoken through Hayne, the Northeast through Webster. What would be the verdict of the West? The verdict soon came,
and with unmistakable clarity, from no less person than the President
himself. An anniversary dinner was set for Jefferson's birthday, April 13,
1830, which all the leading Democrats were to attend. The nullificationists, with curious lack of insight, believed that the President was with
them, and they arranged a program filled with nullification sentiments
that they expected him in some fashion to approve. Well advised as to
their plans, and fully decided as to what part he would play, the President
rose at an opportune moment, and with his eyes on Calhoun proposed a
toast:

"Our Federal Union — it must be preserved!"

Calhoun countered skillfully:

"The Union — next to our liberty, the most dear!"

But the President's speech had made it clear that his states'-rights views went to no such lengths as those of Calhoun and Hayne. Nor could the attitude of the West, which the President could be depended upon to reflect with rare accuracy, be longer open to doubt. The South must stand alone in its support of nullification; the North and the West would stand together against it.

This alliance was accomplished, however, only at the expense of a rift in the Democratic Party. The truce between the followers of Jackson and the followers of Calhoun was now at an end. Taking advantage of a squabble among the Cabinet wives over the social recognition to be accorded the former Peggy O'Neill, dashing daughter of a Washington tavernkeeper, but now the wife of John H. Eaton, Secretary of War, Jackson persuaded his entire Cabinet to resign, and when their successors were appointed the Calhoun element in the party was ignored. An open rupture with Calhoun himself was precipitated when the President learned that years before Calhoun, while a member of Monroe's Cabinet, had favored the public censure of Jackson for his course in Florida. Thereafter it was generally understood that Van Buren, not Calhoun, would receive the President's support for the succession when Jackson's term of office came to a close.

Jackson's break with Calhoun

The final test of the doctrine of nullification was yet to come. In December, 1831, Jackson urged Congress, in view of the rapid reduction of the national debt that the heavy revenues had made possible, to undertake a revision of the tariff. The South insisted upon radically lower duties, but the Northeast and the Northwest, standing together under the leadership of John Quincy Adams, now a member of the House, and Henry Clay, now a member of the Senate, achieved in July, 1832, another victory for protection. The response of South Carolina to this challenge was all that Calhoun could have asked. Nullification became the issue upon which a legislature was chosen in the fall of 1832, and, upon the recommendation of the governor, the new legislature promptly called a convention to deal with the emergency that confronted the state. Delegates were chosen, the convention met, and on November 19, 1832, by a vote of 136 to 26, it declared the tariffs of 1828 and of 1832 "null, void, and no law, nor binding upon this State, its officers, or citizens." Furthermore, federal officers were forbidden to collect customs in South Carolina after February 1, 1833, and any federal action designed to coerce the state into obedience of the nullified laws was declared to be not only null and void, but also "inconsistent with the longer continuance of

Nullification put to the test

South Carolina in the Union." Calhoun now resigned as Vice-President, was promptly chosen to the Senate, and made ready to defend the course of action that he had led his state to pursue.

Jackson did not hesitate to take up the gauntlet that the nullificationists had thrown down. He reinforced the garrisons in Charleston Harbor, issued a proclamation denouncing nullification, asked, and obtained, from Congress authority to use force, if necessary, in the collection of the duties. But he also urged the South Carolinians to reconsider their action, and in the interest of harmony he encouraged his friends in Congress to seek a downward revision of the tariff. Finally, with no less person than Henry Clay leading the way, a compromise tariff bill was rushed through Congress early in 1833. This measure, which even Calhoun supported, somewhat enlarged the free list, and provided for the gradual reduction of such duties as remained until at the end of nine years no rate should exceed twenty per cent. A peaceful solution was now in sight, for with the obnoxious tariff of 1832 repealed, the nullification ordinance could be withdrawn. On March 11, 1833, this action was taken.

The Tariff of 1833

Both sides claimed the victory. The nullificationists pointed out that their firm stand had won a concession on the tariff that could otherwise never have been obtained. The nationalists maintained that through Jackson's firm course the doctrine of the supremacy of the Union had been singularly vindicated. In a sense both contentions were correct. But it was the threat of secession and the danger of Civil War rather than the resort to nullification that had led to the passage of the Compromise Tariff; while Jackson's ardent defense of the Union was somewhat qualified by his increasingly evident desire to interpret strictly the powers conferred upon it by the Constitution.[1]

---

[1] B. M. Rich, *The Presidents and Civil Disorder* (1941), begins with the Whiskey Rebellion and carries on through. W. B. Hatcher, *Edward Livingston: Jeffersonian Republican and Jacksonian Democrat* (1940), is a scholarly biography. Dorothy G. Fowler, *The Cabinet Politician: The Postmasters-General, 1829–1909* (1943), sheds light on the problem of patronage disposal. Arthur M. Schlesinger, Jr., *The Age of Jackson* (1945), is a brilliant re-evaluation.

13

The Panic of 1837

ALMOST as spectacular as his conflict with the nullificationists was Jackson's war on the Bank of the United States. This institution, operating after 1822 under the presidency of Nicholas Biddle,[1] a wealthy and aristocratic Philadelphian, was in a flourishing condition when Jackson took office. Its cautious conservatism satisfied the eastern industrialists and silenced the criticism of many states'-rights Southerners, who on principle could not bring themselves to approve it. Its charter rights would last until 1837, and the chances that the privileges it enjoyed would be renewed for another twenty years seemed excellent. The bank, however, did not lack for critics, particularly in the West. It had unhesitatingly made use of its powerful position to restrain state banks from indulging in dubious practices, such as issuing more paper money than their resources warranted and lending freely on insufficient security. It thus won the resentment, not only of all state bankers with "wild-cat" tendencies, but also of the many disappointed customers of state banks, who were given to understand that the real reason they could not renew old loans or negotiate new ones lay in the policy of the Bank of the United States. The bank was itself a good collector, and by its numerous foreclosures had raised up an equally numerous company of enemies. There were those, too, who had begun to think that the whole banking business was essentially dishonest, and ought to be outlawed. One such was Jackson himself, who told Biddle, "I do not dislike your bank more than all banks, but ever since I read the history of the South Sea Bubble, I have been afraid of banks."

The Bank of the United States

Jackson's known hostility to the B. U. S., as it was generally called, although not much in evidence at first, was a matter of much concern to Biddle, whose peace of mind was by no means improved when the President hinted broadly that places for good Jacksonian Democrats should be found on the bank's payroll. Biddle did not hesitate to make a number of Jackson men directors

Jackson's war on the Bank

[1] *The Correspondence of Nicholas Biddle Dealing with National Affairs, 1807–1844*, edited by R. C. McGrane (1919), supplements admirably the numerous secondary accounts that deal with the bank.

of branch banks, but he was unwilling to subject the welfare of the bank more fully to the hazards of the spoils system. His nervous apprehension, however, led him to seek the favor of Congress in a way almost equally open to question. Previous to the election of Jackson, the bank had lent to congressmen only when such a course seemed warranted as a strictly business proposition; but, beginning with 1829, this policy was unmistakably relaxed. Also, it lent with similar freedom to powerful newspaper editors, and it paid a generous retainer each year to its leading attorney, Senator Daniel Webster.

Jackson's war on the bank was precipitated by the ill-advised action of Webster and Clay, who persuaded Biddle to bring forward a request for the recharter of the bank along existing lines well before the election in 1832. They were convinced — correctly, as the event proved — that Congress would pass such a bill, and they thought it shrewd politics to force upon Jackson the alternative of signing a measure he disliked, or taking the responsibility for what, in their opinion, would be an unpopular veto. Clay was early in the field as the candidate of the National Republican Party in 1832, and he felt especially confident of victory in case he could make an issue of the President's antagonism to the bank. All went substantially as the conspirators had planned. In the summer of 1832 the Senate, by a vote of 28 to 20, and the House by a vote of 109 to 79, passed the bank bill, and Jackson's veto was quickly forthcoming. The bank, he argued, was un-American because of its large number of foreign stockholders; it was undemocratic because it concentrated vast and monopolistic "power in the hands of a few men irresponsible to the people"; and it was unconstitutional because its charter was neither a "necessary nor proper" exercise of the authority delegated by the states to Congress.[1]

Jackson's message was couched in language well calculated to appeal to the patriotism and self-interest of the masses, and it showed deliberate deference to the states'-rights prejudices of the South. It may not have shown a keen understanding of banking and finance, but it was far shrewder politics than the more elaborate schemes of Webster and Clay. The issue in the election became for the ordinary voter not so much the success or failure of the bank, as Clay had intended, but rather the success or failure of Andrew Jackson, champion of the common man. Jackson and his advisers had grasped the fact, far more clearly than their opponents, that elections were won by the votes of the people rather than by the good opinion of thoughtful men. Issues to be effective must be dramatized and simplified.

A new charter vetoed

[1] Ralph C. H. Catterall, *The Second Bank of the United States* (1903), recounts the history of the Bank in detail.

In this campaign, for the first time in American history, an organized third party put in its appearance. The Anti-Masonic Party, as it was called, originated in western New York, a region still distinctly frontier in character. Secret societies in this demo- **Anti-Masonry** cratic community were regarded with much disfavor, partly, no doubt, because only a few could afford membership in such organizations, and partly because of the fantastic exaggerations that gained currency with regard to the oaths sworn and the secrets kept. In 1826 one William Morgan, a citizen of Batavia, New York, and a former Mason, published a pamphlet in which he claimed to have revealed the secrets of Masonry. When, shortly afterwards, he disappeared under conditions that suggested foul play, the Masons were held responsible and a furor of protest arose against the Masonic fraternity in particular and, for good measure, all other secret societies also. The contagion spread rapidly throughout central and western New York, across the borders into Pennsylvania and Vermont, as far east as Massachusetts and as far west as Ohio.

For a time Anti-Masonry was a social upheaval rather than a political movement, but shrewd anti-Jackson politicians — such men as Thurlow Weed and William H. Seward in New York, and Thaddeus Stevens in Pennsylvania — soon found ways to make Anti-Masonry serve their purposes. The President himself was a Mason, and it was easy to find fault with state and local administrations that were dominated by Masons. They appealed to religious prejudice, and saw in even the small number of Catholic immigrants who were coming to the United States (most of whom voted the Democratic ticket) a menace to the liberties of the Republic. Finally, they widened their program to include practically all of Henry Clay's American System. With the election of 1832 in sight the Anti-Masonic leaders took the unprecedented step of calling a national nominating convention to select their candidate for the Presidency, and in September, 1831, their convention, meeting at Baltimore, chose William Wirt of Virginia to lead them, and Amos Ellmaker of Pennsylvania for second place. Wirt's friendship and admiration for Clay were well known, and it was the Anti-Masonic hope that all anti-Jackson men would support him.[1]

But the Anti-Masonic movement failed completely to divert attention from the main contest, which was between the National Republicans, with Clay as their candidate, and the Democrats, with Jackson as theirs. Both parties, however, followed an Anti- **Election of** Masonic precedent in calling together national nominating **1832** conventions for the selection of presidential and vice-presidential candi-

---

[1] Charles McCarthy, *The Antimasonic Party: A Study of Political Antimasonry in the United States, 1827–1840* (1903); S. R. Gammon, *The Presidential Campaign of 1832* (1922).

dates. Such a direct consultation of the popular will was quite in line
with the current conception of democracy, and neither party dare overlook the opportunity of thus cultivating the favor of "King Numbers."
In December, 1831, the National Republicans, also meeting at Baltimore, nominated Clay for President, and John Sergeant of Pennsylvania
for Vice-President; and in May, 1832, the Democrats, at the same place,
endorsed the "repeated nominations" which Jackson had received "in
various parts of the Union," and chose Martin Van Buren of New York
as their candidate for Vice-President. The nomination of Van Buren was
in strict accordance with Jackson's desires, but was so lacking in popular
appeal that in the hope of giving a contrary impression, a rule was devised whereby a candidate to be nominated must receive "two-thirds of
the whole number of votes in the convention." Van Buren, thanks to the
persuasive efforts of the President's friends, received well over this number, and for a hundred years the "two-thirds rule" remained the practice
of Democratic national conventions.

The election resulted in an overwhelming victory for Jackson. In
New York, Ohio, and elsewhere the National Republicans and the Anti-
Masons supported the same electoral tickets, and in general
Jackson's
victory
the Wirt candidacy was used to promote Clay's chances of
victory. Nevertheless, in the popular vote Jackson triumphed by 687,502 to 530,189 for Clay and Wirt combined, while in the
electoral college the vote was 219 for Jackson to 49 for Clay. Only half
the states of New England stood by Clay; Vermont cast her seven votes
for Wirt, while Maine and New Hampshire gave comfortable majorities
for Jackson. In South Carolina, where the legislature still chose presidential electors, the nullificationists retained their majority, and gave
the eleven votes of the state to John Floyd of Virginia. Jackson's re-
election was essentially an endorsement of the popular principles of government for which he stood. The Bank issue, quite as Biddle and Clay
had intended, received much attention during the campaign, but in
general the people voted for or against Jackson rather than for or against
the Bank of the United States. It is difficult to escape the conclusion
that Jackson would have won by about the same majority had he signed
the Bank bill instead of vetoing it.

It was natural, however, that the President should interpret his
re-election as a mandate against the recharter of the Bank. But he was
far too impatient to await its orderly demise, and deter-
The removal
of deposits
mined to cripple it at once by withdrawing from its possession the deposits of the United States government, some
ten or twelve million dollars. Power to withdraw the deposits was
vested, however, not in the President, but in the Secretary of the Treas-

ury, who was authorized to take such action only in the event that he considered the Bank an unsafe place for the government's funds. To get his way Jackson found it necessary to promote one Secretary of the Treasury to be Secretary of State, and to remove his successor outright. But the next Secretary of the Treasury, Roger B. Taney of Maryland, was a states'-rights Jeffersonian Democrat of the old school who believed the bank unconstitutional, and did not hesitate to issue the order which Jackson desired.[1] Thereafter the United States drew upon its deposits in the bank to meet its obligations, but placed all newly collected tax money in selected state banks — "pet banks," as they were called — whose importance increased as that of the Bank of the United States declined.

Jackson's war on the bank ushered in a period of great financial uncertainty. In the Northeast a money famine occurred, for the number of pet banks located in the agricultural South and West was proportionately too large, and in the industrial Northeast much too small. But the West, which was already on the verge of a boom, seemingly prospered as never before. Here the declining power of the Bank of the United States emboldened state bankers of wildcat tendencies to indulge their long-suppressed desires to issue more currency and to extend their loans. Eastern state bankers were for the most part conservative, and refused to expand their business more than their resources warranted, but the number of wildcatters in the West steadily increased. Furthermore, a whole host of new state banks put in their appearance. What was happening can best be set forth as follows:

State banking methods

STATE BANKING IN THE UNITED STATES

Year	Number of Banks	Capital*	Circulation*	Loans*
1829	329	110.2	48.2	137.0
1834	506	200.0	94.8	324.1
1836	718	251.9	140.3	457.5
1837	788	290.8	149.2	525.1

* In millions of dollars.

So marked an inflation of money and credit was certain to result in some form of speculation, and with the chief incidence of inflation in the West this meant primarily speculation in land. Purchases of government land far outran any reasonable demand, and the same plots were often sold and resold several times without once being held by anyone who expected to till them. Government sales of public lands rose from four million acres in 1834 to fifteen millions in 1835, and to twenty mil-

---

[1] Taney was later chosen by Jackson to succeed Marshall as Chief Justice. See C. B. Swisher, *Roger B. Taney* (1936); C. W. Smith, Jr., *Roger B. Taney: Jacksonian Jurist* (1936).

lion in 1836. It was during this period that the phrase "doing a land-office business" entered the American vernacular. The changed banking habits of the United States government added unneeded fuel to the flames. Receipts from the public lands rose from $4,857,000 in 1834 to $24,877,000 in 1836, and most of this money was deposited promptly in pet banks. These institutions then lent the money out again, all too frequently to speculators who bought more land, only to increase thereby the surplus in the treasury, which must make still more deposits in the pet banks, to be lent out again for speculation, and so on in a vicious circle.

The unhealthiness of this situation was not lost on Jackson, who finally decided that the practice of accepting bank notes in payment for public lands must stop. Jackson's decision was embodied in the famous "Specie Circular," which his Secretary of the Treasury issued in July, 1836, to take effect after, rather than before, the election of 1836. From that time forward all payments to the United States for public lands must be made in gold or silver. Since the state banks had little or no hard money available, the "Specie Circular" meant an end to the speculation, and, as matters turned out, a beginning of depression. Congressmen railed violently at the President's policy, and there were many who proved themselves poor prophets by predicting that it would never go into effect.

The Specie Circular

Meantime the treasury was seriously embarrassed by its mounting receipts. In 1835 the last dollar of the public debt was paid off, and the treasury needed only enough money to pay current expenses. At the peak of the speculation, however, the revenues from the public lands were alone sufficient to meet the entire cost of the national government, but by that time the tariff was also bringing in startlingly large sums. The Compromise Tariff of 1833, because it provided for a gradual scaling-down of rates, was expected to produce less revenue as time went on rather than more; but the exact reverse proved to be true. The huge speculative profits that were being made in western lands, and the stimulating effects of inflation on business generally, fostered a spirit of extravagance that was reflected in the heavy purchases of foreign goods. Tariff receipts which had stood at only about sixteen millions in 1834 were half again as large by 1836, and, like the receipts from the public lands, sufficient in themselves to pay the full costs of the national government.[1]

Various projects were brought forward to rid the treasury of its surplus revenue. Most debated was Clay's plan for the distribution of the proceeds of the sales of public lands among all the states, but the Presi-

[1] A. M. Sakolski, *The Great American Land Bubble* (1932); M. S. Wildman, *Money Inflation in the United States: A Study in Social Pathology* (1905).

dent's known antagonism to such a measure prevented its adoption.
Others took seriously a suggestion that Jackson himself had
once made, and urged that all the surplus funds of the govern-   Distribution
ment, regardless of their origin, should be distributed among   of the
the states; but again the President objected, not because   surplus
he opposed such a course on principle, but because he questioned whether
Congress had the necessary authority under the Constitution to take
such action.   Finally, to satisfy the President, it was agreed that the
money should be distributed among the states as a loan rather than as a
gift, and in June, 1836, such a bill became law.   According to this act,
whatever money in excess of five million dollars was in the treasury on
January 1, 1837, was to be apportioned among the states in accordance
with their representation in the electoral college, and paid over to them
during the year in four quarterly installments.

The national government might far better have held on to its funds.
Already many of the states, particularly the new states in the West, had
embarked upon extensive programs of internal improvement, and had
borrowed heavily for the purpose, frequently from foreign investors who
were soon to learn to their sorrow that the credit of the United States
and of the various American states were two different things.   Dazzled
by the prospect of receiving generous subsidies from the national government, some states redoubled their extravagance; by 1837 the total state
indebtedness had reached $170,000,000, for the times a prodigious sum.[1]

English exporters, who noted as early as 1836 that the balance of trade
was running strongly against the United States, were among the first
to foresee a collapse of American prosperity.   As a result
of their fears, the Bank of England raised its discount rates,   Panic of 1837
and English merchants refused new credits to American
customers.   Thereupon American importers, since the foreign balance
could be met only in hard money, deluged their bankers with requests
for specie, requests that could not possibly be met in full, for American
specie in great quantities had already been drained out of the country.
By this time speculators in land, whose efforts to secure the withdrawal
of the Specie Circular had proved unavailing, were also frantically demanding gold from the hard-pressed bankers.   To make matters still
worse, the pet banks, supposedly the strongest in the country, were given
a body blow by the Distribution Act, which required them to return the
surplus government funds they held on deposit.   Payment of the first
installment, January 1, 1837, caused them great embarrassment, and the
second, on April 1 following, brought almost immediate disaster.   Bank
failures now came thick and fast, and in May, 1837, every bank in the

[1] E. G. Bourne, *The History of the Surplus Revenue of 1837* (1885).

United States suspended specie payment. Notes of the failed or failing banks became virtually worthless, and the public took enormous losses. Meantime, many English exporters, unable to collect on the debts owed them by Americans, had also been forced into bankruptcy. Their failure brought down, in turn, the English merchants and manufacturers who furnished goods for the American market. Soon both England and the United States were plunged into the depths of a thoroughgoing economic depression.[1]

It would not be fair to say that Jackson's war on the Bank of the United States was wholly responsible for the panic of 1837. Doubtless the West would have developed with dangerous rapidity under any circumstances; internal improvements, particularly the building of canals, were already an obsession when the "war" began; over-expansion of cotton planting in the South and of manufacturing in the Northeast could hardly have been forestalled. But Jackson's crude handling of public finance certainly stimulated the boom, and accentuated the crash. Fortunately for his popularity, he left office a few weeks before the panic broke. As for the Bank of the United States, it secured a charter from the state of Pennsylvania, and continued in operation until 1841, when it failed.

Causes of the panic

Jackson's administration was primarily concerned with domestic affairs, but in the handling of American foreign relations it witnessed an abrupt break with the past. The men whom Jackson appointed to office were little schooled in the niceties of European diplomacy, and their "shirt-sleeve" methods proved most exasperating to Europeans. Nevertheless, the results were usually gratifying. Determined to end once and for all British discriminations against American trade in the West Indies, Jackson asked and received from Congress authority to admit British ships bound from the West Indies to American ports, on whatever terms West Indian ports were open to American ships. As a result of this direct move, an agreement was soon reached that permitted the same freedom of trade between the United States and the British West Indies that existed between the United States and Great Britain.[2] Another problem that confronted Jackson was the non-payment by France of the "spoliation claims," long demanded in consideration of the losses which Napoleon, in his vain effort to enforce the Continental System, had inflicted upon American shipping. Under strong pressure from Jackson a settlement was agreed upon in July, 1831, whereby the United States was to be paid twenty-

"Shirt-sleeve diplomacy"

---

[1] R. C. McGrane, *The Panic of 1837* (1924), treats of the depression and its causes with commendable directness and brevity.

[2] F. L. Benns, *The American Struggle for the British West India Carrying Trade, 1815–1830* (1923).

three and one-half million francs in six equal installments, beginning in February, 1833. But the French Chamber of Deputies refused to appropriate the funds, and Jackson denounced in brutally plain words this violation of a solemn agreement. For a time feeling between the two countries was at white heat, but at length the Chamber was induced to vote the necessary sums on condition that the President would apologize for his blunt threats. When Jackson said that he had meant no insult, the money was finally paid over.[1]

Jackson also was confronted with the difficult task of maintaining peaceful relations with Mexico while the independent state of Texas was in process of formation. In Spanish times Moses Austin, a Texas resident of Missouri, sought and obtained permission to lead a group of colonists to Texas, and a few years later his son, Stephen F. Austin, won from the new revolutionary government of Mexico confirmation of the privileges the Spanish had extended to his father. A nucleus of settlement from the United States speedily appeared at San Felipe de Austin, and in 1824 a general colonization law welcomed other American settlers in. By 1830 about twenty thousand former citizens of the United States, owners of perhaps a thousand Negro slaves, were residents of Texas.[2]

Inevitably trouble developed between the Texans and their Mexican overlords. The former were constantly irritated by the fact that Texas was not a separate and self-governing state of Mexico, but was joined to the neighboring state of Coahuila on terms that ensured to the native Mexicans a permanent majority in the state legislature. They were skeptical, too, of the semi-feudal land titles they had received; they were not all good Catholics, as the law presumed them to be; and they longed sentimentally to be within the boundaries of the United States. Both before and after Jackson became President the American government tried repeatedly to purchase Texas, but the Mexicans, both officially and unofficially, resented warmly all such suggestions. In 1830 further immigration into Texas was prohibited and the importation of Negro slaves was forbidden. Practically prohibitive duties were placed on imports from the United States, and Mexican officials supported by Mexican soldiers were sent to the border to enforce the regulations.

Almost unavoidably the Texans were soon involved in revolutionary activities. At first they took sides with a Mexican rebel, Santa Anna, but when he triumphed, they found themselves no better off than they had been before. Finally, they decided to follow the well-known precedents of the American Revolution, and in March, 1836, declared their inde-

[1] G. A. King, *The French Spoliation Claims* (1912).
[2] E. C. Barker, *The Life of Stephen F. Austin, Founder of Texas, 1793–1836* (1925).

pendence of Mexico. By this time war had already begun, and Santa Anna was sweeping northward with so many troops at his command that the Texans should have been easily overwhelmed. But at San Jacinto, on April 21, 1836, the Mexicans were disastrously defeated by a Texas army under the command of General Sam Houston, and from this time forward Mexican authority in Texas was at an end.

As long as the Texas revolution was in progress, the government of the United States preserved an air of neutrality, although it made little effort to restrain the American public from giving aid and comfort to the Texans. With Texas as an independent republic, however, Jackson would gladly have favored annexation, had it only been feasible politically. But many Northerners were by this time on record against the acquisition of any new territory open to slavery, while the Mexican government threatened war in case annexation should be attempted. Under the circumstances the Jackson administration did as little about Texas as possible; not until the day before Jackson left office was the Republic of Texas so much as recognized by the United States.

The election of 1836 found the opposition to Jackson strong, but divided. The National Republicans, led by Henry Clay, included within their membership the "better classes" of the Northeast, most of whom were interested, directly or indirectly, in manufactures, and therefore in favor of a protective tariff. They deplored also Jackson's war on the Bank, and they welcomed cordially the support of such Westerners as were offended by his Maysville veto. After their devastating defeat in 1832 the Anti-Masons very generally went over to the National Republicans. This accretion was a matter of great importance, for it brought to the party an enthusiastic rural following, and an atmosphere of democracy that it otherwise would have lacked. Southerners who opposed Jackson still thought of themselves as Democrats, but they could have little sympathy with National Republicanism as long as its cardinal tenets were a national bank, a protective tariff, and a national program of internal improvements. Lacking all other bonds of unity, anti-Jackson men could at least agree in their denunciation of the "Tory" policy of vesting too much authority in the President, whom they sometimes characterized as "King Andrew I." It became the fashion in some circles for the opponents of Jackson to speak of themselves as "Whigs."

The weakness of the Whigs lay in their lack of cohesion. They did not dare to have a national convention, for their leaders doubted whether they could agree either on candidates or platform. To oppose Martin Van Buren, whom Jackson forced the Democrats to nominate as his successor, the Whigs decided that there should be as many candidates as the

various sections might choose to support. The election of 1836 was thus
a kind of free-for-all. Tennessee presented a life-long Democrat, Judge
Hugh L. White; Massachusetts nominated Daniel Webster; a Pennsylvania state convention presented William Henry Harrison; and South
Carolina, where the legislature still chose electors, cast her vote for
Willie P. Mangum. But in the fall of 1836 the country was still prosperous, and all four candidates were not enough to defeat Van Buren, who
received 170 electoral votes to 73 for Harrison, 26 for White, 14 for Webster, and 11 for Mangum. The selection of the Vice-President, for the
first and only time in the history of the United States, went to the Senate,
which chose Richard M. Johnson of Kentucky, the Van Buren candidate.
Jacksonian Democracy had triumphed, but the margin of victory was
uncomfortably narrow.

Martin Van Buren (1782–1862),[1] to whose lot fell the task of guiding
the United States government through the period of depression, was by
no means lacking in political experience. He was of Dutch
descent, but hardly of the Hudson Valley aristocracy, for   **Martin Van**
his father was only a poor farmer and tavernkeeper of   **Buren**
Kinderhook, New York. Young Van Buren's formal education was
limited, but in spite of this handicap he won success both in the law and
in politics. Unusually adroit in his dealings with men, he was the recognized leader of a little group known as the "Albany Regency," which
directed the policies of the Democratic Party in New York. By 1828, the
year Jackson was elected to the Presidency, Van Buren had achieved the
governorship, but he resigned to enter Jackson's Cabinet as Secretary
of State. He was far more conciliatory than his chief in his personal
relationships, but he lacked popular appeal, and it was only because of
the President's favoritism that the "Little Magician" won the succession.

Van Buren had barely taken office when the panic of 1837 broke upon
the country. That this was a political as well as an economic calamity he
was too shrewd a politician not to note, but it is doubtful
whether any President of the period would have conceived   **The independ-**
it to be his duty, as both Hoover and Roosevelt held it to be   **ent treasury**
theirs a century later, to take the lead in restoring prosperity. The depression was an affliction of the business world, and business would have
to work out its own salvation. Van Buren did feel obliged, however, to
try to put the government on a sound financial basis, and with this in
mind he called a special session of Congress for September, 1837. He

[1] *The Autobiography of Martin Van Buren*, edited by John C. Fitzpatrick (1920), is a
document of great value, although it was never completed. The standard biography of
Van Buren is E. M. Shepard, *Martin Van Buren* (1888). See also Holmes Alexander, *The
American Talleyrand: The Career and Contemporaries of Martin Van Buren* (1935).

urged first that the law calling for the distribution of the surplus be repealed, and in this Congress promptly followed him. But his most cherished plan, the establishment of an independent treasury, was violently opposed, and its adoption long delayed. Van Buren recommended that for the future the United States Treasury should have no dealings whatever with banks, whether national or state. Strong vaults, or subtreasuries, should be constructed in the various cities and placed in charge of government officials, who should receive and disperse government funds on a strictly specie basis. Thus the government would run no risk of losing its money by depositing it in banks, nor would it contribute indirectly and unintentionally to such an overexpansion of bank credit as had preceded the panic of 1837.[1] This measure gave the Whigs something concrete to talk against, whatever their financial views, and it was not until 1840 that the advocates of the sub-treasury succeeded in obtaining the required majorities in both houses of Congress. The sub-treasury debate served also to emphasize the existence within the Democratic Party of two diametrically opposed factions, the "Loco-Focos," who particularly in New York were noisily opposed to banks and rejoiced to see the United States sever all connections with banking institutions, and the more conservative Democrats who resented Jackson's ignorance of finance, and believed banks of some kind to be a necessity.

With the national government completely divorced from the banking business, it became necessary for the states and private individuals to

State banking methods

work out a banking system that would meet the needs of the country. Several western states experimented with state-owned banks, patterned after the bank of the United States, but with a few exceptions these banks soon met disaster. Better results were obtained by instituting reforms in the existing banking system. In New England, for example, a kind of clearing house was devised which made possible the redemption in Boston at par of notes issued by sound country banks. In New York state-chartered banks were obliged to contribute a certain percentage of their incomes to a common safety fund, the purpose of which was to ensure that all bank notes should be redeemed at par. More important still was the adoption in the same state of the principle of "free banking"; that is, the enactment of a state banking law under the terms of which any individual or group was "free" to start a bank so long as the stipulations of the law were met. This eliminated the chance for political jobbery, by means

[1] David Kinley, *The Independent Treasury of the United States and Its Relations to the Banks of the Country* (1910). A short account of the money and banking situation in the United States during these years is available in Horace White, *Money and Banking, Illustrated by American History* (1895). This book has been repeatedly revised, and has gone through many editions.

of which so many unsound banks had previously been chartered. By following such precedents the various states were soon able to provide a banking system which, if not wholly satisfactory, at least enabled the country to carry on its business.[1]

Many of the states, however, were long troubled by the debts they had incurred during the boom period. Little of the money they had so freely lavished upon canals and other works of internal improvement had been raised by taxation; most of it had been borrowed on the assumption that profits from the works undertaken would ultimately pay off the debt. Also, some western and southern states, notably Louisiana, Alabama, and Mississippi, had borrowed the capital for their ill-fated state-owned banks. Overwhelmed by the depression, and utterly unable to meet their obligations by taxation or by further borrowing, several states, notably Mississippi, Louisiana, Maryland, Pennsylvania, Indiana, and Michigan, frankly repudiated their indebtedness. The blow which this action dealt to American credit abroad was long felt. Some of the defaulting states repented and paid off their obligations in whole or in part, but others remained obdurate, and their debts were never paid. Urgent pleas, emanating mainly from the solvent states, that the federal government save American credit by assuming all state debts, came to nothing.[2]

Repudiation of state debts

The reverses experienced by the states in their efforts to finance banks and internal improvements made a lasting impression upon the public mind. One after another the projects so initiated found their way into private hands or were abandoned altogether. The conviction grew that the state might better withdraw completely from the field of business, and leave the carrying-out of even such expensive enterprises as canals and railroads to private initiative. Many of the new state constitutions, so common during this period, limited closely the amount of indebtedness the state might incur. Also, general laws of incorporation, in which the privilege of limited liability for stockholders was reluctantly conceded, encouraged private corporations to take over much of the work that the states had previously felt obliged to do.

State withdrawal from business

The political effect of depression is usually adverse to the party in power, whichever it is and whatever it does. The Whig orators, led by Clay, Adams, and Webster, pointed to the hundreds of closed factories, the thousands of unemployed men, the collapse of cotton prices in the South and of land prices in the West as evidence of the mistaken policies that the Democratic Party

Attack on Van Buren

---

[1] D. R. Dewey, *State Banking before the Civil War* (1910).

[2] For details on this subject see W. A. Scott, *The Repudiation of State Debts* (1892); and R. C. McGrane, *Foreign Bondholders and American State Debts* (1935).

had pursued.   Not an opportunity was lost to discredit the unfortunate Van Buren, who was held responsible not only for his own faults, but also for those of his subordinates.   An expensive Indian war, fought to effect the removal of the Seminoles from Florida, was branded as a pro-slavery extravagance, while the President's failure to work for the annexation of Texas was cited as unmistakable proof of his anti-slavery views.   It was no surprise to anyone when the administration lost control of both houses of Congress in 1838, and the Whigs were confident of victory if they could only hold together during the campaign of 1840.

The experience of 1836 had made it obvious that a common candidate would have to be agreed upon if Van Buren's defeat were to be accomplished, so a Whig convention was called to meet at Harrisburg, Pennsylvania, in December, 1839.   Henry Clay was the outstanding Whig leader, but his political principles were too well known, so the Whigs finally nominated William Henry Harrison of Ohio (1773–1841), who owed his popularity mainly to his military service in the War of 1812, and had demonstrated in the election of 1836 that he could win support.   Harrison's long association with the West was deemed an advantage, for he could be played up as the representative of the common man, quite as Jackson had been in 1828.   The observation of a disappointed adherent of Henry Clay's, that if Harrison could only be given a pension and a barrel of hard cider he would gladly retire to a log cabin for the rest of his days, gave Whig orators the chance to feature Harrison as the "log-cabin, hard-cider candidate" of the masses against the aristocratic Van Buren.

Election of 1840

> Let Van from his coolers of silver drink wine,
> And lounge on his cushioned settee;
> Our man on his buckeye bench can recline.
> Content with hard cider is he!

For Vice-President the Whigs nominated John Tyler of Virginia, not only as an appropriate concession to the South, but also as a gesture of good-will to his close personal friend, Henry Clay, whose disappointment at being passed over in favor of Harrison was extreme.   The Whigs presented no platform, for their leaders knew full well that they could never agree upon one.   In a campaign of hokum never since surpassed, they succeeded completely in their undertaking.   Van Buren lost by an electoral vote of 234 to 60.   The popular vote, however, was surprisingly close, for Harrison received less than 150,000 majority out of over 2,400,000 votes cast.[1]

[1] A. B. Norton, *The Great Revolution of 1840* (1888), preserves much of the picturesque character of this campaign.   The troubled career of the Whig Party is entertainingly set forth in John Fiske, *Essays Historical and Literary* (2 vols., 1902), I.   See also A. C. Cole, *The Whig Party in the South* (1913); and H. R. Mueller, *The Whig Party in Pennsylvania* (1922).

The Whig leaders, particularly Webster and Clay, took it for granted that they would be called upon to guide the new administration, and all started off well enough. Harrison chose Webster to be Secretary of State, and gave most of the other places in his Cabinet to the friends of Henry Clay. Clay himself retained his seat in the Senate, and prepared to push through a Congress that the election had made overwhelmingly Whig his long-delayed American System. Unfortunately, however, the President, who was more than sixty-eight years of age at the time of his inauguration, did not long survive that event. Thousands of Whig office-seekers, bent upon replacing the "rascally Democrats" at once, thronged into the capital and gave him no peace. With his strength thus overtaxed, he failed to throw off a severe cold contracted the day of his inauguration, and a month later he was dead.

Death of Harrison

John Tyler (1790–1862)[1] was a Virginia aristocrat who had long been known for the pronounced views he held and the determination with which he held them. As a member of the Virginia state legislature, of the national House of Representatives, and finally of the United States Senate, he had gone on record repeatedly on all the important issues of the day. He was uncompromisingly opposed to a protective tariff, to a national bank, and to internal improvements at national expense; and he was equally ardent in his defense of states' rights, slavery, nullification, and expansion. He had, too, a kind of vanity in his views and a touchiness about them that made it extremely difficult for him to compromise. He retained Harrison's Cabinet, however, and was as conciliatory toward the Whig leaders as he knew how to be.

John Tyler

When Congress met in special session the last of May, 1841, Henry Clay was on hand as a member of the Senate with a series of demands that in the main satisfied the Whig majority: (1) repeal of the Sub-Treasury Act, (2) a third Bank of the United States, (3) a higher tariff, and (4) the distribution among the states of the proceeds from the sales of public lands. As these measures, one after another, came before him Tyler consulted his conscience. He agreed to the repeal of the Sub-Treasury Act, but twice vetoed a plan to establish a new Bank of the United States, and Congress refused to override his vetoes. He signed the distribution bill only after an amendment had been attached to it which stipulated that, in case the tariff duties were raised above the twenty per cent maximum set by the Tariff of 1833, distribution should cease. Then he signed a bill to raise the tariff because he believed that the treasury required the money — an act that totally nullified distribu-

[1] O. P. Chitwood, *John Tyler, Champion of the Old South* (1939), is sympathetic but impartial.

tion. The tariff of 1842, which restored duties to about the level of the act of 1832, was in reality protective in character — about the only real success that Clay achieved. Two other measures were designed primarily to alleviate the existing economic distress. One was a bankruptcy act which debtors promptly used so freely that the same Congress which enacted it also repealed it. The other was a pre-emption act, which western members succeeded in attaching to Clay's distribution bill before it became law. After its passage the "pre-emptors" of Indian lands, or lands of the United States not yet opened to settlement, were assured that, in case they were actual residents on their claims and had made slight improvements, they might, when the government offered the land for sale, buy in as much as one hundred and sixty acres at the minimum price. It was frankly admitted that this law would probably encourage those who suffered from the depression to seek their salvation in a move to the West.[1]

The West as a haven of refuge was discovered, however, long before it received this legislative blessing. During the boom period two new western states, Arkansas (1836) and Michigan (1837), were admitted to the Union, and in the next few years their population increased with great rapidity. So also did the population of all the western states where cheap lands were still available. But the most startling development occurred in the territories that were soon to become the states of Wisconsin, Iowa, and Minnesota. Here land was still to be found that government surveyors had not entered, and here squatters by the thousands took claims which for the time being cost them nothing. Here many of the unemployed found employment, and at the same time created by their efforts a new market for the goods which the older sections so much needed to sell.

Growth of the West

The conflict between Tyler and Clay wrecked all hope of Whig harmony. At Clay's behest the entire Tyler Cabinet, with the exception of Webster, resigned, and the President was formally read out of the party. Naturally the unseemly dissension at Washington had an adverse effect on the voters, and in the elections of 1842 the Whigs lost their majority in the House of Representatives, although they still controlled the Senate. Clay himself dramatically retired to private life. His farewell speech to the Senate moved many of his auditors to tears, and even won a warm handclasp from his arch-enemy, Calhoun. Everyone knew, however, that in spite of his apparent renunciation of politics he would be a candidate for the Presidency in 1844. Meanwhile, with Congress divided, Clay in retirement,

Whig dissensions

---

[1] G. M. Stephenson, *The Political History of the Public Lands from 1840 to 1862* (1917), begins about where Wellington's book leaves off.

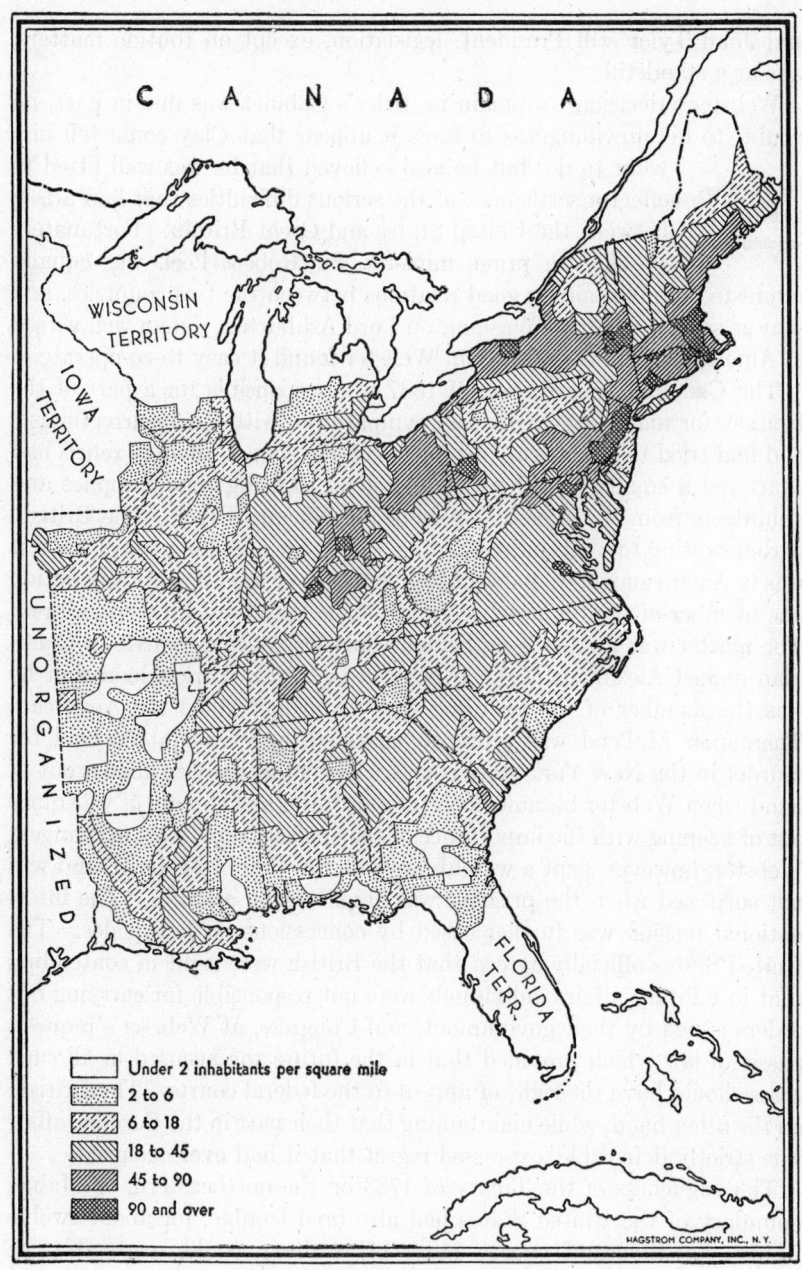

CANADA

WISCONSIN
TERRITORY

IOWA
TERRITORY

UNORGANIZED

FLORIDA
TERR.

Under 2 inhabitants per square mile
2 to 6
6 to 18
18 to 45
45 to 90
90 and over

HAGSTROM COMPANY, INC., N.Y.

DENSITY OF POPULATION IN 1840

and John Tyler still President, legislation, except on routine matters, was at a standstill.

Webster's decision to remain in Tyler's Cabinet was due in part, no doubt, to his unwillingness to have it appear that Clay could tell him what to do; but he also believed that he was well fitted to effect a settlement of the serious difficulties that had arisen between the United States and Great Britain. Fortunately the British prime minister, Sir Robert Peel, was equally interested in maintaining good relations between the two countries, and sent as special envoy to Washington Lord Ashburton, a man well versed in American matters with whom Webster found it easy to co-operate.

The Webster-Ashburton negotiations

The Canadian insurrection of 1837 was responsible for a part of the trouble, for many Americans had sympathized with the insurrectionists and had tried to help them. On one occasion some Canadian rebels had chartered a small steamship, the *Caroline*, to bring them supplies and volunteers from the American side of the Niagara River. The British, perhaps owing to a misunderstanding, seized the offending vessel when it was in American water, and sent it in flames over the falls. In this action one member of the *Caroline's* crew was killed, and several were injured. The matter was further complicated when in November, 1840, a Canadian named Alexander McLeod boasted in a New York saloon that he was the member of the boarding party who had killed the American. Thereupon McLeod was promptly arrested, and brought to trial for murder in the New York state courts. The situation was almost out of hand when Webster became Secretary of State, and threats of war quite out of keeping with the importance of the episode were freely exchanged. Webster, however, kept a watchful eye on the trial of McLeod, and was not surprised when the prisoner was acquitted on an alibi. The international tension was further eased by concessions on both sides. The United States officially agreed that the British were right in contending that in military affairs individuals were not responsible for carrying out orders issued by their government, and Congress, at Webster's request, passed a law which provided that in the future the accused in all such cases should have the right of appeal to the federal courts. The British, on the other hand, while maintaining that their part in the *Caroline* affair was strictly defensible, expressed regret that it had ever occurred.

The vagueness of the Treaty of 1783 on the northeastern, or Maine, boundary of the United States had also bred trouble, for about twelve thousand square miles of territory could reasonably be claimed by both Canada and the United States. Clashes between American and Canadian lumberjacks in the disputed area led by the end of the eighteen-thirties to what, with ample

Boundary disputes

exaggeration, was called the "Aroostook War." [1] Fortunately the governors of Maine and New Brunswick were able in 1839 to agree upon a *modus vivendi*, and early in 1842 Webster and Ashburton negotiated a settlement that gave the United States a little more than half of the territory in dispute. Two other minor boundary disputes were settled in the same treaty. The northern boundary of New York, it had been discovered, had been incorrectly surveyed, but Webster and Ashburton wisely agreed to accept as the international boundary the old line, which had been marked off originally in 1774. Also, the boundary west from Lake Superior through the Lake of the Woods, which had been inadequately defined in earlier negotiations, was reconciled with existing geographic information. West of the Lake of the Woods to the Rockies the Canadian-American boundary took the form that it still retains, but Webster and Ashburton felt no call to settle the Oregon question.

Probably as a result of the *Caroline* affair, it was decided to include in the treaty an article on extradition, something wholly lacking in Anglo-American relations since the expiration of the Jay Treaty. Seven crimes were listed, "murder, or assault to commit murder, or piracy, or arson, or robbery, or forgery, or the utterance of forged paper," for which extradition was to be required. Embezzlement, unfortunately, was not included, and for a long time the phrase "gone to Canada," implied in the American vernacular that the traveler was guilty of this crime. Later, however, the list of extraditable offenses was greatly extended.

Another subject that the treaty dealt with was the international slave trade. In 1807 Great Britain, and the following year the United States, had declared this trade illegal, and in a short time practically all the other civilized nations of the world had done likewise. But as long as slavery existed anywhere, *The slave trade* there were bound to be those who were willing to take the risk of breaking the law. Great Britain, with a navy far superior to that of any other power, took the lead in efforts to suppress this nefarious trade, and succeeded in obtaining from many countries permission to visit and search suspected vessels, regardless of the flag they happened to fly. This policy, however, ran counter to a strong American prejudice, and when American ships were so molested the United States entered vigorous protests. Not without considerable difficulty, Webster and Ashburton at length agreed that both powers should keep strong naval forces off the coast of Africa, the two squadrons to co-operate whenever occasion demanded. This agreement was reasonable enough, but the United States

---

[1] On Anglo-American relations during this period the following books should be consulted: O. E. Tiffany, *Relations of the United States to the Canadian Rebellion of 1837–1838* (1905); J. F. Sprague, *The Northeastern Boundary Controversy and the Aroostook War* (1910); and H. S. Burrage, *Maine in the Northeastern Boundary Controversy* (1919).

failed to maintain its proper quota of ships in African waters, and until the time of the Civil War the American flag continued, unfortunately, to be used freely by ships engaged in the slave trade.

Webster and Ashburton were also forced by circumstances to try to smooth out irritations that had arisen because of the practice, common along the Atlantic seaboard, of transporting slaves by sea **The Creole affair** from one part of the United States to another. On several occasions ships engaged in this maritime domestic slave trade were compelled because of storms or other exigencies to put in at some British West Indian port, whereupon the slaves they carried were promptly set free by the British authorities. In 1841 the *Creole* case brought this matter to a dramatic head. The *Creole* was an American ship bound from Virginia to New Orleans with a cargo of one hundred and thirty-five slaves. During the voyage the slaves engaged in a successful mutiny, killing one person and wounding several others, and then took the ship into the British port of Nassau, where, with the exception of those held responsible for the murder, they were given their freedom. On this case Webster and Ashburton were unable to reach a final agreement, but Ashburton accepted the principle that there should be "no officious interference with American vessels driven by accident or by violence" into British ports, and in 1853 a British umpire, Joshua Bates, to whom the case had been submitted for arbitration, awarded the United States damages of $110,330.[1]

---

[1] A. B. Corey, *The Crisis of 1830–1842 in Canadian American Relations* (1941), is a useful monograph. O. D. Lambert, *Presidential Politics in the United States, 1841–44* (1936), explains Tyler's record on the score of personal ambition. Two biographies of Harrison attempt, without notable success, to build up the old general: J. A. Green, *William Henry Harrison: His Life and Times* (1941); and Freeman Cleaves, *Old Tippecanoe: William Henry Harrison and His Time* (1939).

14

The Awakening of the American Mind

THE United States during and immediately following the Jacksonian era was the scene of a series of remarkable transformations. Democracy in government became for the nation and for most of the states a fact as well as a theory; the multiplication of canals, turnpikes, steamboats, and railroads wrought a revolution in transportation; the industrialization and consequent urbanization of the Northeast progressed with startling rapidity; the triumph of "King Cotton" was duly celebrated in the South; the advance of the western frontier continued through good times and bad. Quite as striking, and quite as characteristic of' the age, were the stirrings that the new scene awakened in the American intellect. During this period inventive genius was strangely stimulated, literary talent rose to unprecedented heights, and many crusades for the righting of ancient wrongs swept through the land.[1]

It is easier to produce evidence of this spiritual ferment than to explain how it came about. The growing wealth of the young nation may have had something to do with it. Wealth meant, at least for a few, freedom from ordinary labor, and the leisure to read and think. And yet comparatively little of consequence was accomplished directly by the leisure class; most of the striking achievements of the period were made by men and women who had to earn their own livings. Possibly the chief contribution of the well-to-do was to create demands, spiritual no less than material, that others less favored would seek to supply. Closer contacts with European culture had also an invigorating influence upon trends of thought in the United States. Foreign travel, which had been at low ebb from the time of the American Revolution to the close of the War of 1812, slowly revived; more European books were imported and read; European criticisms of the United States, while seemingly scorned, were nevertheless taken

Intellectual activity

---

[1] A general picture of the period is given in C. R. Fish, *The Rise of the Common Man, 1830–1850* (1927). More colorful, but marred somewhat by their flippant style, are E. Douglas Branch, *The Sentimental Years, 1836–1860* (1934); and Meade Minnigerode, *The Fabulous Forties, 1840–1850* (1924).

deeply to heart; European ideas that were applicable to American conditions were quickly detected and freely appropriated. But the seething, restless, growing American nation was, after all, its own irresistible challenge to thought. The physical needs of so vast and so new a country commanded the best that inventive genius could supply; and the unique character of the American experiment ensured that alert and inquiring minds would seek to understand it, to explain its implications, to direct its course for the future.

Fortunately the United States was not wholly without an intellectual tradition. New England from its beginnings had had a high regard for learning; it had taken great pride in its schools and colleges; **Leadership of New England** it had required its clergy to become masters of an intricate system of theology. New-Englanders, moreover, were not confined to New England, for in every generation their migratory propensities had taken some of them to nearly every part of the country. Tenacious of their views and born propagandists, they introduced wherever they went New England ideas, New England ways of doing things. Particularly in the West, where a materialistic point of view was naturally prevalent, the New England emigrants exerted a strong leavening influence. Nor were they content merely to uphold the cultural traditions they had inherited; they kept in constant touch with developments in their old homes, and passed on to the rest of the country the new impulses they received. Thus New England became a kind of intellectual capital toward which the whole country looked for leadership.

The thoroughgoing democratization of the newspaper, which took place during this period, helped immeasurably to facilitate the spread of new ideas. In an earlier age only the upper classes could **Newspapers** afford the luxury of a newspaper subscription, but from the eighteen-thirties on almost anyone who could read could enjoy that privilege. No one editor could claim the chief credit for this revolutionary change, but a New-Yorker named Benjamin H. Day, who began in 1833 to sell his paper, the *Sun*, at a penny a copy, had something to do with it. Day further extended his subscription list by making the *Sun* sensational enough to interest even the dullest-witted reader, and because his paper reached so many people he could exact a heavy tribute from the advertisers. His methods were imitated by James Gordon Bennett, who in 1835 began the publication of the *New York Herald*, and by Horace Greeley, who six years later established the *New York Tribune*. Conservative editors and readers at first held the penny papers in great contempt, but the efforts of the latter to increase their circulation led them to present controversial news with an impartiality that even the intelligent public came to respect. In time the higher-priced newspapers were forced either to suspend publication or to reduce their prices. It is also worth noting that the rapid improvement of the national system of transportation enabled the leading papers to extend greatly the radius of their circulation. Not only the New York journals, but such papers also as the *Boston Evening Transcript*, the *Philadelphia Ledger*, and the *Springfield* (Massachusetts) *Republican* exerted far more than a merely local influence. Very often for the distant readers weekly editions took the place of the ordinary daily.[1]

Magazines as well as newspapers enjoyed an astonishing vogue. Possibly a hundred such publications existed in 1825, but a generation later there were six or eight times that number. Most of these periodicals, like their predecessors, were both local in character and extremely short-lived, but a few of them, *Graham's Magazine*, the *Knickerbocker Magazine*, and the *Southern Literary Messenger*, for example, were during many years widely read. They printed articles of nearly every sort and kind — critical essays, sermons, stories, poems, and travel accounts — and played an important part in the formulation of American taste and opinion. Through the magazines American readers made the acquaintance of such writers as Edgar Allan Poe, William Cullen Bryant, Henry Wadsworth Longfellow, and James Fenimore Cooper, not to mention many contemporary English authors whose works, for lack of an international agreement as to copyrights, were frequently pirated. Of especial appeal to American women was *Godey's Lady's Book*, founded in 1830, which supplied not only a somewhat saccharine type of literature, but also the latest word on feminine fashions, good morals, and good manners. Its publisher, Louis A. Godey, became for his times a very rich man. His magazine and many others, also, were plentifully supplied with really excellent woodcut or metal illustrations.[2]

Lyceums vied with newspapers and magazines in giving the public something to think and talk about. Inaugurated at Millburg, Vermont, in 1826, the lyceum movement soon became nation-wide in its scope, and successfully stimulated the presentation of lecture courses far and wide. Some of the lyceums — for example, the Lowell Institute of Boston, which received in 1836 a bequest of a quarter of a million dollars — were well supplied with funds, but most of them

[1] Of recent years the history of American journalism has attracted much attention. Useful manuals are W. G. Bleyer, *Main Currents in the History of American Journalism* (1927); and J. M. Lee, *History of American Journalism* (1917). On the value of the newspapers as historical sources see Lucy M. Salmon, *The Newspaper and the Historian* (1923).

[2] F. L. Mott, *A History of American Magazines, 1741–1850* (1930), brings out clearly the importance of the magazines from the point of view of the social historian. See also Algernon de Vivier Tassin, *The Magazine in America* (1916).

depended for their support upon the willingness of large numbers of citizens to pay small sums to hear the addresses of famous men and women. The stipends which the lecturers received, while often extremely modest, were sufficient to aid many intellectuals in the sometimes difficult task of eking out a living. Naturally not every lecturer had a worth-while contribution to make, but such a man as Ralph Waldo Emerson, whose lecture tours were frequent and extensive, was known to accept as little as five dollars for delivering·an address in some remote frontier village. It is difficult to estimate the influence of the lyceum movement, but it must have been considerable. The lyceums offered a platform to every celebrity with a talent for public speaking, and to every earnest apostle of reform. Like the newspapers and the magazines, they were both a cause and a result of the intellectual and moral awakening that was so characteristic of the age.

Not in America alone, but throughout the civilized world, this period was remarkable for its inventions.[1] One by one the machines that were **Inventions – the telegraph** necessary to complete the Industrial Revolution were brought to a fair degree of perfection and started on their course. In this work Americans, well aware of the need of annihilating distance in a country so large as their own, and faced by a chronic shortage of labor, played an honorable and important part. Outstanding among them was Samuel F. B. Morse, a painter and sculptor of New England origin who had twice spent long periods abroad. In 1832, as he was returning to the United States the second time, he talked with his fellow passengers aboard the ship *Sully* about some electrical experiments then being made in France, and conceived the idea of the electromagnetic telegraph. On his arrival in the United States he assumed a professorship to which he had recently been elected in the University of the City of New York, but he spent much of his time in experimentation. By 1835 he had a mile of telegraph wire in a room at the university, over which he was transmitting messages successfully. It was not until 1843, however, that he obtained an appropriation of thirty thousand dollars from Congress to build an experimental line from Washington to Baltimore. On May 1, 1844, with the line complete to Annapolis, the first news message was sent over the wires. The invention met so obvious a need that its use became general almost at once. By 1850 the settled portions of the country were well supplied with telegraphic communications, and in 1858 a cable was successfully laid across the Atlantic.

Of tremendous importance to agriculture was the work of Cyrus Hall

---

[1] George Iles, *Leading American Inventors* (1912); Holland Thompson, *The Age of Invention* (1921); Carleton Mabee, *The American Leonardo: A Life of Samuel F. B. Morse* (1943).

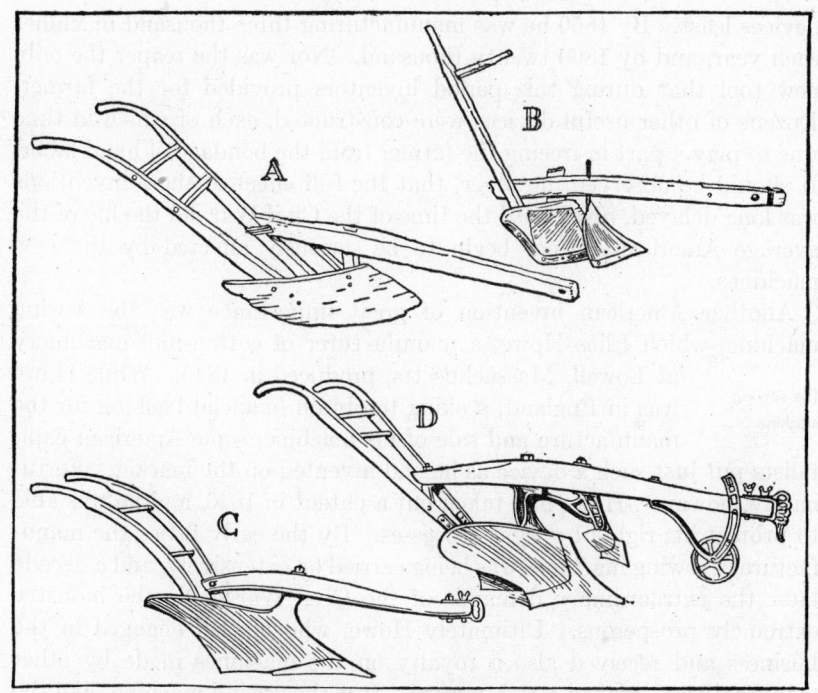

EVOLUTION OF THE PLOW

A. Colonial plow made of wood. B. One-handled colonial plow with iron point and iron-protected side. C. First iron plow cast in more than one piece. D. Plow with first chilled steel mold-board.

McCormick,[1] a back-country Virginian of Scotch-Irish descent, who in 1831 produced a successful reaper. His father, Robert McCormick, had long sought to construct an improved harvesting machine, and had made extensive experiments which his more successful son had been able to utilize. In 1834 young McCormick patented his device, but he was not well enough satisfied with it to attempt its manufacture and sale until he had worked for several years upon improvements. With better business ability than is given to most inventors, he succeeded ultimately in putting on the market a machine which contributed greatly to the revolution in methods of farming that characterized the middle years of the nineteenth century. Sound judgment led him to establish his headquarters in the West, first at Cincinnati (1845) and then at Chicago (1847), where the demand for agricultural machinery would be greatest and the opposition to new

The McCormick reaper

[1] W. T. Hutchinson, *Cyrus Hall McCormick* (2 vols., 1930–35).

devices least. By 1850 he was manufacturing three thousand machines each year, and by 1860 twenty thousand. Nor was the reaper the only new tool that during this period inventors provided for the farmer. Dozens of other useful devices were constructed, each of which in time was to play a part in freeing the farmer from the bondage of hand labor. It should be observed, however, that the full effect of these inventions was long delayed. Not until the time of the Civil War did the life of the average American farmer begin to be seriously affected by the new machines.

Another American invention of great importance was the sewing machine, which Elias Howe, a manufacturer of cotton-mill machinery at Lowell, Massachusetts, produced in 1845. While Howe

The sewing machine

was in England, seeking to obtain financial backing for the manufacture and sale of his machine, some American capitalists put just such a device as he had invented on the market. Fortunately, however, Howe had taken out a patent in 1846, and he was able to protect his rights by legal processes. By the early fifties the manufacture of sewing machines was being carried on extensively, and a decade later the extraordinary demands of the Civil War made the industry extremely prosperous. Ultimately Howe, who himself engaged in the business and received also a royalty on the machines made by other manufacturers, reaped a rich reward. But the sewing machine, like the reaper, was of far greater benefit to a subsequent generation than to the one that produced it.

Several other products of the American inventive genius deserve to be mentioned. In 1830 Samuel Colt, a sixteen-year-old Connecticut lad who had shipped as a sailor from Boston to Calcutta, whiled away his time on the voyage by whittling out a wooden model of a revolving pistol. In 1835 he patented his "revolver" in England, and next year in the United States. By 1838 a company at Paterson, New Jersey, had begun its manufacture. It is difficult to imagine what the history of the Great Plains, just then beginning, would have been like without Colt's invention. In 1836, another Connecticut Yankee, Charles Goodyear, made his first important discovery of an improved treatment for the surface of Indian-rubber products. Some years later he perfected the vulcanizing process, and thus "gave a substantial basis to an industry built on American brains rather than material resources." [1] In 1846 Richard M. Hoe, a New York City manufacturer of printing materials, produced for the use of the *Philadelphia Ledger* the first steam cylinder press. Faster presses were an absolute necessity if the demand for more and more newspapers was to be met, and improvements upon Hoe's in-

[1] Fish, *Rise of the Common Man*, p. 102.

vention made during the next few years, enabled the publishers to print an almost incredible number of papers in a minimum length of time.[1]

Americans also showed great resourcefulness in improving and adapting to different conditions inventions that were introduced from abroad. This was true of the English locomotive, which had to be made lighter and speedier to meet American needs, and of numerous details in the way of railroad equipment. It was true of most of the machinery used in American factories and foundries, of the development of the photograph from the French "daguerreotype," of the "loco-focos," or friction matches, which were invented in Europe but first patented in America. Heating and cooking stoves, which had ancestors on both sides of the Atlantic, were made sufficiently practical during the period to cause the closing-off of many handsome fireplaces. By the middle of the century furnaces and plumbing were being installed, whale-oil lamps were replacing candles, gas-lighting systems were spreading from city to city, tinware was being substituted for costlier copper and iron kitchen utensils, woven carpets were sharing the honors with the old-fashioned rag rugs, and wallpaper was coming into general use. At least for the city dweller, life was becoming increasingly comfortable.

Most American inventions were made to meet an obvious need, and the inventors achieved results, as a rule, only by a persistent application of the trial-and-error method. More scientific advances, however, were by no means lacking.[2] Chief among these should be listed the use of anesthetics in surgery, which a Georgia physician, Doctor Crawford W. Long, proved to be practicable as early as 1842. He did not publish his findings for some years, however, and in the meantime two New England dentists, Doctor Horace Wells of Hartford, Connecticut, and Doctor W. T. G. Morton of Boston, achieved similar results. American scientists also made available much descriptive data. During these years Louis J. R. Agassiz, a French-Swiss immigrant who became a Harvard professor, made important contributions, based upon observations in America, to the world's knowledge of geology and zoology. J. J. Audubon, born in Haiti, the son of a French naval officer, and educated as an artist in France, made the United States his home, and devoted his life to the observation and description of the birds of America. Notable also was the work of Joseph Henry, a physicist, and the first head of the Smithsonian Institution, a foundation made possible by an Englishman's eccentric bequest of a half-million dollars to the United States govern-

Scientific advances

---

[1] Robert Hoe, *A Short History of the Printing Press and the Improvements in Printing Machinery* (1902).

[2] E. S. Dana and others, *A Century of Science in America* (1918).

ment "for the increase and diffusion of knowledge among men." Other American scientists who won distinction were Asa Gray in botany, James Dwight Dana in mineralogy, Ormsby M. Mitchell in astronomy, and Benjamin Silliman in geology. Silliman, a professor at Yale, was not content merely with his teaching and research, but carried to the country by means of popular lectures information about the work the scientists were trying to do.

The period witnessed also a remarkable outburst of literary activity. Foremost among the writers of the time was Ralph Waldo Emerson

Emerson

(1803–82), a philosopher and poet whose influence upon his fellow men was little short of phenomenal.[1] Emerson was descended on his father's side from a long line of New England preachers, and was thus "born to be educated." He attended the Boston Latin School, was graduated in 1821 from Harvard College, taught school, studied theology, and accepted a Unitarian pulpit. He was soon convinced, however, that "to be a good minister one must leave the ministry," and acted accordingly. Late in 1832 he sailed for Europe, where he met many prominent men of letters, among them Coleridge, Wordsworth, and Carlyle. On his return to America a few years later he began to formulate, first in sermons and lectures, and then in books of essays, his doctrine that "God is in every man." Through his reading and his European contacts he had absorbed the philosophy of the German idealists. Like them, he deduced from the teachings of Kant that the world of experience revealed a realm of the spirit. The visible world of the senses was, as he expressed it, only an "apparition of God." There was much to be learned from Nature, for whose teachings he sought to be a "transparent eyeball." The deepest truths, he held, came unbidden and unsought to the receptive human soul. "To believe in your own thought ... is genius." Always professing confidence in the infinite possibilities of man, Emerson found a firm basis for his reasoning in the society he saw about him. Here man was accomplishing new things, building a new civilization. Material progress must be matched by spiritual progress. American thinkers, like American men of action, must strike out for themselves along original lines. "Our day of dependence, our long apprenticeship to the learning of other lands, draws to a close," he told the Phi Beta Kappa Society of Cambridge in 1837. "Let us have done with Europe and dead cultures, let us explore the possibilities of our own new world."

Other young Americans of this generation were profoundly influenced

---

[1] A satisfactory biography is O. W. Firkins, *Ralph Waldo Emerson* (1915), but the interested reader will examine also *The Journals of Ralph Waldo Emerson, with Annotations*, edited by E. W. Emerson and W. E. Forbes (10 vols., 1909–14).

by German idealism, some from having read Coleridge and Carlyle, its leading English proponents, some from having studied in the German universities. In Boston, from 1836 to 1843, a small group of these like-minded men, Emerson among them, met together informally in what they called the Symposium, or sometimes, after Henry Hedge, their leader, "Hedge's Club." To outsiders, however, members of the group were generally known as "transcendentalists," and their version of Kant's philosophy as "transcendentalism." [1] In 1838 they brought out a series of volumes known as *Specimens of Foreign Standard Literature,* and in 1840 they began the publication of a magazine called the *Dial,* through which many of Emerson's writings reached the public. Nearly all of the original transcendentalists became nationally prominent: Henry Thoreau as one of the few really great masters of English prose; Bronson Alcott, Theodore Parker, and James Freeman Clarke as preachers and lecturers; George Ripley and Margaret Fuller as editors and literary critics; George Bancroft as historian. The transcendentalists dreamed of an America which should live up to its opportunities, and, because they thought that it so often failed to do so, they criticized it scathingly. In 1840 some of them, hoping to show how "a system of brotherly co-operation" might be substituted for "one of selfish competition," took part in the establishment of Brook Farm, near West Roxbury, Massachusetts. Here all property was held in common, labor was equally shared, and much time was allotted to social and literary activities. The experiment lasted for several years, and, because of the prominence of its originators, it attracted much attention. The transcendentalists, however, should not be thought of as communists. Their interest was primarily in the individual, and in the full development of his capabilities. Their emphasis upon the dignity of human nature and the perfectibility of man was generally regarded with favor by the public, for it was easy enough to see in such doctrines a kind of justification of American democracy.

The writings of the transcendentalists constituted only a fraction of the literary achievements of New England during the middle decades of the nineteenth century. Indeed, the contrast in this respect between the years before and the years following 1830 was so striking that the term "New England Renaissance" soon came to be applied to the literary activities of the period. The blight of Calvinistic theology, which assured mankind of its total

The "transcendentalists"

The "New England Renaissance"

---

[1] O. B. Frothingham, *Transcendentalism in New England: A History* (1876); H. C. Goddard, *Studies in New England Transcendentalism* (1908); H. S. Commager, *Theodore Parker* (1936). Among the most useful general treatises on American literature are Russell Blankenship, *American Literature* (1931); Bliss Perry, *The American Spirit in Literature* (1918); *The Cambridge History of American Literature,* edited by W. P. Trent and others (4 vols., 1917–21).

depravity and its helplessness without the saving grace of God, is generally regarded as the chief reason for the stifling of nearly every creative
impulse in the earlier years of the century. So Emerson maintained
when he wrote that "from 1790 to 1820 there was not a book, a speech, a
conversation or a thought" in the whole state of Massachusetts. But
Emerson exaggerated. New England under the sway of the Calvinists
may have reflected chiefly upon its sins, but at least it reflected. Out of
these reflections came the Unitarian and Universalist revolts in religion,
the New England renaissance in literature, and a remarkable drive for
social reform. New England minds may have been slow to open to new
ideas, but at least the minds were there, and ultimately some of them did
open. The soil which produced such men as Emerson, Thoreau, Longfellow, Whittier, Holmes, Hawthorne, Lowell, Bancroft, Prescott, Motley, Garrison, and Phillips could hardly have been as barren as it has
been pictured.[1]

Whatever Americans of the present time may think, Henry Wadsworth Longfellow (1807–82) was a great poet to Americans of his own
age. Longfellow was born in Portland, Maine, and was

Longfellow graduated from Bowdoin College, where he soon became a
professor of modern languages. In 1835 he was appointed to a similar
post at Harvard University, and from that time on he was closely identified with the aristocracy of Cambridge and "Back Bay" Boston. Longfellow's poetry was much affected by the cloistered life he led. Twice he
made long visits to Europe, but most of his time he spent in the spacious
mansion at Cambridge which Washington had used as headquarters
during the first year of the American Revolution. In his poetic forms
Longfellow followed European precedents, and he often made use of
European themes; indeed, some of his best work is to be found in his
translations of European writers. But he also used American themes,
such, for example, as in *Evangeline*, the *Courtship of Miles Standish*, and
Hiawatha, although in such a restrained, drawing-room manner that
the principals concerned could hardly have recognized themselves.
Longfellow's incurable romanticism, his aloofness from the sometimes
painful realities of life, and his gentle, soothing rhymes appealed greatly
to the American masses. His poetry matched exactly the popular conception of what poetry should be; ordinary men were deeply gratified to
see how easily they could understand and appreciate it.

Less able than Longfellow, but freer from the charge of artificiality,
was the Quaker poet John Greenleaf Whittier (1807–92). He was born
in Haverhill, Massachusetts, of Quaker parents, and he was himself a

[1] Van Wyck Brooks, *The Flowering of New England* (1936), is a work of exceptional
charm.

lifelong member of the Society of Friends. As a boy he worked on his father's farm and sometimes sent verses to the local news- Whittier paper. His first publication of consequence, *Legends of New England* (1831), exploited themes with which he had a natural intimacy, but he was soon caught up in the anti-slavery crusade, and turned his talent to the furthering of that cause. He advocated, as a Quaker would, the overthrow of slavery by pacific means, but he portrayed its evils in verse vivid enough to gratify the most earnest believer in more direct action. His "Ichabod," a scathing denunciation of Webster for support-ing the Compromise of 1850, reveals clearly his intransigeance. Once the battle for abolition was won, Whittier grew pleasantly reminiscent of by-gone days in New England, and preserved his memories in such poems as *The Barefoot Boy, Snow-Bound,* and *The Tent on the Beach.* His output was more limited than Longfellow's, and his poetic competence less marked, but his influence upon the course of events was far greater.

Among the other outstanding writers of the New England Renaissance were Nathaniel Hawthorne (1804–64), Oliver Wendell Holmes (1809–94), and James Russell Lowell (1819–91). Hawthorne be- Hawthorne, gan his literary career with *Twice-Told Tales,* a modern ver- Holmes, sion of classical myths which he published in 1837, but his Lowell later works centered about American themes. In *The Scarlet Letter,* a story of early New England Puritanism, he drew a powerful indictment of the moral values of his ancestors; in *The House of the Seven Gables* and *The Blithedale Romance* he dealt with the influences that had shaped the lives of those about him. His artistry with words and his deep psychological insight gave his writings a permanent value, although he was unable to make a living from them, and had to piece out his in-come by holding minor political offices. Holmes is known for his poetry no less than for his prose, but for his wit and humor most of all. He hated Calvinism cordially, but he could still celebrate its collapse in the perennially amusing *Wonderful One-Hoss Shay.* His *Autocrat of the Breakfast-Table,* and its numerous sequels, showed him to be a past master of the worldly lore and native drollery of the Yankees. Lowell, like Holmes, was remarkable for his versatility. A New England Brah-min, he nevertheless expressed himself admirably in dialect poems, such as the *Biglow Papers,* many of which, like the poems of Whittier, had a definite anti-slavery bias. But Lowell was also a political essayist of note, a professor in Harvard University, editor for several years of the *Atlantic Monthly,* and later one of the editors of the *North American Review.* His services to letters and politics were recognized after the Civil War by two diplomatic appointments, first as minister to Spain, and later as minister to Great Britain.

Any survey of literary New England during the middle period would be incomplete without mention of its able group of historians.[1] The name of Jared Sparks (1790–1866) naturally heads this list.

New England historians

Like so many scholars of his time, Sparks turned his hand to many things. He occupied a Unitarian pulpit, edited the *North American Review*, was for ten years a professor of history at Harvard University and for three years its president. He was one of the first to recognize in the history of the United States a theme of consequence that must no longer be neglected, and he early set himself the task of collecting the records from which at least an important part of this history could be written. In 1830 he published twelve volumes of the *Diplomatic Correspondence of the American Revolution*; several years later twelve more, the *Writings of George Washington*; then within the decade another dozen, the *Works of Benjamin Franklin*. He also found time during his busiest years to edit a twenty-five-volume *Library of American Biography*, for which he himself wrote many of the sketches, and later in life to bring out four valuable volumes of *Correspondence of the American Revolution*. As an editor he took greater liberties with an original text than would now be regarded as proper, but the debt historians owe him is very great.

George Bancroft (1800–91), like Sparks, saw significance in the history of his own country. A graduate of Harvard, he spent five years in the universities of Germany and came back to the United States well grounded in the principles of historical method. But Bancroft's love of country, and his devotion to the principle of democracy in government for which it stood, led him to saturate his work with a patriotic fervor that today would be regarded as bad form. For half a century he occupied himself with the writing of a monumental *History of the United States*, which from the first volume, published in 1834, to the twelfth, published in 1882, idealizes and overstates the American case on nearly every page. Throughout the colonial period, with which Bancroft was chiefly concerned, the colonists in all contentions with the mother country were always right, the British always wrong. The reader gets the unmistakable impression that Bancroft wrote primarily to justify American democracy, to prove the success of the American experiment. For historians of a later generation such a work has little value; but for Americans of Bancroft's time this flattering point of view gave great satisfaction, and Bancroft's popularity was tremendous.

Two other New England historians, William H. Prescott (1796–1859) and John Lothrop Motley (1814–77), looked beyond the borders of the United States in search of more romantic materials than the history of

[1] J. S. Bassett, *The Middle Group of American Historians* (1917).

their own country afforded. Prescott found what he wanted in the history of Spain and of the Spanish empire in America. His *History cf Ferdinand and Isabella*, published in 1838, won him an enviable reputation both at home and abroad, a reputation which grew as one important work — the *Conquest of Mexico*, the *Conquest of Peru*, and a *History of Philip II of Spain* — succeeded another. Motley interested himself in the history of Holland, and after a long period of research produced in 1856 his *History of the Rise of the Dutch Republic*, and in 1861 the first half of his *United Netherlands*. Greater than either was Francis Parkman (1823–93), who, after an initial work, the *Oregon Trail* (1846), in which he related his own experiences during a trip to the West, fixed upon the French in North America as the theme he wished to develop. But most of Parkman's books were written and published in the years following the Civil War, and they belong, therefore, in point of time, if not in spirit, to the later period.

While the leadership of New England in the world of American letters was incontestable, writers of distinction were also to be found in other parts of the country. Washington Irving (1783–1859), who returned to New York in 1832 after a residence of seventeen years abroad, sought with some success to catch the spirit of the untamed West in his *Tour of the Prairies*, *Astoria*, and *Adventures of Captain Bonneville*. During his later years he wrote a monumental *Life of Washington*, which was more admired by his contemporaries than by their descendants. James Fenimore Cooper (1789–1851), another New-Yorker, found a field for his imagination in the North American Indian, and his *Leather-Stocking Tales* are still read. William Cullen Bryant (1794–1878), a New England boy who won fame in New York and for half a century was editor of the New York *Evening Post*, wrote verse of enduring charm. Herman Melville (1819–91) told with rare vividness tall tales of the sea. His *Moby Dick*, the story of a "strange, fierce white whale" and his enemy, Captain Ahab, is one of the world's greatest romances. Walt Whitman (1819–92) more than any other writer caught the spirit of his times, and reflected it in verse forms that were as new and unpredictable as the civilization he delighted to honor. His *Leaves of Grass* registered a more complete break with European tradition than anything that had come out of New England, and the freedom and gusto with which he expressed himself set important precedents for the coming age.

Edgar Allan Poe (1809–49) defies classification both as to time and place. He was not much concerned with the problems of his own, or any other, generation, and while the South claims him, he was born in Boston and spent much of his time in New York. Virginia was his home,

Writers of the middle states

however, as nearly as he had one, and for a number of years he edited
the *Southern Literary Messenger*. Undoubtedly a psycho-
Edgar Allan
Poe
pathic case himself, he was interested in the weird and abnormal to a startling degree, but he had such a sure eye for beauty
and for perfection of form that he ultimately won the admiration of even
the most conventional. Although he mastered better than any of his
predecessors the technique of the short story, particularly the detective
story, his chief title to fame rests upon his poetry. Such poems as *The
Raven*, *The Bells*, and *Annabel Lee* remain unsurpassed for their haunting
melodies and their technical perfection.

The ante-bellum South produced no other writer even faintly comparable to Poe, but it did not lack for stars of a lesser magnitude. William Gilmore Simms (1806–70), a persistent and often suc-
Southern
writers
cessful imitator of such English writers as Byron and Scott,
published over a hundred volumes of verse and prose before
the Civil War. Like so many other Southerners of his time, he turned
whatever talent he possessed to a militant defense of the institution of
slavery. Henry Timrod (1829–67) and Paul Hamilton Hayne (1830–86)
wrote enchanting, but not very enduring, poetry. William J. Grayson
(1788–1863) defended slavery in a long poem, *The Hireling and the Slave*,
which effectively contrasted the unhappy lot of the wage-slave in the
northern mines and factories with the carefree life of the bond-slave of
the South. John Pendleton Kennedy (1795–1870) revealed in vivid
prose pictures the charm of plantation life in Old Virginia, but he held
no brief for slavery.

It is a curious fact that the literary activities of the years following
1830 were in nowise paralleled by similar successes in the realm of the
arts. Indeed, the period witnessed a definite decline in such fields as
painting and architecture, fields in which during the early years of the
Republic promising beginnings had seemingly been made. The blame
for this state of affairs is usually placed on the triumph of democracy
— a triumph which exalted the taste of the ordinary man, however
execrable it might be, to a parity with the taste of the élite. But this
explanation is not entirely satisfying, for by the same reasoning a dearth
of good literature should also have developed. One might rather suppose that the artists found it more difficult than the men of letters to
keep abreast of the Industrial Revolution. The traditions that bound
them were more rigid than literary forms; the materials they worked
with were less plastic than words. Not only in the United States, but
throughout the civilized world, the arts were at low ebb during the middle decades of the nineteenth century. Everywhere those who looked
only to the past for guidance failed to catch the spirit of the new age,

while those who broke with the past and began to experiment made many false starts.

American architecture throughout this period was strikingly free from originality. The classical vogue that Jefferson had done so much to introduce still flourished, and totally irrelevant replicas of early Greek temples were everywhere in evidence. For *Architecture* public buildings the favorite design was a combination of dome and portico that was not often strikingly successful. Dwelling-houses were apt to reveal the old Georgian influence of the colonial period, although there was much rule-of-thumb modification, and, as time went on, an unmistakable tendency to copy anything that anybody had ever done anywhere. About the middle of the century American builders began to follow European architects in a furious revolt against classicism. Gothic forms were revived, excessive ornamentation replaced simplicity, and a kind of general pandemonium broke loose. This freedom was necessary, no doubt, if any really important new note was to be struck, but at least until well toward the end of the century the search was conducted in vain.[1]

Buildings are a necessity, and architecture of a kind is therefore indispensable in any age, but the same can hardly be said of painting and sculpture, which throughout the period under review were almost non-existent in the United States. Portrait painters *Painting and sculpture* there were, but they showed little of the distinction that had characterized the post-Revolutionary artists, and the beginnings of photography soon dealt their craft a serious blow. A group of landscape painters, known generally as the "Hudson River School," called attention to the beauty of American scenes, and genuinely sought to reproduce what they saw rather than what artists were traditionally supposed to see. But their technique was European, not American, and their achievements hardly above mediocrity. American sculptors had even less to their credit. What few of them there were clung tenaciously to the classical traditions, and did their best to make American politicians look like Roman emperors in disguise. Horatio Greenough, designer of the Bunker Hill Monument, carved from Italian marble a heroic statue of Washington, scantily clad and seated on a throne, which fortunately was soon relegated to storage in the Smithsonian Institution. The "Greek Slave" by Hiram Powers attracted much attention, mainly perhaps because it was a nude female figure, and most Americans had been taught to identify nudity with naughtiness. Powers's extraordinary daring came doubtless from his long residence in Florence, Italy. A fad for waxwork was widely followed, and some really exquisite modeling was done,

[1] T. E. Tallmadge, *The Story of Architecture in America* (1927).

mostly by women of leisure, who also busied themselves successfully
with many other varieties of "fancy work." [1]

Americans of the period were by no means uninterested in music, although in this respect dependence on Europe remained marked. Musi-

Music   cal societies were common to the larger cities, European
artists often made American tours, a few symphony orches-
tras were organized, and attempts to produce opera, mainly Italian, were
not unknown. But American composers of music were neither numerous
nor of profound ability, although some of their work lives on. The
hymns of Lowell Mason (1792–1872), for example, are familiar to nearly
every American churchgoer, and their publication contributed materially
to the popularity of congregational singing. Mason is also to be remembered for his success in introducing the teaching of music into the public
schools. Stephen C. Foster (1826–64), a native of Pennsylvania who
knew little of the South or, for that matter, of formal music, wrote both
the melodies and the words of dozens of songs which reflected admirably
the tempo of southern plantation life, and won an enduring popularity
in all parts of the country. Foster's songs, and many others like them,

[1] Suzanne La Follette, *Art in America* (1929); Charles H. Caffin, *The Story of American
Painting* (1907); Lorado Taft, *The History of American Sculpture* (1903); Porter Butts,
Art in Wisconsin — The Art Experience of the Middle-West Frontier (1936).

INVENTIONS

*Americans have contributed many inventions of great importance to human progress.
Most of these have served to meet some insistent practical problem, such as the separation of the cotton seed from the cotton fiber in which it grows.*

The cotton gin was invented by ELI WHITNEY (1765–1825), *a Yankee graduate of
Yale College, who spent some time in Georgia at the home of General Greene's widow.
This invention had much to do with turning the South into the "Cotton Kingdom,"
saving slavery from speedy extinction, and paving the way for the Civil War. (From
"Harper's Weekly," December 18, 1869.)*

The reaper was invented by CYRUS HALL McCORMICK (1809–84), *a Virginian.
Together with other agricultural implements it revolutionized farming methods in
America. (Courtesy of International Harvester Co.)*

The six-shooter was the brain child of SAMUEL COLT (1814–62), *a runaway sailor
boy from Connecticut, who whittled out the original model from wood. Without the
revolver the history of the Great Plains could never have been the same. (Courtesy of
Colt Firearms Co.)*

The sewing machine was invented by ELIAS HOWE (1819–67), *of Massachusetts,
for whom it made a fortune. (From "Appleton's Journal," October 16, 1869; photo
from Culver.)*

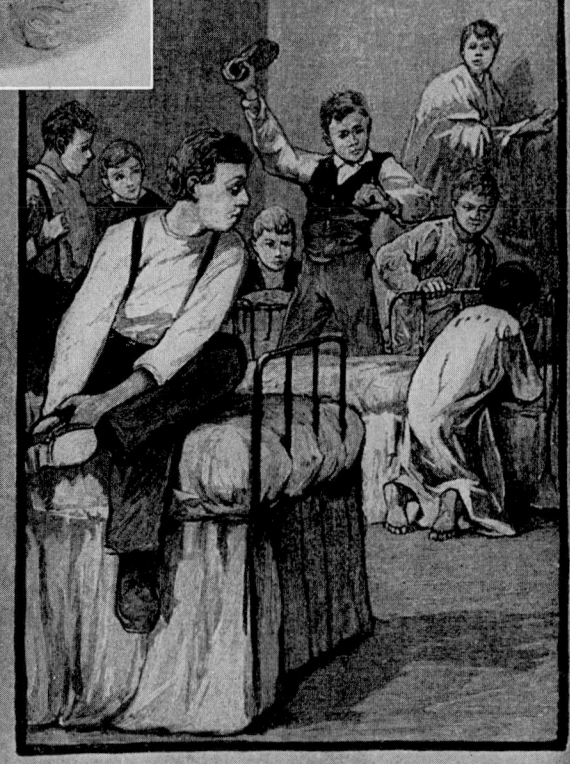

Tom. For some time his excitement and the flood
of memories which chased one another through his
brain, kept him from thinking or resolving. His
head throbbed, his heart leapt, and he could hardly
keep himself from springing out of bed and rushing

frequently reached the public first through black-face minstrel shows, which then enjoyed a great vogue. The Negroes themselves, who sang while they worked, and whose talent for music was very great, were doubtless the originators of many of the melodies that these songwriters exploited.[1]

Owing partly to frontier conditions and partly to the hostility of New England Puritanism, the American theater was slow to develop. During the colonial period small beginnings were made in some of the coast cities, but both the plays and the players were **The theater** English, and the response to their efforts was not always cordial. Even after the Revolution the theater in the United States was for a long time an alien rather than a native institution. By the thirties and forties, however, most of the large towns and cities had stock companies with which well-known actors or actresses on tour co-operated in the production of plays. The tendency to rely mainly upon English stars was a serious handicap to the development of native talent, but a few Americans rivaled the best of the visitors in popularity. Chief among the American stars were Edwin Forrest and Edwin Booth, whose greatest successes were in Shakespearean rôles, and Charlotte Cushman, whom the public liked best as Lady Macbeth or Meg Merrilies.

[1] J. T. Howard, *Our American Music, Three Hundred Years of It* (1931); N. I. White, *American Negro Folk-Songs* (1928); Carl Wittke, *Tambo and Bones* (1936).

MAGAZINES AND SCHOOLBOOKS

"Godey's Lady's Book" influenced feminine styles and thought in the United States from 1830 to 1898. Its purpose, according to its creator, Louis A. Godey (1804–78), who amassed a large fortune from his venture, was to bring "unalloyed pleasure to the female mind." This it seems to have done. To quote one observer, "The stories and poems were read and reread and cried over, the fashions were studied and copied, the engravings were cut out and framed, and the editor's advice was considered the final pronouncement." The circulation of the magazine reached 150,000 — for the time a tremendous figure — and prominent American writers, men as well as women, were delighted to appear in its columns. This illustration from a "Godey's Lady's Book" shows costumes of about 1860. (Photo from Brown Bros.)

The McGuffey Readers, according to Mark Sullivan, were probably read by "at least half the school children of America, from 1836 to 1900." William Holmes McGuffey (1800–73), their compiler, invariably chose selections that had not only a subject but also an object. The selection on this page from a McGuffey Reader is from "Tom Brown's School Days." The preachments of the selections did much to set the pattern of nineteenth-century America's taste in literature, its standards of moral conduct, and its attitude toward life in general. (Photo from Culver.)

The theater of this period was more famous for its actors than for its playwrights. Ears attuned to the resonant oratory of Daniel Webster and Henry Clay asked nothing better than to listen to the long declamations of Shakespearean characters, and the steady devotion of theatrical patrons to the classics tended to discourage the writing of new plays. To this rule, however, there were important exceptions. George Henry Boker's *Francesca da Rimini*, for example, won an enduring place in dramatic literature, and Cora Mowatt's *Fashion, or, Life in New York*, burlesqued so successfully the social pretensions of the times that it has had numerous popular revivals. Current English plays also enjoyed a considerable popularity in the United States. One of them, Tom Taylor's *Our American Cousin*, ran one hundred and forty nights at Laura Keene's New Theater in New York. It was during a performance of this play at Ford's Theater in Washington that Abraham Lincoln was assassinated. His assassin, John Wilkes Booth, a younger brother of Edwin Booth, and also an actor, fancied that by this deed he would redress the wrongs done the South.[1]

Possibly an acute sensitiveness to music and the arts was too much to expect of an age that centered so much attention upon the lot of the common man. Above all else this was a period which pro-

The idea of progress

claimed his importance and sought to meet his needs. Jacksonian democracy was founded on the principle that one man was as much worth while as another, Unitarian theology saw in even the humblest of God's children a spark of the divine; and, long before the publication of Darwin's *Origin of Species* in 1859, the idea of evolution, at least in so far as it implied the doctrine of human progress, was beginning to find able defenders on both sides of the Atlantic. "Progressive development does not end with us," wrote Theodore Parker, the transcendentalist divine, "we have seen only the beginning; the future triumphs of the race must be vastly greater than all accomplished yet." Society in an age that believed so intensely in the capacity of mankind for improvement could not fail to become increasingly aware of the evils with which it was afflicted, and to seek for remedies. In precisely the same spirit religion discarded some of its formalism and "otherworldliness" in order to concern itself more with the necessity of making this world "a better place to live in." Writers developed their talents, more often than otherwise, as the advocates of worthy causes. Humanitarian reformers of every kind got a hearing, and with surprisingly few exceptions a following as well.

The rapid advance of the factory system in the American Northeast

---

[1] O. S. Coad and Edwin Mims, Jr., *The American Stage* (*The Pageant of America*, xiv, 1929).

presented the country with a serious labor problem. Under the vanishing domestic system apprentices and journeymen could hope to rise ultimately to the status of master craftsmen and employers, but only rarely was it possible under the new system for a workman to climb into the capitalist class. As the number of employees under a single management grew greater, the line of cleavage between the two classes grew deeper. Moreover, the employer was no longer aware of the conditions under which his employees lived, and he was often little concerned about the conditions under which they worked, so long as the profits of the factory remained good. Competition among manufacturers was keen, and the need of keeping down labor costs led frequently, especially in the textile mills, to the employment of women and children. Long hours of labor were required in the early factories — "from dawn to dark," or from thirteen to fifteen hours a day, was not unusual. Since most of the original "hands," or operators, had been recruited from the farms, where these long working hours had been the rule, the laborers at first saw no reason to protest. But some of them, at least, soon came to realize that the varied outdoor labor of the farm was one thing, and the monotonous indoor labor of the factory quite another. Many of the factories were badly lighted, poorly ventilated, and dangerous to life and limb. Children were given little if any opportunity for schooling, women were kept away from the duties of the home, heads of families were often unemployed because of the unfair competition of women and children.

As the lot of the laborer grew harder, the strength of the employer grew greater. During the decade of the twenties American manufacturers increased their output six times over, while by 1830, with a total investment about one-fifth as great as that of all the southern plantations combined, they were turning out goods worth one and one-half times as much. Their importance to the society in which they lived won quick acclaim. To the wealthy manufacturers the lawyers looked for fees, the ministers for salaries, the colleges for endowments, the shopkeepers for goods on credit. For all such dependents the prosperity of the manufacturers was a matter of vital importance. Even the farmers, who supplied the foodstuffs to the factory towns, and the laborers themselves, who had no other means of subsistence than their factory jobs, generally accepted the manufacturer's point of view. His will became the will of the community. If protective tariffs were required to make him prosperous, then protective tariffs must be obtained. If the cost of labor must be cut, then the laborer must somehow bear the burden.

Such a thoroughgoing denial in practice of the democratic tenets of the age should have aroused criticism sooner than it did. But the right of individual freedom was a heritage no less prized by Americans than democracy itself. An employer, according to this tradition, must be left free to conduct his business as he chose; an employee must be equally free to accept or reject the contract he was offered. When, early in the nineteenth century, artisans in some of the larger cities sought through unions to force their employers to raise wages, public opinion rallied strongly to the support of the employers. Courts which made use of the English common law to punish strikers for "conspiracy to raise wages" were applauded. Labor organizations of every kind were bitterly condemned, but associations of employers, designed to keep the laborers in their places, won hearty approval.

In spite of these obstacles the country witnessed during the decade that preceded the panic of 1837 a well-defined and relatively successful labor movement.[1] The leadership of this movement came from the artisans rather than from the factory hands, but the benefits were shared quite generally by all types of laborers. Prior to 1827 a few labor organizations patterned upon those of England had been formed in the United States, but they were merely local trades unions; that is, membership in a union was confined to a single city and a single craft. But in the year mentioned the failure of a carpenters' strike in Philadelphia led to the formation of the Mechanics' Union of Trade Associations, a federation of many trades unions. By thus combining forces the Philadelphia workingmen found that their power to exert pressure upon their employers was enormously increased. Strikes, when supported by the city federation, had a good chance to win, and the political influence of so large a group of voters was not to be despised. Soon other cities were similarly organized, and from 1834 to 1837 a somewhat imperfect national federation held annual meetings.

A labor movement

The city federation revealed a strong penchant for political action. The recent widening of the suffrage had made voters of the workingmen, and the possibility of turning this newly won weapon to good purpose was too obvious to be overlooked. The laws, laboring men held, had long been made by the well-to-do, or by their satellites, and the lawmakers had shown little concern for the workers. Mechanics' lien laws, free schools supported by public taxes, the abolition of imprisonment for debt, and the abolition of chartered monopolies were among the demands of the Philadelphia workingmen, who for four years, beginning in 1828, regularly nominated candidates for office. During the same period a Workingman's Party was active in New York, and in 1830 its candidate

---

[1] Useful summaries are contained in Mary R. Beard, *A Short History of the American Labor Movement* (1920); and Selig Perlman, *A History of Trade Unionism in the United States* (1922). For fuller accounts see J. R. Commons and Associates, *History of Labour in the United States* (4 vols., 1918-35).

for governor polled a total of three thousand votes. Not only in Phila-delphia and New York, but in many other cities also, workingmen's parties existed, and steps were even taken toward the formation of a national labor party. This promising third-party movement was under-mined and defeated by the old parties only at the cost of taking over and putting into effect many of the reforms which the workingmen demanded.

To supplement their political activities the workingmen resorted also to strikes. These were particularly numerous during the four years of lush prosperity, 1833–37, when, according to Professor Channing, there were no less than one hundred and sixty-eight such conflicts in the United States. Of this number one hundred and three were held to secure higher wages, and twenty-six for a ten-hour day. Strikers also demanded what came later to be called the "closed shop"; that is, the employment of union men only, and the ex-clusion of non-union men. Even the factory operatives, who had at first taken little part in the labor movement, now began to strike. Through these direct methods the workingmen gained some victories, although the courts remained on the whole hostile, and could be used by employers to hamper the strikers. In 1842, however, the Massachusetts Supreme Court relaxed the rule of conspiracy to the extent of holding that labor organizations might legally seek to advance wages "by rules binding solely on members." By this time, however, strikes were infrequent and the labor movement at low ebb; indeed, lack of employment after the panic of 1837 led to the disintegration of many unions and the temporary cessation of labor activities.

The untimely decline of this first American labor movement did not prevent it from winning many substantial victories for the workingmen. A number of the strikes for a ten-hour day were successful, and the demand for shorter hours attracted much favorable comment, even outside labor circles. Politicians were not slow to catch the drift of public opinion. In 1840 President Van Buren proclaimed the ten-hour day in effect on all public works conducted by the national government. In 1847 the state of New Hampshire legalized the ten-hour day "except in pursuance of an express contract requiring greater time." Other states followed this precedent, employers reluctantly swung into line, and by the time of the Civil War the ten-hour day was general throughout the country, although longer hours were by no means unknown, particularly in New England, where in most of the factories a twelve-hour day was still required. During these same years several other labor demands were materially advanced. In nearly all the states new mechanics' lien laws were passed which gave the claims of laborers for wages precedence over the claims of those who merely furnished materials. Imprisonment for debt, a practice still so common that in 1830 there were, according to reliable estimates, no less than seventy-five thousand persons thus imprisoned in the United States, was abolished throughout the North by 1840, although in the South it continued down to the time of the Civil War. Also, laws designed to safeguard the life and health of factory workers were enacted with increasing frequency.

Many thoughtful Americans (among them most of the New England transcendentalists), although not themselves of the laboring class, sympathized deeply with the efforts of the workers to help themselves, but feared that the remedies proposed would prove to be mere palliatives, and of no permanent value. These high-minded observers sought instead to find some formula by which society could be remade with the evils from which it suffered left out. Since the Industrial Revolution, which was mainly responsible for the existing state of affairs, had come sooner to Europe than to America, Europeans had anticipated Americans in thinking and writing about this problem. American reformers, therefore, were not obliged to rely wholly upon their own observation and reflection in the formulation of their ideas. Borrowing freely from such European theorists as Saint-Simon, Fourier, Robert Owen, and Karl Marx, they attacked the principle of competitive individualism, and sought to substitute for it some collectivist scheme that would improve the lot of the ordinary man. They watched with eager eyes the results of the communistic experiments which Robert Owen staged at New Lanark, Scotland, New Harmony, Indiana, and elsewhere. They tried many experiments of their own, such, for example, as the one at Brook Farm, already noted. As utopian reformers they failed, but as agitators for the amelioration of the workingman's lot they made a notable impression. Individualism was too deeply rooted in the American mind to be eradicated, but Emerson's contention that "a man has a right to be employed, to be trusted, to be loved, to be revered," was quite in keeping with the currents of the age.

Both the workingmen and their allies, the humanitarian reformers, were earnest advocates of free public education. To the workingmen the necessity of equal educational opportunities for the children of rich and poor alike seemed absolutely essential; otherwise the caste lines between the two classes, already marked, would soon become complete and thoroughgoing barriers. The ordinary workingman, however, could not afford to pay for the education of his children; indeed, he often found it necessary to put them to work because he needed their wages, and thus to compound the evils from which he suffered. For child labor, at least in certain industries, kept wages low, and even deprived adults of the opportunity

The demand for free schools

to labor. Workingmen, therefore, united in the demand that the state accept the full responsibility of providing schools at public expense. Taxes for such a purpose, they claimed, were quite as just a public obligation as taxes for any other purpose. The humanitarian reformers carried the argument even further. From their point of view, every man had a right to an education; moreover, in a democracy such as the United States, where, at least in theory, the people ruled, obviously the government must take pains to ensure that its rulers were educated. On the strength of this argument even taxpayers were persuaded that the taking of one man's property to educate another man's children was not so bad as it seemed.

As a matter of fact, the old idea that education was a class prerogative to which ordinary men had no right to aspire had always been somewhat on the defensive in America. Even in the seventeenth century, the Puritans in New England, the Dutch in New York, and the Quakers in Pennsylvania had in varying degrees accepted the responsibility of providing education for the masses, and had passed the tradition down to later generations. In the time of the Confederation the original states had not hesitated to include in the Northwest Ordinances of 1785 and 1787 provisions that obliged the new western states to establish, at least on paper, systems of free public schools. But in every part of the country the difference between precept and practice was considerable. Elementary schools, supported in whole or in part, did exist in the Northeast, particularly in Massachusetts and New York, but they were rarely as good as the private schools to which those whose means permitted preferred to send their children. Moreover, the public schools were often regarded as charity, or "pauper," schools, provided out of tax money (as also were poorhouses) only for those who had no alternative but to use them. In the South, country life made the problem of schooling difficult at best, and the planters were usually content to solve it in their own way for their own children, and to let the rest do without. In the West, the generous grants of school lands were received with much favor, and the obligation to provide free schools was cheerfully accepted, but the schools were slow to materialize. School lands brought slender revenues, and the taxable resources of the new states were always overstrained.

There was need, therefore, of a crusade to secure free public instruction, in fact as well as in theory, and the crusaders were not lacking. Two principles had to be established; first, that the maintenance of a school system must be required of every community; and second, that the schools so established must be equally open to all children, regardless of the ability or the inability of

Educational reformers

their parents to pay tuition. The second principle was embodied in a law which passed the legislature of Pennsylvania in 1834, and which the young Anti-Masonic leader, Thaddeus Stevens, helped save from repeal. The first principle, long established in Massachusetts, was there made thoroughly effective by the work of Horace Mann, who from 1837 to 1848 was secretary of the state board of education. Henry Barnard of Connecticut pioneered in the study of European educational systems with a view to their application in the United States.[1] From such beginnings as these, particularly from the activities of Horace Mann, whose annual reports were studied far and wide, the American system of public schools was soon to grow. Well before the Civil War every northern state was attempting to provide elementary schools at public expense in every community, and important experiments were being made with public high schools. In general, however, private "academies" bridged the gap between elementary and college education, while the zeal of religious denominations, more often than otherwise, provided the colleges. In the South, where both elementary and secondary schools were frequently lacking, the efforts of Thomas Jefferson in behalf of nonsectarian higher education bore fruit when the University of Virginia opened its doors in 1825. Not until 1842, however, was the first of the western state universities, Michigan, able to receive students. By 1850 no less than fifteen such universities had been founded, nearly all of them in the South or the West.

No less important than the wider extension of educational opportunities was the change in the content of the instruction offered. Except for Noah Webster's *American Speller*, published in 1783, and Schoolbooks Jedediah Morse's *American Geography*, published in 1789, the schools of the United States had been compelled to rely mainly upon reprints of European textbooks. When, therefore, a Connecticut Yankee named Samuel Griswold Goodrich began to publish in 1827 his definitely American "Peter Parley" texts, they filled a real need. Goodrich, according to Professor Channing, wrote or edited about one hundred and seventy volumes, most of which bore the name Peter Parley in the title. Among his collaborators was Nathaniel Hawthorne, whose authorship of *Peter Parley's Universal History on the Basis of Geography*, which appeared in 1837, is well attested. The Peter Parley books were not notable, as a rule, either for literary merit or for high standards of scholarship, but they covered a wide variety of subjects, and they provided a medium of instruction precisely fitted to the requirements of the times. Goodrich estimated that not less than seven million copies of

---

[1] B. A. Hinsdale, *Horace Mann and the Common School Revival in the United States* (1898); Will S. Monroe, *The Educational Labors of Henry Barnard* (1893).

his books were sold in the United States, a record that would seem more startling but for the fact that the total sales of Webster's *Speller* probably reached fifty millions.

Competition for the Peter Parley readers was soon furnished by the *Eclectic Series*, compiled by William Holmes McGuffey.[1] These readers not only introduced the youth of America to the best in English and American literature, but contrived at the same time to drive home deftly the moral precepts of the Victorian Age. So popular were the selections that they were repeated in other series, such as the *National Readers* and *Lippincott's Readers*, and probably Mark Sullivan is correct in his opinion that they did much to set the pattern of American thought far down into the twentieth century. In 1828 Noah Webster, whose standardization of English spelling was already taking effect, published his great two-volume *Dictionary of the English Language*. This work, revised and republished in 1840, defined thousands of words that had never before been noted in any English dictionary, and set important precedents in pronunciation. Armed with these new tools of instruction, American teachers, particularly in the elementary schools, became increasingly effective. Largely through the leadership of Horace Mann, who in 1839 induced the state of Massachusetts to establish a normal school at Lexington, efforts were even begun to provide at state expense for the professional training of teachers.

The strongly classical bent of the academies, high schools, and colleges was destined to endure with but slight variation until the time of the Civil War.[2] Classes in Latin, Greek, and mathematics absorbed the bulk of the student's time, although such new subjects as modern languages and natural science won places of importance in some curriculums. The instruction was often mediocre or worse. College students, eager to concern themselves with topics of current interest, sometimes learned more from the debates and oratorical contests which literary societies and fraternities delighted to sponsor than from their classroom exercises. Few went to college except those who wished to enter one of the three learned professions, the ministry, the law, and medicine; and many entered these professions without the benefit of college, or even secondary, training. Separate divinity, law, and medical schools were fairly common among the older colleges and universities by the middle of the century, but the instruction offered, particularly for the medical students, was extremely meager. In general, the importance of higher education was not fully recognized by

Higher education

[1] H. H. Vail, *A History of the McGuffey Readers* (1910).
[2] C. F. Thwing, *A History of Higher Education in America* (1906); D. G. Tewksbury, *The Founding of American Colleges and Universities before the Civil War* (1932).

Americans before the Civil War. Students with a real thirst for learning found it necessary, as a rule, to spend some time in Europe. The emancipation of women from the restriction that a man-made world had placed about them enlisted the efforts of a notable company of American reformers. On both sides of the Atlantic cus-

Women's rights

tom had long decreed that woman's place was in the home. The education of women, therefore, except in so far as it might be of use in better fitting them for their domestic duties, was regarded as unnecessary, and even unwise. Girls who were fortunate enough to receive more than an elementary education attended female seminaries or finishing schools, where religion, morality, and the social graces, including music and art, were given primary consideration. Before the eighteen-thirties not a college or university in the United States had opened its doors to women, and every other approach to the learned professions was similarly restricted to men. Also, the legal status of woman was definitely inferior to that of man: she might not vote; control of her property passed at the time of marriage to her husband; in certain matters the husband answered to the law for the conduct of his wife; legal responsibility for the children of a marriage was vested exclusively in the father.

While American men treated women with a deference that excited the comment of European travelers, the women themselves had to take the lead in the crusade for women's rights. And of these women

Women as reformers

many were led to embrace the feminist cause mainly through their interest in other reforms. So deep-seated was the prejudice against women in any public capacity that male reformers sometimes refused to accept the assistance of women, except in a definitely humble and secondary capacity. For example, eight women delegates to a World's Anti-Slavery Convention, held in London in 1840, were denied admission solely because they were women. Two of the excluded delegates were Lucretia Mott and Elizabeth Cady Stanton, both of whom then realized that if women were ever to accomplish anything as reformers they must first achieve a more honorable status for themselves. In this sentiment they were supported strongly by such other able women as Frances Wright, a Scotswoman who on her second trip to America in 1825 had remained to work against slavery and on behalf of the emancipated slave; Lucy Stone, one of the first to demand equal suffrage; Margaret Fuller, the brilliant literary editor of the *New York Tribune*, who in 1844 published a scandalously frank book, *Women in the Nineteenth Century*; Doctor Elizabeth Blackwell, who won admission to the medical profession against almost insuperable obstacles; Dorothea L. Dix, whose primary passion was the reform of prisons and insane asylums; and Mrs. Antoinette Louisa Brown Blackwell, pioneer woman preacher.

While the feminist movement was greeted with much ridicule and was not wholly successful until well after the Civil War, some promising beginnings were made.[1] High schools and normal schools for girls became increasingly common, and teaching in the elementary schools was soon recognized as almost a woman's monopoly. In 1833 Oberlin College, a Congregationalist institution, recognized two reform movements at once by opening its doors to women and Negroes. Coeducation was permitted by Antioch College in 1853, by the University of Iowa in 1858, and in due time by most of the state-supported schools. A little later many strictly women's colleges were founded. Women also made definite headway against the prejudice which had so long barred them from appearance on the public platform. A few of them were licensed to preach; and by persistent effort many more won toleration, then approval, as lecturers. In their contest for equality before the law the women scored victories in a few states, mainly with respect to the right of married women to hold property separately from their husbands. For the most part, however, the reforms they sought were delayed until after the Civil War, and the suffrage cause was not won until the adoption of the Nineteenth Amendment in 1920.

Among the causes, other than that of their own emancipation, to which the women reformers were deeply devoted was temperance.[2] Hard drinking was an English tradition which had been easily transplanted to America and had flourished in the new environment. There was some variation, however, in the types of beverages consumed. English ale, which was of limited potency and required considerable skill to brew, was discarded in favor of the remarkably effective whiskey, which almost any frontiersman knew how to distill. Likewise imported wines, except for the use of the very rich, gave way to more primitive drinks, such as hard cider. Statistics on the consumption of liquor in the United States during these early years are not available, and the testimony of temperance reformers is not to be trusted, but it is safe to say that drinking was almost universal, among women as well as men, and that public drunkenness, at least for men, was no disgrace. Even ministers were apt to exhibit a degree of conviviality at ordination ceremonies, conferences, and college commencements that later generations would have regarded with astonishment.

Temperance reform

---

[1] This subject is best approached through its plentiful biographic and autobiographic literature. See, for example, Katharine S. Anthony, *Margaret Fuller; A Psychological Biography* (1920); Margaret Fuller [Ossoli], *Women in the Nineteenth Century* (1855); Elizabeth Blackwell, *Pioneer Work for Women* (1914); W. R. Waterman, *Frances Wright* (1924); Francis Tiffany, *Life of Dorothea Lynde Dix* (1890); and Elizabeth Cady Stanton, Susan B. Anthony, and others, *History of Woman Suffrage* (6 vols., 1889–1922). The last mentioned is an important source-book for all the major reform movements of the nineteenth century.

[2] J. A. Krout, *The Origins of Prohibition* (1925).

In its early phases the temperance movement was directed against obvious excesses. Scripture was abundantly available for quotation against drunkenness, and preachers, particularly in the evangelical churches, were fond of quoting it. Women who suffered because of the intemperance of their mates, or who saw the suffering which intemperance inflicted upon other women, bestirred themselves against the evil. A few far-seeing humanitarians connected drunkenness with poverty and crime, and sought by promoting temperance to effect a more fundamental reform. Even before 1830 many local temperance societies had been formed, particularly in New England, and by 1833 a United States Temperance Union joined these locals into one national organization. These early reformers, as the name they took indicated, were primarily interested in temperance rather than in total abstinence; but views of so moderate a nature could hardly survive in an age which responded so cordially to the teachings of extremists. During the eighteen-thirties the temperance movement was practically taken over by the teetotalers. For more than twenty years orators such as John B. Gough and Father Theobald Matthew denounced drinking as a crime against society; writers such as Lucius M. Sargent, with his six volumes of *Temperance Tales*, and Timothy Shay Arthur, with his even more effective *Ten Nights in a Bar-Room*, portrayed the decay of the individual who indulged in drink; and artists, more numerous than talented, provided pictures and cartoons that left nothing to the imagination. This campaign of education was strikingly successful. Individuals by the tens of thousands gave up the use of liquor, churches set more rigorous standards of conduct for the clergy and often also for the laity, and excessive drinking fell into general disrepute.

Efforts to diminish the temptation that led to the downfall of so many youths, and that made so difficult the regeneration of addicts, suggested naturally an appeal to the power of the state. To the New-Englanders, who stood in the vanguard of the movement, such an appeal was no confession of failure. Brought up, as most of them were, on the tradition that the state was properly charged with the duty of protecting the morals of the people, they could not overlook so effective an ally. Laws were demanded, and were frequently obtained, to license the liquor traffic, to hamper it with heavy taxation, and even to prohibit it altogether. State-wide prohibition of a sort was first adopted by Maine in 1846, under the influence of Neal Dow. Ohio followed in 1850, and perhaps a dozen other northern states had enacted prohibition laws before the Civil War. None of these laws was as effective as its advocates had hoped, and most of them were repealed during the Civil War period. The South, which in later years was to champion

Prohibition

the prohibition cause so enthusiastically, was at this time totally un-interested.

It would be difficult to call the roll of the reform movements of the eighteen-thirties and forties with any assurance that all of them would be included. During these years the very word "reform" had an almost irresistible charm for multitudes of Ameri- A reform era cans, and the mere adoption of that label was sufficient to secure a following. Not only in the United States, but throughout the civilized world, the "man of sensibility" was at the crest of his power, seeking out wrongs, striving earnestly to right them. Many reform movements came to America from Europe; others originated on both sides of the Atlantic at about the same time. The rigors of penal codes, although much modified since colonial times, were still open to attack by reformers, who objected to the long sentences meted out for trivial offenses, and to the overfree use of the death penalty. The barbarities common to prisons, insane asylums, and almshouses needed only to be revealed to arouse a feeling of horror, and a demand for change. Probably Dorothea L. Dix, the leading advocate in the United States of this type of reform, saw more of her ambitions realized than any other reformer of the period. New plans of dealing with convicts, designed not so much to punish as to reform them, were tried out with some success, and the idea that the mentally afflicted were entitled to hospitalization and medical treatment was almost universally accepted.

The sufferings incidental to war, while somewhat disguised by the glamour of patriotism, were also recognized, and the problem attacked at its source by concerted efforts to prevent the outbreak of war. As early as 1815, the formation of local organiza- The peace movement tions devoted to the cause of peace had begun in the United States, and in 1828 about fifty of them joined hands to found the American Peace Society, which for decades not only carried on within the United States a steady propaganda for peace, but co-operated also with similar organizations abroad. An American peace plan was formulated which called for regular world congresses to codify international law, and a world court to apply it.[1] Unhappily the peace movement was unable to sustain the shock of the wars which soon engulfed both Europe and America, and naturally the interest of reformers turned during the war-torn decades of the eighteen-fifties and sixties from the highly academic problem of world peace to the more pressing necessity of ameliorating the horrors of the battlefield.

[1] Two excellent books on this subject are Merle E. Curti, *The American Peace Crusade, 1815–1860* (1929); and W. Freeman Galpin, *Pioneering for Peace: A Study of American Peace Efforts to 1846* (1933). More general in scope is Merle E. Curti, *Peace or War — the American Struggle, 1636–1936* (1936).

With the spirit of humanitarian reform so thoroughly unleashed, it was unthinkable that the continued existence of African slavery in the American South could long be overlooked. Ever since the time of the French Revolution slavery had been generally frowned upon by world opinion, and its extinction had proceeded with such rapidity that by the middle of the nineteenth century the southern states of the United States shared only with Brazil and the Spanish colonies the doubtful honor of being the last strongholds of slavery in the civilized world. That many people in the United States were opposed to slavery became abundantly apparent during the debate on the admission of Missouri, and the Missouri Compromise, which actually permitted the further spread of slavery, by no means satisfied them. Benjamin Lundy, a Quaker emancipationist, published from 1812 to 1836 a periodical known as *The Genius of Universal Emancipation.* Lundy's Fabian tactics and mild manners, however, did not satisfy William Lloyd Garrison, a young enthusiast of Newburyport, Massachusetts, who proposed instead a crusade "as harsh as truth" and "as uncompromising as justice." With the first issue of Garrison's newspaper, the *Liberator,* published in Boston on January 1, 1831, the abolitionist movement may properly be said to have begun. So completely did this reform take the center of the stage that all others soon seemed insignificant in comparison; indeed, the slavery issue was destined to shape the course of American politics for more than a generation, and to leave a legacy of unsolved problems that were to plague many generations to come.[1]

Slavery a natural target

[1] The whole history of ideas in America is covered in Merle Curti, *The Growth of American Thought* (1943). R. H. Gabriel, *The Course of Democratic American Thought* (1940), is a series of brilliantly conceived essays. Max Berger, *The British Traveller in America, 1836–1860* (1943), summarizes the best foreign comment from British sources. F. L. Mott, *American Journalism: A History of Newspapers in the United States* (1941), is excellent. A. T. Gardner, *Yankee Stonecutters: The First American School of Sculpture, 1800–1850* (1945), explores a somewhat neglected subject.

There are numerous admirable biographies of interest in connection with this chapter. Among the best of them are: Mason Wade, *Margaret Fuller, Whetstone of Genius* (1940); R. B. Nye, *George Bancroft, Brahmin Rebel* (1944); Oliver Carlson, *The Man Who Made News: James Gordon Bennett* (1942); R. W. Leopold, *Robert Dale Owen: A Biography* (1940); Helen E. Marshall, *Dorothea Dix, Forgotten Samaritan* (1937); A. J. G. Perkins and Theresa Wolfson, *Frances Wright, Free Enquirer* (1939); A. M. Schlesinger, Jr., *Orestes Brownson: A Pilgrim's Progress* (1939); H. S. Canby, *Walt Whitman* (1943); H. S. Commager, *Theodore Parker; Yankee Crusader* (1936).

On various aspects of social history, see Alice Felt Tyler, *Freedom's Ferment: Phases of American Social History to 1860* (1944); Blake McKelvey, *American Prisons: A Study in American Social History Prior to 1815* (1936); W. F. Norwood, *Medical Education in the United States before the Civil War* (1944); S. L. Jackson, *America's Struggle for Free Schools: Social Tension and Education in New England and New York, 1827–42* (1941); A. M. Schlesinger, *Learning How to Behave: A Historical Study of American Etiquette Books* (1946); Bernard Jaffe, *Men of Science in America* (1944).

15

Slavery and Abolition

BY THE time Garrison had opened his abolitionist crusade the institution of slavery, which had once seemed well on the way toward extinction, was more deeply entrenched in the South than ever before. The chief reason for this change, as already noted, was the insatiable demand for American cotton, an The "Cotton South" article which, as experience had amply demonstrated, could be profitably grown by means of slave labor. Under pressure of the world's need for cotton, the South produced nearly twice the amount of that commodity in 1830 that it had produced in 1820, fully twice the amount in 1840 that it had produced in 1830, and more than three times the amount in 1860 that it had produced in 1840. Cotton exports during these years showed similar gains, until by the time of the Civil War well over half the value of American goods shipped abroad was in cotton. A broad belt of southern land, ranging in width from about five hundred miles in the Carolinas and Georgia to six or seven hundred miles in the Mississippi Valley, was devoted primarily to cotton culture. Other crops were grown in this region, particularly foodstuffs, and not all the land was suited to cotton-growing; but the chief wealth of the "lower South" came from cotton. In this region, too, the majority of the Negro slaves were congregated. Such states as Virginia and Kentucky, for example, which depended far more upon tobacco-growing and general agriculture for their prosperity than upon cotton, sold great numbers of their slaves "down South," where the demand for "cotton hands" was always good. Slaves were used profitably also, although in smaller numbers, in the Carolina-Georgia rice fields along the coast, and in the production of Louisiana sugar-cane.[1]

The demand for slave labor in the lower South led both to an increase in the southern slave population and to an advance in the price of slaves. Between 1820 and 1860 the number of slaves in the South grew from

[1] M. B. Hammond, *The Cotton Industry* (1897), is an excellent short treatise. On slavery the literature is voluminous, but the two books by U. B. Phillips, *American Negro Slavery* (1918), and *Life and Labor in the Old South* (1929), summarize the principal results of recent scholarship.

about a million and a half to nearly four million, but in spite of the increased supply the price of a good field hand mounted in the
Growth of
slavery
same years from three or four hundred dollars to a thousand
dollars or more. So great, indeed, was the demand for slaves
that their importation, although forbidden by law, was carried on sur-
reptitiously until the outbreak of the Civil War, while freed Negroes
living in the South were in some danger of being kidnaped and sold
back into slavery. The greatest increases in slave population were
naturally in the states of the new Southwest, where cotton culture was
making its most rapid strides.

The ownership of slave property in the South was confined to a relatively small number of whites. On the eve of the Civil War probably
not more than four hundred thousand southern families — approximately one in four — held slaves. Furthermore, at least two-thirds of
these families held fewer than ten slaves each. The number of great
planters — men who owned fifty or more slaves and proportionately large
holdings of land — was probably not above six or seven thousand. Some
planters numbered their slaves by the thousand and their acres by the
tens of thousands, although such instances were the exception rather
than the rule.

The small farmers who lived in the cotton belt, both those who owned
slaves and those who did not, raised a considerable part of the cotton
crops; but the chief profits of the industry were reserved for the great
planter. He was in a far better position than his less prosperous neighbors to practice scientific agriculture, his expenditures bulked less than
theirs in proportion to his receipts, and he generally owned the most
fertile lands. The farmers, however, saw eye to eye with the planters
in all matters pertaining to slavery. Poor men looked forward to the
time when they would become slaveholders; and the owners of a few
slaves aspired to be the owners of many. What seemed good to the
great planter seemed good, therefore, to the rank and file of southern
farmers, for they tended to think of themselves not so much as what
they were but as what they aspired to become. Thus the great planter
and his ways occupy a place in the history of the South quite out of
proportion to the numerical strength of the planter class.

The plantation owner was first and foremost a manager. Ordinarily
a single plantation, which rarely exceeded a thousand acres in size,
commanded his entire energies; but if, as sometimes was
The planta-
tion system
the case, he owned many plantations, he delegated authority to a hierarchy of stewards and overseers who carried
out his orders. Altogether too many of these underlings possessed faults
of character which unfitted them to be farmers and planters in their

own right, and the relations between master and slave were apt to be far more pleasant than the relations between these white employees and the slaves whose work they supervised. Practically all of the manual labor of a plantation was done by the slaves. Most of the slaves, of course, were field hands, but every plantation had its quota of skilled workers, such as blacksmiths and carpenters, while a favored few were selected for domestic service in and about the master's house. Sometimes Negro foremen, or "slave drivers," were placed in charge of small gangs of slaves. Frequently these drivers, themselves freed from the necessity of labor and empowered to inflict corporal punishment upon those who worked under them, were more oppressive than the whites. Field labor was accomplished by the gang system, in which a driver kept a group of slaves at work on a given task under fear of the lash, or by the task system, in which each individual was given a certain amount of work to do in a given period of time and left free to finish it as he chose, provided only that he did his work well. Any extra time the slave earned by rapid work was his to while away.

The lot of the slave on the southern plantation was ordinarily quite tolerable. As a valuable piece of property, his good health was a matter of considerable consequence to his master. He was well *The slave* fed, although no particular pains were taken to vary his diet from the standard corn bread and fat pork that was regarded as entirely adequate to sustain life. In case of illness he was usually cared for by the same physician that attended the master and his family. His living quarters, usually located not far from the "big house" of the planter, were apt to be primitive, but they afforded protection from the wind and the rain, and were ordinarily provided with fireplaces and a plentiful supply of fuel for use in cold weather. The slave's clothing was coarse enough, and in summer he was not expected to wear very much, but he was about as well clad as southern whites of the lower class. By and large, the conditions of his life represented a distinct advance over the lot that would have befallen him had he remained in Africa.

Indeed, the slaves got much positive enjoyment out of life. Extremely gregarious, they delighted in the community life of the plantation, and on special occasions were permitted to indulge in picnics, barbecues, and various other types of celebration. They loved to sing and dance, and contributed ideas along both lines that the whites, at least of a later generation, were not too proud to appropriate. They were generally blessed with a keen sense of humor; they rarely fretted, when treated well, because of their state of bondage; and they were often deeply devoted to their master and his family. Small children, regardless of color, played together freely, and the affection of white boys and girls for their Negro nurses, or "mammies," was proverbial. The slaves were deeply religious, and almost universally accepted Christianity, usually as interpreted by one of the more emotional denominations, such as the Methodists and the Baptists, whose camp-meetings, revivals, and baptizings gave them unbounded joy. A few Negroes were taught to read, but most of them acquired by word of mouth rather than by reading a considerable knowledge of the Bible and of Christian theology. Their devotions were extremely picturesque, and their moral standards sufficiently latitudinarian to meet the needs of a really primitive people. Heaven to the Negro was a place of rest from all labor, the fitting reward of a servant who obeyed his master and loved the Lord. Negroes sometimes worshiped separately from the whites, and sometimes they were assigned seats in the galleries of the white people's churches. More or less formal marriages among slaves were encouraged by some masters, although cohabitation without marriage was regarded as perfectly normal, and a certain amount of promiscuity was taken for granted. Slave women had no chance to resist the advances of white men, as their numerous mulatto progeny abundantly attested.

Nevertheless, the privileges of the slave were strictly limited. Each southern state had a "slave code," which gave the sanction of law to the practices that experience had proved to be of value in

Slave discipline

keeping the slave population in order. Even minor offenses were punishable by law, but in all save the most exceptional cases the master usually chose to mete out justice himself. Whippings were permissible at his discretion, or at the discretion of those to whom he delegated authority, although it was a punishable crime to beat a slave to death. Some masters, and many of their subordinates, were excessively cruel, although punishment so severe as to unfit the slave for labor was an expensive indulgence which not many masters would either practice or permit. Slave crimes of a serious nature, such as murder, rape, theft, and conspiracy to revolt, were punishable by death, but their concealment by masters who feared the inconvenience and possible property loss involved was not uncommon. Exacting masters were much troubled by runaways, or so the advertisements in southern papers seem to show. Attempts at insurrection were extremely rare, although in the regions where the blacks far outnumbered the whites, the latter sometimes suffered acutely from an unconfessed fear of what their slaves might do. In 1831 a serious slave uprising, led by a trusted Negro preacher named Nat Turner, occurred in Virginia. Some fifty-five whites, mostly women and children, were killed. Turner, and nearly all the other participants in this insurrection, suffered death or worse for their crime, but the incident served to unsettle the good relations between many southern masters and their slaves for years to come.

Undoubtedly the most unlovely aspect of slavery was the slave trade.[1] As already noted, the international slave trade was outlawed in 1808, and after 1820 it was punishable as piracy, but the right to buy and sell slaves within the United States, and to transport them from one slave state to another, remained unimpaired. During the years that the cotton lands of the newer South — from Alabama to Texas — were being opened up, this domestic slave trade came to assume extraordinary importance. Not only did the planters of the Gulf states need more and more slaves, but it was also a fact that the upper South was being confronted with an oversupply of slave labor. Tobacco-raisers in such states as Maryland, Virginia, and Kentucky were suffering from the continued exhaustion of the soil, from the decline of their export trade which began with the Embargo and the War of 1812, and from the competition of Latin-American producers. Under such circumstances the natural increase of their slave population would have amounted almost to tragedy except for the opportunity to sell their surplus hands down South to work in the cotton fields. Except in the case of refractory and objectionable slaves, however, reputable masters often hesitated to dispose of their human property by sale, and many cases are on record where planters allowed themselves to become "slave poor." Other slaveholders were not so squeamish, and bankruptcy or death often accomplished what the best-intentioned master hoped to avoid. Sometimes planters or farmers went as permanent emigrants from the old South to the new, and took their slaves along to be disposed of in whole or in part as necessity required; but far more frequently the slaves were transported from the one region to the other by slave-traders, who bought and sold them strictly with an eye to profit. In 1836, the peak year of this traffic, the number of slaves sold South, or taken there by their masters, from Virginia alone reached the astounding figure of one hundred and twenty thousand. In the eighteen-forties and fifties a revival of agriculture took place in the upper South, due in part to the discovery of better methods of curing tobacco, and in part to the introduction of new and superior varieties. This served to check the domestic slave trade to some extent, but by no means to destroy it. Down to the time of the Civil War there were many planters in the upper South who, whether they would admit it or not, were engaged primarily in the business of raising slaves for sale.

The slave-trader was nevertheless an object of well-nigh universal disdain throughout the South. His business was brutalizing in the

The slave trade

[1] Frederic Bancroft, *Slave-Trading in the Old South* (1931).

extreme, for he was called upon constantly to engage in the separation of families, and to maintain discipline under adverse circumstances over slaves who in many instances were selected for sale precisely because they were hard to discipline. Few high-minded men would engage in such a business, and those who did were usually corrupted by its demands. The typical slave-trader was coarse and ill-bred, intemperate of speech and habits, and callous to the opinions of his fellow men. To succeed among ruthless competitors he learned to drive close bargains and became as adept at covering up the defect of his Negroes as ever was the Yankee horse-trader in making light of blemishes in horseflesh. Slave-traders were rarely accepted into polite southern society; indeed, they were treated as outcasts even by those who had to deal with them. The social status of bootleggers during the prohibition era was, on the whole, well above that of the slave-trader in the pre-Civil War South.

The slave-trader

The collection of a group of slaves and their shipment to the lower South afforded many painful spectacles. Pending shipments, they might be herded together in stockades, locked up in warehouses, or jails, or occasionally cared for decently in taverns. Frequently they were marched overland in coffles to their destination, although the trader also made good use of river steamers and ships engaged in the coastwise trade.

In the final disposal of slaves, the auction-block was frequently resorted to. The slave-trader availed himself, however, of every opportunity to sell, and stops along the route of march, or at wharves, were duly utilized for the cultivation of purchasers. Sometimes slaves were hired out for long or short periods of service, in which case the employer succeeded to the disciplinary authority of the master. Hired slaves were more apt to be overworked and mistreated than slaves directly under the control of their masters.

Such was the institution upon which Garrison and the abolitionists opened their attack.[1] They knew little about it at first hand, but they sought and found an abundance of ammunition to use. Stories of atrocities committed against slaves, such as brutal whippings, the breaking up of slave homes, enforced immorality, and the like, were constantly drifting northward, stories which lost nothing in the telling. These tales were picked up indiscriminately by abolitionist editors and orators who were eager to

The abolitionist attack

---

[1] The work of Garrison is told in detail, and probably with overemphasis on his importance to the movement, by Wendell Phillips Garrison and Francis Jackson Garrison, *William Lloyd Garrison* (4 vols., 1885–89). The significance of the western group of abolitionists is set forth, perhaps with equal overemphasis, by Gilbert H. Barnes, *The Anti-Slavery Impulse, 1830–1844* (1933). For further evidence on the subject, see also the *Letters of Theodore Dwight Weld, Angelina Grimké Weld, and Sarah Grimké, 1822–1844*, edited by Gilbert H. Barnes and Dwight L. Dumond (2 vols., 1934).

believe the worst about slavery and who used, as if they were typical, stories which had to do with highly exceptional occurrences. The abolitionists were not limited, however, to the recital of wrongs done the slaves. They regarded the institution at its best as morally indefensible. Slaves were men, and no man, according to the abolitionist argument, had the right to hold a fellow man in bondage. On this ground the abolitionists rejected totally the idea of compensated emancipation. The slave-owner was a criminal; why pay him for his crime?

The abolitionist doctrines struck a responsive chord in many northern hearts. Humanitarian reformers could not logically resist them. Many New-Englanders, angered by the vicious attacks upon their section that nullificationist orators delighted to make, retaliated, perhaps unconsciously, by going over to the abolitionist camp. The Quakers had always regarded slavery as immoral, and great numbers of them found the transition from passive to active opposition extremely easy to make. Most of the northern evangelical churches, particularly the Methodist and the Baptist, began to lean in the direction of abolition. Among the abolitionist orators, Wendell Phillips, scion of an aristocratic Boston family, was pre-eminent. Not since the days of Patrick Henry had American audiences been treated to such fervid appeals as fell from his lips. Two South-Carolinians, Sarah and Angelina Grimké, went North to Philadelphia, joined the Society of Friends, and devoted their lives to the anti-slavery crusade. Theodore Dwight Weld, a Westerner who became the husband of Angelina, is thought by many to have done more for the cause of abolition than Garrison himself. Lucretia Mott, a Philadelphia Quakeress, overcame valiantly the obstacles placed in the way of women orators, and lectured far and wide in behalf of abolition. Gerrit Smith, an up-state New-Yorker of considerable wealth, devoted both his time and his fortune to the cause. Unnamed hundreds of workers spread the abolitionist doctrines among their neighbors, and, translating word into deed, established many lines of secret stopping-places, or "underground railroads," by means of which fugitive slaves could be passed along from the southern states to Canada and freedom.[1]

The abolitionists lost no time in perfecting an organization. Their first local association was formed in 1831. The next year a New England Anti-Slavery Society was functioning, and in 1833 a convention at Phil-

[1] The abolitionist leaders have nearly all attracted biographers, among them Lorenzo Sears, *Wendell Phillips, Orator and Agitator* (1909); Catherine H. Birney, *The Grimké Sisters, Sarah and Angelina Grimké* (1885); Anna D. Hallowell, *James and Lucretia Mott, Life and Letters* (1884); O. B. Frothingham, *Gerrit Smith* (1878); H. S. Commager, *Theodore Parker; Yankee Crusader* (1936); and William Birney, *James G. Birney and his Times* (1890). For more general accounts, see A. B. Hart, *Slavery and Abolition* (1906); Jesse Macy, *The Anti-Slavery Crusade* (1919); and W. H. Siebert, *The Underground Railroad from Slavery to Freedom* (1898).

adelphia launched the American Anti-Slavery Society. A division in
this society occurred in 1840, however, mainly because
Abolitionist Garrison and a few other extremists were unwilling to stoop
organization
to the level of party politics. Slavery was recognized by the
Constitution of the United States, a fact which, according to Garrison,
made that document "a covenant with death and an agreement with
hell." Theodore Parker, ardent abolitionist and the most eminent
preacher of his time, prided himself on his unwillingness even to cast a
vote under the authority of such a government. But to the rank and
file of abolitionists, the obvious way to promote their cause was through
united political action. The actual abolition of slavery was conceded
to depend upon the individual states where anti-slavery majorities could
not soon be achieved, but the national government had authority to
abolish slavery in the District of Columbia and to put an end to the
interstate slave trade. To promote these ends, as well as to work toward
the eventual abolition of slavery in every state, the Liberty Party was
formed shortly before the election of 1840, and James G. Birney was
selected as its candidate for President. Birney was a Kentuckian by
birth, who after spending many years as a planter in Alabama, had
freed his slaves and come North to work against slavery. For a time he
published an abolitionist paper, *The Philanthropist*, at Cincinnati, but
in 1837 he became secretary of the American Anti-Slavery Society and
removed to New York. In the election of 1840 he polled a total of
about seven thousand votes.

The abolitionists had made greater progress, however, than this small
vote seemed to indicate. Their arguments had stirred up much feeling
against slavery throughout the North, and had convinced many people
who were unwilling to vote the abolitionist ticket that the slavery system must ultimately be overthrown. Furthermore, the prestige of the
southern planters, who traditionally had occupied a prominent place in
national affairs, was seriously damaged. Northern farmers came to
suspect southern leadership of working against the interests of the small
free farmer and solely for the interests of the slaveholding planter.
More and more the conviction grew that slavery at least ought not to
expand, that the newly opened lands of the West should be reserved
for the use of free farmers and should be denied forever to slaveholders.
Partly with this idea in view, and partly also because of the obvious
evils it bred, opponents of the domestic slave trade also increased steadily in numbers.

Perhaps the abolition of slavery in the District of Columbia won
more support than any other abolitionist tenet. Northern members of
Congress were increasingly sensitive to the existence of slavery in the na-

tional capital, and to the necessity of witnessing day by day the public buying and selling of slaves. Floods of abolitionist petitions, most of them praying that slavery be abolished in the district, cluttered up their mail, and many congressmen took pleasure in presenting them. The southern members, however, were deeply offended at these memorials, and in 1836 they persuaded the House to pass a "gag rule" that required all such petitions to be laid on the table without debate. This action was construed by ex-President John Quincy Adams, who represented a Massachusetts district in Congress, as a direct violation of the constitutional right of petition, and he fought against it with all his might. While not himself actually an abolitionist, his constant appearance as a defender of abolitionist petitions tended to identify him with the anti-slavery movement, and to clothe it with increasing respectability. In 1844 his efforts were crowned with success, and by a vote of 108 to 80 the obnoxious rule was repealed. But the abolition of slavery in the District of Columbia awaited the verdict of the Civil War.

Slavery in the District of Columbia

Regardless of the headway they made, the abolitionists were cordially disliked in the North as well as in the South. As individuals they were, like so many professional reformers, apt to be extremely irritating to their less conscience-smitten fellow men. Moreover, the indifference of the extremists among them to the Constitution, and their openly expressed willingness to see the slave-owning South outside the Union, was thoroughly resented by a generation which held both the Constitution and the Union in the deepest reverence. Business interests took fright at the abolitionist propaganda. Northern manufacturers were making good profits from southern trade; with higher tariffs, they stood a chance to make even better profits. Abolitionist activities might imperil the trade relations between the sections, lessen the chance of raising duties against foreign goods, destroy the business value of the Union. Many Northerners, moreover, were themselves ex-Southerners or the descendants of Southerners, and they agreed whole-heartedly with the southern contention that the only proper status for the Negro was slavery. With this view many other Northerners, not themselves of southern descent, were inclined to agree, because of unpleasant contacts they had had with freed Negroes in the North. In fact, most of the anti-slavery crusaders, particularly in the early years of the movement, were subjected to frequent outrages, the offices of abolitionist newspapers were repeatedly sacked, and at least one abolitionist editor, Elijah P. Lovejoy of Alton, Illinois, was put to death at the hands of a pro-slavery mob.

Opposition to the abolitionists

But the unpopularity of the abolitionists in the North was a mild

thing indeed compared with the venomous hatred they provoked in the
South. Losses from runaway slaves became increasingly

Southern
reaction to
abolitionism

serious, and for these losses southern masters, with good
reason, held the abolitionists responsible. Abolitionist
literature, some of which deliberately suggested to the slaves,
by means of cartoons and otherwise, the possibility of running away,
flooded the South in spite of the best efforts of Southerners to keep it out.
The efficiency of the underground railroad, over which unnumbered
thousands of Negroes traveled to freedom every year, was spread assiduously by word of mouth. Southerners believed also that the abolitionists were doing their best to promote Negro insurrections in the
South, and occasional unguarded utterances on the part of a few extremists gave color to this charge. The *Liberator*, for example, once
wished "success to all slave insurrections," and quoted approvingly the
statement of an Englishman who said, "Southern slaves ought, or at
least have a right, to cut the throats of their masters." Nat Turner's
Rebellion, occurring as it did at about the same time that the abolitionist crusade began, was soon very generally, although quite incorrectly,
ascribed to northern anti-slavery propaganda. But more galling even
than property losses or the fear of insurrection were the abolitionist
denunciations of slave-holders as the lowest type of criminals. Slavery,
according to Garrison, was a "damning crime," and slave-holders were
the "meanest of thieves and the worst of robbers.... We do not acknowledge them to be within the pale of Christianity, of republicanism,
or humanity." The southern planter, who was traditionally proud of his
reputation and resented hotly any charge against his personal honor,
could not let such epithets pass unchallenged; and he was particularly
incensed to have them flung at him by un-Christian Unitarians from a
region notorious for its tight-fisted money-changers.

Coincident with the rise of abolitionism came the almost complete
subsidence of southern interest in emancipation. It was generally
alleged that this change of sentiment in the South was due mainly to
resentment against the northern anti-slavery propaganda, but a better
argument can be made in support of the theory that the increasing
profits of slavery had already sapped the vitality of southern emanci-
pationism. Whatever the reason, such projects as contemplated emancipation and the return of freed Negroes to Africa no longer received
southern approbation. The last significant southern debate on the subject of slavery occurred in the Virginia legislature of 1832, immediately
following Nat Turner's Rebellion, an incident which few Southerners
had as yet thought to blame on the northern abolitionists. During the
debate the institution of slavery was subjected to the most searching

criticism; slavery, according to one member, was "the heaviest calamity which has ever befallen any portion of the human race," and according to another was "a curse upon him who inflicts as upon him who suffers it." But the legislature finally refused to take action, and within a few years hardly a Southerner of consequence could be found who would not spring to the defense of slavery.

Furthermore, every possible effort was made throughout the South to suppress all agitation in favor of emancipation, and in particular to prevent the delivery of the abolitionist tracts that the mails of the United States brought in. In 1835, after a Charleston, South Carolina, mob had burned a sack of abolitionist literature, the Postmaster-General ruled that local postmasters might refuse to deliver such mail if they believed it to be of an incendiary nature. Although this ruling was soon rescinded, many southern postmasters continued to abide by it, and many other obstacles to the spread of abolitionist propaganda in the South were devised. The individual who failed to destroy such literature immediately on its receipt was subjected to social ostracism, northern states were threatened with an economic boycott if they permitted its publication within their borders, and efforts were made, more spectacular than successful, to secure the extradition for trial in the South of objectionable northern editors.

At length, arguments were adduced to prove that slavery, far from being an evil, was actually a positive good. Of all the pro-slavery philosophers probably Thomas Roderick Dew, professor of history, metaphysics, and political law in the College of William and Mary, and afterward its president, was the most systematic and effective. Dew had obtained his education in Germany, where he was impressed by the open recognition of the inequalities of man, and the inevitability of a stratified society. Instead of apologizing for what he found in the South, he defended it. The great planters, because of their superior education, ability, and property, stood rightly at the head of southern society; next to them in rank were the small landowners, the traders, and free laborers; at the bottom of the ladder were the slaves. "It is the order of nature and of God," he claimed, "that the being of superior faculties and knowledge, and therefore of superior power, should control and dispose of those who are inferior. It is as much the order of nature that men should enslave each other as that other animals should prey upon each other." Dew's arguments were set forth in pamphlet form as early as 1832, and were repeatedly reprinted.[1] He was ably seconded by Chancellor William

The pro-slavery argument

---

[1] Chancellor Harper and others, *The Pro-Slavery Argument* (1852), contains Dew's Essay. See also William S. Jenkins, *Pro-Slavery Thought in the Old South* (1935). By all

Harper of the Supreme Court of South Carolina, who published in 1838 a *Memoir on Slavery* that was quoted as authority throughout the South. About the same time John C. Calhoun gave it as his opinion that the South had no reason to be ashamed of slavery, and added that "There never has yet existed a wealthy and civilized society in which one portion of the community did not in fact live on the labor of the other." Professional men of every kind, particularly the preachers and the politicians, took up the argument, and boldly proclaimed the virtues of the South's most distinctive institution.

The idea that slavery was ordained of God was particularly comforting to the people of the South, most of whom were devoutly orthodox in their religious views. The Fourth and the Tenth Commandments, which referred to man-servants and maid-servants as of the same status as slaves, clearly gave the stamp of divine approval to slavery. Abraham, Isaac, and the other patriarchs had held slaves, and Saint Paul had enjoined servants to be obedient to their masters. Moreover, it was a particularly happy dispensation of Providence which brought heathen Africans to America, where they might learn the truths of Christianity. But for the institution of slavery they might still be outside the pale of Christian influence.

Slavery was also defended as a benevolent institution in which the relationship between capital and labor was more kindly than could be found anywhere else in the world. The master must care for the slave in sickness as well as in health, in childhood and old age no less than in his prime. The master must not overwork his slave, for to do so would impair the slave's value. Compared with the wage-slave system of the industrial North and of Europe, where, it was asserted, men, women, and children were worked to death in mines and factories, and where the aged, the ill, and the incompetent were ruthlessly discharged, the slavery system could be made to appear as "a beautiful example of communism, where each one receives not according to his labor, but according to his wants."

The claim that slavery as an economic device was also ideally suited to the South was continually made. Dew was not in the least embarrassed by the fact that Virginia piled up excellent profits each year from slave-breeding. Without that prop to its economic structure, he maintained that the Old Dominion would soon become a "howling wilderness." Less specious were the arguments of the eminent southern agriculturalist, Edward Ruffin, who pointed out

The economics
of slavery

odds the best brief treatment of this subject is William E. Dodd, *The Cotton Kingdom* (1919). Of great value also in this connection, is his *Expansion and Conflict* (1915). W. G. Brown, *The Lower South in American History* (1902), recovers much of the emotional fervor that was characteristic of the defenders of slavery.

the economic advantage in large-scale production and in the wholesale purchasing of supplies made possible by the slavery plantation system.[1] Furthermore, slave labor could be specialized at the will of the planter and in accordance with the aptitudes of the slaves, while the expensive struggles between capital and labor that had come to be characteristic of the free-labor system could be avoided. Some insisted that the drudgery required for the production of tobacco, rice, sugar-cane, and cotton could never be provided in sufficient amount by free men; and according to one observer, the North was as much benefited by the slave-labor system of the South as ever was the South itself. Northern manufacturers could count on the plantation South both as a steady source of supply for raw materials and as a market for northern goods.

As a matter of fact, the economic disadvantages of slave labor were becoming plain enough to those who wished to observe them. The South, thanks in considerable part to the limitations of the slave, was overspecialized. It produced only what the slave could produce profitably, and to an increasing extent this meant cotton. Even foodstuffs, which could be, and ordinarily were, grown on every southern farm and plantation, were frequently produced in such meager quantities that importations from the North had to be made. The prosperity of the South thus rose and fell with the proceeds from its money crops. Cotton was "King," but an off year, or a serious drop in price, meant widespread disaster. Moreover, the returns of the southern planter were far too small in proportion to his investment. Much of his capital was tied up in the ownership of labor, a situation which the northern employer of free labor did not confront. Much capital had to be invested also in land, the price of which, thanks to the competition among planters for good cotton land, soared frequently to absurd figures. On a much smaller investment the successful northern industrialist made far greater profits.

Doubtless the worst feature of the system of slavery was that its rather scanty profits were absorbed by so small a number of planters. Ruffin was right in his contention that large-scale production was more profitable economically than small-scale production. But the bulk of the people of the South belonged to the small planter and the farmer class. They had no choice but to compete with the large planter on terms that made him comfortable, but made them permanently poor. It was on this account that tens of thousands of Southerners who had no slaves or only a few

Effect of slavery on the whites

[1] Avery O. Craven, *Edmund Ruffin, Southerner, A Study in Secession* (1932), is of broader scope and interest than the title indicates. See also, by the same author, *Soil Exhaustion as a Factor in the Agricultural History of Virginia and Maryland, 1606-1860* (1926).

slaves fled to the free states of the old Northwest, or to such portions of the slave states as the plantation system was unable to follow them to. Not only did the South lose a steady stream of emigrants to the North; it failed also, because of slavery, to attract immigrants, as the North was doing, from outside the United States. The effect of slavery upon the rank and file of the native southern whites was also unfortunate. They tended to regard physical labor, because it was the customary lot of slaves, as essentially menial and degrading. The leisure class thus came to include many who might have fared far better had they been less opposed to work, and who made little or no contribution to the welfare of their section.

Undoubtedly the flaws in the slave-labor system were too numerous and too serious for slavery to have survived indefinitely. The leaders of southern opinion were temporarily deceived, however, by the advent of King Cotton, and as a consequence came boldly to the defense of the South's "peculiar institution." The attack of the abolitionists gave them an excellent opportunity to transform their apologies for slavery into a determined insistence on its righteousness and the desirability of its permanence. Thus the scene was being rapidly set for an "irrepressible conflict" between North and South — a conflict that would soon rock the Union to its very foundations.[1]

---

[1] The best book on slavery is J. H. Franklin, *From Slavery to Freedom: A History of American Negroes* (1947). Frank Tannenbaum, *Slave and Citizen: The Negro in the Americas* (1947), is a comparative treatment of North and South America. The southern point of view on abolition is given in Harvey Wish, *George Fitzhugh: Propagandist of the Old South* (1943); Clement Eaton, *Freedom of Thought in the Old South* (1940); A. V. Lloyd, *The Slavery Controversy, 1831–1860* (1939); and R. H. Taylor, *Ante-Bellum South Carolina* (1942). D. L. Dumond, *Antislavery Origins of the Civil War in the United States* (1939), features the record of the western abolitionists. On the freed Negro, see L. P. Jackson, *Free Negro Labor and Property Holding in Virginia* (1942); and J. H. Franklin, *The Free Negro in North Carolina, 1790–1860* (1943).

16

Manifest Destiny

UNTIL the late eighteen-thirties and the early eighteen-forties, the people of the United States took it for granted that the growth of the populated area of their country would be hedged in by certain obvious limits. They had foreseen for some time that the **The American frontier** frontier of population would advance steadily into the upper Mississippi Valley and that it would reach, and perhaps cross, the international border to the Southwest, but they had no idea that the region west of Missouri, which was labeled on the maps the "Great American Desert," would ever be desired for settlement. The only significant changes they anticipated were in the international boundaries. They expected the United States to acquire sole title to at least a part of the Oregon country, and they recognized also that the southwestern boundary, made in 1819, might have to be revised. But they never dreamed that the distant regions of the farther West would ever be settled by whites.

One of the circumstances that served to provide Americans with a new vision of expansion was the opening of the Santa Fe Trail. On the upper Rio Grande, separated by a long desert trip from Mexico **New Mexico** City, the Spanish had established outposts at about the same time the English were founding Jamestown. As long as this area remained a part of New Spain, all efforts on the part of Americans to trade with it were thwarted by Spanish officials, but the Mexican Revolution brought a change of policy. After 1822, when William Becknell returned to the Missouri settlements from the first profitable trip to Santa Fe, caravans of American traders crossed the "Desert" each year for more than two decades. Sometimes their profits were excellent. The expedition of 1824, for example, consisting of eighty-one men with thirty thousand dollars' worth of merchandise in twenty-five wagons, brought back one hundred and eighty thousand dollars in gold and silver, in addition to ten thousand dollars' worth of furs, and some mules.[1]

[1] Josiah Gregg, *Commerce of the Prairies, or the Journal of a Santa Fe Trader* (1844), is a classic on this subject. For a recent popular account see R. L. Duffus, *The Santa Fe Trail* (1930). On the general subject of expansion during this decade, the best work is G. P. Garrison, *Westward Extension* (1906).

THE WESTERN TRAILS

The total volume of trade down the Santa Fe Trail was never very large, and the number of traders engaged in it probably did not average many more than a hundred a year. Nevertheless, the opening of a new trail into the Far West was, at least to the people of the Mississippi Valley, an event of real significance. The Santa Fe Trail Traders who were oftentimes themselves also farmers were not slow to observe that the land along the first lap of the journey was good land, and that heavy rainfall sometimes impeded their progress. As their interest grew, they persuaded Congress to survey the trail, and they sometimes obtained military escorts to accompany and protect their caravans. When in 1843 Santa Anna, the Mexican leader, put an end to the trade, they and the whole country with them were deeply shocked, and even its reopening a year or two later did not serve to destroy the impression that "manifestly" this whole region ought to be a part of the United States.

Meantime, the Oregon Trail had opened to American eyes a new vision of the possibilities of the Far Northwest.[1] The origins of this route to the West are somewhat obscure, but by the eighteen-thirties Indian traders bound for the Far Northwest had settled upon it as the easiest way through. It led, not without many variations, from the bend of the Missouri to the bend of the Platte, out the latter stream and its north fork to what is now southern Wyoming, through South Pass, an easy divide in the mountains, to the Snake Valley, then by a cut-off to the Columbia. The region in which it terminated, as everyone knew, was in dispute between Great Britain and the United States. Whatever claims Spain might once have had, the United States had acquired by the Florida Treaty of 1819; and whatever rights Russia might once have had, the British had acquired by an agreement as to the Alaskan boundary in 1825. Eventually, it was well understood, the Oregon country must all go to the United States or to Great Britain, or be divided between the two. But with settlement almost non-existent and with traders sparse, that problem, most people assumed, could wait.

Rivalry between British and American fur-traders, however, did not wait for long.[2] The British interests, united after 1821 under the exclusive control of the Hudson's Bay Company, were ably commanded

---

[1] Joseph Schafer, *A History of the Pacific Northwest* (1905), furnishes an excellent guide to the history of this section. Katharine Coman, *Economic Beginnings of the Far West* (2 vols., 1912), is interesting and informative. Francis Parkman, *The California and Oregon Trail* (1849), has gone through innumerable editions under a shorter title, *The Oregon Trail*, and is as authentic as it is interesting. A recent account is W. J. Ghent, *The Road to Oregon* (1929).

[2] H. M. Chittenden, *The American Fur Trade of the Far West* (3 vols., 1902), is the standard authority on this subject. Useful, also, is K. W. Porter, *John Jacob Astor, Business Man* (2 vols., 1931). For McLoughlin's career see F. V. Holman, *Dr. John McLoughlin, the Father of Oregon* (1907).

by Doctor John McLoughlin, the "King of Old Oregon," and carried on a profitable trade. But McLoughlin's agents on their adventures into the Rockies were soon reporting contacts, and even conflicts, with American traders. Private adventurers also, among them Captain Benjamin L. E. Bonneville, a Regular Army officer on leave, and Nathaniel J. Wyeth, a Boston ice merchant, both of whom led expeditions into the Far Northwest, brought to McLoughlin's attention the imminence of strenuous American competition. By the year 1832 it was abundantly evident that "joint occupation" was soon to be given a real test.

Rivalry in Oregon

And yet the conflict, when finally it came, was less the work of fur-traders than of missionaries. By the eighteen-thirties most American religious denominations had developed a keen interest in foreign missions, and had recognized, somewhat belatedly, that the Indian tribes offered a suitable field for such labors. The Methodists in 1833 sent out their first missionary to the Oregon country, Jason Lee. Close on the heels of the Methodists came the Presbyterians, whose ablest representative, Marcus Whitman, appeared on the scene in 1836. By the end of the decade the American Catholics also were represented in the person of Father Pierre Jean de Smet, a Belgian Jesuit from St. Louis. Conflict among the rival denominations

Missionaries to Oregon

LITERARY FIGURES

The name of RALPH WALDO EMERSON (1803–82), *New England poet and philosopher, heads almost any list of the men who most influenced thoughtful Americans of the nineteenth century.*

HENRY WADSWORTH LONGFELLOW (1807–82), *beloved and genial author of dozens of tuneful poems, was long regarded by Americans as their greatest poet, although literary criticism today assigns him a somewhat lesser place.*

EDGAR ALLAN POE (1809–49) *was remarkable both as a poet and as a writer of short stories. He had an affinity for weird and gloomy themes and developed a style that suited them.*

HENRY THOREAU (1817–62) *wrote exquisite prose as well as poetry and is best remembered for his "Walden," "a book in praise of life rather than Nature . . . a book of social criticism as well."*

WALT WHITMAN (1819–92), *at first spurned because of his unconventionality, was honored before his death as the greatest "poet of democracy."*

SAMUEL LANGHORNE CLEMENS (1835–1910) *was "Mark Twain." Missouri-born and thoroughly western in his point of view, he wrote in a breezy and humorous style that delighted his contemporaries.*

LONGFELLOW

THOREAU

EMERSON

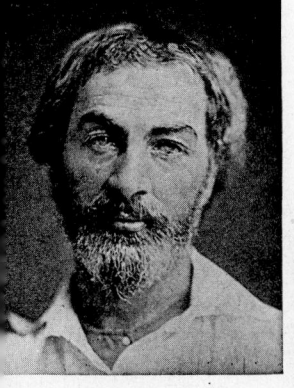

WHITMAN

CLEMENS

POE

HARRIET B. STOWE

LUCRETIA MOTT

LUCY STONE

SUSAN B. ANTHONY

DOROTHEA DIX

JANE ADDAMS

was at first avoided, for the Methodists chose the Willamette Valley as their headquarters, the Presbyterians the region where the Snake enters the Columbia, and Father de Smet the mountains and plains still farther inland. The great majority of McLoughlin's traders, however, were Catholics, and the French-Canadian priests who came out at about this same time to minister to their needs worked at will among all the Indians. Religious rivalry thus began to take on a nationalistic bias.

The real trouble came, however, from the fact that many of the Methodist and Presbyterian missionaries became so actively engaged in agriculture that they almost forgot the spiritual needs of the Indians. In 1844 the Methodists, convinced that the sending of missionary money to Oregon under the circumstances was a scandal, closed down their Willamette mission. Well before this time, however, the far more interesting news that there was good farming land in Oregon had spread far and wide, and after 1841 hundreds of emigrants gathered each spring at Independence, Missouri, to make the long journey by covered wagon into the new frontier. To watch over the growing American colony, the government of the United States in 1842 sent out Doctor Elijah White, ostensibly as an Indian agent, and that year John C. Frémont, son-in-law of Thomas Hart Benton, began an official survey of the Oregon Trail. A

LEADERS AMONG WOMEN

The rôle of women in American history has been generously underestimated. Besides the potent influence they have exerted upon leaders among men, they have themselves furnished much direct leadership in the field of humanitarian reform.

DOROTHEA LYNDE DIX (1802–87) *was deeply distressed as a young woman by the cruel and unintelligent handling of the insane and feeble-minded in American jails and asylums. During a long lifetime she "devoted the vigor of a sound mind to the lessening of the anguish of unsound ones." (Photo from Culver.)*

LUCRETIA MOTT (1793–1880) *was a Quaker preacher. She was early prominent in anti-slavery circles, but her exclusion in 1840 from a World's Anti-Slavery Convention at London, merely because she was a woman, led her to espouse also the cause of woman suffrage.*

LUCY BLACKWELL STONE (1818–93) *was another anti-slavery agitator and suffragist. She was married to Dr. Henry B. Blackwell, but in an age when such independence was rare she retained her maiden name.*

HARRIET BEECHER STOWE (1811–96) *wrote "Uncle Tom's Cabin, or Life Among the Lowly" (1852), the most powerful anti-slavery tract ever published.*

SUSAN BROWNELL ANTHONY (1820–1906) *exerted herself for the emancipation of women along many lines, including the privilege of coeducation as well as woman suffrage.*

JANE ADDAMS (1860–1935), *for many years head resident of Hull House, Chicago, sought to change the crime-breeding conditions of modern city slums.*

year later the Americans in Oregon held a convention to inaugurate the well-known process of establishing self-government. It was evident that joint-occupation had about run its course, and that the issue of whether Oregon should be British or American would have to be faced.

Even in California, where Spanish outposts antedated by a few years the American occupation, the workings of "manifest destiny" were becoming apparent.[1] Spanish penetration had begun here

California

when the officials of New Spain sought, by sending missionaries, soldiers, and a few colonists to California, to forestall British and Russian advances down the Pacific coast. The civilians were mostly ranchers who, with the aid of a rich soil and an easy climate, could produce great herds, but could find no way to market them. The missionaries, conscientious Franciscan friars, were content to establish self-sufficient communities. They converted the natives, taught them numerous arts and crafts, and from a score of picturesque centers ruled their flocks benevolently. Neither the civilians nor the missionaries expected much but trouble from their venal political leaders, or from the soldiers upon whom their authority depended. Unfortunately both the Spanish and the Mexican overlords insisted upon regarding the missions as merely temporary affairs which, whenever the Indians were sufficiently civilized, should be broken up. Soon after the revolt from Spain the Mexican government attempted to put this policy into effect, but the disorder that followed was so great that an effort was made to restore the old system. But this also failed. Deprived of the protection of the friars, the Indians were usually obliged to revert to the wild life from which they had come.

The uneasiness of California society was not lessened by the presence of a constantly increasing number of non-Mexican residents. One such was Thomas O. Larkin, a former citizen of Massachusetts and of South Carolina, who in 1822 opened a store in Monterey. Occasionally, also, seamen deserted from ships that put into California harbors, and more important still, a few immigrants began to trickle in from the American frontier, lured on, no doubt, by the spreading tales of California's unclaimed, fertile acres. By 1845 there were no less than seven hundred Americans in California out of a total white population of about ten times that number. Sutter's Fort on the American River furnished a convenient haven of refuge for these newcomers from the "States." Here a German-Swiss named John A. Sutter had established himself in 1839,

---

[1] California before the Forty-Niners is excellently portrayed in H. E. Bolton, *The Spanish Borderlands* (1921); C. E. Chapman, *A History of California: The Spanish Period* (1921); and J. W. Caughey, *California, the Romance of a Great State* (1940). H. H. Bancroft, *History of California* (7 vols., 1884–1900), is of uneven merit, but a great storehouse of information.

had gathered about him such of the Indians as would accept his protection, and on a large land grant obtained from the Mexican authorities had created a kind of feudal barony.[1] Sutter never failed to give aid and encouragement to the tired travelers who had crossed the California trail, and he even pointed out lands to them that they might safely appropriate. That the American government was also interested in California became clear in 1842 when Commodore ap Catesby Jones, in command of the American Pacific squadron, landed a force at Monterey, took possession of the public property, and ran up the American flag. Jones had acted on the assumption that the British were about to seize California, and he had orders to prevent anything of the kind from happening. When he learned that there were no British about he withdrew, but his act revealed plainly the ultimate goal of his government. Two years later Larkin was designated American consul at Monterey.

Much as the American public was interested in New Mexico, Oregon, and California, the place where "manifest destiny" was most clearly at work was Texas.[2] Here in the "Lone Star State" lived far more Americans than in all the other coveted regions com- | Texas bined. Furthermore, the United States had had a claim to Texas before 1819, and had renounced it only in order to obtain Florida. The issue could therefore be made to appear not so much annexation as reannexation. Texas had made good its independence, and had been recognized by the other governments as well as by the United States. It was in actual fact no longer a part of Mexico, whatever the Mexican officials might claim. The Texans themselves, with relatively few exceptions, desired annexation, and stood ready to see it accomplished on any reasonable terms. Why should the United States hesitate longer? To do so might even force the Texans into a dangerous alliance with Great Britain.

Only the growing distaste in the North for the addition of more slave territory to the Union stood in the way of the annexationists, and neither John Tyler, President of the United States after the death of Harrison, nor his Secretary of State, John C. Calhoun, who took office in 1844, felt obliged to conciliate anti-slavery men anywhere. As a result a treaty was signed on April 12, 1844, between the United States and the Republic of Texas which provided that Texas should become a territory of the United States. The Senate rejected this treaty, but the election of 1844

---

[1] Julian Dana, *Sutter of California* (1936).

[2] N. W. Stephenson, *Texas and the Mexican War* (1921), is an adequate short account. On the diplomatic side, see Jesse S. Reeves, *American Diplomacy under Tyler and Polk* (1907). More exhaustive is G. L. Rives, *The United States and Mexico, 1821–1848* (2 vols., 1913). A special phase of the subject is treated in E. D. Adams, *British Interests and Activities in Texas, 1838–1846* (1910).

was at hand, and annexation became at once a dominant issue in the campaign.

This was no fault, however, of Henry Clay, prospective Whig candidate, and Martin Van Buren, prospective Democratic candidate, both of whom came out openly against annexation. But the Whigs, although nominating Clay unanimously, made no mention of Texas in their platform, while the Democrats pointedly passed over Van Buren and nominated instead James K. Polk of Tennessee, whose devotion to annexation was unquestioned. Further, the Democratic platform urged "the reoccupation of Oregon and the reannexation of Texas," while the possibility of acquiring New Mexico and California, if unmentioned, was by no means overlooked. Quite in keeping with his character as a compromiser, Clay attempted to qualify his prenomination statement during the campaign, but Polk was under no such handicap, and it became increasingly plain as the campaign wore on that the public had little disposition to impede "manifest destiny." Such slogans as "Fifty-four forty or fight" and "All of Oregon or none" seemed to indicate that the expansionist issue far outweighed in importance the anti-slavery argument against adding slave territory to the Union. Some of the abolitionists supported James G. Birney for President as the candidate of the newly-formed Liberty Party, and thus perhaps contributed to the election of Polk, who won by a slender majority. But Polk's triumph was nonetheless complete. Relatively unknown — the first "dark horse" candidate — he had defeated the outstanding politician of his time, and he had carried with him into office a Democratic majority in both houses of Congress. The mandate of the electorate in favor of expansion was perfectly clear.

Election of 1844

With this reassuring popular verdict, steps were taken toward the annexation of Texas even before Polk became President. In accordance with a scheme long advocated by Tyler, a joint resolution, passed in the House by a vote of 120 to 98 and in the Senate by a vote of 27 to 25, Texas was invited to become a state in the Union on condition that it should (1) present a constitution acceptable to Congress, (2) agree that at some future time it might be subdivided into as many as five states, (3) pay its own war debt, and (4) retain its own public lands. Assurance that the institution of slavery would not be disturbed was given by extending the terms of the Missouri Compromise to apply to Texas as well as to the Louisiana Purchase. Three days before he left office, March 1, 1845, Tyler signed this resolution, and at once dispatched a courier to notify the Texas authorities. It was not long before the Lone Star State had signified its willingness to exchange independence for membership in the American Union, but formal admission was not accomplished until December 29, 1845.

The new President, James Knox Polk (1795–1849),[1] was a North-Carolinian by birth, but had served seven terms in the House as a representative from Tennessee, and one term as governor of the same state. During the time he was President he kept a *James K. Polk* diary which reveals him as a hard-working, conscientious executive who believed it to be his foremost duty to carry out the will of the people as expressed in the late election. He had no taste for war, and earnestly sought to avoid it; but the annexation of Texas he regarded as both a necessity and a right. The United States and Texas, he maintained, were "independent powers competent to contract, and foreign nations have no right to interfere with them or to take exceptions to their reunion." As for Oregon, he declared pointedly that "to us belongs the duty of protecting" our emigrants "wherever they may be upon our soil."

In spite of the warlike talk in which his adherents had indulged, Polk hoped for peace, and in the case of Oregon he was willing to compromise. To this end he suggested that the United States would be willing to accept the forty-ninth parallel as the international *Agreement over Oregon* boundary. After some diplomatic sparring a treaty was signed on June 15, 1846, which accepted the line Polk had proposed, except that all of Vancouver Island should go to the British. With respect to Mexico, Polk tried to buy peace. For full acknowledgment of the Rio Grande boundary, he authorized his minister to Mexico, John Slidell of Louisiana, to promise that the United States would assume all damages due American citizens from Mexico. For the rest of New Mexico, the United States would pay five million dollars in cash. As for California, "money would be no object." But Slidell found no one in Mexico who would dare to deal with him, and in March, 1846, returned to the United States with nothing accomplished.

Meantime, on Polk's orders, American troops under General Zachary Taylor had occupied territory "near the Rio Grande del Norte" in order to be able to "protect what, in event of annexation, will be our western frontier." But nothing happened, even after *War with Mexico* the troops, at Polk's insistence, had advanced in January, 1846, to the very banks of the Rio Grande. Impatient of further delay, Polk prepared a message to Congress early in May, 1846, in which he recited the failure of the Slidell mission, and recommended war to bring the Mexicans to terms. Before this message was sent, news arrived in Washington that fighting had broken out between Taylor's troops and the Mexicans along the border. Polk, therefore, rewrote his message in

[1] E. I. McCormac, *James K. Polk* (1922), is a model biography. The careful student will wish to examine also *The Diary of James K. Polk, during his Presidency, 1845 to 1849*, edited by M. M. Quaife (4 vols., 1910).

such a way as to put the blame for starting hostilities upon the enemy. On May 11, 1846, he told Congress that "war exists, and, notwithstanding all our efforts to avoid it, exists by the act of Mexico herself." Thus encouraged by the President, Congress promptly put through a declaration of war by a vote of 40 to 2 in the Senate, and 174 to 14 in the House, authorized the raising of a volunteer army of fifty thousand men, and appropriated ten million dollars to pay the costs of the military venture upon which the country now embarked.[1]

For a time the war spirit remained high, but presently strong opposition began to develop. The attack upon a weaker neighbor was criticized as unworthy of the national honor. The Democrats were charged with fomenting war in order to gain glory enough to enable them to win the next election. Anti-slavery men, already deeply distressed at the annexation of Texas, were sure that a southern conspiracy existed to extend still further the area open to slavery. The Whig Party, always in danger of dissolution because of the discordant views of its members, found a new source of dissension. The "cotton" Whigs, mostly from the West and South, supported the war now that it had begun, while the "conscience" Whigs, mainly from the Northeast, branded it as an inexcusable blunder that ought to be abandoned at once, with apologies and reparations to Mexico.

Perhaps an even more potent cause of opposition came from the fact that the war was by no means easy to win. Advancing southwestward into Mexico, General Taylor captured Matamoras, but was held up by three days' hard fighting (September 21–23) before he could take Monterey. Pushing forward slowly, he was presently confronted by a large Mexican army under Santa Anna, which he defeated with considerable difficulty at Buena Vista (February 22–23, 1847). Taylor's tactics, probably for good reason, had not pleased Polk, but "Old Rough and Ready," as the General was called, had captured the American public, and could not be superseded. Polk therefore determined to shift the main attack on Mexico to Vera Cruz on the eastern coast. With General Winfield Scott in command, an American expeditionary force successfully invested Vera Cruz in March, 1847, and after six months of hard marching and fighting captured the Mexican capital. Meantime a small military force from the Missouri border under Colonel Stephen W. Kearny had taken Santa Fe, and had advanced into California. There Kearny saw some fighting, although American naval units under Commodore R. F. Stockton, with

Campaigns of the Mexican War

---

[1] Justin H. Smith in his two books, *The Annexation of Texas* (1911), and *The War with Mexico* (2 vols, 1919), covers this phase of American history in detail. He is at pains to show that the United States was not wholly to blame for the war.

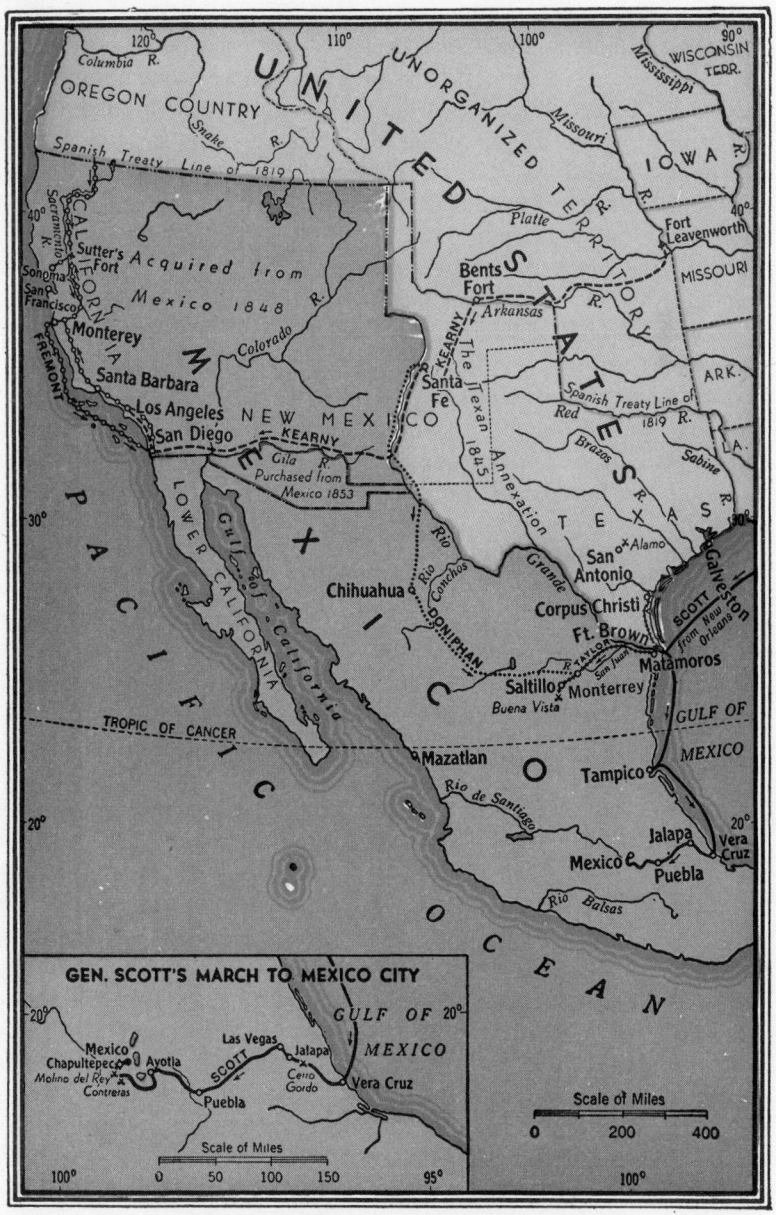

THE WAR WITH MEXICO

some assistance from John C. Frémont, the explorer,[1] and from a "Bear Flag" revolution staged by Americans resident in California, had already put a virtual end to Mexican rule.

During his advance on Mexico City Scott had been accompanied by an employee of the American State Department, Nicholas P. Trist, who was authorized to negotiate for peace. Trist's talents proved to be decidedly limited, and Polk finally deprived him of all authority and ordered him to return to the United States. But with the war won Trist, in cheerful disregard of the President's instructions, negotiated the treaty of Guadalupe Hidalgo, February 2, 1848. By its terms Mexico accepted the Rio Grande boundary, and ceded New Mexico and California, including all the territory that lay between them, to the United States. The United States, in return, made a cash payment of fifteen million dollars to Mexico, and agreed to the cancellation of all claims due from Mexico to American citizens, claims which the United States government itself now undertook to satisfy to the extent of three and a quarter million dollars. It was an expensive peace, considering that the United States was in position to demand what it liked, but Polk accepted it, and sent the treaty to the Senate, where it was ratified by a vote of 38 to 14.

Treaty of Guadalupe Hidalgo

It was the irony of fate that the treaty added to the United States a colony of religious refugees who had sought to put persecution behind them by crossing the American border into Mexico. The Mormons had originated in western New York during the late eighteen-twenties when that region was still sparsely settled. The prophet of the new religion, Joseph Smith, proclaimed doctrines that differed only a little from the numerous other Christian sects that during this same period were springing up all along the frontier. His "Church of Jesus Christ of the Latter Day Saints" accepted the teachings of the Bible, but received added inspiration from the *Book of Mormon*, which had been revealed to Smith in a miraculous fashion, and from other "revelations" which came to him from time to time. The chief distinction of the church was its centralized economic life, which contrasted markedly with the "rugged individualism" of the ordinary frontiersmen, and put the latter at a certain disadvantage. Retreating before strong opposition, the Mormons first made Kirtland, Ohio, their residence, then Independence, Missouri, then a station they called "Far West" in Clay County, Missouri, then Nauvoo, Illinois, a small city on the left bank of the Mississippi River nearly opposite the mouth of the Des Moines. At Nauvoo the inevitable outbreak of "Gentile" antagonism was heightened by talk of polygamy among the church leaders, and schism rent the church itself. Eventually Smith was arrested, then taken from jail and lynched.

The Mormons

[1] Allan Nevins, *Frémont, The West's Greatest Adventurer* (2 vols., 1928).

Smith's successor, Brigham Young, decided reasonably enough that the only hope of peace for the Mormons lay outside the boundaries of the United States, and after a visit to the West picked the Great Salt Lake basin as the best available site for the new colony. Even before this site was selected, the Mormons were on the move across Iowa to Council Bluffs, where they established "Winter Quarters" in 1846, preparatory to the great migration that was to begin the following spring. By September, 1847, the advance guard had reached the Great Salt Lake, and for many years thereafter the "Mormon Trail," which lay to the north of the Platte River, was the scene of a steady migration. Salt Lake City grew with astonishing rapidity and soon became, to the very great profit of the Mormons, a convenient stopping-point on the way to California. The success of the colony, however, was due primarily to the sound judgment and the extraordinary executive ability of its leader, Brigham Young. He it was who planned the migration, supervised the settlement of the newcomers, introduced irrigation, and in many other ways warded off the misfortunes that might otherwise have befallen so large a company in so difficult an environment. His dictatorship was virtually unquestioned.[1]

Polk's policy of expansion was carried through well before his term of office was over, and without a serious failure. He obtained all of Oregon to which he could reasonably lay claim, ensured the permanence of the annexation of Texas, and took one-third of the territory of Mexico in order to advance the boundary of the United States to the Pacific in the Far Southwest, as it had already been advanced in the Far Northwest. Important settlements had been made in every section of the new acquisitions — in Oregon, in California, in New Mexico, and, thanks to the Mormon migration, in what was soon to be known as Utah. Well-defined trails crossed the continent to the Southwest, to the Northwest, and in between. Much of the western country was still regarded as uninhabitable, but such guides as Kit Carson, who accompanied Frémont on some of his explorations and showed Kearny the way from Santa Fe to California, and Jim Bridger, who helped Brigham Young locate the Great Salt Lake basin, were fast dispelling its mysteries.

Polk's achievement

While Polk's main concern as President was expansion, he was able during the first half of his administration to redeem two of his party's pledges on domestic affairs. The Walker Tariff, a measure that again turned the country away from protection and toward the principle of a

---

[1] M. R. Werner, *Brigham Young* (1925); W. A. Linn, *The Story of the Mormons* (1902). Two general histories of the American frontier, which recount the Mormon epic, are R. E. Riegel, *America Moves West* (1930); and E. Douglas Branch, *Westward* (1930).

tariff for revenue only, he signed on July 30, 1846. The enactment of the lowered rates met much opposition from the industrial interests of New England and the middle Atlantic states, but significantly it won support from the West as well as from the South. The second of the Democratic pledges which Polk carried through was the re-establishment by act of Congress, signed August 6, 1846, of the independent, or Sub-Treasury, system that had been discontinued early in the preceding administration.

Far more exciting than either the tariff or the Sub-Treasury was a question that began to be raised as soon as war broke out with Mexico. Should slavery be permitted to expand into the territory soon to be acquired? This issue was formally presented to Congress as early as August, 1846, when David Wilmot, an anti-slavery Democrat from Pennsylvania, proposed an anti-slavery amendment to a bill appropriating money for the purchase of territory from Mexico. According to the "Wilmot Proviso," which failed of passage, "neither slavery nor involuntary servitude" was ever to be permitted in any territory so acquired. The "Wilmot Proviso" was debated, not only in Congress, where for years it was proposed as an amendment to any relevant measure, but throughout the country at large. Northern anti-slavery men maintained that Congress was legally competent to exclude slavery from the territories of the United States, and should exercise its right at once. Southern extremists took the opposite view, and held that the Constitution, because it recognized and protected slavery in some of the states, must be construed to protect slavery also in the territories, for otherwise the property rights of slave-owners would be discriminated against in a region which was the joint possession of all the states. Still others were ready to compromise. Some said that the Missouri Compromise line should be extended all the way to the Pacific; others, that the new territories to be formed in the West should decide for themselves whether they should be free or slave. This latter idea, known generally as "squatter sovereignty," was suggested first by Lewis Cass of Michigan, but it was later taken up by Stephen A. Douglas of Illinois, who renamed it "popular sovereignty," and won for it many adherents.[1]

The obvious determination of the northern anti-slavery forces to keep the South's "peculiar institution" out of the Mexican cession drove southern extremists to a frenzy of anxiety. They knew that in population the North was drawing farther and farther away from the South, while unless new territory open to slavery could be acquired, the balance of the sections in the Senate would soon be broken. Iowa and Wisconsin,

The Wilmot Proviso

---

[1] At this point the scholarly and exhaustive work of James Ford Rhodes, *History of the United States from the Compromise of 1850* (9 vols., 1893–1922), begins to be of use. While Rhodes has been corrected at many points, his history of the Civil War period is still indispensable for the serious student.

admitted in 1846 and 1848, respectively, would serve as numerical offsets to Florida and Texas, admitted in 1845, but Minnesota could not long be held out of the Union, and the Oregon country offered a still further opportunity for the creation of new free states. Southern members of Congress, in a vain attempt to extend the Missouri Compromise line to the Pacific, held up the organization of a territorial government in Oregon for two years, but were at length compelled to capitulate, and Oregon became a free territory in 1848, with no pledges given. Thereafter threats of secession were made with ever-increasing boldness.

The issue raised by the Wilmot Proviso was so fraught with peril to the Union that both the Whigs and the Democrats evaded it during the campaign and election of 1848. The Democrats made no reference in their platform to the status of slavery in the territory acquired from Mexico, and turned to the North for their presidential candidate, Lewis Cass of Michigan. The Whigs, even more cautious, adopted no platform, and presented as their candidate General Zachary Taylor, the "hero of Buena Vista," who by a lucky chance happened to be from Louisiana, and to own three hundred slaves. For second place on their ticket, the Whigs chose Millard Fillmore, an obscure politician from western New York. But this flouting by the older parties of the only real issue before the country led to the union of all anti-slavery men, of whatever gradations of opinion, in support of a new "Free-Soil" Party, which called eloquently for "Free Soil, Free Speech, Free Labor, and Free Men." To win the votes of the strong anti-Polk faction among the northern Democrats, the third party leaders chose as their standard bearer ex-President Martin Van Buren of New York, whose refusal to countenance the annexation of Texas had not only lost him the Democratic nomination in 1844, but had also won the enthusiastic applause of all good anti-slavery men. During the campaign the Free-Soilers emphasized primarily the necessity of keeping the lands of the West out of the clutches of the southern slaveholders in order to make them available for the use of small free farmers, but their ticket, which included Charles Francis Adams, son of John Quincy Adams, as candidate for Vice-President, was generally supported by anti-slavery advocates, even those who based their opposition strictly upon moral grounds.

The strength of the Free-Soil movement was revealed when the election returns came in. The new party had polled nearly three hundred thousand votes, had won the balance of power in a dozen states, and, for good or ill, had drawn enough votes from the Democratic column in New York to throw that state, and the election, to Taylor. The thirteen Free-Soilers chosen to the National House of Representatives were a

Election of 1848 (margin note)

power to be reckoned with, for no party had a majority in that branch of Congress. In the Senate, which was Democratic, John P. Hale already represented New Hampshire, and the legislature of Ohio sent Salmon P. Chase, whose anti-slavery views were almost equally radical, to join him. The one lesson that the election seemed to teach was that the effort to avoid the slavery issue could not long be successful. The nation was at last face to face with the necessity of deciding upon the status of slavery in the territory acquired from Mexico.

The discovery of gold in California early in 1848, and the subsequent gold rush, introduced a new element into the situation. Polk himself, in his annual message to Congress of December, 1848, con- Gold in firmed the news that had long since traveled far and wide — California there was gold — much gold — in California. Immediately thousands of men from every part of the United States left for California at the earliest possible opportunity.[1] "The world seems divided into two classes," wrote William H. Seward, "those who are going to California in search of gold, and those going to Washington in quest of office." Gold seekers who could not afford to do otherwise took the long journey overland by covered wagon; others took ship around Cape Horn; still others went expensively and with great danger to their health by way of the Isthmus of Panama. Agitation at once set in for the building of a Panama Canal, and to promote this venture the United States and Great Britain, in the Clayton-Bulwer Treaty of 1850, accepted joint responsibility for any such venture that might be undertaken. Meantime, not the United States alone, but the whole world caught the gold-fever, and a huge polyglot population descended upon California. San Francisco, a city of tents and shacks, grew prodigiously; burned down, and grew again. To handle so bewildering a situation, the temporary military government was totally inadequate. Men went armed as a matter of course, fatal shootings were common and rarely investigated, voluntary associations kept what order they could. The need of an adequate and authoritative civil government was obvious, and was keenly felt.

It devolved naturally upon the new President, Zachary Taylor (1784–1850), to take the initiative in seeking a solution for this pressing problem. Taylor was a Virginian by birth, but he grew to man- Zachary hood in frontier Kentucky, and from his youth up was an Taylor officer in the regular army. He was in no sense a politician, but he was honest and forthright, well accustomed to meeting emergencies, and unembarrassed by the necessity of making a sudden decision.

[1] R. G. Cleland, *A History of California; The American Period* (1922), is excellent. Readable, and probably true enough in the picture, is S. E. White, *The Forty-Niners* (1920). The hardships of the pioneers who traveled overland to California are graphically told by means of a synthetic diary in A. B. Hulbert, *Forty-Niners* (1931).

His solution for the problem of government in the newly acquired territory was simple. Let the people of California and New Mexico organize state governments, and decide for themselves whether to be slave states or free states. Heedful of the President's advice, the Californians in 1849 drew up a constitution, elected state officers, and took over the government of their self-created state. New Mexico, with less occasion for haste, was not ready with its constitution for a year later. Even the Mormons caught the contagion, drew up a constitution for a proposed state of Deseret, and with Brigham Young as their duly elected governor, applied for admission to the Union. But to the immense chagrin of the pro-slavery politicians, all three of the prospective states proposed to exclude slavery from their borders.

Had Taylor been more experienced in politics, he might have known that Congress would never permit him, unaided, to resolve the dispute over slavery in the newly acquired territory. Furthermore, the Congress that convened late in 1849 was one of the ablest that had ever been chosen. This was in part due to the fact that it was a kind of meeting-point of two generations. In it sat the three great statesmen of the preceding era: Daniel Webster, John C. Calhoun, and Henry Clay. But its roster contained also the names of many men whose careers were before them, such as Salmon P. Chase, William H. Seward, Thaddeus Stevens, Stephen A. Douglas, Jefferson Davis, Alexander H. Stephens, and Robert Toombs. Naturally such a Congress proposed to have a hand in the matter, and all eyes turned for leadership to the aged Henry Clay, whose reputation as a compromiser was justly great. Throughout his life he had never held so tenaciously to any principle that under sufficient pressure he had found himself unable to give it up.

It is not fair, however, to assign the whole credit for the Compromise of 1850 to Henry Clay. Other men, notably Stephen A. Douglas, had an important part in its making, and during the long debate over the Wilmot Proviso a multitude of political theorists had set forth the various possibilities of compromise. It was Clay, however, who presented to the Senate the elaborate series of resolutions that was to form the basis of compromise, and it was Clay's well-established reputation that won for them an instant hearing. The resolutions sensibly did not stop with the question of slavery extension, but included also all the other phases of the slavery problem with which the public mind was vexed. Clay hoped that his plan would restore "the peace, concord, and harmony of the Union" for another thirty years, the length of time that the Missouri Compromise had lasted. On January 29, 1850, he asked the Senate to consider the following suggestions:

The Compromise of 1850

1. Permit California to enter the Union as a free state.
2. Establish territorial governments without any restriction as to slavery in the rest of the territory acquired from Mexico.
3. Set reasonable limits to the western boundary of Texas.
4. Assume the public debt of Texas contracted prior to annexation, on condition that Texas relinquish her claim to any part of New Mexico.
5. Agree that slavery in the District of Columbia may not be abolished without the consent of Maryland, and of the people of the district, and without just compensation to the owners of slaves.
6. Prohibit the slave trade in the District of Columbia.
7. Enact a more stringent fugitive slave law.
8. Assert that Congress has no power to interfere with the slave trade between the states.

The debate that these resolutions precipitated in the United States Senate ranks justly as one of the greatest in American legislative history. Clay led off in a defense of the Compromise that was less an exposition of its provisions than an appeal to Congress and the country to quiet the clamor over slavery, and thus to save the nation from the unnecessary chaos of civil war. To his support came his old rival for preferment within the Whig Party, Daniel Webster, who argued that the prohibition of slavery in New Mexico was an unnecessary taunt and reproach to the South, for in that alien soil, he claimed, slavery could never survive. Why "re-enact the will of God?" Webster's "Seventh of March" speech on the Compromise justly ranks as among the greatest of American orations. But neither of these giants, nor the lesser men who followed in their train, were able to win over the extremists. John C. Calhoun, so old and ill that his address had to be read by a colleague, accused the North of intending to destroy "irretrievably the equilibrium between the two sections." [1] William H. Seward, the young Senator from New York, denounced with equal vehemence the transplantation of slavery into new soil, asserted that emancipation was both inevitable and near, and urged that its peaceful consummation be not impeded by new pro-slavery laws.

Meantime, majority sentiment throughout the country began to assert itself unmistakably in favor of some sort of compromise. Business men, thanks to the flow of gold from California and the increasing demand for railways, enjoyed a degree of prosperity unparalleled since the panic of 1837. Farmers benefited materially from the strong foreign demand for American grain that followed the repeal of the Corn Laws in England, and commercial interests, already flourishing because of the pre-eminence of the American-built clipper ship, were still further stimulated by the low rates of the Walker Tariff. Laborers drew high wages and could count on

Sentiment for the Compromise

---

[1] A sympathetic view of Calhoun is given in W. E. Dodd, *Statesmen of the Old South* (1911).

steady employment. Such prosperity was far too precious to be disturbed by an academic dispute over slavery. Particularly were the northern manufacturers eager to ensure the permanence of their southern markets by conciliating the South; while southern producers were by no means happy at the prospect of secession, with its inevitable disruption of their normal lines of trade.

As the favorable reaction of the country was sensed, the desire of Congress to accept some form of compromise became increasingly apparent. Even so, there were serious obstacles to be surmounted.

Death of Taylor

Most baffling, apparently, was the unrelenting opposition of President Taylor, who seemed determined to pursue his own course without regard for the wishes of Congress. But in July, 1850, the President was taken suddenly ill, probably of typhoid fever, and within a few days he was dead. The new President, Millard Fillmore (1800–74), was known only as a successful lawyer from Buffalo, New York, who had served several terms in the state legislature and in Congress. Early in his career he had won some distinction by pushing through the New York legislature an act for the abolition of imprisonment for debt; later, as a member of Congress, he had much to do with the writing of the Tariff of 1842. When nominated for the Vice-Presidency he was generally regarded as an anti-slavery man, but the debates in the Senate on the Compromise measures, to which he listened as presiding officer, seem to have impressed upon him the urgent necessity of conciliating the South. On succeeding to the Presidency he at once put himself into the hands of Clay, formed a new cabinet with Webster at its head, and gave his undivided support to the proposed plan of compromise.

Most of Clay's original proposals found their way first into three, and finally into five, separate measures, a device which permitted each measure to pass with a different majority. It thus came

The Compromise adopted

about that the Compromise of 1850, as finally passed by Congress and signed by the President, was complete in five laws: (1) California was admitted as a free state; (2) New Mexico was created a territory without the Wilmot Proviso, and the claim of Texas to New Mexican territory was indemnified by the payment of ten million dollars from the federal treasury; (3) Utah was created a territory without the Wilmot Proviso; (4) more stringent provision was made for the rendition of fugitive slaves; and (5) the slave trade was abolished in the District of Columbia. Actually only four senators voted for every one of the five measures, although several others, including Clay and Douglas, would have done so had they not been unavoidably absent when some of the votes were taken. Indeed, in both houses of Congress the majorities in favor of the various compromise bills were in no two instances identical.

For a time it seemed that the Compromise, which by the admission of California at last upset the balance of sections in the Senate, might fail to satisfy the South.[1] In four states, Georgia, Mississippi, Alabama, and South Carolina, special state conventions were held to consider the advisability of immediate secession, but only in South Carolina were the secessionists able to command a majority. On second thought the people of the South made up their minds to accept the Compromise; even the South-Carolinians were unwilling to risk secession without the support of other southern states. The "Georgia Platform," which looked upon the Compromise as a "permanent adjustment of the sectional controversy," best expressed the southern point of view. But the North was warned that "upon the faithful execution of the Fugitive Slave Bill depends the preservation of our much-loved union."

But the Fugitive Slave Act was gall and wormwood to the anti-slavery people of the North. It denied the right of trial by jury to the fugitive, refused him the privilege of testifying in his own behalf, and virtually required that he be turned over to anyone who claimed him. Federal marshals and their deputies were enjoined, under threat of heavy penalties, to make unusual exertions to capture fugitives, and anyone aiding in the escape of a slave was liable to a fine of not more than one thousand dollars or imprisonment not to exceed six months, in addition to civil damages of one thousand dollars to the owner of the slave. These terms, quite obviously, were not dictated merely by the desire to secure the return of fugitive slaves. They were, and they were meant to be, as Rhodes says, "a taunt and reproach to that part of the North where the anti-slavery sentiment ruled supremely." But even this thoroughly obnoxious act was insufficient to keep the North from rallying to the support of the Compromise. Business interests were enthusiastically for it, able lawyers defended it as constitutional throughout, and the promise of the politicians that it had settled the issue of slavery with finality was accepted with a feeling of great relief. Peace and prosperity lay ahead.

The presidential election of 1852 served as a kind of popular referendum on the Compromise. The Democratic nominee, Franklin Pierce of New Hampshire, another "dark horse," had given his unqualified endorsement to the Compromise, while the convention which nominated him had announced its determination to "resist all attempts at renewing, in Congress or out of it, the agi-

Election of 1852

[1] The persistence of secessionist sentiment is well set forth in the following works: P. M. Hamer, *The Secession Movement in South Carolina, 1847–1852* (1918); M. J. White, *The Secession Movement in the United States, 1847–1852* (1916); and R. H. Shryock, *Georgia and the Union in 1850* (1926).

tation of the slavery question." The Whigs, on the other hand, because many of their ablest leaders had opposed the Compromise, were unable to take so bold a stand. They "acquiesced in" the Compromise, but they refused to renominate Millard Fillmore, the President whose signatures had made it possible, and turned instead to General Winfield Scott, whose reputation, like Taylor's, grew out of the Mexican war, and whose views on the Compromise were unknown. The issue before the electorate was thus primarily Franklin Pierce and the Compromise, or General Scott and uncertainty. A third alternative was offered by the Free-Soil candidacy of John P. Hale, but four years of Whig supremacy had brought the Van Buren Democrats back into the party fold, so that the Free-Soilers polled little more than half the numbers of votes in 1852 that they had polled four years before. The popular verdict was plain. The Democrats carried twenty-seven states, and the Whigs only four: Massachusetts, Vermont, Kentucky, and Tennessee. Pierce's electoral vote was 254 to Scott's 42. Indeed, the Whig Party, which throughout its existence had rarely been more than an "organized incompatibility," collapsed under the blow, and was never again strong enough to contest a presidential election. For the time being an overwhelming majority, both North and South, chose to believe that the slavery question was permanently settled.[1]

[1] A. K. Weinberg, *Manifest Destiny* (1935), traces American expansionism from its earliest beginnings. L. R. Hafen and C. C. Rister, *Western America* (1941), covers fully the subjects discussed in this chapter. Bernard De Voto, *The Year of Decision, 1846* (1943), is dramatic and exciting.

On California, see R. G. Cleland, *From Wilderness to Empire: A History of California, 1542–1900* (1944); J. W. Caughey, *Hubert Howe Bancroft, Historian of the West* (1946); Irene D. Paden, *The Wake of the Prairie Schooner* (1943); J. H. Kemble, *The Panama Route, 1848–1869* (1943); J. H. Jackson, *Anybody's Gold* (1941).

On Texas, see R. N. Richardson, *The Lone Star State* (1943); J. W. Schmitz, *Texas Statecraft, 1836–1845* (1941); W. R. Hogan, *The Texas Republic* (1946); Jim Dan Hill, *The Texas Navy* (1937); Marquis James, *The Raven, A Biography of Sam Houston* (1929).

On Oregon, see M. C. Clay, *Winning Oregon* (1938); C. M. Drury, *Marcus Whitman, M.D.* (1937).

On Taylor and Scott: Holman Hamilton, *Zachary Taylor* (1941); Brainerd Dyer, *Zachary Taylor* (1946); C. W. Elliott, *Winfield Scott* (1937).

Allan Nevins, *Ordeal of the Union* (2 vols., 1947), reviews in extraordinary detail the events of the decade immediately following the war with Mexico.

17

Peace and Prosperity

THE prominent place that the slavery dispute occupied in American politics during the two decades preceding the Civil War has tended to divert the attention of historians from other subjects of equal, or even greater, significance. During these same years transportation was revolutionized by the construction of railways, industry and commerce expanded with phenomenal rapidity, agriculture began its far-reaching shift from traditional to more businesslike methods, a new flood of European immigrants swept over the country, and the final conquest of the Far West was definitely assured. Contemporary political leaders, who, in the light of these momentous changes, sought to bury the slavery issue, hardly deserve the scorn that some historians have heaped upon them. Could their efforts have been crowned with success instead of failure, the public mind would have been left free to recognize and wrestle with the issues precipitated by the economic revolution, while slavery in time might well have disappeared without resort to war.

Undoubtedly the greatest factor in transforming American society during this period was the railroad.[1] Up to about 1840 this means of transportation was still in the experimental stage, and the building of a railroad was a choice of desperation to be resorted to only where engineering difficulties made a canal impossible. Among these unwilling experiments were the Baltimore and Ohio, which opened a few miles to traffic in 1830, and the Charleston and Hamburg, which in 1833, with its 137 miles of track across the state of South Carolina, was the longest railroad in the world. Short lines were built, also, to facilitate trade between the principal cities of the country and their respective outlying districts. Philadelphia, for example, was soon connected by rail with the coal-mining regions of central Pennsylvania. By

The railroad

[1] An excellent short history of American railroad-building is John Moody, *The Railroad Builders* (1919). An early assessment, still useful, is C. F. Adams, Jr., *Railroads: Their Origin and Problems* (1878). See also B. H. Meyer, C. H. MacGill and others, *History of Transportation in the United States before 1860* (1917); Edward Hungerford, *The Story of the Baltimore and Ohio Railroad, 1827–1927* (1928); F. W. Stevens, *The Beginnings of the New York Central Railroad* (1926).

the year 1840 the total railroad trackage of the country had reached 2818 miles.

From the operation of these early railroads, short and disconnected as they were, many valuable lessons were learned. The use of horses and sails for motive power was quickly discarded in favor of steam locomotives similar to those built by George Stephenson, the English inventor, but lighter and speedier. Unsubstantial wooden rails, protected only by thin iron straps, gave way to far more durable iron rails. Dizzy curves and steep grades, so characteristic of the early roadbeds, tended to disappear, while wooden cross-ties, designed to ensure that the two lines of rails should remain at all times equidistant, replaced the more uncertain separate foundations. Low four-wheeled trucks, pivoted beneath each end of a freight or passenger car, made the rounding of curves less hazardous, and pointed the way to a complete abandonment of the stagecoach and rail-wagon appearance of the first "rolling-stock." Coal began to replace wood as fuel, partly to save the time consumed in "wooding-up" at frequent intervals, partly to allay the irritation of passengers whose clothing caught fire from the steady stream of sparks that a wood-burner always emitted. Also, the necessity of railroad companies to manage the traffic was quickly demonstrated. On some of the early roads anyone with a proper conveyance was permitted to use the rails just as he might have used a toll road, but endless confusion resulted; moreover, the cost of locomotives and cars was beyond the means of the ordinary individual. It soon became the practically universal custom, therefore, for the owners of the road also to own and operate the equipment. For this service they exacted whatever charges they saw fit, but as "common carriers" they were under obligation to accept for shipment anything within reason presented to them for that purpose.

The second decade of railroad history saw the mistrust with which the new means of transportation had at first been viewed replaced by a deep and abiding faith. Accidental connections — such, for example, as made possible all-rail transportation from Boston to Albany after 1841 — added tremendously to the business of the connecting lines, and pointed the way to future development. The significant part that the railroads might play in linking the East and the West together became apparent in 1842, when a series of seven or eight local lines furnished an alternative route to the Erie Canal across the state of New York. The combinations of all such roads into one through route, while delayed in this case until the emergence of the New York Central in 1853, was a logical next step. By that year three other lines connected the eastern seaboard with the West: the Erie, completed through southern New York in 1851; the Pennsylvania, opened all the

THE EVOLUTION OF LAND TRANSPORTATION IN AMERICA

way to Pittsburgh in 1852; and the Baltimore and Ohio, which reached
its western objective in 1853. Within the West itself the railroad was
hailed as the long-sought solution to the problem of land transportation,
and innumerable ambitious projects were begun. Such cities as Memphis, Chicago, and St. Louis, eager to become important as railroad centers, held railroad "conventions" to arouse enthusiasm. Hastily built
local lines were soon succeeded by through routes, such as the Michigan
Central and the Michigan Southern, which reached Chicago in 1852, and
the Rock Island and Chicago, which connected the Great Lakes with the
Mississippi River in 1854. Next year through rail connections were
established between New York and St. Louis.

The task of providing funds for these extensive enterprises taxed the
resources of the railroad promoters to the limit. The earlier roads, when
not actually owned and operated by some state, could ordi-
Railroad   narily depend upon a loan of the state's credit or a generous
finance   state subscription to railroad stock. But as already noted,
this policy was very generally discredited after the financial disasters
that overtook the states during the panic of 1837. Railroad lobbyists
were able, however, to get direct aid from a few states, and they became
extremely adept at securing from all the states valuable privileges and
immunities for the companies they represented. They also induced
cities and counties that lay along the route of a proposed line to vote
large sums to the coveted railroad, either as outright gifts, or as loans, or
as subscriptions to stock. Skillful, if none too scrupulous, salesmen persuaded private investors, foreigners as well as Americans, to buy large
blocks of railroad securities. Finally, the politicians who sympathized
with the aims of the railroads won from Congress grants of federal land
to be used in aid of railroad-building. The first such grant was obtained
in 1850 for the Illinois Central Railroad by Senator Stephen A. Douglas.
According to this act, three square miles of land in alternate sections on
each side of the proposed line were granted to the state of Illinois for
transfer to the railroad as fast as construction was completed. To secure
the necessary political support for this measure, similar grants had to be
made available for a railroad from the Ohio River to Mobile; and thereafter land grants were generally allotted to any railroad projected in a
region where the government still owned land. Between 1850 and 1860
about twenty million acres of public land was handed over in this manner
to the railroads.

Under these circumstances the conquest of the country
Railroad   by the railroads proceeded with astonishing rapidity. The
expansion   amount of trackage increased from 2818 miles in 1840 to 9021
miles in 1850 and to 30,626 miles in 1860. By the last-mentioned year

the Northeast alone had 9500 miles of railroads, more than the whole country had possessed ten years before. Practically all the important eastern cities were connected by rail, and many of them had also direct connections with the West. The most feverish building, however, had taken place in the Northwest. By 1860 this section, which before the panic of 1837 had hardly a mile of railroad in effective operation, had 11,078 miles to its credit, more than one-third of the total trackage of the country. Chicago, thanks mainly to its natural advantages as a railroad center, had grown from a town of 4000 inhabitants in 1840 to 29,000 in 1850, and to 109,000 in 1860. Inland cities, such as Indianapolis, had achieved an importance that without the railroads could scarcely have been imagined. Railroad connections between the Great Lakes and the Ohio-Mississippi River system put the western canals virtually out of business, and stimulated tremendously the growth of such cities as Cleveland, Cincinnati, and Milwaukee, which could serve as links between the waterways and the rails. By 1855 the Mississippi River had been bridged; by 1857 the railroad frontier had reached the Missouri River at St. Joseph. In the South, railroad-building lagged perceptibly.[1] This section, with its extensive coastline and its numerous navigable rivers, stood far less in need of railroads than the Northwest; moreover, whatever surplus capital the South could command was generally invested in plantations and slaves. Nevertheless many short lines were built, and a few of sectional importance. By 1860, both Norfolk, Virginia, and Charleston, South Carolina, were connected through Chattanooga, Tennessee, with the Mississippi River at Memphis; and the Mississippi itself was paralleled from the Ohio to the Gulf. With 10,048 miles of railroads the South was only slightly ahead of the Northeast in total mileage, although, in view of its greater distances, the effectiveness of its railroads was far less marked. The Northeast on the eve of the Civil War had about twice as much railroad trackage per square mile of land as the Northwest, and four times as much as the South.

RAILROAD MILEAGE IN THE UNITED STATES, 1830–1865

Year	Miles	Year	Miles
1830	32	1850	9,021
1835	1,098	1855	18,374
1840	2,818	1860	30,626
1845	4,663	1865	35,085

One of the most striking developments that a railroad map of 1860 reveals is the drawing together of the Northeast and the Northwest. So closely connected, indeed, were the railroads of these two sections that

[1] U. B. Phillips, *A History of Transportation in the Eastern Cotton Belt to 1860* (1908).

they appear to be, as to all practical purposes they were, one network. With ever-increasing ease the produce of the Northwest found its way to the consumers of the East and to the eastern seaports for transshipment to Europe. Similarly the eastern manufacturers found in the expanding Northwest a gratifying market for the output of their factories. The southern railroads, on the other hand, were not yet integrated with the railroads of the rest of the country. Because so many of them had been built primarily as a means of supplementing waterways, they lacked even sectional unity, and they made contact with the northern railroad system at only three widely separated points.

In spite of the mounting significance of the railroads, the western waterways long remained a major factor in the communications system of the country. Until the railroads appeared, the river steamboats had no transportation rivals in the West, and for years after the coming of the roads the Mississippi River continued to carry an enormous volume of traffic. Great shipyards were located at St. Louis, Cincinnati, and Louisville which turned out huge and speedy craft to carry grain and merchandise downstream, cotton, rice, and sugar upstream, and a steady flow of passengers both ways. By means of these boats the northern farmers found a needed outlet for their produce in the South; southern cotton-planters saved money by buying foodstuffs from the Northwest instead of raising their own; both farmers and planters had more funds to use in the purchase of eastern manufactured goods. Some of the boats were incredibly swift — the best of them made the twelve or thirteen hundred miles from New Orleans to St. Louis in four days, or even less. By the fifties well over a thousand steamboats plied the Mississippi and its tributaries, and since the cost of the larger boats ran to about fifty thousand dollars each, this represented a sizable investment. Cargoes valued at two hundred and fifty thousand dollars each were not unknown. To the upper Mississippi and its tributaries, steamboats brought the blessings of swift transportation long before the railroads arrived,[1] and far out on the upper Missouri fur-traders, too, had their steamboats. Indeed, this elaborate system of river communications seemed so essential to the life of both the Northwest and the South that the prospect of its separation from New Orleans, the head of the river traffic, was one of the worst of the nightmares associated with secession. But the steamboats not only solved a problem of transportation for the West; they created also a way of life and a cast of characters that happily Mark Twain's *Life on the Mississippi* has preserved intact for the wonderment of posterity.

The revolution in means of communication that took place during this

Western steamboating

[1] William J. Petersen, *Steamboating on the Upper Mississippi* (1937).

NINETEENTH-CENTURY IMPROVEMENTS IN WATER
TRANSPORTATION

period extended unabated to the high seas. American shipbuilders contributed during the eighteen-forties the fleet clipper ship,
Ocean trans- which with a fair breeze could make better time than the
portation
              early steamships, and under normal circumstances could
make three trips to Europe while an ordinary ship was making two.[1]
Partly because of the superiority of these ships, partly because of recur-
ring wars both in Europe and in Asia, American ships for a few years
carried a far greater proportion of the world's commerce than had ever
been the case before. During the decade 1850–60, about seventy per
cent of the total foreign trade of the United States was carried in ships
that flew the American flag, while in the year 1853 alone, according to a
reliable estimate, the total tonnage carried by American ships exceeded
that of the British by no less than fifteen per cent. About 1855, however,
the American clipper ship began to be superseded by the British-built
iron steamer, which could cross the Atlantic in less than two weeks' time.
Backed by adequate government subsidies, the British steamers soon
made heavy inroads upon the American carrying trade. To meet this
competition several American steamship companies, which had been
organized during the forties, were for a few years voted subsidies by Congress, but they proved to be unable to hold the trans-Atlantic trade
against the British. Their importance in the coastwise trade, however,
which was closed to foreign vessels, became very great. From the point
of view of efficiency in transportation, it mattered little whether the
commerce of the United States was carried in British or American bot-
toms. What was of far greater significance was the fact that ocean lanes
were being multiplied, and the time of transit was being lessened. Just as
the railroads within the country were bringing its various sections closer
together, so the clipper ships and the steamers tended to bring the United
States into closer contact with the outside world.

Easier means of communication had much to do with the growth of
industry in the United States during this same period.[2] The use of
              power machinery in manufacturing had made steady prog-
Manufacturing
              ress during the first four decades of the nineteenth century,
but the difficulties experienced in transporting goods to market had kept
down the size of American factories and the amount of their output.
Not until the advent of the steam locomotive did the full effects of the
Industrial Revolution begin to be felt in the United States. Then facto-

---

[1] A. H. Clark, *The Clipper Ship Era, 1843–1869* (1910); C. C. Cutler, *Greyhounds of the Sea: The Story of the American Clipper Ship* (1930); Ralph D. Paine, *The Old Merchant Marine* (1919).

[2] All of the short manuals of economic history are full at this point. See especially E. C. Kirkland, *A History of American Economic Life* (1932). V. S. Clark, *History of Manufactures in the United States, 1607–1860* (2 vols., 1916–28), is a good general account.

ries that had previously depended on serving only a local market began suddenly to expand, while others, less fortunately situated, began to decline materially in importance, and even to disappear. Regardless of the number of factories, the total annual output of manufactured goods mounted rapidly. By 1850, the first year in which the federal census attempted to ascertain accurately the amount of manufacturing that went on in the United States, the total value of manufactured goods, $1,055,500,000, exceeded slightly the total value of agricultural products, $994,000,000. Ten years later the figures were $1,885,862,000 for manufacturing and $1,910,000,000 for agriculture; but the ascendancy that agriculture thus seemed to have regained proved short-lived, for all subsequent census statistics, showed manufacturing far in the lead.

Not only improved means of transportation, but many other factors also tended to promote the growth of American industry. The liberal patent system of the United States, which guaranteed to patent-holders a long-time monopoly upon the manufacture, use, and sale of their inventions, encouraged American inventors to devise many labor-saving machines for use in the factory or on the farm, as well as a great variety of articles for the comfort and satisfaction of individuals. A rising standard of living meant also the manufacture and sale in quantities to the ordinary man of the one-time luxuries of the rich. Moreover, the United States was growing rapidly in population, both from the ordinary natural increase and from a new wave of immigration; hence the needs of ever greater numbers of people had to be met. Prosperity meant that nearly everyone had the means with which to buy. Wages were good; agricultural products, thanks in part to the repeal of the Corn Laws in England and in part also to the mid-century European wars, brought high prices; newly mined gold and silver paid the bills of the Far West.

American manufacturing, in spite of its rapid growth, still showed many of the characteristics of youth. The concentration of factories at strategic centers had only begun, and there was in conse- **Manufacturing** quence a far greater diffusion of manufacturing industries **practices** than was later the case. While New England and the middle Atlantic states maintained their early lead in manufacturing, small factories of one kind or another were apt to be found in any part of the country, even in the South and along the frontier. A second characteristic of youth was the close restriction of American manufacturing to the use of such raw materials as were produced within the country: comparatively little was imported in order to be manufactured. American grain was turned into flour and meal, American forests into sawed lumber, American cotton into cotton goods, American wool into woolen goods, American iron ore into iron products, and so on. Also, with some minor excep-

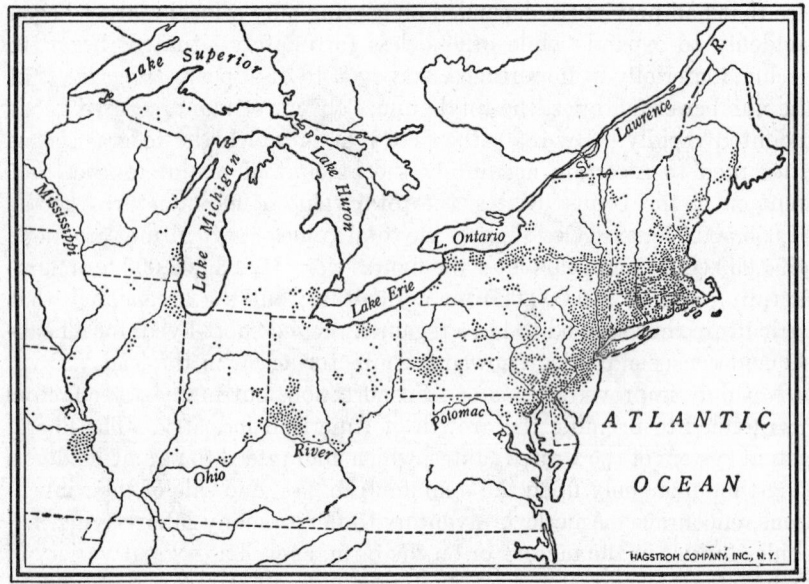

THE LOCATION OF FACTORIES IN NORTHERN
UNITED STATES, 1860

tions, the entire output of the American factories was consumed in the
United States, and that without fully satisfying the demand. American
cotton mills turned out enough cotton goods of the coarser grades, and a
little to spare, but the finer grades still had to be imported from Europe.
American woolens fell still further short of supplying the domestic demand, for the American woolens manufacturers were handicapped not
only by their inability to compete with the English in producing fine
fabrics, but also by an inadequate American supply of raw wool. The
use of anthracite coal and of coke as fuel greatly stimulated the iron industry and pointed the way to a phenomenal development, but the heavy
demands of the railway age were greater than the American supply could
meet. With reference to many minor industries the situation was not
far different.

The high degree of prosperity that American manufacturers enjoyed
during these years was achieved in spite of the relatively low duties of
the Walker Tariff. Naturally, the fact that importers were
The tariff   able to throw upon the American market a plentiful supply
of foreign-made goods was not at all relished by the manufacturing interests. Demands for higher duties in order to promote the more rapid
expansion of American industry were persistently voiced, particularly by

representatives of the northeastern states, where most of the factories were located. Until the time of the Civil War, however, all such demands were foredoomed to failure. Both the South and the West profited from the low duties, and a coalition of southern and western politicians ruled the country. Indeed, in 1857 the rates of the Walker Tariff were still further reduced.

Circumstances conspired to make this period one of extraordinary prosperity for the cotton-growers of the South.[1] The steady fall in the price of cotton that had at first accompanied the expansion of cotton-growing was arrested in the forties and reversed in the fifties. From an all-time low of less than six cents a pound in 1845, the price of cotton rose to an average of between ten and eleven cents throughout the fifties, and to nearly fourteen cents in 1857. Nor was this change in price due to any curtailment of production, for each year saw a sizable increase in the acreage devoted to cotton culture. Rather, the world demand for cotton had been immensely accelerated. Improvements in textile machinery now made possible the manufacture of cotton goods for sale at so low a price that even the humblest Asiatic or African could afford to buy. American manufacturers, after meeting practically the entire domestic demand for cheap cotton cloth, were able to export a considerable excess to the Orient; English manufacturers, ensured by the repeal of the Corn Laws against the danger of having to pay high wages to their operatives, sought and found new markets everywhere in the world; French manufacturers, while definitely less flourishing than their British competitors, were by no means idle. Manufacturers everywhere turned to the American South for their raw cotton, for nowhere else could they find an abundant supply of comparable quality. To meet this tremendous demand practically all the land of the South that was suited to cotton culture was used for that purpose. Indeed, except for cotton and tobacco the production in the South of every important crop failed during the fifties to keep pace with the growth of the population. But the cotton crop, which had risen from 1,500,000 bales in 1840 to 2,500,000 bales in 1850, reached the enormous total of 5,300,000 bales in 1860 — seven-eighths of the world's supply.

The profits of cotton-growing

Less frequently noted is the fact that during these same years a renaissance of tobacco-growing made the states of the upper South more prosperous than they had been for years.[2] This was due in part to the increased demand of a growing world population, in part to the introduction of new species and to improved methods of cultivation and manufacture. In 1849 the tobacco crop of

Tobacco-growing

---

[1] L. C. Gray, *History of Agriculture in the Southern United States to 1860* (2 vols., 1933).
[2] Meyer Jacobstein, *The Tobacco Industry in the United States* (1907).

the United States amounted to less than 200,000,000 pounds; ten years later it was nearly 430,000,000 pounds. Virginia and Kentucky were the greatest tobacco-growing states, but other states also, notably Maryland, Tennessee, and Missouri, contributed large quotas. Indeed, every state in the Union, North as well as South, grew some tobacco, although the cotton states during this decade grew proportionately less tobacco than they had ever grown before.

While tobacco was second in value only to cotton among the crops that the South produced, it was a rather poor second. Throughout that section the saying that "Cotton is King!" went unchallenged. Southerners were proud of the fact that the world depended upon them almost exclusively to supply one of the primary necessities of civilization; they relished the thought that without their help the wheels of industry in the North and in England would scarcely turn; they never forgot that the export of cotton paid more than half the bills contracted by the United States abroad. On one score, however, they confessed some embarrassment. The world's need for cotton would continue to mount, but by the end of the fifties the South's ability to meet that need would be taxed to the limit. Practically all available cotton-growing land was already in use, and in the older states continual planting of the same crop had almost exhausted the soil. New cotton lands must be found. If they did not exist within the United States, why not expand the national borders to include them?

In the general reign of plenty the small farmer of the Northwest was by no means forgotten. The steady growth and population meant for him, too, an increased demand to satisfy. Eastern farmers were unable to meet in full the needs of their new industrial centers for foodstuffs, but the western farmer, thanks to the improved means of transportation that the railway age introduced, was able to flood the eastern markets with his produce. Southerners, also, owing to their increasing concentration upon cotton and tobacco, consumed an ever-growing quantity of northwestern farm products. For this intersectional trade the Mississippi and its tributaries still furnished a cheap and easy means of transportation; and it is worth noting that nearly all the northern goods sent down the river in the years immediately preceding the Civil War found a market in the South itself. The export of northern grain and flour from New Orleans, once deemed so important a factor in the economic life of the Northwest, dwindled to insignificance in comparison to the domestic trade. This did not mean, however, that exports of northwestern products were not being made, for during the middle years of the century the need of Europe for American foodstuffs was considerable. But grain and flour

The northwestern farmer

destined for a foreign market now went by rail to the eastern ports for
transshipment, instead of by river boats, as formerly, to New Orleans.
These overseas sales, while not very great in comparison to the total output of the American farms, were sufficient most of the time to absorb the
excess not needed for domestic consumption. Particularly during the
Crimean War, 1853–56, the European demand was great and the prices
paid were correspondingly high. Stimulated by the new prosperity, the
population of the Northwest grew with amazing rapidity. Frontier conditions in central Illinois, Missouri, Iowa, and southern Wisconsin tended
to disappear, and in 1858 a new northwestern state, Minnesota, was
added to the Union.

That a revolution in agriculture had begun — a revolution soon to be
particularly significant for the new Northwest — was perhaps less apparent to contemporaries than to later generations.[1] Farmers were no longer so strictly concerned, as they once had The revolu-
been, to produce upon their own farms all the necessities of tion in agri-
life for themselves and their families. In earlier times they culture
had taken their own corn and wheat to a near-by mill to be ground into
the very flour from which the bread they ate was to be made. They had
shot or butchered their own meat, had clipped with their own hands the
wool that ultimately through home manufacture provided the clothes
they wore, had built their own houses, sheds, and fences from timber cut
on their own property, and in a great variety of other ways also had met
their own needs without help from the outside. But the self-sufficient
farmer was rapidly becoming a thing of the past. New agricultural machines, such as the reaper, enabled him to produce far more of certain
commodities than he could hope to use. New means of transportation,
especially the railroads, enabled him to ship his excess to market. With
the proceeds from the sale of his crop he could now buy many of the
things he had formerly found it necessary to make for himself or go
without. He could, and did, begin to specialize in farming, even to the
extent of producing only one kind of crop. His farm became a kind of
factory from the profits of which he lived. No longer was he independent
of the rest of the world, for he must sell to it, and he must buy from it.
His purchases stimulated manufacturing, and the growth of manufacturing provided him with new markets. Northwestern farmers, while grateful for the markets that the cotton- and tobacco-growers of the South
were also providing, were increasingly conscious of the greater purchasing
power of the industrial Northeast. The bond of union that was being

---

[1] A. H. Sanford, *The Story of Agriculture in the United States* (1916); P. W. Bidwell and
J. I. Falconer, *History of Agriculture in the Northern United States, 1620–1860* (1925);
U. P. Hedrick, *A History of Agriculture in the State of New York* (1933).

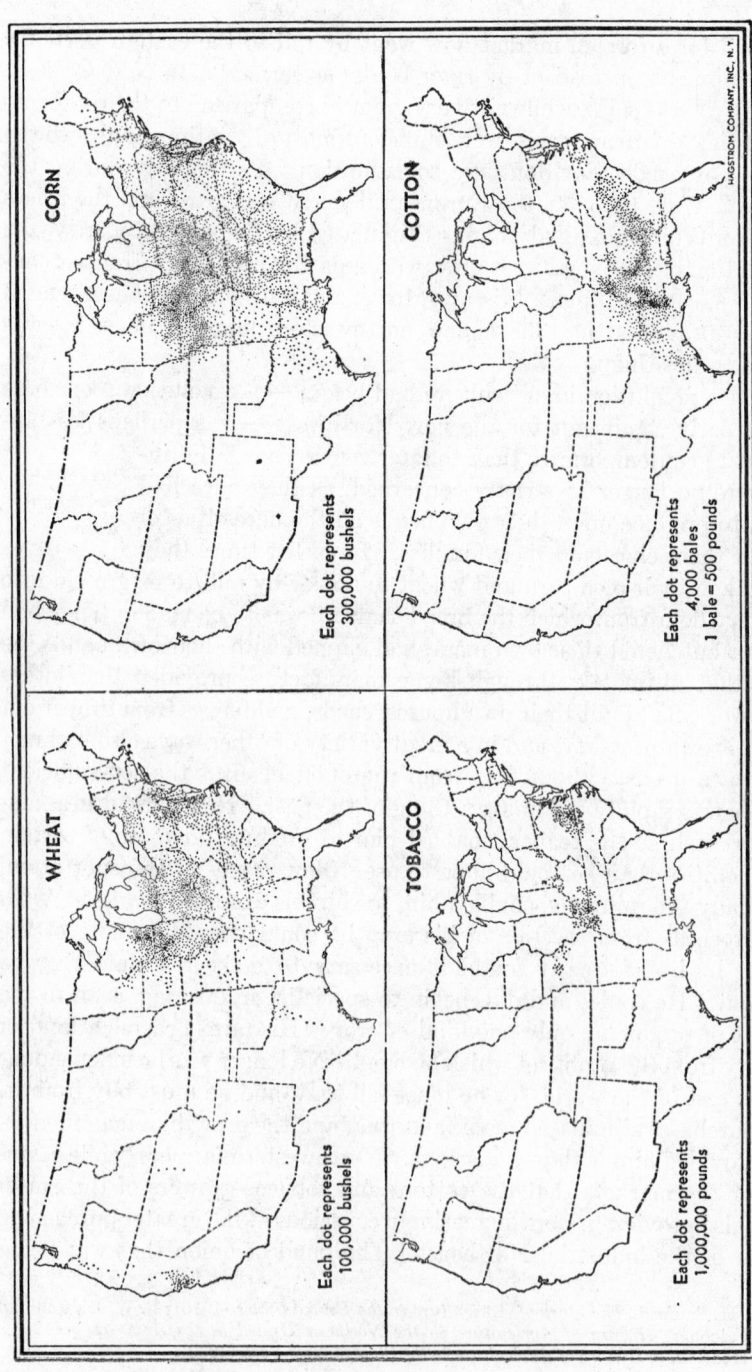

CORN — Each dot represents 300,000 bushels

COTTON — Each dot represents 4,000 bales 1 bale = 500 pounds

WHEAT — Each dot represents 100,000 bushels

TOBACCO — Each dot represents 1,000,000 pounds

HAGSTROM COMPANY, INC., N. Y.

THE DISTRIBUTION OF FARM PRODUCE IN THE UNITED STATES, 1859

cemented between these two sections would soon be strong enough to meet the test of civil war.

The rich natural resources of the United States were already contributing generously to what President Pierce chose to call "the light of our prosperity." Precious metals had much to do, although by no means everything, with making the population of California four times as great in 1860 as it had been in 1850. Magnificent virgin forests in the upper Mississippi Valley furnished an almost limitless supply of lumber to the prairie states below. The lead mines of northwestern Illinois and southwestern Wisconsin, once worked by the Indians, now made profits for the whites. Coal and iron ore were found conveniently close together in central and western Pennsylvania. The first oil well was drilled in 1859, near Titusville in northwestern Pennsylvania. *Exploitation of mineral resources*

It is not surprising that the United States, as "the land of opportunity," attracted during these prosperous years a great host of European immigrants. The impact of the Industrial Revolution upon Europe had not been without its unfortunate aspects. *Immigration* Those left unemployed by the introduction of labor-saving devices found great difficulty in obtaining re-employment. Also, profound political disturbances, such as the Chartist movement in England and the revolutions of 1848 on the Continent, accompanied the changing economic order. For those who wished to flee this turmoil, Europe had no adequate outlet of its own, but this defect the United States was fortunately in good position to remedy. Its industries were new, and could profitably absorb both skilled and unskilled European workmen. Its frontier, capable seemingly of an almost indefinite expansion, could give homes not only to its own needy millions, but to millions of Europeans as well. Before 1840 the number of immigrants who came to the United States each year was an almost negligible figure, twenty-three thousand in 1830, and eighty-four thousand in 1840; but between 1845 and 1855 the average number of newcomers admitted annually had risen to not less than three hundred thousand. They came from many lands, but, owing to special circumstances, from Ireland and Germany far more than from all other countries combined.[1]

Unlike the Scotch-Irish who came to the United States from the north of Ireland during the eighteenth century, the new Irish immigrants came from the southern counties of Ireland; they were Celtic in origin rather than Teutonic, and Roman Catholic *The Irish* in religion rather than Presbyterian. Their incentives for leaving Ireland

[1] G. M. Stephenson, *A History of American Immigration, 1820–1924* (1926), is the most satisfactory book on this subject. A special study of unusual merit is T. C. Blegen, *Norwegian Migration to America* (2 vols., 1931–40).

were numerous: political oppression, whether real or fancied, absentee landlordism, overpopulation, and above all a series of devastating famines that began with the failure of the potato crop in 1845. Deaths by starvation during these hard seasons were pitifully frequent, and those who were able to leave for a land of plenty such as America availed themselves of the first opportunity. Shipping companies cut the cost of transportation to a figure lower than had ever been known before, herded the immigrants together in stifling holds, and made a rich harvest from their enterprise. The Irish landed virtually destitute at Boston, New York, and other eastern ports, and went to work at small wages in the factories, on the railroads, or wherever their help was needed. Thousands of Irish girls found employment as domestics. Soon nearly every city had its "Shantytown" where the newly arrived Irish lived in quarters even more squalid than those they had known in Ireland, and prospered on incomes that to the native Americans seemed ridiculous.

The reasons for the German migration were somewhat analogous. In the vanguard were the political refugees, liberals who had taken a part in the revolutions of 1848, only to lose out in the end **The Germans** before the forces of reaction. Some men of this type, Carl Schurz and Franz Sigel, for example, soon achieved a greater prominence in their adopted land than they had ever known in Germany. Still others left to avoid the compulsory military service required by most German princes, and others to get away from distressing economic conditions for which no remedy seemed available. The success of the English manufacturers with factory-made textiles brought ruin to the numerous German household producers of linen, while crop failures in the Rhine Valley and a losing struggle to hold the English grain market meant critical times for agriculture.

The average German immigrant was a little higher in the social scale than his Irish contemporary, and had often saved enough money to get a start in the new land. Sometimes he went into business, and whole cities, such as Cincinnati, St. Louis, and Milwaukee, soon exhibited many of the characteristic qualities of the Germans. More frequently he bought himself a farm and, unaccustomed to the thriftless methods into which an abundance of rich soil had betrayed the native Americans, he farmed carefully and prospered inordinately. Unlike the Irish, the Germans rarely settled in the East, but went instead to the Middle West, where lands were cheaper and opportunity more abundant. For a generation or more they continued to speak the German language, and they clung tenaciously to the manners and customs of their European homes. Great lovers of music and of good-fellowship, each German community was apt to have its *Liederkranz*, its *Turnverein*, and its *Biergärten*. In Wisconsin the German influence was so pronounced that there was talk of making the state over into an ideal German commonwealth.

Politicians in search of new issues, after the Compromise of 1850 had made a truce over slavery, were quick to discover in the immigrant a menace to American institutions. Port cities and the districts adjacent to them complained bitterly of the pauper population that the immigrant tide forced upon them. Religious zealots professed alarm at the presence of a rapidly growing Roman Catholic element in a country that had always before been dominantly Protestant. American workmen complained that their wages were being beaten down and their jobs actually taken away from them by their alien competitors. Southerners were deeply concerned because the foreigners, unaccustomed to slavery in their former homes, consistently avoided the slaveholding South and helped to swell the already alarming lead of the North in population. Good citizens generally recognized the natural prejudices that must be overcome in order to assimilate fully the clannish Irish and the self-sufficient Germans. Not only must the difficult barriers of race and religion be surmounted, but different political traditions must somehow be reconciled. Some of the Germans, thoroughly imbued with the revolutionary doctrines that had precipitated the revolutions of 1848, even dared to propose radical changes in the American form of government.

Native Americanism

The first impulse of the politicians, however, was to cater to the foreign vote. Aliens were permitted to exercise the suffrage after an extremely short period of residence, German and Irish names appeared on almost every ballot, and naturalized citizens were showered with political favors. In this contest for foreign support the Democrats completely eclipsed the Whigs, whose well-established conservatism repelled both the poverty-stricken Irish and the liberal-led Germans. Indeed, the Whigs might well have seized upon the anti-foreigner issue, but their party was already too moribund to take a pronounced stand on anything. It fell out, therefore, that a new party was formed precisely for this purpose. Its origins lay in a succession of anti-foreigner and anti-Catholic secret societies, culminating in the Order of the Star-Spangled Banner, and finally in the "Know-Nothing," or American, Party.[1] The Know-Nothings, careful always to keep their decisions secret, and professing to "know nothing" about what they intended to do, carried many local elections in such immigrant centers as Massachusetts, Pennsylvania, and New York.

[1] Two useful state studies of this subject are L. F. Schmeckebier, *History of the Know-Nothing Party in Maryland* (1899); and L. D. Scisco, *Political Nativism in New York State* (1901). See also R. A. Billington, *The Protestant Crusade, 1800–1860* (1938).

In their search for an attractive issue to keep the mind of the public off the slavery question, the Democrats tried repeatedly to rekindle the interest in expansion that had brought them such success

Expansion as a political issue in the election of 1844. President Pierce apparently hoped to make the acquisition of Cuba the outstanding achievement of his administration, even if it cost a war with Spain. His ministers to Great Britain, France, and Spain (James Buchanan, John Y. Mason, and Pierre Soulé), when charged with the task of formulating the American program, brought forth the famous "Ostend Manifesto," stating that the United States should first seek to buy Cuba from Spain, but failing that, should take it by force. But this bit of international bad manners came to nothing, for Spain refused to sell, and the United States, already embroiled with the slavery issue, avoided the risks of a foreign war by disavowing the action of its ministers. The sole tangible result of all the expansionist propaganda was the purchase in 1853 from Mexico for ten million dollars of a sandy triangle south of the Gila River. Surveyors claimed that this territory, generally called the "Gadsden Purchase," would be needed in case the United States ever wished to construct a railroad along a southern route to California.

More successful were the efforts of the administration to smooth the way for American traders in the Far East. Ever since 1784, when the *Empress of China* set sail under the Stars and Stripes from

Commerce with the Orient New York for Canton, a small but lucrative oriental trade had been maintained, and in 1844, following the Opium War between England and China, the United States had been accorded by formal treaty the same commercial privileges that the English had won by force. But in China the Americans furnished only weak competition for the better-established Europeans, so the American government determined to open a new field for commercial activities in the "Hermit Kingdom" of Japan. With this end in view, and also to persuade the Japanese not to mistreat American seamen shipwrecked on their shores (as was their custom), Commodore Matthew Perry visited Japan in 1854 with the largest fleet the United States had ever assembled in Asiatic waters. Overawed by so great a show of force, the Japanese government agreed to open two ports to American traders, to permit an American consul to reside at one of them, and to accord protection to American seamen left in distress upon Japanese shores. A trade treaty with Siam, concluded in 1856, and an unsuccessful project for the annexation of Hawaii, called further attention to the Pacific interests of the United States.

But in spite of every effort to supplant it with something else, the slav-

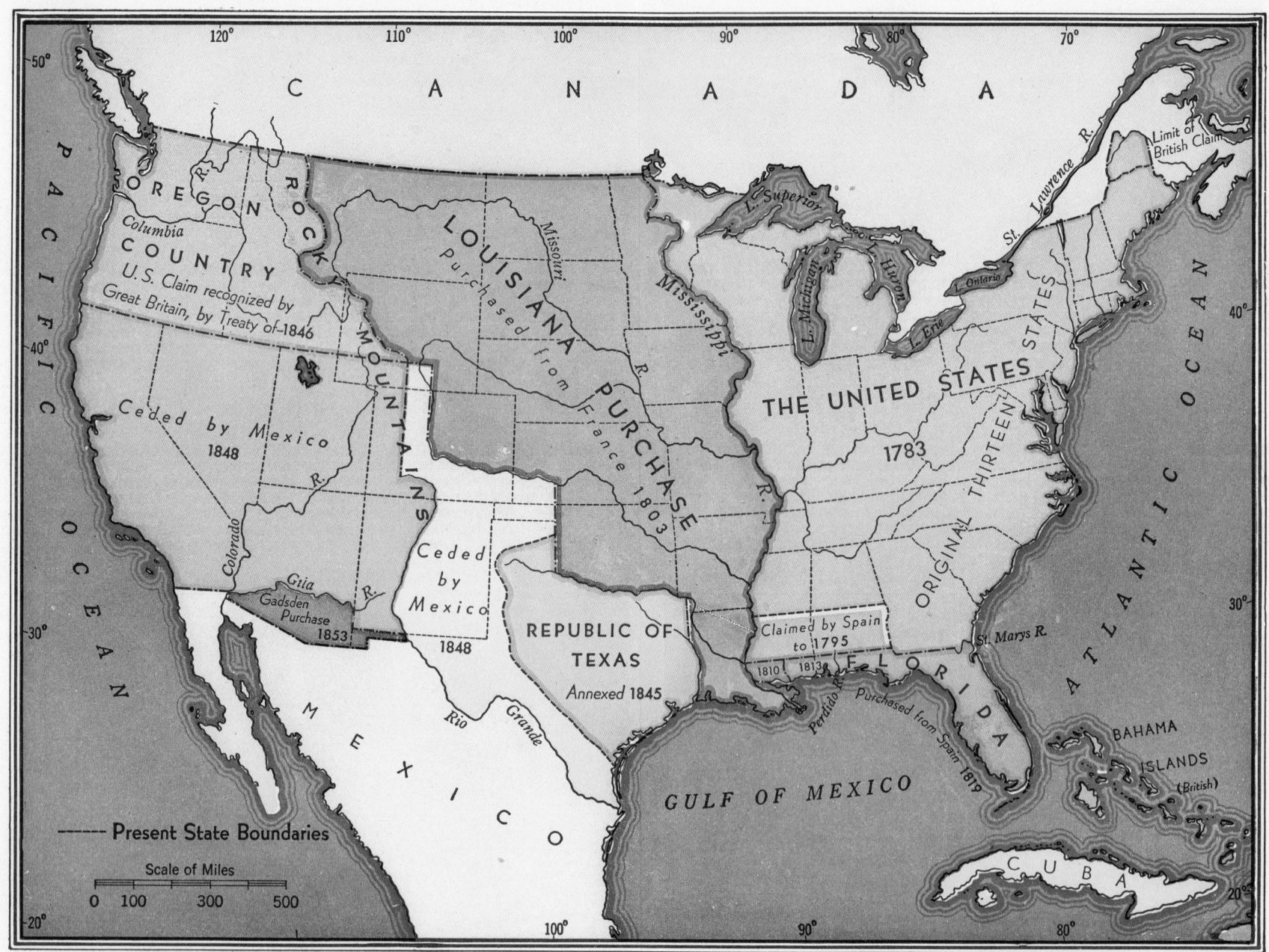

THE EXPANSION OF THE UNITED STATES

ery issue would not down. Know-Nothingism won a strong following in the South, where there were no foreigners, because the inrush of immigrants was strengthening the North, and loomed, therefore, as a potential threat to slavery. Expansion was denounced in the North as a means of adding more slave

Vitality of the slavery issue

territory to the Union. Abolitionists proved that the Fugitive Slave Act was being used as a means of kidnaping northern free Negroes and selling them into slavery. Anti-slavery men in the North gave systematic aid to runaway Negroes. The evangelical churches, long since split over the morality of slavery, continued, in spite of the political truce, to debate the issue.[1] Most important of all, Harriet Beecher Stowe's *Uncle Tom's Cabin*, which appeared in book form in 1852, swept the North. Three thousand copies were sold the first day, and three hundred thousand copies before the end of a year. As a novel, the book left much to be desired, but as a moral indictment of slavery it was tremendous. Dramatized, and played before enthusiastic audiences throughout the North, it made converts for the anti-slavery cause even among those who could not or would not read. But nowhere in the South was *Uncle Tom's Cabin* either played or read. Below the Mason and Dixon Line it won only fiery denunciations.

Under these circumstances it is hardly fair to place the entire blame for the reopening of the slavery dispute upon the shoulders of Stephen A. Douglas (1813-61) of Illinois. It is a fact, however, that in 1854 Douglas did sponsor a measure, the Kansas-Nebraska Act, which embodied a plan for the further expansion of

The Kansas-Nebraska Act

slavery, and which could therefore be construed as unsettling the delicate balance that the compromise measures of 1850 had established. But the time was ripe for such a step, and if Douglas had not been the first to suggest it, in all likelihood someone else would have done so at a not much later date. Douglas was of New England origin, but had come to Illinois when only twenty years of age, and was now the idol of the boastful, untutored, expansionist Illinois democracy.[2] In the Senate since 1847, he had won his greatest victory in 1850, when he had persuaded Congress to adopt the policy of liberal grants of land to the states in aid of railroad building. The resultant rapid construction of the Illinois Central and other roads made Chicago the "metropolis of the West," and put into Douglas's head the idea of a still more ambitious project, a land-grant

---

[1] J. N. Norwood, *The Schism in the Methodist Episcopal Church, 1844* (1923), shows the disruptive forces at work in a single denomination. See also H. K. Rowe, *The History of Religion in the United States* (1924).

[2] The histories of the period all give much attention to Douglas. T. C. Smith, *Parties and Slavery* (1906), is extremely useful. The most scholarly biographies of Douglas are Allen Johnson, *Stephen A. Douglas: A Study in American Politics* (1908); and George Fort Milton, *The Eve of Conflict: Stephen A. Douglas and the Needless War* (1934).

railroad west from Chicago all the way to the Pacific. The idea of a transcontinental railroad was nothing new, nor even the idea of financing it by means of a land grant. But what Douglas realized was that to build such a road where he wanted it the Indian country west of the bend of the Missouri would have to be surveyed and opened for sale. To facilitate this, he determined that the whole region should promptly be organized as a territory.

Promoters of a transcontinental railroad to connect California with the rest of the Union had persuaded Congress, as early as 1853, to appropriate one hundred and fifty thousand dollars to be used by the Secretary of War in surveying a number of alternative railroad routes across the western half of the continent. In due

Railroad surveys of 1853

time the surveyors reported that, at least so far as the engineering problem was concerned, a northern, a southern, and one or more central routes were equally feasible. Conditions seemed to favor the southern route, where the Indian menace was less pronounced, and where land grants, either from the state of Texas or from the United States, would be available for the entire distance. Douglas's plan was to overcome this handicap to the northern route by persuading Congress to organize the territory west of the Missouri River. As early as 1853 a bill to create the territory of Nebraska passed the House of Representatives, but failed to make further progress. Thereupon Douglas, who fortunately for his project was chairman of the Senate committee on territories, offered the South a tempting bait. Let there be *two* territories in the unopened region, Kansas and Nebraska, and extend to this area the principle of the Compromise of 1850 which permitted each territory to decide for itself whether it should be free or slave. Thus by means of "popular sovereignty" the South might open new territory to slavery, while the North (although Douglas said nothing of this) stood a chance to win the railroad. Almost as one man southern Representatives and Senators rose to Douglas's bait, and the Kansas-Nebraska Act became a law in 1854. To please the Southerners, Douglas had even incorporated in the bill the repeal of the Missouri Compromise.

The debate over this measure revived all the bitterness of the years that had preceded the Compromise of 1850. Practically all the northern Whigs and many northern Democrats opposed it. Douglas was accused of undoing the sectional truce in order to gain

Party chaos

southern votes for his presidential candidacy in 1856, and he may have had such a thought in mind. But undoubtedly he was interested in the railroad land grant the act might promote, he knew that many Missourians were eager to see the territory west of their border opened to slavery, and he believed the settlement of the area concerned could not long be

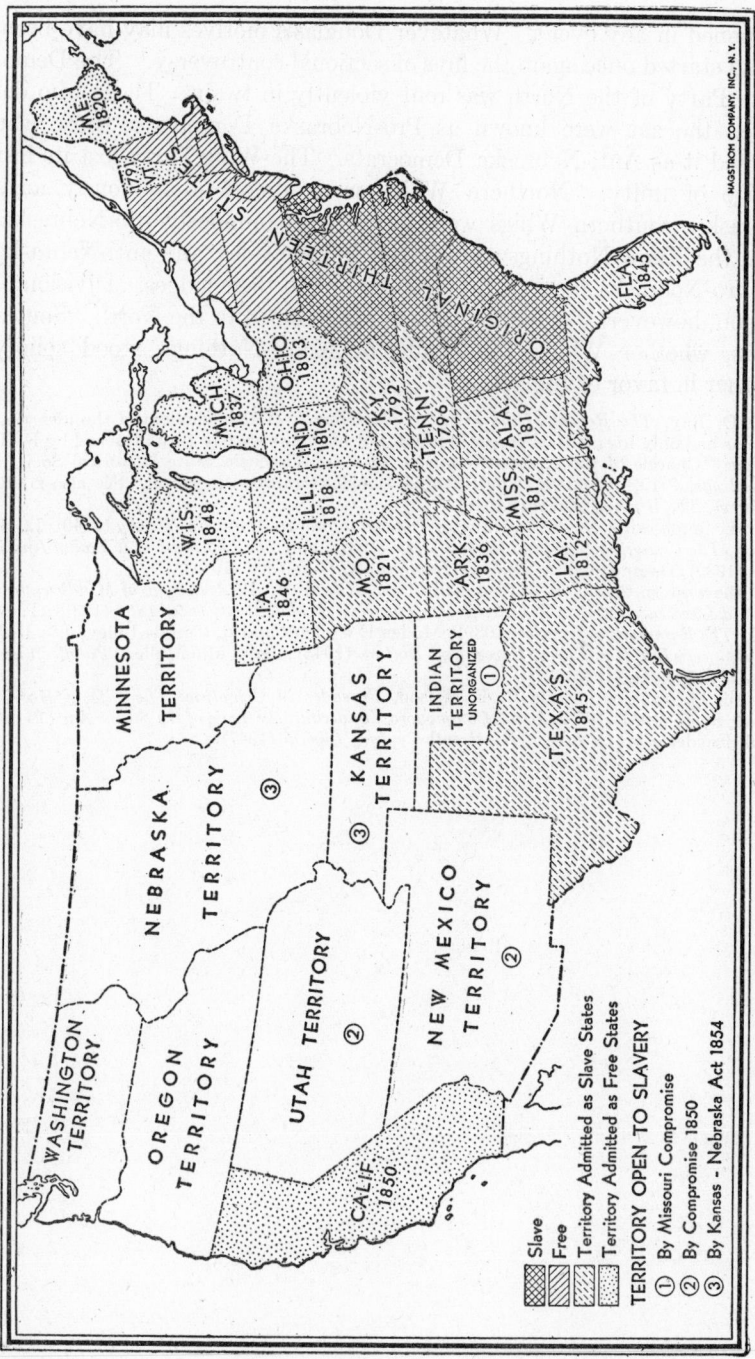

TERRITORIAL ORGANIZATION OF THE UNITED STATES IN 1854

ME.
1820

WIS.
1879

ORIGINAL THIRTEEN STATES

FLA.
1845

MICH.
1837

OHIO
1803

KY.
1792

TENN.
1796

ALA.
1819

WIS.
1848

ILL.
1818

IND.
1816

MISS.
1817

IA.
1846

MO.
1821

ARK.
1836

LA.
1812

MINNESOTA
TERRITORY

KANSAS
TERRITORY

INDIAN
TERRITORY
UNORGANIZED
①

TEXAS
1845

NEBRASKA   TERRITORY

③

③

WASHINGTON
TERRITORY

OREGON
TERRITORY

UTAH TERRITORY

②

NEW MEXICO
TERRITORY

②

CALIF.
1850

MAGSTROM COMPANY, INC., N. Y.

Slave
Free
Territory Admitted as Slave States
Territory Admitted as Free States
TERRITORY OPEN TO SLAVERY
① By Missouri Compromise
② By Compromise 1850
③ By Kansas - Nebraska Act 1854

postponed in any event. Whatever Douglas's motives may have been, he had started once again the fires of sectional controversy.[1] The Democratic Party of the North was rent violently in twain. Those who defended the act were known as Pro-Nebraska Democrats; those who opposed it as Anti-Nebraska Democrats. The Whig Party lost its last vestige of unity. Northern Whigs were almost unanimously anti-Nebraska; southern Whigs were quite as unanimously pro-Nebraska. Even the Know-Nothings were forced to take sides, and anti-Nebraska and pro-Nebraska factions brought discord to their lodges. Division of opinion, however, was for the time being confined to the North. Southerners, whether Whigs, Democrats, or Know-Nothings, stood solidly together in favor of the act.

[1] P. O. Ray, The 'Repeal of the Missouri Compromise (1909), challenged the idea that Douglas had only his political career in mind; but his views were in turn attacked by F. H. Hodder, "Genesis of the Kansas-Nebraska Act," in Wisconsin State Historical Society, Proceedings, 1912, pp. 69–86, who featured Douglas's railroad interests. See also G. R. Gaeddert, The Birth of Kansas (1940).

On the immigrants, see M. L. Hansen, The Immigrant in American History (1940); L. M. Larson, The Changing West and Other Essays (1937), and The Log Book of a Young Immigrant (1939); Oscar Handlin, Boston's Immigrants, 1790–1865 (1941).

On the western theme: J. T. Flanagan, America Is West: An Anthology of Middlewestern Life and Literature (1945); H. C. Hulbert, The Older Middle West, 1840–1880 (1936); T. D. Clark, The Rampaging Frontier (1939); Madge E Pickard and R. Carlyle Buley, The Midwest Pioneer: His Ills, Cures, Cares, and Doctors (1945); Jerry MacMullen, Paddle-Wheel Days in California (1944).

Useful biographies include R. F. Wilson, Crusader in Crinoline: The Life of Harriet Beecher Stowe (1941); W. J. Lane, Commodore Vanderbilt: An Epic of the Steam Age (1942); Frank Freidel, Francis Lieber, Nineteenth Century Liberal (1947).

18

The House Divided

THE UNITED FRONT achieved by the opponents of slavery extension during the debate on the Kansas-Nebraska Act led almost immediately to the formation of the Republican Party. The exact origins of this party are hard to trace, for the movement was almost spontaneous, but certainly the middle-western small farmers, who believed that the lands of the new frontier should belong to them and their kind rather than to the southern slaveholders, deserve much of the credit. At Ripon, Wisconsin, February 28, 1854, an "Anti-Nebraska" mass meeting revived the name Republican; at Jackson, Michigan, July 6, 1854, the first state-wide Republican organization was launched. By November, when the mid-term state and congressional elections were held, Republican tickets, or their equivalent under a different name, challenged the Democrats in every northwestern state, and won far more often than they lost. In the Northeast the emergence of the new party was not quite so speedily accomplished, for there both the Whigs and the Know-Nothings clung tenaciously to life. But by the fall of 1855, when Seward, the leading anti-slavery Whig, came over to the Republicans, the new party was safely out of the third-party status. Eastern Republicans, while embracing within their numbers many former abolitionists, were often quite as much anti-southern as anti-slavery. They believed that the hold of the southern leaders on the national government should be broken, and since new slave states meant more pro-southern votes in Congress they felt obliged to oppose their creation.

Everywhere in the North the rise of the Republicans did serious damage to the Democrats. States that had once been safely Democratic began to elect Republican legislatures and Republican state officers. Douglas himself, the outstanding leader of the Democrats and the author of the Kansas-Nebraska Act, suffered an alarming loss of popularity. Denounced as a traitor for his reopening of the slavery dispute, he was compared to Benedict Arnold and Judas Iscariot. He could have traveled, he later admitted, "from Boston to Chicago by the light of his own burning effigies." In Chicago, where his popularity had once been unbounded, he was greeted with groans and hisses by an unruly audience that finally drove him in a temper from the platform. In the South, however, his popularity increased, and the Democratic Party gained notably at the expense of the Whigs. Some of the latter, unable to join hands so suddenly with their former adversaries, broke the fall by becoming "Know-Nothings," or Americans, for a season. The Democrats could not yet count upon a "solid South," but it was on its way.

The real test of popular sovereignty as a remedy for the sectional controversy over slavery came in Kansas. The Iowans and other

Kansas

Northerners who were moving into Nebraska were certain to exclude slavery from that territory at the first opportunity, and did so; but Kansas was no sooner organized as a territory than rivalry broke out between anti-slavery Northerners and pro-slavery Southerners to see who should settle it. Normally Missourians, who presumably were in favor of slavery, would have furnished the greater proportion of the settlers, but to head off this "normal course of events" anti-slavery groups throughout the North, even in New England, organized to send men to Kansas who would vote their way. Soon a stream of determined free-soilers began to descend upon the new territory. Faced by this emergency, the South, with far less man-power to mobilize, relied mainly upon pro-slavery Missourians, who could easily appear in greater numbers on election days than at other times. With instinctive common sense, the bona-fide pro-slavery and anti-slavery emigrants to Kansas settled at a considerable distance from each other. Most of the pro-slavery men settled close to the Missouri River, and founded such towns as Atchison and Leavenworth. The anti-slavery men, on the other hand, went farther into the interior, where they founded Lawrence and Topeka.[1]

The situation in Kansas could hardly have been more completely mishandled. The President of the United States, Franklin Pierce

Franklin Pierce on Kansas

(1804–69), was not to be depended upon in such an emergency. Handsome, a good lawyer, and a polished public speaker, he had entered the Presidency with the hearty good-will of almost the entire American public. Judging from his record as a member for short terms each in both houses of Congress and as a volunteer officer in the Mexican War, there was good reason to suppose that, in spite of his relative obscurity, he would rise to the requirements of his high office. But these expectations were

[1] W. E. Miller, *The Peopling of Kansas* (1906); L. W. Spring, *Kansas: the Prelude to the War for the Union* (1885).

doomed to quick disappointment. Eager to please, he was always in an agony of indecision, for whichever way he decided someone would be offended: he was known, on occasion, to promise the same office to two different applicants. Such a weakling was bound to be at the mercy of the strongest-willed of his advisers, among whom pro-slavery extremists were usually dominant.[1] Andrew H. Reeder of Pennsylvania, the first territorial governor Pierce appointed for Kansas, turned out to be more interested in land speculation than anything else, but the two elections held during his term of office, one for delegate to Congress and one for members of the territorial legislature, were won by the pro-slavery faction with the assistance of large numbers of Missourians who crossed the border for the purpose. Disgruntled because the legislature would not locate the capital at a town-site in which he had a speculative interest, Reeder eventually went over to the anti-slavery side, and was removed from office by Pierce. The second governor, William Shannon of Ohio, was strongly pro-slavery in his sympathies. It was early apparent that "popular. sovereignty" in Kansas was not meant to enable the anti-slavery settlers to have a chance.

When the anti-slavery Kansans realized the hopelessness of trying to win a territorial election, they decided to follow the precedent recently set by California for establishing a state government in advance of congressional permission. Accordingly they elected delegates to a convention which met at Topeka, October 23, 1855, and drew up a free state constitution. Before the end of the year this document was submitted to the people at the polls, and, since the pro-slavery faction did not participate in the election, was adopted by a one-sided vote. Under its terms a governor and legislature were promptly chosen, and Congress was petitioned to admit Kansas as a state. This action President Pierce denounced as treasonous. The pro-slavery territorial government, he told Congress, was the only lawful government in Kansas, and as such was deserving of the full support of the United States.

The Topeka Constitution

Douglas had claimed that popular sovereignty would exile the debate over slavery from the halls of Congress, and put it where it belonged, in the territories themselves. But this theory did not work out in practice, for Congress had now to decide whether to recognize the pro-slavery territorial government or admit Kansas as a free state. The debate was hot in both houses, but on May 19–20, 1856, it reached a climax in the Senate when Charles Sumner of Massachusetts spoke at length on the "Crime against

Brooks's attack on Sumner

---

[1] R. F. Nichols, *Franklin Pierce* (1931). See also, by the same author, *The Democratic Machine, 1850–1854* (1923).

Kansas." During this address he cast serious aspersions upon the name of Senator Andrew P. Butler of South Carolina and upon the fame of the state Butler represented. These remarks were avenged two days later by Representative Preston Brooks, a relative of Butler's and also a South-Carolinian, in a singularly brutal attack. While Sumner was sitting at his desk in the Senate, Brooks approached him carrying a heavy gutta-percha cane, and after denouncing him for his slanders, beat him over the head until he fell insensible to the floor. Because of his injuries, Sumner was for years absent from his seat in the Senate, but Brooks, after resigning his seat in the House, was not only promptly re-elected, but was also showered with gifts of canes from the usually more chivalrous South. It was obvious that the slavery issue had never been more insistently in national politics.

In Kansas, meantime, "border ruffians" from Missouri bent on violence were being met in kind by free-state men from the North. **"Bleeding Kansas"** Henry Ward Beecher had counseled sending Sharps rifles to the anti-slavery emigrants, and such weapons, generally known as "Beecher's Bibles," were soon in use. When a pro-slavery mob, called by courtesy a "posse," assisted in the arrest of the free-state officers at Lawrence by sacking that city, John Brown of Osawatomie, an abolitionist fanatic, contrived to bring about the murder of five pro-slavery settlers in reprisal. The "Civil War in Kansas" that followed possibly cost the lives of two hundred citizens. It was ended by a new governor, John White Geary, who invoked the aid of federal troops to restore order, but not until "Bleeding Kansas" had become the leading issue in the presidential campaign of 1856.

Despite the turmoil that popular sovereignty had produced in Kansas, the Democratic National Convention declared that this principle **Election of 1856** furnished "the only sound and safe solution of the slavery question." For its nominee, however, it chose James Buchanan of Pennsylvania, whose absence from the country as minister to England had saved him the commitments that Pierce and Douglas had been obliged to make. The Republicans, as eager to serve availability as the Democrats, overlooked the claims of Seward and Chase, their best-known leaders, to choose as their standard-bearer John C. Frémont, the glamorous "Pathfinder of the West." Their platform revived the Free-Soil doctrine that Congress had the constitutional right and the moral duty to prohibit the expansion of slavery into any of the territories of the United States. The Americans, or Know-Nothings, and a remnant of the Whigs held separate conventions, but nominated the same candidate, ex-President Fillmore, and adopted platforms that sought in the main to avoid sectionalism by an insistent demand for the preservation of the Union. The Republicans made a whirlwind campaign, patterned on the Whig tactics of 1840, but the country was frightened by the specter of disunion, and the Democrats won an unexpectedly easy victory. Eleven northern states cast 114 votes for Frémont, but five northern states and every southern state but one cast a total of 174 votes for Buchanan. While the American Party furnished strong opposition to the Democrats in the South, Fillmore carried only one state, Maryland, with 8 electoral votes. Both houses of Congress were safely Democratic.

James Buchanan (1791–1868) [1] was nearly sixty-five years of age when he assumed the Presidency, and, unlike Pierce, he had had ample experience in politics. Before he became minister to Eng- James land, he had served for ten years in the House of Repre- Buchanan sentatives, had been minister to Russia, member of the United States Senate for two decades, and Secretary of State under President Polk. His opposition to the Wilmot Proviso and his ardent championship of expansion marked him as a "dough-face," that is, a "northern man with southern principles." Beyond a doubt he was devoted to the Union, but the conservatism of old age tended to confirm him in the belief that the only way to preserve the Union was to permit the southern leaders to have their way.

Two days after Buchanan's inauguration the Supreme Court of the United States handed down a decision in the case of *Dred Scott vs. Sanford* that put a new aspect upon the dispute over slavery in the territories. This decision did not come un- Dred Scott solicited. The Kansas-Nebraska Act had assumed that case the Supreme Court might have a final word to say on the subject; and Southerners, confident that the Court would be on their side, were eager for its pronouncement. Even the President-elect, shortly before his inauguration, seems to have used his influence to swing a wavering justice into line. Seven of the justices were Democrats, one was a Whig, and one a Republican; and of the seven Democrats five were from the South. Surely such a Court would end for all time the Republican pretension that Congress had a right to exclude slavery from the territories. No doubt the majority of the Court, including the venerable Chief Justice Taney, were genuinely persuaded that the weight of their opinion would be sufficient to bring the heated controversy to an end.

The Dred Scott case offered a satisfactory opportunity for the Court

---

[1] G. T. Curtis, *Life of James Buchanan* (2 vols., 1883). Many interesting letters bearing on the Buchanan administration are printed in *Robert Tyler, Southern Rights Champion, 1847–1866*, edited by Philip G. Auchampaugh (1934).

to declare itself.[1] Dred Scott was a Negro who until 1834 had legally
been held in bondage in the slave state of Missouri. After that date
his master, an army surgeon, removed, taking Dred with him, first to
Illinois, a free state, and then to Wisconsin Territory (later Minnesota)
where, under the terms of the Missouri Compromise, slavery was also
forbidden. Ultimately Dred was brought back to Missouri. Here he
was induced by some interested abolitionists to bring suit for his freedom on the ground that his residence in free territory had set him free.
The case attracted much attention, and ultimately Scott was sold to a
New-Yorker named Sanford so that it could be transferred to the
federal courts. By 1856 it was before the United States Supreme Court,
where it was twice argued. When Buchanan was inaugurated in March,
1857, he referred to the forthcoming opinion with the hope that it would
settle with finality the status of slavery in the territories.

Chief Justice Taney spoke for the seven Democratic justices. First
of all, he denied emphatically the right of the lower federal court to
assume jurisdiction in the case. Dred Scott, said the Chief
Justice, was not a citizen of Missouri within the meaning
of the Constitution; hence he could neither sue nor be sued
in the federal courts. This opinion the Court might have based, as
some of the assenting justices would have been more content to do, on
the ground that Dred Scott, whatever his status in Illinois or Wisconsin
territory, was at the time he brought suit a slave in Missouri, and so
not a citizen. But the Chief Justice argued instead that Negroes of
slave descent, as an inferior order of beings, were not and could not
possibly become citizens of a state. He pointed out further that Dred
Scott's residence in territory north of the Missouri Compromise line
could not have made him free, for Congress, he said, had exceeded its
authority in forbidding slavery in that part of the Louisiana Purchase
north of 36° 30′. Slave property in the territories was as much protected
by the Constitution as any other kind of property. The Missouri Compromise had therefore been unconstitutional, and Dred Scott was no
less a slave in a supposedly free territory than in Missouri. Southern
extremists could ask no more. The Chief Justice had accepted their
position in full. It is worth noting, however, that the reasoning of
Taney was questioned, even by some of his Democratic associates,
while the two other justices, Curtis of Massachusetts and McLean of
Illinois, filed vigorous dissenting opinions.

Taney's opinion

---

[1] G. T. Curtis, *Constitutional History of the United States* (2 vols., 1889–96), contains a
chapter on this subject. The traditional account is significantly amended by F. H. Hodder, "Some Phases of the Dred Scott Case," in the *Mississippi Valley Historical Review*,
vol. xvi, pp. 3–22. See also E. S. Corwin, "The Dred Scott Decision," in the *American
Historical Review*, vol. xvii, pp. 52–69. The decision itself, *Dred Scott vs. Sandford*, may be
found in 19 Howard, 393. Curiously Sanford's name is here misspelled.

It was idle to suppose that a decision so partisan from a Court so divided could settle anything with finality. The Republicans refused to concede that the status of slavery in the territories had actually been before the Court at all. If Dred Scott was not a citizen, that fact alone required demonstration. All the rest of the argument was irrelevant and gratuitous, or as the lawyers put it, *obiter dicta*. Southern Democrats, on the other hand, were greatly elated by the stand the Court had taken. They denied indignantly, and with fair logic, the argument that the status of slavery in the territories had not properly been before the Court. The decision, they insisted, had settled that matter for all time. Slavery must now be allowed to spread freely into all the territories. The Northern Democrats were in a sorry plight. They could not easily condemn the decision of a Democratic Court, but those of them who thought the matter through realized that Douglas's doctrine of popular sovereignty, to which they had pinned their faith, could not easily be reconciled with Taney's opinion. If slavery could not be excluded from a territory by law of Congress, how then could the legislature of a territory, which owed its authority to Congress, exclude slavery? For the moment, however, they refused to admit the contradiction and said little about it.

Once more the attention of the country turned to Kansas. Eager to prevent a recurrence of trouble in that quarter, President Buchanan persuaded Robert J. Walker of Mississippi, a man of far greater ability than could ordinarily be obtained for such a post, to accept the governorship of the new territory. Walker promptly called an election for delegates to a constitutional convention, and urged the free-state men to participate. This, however, they refused to do, for they felt little confidence in the fairness of the Buchanan administration, whose agent Walker was. In consequence, the pro-slavery element carried the election overwhelmingly, and in October, 1857, a convention held at Lecompton framed a pro-slavery constitution. Determined to take no chances, the Lecompton convention failed to give the voters an opportunity to reject the document it had framed, but provided merely that they might vote for or against the further introduction of slaves. Whichever way the vote went, slavery in Kansas would be fully protected. Undeceived by this ruse, the free-state men again refused to vote, so that the constitution was carried with the more extreme pro-slavery clause. In the fall elections for a territorial legislature, however, the free-state men not only voted, but thanks to the rejection by Governor Walker and the territorial secretary of many fraudulent votes, they won. Thereupon the legislature resubmitted the Lecompton constitution, this time with the full alterna-

Events in Kansas

tive of adoption or rejection. Now the pro-slavery men refused to vote, so that the constitution that had just been so easily ratified was almost unanimously rejected. But the relative strength of the two sides was clearly revealed. In support of the Lecompton constitution the pro-slavery forces had cast only 6226 votes, whereas the free-state men only a few weeks later had cast 10,226 votes against it. That Kansas wished to be free and not slave was fully apparent to any unprejudiced observer.

Unhappily, President Buchanan could not be so described. His most trusted advisers were Southerners, and ordinarily he reflected their views. In November, 1857, he forced Walker out of office because the governor's rejection of fraudulent pro-slavery votes had given the legislature of Kansas to the free-state men. Moreover, in December, 1857, when Congress convened, the President made clear his desire to see Kansas admitted promptly as a slave state. Two months later he submitted to Congress the now thoroughly discredited Lecompton constitution, and urged its acceptance. All this was too much for Douglas. His doctrine of popular sovereignty rested upon the assumption that a majority, even in a territory, had the right to decide for or against slavery, and now the President proposed to make Kansas a slave state against its clearly expressed will. This travesty upon popular sovereignty Douglas denounced with all the vigor at his command. Such a course required courage of a high order, for it meant for the Illinois senator not only a break with the administration, but also the certain loss of his recently won popularity in the South. Many other northern Democrats agreed with him, however, and while the President was able to force his policy upon the Senate, he failed with it in the House. Eventually a compromise measure, the English bill, offered Kansas statehood under the Lecompton constitution in case a majority of the voters approved that document, but again the Kansans voted the obnoxious constitution down.

Meantime the panic of 1857 had burst upon the country, and had left in its train a trying period of economic depression.[1] The prosperity of the early years of the decade had carried with it the germs of its own dissolution. The success of the railroads tempted them to an unreasonable overexpansion. Lines were built into unsettled areas where for years to come there could be little hope of profits. Manufacturers, likewise, eager to keep pace with the ever-growing markets, were soon well ahead of them. Producers of foodstuffs were lulled into a false sense of security by the abnormal demand

Douglas on Kansas

The panic of 1857

[1] G. W. Van Vleck, _The Panic of 1857: An Analytical Study_ (1943).

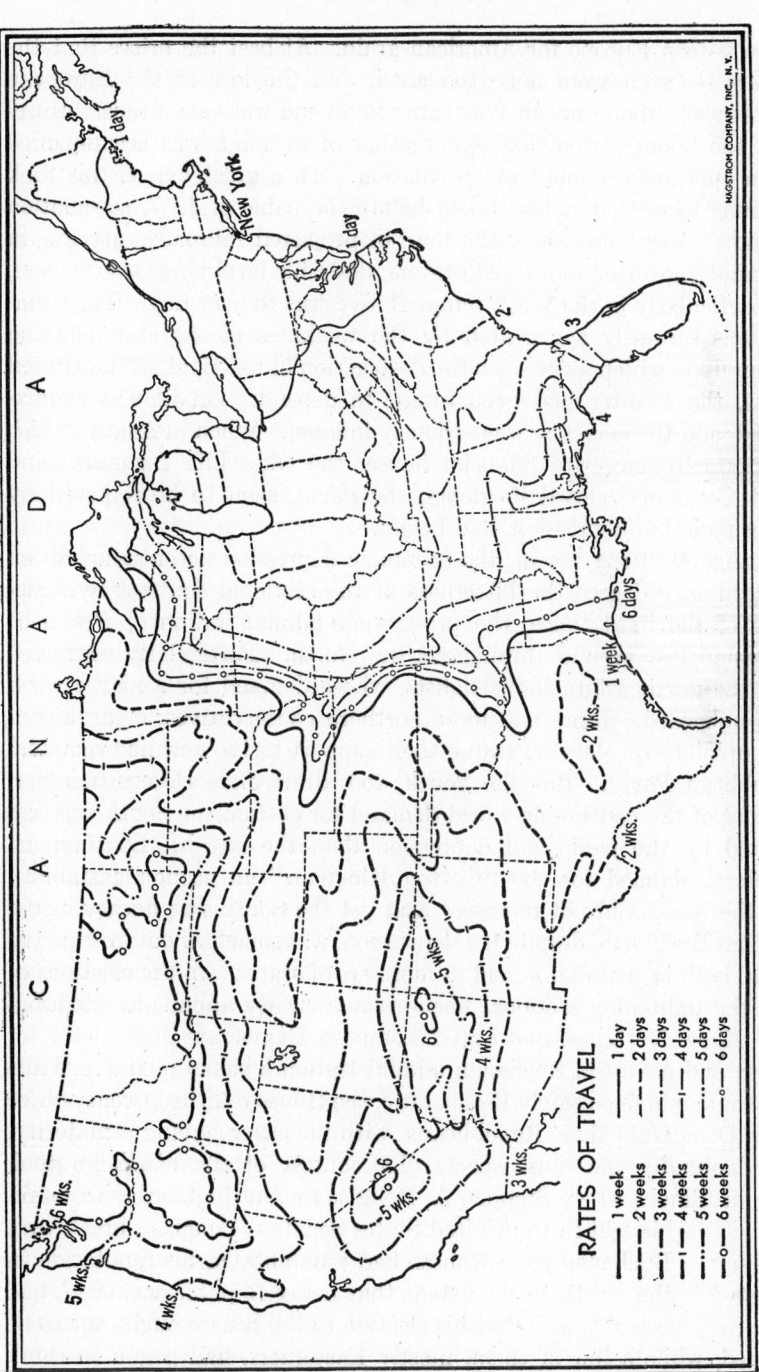

RATIO BETWEEN TIME AND DISTANCE OF TRAVEL FROM NEW YORK IN 1860

Courtesy of the Carnegie Institution of Washington and the American Geographical Society of New York

of a war-torn Europe for American grain. At best the prices that the farmers received were none too good, and the loss of the European market when the Crimean War came to an end was calamitous. Moreover, the boom period, like every other of its kind, was accompanied by an enormous amount of speculation. To a great extent this took the same form that it had taken before the panic of 1837, speculation in land. Town sites along the lines of projected railroads, city lots in the rapidly growing industrial centers, desirable farm lands everywhere, but particularly in the West, tempted investors to over-buy. The situation was seriously aggravated by the weakness of the state-banking system upon which, ever since the destruction of the Bank of the United States, the country had been forced to depend. Credit was overextended, and the currency was seriously inflated. When in August, 1857, a supposedly powerful financial house, the Ohio Life Insurance and Trust Company, closed its doors, the panic, soon to be followed by a long period of depression, had begun.

Strange as it may seem, the economic depression accentuated to an extraordinary degree the bitterness of the sectional controversy. Because of the hard times, the pro-slavery administration of President Buchanan lost ground throughout the North. Particularly aggrieved were the northeastern industrialists, whose demand for a higher tariff went unheeded. More and more northern conservatives, regardless of their opinions on slavery, swung their support to the new and sectional Republican Party. But the South, too, drew more closely together. Because of the continuing world demand for cotton, the South was less affected by the panic and depression than the North. Southerners, therefore, claimed for the "Cotton Kingdom" an economic stability that the North did not possess. And yet the South was uneasy in the fact that the North, despite the depression, was somehow outgrowing the South, both in population and in numbers of states. In the elections of 1858 the tightening sectional lines became clearly apparent. Republicans, Know-Nothings, and anti-Lecompton Democrats drew closer together, and gave the Buchanan administration a sharp rebuke. While the Senate remained safely Democratic, the House returned twenty-three fewer Democrats than Republicans, with no party having a majority.

Undoubtedly the most spectacular contest of the campaign took place in Illinois, where Stephen A. Douglas fought desperately to retain The senatorial election in Illinois his seat in the United States Senate. Douglas's break with Buchanan over Kansas had rehabilitated his reputation in the North to the extent that many Republicans, even, had begun to say that his election to the Senate ought not to be opposed, while a few of them, mostly Easterners, had begun to think of him as a possible Republican candidate for the Presidency in 1860. But the Illinois Republicans, who knew Douglas for himself as well as for the enemies he had made, had no such notions. To oppose Douglas they settled upon Abraham Lincoln, a Springfield lawyer who was well known throughout the state for his political sagacity and his forceful public speaking.[1] Lincoln had served one term in Congress during the Polk administration, he had barely missed election to the United States Senate by an anti-Nebraska legislature in 1855, and he had received strong support for the vice-presidential nomination on the Frémont ticket in 1856. Far from being an obscure backwoodsman, he was the best man the Republicans of Illinois could put forward against Douglas, as the Senator himself well knew. In accepting the nomination, Lincoln made a prophetic statement:

> "A house divided against itself cannot stand." I believe this government cannot endure permanently half slave and half free. I do not expect the Union to be dissolved — I do not expect the house to fall — but I do expect it will cease to be divided. It will become all one thing or all the other. Either the opponents of slavery will arrest the further spread of it, and place it where the public mind shall rest in the belief that it is in the course of ultimate extinction; or its advocates will push it forward till it shall become alike lawful in all the States, old as well as new — North as well as South.

Then, as if to defend this radical doctrine, he promptly challenged Douglas to a series of joint debates, a challenge that Douglas was delighted to accept.

The Lincoln-Douglas debates attracted widespread notice, not only in Illinois, where eager throngs attended them, but throughout the nation at large. Douglas was the outstanding northern Democrat, and his political life was at stake. More than that, if he lost, the northern Democracy had little chance to retain a place in the party councils; if he won, his title to the Democratic nomination in 1860 could scarcely be denied. Lincoln was hardly known outside of Illinois, but his bold words, and his temerity in challenging the able Douglas to a joint debate, awakened an interest in him that grew as the debate went on. Two points Lincoln succeeded in making with telling effectiveness. One was that Douglas, to use his own words, did not care "whether slavery was voted down or voted up." The Republican Party, on the whole, did care, and by emphasizing Douglas's lack of interest in the morality of slavery, Lincoln disqualified him for Republican support. The other telling point was the essential contradiction between Douglas's doctrine of popular sovereignty and the Dred Scott decision. Douglas attempted to reconcile the two

The Lincoln-Douglas debates

---

[1] A. J. Beveridge, *Abraham Lincoln, 1809–1858* (2 vols., 1928), is the most scholarly study of Lincoln's early career.

in his Freeport speech by asserting that a territorial legislature could refuse to enact friendly legislation — a slave code — and so might effectively exclude slavery regardless of the Supreme Court. This clever dodge, which Lincoln had not failed to foresee, cost Lincoln the election, for it satisfied the Democracy of Illinois. But whatever lingering hope Douglas might have had of southern support was not long in disappearing. Completely entranced with Taney's reasoning, the South was ready to demand the last measure of "protection for our slave property in the territories." The wedge between the northern and southern wings of the Democratic Party was thus driven deeper than ever.

After the elections were over, the sectional dispute raged on with ever-increasing acrimony. Whatever the North desired, Congress, unchanged in personnel until after the fourth of March,
John Brown again was at great pains to deny. Buchanan would have liked a higher tariff to please the Pennsylvania manufacturers, but the southern leaders would have none of that. The Pacific railroad project, upon which the North had now set its heart, and the Homestead Bill, long demanded by western farmers and eastern laborers, were both done to death. Southern orators waxed eloquent over the lax enforcement of the Fugitive Slave Act, and denounced vehemently the "personal-liberty laws" by which some northern states had circumvented it. Northern orators railed at the repeated violations in the South of the federal law against the importation of slaves. As if matters were not bad enough already, John Brown of Osawatomie re-emerged, this time in West Virginia, with a plot to capture the Harper's Ferry Arsenal, and so to provide the arms necessary for a slave insurrection. On the night of October 16, 1859, with only eighteen followers, he took the Arsenal, only to be captured a little later by Colonel Robert E. Lee, in command of a detachment of United States Marines. After a fair, if somewhat early, trial for treason, Brown was found guilty, condemned, and executed. Responsible Republican leaders were quick to denounce his mad act, but many Northerners, unmindful of what a slave insurrection would have meant, agreed with Emerson that Brown had "made the gallows glorious like the cross."[1]

Three days after the death of John Brown, on December 5, 1859, the Congress elected in 1858 convened for its first session, and plunged into a long contest over the speakership. During this contest,
Helper's Impending Crisis which resulted eventually in the choice of a Republican, the Democrats made much of the fact that a book by Hinton R. Helper, *The Impending Crisis in the South*, had received

---

[1] J. C. Malin, *John Brown and the Legend of Fifty-six* (1942), is a work of outstanding scholarship. See also O. G. Villard, *John Brown, 1800–1859* (1910).

official endorsement by the Republicans in the campaign of 1858. Helper was a non-slaveholding North-Carolinian whose book attempted to demonstrate that the deep poverty of his class was due to slavery, which he therefore opposed on economic grounds. The Republicans had claimed that they would not attack slavery where it already existed, but had they not done just that in approving Helper's book? Sectional feeling became increasingly tense. According to one congressman, every man in both houses was "armed with a revolver — some with two — and a bowie knife." Even so, only a presidential veto prevented the enactment of a homestead law, something that at least one Southerner, Andrew Johnson of Tennessee, had long urged. But in the main this was a northern measure, the near-passage of which indicated clearly the growing power of the North in the Union.

Under the circumstances the presidential campaign of 1860 aroused the most intense interest throughout the country. Meeting at Charleston, South Carolina, in April, the Democratic National Convention failed after ten days of balloting to make a nomination, and adjourned to meet in Baltimore later in the month. There, after a few preliminaries, it divided. One faction, composed mainly of northern delegates, nominated Douglas and stood by popular sovereignty. The other, composed almost exclusively of Southerners, nominated John C. Breckinridge of Kentucky, and called for the protection of slavery in all the territories. During that same month the Republicans met at Chicago, with William H. Seward of New York as the leading candidate. But the West was regarded as far more debatable ground than the East, and in recognition of this situation the nomination went on the third ballot to Abraham Lincoln of Illinois. The Republican platform was intensely nationalistic, not only in its denunciation of southern threats of disunion, but also in its advocacy of national action to satisfy the demands of its adherents. The advance of slavery into the West must be halted, imposts "to encourage the development of the industrial interests" must be levied, a satisfactory homestead law must be enacted, the existing liberal naturalization policy must be maintained, and a railroad to the Pacific (advocated also by both Democratic platforms) must be built — all by authority of the national government. Still a fourth ticket was placed in the field by the Constitutional Union Party, which was composed of the Whig-Know-Nothing remnants that had nominated Fillmore four years before. Recognizing "no political principle other than the Constitution of the country, the union of the States, and the enforcement of the laws," theirs was primarily a party of conciliation and compromise. To emphasize their intersectional appeal, they offered a

Election of 1860

Southerner, John Bell of Tennessee, for President, and a Northerner, Edward Everett of Massachusetts, for Vice-President.[1]

The campaign and election served only to emphasize how deep the line of cleavage between the sections had become. For all practical **The contest in the North** purposes two separate contests were being held, one in the North and another in the South. The only candidates to figure seriously in the northern balloting were Lincoln and Douglas, and the issue between them was clearly: Should the North use its numerical majority to force upon the South the nationalistic program called for in the Republican platform? With this program Douglas and the northern Democrats found little fault. But they realized, as seemingly the Republicans did not, the serious consequences that might result from forcing the northern point of view upon the South. They knew that the southern threats of secession were far from meaningless, and that if the North insisted upon pressing its advantage a disruption of the Union was in sight. When the votes were counted, it was apparent that the Republicans, who stood ready to give the North what it wanted regardless of consequences, had carried everything before them. Lincoln won every northern state except New Jersey, and there he received four out of the seven electoral votes. With the admission of Oregon in 1859, the free states numbered three more than the slave states and cast half again as many electoral votes. Thus Lincoln was elected, although he had received not a single electoral vote from a southern state. In ten southern states his name had not even appeared on the ballot.

In the South the contest lay between Breckinridge on the one hand and either Bell or Douglas on the other. Here the question at issue **The contest in the South** was, Should "southern rights" be maintained, even at the cost of secession and possible civil war? "Southern rights" meant vaguely whatever the individual who used the term wished it to mean, but the fundamental idea was the right of the South to some kind of constitutional protection from the tyranny of a northern majority. The election of Lincoln, southern extremists contended, would in itself constitute so flagrant an invasion of "southern rights" as to justify the southern states in seceding immediately from the Union. The party that supported Lincoln lay wholly in the North, and its triumph, they genuinely believed, would be but a prelude to the complete domination of the South by the North. Against this radical point of view, the adherents of Bell and Douglas urged an intermediate course that would save the Union, but in the South as in the North the more aggressive policy won. Eleven out of the fifteen slave states voted

---

[1] E. D. Fite, *The Presidential Campaign of 1860* (1911), and R. H. Luthin, *The First Lincoln Campaign* (1944), offer differing interpretations.

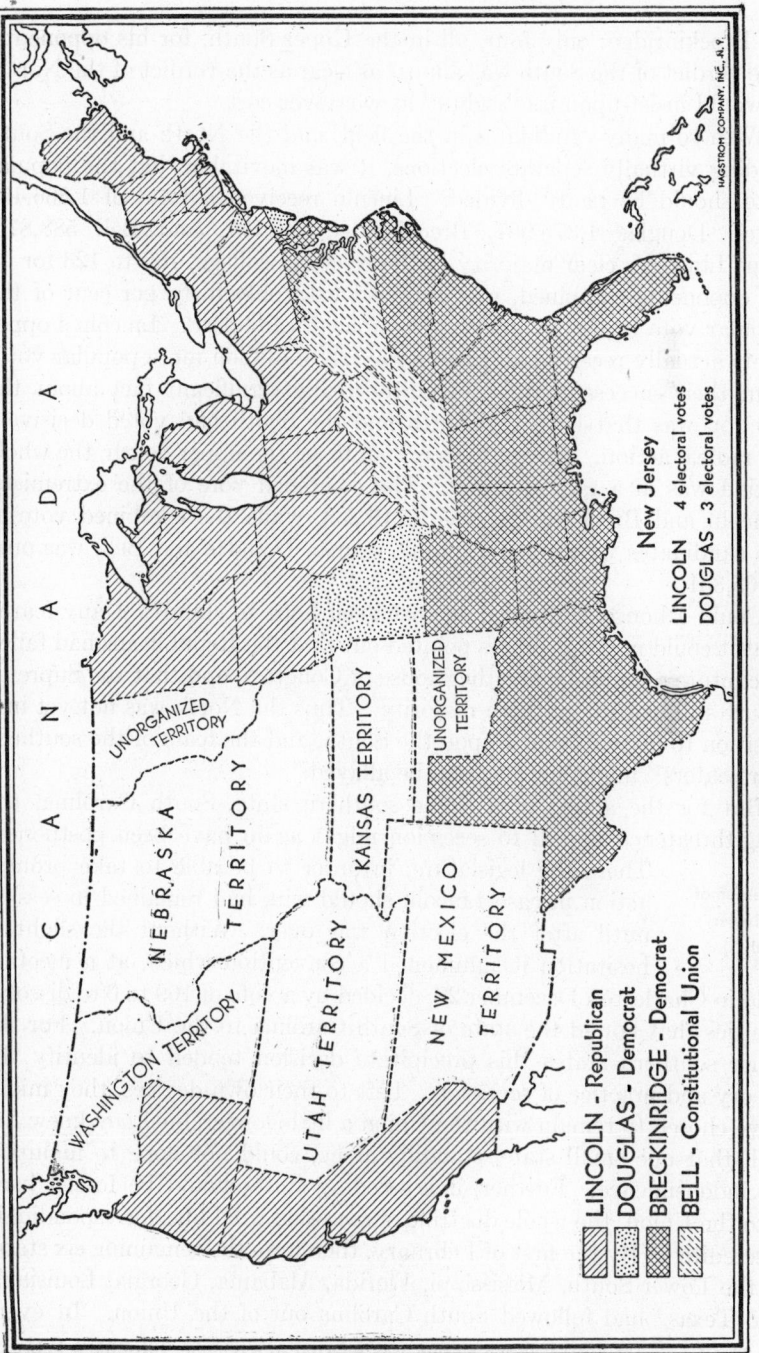

ELECTION OF 1860, BY STATES

New Jersey

LINCOLN — 4 electoral votes
DOUGLAS — 3 electoral votes

LINCOLN - Republican
DOUGLAS - Democrat
BRECKINRIDGE - Democrat
BELL - Constitutional Union

CANADA

UNORGANIZED TERRITORY

WASHINGTON TERRITORY

NEBRASKA TERRITORY

UTAH TERRITORY

KANSAS TERRITORY

NEW MEXICO TERRITORY

UNORGANIZED TERRITORY

HAGSTROM COMPANY, INC., N. Y.

for Breckinridge; only four, all in the Upper South, for his opponents. The verdict of the South was almost as clear as the verdict of the North. It would insist upon its "rights" at whatever cost.

With so many candidates in the field, and the North and the South holding virtually separate elections, it was inevitable that the popular vote should be badly divided. Lincoln received a total of 1,866,452 votes, Douglas 1,376,957, Breckinridge 849,781, and Bell 588,879. Thus Lincoln's clear majority in the electoral college, 180 to 123 for all his opponents combined, was obtained with only forty per cent of the popular vote being cast for the Republican candidate. Lincoln's opponents actually received all together nearly a million more popular votes than their successful rival. But the really significant fact about the election was that both the North and the South had voted decisively for radical action. Except for a few states of the upper South, the whole nation was in a radical mood. The combined vote of the extremists, Lincoln and Breckinridge, was 2,716,233, while the combined vote of the candidates who urged a middle course, Douglas and Bell, was only 1,965,331.

Could a house so divided against itself hope to stand? Many feared that it could not, but others pointed out that the Republicans had failed to capture a majority in either house of Congress, and that the Supreme Court still had its southern majority. Thus the North was not yet in a position to force its views upon the South, and the fears of the southern "fire-eaters" might for a season be allayed.

But for the action of a single southern state, South Carolina, the long-threatened appeal to secession might again have been postponed. There the legislature, in order to be able to take prompt action in case Lincoln should win, had remained in session until after the election was over. Without the slightest hesitation it summoned a convention which, at a meeting held in Charleston December 20, decided by a vote of 169 to 0 to dissolve the ties that bound the state of South Carolina to the Union. For the other southern states this precipitate decision tended to identify the theory and practice of secession. Left to their own devices, they might have chosen to remain with the Union a little longer, but they knew full well that one small state, standing alone, could not hope to maintain its independence. Further, if a seceding state should be forced back into the Union, the whole doctrine of secession would be correspondingly discredited. By the first of February, therefore, the remaining six states of the Lower South, Mississippi, Florida, Alabama, Georgia, Louisiana, and Texas,[1] had followed South Carolina out of the Union. In every

Secession of the Lower South

---

[1] The decision of the Texas convention was referred to a popular vote taken February

one of these states, however, a determined minority had urged insistently that the time for secession was not yet ripe.

Secession was but a means to an end, and the desired end was a united southern confederacy. Early in February a "congress" of delegates, chosen for the purpose by the several secessionist conventions, met at Montgomery, Alabama, to establish the new nation. On February 8 this congress adopted for the Confederate States of America a hastily devised provisional constitution; next day it chose as President and Vice-President, respectively, Jefferson Davis of Mississippi and Alexander H. Stephens of Georgia; and thereafter it remained in session long enough to act as a legislature for the provisional government and to draw up a permanent constitution.[1] Throughout these proceedings the delegates were acutely conscious of the parallel between what they were doing and what their forefathers had done in severing the ties that had bound the colonies to the mother country. They issued no common declaration of independence, but in spite of their lip service to the doctrine of secession they found the real justification of their course in the right of an oppressed people to revolt.

Jefferson Davis (1808–89),[2] upon whose shoulders now devolved the political leadership of the Confederacy, was a Kentuckian by birth, a graduate of West Point who had seen active military service on the frontier and in the war with Mexico, and a Mississippi cotton planter who had long been active in national politics. He was regarded as less radical than many other Southerners, notably R. B. Rhett of South Carolina, who as one of the most persistent advocates of secession was bitterly disappointed not to be the first President of the Confederacy. Unlike Rhett, whose states'-rights views outlasted secession, Davis was essentially a southern nationalist, and set himself the task of building a new nation. His failure was due in part, no doubt, to his own shortcomings. He had an exaggerated idea of his military ability, and often gravely handicapped his generals by dictating to them, or interfering with their plans. He was not a good judge of men, and surrounded himself with mediocre subordinates when he could have had the best talent of the South for the asking. He was proud to the point of arrogance, and his overbearing attitude toward

Jefferson Davis

23, so that technically Texas was not out of the Union until that time. Dwight L. Dumond, *The Secession Movement, 1860–1861* (1931), treats the movement for secession comprehensively and sympathetically.

[1] This document was submitted in March, and ratified in April. It closely resembled the Constitution of the United States.

[2] Probably the best biography of Davis is W. E. Dodd, *Jefferson Davis* (1907). In this connection, however, it is well to consult such sources as Mrs. Jefferson Davis, *Jefferson Davis, Ex-President of the Confederate States of America; a Memoir* (1890); and Jefferson Davis, *Rise and Fall of the Confederate Government* (2 vols., 1881).

those who held opinions at variance from his own often cost him dear.

Northern opinion on secession, meantime, showed little realization of the seriousness of the situation. Some said that the overheated southern tempers would soon cool, and the South would then return to the Union; others that a "reconstruction" of the Union by means of such a compromise as had been worked out in 1850 should be undertaken; still others, including most of the abolitionists, that it was probably a good thing to have the Lower South out of the Union. Above all else the North seemed determined that there should be no civil war. Horace Greeley, editor of the *New York Tribune*, maintained that the proper policy was to "let the erring sisters go in peace." James Buchanan, President of the dissolving nation, held that while secession was unconstitutional, so also was the coercion of a state. Therefore, he could never lead the North into war to conquer the South. Still an incorrigible "doughface," the President told Congress that the blame for the existing sectional controversy rested entirely with the North, and urged the adoption of an "explanatory amendment" to the Constitution which would yield every disputed point to the South.[1]

Nevertheless, the President faced a most embarrassing situation in Charleston Harbor. There Major Robert Anderson, in command of a small federal garrison, had removed his troops from the mainland to an island fortification in the mouth of the harbor, Fort Sumter. Buchanan at first sought only to maintain the *status quo*, but the withdrawal of many Southerners from his Cabinet brought to the fore a group of strong Unionists who finally persuaded him to reinforce Sumter. On January 8, 1861, he sent the *Star of the West*, a merchant steamer, to Charleston Harbor, with two hundred soldiers aboard. But when three days later the vessel attempted to enter the harbor, she was met by the fire of state batteries, and turned back to New York without discharging her errand. This attack on the *Star of the West* was in reality an act of war, but the President chose to ignore it, and during the remainder of his administration he made no further effort to aid Anderson.

Congress, meantime, was hard at work on a plan of compromise by which the Union might be preserved. The leadership of this movement was assumed, appropriately, by Senator John J. Crittenden of Kentucky, the successor to Clay's seat in the Senate, and to the Clay tradition of compro-

Northern opinion on secession

Fort Sumter

The Crittenden compromise

---

[1] A sincere, and at points convincing, apology for Buchanan is made by Philip G. Auchampaugh, *James Buchanan and his Cabinet on the Eve of Secession* (1926). On the attitude of the North, in general, toward secession, see Mary Scrugham, *The Peaceable Americans of 1860–1861* (1921).

mise. Two days before the secession of South Carolina, Crittenden introduced into the Senate an elaborate set of resolutions which provided for the prohibition of slavery in all territory of the United States, "now held or hereafter acquired," north of 36° 30', and protected it south of that line; set drastic limits on the right of Congress to abolish slavery in the District of Columbia and in other territory under its control; guaranteed the preservation of the domestic slave trade; and required the federal government to compensate the owners of rescued fugitive slaves. These and all other plans of compromise were now brought before a Senate committee of thirteen, headed by Crittenden, and so selected as to represent every section and party. For a time it seemed as if the Crittenden plan would be endorsed by the committee, but Seward, the leading Republican member, quite properly sounded out Lincoln, and found the President-elect opposed to any compromise that would permit the spread of slavery. Thereafter, the Republicans voted unanimously against the proposed 36° 30' dividing line, and the committee reported back to the Senate that it could not agree.

Other efforts to devise a satisfactory compromise also failed. A House committee proposed (1) an amendment to the Constitution that would safeguard slavery where it already existed, (2) a recommendation that the northern states repeal the "personal-liberty laws" by means of which they interfered with the capture of fugitive slaves, and (3) the admission of New Mexico, "with or without slavery." But this plan was as unsatisfactory to the representatives of the cotton states as the Crittenden plan had been to the Republicans. Both houses of Congress, however, voted to submit a thirteenth amendment to the Constitution for the protection of slavery in the existing slave states — a far cry from the Thirteenth Amendment that eventually was adopted. With the failure of compromise in Congress, the Virginia legislature invited the states to send delegates to a great peace convention, to open in Washington, February 4. Twenty-one states responded favorably, but the convention found little new to suggest, and its recommendations were promptly rejected by the Senate. The impasse between North and South seemed complete.[1]

Other efforts at compromise

[1] General works covering the period include H. H. Simms, *A Decade of Sectional Controversy* (1942); Avery O. Craven, *The Coming of the Civil War* (1942); Homer C. Hockett, *The Constitutional History of the United States, 1826–1876* (1936). Useful biographies are H. L. Stoddard, *Horace Greeley: Printer, Editor, Crusader* (1946); J. B. Ranck, *Albert Gallatin Brown, Radical Southern Nationalist* (1937); B. W. Palmer, *Marshall and Taney, Statesmen of the Law* (1939); R. M. McElroy, *Jefferson Davis, the Unreal and the Real* (2 vols., 1937).

19

The Appeal to Arms

As THE TIME for Lincoln's inauguration approached, all eyes turned
toward the ungainly Westerner upon whose shoulders the crisis was so
soon to devolve. Abraham Lincoln (1809–65) [1] was born in
Kentucky, the descendant of several generations of American frontiersmen. His father, Thomas Lincoln, was only a child when
his grandfather, Abraham Lincoln, met death at the hands of the Indians.
Grown and married, Thomas Lincoln made two typical pioneer "moves"
to the West, first to Indiana, and later to Illinois. Thus repeatedly
transplanted, the boy Abraham obtained only the slightest schooling, but
he read all the books he could get hold of, and he ultimately learned
enough law to meet the modest requirements of the West for admission
to the bar. He possessed a native shrewdness that stood him in good
stead on all occasions, and he developed a capacity for logical thinking
and for the accurate expression of his thought that would have been
remarkable in any age or place. A thoroughgoing Westerner, he instinctively idealized both nationalism and democracy, and he resented
deeply the determination of the southern leaders to rule the nation with
or without a majority, or else to ruin it. Well above the average height
and homely to the point of fascination, he affected the stoop-shouldered
posture and the loose-jointed shambling gait that western lawyers generally mistook for dignity. He knew little or nothing of the polite usages
of eastern society, and to those who were more sophisticated the essential gentility of his nature was often obscured by his uncouth manners,
his off-color jokes, and his easy familiarity.

During his months as President-elect, Lincoln had studiously avoided

---

[1] The most useful historical biography of Lincoln is Lord Charnwood, *Abraham Lincoln*
(1916). This may be supplemented on the personal side by N. W. Stephenson, *Lincoln*
(1922); and W. E. Barton, *The Life of Abraham Lincoln* (2 vols., 1925). The most voluminous biography of Lincoln, John G. Nicolay and John Hay, *Abraham Lincoln; A History*
(10 vols., 1890), is a detailed chronicle of the political events of the Civil War period. Carl
Sandburg, *Abraham Lincoln, the Prairie Years* (1926), and *Abraham Lincoln, the War Years*
(1939), present a picture that is convincing in spite of the author's indifference to accuracy
in detail.

any public expression of opinion, and the country awaited eagerly his announcement of policy. This statement he properly decided to reserve for his inaugural address, but when crowds gathered around his train on the long journey to Washington he unfortunately felt obliged to talk to them. Unskilled in the art of concealing his thoughts, and yet strongly desirous of setting the public mind at ease, he resorted to ambiguous and sentimental remarks that made some men wonder if he really understood the situation at all. But his inaugural address presented a calm, cogent argument against the constitutional right of secession that could scarcely have been improved upon. More than that, he left the South no alternative but to return to the Union, or else fight to stay out. He declared it his intention to execute the federal laws in all the states, to "hold, occupy, and possess the property and places" belonging to the United States, and to collect as usual the duties and imposts. "In doing this," he reasoned, "there needs to be no bloodshed or violence; and there shall be none, unless it be forced upon the national authority."

Lincoln's inaugural address

Lincoln had stated his policy with candor, but for the first few weeks his administration was in too chaotic a condition to do more than mark time. The President himself, never an efficient administrator, was overwhelmed by insistent office-seekers, and confused by the preponderance of new and inexperienced men among his subordinates. Some members of his Cabinet were not fully loyal to their chief. Four out of the seven, Secretary of State Seward, Secretary of the Treasury Chase, Secretary of War Cameron, and Attorney-General Bates, had hoped for the nomination that Lincoln had won. Two of them, Seward and Chase,[1] were fully convinced that in ability they far outranked the new President; and Seward, in an amazing document written four weeks after the inauguration, actually offered to take over the government. Fortunately, Lincoln did not choose to abdicate his duties, and with that extraordinary magnanimity for which he soon became famous made no effort to discipline his presumptuous Secretary.

It was the Sumter situation that finally forced Lincoln to act. Either he must furnish Major Anderson with supplies, or else permit the evacuation of the post; and approximately the same situation existed at Fort Pickens in the harbor of Pensacola, Florida. To relieve these garrisons might mean war; failure to do so would amount to a tacit recognition of the Confederacy. At length Lincoln, in spite of the disapproval of most of his Cabinet, ordered relief expeditions to both garrisons. The one sent to Fort

Sumter fired on

[1] Frederic Bancroft, *The Life of William H. Seward* (2 vols., 1900); A. B. Hart, *Salmon Portland Chase* (1899).

Pickens was entirely successful, and that post was saved to the North throughout the war, but the mere news that Sumter was to be reprovisioned led the Davis government to order its bombardment. On the morning of April 12 this order was executed, and after defending his post gallantly for more than a day Major Anderson surrendered. On Sunday afternoon, the fourteenth of April, with the relief ships standing helplessly by, he abandoned the fort "with colors flying and drums beating, bringing away company and private property, and saluting my flag with fifty guns." No one had been killed on either side, but the South had served notice by the incident that it meant to accept Lincoln's challenge, and would fight to stay out of the Union.[1]

Whatever the earlier sentiments of the North may have been, the reception of the news from Sumter made it clear that an overwhelming majority of the people in the free states were ready to fight to save the Union. Such prominent Democrats as ex-Presidents Pierce and Buchanan and Senator Stephen A. Douglas came out unqualifiedly for union, and the common people of all parties echoed their sentiments. Not every individual had been swayed to his decision by the same considerations. Abolitionists undoubtedly saw in the coming struggle a long-coveted opportunity to destroy African slavery. Northeastern industrialists feared the loss of southern cotton for their mills and southern markets for their goods. Northwestern farmers believed, probably without foundation, that the Mississippi outlet was essential to their prosperity, although there is no question but what they profited greatly from trade up and down the river with the South. Thoughtful men in every section saw that secession would leave more problems unsettled than it could possibly settle. Who should have the territories? What should be done about fugitive slaves? Would secession stop with the withdrawal of the South, or would there be eventually a Pacific confederacy, and a northwestern confederacy? How would a divided nation maintain the Monroe Doctrine and the doctrine of isolation? Could a democracy, such as existed in the United States almost alone among the nations of the world, ever endure anywhere if the American experiment failed? Certainly this last question agitated Lincoln far more than any other.

Temporary unity in the North

> For my own part [he told his private secretary], I consider the central idea pervading this struggle is the necessity of proving that popular government is not an absurdity. We must settle this question now, whether, in a free government, the minority have the right to break up the government whenever they choose. If we fail, it will go far to prove the incapability of the people to govern themselves.

[1] G. F. Milton, *Conflict; the American Civil War* (1941).

Before the bombardment of Sumter the eight slave states of the Upper South had steadfastly refused to leave the Union. Ties of blood and of interest bound them no less to the North than to the South; war, if it came, would surely make them a battle-ground. From their point of view the retention of the Union as it was, or its "reconstruction" in such a way as to satisfy the seceding members, was far preferable to dismemberment. In all of them, however, the right of secession was generally conceded, and a strong minority favored putting the right into practice. When war between North and South became a certainty, this minority was quickly transformed into a majority in four of the border states — Virginia, North Carolina, Tennessee, and Arkansas. Three others — Delaware, Maryland, and Missouri — decided definitely to remain with the North. Kentucky for a time attempted an impossible neutrality, but Lincoln, with excellent judgment, allowed the Confederacy to trespass first upon its soil, whereupon Kentucky also fell to the Union. Another important victory for the North was won when a block of forty-six counties in the mountains of northwestern Virginia refused to follow the rest of the state out of the Union, and by somewhat irregular methods became the independent loyal state of West Virginia, which Congress in June, 1863, belatedly admitted to the Union.[1] In all the border states sentiment was divided, and most of them furnished recruits for the armies of both North and South. While in a general way it is not inaccurate to speak of the "war between the states," in the border area it was a true "civil war," with brother sometimes pitted against brother, and father against son.

The border slave states

In the division of forces the North fared far better than the South. Eleven states left the Union; twenty-two (or counting West Virginia, twenty-three) remained loyal to it. Of the territories, only New Mexico and the Indian country to the west of Arkansas fell to the South, and this whole region was quickly reconquered. The North got all the rest, and from it admitted Kansas (1861) and Nevada (1864) to statehood. In population the North outnumbered the South, 22,000,000 to 9,500,000, while the relative fighting power of the South was still further lessened by the fact that about 3,500,000 of its people were slaves. As events proved, however, nearly all of the slaves remained loyal to their masters throughout the war, and, although they were not used by the South as soldiers, their labor, both at home and at the front, released a far larger proportion of southern white population for military service than could otherwise have been available.

The division of forces

A disproportionately large share of the economic resources of the

---

[1] C. H. Ambler, *Francis H. Pierpont: Union War Governor of Virginia and Father of West Virginia* (1937).

nation lay in the northern states and territories. The known mineral deposits of the country — coal, iron, copper, precious metals — were located almost entirely in the North. Ninety-two per cent of the manufacturing of the country was carried on in the North, and its iron foundries, textile mills, tanneries, etc., had only to be expanded to meet the unusual demands of war. The South, on the other hand, expected to import the greater part of its manufactures, including the *matériel* of war, a task that would have been easy enough had the North done nothing to prevent the exportation of cotton in payment; for, as already noted, the South had a virtual monopoly on the world's supply of raw cotton. Neither side suffered for lack of foodstuffs, although southern armies and southern cities sometimes went hungry because of transportation difficulties. Of tremendous importance in determining which side would win the war was the railroad supremacy of the North. With nearly two and a half times as many miles of railroad as the South, and with the northern railroads far more strategically located than the southern, the advantage of the North in this all-essential factor was decisive.

Nearly all of the property of the United States government that possessed military value went to the North. The South took over the Norfolk Navy Yard, Harper's Ferry, and the other southern arsenals, the sub-treasury and mint at New Orleans, and a few coast defenses; but the North got practically all the rest, including almost every ship in the United States Navy. It was long charged that John B. Floyd of Virginia, who was Buchanan's Secretary of War until the closing days of 1860, deliberately transferred enough arms from northern to southern arsenals to give the South an undue advantage in this particular. Some such transfers were made, but it is improbable that Floyd, who until close to the end of his term was strongly opposed to secession, could have had the motive imputed to him. Furthermore, the transfers that took place actually left the southern states short of their proper proportion of federal weapons. Just before he left office, Floyd did issue some unreasonable, and possibly treasonous, orders for the shipment of ordnance from northern factories to points in the South, but these orders were immediately countermanded by his successor. In point of fact, neither side possessed enough reliable weapons at the time the war broke out to constitute any real menace to the safety of the other.

The United States had a regular army at the beginning of the war of about sixteen thousand men, and a navy of ninety ships manned by a total of perhaps nine thousand men. The enlisted men in both branches of the national defense remained, with but rare exceptions, loyal to the North, but at least one-fourth of the officers resigned their commissions and tendered their services to the South. Unfortunately

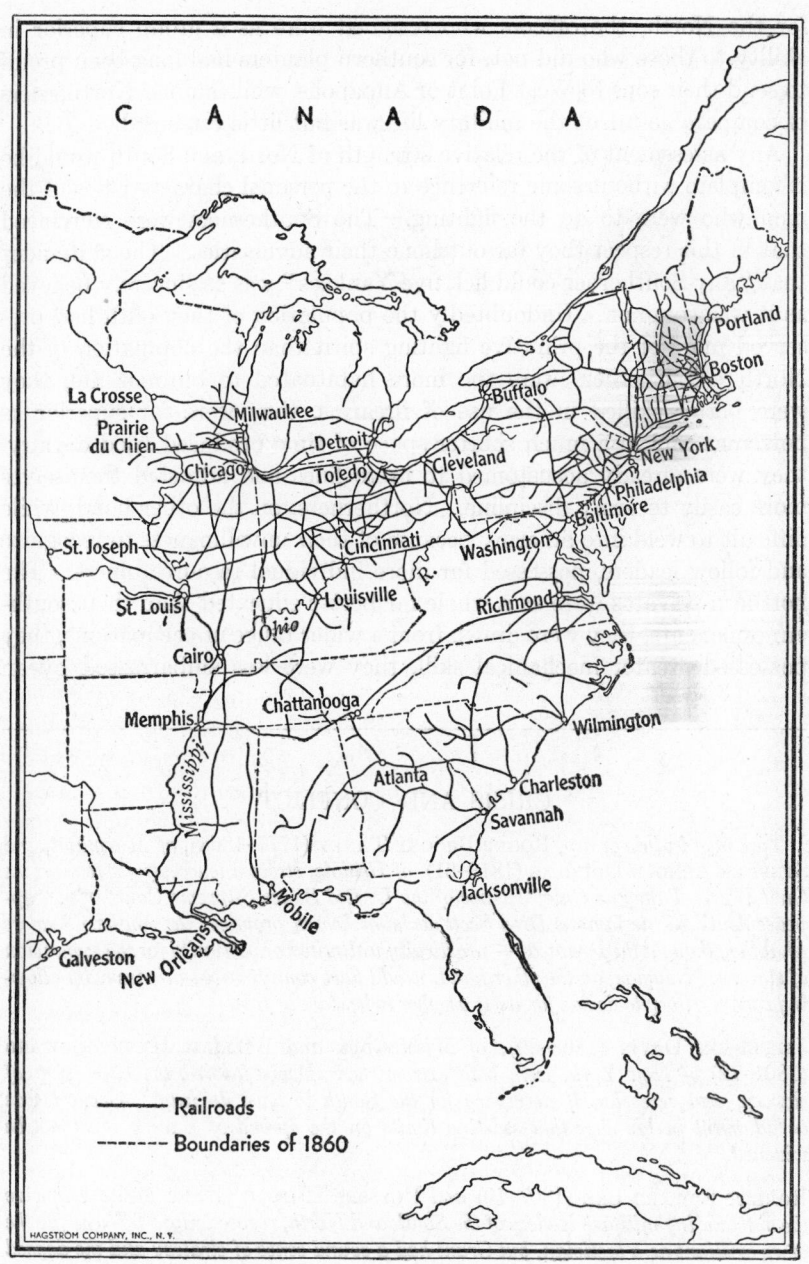

RAILROADS IN THE UNITED STATES, 1860

for the North, the officers who resigned were as a group superior in ability to those who did not, for southern planters had long been proud to send their sons to West Point or Annapolis, while among Northerners of comparable talent the military life was but little esteemed.

Any assessment of the relative strength of North and South would be incomplete without some reference to the personal characteristics of the men who were to do the fighting. The Southerners were convinced that in this respect they far outshone their adversaries. The statement that "any Southerner could lick five Yankees" was as sincerely believed as it was common. Undoubtedly the population of the South had preserved more of the primitive fighting spirit than the population of the North. Southerners were the more habituated to outdoor life, they were better skilled in the use of firearms, they were far superior as horsemen and in a much shorter space of time produced good cavalry, they were already accustomed to caste lines and adjusted themselves more easily to army discipline. Northerners, on the other hand, while difficult to weld into an army because of their unwillingness to recognize and follow leaders, possessed far more individual resourcefulness. The northern privates were as a whole far better educated than their southern opponents, they were drawn from a wider range of occupations, they possessed greater mechanical skill, they were less embarrassed by an

---

CRISIS AND CONFLICT

Two men in this group, ROGER BROOKE TANEY (1777–1864), *of Maryland, and* STEPHEN ARNOLD DOUGLAS (1813–61), *of Illinois, strove unsuccessfully to avert the Civil War. Taney as Chief Justice of the United States Supreme Court tried "appeasement" in his famous Dred Scott decision, which promised the southern leaders what they thought they wanted — practically unlimited opportunity for the expansion of slavery. Douglas, on the other hand, would have compromised this issue by allowing each territory to decide for itself whether to be slave or free.*

JEFFERSON DAVIS (1808–89), *of Mississippi, and* WILLIAM HENRY SEWARD (1801–72) *of New York, were both extremists. Davis favored the expansion of slavery, and secession if necessary for the South to have its way. Seward was as adamant in his view that existing limits on the spread of slavery must not be widened.*

ROBERT EDWARD LEE (1807–70) *and* ULYSSES SIMPSON GRANT (1822–85) *were the outstanding military leaders of the South and North, respectively. Lee was far the more brilliant as a tactician, but Grant had a sound sense of strategy and the dogged determination necessary to win.*

LEE

DAVIS

SEWARD

DOUGLAS

TANEY

GRANT

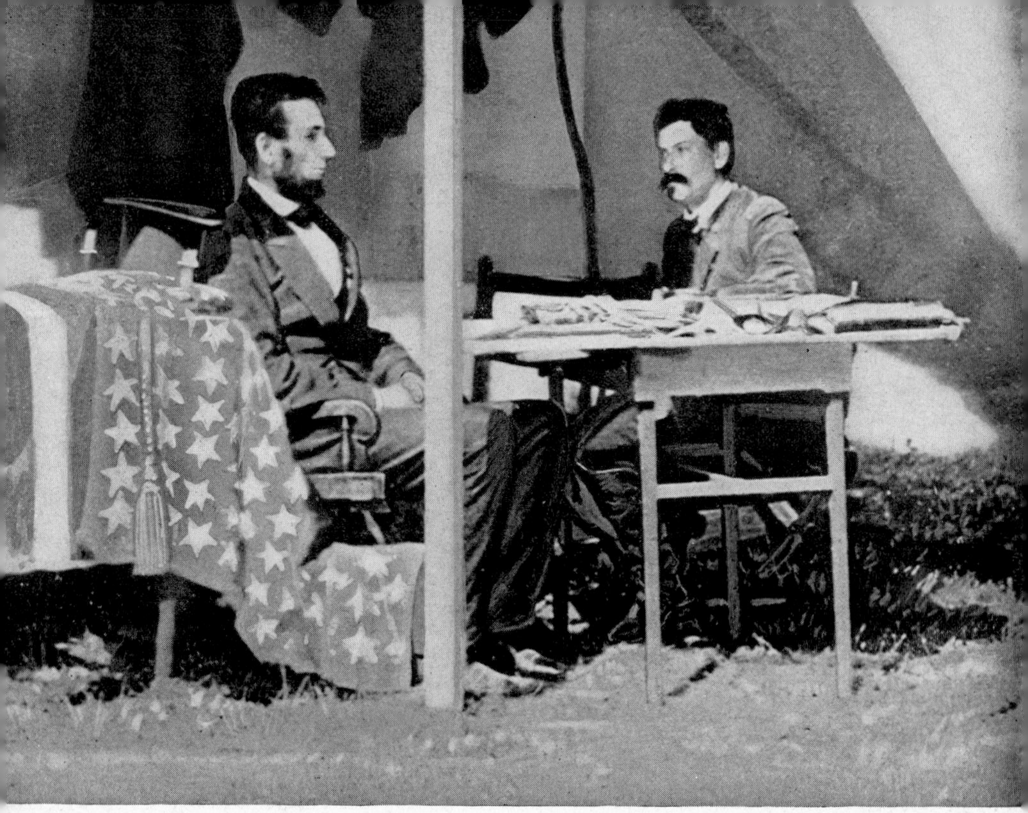

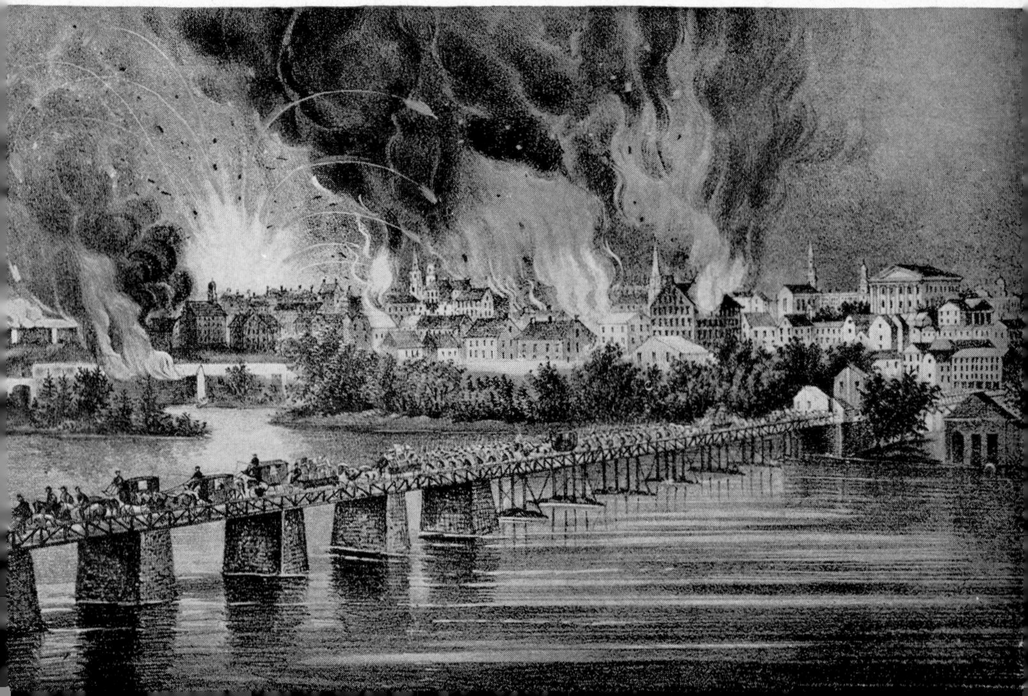

unusual situation. All of which was hardly sufficient to overcome the handicap of fighting in an alien climate and over terrain that neither they nor their officers knew anything about.

The "preponderating asset of the North" turned out to be Lincoln himself. This was not because he possessed any intuitive military understanding that was of use to his generals; indeed, his ideas on strategy were quite as naïve as those of any other Lincoln civilian. Nor was he at first a notably good judge of military men. His strength lay in his extraordinary understanding of the feelings and prejudices of the masses, without whose support the war could never have been won. He realized, more fully than most of his advisers, that when a democracy goes to war military efficiency is of no avail without the backing of public opinion. Every such war has, therefore, its political no less than its military side; and it was in the management of the political side of the struggle that Lincoln's genius was mostly clearly manifest.

What Abraham Lincoln, the politician, was to the North, Robert E. Lee (1807–70),[1] the soldier, was to the South. The two men could

[1] W. E. Dodd, *Lincoln or Lee* (1928), is an interesting interpretation. Sir Frederick B. Maurice, *Robert E. Lee, the Soldier* (1925), is useful, but has been supplanted, together with all other biographies of Lee, by Douglas Southall Freeman, *R. E. Lee: a Biography* (4 vols., 1934–35), a work of extraordinary merit.

CIVIL WAR SCENES

This is an official photograph of Lincoln and General McClellan. In wartime the relationship between the civilian chief of state and his principal military subordinate is a problem of critical importance. In spite of what the picture seems to indicate, in the early days of the Civil War, when Lincoln was President and McClellan commander of the Army of the Potomac, this relationship could hardly have been worse. Later on in the war, when Grant was in command, the relationship between the President and his chief general closely approximated the ideal and had much to do with the success of the northern armies. (Photo by Brady from Culver.)

This Currier & Ives print shows the fall of Richmond in April, 1865. Notice the coaches and soldiers on the bridge. During the entire four years of the war the Army of the Potomac had the capture of Richmond as its principal goal. This was perhaps poor strategy, for the destruction of Lee's army was the really important thing. Finally Grant took Richmond by approaching it from the south, by way of Petersburg. The long-delayed occupation of the Confederate capital by northern troops foretold an immediate end to the war. (Photo from Bettmann.)

hardly have stood in greater contrast with each other. Lee was of the
Virginia gentry, a patrician to his fingertips, and a military

Lee

genius. The son of General Henry Lee, who had served under
Washington during the Revolution, his "strong hereditary claims on
the country" had helped him obtain a cadetship at West Point in 1825,
where four years later he was graduated, second in his class. As Captain Lee, he was General Scott's chief of staff in Mexico, and out of that
campaign he won no less than three brevets — major, lieutenant-
colonel, and colonel — for gallant service in the field. Always a favorite with General Scott, who believed him the ablest officer in the army,
he was undoubtedly the first choice of both Scott and Lincoln for the
active command of the United States Army; a week before the bombardment of Sumter, Francis P. Blair, speaking unofficially for the
President, actually offered Lee this post. But Lee, to use his own words,
"declined the offer he made me, stating as candidly and as courteously
as I could, that though opposed to secession and deprecating war, I
could take no part in an invasion of the Southern States." He was
deeply distressed at the thought of fighting against the United States,
but he regarded it as his duty, in case Virginia seceded, to draw his
sword in defense of his native state. As handsome as Lincoln was
homely, and steeped in the chivalry of the Old South, he was the perfect
embodiment of the rôle he was chosen to play. Had he cast his lot
with the North instead of the South, it is hard to see how the struggle
could have been so long drawn out.

Had lack of preparedness alone been a sufficient deterrent, there would
have been no war between North and South in 1861.[1] In a military
sense neither side was ready for war; indeed, except for

**Lack of
preparedness**

some eleventh-hour activities in the South, it could almost
be said that neither side had given any very serious consideration to the military problem. The regular army of the United
States was not only insignificant in size; it was divided up into a multitude of tiny garrisons, most of which were located along the Indian
frontier, and could be withdrawn only at the risk of an Indian uprising.
The organized state militia, which was the second line of defense for
the North and the beginning and end of southern preparedness, consisted of a few companies of volunteers to each state, imperfectly armed
and inadequately drilled. Probably the total number of such militiamen in the loyal states on the eve of the war was less than ten thousand,
and in the seceding states even less than that. When Lincoln, on

---

[1] F. L. Huidekoper, *The Military Unpreparedness of the United States* (1915), is amply
convincing on this point. For the creation of the armies of the Civil War, see F. A. Shannon, *The Organization and Administration of the Union Army, 1861–1865* (2 vols., 1928);
and A. B. Moore, *Conscription and Conflict in the Confederacy* (1924).

April 15, 1861, issued his call for seventy-five thousand state militia, and Davis shortly afterward countered with a somewhat similar request for one hundred thousand, both men knew that they were asking for units that did not exist. Before there could be any war, volunteers must be obtained, armed, and organized into armies. This situation, more than anything else, accounts for the slow beginning of military operations, and the uncertainty and delay that characterized the first campaigns. Not until well toward the middle of the war did the armies of North and South confront each other as dependable fighting machines.

Lincoln's first call for troops, issued under an antiquated militia law, asked for a specified number of regiments from each state. Since none of the states had anywhere nearly enough organized militia to fill its assigned quota, each loyal governor was forced in turn to issue his own state-wide call for troops. He was in no better position, however, than the President to accept individual volunteers, so he in turn passed on this task to the various communities of the state. There local leaders promptly assumed the responsibility thrust upon them, called patriotic mass meetings where "muster-rolls" could be started, and as soon as a company was filled offered its services to the state. Company officers were invariably elected by the volunteers themselves, but regimental officers were usually chosen by the governor. At the state capitol, or some other prescribed rendezvous, the companies were assembled into regiments, furnished with whatever equipment the state was able to obtain, and then promptly turned over to the national government. Within a remarkably short space of time the troops thus raised far exceeded the number Lincoln had called for; but in spite of frantic purchases abroad by both state and national governments, the supply of arms was totally inadequate, and the uniforms, whenever they existed at all, presented an astonishing variety of colors and patterns. Few of the recruits knew even the barest rudiments of military drill, and the officers, selected usually because of their political or social prominence, were almost as ignorant of military matters as the men they attempted to command.

How the armies were raised

The law cited by Lincoln to authorize his call for state militia limited their term of national service to ninety days, but the President was not so short-sighted as to believe that in that time the war would be over. Encouraged by the response of the country to his first call, he issued another on the third of May following which asked for forty-two thousand volunteers to serve for three years, and directed an increase of eighteen thousand men in the regular army. Since the Constitution gives to Congress, rather than to the President, the right to raise armies, it is hard to see how this second call could have been constitutional. Lincoln himself was under no illusions about his action, and when Congress met on July 4 he asked (and subsequently received) its official ratification of what he had done. Convinced by that time more than ever that the war would be a serious struggle, he asked also for a volunteer army of at least four hundred thousand three-year men. Congress granted him five hundred thousand.[1]

The public, however, expected a speedy conclusion of the war, and called for a battle to end it. With the secession of Virginia, the Confederate capital was removed to Richmond, about a hun-
"On to Richmond" dred miles from Washington, while Confederate soil was no farther away than just across the Potomac. Only a few weeks were required to assemble at Washington a Union army of some thirty-six thousand men, and inevitably the battle-cry was raised, "On to Richmond!" The unhappy result was the first battle of Bull Run, fought on the twenty-first of July. By methods not unlike those used in the North, the Confederacy had accumulated a plentiful supply of raw recruits, and General Lee, soon to become the chief military adviser of President Davis, had stationed two sizable detachments, one under General Pierre G. T. Beauregard and the other under General Joseph E. Johnston, within a few days' march of Washington. The Union commander, General Irvin McDowell, had laid his plans well, but his untrained men were unable to follow them. He attacked Beauregard's men a few miles north of Manassas Junction and might have won but for the fact that Johnston's troops eluded the Union force sent to guard them, and joined Beauregard. In an hour after this news spread, the Union army was in full retreat toward Washington. Elated by their easy victory, some of the Confederate soldiers went home thinking the war was over.

But the battle had taught the North that war could be waged successfully only by prolonged preparation, and a "second uprising" gave
The Union volunteers Lincoln all the three-year men he asked for, and many more. In raising and organizing these troops, the precedents already set in calling out the state militia were closely followed. Quotas were assigned to the various states, upon whom the primary task of obtaining recruits thus devolved. Communities then vied with one another in the heartiness of their response to the governor's call. Officers from the grade of colonel down were commissioned by the governors, although in practice company officers were usually chosen by

---

[1] Two excellent but very different studies of the Civil War are Carl Russell Fish, *The American Civil War: An Interpretation* (1937); and James G. Randall, *The Civil War and Reconstruction* (1937).

the men themselves, and their choices merely ratified by the governor. Care was taken to obtain if possible at least one officer to a regiment who had had some military training, and for this purpose the presence in the northern states of many immigrants who had seen service in Europe proved to be a great advantage. General officers were appointed by the President, by and with the advice and consent of the Senate. This system of recruiting was admirably devised to capitalize fully the existing mass enthusiasm, for the young men of each community could enlist together with the knowledge that they would probably serve together throughout the war. Often they even knew in advance the officers under whom they would serve. But the system also had its disadvantages. When, as frequently happened, certain units took most of the punishment in a given engagement, it followed that the communities from which the men came were correspondingly hard hit. Had the men for each unit been drawn from many different places, the losses would have been more evenly distributed. The problem of replacements was still more perplexing. New companies and new regiments, with a whole new complement of officers, were far easier to raise than an equal number of men for old units that had been decimated by battle losses or disease. Another misfortune was that the War Department chose to keep the regular army intact rather than to distribute it among the volunteer troops to assist in their training. But the President chose many regular army officers for high command in the volunteer army, and it was due mainly to their work that the raw recruits ultimately attained a fair degree of military efficiency. By the spring of 1862, with well over six hundred thousand volunteers accepted, the War Department felt that enough troops had been raised to win the war, and stopped recruiting.

To reorganize the badly beaten "Grand Army of the Potomac," General George B. McClellan was called to Washington. McClellan was a former regular army officer who as a major-general of Ohio volunteers had scored some small but spectacular successes McClellan in the occupation of West Virginia. He proved to be an admirable drillmaster, and in a short time brought order out of chaos. By the end of the summer he had no less than one hundred thousand men at his disposal, all well disciplined, well equipped, and reasonably well drilled. The pride of the North in its new army, and in the general who had produced it, was very great. When Scott resigned in November, McClellan was made commander-in-chief of all the Union forces, and confidence that he would soon bring the war to a successful conclusion was high. But as month after month wore on, and nothing was accomplished, the watchword "All quiet along the Potomac" began to sound like a reproach to the entire country. McClellan's great defect, it soon appeared, was his excess of caution.[1] While he was developing a Union army, General Johnston was doing the same thing over in Virginia for the Confederates. But whereas Johnston's army was never anywhere nearly as strong as his own, McClellan always insisted that the exact opposite was true, and, fearful of another Bull Run, he steadfastly refused to move. Not until March, 1862, after the President had issued express orders commanding it, did he begin his advance.

The general strategy of the war soon became fairly obvious to all the participants. Since the South could ask nothing better than to be left alone, the North, in order to win, must take the aggressive and wage a war of conquest. The existence of the Appalachian mountain barrier ensured that there would be two battlefronts, one to the east, and one to the west. A third, and extremely important, theater of war lay on the high seas. The South, because of its primarily agricultural economy, must depend to a great extent for its munitions of war upon importations from Europe. To pay for these supplies, it would seek to export cotton, and possibly to a lesser extent tobacco and sugar. If, therefore, the North could blockade the South, and could effectively prevent trade between the Confederacy and the outside world, victory would soon crown the northern arms. The armies of the East and of the West, advancing simultaneously into the lower South, would ultimately join forces, crush out the last vestige of opposition, and restore the supremacy of the Union. The hope of the South, on the other hand, lay in breaking the blockade, and in maintaining armies in the field large enough to hold the invaders at bay. The South did not so much need to win victories as to keep the North from winning victories.

The blockade of the southern coast was decided on immediately after the fall of Sumter. Davis conveniently prepared the way for the introduction of this policy by a proclamation of April 17, 1861, in which he authorized privateers to prey upon the commerce of the United States. Two days later Lincoln retaliated by declaring a blockade of all the ports from South Carolina to Texas, and when Virginia and North Carolina seceded, he added their ports also. At first only a "paper blockade," ships of every sort and kind were pressed into service as blockaders, and by the time the war was six months old the South had begun to feel the results. Such items as tea, coffee, soap, candles, and matches brought extremely high prices, and were hard to get at any price. Medical supplies fell desperately short of the demand.

---

[1] This judgment is confirmed, rather than confuted, by McClellan's autobiography, *McClellan's Own Story* (1887). An interesting character sketch of McClellan is in Gamaliel Bradford, *Union Portraits* (1916). See also W. S. Myers, *George Brinton McClellan: a Study in Personality* (1934).

Because of the lack of print paper, newspapers found it necessary to reduce the size of their issues, and sometimes to print them on brown wrapping paper. Because of the shortage of drygoods, homespun gained steadily in popularity, and women accepted as a patriotic duty the necessity of wearing out-of-date garments. It was impossible, however, until the very close of the war to make the blockade fully effective. Fleet blockade-runners, usually of British origin, repeatedly got through the blockading squadrons, and at ports in the West Indies and the Bahamas exchanged the produce of the Confederacy for European goods, mostly *matériel* of war. Thanks to these supplies, Lee at Gettysburg, after two years of war, had almost, if not quite, as good artillery as his northern opponent.

Hopeful that the need of the outside world for cotton would bring European nations, particularly England, to their aid, the Confederate leaders were at first inclined to regard the blockade with a certain degree of equanimity. The old illusion that cotton was king died hard; surely the navies of England and **The clash of ironclads** France must soon break the blockade and open the southern ports. When this hope failed to materialize, however, and the pressure of the blockade became increasingly irksome, the South took steps to help herself. Out of a northern frigate, the *Merrimac*, abandoned and sunk at Norfolk, Confederate shipbuilders constructed a low-lying iron-clad ram, the *Virginia*, which in March, 1862, was sent against the blockading squadron at Hampton Roads. There the *Virginia* (usually called the *Merrimac*) had everything its own way until the appearance of a northern ironclad, the *Monitor*, which a Swedish engineer, John Ericsson, had induced the northern government to construct. In the duel that followed, neither ship was able to do serious damage to the other, and the *Virginia* at length withdrew, never again to figure in the war. The engagement marked a turning-point in naval history, for it proved that the old-fashioned wooden ships were obsolete. But it did nothing to aid the Confederacy, for the North was able to multiply the number of *Monitors* at will, while the South could not produce another *Virginia*.[1]

The South did succeed, however, in harassing the trade of the North by means of commerce-destroyers. Nineteen of these vessels, of which the most famous was the *Alabama*, got to sea. Nearly all of them were British-built, manned chiefly by British subjects and outfitted from British ports, but they were officered **Commerce-destroyers** by the Confederacy, and, acting on its authority, they destroyed a total

---

[1] The definitive work on this subject is J. P. Baxter, 3d, *The Introduction of the Ironclad Warship* (1933). On the naval activities of the Confederacy, see J. T. Scharf, *History of the Confederate States Navy* (1887).

of over two hundred and fifty northern merchant ships. Their exploits struck an almost fatal blow to the American merchant marine, for the risk of destruction and the consequent high insurance rates led American shipowners to dispose of the bulk of their holdings to foreigners, whereupon the ships were transferred to foreign registry. Commerce between the United States and the outside world was not seriously interrupted, but because of the commerce-destroyers such trade tended increasingly to be carried on under a foreign flag.

The commerce-destroyers were built for speed rather than for heavy fighting, and they proved to be of no value in breaking the blockade. In the spring of 1863, however, it became known that the same English firm that had built the *Alabama* for the Confederacy was now engaged in the building of two heavy ironclad rams for use in bringing the blockade to an end. Had these "Laird rams" been permitted to sail, they might well have succeeded in opening up a number of southern ports, but the vigorous protests that the United States launched with the British government, backed up by the threat of a war that the British ministry had decided to avoid, caused orders to be issued for their restraint. With the failure of this scheme, the last serious effort of the South to break the blockade came to nought.

The war in the West got off to a somewhat better start than the war in the East. Here the first objective seemed to be to clear the Confederates from the state of Missouri. This was almost accomplished by General Nathaniel Lyon, who about a month before Bull Run defeated a small secessionist force under General Sterling Price at Boonville, Missouri. But Lyon's defeat and death at the battle of Wilson's Creek, August 10, 1861, left southern Missouri in Confederate hands until the following spring. Then Union forces at Pea Ridge, Arkansas, May 5–8, 1862, won a victory that drove the Confederates far to the south of the Missouri-Arkansas border.

After the death of Lyon, the war in the West was placed in charge of General John C. Frémont, with headquarters at St. Louis, but Frémont's incompetence led to his speedy replacement by General Henry W. Halleck, a graduate of West Point who had left the army to become a lawyer. Halleck was far from brilliant, but he was soon able to report advances along the Mississippi, Tennessee, and Cumberland Rivers, which almost parallel each other for a hundred miles south of the Ohio. At Columbus and Island No. 10 on the Mississippi, at Fort Henry on the Tennessee, and at Fort Donelson on the Cumberland, General Albert Sidney Johnston, the Confederate commander, had made every effort to prepare for the Union attack. Early in February General Ulysses S. Grant,

The Laird rams (margin note)

The war in the West (margin note)

supported by a Union flotilla of gunboats under Flag-Officer Andrew H. Foote, advanced against Fort Henry. On February 6, after hard fighting, the fort surrendered to Flag-Officer Foote an hour and a half before Grant's army arrived on the scene. On February 16 another joint army and gunboat attack under the same officers brought a like fate to Fort Donelson. These victories forced Johnston to abandon his northernmost hold on the Mississippi River at Columbus, and his headquarters at Nashville on the Cumberland. The way seemed well prepared for a Union invasion of western Tennessee.

Ulysses S. Grant (1822–85) [1] was the son of an eccentric and unprosperous Ohio tanner. Accident rather than ability won him an appointment to West Point in 1839, where, to use his own words, he "never succeeded in getting squarely at either end of my class, in any one study, during the four years." Among the thirty-nine members of the graduating class of 1843, reputed to have been unusually weak as a whole, he ranked twenty-first. Commissioned a second lieutenant of infantry, he emerged from the Mexican War only a first lieutenant, and in 1854, as a captain, resigned his commission rather than face a court-martial on the charge of drunkenness. The years of poverty and failure that followed sapped Grant's confidence in himself, but in 1861 his military experience was too valuable to be overlooked, and by August, as a brigadier-general, he was in command at the strategic point of Cairo, Illinois. There his good judgment in occupying Paducah on the Kentucky side of the Ohio, and his success in ousting the Confederates from Belmont on the Missouri side of the Mississippi, marked him as the man to lead the attacks on Forts Henry and Donelson. Time proved that Grant had qualities of tremendous importance to the Union cause. He knew sound advice when he heard it, and was humble enough to accept it. He had a dogged determination, amounting almost to an obsession, never to turn back once he had decided on a given course of action. He chose his subordinates with skill, made his decisions with a degree of speed and accuracy that increased as the war wore on, and accepted without hesitation every new responsibility that was thrust upon him. Grant's victory at Donelson, where he refused to consider any terms except "unconditional surrender," won him a sobriquet that followed him all through the war. In "Unconditional Surrender" Grant the North found its first and most authentic hero. He was promptly promoted to the rank of major-general.

Grant's triumph at Donelson was soon somewhat eclipsed by his close

Grant

[1] *The Personal Memoirs of U. S. Grant* (2 vols., 1885–86) gives a remarkably clear picture of Grant's military career. A satisfactory biography, both military and political, is L. A. Coolidge, *Ulysses S. Grant* (1917).

escape from defeat at Shiloh, near the Tennessee-Mississippi border, where his troops were surprised and attacked by the Confederates on the early morning of April 6, 1862. During the first day of the battle, Grant's army was almost driven into the Tennessee River, but the arrival of reinforcements the second day enabled the Unionists to recover their lost ground and to force the Confederates back into Mississippi. The battle of Shiloh cost the Confederates the life of their commanding officer, General A. S. Johnston, an irreparable loss. His successor, General Beauregard, made Corinth, Mississippi, his headquarters, but was forced to abandon that point in May when the Union army, with Halleck now in personal command, advanced in overwhelming numbers. Fortunately for Grant, of whom Halleck seemed to be jealous, Halleck was rewarded for his success in the western theater by being taken to Washington as general-in-chief of all the Union armies. Meantime there had been spectacular fighting on the Mississippi River. Union troops and gunboats had taken Island No. 10 from the Confederates, and had defeated a Confederate flotilla near Memphis, where Grant soon made his headquarters. On the lower Mississippi, Admiral David Glasgow Farragut [1] ran the strong defenses at the mouth of the river, took New Orleans on April 28, and penetrated upstream as far as Vicksburg. By the end of the year it was apparent that Grant had his eye on that stronghold, but during the winter little of consequence could be accomplished.

The River War

While the North was scoring these moderate successes in the West, the South was piling up victory after victory in the East. McClellan's plan of campaign was to transport his army by water to the peninsula that lay between the York and James Rivers, and then to advance westward to Richmond. This was no doubt sound strategy, but it worried the politicians in Washington, who insisted that a part of McClellan's army be kept directly between Washington and the enemy. Obliged against his better judgment to submit to this division of his forces, McClellan, with nearly twice as many men under his command as the Confederates could bring to bear against him, bemoaned his lack of strength, and failed to take Richmond, although he came within four and a half miles of the city. In the famous Seven Days' Battles, Lee, who succeeded General J. E. Johnston in field command when the latter was wounded, decisively defeated McClellan and forced him to withdraw to the protection of the Union gunboats on the James River. McClellan then proposed, again with sound strategy, to remove his army to the south bank of the James River, and, by threatening the railroads that brought supplies from the

Northern defeats in the East

[1] A. T. Mahan, *Admiral Farragut* (1892).

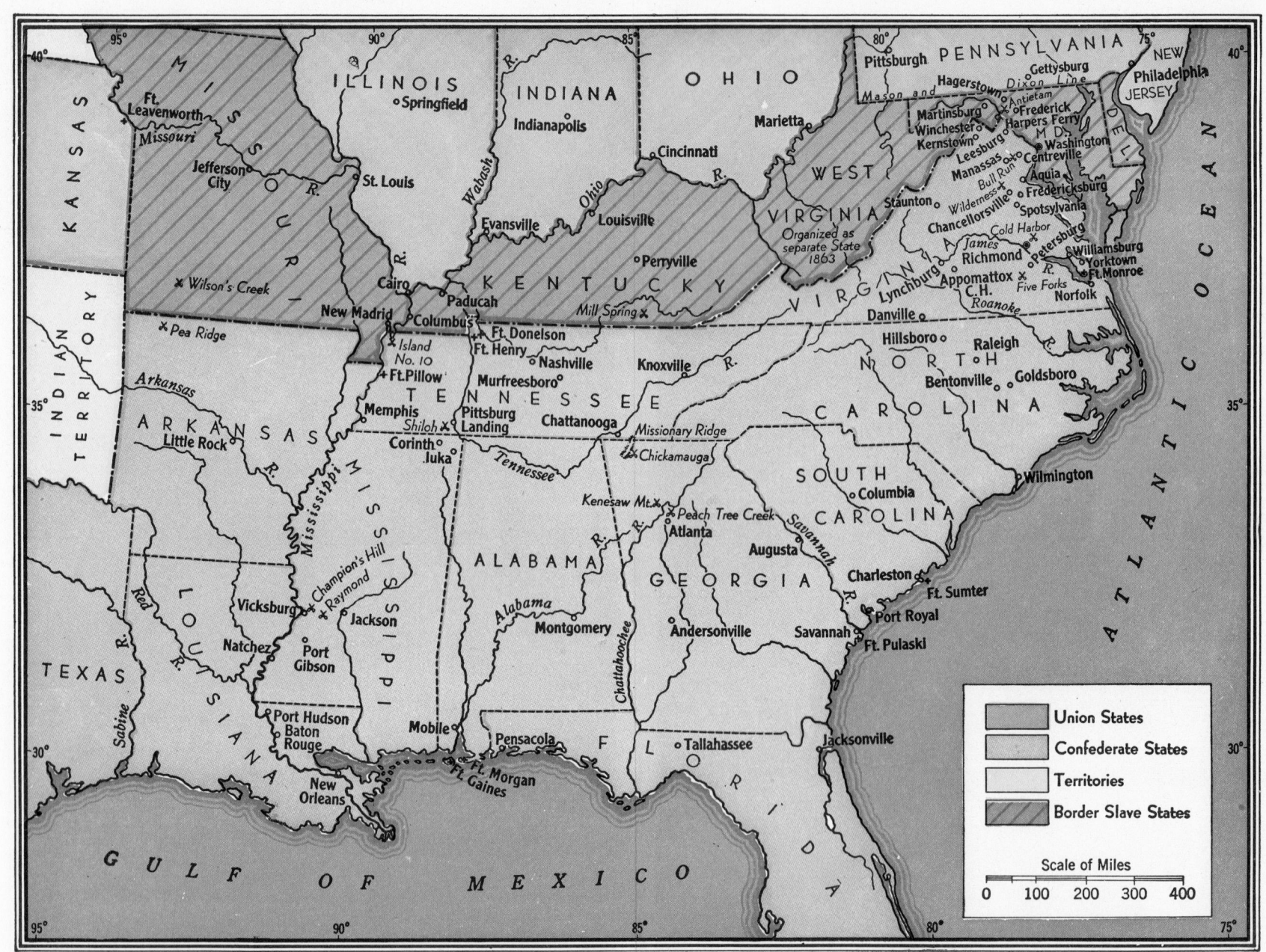

THE CIVIL WAR, 1860–1865

south to Richmond, to force the Confederates to abandon their capital. Later on Grant was to follow precisely this plan through to success, and with the full support of Lincoln, but the President had not yet learned to disregard his civilian strategists; moreover, Halleck was by this time in Washington as general-in-chief, and his advice, rather than McClellan's was followed. McClellan was not actually removed from command, but Halleck brought General John Pope from the West to head a new venture directly toward Richmond from Washington, built up Pope's army at the expense of McClellan's, and ordered McClellan back to the Potomac. Thereupon, Lee turned his attention to Pope, whom he completely outmaneuvered and defeated at the second battle of Bull Run, August 30, 1862. The rout of the Union forces was almost as complete as McDowell's army had suffered at the same place the year before.

Pope's disaster brought McClellan back into favor again, but before the Union forces could be fully reorganized, Lee crossed the Potomac from Leesburg, Virginia, to Frederick, Maryland, and headed toward Pennsylvania. McClellan gave chase, and *Antietam to Gettysburg* at the battle of Antietam, September 17, failed to win a complete victory, but at least turned Lee back to Virginia. Had McClellan been as good a field commander as he was a drillmaster and organizer, Lee's defeat at Antietam would have been a rout. This Lincoln knew, and he therefore began his long and disheartening search for a general whom he could trust. His first choice, General Ambrose E. Burnside, proved his incompetence at Fredericksburg, December 13, in one of the bloodiest and most disastrous defeats of the war. Burnside was then succeeded by "Fighting Joe" Hooker, an able soldier whom the men liked, but a caustic critic of his superiors. At Chancellorsville,[1] early in May, 1863, Lee defeated Hooker as decisively as he had defeated Burnside, but Lincoln delayed making another choice until Hooker himself was ready to resign. This happened shortly after Lee had again crossed the Potomac heading northward into Pennsylvania with Hooker paralleling his movements somewhat to the east. Halleck, whose incompetence Lincoln had not yet fully divined, had doubtless provoked Hooker into resignation, but Lincoln let Hooker go, and gave the command to General George G. Meade just as the greatest battle of the war was shaping up, at Gettysburg, Pennsylvania. Here, after three days of intense fighting, July 1–3, 1863, the Union army won a signal victory. The most spectacular phase of the fighting came the third day, when Lee sent General George E. Pickett with ten thousand men directly against the Union

[1] G. F. R. Henderson, *Stonewall Jackson and the American Civil War* (2 vols., 1898), is one of the best military biographies ever written. Jackson was mortally wounded at Chancellorsville, but his brilliant tactics had made Lee's victory possible. See also D. S. Freeman, *Lee's Lieutenants: A Study in Command* (3 vols., 1942–44).

center. Three-fourths of Pickett's men fell dead or wounded, and next day Lee began his retreat to Confederate soil. Meade's forces were too badly mauled to take full advantage of the victory they had won, and Lee escaped, but with this battle the tide seemed definitely to have turned in favor of the North.

From the West also came news of a Union triumph. There Grant had been wrestling for months with the difficult problem of taking Vicksburg. Finally he had transported his army to the west bank of the Mississippi, marched it thirty miles to the south, then re-crossed the river and advanced northward to invest the city. After several hard-fought battles, Grant settled down in May, 1863, to the siege of Vicksburg, which ended in its surrender, July 3, while Meade was winning at Gettysburg. Shortly afterward, the safe descent of a commercial steamboat from St. Louis to New Orleans justified Lincoln's observation that "the Father of Waters again goes unvexed to the seas." More important than the opening of the Mississippi was the fact that the Confederate states to the west of the river were now virtually out of the war.

Vicksburg

The fighting now shifted to eastern Tennessee, where the Union objective was to take Chattanooga, and so cut squarely in two the only continuous railroad from the East to the West that the Confederacy possessed. At the desperate and bloody battle of Murfreesboro, fought on the last day of 1862 and the first two days of 1863, a Confederate army under General Braxton Bragg successfully halted the Union advance under General William S. Rosecrans. But the next spring and summer, by somewhat the same type of maneuvers that Grant had used at Vicksburg, Rosecrans drove Bragg out of Chattanooga, and on September 9 occupied the city. A little later, however, on September 21-24, Bragg badly worsted Rosecrans at the battle of Chickamauga, and cut off Union communications from Chattanooga to the outside world, except for a narrow mountain wagon-road. General Grant, whose exploits at Vicksburg had by this time led to his being made supreme commander in the West, now appeared in Chattanooga to straighten things out. The battle of Chattanooga, which followed on November 24-25, was a decisive Union victory, and Bragg was sent in full retreat toward Atlanta.

Chattanooga and Chickamauga

Grant's victories at Vicksburg and Chattanooga marked him as the man so sorely needed to take supreme command of all the Union armies, East as well as West. Congress, therefore, promptly revived the grade of lieutenant-general, and Lincoln as promptly nominated Grant for the place. By March, 1864, the nomination had been confirmed, and the new com-

Grant in supreme command

mander-in-chief was in Washington to assume his responsibilities. His modesty and tact won him many friends. Halleck was consoled for the loss of his title as general-in-chief by being made Grant's chief of staff, and Meade, who after Gettysburg had spent the rest of the year in a fruitless game of hide and seek with Lee, was left in command of the Army of the Potomac. Grant made it clear, however, that he had no intention of remaining in Washington as an "armchair" general, and the first hard fighting of the spring found him riding side by side with Meade to direct the operations of the Army of the Potomac. If the war was to be won, Lee must be beaten, and Grant rightly concluded that his first duty was to match his wits with Lee's.

The first results were far from reassuring. Grant with an army twice the size of Lee's felt free to advance directly toward Richmond, but early in May, 1864, at the bloody battle of the Wilderness he tried in vain to beat Lee back. Undismayed by his defeat, he wheeled his columns to the left, and began again his southward march. Again Lee blocked his way, and at Spotsylvania, May 8–12, prevented a Union break-through. Grant's determination to "fight it out along this line if it takes all summer" led to another bloody defeat at Cold Harbor, June 1–3, after which he turned to McClellan's strategy, and began an advance on Richmond south of the James River by way of Petersburg.

Meantime the western army, now under General W. T. Sherman,[1] was advancing southward from Chattanooga to Atlanta. The Confederates, commanded by General J. E. Johnston, who had succeeded Bragg after the battle of Chattanooga, artfully impeded the invader's progress. But the superior resources of the North were now beginning to count, and Johnston, like Lee, was badly outnumbered. Sharp fighting occurred at many points along the route, and it was not until September 2 that the Confederates, now under the command of John B. Hood, abandoned Atlanta. Sherman, believing "war and individual ruin" to be synonymous terms, left a trail of desolation wherever he went. Atlanta was burned, and on the fifteenth of November Sherman began an advance "from Atlanta to the sea" that devastated an area in central Georgia three hundred miles long and sixty miles wide. On the tenth of December he arrived at Savannah, only to begin shortly afterward a march northward through the Carolinas to join Grant. Here he was again confronted by Johnston, who at Bentonville, North Carolina, March 19–21, 1865, gave battle, but with such odds against him that he had no chance to win. Some time before this (December 15–16, 1864) the remnants of the Confederate army commanded by Hood had been defeated and scattered

Sherman in Georgia

---

[1] Lloyd Lewis, *Sherman, Fighting Prophet* (1932), is an excellent popular biography.

by Union forces under General George H. Thomas near Nashville. The
final phase of the war was at hand.

Ever since the summer of 1864, Grant had been engaged in the
dreary business of besieging Petersburg and Richmond. For a while
Lee successfully used the Shenandoah Valley for diversions,
Appomattox but victories won by General Phil Sheridan over General
Jubal Early in the fall of 1864 put an end to that. By the spring of 1865,
Lee's position was extremely precarious. Finally, following the battle
of Five Forks, April 1, 1865, Lee abandoned both Petersburg and Richmond, only to discover that Sheridan's cavalry was on one side of him
and Grant's infantry on the other. By this time his army had dwindled
to less than thirty thousand men, whereas Grant had more than one
hundred thousand, and Sherman with still other thousands was approaching from the south. There was nothing left for Lee to do but to
surrender, and this he did at Appomattox, April 9. Grant's terms were
magnanimous. All the Confederate troops, officers as well as men, were
to be paroled under promise not to serve against the United States again
until exchanged; all military stores and arms, except the sidearms of
officers, were to be surrendered; the mounted Confederates, who unlike
the Union cavalry owned the horses they rode, were to be allowed to keep
their mounts. Learning that Lee's men were desperately short of food,
Grant also ordered that rations for twenty-five thousand men, approximately the number of troops Lee had surrendered, should be sent to the
former enemy at once. Johnston, whose army was now "melting away
like snow before the sun," realized that further resistance was useless and
soon surrendered to Sherman on the same terms that Grant had given
Lee. One by one the lesser bodies of Confederate troops laid down their
arms, and on May 10 Jefferson Davis himself was captured. The Confederate States of America had ceased to exist.

The Union was saved, but at a fearful cost. For four years great
numbers of men had been taken by both sides from productive employment and had been turned into efficient engines of destruc-
Losses of tion. The armies of the Civil War were not large, judged by
the war present-day standards, for only rarely did a general have
mobile units of as high as one hundred thousand men under his command.
But considering that the combined population of North and South approximated only about thirty-two millions, the man-power that had
been mobilized was impressive. The total number of enlistments in the
Union army had been about 2,900,000; in the Confederate army about
1,300,000. But because these figures take no account of short-term enlistments they fail to give an accurate picture of the relative strength of
the two armies. A careful student of the subject, Thomas L. Livermore,

computes that the Union army was equivalent to about 1,500,000 men serving for three years, and the Confederate army on the same basis, to about 1,000,000 men. These statistics are doubtless inaccurate, and the confused state of the records makes it virtually impossible to estimate the actual number of individuals who served on one side or the other. The death-toll was terrific. For the Union army, counting those killed or mortally wounded in battle, and those who died from sickness or other causes, Livermore sets the figure at about 359,000 and for the Confederate army at about 258,000. Among the survivors were thousands who were maimed for life, and other thousands whose health was permanently undermined.[1]

In spite of the enthusiasm that had at first moved more men to join both armies than the two governments were able to make over into soldiers, the volunteering principle failed, unaided, to supply the huge armies that had somehow to be raised. Loath to resort to conscription, both North and South first tried to encourage enlistments by offering bounties. Many of the southern troops had enlisted for one year only, and late in 1861 they were offered a bounty of fifty dollars and a sixty-day furlough to re-enlist. The North went much farther. From the beginning of the war it offered a cash bounty of one hundred dollars to every volunteer, and in 1863 it raised the sum to three hundred and two dollars for new recruits, and four hundred and two dollars for veterans who would re-enlist. Even so, conscription was not to be forestalled for long.

The South invoked it first. Comparatively few of the twelve-months troops accepted the bounty-furlough offer, and in the spring of 1862, with the northern drives beginning, something had to be done to keep them in the army. Accordingly, on March 28, 1862, President Davis was authorized to disregard all short-term enlistments and retain everyone then in the service for three full years from the date of his original enlistment. Also, he might conscript for a like period all white males between the ages of eighteen and thirty-five. Six months later the age limit was raised from thirty-five to forty-five, and in February, 1864, conscription was made applicable to all between seventeen and fifty. In the closing months of the war many Southerners, including General Lee, believed that the slaves should be offered their freedom to enlist, and on March 13, 1865, the Confederate Congress actually passed such a law. But the measure came too late to be of any use. In the earlier conscription laws, liberal exemptions were

Conscription in the South

---

[1] T. L. Livermore, *Numbers and Losses in the Civil War in America, 1861–1865* (1901). These figures, it is only fair to state, are hotly contested. Probably it is impossible to compile anything like exact statistics.

permitted, but toward the end these were whittled down to extremely narrow limits.

The North was a year later than the South in resorting to conscription, and when on March 3, 1863, a draft act was finally passed, it differed materially from the southern conscription laws. The pur-
The northern draft
pose of the northern act was primarily to stimulate enlistments. Only when a given district had failed to produce its assigned quota of troops by volunteering was the draft to be applied. It was thus made a point of honor for a state or a city or a county to supply all the soldiers required of it by means of volunteering, and without resort to the draft. All the able-bodied citizens, and all aliens who had declared their intention of becoming citizens, between the ages of twenty and forty-five were enrolled by districts, roughly resembling the congressional districts, and in assigning quotas to each district the President was to take into consideration the number of volunteers it had already furnished. Many whole states were able to escape the draft altogether, and the number of men forcibly inducted into the northern army was trifling.

But the stimulation to enlistment was very real. Bounties were raised to fantastic figures as states, counties, and cities vied with one another for volunteers. In some districts the total amount of bounty-money that a man who enlisted could claim ran to over a thousand dollars. Immigrants, particularly those coming from Ireland, were often persuaded to enter the army as a means of getting a start in the new land. So generous were the rewards that a class of "bounty-jumpers" arose, whose business it was to enlist and collect the bounty, then desert and re-enlist as often as possible.[1] Lincoln's tender-heartedness caused him to pardon many such deserters, and deeply irritated the draft authorities. But whatever the defects of the system, the draft and the bounties worked relentlessly to keep the Union armies full. Generous exemptions were allowed, and at first a man who was drafted could escape service either by paying three hundred dollars or by hiring a substitute. This provision, which led to the charge that the struggle was a "rich man's war but a poor man's fight," was soon abolished, and a like provision in the southern conscription law went the same way.

In both North and South the attempts to enforce conscription met forcible resistance. In the North serious "draft riots" occurred in New York City and elsewhere during the summer of 1863. In
Resistance to conscription
the South resistance was strongest in the mountain regions where the Confederate cause was never popular, and among the states'-rights extremists, who thought that in conscripting an army

---

[1] Ella Lonn, *Desertion during the Civil War* (1928).

the southern government was exceeding its powers. In several southern states, particularly in Georgia, where Governor J. E. Brown definitely branded the conscription law as unconstitutional, and in North Carolina, where the legislature added at will to the exempted classes, the execution of the law was somewhat impeded. On the whole, however, resistance to conscription, both North and South, was ineffective. Thanks to these measures the South put practically its entire man-power into the field, and the North drew as heavily upon its man-power as was necessary to win the war.[1]

[1] J. G. Randall, *Lincoln the President: Springfield to Gettysburg* (2 vols., 1945), is a work of notable merit. See also W. E. Baringer, *Lincoln's Rise to Power* (1937), and *A House Dividing: Lincoln as President Elect* (1945); D. M. Potter, *Lincoln and his Party in the Secession Crisis* (1942); W. B. Hesseltine, *Lincoln and the War Governors* (1948); H. J. Carman and R. H. Luthin, *Lincoln and the Patronage* (1943); G. F. Milton, *Abraham Lincoln and the Fifth Column* (1942).

On the Confederate side: R. W. Patrick, *Jefferson Davis and his Cabinet* (1944); J. K. Bettersworth, *Confederate Mississippi* (1943); Ella Lonn, *Foreigners in the Confederacy* (1940); B. I. Wiley, *The Life of Johnny Reb* (1943); R. D. Meade, *Judah P. Benjamin, Confederate Statesman* (1943); Rudolph Von Abele, *Alexander H. Stephens: A Biography* (1946).

Useful military biographies include H. J. Eckenrode and Bryan Conrad, *George B. McClellan, The Man Who Saved the Union* (1941); W. H. Hebert, *Fighting Joe Hooker* (1944); W. W. Blackford, *War Years with Jeb Stuart* (1945); R. S. Henry, *"First with the Most" Forrest* (1944); F. H. Harrington, *Fighting Politician: Major General N. P. Banks* (1948).

On the naval side: Jim Dan Hill, *Sea Dogs of the Sixties* (1935); C. L. Lewis, *David Glasgow Farragut, Our First Admiral* (2 vols., 1941–43); W. A. Roberts, *Semmes of the Alabama* (1938); R. S. West, Jr., *Gideon Welles, Lincoln's Navy Department* (1943).

L. M. Hacker, *The Triumph of American Capitalism* (1940), construes the Civil War as a victory for industrial capitalism. Margaret Leech, *Reveille in Washington, 1860–1865* (1941), gives a vivacious account of Washington society during the war.

20

Behind the Lines

WHEN the Civil War broke out the North had not fully recovered from the depression that had followed the panic of 1857, and for a time business interests were more frightened than stimulated by the clash of arms. By the summer of 1862, however, a surge of prosperity had put in its appearance that was to outlast the war. The returns of agriculture were phenomenally good, manufactures flourished as never before, railroads rolled up huge wartime profits, and business generally enjoyed a "boom." [1]

Prosperity for the northern farmer was in part a result of the abnormal demands of war. With millions of men under arms the government became a dependable and generous purchaser of every kind of foodstuff, and its equally great need of woolen goods and leather strengthened the market also for raw wool and hides. Probably the sales that the farmers made directly or indirectly to the government more than offset the losses sustained by wartime interference with sales to the South. And, as a matter of fact, much of this intersectional trade persisted in spite of the war, and in spite of the half-hearted efforts of the government to suppress it.

War and prosperity

Almost equally important, however, was the chance that forced Great Britain during these critical years to import from the United States a large proportion of its wheat. For some time the British farmer had failed to supply the United Kingdom with all the wheat it needed, but in the early years of the Civil War a succession of crop failures made the deficiency abnormally large. Ordinarily the British shortage in wheat had been made up by importations from the Continent, from South America, or from Egypt, but these sources of supply now proved to be insufficient, and the importation of wheat from the United States became

---

[1] E. D. Fite, *Social and Industrial Conditions in the North during the Civil War* (1910), is an excellent analysis of the causes of northern prosperity. A. C. Cole, *The Irrepressible Conflict, 1850–1865* (1934), is of equal merit and wider scope. It covers the social and economic history of both North and South in the decade before as well as during the war. Useful short accounts are F. L. Paxson, *The Civil War* (1911); J. F. Rhodes, *History of the Civil War* (1917); and N. W. Stephenson, *Abraham Lincoln and the Union* (1918).

a virtual necessity. During the three-year period 1861–63, northern farmers actually furnished more than forty per cent of the wheat and flour imported into Great Britain, and the total export of wheat from the United States rose to well above fifty million bushels annually, three times the normal amount.

Several circumstances conspired during these same years to make possible the needed expansion of American agriculture. In the first place, it was possible to increase the acreage under cultivation almost at will. All along the frontier, and elsewhere, good land that had remained unworked or unappropriated **Agricultural expansion** was pressed into service. Moreover, with the South out of the Union, a homestead law, so long the goal of believers in free land, was speedily enacted (1862). Thereafter any person who was the head of a family, or had arrived at the age of twenty-one years, whether a citizen of the United States or an alien who had declared his intention of becoming a citizen, might take up a quarter section of public land, and, after having lived upon it for five years and improved it, might receive full title to it virtually free of charge. Comparatively little use was made of this law during the war, although under its terms thousands of acres of new land were placed under cultivation, immediately after the war ended, all along the "middle border," in Iowa, Kansas, Nebraska, and Minnesota.

Very important also was the rapid introduction of labor-saving farm machinery. Such valuable aids to farming as the improved plow, the corn-planter, the two-horse cultivator, the mower, the reaper, and the steam thresher had all been invented before the Civil War, but it took the acute shortage of man-power that resulted from placing millions of men under arms to induce farmers to give up their old-fashioned methods and make use of the new tools. Before the war, with farm labor relatively cheap and plentiful, the farmer had seen little point to labor-saving machinery. But when he was faced with the alternative of losing his crops or using the machines, he used the machines. A reaper operated by one man could cut ten or twelve acres of grain in a day, whereas the best a man could hope to do with an old-fashioned back-breaking cradle was an acre and a half. By utilizing the new implements the northern farmer was able to take care of a vastly increased acreage without serious difficulty. Even women and children could operate many of the machines, and in innumerable instances they were called upon to do so. By 1865 it was estimated that not less than two hundred and fifty thousand reapers were in use in the United States.[1]

Of some assistance also was the trend toward more scientific methods

[1] H. N. Casson, *The Romance of the Reaper* (1908); Joseph Schafer, *A History of Agriculture in Wisconsin* (1922).

of farming. The states that lay to the east of the virgin lands of the
frontier were soon aware that they suffered from certain
obvious disadvantages. Their soil would not, unaided,
grow such crops as the newer states could produce. In the
older states, particularly, much of the land had been
"cropped to death." Discerning men, mostly Easterners, had begun
well before the Civil War to advocate the scientific study and teaching
of agriculture, but legislative response to their pleas, curiously, came at
the outset more from the West than from the East. In 1857 Michigan
established the first state college of agriculture, only to be emulated in
quick succession by Iowa in 1858, and Minnesota in 1859. By the latter
date Justin S. Morrill of Vermont, chairman of the House Committee
on Agriculture, had pushed through Congress a measure for the granting
of public lands to each of the states as an endowment for agricultural
education. But Buchanan vetoed the bill, and it was not until 1862,
with Lincoln in the presidential chair, that the Morrill Act was placed
on the statute-books. Each state, according to the new law, was granted
as many times thirty thousand acres of public land as the number of
senators and representatives it elected to Congress. Thus stimulated,
the establishment of agricultural colleges, or of agricultural departments
in state-supported universities, spread rapidly from state to state. The
wartime character of the Morrill Act is attested by the fact that the
measure required that courses in military training be offered by each
of the educational institutions that received benefits under the terms of
the act.

The Morrill
Land Grant
Act

Another factor, probably of far greater importance than agricultural
education in promoting the welfare of northern agriculture during the
Civil War, was the weather. Year after year ideal climatic conditions
prevailed over the greater part of the North. The total wheat production
of the loyal states and territories rose from 142,000,000 bushels in 1859
to 187,000,000 in 1862, and to 191,000,000 in 1863. This was the banner
year for wheat, but the general level of production for all agricultural
commodities remained high throughout the entire war. With inflated
prices, and with adequate transportation facilities available both by
land and by sea, the American farmer enjoyed a degree of prosperity
that he had never known before.

Much as agriculture profited from the war, the stimulus given by the
struggle to manufacturing was even greater. The armies required huge
quantities of manufactured goods of every sort and kind —
clothing, boots and shoes, hats and caps, blankets, wagons,
arms and ammunition, ready-to-eat rations, and innumerable other items. To meet these needs old factories were remodeled and

Wartime
manufacturing

expanded and new factories were built. As was the case with the farmer, the manufacturer had only to make use of inventions already at hand in order to increase his output. Possibly of all machines the sewing machine helped him most. By use of it whole uniforms, and many other types of garments, could be turned out in far greater quantity and with far less hand labor than had ever been possible before. The war, indeed, changed the clothing habits of masculine America completely. For the average male citizen ready-made suits permanently replaced suits made at home or at the local tailor shop. Out of the war, too, came the habit of using such factory-made items as shoes, caps, socks, and prepared foods. It is not too much to say that the war brought to an end the last remaining survivals of the domestic system of manufacture in the United States. Manufacturers whose fortunes were founded on government contracts saw their wealth continue to increase after the war, for the changes in customs that the war promoted enabled them to sell with equal advantage to the civilian population.

What came in later times to be called the "heavy industries" profited enormously from the war. Purchases of munitions abroad practically ceased after the first year because of the rapidity with which American factories supplied the government's needs. The new iron works, gun factories, and powder plants that came into existence were for the most part the results of private initiative, but the government itself went as deeply into the business of manufacturing war materials as public opinion would permit. Before the end of the war, for example, the government arsenal at Springfield, Massachusetts, was producing a thousand rifles a day. Railroad-building, which was resumed in the North after the outbreak of the war, and the continual need for railroad repairs, did much for the manufacturers of iron and steel. They were helped, also, by the demand for ironclads that set in after the battle between the *Monitor* and the *Virginia*.

High tariffs ensured the northern manufacturers against the dangers of European competition. A protectionist policy had been demanded by the Republican national platform in 1860, and a higher schedule of tariffs, sponsored by the same Justin S. Morrill who gave his name to the act for the stimulation of agricultural education, was placed upon the statute-books two days before Buchanan left office. This speedy answer to the prayers of the protectionists was made possible by the withdrawal from Congress of the delegations from the seven seceding states of the lower South, and by the fact that President Buchanan was no longer unmindful of the wishes of the manufacturers within his home state. The original Morrill Tariff Act was repeatedly revised upward during the war, until by 1864 the

The Morrill Tariff Act

average of duties levied on imports had reached forty-seven per cent, the
highest thus far in the history of the nation. The significance of this
development can scarcely be overemphasized. A policy which the South
had persistently blocked in the years preceding the war became an ac-
tuality during it, and, as subsequent events were to prove, remained as a
permanent fixture in American political and economic life.

An important component part of northern wartime prosperity was the
production of a sufficient quantity and variety of raw materials to satisfy
the needs of the northern manufacturers. The mining of
Exploitation   coal, which was not only a lucrative industry in itself but
of natural
resources   served also as a kind of measuring-stick for the progress of
the factory system, increased threefold, and the production
of such basic items as iron ore, copper, salt, and petroleum reached unprecedented heights. Lumber also was in great demand, and the forests
of the Great Lakes region, of Maine, and of New York were exploited as
never before. Wool-growers found a ready market for all the wool they
could grow, and by 1865 were producing annually two and one-third
times as much wool as in 1860. The only commodity that the northern
manufacturers experienced serious difficulty in obtaining was cotton,
and there was enough trading through the lines, both licensed and illicit,
to hold this shortage to a minimum.

Another important source of northern prosperity lay in the output of
the gold and silver mines of the Far West. While the flow of precious
metals from the mines of California was somewhat diminished during
the war, new mines were opened up in various parts of the Rocky Mountains area — particularly in the regions later known as Colorado, Nevada, Arizona, and Montana — that more than made up for this loss.
Millions of dollars' worth of gold and silver thus flowed into the national mints at a time when the nation's need for hard money was
greatest.

Indeed, from whatever angle the subject is viewed, the wartime
prosperity of the North was phenomenal. Its railroads, overbuilt during the fifties, were turned into profitable investments by
Business   the heavy traffic of the war, and the railroad mileage of both
activities
the Northeast and the Northwest had to be substantially
increased to carry the load. Internal waterways — the Great Lakes, the
western rivers, and the canals — did an enormous volume of business.
Financial institutions, which at the outset of the war had seriously missed
the patronage of the South, found a more than adequate compensation
for this loss in the expanding commercial activity of the northern states.
The northern merchant marine, as already noted, was virtually ruined
by the war; but this involved little loss of capital, for most of the ships
were sold, not sunk, and the proceeds from their sale were invested in

such lucrative securities as government bonds, manufacturing concerns, and railroads. From one point of view, American shippers were fortunate in leaving the field of ocean transportation at this particular time. Wooden ships were soon to be replaced by ships of iron and steel, and many American firms sold out just in time to escape the cost of extensive replacements.

The profits of war bred a spirit of extravagance and frivolity among the non-combatants of the North that contrasted oddly with the long casualty lists displayed as a regular part of the daily news. Social life reached a dizzy whirl, with more parties and dances, theaters and circuses, minstrel shows and musicales than ever had been known before. Public interest in sports tended to grow rather than to diminish, and to such standard outlets of the sporting instinct as horse-racing and prize-fighting were added the crude beginnings of baseball, soon to be the favorite game of the nation. The *nouveaux riches*, of whom every community had its quota, spent so lavishly as to win the contempt of more sober-minded citizens. Their purchases of foreign luxuries, rather than imports needed for the prosecution of the war, resulted in an unfavorable balance of trade with Europe that sent $54,000,000 of American gold abroad in 1863 and $91,000,000 in 1864. Prosperity, however, was not evenly divided, and labor in particular failed to obtain its proportionate share. With prices rising steadily throughout the war, wages rose also, but never rapidly enough to keep pace with the cost of commodities. According to a statement published by the *Springfield Republican* in 1864, many of the factories whose profits during the war had been "augmented beyond the wildest dreams of their owners" paid their laborers only from twelve to twenty per cent more than before the war. "There is absolute want in many families, while thousands of young children who should be at school are shut up at work that they may earn something to eke out the scant supplies at home." As a consequence of such tactics on the part of employers labor disorders were frequent, and a strong impetus was given to labor organization.

If the war brought prosperity to the North, it brought little but adversity to the South.[1] With the welfare of the section so intimately bound up with cotton culture, the failure of southern cotton to find a normal market was simply catastrophic. The southern government, gambling on the hope that European nations would come to the aid of the South whenever

Wartime extravagance

Downfall of "King Cotton"

[1] An important, but difficult, book is J. C. Schwab, *The Confederate States of America, 1861–1865: A Financial and Industrial History of the South during the Civil War* (1901). A simpler story is told in N. W. Stephenson, *The Day of the Confederacy* (1919).

European mills faced a serious enough cotton shortage, tried in the early months of the war to prevent the shipment of cotton abroad. Cotton-planters were even urged to destroy their crops as the best insurance against exportation, and it is estimated that this mistaken policy cost the South about a million bales of cotton. Had exportation been stimulated rather than discouraged, the South might have built up credit abroad for subsequent use, but faith in the power of "King Cotton" clouded the judgment of the southern leaders.[1] By 1862 the southern government was ready to reverse its cotton policy, but by that time the northern blockade held shipments to a minimum. The effectiveness of the blockade may be estimated from the fact that the price of cotton in Liverpool rose from fourteen cents in 1861 to fifty cents in 1865. Trade between the lines helped the South and the cotton-planter to some extent, especially after the northern armies had penetrated far into the southern states. In exchange for cotton and tobacco, southern traders received salt, clothing, foodstuffs, and even war materials. Naturally much of this trade was accomplished by means of the most demoralizing bribery and corruption.

The break with the North, followed by the blockade, forced the South to attempt a far greater diversity of economic life, both agricultural and industrial, than it had known before the war. Foodstuffs were grown instead of cotton, salt-works[2] were established wherever the resources justified, while cotton mills, boot and shoe factories, munitions plants, and the like were started up in spite of inadequate capital, defective machinery, and poorly trained workers. The difficulties experienced by the South in its effort to achieve self-sufficiency, however, were too great to be overcome in a short space of time, and as the war wore on, both soldiers and civilians were frequently called upon to endure the greatest extremes of privation. While the North was pushing forward relentlessly to the factory system, the South was compelled to resort more and more to household manufacture. The breakdown of southern transportation, particularly the railroads, which the South was utterly unable to keep in repair, served to compound the confusion. The suffering endured by northern prisoners in southern prison-camps was due far more to this confused economic situation than to any deliberate intent on the part of the jailers.[3]

But even the hard-pressed South was not without its war profiteers.

Southern manufacturing

[1] F. L. Owsley, *King Cotton Diplomacy* (1931); James A. B. Scherer, *Cotton as a World Power: a Study in the Economic Interpretation of History* (1916).

[2] Ella Lonn, *Salt as a Factor in the Confederacy* (1933). The trials of the war-torn South are well told in M. P. Andrews, *The Women of the South in War Times* (1920).

[3] W. B. Hesseltine, *Civil War Prisons — a Study in War Psychology* (1930); C. H. Wesley, *The Collapse of the Confederacy* (1922).

Most of those who made money out of the war were associated in some fashion or other with blockade-running, from which the returns were frequently spectacular. Money inflation tempted also to speculation, a passion which, according to Jefferson Davis, "seduced citizens of all classes from a determined prosecution of the war." The southern *nouveaux riches*, while more limited in their opportunities than those of the North, did not hesitate to make whatever vulgar display of their wealth they could, and the social life of such cities as Charleston and Richmond kept up an appearance of gaiety to the very end.

Once prosperity was in the saddle, the North had little difficulty in financing the war. At the outset, however, the credit of the northern government was at low ebb, the treasury was empty, and the banks of the country were so skeptical of the outcome that they soon suspended specie payments. Secretary of the Treasury Chase had little acquaintance with finance, and was so fearful of the political effects of taxation that he proposed to pay the cost of the war mainly from loans. At first he was compelled to pay ruinous rates to obtain money — on one occasion as high as 7.3 per cent — but with the assistance of Jay Cooke,[1] a Philadelphia banker, he succeeded in floating loans that totaled by the end of the war well over two billion dollars. Cooke popularized the bond issues, and besides making the public see that they were a good investment, he played most successfully upon the patriotic motive. People bought bonds to help the government as well as to help themselves. Cooke himself profited considerably from his undertaking, for the government allowed him a commission of one-half of one per cent on all the sales he made up to ten million dollars, and three-eighths of one per cent on all sales above that amount.

While loans were the chief reliance, the government resorted also to far heavier taxation than the people of the United States had ever before been called upon to pay. In 1862 excises were levied upon a remarkable variety of articles, businesses, occupations, and activities. This tax levy, according to James Ford Rhodes, "might be briefly described with a near approach to accuracy as an act which taxed everything." [2] Even lawyers, physicians, and dentists were required to buy licenses, and such articles as liquor, tobacco, carriages, yachts, billiard-tables, and plate carried heavy duties. Manufacturers were required to pay a tax for the privilege of manufacturing, and the articles they manufactured were also taxed. Railroads, steamboats, toll-

Southern profiteers

Northern war-time finance

Northern taxation

---

[1] E. P. Oberholtzer, *Jay Cooke, Financier of the Civil War* (2 vols., 1907).

[2] *History of the United States*, IV, p. 58.

bridges, savings banks, insurance companies, and the like paid a three per cent duty on their gross receipts. Multifold as these taxes were, they did not produce a great revenue. Even with the help of increased rates, levied in 1864, the total receipts from all such sources during the war barely passed the $300,000,000 mark. An income tax, which began in 1861 as a three per cent tax on all incomes above $800, and was later so modified as to tax incomes between $600 and $5000 at the rate of five per cent, and all higher incomes at the rate of ten per cent, was even less successful as a revenue measure, for it brought in a total of only $55,000,-000. Still these were large sums to a people quite unused to federal taxation. Tariff levies, pushed steadily upward as an offset to the internal taxes that protected interests were required to pay, also netted the government more than $305,000,000 during the four years that the war lasted.

But neither the loans nor the taxes sufficed to keep the government supplied at all times with ready cash, and as a result several issues of
Greenback issues paper money were authorized by Congress. Between February, 1862, when the first of the "legal tender" acts was passed, and March, 1863, the date of the last, a total of no less than $450,000,000 in fiat money was ordered printed. Of this sum $431,000,000 was outstanding at the close of the war. Back of the "greenbacks," as the public promptly dubbed these notes, there lay no gold reserve, but only the good faith of the government. Since they were by law made legal tender for all debts, public and private, except duties on imports and interest on the public debt, they constituted in fact a forced non-interest-bearing loan that the government as an emergency measure exacted from the people.[1]

A National Bank Act, passed in 1863 and amended in 1864, provided the nation with yet another type of paper money: the national bank-
The National Bank Act note. According to this measure, any association desiring to do a national banking business and possessed of the minimum capital ($50,000 for cities of less than 6000 inhabitants, $100,000 for cities of from 6000 to 50,000, and $200,000 for larger cities) was entitled to a national charter of incorporation. Partly as a means of stimulating the market for United States bonds, the law provided that one-third of the capital of such a bank must be invested in national securities, but it was also stipulated that, by depositing these bonds with the United States Treasurer as security, the bank should be entitled to receive in exchange "circulating notes equal in amount to ninety per centum of the current market value of the United States

[1] W. C. Mitchell, *A History of the Greenbacks with Special Reference to the Consequence of Their Issue, 1862–1865* (1903).

bonds so transferred and delivered." It was hoped at first that the state banks would quickly convert themselves into national banks, but when this failed to materialize, Congress levied in 1865 a ten per cent tax on all state bank-notes. While this law did not destroy state banking, it did, as was intended, tax state bank-notes out of existence, so that one of the legacies of the Civil War was a national currency, composed in part of greenbacks and in part of national bank-notes. By the end of 1865 the national bank-note circulation had reached more than $200,000,000. The bank-notes were not "legal tender," as were the greenbacks, but the two types of paper money depended in the last analysis upon the credit of the national government, and circulated at the same value.

Since the government had been forced to suspend specie payments early in the war, none of this paper money was worth its face value in gold. Two main factors controlled the value of a paper dollar: (1) the amount of paper in circulation, and (2) the success or failure of the Union armies at the front. During *Currency depreciation* the dark days of 1864, when it appeared that even the tenacity of Grant might prove insufficient to win the war, the value of the paper dollar, as expressed in terms of gold, dropped to thirty-nine cents, and even at the close of the war it stood at only sixty-seven cents. Even fractional currency was driven out of circulation as the premium on precious metals mounted, and the Treasury was forced to issue paper half-dollars, quarters, dimes, five-cent and three-cent "shinplasters," as the small-sized notes were called. The paper dollars themselves, as well as the notes of larger denominations, were of generous dimensions — about twice the size of the currency now in circulation. Their fluctuating value caused an equivalent fluctuation in prices that netted huge fortunes to speculators. While the wages of laborers rose slowly to meet the new price-levels, the salaries of "white collar" workers proved to be extremely resistant to change. Soldiers, also, fought on at thirteen dollars a month until late in the war, when their pay was raised to sixteen dollars. The generous bounties paid for enlistments served, however, to correct this inequality.

In addition to the official expenditures of the United States government for the winning of the war there was an unknown amount of assistance given to the cause by private individuals. In the early weeks of the struggle the outfitting of soldiers was often *Private benevolence* paid for by patriotic men or groups, some of whom neglected to bill the government for their expenditures. The families of soldiers were in innumerable instances cared for by relatives and neighbors. Ladies' Aid Societies in nearly every village sewed and knit and made bandages for the "boys in blue." A group of humanitarians, led by

Henry W. Bellows and Frederick Law Olmsted, organized early in 1861 the United States Sanitary Commission to aid in the care of the sick and wounded. This society, which the United States government recognized with some reluctance, co-operated effectively with the hopelessly overworked Medical Bureau of the army, and raised millions of dollars in gifts for the purpose.[1] "Sanitary fairs" were held all over the country to stimulate the collection of funds, and from the larger cities and from California huge sums were obtained. Pacific coast communities consciously atoned in this way for their inability to contribute their proper proportion of men to the northern armies. So sustained, the Commission became "a great machine running side by side with the Medical Bureau wherever the armies went." Another private organization, the United States Christian Commission, sought to promote the spiritual well-being of the soldiers by distributing tracts, holding religious services, and relieving in numerous practical ways the "intolerable ennui" of camp life.

The South, in its efforts to finance the war, was driven rapidly from one makeshift to another. The United States mint at New Orleans and the United States customhouses that were seized provided

Southern finance

the Confederacy with perhaps a million dollars in greatly needed specie, and the confiscation of private debts owed by southern citizens to northern creditors also helped. Bond issues were floated, both by the Confederacy and by the several Confederate states, but the limited credit resources of the South were soon dried up. The best results were obtained when the bonds were made payable in produce. In this fashion the southern government came into the possession of large quantities of cotton, tobacco, and other staple commodities, some of which it was able to market, and some of which it pledged as security for a small loan floated in Europe in 1863. Taxation turned out to be almost as fruitless as borrowing. An attempt to levy a direct tax through the instrumentality of the states netted as little real money as the similar efforts of the United States Congress during the Confederation period. Thereafter, the example set by the northern government of levying excises, licensing occupations, and taxing incomes was tried, but with comparatively slight success. One unique feature of the southern taxation program, a ten per cent tax on farm produce, to be paid in kind, proved to be of great assistance to the Confederate armies. It was excessively unpopular, however, and the charge of unconstitutionality was persistently hurled at this and all other effective means of taxation. The

[1] Charles J. Stillé, *History of the United States Sanitary Commission* (1866), is almost a contemporary account. See also W. E. Barton, *The Life of Clara Barton, Founder of the American Red Cross* (1922).

total receipts of the Confederacy from all tax sources has been estimated at about one hundred million dollars.

The inadequacy of the sums realized from bond issues and taxation drove the Confederacy early in the war to a chief reliance upon printing-press money. Notes were issued by the Confederate Treasury in a steadily increasing volume until before the end of the war more than a billion dollars of such money was in circulation. In addition, states, municipalities, and private corporations also put out issues of paper that passed for money. The depreciation that inevitably set in as the amount of fiat money increased, and the prospect of Confederate victory dimmed, far outran the depreciation of the northern greenback. By the summer of 1863 the Confederate dollar was worth only twenty-five cents in gold; a year later it was worth less than five cents; by the end of the war it was valueless. Southerners of small incomes suffered the acute distress usually attendant upon such extremes of money inflation, but a few skillful speculators made comfortable fortunes. Northern greenbacks, smuggled through the lines, were eagerly received, and circulated at a tremendous premium.

The confidence of the South that European intervention on behalf of "King Cotton" would be the decisive factor in the war made diplomacy a major concern on the part of both belligerents from the very beginning. Every move of the southern government was designed to promote intervention, while the fondest hope of the northern government was to prevent it. In the diplomatic battle of wits the South, with leaders more experienced in international relations than the northern Republicans could command, should have had the advantage, but the southern government failed to live up to its opportunities. Davis's two secretaries of state, R. M. T. Hunter and Judah P. Benjamin, were second-rate men who had no particular aptitude for the post assigned them, and were quite outmatched by Seward. William L. Yancey, the first Confederate commissioner to England, quickly lost heart and came home. He was succeeded by James M. Mason, who was well received by the British aristocracy, but made little headway with the British government. In France, John Slidell did better, but there was little that France could do to aid the Confederacy without the approval of England, who as "mistress of the seas," and the chief foreign consumer of southern cotton, had to make the decision for or against European intervention in the American war.[1]

"King Cotton" diplomacy

[1] Numerous studies have been made on the foreign relations of both North and South. Among the best are the following: E. D. Adams, *Great Britain and the American Civil War* (2 vols., 1925); Donaldson Jordon and E. J. Pratt, *Europe and the American Civil War* (1931); W. R. West, *Contemporary French Opinion on the American Civil War* (1924); J. M. Callahan, *The Diplomatic History of the Southern Confederacy* (1901).

English sympathy at the outset of the war seemed definitely to lean toward the South. The Tory aristocracy, which understood and appre-
English atti-   ciated the kindred southern planter class, looked forward
tude toward   with satisfaction to the possible downfall of democracy any-
the American   where. Many English liberals also favored the South, for
Civil War   their favorite doctrine was then free trade, and the South
seemed to be definitely committed to a free-trade policy, while the North had just inaugurated a program of protection. Moreover, the right of revolution was a part of the Whig tradition. By the "Glorious Revolution" England had been freed from the tyranny of the Stuarts, and by the American Revolution the colonies had rightfully won their independence, while at the same time bringing deserved discredit upon the attempt of an English king to establish personal rule. If, therefore, the southern people wished to be free, they had the right to be free. Possibly among Whig manufacturers this argument was duly strengthened by the reflection that a direct exchange of southern cotton for English manufactures would be greatly facilitated by the success of the southern arms. Diplomats of both parties saw a probable advantage for England in the division of the United States into two contending powers.

The North, however, was not without its friends in England. Such reformers as John Bright and Richard Cobden, although distressed at the newly adopted tariff policy of the United States, saw clearly that a northern victory must result in the abolition of slavery. With the issue thus reduced to a struggle between free labor and slave labor, their sympathies could lie only with the North. Lincoln's early insistence that the war was one for the preservation of the Union, and not for the abolition of slavery, was somewhat confusing to many Englishmen, but when at last he issued his Emancipation Proclamation, the number of northern sympathizers was greatly increased, particularly among the lower classes. The workingmen of Manchester, in spite of the suffering that the failure of the American cotton supply had caused them, congratulated Lincoln upon his stand, and urged him to complete "the erasure of that foul blot upon civilization and Christianity — chattel slavery." To some extent, perhaps, British sympathy for the North was purchased by the greater need for northern wheat than for southern cotton; and there can be no doubt that the profits of neutrality were widely regarded as preferable to a hazardous war on behalf of southern independence. At all events, well before the end of the war the weight of British opinion had shifted to the side of the North.

Northern anxiety as to the course Great Britain meant to pursue became acute as early as May, 1861, when the British government issued a proclamation of neutrality with respect to the American war. This action, because it accorded to the South the status of belligerent, was regarded by the North as deliberately un-friendly, for at the time the northern government still main-tained that the uprising in the South was no more than an insurrection, and was therefore of no concern to outside nations. The British contention, however, that the struggle was in reality a war was in closer accord with the facts. Indeed, Lincoln himself, in ordering a blockade of the southern coast, had already unwittingly recognized the belligerency of the South. Probably the British proclamation was not meant to be unfriendly, but was designed merely to serve notice that the two contending parties would be expected to observe the customary rules of war. Nevertheless the fact that it was issued just before the arrival in England of Charles Francis Adams,[1] whom Lincoln had sent as minister from the United States, confirmed Northerners in their sus-picion that the sympathies of the British government lay with the South. Otherwise, they argued, Adams would at least have been given an op-portunity to present the northern point of view. Northern fears that the recognition of southern belligerence would ultimately be followed by the recognition of southern independence proved to be unfounded.

British recognition of southern belligerency

Late in 1861 an incident occurred that almost precipitated war be-tween the United States and Great Britain. When the news reached Captain Charles Wilkes of the United States frigate *San Jacinto* that the two Confederate commissioners, Mason and Slidell, were aboard a British mail steamer, the *Trent*, bound from Havana to Southampton, he promptly intercepted the neu-tral ship, arrested the Confederate commissioners, and took them to Boston. Wilkes's action was totally without official authorization, and was much the same sort of high-handed procedure that the United States had protested against when practiced by Great Britain before the War of 1812. But the northern public went wild with joy at the news, and Con-gress voted Wilkes the thanks of the nation for his exploit. British re-action was similarly excited, and the demand of the British government that Mason and Slidell be released and a suitable apology made was fully supported by public opinion. To emphasize the gravity of the situation, the British navy was put on a war footing and eight thousand troops were sent to Canada. In reply Seward failed to make a very emphatic apology, but he sensibly surrendered the prisoners, and so averted war.[2]

The Trent affair

The blockade of the southern coast that the North maintained caused

---

[1] C. F. Adams, Jr., *Charles Francis Adams* (1900).

[2] T. L. Harris, *The Trent Affair* (1896).

far less friction with the British government than might have been expected. Even the American doctrine of continuous voyages, which led at times to the capture of British ships bound from one British port to another, was allowed to pass unchallenged. Great Britain wisely offered little objection to practices that she herself might use to advantage as a belligerent. But the British idea of neutral duties sorely taxed the patience of the United States. The Confederate commerce-destroyers were British built and operated from British ports. For their depredations the American government proposed to collect damages, and after the war succeeded in doing so. The Laird rams, had they been permitted to sail, might have raised the blockade, but, fortunately, when it became clear that their departure from British waters would mean war between the United States and Great Britain, they were not permitted to leave port. The British government may also be credited with having restrained Napoleon III of France from interference in the American war. Napoleon did offer mediation, significantly right after Fredericksburg, but he never dared recognize the independence of the South, and he was compelled to content himself with the working-out of his project for the virtual acquisition of Mexico.

Destruction of northern commerce

That venture was made possible in October, 1861, when Great Britain, France, and Spain agreed to joint intervention in Mexico to protect the

---

RECONSTRUCTION ERA

ANDREW JOHNSON (1808–75), *of Tennessee, seventeenth President of the United States, made a valiant, but not very successful, attempt to preserve home rule for the South during the reconstruction period. Senator* CHARLES SUMNER (1811–74), *of Massachusetts, and Representative* THADDEUS STEVENS (1792–1868), *of Pennsylvania, were the two members of Congress most responsible for taking the process of reconstruction out of the President's hands.*

ROSCOE CONKLING (1829–88), *of New York, and* JAMES G. BLAINE (1830–93), *of Maine, were rivals for the leadership of the Republican Party after the passing of Stevens and Sumner. Conkling's followers called themselves "Stalwarts" and derided Blaine's supporters as "Half-Breeds." The bad feeling between the two factions probably cost Blaine the Republican nominations in 1876 and 1880, as well as the election when he was nominated in 1884.*

RUTHERFORD B. HAYES (1822–93), *of Ohio, nineteenth President of the United States, was the upright and courageous, but not very politic, successor of President Grant. He restored home rule to the South, backed the resumption of specie payments, and made an earnest attempt to reform the civil service.*

JOHNSON

STEVENS

SUMNER

HAYES

CONKLING

BLAINE

"persons and properties of their subjects." After the seizure of several Mexican customhouses, Great Britain and Spain reached agreements with the Mexican government, and withdrew from the enterprise, but Napoleon ordered his army to Mexico City, called an assembly of pliant "Notables," and with their consent placed the Archduke Maximilian of Austria upon an imperial Mexican throne. A more complete violation of the Monroe Doctrine could scarcely have been imagined, but as long as the United States was torn by civil strife Napoleon knew that he had nothing to fear from north of the Rio Grande. Secretary Seward did not fail to register a vigorous protest, however, and after the defeat of the South, Napoleon found it expedient to recall his troops from Mexico. The fall of Maximilian's government then followed as a matter of course.

French intervention in Mexico

Other European nations showed comparatively slight interest in the American Civil War. Spain, with the United States unable to do more than enter a formal protest, did indeed attempt to reannex Santo Domingo, but by 1865 active native opposition had forced her to abandon the project. Russia and Great Britain were on bad terms, and the appearance of two Russian fleets in American waters during 1863 was generally interpreted in the United States as a gesture of friendship toward the North. More probably the Russians were simply stationing their ships where they could most damage British commerce in case war

---

THE FAR WEST

American frontiersmen have always shown themselves equal to the problem of house construction, no matter how primitive the conditions that confronted them.

When settlement was in forested areas, the log cabin, such as that in the first picture, was the ordinary pioneer dwelling. This was not an original American idea, but was borrowed from the Swedish colonists on the Delaware, who had been accustomed to such houses in the old country. (Currier & Ives print of a log cabin in the Rockies, 1871 — photo from Bettmann.) The sod house, shown in the second picture, was, however, a strictly American invention. Out on the prairies, where there were few trees, the slabs of grass turned up by breaking plows could be used instead of logs to build walls. (Photo from Brown Bros.)

The building of the first transcontinental railroad taxed the engineering resources of the eighteen-sixties to the limit. Two companies, the Union Pacific, building westward from the Missouri River, and the Central Pacific, building eastward from the Pacific Coast, carried on the work. Neither road was built according to specifications that would be regarded as necessary today, and both took curves and grades with the greatest unconcern. (Photo from Bettmann.)

should break out, but the purchase of Alaska from Russia in 1867 was frequently justified in the United States on the grounds that Russia had once been a friend in time of need. That Alaska would ever be worth the price paid ($7,200,000), few were then able to see.[1]

More important to the governments of both North and South than problems of diplomacy were the political dissensions that existed within their own borders. While the South was far more united than the North, the Davis administration lost steadily in popularity. Extreme states'-rights advocates saw in Davis's southern nationalism nothing less than an organized effort to establish a centralized despotism upon the ruins of the states. Conscription, too, because it was an act of the central government, was denounced for its encroachments upon the reserved rights of the states. Each effective tax measure raised up a crop of enemies who took refuge behind the well-worn screen of unconstitutionality. And finally, the horrors of war and the increasing probability of a northern victory brought forth not only critics of the government, but also a large crop of defeatists who were always about ready to give up. Party lines were not clearly drawn in the Confederacy, but the congressional elections held in the fall of 1863 placed the Confederate Congress definitely in the hands of the anti-administration forces. From that time to the end of the war, Davis was unable to count upon firm legislative support.

Politics in the South

In the North discontent with Lincoln's administration, and dismay at the prospect of a long fratricidal war, had become abundantly apparent before the first summer was over. To hold a maximum number of northern Democrats to the support of the war, the Republicans in the fall of 1861 quite generally gave up their party name and nominated such state and local tickets as were required under the Union banner. That year satisfactory Union majorities were attained, but by 1862 opposition to the war in the North was open and active. Lincoln was accused of ordering arbitrary arrests, and of suspending the writ of *habeas corpus* without adequate constitutional warrant. Military courts took action against civilians even when regular civil courts were open for business. In May, 1863, Lincoln approved the arrest and conviction by court-martial of Clement L. Vallandigham of Ohio, leading Democratic critic of the administration's war measures. In this case, however, Lincoln commuted the sentence of close confinement until the end of the war to banishment to the Confederacy, and so branded Vallandigham with treason. On the question of freedom of the press the President's course was hardly open to criticism. When the military authorities attempted to suppress the New York *World* and the Chicago *Times*, he promptly reversed their orders.

Politics in the North

[1] B. P. Thomas, *Russo-American Relations, 1815-1867* (1930).

Radical Republicans who wished the more vigorous prosecution of the war were almost as great a trial to the President as pacifistic Democrats. A Joint Committee on the Conduct of the War, created by Congress in April, 1862, did its best to take over the actual direction of military affairs. One policy on which the "radicals" were extremely insistent was the emancipation of the slaves, but this Lincoln refused at first to countenance because of the damage it would do the Union cause in the loyal slave states, and in Democratic circles generally. His "paramount object," he told Horace Greeley, was to save the Union, and not to free the slaves. Nevertheless, the time came when Lincoln was obliged to yield to abolitionist pressure. Runaway slaves fled to the Union armies, where according to General Benjamin F. Butler they became "contraband of war." What should be done with them? Were they slave or free? Two of Lincoln's generals, John C. Frémont and David Hunter, issued premature emancipation proclamations for the regions under their military command, orders which Lincoln felt obliged to reverse, but knew that he could not long oppose. Lincoln would have preferred to work toward some system of gradual emancipation, but the time came when he must either free the slaves or alienate the majority of his own party. He knew, too, that if freedom for the slaves were made one of the northern objectives in the war, there would be an immediate end to the danger of foreign intervention. His mind made up, he waited two full months longer before he acted, so that the winning of a Union victory (Antietam, September 17, 1862) could be cited as proof that his course was not a choice of desperation. Then, on September 22, 1862, he issued his preliminary Emancipation Proclamation. Claiming the right as commander-in-chief of the army and navy, he promised that "on the 1st day of January, A.D. 1863, all persons held as slaves within any state or designated part of a state the people whereof shall then be in rebellion against the United States shall be then, thenceforward, and forever free." [1]

Emancipation

Lincoln, like Davis, was soon obliged to confront a Congress steadily less friendly to his administration. "Union" tickets in 1862 drew many war Democrats into collaboration with the Republicans, but many others refused either to leave their party or to permit it to remain dormant for the duration of the war. Some Democrats objected to Lincoln's dictatorial course and criticized his lack of military success. Others held that the Emancipation Proclamation had turned a war to save the Union into a war to free the slaves, something they were utterly unwilling to fight for. Unfortunately

The "Copperheads"

[1] T. Harry Williams, *Lincoln and the Radicals* (1941), is an admirable study of Lincoln's difficulties with the Committee on the Conduct of the War.

Douglas, who had loyally supported the war, died unexpectedly in June, 1861, and left the northern Democracy virtually leaderless. This permitted the rise of such pacifist leaders as Vallandigham, whose extreme opposition to the war was notorious. Helped along by the lack of Union victories, the Democrats in 1862 won the ascendancy in many states that had supported Lincoln two years before, and came within perilously few votes of winning the national House of Representatives. Strongly "Copperhead" legislatures chosen that year in Indiana and Illinois almost withdrew those states from support of the war, but the resourcefulness of the two governors concerned, Oliver P. Morton of Indiana and Richard Yates of Illinois, was equal to the emergency.

The "Copperheads," as peace-at-any-price men came to be called, won many recruits after the passage of the Draft Act in 1863. Banded together into secret societies with such high-sounding names as "Knights of the Golden Circle," they plotted much mischief and performed a little. They were accused of assassinating enrolling officers, of fomenting draft riots, of encouraging soldiers to desert, of giving aid and information to the Confederacy, of helping captured Confederate prisoners to escape. To counteract such activities, "Union Leagues" were formed, and during the last two years of the war an unknown number of individual assaults and reprisals took place.[1]

The occasional elections that were held in the fall of 1863 revealed, however, an unmistakable trend back to the support of the administration. In nearly every instance the Unionists showed greater strength than the Democrats, although by majorities that were not always large. This change of sentiment was due primarily to the victories at Gettysburg and Vicksburg, but even those successes were insufficient to quiet the peace-at-any-price men, whose numbers, particularly in the states that bordered on the Ohio River, were very great. In Ohio a governor had to be chosen, and Vallandigham himself, still an exile but by that time in Canada, won the Democratic nomination. But he was decisively defeated by the Unionist candidate, John Brough, a former Democrat.

The effect of Union victories

The presidential campaign of 1864 began during the darkest days of the war when long casualty lists and infrequent victories made the Lincoln administration extremely vulnerable. Radical Republicans would have been willing to discard Lincoln for one of their own number, and some of them supported a movement that culminated in the nomination of John C. Frémont by a mass convention held in Cleveland, May 31, 1864. But the renomination of Lincoln was decided upon as the sounder strategy, and Frémont withdrew. For Vice-

Election of 1864

[1] An excellent discussion of Copperheadism is contained in W. D. Foulke, *Life of Oliver P. Morton* (2 vols., 1899).

President, at Lincoln's insistence, the Union Party (the name Republican was still carefully avoided) named Andrew Johnson of Tennessee, a War Democrat who had no Republican connections whatever. The Democrats made an undignified straddle. For President they chose General McClellan, whose loss of favor with the Lincoln administration had made him a kind of Democratic rallying-point, while at the same time writing a peace-at-almost-any-price platform.[1] McClellan accepted the nomination, but denounced the platform. "No peace," he asserted, "can be permanent without union." For a while it seemed that surely Lincoln would lose, but northern victories changed the situation, and the Union ticket won. The electoral vote showed 212 for Lincoln to 21 for McClellan, but the popular vote was very close. In New York, for example, Lincoln's majority was less than 7000 out of a total of 730,000.

By Inauguration Day, March 4, 1865, the war was nearly over, and Lincoln promised, "with malice toward none, with charity for all ... to bind up the nation's wounds." But he was not permitted to have a part in the work of restoration, for on the follow- **Death of Lincoln** ing April 15, less than a week after Lee's surrender, he was dead. His assassination, coming as it did at the very hour of victory, forced a reappraisal of his capacities, with the result that his name and fame were soon coupled in the public mind with Washington's.[2] Even *Punch*, the English periodical, which had repeatedly heaped ridicule upon him, made the following graceful recantation:

> Beside this corpse that bears for winding sheet
> The Stars and Stripes he lived to rear anew,
> Between the mourners at his head and feet,
> Say, scurrile jester, is there room for you?
>
> Yes, he had lived to shame me from my sneer,
> To lame my pencil and confute my pen;
> To make me own this hind of princes peer,
> This rail-splitter a true-born king of men.

Lincoln and his contemporaries interpreted the victory of the North as primarily a triumph of nationalism over states' rights. That the Union was now in fact "one and indivisible," whatever theoretical views some individuals might continue to hold, **Significance of the Civil War** was generally acknowledged, even by the defeated South. Incidentally, the institution of slavery, which had made the doctrine of states' rights its chief constitutional defense, was also brought to an end. While the Emancipation Proclamation had applied only to those states and parts of states that on January 1, 1863, were still at war

[1] E. C. Kirkland, *The Peacemakers of 1864* (1927); E. J. Benton, *The Movement for Peace Without Victory During the Civil War* (1918).

[2] Lloyd Lewis, *Myths after Lincoln* (1929), shows the beginning of the apotheosis of Lincoln· and Roy P. Basler, *The Lincoln Legend* (1935), its continuation.

with the United States, the momentum that Lincoln's action gave to the abolition movement was too great to be stopped. State action in Missouri, West Virginia, Maryland, Tennessee, and Louisiana had abolished slavery within their respective borders by the time the war was over. Meantime, a movement to write abolition into the national Constitution had gathered headway, and in January, 1865, Congress submitted to the states the Thirteenth Amendment, which forbade slavery or involuntary servitude, except as a punishment for crime, within the United States, or any place subject to its jurisdiction. By the end of the year this amendment had become a part of the Constitution. Whether a long civil war was necessary to secure the triumph of nationalism over states' rights and of abolitionism over slavery may well be doubted. Probably, with more skillful handling of a few crises, both ends might ultimately have been achieved without resort to war.

A factor not fully understood at the time, and possibly overemphasized today, was the commanding importance that the new industrial interests won during the course of the struggle. War profits compounded the capital of the industrialists and placed them in a position to dominate the economic life, not only of the Northeast where they were chiefly concentrated, but also of the nation at large. With the southern planters removed from the national scene, the government at Washington tended more and more to reflect the wishes of the industrial leaders. The protective tariff, impossible as long as southern influence predominated in national affairs, became the cornerstone of the new business edifice, for by means of it the vast and growing American market was largely restricted to American industry. Transcontinental railroads, designed to complete the national transportation system, were likewise accorded the generous assistance of the government, while a national banking act and a national currency facilitated still further the spread of nation-wide business.

Industrial supremacy

The Northwest, where industry was definitely subordinate to agriculture, profited less from the war than the Northeast, but Westerners applauded the passage of the Homestead Act, which threw the national domain open to settlers, and they were for a time as eager as the Easterners to accelerate the expansion of the railroads. By assisting in the defeat of the South, however, the Northwest had unknowingly sacrificed a valuable ally. Before the war the two agricultural sections had repeatedly stood together, first against the commercial, and later against the industrial, Northeast. Now, with the weight of the South in the Union immensely lessened, the Northwest was left to wage its battles virtually alone. For more than a generation after the war, with eastern men and eastern policies in the ascendancy, American industry steadily consolidated the gains it had made.

21

The Problem of the South

WITH the spring of 1865 the American Civil War had worn itself out, but the tardy arrival of peace introduced other difficulties more appalling, perhaps, than the nation had ever faced before. The South, after four years of warfare within its borders, was not only defeated; its whole pattern of social organization lay in hopeless ruins. How were the people of the New South to live? What was to be the status of the freedmen? When and how were the normal processes of government to be resumed? Nor were the problems of the day confined wholly, or even mainly, to the South. The government of the United States, and, indeed, the governments of the northern states also, had become accustomed to the exercise of unusual wartime prerogatives. Were these practices to become permanent, or were they to be trimmed to fit the needs of peace? A million men were under arms. How could their speedy absorption into the ordinary walks of life be best facilitated? A huge national debt, an inflated currency, an overgrown system of taxation were parts of the inevitable legacy of war. What should the new financial picture be like? Manufactures of many sorts and kinds, stimulated by war orders and war profits, had reached a phenomenal development. Could their prosperity be preserved with the nation at peace? Agriculture, too, particularly in the Northwest, had expanded abnormally. How were the farmers to find markets for their produce? Less tangible, but no less important, the peoples of North and South for full four years had unbridled their prejudices, each against the other, and had carefully nourished their hatreds. How were the two parts of the restored Union ever to become one again in spirit? How could they learn to forgive and forget?

"Reconstruction" is the label that historians have generally applied to these post-war years. The word gained currency on the eve of the Civil War, when a "reconstruction of the Union" that would satisfy the South was often suggested as an alternative to secession. It was applied during and immediately after the war to the "reconstruction" of loyal governments in states from

Post-war problems

Reconstruction

which secessionist officials had fled. As a descriptive term it leaves much
to be desired. Neither the pre-war South nor the pre-war Union could
ever be rebuilt or restored. Out of the ordeal of war and its aftermath
there emerged a new nation, a nation so different from the old that the
term "revolution" would scarcely overstate. But "reconstruction" has
the sanction of long usage, and, properly redefined, it may still be permitted to serve. In a narrow sense, "reconstruction" means the process
by which state government was revived in the South; broadly speaking,
it must include all the drastic transformations of the period, both North
and South.

Four years of warfare had left their marks upon the South.[1] Armies
had marched, camped, foraged, and fought in practically every southern
state, and in some of them almost continuously. Sherman's

Conditions in the South
exultant report of the desolation wrought by his column on
the way from Atlanta to the sea speaks for itself:

> We have consumed the corn and fodder in the region of country thirty miles
> on either side of a line from Atlanta to Savannah as also the sweet potatoes,
> cattle, hogs, sheep and poultry, and have carried away more than 10,000
> horses and mules as well as a countless number of slaves. I estimate the
> damage done to the State of Georgia and its military resources at $100,000,-
> 000; at least $20,000,000 of which has inured to our advantage and the
> remainder is simple waste and destruction.

As Sherman's army turned northward into South Carolina, it vented its
fury upon the state that most Northerners held responsible for starting
the war. Carl Schurz reported, from observations made six months
later, that the countryside along the "track of Sherman's march"

> looked for many miles like a broad black streak of ruin and desolation — the
> fences all gone; lonesome smoke stacks, surrounded by dark heaps of ashes
> and cinders, marking the spots where human habitations had stood; the
> fields along the road wildly overgrown by weeds, with here and there a sickly
> looking patch of cotton or corn cultivated by negro squatters.

Traveling through Virginia in October, 1865, Alexander H. Stephens
wrote in his diary: "The desolation of the country from Alexandria to
near Charlottesville was horrible to behold." Around Petersburg, where
the forces of Grant and Lee had fought under conditions resembling
modern trench warfare, farmers were stopped in their plowing by the
quantity of metal they found in the ground, and the stench of death
ended only with the autumn frosts. The Shenandoah Valley was so

---

[1] An excellent picture of post-war conditions in the South is contained in W. L. Fleming,
The Sequel of Appomattox (1919). E. P. Oberholtzer, *A History of the United States since
the Civil War* (5 vols., 1917-37), begins at this point to be useful. W. A. Dunning, *Reconstruction, Political and Economic* (1907), set a pattern for historical thinking on the problem that has only recently been challenged.

thoroughly denuded that, in accordance with Sheridan's promise "a crow could not fly over it without carrying his rations with him." Several years after the war an English traveler in America found the Valley of the Tennessee little better:

> It consists for the most part of plantations in a state of semi-ruin, and plantations of which the ruin is total and complete.... The trail of war is visible throughout the valley in burnt-up gin-houses, ruined bridges, mills, and factories, of which latter the gable walls only are left standing, and in large tracts of once cultivated land stripped of every vestige of fencing. The roads, long neglected, are in disorder, and having in many places become impassable, new tracks have been made through the woods and fields without much respect to boundaries. Borne down by losses, debts, and accumulating taxes, many who were once the richest among their fellows have disappeared from the scene, and few have yet risen to take their places.[1]

The sight of Charleston, once the proudest city of the South, moved the war-hardened Schurz to rhetoric:

> There was no shipping in the harbor except a few quartermaster's vessels and two or three small steamers. We made fast to a decaying pier constructed of palmetto-logs. There was not a human being visible on the wharf. The warehouses seemed to be completely deserted. There was no wall and no roof that did not bear eloquent marks of having been under the fire of siege guns.... Nothing could be more desolate and melancholy than the appearance of the lower part of the city immediately adjoining the harbor. Although the military authorities had caused the streets to be "policed" as well as possible, abundant grass had still grown up between the paving stones. The first living object that struck my view ... was a dilapidated United States cavalry horse bearing the mark I.C. — inspected and condemned — now peacefully browsing on the grass in a Charleston street. A few cows were feeding in a vacant lot near by, surrounded by buildings gashed and shattered by shell and solid shot. The crests of the roofs and the chimneys were covered with turkey-buzzards, who evidently felt at home, and who from time to time lazily flapped their wings and stretched their hideous necks. Proceeding higher up into the city, we passed through a part of the "burned district," looking like a vast graveyard with broken walls and tall blackened chimneys for monuments, overtopped by the picturesque ruins of the cathedral.[2]

Many another southern city had been similarly despoiled. Columbia, the thriving pre-war capital of South Carolina, was the customary "mass of blackened chimneys and crumbling walls." The fire that destroyed it had swept eighty-four blocks, and had consumed every building for "three-fourths of a mile on each of twelve streets." Atlanta was a riot of tangled brick and mortar, charred timbers, and rubbish. "Hell has laid her egg," one Georgian observed, "and right here it hatched."

---

[1] Robert Somers, *The Southern States Since the War, 1870–71* (1871), p. 114. This is typical of the great mass of travel literature on the South.

[2] From *Reminiscences*, vol. III, by Carl Schurz (copyright, 1906, 1908, 1935. Reprinted by permission of Doubleday, Doran and Company, Inc.), p. 165.

Mobile, too, had suffered from fire and had fallen into "torpor and decay." Galveston was described as "a city of dogs and desolation."

The havoc that the war had wrought on the South's transportation system was one of the worst of the calamities from which it suffered.

Transportation

Columbia, South Carolina, had been a railway center before the war, with five lines converging upon it. By the time Sherman's troops had departed, the tracks had been torn up for thirty miles in every direction. Rolling stock was left standing in the fields to be used by the homeless as dwellings. Rails were heated in the middle and twisted fantastically around trees. Similar thoroughness had characterized railroad destruction in Georgia, Mississippi, and various other parts of the South, while the wear and tear of wartime usage without adequate repairs had made the railroads outside the devastated regions almost as worthless as those within. Before the war river traffic had played a large part in moving the produce of the South. Now river channels were blocked, steamboats were destroyed, and wharves were missing. Seaports, so essential to the trade of the pre-war South, were in similar disarray. Country roads were non-existent or worse; bridges were gone; horses, mules, oxen, carriages, wagons, and carts had all too frequently been commandeered by the troops of North or South.

Property losses suffered in the states of the former Confederacy should include numerous other items. The Confederate bonds, both

Southern losses from war

state and national, into which much southern capital had gone, had ceased altogether to be of value. So also had Confederate currency. Banks were closed; factories were idle; land values had toppled to nearly nothing; business in general was shattered. Property in slaves, which before the war accounted for so much of the South's wealth, was completely wiped out. Worse still, confiscation, contrary to a common opinion, took a heavy toll from the scanty resources of the defeated states. President Johnson tried to prevent this by ordering, in an amnesty proclamation issued May 29, 1865, that no further seizures of private property be made, and his Attorney-General helped still more by ruling that private property already seized must be restored to anyone who had received a presidential pardon. But it was generally agreed that the property of the Confederate government was now the property of the United States, and that all such property must be located and attached.

It was from the attempt to seize this public property that the South came to know what confiscation might mean. Agents of the Treasury

Confiscation

Department, sent South on a twenty-five per cent commission basis to locate the 150,000 bales of cotton that the Confederate government was supposed to have had on hand at the close of the war, developed a tendency to take whatever cotton they happened to find, and to turn over to the United States only such of their takings as they saw fit. "I am sure I sent some honest cotton agents South," Secretary of the Treasury McCulloch admitted ruefully, "but it sometimes seems doubtful whether any of them remained honest for long." Not only cotton, but livestock, tobacco, rice, sugar, or anything of value was seized by individuals who represented themselves as agents of the United States. The total sum realized by the Treasury from seizures was $34,000,000, a considerable part of which was later returned. But this sum represents only a fraction of the damage done. With laudable candor Secretary McCulloch reported in 1866:

> Contractors, anxious for gain, were sometimes guilty of bad faith and peculation, and frequently took possession of cotton and delivered it under contracts as captured or abandoned, when in fact it was not such and they had no right to touch it. . . . Residents and others in the districts where these peculations were going on took advantage of the unsettled condition of the country, and representing themselves as agents of this department, went about robbing under such pretended authority, and thus added to the difficulties of the situation by causing unjust opprobrium and suspicion to rest upon officers engaged in the faithful discharge of their duties. Agents, . . . frequently received or collected property, and sent it forward which the law did not authorize them to take. . . . Lawless men, singly and in organized bands, engaged in general plunder; every species of intrigue and peculation and theft were resorted to.

In assessing the damage done the South by the war, the personal element must not be ignored. Perhaps a quarter of a million soldiers and an untold number of civilians lost their lives because of the clash of arms. Among those who perished were a large portion of the natural leaders of the South — men who, had **The southern people** they lived, could have helped most during the trials of the reconstruction era. Many of the survivors were themselves immeasurably the worse for their experiences; even when they were not maimed or broken in body, men trained in the school of war could never be quite the same as if trained in the normal pursuits of peace. As for the Negroes, the boon of freedom was not without its unfortunate consequences. Before the end of the war about 180,000 of them had been enrolled as free soldiers in the United States Armies, others were merely camp-followers and refugees. The downfall of the Confederacy plunged all the rest into freedom — a state of society for which they were almost totally unprepared. As slaves, they had looked to their masters for food, shelter, and protection. As free men they had little idea how to provide such things for themselves. Freedom meant freedom from work, and the right to leave the plantation at will; that it might carry with it unpleasant responsibilities few of the Negroes were able to understand. Some stayed with the old masters and worked on as if nothing had happened; others wandered away to places they had never seen before. During the spring and summer of 1865 they could be found in bands like gypsies, roving the country, and emulating Sherman's "bummers" in their search for food. From one point of view the abolition of slavery had cost the South nothing. The Negroes were still there, and they could do as much work as ever before — if only they would. But the evidence compounded that most of the ex-slaves, temporarily at least, had no will to work. And with the blacks constituting nearly forty per cent of the total population, this was a frightfully serious matter.[1]

At the present time the people of the United States, or of any other great power, if confronted with such a condition as existed in the South of 1865, would take it for granted that the government must
National policy play the principal part in restoring the economic life of the war-stricken section. In the middle of the nineteenth century, however, there were few who would have thought of such a thing. The "less government the better" was still the dominant philosophy, not only of the Democrats, but also of the great majority of the Republicans; indeed, the doctrine of rugged individualism, whether derived from the experience of the American frontier, or from the writings of European savants, or from both, was never more universally accepted. In the main, therefore, the economic problems of the South were regarded as the concern of individuals, rather than of the government, and in their solution the government gave only incidental assistance.

The necessity of direct aid for the freedmen, however, was something that could not easily be overlooked. The power of the national government had been used to free the slaves; hence the Negroes,
The Freedmen's Bureau now that they were free, had become in a sense the wards of the nation. The freedmen themselves were by no means unaware of this obligation. Just as their masters had cared for them in the past, so now they expected their "deliverers" to look after them. That Congress was ready to accept such responsibility, at least for a limited time, was shown by the passage in March, 1865, of an act creating the Freedmen's Bureau. This organization, which was to last for a year after the close of the war, was to be set up in the War Department under a commissioner appointed by the President, and an assistant commissioner for each of the insurrectionary states. It was authorized to distribute "such issues of provisions, clothing, and fuel" as might be necessary to relieve the "destitute and suffering refugees and

[1] W. E. B. DuBois, *Black Reconstruction* (1935), and A. A. Taylor, *The Negro in South Carolina During the Reconstruction* (1924), present the problem from the Negro's point of view. See also B. G. Brawley, *Social History of the American Negro* (1921), and G. W. Williams, *History of the Negro Race in America* (2 vols., 1882).

freedmen and their wives and children." It had also the right to take over any land within the designated states that had been abandoned by its owners or confiscated by the United States, and to distribute it in tracts of forty acres or less, on a three-year rental basis, to "loyal refugees and freedmen."

Under the leadership of General Oliver O. Howard, an able and conscientious man, the Freedmen's Bureau went promptly to work.[1] Its agents soon penetrated to every portion of the South, and were kept busy, for a time, distributing the bare necessities of life to hundreds of thousands of needy, white as well as black. Without this assistance there can be no doubt that many of both races would have starved to death; or, one might properly say, many more might have starved than did. The Bureau also made a laudable effort to provide its dependents with medical care and hospitalization, but among the Negroes, who knew so little about how to take care of themselves, illness took a frightful toll. The mortality among Negro children, who in slavery times would often have been nursed through their illnesses by the plantation mistress herself, but now had to depend upon the pitifully inadequate ministrations of their parents, was particularly appalling.

The plan to distribute abandoned land to the freedmen led to an unfortunate misunderstanding. It was inferred at first that all land "abandoned" because its owners had left it for Confederate service would be available for distribution, but President Johnson's policy permitted the pardoned owners of such property to recover it. The result was that the Bureau had comparatively little land of value to give away. The Negro, however, got the impression, often deliberately spread by unscrupulous agents, that each freedman would soon be given "forty acres of land and a mule." Some included, for good measure, a white man to do the work. With so rosy a prospect for the future, and an abundance of free rations for the present, many of the Negroes found it difficult to see why they should do more than await the day of "jubilee." For some of them this day was dated. On January 1, 1866, they believed, the redistribution of land would take place.

"Forty acres and a mule"

In noting the governmental assistance given to the South after the war, one should remember the army of occupation. For several years detachments of Federal troops were not far away in any part of the South, and there were regions in which the hated "blue-bellies," as they were inelegantly termed, were very numerous. The northern army, always abundantly provided with ra-

The army of occupation

[1] The Freedmen's Bureau has been the subject of many historical studies. Among the best are Paul S. Peirce, *The Freedmen's Bureau* (1904), and Laura J. Webster, *The Operation of the Freedmen's Bureau in South Carolina* (1916).

tions, clothing, and other supplies, shared its plenty with the destitute. This was the more natural because some of the Federal troops were themselves Negroes. When the war ended, most of the whites in the Federal army had taken the first opportunity to be "mustered out," but the Negroes had shown no such eagerness, and many of them were allowed to remain in the service. The soldiers, whether white or black, had money to spend, and the government spent still larger sums for their maintenance. Directly or indirectly, the army thus contributed an appreciable amount to the economic rehabilitation of the South.

One other item of governmental aid to the South deserves mention, and that, curiously, was given to the southern railroads.[1] While northern troops accounted for an enormous amount of railroad destruction, it is also a fact that wherever the operations of the Federal army required the reconditioning of the railroads, that, too, was done. In those portions of the upper South that the North had long held, the railroads were actually left in better condition than they were found. At the end of the war the United States War Department even went so far as to take over and reorganize some of the bankrupt railroad companies, and then, with "loyal" boards of directors assured, to return them to their owners.

Private benevolence added a little to the aid given by the government. The Negroes, naturally, were the recipients of much such attention.

Private benevolence   Even before the end of the war the American Missionary Association, for example, had begun a work among them that led to expenditures after the return of peace of about $100,000 annually, mostly on Negro education. Also, the churches of the North sent a sizable army of missionaries, preachers, and teachers into the South. At first many such individuals assumed that the collapse of the Confederacy meant that the separate southern churches would also cease to exist, and that reunion under northern domination would follow immediately, with themselves in prominent positions. This failed to happen, but the missionary zeal of the northern workers found a ready outlet in helping the Negroes adjust themselves to freedom. They induced most of the ex-slaves to separate from the churches of their former masters, and to form new churches of their own. They used northern missionary money to build and maintain Negro churches and schools, and to care for the needy. Among the most active in this respect were the agents of the Freedmen's Aid Society of the Methodist Episcopal Church, but similar work was supported by the Baptists, the Presbyterians, and many other denominations.

Philanthropy, although then in its infancy, furnished another source

[1] Carl Russell Fish, *The Restoration of the Southern Railroads* (1919).

of outside income to the South. The most notable donation of money came from George Peabody, who gave the income from a fund of two million dollars, or more, "to the suffering South for the good of the whole country." The Peabody Education Fund was wisely administered, and proved to be an effective aid to the establishment of better common schools in the South. The Negroes themselves were pathetically eager for book-learning, and flocked into whatever schools were provided for them. Most of them, however, showed no great proficiency beyond the elementary stages, and the wisest of their advisers were soon counseling them to seek vocational training rather than the higher learning, including Greek and Latin, that altogether too many of them craved.

Philanthropy

Southerners were at first hopeful that a great outpouring of northern capital would aid in the rehabilitation of the South, but in this they were to be sadly disappointed. Northern investors did, indeed, buy southern railway securities in sufficient amounts to make possible a rapid recovery on the part of the southern railroads, and they also purchased, to their later regret, the new bond issues of the southern states. But their southern investments went little further. The North, with its own fields of endeavor to look after — industrial expansion, agricultural extension, the building of transcontinental railroads, the development of the mining and ranching West — had little left to risk in a region where political conditions were disturbed and a racial conflict was in the making. Thrown back upon its own meager resources, the South made numerous small beginnings in the lumbering industry, in the manufacture of tobacco, in the establishment of cotton mills, in the exploitation of its resources in coal and iron, as well as in the restoration of its agricultural activities, particularly the growing of cotton, which became again, as before the war, its chief concern.

Scarcity of capital

Fortunately for the South the world had need of cotton, but to restore production was no easy matter. Seed was lacking, tools and machinery were worn out, horses and mules were scarce, and the labor supply was an unknown quantity. Many Southerners, convinced that without slavery the Negroes could never be induced to work, hoped to devise some scheme for sending them back to Africa or to the West Indies; and still more believed that the salvation of the South lay in replacing or supplementing Negro labor with that of immigrants from Europe or elsewhere. But the Negroes would not go and the immigrants would not come. Some of the planters attempted to revive the old plantation system on the basis of free labor. Backed with whatever money the promise of cotton enabled them to borrow in Europe or in the North, they offered the Negroes wages to return to their former

Cotton culture

duties. Such a transaction was apt to be carefully watched by the Freed-men's Bureau, which usually insisted on a written contract, with the amount of wages and the conditions of labor carefully set down. It was not the planter, however, who broke the contract, but the freedman, who rarely saw point to working after he had earned a few dollars. Delayed wages were sometimes tried, but with equally indifferent results. Other planters offered laborers a share in the annual proceeds of the plantation, but this system, likewise, proved defective. The freedmen resented the necessity of working in gangs, as in slavery times, and even more, the existence of anything bordering on oversight.

In the end the plantation system had to go, and in a sense the promise of "forty acres and a mule" was realized. The planters found by experi-

The southern
tenant system

ence that only when they split up their land into small plots, with a Negro, or it might be a white tenant, in charge of each, could they obtain satisfactory results. Each tenant had usually to be supplied with not only his mule, but his seed, his tools, and his living until the crop was harvested; all this the landlord either furnished directly, or by obtaining credit for his tenants at one of the numerous "country stores" that sprang up all over the South. A crop lien secured both the landlord and the storekeeper against loss. As a rule the tenant turned over from a third to a half of his produce to the landlord as rental, and all the rest went to repay his debts; but by working along on his own time in his own way he at least produced a part of a crop. His status, bound as he was by his crop lien, lay somewhere be-tween slavery and freedom, but it amounted, perhaps, to as great a change as his limited experience would permit. The first few crops after the war, with the Negroes unsettled and the Freedmen's Bureau at hand to back them up in fantastic demands, were miserable failures, but by 1869 a cotton crop worth a quarter of a billion dollars was marketed. From that time forward the acute poverty of the South began to abate.[1]

So much attention has been focused upon the Negroes, whether slave or free, that the rôle of the small white farmer of the South has rarely

The white
farmer

received the prominence that it deserves. Even before the Civil War white labor accounted for a considerable part of the South's crop of cotton, and after the war the proportion tended to increase. In general the land worked by the whites in the time of slavery was inferior to that included in the great plantations and worked by slaves. But after the war the planters were glad to obtain tenants, white as well as black, and they often found it necessary to sell a part, or even all, of their holdings. Independent ownership was greatly

[1] M. B. Hammond, *The Cotton Industry* (1897), is a book of enduring merit. Consult also R. P. Brooks, *The Agrarian Revolution in Georgia, 1865–1912* (1914).

stimulated by the low prices that landowners were obliged to accept. Land that had been worth from twenty to thirty dollars an acre before the war sold for from three to five dollars an acre after the war, and sometimes for less. Many of the whites who had owned poor land before, or no land at all, took advantage of this remarkable opportunity to buy. In ten years, according to the census of 1870, the number of farms in South Carolina had increased from 33,000 to 52,000; in Mississippi, from 43,000 to 68,000; in Louisiana, from 17,000 to 28,000. In the other southern states the figures, while not so striking, show the same general trend. Some of the new landowners were Negroes, but their holdings were generally very small, and most of the land that changed hands went to whites. A considerable number of Northerners were attracted into the South by the low prices of land, but most of them were unable to adjust themselves satisfactorily to the new environment.

While cotton was the best money crop of the South, it must not be forgotten that southern agriculture, both before and after the war, produced some of nearly everything that can be grown on farms. Rice culture, which had been an important activity *Rice, sugar, and tobacco* in South Carolina and Georgia before the war, showed in those states few symptoms of revival, but in Louisiana the production of both rice and sugar-cane was successfully undertaken. Tobacco-growing in the upper South made rapid headway, particularly in Kentucky, where the crop increased from 54,000,000 pounds in 1865 to 103,-000,000 pounds in 1871.[1] In the states where cotton had never been "king," and where in consequence the concentration of Negroes had been less marked, the problem of restoring normal production was far more easily solved. After the first two or three hard years, livestock and foodstuffs could be found practically anywhere in abundance.

Unfortunately, the valiant efforts of the South to work out a new economic system proved to be of far less concern to the national government than the strictly political problem. Even in this field, little "post-war planning" had been undertaken, although Lin- *Lincoln's plan of reconstruction* coln had been obliged as early as 1862 to appoint military, or provisional, governors for states occupied mainly by Union troops, and to devise a system for the establishment of civil government within their borders. In December, 1863, he set forth in detail a generous plan of reconstruction. With some reasonable exceptions, it promised pardons to all residents of conquered states who would take a prescribed oath of allegiance to the United States, and, whenever in any state as many as one-tenth of the number of persons who had voted in 1860 should

[1] Meyer Jacobstine, *The Tobacco Industry in the United States* (1907); B. W. Arnold, *History of the Tobacco Industry in Virginia from 1860 to 1894* (1897).

take the oath, a civil government was to be inaugurated which the President bound himself to recognize "as the true government of the state." Operating under this plan, three states, Tennessee, Louisiana, and Arkansas, succeeded during the year 1864 in re-creating state governments, and were accorded presidential recognition. The President also recognized a loyal, although decidedly impotent, government in Virginia that throughout the war had maintained a precarious existence at Alexandria.[1]

Lincoln's easy plan for the formation of new, and supposedly loyal, governments in the South was resented by many congressmen, even of the President's own party. They feared that such magnanimous terms might produce a combination of ex-secessionists and ex-Copperheads that would eventually oust the Republicans from control of the national government. They branded the President's failure to consult Congress on so important a matter as "executive usurpation," and in July, 1864, pushed through Congress the Wade-Davis Bill as a substitute for the President's plan. This bill failed because of a pocket veto, but Lincoln in a formal proclamation described it as "one very proper plan for the loyal people of any state choosing to adopt it." Undoubtedly Lincoln would have made some kind of terms with the congressional opposition had he lived, but at his last cabinet meeting he expressed his desire to "reanimate the states" before Congress should meet again.

Lincoln's death brought to the Presidency a man whom the Radicals, as the Republican extremists were generally called, felt certain they could use. Andrew Johnson (1808–75) was both a Southerner and a Democrat, but he was not of the southern ruling caste, and as a fairly typical representative of the poorer people of the South he was a bitter opponent of the southern aristocrats. Born in North Carolina, he had migrated at an early age to Greeneville, Tennessee, where he worked at his trade as a tailor, and ultimately became the proprietor of a moderately prosperous tailor shop. Even as a youth he was interested in oratory, and his love of argumentation seems to have furnished the stimulus that drove him persistently forward in his quest for learning. As a highly effective rough-and-tumble debater, he drifted easily into politics — a Democratic denouncer of the aristocratic Whigs — and for twenty years before he became President he had been a power in Tennessee politics. Although he had voted for Breckinridge in 1860, he had utterly refused to become a party to the destruction of the Union, and alone among the senators from the seceding states had stayed at his desk in the Senate. Johnson's obstinacy and tactlessness

Andrew Johnson

[1] J. W. Patton, *Unionism and Reconstruction in Tennessee* (1934); J. R. Ficklen, *History of Reconstruction in Louisiana* (1910); T. S. Staples, *Reconstruction in Arkansas* (1923); H. J. Eckenrode, *Political History of Virginia During Reconstruction* (1904).

were not unknown, and, except for his devotion to the Union, his political principles were far removed from the majority of those who had voted for him. But the Radicals believed that because he shared their hatred of the southern leaders he would become a pliant tool in Radical hands.

It soon transpired that Johnson, from the Radical point of view, was quite as untrustworthy as Lincoln. The southern aristocrat, he quickly noted, was at the moment as penniless and powerless as his humblest neighbor. As a Southerner, he knew also how unprepared the ex-slave was for the duties of citizenship, and he cherished as deeply as any aristocrat the right of the states to deal with internal problems without undue interference from the national government. And so he not only kept Lincoln's Cabinet, but he also accepted as legal the loyal governments that Lincoln had recognized in the South, and during the summer of 1865 began a process of reconstruction of his own that was as breathtaking in its generosity as anything Lincoln himself could have devised.[1]

Johnson's plan was to appoint in each of the unreconstructed states a provisional governor — a local man, not an outsider — who would call together a constitutional convention. The delegates to this convention were to be chosen by such of the members of the old white electorate as were now ready and willing to take the oath of allegiance to the United States. The constitutional conventions on assembling were required (1) to invalidate their old ordinances of secession, (2) to abolish slavery, and (3) to repudiate all debts contracted in order to aid the Confederacy in its prosecution of the war; but otherwise they were as free as any other such conventions to write into their constitutions whatever they chose. Johnson specifically acknowledged that it was their privilege to decide who should vote and who should hold office, but he let it be known privately that, for the effect such action would have upon the northern Radicals, he hoped that Negroes who could read and write, or who owned a small amount of real estate, would be permitted to vote. With their constitutions rewritten, the states might elect their own governors, legislators, and other officers, and resume their place in the Union. Naturally this plan was enthusiastically accepted by the southern states, and was carried through with a maximum of speed. Before the end of the year 1865, the President was able to tell Congress that only in Florida and Texas was the work of restoration incomplete, and that in these states it would be finished soon. None of the states, however, saw fit to take Johnson's advice about

Johnson's plan of reconstruction

---

[1] The career of Andrew Johnson has been generously re-estimated. Claude G. Bowers, *The Tragic Era* (1929), is extremely readable but somewhat overdrawn. George Fort Milton, *The Age of Hate* (1930), is eminently fair. Less satisfactory in the order mentioned are R. W. Winston, *Andrew Johnson, Plebeian and Patriot* (1928), and L. P. Stryker, *Andrew Johnson* (1929).

Negro voting, and most of them chose their old secessionist leaders to represent them again in the Senate and House of Representatives at Washington.

The President's defense of what he had done was presented in an able message to Congress, the happy phraseology of which was due to the skillful pen of George Bancroft, the historian. The meaning of the message, however, was the President's own. In it he maintained, more insistently than Lincoln had thought advisable, that the southern states, as such, had never ceased to exist, but had merely been in a state of suspended vitality. It had been his duty to assist in restoring them to their rightful energy, and this duty he had performed as "gradually and quietly" as possible. Inasmuch as he had found no constitutional warrant to do otherwise, he had left with the states themselves the problem of enfranchisement of the freedmen. As for the delegations that the restored states had sent to Congress, he believed that the adoption of the Thirteenth Amendment warranted their reception, but of this each house of Congress must judge for itself. That Congress had no notion of being bound by the President's action was at once apparent. A "Joint Committee on Reconstruction," composed of nine representatives and six senators, was promptly created with authority to inquire into the condition of the former Confederate states, and to ascertain whether they were entitled to representation in Congress.

Opposition to the President's policy toward the South was most effectively voiced in the House by Thaddeus Stevens (1792–1868), a Pennsylvania representative whose political career dated as far back as the Anti-Masonic Party, in which he was prominent.[1] Stevens had long hated the institution of slavery, and before the war had opposed all concessions to the slaveholders. His ill-temper toward the South continued during and after the war, and his resentment toward Lincoln's easy plan of reconstruction was widely known. The southern states, he held, were no longer states, but only "conquered provinces" with which Congress might deal as it chose; Lincoln's pocket veto of the Wade-Davis Bill was nothing less than "infamous." Lame from his birth, old and perilously ill, unmarried and cared for only by a faithful colored housekeeper, his one passion became the ruthless punishment of the South. Congressmen had already learned to fear his lashing tongue, and he proposed to destroy Johnson, whose easy terms of reconstruction he despised.

Thaddeus Stevens

No less the enemy of Johnson than Stevens was Charles Sumner

[1] Richard Nelson Current, *Old Thad Stevens* (1942), is a sympathetic attempt at reevaluation of Stevens's career. Older studies of some merit are James A. Woodburn, *The Life of Thaddeus Stevens* (1913); Samuel W. McCall, *Thaddeus Stevens* (1899); T. F. Woodley, *Thaddeus Stevens* (1934).

(1811–74), the Republican senator from Massachusetts whose body still bore the marks of Preston Brooks's assault.[1] His whole life long Sumner had been a favored member of the Boston intelligentsia. He was a graduate of Harvard, a student of history and the classics, a friend of nearly every New Englander who had won distinction in the realm of literature, and a European traveler whose *entrée* into the highest political and intellectual circles was never denied. The soul of honor, and upright to a fault, he was vain of his own abilities, and utterly contemptuous of lesser mortals. He had always opposed slavery, and he now opposed the immunity from punishment that presidential reconstruction had offered the South. In his opinion the seceding states, by their treasonous acts, were guilty of "state suicide." Because they had ceased to exist as states, Congress had the same authority over them that it had always exercised over the territories. A firm believer in political equality for all men, he urged Negro suffrage as a primary condition for the reconstruction of the seceded states.

Charles Sumner

Unfortunately, the state governments set up under Johnson's plan gave unintended assistance to Stevens and Sumner in their war on the President. Realizing far better than the Northerners the great gap that lay between slavery and freedom, the restored states had enacted "black codes," or "black laws," that prescribed an inferior legal status for the ex-slaves. At best these laws were meant to protect the Negroes from their own ignorance and helplessness; at worst they were meant to keep them at work and to circumscribe their freedom as much as possible. In the North they were very generally denounced as evidence that the South had no notion whatever of living up to the terms of the Thirteenth Amendment. Radicals could also point to the prevalence of racial conflicts in the South, particularly between the lower-class southern whites and the Negroes, whose long-standing hatred for one another was greatly aggravated by emancipation. They complained, too, that cordial hatred of the North was freely expressed, and Carl Schurz, whom the President himself had sent on a tour of the South, found the South was in no wise repentant, and still regretful that it had lost the war.[2]

The "black codes"

The first important test of strength between the forces led by the Pres-

[1] Moorfield Storey, *Charles Sumner* (1900), is a satisfactory biography, but see also E. L. Pierce, *Memoir and Letters of Charles Sumner* (4 vols., 1877–93). Excellent short sketches of the leading participants in American history are to be found in the *Dictionary of American Biography* (20 vols., 1928–36), edited by Allen Johnson and Dumas Malone.

[2] Schurz's "Report on Conditions in the South" is published in Frederic Bancroft (editor), *Speeches, Correspondence and Political Papers of Carl Schurz* (6 vols., 1913), I, 279–374. Paul H. Buck, *The Road to Reunion, 1865–1900* (1937), traces with impartial hand the slow process of reconciliation between the victorious North and the defeated South.

ident and those led by Stevens and Sumner came over the Freedmen's
Bureau. Should this organization be allowed to live longer

The Freedmen's Bureau Bill

than the year after the war for which it had originally been created? The Radicals hoped to continue the Bureau, and through it to make the Negroes into loyal supporters of the national government and the Republican Party. But Johnson with his states'-rights views was ready to turn the whole Negro problem over to the states. On this issue, which was carefully chosen, an overwhelming majority in Congress favored the Radicals, so a Freedmen's Bureau Bill such as they desired soon reached the President's desk. As anticipated, he vetoed it, but to the dismay of the Radicals the Senate, with only a few votes to spare, sustained the veto. This development greatly elated Johnson, for he believed now that by use of the veto power he would be able to kill all legislation hostile to his plan of reconstruction. But in this he was mistaken. Always tactless, he took occasion to denounce the Radical leaders by name, and to cast aspersions on their loyalty. As a result, when a Civil Rights Bill, which declared Negroes to be citizens of the United States and guaranteed them equality before the law, passed Congress and received a veto, many who had formerly supported Johnson turned against him. This time the veto was not sustained, the bill became a law in spite of the President's opposition, and the Radical triumph was complete. To show exactly how matters stood, Congress now revived the Freedmen's Bureau Bill in slightly altered form, and passed it over the President's veto. Thus it seemed apparent that the Radicals, if they chose, could undo the President's plan of reconstruction, and substitute for it one of their own.

This was exactly what the Joint Committee on Reconstruction had decided to do. After a spectacular sequence of hearings, it proposed in

The Fourteenth Amendment

the early summer of 1866 a Fourteenth Amendment to the Constitution which, after some revision in the Senate, was duly submitted to the states for adoption. The first section of the amendment, which virtually restated the terms of the Civil Rights Bill, declared all persons born or naturalized in the United States to be citizens of the United States, and forbade the states to abridge in any way the privileges and immunities of such citizens, or to "deprive any person of life, liberty, or property without due process of law." The second section, to the disappointment of such extremists as Stevens, did not require Negro suffrage, but provided that a state which denied the suffrage to any of its male inhabitants over twenty-one years of age, "except for participation in rebellion or other crime," would have its basis of representation in Congress and in the Electoral College correspondingly reduced. The third section was designed to make ineligible for officeholding all ex-Confederate leaders, regardless of whatever presidential pardons they might have received. The fourth section provided that the debt of the United States, incurred to preserve the Union, should never be questioned, while the debt of the southern states and the Confederacy, incurred to destroy it, should never be paid. A fifth section gave Congress the power to enforce the amendment by appropriate legislation.

By the time this amendment was drafted, the mid-term congressional elections of 1866 were close at hand, and Congress refused to proceed further with its work until the people had been heard from. Would the country back up the President and his plan of reconstruction, or would it give Congress a mandate to go on with the program it had begun in submitting the Fourteenth Amendment? Congress declared one southern state, Tennessee, which alone among the ex-Confederate states had ratified the Fourteenth Amendment, to be fully restored, but left the status of the other ten in doubt until after election. The President cheerfully accepted the challenge of the Radicals, made every effort to revive the Union Party, on whose ticket he had been elected to the Vice-Presidency, and even took a speech-making "swing around the circle" to Chicago and back. The Radicals were equally active and, as events proved, far more effective. They impressed northeastern industrialists with the danger of low-tariff legislation in case the Southerners should return unhumbled to a place of importance in the government; they charged that ex-Copperheads and ex-secessionists might either repudiate the national war debt or pay it off in depreciated paper currency; they made all manner of fun of the President whose speeches were invariably intemperate, and often in bad taste. By the time the election was held, its outcome was no longer in doubt. The Radicals carried both houses of Congress by staggering majorities, and the total defeat of the President's program was assured.

When Congress convened in December, 1866, it promptly laid out a plan of reconstruction far more radical than anything embodied in the Fourteenth Amendment. It proposed, in spite of the fact that two years had elapsed since the end of the war, to undo as completely as possible all that Lincoln and Johnson had done to restore normal civil government in the ten southern states unrecognized by Congress. Military rule was to be resumed, with the South divided into five military districts and an officer of the United States Army not below the rank of brigadier-general in charge of each. Each general, duly supported by an adequate military force, must register all the legal voters, excluding all who had ever been disfranchised for dis-

Election of 1866

Radical reconstruction

loyalty, and admitting Negroes on the same basis as whites. He must then call upon these voters to elect a constitutional convention, which should draw up a new constitution providing for Negro suffrage. If, on submission to the voters, this constitution should receive a popular majority, the general in charge should order the necessary elections to put it into effect; whereupon, if Congress should approve the new constitution, and if the legislature of the state should adopt the Fourteenth Amendment, and if as many as three-fourths of all the states should ratify the Fourteenth Amendment and so make it a part of the national Constitution, then and not until then should the representatives and senators of each restored state be considered eligible for admission to the two houses of Congress; and then, and not until then, should Federal troops be withdrawn from the state's borders. Furthermore, each of the newly chosen representatives and senators must be able to take the so-called "ironclad oath" that he had never given voluntary aid to the Confederacy.

The key to this plan of reconstruction was of course Negro suffrage. By giving the blacks the vote and by denying it to many whites the Radicals hoped to make sure that the southern states would long remain true to the Republican Party. They feared that, without such a provision, the Democratic Party might not only win the ascendancy in the South, but in the national government as well. Education of the Negroes in the belief that their freedom depended upon the preservation of Republican rule was well along, and the new scheme would give abundant time to complete the process.

Although Congress could now count on being able to pass any legislation it chose over the President's veto, the Radicals decided that they had had enough of Johnson, and would use their power to remove him from office. By the Tenure of Office Act, passed early in 1867, Congress made it a misdemeanor, punishable by fine and imprisonment, for the President to remove civil office-holders without the consent of the Senate. This law was designed not only to save from dismissal such Radical officials as had not yet been removed, but also because of its doubtful constitutionality to tempt the President to challenge it, and so to open the way for his impeachment. Johnson was ordinarily extremely scrupulous in the execution of the numerous laws that Congress kept passing over his veto, but he was finally irritated into a near-violation of the Tenure of Office Act. Edwin M. Stanton, the Secretary of War who had served under Lincoln, continued under Johnson, but soon went over in principle to the Radicals, for whom he became a kind of spy in the President's household. Finally the President could stand it no more, and in August, 1867, asked Stanton to resign. Stanton

Impeachment of Johnson

refused, whereupon Johnson suspended him from office, and as the law required asked the Senate's consent for his removal. This the Senate refused to give, and Stanton resumed his duties. Thoroughly outraged, Johnson now attempted to remove Stanton from office, although Stanton defiantly refused to yield possession. The Radicals, now in high glee, voted impeachment charges against the President in the House of Representatives, and as prescribed by the Constitution brought him to trial before the Senate. That the trial was purely political, few denied, and when the vote was taken seven Republican senators joined with twelve Democrats in voting for acquittal. Thus, by the narrow margin of one vote (35 to 19) the President was left in possession of his office. Technically, he had probably not violated the Tenure of Office Act at all, for that law seemed to contemplate the removal of Cabinet members appointed by a *preceding* President, and Lincoln, not Johnson, had appointed Stanton. After the failure of the impeachment proceedings, Stanton retired from office, and was succeeded by General J. M. Schofield.[1]

[1] R. N. Current, *Old Thad Stevens: A Story of Ambition* (1942), is objective and critical, and does much to rehabilitate Stevens's reputation, especially in his earlier years. F. B. Simkins, *The South Old and New, 1820–1942* (1947), follows the main currents of southern history. V. L. Wharton, *The Negro in Mississippi, 1865–1890* (1947), is a modern re-interpretation.

22

Radical Reconstruction

THE PROCESS of Radical reconstruction did not really begin in the South until two years after the end of the war. This was one of the reasons why it was so hard for the southern people to endure. At the end of the war they had expected harsh terms and were psychologically prepared to suffer them. Instead, they had been permitted to re-establish and maintain their own civil administrations without undue outside interference; then, to their great distress, the slate was wiped as clean as possible in 1867, and another beginning made, this time fully as harsh as had been anticipated before, and far less warranted.

In conformity with the Reconstruction Acts that Congress had passed over his veto, President Johnson placed a high-ranking army officer in charge of each of the five reconstruction districts of the South. These military overlords lacked nothing in authority, for they were set above existing state governments, which they might use or ignore as they chose. They had the power to make arrests, to conduct military trials, and to carry on as they saw fit the ordinary processes of civil government. Their main business was, of course, to organize new state governments according to the plan Congress had laid down. The first step in the process was to register the voters, a task that presented many difficulties. Army officers, Freedmen's Bureau agents, and loyal citizens generally, among them many Negroes, were made members of the registration boards. Eligible whites, although admonished by many of the best-beloved southern leaders to roll up the largest possible majorities for their race, were reluctant to register, but the Negroes presented themselves gladly.

Military rule in the South

Immediately at the close of the war, many Southerners had had no very great fear of Negro suffrage, believing that the blacks could be persuaded to vote as their former masters directed. Indeed, one of the most telling of the arguments made against giving the freedmen the vote was based on precisely this premise. It was a well-known fact that the Negro population was concentrated in the best cotton-growing areas where before the war the

Southern opinion on Negro suffrage

great planters had held sway. Sometimes in these "black counties" the number of Negroes far exceeded the number of whites, although in the less favored "white counties" of the interior the exact reverse was true. And so it could be maintained that, in case the few favored whites of the "black counties" were aided by Negro votes, they could control the various state governments in complete disregard of the far larger number of whites in the back-country. Negro suffrage was thus feared, not so much for itself as for the danger it might involve of turning the South back to the rule of the old pre-war plantation aristocracy.

The northern Radicals, however, had taken great pains to wean the Negroes away from their natural allegiance to their former masters. Working mainly through the Union League, a private organization that during the war had existed to disseminate northern propaganda, but that after the war had turned its **The Union League** attention to the Negro problem, they taught the freedmen that their former masters were not to be trusted, and that in all political matters they must rely strictly upon Republican advisers. To make the League the more appealing to the blacks, it was converted into a kind of lodge, with an elaborate ritual and much ostentatious ceremony. Soon, with the aid of the northern soldiers stationed in the South and the agents of the Freedmen's Bureau, the League organizers had most of the Negroes under their control, so that when the time came for registering them as voters there was no question but what they would both register and vote as the Radicals desired.

Slowly and painfully the reconstruction process worked itself out. Since the new electorates included so many Negroes — in five out of the ten states more than half of the voters — the conventions that were chosen in 1867 and 1868 contained in every in- **Carpet-bag rule** stance a large block of Negro delegates. The leaders, however, turned out to be mainly Northerners, men who had come South with the army, or with the Freedmen's Bureau, or merely to fish in troubled waters. These "carpet-baggers," as they came to be called, were usually dependable Radicals who willingly carried out the wishes of the Radicals in Congress. In each convention there was a considerable . sprinkling of southern whites, among whom those who were willing to follow the lead of the Northerners were called "scalawags." The new constitutions, in spite of their origin, contained some admirable provisions. They looked forward to the establishment of far better public-school systems than the South had ever known before — an end eagerly sought by the Negroes, who regarded their lack of education as the most serious obstacle they confronted in their struggle for racial equality. They also copied the latest reforms in systems of taxation and finance, of local government, and of judicial organization that had found their way into northern state constitutions, but had not previously been current in the South. Such reforms, however, were small compensations to the dispossessed Southerners for the prospect of "carpet-bag rule" that the suffrage provisions of every constitution seemed to make certain. Some of these provisions were even more drastic than those which Congress had prescribed. Nor could the various attempts to insure social as well as civil and political equality between the races be viewed with equanimity.

Eventually each of the southern states was obliged to accept a "carpet-bag" constitution, although in Mississippi and Alabama the first such documents failed of adoption at the polls. The first state to complete the process prescribed by Congress was Arkansas, which in June, 1868, was readmitted to the Union. The last was Georgia, which after much tribulation was reinstated only in July, 1870. Seven out of the ten states were hurried through in time to make doubly certain the election of a Republican President in 1868, and to send almost solidly Republican delegations to Congress. Reconstruction was now technically over, but the opposition to carpet-bag rule in the South was so strong that from many of the conquered states the central government dare not withdraw its troops.[1]

The complete triumph that Congress had scored over the President in pushing through its program of reconstruction against his will found an interesting parallel in the humiliation by Congress of the Supreme Court. In 1866 that tribunal had held in *Ex parte Milligan* that trials of civilians by military courts were illegal in regions where the civil courts were open for business. This decision cast serious doubt upon the legality of the whole system of military rule upon which the Radicals proposed to base their plan of reconstruction, and Republican denunciations of the Supreme Court went to violent extremes. To discipline the Court, and also to prevent Johnson from making appointments to it, Congress enacted a law in July, 1866, which provided that the next two vacancies among the associate justices should not be filled, and that the number of judges should ultimately become seven instead of nine. The Republican majority in the House of Representatives also passed a measure which would have

Congress humiliates the Supreme Court

---

[1] Of the many state histories of reconstruction the least biased and best is F. B. Simkins and R. H. Woody, *South Carolina During Reconstruction* (1932). Others of merit, most of them reflecting a more or less official "southern white man's" point of view, are J. W. Garner, *Reconstruction in Mississippi* (1901); J. G. de R. Hamilton, *Reconstruction in North Carolina* (1914); W. W. Davis, *The Civil War and Reconstruction in Florida* (1913); W. L. Fleming, *Civil War and Reconstruction in Alabama* (1905); E. M. Coulter, *Civil War and Readjustment in Kentucky* (1926); C. Mildred Thompson, *Reconstruction in Georgia, Economic, Social, Political, 1866–1872* (1915); C. W. Ramsdell, *Reconstruction in Texas* (1910); Ella Lonn, *Reconstruction in Louisiana after 1868* (1918).

required a two-thirds majority of the justices to declare a law of Congress unconstitutional, but on this proposal the Senate failed to take action. Congress, however, did forbid the Court to receive appeals from the lower courts in cases involving the right of *habeas corpus*. Reeling under these blows, the Court took pains to avoid as completely as possible all decisions that might offend Congress, although in the case of *Texas vs. White* (1869) it went on record as favoring the Johnson theory that the southern states, in spite of their acts of secession, had never legally ceased to exist.

The first elections in the reconstructed states resulted in the choice of a dubious array of officials. The highest places went mainly to Northerners who had not become residents of the South until after the war, and who had frequently seen it for the first time as members of the Union army. Lesser offices were *Elections in the South* held almost exclusively by Negroes, scalawags, and carpet-baggers. One Negro became lieutenant-governor of Louisiana, another secretary of state in South Carolina. Negroes were numerous in every legislature, and in South Carolina they outnumbered the whites eighty-eight to sixty-seven. Most of the office-holders were men of little property. In Louisiana only ten members of the legislature were taxpayers; in South Carolina the total taxes paid by the members of both houses were less than seven hundred dollars; in Georgia, they were less than one hundred dollars. Most of the Negroes and many of the whites chosen to office, including even judicial positions, were utterly illiterate.

The inevitable result of entrusting the powers of government to such persons was an orgy of corruption.[1] Private enterprises, such as railroad and canal companies, were expected to pay sizable bribes in order to secure charters, and, indeed, in order to carry on their legitimate business. If any enterprise happened to be *"Carpet-bag" excesses* thoroughly dubious, however, the chances were good that public money or public credit would be generously voted toward its support. Contracts were let to favorites at ridiculously high figures, and the public servants responsible took a cut of the profits. Public printing in Louisiana during a three-year period cost approximately a million and a half dollars a year, about seven hundred thousand of which was paid in two of these years to a newspaper belonging to the governor of the state, H. C. Warmoth, whose private fortune, incidentally, rose to a tidy sum

---

[1] James Pike, *The Prostrate State: South Carolina Under Negro Government* (1874; new edition, 1935), is a classic picture. Another excellent contemporary account is Charles Nordhoff, *The Cotton States in the Spring and Summer of 1875* (1876). For later opinions see W. F. Nowlin, *The Negro in American National Politics* (1931); Charles S. Johnson, *The Negro in American Civilization* (1930); and A. A. Taylor, *The Negro in the Reconstruction of Virginia* (1926).

before he left office. Worthless real estate, acquired for next to nothing, was sold by connivance to states or municipalities for prodigious figures. A single session of the carpet-bag legislature in Louisiana cost nearly a million dollars, whereas before the war the cost of a session had never been more than one-tenth that amount. What happened to this money was explained by a governor who had good reason to know the facts:

> It was squandered in paying extra mileage and per diem of the members for services never rendered; for an enormous corps of useless clerks and pages, for publishing the journals of each house in fifteen obscure parish newspapers, some of which never existed, while some never did the work; in paying extra committees authorized to sit during the vacation and to travel throughout the state and into Texas; and in an elegant stationery bill which included ham, champagne, etc.

The rule of the carpet-baggers raised tax-rates to figures never known before, and piled up debts which most of the southern states felt obliged later on to repudiate; but it must not be forgotten that such political depravity was no monopoly of the South. In New York, for example, during this same period, the Tweed Ring reduced graft to a science that the carpet-baggers might well have envied, while the word "racketeering," with all of its relevant connotations, was the product of a much later age. Of all those who participated in the work of Radical reconstruction the Negroes were the least to blame for its excesses. Only a few of them understood what was being done, and only a few of those who did were shrewd enough to line their pockets with plunder. For the most part they were but helpless victims of the conscienceless rogues who controlled them.

Strange as it may seem, there was a brighter side to the rule of the carpet-baggers. They and their allies represented, however crudely, the underprivileged classes in southern society, and they inaugurated many policies that were designed to better the lot of the ordinary man. Free public schools for the children of both races were generously supported, although with little regard for available taxation resources.[1] The tax burden itself, unreasonable as it became, was distributed with better regard for ability to pay than formerly. Poor relief had never been less neglected, and the rebuilding of roads, bridges, and public buildings that had been damaged or destroyed during the war was carried forward with little regard for expense. Most of all, the taste of democracy that the lowly of both races obtained was not soon forgotten. The rights of the Negroes were soon curtailed, but the incentive remained, at least with some of them, to win back by merit privileges that they had lost because they had been given

Contributions of the carpet-baggers

[1] E. W. Knight, *The Influence of Reconstruction on Education in the South* (1913).

them too soon. As for the poorer whites, from whose ranks many of the "scalawags" had been recruited, they were never again quite so inarticulate as they had been in the days before their kind had sat in the seats of power.

The later phases of reconstruction were carried through under the administration of General Grant, whom the Republicans nominated for the Presidency, and elected, in 1868. Before the war Grant had been a Democrat if he had been anything, and for a time after the war it was not known which party nomination he would accept. But he had trouble with Johnson, and long before the Republicans held their convention was high in the counsels of the Radicals. On the first ballot every one of the Republican delegates voted for Grant. For Vice-President, the convention chose Schuyler Colfax of Indiana, a dependable Radical who had proved his worth as Speaker of the House. Throwing off the Unionist disguise they had worn so willingly during the war, the Republicans with this campaign took back their pre-war name, and made the carrying through of Radical reconstruction their principal tenet. On Negro suffrage, however, their course was devious. While insisting that it was a necessity in the South, they held that in the North it was a matter for each state to decide for itself.[1]

Campaign of 1868

Logically the Democrats should have nominated Johnson, but his record of political ineptitude turned them instead to the far more available Horatio Seymour, able war governor of New York. For Vice-President they named Francis P. Blair, Jr., of Missouri, perhaps their most violent critic of Radical reconstruction. Their opposition to that policy was also registered unmistakably in their platform, which declared that Congress, instead of restoring the Union, had, "so far as in its power, dissolved it, and subjected ten states, in the time of profound peace, to military despotism and Negro supremacy." The platform also gave its approval to the theory advocated by George H. Pendleton of Ohio that the Civil War bond issues should be paid off in greenbacks, whenever the letter of the law would permit, instead of gold. But the "Ohio idea," as this "soft-money" theory was called, did not meet the approval of Seymour, and was more or less ignored during the campaign.[2] The real issue was Radical reconstruction, and the opposition to what Congress had done was far greater than the face of the electoral returns revealed. Eight states, including New York and New Jersey, voted for Seymour, while in most of the twenty-six that voted for Grant the Democratic

[1] The Fifteenth Amendment was not submitted until after the election. Then, in spite of this plank in the Republican platform, the Radical leaders maintained that the election of Grant amounted to a mandate to write Negro suffrage into the Constitution.

[2] M. S. Wildman, *Money Inflation in the United States* (1905); W. C. Mitchell, *History of the Greenbacks* (1903).

minorities were far too large for Republican comfort. In a total popular vote of nearly six millions, Grant's majority was only about three hundred thousand, and far more than that many Negroes had voted! Of the total white electorate, therefore, clearly Grant was a minority choice. The electoral returns gave Grant 214 votes to Seymour's 80. Both houses of Congress remained in the hands of the Radicals, but the death of Stevens, late in the summer of 1868, had deprived them of their most competent leader.

Some of the very qualities that had made Grant the soldier a success, made Grant the politician a sore trial to his colleagues and to his country.[1]

Grant the politician

In the army most of the men he liked he trusted, and because the men he felt drawn to instinctively were generally good soldiers, they rarely betrayed his trust. In politics he met a different breed. Those he liked he trusted, but his instincts often played him false. In the army, Grant had learned to stand loyally behind his subordinates, regardless of popular criticism. In politics, this trait sometimes made him the last to recognize that one of his appointees was a rogue. In the army, when counsels were divided, he had often been compelled to think things out for himself, and to follow his own course. In politics, where his counsels were usually divided, his lack of expert knowledge sometimes made his independent judgments ridiculous. Years of political experience taught him something, and he left office a better politician than when he entered it; but there may be some significance in the fact that, ever since his time, the people of the United States have steadfastly refused to elevate a professional soldier to the Presidency.

In making the numerous appointments that fell to his lot as President, Grant showed an extraordinary capacity for political bungling. His first Cabinet was an odd assortment of political misfits that shrewd politicians soon found means to eliminate; not one of Grant's original appointees served longer than a year. By a stroke of good luck, Hamilton Fish of New York, an excellent choice, became Grant's second Secretary of State after the first, Elihu B. Washburne, had been made minister to France. Nor was Grant much more to be trusted in his selections for lesser offices. He was at great pains to take care of many indigent friends and relatives, but after that was accomplished he fell easily into the hands of the Radical leaders, and followed their advice almost exclusively. A small but influential group of civil service reformers — such men as E. L. Godkin of the New York *Nation*, George William Curtis of *Harper's Weekly*, Thomas A. Jenckes, a representative from Rhode Island whose study of

---

[1] W. B. Hesseltine, *Ulysses S. Grant, Politician* (1935), traces with a sure hand the progress of Grant's political career.

the English civil service had made him an ardent advocate of reform, and Carl Schurz, now United States Senator from Missouri — finally induced Congress in 1871 to set up a Civil Service Commission, of which Curtis became head. But this was done mainly to catch reform votes in the election of 1872, and after election the Commission was allowed to die for lack of Congressional appropriations.

The "sound-money" men who hoped for help from the Grant administration fared far better than the civil service reformers. They claimed that the election of 1868 constituted a mandate to save the country from the "Ohio idea," according to which billions of greenback dollars might conceivably be printed to pay off the national debt. One of the first measures to pass Congress, in March, 1869, pledged the United States to redeem its bonds "in coin or its equivalent," a phrase which Grant's and successive administrations interpreted to mean "in gold." Thus bonds that had been paid for in depreciated greenbacks were to be redeemed in dollars that were worth up to twice as much as the dollars originally lent the government. A refunding act, passed in July, 1870, provided for the systematic refinancing of the national debt on a long-term basis. Quite properly, in view of the friendly attitude the government had taken toward its creditors, the new bonds carried a much lower rate of interest.

The "Ohio idea"

What to do with the greenbacks that had been so freely issued during the Civil War, and that were still in circulation, was another serious problem. In Johnson's administration the expedient of reducing them in quantity, in order ultimately to raise their value to a parity with gold, had been tried, but the outcry from the country when prices began to drop was so great that Congress in 1868 called a halt. At the time Grant became President the greenback circulation stood at $356,000,000, far more than the government had, or could easily get, the gold to redeem. For the moment it seemed inexpedient to work for the resumption of specie payments, but "sound-money" men looked forward anxiously to the time when a greenback dollar should be equal in value to a gold dollar.

In February, 1870, the Supreme Court became involved in the matter. In the case *Hepburn vs. Griswold*, it reached the unexpected conclusion that the "legal-tender" quality with which Congress had endowed the greenbacks was unconstitutional to the extent that it applied to debts contracted before the passage of the acts in question. The opinion of the Court, delivered by Chief Justice Chase, was reached by a four-to-three vote. Had this decision been allowed to stand, it would have added merely one more element of instability to the already unsatisfactory monetary situation, but a combination of circumstances enabled the Court to reverse itself the following

The legal-tender cases

year. With Johnson out of the way, Congress had again raised the number of justices to nine, and on the very day that the Hepburn case was
decided, President Grant had sent to the Senate the names of two new
justices, who, shortly after their confirmation, joined with the minority
of the Hepburn decision to affirm by a five-to-four vote the constitutionality of the legal-tender clause. It has often been argued that the Court
was deliberately packed to bring about this reversal, but the general
consensus of opinion among historians seems to be that Grant had decided on his nominations without particular reference to the greenback
decision. That the prestige of the Court suffered considerably from the
proceedings, however, can hardly be denied.

In the campaign of 1868 the Republicans had definitely committed
themselves to the reduction of taxation, a policy which, in fact, was
already under way. Just before the end of the war, Con-
Reduction
of taxes   gress had authorized the appointment of a special commission to study how new revenues might be obtained, but by
the time the appointments were made the war was over. The commission, therefore, turned its attention to the problem of how the tax burden
might best be reduced, and so impressed the Secretary of the Treasury
with its diligence that when its term had expired he kept on its able
chief, David A. Wells, as "special commissioner of the revenue." Both
the commission and the special commissioner advised the gradual reduction of tariffs and excises, and on the latter subject Congress responded
willingly. When Grant became President, however, many of the war
taxes were still in force, so in July, 1870, an act was passed which eliminated most of the "nuisance" taxes, restricted the internal revenues to a
small number of articles, such as liquor and tobacco, and greatly reduced
the income tax, which, two years later, was abolished entirely.

For a long time efforts to lower the tariff met with successful opposition
from those who profited from the high rates, and during Johnson's term
Tariff   Congress was actually persuaded to raise the duties on raw
legislation   wool, woolen goods, copper, and copper ore. Not until 1872
were the first real reductions made. At that time many non-
protective duties, such as those on tea, coffee, spices, and various raw
materials, were lowered or abolished, and a ten per cent cut was reluctantly conceded for a few carefully chosen duties on manufactured
articles.

It was the irony of fate that Grant, who had shown at the end of the
Civil War his thorough sympathy with the prostrate South, should have
been President during the worst excesses of carpet-bag rule. But such
was the case. With the co-operation of the army assured, detachments of
soldiers were always available to put down revolts, real or fancied, and to

sustain the carpet-baggers. States that showed signs of going over to the Democrats were apt to be subjected to a congressional investigation, and then dealt with most drastically. On several occasions, for example, military officers deliberately purged southern legislatures of undependable members. Some of the carpet-bag governors also made use of Negro militia, whose chief duty, apparently, was to terrorize "disloyal" whites.

It was inevitable that violence of this sort would beget similar violence. As early as 1866 a group of young men who had lately been soldiers in the Confederate army organized, at Pulaski, Tennessee, a secret society, which, from the Greek word κύκλος, meaning circle, they called the Ku Klux Klan.[1] The society at first spread slowly, and seemed as barren of any real reason for existence as most such societies; but the mysterious name, and the equally mysterious letters, K. K. K., that stood for it, were soon utilized to frighten the Negroes. Before long night riders in various disguises, such as ghostly gowns, false faces, and tails, were visiting the cabins of bothersome Negroes, breaking up meetings of the Union League, beating up Negro militiamen, frightening black Republicans away from the polls, and occasionally attacking both scalawags and carpet-baggers. As soon as the vigilante possibilities of the Klan were realized, it grew like wildfire, and was paralleled by numerous similar organizations such as the Knights of the White Camellia, the Constitutional Guards, the Pale Faces, and the Knights of the Rising Sun. By the year 1869 these various orders had covered the South with their activities, and had attracted to membership, or to imitation, which amounted to much the same thing, men who would stop at nothing. Murders now replaced whippings as a common proceeding, and the most fiendish acts of torture were by no means rare. Horrified at the turn events had taken, and certain that such an opportunity for reprisals would not long be neglected, the responsible heads of the various orders, as early as the spring of 1869, did everything they could to disband them. But the worst of the "midnight banditti" continued their activities unabated.

Congress replied to the Ku Klux challenge with a series of drastic enforcement acts, which laid down heavy penalties for all found guilty of using force, bribery, or intimidation to prevent citizens from voting, and listed as high crimes subject to severe penalties the various activities of the Klan, such as forming conspiracies, wearing disguises, resisting officers, and intimidating witnesses. The President was also authorized to suspend the writ of *habeas corpus* wherever he deemed such action

The Ku Klux Klan

---

[1] J. C. Lester and D. L. Wilson, *Ku Klux Klan, Its Origin, Growth and Disbandment* (new edition, 1905); Susan L. Davis, *Authentic History, Ku Klux Klan, 1865–1877* (1924); W. G. Brown, *The Lower South in American History* (1902); W. A. Sinclair, *The Aftermath of Slavery* (1905); S. F. Horn, *Invisible Empire: the Story of the Ku Klux Klan* (1939).

necessary to suppress "armed combinations" in rebellion against the authority of the United States. Grant knew precisely how to enforce such measures, and did it thoroughly. He singled out for an example nine counties in South Carolina where the lawlessness had been most marked, suspended the writ of *habeas corpus* within their borders, and brought hundreds of law-breakers to trial. Federal troops stood by to see that the courts were left free to do their work, and in less than two years United States judges in South Carolina imposed heavy sentences upon eighty-two persons for violation of the acts. The example proved effective, and in part on this account the number of outrages attributed to the Klan declined sharply from this time on. A congressional committee, appointed to investigate "affairs in the late insurrectionary states," and generally known as the Ku Klux Committee, was able to show that many of the excesses complained of did exist. But its reports, in twelve large volumes, also brought home for the first time to many Northerners the disabilities under which the South was laboring, and helped pave the way for a change of policy.

Ultimately the attempts of Grant and the Radicals to maintain Republican majorities in the South came to nought. Southerners, bent on the restoration of home rule in the South, learned to stop short of violence in their efforts to restrain the Negroes from the exercise of their newly acquired political rights, but they often found more peaceable means quite as potent. Also, the pressure of northern opinion for greater leniency toward the South forced Congress to pass an Amnesty Act, in May, 1872, that reduced the number of ex-Confederates excluded from the suffrage to about five hundred. Gradually, in state after state, Democratic majorities took over the administration of government, carpet-baggers were expelled, and great numbers of Negroes ceased to vote. The chief legacy of reconstruction, from the party point of view, was the emergence of the "Solid South." Thereafter a vast majority of the southern whites, scalawags along with the rest, felt obliged, regardless of important political differences, to stand together as members of the Democratic, or "white man's," Party. Thus Radical reconstruction, instead of producing a solidly Republican South, as had been intended, produced instead a solidly Democratic South.

By the year 1872 the opponents of Radical reconstruction within the Republican Party itself had come to be embarrassingly numerous, and to have a name. As "Liberals," or "Liberal Republicans," they stood ready to leave the party, if necessary, in order to prevent the further punishment of the South. This movement for reform started in Missouri, as an effort to get rid of some of the unreasonably vindictive provisions that a state constitution, adopted in 1865, had aimed at all citizens who had been southern sympathizers.[1] Such persons were not only denied the right to vote and to hold office, but they might not so much as act as trustees, practice law, teach, preach, or solemnize marriages. In the election of 1870 the Missouri Liberals, with the assistance of the Democrats, drove the Radicals from power and excised the offensive clauses from the state constitution. Soon the movement became national in scope, and numbered among its adherents such prominent citizens as Horace Greeley, editor of the New York *Tribune*, Carl Schurz, United States Senator from Missouri, and Charles Francis Adams, distinguished son of one President and grandson of another. Opposition to "Grantism" went much further with some Liberals than mere denunciation of the administration's southern policy. Civil service reformers hoped for the day when appointments would be made on merit, and tariff reformers were determined that through Liberal auspices they should scale down the high protective duties that had lasted on after the Civil War.

When it became apparent that the Radicals intended to renominate Grant, a split in the Republican Party was assured. A national convention, called by the Missouri Liberals, met in Cincinnati, May 1, 1872, and nominated Horace Greeley for the Presidency, with B. Gratz Brown of Missouri as candidate for Vice-President. Greeley was unfortunately a high-tariff man, so his selection failed to satisfy a large faction among the Liberals who had hoped for tariff reform. Curiously, however, it did not alienate the southern Democrats, who remembered that in 1867, when Jefferson Davis was being held under an indictment for treason, Greeley had signed the ex-Confederate's bail-bond. It was hard for the northern Democrats to accept an old enemy as their leader, but they knew that the only way they could hope to defeat Grant was by joining forces with the Liberal Republicans, and were obliged to act accordingly. When the Democratic convention met, it accepted both Greeley and the platform upon which he had been nominated. That document was sufficiently forthright in its criticisms of Radical reconstruction and the spoils system, but in deference to Greeley's views it dodged the tariff issue as completely as possible. The Liberal campaign, earnest and purposeful as it was, failed completely to stop Grant. He was not only renominated by the Republicans, but was also triumphantly re-elected. Greeley carried two states of the Lower South, Georgia and Texas, and four border

Election of 1872

[1] E. D. Ross, *The Liberal Republican Movement* (1919), and T. S. Barclay, *The Liberal Republican Movement in Missouri, 1865–1871* (1926), trace the revolt against "Grantism" from its origins.

states, Missouri, Tennessee, Maryland, and Kentucky, but Grant won all the rest. The cartoons of Thomas Nast heaped insults upon the eccentric Greeley during the campaign, but Greeley's death shortly after the election probably came less from this humiliation, as often asserted, than from his strenuous speech-making tours, his disappointment at the election result, and his grief over the death of his wife.[1]

The scandals that were to make Grant's régime notorious for its corruption had already begun when he took the oath of office for the second time. One of the worst of them, the infamous "gold conspiracy," was engineered in 1869 by two speculators, Jay Gould and James Fisk, with the effective, although unintended, assistance of the President himself. While gold did not then circulate as money, it was in constant demand for adjusting international trade balances and for other legitimate purposes. To meet this demand the United States Treasury was accustomed from time to time to sell gold, but Gould managed to persuade Grant that in order to raise farm prices this should be stopped. Knowing that a treasury order to this effect was about to be given, Gould and Fisk "cornered" the existing small supply of available gold, and between September 20 and 24 drove the price from 140 to $163\frac{1}{2}$. The result was a short but violent stock exchange panic, and serious embarrassment, even bankruptcy, for many legitimate businesses. Finally an emergency order from the President, who at last saw that he had been duped, permitted the Treasury to sell gold, and brought the price down.

The Grant scandals

The building of the Union Pacific Railroad, which Congress had chartered during the Civil War, brought forth another precious scandal that the country learned about in 1872. The Crédit Mobilier was a construction company, so designed as to permit a few Union Pacific stockholders, who were also stockholders in the Crédit Mobilier, to drain off huge profits from construction contracts. Since a principal source of revenue for the railroad was bonds given it as a subsidy from the United States government, an effort was made to "fix" congressmen by selling them Crédit Mobilier stock at a generous discount. Oakes Ames, a congressman from Massachusetts, acted as agent for the company, and was able to induce many prominent politicians, among them Vice-President Colfax, to accept his favors. The congressional investigation which exposed the scandal tarnished a number of reputations, although to the public the holding of Crédit Mobilier stock was seemingly less reprehensible than the attempts made by some congressmen to conceal such holdings.

During Grant's second administration one unpalatable revelation suc-

---

[1] Horace Greeley, *Recollections of a Busy Life* (new edition, 1930), is a fuller revelation of Greeley's character than is found in any other work.

ceeded another with disheartening regularity. Congressmen in 1873 voted themselves a fifty per cent increase in salary, with back pay for two years. Naturally, this "Salary-Grab" Act was severely criticized, and was almost immediately repealed. The Treasury Department furnished another scandal when in May, 1874, it was disclosed that one John D. Sanborn had collected some $427,000 of overdue revenue, and had received for his services a commission of fifty per cent. To escape formal censure for allowing such a practice, William A. Richardson, Grant's second Secretary of the Treasury, was obliged to resign. Before another year was up, Grant's third Secretary of the Treasury, Benjamin H. Bristow, had uncovered a "Whiskey Ring," composed of revenue officers and distillers who had conspired to defraud the government out of a part of the excise on liquor. Even Grant's private secretary had accepted favors from the "Ring," and the President himself, while meaning no harm, had taken presents that a keener sense of propriety would have led him to refuse. To cap the climax came the tale, ultimately proved true, that Grant's current Secretary of War, W. W. Belknap, had received through his wife as intermediary a total of $24,450, as the price of keeping in office a post-trader at Fort Sill in the Indian Territory. Belknap escaped removal from office by impeachment only by resigning.

The foreign policy of the Grant administration was far better handled than its domestic affairs.[1] Grant did indeed create a near-scandal by his unflinching determination to annex the republic of Santo Domingo to the United States, but his efforts in this direction were fortunately overruled by the United States Senate. Highly creditable, however, was the settlement of all outstanding disputes between the United States and Great Britain. The most serious of these troubles came from the lax interpretation of neutral duties that had characterized British policy during the Civil War. Soon after that war had ended, the United States had an opportunity to demonstrate that its stricter view of neutrality might be of use to the British. At that time the Fenian Brotherhood, an organization of Irish-Americans whose ultimate goal was freedom for Ireland, not only planned an invasion of Canada from American soil, but in June, 1866, actually crossed the border in some force and fought a battle with Canadian volunteers. Possibly the American government should have forestalled this "invasion," but having failed in that it did the next best thing. It promptly arrested the Fenian leaders, seized their collections of supplies, and strengthened the border garrisons so as to prevent any further such happenings. This episode may have had something to do with the increasing

Grant's foreign policy

[1] Allan Nevins, *Hamilton Fish; The Inner History of the Grant Administration* (1936), gives a satisfactory account of Grant's diplomacy.

willingness of the British to accept responsibility for the depredations committed by the *Alabama,* and other Confederate commerce-destroyers, and to arrange for the arbitration of all unsettled controversies.[1]

The tactful diplomacy of Grant's Secretary of State, Hamilton Fish, finally resulted in the signing of the Treaty of Washington in 1871. In this treaty the British government definitely expressed its

The Geneva awards

regret for the "escape" of the Confederate cruisers, accepted as binding a set of rules that amounted to a clear confession of unneutral action, and agreed to submit the matter of damages to an arbitration tribunal of five, one each to be chosen by the United States, Great Britain, Italy, Brazil, and Switzerland. Meeting at Geneva the *Alabama* Tribunal, as it was often called, awarded to the United States damages of $15,500,000, a sum so large as to arouse indignant protests in England. Nevertheless, full payment was made, and the United States did the best it could to reimburse the individuals who had suffered the losses. Other settlements provided for in the Treaty of Washington resulted in money payments to Great Britain by the United States. For damages suffered by British subjects during the Civil War an arbitration commission awarded Great Britain nearly $2,000,000. For the special favors American fishermen enjoyed in British North American waters, another commission ordered the United States to pay Great Britain $5,500,000. The exact boundary between the United States and British Columbia in Puget Sound was settled, mostly in favor of the United States, by a referee, the German Emperor.

The numerous settlements reached under the terms of the Treaty of Washington emphasized once more to the two English-speaking nations, and for that matter to many others, the advantage of peaceful over warlike methods in adjusting international disputes. For the third time, once soon after the War of 1812, once in the forties under the leadership of Webster and Ashburton, and now once again during the seventies, Great Britain and the United States had made differences of far greater consequence than those which often resulted in war the subjects of successful negotiation. Such a succession of precedents, as subsequent events have proved, could not easily be broken.[2]

[1] See in this connection S. F. Bemis (editor), *The American Secretaries of State and their Diplomacy,* VII, 165 ff.

[2] E. M. Coulter, *The South During Reconstruction, 1865–77,* is a recent revaluation. Willie Malvin Caskey, *Secession and Restoration in Louisiana* (1938), is primarily political. Henry Lee Swint, *The Northern Teacher in the South, 1862–1870* (1941), describes an interesting phase of carpetbag history. G. W. McGinty, *Louisiana Redeemed: The Overthrow of Carpetbag Rule, 1876–1880* (1941), continues the reconstruction story beyond the end of carpetbag rule. On the revenue problem, see H. R. Ferleger, *David A. Wells and the American Revenue System, 1865–1870* (1942).

23

A Business Cycle

THE economic background of reconstruction, so far as the North was concerned, was a business boom. After the Civil War, no less than during it, the South knew little prosperity, but the flush times that began in the North while the war was on continued unabated for over eight years. There were many reasons why this should have been so. The greenbacks, despite earnest efforts on the part of Secretary of the Treasury McCulloch to reduce them in quantity and so to raise their value, remained in circulation, and thus the cutting of prices and wages that would certainly have occurred had they been withdrawn was avoided. Capital was abundant. War profits had been handsome, and graft at the expense of the government so common as scarcely to excite comment. About two billion dollars' worth of United States bonds were outstanding, and regardless of how cheap the money with which they had been purchased, both interest and principal were payable in gold. Capital so invested multiplied with startling rapidity. Gold and silver poured in from the western mines. European investors readily purchased large blocks of American securities. Banks, with credit so inflated, flourished as never before. Not until 1864 had the national banking system, created during the war, really begun to function, but by 1865 there were more than fifteen hundred national banks scattered throughout the country, with a bank-note circulation that was soon almost to equal that of the greenbacks.[1]

Under these circumstances it is not surprising that manufacturing lost none of the momentum it had accumulated during the war. The United States, indeed, became a sort of paradise for industrialists. A dependably high tariff assured them of the **Rise of big business** right to exploit the steadily growing American market, while soldiers returning from the war and immigrants streaming in from Europe supplied a comfortable abundance of labor. One by one the high records of production set up during the war fell below the higher records that came with the first five years of peace. The results were nothing

[1] Allan Nevins, *The Emergence of Modern America, 1865–1878* (1927), furnishes a well-balanced account of the social readjustments made during this period.

less than revolutionary. Before the Civil War the United States had been primarily a nation of farmers, but agricultural America had no chance to keep up the pace being set by industrial America; Jefferson's dream of a nation composed mainly of small free farmers had faded before the realities of the machine age. The America of the future was to be less rural than urban, more factory than farm. The black belt of the cotton kingdom was to recede in importance before a northern black belt, traced by the smoke of factory chimneys, a belt that ultimately was to extend far into the South itself.

Closely identified with almost every aspect of these revolutionary changes was the production of steel. Before the Civil War the high cost of steel confined its use to the manufacture of such small **The romance of steel** articles as tools and cutlery in which quality was demanded regardless of price. That anything so bulky as railroad rails, or the heavy locomotives that ran on the rails, should ever be made of steel rather than of iron seemed utterly fantastic. All this was changed as the result of a remarkable discovery made independently and at about the same time by an American, William Kelly, and an Englishman, Henry Bessemer. Kelly, a resident of Eddyville, Kentucky, who made wrought-iron sugar kettles for his neighbors, observed one day that the effect of an air-blast on molten iron was to make it white-hot. From this he readily deduced that the molten metal itself contained enough carbon to burn out its impurities, if only a strong blast of air could be directed against it. Plainly this "air-boiling" process, if only it could be made practicable, would tend to eliminate the expensive use of charcoal, and so greatly reduce the cost of refinement. In a series of experiments, carried on between 1851 and 1856, Kelly demonstrated the soundness of his idea, although his patrons obstinately insisted upon wrought-iron kettles made in the old-fashioned way.

In 1856 the Englishman, Bessemer, who had been carrying on similar experiments, announced the successful application of a "fuel-less" process, and obtained a United States patent upon it. **The Bessemer process** Kelly, however, soon convinced the Patent Office that he was the original inventor, and it was some time before the conflicting interests could be reconciled. Before the Civil War ended, successful efforts were being made within the United States to make commercial use of the "Bessemer process," as it was generally called, and in 1866 one Alexander Lyman Holley, by obtaining the right to use both the Bessemer and the Kelly patents, paved the way for a phenomenal development. Within a few years the number of Bessemer steel works in the country could be counted by the dozen, and the price of steel had dropped to a figure that made its use instead of iron entirely practicable

Another new method of producing steel, known as the "open-hearth" process, was introduced into the United States from Europe in 1868 by Abram S. Hewitt, who shared with his father-in-law, Peter Cooper, control of the New Jersey Steel and Iron Company at Trenton.[1] Ultimately far more open-hearth than Bessemer steel was to be made, but until well toward the end of the century Bessemer steel cost less to produce, and so enjoyed a great advantage. Naturally the steel industry, like the iron industry, tended to concentrate in Pennsylvania, where both iron ore and coal were found in great abundance; but by 1873 the Michigan iron mines, little used before the Civil War, were furnishing more than half of the ore supply.

The steel industry was to produce many great names, but none more glamorous than that of Andrew Carnegie (1835–1919), the Scottish immigrant lad whose career became an almost perfect pattern for the typical American success story. The son of a Andrew Carnegie humble, but by no means unintelligent, Dunfermline weaver, young Carnegie was brought to America in 1848 by his parents

[1] Allan Nevins, *Selected Writings of Abram S. Hewitt* (1937), contains an illuminating report by Hewitt, as commissioner to the Paris Exposition in 1867, on "The Production of Iron and Steel in Its Economic and Social Relations." See also by the same author, *Abram S. Hewitt, with Some Account of Peter Cooper* (1935).

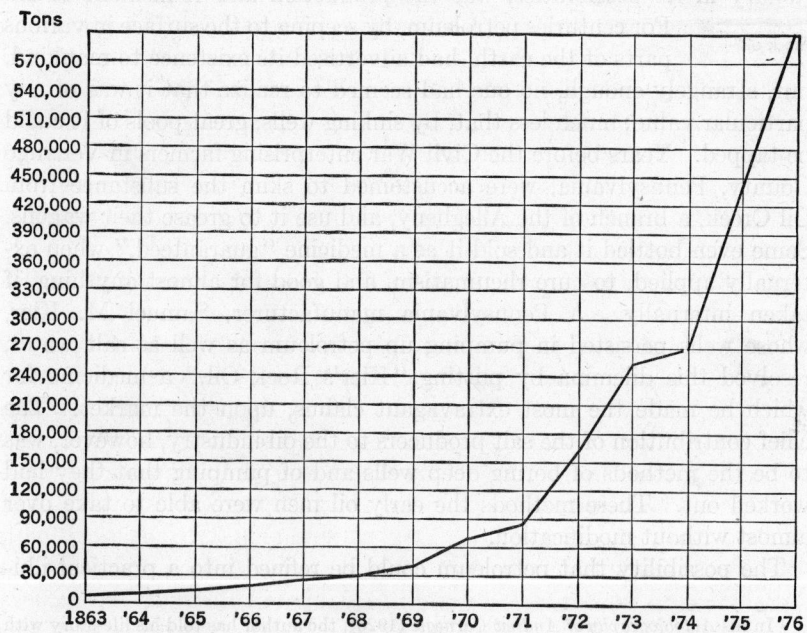

PRODUCTION OF STEEL IN THE UNITED STATES, 1863–76

in the proverbial quest of opportunity. He found it, first as a bobbin-boy at a dollar and twenty cents a week in a western Pennsylvania cotton factory, then as a messenger at two dollars and a half a week in a Pittsburgh telegraph office. Soon he was a telegraph operator, one of the first to learn to read "by sound" the messages that came over the wire, and a little later, as much because of his personal charm as because of his outstanding proficiency, the private secretary of Thomas A. Scott, a Pennsylvania Railroad official. From that position to railroading was an easy transition; and then from railroading to bridge-building, where he made a specialty of supplanting outmoded wooden construction with iron. Astoundingly versatile, he pursued many side lines, nearly all of which turned out well. He built bridges, made money out of oil, and sold railway bonds in Europe — all at the same time. On one of his trips to England he saw steel being made by the Bessemer process, and returned to the United States determined to put "all of his eggs in one basket," the manufacture of steel. By 1873, the date when he opened the J. Edgar Thomson Steel Mills — named after the president of the Pennsylvania Railroad, an associate in the project — his career as a steel magnate had begun.[1]

No less startlingly new than the steel industry, and almost as revolutionary in its possibilities, was the production and refinement of oil.

"Rock oil"   For centuries petroleum, by seeping to the surface in various parts of the earth, had advertised its existence to mankind, but, strangely enough, no one had seemed to realize that it was of any particular value; much less that, by sinking wells, great pools of it could be tapped. Years before the Civil War enterprising farmers in Venango County, Pennsylvania, were accustomed to skim the substance from Oil Creek, a branch of the Allegheny, and use it to grease their wagons. Some even bottled it and sold it as a medicine "guaranteed," when externally applied, to cure rheumatism, and good for almost anything, if taken internally. A Pennsylvania manufacturer, Samuel M. Kier, whose wells persisted in pumping up petroleum as well as salt water, resolved this dilemma by putting "Kier's Rock Oil," a medicine for which he made the most extravagant claims, upon the market. The chief contribution of the salt producers to the oil industry, however, was to be the methods of boring deep wells and of pumping that they had worked out. These methods the early oil men were able to take over almost without modification.

The possibility that petroleum could be refined into a practical illu-

---

[1] In his *Autobiography of Andrew Carnegie* (1920), the author has told his life-story with few reservations. See also J. K. Winkler, *Incredible Carnegie: the Life of Andrew Carnegie* (1931).

minant was not unrealized by the versatile Kier, who made some significant experiments along that line, but the chief credit for
this epochal discovery belongs to a graduate of Dartmouth   Oil for
College, named George H. Bissell, who remembered, curi- illumination
ously, some of the experiments with crude oil that one of his teachers had
made. Convinced that ultimately he could supplant the old-fashioned
tallow candles and whale-oil lamps with something far superior, Bissell
leased some land in western Pennsylvania, and sent a sample of the oil it
produced to Benjamin Silliman, Jr., professor of chemistry in Yale College, for analysis. In a memorable document, written in 1855, Silliman
reported that an excellent illuminant could be made from petroleum, that
the cost of refinement would be slight, and that from it a number of
important by-products, such as naphtha and paraffin, could also be
recovered. Bissell now turned promoter, won sufficient support from
capitalists to begin operations, and sent Edwin Drake with the standard
equipment for opening a salt-well out to Titusville, Pennsylvania, to
drill for oil. In August, 1859, "Drake's folly," as the incredulous natives called this venture, was producing oil at the rate of twenty barrels
a day.

What followed was hardly less tumultuous than a gold rush. That
fabulous sums were to be made from oil, few could deny, and the venturesome flocked to western Pennsylvania by the thousands.
Farmers who had known only the extreme of poverty sold   The petroleum
their land for fantastic prices, or, by good luck, sometimes   industry
became part owners in oil wells that speedily made them rich. Oil der-
ricks dotted the landscape; crossroads became towns, and towns became
cities, almost overnight. Pittsburgh, and other strategic centers, found
a new source of wealth in the business of oil refining, while the whole
country bought the new "coal-oil" lamps, and began to sit up nights.
Inasmuch as almost anyone with a little capital could make a start in the
oil business, competition for a while was utterly unrestrained. On this
account, and also because of the unpredictable nature of both the supply
and the demand, the prices of crude oil and of kerosene varied from year
to year, from month to month, and even from day to day. Fortunes
were lost as well as made. Nevertheless, by 1864 the oil fields around
Titusville had expanded to four hundred square miles, and by 1872 not
only western Pennsylvania, but parts of West Virginia and Ohio also,
were included within the two thousand square miles in the United States
devoted to the production of oil. With a total output to date of nearly
forty million barrels, the petroleum industry had in a dozen years
climbed to a place of high prominence in the nation's business. In a
single year, 1871, foreign purchasers took over one hundred and fifty

thousand gallons of American oil, making this commodity the fourth largest item among the country's exports.

Inextricably intertwined with the history of oil refining in the United States is the name of John D. Rockefeller (1839–1937), a native of Rich-

John D.
Rockefeller

ford, New York, who had moved with his parents to Cleveland, Ohio, when he was thirteen years old. Young Rockefeller had only a common-school education, but he early exhibited extraordinary business talent. Before he had reached his majority he had become a partner in a produce commission firm that took excellent profits, particularly after the outbreak of the Civil War. Shrewd, calculating, and thrifty, he made up his mind in 1862, while other young men of his age were patriotically going off to war, that the "coal-oil" business had a future worth sharing. With characteristic good judgment he first backed a refinery that the inventive genius of one Samuel Andrews had provided with a highly improved process; then, at the end of the war, when it was apparent that he had made no mistake, he gave up his commission business, formed a partnership with Andrews, and started out as an oil refiner on his own. By this time the two chief western centers for the refining of oil were Pittsburgh and Cleveland, but the advantage, as Rockefeller sensed, lay with Cleveland, which had easy access, both by water and rail, to the East no less than to the West, whereas Pittsburgh, for its eastern market, was wholly dependent upon the Pennsylvania Railroad. Five years later, reinforced by two new allies, H. M. Flagler and S. V. Harkness, Rockefeller had founded the Standard Oil Company of Ohio, which that year refined four per cent of the nation's total output.[1] By 1872, with monopoly as his goal, he had acquired twenty out of the twenty-five refineries in Cleveland and was laying plans for further conquests that within a decade were to bring him control over ninety per cent of the oil refineries of the country.

It would be difficult to maintain the thesis that the Civil War was in any fashion responsible for the steel or oil industries. Indeed, the de-

The Civil War
and American
industry

velopment of steel manufacturing in the United States was doubtless retarded because of the necessity of keeping up the flow of the standard iron products demanded by the war, and it is quite possible that the uses found for oil might have been greater had the nation been at peace. Wartime necessities, however, acted as a powerful stimulus to many other industries, such, for example, as meat-packing, flour-milling, and the manufacture

[1] Ida M. Tarbell, *The History of the Standard Oil Company* (2 vols., 1904) was an early attempt at muckraking, but of reasonable accuracy. Allan Nevins, *John D. Rockefeller* (2 vols. 1940), corrects and expands her account. The rise of the great industrialists is told in journalistic style by Matthew Josephson, *The Robber Barons* (1934).

of prepared foods, textiles, and leather goods. And yet it is impossible to believe that these developments would not have come, more slowly, to be sure, but quite as certainly, had there been no war. Undoubtedly the Civil War greatly accelerated the economic revolution in the United States, and greatly promoted the change of emphasis in the nation's business from agriculture to industry. But this transformation only accompanied and followed the war; it was not caused by it. Furthermore, such evidence as is sometimes adduced to prove that the Civil War was primarily the result of a conspiracy of industrialists bent on obtaining longer profits is not convincing. The industrialists made much of the advantage that the war offered them, and after the war was over they enjoyed a tremendous prosperity; but there is no reason to suppose that the war was essential to their triumph, or that they thought of the struggle in any such light.

It would be impossible even to list all of the industries that were transformed in the years following the Civil War from small and local businesses to great nation-wide concerns, some with steadily growing markets abroad. In addition to those noted, mention should be made, however, of refined sugar; intoxicating beverages, particularly whiskey and beer; pottery, glass, and enameled wares; clocks and watches; organs and pianos; stoves and hardware; farm machinery; and building materials. All these expanding activities widened the base of industrial operations to include the meat-packers of Kansas City, the millers of Minneapolis, the watch-makers of Elgin, Illinois, and the farm-implement manufacturers of Moline, in the same state. No longer could it be said, without ample qualification, that the West was merely an agricultural section.[1]

Labor for the new factories was recruited both at home and abroad. As the war ended, an occasional ill-starred prophet arose to predict that the great armies of the North could never be peacefully disbanded; either they must remain in service to lay the basis of a military dictatorship, or they must dissolve into an army of the unemployed to spread disorder throughout the land. Both guesses were wrong. The soldiers, as fast as they could be mustered out, rejoiced to abandon military for civilian life. Many returned to the pursuits they had left when they went to war, many followed the frontier into the West, and many found work in some department of the rapidly expanding industrial life of the times.

Employers could count also upon a steady influx of immigrants from

Ex-soldiers as workers

[1] Nearly every industry has attracted its historian; for example: F. J. Allen, *The Shoe Industry* (1916); A. H. Cole, *The American Wool Manufacture* (2 vols., 1926); M. T. Copeland, *The Cotton Manufacturing Industry of the United States* (1912).

Europe who were conditioned to a lower wage scale and lower standards
of living than most native Americans were willing to tol-
Immigrants erate. So economical was it to employ these immigrants
that manufacturers sometimes combined to send agents abroad to
recruit the supply. Such urging, however, was of far less consequence
than the general dislocations in Europe resulting from the economic
revolution. Men thrown out of work, or unable to find it, looked long-
ingly toward the greater opportunities of America, which the diminishing
cost of ocean transportation brought more and more frequently within
their grasp. During the first two years of the Civil War, immigration had
fallen off precipitately, but by 1863 confidence in the future of America
had revived, and the number of newcomers had swelled to a figure greater
than had crossed the Atlantic in any one of the three years preceding the
war. Official stimulation came from the American side, both by way of
liberal bounties for those who would volunteer to serve in the army, and
by an immigration act, passed in 1864, which allowed the importation of
laborers under contracts not particularly different in principle from the
contracts that in colonial times had brought so many indentured servants
to America. In 1865 a quarter of a million immigrants landed on American shores, and three years later the annual total had reached 326,000,
well above the average for the eighteen-fifties. By 1873 when more than
460,000 aliens entered the country, the immigrant tide broke all preceding records. The census of 1870, which counted 38,558,371 people in the
United States, described 2,314,000 of them as immigrants who had arrived during the sixties; while five years later the total number of foreign-
born in the population was set at 7,500,000.

The great bulk of this immigration came, as before the war, from the
British Isles and from Germany, but some notable new trends were in
evidence. Immigration from Ireland, although still heavy, never again
reached the startling totals of the forties and fifties, and was even exceeded during the seventies by the numbers coming from England.
From Norway, Sweden, and Denmark came also a Scandinavian migration that in the first half of the seventies averaged not less than
twenty-five thousand a year. Most of the Scandinavians went to Illinois, Wisconsin, and the states of the new Northwest, particularly Minnesota. By no means less significant was the arrival of smaller numbers
of Slavs and Italians from eastern and southern Europe, the vanguard of
a mighty host.[1]

[1] The literature of this subject is voluminous. The most recent and best of the single-
volume studies is Carl Wittke, *We Who Built America, the Saga of the Immigrant* (1940),
but G. M. Stephenson, *A History of American Immigration, 1820–1924* (1926), is also a
convenient summary. Racial groups have nearly all drawn their historians, but two notably excellent books are Theodore C. Blegen, *Norwegian Migration to America, 1825–60*
(1931), and by the same author, *Norwegian Migration to America: the American Transition*
(1940).

It is not too much to say that the common denominator for all these remarkable transformations was to be found in the rapidly expanding railroad system of the country. The steel manufacturers found their greatest market in supplying steel rails and **Railroads** other new equipment for the railroads; the oil men at first depended upon the railroads for the transportation of the crude oil that they refined no less than for the refined oil that they sold; the packers owed their very existence to the facilities that the railroads provided them; industrialists of every kind saw their establishments grow in direct ratio as the railroads grew.

Greatly overbuilt before the Civil War, the railroads of the country enjoyed a tremendous prosperity while the war was on. Rates soared, except where the competition of the Great Lakes and the Erie Canal kept them down, and companies that had never made profits before now felt obliged to disguise their heavy earnings by issuing stock dividends. Railroad managers, as long as they could count on a wartime abundance of traffic, showed little interest either in new construction or the improvement of their equipment. Indeed, by 1865 the number of railroad accidents due to avoidable defects in roadbeds and rolling stock had reached the point where the public would no longer have tolerated such neglect except for the immunity to tragedy that accompanies war. With the return of peace the time was ripe for the renovation of the old roads and the building of new ones. Capital for the purpose was easily obtained by Jay Cooke and other promoters, who convinced the public that railroad securities were among the safest as well as the most profitable of investments.

The government itself, particularly by its generous subsidies to the building of transcontinentals, did much to stimulate the railroad boom. This policy, contemplated for many years before the war broke out but postponed because of southern opposition, **The** was inaugurated in 1862 when Congress chartered the Union **first trans-** and the Central Pacific Railroads. In addition to the origi- **continental** nal reasons for building a transcontinental road, proponents could now cite the necessity of connecting California closely enough to the Union to insure its loyalty for all time to come. The Union Pacific was to build westward from Omaha, Nebraska; the Central Pacific, eastward from Sacramento, California. Each company, after the completion of an initial forty miles of track, was eligible to receive from the government, for each mile of track laid, ten square miles of land in alternate sections, checkerboard fashion, along the right of way; and also, for each mile of track laid, the loan of sixteen, thirty-two, or forty-eight thousand dollars (for plains, foothills, or mountain country, respectively) in government bonds. Generous as these offers seemed, they proved to be inadequate to attract the modest sums necessary to build the first essential divisions of forty miles each, so in 1864 Congress amended the original terms. The government now doubled the land grant, accepted a second mortgage for the loans it made, and permitted the companies to borrow private capital, up to the amount of the government loans, on first-mortgage bonds. The prospect of title to nearly twenty million acres of land and loans amounting to about sixty million dollars proved to be a sufficient inducement to moneylenders, and building soon began in earnest. At first it was stipulated that the eastern boundary of California should be the dividing line between the two roads, but ultimately they were permitted to race for distance, and in 1869, when they met near Ogden, Utah, the Union Pacific had laid 1086 miles of track and the Central Pacific 689.

Unfortunately the building of both roads was accompanied by the most shameless profiteering. In each case the device of a construction
Profiteering   company, controlled by the leading stockholders of the
railroads concerned, was utilized to drain off through unreasonably high contracts all possible profit from the building of the road. The Crédit Mobilier of America served this purpose so well for the Union Pacific that it received, according to a congressional committee, a total of $73,000,000 for construction that cost about $50,000,-000. In one year, 1868, the favored holder of Crédit Mobilier stock took dividends amounting to 230 per cent in first-mortgage bonds, 515 per cent in Union Pacific stock, and 60 per cent in cash. The construction companies that did the work for the Central Pacific were two in number. At first the firm of Charles Crocker and Company received the contracts, but Crocker's close connection with the Central Pacific was so well known that in 1867 a new firm, the Contract and Finance Company, was formed. The two Central Pacific construction companies did even better for their stockholders than the Crédit Mobilier was able to do for its, for their profits on an investment of $121,000,000 amounted to $63,000,000. Most of this sum went to the four leading officials of the Central Pacific, Leland Stanford, Collis P. Huntington, Charles Crocker, and Mark Hopkins. Unlike the original owners of Union Pacific stock, most of whom sold out their holdings as soon as the road was built, the original Central Pacific group operated their road for many years, and took excellent profits from it. Each of the four mentioned left a fortune at his death of forty million dollars, or more.[1]

---

[1] The building of the Union Pacific has attracted many historians, among them; G. M. Dodge, *How We Built the Union Pacific Railway* (1910); John P. Davis, *The Union Pacific Railway* (1894); E. L. Sabin, *Building the Pacific Railway* (1919). On the Central Pacific see the extremely lively and interesting Oscar Lewis, *The Big Four; the Story of Huntington, Stanford, Hopkins, and Crocker* (1938).

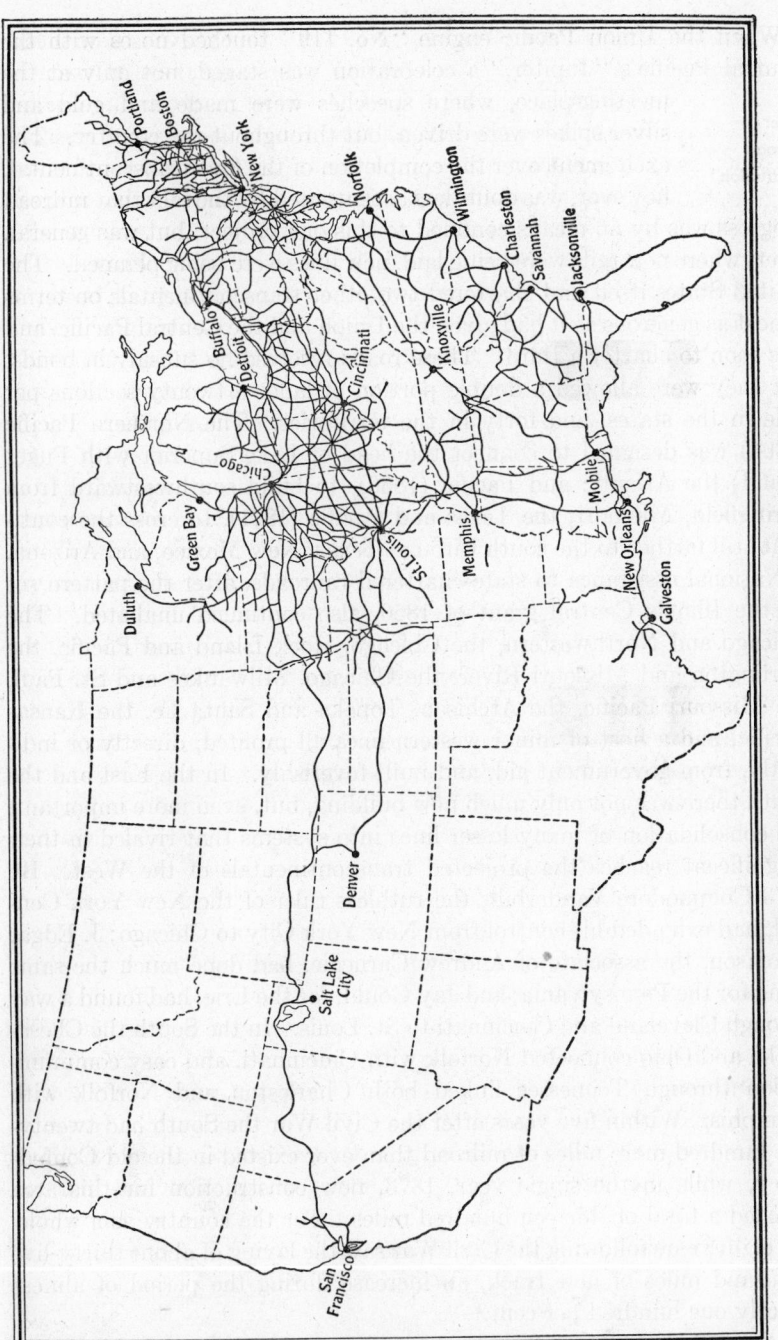

THE AMERICAN RAILROAD SYSTEM, 1870

When the Union Pacific engine "No. 119" touched noses with the Central Pacific's "Jupiter," a celebration was staged, not only at the meeting-place, where speeches were made and gold and silver spikes were driven, but throughout the country. The excitement over the completion of the first transcontinental, however, was doubtless accentuated by the fact that railroad progress was by no means confined to this one project, but was general. Everywhere new rails were being laid, new lines were being planned. The United States itself had chartered two other transcontinentals on terms almost as generous as it had given the Union and the Central Pacific, and was soon to charter a third. These roads received no subsidy in bonds, but they were allowed a double portion of land — twenty sections per mile in the states, and forty in the territories. The Northern Pacific (1864) was designed to connect the head of Lake Superior with Puget Sound; the Atlantic and Pacific (1866), to build southwestward from Springfield, Missouri; the Texas and Pacific (1871), to cross the continent still farther to the south through Texas, New Mexico, and Arizona.

Other railroad construction

National assistance to state-chartered railroads, after the pattern set by the Illinois Central grant of 1850, also continued unabated. The Chicago and Northwestern, the Chicago, Rock Island and Pacific, the Burlington and Missouri River, the Chicago, Milwaukee and St. Paul, the Missouri Pacific, the Atchison, Topeka and Santa Fe, the Kansas Pacific, and a host of minor western lines all profited, directly or indirectly, from government aid, and built feverishly. In the East and the South there was not only much new building, but, even more important, the consolidation of many lesser lines into systems that rivaled in their magnificent reaches the projected transcontinentals of the West. By 1873 Commodore Vanderbilt, the ruthless ruler of the New York Central, had extended his control from New York City to Chicago; J. Edgar Thomson, the associate of Andrew Carnegie, had done much the same thing for the Pennsylvania; and Jay Gould, for the Erie, had found a way through Cleveland and Cincinnati to St. Louis. In the South the Chesapeake and Ohio connected Norfolk with Cincinnati, and easy communication through Tennessee linked both Charleston and Norfolk with Memphis. Within five years after the Civil War the South had twenty-five hundred more miles of railroad than ever existed in the old Confederacy, while in the single year, 1873, new construction for this area reached a total of thirteen hundred miles. For the country as a whole, the eight years following the Civil War saw the laying of about thirty-five thousand miles of new track, an increase during the period of almost exactly one hundred per cent.[1]

[1] Among the best books on the railroad expansion of this period are John Moody, *The Railroad Builders* (1919); Robert E. Riegel, *The Story of the Western Railroads* (1926); and Glenn Chesney Quiett, *They Built the West* (1934).

A great variety of improvements kept pace with the new construction. In 1864 George M. Pullman built his first sleeping-car, the "Pioneer A," at a cost of twenty thousand dollars, and a few years later he was actively at work on separate dining-, drawing-room, and reclining-chair cars. In 1868 George Westinghouse demonstrated on a Pennsylvania passenger train his epoch-making airbrake, a device which by 1872 became an automatic appliance. During these years steel rails were introduced, although a heated debate continued for some time as to the relative merits of iron and steel for this purpose, and it was not until 1877 that the rapid replacement of iron by steel began. As the roadbeds were improved, heavier locomotives and rolling stock were built and a uniform gauge of four feet, eight and one-half inches — the gauge used by the Union Pacific — came into general use. Terminal facilities were greatly improved, union stations made easier the transfer of passengers, and extensive freight yards expedited the traffic in "through freight." Long bridges, after the beginning of work on the Brooklyn Bridge in 1866, became a sort of passion. In 1869 the Missouri River was bridged at Kansas City, and in 1872 at Omaha. Between 1867 and 1874 James B. Eads built the famous bridge that bears his name across the Mississippi at St. Louis. John A. Roebling, the man who planned the Brooklyn Bridge, had first spanned the Ohio River at Cincinnati. These great bridges, and numerous lesser ones, enormously enhanced the speed and ease of railroad transportation.

Railroad improvements

Overinvestment in railroads, many of which, especially in the West, were built into unpopulated regions where for years operations could be carried on only at a loss, together with the wildest sort of speculation in railroad securities, had much to do with bringing the period of prosperity to a close. During these years the amount of capital invested in railroads alone had reached a billion dollars, while other huge sums had gone into the development of the new American industries. Capital from abroad amounting to over a billion and a half dollars had been borrowed to carry on the expansion, and interest charges of eighty million dollars annually had to be met. To pay these charges, and to remedy an adverse balance of trade, more gold had to be sent abroad each year than the United States could well spare. The new national banks yielded to the temptation to overextend their loans, and in the five years preceding 1873 let out many times as much money as they took in by way of new deposits. Insurance companies were hard hit by the Chicago Fire of 1871, which cost them $200,000,000, and the Boston Fire of 1872, which added another $73,000,000 to the bill they had to pay. Conditions in Europe were similarly gloomy, and a sharp panic on the Vienna Bourse in May, 1873, inaugurated a general European depression that could not long be kept from America.

On Thursday, September 18, 1873, the banking firm of Jay Cooke and Company closed its doors in New York, Philadelphia, and Washington. Cooke's fame had risen during the Civil War with his successful flotation of the bond issues by which the North financed its operations. After the war he turned his attention to railway securities, and again demonstrated his ability to win the confidence of investors. In attempting to back the Northern Pacific Railroad, however, he met with disaster. The huge sums needed for this undertaking could not be obtained without European assistance, and after the outbreak of the Franco-Prussian War in 1870 foreign capital became harder and harder to get. The result was that Cooke tied up so much of his firm's resources in advances to the railroad that his partners, without his knowledge or consent, finally took the drastic step of closing. Already a number of bankruptcies had made the business world nervous, and on the day before Cooke's failure there had been a ruinous decline in values on the New York Stock Exchange. But no one dreamed that the firm of Jay Cooke and Company, long regarded as the last word in financial solvency, was in danger. Hence, when the suspension was announced, the Exchange was immediately thrown into a panic so severe that, in comparison, the disturbance of the preceding day looked like nothing at all. Two days later, with the price of stocks still going down, the Exchange was closed, and it remained closed for ten days. Bankruptcies followed thick and fast, factories shut down, business came to a standstill; a depression that was to last for nearly six years had begun. Thus dramatically did the "boom" that the Civil War unleashed come to its inexorable end.[1]

One notable reaction to the monopolistic tendencies that had accompanied the business boom, and that became even more apparent during the hard times that followed, was a violent attack on the railroads. As a matter of fact, they were not particularly more reprehensible in their conduct than other big businesses, but their public nature made their behavior more easily observable; moreover, with the railroads, sooner than with most other enterprises, the breakdown of the competitive system was fully apparent. Among the first to protest against railroad extortions were the grain-growers of the upper Mississippi Valley, whose dependence upon the railroads was well-nigh complete. Only by means of the railroads could they ship their produce to market; only in the same fashion could they obtain from the outside world the manufactured articles they had to have. Inasmuch as the number of regions served by competitive lines was few indeed, the ordinary farmer had no choice but to use the road that ran

Side notes: Failure of Jay Cooke and Company; Attacks on the railroads

[1] Henrietta M. Larson, *Jay Cooke: Private Banker* (1936), is useful in this connection.

nearest his farm. Competition was a myth; the railroads regularly charged "all the traffic would bear," and dictated at will the terms on which they chose to serve their patrons. Elevators and warehouses, often owned or controlled in turn by the railroads, did likewise; and middlemen, themselves compelled to pay a heavy toll in freight to the roads, were not far behind. Efforts to "get another railroad" so as to restore competition rarely availed; more frequently companies that had once been competitive joined forces and ceased to compete.

Ripe for an organized revolt, the farmers of the Northwest found in the Patrons of Husbandry, or the Grange, as it was more frequently called, the tool they needed. The founder of this order, Oliver Hudson Kelley, a government clerk at Washington, had intended it to be a farmers' lodge with an attractive secret ritual that might induce the farmer and the farmer's wife, who was also eligible to membership, to listen to expositions of the latest ideas on scientific farming. Founded in 1867, the order began to grow only in the early seventies when the northwestern farmers seized upon it as a means of attacking the railroads. Then Granger orators inflamed public opinion against the railroads, and the Granger organization cleared the way for action.[1]

The Granger idea — that the state should regulate the railroads, if necessary to the point of fixing maximum rates — was older than the movement. Toyed with gingerly in Massachusetts, its real beginning was in Illinois, where during the late sixties laws were passed to restrain both the elevators and the railroads. These early measures proved unavailing, but a new state constitution, adopted in 1870, specifically stated:

> *Section* 15. The General Assembly shall pass laws to correct abuses and to prevent unjust discrimination and extortion in the rates of freight and passenger traffics on the different railroads in this state, and enforce such laws by adequate penalties, to the extent, if necessary for that purpose, of forfeiture of their property and franchises.

With a similarly strong mandate to regulate warehouses, the Illinois legislature of 1871 promptly established maximum rates for the transportation of passengers, required that freight charges should be based entirely upon distance traversed, provided regulations for the storing and shipping of grain, and created a state board of railroad and warehouse commissioners charged with the duty of enforcing the laws. Against these measures the railroads made a determined, and at first a successful, fight, for on the first test case the Supreme Court of Illinois held the laws to be unconstitutional. But the Grangers, now thoroughly aroused, promptly voted one of the judges who had held against them

---

[1] This movement is fully covered by Solon J. Buck, *The Granger Movement* (1913) and less extensively by his *The Agrarian Crusade* (1921).

out of office, and replaced him with a judge who shared their views. The result was that in 1873 a new law, better drawn but designed to effect the same ends, was sustained.

Meantime the Grangers, bent on using the power of the state to curb the railroads, had gone into politics throughout the Northwest. Some-

The Granger movement

times they were content merely to vote for Republicans or Democrats who shared their views, but frequently they chose third-party candidates on separate "Anti-Monopoly" or "Independent" or "Reform" tickets. Independence Day, 1873, was long remembered as the "Farmers' Fourth of July," for on that day hundreds of Granger audiences gave their approval to a *Farmers' Declaration of Independence*, which repeated in well-worn phraseology the grievances from which farmers suffered, and announced in no uncertain way their determination to find relief. Presently Granger legislatures had enacted, not only in Illinois, but also in Wisconsin, Minnesota, and Iowa, measures of drastic regulation for railroads and warehouses. In each instance litigation followed, and the railroads, despairing of aid from the Granger-minded state courts, at length took their cases to the federal courts. The Granger laws, railroad attorneys claimed, were impairments of contracts that the states had already made in granting charters to the railroads, and they provided for the taking of private property without due process of law. But in the spring of 1877, the United States Supreme Court ruled against the railroads in a series of decisions, the most important of which were *Munn vs. Illinois* and *Peik vs. the Chicago and Northwestern Railroad*. Thus the "right of a state to regulate a business that is public in nature though privately owned and managed" won striking vindication, and a weapon was forged with which, it was hoped, not only the railroads but other monopolistic enterprises also could be attacked. Most of the early Granger laws were defective and had to be repealed, but the principle on which they were founded endured, and before long railroad and warehouse commissions were hard at work in nearly every state. Moreover, it was this same principle that underlay the resort to governmental regulation later on in many other fields of business endeavor. Presently both states and nation were to regard the protection of the individual from corporation exploitation as one of the most important of their functions.

The Granger movement, although short-lived, left other legacies besides the point of law it had made. Convinced that they were being

Granger contributions

robbed by manufacturers and middlemen, the Grangers made strenuous efforts to establish co-operative farm-implement factories, elevators, creameries, and general stores. They experimented with purchasing agencies, and tried out co-operative selling. Many of these ventures were unsuccessful, not so much because they were wrong in principle as because of the inexperience and mismanagement of the men who were placed in charge. These business failures, more than anything else, account for the sudden decline in Granger popularity about 1876, and the relegation of the Patrons of Husbandry once more to the inconspicuous rôle of a farmers' lodge. But the farmers who had participated in the movement did not soon forget the fright they had given the politicians by their independence, the victory they had won over the railroads, and the good times they had had at lodge meetings and picnics. Also, the occasional surviving co-operatives paved the way for an important development later on.[1]

[1] Thomas C. Cochran and William Miller, *The Age of Enterprise: A Social History of Industrial America* (1942), is a left-wing view of the development of big business. On oil, see Paul H. Giddens, *The Birth of the Oil Industry* (1938), and *The Beginnings of the Petroleum Industry: Sources and Bibliography* (1941). Biographies of industrialists include H. O. Evans, *Iron Pioneer: Henry W. Oliver* (1942); J. K. Winkler, *Tobacco Tycoon: The Story of James Buchanan Duke* (1942); Harper Leech and John Carroll, *Armour and his Times* (1938). D. B. Steinman, *The Builders of the Bridge* (1945), is the story of John Roebling and his son.

24

American Society During the Depression

THE sudden descent from post-war prosperity to post-panic adversity plunged the American people into an atmosphere of the deepest gloom. Critics of American society had not been lacking while times were good, but their comments, all too frequently, had fallen on deaf ears. Now, with each succeeding year a little harder than the one that had gone before, the apostles of pessimism reigned supreme. Long and earnestly they dwelt upon the sins of society, the wickedness of business, and the total depravity of the politicians. Could the United States hope to survive the moral collapse it had suffered? [1]

There was reason for the gloom. America had long been regarded as the land of opportunity, but a trip through the slum district of any

American slums

great American city seemed to show rather that it was the land of want. In New York City, out of a hundred thousand slum-dwellers, twenty thousand lived in cellars; in Boston, one-fifth of the total population lived in flimsy, overcrowded tenements. Unemployment estimates for the country at large revealed that from two to three million people were out of work, and for most of these the long, expensive trip to the "free lands" of the West completely closed that "safety-valve." Wages dropped precipitately, woman and child labor were ruthlessly exploited, actual starvation was by no means unknown. Everywhere, but most of all in the crowded city centers where ignorance of the simplest sanitary precautions was rivaled only by indifference to those that were known, preventable diseases, such as smallpox, typhoid, and typhus, took a heavy toll. Always such suffering fell heaviest upon the poor. At any given time three-fourths of the sickness and death in New York City was furnished by the less-favored half of the population.

Hardly less distressing than the plight of the poor was the vulgar ostentation of a small army of *parvenu* rich.[2] War profiteers, successful specu-

---

[1] Don C. Seitz, *The Dreadful Decade* (1926), makes no effort to avoid overstatement.

[2] Gustavus Myers, *History of the Great American Fortunes* (3 vols., 1910), shows little sympathy for its subject.

lators, oil men and miners who had "struck it rich" flocked to the cities to display their wealth. Few of them could approximate the extravagances of the notorious Jim Fisk, but many of them tried. Fisk, at the height of his glory, had sumptuous offices in "Castle Erie," a huge marble building on Eighth Avenue in New York that also housed his privately owned and operated Grand Opera House. From his theatrical stars and dancers, many of whom were imported, he recruited a harem that might well have been the envy of an Oriental potentate. The chief recipients of his favor lived in palaces, and fared forth in handsome carriages, drawn sometimes, when Fisk went along, by three teams of fine horses, whites to the left and blacks to the right. Among Fisk's other fancies were canary birds, hundreds of which, in gilded cages, adorned his rooms, and the well-appointed steamboats that he also owned and loved. On occasion he would dress himself up in the gold lace of an admiral's uniform, and once, when so arrayed, he contrived to receive President Grant. The colonelcy of the Ninth Regiment of the New York National Guard, a position he obtained by means of generous gifts, furnished him another opportunity to indulge his penchant for gaudy pageantry. During the summer of 1871 he took the entire regiment to Boston at his own expense to celebrate the anniversary of the battle of Bunker Hill. He died on January 7, 1872, from bullet wounds inflicted by one of his own kind, Edward S. Stokes, a "business and amatory rival." Stokes, for his crime, was sentenced to four years in the penitentiary at Sing Sing, but there he received many special privileges, such, for example, as being permitted to drive about after night with the span of horses he kept for the purpose at a local livery stable. On his release he became the proprietor of the Hoffman House at Broadway and Twenty-Sixth Street, New York, a hotel chiefly noted for the daring paintings on its barroom walls.[1]

The newly rich

While the loose living of a Jim Fisk could hardly be said to reflect against the character of the American people as a whole, there was an abundance of other evidence at hand for the use of alarmists who held that morality "to a fatal extent" had broken down. It was disheartening to have the name of the leading preacher of the time, Henry Ward Beecher, bandied about among the unregenerate because of an affair he was alleged to have carried on with a woman of his congregation. Beecher was probably innocent, but in any event the conspiracy to disgrace him and the long trial it involved were ugly enough. Conventional citizens were shocked, in a day when divorce had not yet become a national pastime, at the ease and frequency with which marriages were annulled under the lax laws of two offending

Moral laxity

[1] R. H. Fuller. *Jubilee Jim; the Life of Colonel James Fisk, Jr.* (1928).

states, Connecticut and Indiana. From West Virginia to Arkansas, the region over which the Civil War had been fought, bands of ruffians continued their wartime habits, and for years escaped arrest. Most noted of these outlaws was Jesse James, who in 1872 robbed the Kansas City Fair of ten thousand dollars, and until the time of his death a decade later kept the Kansas-Missouri border in a state of frightened expectancy. City gangs likewise defied the law, and committed depredations that would have taxed the talents of twentieth-century racketeers.[1] Gambling, particularly in the cities and along the frontier, flourished covertly or openly as the taste of the community preferred. The State of Louisiana raised money by a lottery. Prostitution was railed at and preached against, but flaunted itself in every sizable town. Intemperance was the commonest vice of all, and since the Civil War had seemingly been definitely on the increase. During the war most of the state prohibition laws had been repealed, while the national government, by placing a tax on intoxicants, had, in a sense, given the liquor traffic its blessing. Saloons, as the places where liquor was sold came universally to be called, were outfitted with clublike attractiveness and their popularity is attested by the fact that the total capital invested in the liquor business grew from $29,000,000 in 1860 to $193,000,000 in 1880. Most of the immigrant groups gave the liquor interests their enthusiastic support.

The sordidness of business during the post-war years was another subject that aroused the anxiety of thoughtful critics. The well-nigh universal devotion of Americans to the pursuit of wealth
Business ethics was in itself a heavy curse, but the devious means that men used to gain their ends hit at the very foundations of society. In part this alarming laxity of conduct could be blamed upon the war itself, which, for literally millions of young Americans, had stood in lieu of a college education. As students of war they had been taught to deceive the enemy, to take his property, to destroy, and to kill; as graduates of such a course they sometimes failed to perceive that the virtues of war were not also the virtues of peace. Furthermore, with business expanding so rapidly, executive experience of any kind was in great demand. American capitalists had not often gone to war themselves, but when peace was restored they made good use of the war-trained heroes. Army officers were, after all, trained executives, and the high-ranking officer who was not promptly solicited to accept a "business opening" was rare indeed.

It would be a mistake, however, to blame the war for every evil practice of the business world. Far more important was the utter novelty of

[1] Herbert Asbury, *The Gangs of New York; an Informal History of the Underworld* (1928).

large-scale business operations. Before the Civil War most American businesses were relatively small, and their fields of activity were local. Standards of conduct existed which the prudent business man, to retain the good-will of his customers and the public, felt obliged to recognize. But for large-scale business no code of ethics had yet been evolved. With monopoly, or at least near-monopoly, as the goal, the struggle for survival among competitors was intense, and as a rule only the ruthless had a chance to win. The law offered no restraint, for, since similar problems had never before been faced, laws to meet them had never been devised; furthermore, as business organizations grew in size and power they found that they could, when they chose, have a hand in both the making and the enforcement of laws. The situation was not unlike that on the high seas in the days when piracy and buccaneering, unchallenged by international law, amounted almost to legitimate occupations.[1]

Corporation methods of finance offered an opportunity, never long neglected, for astounding frauds in the issuance and manipulation of stocks and bonds. "Wildcat" or "blue-sky" securities were easily sold to a public made gullible by the unprece- *Corporation finance* dented number of fortunes that the "boom" times actually produced. Oil companies were organized that never drilled a well, mining companies that never sunk a shaft, railroad companies that never laid a rail, all for the sole purpose of separating careless investors from their savings. General Robert C. Schenck, an ex-congressman from Ohio whom Grant sent as Minister to England, gave his support to the promoters of a mining venture that sold fifty thousand dollars' worth of worthless stock to British investors.[2] General George B. McClellan, more innocently, backed a ten-million-dollar corporation that proposed to exploit a mythical diamond and ruby field in California.

Even the more substantial corporations were frequently led to "water" their stock and to incur bonded indebtedness altogether out of proportion to their assets. Daniel Drew, a pious old fraud who hoped to purchase pardon for his sins by making generous pledges, mostly never paid, to Drew Theological Seminary, wormed his way into the directorate of the Erie Railway, became its treasurer, and for years manipulated the price of its stock in such a way as to enhance his private fortune. According to a current Wall Street saying: "Dan'l says up — Erie goes up. Dan'l says down — Erie goes down. Dan'l says wigglewaggle — Erie bobs both ways." In 1868 Cornelius Vanderbilt, who already controlled the New York Central and the Hudson River Railroad, proposed to add the badly wrecked Erie to his domain. A battle royal followed in

[1] F. C. Sharp and P. G. Fox, *Business Ethics; Studies in Fair Competition* (1937).
[2] Schenck further distinguished himself by writing a treatise on poker-playing.

which Drew, supported by his apt "pupils," Jay Gould and Jim Fisk, finally won. To do so, however, Drew and his associates found it necessary to issue fifty thousand shares of fraudulent stock, to flee to New Jersey to escape arrest, and to bribe the New Jersey legislature to legalize their transaction. But Drew's luck did not last. His two "pupils" raised the price of Erie stock by sales abroad, thanklessly cornered their teacher, and trimmed him of a million and a half. The Panic of 1873 also hit him hard, and by 1876 he was bankrupt with liabilities of over a million dollars and no assets to speak of. Long a target of reproach, he died three years later with none to mourn his passing.[1]

Not many types of sizable business enterprise came through the cycle of boom and depression with clean records. Three New York savings banks failed in 1872 under the most scandalous circum-

Bank failures

stances; while small investors suffered acutely, the former bank officials continued to live in luxury. During the first eight years of the seventies, twenty-eight New York life insurance companies either failed outright, or avoided failure by amalgamation with some stronger concern. Losses to policy-holders amounted to a nominal total of $159,000,000 insurance. Even the solvent companies unblushingly "froze out" aged and undesirable policy-holders, usually by increasing rates. "The whole chapter," said the *Commercial and Financial Chronicle*,[2] "is so dark a record of betrayal of corporate trust — incapacity being so blended with dishonesty that it is impossible to separate them — that if we had the space and the data, we should not have the desire to expose its details."

Whatever the shortcomings of business may have been, they met their match in politics. The Grant administration was known, even before it had ended, as the most corrupt that the Republic had yet

Political scandals

experienced. Reconstruction, with its attempt to perpetuate the rule of the northern Radicals by forcing Negro rule upon the South, would have been a scandal even if honestly carried out, but the number of honest officials in the "carpet-bag" South seems to have been negligible. And yet the scandals that rocked the country were as frequently associated with the North or the West as with the South. The Crédit Mobilier, the Whiskey Ring, the frauds in the Indian service, and the Salary Grab Act had no southern or reconstruction connotation whatever. In the fields of state and local government political degradation reached its lowest depths. The spoils system, everywhere deeply entrenched, had produced an unsavory set of petty party "bosses,"

---

[1] Bouck White, *The Book of Daniel Drew* (1910), and A. D. H. Smith, *Commodore Vanderbilt* (1927), are true in the picture if not in every detail.

[2] April 19, 1879.

each presiding over his county or city or state because, by fair means or foul, he had gathered into his hands the disposal of the "patronage." Working together as a party "machine," the bosses could levy assessments, win elections, reward the faithful, punish the disobedient, and, if they chose, line their pockets with public money and exact a heavy toll from business.

As befitted its size and prominence, New York City furnished the country with the outstanding example of municipal corruption. There the Tammany Society, a political organization that dated back to the eighteenth century, controlled the local machinery of the Democratic Party, and regularly rolled up huge majorities for the Democratic ticket. Tammany Hall, as the society was usually called (after its meeting-place on Fourteenth Street), won the support of the masses by providing them with a kind of unofficial social insurance. Tammany leaders in each ward made it their business to find jobs for the unemployed, to relieve the needy, to care for the sick, to aid the newly arrived immigrants in their efforts to become adjusted. In return for all this, Tammany chiefs expected and obtained unquestioning political support. When extra votes were needed, wholesale frauds were easily possible, for the election machinery was in Tammany hands. In the election of 1868, for example, it was generally believed that the returns from New York City and Brooklyn were held back until the rest of the state could be heard from so that enough votes could be cast for John T. Hoffman, the Tammany candidate for governor, to insure his election.

When Grant became President of the United States the "Grand Sachem" of Tammany Hall was William M. Tweed, a thoroughgoing corruptionist who had worked his way up in politics from membership in a volunteer fire department. Tweed's opportunity for wholesale graft came after he and his associates by the most barefaced bribery had secured from the state legislature a city charter that was specifically designed to enable them to avoid responsibility for their crimes. The principals of the "Tweed Ring" were "Boss" Tweed himself, whose presidency of the board of supervisors of New York County (coterminous with New York City) had obvious possibilities; A. Oakey Hall, the mayor, an aspirant for social recognition whose fastidious appearance won him the sobriquet, "Elegant Oakey"; Peter B. Sweeny, treasurer of both city and county, useful not only because of his position, but also because of his unquestioned ability as a lawyer; and Richard B. Connolly, the controller, otherwise and appropriately known as "Slippery Dick." In 1869 this disgusting crew began a series of peculations that mounted year by year until at the height of their power they were dividing among themselves and their

The Tweed Ring

confederates eighty-five per cent of the total expenditures made by the city and county. Tweed received as his share twenty-four per cent of the "take," and the rest was apportioned out according to a prearranged plan. The actual cost of maintaining the city's armories, for example, totaled for a given period $250,000, but the amount paid out allegedly for that purpose was $3,200,000. A courthouse was built that cost about three million dollars, but the county's books showed expenditures for that purpose of about eleven millions. The plastering of this building alone cost the taxpayers $2,870,464.06, and its carpeting $350,000, "enough to cover the whole City Park three times." During a period of thirty months the city and county printing bill ran to over seven million dollars. Probably the total loot taken by the Tweed Ring reached a hundred million dollars.[1]

At last, scathing editorials in the *New York Times*, and cartoons by Thomas Nast in *Harper's Weekly*, began to take effect, and the public

The ring broken up was aroused. George Jones, the owner of the *Times*, was offered a million dollars to quiet his paper; Nast, a half million to go to Europe and cease his campaign of carica-

[1] Rhodes, VII, and Oberholtzer, II, cover this subject with generous detail.

"WHO STOLE THE PEOPLE'S MONEY ?"

THE TWEED RING
Cartoon by Thomas Nast

ture.[1] Long baffled for lack of direct evidence, the *Times* finally had the proofs it wanted put into its hands by an insider with a grievance. The exposure that followed was complete and devastating; the more so when the efforts of Tweed, Hall, and Sweeny to lay the entire blame on Connolly drove the latter to open his records to the reformers. Under the brilliant leadership of Samuel J. Tilden and Charles O'Conor, they were able by the end of 1872 to drive every member of the "ring" out of office. Tweed himself died in jail.[2]

The national rejoicing that Tweed had at last been brought to bay was tempered by the reflection that his misconduct differed only in degree from what went on almost everywhere. James Russell Lowell well expressed the national sense of humiliation when he wrote, apropos of the opening of the Centennial Exposition at Philadelphia:

> Columbia, puzzled what she should display
> Of true home-make on her Centennial Day,
> Asked Brother Jonathan; he scratched his head
> Whittled awhile reflectively, and said,
>
> .   .   .   .
>
> Show your State Legislatures; show your Rings;
> And challenge Europe to produce such things
> As high officials sitting half in sight
> To share the plunder and to fix things right;
> If that don't fetch her, why you only need
> To show your latest style in martyrs — Tweed.
> She'll find it hard to hide her spiteful tears
> At such advance in one poor hundred years.

Lowell's bitter sarcasm well expressed the feeling of hopelessness that overcame so many Americans when they saw depression added to the lengthening list of their nation's woes. Nevertheless, there was a brighter side to the picture, even if most men failed to see it. The United States could not have been wholly bad; if so it would have produced fewer Jeremiahs. There is an element of hope in the recognition of an existing evil, and the number of Americans who now sprang forward to denounce the shortcomings of their nation and their fellow citizens was so great as to constitute in itself good evidence that the times were not altogether out of joint. Three of these unconscious optimists, Edwin Lawrence Godkin, George William Curtis, and Carl Schurz, deserve particular mention. A nation that could list

A brighter side

---

[1] A. B. Paine, *Thomas Nast, His Period and His Pictures* (1904), reproduces many of these cartoons.

[2] Further details on this unsavory story may be found in D. T. Lynch, *"Boss" Tweed* (1927), and M. R. Werner, *Tammany Hall* (1928).

such men among its leaders of thought had no reason to despair. There was yet "balm in Gilead."

E. L. Godkin (1831–1902) was Irish-born but of English stock, the son of a distinguished Protestant clergyman and journalist.[1] Educated for the law, young Godkin chose instead to make journalism his career, and, after a brief connection with the London *Daily News* and the Belfast *Northern Whig*, he emigrated in 1856 to America. Here he at once made friends, and forged ahead so rapidly that in 1865, when he was not yet thirty-four years of age, forty interested stockholders subscribed one hundred thousand dollars with which he was to start a weekly newspaper, the *Nation*. Despite many early financial embarrassments, the venture succeeded beyond its founders' highest hopes, and the *Nation* came to exercise an influence upon American life second to none. According to James Bryce, it was "the best weekly not only in America but in the world." Its pronouncements were awaited eagerly by ministers, editors, and minor publicists who pushed the radius of its influence far beyond the number of its readers. Godkin fearlessly attacked every evil that he saw, and aimed his most barbed shafts at the venal politicians whom the spoils system had foisted on the country. He stood steadfastly for a sound-money policy, but he denounced scornfully the business rascality that the age produced. He saw, far more clearly than if he had been a native American, the elemental flaws in American society, and bitingly headed an editorial on the Beecher trial "Chromo Civilization." Ruefully he pointed out what the witnesses revealed about American "ways of living, standards of right and wrong, traits of manners, codes of propriety, religious and social ideas." Floral tributes sent by Beecher's congregation to grace the trial he likened to "wreaths round the manhole of a sewer."

George William Curtis (1824–1892) was a New Englander by birth who had come to New York City as a boy.[2] He maintained the best traditions of Puritan New England: read Emerson, lived for a while at Brook Farm, and before the Civil War wrote several books of travel and criticism. Stirred deeply by the war, he became in 1863 editor of the strongly pro-northern *Harper's Weekly*, which, in the ascendancy it soon gained over men's minds, was rivaled only by its more strictly intellectual contemporary, the *Nation*. Allotting generous space to pictorial representation of current events, frequently drawn on the spot, and featuring the cartoons of Thomas Nast, *Harper's Weekly* appealed to a far wider audience than the *Nation*; nor was it, out of deference possibly to the publishers' profits,

E. L. Godkin [side note]

George William Curtis [side note]

---

[1] Rollo Ogden (editor), *Life and Letters of Edwin Lawrence Godkin* (2 vols., 1907).

[2] Edward Cary, *George William Curtis* (1894).

so avowedly militant in its advocacy of reform. Curtis's influence, however, was exerted from the lecture platform almost as actively as from the editor's desk. Scores of audiences heard his lecture on "Political Infidelity," but he did not always deal exclusively with politics. Concerned because American materialism was deadening the moral sensibilities of the people, he once cried out:

> Are we satisfied that America should have no other excuse for independent national existence than a superior facility of money-making? Why, if we are unfaithful as a nation, though our population were to double in a year, and the roar and rush of our vast machinery were to silence the music of the spheres, and our wealth were enough to buy all the world, our population could not bully history, nor all our riches bribe the eternal justice not to write upon us: "Ichabod, Ichabod, thy glory is departed."

Carl Schurz (1829–1906), like Godkin, was alien-born. His father, a small-town German schoolmaster, made every sacrifice in order to permit young Carl to work for a doctor's degree in history at the University of Bonn. Here the boy was caught up, along *Carl Schurz* with many other student liberals, in the revolutionary movements of 1848–49, joined the rebel forces, and escaped capture only by fleeing to France. Later he went to Switzerland, where many other German refugees had gathered, and where he might have remained but for his determination to rescue one of his Bonn professors, Gottfried Kinkel, who was under sentence of imprisonment for life at Spandau, near Berlin. The exciting story of Kinkel's rescue by Schurz, and of their joint flight to England, is not often paralleled except in fiction, but much of the rest of Schurz's life also reads like a romance. He tried living in France, only to be expelled as a dangerous radical, and at last sailed for America where, naturally, he joined the German colony in Wisconsin. Because of his intense interest in liberal democracy, he was soon drawn into politics, and his anti-slavery sentiments made him a Republican. A born orator, he spoke not only in German, but had soon acquired such facility in the use of English that his assistance in campaigns was in great demand. He fought loyally in the Civil War, from which he emerged a major-general, and after the war made an official tour of the South at the behest of President Johnson. In 1867 he became part owner and editor of a German-language newspaper, published at St. Louis, and was soon in the thick of the fight for Liberal Republicanism. By the time he went to the United States Senate in 1869 his Americanization was thoroughgoing and complete. Like Lincoln, he was intensely interested in proving that democracy as a form of government was fit to survive, and the venality of the spoilsmen who stood ready to betray it for a price drove him to the highest invective. When he spoke in the Senate the galleries were packed, and when he took to the lecture platform, as he often did, great crowds came out to hear him.[1]

In the business and political world the work of such men as Godkin, Curtis, and Schurz was not wholly without effect. Political scandals were ruthlessly exposed, and sometimes, as in the case of Tweed, the guilty parties were punished. A governor in Nebraska and a state treasurer in Minnesota were impeached and removed from office. A member of the Kansas legislature laid on the speaker's desk seven thousand dollars that he had been paid to vote for the re-election of Samuel C. Pomeroy to the United States Senate, and Pomeroy was not re-elected. The Whiskey Ring was put out of business; thievery in the Indian service was restrained; wholesale attempts to bribe Congress, as in the Crédit Mobilier, were not again attempted; alien rule in the South and the corruption it bred were soon overthrown. Most significant of all, the state served notice through the Granger movement that it could and would use the power of government, honestly administered, to restrain whatever practices of big business, particularly the railroads, seemed to interfere unjustly with the personal and property rights of the individual.

Even more noteworthy than all these efforts to purify politics and to regulate business were the spiritual strivings of a people, now acutely conscious of its shortcomings. The success of the American experiment in democracy depended in the last analysis upon the character of the individual citizens who made up the population. If the citizens were honest, capable, and intelligent, the future of the nation, however much it might be temporarily eclipsed by the depression, was bright; but if the citizens were unworthy, prosperity itself could not dispel the gloom. Out of such heart-searchings there came a significant educational renaissance, a renewed interest in literary activity, and a wholesome enthusiasm for humanitarian reform.

With respect to public elementary education, the Civil War, at least so far as the North was concerned, merely interrupted a trend of development that had begun long before. After the war, as before, the "little red schoolhouse," or its equivalent, continued to be the chief citadel of rural education, and from its lowly rostrum young men and maidens, only a little older than the "scholars" they taught, dispensed knowledge of the "three R's" — reading, writing, and arithmetic. In the towns and villages, buildings of several "rooms" could be found, and the process of separating the various "grades" from one another, with a teacher for each, was an ideal more and more frequently attained. Most rapid progress, however, was

Educational advances

---

[1] C. V. Easum, *The Americanization of Carl Schurz* (1929), treats of his pre-Civil War career; Joseph Schafer, *Carl Schurz, Militant Liberal* (1930), of his whole life.

made in the cities, where new ideas in education did not put so severe a strain upon taxable resources. In 1873, for example, St. Louis, following the lead of Mrs. Carl Schurz, whose efforts to introduce the European kindergarten idea into America antedated the Civil War, accepted the innovation, and so began a movement that was soon to spread to the whole country. The rapid multiplication of tax-supported normal schools (of which there were only twelve when Lincoln was inaugurated) served greatly to improve the quality of instruction: teachers who themselves had no opportunity to attend such schools learned the latest methods at summer "institutes," locally provided for the purpose.[1] The spell cast by the Webster spellers and by the McGuffey readers had not yet been broken, but new and better books were being written. Publishers did not long neglect this opportunity for profit, and the means they used to secure "adoptions" sometimes failed to square with the precepts so generously sprinkled through the books they sold. The fact that the several states, operating through local school districts set up by state law, had complete control of educational policy accounts for the wide variety of educational practice in the different parts of the country, but in 1867 the national government took a hand by creating the office of the United States Commissioner of Education, whose business it was "to collect statistics and facts concerning the conditions and progress of education in the several states and territories and to diffuse information respecting the organization and management of schools and school systems and methods of teaching."

Even more striking than the rapid development of the elementary schools was the movement for free public high schools that swept the country during the post-war period, and persisted throughout the dark days of depression.[2] Before the Civil War High schools private academies had generally carried forward the education of such students as intended to enter college; indeed, when the war broke out, there were only about one hundred public high schools in the whole United States. The next few decades, however, witnessed the almost complete elimination of the old-fashioned academy and the substitution in its place of secondary instruction at state expense. By 1870 the country had about five hundred public high schools; by 1880 the number had risen to eight hundred; by the end of the century, to six thousand. With the state so thoroughly committed to expenditures for high schools, insistence upon better qualified teachers was inevitable, and systems of

[1] A comparison of Edward Eggleston, *The Hoosier Schoolmaster* (1871), with Herbert Quick, *One Man's Life* (1925), shows how rapidly conditions were changing.

[2] Two excellent manuals on the general subject of education are E. P. Cubberley, *Public Education in the United States* (1934), and E. G. Dexter, *A History of Education in the United States* (1904).

certification were devised for the purpose of weeding out the unfit. As the children of the masses pushed on into the high schools, revision of the curriculum to meet the needs of those who had no thought of entering college began to be made, although an undue emphasis upon mathematics and the classical languages long persisted. From shorter beginnings the high-school term generally lengthened out to four years, which, together with the eight years usually assigned to the elementary school, provided a total of twelve years' instruction. Eight or nine months of school per year was the customary goal toward which educators worked, but frequently, especially in the country districts, the school year was much shorter. Many of the northern states enacted compulsory education laws of varying terms and efficacy.

In these significant developments the South, necessarily, lagged far behind. What little there was of free public education in the South

Education in the South

before the war had vanished during the conflict, and the freeing of the slaves now placed upon the limited financial resources of the reconstructed states a double burden, schools for the children of the freedmen, and schools for the children of the whites. As already noted, most of the carpet-bag governments made generous legal provisions for education, although the distance between promise and performance was often very great. Nevertheless, to cite a single example, South Carolina by 1876 had a public-school population of fifty thousand whites and seventy thousand colored children as against a total of only twenty thousand in 1860.[1]

Quite the most striking educational development of the times, however, appeared in the field of higher education. It would seem, almost, that from this source Americans expected to draw the inspiration and the information that would confound the critics of democracy and make of the United States a kind of Utopia. Even the uneducated masses showed a touching faith in the power of learning. Education, especially higher education, they tended to regard as an unfailing panacea for all of the ills that beset both the nation as a whole and the individuals that composed it.

The remarkable transformation that came over higher education in the United States during the generation that followed the Civil War

American universities

owed much to the statesmanship of a small group of university presidents. Chief among these, no doubt, was Charles W. Eliot, the brilliant young chemist, who in 1869, when only thirty-five years of age, took the helm at Harvard. Much older, but fully alive to the currents of the age and destined to serve for many years, was Frederick A. P. Barnard, the president after 1864 at

[1] E. W. Knight, *Public Education in the South* (1922).

Columbia. Almost equally noteworthy were such other newly chosen presidents as Andrew D. White of Cornell (1868), James McCosh of Princeton (1868), Noah Porter of Yale (1871), James B. Angell of Michigan (1871), John Bascom of Wisconsin (1874), and Daniel Coit Gilman of Johns Hopkins (1876).[1] Six of these eight men were of New England birth, and all but one of them, McCosh, a Scott from the University of Edinburgh, were graduates of New England colleges. Most of them, according to the prevailing custom of American scholars, had traveled or studied abroad, and possessed a fair familiarity with European university methods. Their concern, however, was neither to preserve the traditional New England college nor to imitate what was being done in Europe. Rather, what they set out to do was to revise the American system of higher education in such a way as to make it fit the needs of a rapidly changing America.

The best efforts of educators would have been in vain but for the liberal financial resources they were able to tap. The profits of the new industrial age were not all put back into business; millions of dollars were poured by philanthropists into education. Be- *Philanthropy* fore the Civil War such a gift as that of Stephen Girard, who at his death in 1831 left two million dollars to found a school for boys in Philadelphia, was so rare as to brand its donor as an eccentric. After the war such gifts became increasingly common, in fact, they were both sought after and expected. In 1865, Ezra Cornell, whose fortune had been made from the electric telegraph, gave a half-million dollars to found Cornell University in Ithaca, New York. In 1873, a similar gift from Cornelius Vanderbilt, the railroad magnate, made possible the establishment of Vanderbilt University in Nashville, Tennessee. Three years later, Johns Hopkins University opened its doors because a rich merchant, banker, and railroad director of Baltimore had endowed it with property worth four and one-half million dollars, and his name. Supplemented presently by the outpourings of such philanthropists as John D. Rockefeller, Andrew Carnegie, and Edward Stephen Harkness the total endowment of colleges and universities in the United States ultimately reached enormous figures. The resources of Harvard, for example, amounted to only two and one-half million dollars when Eliot became its president in 1869; two-thirds of a century later this sum had grown to one hundred and thirty millions.[2]

A powerful stimulus to higher education at public expense came from the generous gifts of land made by the federal government to the states

---

[1] Fabian Franklin, *The Life of Daniel Coit Gilman* (1910), furnishes an excellent insight into the way in which a great university was built.

[2] C. F. Thwing, *A History of Higher Education in America* (1906).

under the terms of the Morrill Act of 1862. Each state, in return for a land subsidy of as many times thirty thousand acres as it had senators and representatives, was required within five years to establish at least one college which, "without excluding other scientific and classical studies," would "teach such branches of learning as are related to agriculture and the mechanic arts." The law provided also that whenever any of the land so given should be sold, the principal must be kept intact, and only the interest used; furthermore, depletions in the fund must be made good by legislative appropriation. Unfortunately the original law failed to specify a minimum price per acre below which lands might not be sold, and the correction made in 1889 that fixed a minimum of ten dollars per acre came too late to do much good. Nevertheless, the sums realized by the states were considerable, and in a few instances they were about all that could have been expected. Ezra Cornell, for example, so successfully located and sold the lands handed over by New York to the university that bore his name that he was able to pile up for it an endowment of five and one-half million dollars.

Federal Landgrants

Hardly less important than the financial aspect of the Morrill Act was the obligation it laid upon the states to support a greatly extended program of higher education. The intent of the law was clearly to place a college course within the reach of anyone who wanted it, and to make this privilege a charge on government. Nevertheless, state after state revised its educational system in order to meet the terms of the act. Many states used their grant to help along, or sometimes to found, a single state university; others showed a preference for separate colleges of agriculture and engineering; only a few attempted in any way to dodge the issue. Once a college or university was accepted as a financial responsibility of the state, it could almost certainly count upon annual legislative appropriations to keep it alive and growing. Many of the western state universities, notably Wisconsin, Illinois, Minnesota, and California, rose to prominence as a result of the Morrill Act, and ultimately not less than sixty-nine "landgrant colleges" profited from its terms.

State-supported universities

But the changes that came over higher education during these years went far deeper than mere size and numbers; no less in the endowed than in the state institutions there came a determined break from the traditional idea of what a college course should be. The backbone of the old curriculum had been the classical languages and mathematics, with somewhat less attention to such subjects as ethics and rhetoric. Courses in the modern languages and history were occasionally tolerated, and a little science, with the

Changes in the curriculum

laboratory work confined to what experiments the professor could do in the presence of the class. Most of the teachers were all-around scholars who were as much at home with one subject as with another. Indeed the "chairs" that some of them occupied were veritable benches of learning; one heroic Columbia professor taught mental and moral philosophy, English literature, history, political economy, and logic. But the old curriculum bore scant resemblance to the new civilization that was growing up outside the college walls. Its drill on the classics and its moralistic, theological bent were designed at best only to fit the needs of the few — most of whom expected to enter some "learned" profession — rather than the many, most of whom in the new age were destined for decidedly materialistic careers. If higher education was to be opened to the masses, then its content must be such as would have meaning for them. There was, moreover, an infinite quantity of new data to be evaluated and assimilated into the scholar's store of knowledge. An economic revolution was in process that the colleges and universities had all but ignored, while every field of science cried out for further exploration and investigation.

Under the leadership of President Eliot, Harvard University began to emphasize the right of a student to have some voice in the selection of his course of study. In most colleges the studies were rigidly prescribed, but Harvard's experiments with "electives" *The elective system* during the sixties convinced Eliot that the elective principle was the correct one upon which to build a new curriculum. Year after year the number of "prescribed" courses was cut down and the number of "electives" was lengthened. This process served a double purpose. On the one hand, it permitted the student to escape from subjects for which he lacked interest or aptitude; on the other, it permitted the indefinite expansion of the number of "subjects" that a given institution might offer. Once more, as in the Middle Ages, the totality of knowledge became the university's goal, rather than merely the set pattern of disciplines that tradition had developed; and an infinite number of subjects that previously had been regarded as well beyond the pale of educational respectability — some of them frankly "bread-and-butter" courses — began to enter the curriculum. The elective idea spread like wildfire all over the country, and awakened both enthusiastic approval and fierce denunciation. President McCosh of Princeton was among the skeptics, and on one occasion he met President Eliot in a public debate on the topic. Critics of the new system complained, as Henry Cabot Lodge said later, that it permitted students "to escape without learning anything at all by a judicious selection of unrelated subjects taken up only because they were easy or because the burden imposed by those who taught them was light." But, for good or for ill, electives had come to stay, although most institutions ultimately insisted upon a central core of "required" subjects.[1]

Quite as revolutionary as the elective system was the equally determined insistence upon technical and professional training. The Morrill Act gave a great stimulus to agricultural education, and as time went on more and more students who were primarily interested in the problems of farming began to put in their appearance. For a long time, however, the agricultural colleges were decidedly on the defensive because of their low enrollment. The University of Wisconsin, for example, had only one graduate in agriculture by 1880. Nevertheless, the building up of a staff of experts went on, and ultimately the public realized that the agricultural colleges reached a far wider field than the small number of students who attended them. Remarkable progress was made in the investigation of such subjects as the diseases of plants and animals, the proper treatment of soils, and the selection of seeds. All this information was passed along in one fashion or another to the farm population, and the schools themselves became headquarters not so much for the training of farmers as for the training of experts to advise the farmers. The Morrill Act did a similarly important service for engineering, particularly with respect to the more practical aspects of the subject. Courses in mechanical and civil engineering, mining and metallurgy, and architecture were established which presently produced sufficiently well-trained graduates that the business world was eager to obtain their services.

Technical and professional schools

Perhaps the most astonishing development of all began in the medical schools, which before the Civil War had been nothing less, according to one authority, than a "social disgrace." Most of these early institutions existed to make what little money they could out of the students who patronized them, and the so-called "doctors" they turned out were quite definitely a liability to society. Even at Harvard, which possessed one of the best of the medical schools in the country, the student who took two lecture courses for a term less than four months in length was entitled to his degree if he could prove that his total medical experience ran to three years, and could pass a simple examination. Written examinations were said by the head of the school, as late as 1870, to be out of the question, because "a majority of the students cannot write well enough." President Eliot had much to do with the progress that Harvard made in medical education, and

Medical education

---

[1] Charles W. Eliot, *A Late Harvest* (1924). Many of the great universities have produced their historians, among them F. P. Keppel, *Columbia* (1914); J. H. Gardiner, *Harvard* (1915); Elizabeth H. Haight and J. M. Taylor, *Vassar* (1915); J. F. A. Pyre, *Wisconsin* (1920); Jonas Viles, *The University of Missouri* (1939).

that was soon communicated to other colleges. Supported by Oliver Wendell Holmes, whose service to American medicine ranks parallel to his service to American literature, Eliot insisted upon actual attendance for the three-year period, together with laboratory and clinical training. Drawing freely upon the superior knowledge and techniques of European scientists, American medical scholarship was soon to be fully abreast of the times.

What was being done for the teaching of medicine was also being done for the law. Instead of a few months' cramming, law students were now introduced by Dean C. C. Langdell of the Harvard Law School to the "case method," by which they were required to dig out for themselves the rules of law that had grown out of judicial decisions. Here again, as with the colleges of arts and sciences when the elective system was introduced, there arose from conservative sources a great outcry of opposition, but the new method had come to stay, and in the course of time was adopted by practically every reputable law school in the country. As with medicine, the course was lengthened, standards were raised, and competent scholars were engaged to devote their full time to teaching.

Perhaps the best evidence that American scholarship was reaching maturity was supplied by the establishment of a considerable number of graduate schools. Prior to this time the determined devotee of learning had little recourse from the requirement of study abroad. American scholars were European made. Some *Graduate schools* obtained their training in England, but an apparent disdain on the part of English savants for Americans who pretended to scholarship led the latter to prefer the Continent, especially Germany, where they were more cordially received.[1] When the time came for the establishment of American graduate schools, therefore, it was the German, not the English, model that was followed; and presently the Ph.D. (Doctor of Philosophy) degree, virtually unknown in England, was to become in America, as in Germany, the heart's desire of every budding young scholar. The first Ph.D. ever conferred in America was given by Yale in 1861, but it was not until ten years later that the Yale graduate school was organized. By 1872 Harvard had established a graduate school, and in 1876 Johns Hopkins University sought to set a new precedent by making graduate work its main concern. Before long even the new state universities of the West were emphasizing the importance of research and the training of scholars, and the day had passed when the only possible place to do advanced work was in Europe. According to President Ira

---

[1] C. F. Thwing, *The American and the German University* (1928), shows the Teutonic influence upon American educational development.

Remsen, Gilman's successor at Johns Hopkins, there had been in 1850 only eight graduate students in the whole United States; by 1875 this number had risen to 399; by the end of the century it was 5668.

The new emphasis on intellectual achievement was revealed also in the activities of a small but able group of scholars. Major J. W. Powell, a war veteran who served for a time as a professor in Illinois Wesleyan University, established his reputation as a geologist by an exploration in 1869 of the Grand Canyon of the Colorado that led presently to its systematic survey under the auspices of the Smithsonian Institution. In 1879 Powell became director of the United States Bureau of Ethnology, and a year later of the United States Geological Survey. During the same period Lewis Henry Morgan, who had won fame even before the Civil War for his studies of the Iroquois Indians, brought out two notable works, *Consanguinity and Affinity* (1868) and *Ancient Society* (1877), which still rank among the most distinguished of the writings of American anthropologists. During these years also Othniel Charles Marsh, professor of paleontology at Yale after 1866, made a number of dangerous but fruitful expeditions into the Rocky Mountain region, and as vertebrate paleontologist for the United States Geological Survey discovered more than a thousand new fossil vertebrates. Other names of note were Simon Newcomb, the astronomer, Benjamin Peirce, the mathematician, and John Fiske, the philosopher. Fiske, as an ardent disciple of Herbert Spencer, did much to popularize in America the Darwinian views on which Spencer's *Synthetic Philosophy* was based; and when, years later, he turned to the writing of American history he treated that subject as a strictly evolutionary process.[1] At best, however, the list of American scholars was not a long one. According to one authority, for every work of research published in the United States during this period not less than fifty appeared in Europe. What interested Americans more than research was the widening of educational opportunity so that everyone might have his chance at learning. The deepening process could wait.

Even the women shared in the new opportunity. Their right to equal treatment in elementary and secondary schools was fairly well acknowledged before the Civil War, but their chance of obtaining instruction on the college level remained slight. In 1865, however, Vassar opened its doors at Poughkeepsie, New York, as a strictly women's college, only to be followed a decade later by Wellesley, not far from Boston. Both institutions struggled along for years without adequate endowments and without adequately prepared students — "between the devil of bankruptcy and the deep sea of the

Science and philosophy

Education for women

[1] J. S. Clark, *The Life and Letters of John Fiske* (2 vols., 1917).

young ladies' seminary."[1] In 1875, Smith College, with a gift of $365,-
000 from Sophia Smith of Hatfield, Massachusetts, to found an institution that would provide educational opportunities for young women
equal to those available for young men, opened at Northampton, Massachusetts, with only fourteen freshmen. Each year it admitted a new
class, but continued to insist on adequate preparation, however small the
numbers. When Bryn Mawr was established in the eighties, near Philadelphia, enough young women were being fitted for college work that the
battle for high standards had no need to be fought over again. The beginnings of Radcliffe College go back to 1879 when the "Annex" at
Harvard offered its first courses for women.

It was not through women's colleges, however, but through co-education that most American women were to get their chance at a college
course. The demand for co-education antedated the Civil
War and was for a long time closely connected with the   Co-education
movement for women's rights. After the war it grew mainly as an
economical and common-sense western idea. Reassured by the experiments of Oberlin, Antioch, and Iowa, all of which had admitted women
along with men before the Civil War, the University of Wisconsin set up
a special normal department for women in 1863, and was presently drawing no distinction between men and women students. Ohio State University admitted women from its beginning in 1870. Other western
universities fell into line, and with them the small denominational colleges, not only in the West, but to a considerable extent also in the East
and even in the South. While co-education thus promptly became the
rule in the West, the number of skeptics in the older sections of the country was great, and in the South separate state institutions for women were
often established as a lesser evil.

Higher education for the Negro made progress in 1867 with the incorporation of Howard University in Washington, named after one of its
most active promoters, General O. O. Howard of the Freedmen's Bureau; and in quick succession such other institutions   Negro
as Fisk University in Nashville, Straight University in New   education
Orleans, and Shaw University in Raleigh began to function. For these
and similar schools northern philanthropy retained for a time a certain
fondness, born of the abolitionist crusade. The Peabody Fund, already
mentioned, was administered mainly with a view to the improvement of
common schools for Negroes, but the Peabody Normal College in Nashville, which it aided generously, also served notably the cause of education among the whites. Unfortunately the Negroes at first thought of

---

[1] F. L. Paxson, *Recent History of the United States* (new edition, 1937), p. 52. See also
A. C. Cole, *A Hundred Years of Mount Holyoke College* (1940).

education, particularly higher education, primarily as a means of escape
from manual labor, and showed little interest in substituting for Latin
and Greek the more "practical" subjects that were crowding into the
curriculums of the northern colleges and universities. Nevertheless, the
Hampton Normal and Agricultural Institute, which opened at Hampton,
Virginia, in 1870 with funds provided by the American Missionary Association, struck out along new and bold lines. Its purpose was to
emphasize the dignity and importance of skill in labor with the hands,
and to prepare its students as well as might be for the type of work that
was actually available to them in the South. Means were provided at
the Institute whereby the poorer students might "work their way
through," and in 1872 Hampton's most distinguished student, Booker
T. Washington, walking and begging rides to make a five-hundred-mile
journey from his home in West Virginia, arrived with fifty cents in his
pocket to take advantage of the opportunities that the Institute offered.
Less than ten years later, Washington was chosen to head a school for
Negroes at Tuskegee, Alabama, that under his leadership was soon to
rival Hampton in its success with the same type of instruction.[1] Critics
of so much emphasis upon industrial education for the Negroes complained that such training was designed merely to keep the colored race
in a permanently inferior status, but in the main the aims and efforts of
Hampton, Tuskegee, and their imitators were applauded by both Negroes and whites. Probably the gradual easing of the tension between
the two races owed much to the activities of these institutions.

The Civil War dealt harshly with American literary talent. The old
generation of American writers — Emerson, Longfellow, Lowell, Whittier, Bryant, Holmes — lived on and continued to write, but
the roar and bustle of the new age had passed them by. The
America they represented was dead and gone. This was not
true of Walt Whitman, perhaps, whose *Leaves of Grass* was presently to
become, according to one opinion, the "Bible of democracy," but the
hiatus between the old generation and the new was nevertheless well
marked. The period represented politically by the Civil War and reconstruction was one of stalemate for American letters. Whether this was
because too many men of potential literary genius perished on the battlefield, or because the martial spirit dulled the interest of Americans in
bookish pursuits, will never be known. "For ten years," said a discouraged observer, "the new generation read nothing but newspapers."

That a new day was soon to dawn became evident when the literary
world discovered that Samuel Langhorne Clemens (1835–1910), better

*American
letters*

---

[1] Booker T. Washington, *Up From Slavery* (new edition, 1937), is one of the most significant of Negro autobiographies.

known by his pen-name, Mark Twain, had more to his credit than an irreverent, western sense of humor.[1] Definitely out of line with the American literary tradition was Mark Twain's birthplace, the western town of Florida, Missouri. Quite as unorthodox was his education, which, to begin with, was derived less from the ungraded school which he attended than from the Mississippi River, which flowed by the town of Hannibal, Missouri, where he spent his boyhood. Always fascinated by the river, and curious about the unknown world from which its steamboats came and into which they went, young Clemens, after spending a few years as an itinerant printer, apprenticed himself to a river pilot, and learned the river "by heart" from St. Louis to New Orleans.

Mark Twain

> In that brief, sharp schooling [he wrote later] I got personally and familiarly acquainted with all the different types of human nature that are to be found in fiction, biography, or history. When I find a well-drawn character in fiction or biography, I generally take a warm personal interest in him, for the reason that I have known him before — met him on the river.

Clemens's career as a river pilot was cut short by the Civil War in which he fought for two full weeks as a Confederate bushwhacker. His heart was not in the fray, and his sympathies ultimately turned to the North. Before the summer of 1861 had ended, he was on his way to Nevada, and by the time the war was over, he had seen most of the mining West, making his way about by reporting for various newspapers. A visit to Hawaii in 1866 gave him the material for a story published in *Harper's Magazine* that same year, and set him to lecturing. Immensely successful with Pacific Coast audiences, he soon had the means to return by way of New York and Panama for a visit to his old home, to make a trip to Europe, and to establish himself in a new home at Hartford, Connecticut.

His writings, based upon his varied experiences and interpreted by the lore he had learned on the river, came thick and fast. *The Celebrated Jumping Frog of Calaveras County, and Other Sketches* (1867), was sheer hilarity; *Innocents Abroad* (1869) became immediately a best-seller because of the fun it poked at the tourist's Europe; *Roughing It* (1872) introduced Easterners to a Far West that was immensely interesting and vital, although in writing it Mark Twain undoubtedly followed the advice he later gave to Rudyard Kipling, "Young man, first get your facts; then distort them as you please"; *The Gilded Age* (1874), written in collaboration with Charles Dudley Warner, satirized skillfully the

---

[1] A. B. Paine, *Mark Twain: A Biography* (3 vols., 1912), and *A Short Life of Mark Twain* (1920), are the best works to consult, but Bernard De Voto, *Mark Twain's America* (1932) is also useful.

corrupt politics, ruthless fortune-chasing, and social bankruptcy of the reconstruction era; *Life on the Mississippi,* published first as a series of articles in the *Atlantic Monthly* for 1875, preserved for all time what Mark Twain knew so well about the fast-ebbing civilization that had centered about the river; *Tom Sawyer* (1876) recovered the scenes of the author's childhood in what William Dean Howells called "the best boy story ever written"; and for a generation longer the list continued to grow. Europeans sooner than Americans recognized that Mark Twain's books had literary merit as well as humor; that in a manner quite at variance with respectable tradition they set forth themes that were equally new. Brahmin Boston, still the self-confessed literary capital of America, was slow to acknowledge that this upstart Westerner was a man of parts, but on December 17, 1877, when the *Atlantic* gave a dinner in honor of Whittier's birthday, Mark Twain was invited to make one of the main addresses. Unfortunately, he resorted to a type of burlesque better suited to the West than to his hearers, who were definitely unamused. But the recognition he had at last received was not recalled.

Mark Twain was not so much the founder of a new school of American writers as he was the ablest representative of a considerable group of

Other western writers

Westerners who exploited the frontier theme in literature well before Frederick Jackson Turner had introduced it to the historians. Far-famed also was Bret Harte, who, although a New Yorker by birth, grew up in California while the spirit of lawlessness was still strong in the mining camps, and with a vividness that has seldom been surpassed described that West in such stories as "The Luck of Roaring Camp" and "The Outcasts of Poker Flat," both of which were published in the *Overland Monthly* during 1868. Harte also stooped sometimes to the writing of charming doggerel, such as the tale of the "Heathen Chinee" whom two white men tried unsuccessfully to cheat at cards:

> Which is why I remark,
> And my language is plain,
> That for ways that are dark
> And for tricks that are vain,
> The Heathen Chinee is peculiar.

Joaquin Miller, born a Hoosier, was taken to Oregon as a child, saw life as a gold miner, soldier, journalist, lawyer, and judge, but won distinction mainly as a minor poet of the West.

William Dean Howells

The period of the seventies witnessed the rise of numerous "local-color" writers from other sections of the country also. William Dean Howells, an Ohioan, went East instead of West, and from the time of the Civil War to the end of the century he was connected in an editorial capacity successively with the *Nation*, the *Atlantic*, and *Harper's*.[1] While he wrote of the East, he never forgot the experiences of his youth, and he featured in his writings the problems of adjustment that confronted one who came from a primitive to a cultured environment. Howells's fame rests mainly upon a long and distinguished sequence of novels, beginning with *Their Wedding Journey* (1871), *A Chance Acquaintance* (1873), and *A Foregone Conclusion* (1875). Edward Eggleston, a Methodist "circuit-rider" who had experienced much of what he wrote, portrayed in his first and best novel, *The Hoosier Schoolmaster* (1871), the quaint country life of southern Indiana. Mention also should be made of George W. Cable of New Orleans, whose *Old Creole Days* appeared in 1879, and Sarah Orne Jewett of Maine, whose exquisite delineations of New England character were printed first as stories in the *Atlantic*, and were later collected into books, *Deephaven* (1877) and *Country Byways* (1881). In these years, too, Henry James, who "was born an American and died an Englishman," began with his *Roderick Hudson* (1875) and *The American* (1876) to write finely spun novels dealing with the contacts of Americans with European sophistication.

Paralleling the educational and literary achievements of the post-war period came a definite upsurge of humanitarian reform. To a great extent this can be accounted for on the ground that exactly such an interest had preceded the Civil War, and that with the war and the immediate problems it raised out of the way, *Humanitarian reform* the old desire to better the lot of the unfortunate reasserted itself. It should not be forgotten, however, that the work of such organizations as the United States Sanitary Commission and the United States Christian Commission had done much to keep alive the humanitarian spirit, even while the war was on; and that the crying needs of the freedmen had made for an awareness of the problems that confronted downtrodden humanity, whether white or black.

Among the many factors that contributed to the popular interest in humanitarianism doubtless the religious revival that swept through Protestant America during these years was one of the most important. Poured forth from thousands of pulpits, the *Moody and Sankey* doctrine that the depression was but a just judgment upon men for their sins produced a multitude of penitents. Rivalry with the Catholics and the Jews, whose numbers were being enormously increased by immigration, and rivalry among the various Protestant denominations themselves spurred on religious workers to greater and greater

---

[1] W. D. Howells, *Years of My Youth* (1916). For a general survey see F. L. Pattee, *A History of American Literature Since 1870* (1915).

activity. Leadership was furnished, less by the great preachers of the day, such as Henry Ward Beecher and Phillips Brooks, than by the evangelists, among whom Dwight L. Moody, the exhorter, and Ira D. Sankey, the singer, were pre-eminent.[1] In 1875 Moody and Sankey, just returned from a series of successful revivals in the British Isles, began a meeting in Philadelphia that lasted three months, and then went on to New York, Chicago, Boston, and other great cities; in Chicago for four months their "tabernacle" was crowded daily by an audience of from five to ten thousand persons. The narrow and traditional doctrines of these evangelists, and of the host of lesser lights who imitated them, had but little direct bearing upon the social problems of the current age, but they at least extolled the Christian virtues and filled "converts" with an earnest if unguided desire to better the lot of their fellowmen.

Far more conscious than the churches of the needs of the time were the Young Men's and Young Women's Christian Associations, both of which dated back to the middle of the century, but began to be really effective only during the seventies. Religion, for them, meant wholesome recreation, study classes, and even musicales, far more than the inculcation of Christian theology. Immediately effective among the submerged classes was the Salvation Army, which invaded the United States from England in 1879, and soon extended its interest from saving the souls of the down-and-out to an extensive program of social activity. Quite at the other extreme of society was Christian Science, a new religious sect that took its tenets from *Science and Health*, a book published by Mrs. Mary Baker G. Eddy in 1875. Rejecting medicine, and claiming for the mind a complete superiority over matter, the Christian Scientists preached a doctrine that wrought many cures among those whose nerves were unstrung by the increasing tempo of civilized life; its influence, also, reached over into other denominations and into medicine itself. More and more, at least in sophisticated circles, people were prone to admit that a vigorous will had much to do with the attainment of happiness and health.[2]

Practical Christianity

One shocking cause of unhappiness and ill-health was intemperance, a vice that the Civil War, as already noted, had done much to promote. At the end of that struggle only two states, Maine and Massachusetts, remained true to their earlier stand for prohibition, and in 1868 Massachusetts voted in favor of the licensing system. Representatives of the old school of temperance reformers, such as

The W.C.T.U.

---

[1] Gamaliel Bradford, *D. L. Moody* (1927), is an understanding study. See also F. G. Beardsley, *A History of American Revivals* (1912).

[2] For a favorable view, see Sibyl Wilbur, *The Life of Mary Baker Eddy* (1929). More critical are E. F. Dakin, *Mrs. Eddy* (1930), and L. P. Powell, *Mary Baker Eddy* (1930).

John B. Gough, were still at work, but it was clear that their efforts alone would avail little against the effective organization that the liquor interests were able to achieve. In 1867, a National Brewers' Congress openly went on record against the election of any candidate to office, whatever his party, in case he showed himself favorable to the cause of total abstinence, and very generally the cause of one liquor dealer became the cause of all. Faced by this situation the evangelical churches, especially the Methodists, the Baptists, and the Presbyterians, presented a united front against the "Demon Rum," and began to urge such measures as the raising of license fees to liquor dealers, local option for towns and counties, and the revival of state-wide prohibition. A few gave their votes to the Prohibition Party, which was founded in 1869, but by far the greater number stood steadfastly by their old party affiliations regardless of their interest in the temperance cause. Outside the churches, the most effective organization of temperance advocates was the Women's Christian Temperance Union, which, founded in 1874, campaigned energetically, with Frances E. Willard of Evanston, Illinois, as its leader, for temperance instruction in the schools and the better awakening of the public to the evils of intemperance. By the end of the seventies the temperance forces could point to only a few victories, but their confidence in the future was complete.[1]

Because women seemed to be more easily aroused against intemperance than men, temperance advocates very generally favored the "emancipation of women," particularly with respect to conferring upon them the right to vote. The woman suffrage **Woman suffrage** movement, like the temperance movement, had attracted attention long before the Civil War, but the attainment of suffrage by the illiterate freedmen of the South had spurred the women reformers on to renewed activity. Surely women were as fit to cast their ballot as exslaves. Led by such intrepid workers as Susan B. Anthony and Elizabeth Cady Stanton, and joined by a host of professional reformers who before the Civil War had centered their attack upon slavery, the suffragists made a little progress. A few states reluctantly conceded to women the right to vote in school elections, and far out in the West the two territories of Utah and Wyoming established complete political equality. Eventual victory for the suffragists was forecast by the increasing freedom with which women attended college, entered such professions as the ministry, the law, and medicine, and organized Women's Clubs.[2]

---

[1] Frances E. Willard, *Glimpses of Fifty Years* (1889); Ray Strachey, *Frances Willard; Her Life and Work* (1912).

[2] Elizabeth Cady Stanton and others, *History of Woman Suffrage* (6 vols., 1881–1922). neglects few aspects of the movement.

That the zeal for reform, so characteristic of Americans during the generation preceding the Civil War, had been eclipsed rather than destroyed by that struggle was apparent in a multitude of ways. Dorothea L. Dix, to mention a single name, laid down her war work only to resume her earlier efforts for the improvement of conditions among criminals, paupers, and the insane. In state after state boards of charities were set up to deal with the problem of relief. State schools for the deaf and the blind were established, and occasional efforts were made to deal separately with the problem of juvenile delinquency. In Massachusetts, for example, an industrial school for delinquent girls was opened during the seventies at Lancaster. Even the humane treatment of animals was demanded, and an American Society for the Prevention of Cruelty to Animals, founded in 1866 by Henry Bergh on the model of the British Royal Society for the same purpose, made rapid progress. Through its efforts American children by the million read the well-told tale, *Black Beauty* (1877), by Anna Sewell, an English writer; more important still, the Society interested itself in the well-being of children as well as animals, and did much to rescue the unfortunate from conditions that were sure to drag them down. All such efforts, however, were at best only piecemeal, and comparatively little thought was given to the underlying causes of insanity, poverty, and crime. Some light was shed on the subject by the work of R. L. Dugdale, *The Jukes: A Study in Crime, Pauperism, Heredity, and Disease* (1877), which traced the history of a feeble-minded and diseased family that had cost the state of New York a million dollars since 1800.

Other reformers

Probably only a few Americans were able to take comfort during the dismal years of depression from the fact that an educational and literary renaissance seemed imminent, or that their humanitarian instincts were still alive, but a great many had their faith in their country restored by a visit to the Centennial Exposition, held in Philadelphia from May to October, 1876. Similar "world's fairs" had recently been staged in Europe, notably at London, Paris, and Vienna, but the Philadelphia Exposition was the first ever to be undertaken in the United States. Preparations for it had been begun before 1873, and in spite of bad business conditions the project was not abandoned. Interested individuals gave heavily of their time and money, the city of Philadelphia contributed generously, and still further assistance was obtained from the various states and from the government of the United States. The railroads, famishing for lack of business, offered greatly reduced rates to Philadelphia, and from all over the country the people came. By the time the Exposition closed, more than nine million visitors had entered its gates, and on a single day as

The Centennial Exposition

many as 275,000. With total receipts of $3,000,000 the fair was a brilliant financial success.

Compared with later exhibitions, the Philadelphia Centennial had little to offer. Its architecture was mediocre, and its art exhibits, while representative of the best that the United States could then supply, suffered from the unwillingness of foreign nations to send their treasures to America. England, however, was more generous than her Continental neighbors, and for the first time thousands of Americans were able to view the works of such masters as Gainsborough and Reynolds. English furniture and household decorations, German porcelain, French textiles, Japanese bronzes and lacquer wares, and Indian shawls and jewels were also freely displayed. These foreign exhibits greatly impressed the common run of visitors, whose provincialism had always made them slow to recognize that Americans in some ways might possibly be excelled by foreigners. Such exhibits also definitely stimulated interest in foreign lands, and more than ever before Americans began to find opportunity for travel abroad.

The greatest success of the fair was along materialistic rather than artistic lines. Its very size was impressive. The Main Building, covering twenty acres of land, was reputed to be the largest building in the world. Numerous other buildings, four of them Successes of also of large dimensions, occupied an enclosure of two hun- the fair dred and thirty-six acres in Fairmount Park, overlooking the Schuylkill River. Machinery Hall housed a magnificent Corliss engine and numerous other symbols of the triumphs of American industry. When it came to commercial and industrial exhibits, European nations, eager to advance their trade in America, vied with the United States in the richness of their offerings, but Americans were able to feel pleasantly elated as they observed that in such matters as these their own country was more often than otherwise in the lead. The agricultural exhibit opened the eyes of farmer visitors to the possibilities of scientific agriculture; the educational exhibit forced the attention of educators to the progress that was being made in educational methods both at home and abroad; the Woman's Pavilion presented in a full acre the products of feminine industry; the mining and mineral exhibit revealed effectively the tremendous resources of the Far West.

Americans who visited the fair returned home with far more faith in the future than they had had before. After all, the depression could hardly be so dark as it seemed if so many persons could afford the trip to Philadelphia. Nor could an America that in a hundred years had made such marked advances be forever arrested in its progress by a single unfavorable turn of the business cycle. As for the mediocrity of American painting, sculpture, and architecture, most Americans were not aware of any shortcomings in what they saw and were surprised and pleased, rather, that so much was being done by their fellow countrymen along these lines. The years that followed 1876 saw a veritable rash of centennial celebrations, as one important anniversary after another recalled the times in which the foundations of the Republic had been laid. It might not be flattering to compare Grant, Blaine, and Ben Butler with Franklin, Jefferson, and Washington, but it was true, nevertheless, that since the time of the "founding fathers" the United States had conquered a continent, had exchanged economic dependence upon Europe for a remarkable degree of self-sufficiency, and had at least begun to create a civilization of its own. The cloud of depression was still dark, but the silver lining was in sight.[1]

[1] On educational aspects of the period, see John C. French, *A History of the University Founded by Johns Hopkins* (1946); Ferris Greenslet, *The Lowells and their Seven Worlds* (1946); Carl L. Becker, *Cornell University: Founders and Founding* (1943); E. D. Ross, *Democracy's College: The Land Grant Movement in the Formative Stage* (1942); John Ise, *American Federal Land Policy* (1928); Paul W. Gates, *The Wisconsin Pine Lands of Cornell University: A Study in Land Policy and Absentee Ownership* (1943).

The twilight of literary New England is entertainingly portrayed in Van Wyck Brooks, *New England: Indian Summer, 1865–1915* (1940).

For the life story of a great Negro scientist, see Rackham Holt, *George Washington Carver: An American Biography* (1943).

On religion and reform: Mary Gray Peck, *Carrie Chapman Catt: A Biography* (1944); Mary Earhart, *Francis Willard: From Prayers to Politics* (1944); Sherwood Eddy, *A Century with Youth: A History of the Y.M.C.A. from 1844 to 1944* (1944).

25

The Far Western Frontier

THE exciting events of the Civil War and reconstruction, followed as they were by the manifold calamities of depression, served somewhat to obscure the importance of what was happening far out on the western frontier. Americans were accustomed to **The Far West** an advancing frontier — there had always been one; but this last American frontier differed markedly from all the rest. As Professor Webb so aptly points out, civilization east of the Mississippi proceeded comfortably into the West on three legs — land, water, and timber. But beyond the Mississippi on the Great Plains, two of these legs, water and timber, gave out, and thereafter civilization limped along as best it could on only one leg — land.[1] This newest West was a frontier of miners and cattlemen rather than of farmers, a frontier where mounted Indians fought desperately and sometimes successfully to hold back the tide of white invasion. Moreover, it was all that was left of the area within the national boundaries for civilization to conquer. The end of the frontier process, which from the beginning had been a kind of common denominator of American history, was in sight.

Within a few years after the "forty-niners" had invaded California, they and their successors had exhausted practically all of the free gold that that region had to offer. California mining then be- **California** came a capitalistic enterprise; expensive machinery was re- **prospectors** quired to do the work that formerly anyone with a shovel and a "washbowl" felt himself adequately equipped to do. As this situation unfolded, some of the adventurers turned to agriculture for a livelihood, others went back to the "States," and still others became "prospectors," men who searched the mountains for signs of gold, and sometimes made a "strike." These prospectors went everywhere, for gold had a way of appearing in the most unlikely places. Not content with having prospected every bleak plateau and every hidden valley of the

---

[1] W. P. Webb, *The Great Plains* (new edition, 1936). Webb perhaps overemphasizes the contrasts between the plains and the earlier frontiers, but many marked differences did exist.

Rocky Mountains, they found their way to such distant regions as South Africa and Australia, and there, too, they discovered gold. Only rarely did one of them acquire wealth, but thanks to their efforts the world's supply of gold was soon to be doubled.[1]

The Pike's Peak gold rush, which occurred just a decade after the rush to California, laid the basis of Colorado. As compared with the forty-niners, the fifty-niners had an easy time of it. Those who came from the East had less than half as far to go, they had no mountains to cross, and the trail which they followed was well supplied with ferries, merchants, and even stage-coaches. Denver arrived full-grown almost overnight, and within a matter of weeks other mining camps in the "hills," such as Central City and Idaho Springs, achieved sizable proportions. Horace Greeley, of the New York *Tribune*, who went out merely to see what a gold rush was like, vividly described one of these early camps:

Colorado

> As yet the entire population of the valley sleeps in tents or under booths of pine boughs, cooking and eating in the open air. I doubt that there is ... a table or chair in these diggings, eating being done on a cloth spread on the ground, while each one sits or reclines on mother earth.

Far sooner than in California the free gold of Colorado gave out, and for a time it even seemed as if no permanent settlement might result. Covered wagons that had gone west displaying the hopeful legend, "Pike's Peak or Bust," returned east by the same route with the label changed to read, "Busted, by gosh." Some, however, stayed on, as in California, to farm; as early as the summer of 1859 radishes, lettuce, onions, and peas brought high prices on the Denver market. Native grasses were cut for hay; claims were staked out and claims clubs formed; irrigation, after the manner of the Mormons in Utah, was introduced. Soon capitalistic mining replaced the crude efforts of the first comers, and such "valley" towns as Golden, Colorado City, and Pueblo showed sure signs of permanence. Efforts to follow the example of California in making a new state without going through the customary territorial stage came to nought, although an unauthorized Territory of Jefferson existed for a few months. In 1861 Congress made Colorado a territory, and a few years later, in order to obtain more Unionist senators and representatives in Washington, would have admitted it as a state. This offer, however, was wisely declined, for as late as 1870 the population of Colorado was only 40,000. Admission as the "Centennial State" came finally in 1876. Shortly afterward the exploitation of silver mines around Lead-

---

[1] LeRoy R. Hafen and Carl Coke Rister, *Western America* (1941); Harold E. Briggs, *Frontiers of the Northwest* (1940).

ville inaugurated an era of prosperity that the region had not known before.[1]

While the rest of the country resounded to the din of Civil War, the mineral empire of the West expanded with unconcerned rapidity. Close on the heels of the Pike's Peak gold rush came a similar rush to the western part of what is now Nevada, where gold had been discovered along the main trail to California. The famous Comstock Lode, discovered in the spring of 1859, brought in no less than fifteen million dollars' worth of gold and silver in a single year. Located in the heart of a desert, a less auspicious place for the development of a new area of settlement could hardly have been imagined, but such was the richness of the mines that adventurers by the thousand flocked in from California and Oregon to the West, as well as from the settled regions of the East. Such towns as Carson City and Virginia City fantastically flaunted their wealth in the face of a desert where water was almost as dear as the other liquid refreshments the miners so liberally consumed. In 1861 Congress made Nevada a territory, and three years later, with a population probably greater than it possesses at the present time, Nevada accepted the same hasty offer of statehood that Colorado rejected. Unlike most of the mining regions, the opportunities for agriculture in Nevada were for a long time negligible, and the prosperity of the new state was limited almost exclusively to the exploitation of its mineral resources.[2]

Nevada

After the opening of Nevada, mining booms came thick and fast. In the vicinity of Lewiston, Idaho, then a part of Washington Territory, gold was found in 1860, and next year the inevitable boom occurred. As news of new strikes came in, the miners rushed from place to place founding, as they went, such permanent settlements as Florence and Boise City, but leaving often as suddenly as they had come. "The Idaho miners," said H. H. Bancroft, "were like quicksilver. A mass of them dropped in any locality, broke up into individual globules, and ran off after any atom of gold in their vicinity. They stayed nowhere longer than the gold attracted them." In 1863 the Territory of Idaho was created, but by that time the miners had crossed the Bitter Root Mountains to lay the foundations of Montana. Such mining centers as Bannack City, Virginia City,

Mining booms in the Northwest

---

[1] LeRoy R. Hafen, *Colorado — The Story of a Western Commonwealth* (1933). Ina Faye Woestemeyer and J. M. Gambrill, *The Westward Movement* (1939), contains many excellent readings on the history of the West.

[2] Mark Twain, *Roughing It* (1872), gives a classic picture of early days in Nevada; William M. Steward, *Reminiscences* (1908), is more interesting than accurate; H. H. Bancroft, *History of Nevada, Colorado and Wyoming* (1890), supplies much useful information; C. H. Shinn, *The Story of the Mine* (1901), is mainly the story of the Comstock Lode, which is also described vividly in C. B. Glasscock, *The Big Bonanza* (1931).

Deer Lodge, and Missoula not only drew population away from the farther western camps, but also attracted newcomers from the East, many of whom came up the Missouri River to Fort Benton, which in high water could be reached by steamboats. Among those who came were a number of refugees from the guerrilla warfare that raged along the Kansas-Missouri border during the Civil War, and others who preferred the hazards of the mines to the prospect of being drafted into the army. In 1864 Montana was separated off from Idaho as an independent territory.[1]

During this same period the Far Southwest, too, had its mining booms. The mineral resources of New Mexico, twin territory with Utah, had long been known, but the Spanish-Mexican population, located mainly in the upper Rio Grande Valley, subsisted upon agriculture and ignored the mines. The Americans, however, reopened the ancient diggings near Tucson and Tubac, and found placer gold in considerable quantities in the valley of the lower Colorado. When in 1862 Colonel James H. Carleton attempted to lead a column of eighteen hundred Californian volunteers to the aid of the Union forces in New Mexico, he was plagued by desertions to what he described as "one of the richest gold countries in the world." Thus another mining boom got under way, and in 1863 Congress, as usual, obliged by creating out of the western half of New Mexico the new Territory of Arizona.

The Far Southwest

The prosperity of these new mountain territories varied markedly in the years that followed the war. As long as the Comstock Lode continued to yield up its riches, Nevada fared best, but by 1880 this magnificent deposit had been worked out, and the desert cities faded as rapidly as they had bloomed. Stocks in Nevada mines valued at $393,000,000 in 1875 could be bought five years later for $7,000,000. The fate of the mines in Colorado, where the quartz lodes could be reached and reduced only with the aid of heavy financial outlays, fluctuated according to the availability of capital and the intelligence with which it was utilized. In Idaho and Montana the fortune hunters of 1866 numbered probably thirty and forty thousand respectively, but the census of 1870 found that only half that many had seen fit to remain. A dozen years later, the opening of rich copper mines near Butte, Montana, ushered in an era of unprecedented prosperity for that region which the exploitation of other base metals, such as lead and zinc, handsomely reinforced. Ultimately the world's largest copper smelters were to be located at Anaconda, Montana. In the Southwest the exhaustion of placer gold brought the

---

[1] W. J. Trimble, *The Mining Advance into the Inland Empire* (1914), is a work of dependable scholarship.

Civil War boom to a quick conclusion, and, in the years that followed, the warlike nature of the Apache Indians tended to discourage even the prospectors. Here, as in Montana, copper presently became a more important product than gold. None of the other mountain territories achieved the prosperity that came to Utah, where the Mormon leader, Brigham Young, urged the saints to eschew mining and devote themselves to agriculture. Indeed, hard as was the lot of the farmer in these regions of inadequate rainfall, Indian raids, and grasshopper plagues, the prosperity of any territory could almost be measured by the number of its inhabitants who forsook the mines for the farms.[1]

Social conditions on the mining frontier differed little from place to place. Most mining towns consisted of a single long crooked street that followed, and occasionally crossed, a mountain stream. Horses hitched along the street testified to the almost universal dependence upon horseback means of communication, *The mining towns* and no other criminal was so utterly despised or so certainly punished as the horse-thief. Most of the houses were hastily improvised, one-roomed, one-storied structures, the kind that frequently appear near city dump heaps. Invariably the most pretentious buildings were occupied by saloons and gambling-houses, to which the men turned for amusement after the hard and lonely labor of the mines. Few women reached the early mining camps, and those who came were usually of easy virtue. Drunkenness and debauchery were too common to attract much notice, and for a long time individual vengeance provided almost the only punishment that was meted out for crime. Medical help for the sick and injured was of the crudest sort, or, more likely, was altogether missing, and the death rate was high. The romance of the mines, so dear to the heart of the fictionist, was built on the slenderest possible basis of fact.[2]

The business of supplying the mining camps with the necessities of life and of transporting to the East the product of the mines soon reached formidable proportions. Stage-coaches and freight-wagons made their appearance on the western plains during the *Staging and freighting* fifties, and by the time the Civil War ended there were few places too remote for them to reach. As early as 1857, when the United States government asked for bids to carry the mail to California, there was no dearth of plains express companies ready to do the work. The contract went to John Butterfield, whose "Overland Mail" operated until 1861 along the southern route, and thereafter by the central route.

---

[1] An interesting popular account of the mines is G. C. Quiett, *Pay Dirt, a Panorama of American Gold Rushes* (1936).

[2] C. H. Shinn, *Mining Camps: A Study in American Frontier Government* (1885).

During the years 1860–61 the firm of Russell, Majors, and Waddell, without a government subsidy, relayed light mail by "pony express" from St. Joseph, Missouri, to Sacramento, California, in less than two weeks. The pony express and the company that backed it were put out of business by the completion of a telegraph line to the Pacific in 1861, but stage-coach connections, with the aid of generous mail contracts, continued to be multiplied so that by 1866 Ben Holladay, into whose monopolistic grasp most of the western routes had fallen, could claim a total of five thousand miles of stage-lines. That same year Holladay sold out to Wells, Fargo, and Company.[1]

Travel by western stage was an experience not to be forgotten. The stage itself, with its high, heavy wheels, its wide, thick tires, and its sturdy leather thorough-braces instead of springs, was no western invention, but rather the product of centuries of experience. It was equipped with three inside seats for passengers, an outside front seat for the driver, and a rear container for baggage. Painted a bright red or green, and drawn by two or more teams of horses, it bowled along the prairies, forded bridgeless streams, ignored wind, sand, and dirt. Dangers abounded from the charges of angry buffaloes, from attacks by hostile Indians, from robberies in a region that long knew no law. Passage through these hazards from the Mississippi to the Pacific cost about two hundred dollars, with corresponding charges for shorter distances. One articulate traveler, a certain Demas Barnes, who took the stage to Denver in 1865, described his trip as follows:

> It is not a *pleasant*, but it is an *interesting* trip. The conditions of one man's running stages to make money, while another seeks to ride in them for pleasure, are not in harmony to produce comfort. Coaches will be overloaded, it will rain, the dust will drive, baggage will be left to the storm, passengers will get sick, a gentleman of gallantry will hold the baby, children will cry, nature demands sleep, passengers will get angry, the drivers will swear, the sensitive will shrink, rations will give out, potatoes become worth a gold dollar each, and not to be had at that, the water brackish, the whiskey abominable, and the dirt almost unendurable. I have just finished six days and nights of this thing; and I am free to say, until I forget a great many things now visible to me, I shall not undertake it again.[2]

Freighting on the western plains was no less important than staging. Little of this went through to the Pacific coast, for water transportation served that purpose better, but the great interior region opened up by the mines was served, for the most part, by slow-moving freight-wagons, drawn by ox teams from such Missouri River towns as Inde-

---

[1] Paxson, *Last American Frontier*, already cited, contains much interesting detail. See also Emerson Hough, *The Passing of the Frontier* (1921).

[2] D. E. Clark, *The West in American History* (1937), p. 517.

pendence, Leavenworth, Nebraska City, and Omaha. After the building of the Union Pacific the freight-wagons, and the stages also, took off into the interior from such railroad stations as lay nearest the desired destinations, but in any event huge freight charges had to be paid. According to a reliable estimate the total freight bill of the mountain towns for one year, 1866, was $31,000,000. High prices gave merchants a chance for long profits, and laid the basis for many pioneer fortunes, such, for example, as those amassed by the Creighton brothers of Omaha, and William A. Clark of Montana. Demas Barnes was much impressed with the freighting activities he witnessed:

> The great feature of the Plains is the transportation trains, usually consisting of thirty to fifty wagons, five yoke each. . . . As they wind their slow course over the serpentine roads and undulating surface in the distance, a mile in extent (I saw one train five miles long), the effect is poetic, grand, beautiful. They select a high position for camping, draw the wagons in a circle, enclosing say a quarter, half, or full acre, the exterior serving as a fort, the inside as a camp, and a place wherein to drive the animals in case of danger, and to yoke or harness them for the next trip. One of these camps, seen at sundown, with night fires kindled, and from five hundred to a thousand head of animals feeding near by, is well worth a long visit to behold.

The traffic of the plains, particularly the cargoes of gold that the stage-coaches took out, led inevitably to many robberies. Gangs of "bad men," drawn together to live by their wits rather than by their labor, terrorized the stage-routes, and took

Lawlessness

a heavy toll, not only in gold but also in lives. The gang led by Henry Plummer of Montana during the sixties was guilty of over a hundred known murders and an untold number of robberies. In Montana, as in California, vigilantes, administering lynch law, finally put the disorderly elements of society out of business. One might note, indeed, four stages of development on any given mining frontier: (1) peaceful exploitation by the original prospectors; (2) the mining "boom," with its full quota of violence and crime; (3) the establishment of vigilance committees to punish the worst criminals and to introduce a reign of law; and (4) the creation of regular legal governments. In many instances, however, the third and fourth stages were reversed. Legal government in Montana, for example, preceded the work of the vigilantes; Plummer himself was a sheriff, and local government throughout the territory was in the hands of the "bad men" until the vigilantes broke their power.[1]

In 1876, the last great mining boom of the West broke forth in the

---

[1] N. P. Langford, *Vigilante Days and Ways* (1912), is a vivid first-hand account.

Black Hills region of southwestern Dakota Territory — a wild, barren
region, long suspected of harboring gold. Deadwood, the
principal city, lay in the heart of a wilderness, and depended
for the necessities of life upon stage-coaches and freighters
from Bismarck to the east and Cheyenne to the south. Bandits and Indians were plentiful, but Wells, Fargo, and Company carried out the gold
in steel-lined, heavily guarded coaches that were not lightly attacked.
In a single trip, July, 1877, $350,000 in gold was taken out, and before the
stage-line surrendered its business to the railroad, the grand total of
such shipments had reached $60,000,000.[1] Deadwood, as the chief
supply station for the various mining camps near-by, built up a lively
prosperity. Here, too, gathered a notable array of gamblers and outlaws, the backwash of all the mining booms; among them, "Wild Bill"
Hickok, who shot from the hip and rarely missed his mark, and "Calamity Jane" Canary, a colossal sinner whose fame spread far and wide.
Deadwood was more sophisticated than most of the early mining towns,
and boasted, along with its gambling-houses and saloons, several
theaters, particularly the *Gem*, which provided living quarters for its
players, and produced numerous plays of merit. During one season,
before street-carnivals, dance-halls, and bar-room singers put the theater
out of business, the *Mikado* had a run of one hundred and thirty
nights.

> *The Black Hills*

For all its seeming tumult, life in the mining camps was founded upon
a sound substratum of common sense. Lawlessness eventually was
curbed, and the normal institutions of government were
evolved. Agriculture, even under the most adverse circumstances, was speedily introduced. Rule-of-thumb arrange-
ments — such, for example, as those which enabled the discoverer of a
mine to "stake out his claim," or the first farmer to use the waters of a
given stream for irrigation purposes to have a "priority right" over all
others — presently received the sanction of law. More women came in,
and with them schools, churches, and the amenities of life. Frontier
characteristics gradually gave way before the advance of civilization:
the individualism of the early miners to the co-operative, capitalistic
enterprises that were required to carry on their work; the actual democracy of the boom days to the astounding inequalities between those who
"struck it rich," and those whose poverty endured; the radicalism of a
new society to the conservatism of one that approached middle age.
And yet, the social inheritance from the mining frontier could hardly be
called negligible. Throughout the region first opened by the mines, the

> *Evolution of law and order*

---

[1] Total output of all the western mines, 1860 to 1890, has been set at $1,241,827,032 in
gold, and $901,160,660 in silver.

tendency to paint an overbright picture still reflects the chronic optimism of the prospector, and the ease with which the speculative spirit
is fanned into a flame shows that the gambling instinct is not yet quite
dead. Here, too, where unruly elements from all over the world broke
the "cake of custom" most thoroughly, the old willingness to try anything new remains a hardy perennial. Widely separated from the rest
of the country, and for a long time a law unto itself, the Far West to
this day retains some of its old aloofness — it is a part of the United
States, and yet at the same time apart from it.

Among the inevitable complications that resulted from the opening
of the mining West was the necessity of developing a new Indian policy
for the United States. The old policy of leaving the region
west of the "bend of the Missouri" for the exclusive use of   The Indians
the Indians had broken down badly in the decade before the Civil War.
Thousands of emigrants, crossing the plains to Oregon, to Santa Fe, to
Utah, and to California, came into contact and often into conflict with
the Indians. Demands for protection of the trails led to the establishment of army posts in the Indian country at such strategic centers as
Fort Kearney and Fort Laramie, and to treaties between the United
States and most of the Indian tribes, describing the tribal boundaries,
and authorizing the government to build both roads and posts wherever
it wished. While the Indians received annuities as compensation for
the losses they sustained from the white intrusion, they found the new
agreements far from satisfactory, and frequently forgot their promises
not to molest the emigrants. The requirement of new cessions in Minnesota, in Iowa, in Kansas, and in Nebraska added still further to the
unrest, both on the part of the tribes that had to find new homes, and
on the part of those who had to make room for unwanted newcomers.
Altogether, the time was ripe for trouble from the Indians when the Civil
War broke out, while the combing of the mountains for gold that accompanied the conflict furnished still further cause for alarm.

In 1862 came the first uprising. The Sioux of Minnesota, reduced by
land cessions to a narrow and indefensible reserve along the Minnesota
River, had long suffered from the dishonesty of traders and
government agents. With the regular army garrisons with-   The Sioux
drawn, and their places taken by unsuspecting volunteers,   outbreak in
the Indians' temptation to seek revenge was great. Never-   Minnesota
theless, the trouble, when it came, was precipitated by the unauthorized
action of a few irresponsible braves who on August 18, 1862, murdered
five whites near New Ulm, Minnesota. The white population of the
vicinity, sure that a general attack was impending, fled for their lives,
while the Indians, no less frightened, divided into two groups, one of

which made a hasty retreat to the west, while the other under Little Crow, knowing that the whites would never forgive the murders, took the warpath, burning farmhouses and villages, and killing men, women, and children by the hundreds. In due time the Indians were met by overwhelming numbers of state militia, decisively defeated, and many of them captured. Of the captives some four hundred were tried by court-martial in St. Paul, and over three hundred were sentenced to death. All but thirty-eight of those sentenced were pardoned by President Lincoln, but these unfortunates paid the full penalty for their crime at a great hanging-bee, held at Mankato, Minnesota, the day after Christmas, 1862. Settlers came from far and near to witness the executions, which were made the more weird by the fact that the unhappy Indians during their imprisonment had been converted to Christianity, and had come to be known as the "praying Indians." In 1863 the remnants of the Sioux were harassed by an expedition into Minnesota and Dakota, and the entire Sioux holding in Minnesota was confiscated. Little Crow himself was killed in July, 1863, and his tanned scalp, his skull, and his wrist bones presently became prized exhibits of the Minnesota Historical Society.[1]

[1] W. W. Folwell, *A History of Minnesota* (4 vols., 1921–30), presents faithfully the story of this uprising. See also T. C. Blegen, *Building Minnesota* (1938), a brilliantly written and scholarly textbook.

LEADERS OF REFORM

Of these so-called reformers, SAMUEL J. TILDEN (1814–86) *and* GROVER CLEVELAND (1837–1908), *both of New York, must be described as relatively conservative in their views. Tilden opposed the reconstruction policy of the Republicans, and Cleveland earnestly advocated a low tariff. Cleveland's two terms as President were separated by four years; hence, he is described as both the twenty-second and the twenty-fourth President of the United States.*

WILLIAM J. BRYAN (1860–1925), *of Nebraska, and* JOHN P. ALTGELD (1847–1902), *of Illinois, were much more radical in their views than Tilden and Cleveland, but can hardly be classified as extremists. Altgeld shared most of Bryan's ideas, and, but for the fact that he was born outside the United States, might have been the Democratic nominee instead of Bryan in 1896.*

CARL SCHURZ (1829–1906), *of Wisconsin and Missouri, was extremely independent in his political views and changed his party allegiance many times.* JAMES B. WEAVER (1833–1912), *of Iowa, was the Greenback candidate for the Presidency in 1880 and the Populist candidate in 1892.*

CLEVELAND

TILDEN

ALTGELD

SCHURZ

WEAVER

BRYAN

THE BOSSES OF THE SENATE

The rigorous punishment meted out to the Minnesota Sioux failed to deter the plains Indians from following their example. Among the tribes most affected by the coming of the miners were the Arapaho and Cheyenne, who were persuaded in 1861 to make way for the white advance into Colorado by with-drawing into what was generally known as the Sand Creek Reserve, a barren and gameless tract in the southeastern part of the territory. Sullen and resentful, they began by the spring of 1864 to raid the trails along the South Platte, and to push on down into Nebraska. Companies engaged in staging and freighting were put out of business, settlers and travelers were killed, and the whole frontier as far east as the Blue River was thrown into a panic. Promptly Governor John Evans called out the Colorado militia, but before ordering an attack he urged all peaceable Indians to concentrate in certain designated posts where they would be safe from harm. Not until fall, when the best fighting weather was over, did any considerable number of Indians choose to accept this invitation, but by that time about five hundred of them, including Black Kettle, their leading chief, had reported to Fort Lyons on Sand Creek, and were encamped near-by. As evidence of their peaceful intentions they flew both a white flag and the Stars and Stripes above their camp.

Meanwhile, however, Major-General Curtis of the United States

The Arapaho and Cheyenne

PROBLEMS OF THE EIGHTIES

No doubt the framers of the Constitution intended that the United States Senate should represent the property interests of the nation. Gouverneur Morris, of Pennsylvania, for example, told the Federal Convention that the Senate must be "an aristocratic body," that "it must have great personal property; it must have the aristocratic spirit; it must love to lord it through pride." By the end of the nineteenth century the Senate had become about what Morris had in mind. In state after state the principal industry had come almost to regard a seat in the Senate as its vested right. Election of United States senators by direct ballot instead of election by the legislatures corrected this situation in considerable part.

The Haymarket Riot, which occurred at Haymarket Square, Chicago, May 4, 1886, cost eleven lives and over a hundred injuries. It came as a result of police efforts to disperse a crowd of strikers and strike-sympathizers who had assembled to listen to anarchistic speeches. A bomb thrown from the crowd into the ranks of the police precipitated the fighting. Following the riot, eight Chicago anarchists were brought to trial and convicted of murder, although no evidence was ever produced to show that any of them had had anything to do with making or throwing the bomb. (Both pictures reproduced through the courtesy of the New York Public Library.)

Army, in command of the West, had telegraphed, "I want no peace till the Indians suffer more," and Colonel J. M. Chivington in command of the Colorado militia made ready to oblige him. Although there were bands of Indians still on the warpath, Chivington chose to ignore them, and instead to make a surprise attack upon the camp at Sand Creek. At the break of day, November 29, 1864, with about nine hundred men he fell upon the unsuspecting camp and murdered in cold blood about one hundred men, women, and children. Following the practice of the savages, the soldiers indulged in indescribable mutilations of the dead bodies, the mildest of which was scalping. Next year the government made a new treaty with the Arapaho and Cheyenne, pushing them farther to the southeast, but the Senate failed to confirm it, and the homeless Indians were sometimes guilty of attacks on settlers and travelers. Expeditions against them in 1867 and 1868 culminated in another massacre, this time on the Washita, near the Texas border, where Major-General George A. Custer with a detachment of regulars duplicated Chivington's unsavory exploit (November 27, 1868). Black Kettle himself was slain, and his people at length accepted lands assigned to them in the Indian Territory.[1]

The western Sioux, who ranged north of the Platte and east of the mountains, were deeply disturbed, both by the fate that had overtaken the Arapaho and Cheyenne, and by the advent of mining activities in Montana. When, in 1865, the government decided to open a road along the Bozeman Trail, from Cheyenne northwestward to the mouth of the Rosebud in Montana, the Sioux determined to resist this invasion of their finest hunting-grounds with all their might. That year General P. E. Connor in command of sixteen hundred men, and guided by Jim Bridger, the noted plainsman,[2] marched over part of the route, but was turned back by the Sioux; and in 1866 a second expedition under Colonel H. B. Carrington succeeded only with the greatest difficulty in building Fort Phil Kearny and Fort C. F. Smith to the east of the Big Horn Mountains. Red Cloud, the Indian leader, and his Sioux warriors risked no open fighting, but they continually harassed wood-trains sent out from the forts, and otherwise hampered the operations. On one occasion, a brash young officer, Captain W. J. Fetterman, was dispatched from Fort Phil Kearny to the aid of a wood-train with definite orders not to take the aggressive. New to western fighting and disdainful of Indians, he disobeyed orders, was

The western Sioux [margin note]

---

[1] G. B. Grinnell, *The Fighting Cheyennes* (1915), is among the best of the books on the Indian wars of the plains. See also his more elaborate *The Cheyenne Indians: Their History and Ways of Life* (2 vols., 1923).

[2] J. C. Alter, *James Bridger* (1925), tells the life-story of this typical plainsman. Useful also are the two volumes by Stanley Vestal, *Mountain Men* (1937) and *Kit Carson* (1928).

ambushed, and in the resulting combat (December 21, 1866) every member of his party was slain. Two years later, when the government made peace with Red Cloud and his warriors, it was on condition that the "country north of the North Platte River and east of the summits of the Big Horn Mountains shall be held and considered to be unceded Indian Territory," and that the forts on the Bozeman Trail should be abandoned. This was one of the few instances in American history in which an Indian treaty registered a white retreat.

Meanwhile the government had taken steps toward the formation of a new Indian policy. A congressional Committee on the Condition of the Indian Tribes, created in 1865, visited the West, took full testimony on such gruesome events as the Chivington massacre, and revealed how utterly untenable the status of the Indians had become. Its illuminating *Report on the Condition of the Indian Tribes*, made in 1867, led to the creation of an Indian Peace Commission, composed of three generals and four civilians, whose duty it was not only to stop the Indian wars, but also to work out a permanent solution of the Indian problem. The commission planned two great meetings, one for the southern tribes at Medicine Creek Lodge, near the southern border of Kansas, held in 1867, and one for the northern tribes at Fort Laramie, held in 1868. At these councils treaties were concluded that definitely foreshadowed the reservation system. Confiscation of the western half of the holdings of the Five Civilized Tribes in the Indian Territory, on the ground that the tribes had sided with the Confederacy during the Civil War, made possible the resettlement in that region of the Arapaho and Cheyenne and other plains Indians. In the North the Sioux were left in peaceable possession of southwestern Dakota, and such minor tribes as the Utes, Shoshonis, and Bannocks were concentrated within appropriate narrow limits. Subsidies in the form of annuities, payments for lands, and outright doles helped the dispossessed Indians to eke out a precarious existence, and unconsciously introduced pauperization as a means of insuring docility. A new Board of Indian Commissioners, composed of civilians, was created in 1869 to advise with the Bureau of Indian Affairs, which, since 1849, had been a part of the Department of the Interior. Believing that the Indians could eventually be made over into peaceful and contented farmers, the civilian commissions tried to break down tribal autonomy, and in 1871 they induced Congress to abolish the legal fiction of dealing with the tribes by treaty as if they were foreign nations. This was a definite improvement, but the road to civilization for the Indian was long and hard.[1]

The new Indian policy

---

[1] Among the best of the many popular books on the Indians are Flora W. Seymour, *The Story of the Red Men* (1929), and F. E. Leupp, *The Indian and His Problem* (1910).

By this time most of the Indian fighting was at an end, although occasional outbreaks occurred until as late as 1890. The worst of these
was precipitated by the Black Hills gold rush, which
brought thousands of whites into the heart of the region
reserved for the Sioux. Even before the rush started,
military maneuvers, designed merely to check up on the rumors of gold,
and wholesale frauds, perpetrated systematically at the Red Cloud
Indian Agency, had alarmed the Sioux, and many of them had left the
reservation. Led by two able braves, Sitting Bull and Crazy Horse, the
fugitives ignored all orders to return, and fought bravely when troops
were sent to herd them in. During this campaign General George A.
Custer and his command of over two hundred cavalrymen met the same
fate that Custer had meted out to the Indians on the Washita eight years
before. Lured into an ambush that he should have known enough to
avoid, Custer and his entire command lost their lives. The campaign,
however, could have but one end, and within a short time General Nelson
A. Miles had restored order.[1] Crazy Horse was captured, and Sitting
Bull fled to Canada. In 1877, a somewhat similar uprising among the
Nez Percés of Idaho came to the same inexorable end. Chief Joseph,
the Indian leader, gave a good account of himself, but at length surrendered. "I am tired of fighting," he told his chiefs, "My heart is sick
and sad. From where the sun now stands I will fight no more forever."
Down in New Mexico the Apaches repeatedly gave trouble, and the
campaigns against them amounted almost to wars of extermination.
Not until 1885, when Geronimo, their principal chief, was captured and
exiled to Florida, was a lasting peace established. Trouble broke out
again about 1889 with the Sioux in Dakota. A religious frenzy, based
upon hope for an Indian Messiah, led to demonstrations by Indian
"ghost dancers" that frightened the Indian agents into calling for
troops. Fearful of soldiers' vengeance, many Indians left the reservation,
only to be massacred at the so-called battle of Wounded Knee (December
29, 1890). Two weeks before, Sitting Bull, who in 1881 had returned
to the United States and had been allowed to live with his people, had
lost his life while resisting, or seeming to resist, arrest.

The wars against the Indians, conducted after 1865 exclusively by
regular army detachments, were far from popular with the American
people, and protests against the inhuman treatment that
the tribes received grew more and more insistent. The
publication in 1881 of Helen Hunt Jackson's *A Century of*

Later Indian uprisings

Lands in severalty

---

[1] N. A. Miles, *Serving the Republic* (1911), and G. A. Custer, *My Life on the Plains* (1874),
tell of army life in the Far West, but consult also P. E. Byrne, *Soldiers of the Plains* (1926),
Stanley Vestal, *Sitting Bull* (1932), and Mari Sandoz, *Crazy Horse* (1942). The Custer
Massacre occurred June 25, 1876.

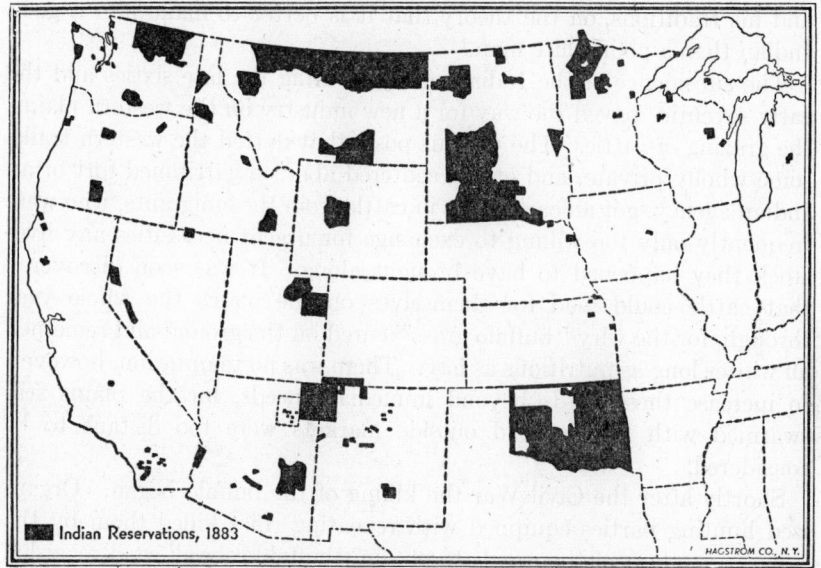

Indian Reservations, 1883

INDIAN RESERVATIONS IN THE UNITED STATES, 1883

Dishonor, with its stinging indictment of the American Indian policy, brought public opinion strongly behind all efforts to alleviate the lot of the Indians. Their retention upon reservations, however, was an obvious necessity, and was long continued. In 1887 the Dawes Act paved the way for the gradual extinguishment of tribal ownership of lands, and the substitution in its place of individual allotments of one hundred and sixty acres each to heads of families, eighty acres each to single adults or orphans, and forty acres each to dependent children. Only a "trust patent" to the land was given at first, and complete ownership was delayed for twenty-five years. In 1906 the Burke Act gave the Secretary of the Interior a discretionary right to lessen the probationary period, and corrected other defects in the original law. Compulsory education for Indian children was introduced in 1891, and full citizenship was conferred in 1924 upon all Indians in the United States. It cannot be said, however, that the government's policy, granted the best of intentions, was an unqualified success. Many of the Indians long retained their tribal identity, and showed remarkable powers of resistance against the white man's way of living. And yet others, particularly in Oklahoma, actually achieved that full equality with whites that was once only the dream of idealists. More recently the makers of Indian policy have shown a tendency to revive the Indians' pride in his tribe and his traditions, on the theory that it is better to make him a good Indian than a poor white man.[1]

The subsidence of the Indian menace during the late sixties and the early seventies paved the way for a new industry on the western plains, the grazing of cattle. The various posts that dotted the western trails, some wholly private, and others centered about a garrisoned fort or an Indian agency, got an early start in cattle from the emigrants, who were frequently only too willing to exchange for urgent necessities any live-stock they happened to have brought along. It was soon discovered that cattle could fend for themselves on the plains the whole year through, for the wiry "buffalo grass" cured on the ground and remained all winter long as nutritious as hay. There was no temptation, however, to increase these herds beyond immediate needs, for the plains still swarmed with buffalo, and outside markets were too distant to be considered.

Shortly after the Civil War the killing of the buffalo began. Organized hunting parties equipped with repeating rifles killed them by the tens of thousands to obtain "buffalo robes," soon regarded **The killing** as almost a necessity in the average American home. **of the buffalo** Others were killed, by Indians and whites alike, for their meat, but often only the tongue and a few choice cuts would be taken, and the rest of the carcass left to rot. Hunters killed them just for the sport of it, although one English sportsman who came to America primarily to hunt buffalo refused to take part in a game that he described about as exciting as shooting cows in a pasture. The building of the Union Pacific Railroad aided the hunters greatly, and divided the buffalo into two herds, one to the north and the other to the south. By 1870 from five to seven million buffalo still existed, but in the succeeding years the slaughter was terrific. The southern herd was gone by 1875, and in 1883 Sitting Bull and his braves destroyed the last sizable remnant of the northern herd. Probably not more than a thousand head were left alive. For years buffalo bones were gathered for shipment by the trainload to eastern factories, where they were turned into fertilizers, or into carbon for the use of sugar refineries.[2]

The passing of the buffalo, unpleasant as it is to contemplate, was not an unmixed evil. The government purposely did nothing to prevent the tragedy, for as long as the herds remained intact the Indians had a sure food supply, and could the more easily defy governmental control. Some of the later Indian uprisings were caused in part by the Indians'

[1] J. B. Nash, *The New Day for the Indians* (1938).

[2] E. D. Branch, *The Hunting of the Buffalo* (1929), possesses literary as well as historical merit.

concern at the threatened destruction of their herds, but once the buffalo were gone the end of Indian resistance had been reached. Furthermore, the disappearance of the buffalo, together with the building of the western railroads and the pacification of the Indians, gave the cattle industry the chance it needed to grow.

In a sense, however, the western cattle industry was already full grown. Its real beginnings were Mexican, rather than American, and dated back for centuries. Both the cattle themselves, and the horses without which the industry would have been vastly different (to say the least), were the descendants of European stock brought over by the Spaniards in the sixteenth century, and allowed to go wild. Survival of the fittest produced by the nineteenth-century cattle that were more noted for their speed and endurance than for tender cuts of beef, each blessed also with an incredible spread of horns. The horses, sprung no doubt from noble Arabian forebears, had developed into sure-footed, quick-witted, wiry broncos, well under a thousand pounds in weight, but ideally suited for riding purposes.[1] The technique of cattle-raising, to the last detail, was worked out in Mexico long before it was introduced into the United States, and was practiced for years in New Mexico, Texas, and California before it was known on the western plains. The cowboy's saddle, bridle, bit, lariat, and spurs were adaptations, for the most part, of equipment used by Spanish cavalrymen, while the "round-up" and the use of "brands" to indicate ownership were early invented to meet obvious needs. The unimportance of the cattle industry for so many years was not due to inability to produce cattle. Anyone in the Southwest with a little ambition could have all the cattle he wanted. What the industry needed was a market for its produce, and until that could be found it remained insignificant.[2]

Attempts to drive Texas cattle to an outside market were made from the time of the Mexican War on, but all such ventures amounted to little until the railroads began to push out across the western plains. Then the idea of the "long drive" from somewhere in Texas to a shipping point in Kansas or Nebraska immediately took hold. Abilene, Kansas, a station on the Kansas Pacific, became noted as early as 1867 as a "cow-town." Here

Beginnings of the cattle industry

The long drive

---

[1] The western Indians early found this out, became expert horsemen, and as such, with their bows and arrows, were more than a match for white cavalrymen with carbines. Only when the six-shooter was invented could the white horseman meet the mounted Indian on equal terms. W. P. Webb, *The Texas Rangers* (1935).

[2] P. A. Rollins, *The Cowboy* (1922), and J. H. Cook, *Fifty Years on the Old Frontier* (1923), give excellent accounts of the origins of the plains cattle industry. Much valuable information is contained also in Emerson Hough, *The Story of the Cowboy* (1897), and in E. D. Branch, *The Cowboy and His Interpreters* (1926).

untold numbers of Texas cattle, driven northward through the Indian Territory, or the "Nation," as cowboys called it, were purchased for the use of the newly established packing-houses. Early each year groups of ranchers who wished to participate in a "drive" rounded up their cattle and threw them upon the trail — a route generally known as the "Chisholm Trail," regardless of where it ran. Grazing the cattle as they went, cowboys moved them slowly northward in herds of two or three thousand head. Such a group required the services of sixteen or eighteen cowboys, a cook with a "chuck-wagon," and a "wrangler" with extra cow-ponies. Trials on the march included the danger of stampedes due to lightning, buffalo, or Indians.

On the "long drive" the cowboy developed those peculiar characteristics that made him, like the fur-trader, the lumberjack, and the prospector, a unique specimen of the American frontier. He found
The cowboy the revolver indispensable to the protection of his herd, and of great advantage in the actual business of herding. Naturally he became a fair marksman. He sang to the cattle, whether to help him bear the loneliness, or to keep the cattle aware of his presence, or to prevent or promote a stampede. The verses he invented were colorful, they told of the life he led, and they became as authentic a part of the American folklore as the songs of slavery and freedom that the southern Negroes sang. In reality, just a "plain everyday bow-legged human," the cowboy's occasional excesses after periods of long riding and lack of sport caught the eye of the fictionist, and were romanticized out of all proportion to the facts. A wanderer, an adventurer, and sometimes a refugee, the cowboy's actual exploits did make good stories, but most of his life was given over to hard and monotonous labor.[1]

The advance of the frontier into Kansas and Nebraska drove the "Chisholm Trail" farther and farther west, and determined the location of new cow-towns to take the place of those enclosed in settled areas. Dodge City, Kansas, for example, soon replaced Abilene as the leading shipping-point for Texas cattle. Settlement interfered with grazing; moreover, the Texas cattle brought with them the germs of the dreaded "Texas fever" to which they themselves had become immune, but which brought almost certain death to other cattle that caught it. Quarantine

---

[1] The following lines are inscribed on a tombstone in the Cemetery at Douglas, Wyoming:

"Underneath this stone in eternal rest
Sleeps the wildest one of the wayward west.
He was gambler and sport and cowboy too,
And he led the pace in an outlaw crew.
He was sure on the trigger and staid to the end,
But he was never known to quit on a friend.
In the relations of death all mankind is alike,
But in life there was only one George W. Pike."

laws were passed that pushed the drive still farther into the west. Also, a new market was discovered when the northern plains had been cleared of buffalo. Northern ranchers, eager to expand their herds, paid good prices for the Texas longhorns, bred them up rapidly by the introduction of blooded cattle from the East, and laid the basis for a short, but spectacular, prosperity. Points on the Union Pacific such as Ogallala and Sidney, Nebraska, were visited by western as well as eastern buyers, and Cheyenne, Wyoming, which had once had no other excuse for existence than the railroad, now found itself the center of an exciting cattle industry. Texas cattle were driven northward as far as Dakota and Montana, and even westward into New Mexico, Arizona, Colorado, and Utah.

The profits of cattle-growing on a well-policed range, for the use of which the government made no charge, and to which, thanks to the railroads, markets were now easily accessible, did not fail to attract capital, not only from the American East, but also from Europe, particularly England. Ranchers, or "cattle-men," as they were called to distinguish them from their employees, the "cowboys," figured that an original investment of five thousand dollars should pay profits of from forty to fifty thousand dollars in four years' time. Ranching companies, some of them with capital investments well up into the millions, were formed to crowd more and more cattle upon the range. Access to water was, of course, essential, and each individual or company engaged in the cattle business took care to obtain title to some land so situated. Here the ranch house and other necessary buildings were located, and from this headquarters operations were carried on over a range bounded by the distance the cattle were willing to travel to water. Large "outfits," as the companies were called, sometimes had access to water at many different places, and companies existed that claimed the grazing rights to strips of land no less than a hundred miles long and fifty miles wide.[1]

The range-cattle industry

The law of the range, like the law of the mining camp, was to a great extent invented to meet the needs of the situation. Stock-growers' associations were formed, at first for mutual protection, but later to work out rules for users of the range that actually had the effect of law. Indeed, the Wyoming Stock-Growers' Association, formed in 1873, came to have more power than the territorial government of Wyoming, which, as a matter of fact, it controlled. The Association promoted community rather than individual round-ups, regulated the use of brands and recorded them, required that "mavericks" (unbranded

---

[1] The best works on the cow country are E. S. Osgood, *The Day of the Cattleman* (1929), and E. E. Dale, *The Range Cattle Industry* (1930), and *Cow Country* (1942).

calves that no longer followed their mothers) should be sold to the highest
bidder and the proceeds paid into the Association treasury, discouraged
overstocking of the range by refusing membership to outsiders, and
made relentless warfare upon all who were suspected of "rustling" (stealing) cattle. Punishment for defiance of the Association might or might
not await court action.

The day of the cattleman soon passed. Trouble with rustlers who
branded mavericks and "worked" (altered) brands cost the ranchers
heavy losses, both in cattle stolen and in fees paid to de-
The passing tectives and inspectors. Trouble with "nesters" (farmers)
of the whose fences interfered with the free access of cattle to
cattleman water-holes not only caused heavy losses in property, but
frequently resulted also in loss of life. Cowboys learned to carry wire-
cutters as part of their equipment; and finally, in self-defense, the cattlemen themselves began to fence the land they used but did not own, only
to have their fences branded as illegal by the United States government,
and ordered down. But the greatest calamity that befell the cattlemen
was the overstocking of the range. By the middle eighties so many
millions of cattle had been turned loose to pick up a living from the plains
that one severe winter was sure to bring disaster, and instead of one such
winter most of the range country saw two, 1885–86, and 1886–87. The
result was wholesale ruin and bankruptcy, and a complete change in the
nature of the cattle industry. After this time, ranchers tended more
and more to raise hay for winter feed, and in general to carry on farming
as well as ranching activities. On many ranges sheep replaced cattle,
although not without resort to actual warfare between sheepmen and
cattlemen. The close-grazing sheep left the range stripped of grass,
so when sheepmen came to stay cattlemen had to fight or leave. In
some of these conflicts, sheep-herders were slain, the wagons that carried
their supplies were burned, and the herds themselves were destroyed.[1]

Short-lived as it was, the range-cattle industry left its mark upon the
West and upon the country as a whole. It did its share to promote
the growth of the meat-packing industry. It made clear the absurdity
for the Far West of land legislation devised to meet the needs of the
eastern half of the continent, and paved the way for important changes,
such as the Desert Land Act of 1877, and the Timber and Stone Act of
1878. It bequeathed to the residents of the plains a breezy, slangy
language, cowboy costumes, "dude" ranches, and rodeos. It lived
persistently in stories of the "Wild West" such as Owen Wister's *The
Virginian,* and the multitudinous works of Zane Grey; in the infinite

---

[1] The story of a typical mountain region which passed through every stage of the frontier
process is told in Charles Lindsay, *The Big Horn Basin* (1932).

number of scenarios derived from them for the use of the motion-picture industry; in the "Wild West" shows first popularized by "Buffalo Bill" Cody; in the solemn melodies and bungling rhymes of the cowboy songs.[1]

> Oh, beat the drum slowly and play the fife lowly;
> Play the dead march as you carry me along.
> Take me to the green valley and lay the sod o'er me.
> I'm just a poor cowboy and I know I've done wrong.

[1] Several collections of these interesting songs exist: John A. Lomax, *Cowboy Songs and Other Frontier Ballads* (1910), and *Songs of the Cattle Trail and Cow Camp* (1920); Badger Clark, *Sun and Saddle Leather* (1936).

The literature of the West is voluminous. Dorothy Gardiner, *West of the River* (1941), features trails and transportation, subjects also treated in J. V. Frederick, *Ben Holladay, the Stagecoach King* (1940); and Everett Dick, *Vanguards of the Frontier* (1941). Much state and regional writing has appeared: O. W. Winther, *The Great Northwest* (1947); P. S. Fritz, *Colorado, the Centennial State* (1941); Effie M. Mack, *Nevada, A History of the State from Earliest Times through the Civil War* (1936); M. G. Burlingame, *The Montana Frontier* (1942); J. K. Howard, *Montana: High, Wide, and Handsome* (1943).

On the Great Plains livestock industry: J. W. Thompson, *History of Livestock Raising in the United States* (1942); Louis Pelzer, *The Cattlemen's Frontier* (1938); Ora Brooks Peake, *The Colorado Range Cattle Industry* (1937).

On Indians: M. F. Schmitt (ed.), *General George Crook: His Autobiography* (1946); R. H. Ogle, *Federal Control of the Western Apaches, 1848–1886* (1940); C. C. Rister, *Border Command: General Phil Sheridan in the West* (1944).

26

From Hayes to Harrison

THE ascendancy of the Republicans in the years that followed the Civil War, already shaken by the excesses of reconstruction and the scandals of the Grant régime, tottered almost to a fall
The disputed election of 1876 with the advent of the depression. The elections of 1874 returned a Democratic majority in the House of Representatives of more than seventy, while in the states, North as well as South, Democrats — ex-Copperheads and ex-Confederates — replaced Republicans with disheartening regularity. As the election of 1876 approached, the nervousness of the Republicans was intense. To many of them the loss of the Presidency seemed almost the equivalent of having lost the war. Not daring under the circumstances to select anyone as a standard-bearer who was even slightly tainted with scandal, the Republican National Convention turned for its nominee to the spotless but relatively unknown Rutherford B. Hayes, an able volunteer officer in the Civil War, and three times governor of Ohio. Such a choice was the more necessary because the Democrats seemed certain to nominate, and did nominate, Samuel J. Tilden, whose part in the overthrow of the Tweed Ring had made him governor of New York. Tilden's name was thus indelibly connected with political reform, a strong attraction for the Liberal Republicans whose return to the fold the Republicans must have to win. More by accident than by conscious planning, both candidates for the Presidency proved to be conservative in their economic views, particularly on the money question. Defeated factions took some comfort, however, from the nominees for the Vice-Presidency, for the Republican candidate, William A. Wheeler of New York, had been a dependable Radical, while the Democratic candidate, Thomas A. Hendricks of Indiana, was an ex-Copperhead of soft-money tendencies. Extremists on the money question gave their votes to a new Independent, or "Greenback," Party, which favored expansion of the currency by the issue of more paper money, and supported the candidacies of Peter Cooper of New York for President and Samuel F. Cary of Ohio for Vice-President. Most voters, however, even if they held

soft-money views, were too enthralled by the main contest to take the Greenbackers seriously.

By the time the election was held, the supremacy of the carpet-baggers had been overthrown in all but three of the southern states, South Carolina, Louisiana, and Florida. It was known in advance that every other southern state would vote for Tilden, and on the evening of election day, November 7, it appeared that these three states, too, were safely in the Democratic column. Since New York and several other northern states had gone Democratic, the election of Tilden seemed assured. But the Republican leaders, confident that they could correct the conduct of the three carpet-bag states, claimed that those states had in reality voted for Hayes and Wheeler, who would thus have 185 electoral votes to their opponents' 184. The electoral contest thus begun rocked the country, and for a time hope of a peaceful settlement seemed faint. Finally Congress decided to refer the double returns received from the carpet-bag states to an Electoral Commission of fifteen, five each from the Senate, the House, and the Supreme Court. By a strict party vote, eight to seven, the Commission gave the election to the Republicans. While on the face of the returns it would seem that the election had been "stolen," as the Democrats charged, no doubt many thousands of Negro voters in the South who had wished to vote for Hayes had not dared to vote at all. The real victory of the election rested less with either party than with the American people as a whole, who, in spite of the tenseness of the situation, kept their tempers, and accepted in good faith the decision that had been reached.[1]

Rutherford B. Hayes (1822–1893), the new President, was Ohio born and educated.[2] As governor of his native state he had made an excellent record: he took his duties seriously, his judgment was good, his word could be trusted, he made appointments for merit even to the extent of naming Democrats to office. During the campaign he astonished reformers by the earnestness with which he denounced the spoils system, and he irritated party regulars by the assertion that "he serves his party best who serves his country best." As President, however, his good intentions frequently betrayed him into bad politics. His cabinet, which was called by some the ablest since Washington's, contained four men who had voted for Greeley in 1872. One of them, the Postmaster-General, was an out-and-out Tilden Democrat from Tennessee, and Hayes had even considered naming

Rutherford B. Hayes

---

[1] The most thorough study of this election is P. L. Haworth, *The Hayes-Tilden Disputed Presidential Election of 1876* (1906).

[2] Hayes has had two excellent biographers, C. R. Williams, *The Life of Rutherford Burchard Hayes* (2 vols., 1914), and H. J. Eckenrode, *Rutherford B. Hayes, Statesman of Reunion* (1930).

General Joseph E. Johnston, the ex-Confederate, as Secretary of War. A man so unversed in political finesse could never become the successful leader of a party, however great his integrity.

The first concern of the Hayes administration was to end the scandal of reconstruction. In Florida, although its vote was counted for Hayes, carpet-bag rule came to an end with the inauguration of a Democratic governor on January 2, 1877. In the two other southern states that were counted for Hayes, South Carolina and Louisiana, Republican state administrations retained power only because they were supported in each instance by small detachments of federal troops. On all sides it was conceded that if these troops were withdrawn, the rival Democratic candidates, whom nearly every white voter had preferred, would promptly seize the reins of power. Regardless of the political consequences, Hayes ordered the removal of the troops. The reaction in Columbia and New Orleans was instantaneous; Democratic officials moved in as Republicans moved out. The "solid South" had become a fact; military reconstruction had broken down. Six years later, when the Supreme Court of the United States ruled in the Civil Rights cases that the Fourteenth Amendment could not be used to restrain individuals from conduct designed to enforce social discriminations against the Negroes, civil reconstruction may be said to have broken down. Within another decade, as one southern state after another began to devise laws that made the Fifteenth Amendment a mockery, the last remnant of political reconstruction faded away.

Restoration of home rule

Hayes's next move was in the direction of civil service reform, but to accomplish much along this line he needed a really effective civil service commission, something Congress refused to give him. Nevertheless, Hayes did what he could, unaided by Congress and with comparatively little help from public opinion, to make good appointments. His record in this respect was the best of any President's since John Quincy Adams, but his occasional mistakes annoyed the reformers, who spoke slightingly of his "opportunities and failures," while his successes won him the undying hostility of the most powerful of the Republican leaders. Early in his administration he engaged in a battle with the Senate over the rule of "senatorial courtesy," according to which every senator of the dominant political party claimed the right to block confirmation of the appointment within his own state of any individual to whom he personally objected. In this fight he won a partial victory. His removal of Chester Alan Arthur, collector of the port of New York, gave great offense to Roscoe Conkling, senator from New York, who succeeded in preventing confirmation of the first man

Civil service reform

Hayes chose for the place. But with the help of Democratic votes Hayes's second nominee was confirmed.[1]

Hayes's tenacious adherence to hard-money views, even in the face of persistent depression, was in keeping with his character. On this issue he saw eye to eye with the leading men of his party, and he approved cordially the action taken by Congress during Grant's administration to bring about the resumption of specie payments. By a law passed early in 1875, before the Democrats took control of the House of Representatives, Congress had authorized the Secretary of the Treasury to prepare for resumption on the first of January, 1879, by building up a gold reserve. John Sherman was chiefly responsible for this measure, and as Hayes's Secretary of the Treasury it fell to his lot to carry it into effect.[2] Backed steadfastly by the President, he sold bonds for gold, and ultimately accumulated a gold reserve of $100,000,000. As this fund grew, confidence that the government would be able to exchange gold dollars for greenbacks on the appointed day grew with it, and the value of the greenback dollar, expressed in terms of gold, also grew. Worth only sixty-seven cents in 1865, the greenback dollars had risen to eighty-nine cents in 1875, to ninety-six cents in 1877, and well before January 1, 1879, to one hundred cents. In 1878 Congress decided that $346,681,016 in greenbacks should remain a permanent part of the national currency, but the existence of the gold reserve made every greenback dollar "as good as gold." Accustomed by long usage to a paper currency, no one cared to make the exchange, and the greenbacks continued to circulate.

Resumption

The steadily appreciating value of the dollar insured comfortable profits to money lenders, particularly those who made long-term loans. For borrowers, however, the situation was far different. The farmer who mortgaged his farm as security for a five-year loan found to his sorrow when the time for payment came that the dollars he had borrowed were worth far less than the dollars with which he must repay. Dearer dollars meant lower prices for the wheat, or corn, or livestock he had to sell. He must therefore in effect pay back not only principal and interest, but enough more to cover the amount which the dollar had appreciated. When he borrowed, a thousand bushels of wheat might equal in value the amount of his loan; when he repaid, it took from twelve to fifteen hundred bushels of wheat to raise the money he needed, and more for interest. Protests against

Soft-money ideas

---

[1] An excellent popular account of the political life of this period is Matthew Josephson, *The Politicos, 1865–1896* (1938).

[2] The active part taken by Sherman in many phases of American politics is told by himself, John Sherman, *Recollections of Forty Years* (2 vols., 1895).

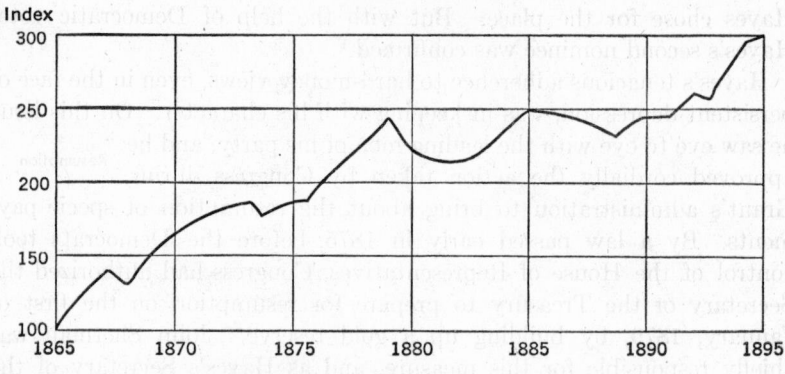

THE APPRECIATING DOLLAR, 1865–95
Based on weighted averages of commodity values. From A. M. Arnett,
The Populist Movement in Georgia (1922) p. 69

dearer dollars and lower prices came thick and fast as one depression
year after another compounded the gloom, and in the West and the
South, where debtors were numerous and creditors were few, soft-money
ideas, such as Pendleton's "Ohio idea," found much favor. In general
the Democratic Party was more hospitable to soft-money views than the
Republican, but in both parties hard-money men, representing the point
of view of eastern creditors rather than of southern or western debtors,
were in the ascendancy. With resumption imminent, the Greenback
Party, founded in 1876, won more and more adherents. In the elections
of 1878, it polled a million votes, as against its eighty thousand of two
years before, and elected fifteen members of Congress.[1]

The success of resumption, and the return of prosperity in 1879, tended
to discredit Greenbackism, and the high-water mark of 1878 was never
attained again. In the meantime, however, a new soft-
Free silver   money panacea had been discovered in what was popularly
known as "free silver." [2] For ages the two precious metals used as
money, gold and silver, had depended for their value, not upon the fiat
of government, but upon commercial demand. By a curious and long-
sustained coincidence the relative value of the two metals had been almost constant; and it took fifteen or sixteen times as much silver to
equal in value a given unit of gold. In early times the slight fluctuation
in the ratio of value between the two metals had been of small concern.

[1] F. E. Haynes, *Third Party Movements Since the Civil War, with Special Reference to
Iowa* (1916), contains a good account of the Greenbackers. See also D. C. Barrett, *The
Greenbacks and Resumption of Specie Payments* (1931).

[2] An excellent account of the rise of the silver issue is given in J. L. Laughlin, *History of
Bimetallism in the United States* (1892).

Methods of refinement and of measurement were too crude to make the variations noticeable, and governments themselves were not above deceiving the public all they could. With the progress of modern science, however, the exact amount of silver and of gold in a coin could be easily ascertained, and nations made an effort to establish coinage ratios that would harmonize with the existing commercial ratio. Always this was difficult, or even impossible, for the commercial ratio was inevitably a variable, while the coinage ratio established by law was a constant. Human nature being what it is, people who knew the difference hoarded the overvalued coins, and spent those undervalued; or, as the ancient Gresham Law expressed it, the cheap money drove the dear money out of circulation. Paper issues, being as a rule less valuable than either gold or silver, rarely had much difficulty in driving both out of circulation. Such had been the case in the United States during most of its history, while during and after the Civil War the rule of the greenbacks and the national bank notes had been supreme.

Hopeful that the time had come at last when a metallic currency could be provided for general use, the Secretary of the Treasury obtained from Congress in February, 1873, a new coinage law. This measure took account of the theory, generally observed in European practice, that only one metal could be used as a standard. Accordingly it dropped the silver dollar, which at the old coinage ratio of sixteen to one contained too much silver to permit it to circulate anyway, from the coinage lists. This was the famous "crime of 1873," committed, according to a generation of silver orators, as the result of an "international conspiracy to demonetize silver." Actually, no one would have thought of branding this law as a crime had not the ratio of value between silver and gold begun suddenly to change. This was due, no doubt, primarily to the huge outpourings of silver mines in the American West, although the diminishing demand throughout the world for the use of silver as money may also have been a factor. Whatever the causes, the trend in the price of silver was steadily downward for the next twenty-five years, a situation which led the despairing silver miners to demand the "free and unlimited coinage of silver at the ratio of sixteen to one" as a remedy. The silver miners were soon joined by the debtor farmers of the Middle West, and to a lesser extent by those of the South, who had no interest in a higher price for silver, but believed that "free coinage," or "free silver," as they termed the desired policy, would mean a cheaper dollar. Former Greenbackers altered their paper-money arguments to fit this new demand. If the government would only take silver from all who offered it, as it still took gold, coin the silver into silver dollars at the rate of sixteen to one, and put the new silver dollars into circulation, the country would have more money and cheaper money, just as surely as if more greenbacks had been issued. Free silver thus became the adopted child of the Greenbackers.

The silver issue continued as a constant factor in American politics for the rest of the nineteenth century, and during Hayes's administration the silver forces won what they mistook at first for a considerable victory. By the Bland-Allison Act,[1] passed in 1878 over Hayes's veto, the Secretary of the Treasury was ordered to purchase each month from two to four million dollars' worth of silver at the market price, and to coin it into silver dollars at the old coinage ratio of sixteen to one. This meant limited coinage, however, instead of unlimited coinage, and while the new silver dollars were made legal tender, Secretary Sherman and others saw clearly that if only they could be backed by gold, as was the case with the greenbacks, they would be "as good as gold." In practice not only Sherman, but his successors also, whether Republicans or Democrats, completely defeated the hopes of the silverites by standing ready at all times to redeem silver dollars, whatever their "intrinsic value," in gold.

The Bland-Allison Act

As the time approached for the election of 1880, it became apparent that the Republicans could count upon that most valuable of all political allies, prosperity. Foreign trade had increased; the United States enjoyed in 1880, not only a greater volume of trade than had ever been recorded in any previous year, but also a favorable balance of trade. Farm prices, particularly wheat and cotton, were up, and manufacturers were reaping rich harvests from the markets provided by a steadily increasing population. A feeling of confidence replaced the feeling of gloom that had characterized the depression years. But could the Republican Party take advantage of the situation? As everyone knew, it was sadly torn by internal strife. At one extreme were the "Stalwarts," hard-boiled realists who believed in practical politics and scoffed at reform. They were led by Roscoe Conkling of New York, whose great ambition at the moment was to nominate for a third term ex-President Grant. Only a little less conservative were the "Half-Breeds," who regarded James G. Blaine, the "man from Maine," as their leader, and were determined to make him President. In addition to these factions there were many Independents, most of whom were more friendly to Blaine than to Conkling, but had little use for either. Finally there was the President himself, who had no wish or hope for renomination, and his insignificant number of friends. It was obvious that only a compromise

Republican dissension

[1] W. V. Byars, *An American Commoner, the Life and Times of Richard Parker Bland* (1900), recounts the successive failures of "Silver Dick."

could save the day, and that the National Convention after many ballots and much heart-burning produced. For President the Republicans chose a "dark horse," James A. Garfield of Ohio, a Blaine man who was satisfactory to the reformers, and for Vice-President, Chester Alan Arthur of New York, Conkling's trusted friend and subordinate. The ticket was as strong as compromise could make it.

The Democrats, quite as badly divided as the Republicans, were less successful in achieving a united front. The northern wing of the party was extremely suspicious, and not a little ashamed, of the southern wing; and *vice versa*. Moreover, in both sections there was internal strife that dated at least as far back as the Civil War. Northern Democrats who had been loyal to the Union during the war had not yet forgiven the "Copperheads" whose desire for peace had almost led them to support the South. Southern Democrats whose devotion to the party stemmed from the leadership of Andrew Jackson had little use for the ex-Whigs and conservative "Bourbons," who now, under the necessity of maintaining white supremacy, called themselves Democrats and sought to monopolize party leadership. Native Americans generally, of whatever section, regretted the dire necessity of cultivating the immigrant vote, particularly the Irish vote, which in many American cities had become a factor to be reckoned with. So long out of power as to have lost its personality, bereft of intelligent leaders, tainted with treason and with pacifism, the Democratic Party floundered helplessly through the campaign. Tilden was too old and too ill to be a candidate, and the nomination went, almost by default, to General Winfield S. Hancock of Pennsylvania, who had won distinction as a Union officer at Gettysburg, and had later pleased the South by the way he conducted himself as military commander of Louisiana during reconstruction. In politics, however, he was only, as one wag expressed it, "a good man, weighing two hundred and fifty pounds." For Vice-President the Democrats named William H. English of Indiana, a political anachronism whose last significant deed had been to promote the admission of Kansas as a slave state during the Buchanan administration. Such a ticket amounted almost to an open confession of political bankruptcy.

As a matter of fact, both parties were completely bankrupt. The issues that divided them were historical merely. The Republican Party had come into existence because of the stand it had taken on slavery, and it had lived on because of its determination to free the slaves, to save the Union, and to punish the South. Its program was now finished and its excuse for existence had disappeared. The Democrats, likewise, had so long centered their attention upon the issues

(margin note: Democratic dissensions)

(margin note: Lack of party issues)

of slavery, the Civil War, and reconstruction that they failed to observe
that the era in which these issues meant anything had rolled by. The
platforms of the two parties in 1880 revealed few real differences of
opinion as to policies and no real awareness of the problems that confronted the nation. Neither Democrats nor Republicans seemed to
sense the significance of the vast transformation that was coming over
business, nor the critical nature of the relationship between labor and
capital, nor even the necessity of doing something definite about civil
service reform, the money problem, and the tariff. The Republican
Party existed to oppose the Democratic Party; the Democratic Party
existed to oppose the Republican Party. Real issues cut across both
parties, and even when recognized, which was rare, had to be evaded or
ignored. When the Republican Convention prepared to adopt the
customary meaningless platitudes about civil service reform, a delegate
from Texas named Flanagan protested in plain language: "What are
we up here for?" What, indeed, if not for the offices?

With issues lacking, the campaign turned on personalities. The Republicans, in rejecting the candidacy of General Grant, had freed themselves of the charge of "Bonapartism." Their nominee was,
Campaign of 1880 to be sure, a Union officer in the Civil War, but he had been,
like Hayes, a volunteer officer, and had won distinction in
politics rather than in the army. The Democrats, on the other hand, in
their effort to shake off the charge of treason, had nominated a professional soldier. If anyone was prepared to play the rôle of "the man on
horseback," it was Hancock, not Garfield. Efforts were made to prove
that Hancock, whose exploits on the battlefield had won him the sobriquet, "the Superb," was in reality a coward, and that Garfield, whose
record was far cleaner than that of most politicians, had been deeply
involved in the Crédit Mobilier and other scandals. Neither charge
carried much weight. Garfield, as a matter of fact, was satisfactory
enough to the reform element in the Republican Party and most Independents gave his candidacy their warm support. The Democratic
platform, written by Colonel Henry Watterson of Kentucky, called for
"a tariff for revenue only." When the Republicans showed a disposition
to press this issue, Hancock declared that it was unimportant because the
tariff was a "local affair." For this statement he was roundly ridiculed,
but he spoke far more truly than he knew. Tariff rates must be levied
by Congress, but they have generally been fixed, item by item, because
of some local demand.

Fought with fury, and as if the result would really be important, the
campaign settled nothing much except that Garfield, not Hancock, was
to be the next President of the United States. The Republican plurality,

out of a total vote amounting to over nine million, was about nine thousand. Neither of the two leading candidates had a ma- jority of all the votes cast, for James B. Weaver of Iowa, the **Election results** Greenback candidate, polled over three hundred thousand votes. The Republicans, however, won enough local victories to enable them to recapture the Senate, and, although the membership of the House was so evenly divided as to leave its control in doubt until Congress actually met, the Republicans were finally able to organize it also. For the first time in six years the Presidency and both houses of Congress were under the control of a single party.

But as events proved, the Republicans failed signally to capitalize upon their victory. Their first misfortune was the death of the young and probably able President they had elected. James A. Garfield (1831–1881),[1] like Abraham Lincoln, was a typical **Death of Garfield** product of the American frontier, but he had lived a generation later than Lincoln and had enjoyed advantages, particularly in education, that Lincoln never knew. He served for a time as a volunteer officer in the Civil War, but after 1863 represented an Ohio district in the lower house of Congress. Here he proved to be a finished debater, a tireless committeeman, and a dependable party regular. His chance at the Presidency came prematurely and unexpectedly, but he had long been marked for preferment. Four months after his inauguration as President, he was shot by a disappointed office-seeker. For weeks he lingered between life and death, but finally on September 19, 1881, he died. It cannot be said that with his passing the country lost a great man, but it can perhaps be said that it lost one who was potentially great at a time when great men in politics were rare.

Garfield's death elevated to the Presidency Chester Alan Arthur (1830–1886),[2] a New York politician whose record made him the despair of the reformers. Early in life Arthur became an organization Republican, and his code of ethics, while calling for the strictest personal honesty, tolerated freely the time-honored custom of rewarding the faithful with the spoils of office. As collector of the port of New York he had, as a matter of course, overstaffed his force with party workers, and he never hesitated to call upon the men who held their positions through his favor to do their full political duty during campaigns and on election days. As President, however, he was scrupulously on guard against criticism. He bore himself with becoming dignity, refused to indulge in a wholesale proscription of Garfield's appointees, took up the

---

[1] T. C. Smith, *Life and Letters of James Abram Garfield* (1925); R. G. Caldwell, *James A. Garfield* (1931).

[2] G. F. Howe, *Chester A. Arthur* (1934), is an excellent political biography.

cudgels in favor of civil service reform, and even tariff revision, with wholly unexpected zeal.

Despite the President's best efforts, Congress showed little disposition to inaugurate any disturbing innovations until after the election of 1882. That year, however, the electorate seemed to register an emphatic rebuke for the ruling party by returning a decisive Democratic majority to the House of Representatives. Was this reverse the result of Republican failure to do something about civil service reform and the tariff? Fearing that this was indeed the case, the Republican leaders in Congress decided to pass laws on both subjects during the "lame-duck" session that began the month after the election and lasted until the fourth of March following. Such a "death-bed repentance" might not be very convincing, but it might in the long run be better than no repentance at all.

With reference to civil service reform the Republicans were obliged to accept the assistance of the Democrats. In fact, it was George H. Pendleton, Democratic Senator from Ohio, who introduced and gave his name to the reform measure which an overwhelming bipartisan majority enacted into law in January, 1883. The Pendleton Act authorized the President to appoint three civil service commissioners, not more than two of whom should belong to the same political party, whose duty it should be to provide "open competitive examinations for testing the fitness of applicants for the public service now classified, or to be classified." Only the lowest offices were at first classified, but the law provided that the President might extend the classified lists at will to include other executive appointees. President Arthur administered the law in complete good faith. He appointed as the first chairman of the commission Dorman B. Eaton, who as secretary of the Civil Service Reform Association had been an ardent advocate of reform. During the first year of its existence the commission was given jurisdiction over about fourteen thousand offices out of a total of one hundred and ten thousand, or about twelve and one-half per cent. In contrast with the British system, which examines a candidate upon what fields he happens to know, the American system is based upon strictly practical tests.[1]

Changes of national administration from Arthur's time on worked to the advantage of civil service reform. It happened that Arthur was succeeded by a Democrat, Cleveland; then Cleveland was succeeded by a Republican, Harrison; Harrison in turn was succeeded by a Demo-

Civil service reform (marginal note)

---

[1] C. R. Fish, *The Civil Service and the Patronage* (1905), is the definitive work on this subject. For the later period it is admirably supplemented by A. B. Sageser, *The First Two Decades of the Pendleton Act* (1935).

crat, Cleveland; and Cleveland, by a Republican, McKinley. Each President, as he was about to retire from office, tended to protect his own appointees by extending the classified lists. Men thus "blanketed" into the civil service were not required to take examinations, but when they died or resigned, their successors received appointments only on recommendation of the commission. By 1893 the number of civil servants under the merit system had reached forty-five thousand; by the turn of the century it was about one hundred thousand; by the time of the first World War nearly half a million — over sixty per cent.

Tariff reform was as long overdue as civil service reform, and in practice it proved to be much harder to accomplish. The slight reductions in the Civil War rates obtained in 1872 were practically wiped out in 1875 on the pretext of the depression, and the Tariff of 1883 duties on a few items, such as molasses and sugar, were actually increased. To the reform demands long voiced by David A. Wells, the nation's outstanding expert on the subject, were now added the arguments of such economists as William Graham Sumner of Yale, and Frank W. Taussig of Harvard; also, the public was becoming increasingly insistent. Finally, on the recommendation of President Arthur, Congress created in 1882 a non-political tariff commission to study the subject, and, in spite of the fact that every one of its nine members was an avowed protectionist, the commission speedily reported back that the existing duties should be cut by as much as twenty per cent. Acting this time without any considerable Democratic collaboration, the Republicans were able to hurry into law before the adjournment of Congress in March, 1883, what one writer has aptly called the "Mongrel Tariff." [1] Partly because of the necessity for haste, partly because of the effective work of the lobbyists, and partly because of the logrolling tendencies of congressmen themselves, the measure failed completely to accomplish the purpose for which it was intended. As Senator Sherman admitted, it "restored nearly all the inequalities and incongruities of the old tariff and yielded to local demands and local interests to an extent that destroyed all symmetry and harmony."

The passage of the "Mongrel Tariff" was not without important political results. Since the Republicans were obliged to defend their handiwork, their party inescapably came to be identified more and more with the policy of protection, whereas the Democrats, who were in duty bound to oppose whatever they could in the Republican program, drifted gradually in the direction of an out-and-out low-tariff policy. When the Democrats in 1883 took control of the House of Representatives, they ignored the claims of Samuel J. Randall, a Pennsylvania protection-

[1] Ida M. Tarbell, *The Tariff in Our Times* (1911).

ist who before 1881 had three times been elected Speaker, in order to
place in that office a dependable low-tariff advocate, John G. Carlisle
of Kentucky.

The campaign and election of 1884 turned less on the tariff, however,
than on the personalities of the two outstanding individuals who contested for the Presidency. The Republicans overlooked
Election of 1884 the claims of Arthur, who had offended the regulars by
vetoing in 1882 an $18,000,000 rivers and harbors ("pork-
barrel") bill, and had never been able to live down his past to the
complete satisfaction of the liberals. Instead, they nominated their
outstanding leader, James G. Blaine (1830–1893),[1] whom Garfield had
made Secretary of State, but whose resignation from that office Arthur
had not hesitated to accept. Blaine was born in Pennsylvania, but had
entered politics in Maine. Unlike most politicians his background was
journalism, rather than the law. When war broke out in 1861, he did
not join the army, but in 1863 entered the national House of Representatives, and remained there until 1876, when he went to the Senate.
During Grant's administration he emerged as the outstanding leader of
the Republican Party. A firm believer in the righteousness of Radical
reconstruction, and a veritable incarnation of Republican prejudice, he
appealed strongly to a party-loving age. Both on and off the platform
he possessed great personal charm, a quality which he used, no less than
Henry Clay, to excite the worshipful support of his followers. Both
in 1876 and in 1880 far more sentiment had existed for Blaine than for
the men the Republicans had nominated, but Blaine's record had
offended the liberals, and lesser lights had won the prize. Even now the
"Mulligan letters," which revealed that Blaine as congressman had
helped obtain a land grant for an Arkansas railroad from which he hoped
to make a financial profit, were flaunted as good reason to keep Blaine in
retirement, but the "Blaine or bust" crowd was not to be denied.

The Democrats, as in 1876, nominated a reform governor of New
York. Grover Cleveland (1837–1908),[2] was born in New Jersey, but
had early removed to New York. After a hard struggle
Grover Cleveland with poverty he had become by 1859 a practicing lawyer
in Buffalo. During the Civil War, when other young men
were joining the army, he borrowed money to hire a substitute because

---

[1] The best biography of Blaine is D. S. Muzzey, *James G. Blaine* (1934). Those written
by Blaine's contemporaries are too prejudiced to be of value. Blaine's own *Twenty Years
in Congress* (2 vols., 1884–86) treats only of his earlier career. See also C. E. Russell,
Blaine of Maine: His Life and Times (1931).

[2] Allan Nevins, *Grover Cleveland: a Study in Courage* (1932), is in reality a well-rounded
history of the period. Useful also is Allan Nevins (editor), *Letters of Grover Cleveland*
(1933). These works completely supplant the earlier lives of Cleveland.

his still meager earnings were needed for the support of his mother and sisters. In 1863 he received a welcome appointment as assistant district attorney, and in 1870 he was not above accepting a nomination as sheriff of Erie County. Elected, he revealed qualities of scrupulous honesty and unflinching courage that soon made him a marked man. He refused to hire a hangman when two murderers were to be executed, and sprang the trap himself. He made life consistently uncomfortable for local crooks and grafters. In 1881, nominated and elected mayor of Buffalo to placate the "better element," he reorganized the city administration, purged it of venal politicians, vetoed dubious measures, and in general endeared himself to reformers. The fame of the "veto mayor" spread, and when in 1882 the New York Democrats needed a candidate for governor with an unimpeachable record, they turned to Cleveland and elected him by a majority of nearly 200,000 votes. As governor, he struggled irritably against a bewildering accumulation of governmental inefficiency or worse, made some progress and many enemies, particularly among the Tammany leaders of New York City. "We love him most for the enemies he has made," General E. S. Bragg told the Democratic Convention of 1884, mindful of Tammany's earnest desire to prevent Cleveland's nomination for the Presidency.

The nomination of Cleveland insured that a large number of Republican liberals, now called "Mugwumps," would swing their support to the Democratic ticket. Ordinarily this would have insured his election by a fairly wide margin, but he happened to be a bachelor, and flaws were uncovered in his private life *Election of Cleveland* which in some minds offset his irreproachable conduct of his public responsibilities. The campaign reached an all-time low in mud-slinging, but the sober second thought of most Americans seemed to coincide with that of a philosophical Mugwump who held that "we should elect Mr. Cleveland to the public office he is so eminently qualified to fill and remand Mr. Blaine to the private life which he is so eminently fitted to adorn." For whatever might be said of Blaine's public record, his private life was blameless. The decision in 1884 was almost as close as in 1880. Cleveland's plurality over Blaine in the country as a whole was only 23,000, and the electoral vote stood 219 to 182. Cleveland carried the solid South, Delaware, Indiana, Connecticut, New Jersey, and New York. All the rest of the states voted for Blaine. The Democrats won control of the House of Representatives by a comfortable margin, but the Republicans retained their majority in the Senate. Benjamin F. Butler, the Greenback candidate, received a total of 175,370 popular votes, and John P. St. John of Kansas, Prohibitionist, 150,369. The Prohibitionist vote in New York State alone ran to over

25,000, another factor in the defeat of Blaine. Had the temperance forces not had a candidate of their own, undoubtedly most of them would have voted for Blaine and against Cleveland, whose bibulous habits were well known.

Cleveland's efforts to inaugurate reforms met many obstacles. He protected the Civil Service Commission all he could, and even extended the classified lists, but in order to avoid an outright revolt within his party he was obliged to yield many non-classified offices to the spoilsmen. He had trouble with the veterans of the Civil War, now organized into a powerful society known as the Grand Army of the Republic, because he stood athwart their desires for more and larger pensions. Already the Arrears of Pensions Act of 1879 had permitted pensioners, whatever their service disability, to recover back payments for the period between the time of mustering out and the time a given pension was granted. The abuse of this privilege angered the President, but he could do little about it; on the other hand, he could, and did, veto a "pauper" pension bill that would have given a pension to all who stood in need of it, regardless of disability. He also vetoed hundreds of the private pension bills that lenient congressmen had long been willing to push through for the benefit of favored constituents who had seen service, but according to the general law were not entitled to pensions. This attitude on the part of the President, together with his willingness to restore to the states from which they had come all captured Confederate battle-flags, won him the undying hatred of the "G. A. R.," sometimes appropriately called the "Grand Army of the Republican Party."

Cleveland's chief bid for reform came during his second administration, when he forced both parties to take their stand on the tariff issue.

Cleveland and the tariff

In his annual message of December, 1887, he dealt exclusively with the tariff, presented a well-reasoned, hard-hitting argument against the existing high rates, and, pointing to the annual surplus of about $100,000,000 brought in each year by the Tariff of 1883, declared: "It is a *condition* which confronts us, not a theory." Thus briefed by the President, the Democratic majority in the House of Representatives, with only four dissenting votes, accepted the low-tariff bill presented by Roger Q. Mills of Texas, chairman of the House Ways and Means Committee. This measure called for reductions from an average level of about forty-seven per cent to an average level of about forty per cent, and placed such items as wool, flax, hemp, salt, lumber, and tinplate on the free list. In response to this Democratic challenge, the Senate Committee on Finance, under the leadership of Senator Allison, presented a sample of what the Republicans would be glad to do if only they could win control of the government in the election of 1888. As passed by the Republican majority in the Senate, the Allison bill proposed to maintain a generally high level of duties, but it insured a smaller revenue by resort to prohibitive duties, by the lowering of excises, and by a cut in the duty on sugar. As anticipated, the House would not accept the Senate bill, and the Senate would not accept the House bill. But as Cleveland had foreseen, both parties had been committed to positions that they could not possibly abandon in the coming presidential campaign.

As was now inevitable, the Democrats renominated Cleveland in 1888, and made tariff reform their principal issue. The Republicans, having lost with Blaine in 1884, turned to one of their lesser lights, Benjamin Harrison of Indiana, who had the triple advantage of a presidential grandfather, residence in a close state, and a clean, if almost empty, political record. The campaign was a revelation to the Republicans, for they learned for the first time how advantageous an issue the tariff could be. Campaign contributions as insurance against Democratic tariff reductions poured into the Republican coffers in a flood. The funds thus collected were used both to carry on an extensive campaign of education, and to get out the vote. For the former purpose Republican orators and publicists made much of the necessity of maintaining the high wages of American labor, something that could not be done, they insisted, if the products of low-paid European labor were admitted freely to American markets. When it came to "getting out the vote," party workers, particularly in the doubtful states, scrupled at nothing. The scandals of the election were so open and notorious as to give great impetus to the movement for the "Australian" system of secret voting, which down to this time had made little headway in the United States. Even so, Harrison won the election by only a slender margin. In the popular vote Cleveland led by more than 100,000, but Harrison carried the crucial states of New York and Indiana, and so amassed 233 electoral votes to Cleveland's 168.

Benjamin Harrison (1833–1901) was designed to be, and as President became, a "dignified figurehead." He was at the time of his nomination a successful lawyer of great party regularity who had served one term in the United States Senate. He was in no sense the leader of his party, and James G. Blaine, whom he made his Secretary of State, completely overshadowed him.[1] Harrison was a good platform orator, but cold in his personal relationships. "Harrison can make a speech to ten thousand men," said one of his associates, "and every man of them will go away his friend. Let him

Election of 1888

Benjamin Harrison

---

[1] A. T. Volwiler, *The Correspondence Between Benjamin Harrison and James G. Blaine, 1882–1893* (1940)

meet the same ten thousand in private, and every one will go away his enemy." His honesty was probably as unimpeachable as Cleveland's, but he lacked Cleveland's forceful nature. During Cleveland's administration the Democratic party leaders, one by one, acknowledged the President's supremacy, whereas Harrison from the beginning of his administration to its end, had far less to do with charting his party's course than many another of lesser rank.

Harrison's record on civil service reform and pensions was by no means as courageous as Cleveland's. Like President Grant, he saw fit to allot many minor offices to his indigent friends and relatives. In making other appointments he leaned on the advice of the politicians, and did what they wanted if he could. His chief contribution to civil service reform was his appointment of Theodore Roosevelt to membership on the Civil Service Commission, an appointment which Roosevelt earned as a reward for serving his party faithfully during the campaign of 1888. As civil service commissioner, however, Roosevelt made it his business to see that no such rewards as he had received were made through the agency of the commission. In the pursuit of this course he soon fell afoul of the President, whom he came to dislike, and of many of the President's friends, but Harrison was nonetheless obliged to retain the obstreperous commissioner in office, and when in 1893 Cleveland became President again he also retained Roosevelt. As for pensions, the G. A. R. got exactly what it wanted in a Dependents' Pension Act, which provided that all veterans of the Civil War who had served for as long as ninety days, and who suffered from any disabling mental or physical ability, should receive pensions of from six to twelve dollars a month, according to the degree of disability from which they suffered. Widows of veterans, if dependent upon their own labor for support, were awarded pensions of eight dollars a month, and minor children, two dollars a month. As a result of this law the number of pensions rose from 489,725 in 1889 to 966,012 in 1893, and the amount of money appropriated for pensions in the same period from $89,000,000 to $157,000,000.[1]

The main business of the Fifty-First Congress was to pass a high protective tariff law, but to accomplish this strictly partisan end political strategy of a high order was required. The Republicans had a majority in each house of Congress, but particularly in the House of Representatives the majority depended upon too few votes for comfort. To expedite the business in hand, the Republican Speaker, Thomas B. Reed of Maine, broke

The
Republican
program

[1] There are two revealing monographs on this subject: J. W. Oliver, *History of the Civil War Military Pensions* (1917); W. H. Glasson, *Federal Military Pensions in the United States* (1918). See also F. H. Heck, *The Civil War Veteran in Minnesota Life and Politics* (1941).

traditional rules right and left. Members present, but not voting, were counted to make a quorum, and a powerful Committee on Rules, of which "Czar" Reed himself was chairman, brought in from time to time whatever special rules were needed to push the Republican program along. To bolster up the Republican majority, especially in the Senate, two new northwestern territories, Wyoming and Idaho, were added to the four, North and South Dakota, Montana, and Washington, that the preceding Congress had authorized to take the steps necessary to become states. Since the voters of this region were predominantly Republican, the control of the Republican Party in Congress was greatly strengthened by their admission. Finally, as a sop to the silver Republicans of the West, who refused to vote for a high tariff until something should be done for silver, the Sherman Silver Purchase Act of 1890 was passed. This measure required the Treasury to buy 4,500,000 ounces of silver a month, the estimated output of all the silver mines in the United States. Not all the silver need be coined, but it was to be paid for in Treasury notes redeemable "in gold or silver coin," and so provided for a substantial addition to the amount of money actually in circulation. Efforts to enact a Federal Elections Bill, or "Force Bill," which would again give the national government control of elections in the South, as during reconstruction, failed; otherwise, the Republicans might have forged a weapon by means of which they could have controlled the national government almost indefinitely.

The McKinley Tariff Act, which became a law on October 1, 1890, was the Republican answer to the prayers, and the contributions, of the American industrialists. It provided first and foremost a set of duties on manufactured articles higher than the American government had ever levied before. Some of these duties turned out to be, as their authors had intended, actually prohibitive; others went to the length of offering protection to nonexistent industries, provided only that responsible persons could demonstrate their intent to begin manufacture. The law also embodied an impressive list of agricultural duties, charged against such imports as eggs, butter, potatoes, wheat, and barley. These items were included primarily for their psychological effect upon the farmer vote. Duties levied upon commodities of which the United States had an excess for export, and the price of which was fixed on the world market, amounted, as was well known, to little more than empty gestures. The reduction of the revenue, deemed imperative by both Democrats and Republicans, was accomplished in part by the discouraging effect on importation of the high duties, but in greater part by placing raw sugar on the free list. This was in effect an aid to the manufacturers of refined sugar,

The McKinley Tariff

whose product was still protected, but who could now buy raw sugar for less, but it was very disturbing to the sugar producers of Louisiana until the idea of a bounty of two cents per pound on all raw sugar of American origin was included. Thus the sugar schedule, figuratively speaking, succeeded in taking money out of the Treasury with both hands. To please the Secretary of State, James G. Blaine, a reciprocity clause was included in the McKinley Tariff, although its provisions were much more restricted than Blaine had hoped. The President was authorized to enforce a specified schedule of tariff rates on items listed as free in case the nations that produced them failed to grant equivalent advantages to American exports.

Public reaction to the behavior of the Fifty-First Congress was far from cordial. Each of its measures made a generous quota of enemies, and the grand total of accumulated grievances grew with each succeeding month. To the effect of the McKinley Bill on the revenue, which was sure to be disastrous, was added the orgy of spending in which Congress permitted itself to indulge. Its lavish appropriations for pensions, river and harbor improvements, federal buildings, coast defenses, and other extravagances led the newspapers to refer to it as the "billion-dollar Congress," a description strikingly lacking in political appeal. Unfortunate as a Treasury surplus might have been, a deficit, even less desirable, appeared to be in sight. Consumers found that the higher rates of the McKinley Tariff meant higher prices for what they had to buy; when its rates were made known, John Wanamaker, Harrison's storekeeper Postmaster-General, with more business than political acumen, openly urged his customers to "buy now, before prices go up." The Force Bill, based as it was upon an attempt to revive sectional antagonisms, was unpopular, North as well as South. As Elihu Root phrased it a little later, the whole country was ready to concede "the failure of the plan formulated at the close of the war to elevate the black man by conferring the suffrage upon him."

Held only a few weeks after the passage of the McKinley Bill, the congressional elections of 1890 showed how unpopular that measure, and the Congress that passed it, had become. Democratic campaigners did not fail to take full advantage of the opportunity to denounce "Bill McKinley and the McKinley Bill." Peddlers were sent through the country, so the Republicans claimed, to offer tin cups at twenty-five cents each and tin pails at a dollar apiece in order to show the rural voters how much the McKinley duties had increased the cost of living. Merchants and salesmen apologized for high prices, whatever the truth might be, on the ground that the new tariff law had made them necessary. The Republicans, with

Elections of 1890

tea, coffee, and sugar on the free list, had hoped to make much of the "free breakfast table," but the fact that the sugar duties were retained for six months after the passage of the bill made this battle-cry seem decidedly premature. When the votes were counted, the Republicans discovered that they had received the most emphatic rebuke in the history of their party. In the Senate the Republican majority was narrowed to eight, and would have been wiped out altogether but for the hold-over senators from the newly admitted states of the Northwest. In the House the Democrats had 235 seats, and the Republicans 88, while nine Farmers' Alliance men, or Populists, refused to vote with either of the older parties. The appearance of this group of independents in Congress marked the beginning of an agrarian revolt in the Middle West and the South, which, with the assistance it received from the silver mining states of the Far West, threatened for a time to bring about a complete realignment of political parties in the United States.[1]

[1] Wilfred E. Binkley, *American Political Parties: Their Natural History* (1948), is an excellent synthesis. Political biographies of consequence include C. L. Barrows, *William M. Evarts, Lawyer, Diplomat, Statesman* (1941); Brainerd Dyer, *The Public Career of William M. Evarts* (1933); L. B. Richardson, *William E. Chandler, Republican* (1940); C. C. Tansill, *The Congressional Career of Thomas Francis Bayard, 1869–1885* (1946), and *The Foreign Policy of Thomas F. Bayard, 1885–1897* (1940); Elmer Ellis, *Henry Moore Teller, Defender of the West* (1941).

27

Capital and Labor

WHILE the depression years of the seventies had called a halt to the rapid expansion of industry in the United States, it was only a temporary halt. Indeed, businesses that escaped annihilation were often the better off for the restraints that the depression imposed upon them. In flush times comfortable profits were too easily achieved; in hard times even small profits were won, more than likely, only as the reward of efficiency. In flush times American manufacturers had depended all too exclusively upon the American market; in hard times they sought to adapt their products to the needs of other lands, and began to sell abroad. Solvent organizations bettered their positions by absorbing their weaker rivals, and by devising trade agreements with their stronger rivals to forestall the menace of cut-throat competition. When, at last, the depression was

---

LEADERS IN INDUSTRY AND FINANCE

CORNELIUS VANDERBILT (1794–1877) *was one of the first of the great industrial pioneers of America. In his early life his principal interest was in steamboating, and by his shrewdness in achieving monopoly wherever his interests led him, he amassed a huge fortune. In his later life he turned to railroads with the same outstanding success. When he died he was worth nearly $100,000,000.*

Four of these men belonged to the same generation: ANDREW CARNEGIE (1835–1919), *steel manufacturer;* J. PIERPONT MORGAN (1837–1913), *financier;* JOHN D. ROCKEFELLER (1839–1937), *oil refiner;* JAMES J. HILL (1838–1916), *railroad builder. Theirs was the age of industrial pioneering in America, and they were only outstanding representatives of a much larger group, men who furnished the economic leadership necessary for the development of the country. (Photo of Carnegie from Keystone; photo of Morgan from Underwood & Underwood.)*

HENRY FORD (1863–) *belongs to a later period. His field of endeavor, as everyone knows, was automobiles. But in the twentieth century, with corporation rather than individual enterprise in the ascendancy, Ford may be regarded as the exception rather than the rule. In a sense, he was the "last of the pioneers."*

FORD

CARNEGIE

HILL

ROCKEFELLER

VANDERBILT

MORGAN

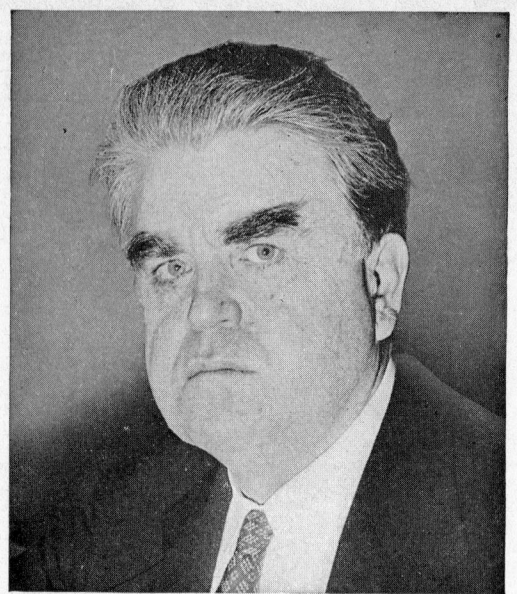

LEWIS

POWDERLY

DEBS

GOMPERS

MITCHELL

GREEN

over, business, particularly big business, was in position to begin another era of spectacular expansion.

As had happened before, the railroads led the way in the new development. Under the leadership for a time of Frederick Billings, and later of Henry Villard, the Northern Pacific was completed in 1883. Although this road was the first to make rapid headway after the depression, it was finished a year too late to be the second transcontinental, for in 1882 the Southern Pacific of California had through trains running over the old Texas Pacific route from San Francisco to St. Louis. Another Southern Pacific route connected at Needles, California, with the Atchison, Topeka, and Santa Fe, which had built westward through Kansas on a state land grant, and from Albuquerque to Needles on the federal grant of the now defunct Atlantic and Pacific. Other western roads — the Burlington, the Rock Island, the Northwestern, the Missouri Pacific, the Denver and Rio Grande, and the Great Northern — extended their lines during these years with the same feverish speed. In the East and the South there was also much new building, and almost equally important, steel rails everywhere replaced iron, and improved rolling stock and other equipment revolutionized the whole process of railroading.[1]

[1] Stuart Daggett, *Chapters on the History of the Southern Pacific* (1922); J. B. Hedges, *Henry Villard and the Railways of the Northwest* (1930); R. C. Overton, *Burlington West* (1942).

LABOR LEADERS

The history of the labor movement in the United States since the Civil War could be written around the lives of these six men. TERENCE V. POWDERLY (1849–1924), *a Pennsylvania machinist, did his greatest work as Grand Master Workman of the Knights of Labor from 1879 to 1893.* SAMUEL GOMPERS (1850–1924) *was a founder of the American Federation of Labor and was its president for forty years. Gompers differed from* EUGENE V. DEBS (1855–1926) *because Gompers did not believe in the organization of labor into a political party and Debs did. Debs was Socialist candidate for President of the United States five times.* JOHN MITCHELL (1870–1919) *was president of the United Mine Workers of America from 1898 to 1908 and won fame by his successful handling of the anthracite coal strike of 1902.* WILLIAM GREEN (1873–) *and* JOHN L. LEWIS (1880–) *were rival labor leaders before and during the Second World War. Green became president of the American Federation of Labor in 1924. Lewis was founder and first president of the Congress of Industrial Organizations, organized after a break from the A.F. of L. in 1936–38. Later, however, Lewis and his union, the United Mine Workers, withdrew from the C.I.O. and sought readmission to the A.F. of L. (Photo of Powderly and Green from Harris & Ewing, of Gompers and Debs from Keystone, of Lewis from Acme, and of Mitchell from Brown Bros.)*

Because of these expensive innovations, statistics on mileage fail to give a complete picture of the railroad development of the period. Nevertheless the statistics are impressive. From 52,000 miles of railroad in 1870 the total mileage in the United States had risen by 1880 to 93,000 and by 1890 to 163,000 — an increase of 70,000 miles in ten years. Construction more than kept pace with the expansion of population. In 1870 the United States had 1380 miles of railroad per million inhabitants; in 1880 it had 1858 miles, and in 1890 it had 2625 miles. By the last-mentioned date the main outlines of the American railroad map were complete; after that date the mileage continued to increase, but such new tracks as were laid served mainly as feeders for existing lines. The age of railroad pioneering was over.

The creation of these great railroad systems was not usually accomplished without the elimination of a multitude of lesser lines. Back in the pre-Civil War era more or less accidental connections had played a considerable part in railroad consolidation. In this way the work of Cornelius Vanderbilt in welding together the New York Central had been greatly facilitated. Panics and periods of depression had also done their bit. During the years following 1857, and even more after 1873, the weaker roads had gone into bankruptcy only to emerge as parts of some stronger, and usually much larger, system. During the depression years of the seventies no less than four hundred and fifty railroads, fully two-fifths of the roads of the country, had suffered this experience. The holding company idea also facilitated consolidation. The Southern Pacific, for example, drew its extensive properties together through a holding company known as the Southern Pacific of Kentucky. The Southern Pacific owned no railroads in Kentucky, but the laws of that state were friendly to its purposes, while incorporation in a state far removed from the scene of the road's activities seemed likely to reduce to a minimum the danger of investigation and regulation. Great sectional systems, by whatever means created, could and did monopolize the business of the region they covered. Within these areas competition was stifled, and only the interposition of governmental authority could prevent railroad monopolies from charging for their services "all the traffic would bear."

Railway consolidations

The Granger movement had called attention to many railroad grievances, and had led to the creation in most of the states of regulatory commissions. These commissions, ill-informed as to the problems that confronted them, and often subservient to the corporations they were supposed to regulate, at first accomplished comparatively little. Knowledge, to be sure, came with the years, but it added nothing to the effectiveness of state regulation;

Railroad regulation

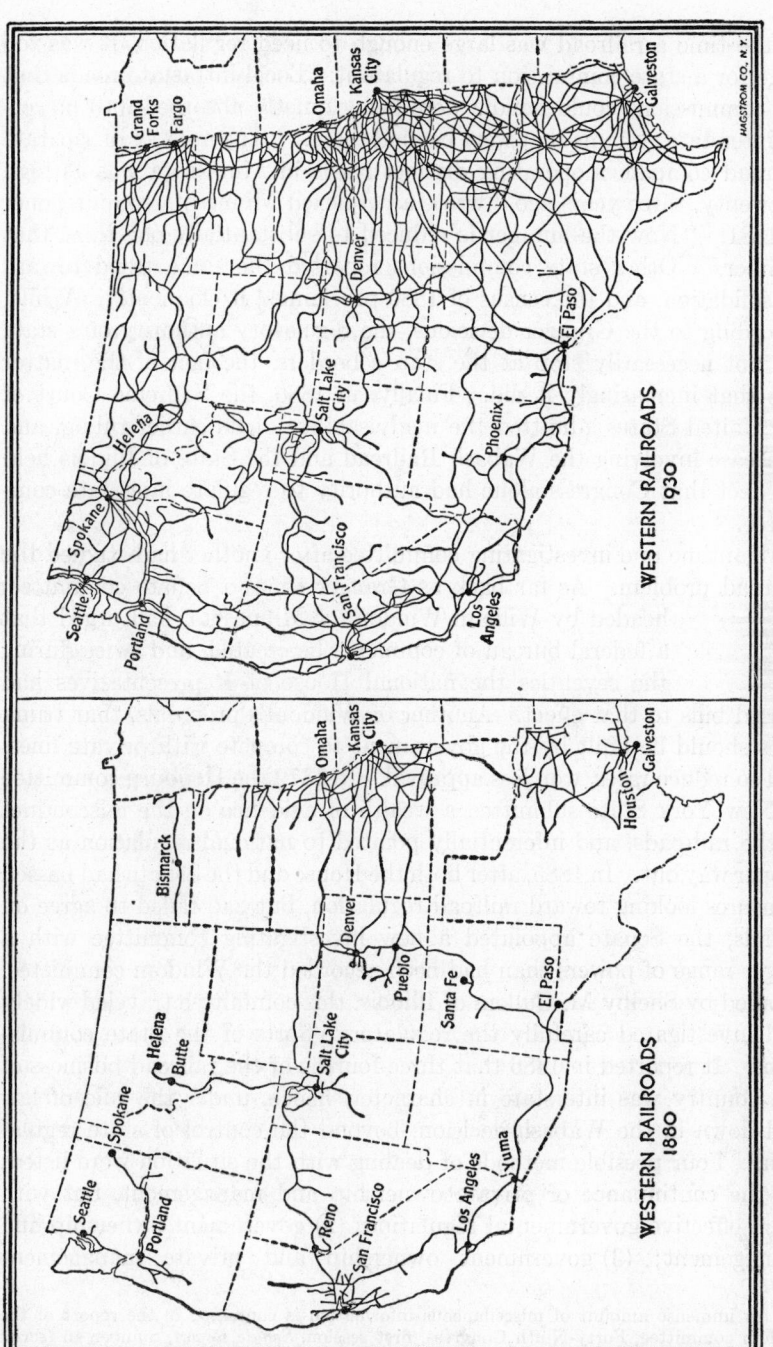

GROWTH OF THE WESTERN RAILROADS

by the time a railroad was large enough to need regulation, it was too large for a state commission to regulate it. Local intrastate roads that the commissions could handle were being quietly absorbed into powerful interstate systems that were beyond them. "The number of separate railroad companies operating distinct roads in Minnesota was as high as twenty, three years ago," wrote a perplexed Minnesota commissioner in 1881. "Now the number is reduced to substantially one third that number." Other state commissions reported the same trend toward consolidation, and the census of 1880 proclaimed it eloquently. While, according to the Granger decisions, the regulatory authority of a state did not necessarily stop at the state's borders, the fact of the matter was that increasingly it did. Finally, in 1886, the Supreme Court of the United States admitted the inadvisability of its earlier ruling, and in a case involving the Wabash Railroad and the State of Illinois held in effect that Congress alone had authority to regulate interstate commerce.

Meantime one investigating committee after another had studied the railroad problem. As far back as Granger times a Senate committee, headed by William Windom of Minnesota, had urged that Investigations a federal bureau of commerce be created, and twice during the seventies the national House of Representatives had passed bills to that effect. Another of Windom's proposals, that trunk lines should be built by the government to compete with private lines, and so reduce rates, won less approval. In 1879 the Hepburn committee in New York State submitted a wealth of evidence on the misconduct of the railroads, and inferentially pointed to national regulation as the proper way out. In 1885, after both the House and the Senate had passed measures looking toward railroad regulation, but had failed to agree on details, the Senate appointed a new investigating committee with a larger range of powers than had been accorded the Windom committee. Headed by Shelby M. Cullom of Illinois, this committee traveled widely and investigated carefully the regulatory efforts of the State commissions. It reported in 1886 that three-fourths of the railroad business of the country was interstate in character, hence, under the rule of law laid down in the Wabash decision, beyond the control of state regulation.[1] Four possible methods of dealing with the situation were listed: (1) the continuance of private ownership and management, but with more effective governmental regulation; (2) government ownership and management; (3) government ownership and private management

---

[1] An immense amount of miscellaneous information is contained in the report of the Cullom committee, Forty-Ninth Congress, first session, *Senate Report*, number 46 (serial 2356).

under public regulations; and (4) government ownership and management in competition with private companies. Noting the widespread opposition throughout the country to government ownership, the committee recommended regulation by the national government as the preferable alternative.

Congress was now ready to act, and in 1887 it established an Interstate Commerce Commission to consist of five members, of whom not more than three might belong to the same political party, to be appointed by the President for six-year terms. The   The I.C.C. law forbade most of the evil practices uncovered by the various investigating committees, and in a sense made national the current trends in state regulation. Rebates, pools, and discriminations were branded as illegal, and the rule that more could not be charged for a short haul than for a longer one over the same line was established. The commission was authorized to investigate complaints against the railroads, and to make decisions which, however, it could enforce only through court action. This provision for a judicial review of its rulings proved to be the undoing of the early commission. Although headed by an eminent ex-judge, Thomas M. Cooley of Michigan, it failed to obtain the judicial backing through which, alone, its decisions could be made effective. Delays and reversals permitted the railroads to operate about as they had operated before. Not until the Presidency of Theodore Roosevelt did the Interstate Commerce Commission become a really effective body.[1]

The trend toward consolidation, so evident in the history of the railroads, was equally apparent elsewhere in the business world. This was due in large part to the transportation revolution that the completion of the railroad system had worked, but a number of other newly devised means of communication were available by the eighties that facilitated almost as much as the railroads themselves the operation of large business units. One of these was the electric telegraph, used for years before the Civil War, but now extended to parallel every railroad right of way and to serve practically every hamlet in the nation. Cable service also had steadily improved. The first transoceanic cable, laid in 1858, had soon been destroyed by the use of too strong electric currents, but by 1866, through the persistent labors of Cyrus W. Field, a better one had been laid, and soon thereafter many others. American businessmen were thus able to keep in as close touch with London as with New York quotations, and to make their plans with a fuller knowledge of world affairs than had ever been possible before.

Of incalculable importance also was the telephone, the invention of

---

[1] The two treatises by W. Z. Ripley, *Railroads: Rates and Regulation* (1912), and *Railroads: Finance and Organization* (1915), best cover these subjects.

Alexander Graham Bell, an American Scot who taught deaf mutes, and
          had interested himself in acoustics. At the Centennial
The telephone Exposition of 1876 Bell exhibited his instruments, and made
          a deep impression on the American public. He was not the
first to study the problem of transmitting human speech by electricity,
nor the only one to find a solution, but he did develop the first practicable telephone.[1] Even so, it was not easy to induce capital to invest in so
fantastic an enterprise, and the successful launching of the telephone
owed much to the organizing genius of Theodore N. Vail, later president
of the American Telephone and Telegraph Company. During the
eighties telephone systems were introduced into virtually every American city, and by the end of the decade no less than 440,000 instruments
were in use. Well before the turn of the century successful long-distance
connections had been generally established.

The significance of the telephone in the business world can hardly be
overestimated. Among other things, it enabled business executives to
keep in close touch with a veritable army of subordinates, and thus
tremendously facilitated the process of consolidation. A natural monopoly, it soon furnished in its own tightly woven business organization
an example that other businesses strove earnestly to follow. Incidentally, it provided at its switchboards a new occupation for women,
and through its rural extensions another effective weapon against social
isolation.

The telephone was only one of the many new uses which electricity
was being made to serve. Wizard of electrical inventors was Thomas A.
Edison (1847-1931), an Ohioan by birth whose formal schooling had
been limited to three months, but whose natural ingenuity has probably
never been surpassed. At fifteen he had learned to send and receive
telegraph messages, but his fondness for experimentation doomed him
to frequent dismissals by irritated employers. In 1879 he made his
first really revolutionary invention, a practicable incandescent light.
Others had already devised the arc light, which served well enough for
street-lighting, but was wholly unsatisfactory for indoor use. By January, 1880, Edison had taken out a patent on his light bulb, which before
long he was able to manufacture, in quantities for commercial use, at
a factory in Harrison, New Jersey. Improvements in generators followed, and soon business houses and even dwellings were depending for
illumination on the new device. The next need was for central electric
power stations, an opportunity for business expansion so fully appreciated that the number of such stations increased from eight in 1881 to

[1] H. N. Casson, *The History of the Telephone* (1910); Catherine Mackenzie, *Alexander Graham Bell, the Man Who Contracted Space* (1928).

2774 in 1898.[1] While Edison, with his numerous inventions, including among others the phonograph, motion pictures, automatic telegraphy, the stock-ticker, and the microphone, ranks as the leading electrical engineer of his time, he was by no means the only one. Soon electric railway systems were banishing horsecars from the city streets, electric elevators were adding innumerable stories to the height of skyscrapers, and electric power was being used to turn a larger and larger proportion of the wheels of industry.

The typewriter met another business need. Its inventor was a Milwaukee printer, Charles Latham Sholes, who as early as 1867 had devised a machine that would write with fair rapidity. Fortunately, a letter written on one of Sholes's typewriters fell into the *The typewriter* hands of James Densmore, a Pennsylvania businessman, and led him to come to the aid of the inventor with money and ideas. Within a decade the collaborators had sufficiently perfected their machine that it was finding its way into business offices, and within another decade it had become a business necessity. Sholes's machine, which was first manufactured commercially by the firm of E. Remington and Son, had many imitators, and by the end of the century nearly a hundred different models were on the market. Like the telephone, the typewriter provided a new gainful occupation for women. Women operators, it transpired, were not only quite as efficient as men, but they could also be hired for less. Soon it was generally assumed that the noun stenographer was feminine gender, and that it referred to any member of the vast army of young women whose skill at shorthand and typewriting made their services indispensable to the smooth functioning of business offices.

A number of other circumstances promoted also the widening of business horizons. Advertising took on new life with the invention of the half-tone process, through which the image recorded by the camera could be inexpensively transferred to print paper. *Nation-wide advertising* Improvements in photography served the same useful end. The cost of job printing was reduced by the invention of the linotype and the monotype, and at the same time the quality was greatly improved.[2] Meantime the United States Post-Office, regardless of deficits, cheapened its rates, and amplified its service. Railroad extensions were followed everywhere by postal extensions. Mail delivery at the door

[1] Ida M. Tarbell, *The Nationalizing of Business, 1878–1898* (1936), reviews admirably these and similar transformations. On Edison himself see F. L. Dyer and T. C. Martin, *Edison, His Life and Inventions* (1929).

[2] Ottmar Mergenthaler, a naturalized American of German birth, invented the linotype in 1885, and Talbot Lanston, a clerk in the Pension Office in Washington, D.C., invented the monotype in 1887. On the general subject of inventions two short treatises are available: Holland Thompson, *The Age of Invention* (1921); and George Iles, *Leading American Inventors* (1912).

was inaugurated in a few American cities as early as 1871, and thereafter was rapidly bestowed upon smaller and smaller communities. Catalogues and printed circulars were accorded special rates to facilitate general distribution. The penny postal card, introduced into the United States from Europe in 1873, brought the cost of personal mail service to an irreducible minimum; but the two-cent letter rate, inaugurated in 1883, was not far behind.

It is not difficult to see why business, with all these aids, became increasingly national rather than local in scope. With nation-wide competition at work only the ablest, the most selfish, and the most unscrupulous of the competitors could survive. Great producers tended to become the cheapest producers, and little companies tended to disappear. Close observers of business trends during the eighties noted that the current formula of business evolution called for a greatly increased output from a steadily diminishing number of plants. In 1880, for example, the nation had 1990 woolen mills, in 1890, only 1311; in 1880 it had 1934 factories that made agricultural implements, in 1890, only 910. During the same decade the number of iron and steel mills decreased by one-third, and the number of leather establishments by three-fourths. In every case, however, the total capital investment and the total output of the industry had vastly increased, while ownership, or at least management, had been concentrated far more rapidly than even the reduced number of plants would indicate. What the nation was witnessing was the emergence of a large number of near-monopolies, each of which aspired to the complete control of some important national necessity.[1]

Tendencies toward monopoly

Public awareness of the situation began with the appearance of an article, "The Story of a Great Monopoly," by Henry Demarest Lloyd, in the *Atlantic Monthly* for March, 1881. Lloyd's article was a scathing attack on the Standard Oil Company, and the deep impression it made was fully attested by the fact that that particular number of the *Atlantic* sold out seven editions. John D. Rockefeller, the guiding genius of Standard Oil, had planned monopoly from the start. The first important step toward this goal, control of the oil-refining business of Cleveland, Ohio, he had accomplished by the time the Panic of 1873 broke. This gave him perhaps one-third of the oil-refining business of the country, and undismayed by the depression he set out to get the rest. Skillful at obtaining financial backing, and always equipped with a large cash balance of his own, he bought up whatever refineries would sell, induced

[1] J. W. Jenks and W. E. Clark, *The Trust Problem* (new edition, 1929). Other interesting surveys are Burton J. Hendrick, *The Age of Big Business* (1920), and John Moody, *The Masters of Capital* (1921). For a more recent interpretation, see T. C. Cochran and William Miller, *The Age of Enterprise* (1942).

others to join forces with him, and drove still others out of business. By the time the depression was over, the Rockefeller interests, with control over all the greatest refineries in New York, Philadelphia, Pittsburgh, Baltimore, and Titusville, had approximated the complete monopoly their leader had sought.[1]

Rockefeller's ruthless methods left him a rich legacy of hatred. The railroads, hard-pressed for business during the depression, had little choice but to give him the rebates he demanded. Shippers less favored either were ruined by the unfair competition or sold out to Standard Oil. When it came to the marketing of oil, Rockefeller gave no quarter. The United States was divided up into convenient sections, each with its agent and subagents, with every agent under instructions to "sell all the oil that is sold in your district." Agents who succeeded in this undertaking were rewarded with higher salaries and promotions; agents who failed were summarily dismissed. Railroad records were spied upon by Standard Oil men so that the business of competitive refineries could be stolen. Price-cutting was carried to any extreme necessary to put a competitor out of business, and as soon as his defeat was assured the price of oil was set again at a figure as high as or higher than before the price-war began. Pipeline companies that carried the crude oil to railway centers, and even hundreds of miles to the refineries, were gathered up by Standard Oil, one by one, usually at its own price. Determined to pay no man profits, Rockefeller built terminal warehouses of his own, established factories to make barrels and other necessary articles, and eliminated hundreds of wholesalers and middlemen. Finally, in order to facilitate centralized control and to insure against unintentional competition among the various Standard properties, the Standard Oil Trust was formed. This device, first adopted in 1879, but revised and more completely applied in 1882, consisted merely of a group of nine trustees to whom was surrendered all the stock of the Standard Oil Company and its various affiliates. Trust certificates were then issued to each Standard stockholder in the proportion of twenty trust certificates for each share of Standard stock. For several years the nine trustees, with John D. Rockefeller at their head, made the decisions for all of the stockholders and all of the companies that were dominated by Standard Oil.

The Standard Oil Company

"This is the original trust," declared a New York committee that in 1888 began the investigation of Standard Oil. "Its success has been the incentive to the formation of all other trusts or combinations. It is the type of a system which has spread like a

The "trusts"

---

[1] J. T. Flynn, *God's Gold; the Story of Rockefeller and His Times* (1932), is exciting and colorful. See also Nevins, *John D. Rockefeller*, already cited.

disease through the commercial system of this country." What the committee charged was fully borne out by the facts. One after another "an incredible number of the necessaries and luxuries of life, from meat to tombstones," had fallen into the hands of some tightly organized little group that frequently only by the most unscrupulous and underhand methods had achieved control. Sugar, salt, whiskey, matches, crackers, lead, cottonseed oil, linseed oil, wire and nails, agricultural machinery, electrical supplies, and a host of other items could be obtained only by paying tribute to some such trust or combine. The exact pattern of the Standard Oil Trust was not always followed, but the results were generally about the same. Sometimes the possession of exclusive patent rights promoted the cause of monopoly, and thus made of the liberal patent laws of the United States a kind of subsidy to big business.[1]

The evils of the "trusts," as the public without much discrimination described all big businesses, became increasingly apparent. Prices were fixed without benefit of competition, and sometimes at higher levels than before the trust was formed. Raw producers were compelled to take what the trust chose to pay, for there was no one else to whom to sell. Labor was forced into line by the closing of troublesome plants, and by the circulation of "blacklists" that made it difficult for agitators to obtain employment. Politicians were influenced by free passes from the railroads, by campaign contributions, and by outright bribes. Oliver H. Payne, treasurer of the Standard Oil Company, was reputed to have spent one hundred thousand dollars to secure the election of his father, H. B. Payne, to the United States Senate in 1886. Powerful lobbies appeared in Washington and in the several state capitals charged with the duty of winning favors from lawmakers and law-enforcers. The Washington lobbyists were sometimes described as the "third house" of Congress. Plants that experience had shown to be well located were enlarged, and others less ideally situated were closed down, without regard to the inevitable unemployment involved or the municipal problems that arose from the concentration of vast numbers of people at whatever centers business leaders deemed strategic. Individual freedom suffered blow after blow as the owners of small establishments became the employees of larger ones, and as the chance to enter business independently grew less and less. Employees were pushed farther and farther from the sight and hearing of employers, and fewer occasions existed for emotions of the "heart" to influence the conduct of businessmen who prided themselves upon their "hard-headedness."

And yet the "trusts" were by no means without their good points.

[1] An admirable history of a developing "big business" is W. T. Hutchinson, *Cyrus Hall McCormick; Harvest, 1856–1884* (1935).

Much of the competition that they eliminated was sheer waste, and without it prices could be, and often were, reduced. Large-scale businesses were usually far more efficient than the small concerns they supplanted, and were able to make money **Advantages of the trusts** out of by-products that the smaller operators were forced to throw away. The packers, for example, claimed that they paid more for a live steer than they received for the dressed meat it yielded. Their profits came from the use they made of horns, hoofs, and other materials that the local slaughter-house wasted. Big business could afford to take heavy initial losses while waiting for ultimate profits. It could bear the cost of advertising and of the slow enlargement of markets. Usually, too, it was better managed, better located, better equipped. Small establishments could not so easily afford to scrap expensive machinery because new inventions made better equipment possible. They could not compete with big businesses in paying salaries to the ablest managers. Even without the cut-throat competition to which they were subjected, many of them would have lost out anyway because of their inefficiency.[1]

As public awareness of the trust problem grew, an insistent demand set in that something should be done about it. This meant, to most Americans, that the government should take action against the trusts, but unfortunately governmental action under **Legal status of the trusts** the existing system was not easily attainable. The Constitution gave the central government only definitely specified powers, and left all others to the states. Since the "founding fathers" had never heard of a trust, the only power to control such organizations that they had lodged with the central government was whatever might be inferred from the right to control interstate commerce. Obviously, the extent to which any such implied power might be exercised would have to be determined by the courts after extensive litigation. The states, on the other hand, had ample power within their several jurisdictions, but their boundaries were too small, for the activities of any important trust extended through many states. Moreover, the requirement of the national Constitution that each state must give "full faith and credit ... to the public acts, records, and judicial proceedings of every other state" had embarrassing possibilities. Under the terms of this clause special favors obtained in one state might easily be interpreted to mean special favors in every state. Another constitutional advantage enjoyed by corporations flowed from the Fourteenth Amendment which required that the states might not "deprive any person of life, liberty, or property, without due process of law." In 1886 the Supreme Court, reversing an earlier

---

[1] John Moody, *The Truth About the Trusts* (1904); W. Z. Ripley, *Trusts, Pools and Corporations* (new edition, 1916); Eliot Jones, *The Trust Problem in the United States* (1921).

ruling, held that the use of the word person in this clause was meant to apply to corporations as well as to individuals.[1] Thus the states, themselves the creators of the corporations, were restrained by the federal government from any measures of taxation or regulation that the courts chose to regard as depriving the corporations of property "without due process of law."

Attempts to restrain the trusts were made nevertheless. Just as the Grangers had invoked to good advantage the old rule of common law that a common carrier was subject to regulation because it was quasi-public in nature, so now the states fell back upon the common-law prohibition of conspiracy in restraint of trade. During the later eighties state after state passed statutes based on this principle. Finally, Congress also fell into line, and on July 2, 1890, the Sherman Anti-Trust Act received the President's signature. This measure, named after Senator Sherman, for no other reason, according to Senator Hoar, "except that Mr. Sherman had nothing to do with framing it whatever," lacked nothing in vigor of language. It branded as illegal "every contract, combination in the form of trust or otherwise, or conspiracy in restraint of trade or commerce among the several states, or with foreign nations." It defined as a misdemeanor any "attempt to monopolize, or combine or conspire with any other person or persons to monopolize, any part of the trade or commerce among the several states or with foreign nations." Penalties for persons held guilty of violating the act were set at a fine not to exceed five thousand dollars, and imprisonment not to exceed a year, one or both, as the court might prescribe. Furthermore, any person injured by means that the act declared unlawful might recover in court "threefold the damages by him sustained."

The Sherman Anti-Trust Act

Enforcement of these acts was quite another matter. A number of suits were lodged by the states, and a few decisions unfavorable to the corporations were obtained. In New York State, for example, the North River Sugar Refining Company, a part of the sugar trust, lost its charter; and in Ohio, the Standard Oil Company was held guilty of attempting "to establish a virtual monopoly." Since the technical trust was so clear-cut a violation of both the common law and the statutes, that type of organization was generally discontinued, but in its place new devices to accomplish the same end were speedily invented. Chief among these was the holding company, through which a controlling fraction of the stocks in a great

Difficulties in enforcement

---

[1] *Santa Clara County vs. Southern Pacific Railroad*, 118 United States Reports, 396. W. P. Webb, *Divided We Stand* (1937), vigorously attacks this extension to corporations of immunities intended, as he believes, only for individuals.

number of enterprises were owned and voted by a single corporation, but many of the trusts chose instead to incorporate as a single great company in the most friendly state they could find. As for the Sherman Anti-Trust Act, for all its brave language, it proved to be unenforceable. Seven out of the first eight attempts to invoke its penalties went against the government, and in the Knight case (1895) the Supreme Court of the United States held that the mere purchase of property, even if it made for monopoly and the restraint of trade, was not in itself illegal; further, that manufacture and production (in this case the refining of sugar) were no part of interstate commerce. Confronted by this rebuff, the government made little further effort to enforce the Sherman Act, and lawyers felt free to advise their clients that the Supreme Court of the United States had conceded the legality of private monopoly.

The increasing concentration of capital that characterized the eighties was accompanied by a steady growth in labor organization. This development was well-nigh inevitable. As the corporations grew in size and strength, the bargaining power of the in- Labor dividual laborer became correspondingly less effective. Con- organization centration gave the employer greater power to oppress, whether by way of low wages, long hours, or bad working conditions. But concentration meant also a diminishing number of employers, and a proportionately larger number of employees. By acting together and bargaining collectively laborers might hope to protect themselves against undue exploitation. This they attempted to do by means of more and stronger trade unions, but even more significantly, by efforts to unite all laborers, of whatever crafts, under one leadership.[1]

Local labor unions had existed in the United States since the early nineteenth century, and the Jacksonian period had witnessed the development of a well-defined labor movement; but the depression that began in 1837 had been disastrous for labor, and Trades unions not until the time of the Civil War was any considerable part of the ground lost regained. During the fifties and sixties a few national organizations, formed by such groups as the printers, the locomotive engineers, and the bricklayers, came into existence, but for a long time none of them succeeded in drawing into its ranks any large percentage of those eligible, while attempts at all-labor organizations were even less satisfactory. In August, 1866, a National Labor Union was formed at Baltimore by a group of seventy-seven delegates, representing a great variety of labor interests. This organization lasted for half a dozen years, sponsored annual labor congresses that were well attended, and

[1] Selig Perlman, *A History of Trade Unionism in the United States* (1922), is compact and dependable.

at one time claimed a membership of 640,000. It was soon drawn off into politics, however, and by 1872 had assisted in the formation of the Labor Reform Party, which survived only one presidential election. What little was left of the National Labor Union crashed with the Panic of 1873, but, while it lasted, it had given the movement for an eight-hour day a good start, and had promoted in a variety of ways the study of labor problems. It furnished, also, an example of concerted action by labor that was not forgotten.

Labor troubles came during the seventies in spite of the fact that labor was as yet imperfectly organized. Some of these disorders might actually have been averted had the unions been strong enough to control their men and to bargain successfully with employers. One of the worst outbreaks occurred in the anthracite coal mining region of Pennsylvania, where for a dozen years after the Civil War the "Molly Maguires," a secret society of terrorists rather than a union, carried more or less legitimate protests against bad working conditions to the worst extremes of violence, and even murder. Finally, in 1877, with the help of a detective named James McParlan, prosecutions and convictions were obtained that brought the outrages to an end, although the need for united action by the miners had by no means disappeared. The railroad strikes that occurred during the summer of 1877 were likewise characterized by much disorder and an unhappy ending. Railroad workers were still unorganized, but a cut of ten per cent announced by the principal northeastern roads led many men to cease work, even without union officers to issue formal strike orders. The efforts of the strikers, however, were unavailing, for at each center of disturbance federal troops were freely used to break the strike. Another example of labor disaffection appeared far out on the Pacific Coast in the area surrounding San Francisco Bay. There the chief difficulties were widespread unemployment and the presence of many Chinese who worked for "coolie wages." But the activities of the leading agitators, who at first seemed headed toward revolution, turned instead to the formation of a local Workingmen's Party, which seemed content with writing some of its principles into the new state constitution that California adopted in 1879.

The need for intelligent leadership, so evident in the labor outbreaks of the seventies, was soon supplied in part by a national organization known as the Noble Order of the Knights of Labor. This society, which was at first a kind of labor lodge, was founded in 1869 by Uriah S. Stephens, a Philadelphia garment-cutter, who provided it with a secret ritual, a password, and a grip. Since the name of the order was at first represented in public notices by five

The Knights of Labor

asterisks, it was long known to the uninitiated as "the five stars." Unlike its predecessor, the Knights of Labor built directly upon the individual, rather than upon existing trade unions. "One big union," to which all workers, skilled or unskilled, should belong, was the ideal; indeed, practically anyone, regardless of race, color, or occupation, could become a "Knight." Under these circumstances members of the more exclusive trade unions, who took pride in their craft skills, tended to hold aloof, and for a decade the growth of the Knights was only moderate. After 1878, however, when Terence V. Powderly (1849-1924) of Scranton, Pennsylvania, became its "Grand Master Workman," the order took on new life.[1] Powderly, as his name would indicate, was of Irish origin, but he was a native American, not an immigrant, born in Carbondale, Pennsylvania. At thirteen years of age he joined the ranks of labor as a switch-tender; later as a Scranton machinist he took so prominent a part in the work of the Machinists' and Blacksmiths' Union that he not only lost his job, but also won a place for his name on an employers' blacklist. This happened in 1873, after which he worked for a time in Ohio and western Pennsylvania, but on returning to Scranton won election as mayor of the city in 1878 on the Greenback-Labor ticket. When later a meeting was held at Reading, Pennsylvania, to reorganize the Knights, Powderly dominated the proceedings, and for the next fifteen years his name and the Knights of Labor were almost synonymous terms. Secrecy was done away with, the name of the order was publicly proclaimed, and Powderly, with only the barest apology of a salary, traveled at his own expense wherever he felt he could gain more recruits for the Knights. From a membership of only 28,000 in 1880 the organization shot forward to 52,000 in 1883, 104,000 in 1885, and perhaps as many as 700,000 by 1886.

The ideals of the Knights were by no means new. They believed, with Edmund Burke, that "When bad men combine, the good must associate, else they will fall, one by one, an unpitied sacrifice in a contemptible struggle." Like the National Labor Union they favored the eight-hour day, the "establishment of co-operative institutions productive and distributive," the use of arbitration as a substitute for strikes, and such legal innovations as were calculated to improve the status of labor. Powderly saw especial virtue in the co-operative idea, and under his urging not less than one hundred and thirty-five such ventures were undertaken, some of which for a time seemed destined to endure. But bad management, internal dissensions, insufficient funds, and cut-

[1] Terence V. Powderly, *Thirty Years of Labor* (1889), recounts the history of the Knights of Labor, as does also somewhat more objectively, N. J. Ware, *The Labor Movement in the United States, 1860-1895* (1929).

throat competition accounted for the undoing of most of them. Labor co-operatives proved to be no less difficult to inaugurate than farmer co-operatives.

In spite of their insistence upon arbitration the Knights became embroiled in a series of violent strikes. In 1884 a business recession set in, accompanied by the inevitable increase in unemployment and in labor unrest. Companies that took advantage of the opportunity to discharge union men, particularly Knights, were sometimes fought successfully by boycotts, but the chief weapon of labor proved to be the strike. By use of it, for example, the Missouri Pacific, early in 1885, was forced to restore a wage-cut made without warning and without even the excuse of declining earnings. Public sympathy was almost unanimously with the strikers, and the company in yielding felt obliged to grant its employees time and one-half for overtime, something the strikers had not even asked. In many minor instances during the middle eighties the Knights helped to win such victories.

Sometimes, however, the outcome was far different. In March, 1886, when a foreman in the Texas and Pacific car shops at Marshall, Texas, was dismissed apparently because he was a member of the Knights of Labor, another important strike occurred. Under the leadership of Martin Irons, some nine thousand shopmen employed on the Gould system (of which the Texas and Pacific was a part) quit work, and attempted by sabotage to make all freight-hauling locomotives unfit for duty. So successful were their efforts that along five thousand miles of railroad in the Southwest freight traffic was at a standstill; only passenger trains carrying United States mails were permitted to move. At first popular hatred for Jay Gould worked in favor of the strikers, but when food shortages began to be felt and factories had to close down for lack of coal, the public had had strike enough. Four state governors, strongly backed by public opinion, ordered the strikers to cease interfering with trains, and Powderly himself, hoping for arbitration, intervened to call a temporary halt. When Gould refused to arbitrate, the strike was resumed with renewed violence, but the public was now so definitely against the strikers that their cause was soon lost.

Strikes of 1886

Excitement over the southwestern railroad strike had scarcely subsided when the May Day strikes of 1886 claimed the attention of the country.[1] The purpose of these strikes, in which perhaps 340,000 men participated, was to promote the cause of the eight-hour day. Although the claim was made that half

The Hay-market riot

[1] Samuel Yellen, *American Labor Struggles* (1936), covers all the important strikes after the Civil War.

the strikers won a reduced work day, an episode that occurred in Chicago, the storm-center of the strike, gave organized labor the most severe set-back it had yet received. Chicago happened to be the headquarters of a small group of foreign-born anarchists who welcomed the opportunity to expound to the strikers, both orally and in print, their principal tenet, the abolition of the state. To promote this end they were ready to advocate, although far less ready to perform, deeds of violence and terror. On the afternoon of May 3, August Spies, anarchist editor of the *Arbeiter Zeitung*, was addressing a meeting of strikers and strike sympathizers on a vacant lot not far from the McCormick Harvester Works, when the police attempted to disperse the assembly. In the ensuing mêlée several strikers were killed, and about twenty were wounded. That night a circular, printed in English and German, called lustily for "Revenge! Revenge! Workmen to arms!" Next day many meetings of protest occurred, the most notable being set for the evening at Haymarket Square, where a crowd of fifteen hundred assembled to listen to speeches by three leading anarchists. Although the crowd was orderly, the police again appeared and attempted to disperse it. This time, however, the officers of the law were met with a bomb that exploded with terrific violence, killing one policeman and wounding many more. Hard fighting followed, and when the casualties were reckoned it was found that of the policemen seven had lost their lives and over sixty had been seriously wounded, while of the civilians, four were dead and about fifty wounded.

The feeling of blind rage with which the public reacted to the "Haymarket riot" demanded victims. Efforts to find the guilty culprits, however, proved singularly unavailing. "For days," wrote one observer, "the police stations were filled with suspected persons, rigorously examined in the method of the third degree; persons for the most part that had no knowledge of the bomb nor of the meeting, nor of anything connected with either, and could not have." At length, for lack of better scapegoats, eight well-known anarchists, including Spies, were marked for trial. Evidence that any one of the eight had had anything to do either with the making or the throwing of the bomb was never produced, but seven of the men were given death sentences, and the eighth, imprisonment for fifteen years. The convictions were made on the assumption that these men, by advocating violence, had influenced some unknown person to throw the bomb, but this was merely an assumption utterly unbuttressed by evidence. It was clear that the men were convicted because of the opinions they held. In general, the public applauded the sentences, and rejoiced when four of the convicted men were hanged. One of the others had managed to blow out his brains with a bomb, and two had had their sentences commuted to life imprisonment. A few hardy souls condemned the whole proceedings as a miscarriage of justice, and in 1893, Governor John P. Altgeld, by pardoning the two men who were serving life sentences, classed himself with this number, an act of courage that wrecked his political career.[1]

It was the irony of fate that the public saw in the Haymarket riot occasion for further condemnation of the Knights of Labor. Actually

Decline of the Knights

the strike for the eight-hour day had been promoted mainly through local trade unions, and Powderly had counseled against it on the ground that the weapon of the strike should not be invoked until all other means of protest had been exhausted. Nevertheless, the Knights had already won a reputation for violence and they received the blame. Anarchists and other advocates of revolution had found it easy to obtain membership in the order and had used its forums to propagate their views. Powderly even charged that an attorney for one group of employers confessed that anarchists had been paid to become Knights so that "they might stir up the devil and bring discredit upon your whole movement." As the control of the central organization over the behavior of the locals disintegrated, strikes were often undertaken "against the advice of the General Executive Board." The result was that skilled workers, alienated by the ruthless way in which the unskilled precipitated conflicts, tended to withdraw from the Knights in order to build up their own trade unions. By 1888 the membership of the Knights of Labor had declined to less than 260,000, and by 1890 to about 100,000. Within a short time the order had disappeared entirely.

Meantime a rival organization, which discarded the "one big union" idea in favor of the older federative plan, had begun to make headway.

The A.F. of L.

The American Federation of Labor, which was founded in 1881 at Pittsburgh as the "Federation of Organized Trades and Labor Unions of the United States and Canada," shortened its name in 1886, and at about the same time began to lengthen its membership list. While individuals, as such, were excluded from membership, almost any kind of labor organization, whether national, state, or local, might belong. The intent of the new order was no less to protect skilled labor from competition by the unskilled than to protect labor as such from the oppression of capital. It had, in fact, no real quarrel with capitalism as an economic system. Its mission, rather, was to insure that labor should share generously in the profits of capitalistic enterprise. To this end it set for itself such definite goals as an eight-hour work day, a six-day work week, a high wage level, greater

[1] Henry David, *The History of the Haymarket Affair* (1936).

security of job tenure, and the elimination of child labor. It showed little interest in the establishment of labor co-operatives, and it convincingly resisted all efforts to make the Federation over into a separate political party. Instead of going directly into politics, it supported candidates and platforms, of whatever party, provided only that they were favorable to the program of the Federation. While it hoped to see labor win most of its victories peacefully, either by obtaining favorable legislation or by collective bargaining with employers, the Federation, like the Knights, was willing in case of necessity to rely on the strike and the boycott. Its organization lent itself admirably to the use of the sympathetic strike, by means of which workers in a related craft, although lacking a grievance of their own, might come to the aid of a striking union. A sizable "war chest," supported by a per capita tax levied on members, enabled the Federation's central board of control to aid unemployed strikers and to prolong any conflict it chose to support.

What Terence V. Powderly was to the Knights of Labor, Samuel Gompers (1850–1924) was to the American Federation.[1] Gompers was born in London, the son of a cigarmaker. At ten years of age he began to learn the shoemakers' trade, but he soon gave that up in favor of his father's trade, because the latter was organized and the former was not. In 1863 he came with his parents to America, and a year later he joined the first cigarmakers' union ever organized in New York City. Always an enthusiastic member, when he grew to manhood he became first the union's secretary and later its president. The training that he thus received was of great significance, for in many ways this local New York cigarmakers' union was a model organization. It followed the British system of benefit payments in case of unemployment, sickness, or death; it tried to encourage skill and intelligence among its members; it gained many of its victories by collective bargaining, by arbitration, and by retaining the good-will and respect of employers. Gompers never forgot this early training, and much of the conservatism of his later career may properly be attributed to it. He was one of the original group of delegates that founded the Federation in 1881, and was even more active in the reorganization of 1886. From 1885 to the time of his death, with the exception of a single year, 1895, he was regularly elected president of the Federation.

Under Gompers's devoted leadership, the Federation scored many successes.[2] It backed the strike for the eight-hour day in 1886, and claimed substantial gains in spite of the unfavorable reaction to the

[1] Samuel Gompers, *Seventy Years of Life and Labor* (2 vols., 1925), is an excellent autobiography. See also R. H. Harvey, *Samuel Gompers* (1935).

[2] The most satisfactory history of the Federation is L. L. Lorwin, *The American Federation of Labor* (1933).

Haymarket riot. It conducted another strike for the eight-hour day in 1890, this time in the carpenters' union, with fairly satisfactory results. It supported innumerable movements, both in the states and in the nation as a whole, that resulted in the enactment of laws favorable to labor. In part through its activities practically every state in the Union was soon equipped with a bureau of labor statistics, and in 1903 Congress went so far as to establish the Department of Commerce and Labor with a seat in the cabinet. The Federation encouraged member unions to set up their own systems for sickness and unemployment benefits, and could soon point to many instances in which its advice had been followed. Its assistance could be counted upon, also, in efforts to secure adoption by employers of the "closed shop," which meant that only union labor might be employed in a given plant, and to eliminate "yellow dog" contracts, by which workers were obliged to agree in advance of employment that they would not join labor unions. From a membership of about one hundred and fifty thousand in 1886 the Federation by 1900 had grown to more than half a million, by 1905 to a million and a half, by the outbreak of the World War to two million. The greatest weakness of the American Federation lay in the fact that it represented only a favored minority of labor. All unskilled workers were excluded from membership, together with all skilled workers who did not belong to a union. Moreover, a number of labor organizations, including the four great railway unions, refused to affiliate with the Federation on the ground that they were able to take care of themselves, and were not eager to accept responsibility for others. The railway unions, however, ordinarily could be counted on to co-operate fully with the Federation.

Closely connected with the labor problem was the new immigration which came to the United States from Europe in an increasing tide from **The new immigration** 1880 on.[1] Easier means of communication had much to do with the acceleration of this long-established migration. The effort that had once been involved in making the trip to America had become for many by the last quarter of the nineteenth century a mere following of the line of least resistance. Steamship companies that wished to fill their holds with immigrants quoted low rates and joined with the American railroads that had land to sell in describing the boundless opportunities awaiting the newcomer on American shores. American industrialists in need of unskilled labor sent recruiting agents abroad to offer wages that to Europeans seemed high, but that to Americans seemed ridiculously low. Immigrants who had

---

[1] J. W. Jenks and W. J. Lauck, *The Immigration Problem* (1912); M. R. Davie, *World Immigration with Special Reference to the United States* (1936).

EUROPEAN IMMIGRATION INTO THE UNITED STATES, 1841–1930
FROM STATISTICAL ABSTRACT OF THE UNITED STATES (1931)

Country	1841–50	1851–60	1861–70	1871–80	1881–90	1891–1900	1901–10	1911–20	1921–30
Austria }	5,074	4,738	7,800	72,969	353,719	592,707	2,145,266	453,649	32,868
Hungary }								442,693	30,680
Belgium			6,734	7,211	20,177	18,167	41,635	33,746	15,846
Bulgaria						160	39,280	22,533	2,945
Czechoslovakia								3,426	102,194
Denmark	539	3,749	17,094	31,771	88,132	50,231	65,285	41,983	32,430
Finland								756	16,691
France	77,262	76,358	35,986	72,206	50,464	30,770	73,379	61,897	49,610
Germany	434,626	951,667	787,468	718,182	1,452,970	505,152	341,498	143,945	412,202
Greece	16	31	72	210	2,308	15,979	167,519	184,201	51,084
Italy	1,870	9,231	11,725	55,759	307,309	651,893	2,045,877	1,109,524	455,315
Netherlands	8,251	10,789	9,102	16,541	53,701	26,758	48,262	43,718	26,948
Norway }	13,903	20,931	109,298	95,333	176,586	95,015	190,505	66,395	68,531
Sweden }				115,922	391,776	226,266	249,534	95,074	97,249
Poland	105	1,164	2,027	12,970	51,806	96,720		4,813	227,734
Rumania				11	6,348	12,750	53,008	13,311	67,646
Russia	551	457	2,512	39,284	213,282	505,290	1,597,306	921,201	61,742
Spain	2,209	9,298	6,697	5,266	4,419	8,731	27,935	68,611	28,958
Portugal	550	1,055	2,658	14,082	16,978	27,508	69,149	89,732	29,994
Switzerland	4,644	25,011	23,286	28,293	81,988	31,179	34,922	23,091	29,676
Turkey (in Europe)	59	83	129	337	1,562	3,626	79,976	54,677	14,659
United Kingdom	1,047,763	1,338,093	1,042,674	984,914	1,462,839	659,954	865,015	487,589	550,804
England	32,092	247,125	222,277	437,706	644,680	216,726	388,017	249,944	157,420
Ireland	780,719	914,119	435,778	436,871	655,482	388,416	339,065	146,181	220,591
Scotland	3,712	38,331	38,769	87,564	149,869	44,188	120,469	78,357	159,781
Wales	1,261	6,319	4,313	6,631	12,640	10,557	17,464	13,107	13,012
Not Specified	229,979	132,199	341,537	16,142	168	67			
Yugo Slavia								1,888	49,064
Other Europe	79	5	8	1,001	682	122	665	8,111	22,983
Total Europe	1,597,501	2,452,660	2,065,270	2,272,262	4,737,046	3,558,978	8,136,016	4,376,564	2,477,853

come to America wrote back to their relatives in glowing terms of the
success they had achieved in the New World, and in many such letters
the passage money was included to bring more immigrants across the
Atlantic. The oppression of minorities in central and eastern Europe,
the desire to escape military service, the official encouragement of emigration as a means of alleviating poverty and unemployment, all sent
their quotas to America. In the decade of the sixties, 2,314,824 immigrants landed at American ports; in the decade of the seventies, in spite
of the depression, the number rose to 2,812,191; and in the decade of the
eighties all previous records were broken by an influx of 5,246,613, an
average of more than half a million immigrants a year. By 1905 the
number of annual entrants had reached a million, and until the outbreak
of the World War in 1914 the avalanche continued.

Far more significant than the actual number of immigrants was their
racial origin. During the first half of the eighties Germany furnished
about one-third of the newcomers, the British Isles and the
Scandinavian countries another third, with most of the rest,
the really "new" immigration, coming from southern and
eastern Europe. In the last half of the eighties the proportion
began to change; from that time on the numbers coming from southern
and eastern Europe rose as those coming from northern and western
Europe fell. By the later nineties the former exceeded the latter in the
proportion of three to two. The descendants of colonial Americans had
long been familiar with immigrants from the British Isles and from
Germany, and they found little difficulty in accustoming themselves to
the Scandinavians. All of these peoples took on American ways with a
minimum of difficulty, and were soon in process of absorption into the
native population. But Italians and Poles, Rumanians, and Ruthenians,
Magyars and Bulgars, Czechs and Croats, Slovaks and Slovenes, Jews
and Greeks seemed somehow vastly different.[1] Most of them went to
work at once in the factories, in the mines, or on railroad construction
gangs. They clung together in racial groups and retained tenaciously
their Old-World languages and customs. They reproduced in American
cities the living conditions of European slums, ideal breeding-grounds
for disease. They fell in easily with city machines, and complicated the
already difficult problem of good city government. They shocked the
dominantly Protestant native Americans with their devotion to Catholicism, whether Roman or Greek Orthodox, or to Judaism. They often
refused to send their children to the public schools, and established in-

Marginal note: Nationalities of the newcomers

[1] R. F. Foerster, *The Italian Emigration of Our Times* (1919); William I. Thomas and
Florian Znaniecki, *The Polish Peasant in Europe and America* (5 vols., 1918–1920); Samuel
Joseph, *Jewish Immigration to the United States from 1881 to 1910* (1914); Jerome Davis, *The
Russian Immigrant* (1922).

stead foreign-language parochial schools. In short, they put every obstacle in the way of the traditional process of amalgamation by means of which, ever since America began, the perpetual problem of immigration had been solved.

Organized labor in the United States was at first hostile to the new immigrants, and attempted to keep them out of the unions. Skilled workmen, however, soon won recognition, and in due time the foreign element began to play an important rôle in the labor world. Unversed in American ways, the newcomers

Labor and the immigrant

sometimes employed in their adopted land the methods of violence they had used against European tyrannies. Each such outbreak increased the dislike of the so-called "native American" for the immigrants, and tended to discredit the labor organizations to which they belonged. From the unions themselves, in self-protection, and from the public in general a demand for the restriction of immigration set in. During the nineteenth century, however, the restrictionists gained only modest victories. In deference to the wishes of the Pacific Coast the Chinese government was persuaded to give the United States the right to "regulate, limit or suspend but not absolutely prohibit" the immigration of Chinese laborers, and in 1882 a Chinese Exclusion Act, based on this principle, went into effect. That same year paupers, criminals, convicts, and the insane were also forbidden entry into the United States. Steamship companies found guilty of bringing such persons into the country were required to take them back again free of charge. More important was the prohibition of the importation of laborers under contract. A comprehensive law, passed in 1891, added to the proscribed lists prostitutes, idiots, polygamists, and persons suffering from certain types of diseases; prohibited under penalty of fine the recruitment of foreign laborers by advertising or solicitation; made a charge of fifty cents against each immigrant admitted; and placed the administration of the law in the hands of a federal superintendent of immigration. Efforts to secure a literacy test, which would have excluded great numbers of immigrants from southern and eastern Europe, but comparatively few from northern and western Europe, culminated in a law that passed Congress in 1897, only to be vetoed by President Cleveland.[1]

[1] C. B. Swisher, *American Constitutional Development* (1943), is particularly good on government and industry. Business histories are becoming increasingly common: R. C. Overton, *Burlington West: A Colonization History of the Burlington Railroad* (1941); James Marshall, *Santa Fe: The Railroad that Built an Empire* (1945); Malcolm MacLaren, *The Rise of the Electrical Industry During the Nineteenth Century* (1943). On labor: Marjorie R. Clark and S. Fanny Simon, *The Labor Movement in America* (1938); H. J. Carman, Henry David, and Paul N. Guthrie (eds.), *The Path I Trod: The Autobiography of Terence V. Powderly* (1944); Ira B. Cross, *A History of the Labor Movement in California* (1935).

28

The Populist Revolt

DISCONTENT with the effects of the industrial revolution upon American life was not confined to labor. The farmers of the country, particularly those of the South and the West, who lived far from the nation's principal markets, showed with each passing decade their increasing dissatisfaction. They believed that they worked harder and longer than any other class, and yet they had less to show for their toil, they insisted, than the humblest city workmen. Why should everyone else prosper, and the farmer be obliged to slave his life away for next to nothing?

The South was not so completely agricultural as it had been before the Civil War. Conscious of the fact that northern industries had

The New South played a principal rôle in the defeat of the South, such southern leaders as Henry W. Grady, able editor of the Atlanta *Constitution,* had made industrialization the principal goal of their section. Of Grady's activities a contemporary wrote, "He did not tamely promote enterprise and encourage industry, he vehemently fomented enterprise and provoked industry until they stalked through the land like armed conquerors." By the eighties a "New South" had appeared some of which was cast in the mold Grady had desired.[1] Particularly was this true of the long tongue of piedmont and mountain country extending southward from the border of Pennsylvania through western Maryland, the Virginias and Kentucky, the Carolinas and Tennessee, into Georgia and Alabama. Throughout this region a new and startling devotion to industry had taken hold. Most of the new factories were concerned with the manufacture of cotton goods, cottonseed products, tobacco, and lumber, but Birmingham, Alabama, became an important center of the iron and steel industry, while the coal fields of the Upper South were exploited, not only for the benefit of southern industry, but also to supply the fuel necessities of industries in many near-by northern cities.

[1] W. B. Hesseltine, *The South in American History* (1943), contains a significant chapter on this subject. Holland Thompson, *The New South* (1919), and P. A. Bruce, *Rise of the New South* (1905), are sympathetic studies.

Most of the southern mills and factories developed along definitely paternalistic lines. Someone had to provide houses for the workers, and the "company" made it its business to provide them. The company likewise opened stores, and in many instances paid the workers in scrip, good at any time for payments to the company, but redeemable in cash only at infrequent intervals. The company also provided such schools and churches as it deemed desirable, and hired both the teachers and the preachers. To the country people who flocked to the mills these acts of forethought were accepted without suspicion. The houses of the mill villages were better than the houses of the farms, the company stores were easy of access, and charged little more, if any, than other stores; while the schools, the churches, and the factories themselves furnished such an opportunity for community life as the workers had never known before. At first labor unions were virtually unknown, and throughout the nineteenth century labor agitators were given little encouragement either by employers or by employees. In the twentieth century, however, unionism took strong hold in the South and worked many changes.

For all the vast transformation wrought by industrialism in southern life, the South at the end of the nineties, as before the war, was still a dominantly agricultural region. In every southern state far more people were engaged in agriculture than in any other occupation, while most of the business and professional classes were dependent upon farm income for their support. The New South, like the Old, had few large cities, and its annual output of manufactured goods actually accounted for only about one-eighth of the nation's total output. Southern cotton was still grown after much the same fashion, by nearly the same types of laborers, in approximately the same regions as before the war. The yield had steadily increased. By 1894 the production of cotton in the South exceeded ten million bales, nearly twice that of the pre-war years. Much the same could be said of tobacco, sugar-cane, cereals, and livestock, but if the total produce of the South had increased, so also had its population. For the great majority of the southern people, the industrial frenzy of the New South was of no direct or immediate consequence.

Southern agriculture

Seventy per cent of the farmers of the South, a generation after Appomattox, were tenants. Of these a large proportion, both black and white, were caught in the meshes of the one-crop, crop-lien system. Cotton in the Lower South, and tobacco in the Upper South, were the "money crops" toward the production of which nearly every farmer felt obliged to devote his principal efforts. Since he had nothing to start with, either immediately after the Civil War or at any time later, he was obliged to pledge a share of his crop to the landlord whose acres he tilled, and to give a lien on the rest to the merchant (often the same person as the landlord) from whom he bought supplies on credit. When at the end of the year the books were balanced he was usually in debt, and according to the law in many southern states, he could not seek another landlord nor trade with another storekeeper until his debts were paid. The result was a system of virtual peonage. The southern tenant farmer was bound to his land almost as effectively as the medieval serf before him.

The one-party system which the reconstruction period had left as a legacy to the South made it extremely difficult for the farmers of that section, whether black or white, to seek through political action the amelioration of their ills. The blacks were virtually disfranchised, and, because of the peculiar distribution of the white population, the power of the lower-class rural whites in politics was far less than their numbers would have justified. The best cotton lands lay along the river valleys and close to the sea, precisely the same lands that had grown the cotton of the pre-war plantation South. Here the Negroes were concentrated, no longer as slaves but as tenants of a favored few of the whites. In these "black belts" the landlords and the merchants, supported by the votes of the townspeople, not only ruled supreme over a population predominantly Negro and non-voting, but exercised also a disproportionate influence in the politics of any given state. Since the assignment of membership in the legislature and of delegates in nominating conventions was according to population, the representatives of the "black counties" could practically always outvote the representatives of the "white counties." And, since white solidarity demanded unfailing support of whatever Democratic candidates were nominated, the "Bourbons" of the "black belt," eager servants of the industrialists, the landlords, and the merchants, maintained their uninterrupted sway. Hardly less than before the Civil War the South remained in the hands of a favored ruling caste. Discontent with such a system, followed by open revolt against it, was sure to come.

Conditions in the West were vastly different from those in the South, but in large areas quite as unsatisfactory from the farmers' point of view. Particularly was this true of the "Middle Border," a region which stretched from the bend of the Missouri to the Rockies, and had been settled almost entirely after the Civil War. This latest "New West" included Kansas, Nebraska, the Dakotas, and parts of Montana.

Note to map on page 557: This map shows the total area from which lands were granted. The shaded portions include (1) both the non-railroad sections and the alternate sections actually taken by the railroads; (2) "indemnity lands" from which the railroads selected grants in case lands near their tracks had already been taken; and (3) lands granted for wagon roads (mostly in Michigan and Oregon). The state of Texas, which owned its own lands, also made extensive grants to railroads.

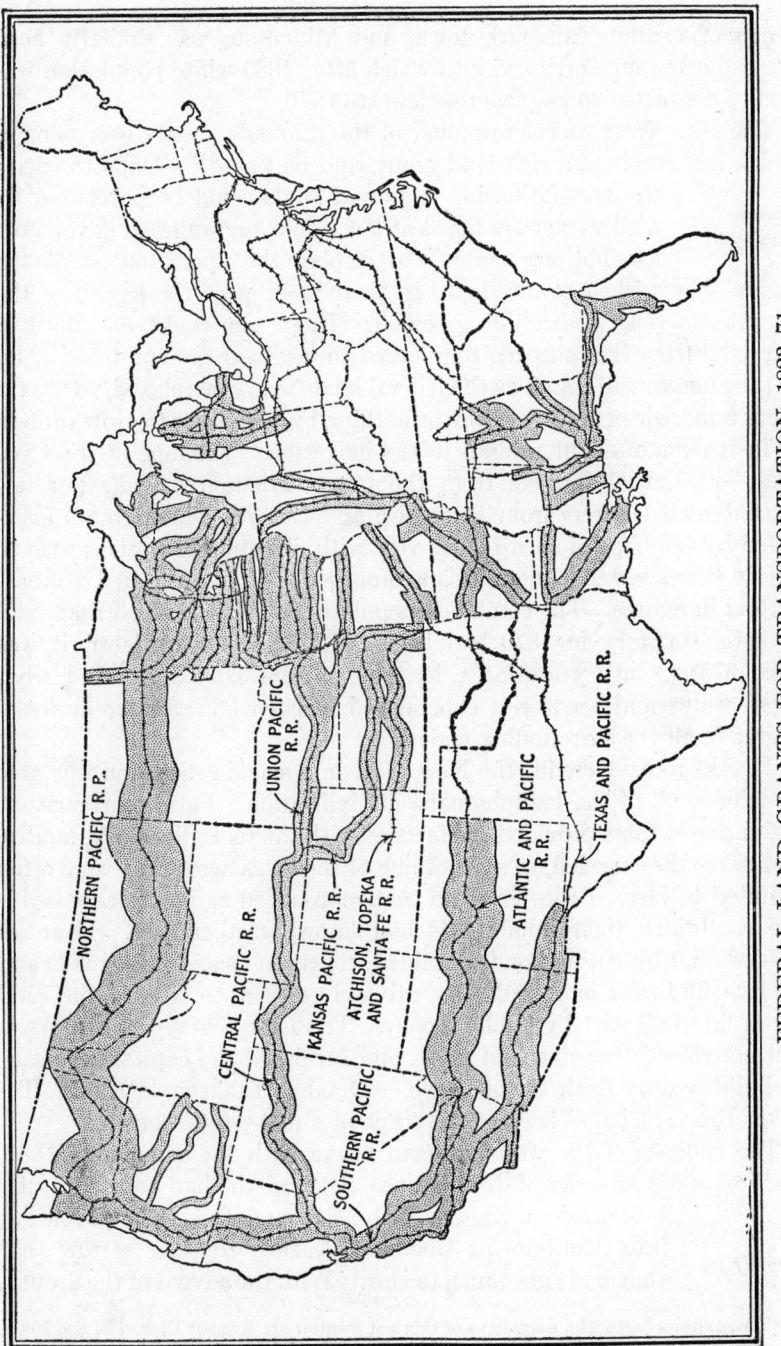

FEDERAL LAND GRANTS FOR TRANSPORTATION, 1823–71

Much of western Missouri, Iowa, and Minnesota was similarly new, while the Indian Territory, into which after 1889 white population was legally permitted to go, was the newest of all.

The New West was the product of the railroads, nearly every one of which had received a rich land grant, and had used its lands to entice the population in. Railroad lands could be purchased by **Another "New West"** settlers on easy terms at low prices, and railroad advertisers left nothing undone to display the opportunities of the region they wished to develop. In their facile pens the legend of the "great American desert" disappeared. Those who could not afford to buy land from the railroads they urged to use their pre-emption rights, to take homesteads, and, as the federal land laws were relaxed, to obtain other hundreds of acres for little or nothing by promising to grow timber, or in regions of slight rainfall to try irrigation. Veterans of the Civil War, substantial farmers from the upper Mississippi Valley, a few discontented laborers from the cities, and European immigrants fascinated by the hope of cheap lands vied with one another in their rush to obtain the riches that the railroads promised. What happened can best be told in figures. The combined population of Kansas, Nebraska, and Dakota Territory in 1870 had been 501,573; ten years later, it was 1,583,675; twenty years later, in 1890, it was 3,030,347. And what these states and territories experienced, occurred in greater or lesser degree in all the surrounding region.

Thanks to easy credit, the New West in a single generation was able to achieve all of the paraphernalia of civilization. Farm mortgages at high interest rates provided the farmers with the tools, livestock, houses, and barns they needed, to say nothing of the extra acres they were often tempted to buy. Cities grew up that reproduced as nearly as possible the conditions their inhabitants had known farther east. Counties needed, and by voting bonds obtained, courthouses and jails, roads and bridges, and even more railroads, privately owned, to be sure, but paid for in no small part by public money. The East believed in the West, was convinced that it would grow, and furnished the capital necessary to build it up. Each sizable town — Omaha, Yankton, Atchison, Topeka, Kansas City — became the scene of a real-estate "boom."

The collapse of the western boom began with the summer of 1887, the first of a long series of dry seasons. Settlers who had gone hopefully into western Kansas, Nebraska, and Dakota, or even out **Western adversity** into Montana or Colorado, learned to their sorrow that they had gone much too far.[1] With the advent of the drouth,

---

[1] Two extremely colorful narratives of this last frontier are Everett Dick, *The Sod House Frontier, 1854–1890* (1937), and H. E. Briggs, *Frontiers of the Northwest* (1940).

moneylenders promptly changed their minds about the future of the
West, and the flow of easy money came to an abrupt halt. The same
covered wagons that had taken the settlers hopefully into the West were
now sometimes turned in defeat and despair toward the East. For there
was no longer another West to which to go. Of mountains and deserts
and arid plains the government still possessed an abundance, but of
land suitable for the traditional types of agriculture perhaps less than
two million acres remained. Henry George was well aware that such a
condition was in sight when he advocated in his *Progress and Poverty*,
published in 1879, a "single tax" on land. "All who do not possess
land," he argued, "are toiling for those who do, and this is the reason
why progress and poverty go hand in hand." Most of the people of the
New West were unaware of George's theories, and if they had known
them, they would not have liked them. What they wanted was a chance
to live through the hard years on the land they had taken, without
danger of foreclosure by the banks, or extortion by the middlemen and
the railroads. Denied the opportunity of flight to another frontier, and
convinced that the ills from which they suffered were not of their own
making, the farmers of the New West, like those of the New South,
were ripe for revolt.

Common grievances acted powerfully to draw the farmers of the two
sections closer together. The western wheat-grower who was convinced
that, unless the price of wheat was as much as a dollar a bushel, he could
not make money, talked the same language as the southern cotton-
grower, who held that any price less than ten cents a pound for cotton
meant disaster. The northern farm-owner who was chronically on the
verge of losing his property to the mortgage-holder was only a trifle
better off than the southern tenant who each year turned over his entire
crop to his creditors only to learn that he was still in debt. The West
had the greater grievance against the railroads. Debts for lands purchased from them were hard to wipe out, and the high cost of transporting bulky western crops to distant markets ate away an alarming proportion of western farm receipts. But the South, no less than the West,
knew how railroad companies watered their stock, granted rebates,
evaded taxation, bought favors with free passes, and mixed business
with politics. Southern farmers, who sold abroad and would have preferred to buy cheap foreign manufactured goods in return, could see
more clearly the disadvantages of the high-tariff system than the farmers of the Northwest, but even the Westerners registered their objections to buying in a tariff-protected market and selling against the
competition of the whole wide world. Both sections recorded heated
protests against the tolls paid to trusts and middlemen, the high taxes

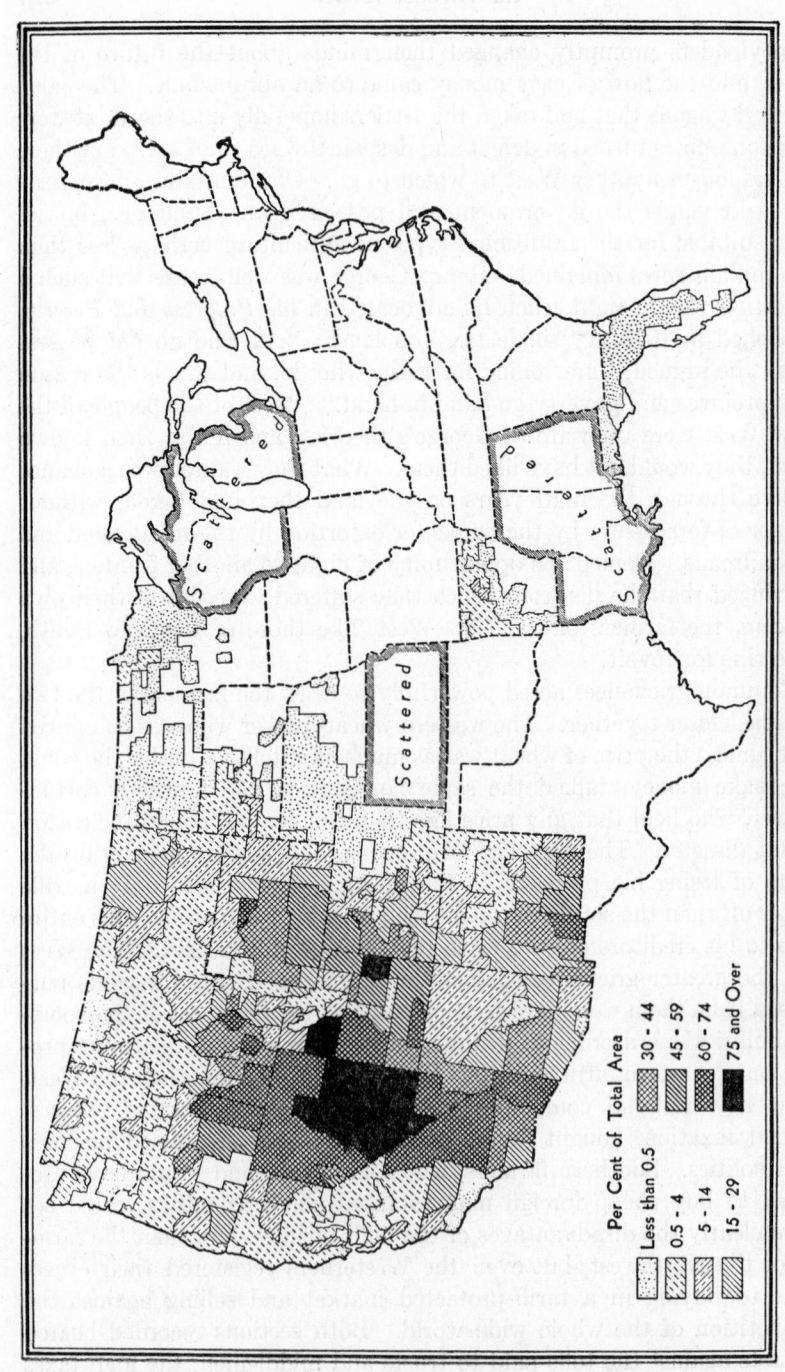

DISTRIBUTION OF PUBLIC LANDS IN THE UNITED STATES, 1929

Per Cent of Total Area

Less than 0.5
0.5 - 4
5 - 14
15 - 29
30 - 44
45 - 59
60 - 74
75 and Over

Scattered

that for farmlands seemed inescapable, and the steadily appreciating value of the dollar. And, although the West knew it best, both sections were seriously affected by the fact that good cheap lands were rapidly disappearing. The prospect of an alliance between the dominantly agricultural sections of the country was by no means an idle dream.

As if to pave the way for a closer union, the distressed farmers of the South and the West had begun during the eighties to organize. Copying somewhat the labor unions, whose occasional effectiveness they envied, they had banded themselves together into farm orders of various names and natures. Most important **The Farmers' Alliances** of these organizations were two great sectional "Alliances," the National Farmers' Alliance representing the Northwest, and the Farmers' Alliance and Industrial Union representing the South. Some of the smaller orders, such as the Grange, which had lasted on in spite of the collapse of the Granger movement, the Farmers' Mutual Benefit Association, and the Patrons of Industry, continued to exist; others were absorbed into one or the other of the two dominant organizations, which, commonly called the "Northern" or "Northwestern" Alliance and the "Southern" Alliance, became the authoritative spokesmen of agricultural discontent.

Circumstances conspired to drive both Alliances, contrary to their expressed intentions, into politics. The Northern Alliance, like the Southern Alliance, made numerous and sometimes successful ventures into co-operative buying and selling, and both **The Alliance in politics** orders earnestly stimulated among their members a wide variety of social and educational activities. But in spite of all such efforts farm prosperity failed to put in its appearance. More and more the conviction grew that the real trouble with agriculture lay in the unfair discriminations from which it suffered. Some sinister force restrained the farmers from the prosperity that their hard labor should have earned. The railroads, the bankers, the manufacturers, and the merchants were somehow robbing the farmers. Only through the power of government could these evil practices be brought to light and corrected, and to influence the government, whether in state or nation, political action was essential.

At first the Alliances sought to achieve their ends by obtaining control of the various state governments. In the South the chief business of the Alliance became the capture of the machinery of the Democratic Party, through which every state government **Alliance successes** was administered, and before the elections of 1890 this process was far advanced. In the Northwest the same policy was for a time given a trial, with the Republican rather than the Democratic Party the chief object of Alliance solicitude, but dissatisfaction with the results, together with the continuing hard times, led to the nomination in 1890 of many third-party tickets. As yet the name of the new party varied from state to state, but the Kansans, seeking to dramatize the battle between the people and the "plutocrats," called their organization the People's Party, a name that won increasing acclaim. "Populist" and "Populism" were natural derivatives.[1] The effectiveness of Alliance activities was mirrored in the election results. In at least four northwestern states, Kansas, Nebraska, South Dakota, and Minnesota, third-party candidates won the balance of power, although in no case did they obtain outright control. In the South, Alliance gains were even more spectacular. Alliance candidates for governor were nominated and elected in three states, South Carolina, North Carolina, and Georgia, while in no less than eight states Alliance-controlled legislatures were chosen. Even in Congress, the evidence of agrarian discontent was emphatically recorded. Two third-party senators, William A. Peffer of Kansas and James H. Kyle of South Dakota, were on hand for the opening session of the Fifty-Second Congress, while eight third-party representatives from the Northwest voted for Thomas E. Watson of Georgia for Speaker. Watson was the only southern Congressman to admit that he was now a third-party man, but among the southern delegations there sat perhaps thirty or forty Alliance members, and many others who were drawn to the Alliance by bonds of sympathy.[2]

To the third-party men of the Northwest the logical next step was the formation of a new nation-wide party of the people, but to Southerners such a course seemed fraught with the greatest of peril. The Democratic Party of the South was primarily a symbol of white supremacy. Democratic rule meant white rule. If the white voters of the South were divided, Negro voting might become common, and the supremacy of the white race would be jeopardized. Perhaps even the horrors of reconstruction might be repeated. Southern Alliance men preferred, therefore, to work within the framework of the Democratic Party, although there was one great objection to such a course. The southern wing of the party, however strong it might become, could hardly hope to dominate the party as a whole. Through an Alliance-controlled southern Democracy a certain amount of useful state legislation might be achieved, but reforms that depended upon nation-wide action would

---

[1] The changing point of view with respect to Populism may be noted by comparing F. L. McVey, *The Populist Movement* (1896), with J. D. Hicks, *The Populist Revolt* (1931).

[2] A model biography of the leading southern Populist is C. V. Woodward, *Tom Watson, Agrarian Rebel* (1938). The development of Populism in the South can be further followed through the several excellent state studies that have appeared: F. B. Simkins, *The Tillman Movement in South Carolina* (1926); J. B. Clark, *Populism in Alabama* (1927); A. M. Arnett, *The Populist Movement in Georgia* (1922); R. C. Martin, *The People's Party in Texas* (1933); W. D. Sheldon, *Populism in the Old Dominion* (1935).

still be out of reach. The so-called "sub-Treasury plan," for example, to which the Southern Alliance was committed after 1889, could never be put into effect without a law of Congress. This plan, much ridiculed then, would seem less radical to a later generation. It called for national warehouses in which non-perishable farm produce might be stored and upon which the owners might borrow from the United States government as much as eighty per cent of the "local current value" of their deposits in Treasury notes, issued for the purpose by the United States government, and providing incidentally an unpredictable amount of money inflation.

Southern reluctance was insufficient to restrain the third-party ardor of northwestern Alliance men, who at a series of conventions beginning with one at Cincinnati, in May, 1891, and ending with a nominating convention at Omaha in July, 1892, formally launched the People's Party as a national organization. **The People's Party**
The Populist platform, written in large part by Ignatius Donnelly of Minnesota, denounced both old parties in vivid rhetoric, and called for revolutionary reforms on the subjects of land, transportation, and finance. Believing, as they did, that the value of the gold dollar had been artificially stimulated to the benefit of the creditor class and to the distress of the debtors, the Populists demanded first and foremost an extensive expansion of the currency — in other words, money inflation. The amount of the circulating medium, they contended, whether by direct paper-money issues or by the "free and unlimited coinage of silver at the ratio of sixteen to one," or by both, should "be speedily increased to not less than fifty dollars per capita." As for the transportation issue, they advocated that the government should own and operate the railroads, and also, for good measure, the telegraph and telephone systems of the country. On the subject of public lands they looked faintly in the direction of conservation by demanding the return to the government by "railroads and other corporations" of all lands received "in excess of their actual needs." Alien landownership the Populists also condemned, and among other reforms favorably mentioned in their platform were the sub-Treasury system, the Australian ballot, a graduated income tax, postal savings banks, shorter hours for labor, the initiative and referendum, election of United States senators by direct vote of the people, and a single term for the President and Vice-President. For their candidates the Populists chose James B. Weaver of Iowa,[1] who had fought for the North in the Civil War, to head the ticket, and James G. Field of Virginia, an ex-Confederate, for second place.

The Populists, while predicting a victory of the "people" over the

[1] F. E. Haynes, *James Baird Weaver* (1919).

"plutocrats" in 1896, hoped only to make a good showing in 1892. Circumstances came ably to their assistance. The Republicans, in spite of the overwhelming rebuke they had received
in 1890, had little choice but to renominate the unpopular
Harrison and to defend the long list of dubious measures, including the
McKinley Act, that were associated with his administration; while the
Democrats, convinced that another battle must be fought over the tariff,
turned for a third time to Cleveland. Signs of dissension in both old
parties were apparent. Three days before the opening of the Republican Convention, Blaine had resigned as Secretary of State and had permitted his friends to work openly, if unavailingly, for his nomination.
Cleveland, likewise, had met with formidable opposition. David B.
Hill of New York had sought in every way to discredit the ex-President
and to take the nomination away from him; moreover, among soft-
money men of the West and the South Cleveland's hard-money views
aroused the strongest antagonism. The Populists went into the campaign as the one party willing to take a radical stand on the money
question. Their free-silver plank provided, as events proved, the one
really exciting issue of the campaign. Cleveland was elected, as had
been anticipated, with 277 electoral votes to Harrison's 145, but for the
first time since the Civil War a third party had broken into the Electoral
College. Weaver's popular vote of over a million won him 22 electoral
votes, all from the silver-mining or farmer-dominated states of the West,
and gave the Populists confidence to believe that with a monopoly of
the silver issue, they could capture the national government in 1896.
Both houses of Congress were safely Democratic, but the Populists
rejoiced in the knowledge that they would be represented by a small but
faithful few in the Senate as well as in the House.[1]

A casualty of the election was the Farmers' Alliance. In the Northwest it was absorbed into and replaced by the Populist Party. In the
South it was torn violently asunder and destroyed by the third-party
issue. The smaller faction, convinced that deliverance for the southern
cotton-farmer was never to be found under the rule of the Democrats,
dared the derision of neighbors and the loss of friends to join hands with
the Populists. The larger faction, equally certain that white supremacy
was still the one issue to which all others must bow, returned to the
Democratic Party.

There is some reason to suppose that, even before his
term of office ended, Harrison had occasion to rejoice in his
defeat. A nightmare of his administration had been the
condition of the "gold reserve." Authorized by the Resumption Act

---

[1] G. H. Knowles, *The Presidential Campaign and Election of 1892* (1942).

of 1875, and painstakingly assembled by John Sherman during Hayes's administration, this fund had originally amounted to only a little more than $100,000,000. With that sum the Treasury had·successfully resumed specie payments in 1879, although the outstanding issues of greenbacks exceeded the gold reserve in the proportion of about three dollars to one. Businessmen assumed, however, that as long as there was $100,000,000 in gold in the Treasury, the gold standard was secure. Each year the operation of the Bland-Allison Act of 1878 added somewhat to the burden borne by the gold reserve, for successive Secretaries of the Treasury invariably adopted the policy of backing the silver dollar, whatever its "intrinsic" value, with gold. But the plentiful revenues and the general prosperity of the eighties steadily increased the gold reserve, until by 1890 the Treasury was able to record that it possessed $190,000,000 in gold, nearly twice the essential minimum.

It was at this point that the financial measures of the Harrison administration began to take effect. In the first place, the McKinley Tariff, as its framers intended, had reduced the annual revenue by about $100,000,000 a year. Secondly, the lavish expenditures of the new administration, particularly for pensions, placed a new and heavy burden upon the Treasury. Thirdly, the Sherman Silver Purchase Act, which replaced the Bland-Allison Act of 1878, not only required the government to purchase nearly twice as much silver as before, but also provided for a new issue of Treasury notes, based on these silver purchases, that all sound-money men agreed must be redeemable in gold rather than in silver. Failure to maintain their parity with gold would mean that the silver standard would succeed the gold standard, and the purchasing power of the American dollar would decline to the commercial value of the silver dollar — a drop of nearly fifty per cent.[1]

Well before the end of the Harrison administration the condition of the Treasury had begun to excite general alarm. By 1892, the Treasury surplus, which recorded the excess of revenues over expenditures, had almost reached the vanishing point. Far more significant was the fact that the last two years had witnessed heavy withdrawals of gold. Faith that the government could redeem its greenbacks and Treasury notes in gold was obviously shaken, for gold flowed steadily out of the Treasury and paper flowed in. By January, 1893, the gold reserve had dwindled to only $108,000,000, and the Harrison administration, in order to stave off the inevitable crisis until after March 4, was driven to heroic measures. Late in January, Harrison's

Condition of the Treasury

---

[1] W. J. Lauck, *The Causes of the Panic of 1893* (1907), blames the panic mainly upon the currency situation. Compare with F. P. Weberg, *The Background of the Panic of 1893* (1929).

Secretary of the Treasury successfully implored the New York banks to exchange $6,000,000 in gold for paper, a sum that kept the gold reserve above the $100,000,000 mark until after Cleveland was inaugurated. But when the Democrats took over the Treasury, they found a gold reserve of only $100,982,410.

By April 21, 1893, within a matter of weeks after the change of government, the gold reserve dropped below the $100,000,000 mark, and the Panic of 1893 was on. Before six months had passed no less than eight thousand business failures, involving liabilities of $285,000,000, were recorded. Four hundred banks, most of them in the West or in the South, closed their doors. Railroads followed each other into receivership in a procession that ended only after 156 companies, among them the Erie, the Union Pacific, and the Northern Pacific, had gone into bankruptcy. Panic conditions lasted throughout the summer, after which the country settled down to the long, hard process of waiting out a depression that was to last four full years.

Panic of 1893

While the condition of the Treasury, which gave rise to the fear that the government would be unable to maintain the gold standard, undoubtedly ushered in the Panic of 1893, there were other reasons in abundance that must be taken into account in explaining both the panic and the depression. Well to the front was the long-standing agricultural distress of the West and the South. For both sections the beginning of the depression might better have been set at 1887 than at 1893. The purchasing power of the stricken sections had steadily declined, and in consequence the earnings of all businesses that depended on farm markets or the handling of farm goods had suffered. The eighties, too, had been a period of overexpansion in industry. The great transcontinental railroads, the huge industrial trusts, and the building of the larger cities and the new cities that they had made necessary had drained dry the investment resources of the nation. Furthermore, the depression, far from being a strictly American affair, was of world-wide dimensions. From 1889 on, and particularly after the so-called "Baring panic" of 1890 in England, all Europe had recorded subnormal business conditions; indeed, one reason for the depletion of the American gold reserve was the withdrawal of foreign capital from investment in America in order to bolster up the waning fortunes of European enterprise.

Repeal of the Silver Purchase Act

Like all depression Presidents before him, Cleveland did not regard the problem of business recovery as a direct concern of government. The depression was a business problem which business itself was obliged to solve. But the money question was a different matter. Failure to maintain the gold standard would have seemed to Cleveland a breach of public faith. Accordingly, he called Congress at once into special session and asked it to repeal the obnoxious Sherman Silver Purchase Act, which in his judgment had done so much to deplete the gold reserve. He could hardly have thought of a better way to alienate the West and the South, where silver orators were gaining converts every day. The debtor farmers, to whom the gold standard meant low prices and continued agricultural distress, had no desire whatever to save it; for them the fifty-cent dollar had no terrors. The silver interests of the Far West were even more violently. opposed to repeal. What silver needed, they insisted, was a larger rather than a smaller subsidy; better still, "the free and unlimited coinage of silver at the ratio of sixteen to one." Congress at length supported Cleveland in his resolve, but only at the cost of a definite split in the Democratic Party. Enough eastern Republicans joined the eastern Democrats to repeal the Sherman Law, but the confidence of western and southern Democrats in the President they had chosen was sadly shaken.[1]

Cleveland's next move alienated the soft-money men still further. In spite of the fact that silver purchases were discontinued, the drain on the gold reserve continued. By October the amount of gold in the Treasury was less than $82,000,000, and before the end of the year it was down to $68,000,000. Faced by this emergency the President, after some hesitation, authorized his Secretary of the Treasury, John G. Carlisle, to invoke the provisions of the still-unrepealed Resumption Act of 1875, and to buy enough gold to maintain the proper reserve. In January, 1894, an issue of $50,000,000 worth of five per cent bonds brought $58,000,000 in gold into the Treasury, but of this sum $24,000,000 was immediately withdrawn, and before the end of the year one more purchase of gold was necessary — an "endless chain," for in each case the gold was hardly in the Treasury until it was drawn out again. To save the situation, Cleveland resorted in February, 1895, to a deal with the Morgan and Belmont banking firms whereby they were permitted to purchase a large issue of four per cent gold bonds at a figure far below the price the issue would have brought on the open market. In return for the handsome profit they were thus assured, the bankers agreed to procure half the needed gold from abroad, and to use their influence to prevent further withdrawal of gold from the Treasury. By thus "selling out to Wall Street," as the enraged silverites described the deal, Cleveland was able to maintain the gold standard, but his popularity with the debtor South and West dropped completely out of sight.

Part of the price that Cleveland paid for maintaining the gold stand-

[1] Robert McElroy, *Grover Cleveland* (2 vols., 1923).

ard was the defeat of his long-cherished plans for a genuine revision downward of the tariff. Of necessity, or so he thought, he had postponed the tariff battle until after the repeal of the Sherman Act. But when that end had been accomplished, his prestige with the silver wing of his party was so impaired that in that quarter his commands were no longer respected. Moreover, the alliance of eastern Democrats and eastern Republicans, originally called into existence against silver, soon found that it could also function effectively on the tariff. The result was a tariff measure, the Wilson-Gorman Act of 1894, so far removed from the party's pledges on the subject that Cleveland called it a "piece of party perfidy," and obstinately refused to sign the bill, although he did permit it to become a law without his signature.

The Wilson-Gorman Tariff

As it passed the House under the leadership of William L. Wilson of West Virginia, scholarly chairman of the Ways and Means Committee, the Wilson Bill was an honest attempt at tariff reduction. In the Senate, however, two eastern Democrats, Brice and Gorman, aided and abetted by log-rolling Democrats from every section, and in particular by the "sugar senators" from Louisiana, joined with the Republicans to attach 633 amendments to the bill, wholly changing its character. The sugar bounty was not revived, but duties that were worth twenty million dollars annually to the Sugar Trust were placed on both raw and refined sugar. Throughout the revised measure the low-tariff principle was all but ignored. Reluctantly the House acquiesced in the wrecking of its work, and the President's attempts at intervention proved unavailing. In general the duties of the Wilson-Gorman Tariff were lower than those of the McKinley Tariff, and not far different from the duties set by the Tariff of 1883. The provision for an income tax, which actually reached the statute books, was declared unconstitutional by the Supreme Court in a five-to-four decision (1895). This was the more remarkable because of the fact that an income tax had been levied and collected during the Civil War without serious question as to its unconstitutionality.

The distress in agriculture that led to the Populist revolt was no more serious than the plight of the city workers during the hard years that followed the Panic of 1893. Industrial depression meant wholesale unemployment, a condition that state and municipal governments were unable to handle effectively and that the national government looked upon as outside its sphere of activity. One violent strike followed another with appalling frequency, and armies of the unemployed repeatedly marched on Washington. Strangely, however, the farmers and the laborers, although they claimed a common enemy, found difficulty in uniting their forces. The Populists were more

Labor disorders

than eager to produce a united front and made earnest overtures to the laborers, but only the old and weakened Knights of Labor, struggling valiantly to stave off the day of dissolution, signified any interest in co-operation. The American Federation of Labor, to which increasingly the labor world looked for leadership, adhered tenaciously to its policy of keeping the labor movement free from party politics. It was deter-mined neither to become a political party nor to be absorbed in one. The disappointment of the Populists at the resultant failure of their new People's Party to become a genuine party of all the people was acute.

In 1892 a strike broke out in the steel industry, then centered com-pactly about Pittsburgh, Pennsylvania, that gave the country a fore-taste of the labor difficulties from which it was to suffer during the depression. The Homestead strike, as this con-flict was called, involved on the one hand the Amalgamated Association of Iron and Steel workers, a well-established labor organiza-tion that had been formed as early as 1876 by a merger of several smaller craft unions, and on the other hand the Carnegie Steel Company, per-haps the most powerful of the several American steel corporations. Carnegie himself was no labor-baiter, and three years before he had agreed to a satisfactory contract with the union, but at the time trouble broke out in 1892 he had gone to Europe, leaving the affairs of the com-pany in the hands of Henry Clay Frick, a man whose detestation of organized labor was open and unconcealed.[1] The chief point at issue be-tween the company and the workers was a proposed reduction in the pay for piece-work. The company argued that such a reduction was justified because more efficient machinery had been installed. The worker who made use of the new tools could turn out more pieces than formerly in a given time without any greater expenditure of energy. Thus, according to the employers, a reduction in the piece-rate could be made without reducing the worker's daily or weekly earnings. The union, however, refused to be persuaded, and held that the real intent of the company was a wage-cut.

When on July 1 the union refused to accept the company's terms, Frick anticipated the strike by closing the Homestead works. Technically, therefore, what followed was the result of a "lockout" rather than a strike. The union at once began to picket the works, while Frick showed that he meant business by surrounding the company's property with a wire fence fifteen feet high and three miles long, and also by ordering three hundred guards from the Pinkerton Detective Agency. The boats which brought the "Pinkertons" to the scene of conflict, however, were immediately attacked by the strikers, and fighting that occurred on

The Homestead strike

[1] George Harvey, *Henry Clay Frick* (1928), throws some light on this subject.

July 6, 1892, resulted in numerous deaths and injuries on both sides. The Pinkertons were no match for the enraged strikers, who captured and disarmed their entire force and, after holding them for a day as prisoners of war, ran them out of town. Frick then appealed to the state for protection, and the governor responded by sending enough militia to turn the little mill town of Homestead into an armed camp. The strikers held out for nearly five months, but at length public opinion turned against them and they resumed work on the company's terms. An important factor in alienating the public from the strikers, whose case at first had aroused considerable sympathy, was the mad attack, by Alexander Berkman, a young anarchist, on the life of Frick. Frick, although seriously injured, soon recovered, and Berkman for his crime spent fifteen years in prison.

Of all the many labor disturbances that punctuated the years of depression the Pullman strike of 1894 was by far the most significant. In 1880 George Mortimer Pullman, the inventor and builder of the Pullman sleeping-car, had established for the benefit of his employees the "model town" of Pullman on the outskirts of Chicago. This project carried paternalism to an extraordinary extreme. Model dwellings were built by the company and rented to employees; company stores were opened at which Pullman employees were encouraged to buy; a company church, a company school, a company park, and a company theater ministered to the various social needs of the community. The entire village, indeed, was owned and operated by the Pullman Palace Car Company as a business investment — a kind of modern feudalism, so critics were accustomed to say. The situation was changed somewhat in 1889 when the village was annexed to Chicago, but for the most part the property rights of the Pullman Company remained undisturbed.

The Pullman strike

Pullman had no use for labor unions, but during the first year of the depression organizers of the American Railway Union made rapid headway with his men. This union was the brain-child of Eugene V. Debs (1855–1926), who was later to become the outstanding leader of the Socialist movement in the United States. Debs was born in Terre Haute, Indiana, of French-Alsatian ancestry, and at the time of the Pullman strike was still less than forty years of age. He had worked in the railway shops of his home town when he was a boy of only fourteen, and at sixteen he had become a locomotive fireman. A passionate defender of the underprivileged and devoted to the union idea, he held high office in the Brotherhood of Locomotive Firemen, and for a time edited *The Locomotive Fireman's Magazine*. He became increasingly impatient, however, with the unaggressive attitude of the railway brotherhoods and the

American Federation of Labor, with which the brotherhoods co-operated, although they would not join it. Convinced that industrial unions were preferable to trades unions and that railroad men should all be members of one organization, in 1893 he founded the American Railway Union, and such was his persuasiveness that within a year the new union had enrolled one hundred and fifty thousand members.

The Pullman strike was precipitated in the spring of 1894 when the Pullman Company, hard hit by the depression, laid off one-third of its men and cut the wages of the rest from thirty to forty per cent. No reductions, however, were made in the rent charged for company houses nor in the price of goods at the company stores. In protest the men quit work, and with the demand for sleeping-cars at a standstill Pullman showed no disposition to call them back.[1] With their credit withdrawn at the company stores, the strikers were on the verge of starvation when the American Railway Union came to the rescue with relief money and with the threat of a boycott against the hauling of Pullman cars. On June 26 Debs ordered the boycott to be applied on all the western railroads, and "A.R.U." men obeyed by cutting out Pullman cars from their trains and leaving them on side-tracks. When boycotters were discharged for such acts, the strike became general, and not Pullman cars alone but whole trains stood on side-tracks. From Cincinnati to San Francisco the effects of the strike were felt. Traffic between Chicago and the West was virtually paralyzed and hoodlums who joined the strikers stooped to every sort of violence, as all the accumulated bitterness and resentment of the unemployed multitudes was poured into the strife. Engines were crippled, freight-cars were overturned and looted, loyal employees were driven from their posts.

The railroad operators, faced by this dangerous situation, would normally have been willing to trust the governor of Illinois — the state most seriously involved — to keep order, if necessary by calling out the militia to aid the civil authorities. But the governor of Illinois happened to be John P. Altgeld, already notorious among conservatives for his pardoning of the Haymarket anarchists. The operators, therefore, demanded that federal troops be brought in, and when Altgeld took no steps in that direction they appealed directly to the President for aid. Cleveland was in a quandary, for while the Constitution authorized the President to protect a state against domestic violence, it expressly stated that such action was to be taken "on application of the legislature, or of the executive (when the legislature cannot be convened)." The legislature of Illinois was not in session and the governor of the state had issued no call for help, but the

Railroad tie-ups

Federal troops

[1] Almont Lindsey, *The Pullman Strike* (1943).

President at length decided that he might intervene on the pretext that the Chicago disorders interfered with the free transport of United States mail. By the fourth of July two thousand regulars, including cavalry and field artillery, had moved into the troubled zone. Having arrived there, they exerted themselves not merely to see that the mails were carried, but also to break the strike. Altgeld protested vigorously that Cleveland's action was unconstitutional and demanded the immediate withdrawal of the federal troops, but Cleveland stood his ground. No doubt Altgeld, had he been given time to do so, would have restored order, but it is by no means certain that he would have tried to break the strike.[1]

Governmental action against the strikers was not confined to the use of troops, for the federal courts soon took a hand. Debs, who had assumed direct supervision of the strike, and several other leaders were arrested by federal officers on the charge of conspiracy to obstruct the mails, and although released on bail were enjoined by Federal Judges Grosscup and Woods against doing anything to prolong the strike. In direct defiance of this order, Debs urged a group of labor leaders on July 12 to promote a general strike by all the labor organizations of the country. Thereupon he and six others were cited for contempt of court and sentenced to six months in jail. Thus summarily removed from the scene of conflict, Debs was left free to read and to think, and when he emerged from confinement he announced his conversion to socialism.[2] His imprisonment served also to call attention to the fact that the courts were not averse to obtaining results by the use of the injunction that they could not so certainly have obtained had the normal procedure of a jury trial been followed. Criticism of "government by injunction" and of the use of the regular army to break strikes was freely expressed. To many the now familiar Populist charge that a corrupt alliance existed between business and government to suppress the liberties of the people seemed only too well substantiated.

Use of the injunction

That another view of the duty of government could be taken was shown by Governor Davis H. Waite of Colorado, whom Populists, with Democratic assistance, had elected in 1892. "It is better," he had said, "infinitely better, that blood should flow to the horses' bridles rather than our national liberties should be destroyed." Known thenceforth as "Bloody Bridles"

"Bloody Bridles" Waite

---

[1] Cleveland's action precipitated a long-drawn-out controversy. The President's case is stated in Grover Cleveland, *The Government in the Chicago Strike of 1894* (1913); but this should be compared with Harry Barnard, *Eagle Forgotten, the Life of John Peter Altgeld* (1938); W. R. Browne, *Altgeld of Illinois* (1924); and Edward Berman, *Labor Disputes and the President of the United States* (1924).

[2] McAlister Coleman, *Eugene V. Debs; A Man Unafraid* (1930), and Floy R. Painter, *That Man Debs and His Life Work* (1929), both review fully Debs's connection with the Pullman strike.

Waite, he did not hesitate to help the striking miners during the so-called "Cripple Creek War" of 1894 instead of giving the customary aid and comfort to the employers. When an army of deputy sheriffs made ready to attack the strikers, Waite called out the entire state militia to preserve the peace, and marched his troops between the opposing forces. Waite was a man of no tact and little judgment, but his attitude, like Altgeld's, gave courage to the forces of labor. Throughout the nineties in Colorado, Idaho, and Montana the Western Federation of Miners battled employers with a degree of violence that bordered on revolution. In May, 1897, the president of this organization urged every union in Colorado and Idaho to arm itself "so that in two years we can hear the inspiring music of the martial tread of 25,000 armed men in the ranks of labor." [1]

Attempts to induce the government to help solve the problem of unemployment by means of work relief, while not entirely unknown, proceeded usually from the minds of men whom the public regarded as "crack-pots." Most famous of these was General Jacob S. Coxey of Massillon, Ohio, a Greenbacker and a Populist, who advocated that Congress should issue $500,000,000 in legal-tender notes to be expended at the rate of $20,000,000 a month on the building of good roads. Wages of one dollar and fifty cents per eight-hour day were to be paid to all who needed employment. Coxey also urged that municipalities desirous of making public improvements should be authorized to issue non-interest-bearing bonds equal to half their assessed valuation. These bonds might then be used as security with the Secretary of the Treasury to obtain loans of legal-tender notes to pay for the construction of schools, courthouses, paved streets, and other worthy projects. Both schemes, on the financial side, were highly inflationary in character, but they aimed at a type of governmental activity that in the next great depression became extremely familiar.

"Coxey's army"

In seeking to promote his ideas Coxey hit upon the expedient of presenting, by means of a march of the unemployed on Washington, a "living petition" to Congress. With the assistance of amused and interested newspaper men, he actually got his march started on Easter Sunday, 1894, and on the first of May following "Coxey's Army," [2] five hundred strong, entered Washington determined to lay its demands before Congress. At the Capitol Coxey and several of his principal adherents suffered ignominious arrest for disobeying an ordinance to keep off the grass. But Coxey's exploit, which attracted wide newspaper attention, was speedily imitated by other marchers, most of whom were stopped far

[1] Louis Adamic, *Dynamite* (1931). This book recounts, with sympathy, the more violent labor outbreaks from the Civil War to the Great Depression.

[2] Donald L. McMurry, *Coxey's Army* (1929), p. 120. This book deals fully with all the various labor "marches" of the period.

short of Washington. These "marches of the unemployed" called striking attention to the acute suffering of labor during the depression, and encouraged the Populists to hope that eventually farmers and laborers would learn to work together. If only such a union could be achieved, they believed that the people, not the plutocrats, would soon rule. Populist strategy called for union through the agency of the People's Party. First the Populists must capture the government, and then, as rapidly as possible, they must put into effect the numerous and complicated reforms of their cherished platform.

As events turned out, whatever union of the working classes was actually accomplished came primarily on the issue of free silver, and more or less without regard for the wishes of party leaders. Propaganda from mine-owners in the silver states of the Far West flooded the country with denunciations of the "crime of 1873" and with innumerable arguments to prove that only "the free and unlimited coinage of silver at the ratio of sixteen to one" was required to restore prosperity. *Coin's Financial School*, a little book written by William H. Harvey and published in 1894, set forth in simple language, and seemingly with unanswerable logic, the doctrines of the silverites. "Professor Coin," as the author called himself, purported to run a school in Chicago for financiers, and the lectures he gave on the money question were recorded in the book. Illustrated with numerous cartoons and diagrams, and sometimes reduced to the simplicity of a dialogue between the "Professor" and his students, the book appealed to an enormous audience. Silver orators, such as William Jennings Bryan, knew its arguments by heart and spread them far and wide. Soon countless thousands had come to believe that an international conspiracy to set gold above silver was at the root of the economic distress from which the nation suffered. The restoration of prosperity need not await the enactment of a long and complicated series of reforms. By the simple expedient of restoring silver to its historic status as money, all wrongs would be righted.

Rise of the silver issue

While the Populists alone were clear-cut in their support of free silver, or bimetallism, as it was sometimes called, there were innumerable converts to this "heresy" in both the older parties. As a result the congressional elections of 1894 turned upon hard times and the unpopularity of Cleveland. The Democrats were no more responsible for the depression than the Republicans, if as much so, but it was their misfortune to be in power when the panic broke, and the Republicans drove home the charge that Democratic supremacy and hard times went together. As a result the Republicans obtained a two to one majority in the national House of Representatives, greatly re-

Elections of 1894

duced the Democratic majority in the Senate, and captured nearly every state government outside the South. The behavior of the Populists during the campaign tended, if anything, to aid the Republicans. In the West the Populists, unable or unwilling to co-operate with the Democrats as fully as in 1892, tended to avoid fusion and to keep "in the middle of the road"; in the South, they unblushingly joined forces with the Republicans. The total Populist vote, however, was more than forty per cent larger in 1894 than in 1892, and enthusiastic Populists cited the rapid rise of Republicanism before 1860 as evidence of what their party could do by 1896. Leading Republicans held a different view of the situation; some of them boasted openly that in 1896 they could "nominate a rag baby and elect it President."

That the original Republican plan for 1896 did not contemplate a straight-out endorsement of the single gold standard was apparent from the record of the candidate slated for first place on the Republican ticket. William McKinley (1843–1901), author of the McKinley Tariff Bill of 1890, and governor of Ohio from 1891 to 1895, was a tariff expert with no deep convictions on the money question. Indeed, in so far as he had committed himself, he seemed to have taken the silver side. In 1878 he had voted for the Bland-Allison Act, and in 1890, when the Sherman Silver Purchase Act was being formulated, he again advocated special favors for silver. As a compromise candidate, satisfactory to both the silver and the gold factions of the party, he seemed ideal, for his leanings toward silver were nicely balanced by the fact that he was a thoroughgoing party regular who could be trusted not to get out of step with the party leaders. His availability for the Republican nomination in 1896 was further emphasized by his creditable record as a Union officer in the Civil War, by his chivalrous devotion to his invalid wife, by his suave and genial manners, and by his abiding friendship with Marcus Alonzo Hanna, Cleveland industrialist and boss of the Republican Party in Ohio. Hanna had the normal attitude of his class toward tariff protection, but his regard for McKinley was personal no less than political. He early made up his mind that McKinley must be the Republican standard-bearer in 1896, and long before the convention met had rounded up the necessary votes.[1]

The steady drift of the electorate toward the free-silver "heresy" upset the Republican plan for a fence-sitting campaign on the money question. Many Democrats, both in the South and in the West, were converted to the idea; others realized that only by embracing it could they prevent

[1] Herbert Croly, *Marcus Alonzo Hanna* (1913), is far superior to any biography of McKinley in its understanding of the forces that shaped McKinley's policies. Thomas Beer, *Hanna* (1929), is also useful.

large numbers of Democrats from going over to the Populists. Shrewd observers could easily foretell that, in spite of the strenuous efforts of President Cleveland and the gold-standard Democrats of the Northeast, the Democratic Party would be forced to include in its platform an uncompromising demand for free silver. Confronted by this situation, the Republican leaders, Hanna among them, finally determined to commit their party to the single gold standard. They could not resist a slight gesture, however, in the free-silver direction. The plank finally adopted opposed the free coinage of silver "except by international agreement with the leading commercial nations of the world," and until that could be obtained pledged the party to maintain the existing parity of all money with gold. On the adoption of the gold plank, a small group of "Silver Republicans," led by Senator Henry M. Teller of Colorado, bolted the convention, presumably with the intention of joining the Democrats in case the Democratic Party endorsed free silver. But the Republican convention stood its ground, nominated McKinley for President and Garret A. Hobart of New Jersey for Vice-President, and adjourned in the hope that Marcus A. Hanna, their new campaign manager, could find the money and the means to restore their party to power.

The action of the Republicans left the Democrats, whose convention met a few weeks later at Chicago, no logical choice but to endorse free silver. The Democratic National Committee, however, was still in the hands of the men who had helped to nominate Cleveland in 1892, and they made a determined effort to halt the trend toward silver. But when their nominee for temporary chairman, David B. Hill of New York, a "gold-bug," was defeated by Senator John W. Daniel of Virginia, a silverite, 556 to 349, it was apparent that the radicals were in control. The platform they presented and adopted (628 to 301) on the money question bore no trace of compromise.

> We demand the free and unlimited coinage of both silver and gold at the present legal ratio of sixteen to one without waiting for the aid or consent of any other nation. We demand that the standard silver dollar shall be a full legal tender, equally with gold, for all debts, public and private, and we favor such legislation as will prevent for the future the demonetization of any kind of legal tender money by private contract.

The Democrats had produced a platform; they were not long in finding a candidate. Before the convention met, the leading aspirant among the silverites was Richard P. Bland, a congressman from Missouri. But Bland's candidacy had awakened little enthusiasm, and many delegates regretted the constitutional provision that alone would keep them from voting for the far more colorful John P. Altgeld of Illinois, a naturalized citizen of German

William Jennings Bryan

birth. Among the numerous minor candidates was William Jennings Bryan (1860–1925) of Nebraska, a young man only thirty-six years of age whose reputation for persuasive oratory was already well known.[1] Bryan had served two terms in Congress, 1891 to 1895, and had once attracted nation-wide attention by a powerful speech on the tariff. During the depression, without actually becoming a Populist, he had taken up with most of the Populist doctrines, particularly free silver. As Ignatius Donnelly, the most famous orator of Populism complained, "We put him to school and he wound up by stealing the schoolbooks."

For months before the nominating convention met in 1896, Bryan had been speaking on free silver to western audiences, and had rehearsed many times the ringing phrases that were to bring him fame at Chicago. Fully conscious of his genius as an orator, he knew in his heart that if he could only find the occasion to make the speech he had learned so well the coveted prize would be his. The opportunity came when he was asked to close the debate on a resolution that would have repudiated free silver and commended the Cleveland administration. Bryan poured forth his soul in "magic words" that met the mood of his audience "to the very full." His speech was not a reasoned defense of the silver cause, and was not meant to be. Rather it was a leader's call to action. His closing words, "You shall not press down upon the brow of labor this crown of thorns, you shall not crucify mankind upon a cross of gold," summarized in a sentence all that had gone before. At that moment, had the convention been given the chance, it would doubtless have nominated Bryan by acclamation. When the proper time came, in spite of the fact that more than a hundred and fifty gold Democrats persistently abstained from voting, Bryan obtained the necessary two-thirds majority after only five ballots. For Vice-President the convention chose Arthur Sewall, a wealthy banker and shipbuilder from Maine.

The plight of the Populists when they learned what the Democrats had done was far from pleasant. The Democratic platform had not only appropriated the silver issue; it had denounced with Populistic fervor the "absorption of wealth by the few," **Plight of the Populists** and had called for a stricter control of trusts and railroads by the federal government. The Democratic candidate, Bryan, was a Populist in everything but name. The Populist leaders, confident that both the Republicans and the Democrats would be captured by the "goldbugs," had set the date of the Populist Convention later than either of the

---

[1] Unfortunately there is as yet no really good biography of Bryan. Probably the most nearly satisfactory is M. R. Werner, *Bryan* (1929). Paxton Hibben, *The Peerless Leader, William Jennings Bryan* (1929), and J. C. Long, *Bryan, The Great Commoner* (1928), leave much to be desired, but are still superior to W. J. and Mary B. Bryan, *The Memoirs of William Jennings Bryan* (1925).

old-party conventions, and had hoped to rally all free-silver men and all reformers to their standard. Now they were faced squarely with the problem of sacrificing their party by endorsing the Democratic nominee or aiding the Republicans by dividing the silver vote. In general western Populists were willing to accept Bryan and join the Democrats, but to southern Populists such a course, involving, as it did, full surrender to a hated enemy, was extremely painful to contemplate. After a heated battle the Populist Convention voted in favor of a compromise. Instead of the wholly unacceptable Sewall, they chose Watson of Georgia as their candidate for Vice-President, but supported Bryan for President. Their hope that the Democrats would "take down" Sewall and replace him by Watson was unrealized, and Bryan was obliged to fight the campaign through with the handicap of two running-mates. As a matter of fact, however, the Populist Party practically dissolved during the campaign. For the next three presidential elections it continued to put tickets in the field, but after 1896 it was never again a serious factor in American politics.[1]

Bryan's matchless oratory and the popularity of his cause put the Republicans, much to their surprise, at an initial disadvantage, but Mark Hanna collected the largest campaign fund that up to that time had ever been available in a national election. Backed by as many millions as he cared to gather, he conducted an elaborate campaign of "education." On the money question, the Republican orators and pamphleteers no doubt had the better of the argument, and they made the most of their advantage. Even among the reformers there was much dissent from the free-silver hypothesis and some genuine dismay at the overemphasis it received. Henry Demarest Lloyd, the author of *Wealth Against Commonwealth* (1894), a powerful indictment of the existing economic order, described free silver as a "fake" and called it the "cowbird of the reform movement. It waited until the nest had been built by the sacrifices and labors of others, and then laid its eggs in it, pushing out the others which lie smashed on the ground." There is truth, too, in the contention of Tom Johnson, perennial mayor of Cleveland, Ohio. He described the election as "the first great protest of the American people against monopoly — the first great struggle of the masses in our country against the privileged classes. It was not free silver that frightened the plutocrat leaders. What they feared, then, what they fear now, is free men." [2]

Campaign of 1896

---

[1] The gold wing of the Democratic Party subsequently held a convention and nominated John M. Palmer of Illinois for President and Simon B. Buckner of Kentucky for Vice-President. Cleveland supported this ticket, but like most of the "Gold Democrats" hoped for a Republican victory. For a colorful account of the campaign see Harry Thurston Peck, *Twenty Years of the Republic* (1907).

[2] Tom L. Johnson, *My Story* (1911), p. 109.

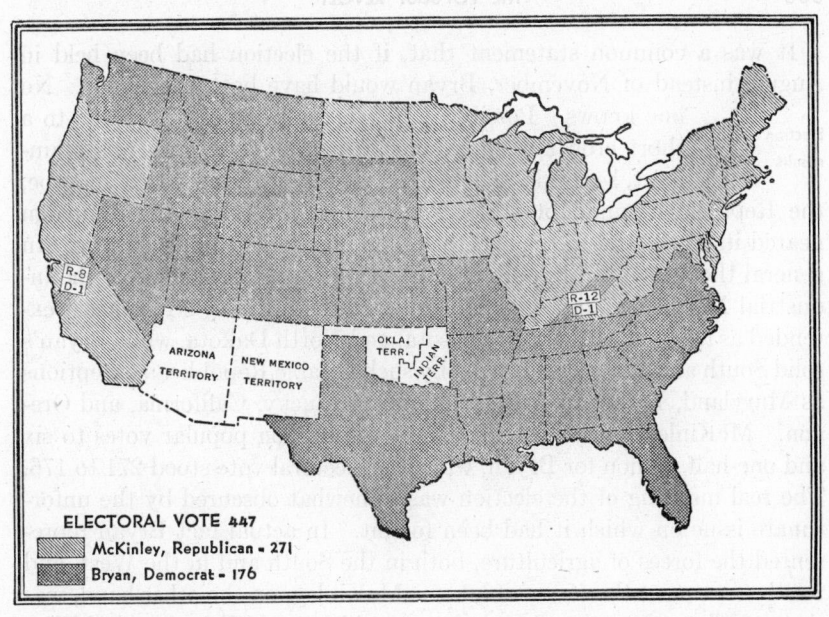

ELECTORAL VOTE 447

McKinley, Republican - 271

Bryan, Democrat - 176

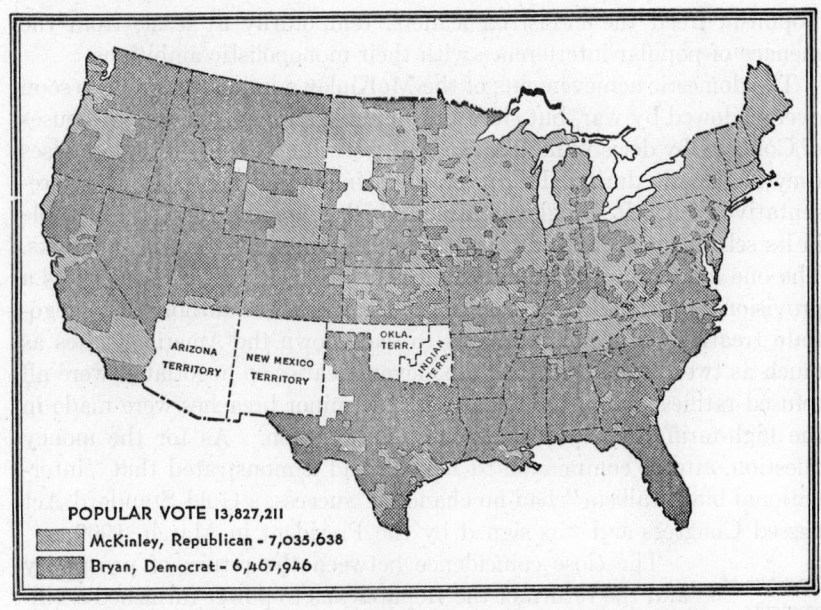

POPULAR VOTE 13,827,211

McKinley, Republican - 7,035,638

Bryan, Democrat - 6,467,946

PRESIDENTIAL ELECTION OF 1896, BY STATES
AND BY COUNTIES

It was a common statement that, if the election had been held in August instead of November, Bryan would have been the victor. No

Election results

one knows. Possibly a rise in the price of wheat due to a short crop abroad, whereas the American crop was abundant, seriously affected the results. However that may be, the Republicans undoubtedly picked up many votes as the campaign neared its close, and in the end they won an overwhelming victory. In general the agricultural South and West supported Bryan, while the industrial Northeast supported McKinley; but McKinley's Northeast extended as far west as Iowa, Minnesota, and North Dakota, while Bryan's solid South and West were broken by such notable Republican exceptions as Maryland, Delaware, West Virginia, Kentucky, California, and Oregon. McKinley received more than seven million popular votes to six and one-half million for Bryan, while the electoral vote stood 271 to 176. The real meaning of the election was somewhat obscured by the unfortunate issue on which it had been fought. In actual fact Bryan represented the forces of agriculture, both in the South and in the West, and to a lesser extent the forces of labor. McKinley, on the other hand, was the candidate of northeastern industry, which, ever since the Civil War, had been well-entrenched in the control of the national government and meant to hold its ground. The defeat of Bryan and the downfall of Populism freed the industrial leaders, temporarily at least, from the menace of popular interference with their monopolistic ambitions.

The domestic achievements of the McKinley administration were soon overshadowed by war, but since the Republicans controlled both houses of Congress by decisive majorities, they were able to redeem the promises they had made during the campaign. Under the leadership of Representative Nelson R. Dingley of Maine a high protective tariff, comparable in its schedules to the McKinley Act, was placed on the statute books. The one faint ray of hope in the measure to low-tariff advocates was a provision for limited reciprocity. The President was authorized to negotiate treaties with foreign nations to scale down the American rates as much as twenty per cent, but the eleven treaties so negotiated were all refused ratification by the Senate. Some minor breaches were made in the high-tariff wall by presidential proclamation. As for the money question, after a commission to Europe had demonstrated that "international bimentallism" had no chance of success, a Gold Standard Act passed Congress and was signed by the President in March, 1900.

The return of prosperity

The close coincidence between the return of prosperity and the return of the Republicans to power furnished a valuable weapon to Republican campaigners for many years to come. It is possible, of course, that the prospect of Republican victory promoted business confidence and led to business expansion. Good times were on the way back, however, even before the election, and it seems reasonable to suppose that the course of events would not have been far different, even if Bryan had been elected. Undoubtedly one reason for the upward surge was an increase in the money supply. It is a curious fact that monetary inflation actually occurred in spite of all the Republicans had done to prevent it, and it occurred in a way they had least expected, by means of an increase in the world's supply of gold. For a quarter of a century before 1890 the amount of new gold mined each year was practically constant. Then a steady increase began which by the end of the nineties had reached spectacular proportions. In the year 1897, approximately twice as much gold was produced as in the year 1890; in 1898 nearly two and one-half times as much. The cyanide process by which more gold was extracted from the ore mined, coupled with new discoveries of gold in Australia, South Africa, and the Klondike, accounted for the increase. Bryan was doubtless right when he first began to assert that the amount of gold in existence was inadequate to transact the world's business, but his arguments were less convincing with each succeeding year. Before Bryan became active in politics American business had to overcome the handicap of a steadily appreciating dollar, which meant also steadily diminishing price levels; by the time Bryan began to run for President, the value of the dollar had begun to diminish, and prices were on the rise. American agriculture no less than industry responded to the stimulus of gold inflation, while in the West the drouth at long last came to an end. Good harvests in America were matched by poor harvests abroad and the price of farm produce began to rise. Presently the Spanish-American War, the Philippine Insurrection, and the Boer-British War each added its quota to the boom that had already begun.[1]

[1] J. F. Rhodes, *The McKinley and Roosevelt Administrations, 1897–1909* (1922), is useful for the inside view of politics it presents, but almost totally ignores economic and social history. H. H. Kohlsaat, *From McKinley to Harding* (1923), is a book of personal recollections by "one who knew." Chester McA. Destler, *American Radicalism, 1865–1901: Essays and Documents* (1946), is thoughtful and provocative. Fred A. Shannon, *The Farmers' Last Frontier: Agriculture, 1860–1897* (1945), presents admirably the economic background of frontier Populism. There are a number of pertinent biographies: F. B. Simkins, *Pitchfork Ben Tillman, South Carolinian* (1944); James C. Olson, *J. Sterling Morton* (1942); R. B. Nixon, *Henry W. Grady, Spokesman of the New South* (1943).

On the "New South," see W. J. Cash, *The Mind of the South* (1941); A. F. Raper and Ira DeA. Reid, *Sharecroppers All* (1941); Virginius Dabney, *Below the Potomac* (1942); T. D. Clark, *Pills, Petticoats, and Plows: The Southern Country Store* (1944).

Earl S. Pomeroy, *The Territories and the United States, 1861–1890* (1947), throws light on a much neglected subject.

29

The Old American Way

BETWEEN 1876, the one-hundredth anniversary of the signing of the Declaration of Independence, and 1889, the one-hundredth anniversary of the inauguration of government under the Constitution, the United States became habituated to centennial celebrations. It was a foregone conclusion, therefore, that so available a date as the four-hundredth anniversary of the discovery of America by Columbus would not be overlooked. As early as 1890 an act was passed by Congress providing for an exhibition, to be held in 1892, that should commemorate the progress of the nation in art, industry, and agriculture. Rivalry for the honor and profit involved in staging the "Fair" was keen between New York, Washington, St. Louis, and Chicago, but Chicago, with a guaranty of ten million dollars, was the successful bidder.

Great were the preparations that were made for what its promoters were pleased to call the "World's Columbian Exposition." In its behalf the ablest of America's artists, under the general direction **The Chicago** of Daniel Hudson Burnham,[1] pooled their talents. Fred- **World's Fair** erick Law Olmsted, the landscape architect who had laid out Central Park, New York; Stanford White, C. F. McKim, R. M. Hunt, and Louis Sullivan, architects; Augustus Saint-Gaudens, Daniel Chester French, Lorado Taft, and Frederick Macmonnies, sculptors; Kenyon Cox, Gari Melchers, and Edwin Blashfield, painters; all these and others contributed of their genius to produce an artistic setting of surpassing beauty for the exhibition. "Look here, old fellows," Saint-Gaudens once told these leaders as they pored together over their plans, "do you realize that this is the greatest meeting of artists since the fifteenth century?" For the site of the Fair ninety acres of Lake Front adjoining the business district of Chicago and six hundred acres in Jackson Park were dedicated. Here, at a cost of twenty-six million dollars, arose a "White City" so breath-takingly beautiful as to win the highest praise, not merely from the multitudes, but also from such professional skeptics and sophisticates as Henry Adams and Charles Eliot Norton. In full

[1] Charles Moore, *Daniel H. Burnham* (1921).

revolt against the grotesque architecture of the "General Grant" period, the planners of the White City adhered closely to classical designs — a confession, in a sense, that America had not yet produced a worth-while native architecture. But as a classical reproduction — "what the Romans would have wished to create" — it was superb.

The Fair was dedicated on Columbus day, October 12, 1892, but it was not officially opened until the following spring. In spite of the depression, twelve million visitors entered its gates, and it was a financial success. Its exhibits well revealed the material and artistic achievements of America and the world, for nearly every foreign nation was represented. The Palace of Fine Arts satisfied Americans that they no longer had need to apologize for the work of their sculptors and painters. Buildings devoted in whole or in part to transportation, manufactures, machinery, electricity, mines and mining, agriculture, horticulture, floriculture, and the liberal arts mirrored the remarkable transformations of the age. The Midway Plaisance, with its exotic "villages," its exciting "Streets of Cairo," its enormous "Ferris Wheel," and its innumerable other amusement features, set the pattern for future American playgrounds. Less talked about than they deserved were the numerous "congresses" that accompanied the Fair. Their purpose was to present the most pressing scientific, literary, and religious problems of the times. A fitting climax to the series of religious congresses was a great "parliament of religions" in which Catholics, Protestants, and Jews rubbed shoulders and exchanged ideas with Buddhists, Confucianists, Mohammedans, and representatives of many other religious sects. Out of the Fair and the congresses Americans got a far better understanding of their country and its place in the world than they had ever had before. They went home to imitate its architecture, to seek for beauty in the replanning of their towns and cities, and to dream dreams, not wholly unrealized, of a more abundant life.

Among the World's Fair congresses the one on history attracted comparatively little attention, but at an evening session, on July 12, 1893, Frederick Jackson Turner, a youthful professor from the University of Wisconsin, read a paper of great importance **Frederick Jackson Turner** on "The Significance of the Frontier in American History." [1] Pointing out that "the germ theory of politics" had been sufficiently emphasized, and that the evolution of institutions along the Atlantic coast was, after all, a fairly "familiar phenomenon," he urged historians of the United States to study the West as well as the East.

---

[1] This essay, together with other interesting material bearing on the so-called "Turner hypothesis," appears in the latest compilation of Turner essays, *The Early Writings of Frederick Jackson Turner* (1938).

American social development has been continually beginning over again on the frontier. This perennial rebirth, this fluidity of American life, this expansion westward with its new opportunities, its continuous touch with the simplicity of primitive society, furnish the forces dominating American character. The true point of view in the history of this nation is not the Atlantic coast, it is the Great West. . . . What the Mediterranean Sea was to the Greeks, breaking the bonds of custom, offering new experiences, calling out new institutions and activities, that and more, the ever retreating frontier has been to the United States directly, and to the nations of Europe more remotely.

Turner's words were heeded, and soon a veritable cult of the West had sprung up among the writers of American history. Sometimes the American Historical Association, founded in 1884 by scholars of unimpeachable eastern connections, was accurately, if facetiously, described as the "Turner-verein." Turner's disciples outdid their master in claiming significance for the frontier, and they often claimed too much. Nevertheless, it seems clear that the influence of a succession of frontiers had much to do with molding the character of American civilization. Years before, E. L. Godkin, editor of the *Nation*, had recognized this fact in an elaborate review of de Tocqueville's *Democracy in America*. The pioneering element, he wrote,

spread itself thinly over a vast area of soil, of such extraordinary fertility that a very slight amount of toil expended on it affords returns that might have satisfied even the dreams of Spanish avarice. The result has been very much what we might have concluded, *a priori*, that it would be. A society composed at the period of its formation mainly of young men, coming from all parts of the world in quest of fortune, released from the ordinary restraints of family, church, and public opinion, even of the civil law, naturally and inevitably acquires a certain contempt for authority and impatience of it, and individualism among them develops itself very rapidly. If you place this society, thus constituted, in the midst of a wilderness, where each member of it has to contend, tools in hand, with Nature herself for wealth, or even subsistence, the ties which bind him to his fellows will for a while at least be rarely anything stronger than that of simple contiguity; and the only mutual obligation which this relation suggests strongly is that of rendering assistance occasionally in overcoming material difficulties — in other words, the simplest bond which can unite human beings. Each person is from the necessity of the case so absorbed in his own struggle for existence, that he has seldom occasion or time for the consideration and cultivation of his social relations. He knows nothing of the antecedents of his neighbors, nor they of his. They are not drawn together, in all probability, by a single memory or association. They have drifted into the same locality, it is true, under the guidance of a common impulse, and this a selfish one. So that the settler gets into the habit of looking at himself as an individual, of contemplating himself and his career separate and apart from the social organization. We do not say that this breeds selfishness — far from that; but it breeds individualism.[1]

Whether Godkin was right or wrong in his explanation of its causes, few will deny the existence among early Americans of a strongly individualistic bent. If, as Godkin held and Turner preached, this emphasis upon individualism proceeded from "the frontier life," then it would seem to follow that the gradual extinction of the frontier would make a difference. Godkin may not have been fully aware of the fact, but by the time he wrote these words the kind of frontier he described was rapidly disappearing. A generation later, when Turner wrote, it was virtually gone. Enormous tracts of unsettled land still existed in the trans-Mississippi West, but most of this land was arid plains or rugged mountains, totally unfitted for the type of agriculture that earlier American pioneers had practiced. Radical changes in methods of farming made possible a long-sustained advance, but by the end of the century the law of diminishing returns had begun to operate. "Free land" still existed in quantities, and settlers who knew no better than to take it could still be found, but for the ordinary farmer who pioneered in the twentieth century the returns were rarely such as might have satisfied "the dreams of Spanish avarice." Rather, they were such as to saddle upon the next generation a vexatious problem of resettlement and relief.

The frontier life

Undoubtedly the diminishing importance of the frontier life had its effect upon the character of American civilization. New forces were now at work that had little to do with the frontier life, except to stifle it. Coincident with the passing of the frontier an economic revolution had occurred that in its transforming influence had affected not only the United States but the whole world besides. Railroads permeated every part of the country, and at both coasts connected with steamship lines that crisscrossed every ocean. Telegraph, telephone, and cable service grew daily more complete. Cheap paper, cheap printing, and cheap postage greatly facilitated the circulation of newspapers, books, periodicals, and advertising literature. Inventions crowded forward in an exciting procession. Big business, equipped and re-equipped with new and then still newer tools, drove little business out of business. New breeds of immigrants flocked in from the Old World to do the hard work of industry. Labor and capital drew apart with an acute class-consciousness that the frontier life had never known. Before this barrage the individualism of log-cabin, covered-wagon days gave way. For the

[1] E. L. Godkin, "Aristocratic Opinions of Democracy," in *North American Review*, C, 194–232 (January, 1865).

few it became an instrument with which to exploit the many; for the many it tended, more and more, to become merely a memory.

Whatever the forces that worked together to shape the pattern of American society in the late nineteenth century, undoubtedly the economic revolution, aided and abetted by the gradual disappearance of the frontier, played a principal part. Responding to the new impetus, an urbanized industrialized society swept rapidly from East to West.[1] Labor, influenced no less by the influx of European ideas than by the influx of European immigrants, tended to subordinate the welfare of the individual to the welfare of the class. Farmers, transformed by the machine age into petty business men who produced primarily to sell, forsook their individualistic traditions to battle co-operatively for their rights through Granges, Alliances, and even a third political party. With the whole nation open, almost equally, to the operation of the same forces, life in the United States became increasingly standardized. Sectional differences and local idiosyncrasies yielded slowly but surely before an insistent demand for uniformity.

Uniformity in American society

Much has been written to show how the coming of the immigrants in the late nineteenth century brought diversity rather than uniformity to the American people. What is sometimes forgotten is that, in spite of the rising immigrant tide, the native Americans continued to be overwhelmingly in the ascendance. During the thirty years preceding 1900 the percentage of native-born inhabitants remained practically constant, varying through four sets of census figures less than one per cent from an average of eighty-six per cent. It is true, of course, that many native Americans — in 1900 about one-fifth of the total population — had at least one immigrant parent; but it is also true, if the matter of ancestry must be fully examined, that all native Americans, except for the Indians, were the descendants of immigrants. Even more to the point is the fact that until the last decade of the nineteenth century the immigrants, numerous as they were, came primarily from the British Isles and Canada, from Germany, and from the Scandinavian countries. In the seventies 82.8 per cent were so classified, in the eighties, 75.6; in the nineties, when the trend from southern and eastern Europe began in earnest, 41.8. During these three decades some 7,834,412 immigrants entered the United States from Canada or from northwestern Europe, as against only 2,953,714 from southern and eastern Europe. The former, as a rule, were quickly and easily assimilated into the American population; a large proportion of them were Eng-

Immigrant influences

---

[1] By all odds the best study of the transformation of American life wrought by the economic revolution is A. M. Schlesinger, *The Rise of the City, 1878–1898* (1933).

THE OLD AMERICAN WAY

lish-speaking on their arrival, and practically all of them made haste to imitate the American way of life. Against the winds of uniformity that were blowing, the nineteenth-century immigrants offered as little resistance as the descendants of the Puritans and the Cavaliers.

In a sense the frontier, while it lasted, had had much to do with the increasing homogeneity of the American people. It had been both a melting-pot and a mixing-bowl. Moreover, every part of the United States, at one time or another, had gone through the frontier process, and the experience had everywhere left its mark — more or less the same mark. Just as the child is father to the man, so the primitive society of frontier times bequeathed a number of its most distinctive characteristics to later generations. Such ideals as flowed from the frontier's love of conquest, of individual freedom, and of equality of opportunity lived on into a period when the actual conditions of life belied them. The frontier might have vanished, but the restless search for greener pastures that it had bred survived.[1]

But if the frontier had promoted homogeneity, the passing of the frontier tended to promote it even more. It is not necessary to believe that while the West was young all of the more aggressive and energetic people went West, leaving to the East only a stagnant and unenterprising lot. Nevertheless, with the *Passing of the frontier* frontier at the vanishing point, with the railroads offering tempting rates, and with opportunity knocking more boldly in the eastern cities than on the western plains, there occurred in the late nineteenth century a remarkable return of the West upon the East. The enterprising Easterner going west was met by the enterprising Westerner going east. Western ideas got a hearing in the East, just as eastern ideas had all along got a hearing in the West. Western leaders in business, in politics, in the professions appeared in every eastern city. Northerners, too, went south, and Southerners went north. The population was mixed up as never before, and the characteristics of one section became increasingly the characteristics of all.

This strikingly homogeneous nature of American society can perhaps be best appreciated when compared with European society during the same period. In Europe only a few hundred miles at most would bring the traveler to a region where the people saluted a different flag, spoke a different language, cherished a different culture. In America, for nearly three thousand miles east and west, and for half that many miles north and south, one met with the same flag, the same language, and essen-

---

[1] An illuminating interpretation of the rôle of the West in American history is contained in F. L. Paxson, *When the West is Gone* (1930). See also D. R. Fox (editor), *Sources of Culture in the Middle West* (1934).

tially the same culture. Minor differences of course endured. New Englanders broadened their *a*'s, did curious things to their *r*'s, and sometimes forgot their final *g*'s. Southerners spoke with a soft and musical drawl that owed something, no doubt, to the influence of a large colored population; certain cities reflected the speech characteristics of a leading immigrant group — Jewish in New York, German in Milwaukee, Swedish in Minneapolis. Only by such trifles as these could the remnants of separate cultural heritages be observed. Far greater differences existed within the compass of the British Isles alone. Americans everywhere tended to talk alike, think alike, act alike.

"After all, business is the biggest thing in this country." So the editor of the Atlanta *Constitution* told his readers on January 8, 1890; and for good measure he added, "Politicians may talk, but businessmen will act, control, and dominate the destinies of this common-sense country." Embryo Populists, whether of the South or of the West, might not have approved the *Constitution*'s cheerful acceptance of this situation, but few would have tried to deny the fact. Business, moreover, was not only the "biggest thing" in the country, it was also the greatest single agency of standardization. More and more the "princes of commerce and industry" thought and planned in national terms. With revolutionary improvements in means of communication at their disposal, they had expanded their interests to include the whole nation. No longer did the manufacturer seek mainly to reach a local market; he must now sell his product in every state and territory of the Union — beyond the national borders if he could. Local natural resources might determine that cotton-factories should dominate in the South, iron- and steel-works in the middle Atlantic states, and flour- and grist-mills in the new Northwest, but dependence upon a nation-wide market was universal. Merchants in every part of the country offered the same types of goods to their customers, and counted upon national campaigns of advertising, paid for by the manufacturers, to stimulate sales. Americans everywhere became accustomed to the same "makes" of washing-machines, farm implements, bicycles, wagons and buggies; wore the same styles of readymade clothes; painted their houses with nationally known brands of housepaint; purchased quantities of patent breakfast foods, patent toothpowder, and patent liniment ("good for man or beast"). Mail-order houses, selling commodities pictured in catalogues at cut-rate prices direct to the trustful purchaser, did a thriving business. Retail prices, in spite of widely divergent transportation costs, varied little from one section of the country to another, and even the methods of doing business became standardized.

Nation-wide business

Industrialism, of course, meant the growth of cities, but this was a development that spread itself with remarkable uniformity the whole country over. While the Northeast led the way in urbanization, other sections of the country showed themselves excellent imitators. The South during and after reconstruction sought eagerly to crowd itself with factories and cities; as Henry Watterson put it, "The South, having had its bellyful of blood, has gotten a taste of money, and is too busy trying to make more to quarrel with anybody." The West, too, from the time of the Civil War on, tried hard to get rid of its overgreat dependence upon agriculture which made no one rich, and to embrace industry which made riches for at least a few. In 1871 the Milwaukee Chamber of Commerce lamented:

> We are sending our hard lumber east to get it back as furniture and agricultural implements, we ship ores to St. Louis and New York, to pay the cost of bringing it back as shot, type, pipe, sheet lead, white lead, paint, etc., we ship away our wool crop and import cloth, carpets, blankets and other fabrics; we give rags for paper, and hides for boots and harness, and iron-ore for stoves — and our consumers all the while are paying the double costs of this unnecessary transportation.

What this chamber of commerce really wanted for Milwaukee was factories, of whatever kind, and Milwaukee soon got them. So also did every other enterprising western city with good railroad or water connections. In 1870 only 20.9 per cent of the American population lived in places of eight thousand inhabitants or more, whereas in 1900 33.1 per cent were so situated. In the East the percentage of city dwellers ran well above this figure; in the South, the Middle West, and the Far West, well below it. But the trend toward urbanization was national, not sectional, and it affected every part of the country.[1]

The new cities and the rejuvenated old ones showed remarkable similarities. According to James Bryce, "American cities with eight or nine exceptions differ from one another only herein, that some of them are built more with brick than with wood, and others more with wood than with brick." The checkerboard of "squares" in which William Penn had laid out Philadelphia became the favorite American pattern for city development, and each new "addition" strove valiantly to be exactly like the rest. Pavements rarely kept up with expansion, and while asphalt and brick won increasing popularity, cobblestone, stone block, wood block, and macadam continued in general use. Telephone, telegraph, and electric light poles and wires, all rare or missing in the seventies, became chronic by the

American cities

[1] Josiah Strong, *The Twentieth Century City* (1898), is a useful study written from the sociological point of view.

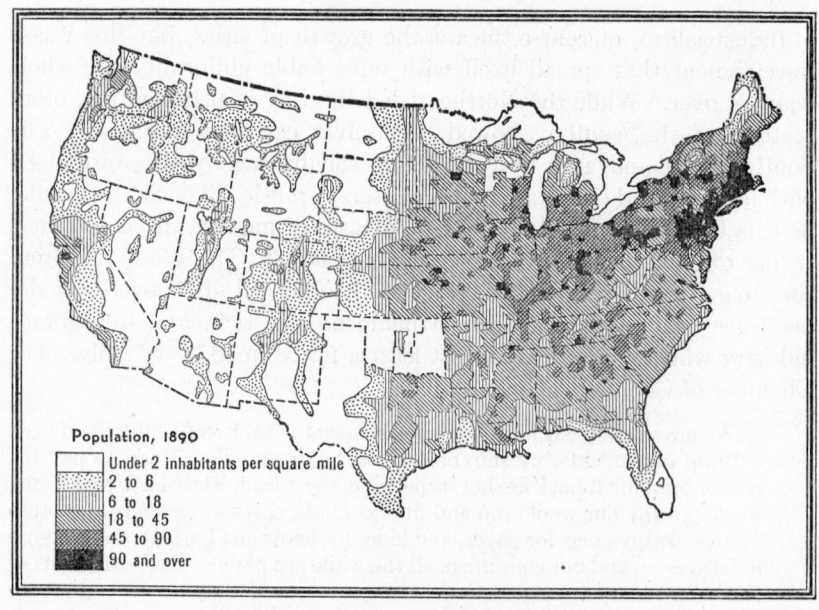

DENSITY OF POPULATION, 1890

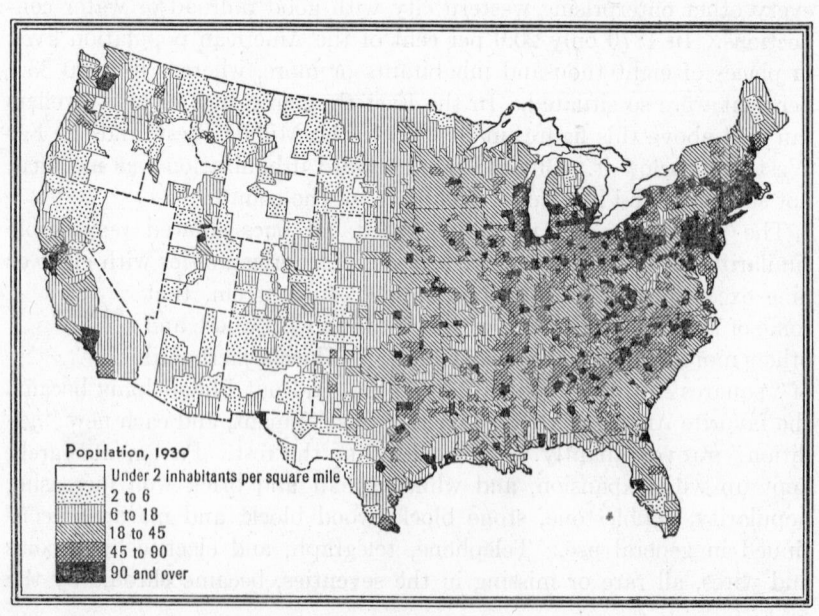

DENSITY OF POPULATION, 1930

nineties, and competed with trees and fences for space at the sides of roads and railroads. Business districts at any given time were everywhere much alike, but each decade saw the height of downtown buildings increase. The first of the skyscrapers, made possible by the use of structural steel and iron, was the ten-storied Home Insurance Building of Chicago, completed in 1885. Thereafter, with one accord, city skylines rose, while traffic congestion increased in spite of the best efforts of horsecars, cable cars, elevated railways, and electric streetcars to keep pace with it. For those who could afford the time and cost of transportation to work, residence districts pushed farther and farther into the surrounding country; for those who could not, apartment houses, tenements, and slum districts were multiplied. Unknown to the cities of the nineteenth century were the long lines of automobiles, the garages, the filling stations, and the motion-picture "palaces" of today. Omnipresent then, but almost obsolete now, were horse-drawn vehicles, livery stables, blacksmith shops, and saloons with shuttered doors. But the uniformity of yesterday is matched only by the uniformity of today.

Behind these externals lay a pattern of life that varied little from city to city. The great majority of city-dwellers were employees of industry or trade, dependent upon wages for their daily bread. From eighty to ninety per cent of them rented the space they lived in. Except in the South, unskilled labor was recruited mainly from the less assimilable immigrant groups, who, at least for a generation, lived in foreign "quarters," and clung tenaciously to their foreign ways. While a few women in the upper strata of society grumbled that the opportunity for "careers" was still in large measure denied them, those on the lower levels suffered no such sorrows. The percentage of women gainfully employed rose from fifteen per cent in 1870 to twenty per cent in 1900. In Philadelphia, by the latter year, one-third of the women (counting girls over ten years of age) worked for wages away from their homes. Wherever it could be used to advantage, child labor was ruthlessly exploited — in the cotton-mills of the South, in the sweatshops of the East, in the packing-plants of the West. The middle classes, who depended upon regular incomes or salaries instead of wages, were for the most part native Americans who had come to the cities from the rural districts. Naturally, most of them retained in the cities the characteristics and customs of country-dwellers, so that American cities in their cultural aspects became, in a sense, merely overgrown country towns. A small fraction of the population enjoyed large incomes, and some of them, particularly the *nouveaux riches*, laid firm foundations for Thorstein Veblen's theory of conspicuous waste.[1]

[1] Thorstein Veblen, *The Theory of the Leisure Class* (1899), launched a strong attack on orthodox economic theories with reference to capital and industry.

It would be a mistake, however, to assume that the United States was merely a nation of cities. More than sixty per cent of the people, as late as 1900, still lived in the country, or in towns of less than **Rural America** four thousand inhabitants. Practically all of these, and many more besides, depended directly or indirectly upon agriculture for their livelihood. Even the cities, in the last analysis, owed much to the farms, for throughout the nineteenth century an abundant farm demand, restricted from foreign purchases by a protective tariff policy, absorbed the products of the city factories, and spared American manufacturers the necessity of finding in foreign markets an outlet for their goods. For agriculture, as for industry, these were revolutionary years. New tools had to be learned and used, new types of crops had to be raised to suit the city markets, experiments with diversification and standardization had to be carried through, a rising price for farmlands had to be faced. Less and less the American farmer farmed according to ritual; more and more he used his intelligence and the reports of scientific investigators to improve his profits. Caught securely in the meshes of the prevailing economic system, he made every effort to understand it and to bend it to his needs. The farmer movements of the period were not the work of wild-eyed radicals; the farm leaders and a host of well-informed followers based their arguments upon reasoning as sound as that which guided the actions of the prudent industrialist. The interests of the farmers perhaps collided with those of the industrialists, but that did not necessarily make the farm policies radical.

Farm life tended gradually to merge with village life. On Saturdays farmers went to town to trade; on Sundays they went to town to church; on other days when work was not too pressing they went to town, with or without excuses. Retired farmers went to town to live and to be visited by their children, who in many cases were now their tenants. Farm boys and girls went to school in town, got jobs in town, and, when they could, set out with the town boys and girls for the city. Farmers and farm wives borrowed from the town the conveniences that the town had borrowed from the city. Steadily, the extreme isolation of farm life broke down — a process that the rural free delivery of mail, rural telephones, rural electrification, the automobile, and the radio were soon to accelerate immeasurably.

Country towns and villages enjoyed an importance during most of the nineteenth century that they have entirely lost today, and were beginning to lose at its close. As centers of trade for the sur-
Town life rounding countryside, they could count upon a certain amount of steady business. The stores might be strung along a single "Main Street," or they might surround a central block on which, in

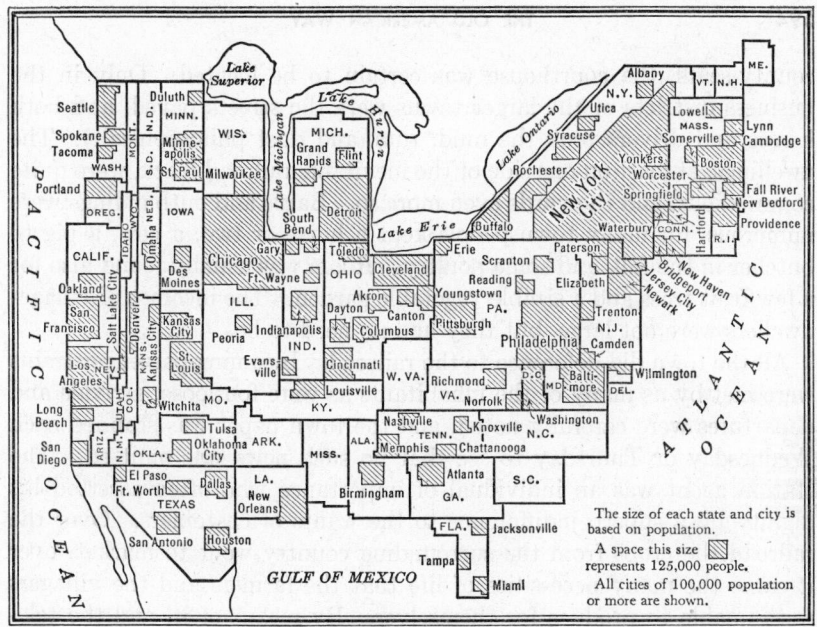

The size of each state and city is based on population.

A space this size represents 125,000 people.

All cities of 100,000 population or more are shown.

Copyright reproduced by permission of Erwin, Wasey & Co., N.Y.

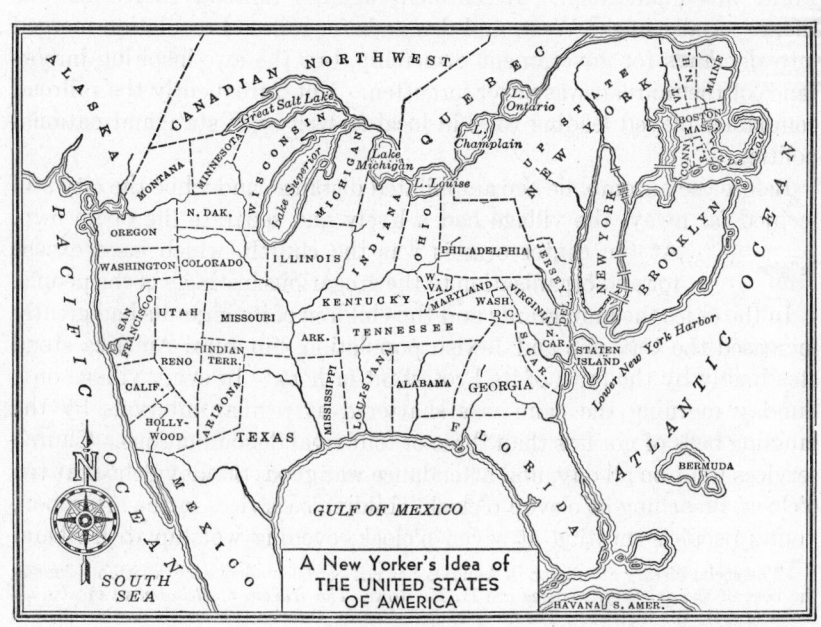

A New Yorker's Idea of
THE UNITED STATES
OF AMERICA

Based on a map copyrighted by Daniel K. Wallingford, N.Y.C.

RELATIVE IMPORTANCE OF CITY AND COUNTRY
POPULATIONS

county-seats, the courthouse was certain to be located. Only in the business districts of the larger towns were the streets paved, and both horses and drivers took the mud, ruts, and dust philosophically. The dwellings, at least on one side of the inevitable railroad track, were quite commodious, and the yards even more so. Barns and outbuildings were numerous, for many townspeople kept a horse or two, a cow, a pig to butcher in the fall, and some poultry. Room was usually found also for a few fruit trees and a sizable vegetable garden. The incomes of village-dwellers were not large, but they had no need to be.

All the town did deference to the railroad. Incoming passenger trains were met by as many of the inhabitants as were footloose, arrivals and departures were carefully noted, and the town paper was scanned each Wednesday or Thursday to see that no such news was omitted. The station agent was an individual of importance who often asserted his dignity by a superb indifference to the wants of customers. Over the railroad the crops from the surrounding country went to market, over it came the many necessities of life that the farmers and the villagers were unable to produce for themselves. By means of it, and the telegraph line that seemed somehow a part of it, contact with the rest of the world was maintained. Resentment against railroad extortions was rife, especially in the West, and demands for railroad regulation merged into demands for government ownership, but the awe-inspiring importance of the railroad was never forgotten. Not infrequently the railroad companies played leading rôles in local as well as in state and national politics.

Before the automobile age annihilated distance, and while the city still seemed far away, the village had a lively and separate life of its own. At the center of this was the church, which gave excuse for and organization to the gregarious instincts of the people.

Religion

In the cities the immigrants and the children of immigrants had greatly increased the Catholic and Jewish population, but rural America stood steadfastly by the faith of its Protestant fathers.[1] In every village on a Sunday morning the calm was shattered at regular intervals by the jangling bells of not less than three or four rival denominations. Church services went on all day, and attendance was good: Sunday School at ten o'clock, preaching at eleven o'clock, children's services in the afternoon, young people's meeting at seven o'clock, evening worship with liberal

---

[1] The social history of religion in America has not yet been adequately written. Among the best of the existing treatises are H. K. Rowe, *The History of Religion in the United States* (1924); W. W. Sweet, *The Story of Religions in America* (1930); H. K. Carroll, *The Religious Forces of the United States* (1912). On the subject of revivals, see F. G. Beardsley, *A History of American Revivals* (1912); G. C. Loud, *Evangelized America* (1928); and H. C. Weber, *Evangelism* (1929). Thomas Beer, *The Mauve Decade* (1926), is smart and cynical on all aspects of the society of the times.

congregational singing at eight o'clock. Weekday services included prayer-meetings on Wednesday or Thursday evening, to which only a handful of the most devout repaired; better-attended meetings of ladies' aid societies, missionary societies, and guilds, all absorbed in money-raising efforts; choir-practice for the faithful, if somewhat storm-tossed, musical contingent; and "protracted meetings," or "revivals," held night after night for several weeks once or twice each year. For these long meetings evangelists who imitated the methods of Moody and Sankey were often called in to aid the local pastors, and with good luck hundreds might be induced to "make their profession of faith." The old emotionalism of the frontier was not quite dead. "Shouting" was not unusual, "conversion" was for many an intensely exciting experience, and preaching reached its climax of success when "not a dry eye was left in the house." A few country churches, each in its mournful setting of tombstones, still managed to survive, as the long rows of teams tied each Sunday to the church's hitch-racks well attested. Farm families, however, preferred increasingly to attend church in town and so the country congregations dwindled.

Theologically speaking, the great problem of the times was the attempt of religion to digest the scientists' doctrine of evolution. For the older generation, of whatever denomination, this was asking a great deal. The idea of an infallible Church or an infallible Book had been too long and too steadfastly maintained to be surrendered without a struggle, and heresy charges drove many of the modernists from their pulpits. But the reasonableness of the evolutionary hypothesis could not be lost indefinitely on a world that owed so much to scientific discovery. Prominent clerics, among them Henry Ward Beecher and Lyman Abbott, attempted to reconcile science and religion, and the popular defense of evolution made by a Scotchman, Henry Drummond, in his book *Natural Law in the Spiritual World* (1884), profoundly impressed the American reading public.[1] For the most part American thinkers, in the struggle over evolution and the literal interpretation of the Scriptures, merely followed the lead of Europeans; if there was an American contribution to the controversy, it was to the effect that, after all, conduct was far more important than belief. Laymen, a little befuddled by the uproar, called for practical rather than theoretical Christianity, adopted as a part of their creed the temperance efforts of the Woman's Christian Temperance Union and the Anti-Saloon League, gave friendly support to the establishment of institutional churches that could minister to the spirit through the flesh,

Science vs. religion

[1] But see also A. D. White, *A History of the Warfare of Science with Theology in Christendom* (2 vols., 1896).

applauded Jane Addams of Chicago and Lillian D. Wald of New York for their settlement work, and held such agencies of "uplift" as lecture courses and Chautauqua programs to be laudable byproducts of Christianity.[1] As already noted, Christian Science, the first new American religion since Mormonism, went to the logical extreme of asserting the complete control of mind over matter. Thus might the spirit itself minister to the flesh, and religion serve the practical purpose of keeping its devotees well.

Undoubtedly public education played an important part in the standardizing process so characteristic of the times. During these years the public-school system achieved the pattern that with only slight variations it has maintained ever since. In the rural districts the one-room country school, ungraded but designed to carry its pupils through the equivalent of eight grades in town, still endured. In the towns and villages an eight-grade elementary school, followed by a four-year high school, was the goal most often set and increasingly attained. State-supported normal schools for the training of teachers, a state-supported college of agriculture, and a state-supported university, which might or might not include the college of agriculture, completed the customary picture. Strangely, forty-five states and several territories, in spite of complete freedom to mold their educational systems as they chose, emerged with essentially the same system. Even the content of public education tended to become fixed. In the rural and elementary schools instruction in the "three R's" reigned supreme without much attention to "extras." High schools, in spite of some commendable efforts to prepare their graduates for life rather than for college, held steadfastly to a curriculum not far different from that of the old academies they supplanted. Practically all of the colleges and universities took up with the elective system that Charles W. Eliot had introduced at Harvard, but the courses thus offered, cafeteria fashion, differed little from campus to campus. Most of the older generation of instructors had been trained in Germany; most of the younger generation at Harvard or Johns Hopkins, the two universities that had pioneered the way for graduate work in America.[2] At the end of the century scarcely a college student anywhere was more than a single generation removed in his instruction from one or the other of these

Public education (margin note)

[1] The growing significance of settlement work is best set forth in Jane Addams, *Forty Years at Hull House* (1935), and Lillian D. Wald, *The House on Henry Street* (1915).

[2] D. C. Gilman, *The Launching of a University* (1906), tells the story for Johns Hopkins, and Henry James, *Charles W. Eliot* (2 vols., 1930), does a similar service for Harvard. On the University of Chicago, which played a worthy part in stimulating graduate study in the West, see T. W. Goodspeed, *William Rainey Harper, First President of the University of Chicago* (1928).

institutions. Students everywhere, thus exposed to about the same educational diet, tended to get about the same results from their college work and to emerge with strikingly similar points of view. Contacts in college with individuals from other parts of the country helped them to "rub off the rough corners," and still further promoted the cause of standardization. Private institutions, even those under religious leadership, shared almost equally, to the dismay of the orthodox, in the standardizing process. The earnest pursuit of truth for truth's sake, regardless of religious, political, or economic prejudices, met occasional set-backs, but the eloquent defense of academic freedom, made by the Regents of the University of Wisconsin in answer to an attack on Professor Richard T. Ely, the noted economist, raised a banner that institutions of higher learning the whole country over were increasingly willing to defend: "Whatever may be the limitations which trammel inquiry elsewhere, we believe that the great State University of Wisconsin should ever encourage that continual and fearless sifting and winnowing by which alone the truth can be found." [1]

Other evidence of the rapid drift toward standardization in American life may be cited almost at will. Improved means of transportation led to the formation of a host of national organizations, each with its annual meeting attended by delegates from the whole country over. Subjected to the same influences, the delegates carried back home the same ideas. Better means of communication led to the astonishing expansion of the Associated Press and other news-gathering agencies, which furnished identical stories to the readers of hundreds of different newspapers and thus laid the basis for a common reaction. The day when an editor such as Horace Greeley of the New York *Tribune* or Charles A. Dana of the *Sun* expressed his personality through his newspaper had long since passed. Among the new editors Joseph Pulitzer of the New York *World*, and William Randolph Hearst of the San Francisco *Examiner*, did indeed introduce an exaggerated type of sensationalism, but their methods were quickly copied by all except a few of the most conservative journals. Newspapers imitated one another in format as well as in content; they not only read alike; they looked alike. Magazines, even of the popular variety, built up national circulations, and promoted whatever cause they served in a national way. Musical "hits" registered in New York were whistled a few days later by the newsboys in every other American city, and within weeks had reached the country towns. Plays that enjoyed a "run" in New York soon took to the road, and were produced also by the numerous stock companies that flourished in the pre-motion-picture age. Chautauqua circuits of popular lecturers

[1] Richard T. Ely, *Ground Under Our Feet — an Autobiography* (1938).

and entertainers were formed to spin around like a top each season until the entire American map had been covered, and all who had ears to hear had heard.

Even sports became nationalized. Baseball, which in any recognizable form had been non-existent before the Civil War, developed during the seventies and eighties into the "great American game,"
Sports with a complicated system of major and minor leagues that every boy and youth in America understood. Football, which was introduced into the United States during the seventies as an adaptation of English Rugby, had by the nineties conquered most of the American colleges and universities. Professional boxing approached the level of respectability when "Gentleman Jim" Corbett won the heavyweight championship in 1892.[1] By this time, too, the bicycle had been tamed, and bicycling had become a fad that women and children as well as men could enjoy. For devotees of the less strenuous life there were such milder activities as lawn-tennis, roller-skating, and croquet. The poor no less than the rich, town- and country-dwellers no less than city-dwellers, found in sports a satisfying refuge from the workaday world, which replaced, in a sense, the excitement once associated with a developing frontier. And, at least for masculine America, the doings recorded on the "sports page" furnished lively topics of conversation when all else failed.

It would, of course, be ridiculous not to concede that striking differences as well as striking similarities have always existed, and will always exist, in a nation as vast as the United States. In many ways, no doubt, the differences were more important than the similarities. But the fact remains that by the end of the nineteenth century, American civilization had achieved a distinct pattern, a pattern quite as unique as that possessed by any other nation. Bryce's *American Commonwealth*, which first appeared in 1888, revealed this pattern with all its faults to thinking Americans. Thereupon the book itself became a powerful agency of standardization. Seized upon as a college text and repeatedly reissued, it served for a generation as the mirror with which Americans viewed themselves. Some of the things they saw they liked and meant to keep; others they definitely did not like and meant to change. In part, at least, out of this new comprehension came the heavy rumblings of reform with which the twentieth century opened.[2]

[1] A. G. Spalding, *America's National Game* (1911); A. M. Weyand, *American Football* (1926); Alexander Johnston, *Ten — and Out* (1927); F. R. Dulles, *America Learns to Play* (1940).

[2] Richard Hofstadter, *Social Darwinism in American Thought, 1860–1915* (1944), explores a most significant field. See also, by the same author, *The American Political Tradition and the Men Who Made It* (1948).

30

The End of Isolation

UNTIL well toward the end of the nineteenth century the foreign policy of the United States reflected primarily the interest of the American people in westward expansion. Washington's doctrine of isolation was designed to keep the new nation free from any European entanglements that might distract its attention **American isolation** from the main business in hand — the conquest of a continent. The Monroe Doctrine, by which European governments were warned to keep out of American affairs, was merely the converse of the same proposition. By it the United States hoped to end for all time the threat of outside interference with the workings of "manifest destiny." The War of 1812 and the war with Mexico were both expansionist wars, and the Civil War was fought, in considerable part at least, to decide whether the North or the South should have the advantage in the formation of new western states. During all these years the United States was busy at home. It cared little about the doings of other nations so long as they showed no desire to block the American policy of expansion. American political development was self-centered and introspective. American economic development was a frantic struggle to exploit the rich natural resources that the continent had divulged, and to satisfy, mainly by domestic production, the needs of a rapidly growing people. American diplomacy, especially during the quarter-century that followed the Civil War, was episodical and inconsequential.

By the last decade of the nineteenth century a change had set in. The era of continental expansion was over, the United States was full grown, the time-honored frontiering process was fading from the picture. Good free lands and good cheap lands were nearing exhaustion. Population penetration into the High Plains and the Rocky Mountain plateau all but eliminated from census maps the zone of uninhabited territory that until 1890 had stretched unbroken from the Canadian to the Mexican border. American industry was catching up on its assignment. Already, for many mines and factories, the time had come when the needs of the domestic market could be fully supplied, with a margin left over for sale abroad.   American capital had been multiplied many times over, and considerable sums now sought foreign investment.   The interest of the United States in itself alone began to give way to an active American interest in the whole wide world.   Isolation had lost its charm; increasingly the American government felt called upon to play an important part in international affairs.

James G. Blaine, twice Secretary of State (1881, 1889–92) has often been spoken of as the "harbinger of the new era." This, no doubt, is an exaggeration, but Blaine did attempt to widen the sphere of American influence to include, in fact as well as in theory, all of the Americas.   Toward European nations with an interest in the western hemisphere, but most particularly toward Great Britain, he adopted an uncompromising, almost belligerent, attitude.   While serving under Garfield, for example, he made a blustering, but unavailing, demand that the British government give up its rights under the Clayton-Bulwer Treaty of 1850 to joint control of any interoceanic canal that should be built.   Likewise, during his second term of office he tried to establish a kind of prescriptive right for the United States to the fur-seal fisheries of the Bering Sea, a contention that a joint Anglo-American arbitration commission was unable to approve. Most important of all, he sought consistently to promote the cause of "Pan-Americanism."

Blaine's foreign policy

Blaine's fondest dream was to induce the Latin-American states of North and South America to enter a kind of informal federation, with the United States, as an interested and friendly "elder sister," at its head. Through such a union Blaine hoped to eliminate wars between the lesser American nations and to promote better commercial relationships between them and the United States.   In pursuit of this goal, it fell to his lot to receive in Washington on October 2, 1889, the representatives of nineteen independent American republics.   Nothing could be accomplished on the important subject of arbitration, but the First Pan-American Congress, as this meeting came to be called, made considerable progress in the discussion of such important problems as the standardization of sanitary regulations, the building of an intercontinental railroad. and the adoption of uniform weights and measures, including a common silver coin.   One permanent result of the congress was the establishment of an International Bureau of American Republics, with headquarters in Washington.[1]

It is possible to discern in Blaine's foreign policy an effort to reserve the Pacific as a region for future American exploitation.   Blaine cultivated good relations with Japan, and at the same time managed to

[1] Alice Felt Tyler, *The Foreign Policy of James G. Blaine* (1927)

keep friendly with China in spite of the deepening antagonism between the two great Oriental nations. Nor was Blaine displeased at the prospect of the speedy annexation to the United States of Hawaii, for generations the chief stopping-place in the mid-Pacific for vessels bound to Asia, and a center of increasing importance for the production of sugar. When Americans in Hawaii staged a revolution with annexation to the United States as their goal, Blaine offered no objections, and a treaty of annexation was actually signed shortly after he left office, but never ratified. Not until McKinley became President, in 1898, was annexation actually accomplished, but Blaine had favored it, and hoped for it.[1] Blaine also sought to retain for the United States a foothold in the Samoan Islands, first tentatively marked out as early as 1872. Both Germany and Great Britain had interests in the Samoans, however, and international rivalry for commercial privileges became acute. A conference of the three contending parties, called by Bismarck, met in Berlin early in 1889, and decided on a tripartite protectorate, which worked badly and was abandoned in 1899. The islands were then divided between the United States and Germany, while Great Britain was indemnified for her withdrawal by title to the Gilbert and Solomon Islands, which had formerly belonged to Germany. These negotiations, from beginning to end, showed small regard for the traditional American doctrine of isolation.

Hawaii and Samoa

While Blaine's policy in the Pacific was later to pay substantial dividends, his plans for Pan-Americanism fell far short of the goals he had set. The United States minister to Chile, Patrick Egan, for whose appointment Blaine was responsible, openly took sides in a Chilean revolution, and even more unfortunately gave his support to the side that lost. While feeling against the United States was still high in Chile, American sailors on shore leave at Valparaiso became involved in street fighting that cost two of them their lives and others serious injuries. By threat of military reprisals, the United States collected an indemnity of $75,000 for this "outrage," and built up an amount of ill-will throughout all Latin-America that could not be measured. These incidents undid nearly everything Blaine had accomplished. Under the terms of the McKinley Act he negotiated a few useful trade treaties, and the First Pan-American Conference set a precedent that later on was to become significant, but for the most part Blaine's high hopes of international accord among the Americas were long to remain unrealized.

Chile

That the aggressive nature of American diplomacy was neither a per-

[1] H. W. Bradley, *The American Frontier in Hawaii; The Pioneers, 1789–1843* (1942), and S. K. Stevens, *American Expansion in Hawaii, 1842–1898* (1945), recount the early history.

sonal policy of Blaine's nor a party policy of the Republicans was made
evident shortly after Harrison left office by Cleveland's
handling of the Venezuelan boundary dispute. The boundary line between Venezuela and British Guiana lay in a
tropical wilderness and had never been properly delimited.

The
Venezuelan
controversy

Long a subject of desultory controversy, the subject became really interesting when the news came out that gold had been discovered in the disputed territory. To Cleveland the prospect of the British government
enforcing its will upon Venezuela, as the American government had
recently enforced its will upon Chile, was extremely disquieting, for he
had made up his mind that in case such action resulted in the taking of
territory that properly belonged to an American nation the Monroe
Doctrine would clearly have been violated. In his message to Congress
of 1894, he therefore expressed his hope that the matter would be arbi-
trated, and Congress by resolution promptly echoed his sentiments.
The English government, however, refused to submit the whole question
to arbitration, although pointing out that it had long been willing to
arbitrate within certain specified limits. This attitude satisfied neither
Cleveland nor his aggressive Secretary of State, Richard Olney, who in a
statement of June 20, 1895, declared that "the United States is practically sovereign upon this continent, and its fiat is law."

At first the British were in no mood to back down, and Cleveland
plainly threatened war. Eventually, however, a plan of arbitration
satisfactory to the United States was accepted, and Americans talked
loudly of their diplomatic triumph. Undoubtedly the British right-
about face was due to other circumstances than the American representations. In particular, a telegram of congratulations, sent by Kaiser
Wilhelm II of Germany to Paul Kruger, the anti-British Boer leader in
South Africa, emphasized the fact that the future enemy of Great Britain
was to be Germany, rather than the United States. Indeed, friendship
with the United States became from this time forward an earnest objective of British diplomacy. The strong stand that the United States had
taken on behalf of a Latin-American republic should have made for
better relations between the United States and her neighbors, also, but
Olney's bombastic words robbed the American victory of its best fruits.
The "Colossus of the North" was still mistrusted.[1]

England was not the only European power, however, whose concern
with American affairs led to diplomatic difficulties with the United States.

Cuba

Spain still held a remnant of her once great American empire,
notably the two islands of Cuba and Puerto Rico just south

---

[1] Henry James, *Richard Olney and His Public Service* (1923), is a good biography. On
the Venezuelan affair see also A. L. P. Dennis, *Adventures in American Diplomacy, 1896–
1906* (1928), and Dexter Perkins, *The Monroe Doctrine, 1867–1907* (1937).

of the Atlantic seaboard of the United States. Cuba had long been a storm-center in Spanish-American relations. Before the Civil War southern expansionists had coveted the island; after the war Cuban insurrectionists had repeatedly sought to involve the United States in their struggles. For ten years, from 1868 to 1878, the island was in constant turmoil, and in 1895 another revolt broke out. This second insurrection came about in no small part as a result of American tariff legislation. The McKinley Act of 1890, which admitted raw sugar free of duty and compensated American growers by a bounty, had enormously stimulated the Cuban sugar industry. Much new foreign capital was poured into Cuban plantations, and for a brief period the island enjoyed unusual prosperity. When, in 1894, the Wilson-Gorman Act again made raw sugar dutiable, Cuban sugar prices declined precipitately, and the era of prosperity vanished as rapidly as it had come. With the American market for other Cuban commodities, notably tobacco, also weakened by the depression, hard times and unemployment provided a convenient setting for insurrection.

It is an exaggeration to speak of the disorder in Cuba that broke out in 1895 as a revolution, although citizens of the United States tended to view it in that light. Maximo Gomez, the Cuban leader, was utterly unable to maintain a government, or even to keep an army in the field. What he promoted was insurrection rather than revolution, and his chief weapon was devastation. Small guerrilla bands, often operating by night rather than by day, destroyed sugar-mills and laid waste plantations belonging to Spanish loyalists. Carrying on at first almost without military equipment, the Cuban *insurrectos* were soon receiving aid from other Cubans who resided in the United States, and from American sympathizers, most of whom thought of Gomez and his guerrillas in terms that might better have been applied to George Washington and the patriot army of 1776. In New York a Cuban junta, which called itself the Cuban government, sold bonds, and with the proceeds bought and shipped arms to the insurrectionary forces.

Nature of the Cuban revolt

Spanish methods of dealing with the insurrection were both brutal and effective. "Butcher" Weyler, the Spanish commander in Cuba, by using "corrals" of barbed wire and blockhouses to separate the more peaceful sections of the island from the more warlike, and by herding all suspects into *reconcentrado* camps, was well along with the task of restoring order when the Cuban situation began to make the headlines in American newspapers. Reporters told lurid tales of the bad conditions they saw, and Americans who resided in Cuba or who visited the island for the purpose corrobo-

Spanish methods of warfare

rated the newspaper accounts. The American public, long unaccustomed to the horrors of war, began to feel that the government of the United States should take a hand in the situation, and do something to "reform" the war. Both Cleveland and McKinley tried hard to keep the peace, and the latter had only this object in mind when he made strong representations to the Spanish government "against the uncivilized and inhuman" conduct of Weyler's campaign.[1] The Spanish government, conscious of the fact that the proximity of the United States to Cuba gave the Americans an immense military advantage, made every effort to comply with McKinley's requests, even ordering the abandonment of the *reconcentrado* policy, and the recall of Weyler. In fact, the American minister to Spain informed his government that the Spanish officials, if given a little time, would agree to whatever demands the United States cared to make.

Whatever chance there was of a peaceful settlement evaporated as a result of two untoward incidents. The first was the publication of a private letter written by de Lôme, the Spanish minister in Washington, to a friend in Cuba. This letter, purloined from the mails and published in the newspapers, described McKinley as a "spineless politician." Inasmuch as the original one-hundred-per-cent American, Theodore Roosevelt, held that the President had "no more backbone than a chocolate éclair," de Lôme's statement may not have been altogether inaccurate, but it was one thing for an American citizen to speak his mind about the President, and quite another for a foreign minister to make such a statement. De Lôme's recall was immediately demanded, and the offending minister resigned. The other unfortunate incident was the destruction of the battleship *Maine* in Havana Harbor, February 15, 1898, with heavy loss of life. That the Spanish government could have promoted such a catastrophe at a time when its officials were making every effort to keep on good terms with the United States seems incredible, but the American public jumped immediately to the conclusion that Spain was responsible. The battle-cry, "Remember the Maine," rent the air, and the demands on Spain made by the American government became more and more peremptory.

It is possible that war might have been averted had McKinley had the same sort of courage that John Adams exhibited in 1798, when he prevented war between the United States and France. Had the President decided to make a firm stand for peace, he would have received the cordial support of Marcus A. Hanna and many another leading capitalist who

The approach of war

[1] Events leading up to the Spanish-American War are well chronicled in F. E. Chadwick, *The Relations of the United States and Spain: Diplomacy* (1909), but some new material is presented in Orestes Ferrara, *The Last Spanish War* (1937). See also Bemis, *American Secretaries of State*, ix.

feared the economic unsettlement that war might bring. But McKinley knew that opposition to following the lead of the plutocrats on this, or any other matter, was already rife among the young Republicans, and he believed that only by yielding to the popular clamor for war could he be certain of holding his party together. Finally, on April 9, the Spanish government, in response to a joint peace plea, delivered by the great powers of Europe to both Spain and the United States, ordered the cessation of hostilities in Cuba and gave in to the American contentions on every essential point. Nevertheless, the President on April 11 sent a war message to Congress. Six days later Congress by joint resolution demanded that Spain withdraw from Cuba, and authorized the President to use the military and naval forces of the United States to effect that end. Expressly disclaiming any intent to add Cuba to the United States, the resolution went on to claim that the people of the island were "and of right ought to be free and independent."

The outbreak of hostilities in this "needless war," as James Ford Rhodes, the historian, later described it, did not take place because of the failure of American diplomacy. War came in spite of the complete success of American diplomacy, and primarily because the American people wanted to have a war. This
A needless war
unnatural craving was in part a legacy of the Civil War, a struggle which for more than thirty years had colored almost every aspect of American thought and action. Veterans of the Civil War were held in honor because of their war record, and particularly in politics they tended to fare better than the men who had stayed at home. As the old soldiers grew older, they forgot the seamy side of war, and told tall tales of heroics and adventure. Young America, typified by Theodore Roosevelt, had grown to manhood on a steady diet of Civil War glorification. It envied the boys in blue or gray, and felt cheated that it had had no chance to win distinction for itself in war. Older America was likewise out to get its thrill — a vicarious and reassuring thrill. It took pride in the great new nation that it had seen emerge, but its faith was somehow tinctured with doubt. Had the United States really arrived as a nation, or was it only on its way? Perhaps by a baptism of blood the country could prove to itself and to the rest of the world that it was really great. If the United States could win a war, who could deny it the high station among the nations of the world to which it aspired? Years later, Theodore Roosevelt recaptured the atmosphere of 1898 when he mourned apologetically, "It wasn't much of a war, but it was the best war we had." America in the spring of 1898 was ripe for any war, and the country's mood was not to be denied.

As the American people entered the war, they were extremely conscious and proud of the new "white navy" by means of which they hoped to win it. The construction of steel ships had begun during the eighties, in part as a means of reducing the ever-vexatious surplus; but even in the "heart-breaking nineties," when funds were low, more and more units were added to the navy. By that time Admiral Alfred Thayer Mahan had begun the publication of a series of books which demonstrated quite conclusively that the influence of sea-power on a nation's destinies, particularly in wartime, was decisive.[1] Mahan made important converts, among them Theodore Roosevelt, whom McKinley appointed Assistant Secretary of the Navy in 1897. In office Roosevelt made a fetish of naval efficiency, and insisted above all else on target practice. Ten days after the *Maine* went down, he took advantage of his superior's absence from Washington to put the entire navy on a war footing. "The very devil seemed to possess him." It was due to Roosevelt's planning, also, that Commodore George Dewey was in command of an American squadron in Asiatic waters — in striking distance of the Spanish fleet in Manila Bay — when war broke out. The stronger portion of the American navy, however, was mobilized off Chesapeake Bay under command of Captain (later Rear-Admiral) William T. Sampson. A new battleship, the *Oregon*, uselessly located in the North Pacific, was ordered to the Atlantic, and on March 19 began a voyage around Cape Horn that for two months consumed the interest of the newspaper-reading public.

The American navy

If the navy was well prepared for war, undoubtedly the army was not. Its 27,000 officers and men were scattered over the country in small garrisons; it lacked a central planning board comparable to the present general staff; its high-ranking officers had age rather than efficiency to commend them. The second line of defense, the National Guard of the states, was of uncertain size and merit, but capable of great expansion in case of need. Everyone took it for granted, however, that if a really important war should develop, a volunteer army, organized along the lines of the Union army in the Civil War, would do most of the fighting. And yet Congress, for all its impatience to get on with the war, did little to make ready for the conflict before it came. Fifty million dollars were appropriated for the national defense in March, 1898, but not until late in April, after the war resolutions had been passed, were extensive army increases authorized. At that time Congress voted an expansion of the regular army to 62,597 men, and the creation of a volunteer army of 125,000. While most of the volunteers were to be raised through the states, as in the Civil War, the law

The army

[1] Harold and Margaret Sprout, *The Rise of American Naval Power, 1776–1918* (1939). Admiral Mahan tells his own story in *From Sail to Steam; Recollections of Naval Life* (1907).

also provided that the President might accept directly into the national service three regiments of volunteer cavalry. This provision was included primarily to enable Theodore Roosevelt, who now resigned as Assistant Secretary of the Navy, to lead a regiment into battle. With the help of Captain Leonard Wood, an officer in the medical corps, Roosevelt brought together a motley array of ex-cowboys, college athletes, and adventurers to form the "First United States Volunteer Cavalry," or, as they were more generally called, the "Rough Riders." Since Roosevelt had had no military experience whatever, he modestly accepted only a lieutenant-colonelcy, while the command of the regiment went to Wood.

The first blow of the war was struck by Admiral Dewey at Manila Bay, into which the American commander had led his little fleet of four cruisers and three minor war-craft on the early morning of May 1. There, in leisurely fashion, with time out for breakfast, Dewey's ships proceeded methodically to the destruction of the Spanish ships, which their commander, Admiral Montojo, who knew full well what was in store for him, had thoughtfully stationed at some distance from the defenses of Manila so that the city might be spared the danger of shell-fire and in shallow water where as many as possible of his men might escape. The Spanish losses in this one-sided battle included three hundred and eighty-one killed, besides numerous wounded, while not an American was killed and only seven or eight were wounded.[1]

Popular rejoicing in the United States on the receipt of the news

Dewey at
Manila

[1] The most entertaining account of the war is Walter Millis, *The Martial Spirit* (1931). The book is undocumented, but in the main shows careful use of source material. F. E. Chadwick, *The Relations of the United States and Spain; The Spanish-American War* (1911), is dependable but dull. J. H. Latané, *America as a World Power, 1897–1907* (1907), is the volume covering the period for the *American Nation* series, and C. R. Fish, *The Path of Empire* (1919), for the *Chronicles of America*. On the battle of Manila Bay, see the *Autobiography of George Dewey* (1916).

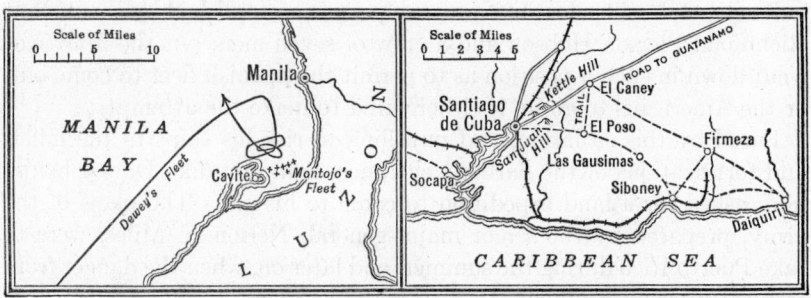

MANILA BAY   SANTIAGO DE CUBA

from Manila Bay was unrestrained, but Dewey's position was in reality far from comfortable. He had possession of the Bay, but not one foot of land. Naturally he lost no time in urging the American government to send an American expeditionary force to his aid, but the needed land forces did not arrive until the end of July. Meantime, Dewey had had a misunderstanding that might have been serious with Admiral Diedrich, commander of a German fleet that had anchored in the harbor, but, thanks to hearty co-operation from a British squadron under Captain Chichester, the affair was settled amicably. When finally General Wesley Merritt, with a force of nearly eleven thousand men, arrived on the scene, the city of Manila was captured with little more than "token" resistance. By that time both the Spanish and the Americans were less worried about each other than about the presence of a large army of Philippine insurgents under Emilio Aguinaldo, a native leader whom the Spanish had once exiled, but whom Dewey had unwisely brought back home. Curiously, the surrender of Manila to the Americans occurred August 14, with both parties unaware of the fact that on the other side of the world, two calendar days before, an armistice had been signed.

Events in the Atlantic theater had moved less swiftly than in the Pacific, but the outcome was quite as decisive. The first concern of the American fleet was to intercept and destroy a Spanish squadron, known to have set sail from the Cape Verde Islands on April 29 bound for American waters. But the Spanish commander, Cervera, succeeded in reaching the port of Santiago de Cuba without once being challenged by the Americans on the high seas. There he was presently blockaded by Admiral Sampson's entire fleet, including the lately arrived *Oregon*. The Spanish ships were no match for the Americans, and Cervera on this account seemed bent on avoiding battle. Sampson's first impulse seems to have been to block the narrow entrance to the harbor by sinking an old collier, the *Merrimac*, in its channel. This feat of seamanship was accomplished by Lieutenant Richmond Pierson Hobson and a crew of seven men, but the *Merrimac* went down in such a position as to permit the Spanish fleet to come out, or the Americans to go in, if either cared to make the attempt.

The Atlantic theater

Faced by this situation, and unwilling to risk his ships to the mines and fortifications of the harbor's entrance, Sampson, like Dewey before him, asked for a land expedition to come to his aid. The plans of the army, prepared by the senior major-general, Nelson A. Miles, were to take Puerto Rico during the summer, and later on, when the danger from tropical diseases would be less, to make a frontal assault on Havana. All this had now to be changed, and an expeditionary force had to be dispatched without further preparations to Santiago. Amidst literally indescribable confusion, some six thousand troops, all from the regular army except Theodore Roosevelt's Rough Riders (without their horses), were dispatched from Tampa Bay, Florida, on June 14, and six days later appeared off Santiago. From their first meeting, General William R. Shafter, in command of the army, and Admiral Sampson, in command of the navy, misunderstood each other perfectly. Nevertheless, the troops somehow got ashore several miles to the east of the harbor, and with the Rough Riders ever in the thick of the fray began an advance that by the first days of July had led them to the storming of San Juan Hill, close to the city's last defenses. By this time, however, the American striking force was almost spent, and the officers in command scarcely knew whether to retreat or to advance. "We are within measurable distance of a terrible military disaster," wrote Theodore Roosevelt.

But as events proved the Spanish were even more thoroughly disheartened than the Americans. Their army was short of ammunition and the city was on the verge of famine. Nothing, it seemed, could halt the American advance. Ultimate surrender was inevitable. Under orders from Madrid, Admiral Cervera *Naval battle of Santiago* made a brave attempt on July 3 to escape with his squadron from the harbor, but American shells set his wooden-decked ships afire, and one after another they had to be beached. When the fight was over, he had lost every ship, and had casualties of four hundred killed and wounded; the American fleet was practically unharmed, and had lost one man killed and one man wounded. At the time the battle began, Admiral Sampson was several miles distant in conference with Shafter, and the highest ranking officer on the scene was Commodore Schley. Before the battle ended, Sampson's flagship was participating in the fighting, and the American ships, with the exception of the one on which Schley was stationed, had throughout obeyed Sampson's orders and ignored Schley's. Nevertheless the debate long raged in the newspapers, "Was it Sampson, or was it Schley?" Theodore Roosevelt's verdict that there was "glory enough for all" probably overstated the facts, and certainly made few converts of partisans.

With Cuba's naval protection gone and communications with Spain cut, there was nothing left for the Spanish government to do but to sue for peace. This it did through the French embassy at Washington, which opened negotiations for an armistice on July *The war ends* 13. Three days later, General Toral, in command of the Spanish forces at Santiago, signed articles of capitulation with Shafter.[1] By this time

---

[1] For those with an interest in military detail, the work of Colonel H. H. Sargent, *The Campaign of Santiago de Cuba* (3 vols., 1907), should prove satisfactory. Joseph Wheeler, *The Santiago Campaign* (1899), and John Bigelow, Jr., *Reminiscences of the Santiago Campaign* (1899), are interesting personal accounts.

General Miles, lest he be too late, was beginning his expedition to Puerto Rico, which, lacking opposition, proved to be in comparison with the Santiago campaign a model of efficiency. The chief purpose of the expedition was to enable the United States with better grace, to lay claim to the island, for the French ambassador soon learned that before the United States would make peace, Spain must agree to withdraw entirely from the western hemisphere. Spanish sovereignty over Cuba must be relinquished, and all the rest of the Spanish West Indies, including Puerto Rico, must be ceded to the United States. On the other side of the world the American government demanded the cession of an island in the Ladrones (midway between Hawaii and the Philippines), and possession of the city, harbor, and bay of Manila, pending determination in the treaty of the "control, disposition, and government" of the Philippines. In view of these somewhat extraordinary territorial demands, the United States promised to waive for the time being "any demand for pecuniary indemnity." On these terms an armistice was signed on August 12, and the war was over.

Commissioners from the United States and Spain met in Paris, October 1, 1898, to work out the details of peace. The American delegation consisted of William R. Day, chairman, who was **Peace negotiations** required to resign as Secretary of State to accept the assignment, three leading senators of whom one was a Democrat, and a prominent Republican newspaper editor. McKinley's instructions gave the commissioners no option as to the expulsion of the Spanish Empire from America, but the Spanish delegation argued plausibly that, inasmuch as there was no government in Cuba worthy of the name, that island should be ceded direct to the United States, which would thereby become responsible for the Cuban debt. The Americans refused this dubious proffer. They agreed that the United States should occupy the island temporarily, but they successfully insisted that Spain should assume the island's debt. The most heated dispute was over the Philippine Islands, which McKinley soon informed the American commissioners they must somehow obtain. Since the total area of the Philippines was seven thousand square miles greater than that of the British Isles, and since in all this vast space the United States had occupied only one city, the demand seemed utterly unjustified on military grounds. Spanish protests were long-drawn-out, and in the end the Spanish commissioners won an extraordinary concession. Without exactly explaining why it was to be done, the United States agreed to "pay to Spain the sum of twenty million dollars within three months after the exchange of the ratifications of the present treaty." Money payments were usually demanded of vanquished powers instead of being accorded to them, but, in view of the extensive territorial cessions the United States had obtained, a money indemnity could hardly have been required. The twenty million dollars was variously explained as representing the difference in value between what the United States had actually conquered and what it insisted on taking, or the investment the Spanish government had made in the Philippines, or what it was worth to the United States in satisfaction just to have a war and win it. On December 10, 1898, the treaty was finally signed, and early next month the President submitted it to the Senate for ratification.

For a time there was danger that the necessary two-thirds majority could not be obtained.[1] Led by the resourceful William Jennings Bryan, "anti-imperialists" gave battle the whole country over against so wide a departure from American tradition as was involved in the acquisition of the Philippines. Not Democrats merely, but many prominent Republicans also, including Senator Hale of Maine and Senator Hoar of Massachusetts, objected strenuously to the terms of the treaty, and when the time came voted against ratification. Speaker Thomas B. Reed was "terribly bitter" in his opposition, and according to Senator Lodge was "saying all sorts of ugly things about the Administration and its policy." Ultimately Reed resigned his seat in the House and retired from politics rather than stand with his party on such an issue. Andrew Carnegie went to Washington and lobbied against the treaty. Strange as it may seem, the man who finally saved the treaty was Bryan. Some attribute this move to his conviction that free silver would not provide the Democrats with a winning issue in 1900, and his desire to supplement free silver with anti-imperialism. Others argue exactly the other way around, that he was eager to prevent imperialism from becoming the principal issue, and wished only to hold the field open for free silver. Whatever his motives, Bryan urged that the proper policy for the moment was to accept the treaty, and then to demand that the Philippines be set free. Without the efforts of the Democratic leader, who conferred in Washington with wavering Democrats and Populists, it seems certain that the administration would have lost. As it was, ten Democrats and eight Populists voted with thirty-nine Republicans to give the treaty one more than the two-thirds majority required for ratification.

From the Spanish-American War the United States emerged as a world power. It had defeated a European nation in war, and it had added to its possessions regions distant enough and different enough that none could deny the existence of an American Empire. Alaska, the

[1] The struggle over ratification is well told in W. S. Holt, *Treaties Defeated by the Senate* (1933).

Hawaiian Islands, the Philippines, Puerto Rico, Guam, all these and a

The United
States as a
world power

number of minor islands, together with the temporary occupation of Cuba, satisfied for the moment the ambitions of the most rabid of expansionists. Of these possessions Alaska and the Hawaiian Islands seemed most easily assimilable. Alaska [1] the United States had owned since 1867, but only since 1896, when gold was discovered in the Klondike, a near-by district in Canada, had the possibilities of "Seward's Folly," been realized. Thereafter, the discovery in Alaska itself of gold and other valuable mineral deposits had proved the acquisition to be an extremely profitable investment. Hawaii, likewise, furnished a worth-while addition to American economic resources, particularly because of the sugar it could produce. In governmental organization both Alaska and Hawaii became territories of the United States after the traditional pattern, although in neither instance was admission to statehood deemed likely.

The Spanish cessions presented many perplexing problems. Cuba had to be occupied, scoured into cleanliness, and provided with a govern-

Freedom for
Cuba

ment before it could be set free. Under General Leonard Wood as governor, and with the assistance of many American medical men, notably Major William C. Gorgas and Doctor Walter Reed, the pacification and sanitation of the island was accomplished with praiseworthy speed. As an incident to this task the mosquito carrier of yellow fever was identified, and the pestilence it spread brought under control. By 1901 the Cubans had formed a constitution, patterned after the Constitution of the United States, and were ready to begin self-rule. Before this could be accomplished, however, they were required by the United States to subscribe to the famous "Platt Amendment," which seriously limited the sovereignty of the new republic. Cuba might not make any treaty that would impair its independence, it must keep its debt within its capacity to pay, it must permit the United States to intervene with force in case that should be necessary to keep order, and it must carry out the plans of sanitation the United States had begun. When an insurrection broke out in Cuba in August, 1906, the United States exercised its right of intervention, and sent William Howard Taft to Cuba to "sit on the lid." For more than two years the American occupation continued. On several other occasions the United States made use of its right of intervention, but in every instance stopped short of annexation.[2]

[1] Jeannette P. Nichols, *Alaska* (1924); J. M. Callahan, *The Alaska Purchase and Americo-Canadian Relations* (1908); W. F. Willoughby, *Territories and Dependencies of the United States* (1905).

[2] R. H. Fitzgibbon, *Cuba and the United States, 1900–1935* (1935); D. A. Lockmiller, *Magoon in Cuba* (1938); Carleton Beals, *The Crime of Cuba* (1933).

The problem of Cuba was as nothing in comparison with the problem of the Philippines, for in annexing the latter the United States acquired also a full-blown insurrection. The Philippine population, which was a mixture of native races and immigrants from the Asiatic mainland, included about seven million Spanish-speaking and Roman Catholic Filipinos, besides perhaps two-thirds of a million wild and uncivilized Igorrotes and Moros. Under Spanish rule the islanders had suffered from neglect, exploitation, and oppression, and, when the war between the United States and Spain broke out, Filipino insurgents were seriously challenging Spanish supremacy. The insurrection was immensely aided by Dewey's return of its exiled leader, Emilio Aguinaldo, whose forces, by the time the United States had acquired title to the islands, actually held the upper hand everywhere except in Luzon. At first the Filipinos had assumed naïvely that the American promise of freedom for Cuba carried with it by implication the promise of freedom for the Philippines. When they learned that the United States had no such intentions, they turned in full force against the new invaders, and for two years and a half fought hard for their independence. Not until October 1, 1901, did the United States find it possible to announce the complete suppression of the insurrection, and for many months longer the facts failed to justify the statement.

The occupation of Puerto Rico involved fewer perplexities than confronted American officials either in the Philippines or in Cuba. The population of the island was less than a million, nearly two-thirds of whom were white, and the rest of Negro extraction. There had been no revolution and no war damage of consequence. American rule was accepted without enthusiasm, but without protest. Even under the military régime rapid strides were made toward the better sanitation of the island, the building of roads, and the re-ordering of public finance. So smoothly was the transition accomplished that as early as April 12, 1900, Congress passed the Foraker Act establishing a civil government for Puerto Rico, the first to be accorded any of the new possessions. The pattern of government thus set for the dependencies was similar to that of the traditional American territory, but with more limited privileges of self-government. Furthermore, residents of the island were not accorded full American citizenship, but were described as citizens of Puerto Rico.[1]

Meantime the people of the United States had had a chance to express

---

[1] Knowlton Mixer, *Porto Rico* (1926). An act of Congress signed March 2, 1917, provided the island with the customary territorial form of government, and declared its citizens to be citizens of the United States. Another act, dated May 17, 1932, substituted Puerto Rico for Porto Rico as the official name of the island.

themselves at the polls on the issue of "imperialism." Republican successes in the elections of 1898 denoted little more than
Election of 1900 general satisfaction at the victories won by Americans in
the war with Spain, but the presidential election of 1900 was
a pitched battle, with the forces favoring annexation of the Philippines
lined up solidly on one side, and those opposed on the other. The Republicans, with William McKinley once more their standard-bearer,
and with Theodore Roosevelt, the hero of San Juan Hill, as their candidate for Vice-President, rejoiced in the "new and noble responsibility"
that had come to the American people, and asserted that "no other
course was possible" in the Philippines than the one that had been taken.
The Democrats, still under the spell of Bryan's oratory, also renominated
their leader of the preceding campaign, but for second place they had
no war hero; only the time-worn Vice-President of Cleveland's second
administration, Adlai E. Stevenson of Illinois. Bryan himself had been
a colonel of Nebraska volunteers, but he had had no such luck with the
War Department in obtaining a chance to fight as had the Colonel on
the Republican ticket. To Bryan, "imperialism" was the "paramount
issue" of the campaign.

Throughout the campaign the debate on imperialism held the center
of the stage. The arguments were not new; they had all been used
while the Treaty of Paris was before the country. Nor was
Imperialism the paramount issue the decision ever in doubt. McKinley, as the cartoonists
so graphically portrayed, always had his "ear to the
ground," and he knew full well that he had read the public
mind aright. Nevertheless, Democratic orators dwelt long upon the
inconsistency of a democracy such as the United States fighting to suppress the ambitions of another people to be free. They cast William
McKinley in the rôle of George III, and Aguinaldo in that of George
Washington. They pointed out the practical difficulties involved. The
United States was wholly without experience in the governing of colonies.
How could it hope to solve the problems of a distant and alien race?
A great navy and a great army would be necessary to protect the new
possessions. Once the United States had depended upon the Atlantic
Ocean and the Pacific Ocean for its defense. But with Asiatic possessions
American military might must be expanded to reach far across the seas.

Republican orators had no difficulty in justifying all that had been
done. The Philippines, they claimed, offered an inviting missionary
field. The United States had at last an opportunity to extend the blessings of American civilization. The Filipinos were not yet capable of
governing themselves; freedom would mean only anarchy and misrule,
or perhaps conquest by some predatory commercial nation, such as

Germany or France. The United States had become a great power, and it must accept the responsibilities of greatness, or as Kipling phrased it, "Take up the White Man's Burden." There would be profits, too, good profits, from colonial trade. Besides, how could the United States be a really great nation if it had no colonies? Other great nations had colonies and were engaged in a mad scramble for more. Why should Americans deny themselves whatever glory colonial possessions would bring?

But it would be a mistake to assume that imperialism was the only issue of the campaign. On free silver and the tariff both parties defended the positions they had taken in 1896, and these issues swayed many voters. Cartoonists made merry with the "hold-your-nose-and-vote" crowd who in the confusion could not escape voting for something they heartily disliked, or against something they heartily approved. Shrewdly, Republican campaigners rang the changes on prosperity all they could, and pressed home the point with such slogans as "The Full Dinner Pail," and "Let Well Enough Alone." A well-filled Republican campaign chest helped even more. When the votes were counted, it appeared that Bryan had carried only the normally Democratic states of the South, and four silver states in the Far West. Even Nebraska deserted him. The popular vote stood 7,219,525 for McKinley to 6,358,737 for Bryan and the electoral vote, 292 to 155. Both houses of Congress were also assured to the Republicans by substantial majorities, and, except in the South, Republican candidates for state office were generally the victors. In so far as an election could decide anything, the country had given its approval to imperialism, the gold standard, and a high protective tariff.

Election results

A problem of imperialism as yet unsettled at the time of the election, was how to reconcile the exigencies of empire with the Constitution of the United States. According to the treaty of cession, "the civil rights and political status of the native inhabitants of the territory... ceded to the United States" were left to the determination of Congress. Did this mean that Congress could do as it pleased without extending the liberties guaranteed by the Constitution to its island possessions, or was the freedom of Congress in this respect as much subject to the Constitution in the new territory as in the old? In other words, as the public phrased the question, Does the Constitution follow the flag?

From the first Congress assumed that it was free from all embarrassing constitutional limitations. In the Foraker Act, for example, it levied a tariff against Puerto Rican imports into the United States equal to fifteen per cent of the regular Dingley rates. If Puerto Rico had become a part of the United States this provision was clearly contrary to the

constitutional requirements that "all duties, imports, and excises shall
be uniform throughout the United States." Obviously, therefore, Congress did not regard the island as a part of the United States in the constitutional sense of the term, nor did the President who signed the law.
But what would be the attitude of the federal courts, which since the
time of John Marshall had felt free to set aside laws of Congress that in
their judgment did not harmonize with the Constitution?

In a series of five-to-four opinions on what came generally to be known
as the "Insular Cases" the Supreme Court decided in 1901 not to interfere with the stand that Congress and the President

The "Insular Cases" had taken. The first of these cases, *De Lima vs. Bidwell*,
was brought by an importer of Puerto Rican sugar against
the collector of the port of New York who *before* the enactment of the
Foraker Act, but *after* the acquisition of Puerto Rico by the United
States, had charged the full Dingley duties. In this case the Court
held that the money collected must be refunded, for Puerto Rico was
no longer foreign territory. In another case, however, *Downes vs. Bidwell*,
where the collections had been made *after* the passage of the Foraker
Act and according to its terms, the Court held that a refund was unnecessary, for Puerto Rico was not exactly a part of the United States. To
eight justices these decisions seemed utterly contradictory, for the result
was achieved by Mr. Justice Brown changing sides, and voting in the
second decision with the four justices who had constituted the minority
in the first decision. The reasoning by which he justified this shift of
opinion no one but himself seemed to understand. But his decision,
that Puerto Rico and the other dependencies were "territory appurte-
nant — but not a part — of the United States," stood. "Mr. Dooley,"
the popular newspaper commentator of the time, probably got the idea
clearly enough when he said: "No matter whether the constitution
follows the flag or not, th' Supreme Court follows th' illiction returns."
In another case, *Hawaii vs. Mankichi*, the Court decided that in the
period after annexation, but before the passage of an organic act of
government, the inhabitants of the Hawaiian Islands could not claim
the right of trial by jury as secured by the Fifth and Sixth Amendments.
The reasoning in this case was even more stratospheric, for the Court
held that the "rights alleged to be violated ... are not fundamental in
their nature."

American colonial policy In one respect American colonial policy showed a remarkable difference from the pattern customary among Euro-
pean nations. Cuba was set free, or at least relatively free,
although the United States, had it chosen to do so, might
easily have retained the island as a dependency. Even the Philip-

pines were promised their ultimate independence, by the Republicans no less than by the Democrats. On this issue the difference between the two parties was merely as to the time when independence should be granted. What the Democrats said should be done immediately the Republicans proposed to do later on, after the Filipinos had obtained sufficient experience in self-government to be ready to cope with the problems of independence. Philippine policy, therefore, worked toward an increasing amount of autonomy regardless of the party in power. McKinley sent William Howard Taft to the Philippines to institute civil government, and under his administration the beginnings of self-rule took place. By 1907 the Filipinos were electing the lower house of their legislature; by 1916, under the terms of the Jones Act, they were permitted virtual autonomy, although during the twenties, with the Republicans again in the ascendancy, some of the privileges acquired while Wilson was President were lost. By 1934, with the Democrats in power, the Tydings-McDuffie Act offered independence after ten years, an offer that the Philippines were ready to accept two years later. At the outbreak of the second World War, the Philippines were scheduled to obtain their independence in 1946.[1]

"Dominion over palm and pine" carried with it also many other familiar aspects of American culture. One of the most important transplantations was the American public-school system. In 1898 perhaps five thousand Filipino children were in school; by 1920, over a million. At first American teachers were placed in charge, but adequately trained Filipinos, many of them educated in the United States, were soon available to take over the work. By 1920 the number of American teachers had dwindled to three hundred, and the English language rivaled the Spanish as the most generally understood tongue in the islands. American notions as to sanitation also reached the Philippines. Smallpox and cholera were stamped out, lepers were isolated in colonies and treated instead of being permitted to roam at will, and the infantile death-rate was sharply reduced. Good roads, too, were built, and improved methods of transportation were introduced. Most significant of all, the modified tariff barriers that had at first restricted trade between the Philippines and the United States soon gave way to virtual free trade, thus opening the rich American markets to Philippine sugar, coconut oil, rice, tobacco, and hemp. The result of this favored economic status was a degree of prosperity such as the Philippines had never known before. Whatever their political

Philippine civilization

[1] Grayson L. Kirk, *Philippine Independence* (1936), is an excellent study of the relations between the Philippines and the United States from 1898 to the enactment of the act of independence. See also Moorfield Storey and M. P. Lichauco, *The Conquest of the Philippines by the United States, 1898-1925* (1926), a strongly anti-imperialistic view.

differences, the economic ties that bound the islands to the United States became closer with each succeeding year. Rich resources in minerals and lumber that might also be sold to American customers were discovered, and plans for their exploitation were laid. It was because these ties would be so hard to break that the probationary period of ten years was stipulated in the Tydings-McDuffie Act.

Prideful Americans recounting the spoils of imperialism were aware of certain minor possessions above which waved the Stars and Stripes. Besides Alaska, the Philippines, and Puerto Rico, the United States had acquired the Hawaiian Islands, with a population of more than one hundred and fifty thousand and enormous sugar-producing possibilities. Not more than one-fifth of the residents of these islands were native Hawaiians; nearly another fifth were Americans; and the remaining three-fifths were Asiatics. Here American investments were important, and the wishes of American residents were given careful consideration. On April 30, 1900, by Act of Congress Hawaii was accorded full territorial status. American sovereignty had also been extended to Tutuila, one of the Samoan Islands in the southern Pacific, to Guam, some fifteen hundred miles east of the Philippines, and to numerous tiny uninhabited islets in the Pacific over which no other nation had chosen to raise its flag. With no form of government prescribed by Congress for these acquisitions, they remained under the absolute control of the President as commander-in-chief of the army and navy. Two other tiny colonies came to the United States as a result of the decision to build a canal across the Isthmus of Panama. The Canal Zone, ten miles wide, obtained by treaty with Panama in 1903, came to be inhabited principally by government employees, and was eventually left to the government of Congress, the President, and the national courts. The Virgin Islands, acquired by purchase from Denmark in 1917, were deemed of value for the proper defense of the Canal. To govern the impoverished twenty-five thousand Negroes and mulattoes who inhabited them, the President was authorized to appoint a governor, subject to the approval of the Senate. The Danish code of laws, already in force, was retained.

Quite as the opponents of imperialism had predicted, the necessity of defending this overseas empire led to a rapid expansion of the military might of the United States. Under Elihu Root as Secretary of War the United States Army underwent a reorganization so thorough that the scandals of inefficiency that marred the prosecution of the war against Spain could not soon be repeated. In keeping with modern practice a general staff was created to take the place of the major-general in command of the army, and to lay plans for the proper defense of the United States and its possessions. By means of the Army War College, established in 1901, and other service schools, an attempt was made also to carry on the military education of officers after they had been commissioned. The size of the army was not greatly increased, but a new militia law, designed to make of the National Guard a more efficient second line of defense, was placed on the statute books in 1903. Even more striking than the reorganization of the army was the rapid expansion of the navy, to which one or two new battleships were added every year. In 1907 President Roosevelt spectacularly advertised the strength of the American Navy by sending a fleet of sixteen battleships, together with the necessary auxiliary craft, on a voyage around the world. Any power critical of American policies — and the President had Japan particularly in mind — might thus see what it would have to deal with should it provoke the United States to war.

Quite as striking a fact as the sudden acquisition of a colonial empire by the United States was the equally sudden subsidence of the imperialistic urge. After the first excitement, interest in the newly acquired possessions diminished, and the public showed not the slightest appetite for more. When the United States entered the World War in 1917, one of the certainties, un- *Declining interest in imperialism* challenged by any political party, was that the American nation would not emerge with more colonies. At the Paris Peace Conference the United States, almost alone among the victors, made no demands for territory, and all efforts to induce the American government to accept colonial mandates came to nought. From the financial point of view colonial empire had proved to be almost a total loss; the Philippines in particular had cost the government huge sums, and had brought in comparatively little by way of profit. This, perhaps, need not have been so; other nations took a heavy toll from their possessions. But neither the American government nor the American people showed great aptitude along this line. Americans with a taste for foreign investments were not lacking, but they made as good profits, if not better, in lands that lay outside the American Empire. Perhaps a distinction should be drawn between possessions acquired in the western hemisphere and those acquired elsewhere, for with the exception of Cuba Americans showed little disposition to dispose of the territories they had taken in the New World. They even acquiesced while their government, under one pretext or another, made virtual protectorates for a time of nations bordering on the Caribbean Sea and adjacent to the Panama Canal. Imperialism close at hand could be more easily reconciled with the traditional idea of American isolation from Old World affairs than imperialism far away, and however much the facts might belie it, the old tradition died hard.

31

Theodore Roosevelt

SIX MONTHS after his second inauguration William McKinley visited the
Pan-American Exposition at Buffalo, New York, and on September 5
made a speech in which he emphasized the end of American
isolation and the importance of reciprocity as a means of
promoting foreign trade. Next day, during a reception, he
was shot by an anarchist who had no other motive for his crime, apparently, than his disbelief in government. For a few days the President
lingered on, but on September 14 he died, and was succeeded by the
youthful Vice-President, Theodore Roosevelt (1858–1919).[1] Well-born,
well-educated, well-to-do, the new President in his youth had disdained
the life of a rich man's son, and in 1881, as a representative in the state
legislature of New York, had entered politics "at the bottom of the ladder." A few years later, however, he thought himself ready to turn his
back on a political career, and began to spend part of each year on a
Dakota ranch. But he consented to make the hopeless race as Republican candidate for mayor of New York in 1886, and he campaigned for
Harrison in 1888 with such earnestness that he was rewarded for his
service to the party by appointment to the Civil Service Commission.
Here for six years he did outstandingly effective work, but in 1895 accepted an even humbler post as president of the New York Police Board,
a position that served greatly to broaden his social horizon. In spite of
his active political life, he wrote extensively, sometimes of his ranch and
hunting exploits, but more often books of American history and biography. His best work was a four-volume series, *The Winning of the West*,
which traced in exciting detail the story of the white man's conquest of
the region from the Appalachians to the Mississippi.

Roosevelt re-entered national politics in 1896 by campaigning for
McKinley with more enthusiasm than his understanding of the money

[1] The only adequately critical biography of Roosevelt is H. F. Pringle, *Theodore Roose-
velt* (1931). Most other writers on Roosevelt are content to expound or elaborate the
"Roosevelt legend," so ably set forth in Theodore Roosevelt, *An Autobiography* (1913),
and J. B. Bishop, *Theodore Roosevelt and His Time Shown in His Own Letters* (2 vols., 1920).
Of this type are W. R. Thayer, *Theodore Roosevelt; an Intimate Biography* (1919); L. F.
Abbott, *Impressions of Theodore Roosevelt* (1919); and W. D. Lewis, *The Life of Theodore
Roosevelt* (1919).

question warranted, and after McKinley's inauguration served as Assistant Secretary of the Navy. As a hero lately returned from the war he was elected governor of New York in 1898, and Vice-President in 1900. Never a dependable regular, and given to impetuous statements on all manner of questions, the new President was immediately suspect by the more conservative element of his party. Indeed, many of them had helped make him Vice-President as a means of insuring an end to his political career.

To the confusion of his critics, Roosevelt took over his new duties in perfect good taste, and even promised "to continue absolutely unbroken the policies of President McKinley." Especially reassuring was his decision to retain McKinley's Cabinet, for whatever his faults McKinley had proved himself to be an able judge of men. Two of the advisers on whom Roosevelt was to depend most, John Hay, Secretary of State, and Elihu Root, Secretary of War, were already in the cabinet, while a third, William Howard Taft, had been picked by McKinley for the difficult task of inaugurating civil government in the Philippines. Roosevelt even sought with some success to appease Mark Hanna, now Senator from Ohio, although, as both knew, the gulf between them on most matters of consequence was very wide. It was inevitable that eventually Roosevelt was to be his own President. For the most part McKinley had been content to follow public opinion, but aggressive leadership was an integral part of the Roosevelt personality. Fortunately the new President embodied to a remarkable degree the interests and prejudices of the average American. When he sought to lead there was no dearth of followers.

Roosevelt as President

Better versed in world affairs than his predecessors, Roosevelt tackled with eager enthusiasm the problems of diplomacy that came before his administration. He found European nations far less contemptuous of the United States than they had been before the Spanish-American War. Germany sent the Kaiser's brother, Prince Henry, on a friendly visit to the United States, France founded some exchange professorships, and Great Britain worked, too openly to succeed, for an Anglo-American alliance. All this good-will was of great importance to the United States in working out its Asiatic policy, for the great powers of Europe, it transpired, were with the exception of Japan also the great powers of Asia.

Already John Hay, as McKinley's Secretary of State, had set himself the task of preventing the dismemberment of China, nearest neighbor of the Philippines, with whom both American and Philippine trade was important. Japan and the nations of Europe had marked out for themselves "spheres of influence" in China, where they enjoyed special "concessions," and which they meant ulti-

The "Open-Door" policy

mately to absorb. Hay's idea was to substitute for this predatory policy an "open door" to world trade in all of China, with each nation respecting the rights and privileges of every other. Ably assisted by Great Britain, Hay had actually persuaded the powers to give lip service to the "open door," although what they actually meant to do was by no means clear. The American Secretary of State found his diplomatic talent taxed to the full when the "Boxer Uprising," an anti-foreigner movement in China, went to such lengths of violence and bloodshed as to insure intervention. Wisely the United States sent its troops along with those of most of the rest of the powers on an international expedition to Peking, which after hard fighting reached the Chinese capital in August, 1900. When order had been restored, Hay used his influence to induce the participants in the affair to accept from China, in compensation for their losses and expenditures, a money indemnity rather than, as some would have preferred, cessions of territory and grants of more special privileges. At all times the "open-door policy" hung on a slender thread, for Hay knew, and most of the nations of the world knew, that the American people were extremely reluctant to use force to sustain it.[1]

The indemnity required of China, $333,000,000 to be paid in thirty-nine annual installments, was large, but it would have been much larger had not the United States made every effort to keep it down. The portion awarded to the United States was $24,440,700, but later investigation showed that the original estimates of American losses had been much too high. Accordingly Congress in 1908, on recommendation of President Roosevelt, reduced the obligation to approximately half its original size, and in 1924 remitted also an unpaid balance of $6,000,000. In appreciation of these friendly acts the Chinese government announced that it would devote the first remission to the education of Chinese students in the United States, and the second, to educational and scientific work in China. For many years Chinese students, supported by "Boxer indemnity" money, were a familiar sight on American campuses, and their absorption of western civilization deeply influenced the course of Chinese development. The handling of the indemnity matter, together with Hay's persistent efforts to preserve Chinese national integrity, caused the Chinese for a generation to regard the United States as a kind of moral, if not political, ally.

The Boxer indemnity

The withdrawal of the expeditionary forces from China was set for the fall of 1901, and was carried out according to agreement by all the nations except Russia, which maintained a special concentration in

---

[1] Hay's work for the open door is best examined in Tyler Dennett, *John Hay* (1933), but W. R. Thayer, *The Life and Letters of John Hay* (2 vols., 1915), is well worth reading. See also Tyler Dennett, *Americans in Eastern Asia* (1922).

Manchuria with a view to exacting further favors from China. To prevent this, only the Japanese were prepared to strike. Japanese students of western civilization had reached the conclusion that the enormous and growing population of Japan could be supported only by the rapid expansion of manufacturing. But Japan lacked the two greatest essentials for a manufacturing nation, coal and iron, both of which China possessed in abundance. Access to these commodities, as well as to Chinese markets for Japanese goods, the Russian advance might eventually block. With the Japanese "life-line" thus endangered, Japanese statesmen made deliberate plans for the expulsion of Russia from Manchuria. On January 30, 1902, Japan signed a treaty of alliance with Great Britain, which stipulated that if either signatory were attacked by more than one power, the other must come to its aid. This alliance permitted the British to concentrate their naval strength in European waters where German might was on the rise, and left Japan free to drive the Russians out of Manchuria without fear of attack from any other power.

Japan's ambitions

The Russo-Japanese War that broke out in 1904 was soon over. It was fought on Chinese soil, although China, strongly supported in' this endeavor by the United States, succeeded in remaining neutral. Naturally American sympathy ran with Japan, for it was the Russians, rather than the Japanese, who had most openly flouted the "open door." Roosevelt even went so far as to send a private warning to France and Germany that if either of them entered the war on the side of Russia he would bring the United States to the aid of Japan. Finally, with the Japanese everywhere victorious and the Russians handicapped by a revolution at home, President Roosevelt offered mediation, and assisted in the making of peace at Portsmouth, New Hampshire, where on September 5, 1905, a treaty was signed. Both parties agreed to evacuate Manchuria, and Japan received, in lieu of an indemnity, the lower half of the island of Sakhalin.

Russo-Japanese War

Once the war was over, the friendly relations between Japan and the United States came to an abrupt end. Japan was offended at Roosevelt for not backing her demand for a money indemnity from Russia; she soon showed that she had no intention whatever of maintaining the open door, either in Korea [1] or in Manchuria; and she was deeply angered by American discriminations against the seventy-five thousand or more Japanese immigrants who, since about 1900, had appeared along the Pacific Coast of the United States. Fully aware of the mounting antagonism between the

The Japanese turn against America

[1] Roosevelt recognized Japan's absorption of Korea in return for a Japanese promise not to interfere with American rule in the Philippines.

two peoples, Roosevelt did what he could to keep the peace. He obtained from the Japanese government a "gentlemen's agreement" whereby Japan herself undertook to terminate the flow of Japanese laborers to the United States; he sent the American battle-fleet around the world in 1907 as a means of revealing the strength of the United States to the Japanese; and he accepted as if it were a sincere document (although he well knew that, as far as Japan was concerned, it was not) the Root-Takahira Agreement of 1908. According to this (1) the two nations asserted a common desire to develop their commerce on the Pacific freely and peacefully; (2) they agreed to maintain "the existing *status quo*" in the Far East, including the open door in China; (3) they stood together in support of the independence and integrity of China; and (4) they promised, in the event of any threat to existing conditions, to consult with each other as to what measures they should take. This polite exchange said all that the United States could ask, but it was utterly unenforceable on Japan, as both governments knew. The United States, without allies and unwilling to have them, was in reality powerless to defend either the open door or the integrity of China.

While the American adventure into Far-Eastern diplomacy was meeting with indifferent success, a gratifying record of triumphs was being established in the western hemisphere. Here the United States was close enough to the problems it attacked to have a better understanding of them, and it ordinarily had no such powerful antagonists to deal with as in the Orient. Furthermore, events soon proved that in all matters of consequence the United States could count with certainty on British support. In the settlement of a dispute over the Alaskan boundary, for example, the British government showed more concern for the maintenance of cordial relations with the United States than for pleading the cause of Canada, a component part of the British Empire. By a somewhat dubious reinterpretation of the treaty line of 1825, agreed upon between Great Britain and Russia, the Canadians had laid claim to a corridor across the Alaskan panhandle that would have given them ocean frontage at the head of the trail to the Klondike. But an Anglo-American commission of six — three Americans, two Canadians, and an Englishman — favored the American side of the controversy, with the English representative voting consistently with the Americans and against the Canadians (1903). Similarly, in deference to the demand from the United States for a strictly American canal through Central America, the British permitted, first the amendment of the Clayton-Bulwer Treaty of 1850, which had given the British equal rights with the Americans in any canal to be constructed, and when the United States Senate proved still

Anglo-American relations

to be unsatisfied, the complete abrogation of the treaty (1901). As a result of the second of these Hay-Pauncefote Treaties, as they were called, the United States was permitted to acquire territory in Central America and to police the canal — a provision that the American government interpreted to mean the right of fortification. The only reservation insisted upon by the British was that the canal, while strictly American, was to be "free and open to the vessels of commerce and of war of all nations ... on terms of entire equality"; nor were there to be any discriminations "in respect of the conditions or charges of traffic." [1]

The significance of this treaty was deeper than most Americans realized. The British government, in granting to the United States a free hand in building the canal, meant to indicate its belief that the friendship between the two nations was permanent and could never be broken. Had the United States been ready to seal the pact by an outright alliance, Great Britain would have been all too willing; as it was she withdrew her fleets from Caribbean waters, and left to the United States the protection of British interests in that region, just as she had turned over some of her Asiatic interests to the protection of Japan after the Anglo-Japanese alliance. While the American public in general distrusted Great Britain, and refused even to consider British friendship desirable, there is some evidence to show that the American government took a far different view of the matter. Since the growing naval strength of the United States came to be based increasingly in Pacific waters, it seems reasonable to suppose that responsible American officials felt satisfied to entrust to the British the policing of the Atlantic.

The building of the Panama Canal, upon which the American government — after some flirtations with the alternative Nicaragua route — had set its heart, required extensive diplomatic preparations also with other American nations. In the eighties a French company headed by Ferdinand de Lesseps had attempted unsuccessfully to build a similar canal, and for its rights and property the United States was willing to pay the sum of forty million dollars. Before this could be done, however, it was necessary to obtain the consent of Colombia, the South American nation through whose territory the canal would be built, for the American plan contemplated real or virtual land-ownership, as well as a permit to build. With this in view, Secretary Hay, using the threat of the Nicaraguan alternative, drove a sharp bar-

The Panama Canal

---

[1] Mary W. Williams, *Anglo-American Isthmian Diplomacy, 1815–1915* (1916); J. H. Latané, *From Isolation to Leadership* (new edition, 1923). In spite of the "entire equality" clause of the Hay-Pauncefote Treaty, Congress in 1912 attempted to exempt American coastwise shipping from the payment of tolls. The British government immediately protested, and in June, 1914, President Wilson persuaded Congress to repeal the exemption. It came out later that this was the price Wilson paid to obtain British support for his policy in Mexico.

gain with Tomas Herran, the Colombian Representative at Washington.
The United States would pay ten million dollars down and an annual
quit-rent of two hundred and fifty thousand dollars for control over a
strip of land six miles wide from Panama to Colón, but exclusive of
those cities. That was all. Furthermore, it was specifically stated
that Colombia might not negotiate with the French company to obtain
a portion of the forty million dollars it was to receive from the United
States. The United States Senate promptly ratified the treaty, but the
Colombian government, which resented both the terms and the manner
in which they had been imposed, refused to ratify.

Impatient to get on with the work, President Roosevelt gave tacit
approval to a suddenly conceived secessionist movement on the part of
the state of Panama — that section of Colombia through which the
canal must be built. This movement was fomented and financed by the
officers of the French company, as Roosevelt well knew, but he was
determined that it should succeed. On the authority of a treaty of 1846
between the United States and New Granada (which became Colombia
in 1863), he held that the United States was bound to protect "the
right of way or transit across the Isthmus of Panama," and to insure
this end instructed American naval units in the vicinity to "prevent the
landing of any armed force with hostile intent, either government or
belligerent." Since the only possible route by which Colombia could
bring troops to Panama was by sea, the proposed revolution took place
on November 3, 1903, without the usual accompaniment of violence
and bloodshed. Three days later, Secretary Hay accorded diplomatic
recognition to the new republic. "I took Panama," Roosevelt is said
to have boasted later.[1]

With Colombia disposed of, and a representative of the French company, Philippe Bunau-Varilla, the first minister from Panama to the
United States, a new treaty, the Hay-Bunau-Varilla Treaty,
Canal
diplomacy
quickly cleared the way for the beginning of canal construction. The United States was permitted to acquire a zone
five miles wide on each side of the canal "as if she were sovereign,"
and to fortify it at will. Panama was to receive an initial payment of
ten million dollars, and two hundred and fifty thousand dollars per year,
beginning nine years after date. The independence of Panama was guaranteed by the United States, but the principles of the Platt Amendment,
including the right of intervention, were applied to the new republic.
As Roosevelt should have foreseen, his imperialistic diplomacy deeply

[1] The best general treatment of this subject is H. C. Hill, *Roosevelt and the Caribbean*
(1927), but see also E. T. Parks, *Columbia and the United States, 1765–1934* (1935); J. F.
Rippy, *The Capitalists and Colombia* (1931); W. D. McCain, *The United States and the
Republic of Panama* (1937).

enraged the Colombians, and made other Latin-American nations fearful of what he might have in store for them. Later, with Latin-American good-will a constant objective of the United States, repeated efforts were made to buy back Colombia's friendship with a money payment, but as long as Roosevelt lived no such movement succeeded. After his death, with Harding as President, a treaty which compensated Colombia for the damage done by a payment of twenty-five million dollars was accepted by both nations. Fear that European syndicates would be able to monopolize the rich oil resources of Colombia to the exclusion of American firms had much to do with converting the United States Senate to the wisdom of such a treaty.

The actual building of the canal was a feat of extraordinary magnitude. At first sanitation threatened to be an even greater problem than excavation, but the work of Colonel W. C. Gorgas in making the canal zone a fit place in which to live was so well done that trouble from that source was soon practically eliminated. Administrative difficulties arising from the fact that Congress insisted on delegating the control of operations to a commission instead of to an individual hampered work for a while, but Roosevelt at length made Major George W. Goethals, an army engineer, chairman of the commission, and extracted a promise from all other members of the commission never to disagree with the chairman. After that the work proceeded satisfactorily, and on August 15, 1914, the first ocean steamer passed through the canal. The cost of building it ran to $275,000,000, which the government raised by floating bonds, together with another $113,000,000 for fortifications; but receipts during the first fifteen years of operation brought in large enough net earnings to meet in full the interest on the bonds floated. Roosevelt always considered the building of the Panama Canal the greatest achievement of his administration.[1]

Before he became President, and with his thoughts on the New York Republican machine, Roosevelt had once quoted an old adage: "Speak softly and carry a big stick, and you will go far." Later this statement was resurrected and fittingly applied to his policy in Latin America. Backed by the new American navy, Roosevelt prepared to enforce the Monroe Doctrine with aggressive determination; some said that he even intended to use it as a cloak for further imperialistic ventures. Certainly he kept persistently in mind the fact that the Panama Canal must be defended at all costs. Because of the canal events in Latin America that in an earlier age might have passed unnoticed now became matters of grave concern.

The "Big Stick" policy

[1] J. B. and Farnham Bishop, *Goethals, Genius of the Panama Canal* (1930); M. D. Gorgas and B. J. Hendrick, *William Crawford Gorgas, his Life and Work* (1924).

The Venezuelan incident of 1902 paved the way for the first official statement of the "big-stick" policy. The State of Venezuela, which bordered on the Caribbean Sea adjacent to the proposed canal, was in trouble with Great Britain, Germany, and other European nations because of the nonpayment of debts owing their citizens. A legitimate difference of opinion existed as to the amounts due, for in some cases no such sums had ever been delivered as were claimed. But the Venezuelan dictator, Cipriano Castro, seemingly had no intention of paying anything if he could avoid it. Finally Great Britain and Germany, mildly supported by Italy, withdrew their legations from Caracas, and by a strong show of force brought Castro to terms. Through the United States he made known his willingness to arbitrate the claims, and eventually the case was settled by the Hague Tribunal. Although Germany was probably following British leadership throughout these proceedings, Roosevelt got the impression that the German government was looking for an opportunity to challenge the Monroe Doctrine, and he seems to have had some dramatic interviews with the German ambassador in Washington. However this might be, when Luis M. Drago, Argentinian Foreign Minister, expressed the opinion that "the public debt cannot occasion armed intervention nor even the actual occupation of the territory of American nations by a European power," Roosevelt was interested, and two years later he countered with what came to be known as the "Roosevelt corollary" of the Monroe Doctrine:

> If a nation shows that it knows how to act with reasonable efficiency and decency in social and political matters, if it keeps order and pays its obligations, it need fear no interference from the United States. Chronic wrongdoing, or an impotence which results in a general loosening of the ties of civilized society may in America, as elsewhere, ultimately require intervention by some civilized nation, and in the Western Hemisphere the adherence of the United States to the Monroe Doctrine may force the United States, however reluctantly, in flagrant cases of such wrongdoing or impotence, to the exercise of an international police power.

Roosevelt's interpretation of the Monroe Doctrine, as events proved, was applied with rigor only in the Caribbean zone, which guarded the eastern approaches to the Panama Canal. Here it supplemented and assisted the defense policy of the United States which maintained that the Caribbean Sea must become as strictly as possible an American lake. Property rights acquired by the United States on the borders of the Caribbean included: (1) Puerto Rico, annexed at the close of the Spanish-American War; (2) the Canal Zone, obtained on terms practically equivalent to annexation; (3) the Virgin Islands, purchased from Denmark in 1917 for twenty-five million

Caribbean control

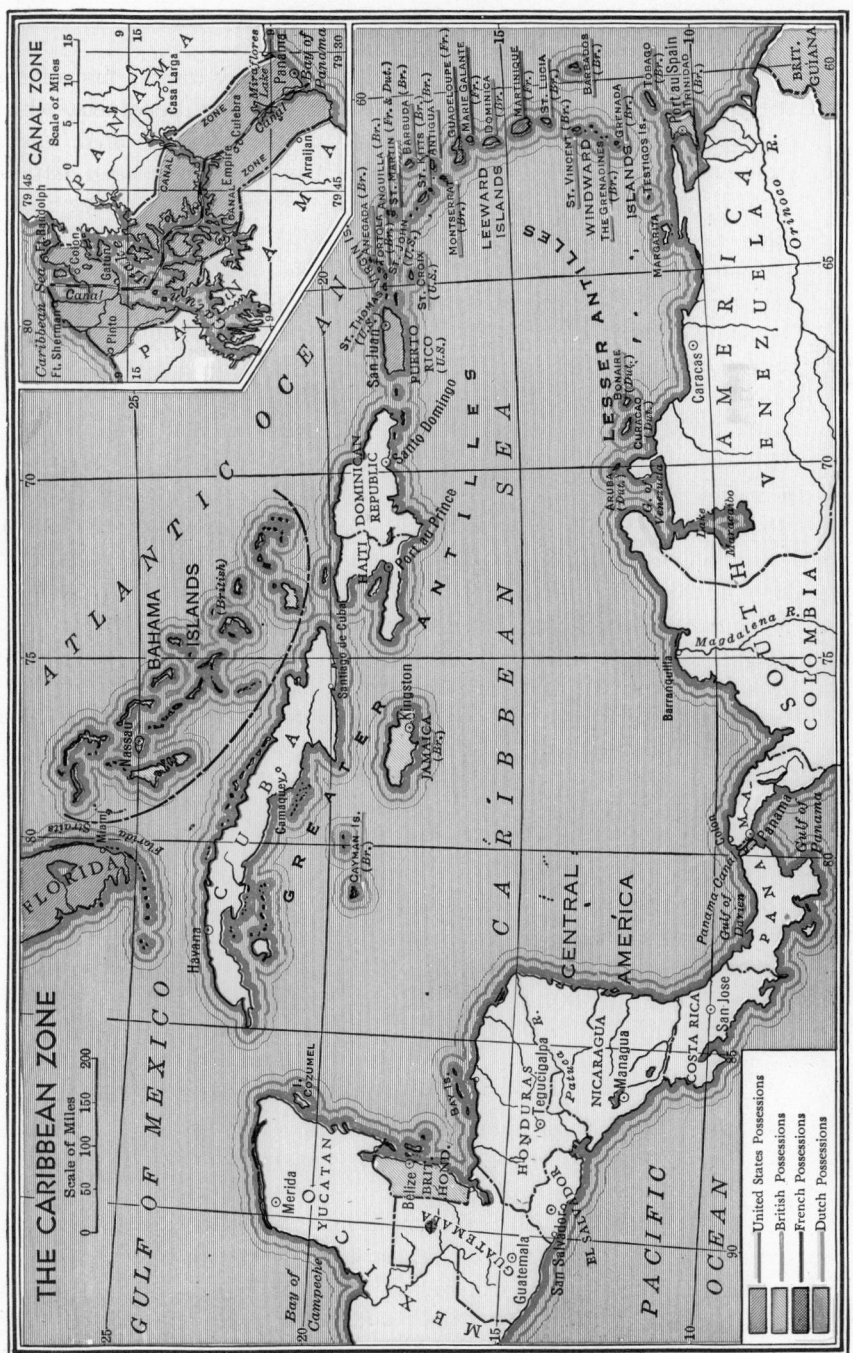

THE CARIBBEAN ZONE
Scale of Miles
0 50 100 150 200

CANAL ZONE
Scale of Miles
0 5 10 15

United States Possessions
British Possessions
French Possessions
Dutch Possessions

dollars, a price utterly out of proportion to their economic value; (4) convenient sites for naval bases at Guantanamo in eastern Cuba, on the Corn Islands off Nicaragua, and elsewhere; and (5) a concession from Nicaragua giving the United States the sole right of constructing a canal through her territory. Cuba and Panama, thanks to the principles of the Platt Amendment, were virtual protectorates of the United States, while the application of the Roosevelt corollary eventually brought the Dominican Republic (1905), Nicaragua (1912), and Haiti (1914) quite as completely within the American orbit. Intervention in the two republics of Santo Domingo began when the United States took over the collection and the administration of the revenues; in Nicaragua, the initial act was the landing of American marines to keep order. In every instance decades elapsed before American supervision, in one form or another, was withdrawn. Other territory in the Caribbean Zone was either in the hands of friendly European nations who made no effort to match the strength of the United States in the region, or of independent Latin-American nations whose conduct was tempered by fear of the "big stick." [1]

The charge was often made that the purpose of American intervention in the Caribbean Zone was primarily to promote the development of American financial interests in that area. It is demonstrable that a great increase in American investments and a somewhat more modest increase in American trade followed in the wake of governmental policy, but it is hard to believe that either Roosevelt or any of his successors were seeking merely to open new fields for American enterprise. Undoubtedly the objectives they had most in mind were the defense of the Panama Canal, the protection of American lives and property already in the troubled areas, and the abatement of governmental nuisances that might conceivably lead to European intervention.

"Dollar diplomacy"

The active participation of the United States in world affairs after the Spanish-American War led many thoughtful Americans to wonder if their nation in its new rôle could hope to escape involvements that would lead to war. With possessions as far away as the Philippines and with interests in every part of the globe, the very idea of American isolation seemed a contradiction. How then could peace be maintained? It did not require much logic to deduce that the surest way to keep the United States out of war was to keep war out of the world, and a strong movement for world peace set in. The First Hague Conference, called by the Czar of Russia in 1899, had already struggled with this problem, and had recommended

The First Hague Conference

[1] Later Caribbean policy can be followed in J. F. Rippy, *Latin America in World Politics* (new edition, 1938); C. L. Jones, *Caribbean Interests of the United States* (1916); C. L. Jones, *The Caribbean Since 1900* (1936); C. L. Jones, *The United States and the Caribbean* (1929).

three means for settling disputes without resort to war: (1) through good offices and mediation, which, when offered by a third party to powers at war or about to go to war, must not be considered an unfriendly act; (2) through international commissions of inquiry, for which so many precedents existed, particularly in the relations between Great Britain and the United States; and (3) through submission to a new court of arbitration to be established at The Hague. To this tribunal each member nation might name as many as four qualified judges, and from the list so obtained nations desiring to arbitrate a given case might pick as many or as few judges as they saw fit. They might define, too, the powers of the arbitrators, but they must consider themselves bound to submit in good faith to the award. The United States not only accepted the recommendations of the Hague Conference, but President Roosevelt submitted the first case for the Hague Tribunal to decide — the Pious Fund controversy with Mexico — and agreed to the decision.

Keyed up to the idea that the United States must play an important part in the preservation of world peace, Roosevelt involved his country more deeply in European affairs than most Americans knew when he participated in the settlement of the Moroccan crisis of 1905–06. This threat to world peace was precipitated when the German Emperor, whose government was distressed at the Franco-British accord in North Africa, and feared that it might mean the exclusion of German commerce from Morocco, made a saber-rattling speech at Tangier in March, 1905. After considerable diplomatic sparring, the Emperor asked Roosevelt to promote the calling of a conference for the settlement of the dispute, and this Roosevelt did. The Conference met at Algeciras in Spain, and, with Roosevelt's assistance, worked out a solution far from pleasing to Germany. For one decision of the Conference, that the port of Casablanca should not be turned over to Germany, Roosevelt took personal credit. He had a deep distrust of Germany, and was strongly opposed to the establishment of a German outpost on the eastern Atlantic close to the Western Hemisphere. Whether or not Roosevelt actually helped avert the outbreak of a general European war, as he thought, may never be known, but undoubtedly his motive was to preserve the peace, and for the time being, at least, the peace was preserved.

The Algeciras Conference

At a second Hague Conference, held in 1907, the United States began a persistent campaign to commit the nations of the world to the settlement of their disputes by peaceful means. The American delegation worked strenuously, although unavailingly, for the creation of an international court of justice, comparable to the United States Supreme Court, to which cases could

The Second Hague Conference

be referred for adjudication. Curiously the Conference spent much of its time in discussing the laws of war, and ultimately submitted its conclusions on many disputed points of land warfare to the nations of the world for ratification. A supplementary naval conference, held in London the following year, adopted a similar codification of the rules of naval warfare, known as the Declaration of London. Both documents failed of complete ratification, but they registered in general the progress of world thought on the subjects with which they dealt, and nations that observed the new rules had less to apologize for than those that did not. The Second Hague Conference drew up also a model arbitration treaty, which all the nations of the world were urged to follow in negotiating treaties with one another. Both under Roosevelt, and under the next two Presidents, Taft and Wilson, the United States worked diligently for arbitration, and it is worthy of note that by 1914 the American government had obtained arbitration treaties of one kind or another with every one of the European nations allied against Germany in the first World War. The nations that became the leading central powers, however, persistently rejected the American proposals.[1]

The aggressive leadership that characterized Roosevelt's handling of foreign affairs was equally evident in the development of his domestic policies. No lawyer, Roosevelt was unimpressed by the traditional allocation of separate powers to the executive, the legislature, and the judiciary. The President, as the head of the government, was in his judgment meant to lead. In matters that required the co-operation of Congress, Roosevelt was not invariably successful, but his administration was characterized, nonetheless, by notable efforts to use the power of the national government in curbing the activities of the great monopolistic enterprises, so much in evidence when he took office.[2]

Economics was definitely not Roosevelt's principal forte, but he would have been blind indeed if he had not recognized in the emergence of "big business" a problem of fundamental importance to his administration. By the beginning of the twentieth century "rugged individualism" had run riot in the United States. In one industry after another great corporations, successfully claiming the rights of persons before the law, had grown to monopolistic proportions. The total capital of million-dollar corporations had increased from $170,000,000 in 1897 to $5,000,000,000 in 1900, and to

The trust problem again

[1] W. I. Hull, *The Two Hague Conferences and their Contributions to International Law* (1908); J. B. Scott, *The Hague Peace Conferences of 1899 and 1907* (2 vols., 1909); Merle Curti, *Bryan and World Peace* (1931).

[2] An excellent short account of twentieth-century American history is D. L. Dumond, *Roosevelt to Roosevelt* (1937). Mark Sullivan, *Our Times*, ii, *America Finding Herself* (1927), is devoted in considerable part to Roosevelt's activities as President.

$20,500,000,000 in 1904. Railway mergers, such as the one by which E. H. Harriman brought the Union Pacific and the Southern Pacific together in 1900, had become the order of the day. Concentration in industry was effected both by means of "horizontal" combinations, through which several industries of the same kind were united, and by means of "vertical" combinations, through which businesses of allied interests joined forces. Of the latter type was the United States Steel Corporation, the first of America's billion-dollar companies, which J. P. Morgan helped knit together in 1901. But what happened to steel happened also in greater or less degree to tobacco, petroleum, sugar, copper, beef, starch, flour, whiskey, and innumerable other commodities. Among the rulers of these great corporations there was a close community of interest, and since most of the mergers were arranged by financiers, a few great banking firms, notably the house of Morgan, came to occupy a commanding position in the nation's business structure.

The trust problem was not new to Roosevelt's time, for during the eighties it had greatly exercised the American public. During the nineties, however, first the depression and then the war tended to eclipse what was going on in the business world. The new awakening was due in remarkable degree to the "muckrakers," a group of energetic journalists who made it their chief concern to discover and exploit in popular articles the seamy side of business behavior.[1] They owed their name to Roosevelt, who was by no means unsympathetic with their work, but who compared some of the most sensational of them to the character in *Pilgrim's Progress* "who could look no way but downward with the muckrake in his hands." A vehicle was available for the muckrakers in the popular magazines that the nineties had produced, *McClure's*, the *Cosmopolitan*, *Everybody's*, the *American*, *Pearson's*, *Munsey's*, the *Arena*, and a number of others. Through these journals, which the public bought and read for the thrill they gave, Ida M. Tarbell exposed the "History of the Standard Oil Company," Lincoln Steffens, "The Shame of the Cities," Thomas Lawson, "Frenzied Finance," Charles Edward Russell, "The Beef Trust," Ray Stannard Baker, "The Railroads on Trial," and so on through an almost interminable list of titles. Unread by the public at large, but of notable perspicacity, were the philosophical treatises of Thorstein Veblen, *The Theory of the Leisure Class* (1899), and *The Theory of Business Enterprise* (1904). Veblen's reasoning provided reformers

The "muckrakers"

---

[1] C. C. Regier, *The Era of the Muckrakers* (1932). The number of the leading muckrakers was surprisingly small, and several of them have left important memoirs. Probably the best of these are *The Autobiography of Lincoln Steffens* (2 vols., 1931), and F. C. Howe, *The Confessions of a Reformer* (1925). On Veblen's contribution, see Joseph Dorfman, *Thorstein Veblen and His America* (1934).

Courtesy of the Minneapolis Journal

"THE DEAD RETURNED TO LIFE"

of the next generation with some of their most cogent arguments against "predatory wealth."

Roosevelt's first action against the trusts was taken in February, 1902, when his Attorney General announced that suit was being brought under the terms of the Sherman Anti-Trust Act to dissolve the Northern Securities Company, through which the year before a merger of three northwestern railroads, the Great Northern, the Northern Pacific, and the Burlington, had been attempted. If the government could induce the United States Supreme Court to support it in this instance, Roosevelt believed that he might later make the Sherman Act a really effective weapon in arresting the trend toward monopoly that had set in. The organizers of the Northern Securities Company, James J. Hill and J. P. Morgan, believed that they had remained within the letter of the law, but a decision of the United States Supreme Court, reached in 1904, by abandoning the reasoning of the Knight case, held quite otherwise. According to the majority of the Court the Northern Securities Company was a violation of free competition within the meaning of the Sherman Act, and must be dissolved.[1]

Northern Securities case

[1] B. H. Meyer, *A History of the Northern Securities Case* (1906); A. H. Walker, *History of the Sherman Law of the United States of America* (1910).

Gleeful at having induced the Court to reverse itself, and acclaimed by the public as a "trust-buster," Roosevelt went ahead with other prosecutions. A total of twenty-five indictments were brought by the Department of Justice during his administration, and in a few instances the government scored victories. Perhaps the most notable of them was the dissolution of the "beef trust," which counted among its sins an agreement whereby six-tenths of the nation's dealers in fresh meat avoided bidding against one another in the purchase of livestock. Eventually Roosevelt came to distinguish between "good trusts," which showed a proper concern for the welfare of the consumer, and "bad trusts," which sought only selfish ends. The latter he prosecuted, the former he let alone. The Supreme Court, in the rule of reason it adopted in 1911, came to about the same conclusion. Only when the monopolistic actions of trusts "unreasonably" interfered with interstate commerce would the Court hold against them. By allowing itself this wide latitude, the Court was free to ignore mere "bigness," while at the same time punishing the misuse of power that great size made possible.

Roosevelt's efforts to obtain regulatory laws from Congress most nearly approached success with reference to the railroads. The Inter-

Railroad regulation

state Commerce Act of 1887 had taken a step in this direction, but its primary purpose after all had been the maintenance of free competition. Even in that sphere the Interstate Commerce Commission, hampered repeatedly by court decisions, had been singularly ineffective, and without a new grant of powers it could never hope to cope with the great mergers that had taken place since its creation. First, the rebate evil was curbed by the Elkins Act of 1903. Then a new Department of Commerce and Labor was set up, within which a fact-finding Bureau of Corporations was designed to ferret out questionable corporation practices. Finally, with strong presidential support, the Hepburn Act, which added immeasurably to the power and prestige of the Interstate Commerce Commission, became law in 1906. No longer did the commission have to go to court to enforce an order; now the carrier had either to accept the rates set by the commission or go to court itself. Furthermore, the law also extended the jurisdiction of the commission to include other common carriers, such as express companies, pipe lines, sleeping-car companies, bridges, and ferries; it forbade the granting of free passes; it prohibited railroads from carrying commodities, except for their own use, that they had produced themselves — coal, for example; and it empowered the commission to prescribe a uniform system of bookkeeping for all railroads, a provision of fundamental importance. Owing to the various methods of accounting in use among the railroads, it had been virtually impossible before this time to arrive at dependable comparative statistics. In order to aid the commission in the discharge of its new duties, its membership was raised from five to seven. Within a few years, under the operation of the new law, the "I.C.C." had not only effected drastic reductions in rates, but it had also won the respect of the public, the courts, and the carriers themselves, who increasingly tended to accept its decisions as final.

The railroads were not the only trusts to feel the force of national regulation. The meat-packers, the food-processors, and the producers of drugs and patent medicines had much to explain when the muckrakers got through with them. Precedents for federal action in this field were not altogether lacking, for laws dating back to the eighties required inspection by the Bureau of Animal Industry of all meats designed for export. This requirement vas extended by a law of 1906 to all meats destined for interstate commerce, and a Pure Food and Drug Act, passed the same year, placed some restrictions, but not nearly enough, on the producers of prepared foods and patent medicines. An amendment to this act, passed in 1911, prohibited also the use of misleading labels, but events proved that the gullible public bought about as freely when the unpleasant truth was printed on the label as when it was not. The real root of the difficulty, fraudulent advertising, escaped unscathed. All such regulation, when undertaken by the federal government, depended for its validity upon the powers of Congress over interstate commerce, and the exact line of demarcation between state and national authority could be drawn only by the courts. Roosevelt, annoyed at the existence of this "twilight zone," strongly favored resolving all doubts in favor of the national government.

Food and Drugs

Always a happy phrase-maker, Roosevelt's insistence on a "square deal" for labor, capital, and the public gave him the advantage of an attractive label for his labor policy. Naturally the rapid development of industrial concentration aroused the fears of labor, and as the strength of organized capital grew, the strength of organized labor grew also. By 1905 the American Federation of Labor claimed for its affiliates a total membership of two millions, with perhaps six hundred thousand unaffiliated but co-operating, union members. Under the circumstances a test of strength between labor and capital was almost inevitable. It came, reasonably enough, in the coal-mining region of Pennsylvania, where in spite of deplorable labor conditions the operators were stubbornly determined to resist reform. Demanding recognition of their union, a wage increase of twenty per

The "square deal"

cent, and a nine-hour day, the anthracite coal miners quit work on May 12, 1902, and at a cost of perhaps a million dollars to all concerned held their lines intact until October 23. John Mitchell, the strike leader, kept his men from violence, and won much sympathy for the strikers' cause. President George F. Baer of the Philadelphia and Reading Coal and Iron Company, who spoke for the operators, was far less skillful. In a letter that he carelessly allowed to fall into the hands of the press he revealed his true sentiments. "The rights and interests of the laboring man," he wrote a supposed sympathizer, "will be protected and cared for — not by the labor agitators, but by the Christian men to whom God in His infinite wisdom has given the control of the property interests of the country."

Finally Roosevelt, fully conscious of the widespread suffering that the coal shortage was sure to bring, used his influence with both parties to the strife in favor of a compromise solution. The miners he found ready enough to talk terms, but the operators, sure that victory was within their grasp, remained obdurate. Only after Roosevelt had threatened to send in a "first-rate general," backed by sufficient federal troops "to dispossess the operators and run the mines as a receiver," would the mine-owners give way. Then, after considerable delay, both sides agreed that a commission of seven, chosen by the President, might settle the dispute. Work was resumed at the mines, and in March, 1903, a decision that in the main favored the miners, was announced. Thus the President had obtained his "square deal" for labor.[1]

Nor was this all. Repeatedly the President recommended to Congress legislation favorable to labor, such as the protection of women and children in industry, limitations on the use of injunctions in labor disputes, and employer's liability laws for workers on interstate railroads. Only the last-mentioned of these recommendations received the favorable action of Congress, and the first such law, passed in 1906, was annulled by the Supreme Court. A law of April, 1908, met the Court's objections. In general Roosevelt's thinking on the labor problem was not far in advance of his times, but it represented a distinct improvement over the positions taken by his predecessors.

Another policy dear to Roosevelt's heart was the conservation of the nation's natural resources. When he became President, the United States was "somewhat in the position of the man who had unexpectedly lost most of his fortune." Its greatest resource throughout its history, or so the people had always thought, had been its vast reservoir of public lands. Now the best of these had been used

Conservation

[1] Elsie Glück, *John Mitchell, Miner* (1929), gives an account of the strike; see also, Harold Howland, *Theodore Roosevelt and His Times* (1921).

up; although at the turn of the century more than five hundred million acres still remained open to settlement, only a small fraction of this vast area could ever be farmed in the traditional American way. Moreover, even after the lands had passed into private or corporate hands the tendency had been to exploit them rather than to preserve their fertility. Millions of acres, particularly in the East and the South, had been returned, thoroughly despoiled, to nature, or could be farmed only by the constant use of fertilizer. What had happened to the lands had happened also in varying degrees to other natural resources. Four-fifths of the nation's forests had been chopped down without thought as to their replacement, and many of those that remained had been acquired by a few large lumber companies bent on using them up. Mineral resources, too, whether of metals, coal, gas, or oil, had been exploited with the utmost wastefulness. Water-power sites, in return for next to nothing, had been allowed to pass into the hands of private companies who had developed their possibilities along profit-making lines, without regard for the destruction of beauty or prevention of floods. By the turn of the century, pessimists were beginning to foretell that the rich resources of the United States would soon be exhausted, and the poverty of the Old World would extend to the New.[1]

Roosevelt set his face steadfastly against this trend of events, and before he left office had begun to achieve results. The Reclamation Act of 1902 put the federal government into the business of building the dams, tunnels, flumes, and ditches necessary for irrigation projects. An Inland Waterways Commission, appointed in 1907, stressed the interrelation of all conservation problems, and urged the President to call a national conference on conservation, to which representatives from all sections and from both parties should be invited. As a result, on May 13, 1908, at the White House Roosevelt met with an assembly of notables that included state governors, cabinet members, Supreme Court justices, members of Congress, businessmen, and a wide range of experts. For three days he kept the conference in session, and from it he obtained support for such important policies as the protection of the water supply of navigable streams, the control of forest fires, government regulation for the cutting of timber, the granting of surface titles to public lands separate from the right to exploit the minerals that lay below the surface, and the withdrawal from entry of lands bearing coal, oil, natural gas, and phosphate. On Roosevelt's order, the Secretary of the Interior added to the forest lands already withdrawn from entry some eighty million acres of coal lands, a million and a half acres of lands adjacent

---

[1] An early and significant study of this subject is C. R. Van Hise, *The Conservation of Natural Resources in the United States* (1910).

to water-power sites, and nearly five million acres of phosphate lands.

There was a direct relationship between Roosevelt's policy of governmental interference in the affairs of business and his policy of conservation. In the former he brought businessmen face to face with the specter of effective governmental regulation, in the latter he served notice that in certain spheres, previously left open to private initiative, the government either would act itself or would permit individuals to act only on terms laid down by the government in advance. The day of rampant individualism was almost done. Perhaps the senior Robert M. La Follette, never a very devoted admirer of Roosevelt, had these considerations in mind when he described conservation as Roosevelt's greatest work. According to the Wisconsin senator, Roosevelt deserved unstinted praise "for staying territorial waste" and for saving the things "on which alone a peaceful, progressive and happy race life can be founded."

Roosevelt as President enjoyed a tremendous popularity. This was due not only to the issues he embraced, but even more to the type of man he was. To a phenomenal degree he exhibited in his personality the traits that the average American most admired; the President, indeed, was the ordinary citizen as he might have appeared under a microscope. What Roosevelt actually became, the ordinary citizen wished to be. Roosevelt's popularity had much to do with the overwhelming victories scored by the Republicans in the four elections (1902, 1904, 1906, 1908) held during his administration, and his renomination and re-election in 1904 was a great personal triumph. To oppose him the Democrats turned that year to a conservative New York judge, Alton B. Parker, whose reliability on all issues affecting business was as dependable as Roosevelt's was uncertain. To clinch the Democratic bid for "Wall Street" support, Parker came out openly for the gold standard, and completely repudiated Bryan's record on free silver. Nevertheless, when the votes were counted it appeared that he had suffered a worse defeat than had been Bryan's lot, either in 1896 or in 1900. The electoral vote stood 336 for Roosevelt and 140 for Parker. Elated by the election returns, Roosevelt immediately issued a dramatic statement that he must have regretted later many times. "The wise custom which limits the President to two terms regards the substance and not the form, and under no circumstances will I be a candidate for or accept another nomination." [1]

Roosevelt's re-election

---

[1] The political history of the period is portrayed without embellishment in F. A. Ogg, *National Progress, 1907–1917* (1918), but with many embellishments in Mark Sullivan. *Our Times*, III, *Pre–War America* (1930), and IV, *The War Begins, 1909-1914* (1932).

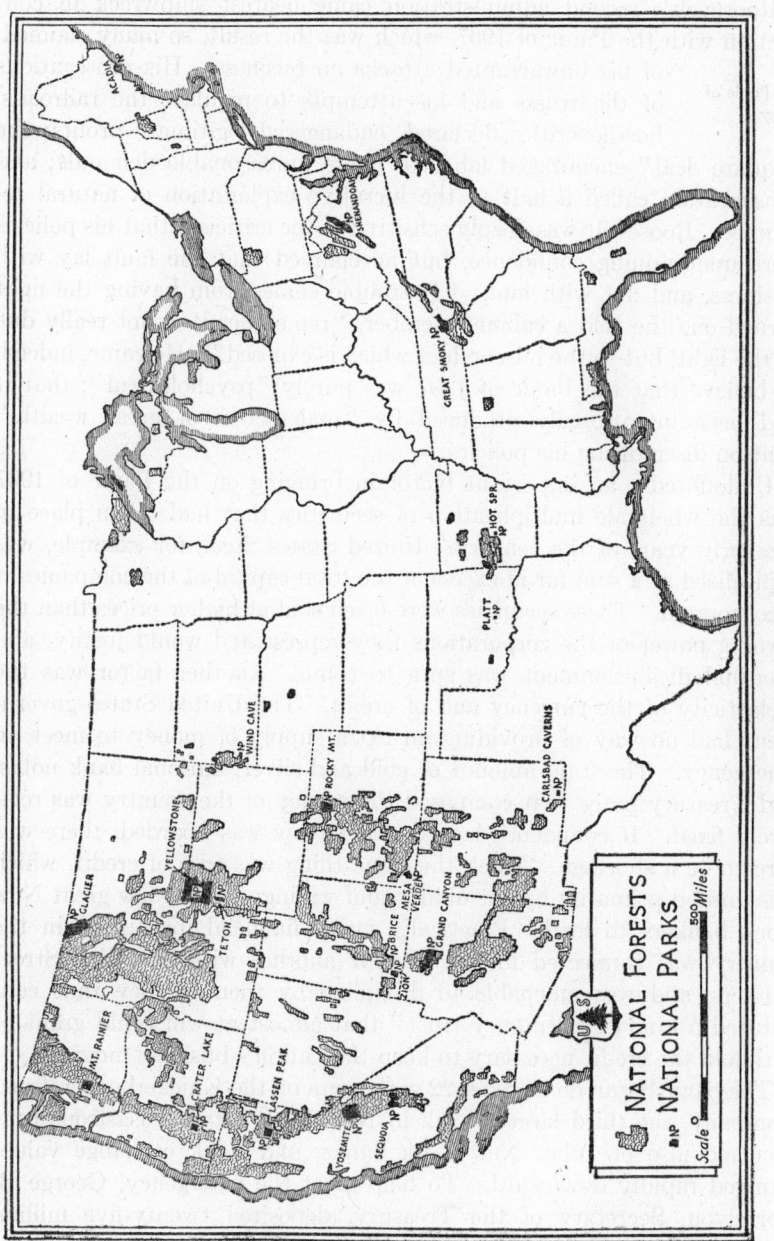

NATIONAL FORESTS AND NATIONAL PARKS

Roosevelt's second administration came nearest shipwreck in connection with the Panic of 1907, which was the result, so many claimed,
of his unwarranted attacks on business. His prosecutions
of the trusts and his attempts to regulate the railroads,
hostile critics declared, endangered legitimate profits; the
"square deal" encouraged labor to make unreasonable demands; and
conservation called a halt to the lucrative exploitation of natural resources. Roosevelt was deeply sensitive to the criticism that his policies
were undermining confidence, but he claimed that the fault lay with
business, and not with him. "If trouble comes from having the light
turned on," he told a cabinet member, "remember it is not really due
to the light, but to the misconduct which is exposed." He came, indeed,
to believe that the Panic of 1907 was purely "psychological"; that it
had been intentionally produced by "malefactors of great wealth,"
bent on discrediting his policies.

The Panic of 1907

Undoubtedly an important factor in bringing on the Panic of 1907
was the wholesale multiplication of securities that had taken place in
the early years of the century. United States Steel, for example, was
capitalized at a sum far in excess of the total capital of the companies it
incorporated. These securities were often sold at higher prices than the
earning power of the corporations they represented would justify, and
eventual disillusionment was sure to come. Another factor was the
inelasticity of the currency and of credit. The United States government had no way of providing an extra supply of money to meet an
emergency. The total amount of gold and silver, national bank notes,
and Treasury notes that composed the money of the country was relatively fixed. If confidence lagged and money was hoarded, there was
sure to be a shortage. Much the same thing was true of credit, which
was limited primarily by the ability and willingness of a few great New
York bankers to lend. Practically every financial institution in the
country was connected in one way or another with the Wall Street
bankers, and was amenable to discipline by them. They thus constituted a kind of a "money trust" that almost at will could grant or
withhold the credit necessary to keep the nation's business moving.

The panic began on October 22 with a run on the Knickerbocker Trust
Company, the third largest bank in New York City. Disastrous runs
occurred also on other New York banks, and stock exchange values
plunged rapidly downward. To help meet the emergency, George B.
Cortelyou, Secretary of the Treasury, deposited twenty-five million
dollars of Treasury funds with hard-pressed New York banks, while
the President, at the suggestion of J. P. Morgan, promised the United
States Steel Corporation immunity from prosecution so that it could

absorb, and save from collapse, the Tennessee Coal and Iron Company. This, Morgan told Roosevelt, was necessary to stave off a really major disaster.[1] As it turned out, the storm was soon over, and in its wake came no long period of depression comparable to the aftermath of 1873 and 1893. Convinced that the panic might have been averted altogether, or at least that its worst effects might have been avoided, had the banking and currency system of the United States been on a sounder footing, Congress in 1908 passed the Aldrich-Vreeland Act which empowered the national banks of the country for a period of six years to issue emergency currency in times of financial stringency. This was but a mere stop-gap. The most important part of the act was the creation of a National Monetary Commission to investigate the currency systems of the world and to lay plans for a thoroughgoing reform in the American system.

Meantime the end of Roosevelt's administration was fast approaching and the election of 1908 was at hand. In spite of Roosevelt's assertion of four years before he was accused of wanting to run again, and certainly many of his admirers would have been delighted to see him have a third term. Nevertheless, Roosevelt had no intention of running again, and to head *The Republicans nominate Taft* off the danger that his devotees might draft him, as they had once done for the Vice-Presidency, he decided to work actively for the nomination of his able Secretary of War and close personal friend, William Howard Taft (1857–1930) of Ohio.[2] Taft's rise up the political ladder had come principally by the appointive route. An honor graduate of Yale, he became successively a judge in the superior court of Ohio, solicitor-general in the federal Department of Justice, federal judge, commissioner to the Philippines and governor-general, and finally Secretary of War. A consistently able administrator and Roosevelt's favorite envoy abroad, he had had what seemed to be an almost ideal training for the Presidency. His personal inclinations lay toward the Supreme Court, but more than once he felt obliged to reject the appointment he craved in the interest of the unfinished business he had in hand. He was a huge man weighing three hundred and fifty pounds, good-natured and affable, and blessed with an infectious chuckle. Earnestly and effectively supported by the President, Taft was nominated on the first ballot by a Republican convention that would have preferred to name Roosevelt.

The Democrats, disastrously defeated four years before with the

---

[1] W. F. McCaleb, *Theodore Roosevelt* (1931), is especially satisfactory at this point.

[2] H. F. Pringle, *The Life and Times of William Howard Taft* (2 vols., 1939), lacks much of the sparkle that makes Pringle's *Roosevelt* so readable, but is an even better study from the point of view of research.

conservative Parker, renominated Bryan, who was still young, vigorous,
and hopeful. Bryan as a favorite Chautauqua orator had
Bryan again probably been heard by more Americans than any other
man in public life, and his adherents gave him the same unstinted devotion that Henry Clay and James G. Blaine had once commanded. In
1906 Bryan had made a trip around the world, had been well received,
and had returned with his self-confidence restored. Ready at last to
admit that free silver was a dead issue, he proposed in August, 1906, a
new program for curbing the trusts. Corporations should be barred
from contributing to campaign funds, interlocking directorates should
be prohibited, and a federal license should be required of all engaged in
interstate business. For the railroad problem he reverted to the Populist
remedy, government ownership, "not as an immediate issue, but as an
ultimate solution of the controversy." The trouble with Bryan's program was that it was so like Roosevelt's; indeed, well before election
time Congress had passed and Roosevelt had signed a measure forbidding
corporations to contribute toward the election of national officers, while
Bryan had temporized still further on the railroad question.

The real issue in the lackadaisical campaign of 1908 was whether
Bryan or Taft could be the better trusted to carry out the Roosevelt
policies. In the end Taft won by an electoral vote of 321
Election of to 162. Besides the "solid South" Bryan carried only
1908 Nebraska, Colorado, and Nevada, but he at least surpassed
Parker's record of four years before. Republican conservatives, looking
carefully into Taft's record as a judge, concluded that they had little
to fear from Roosevelt's political legatee. Later, not without a show of
justice, Bryan complained that the Republicans had enjoyed an unfair
advantage in the campaign. Taft the progressive carried the West,
while Taft the conservative carried the East. Forty-six states participated in the election of 1908; for in 1907 the majority party in Congress
had at last decided that Republican supremacy was well enough established to risk the admission of Oklahoma, an almost certainly Democratic
state. A similar offer to admit New Mexico and Arizona as one state
failed because of the opposition of Arizona to such a scheme.

With the election over, Roosevelt turned his attention to preparations for a great hunting expedition to Africa, upon which he had long
set his heart, and immediately after Taft's inauguration he left the
country, Africa bound. Perhaps he wished his successor to be free from
the handicap of a popular ex-President; or, perhaps he was only seeking
for himself consolation for having lost the Presidency, an office he had
enjoyed to the full every moment he had held it, and could not surrender
without deep pangs of regret that he must somehow conceal.

32

The Progressive Movement

THE Roosevelt era saw the rise of a reform movement in the United States that affected every aspect of American life, state as well as national, social no less than political. Just as had been the case during the Jacksonian period, reform was in the air. Much of the momentum that the reform movement had attained came from the Populists, whose party had practically disappeared by the turn of the century, but whose principles had been espoused alike by Bryan Democracy and Roosevelt Republicanism. The contributions of the muckrakers fed new and exciting fuel to the flames. Possibly most significant of all was the rise of socialism to a position of consequence in the American mind. Socialistic ideas had been brought to the United States, mainly by immigrants from Europe, far back in the nineteenth century, but only on the threshold of the twentieth century had American conditions become sufficiently comparable to those of Europe to make socialism seem plausible to even the least favored of Americans. Organized labor in the United States, although it consistently refused to encourage the formation of a strictly labor, or socialist, party, tended in most other matters to go along with the progress of socialistic thought. During the early nineties a Socialist-Labor Party, founded by Daniel De Leon, made a few converts, but it was less successful than the far more conservative Social Democratic, or Socialist, Party, which for the first time, but by no means the last, nominated Eugene V. Debs for the Presidency in 1900.[1]

The fundamental tenet of the Socialists was the abolition of the capitalist system in order to make way for the ownership by the public of all the means of production and distribution. This end they hoped ultimately to achieve by use of the ballot, rather than by revolution; nor did they "strive to substitute working-class rule for capitalist-class rule, but to free all humanity from class rule and to realize the international brotherhood of man." Pending

The reform spirit

"Socialistic" trends

---

[1] Nathan Fine, *Labor and Farmer Parties in the United States, 1828–1928* (1928), is better on the labor than on the farmer side.

more fundamental reforms, they were willing to support such halfway measures as public works for the relief of the unemployed, the collective ownership of the railroads, public utilities, and all existing national monopolies; the improvement of the industrial condition of the workers; the extension of inheritance taxes; a graduated income tax; woman suffrage; the initiative and the referendum; the abolition of the doctrine of judicial review; the election of judges by the people for short terms; and the enactment of further measures for general education and the conservation of health. Many so-called socialistic policies had an ancestry quite separate from the Socialist Party, but many others were original and seeped gradually over into the old-party platforms.

The most spectacular of the reforms of this period occurred in the realm of state, rather than national, government. Among the state governors Roosevelt had many precursors and imitators, each with a vision of reform. They found the state governments almost completely in the control of whatever big business corporations happened to be most powerful in their particular part of the country. Well-oiled party machines in each state did the bidding of the state "boss," and the "boss" in turn did the bidding of the business interests that furnished the oil for his machine. Speaking before the New York Constitutional Convention of 1915, Elihu Root, an excellent authority, remarked:

> Mr. Platt ruled the state; for nigh upon twenty years he ruled it. It was not the governor; it was not the legislature; it was Mr. Platt. And the capital was not here [at Albany]: it was at 49 Broadway.... The ruler of the state during the greater part of the forty years of my acquaintance with the state government has not been any man authorized by the constitution or by law.... The party leader is elected by no one, accountable to no one, bound by no oath of office, removable by no one.... I don't criticize the men of the invisible government.... But it is all wrong.

For a reformer to be elected to a governorship under such conditions was in itself a revolution; once in office his only chance of remaining there was to break the power of the machine.

Outstanding among the reform governors was Robert M. La Follette (1855–1925) of Wisconsin, a man whose influence upon the course of political events during his lifetime was more fundamental than that of many Presidents. "Fighting Bob," as he came to be called, had entered politics, without benefit of machine assistance, soon after his graduation from the University of Wisconsin in 1879.[1] As county prosecutor of Dane County he made an excellent record, and in 1884 was nominated and elected for the first of three successive terms in the national House of Representatives. He

**Robert M.
La Follette**

---

[1] La Follette's life-history is still best told in his *Autobiography* (1913), but a more objective study of his career is badly needed.

was an indefatigable canvasser, delighted in controversy, and developed political speechmaking into a fine art. Like many another Republican he was left at home by the election of 1890, and but for a controversy with the all-powerful Senator Philetus Sawyer, who was both a politician and a lumber baron, his ambitions for a career in state politics might easily have been gratified. When the Democrats took over the government of Wisconsin in 1891, they found that for years the Republican state treasurers had made a practice of depositing the state's funds, interest free, in certain favored banks. The new attorney-general promptly brought suit to recover this interest money for the state, and Sawyer, because he had acted as bondsman for the treasurers, came in for his share of the trouble. According to the La Follette version of the story, Sawyer attempted through La Follette to bribe the judge before whom the case was to be tried — a Democratic brother-in-law of La Follette's. Deeply incensed, La Follette made the whole matter public, and helped the state recover the funds of which it had been defrauded.

From that time on La Follette was a crusader for reform. Determined to win the governorship, he was repeatedly denied the nomination in spite of a growing popular sentiment in his favor; not until 1900 was he able to line up a majority of the convention delegates. Elected, and twice re-elected, he forced through reluctant legislatures laws for the more effective taxation of the railroads and other corporations; for the establishment of direct primaries through which the people, not boss-ridden conventions, could select their own candidates for office; for the termination of the free-pass evil by prohibiting state officials from accepting them; and for the conservation of the natural resources of the state in forests and water-power. In his quest of good government he enlisted the aid of experts from the University of Wisconsin, whose new president, Charles R. Van Hise, was his close personal friend and his choice for the office. He was instrumental, also, in the creation of a Legislative Reference Bureau through which legislators might obtain expert advice on the drafting of bills.

The "Wisconsin idea," which was fundamentally to free the state from business domination through venal party bosses and to turn over public administration to popularly chosen leaders willing to seek the advice of experts, exactly suited the temper of the times.[1] Other crusaders Other governors in other states duplicated in varying degrees the La Follette record in Wisconsin. In Missouri Joseph W. Folk won public attention as circuit attorney by successfully prosecuting the corrupt ring of St. Louis "boodlers" that for years had fattened on

[1] Charles McCarthy, *The Wisconsin Idea* (1912), is the work of an enthusiastic La Follette supporter. See also Edward A. Fitzpatrick, *McCarthy of Wisconsin* (1944).

municipal graft. As governor for four years after 1905, he sought with moderate success to repeat in the state arena what he had done for his home city. In New York Charles Evans Hughes became a national figure while serving as counsel for a legislative investigating committee that was examining into the methods of the New York life insurance companies. Hughes's sensational disclosures brought about a revolution in the insurance business and led to his election as governor in 1906. Out in California the star of Hiram Johnson began to rise. As early as 1902 he attracted attention as a member of the staff of prosecuting attorneys in charge of some San Francisco "boodling" cases. In 1908 he secured the conviction of Abe Ruef, grafting municipal boss of San Francisco, after Francis J. Heney, the original prosecutor, had been shot in the line of duty. In 1910 Johnson was elected governor, determined above all else to end the domination of the state by the Southern Pacific Railroad.

The roll of reform governors was a long one, including, besides such prominent individuals as A. B. Cummins of Iowa, and John A. Johnson of Minnesota, many lesser lights whose names never became nationally well known. Private individuals, such as William S. U'Ren of Oregon, crusader for "the Oregon system," also took a hand, while the public at large, fully aroused by the revelations of the muckrakers, demanded and obtained results.[1]

The most fundamental of the political reforms effected during these years was the substitution of the direct primary for the convention system of making nominations. Under the old system only

The direct primary a small fraction of the voters, certainly never more than fifteen per cent, attended the original caucuses or "primaries" by which convention delegates were chosen. A large proportion of those who attended were local office-holders and aspirants to office. It was thus easy for the machine to secure a working majority of the delegates to almost every convention, and to put through the "slate" of nominees agreed upon by the leaders in advance. The direct primary, however, substituted voting at the polls by secret ballot for the caucus-convention system, and reduced immeasurably the chances of machine manipulation. Within a comparatively short time after the passage in 1903 of the Wisconsin primary law, similar laws had been enacted by nearly every state in the Union.[2] The results were revolutionary. It would be idle to claim that the direct primaries completely eliminated either business domination of government or the power of venal party

[1] An excellent chapter on reform within the states is contained in D. S. Muzzey, *The United States of America*, II, *From the Civil War* (1933).

[2] A. F. Lovejoy, *La Follette and the Establishment of the Direct Primary in Wisconsin* (1941).

bosses. But the new laws greatly promoted the possibility of successful popular uprisings against corrupt machines, and because of them in state after state men were elected to office who under the old system would never have had a chance.

The initiative and referendum were twin measures of popular government that might be used as clubs over legislatures unresponsive to the popular will. By these devices laws could be initiated by petition, and voted on by ballot. The use of the referen- Initiative
dum for constitutional provisions and for such local legis- and
lation as the flotation of bond issues was by no means new, referendum
but its application to ordinary law-making, coupled with the power of popular initiative was decidedly an innovation. The initiative and referendum were first adopted in South Dakota, in 1898, but obtained their best test in Oregon, where from 1902 to 1910 no less than thirty-two measures were referred to the people for a vote. In Oregon, too, the recall, a measure by which faithless officials, on petition of a stipulated number or percentage of the voters, were required to stand for re-election at special elections, was given a thorough trial. Indeed, "the Oregon system" came to be the term most commonly used to describe the new adventures in popular government. Largely because of U'Ren's effective leadership, Oregon had adopted the Australian ballot in 1891, a registration law in 1899, the initiative and referendum law in 1902, the direct primary in 1904, a sweeping corrupt practices act in 1908, and the recall in 1910. "In Oregon," so it was said, "the state government is divided into four departments — the executive, judicial, legislative, and U'Ren — and it is still an open question who exerts the more power." [1] Within a decade nearly twenty states had the initiative and referendum, and nearly a dozen the recall. Acceptance of "the Oregon system" moved in general from west to east, and in the older states often met unyielding opposition.

That even the federal government might be affected by state reforms was proved when preferential primaries were introduced whereby the voters might express their choices for United States senators. These laws assumed that in senatorial elections state legis- Direct
latures would be guided solely by the popular mandate, and election of
regardless of personal or party considerations would elect senators
the primary winner to the senatorship. The movement for direct election of United States senators dated far back into the nineteenth century, and had won warm support not only from off-color politicians such as

---

[1] A. H. Eaton, *The Oregon System* (1912). See also E. P. Oberholtzer, *The Referendum in America* (1911), and C. A. Beard (editor), *Documents on the State-Wide Initiative, Referendum and Recall* (1912).

the Populists, but from many conservative citizens as well. Four times, in 1894, 1898, 1900, and 1902, the national House of Representatives had supported a constitutional amendment for the direct election of senators, but each time the Senate had refused to concur. Meantime the scandals involved in legislative elections became increasingly more evident. At best state legislation tended to be treated as of secondary importance in years when a senator was to be chosen; at worst open bribery was resorted to by individuals and corporations bent on the success of a candidate friendly to their interests.

Undoubtedly the framers of the Constitution had intended that the upper chamber should represent not merely the individual states, but also the wealth of the nation. They had builded better than they knew. By the twentieth century the United States Senate could be spoken of, not without a semblance of truth, as a "millionaire's club." Men of great wealth aspired to a seat in it as a crowning evidence of success. Corporations with privileges to protect made every effort to secure a senatorship for one of their directors, or at least for one of their attorneys. Party bosses themselves often sought and obtained election to the Senate. The general level of intelligence in the upper chamber therefore was high — has perhaps never been higher — but the senators, so critics insisted, represented the vested interests of the country rather than the people as a whole. Naturally the Senate refused, as long as it dared, to risk the results of popular election. But the preferential primaries, which eventually were adopted by more than half the states, brought about by indirection the change that the Senate had tried to avoid. Further, as popularly chosen senators took their seats, the opposition to direct election was broken down. By 1912 the Senate submitted to the inevitable and agreed to the Seventeenth Amendment, which a year later became a part of the Constitution.

Reforms in the field of municipal government paralleled, but hardly equaled, the reforms being made by the states. The Tammany machine in New York was no worse than many another, only better **Municipal reform** advertised. In nearly every city of considerable size crooked deals in the awarding of contracts and franchises, open or secret alliances with commercialized vice, and the protection of favored classes of criminals who paid well for their privileges were only the worst of the sins of the politicians in charge. As with Tammany Hall, the machine could count on the support of thousands of voters who received in return for their ballots a feeling of security. If a worker lost his job, got into trouble with the law, needed money to meet an emergency, or faced any personal crisis whatever, he went to his local leader for help, and got it. To make surer of success at the polls, however, ballot-boxes were stuffed, returns were falsified, and a thousand irregularities were condoned. Lincoln Steffens's articles made the "shame of the cities" better known than ever before, but reformers had already arisen. In Toledo Samuel M. Jones, better known as "Golden Rule" Jones, made successful war upon the private-contract system, and advocated the municipal ownership of public utilities. Elected to office in 1897, he was repeatedly re-elected, and in 1904 was succeeded by his friend and disciple, Brand Whitlock, who continued the good work. In Cleveland Thomas L. Johnson became mayor in 1901. A convinced "single-taxer," he secured among other reforms a long-overdue reassessment of property values, municipal control of the street-car system, and a three-cent fare. Under his régime Cleveland could claim to be the "best governed city in the United States," a claim that Milwaukee, under the Socialist leadership of Emil Seidel and Daniel W. Hoan, was soon to challenge.[1]

To many thoughtful critics the reform of city government could best be promoted by a change in the system. City administration was primarily a business affair; why should it be hampered by a form of government patterned after that of the United States? Why should the Democrats and the Republicans run opposing tickets for city offices? What difference did it make whether a candidate for mayor or alderman believed in a high tariff or a low tariff, in imperialism or in isolation, in free silver or the single gold standard? In 1901 the city of Galveston, Texas, which the year before had been destroyed by a tidal wave and was in desperate need of efficiency in government, tried to obtain it by turning over the whole problem to a commission of five, each of whom would administer under rules laid down by a majority vote some department of city affairs. Soon many other cities were experimenting with the "commission form" of government, and out of it grew an even more reasonable scheme, the "city manager" plan. This system sought to duplicate the methods of the business corporation. The elected board or commission employed a manager, who ran the city with the same freedom of action that was normally accorded a business executive. Soon hundreds of American cities, large or small, were being administered, usually more efficiently than ever before, by commissions and city managers. Thousands, however, adhered to the old systems, and in all too many instances to the old ways.

The reforms of the Roosevelt era in state and city government greatly facilitated the efforts of those who wished to enlist the aid of the law in the improvement of social conditions. No longer so deferential to the rich man's point of view, and unhampered by the constitutional limita-

[1] The battle for municipal reform may be followed in Lincoln Steffens, *The Shame of the Cities* (1904); Fremont Older, *My Own Story* (1925); C. H. Harrison, *Stormy Years* (1935); ₹. C. Howe, *The City, the Hope of Democracy* (1905).

tions that so restricted the activities of the national government, the states crowded their statute books with laws that had rarely or never been obtainable before. A large part of the new legislation was designed to promote the "square deal" for labor, but other important subjects, particularly the prohibition of the liquor traffic, received careful consideration.

Most important of the new labor legislation, perhaps, was the series of employer's liability, or workmen's compensation, acts that followed Maryland's first feeble beginning in this direction in 1902.

Labor legislation These laws were designed to reverse the old common-law rule that a workman had to prove negligence on the part of his employer in order to obtain compensation for injuries, and that even this might be insufficient if he himself, or any "fellow-servant," had been guilty of contributory negligence. The new principle, which by 1921 had been accepted in all but six states, was that in hazardous occupations the employer was liable for all injuries that occurred to his employees while they were at work. As a result of the new laws millions of dollars were soon paid out each year in benefits to injured workmen or their families.

Efforts were made also to increase the protection given to women and children in industry. Most of the states eventually adopted laws forbidding in certain types of industry the employment of children under fourteen years of age, while laws for compulsory school attendance accomplished the same purpose in another way. Opposition from the southern textile industries caused some of the southern states to lag either in the enactment or in the enforcement of child-labor laws, and as early as 1906 a movement was begun to give Congress authority over child labor by a constitutional amendment. Such an amendment was actually submitted in 1924, but it failed of ratification. Laws limiting the number of hours per day that women and children might be employed, and fixing minimum-wage schedules that they must be paid, were also enacted by some of the states. Attempts to extend these same principles to employed men met with stronger opposition, but a few successes were recorded. In the whole field of labor legislation the United States lagged far behind European nations. Unemployment insurance and old-age pensions, for example, while common enough elsewhere, were hardly more than talked about in the United States.

Attempts by prohibitionists to do away with the liquor traffic dates far back into the nineteenth century, but the era of successful activity began with the formation of the Anti-Saloon League in 1893. This

Prohibition organization received the active support of all the evangelical denominations, and was maintained by the funds its agents were permitted to collect at regular church services. Its methods came to be quite as hard-boiled as those of the politicians with whom it had to deal. It knew one test, and only one test, for fitness to hold office. If a man favored the liquor traffic, the Anti-Saloon League was against him; if he opposed the liquor traffic, the Anti-Saloon League was for him. With a budget that by 1903 had reached four hundred thousand dollars a year, the League was in a position to hire hundreds of organizers and to maintain scores of offices. For a generation, under the leadership of Wayne B. Wheeler and William H. Anderson, it made the issue, "wet" or "dry," take precedence over nearly every other issue in state and local politics. As between low license and high license, the League favored high license. As between high license and "local option," whereby a town or county might vote to exclude saloons, it favored local option. As between local option and state-wide prohibition, it favored state-wide prohibition. And as between state-wide prohibition and national prohibition, it favored national prohibition. Never too squeamish about its methods or its political bedfellows, it took what it could get.

It got a great deal. The liquor business was open to attack for all the same reasons that other big businesses were vulnerable, and for many more besides. A veritable barrage of tracts, sermons, orations, and temperance journals set forth its shortcomings with a degree of passionate intolerance reminiscent of the abolitionists. The efforts of brewers, distillers, and wine-makers to obtain business favors from legislatures, county boards, and city councils were skillfully used to classify the liquor interests with the corruptionists. Local liquor dealers' associations were taunted as defenders of lawlessness and vice, and crooked politics was traced with an unerring eye to the door of the saloon. In the South the mistakes of the Negro were blamed upon liquor, and prohibition was demanded as a necessary preliminary to good relations between the races. While Roosevelt was President the successes of the Anti-Saloon League were mainly confined to the rural districts and were obtained by local option, but before he left office four southern states had voted dry, and within the next few years many others, northern as well as southern, were to follow. By the time the World War broke out, nearly half the people of the United States lived in "dry" territory, while in three-fourths of its total area the saloon had been outlawed. The ratification of the Eighteenth Amendment to the Constitution in 1919 merely completed a process that had been long under way.[1]

Woman suffrage was a companion reform to prohibition. If women

[1] J. A. Krout, *The Origins of Prohibition* (1925); E. H. Cherrington, *The Evolution of Prohibition in the United States of America* (1920); Justin Steuart, *Wayne Wheeler, Dry Boss* (1928).

obtained the vote, so prohibitionists reasoned, they would with certainty aid the temperance cause. In 1869 the Territory of Wyoming had conferred the suffrage on women, and by 1911 six western states, Wyoming, Colorado, Utah, Idaho, Washington, and California, had accepted the innovation *in toto*, while many other states gave women the right to vote in certain elections. Like the prohibitionists the suffragists hoped to crown their efforts by obtaining an amendment to the Constitution that would end the denial of the suffrage to women, and, while adding state after state to their lists of converts, they continued to work on Congress. An outbreak of "militancy," borrowed from Great Britain during the World War, may have had something to do with bringing Congress to yield in 1919. The Nineteenth Amendment became a part of the Constitution in 1920.[1]

Woman suffrage

The movements for prohibition and woman suffrage carried along in their wake a great variety of reforms designed to promote the public health and happiness. New building codes were devised, and public parks and playgrounds were multiplied. Renewed efforts were made to wipe out gambling and prostitution. Special courts were established to deal with the problem of juvenile delinquency. Divorce laws were relaxed. Legal discriminations against women, aside from the suffrage, were brought near the vanishing point. Most of these laws, like prohibition and the labor codes, depended for their constitutionality upon the "police power"; that is, the right of the state to do whatever might be necessary to promote the health, happiness, and morality of its citizens. Such laws frequently interfered seriously with the full freedom of individuals, and led to an enormous amount of litigation. The courts, almost invariably hostile in the beginning, eventually relented, and in nearly every instance granted a grudging approval to the measures that the public desired.

With Roosevelt in the Presidency, the country felt satisfied that the reform spirit was duly represented in national affairs. The accession of Taft, it was confidently predicted, would bring little change. "Never before in our time," said the New York *Tribune*, "has the entry of a new President into office marked so slight a break politically between the present and the past." Unfortunately, Taft was unable to live up to the reputation that Roosevelt had made for him. An able constitutional lawyer, he had more respect for the legislative independence of Congress than Roosevelt had ever had, and often it was the Congress rather than the President who determined the course of national policy. Furthermore, Taft was not a disciple of the "strenuous

Taft as President

---

[1] A. M. Schlesinger, *New Viewpoints in American History* (new edition, 1937), contains an admirable chapter on the "rôle of women."

life," and tended to avoid rather than to embrace political warfare; Roosevelt, on the other hand, was never happier than in the midst of an "elegant row." Before long the public began to grumble that Taft had been elected to carry out the Roosevelt policies, and had "carried them out on a stretcher."

Taft's first failure was with tariff reform, something Roosevelt had never attempted, but had somehow managed to bequeath as one of his policies to his successor. True to a promise made during the campaign, Taft called Congress into special session for March 15, and by April 9 the Payne Bill, providing for **The Payne-Aldrich Tariff** moderate reductions downward, had passed the House. When the bill reached the Senate, it was taken in hand by Senator Aldrich of Rhode Island, chairman of the Senate Committee on Finance, and rewritten to fit the high-protectionist views of the multimillionaire American industrialists, of whom Aldrich himself was one. But Aldrich's plans for the speedy passage of the bill were interrupted by a little group of middle-western Republican insurgents, led by Senator Robert M. La Follette of Wisconsin, who had entered the Senate in 1906. Determined that the bill should not be passed before the public could find out how complete a betrayal it was of the Republican campaign pledges, La Follette, ably assisted by Dolliver and Cummins of Iowa, Beveridge of Indiana, Bristow of Kansas, Clapp of Minnesota, and a few others, studied it by night and debated it by day. They were unable to prevent its passage, but ten of them joined with the Democrats in refusing to vote for it.[1] Known now as the Payne-Aldrich Bill, the measure at length was accepted by the House and approved by the President, who in a speech at Winona, Minnesota, in the fall of 1909 described it as the best tariff bill that the Republican Party had ever passed. This might have been true, but it was small consolation to a public that had come to believe, not without reason, that the tariff was "the mother of the trusts."

Circumstances soon made it appear that on the subject of conservation the new President was no more to be trusted than on the tariff. Taft's Secretary of the Interior, R. A. Ballinger of Washington, felt obliged for strictly legal reasons to restore to private **The Ballinger controversy** entry some waterpower sites in Montana and Wyoming and some coal lands in Alaska. This action was vigorously protested by one of Ballinger's subordinates, Louis R. Glavis, and by the chief of the forestry service, Gifford Pinchot. Taft, after careful investigation, decided that there was nothing against Ballinger, and for their insubordination dismissed both Glavis and Pinchot from office. But to the ever

[1] The two sides of this controversy are well presented in N. W. Stephenson, *Nelson W. Aldrich* (1930), and C. G. Bowers, *Beveridge and the Progressive Era* (1932).

Reproduced by special permission of Herbert Johnson

"PLEASE, MR. ALDRICH"

more hostile public, it appeared that Taft, however well-founded his action, had lined up with the anti-conservationists.

Meantime insurgency had broken out in the House, where a small group of progressive-minded Republicans had discovered that with Democratic co-operation they could outvote the Republican regulars. This power they determined to use against the autocratic sway of the Speaker, Joseph G. Cannon of Illinois, an ultra-conservative who consistently and effectively stood in the way of all progressive legislation. Ably led by Representative George W. Norris of Nebraska, they presented an amendment to the House rules designed to take the appointment of the Rules Committee out of the hands of the Speaker, and to make it elective by the House. With every parliamentary device in his possession, Cannon fought back, but eventually the Insurgent-Democratic combination won out. When the next Congress met, the rules were still further amended. All committees were made elective, with the Ways and Means Committee acting as a committee on committees. The changes wrought were fundamental. No longer could it be said that the Speaker, next to the President, was

Insurgency in the House

Reproduced by special permission of Herbert Johnson

THE COMMON PEOPLE AWAITING T. R.'S RETURN

the most powerful of American officials; moreover, the chief agency for maintaining party discipline in the House was destroyed. More and more members felt free to vote as their consciences or their constituents might direct, regardless of party pressure.

With the Republican Party on the verge of a disastrous split, the interest of the public in Roosevelt's return from Africa became intense.[1]   Finally, the Roosevelt hunting party reached Khartum in the Anglo-Egyptian Sudan on March 14, 1910, and after an extensive trip through Europe, the living Roosevelt, so long a mere memory, reappeared in the United States.   It was soon apparent that the old cordiality between Roosevelt and Taft was gone, although in the campaign of 1910 Roosevelt made every effort to heal

Election of 1910

[1] Teddy, come home and blow your horn,
   The sheep's in the meadow, the cow's in the corn.
   The boy you left to 'tend the sheep.
   Is under the haystack fast asleep.
From *Life*, May 26, 1910, quoted in Mark Sullivan, *Our Times*, IV, 441.

the breach in the party and to bring about a Republican victory. But for once the people would not follow him. They could see no other way to rebuke the Republican conservatives, among whom they now numbered Taft, than by voting the Democratic ticket. As a result, the House of Representatives fell to the Democrats with 229 members to 161 for the Republicans and one for the Socialists, Victor L. Berger of Milwaukee. The Senate remained Republican by a vote of 51 to 41, but this majority was so slender that the insurgents, of whom there were a dozen or more, by voting with the Democrats, could easily overturn it. The conservative Republicans had thus lost control of both houses of Congress. In the states the trend was equally pronounced. Such normally Republican strongholds as New York, Ohio, Massachusetts, Connecticut, and New Jersey, went Democratic by large majorities.

There can be no doubt that the election was intended as a rebuke to the Taft administration, but in many ways it was undeserved. In reality, Taft had carried out the Roosevelt policies with considerable success. He had secured a revision of the tariff, which, however inadequate, was something that Roosevelt had not even dared to attempt. He had prosecuted the trusts with vigor and persistence; before his administration ended he had brought more than twice as many suits against them as were undertaken by Roosevelt. He had sponsored the Mann-Elkins Act of 1910, which greatly increased the powers of the Interstate Commerce Commission, and extended its jurisdiction over railroad terminals as well as telegraph, telephone, and cable communications. He had served the cause of conservation by permitting the purchase by the government of privately owned timber tracts in the Appalachians, by withdrawing oil lands from entry — another thing Roosevelt had never done — and by obtaining from Congress the authority that Roosevelt lacked for withdrawing coal lands, also. Other measures enacted during his administration included the division of the Department of Commerce and Labor into two departments; the establishment of a Bureau of Mines; the improvement of the public land laws; and the enactment of postal savings and parcel post laws.

Much of Taft's unpopularity may be attributed to his political ineptitude, and much of it merely to hard luck. He got little credit for the reforms he had instituted, and much undeserved criticism. He made five wholly admirable appointments to the Supreme Court, but when he promoted a Democrat, Associate Justice White, to be Chief Justice, the Republican regulars were offended, while when he chose Governor Hughes of New York to be an associate justice, Republican progressives said he was merely seeking to

Taft's
bad luck

sidetrack a possible competitor for the 1912 nomination. When reciprocity with Canada, on which Taft had set his heart, was turned down in Canada after acceptance by the United States, Taft got the blame. When Taft's Secretary of State proposed to follow the same tactics in Nicaragua and Honduras that Roosevelt had used in Haiti, he was accused of "dollar diplomacy," an epithet that was used also to describe a plan for the participation by American bankers in a six-power loan to the new republic of China.[1]

The original program of the Republican insurgents was not the formation of a new party, but the capture of the party to which they still belonged. This was made clear as early as January 23, 1911, when a group of them, meeting at Senator La Follette's house in Washington, formed the National Progressive Republican League. Included in their program were the reforms designed to enable the people to defeat boss rule, such as the direct election of United States senators, direct primaries, the direct election of delegates to national nominating conventions, the initiative, the referendum, and the recall in the states, and a thoroughgoing corrupt practices act. On the assumption that Roosevelt would not consider a third term, they rallied around La Follette as the "logical man" to defeat Taft for renomination. But to the intense disappointment of La Follette who claimed that he had been used only as a "stalking-horse," Roosevelt announced on February 24, 1912, that he was ready to throw his "hat in the ring." From this day on the La Follette candidacy was a lost cause, and the progressive wing of the party turned with unbounded enthusiasm to Roosevelt.

The La Follette and Roosevelt candidacies

It soon developed that the ex-President, for all his popular appeal, had entered the campaign too late. The party machine was in the hands of the conservatives, who were determined to renominate Taft. They had already lined up many of the southern delegations which, because they were so largely composed of federal office-holders, could always be trusted to follow the will of the President, and they now made haste to gather in the rest. Elsewhere, in case the old convention system of choosing delegates was in force, the party regulars almost invariably controlled and obediently delivered their delegations to Taft. On the other hand, wherever the new system of preferential primaries existed, Roosevelt generally won; indeed, several states made haste to adopt such laws in order to promote his chances. When the Republican Convention met in Chicago on June 18, it was apparent that the Roosevelt forces were ap-

---

[1] Scott Nearing and Joseph Freeman, *Dollar Diplomacy* (1925); J. G. Reid, *The Manchu Abdication and the Powers, 1908-1912* (1935). American participation in the loan was cancelled by Wilson.

proximately a hundred votes short of a majority. To make up this deficiency, they had brought contests involving about two hundred and fifty seats, some fairly reasonable and others merely for the "moral effect." But the national committee had already turned most of their contests down, and the convention, effectively controlled by a conservative "steam-roller," decided nearly all of them in favor of Taft — a "naked theft," according to Roosevelt. Taft was nominated on the first ballot, although 107 delegates voted for Roosevelt, and 344 sat silent in protest.[1]

Even before the Republican Convention met it was obvious that Roosevelt was in no mood to accept defeat. If he lost the Republican nomination, he would run anyway. On June 22 he told a

The Progressive Party rump convention that met in Orchestra Hall, "If you wish me to make the fight, I will make it, even if only one state should support me." Six weeks later the new Progressive Party met, again in Chicago, to select Roosevelt as its standard-bearer. Already it had a symbol with which to match the Republican elephant and the Democratic donkey — the "bull moose." This was a favorite term with

[1] The stand taken by the national committee is explained and defended in Victor Rosewater, *Back Stage in 1912* (1932).

THE OLD AMERICAN WAY

The old-fashioned country store, like this one of about 1900, was far more than a place for buying and selling. It was a kind of social club. Here farmers and their families came on Saturday afternoons and evenings to meet each other, to exchange gossip, and to discuss the news. Here beside the cracker barrel, into which many an honest hand unhesitatingly strayed, public opinion on national and international problems was formed. Villagers, too, congregated in and about the stores. The talk that went on around the blazing stoves on a cold, stormy day left few subjects of consequence unmentioned. (Courtesy of the "Ladies' Home Journal.")

The New York "East Side" was long regarded as the place where social workers could find all the worst elements of city slums. Here on the streets, at the markets, and in the tenements the newly arrived immigrants got their first acquaintance with the American way of life. Humanitarian reformers have struggled earnestly to improve these conditions, but the field of better housing, basic to any real solution of the problem, has hardly been touched, even by the New Deal. (Photo from Keystone.)

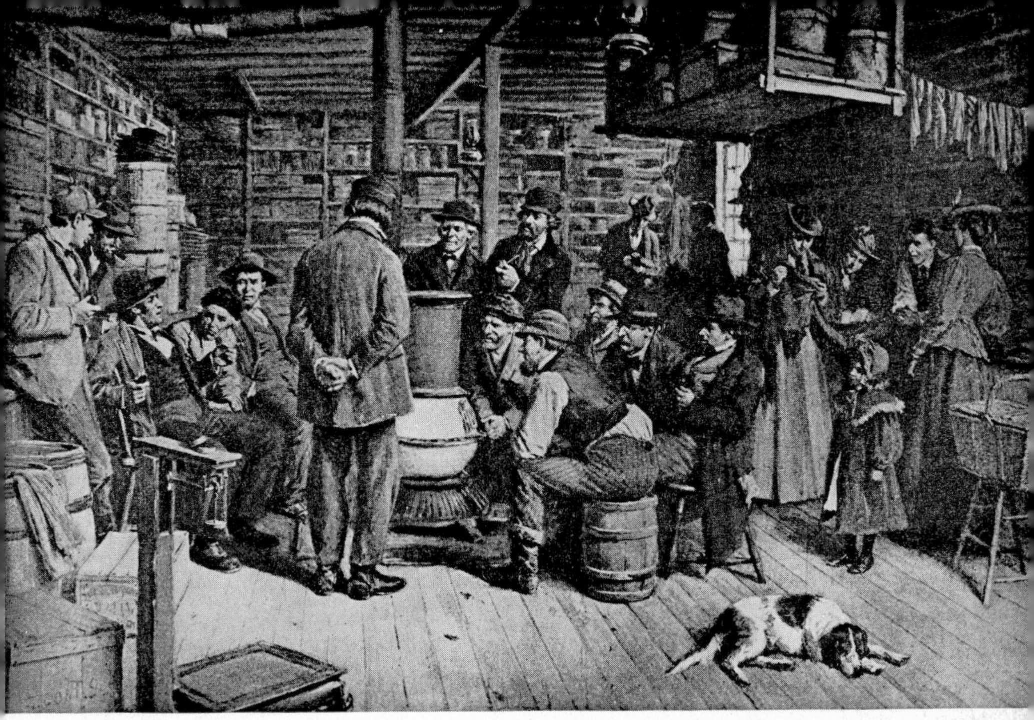

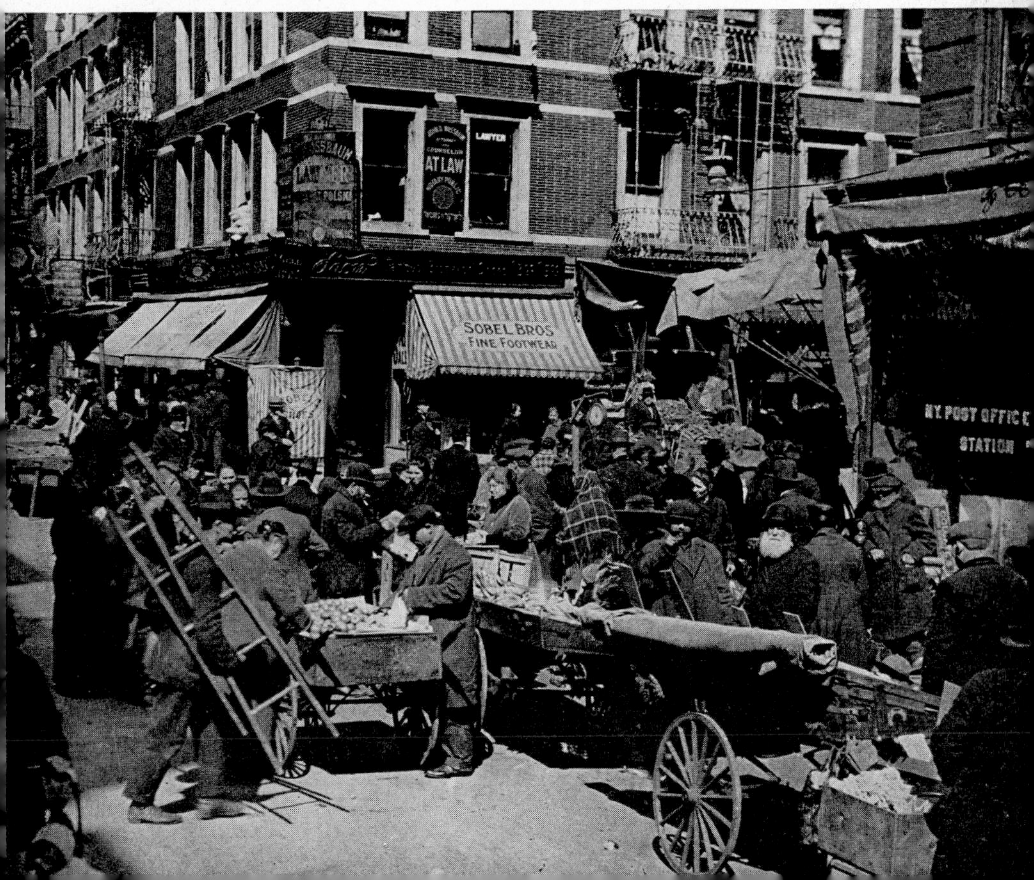
LAWYER
AT LAW
SOBEL BROS
FINE FOOTWEAR
STATION

ROOSEVELT

LA FOLLETTE

NORRIS

HUGHES

TAFT

ROOT

Roosevelt, one he had used as far back as 1900 when he had boasted to Hanna that he was "as strong as a Bull Moose." An enthusiastic audience of twenty thousand people heard the Progressive leader denounce both old parties as "husks, with no real soul within either, divided on artificial lines, boss-ridden and privilege-controlled, each a jumble of incongruous elements, and neither daring to speak out wisely and fearlessly what should be said on the vital issues of the day." On a great variety of issues the new party spoke out. Its trust policy recognized the corporation as "an essential part of modern business," but demanded effective regulation through "a strong federal administrative commission of high standing." It endorsed, too, all the current reforms such as the direct primary, woman suffrage, an easier way to amend the Constitution, tariff revision downward to reasonable protection, better working conditions in the factories, the prohibition of child labor, the better regulation of labor by women, minimum-wage standards, and an eight-hour day in continuous twenty-four-hour industries. Such pronouncements delighted social workers, such as Jane Addams, and gave the new party a crusading character that well became its leader. With a fervor reminiscent of Populism the Progressive Convention sang "Onward, Christian Soldiers," and quoted Roosevelt's challenge to the Taft forces at Chicago: "We stand at Armageddon and we battle for the Lord."

THE ROOSEVELT ERA

The Roosevelt Era produced a notable galaxy of political stars. THEODORE ROOSEVELT (1858–1919), *twenty-sixth President of the United States, was the dominating figure of his age, and one of the most popular of American Presidents.* WILLIAM HOWARD TAFT (1857–1930), *twenty-seventh President, was the unhappy wearer of the Roosevelt mantle. Defeated for re-election in 1912, he returned to political life in 1921, when Harding made him Chief Justice of the United States Supreme Court.*

ELIHU ROOT (1845–1937) *was Roosevelt's second Secretary of State, and later, as the ranking "elder statesman" of the Republican Party, exerted for many years a profound influence upon the course of political events.*

CHARLES EVANS HUGHES (1862–   ), *as reform governor of New York during Roosevelt's administration and later as Secretary of State under Harding and Associate Justice and Chief Justice of the United States Supreme Court, left an indelible mark upon American political life.*

ROBERT M. LA FOLLETTE (1855–1925), *of Wisconsin, and* GEORGE W. NORRIS (1861–   ), *of Nebraska, were both nominal Republicans during Roosevelt's time, but were extremely independent in their views. La Follette in the Senate and Norris in the House led the insurgent movement of the Taft administration.* (*Photos of Hughes, La Follette, and Norris from Harris & Ewing.*)

Meanwhile, the Democrats, convinced that the Republican split would insure their triumph at the polls in November, had met in Baltimore, July 25, to choose their candidate from a long list of favorite sons. After the tenth ballot it seemed certain that Champ Clark of Missouri, Speaker of the House, would be the nominee, for he had obtained a majority of the votes, although not yet a two-thirds majority. But William Jennings Bryan, still the most powerful man in the Democratic Party, switched from Clark to Governor Wilson of New Jersey on the fourteenth ballot. The Tammany delegation from New York had voted for Clark since the tenth ballot, and Bryan's explanation of his conduct was that he could not support anyone who would owe his nomination to Tammany. Cynics insisted that Bryan was only trying to deadlock the convention so that it would again turn to him, but on the forty-sixth ballot it chose Woodrow Wilson.

The campaign provided plenty of excitement and the public enjoyed it thoroughly. The presidential nominees spoke freely and with vigor.

The campaign of 1912

Roosevelt and Taft, throughout the primary contests and on into the election campaign, belabored each other as only two friends fallen out can do. Wilson proved to be an admirable public speaker, and those who bothered to follow what he said must have realized that his interpretation of the Democratic platform furnished a close approximation of what the Progressives believed they were fighting for. The results of the election were what all astute observers were able to foresee. Wilson, with fewer popular votes than Bryan had received in any of his three defeats, amassed an electoral vote of 435 to Roosevelt's 88 and Taft's 8. With the Democrats equally victorious in the congressional and the senatorial elections, the new President would be assured also of a comfortable working majority in Congress. In most of the state contests the Democrats also scored victories, the cleanest sweep their party had made since before the Civil War.

It thus fell out that the reform policies which Roosevelt had begun, and which Taft had sought with only partial success to continue, would

Woodrow Wilson

be carried to fruition, if at all, by a Democratic President. Woodrow Wilson (1856–1924), upon whom this task had devolved, had had an unusual preparation for the Presidency. The son of a prominent southern clergyman, he had given up the law to become a college professor, and as a political scientist at Princeton University had achieved international recognition for his studies in comparative government. Deeply impressed with the vast powers wielded by the prime ministers in Great Britain and elsewhere, he was convinced that the principle of executive leadership must somehow be grafted into the

American system. Roosevelt's expansion of the President's prerogatives were quite in line with Wilson's thinking. "The President," wrote the professor, "is at liberty, both in law and conscience, to be as big a man as he can. His capacity will set the limit." Promoted presently to the presidency of Princeton, Wilson made an effort to democratize the institution that was totally unappreciated by his governing board. Hence, when the Democratic "boss" of New Jersey, in search of window-dressing for his ticket, offered Wilson a nomination as governor in 1910, he accepted gladly, made an earnest campaign, and was elected.[1]

In office, Wilson at once put into effect the doctrine of executive leadership he so long had taught. Why were there party bosses? Because the elected leaders failed to use the powers that were rightly theirs. The governor had power; Wilson used it. He could command the attention of the press; Wilson used that too. With the support of public opinion Wilson soon had the legislature doing the governor's bidding, not the party boss's. In spite of the machine, he saw to it that the laws promised by the Democratic platform were enacted. On pressure from the governor's office, the legislature of New Jersey passed up-to-the-minute reform measures — to establish employers' liability, to punish corrupt practices, to control public utilities, and to reform the ballot. These victories in a state that had long been known as the "home of the trusts," made Wilson a marked man. Adroitly presented to the public outside New Jersey by Colonel Edward M. House of Texas, he had become by the time the Democratic National Nominating Convention met in 1912 the favorite candidate of the liberal wing of his party.[2]

Having achieved the Presidency, Wilson was determined to be the prime-minister type of President. With this end in view he included in his cabinet as Secretary of State the man whose influence with the rank and file of the Democratic Party was still second to none, William Jennings Bryan. Other appointments were made, not only with an eye to the fitness of the candidate, as might have been expected of such a President, but also with an eye to political cohesiveness. It was soon clear that Wilson meant to become the unchallenged leader of his party. He broke a precedent more than a century old by appearing in person to read his messages to Congress, short messages that the public would also read and expect to see

Wilson's view of the Presidency

---

[1] R. S. Baker, *Woodrow Wilson, Life and Letters* (8 vols., 1927–1939), is extraordinarily detailed, and somewhat worshipful. Other biographies of consequence are Josephus Daniels, *Life of Woodrow Wilson* (1924); David Lawrence, *The True Story of Woodrow Wilson* (1924); W. A. White, *Woodrow Wilson* (1924); W. E. Dodd, *Woodrow Wilson and his Work* (1920); Eleanor Wilson McAdoo, *The Woodrow Wilsons* (1937); Edith Bolling Wilson, *My Memoir* (1939).

[2] Decidedly the best history of the Wilson administration is F. L. Paxson, *American Democracy and the World War*, I, *Pre-War Years* (1918).

speedily translated into law. He took the people constantly into his
confidence, and made the most of newspaper publicity. The President,
he had once said, "has no means of compelling Congress except through
public opinion." But he also used his influence directly upon congressmen in personal interviews, and unhesitatingly accorded patronage
favors to the faithful, while denying them to others. Behind the scenes
he relied heavily upon the advice of Colonel House, with whom he discussed all matters of consequence, and Joseph P. Tumulty, his faithful
private secretary, a shrewd and practical politician.

Wilson's first efforts were directed toward the downward revision of the
tariff, an end his predecessor had failed to achieve. Acting under steady

The
Underwood-
Simmons
Tariff

pressure from the White House, the Underwood-Simmons
Tariff Act was ready for the President's signature on October 3, 1913. It was neither a free-trade measure nor a low-
tariff measure, and was not meant to be either. Its schedules
of duties, however, were on the average about ten per cent lower than
those of the Payne-Aldrich Tariff, and it placed a hundred new items,
mostly raw materials or foodstuffs, on the free list. What these duties
might have done for business and for the revenue had times remained
normal will never be known, for the outbreak of war in Europe drastically
reduced importations. For revenue the government was obliged to fall
back on the income tax, made possible by the recent adoption of the
Sixteenth Amendment, and provided for in the Underwood-Simmons Act.
A tax of one per cent was charged against all incomes in excess of three
thousand dollars, or, in the case of married couples, four thousand dollars; while on incomes above twenty thousand dollars a surtax, beginning
with an additional one per cent, was gradually stepped up to a maximum
of six per cent on incomes above five hundred thousand dollars. At the
time these rates were devised the possibilities of the income tax were
only faintly realized, but within a few years it became the chief reliance of
the federal government for revenue.

On the heels of the tariff act came banking and currency reform of a
scale never before attempted in the United States. The National Mone-

The Federal
Reserve Bank-
ing System

tary Commission that Congress had created as a result
of the Panic of 1907 reported in 1912 that the only sure cure
for the financial ills from which the country suffered would
be a centralized banking system, substantially a third Bank
of the United States. The subject was again investigated during the
second half of the Taft administration, this time by a committee of the
Democratic House of Representatives, headed by A. P. Pujo of Louisiana.
The Pujo Committee, while fully convinced that there was a "money
trust" controlled by the whims of a few great bankers, balked at the

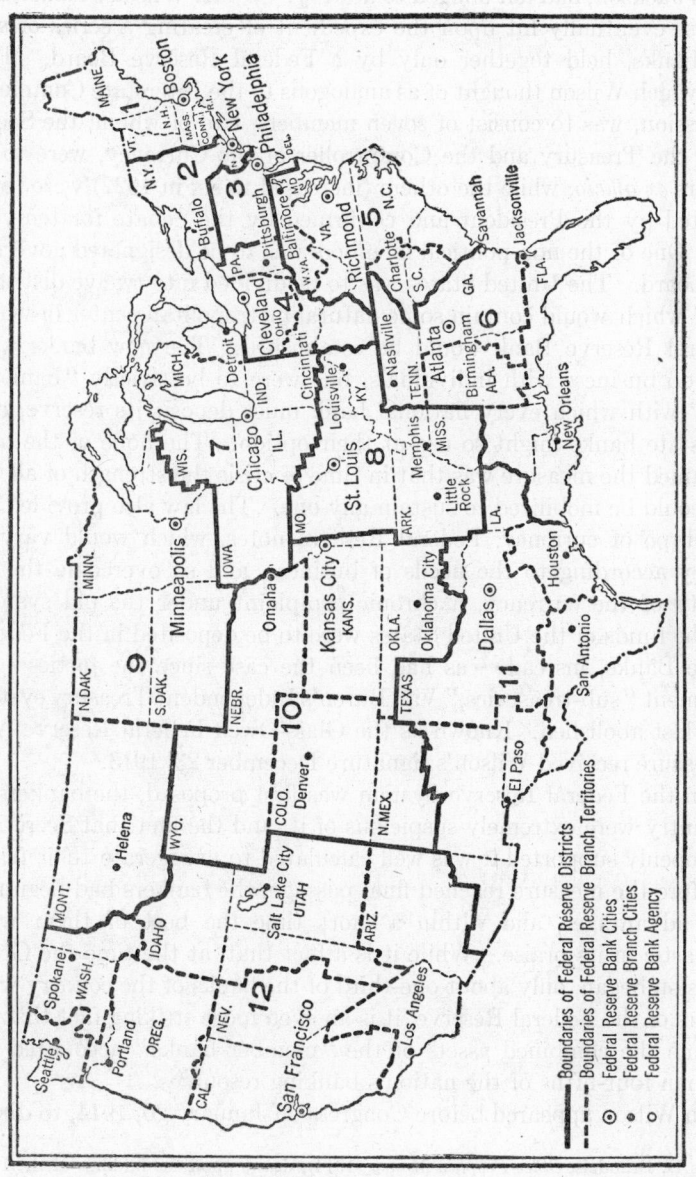

THE FEDERAL RESERVE DISTRICTS

Boundaries of Federal Reserve Districts
Boundaries of Federal Reserve Branch Territories
Federal Reserve Bank Cities
Federal Reserve Branch Cities
Federal Reserve Bank Agency

idea of creating the same kind of bank that a great Democratic President, Andrew Jackson, had felt obliged to destroy.[1] Under Wilson's leadership, Congress eventually hit upon the expedient of creating a series of sectional banks, held together only by a Federal Reserve Board. This board, which Wilson thought of as analogous to the Interstate Commerce Commission, was to consist of seven members, two of whom, the Secretary of the Treasury and the Comptroller of the Currency, were to be members *ex officio*, while the others (increased to six in 1922) were to be appointed by the President and confirmed by the Senate for ten-year terms. One of the non-political members was to be designated governor of the board. The United States was to be divided into twelve districts, each of which would contain some natural metropolitan center in which a Federal Reserve Bank would be established. The new banks were not to do business with individuals, but were to be strictly "bankers' banks," with which every national bank must deposit its reserve, and which state banks might so use at their option. The hope of the men who framed the measure was that in time of crisis the strength of all the banks could be mobilized to sustain any one. The law also provided for a new type of currency, Federal Reserve notes, which would vary in quantity according to the needs of business, and so overcome the inelasticity of the currency, a chronic complaint under the old system. Since the funds of the United States were to be deposited in the Federal Reserve Banks, instead — as had been the case since the forties — in government "sub-treasuries," Van Buren's Independent Treasury system was at last abolished. Known as the Glass-Owen Federal Reserve Act, this measure received Wilson's signature December 23, 1913.[2]

When the Federal Reserve System was first proposed, the bankers of the country were extremely suspicious of it, and the fact that Secretary Bryan openly supported it was well calculated to exaggerate their fears. But before the measure reached final passage, the bankers had begun to see its advantages, and within a short time the best of them were enthusiastic in its praise. While it is a fact that, at the time the Great Depression began, only about one-third of the banks of the country were members of the Federal Reserve, it is an even more striking fact that by that time the combined assets of the "member banks" accounted for more than four-fifths of the nation's banking resources.

When Wilson appeared before Congress on January 20, 1914, to direct

---

[1] Louis D. Brandeis, *Other People's Money* (1914), draws upon the findings of the Pujo Committee to set forth the facts about the existing system of finance.

[2] The literature of this subject is immense, but for the historical student H. P. Willis, *The Federal Reserve* (1915), and P. M. Warburg, *The Federal Reserve System* (2 vols., 1930), will prove satisfactory. Carter Glass, *An Adventure in Constructive Finance* (1927), throws light on the origin of the law.

attention to the trust problem, he had information available that his predecessors had lacked. The nature of modern business had been better studied. The Bureau of Corporations estab- *Wilson's* lished in Roosevelt's time had begun to bear fruit. Eco- *trust policy* nomics had elbowed its way to the front in the colleges and universities as the most significant of the social studies. Wilson knew, better than either Taft or Roosevelt had known, the hopelessness of trying merely to turn big businesses into little businesses. Such efforts were like trying to turn back the clock of time. What Wilson now sought of Congress was a clear definition of what was fair and what was unfair in business activity; further, a more complete recognition of the fact that the government through proper agencies should have the right to enforce the regulations that Congress laid down. Before the mid-term election of 1914, Congress had enacted two significant measures, the Clayton Anti-Trust Act and the Federal Trade Commission Act. The Clayton Act added various new prohibitions to the already long list of forbidden corporation practices, and the Federal Trade Commission Act created a new board of five members to investigate the origin and management of corporations, and to seek the assistance of the courts in putting an end to such "unfair methods of competition in commerce" as it might discover. Some progress was made with the enforcement of these laws during Wilson's first administration, but the work thus begun was adversely affected by the entrance of the United States into the World War. While that struggle was on, there was little attempt to enforce the restrictions of the Clayton Act, and after the Republicans returned to power in 1921, there was little desire to enforce them.[1]

The attitude that the Wilson administration meant to take toward labor was clearly revealed by the incorporation of what labor called its "Magna Charta" in the Clayton Act. Section 6 of the act specifically exempted labor and agricultural corporations *A "Magna* from prosecution under the terms of the anti-trust laws, *Charta" for* while section 20 limited the use of the injunction in labor *labor* disputes, prescribed trials by jury in contempt cases, and legalized such labor weapons as strikes, picketing, peaceable assembly, boycotts, and the collection of strike benefits. The framers of the Sherman Anti-Trust Act had probably not meant to extend its provisions to labor unions, but the courts had read that interpretation into the law. Until the passage of the Clayton Act, labor unions had to take care lest they be held guilty of "interstate boycotting." Judicial obstacles had been placed in the way of nearly every other labor practice also, and "government by injunc-

---

[1] G. C. Henderson, *The Federal Trade Commission* (1924); F. A. Fetter, *The Masquerade of Monopoly* (1931).

tion" had become a truism. The provisions of the Clayton Act were therefore hailed as a great boon to labor, and they were successfully enforced as long as Wilson was President. During the reactionary years of the twenties many of these guaranties were interpreted away by the courts.

The friendliness of the Wilson administration toward labor was manifested in many other ways. A Children's Bureau in the new Department of Labor sought to extend at least as good advice on the care of the nation's youth as the Department of Agriculture had long made available to farmers for the care of livestock. The problem of unemployment was faced courageously, and the employment service offered by the government was greatly expanded. The La Follette Seamen's Act required better physical conditions for ship crews, and ended the tyrannical control over their men that sea-captains had exercised since the days of Captain Bligh. Such measures as these, however, fell far short of the goals set by a small but tempestuous group of extreme radicals. Most difficult of these groups to deal with was the Industrial Workers of the World, commonly called the "I.W.W." or "Wobblies," whose greatest strength was recruited in the Far Northwest. The objectives of the "Wobblies" were frankly revolutionary, and their warlike methods resulted in the passage of criminal syndicalist laws by sixteen states which seriously crippled their activities. Finally, the United States government completed their destruction by bringing to trial some one hundred and thirteen I.W.W. leaders, most of whom were convicted and given long jail sentences. Since many of the radicals were recent immigrants, a strong movement for immigration restriction set in that resulted in the passage of a bill in 1917 which required ability to "read the English language or some other language" for admission to the United States. The measure was passed over President Wilson's veto.

In his inaugural address Wilson had given prominent mention to the needs of agriculture, and had particularly stressed the need of rural credits. The Federal Reserve Act authorized short-term
Rural credits loans up to six months on farm mortgages, but the pressure for long-term loans, by means of which the purchase of farm lands could be financed, grew steadily more insistent. After two years' consideration of the problem, Congress finally agreed to the Federal Farm Loan Act of 1916, which created a farm loan system patterned closely on the model of the Federal Reserve System. A central board consisting of the Secretary of the Treasury and four appointive members was given general control over a dozen Federal Farm Land Banks operating in as many different districts. Out of deference to the wishes of private moneylenders, who objected to the government monopolizing the busi-

ness of supplying rural credits, the law provided also for the establishment of joint-stock land banks, privately financed. By 1930 the two types of banks created by the Federal Farm Loan Act had together lent over two billion dollars to American farmers at interest rates of from five to six per cent.[1]

Before the exigencies of war halted the course of domestic reform the Wilson administration inaugurated another notable policy. Gifts from the federal government to aid the states in such matters as education and internal improvements were almost as old as the Constitution, but throughout the nineteenth century these gifts had been made primarily in the form of land or the receipts from land sales. By the time Wilson became President this source of supply had so nearly approached exhaustion that some new form of subsidy had to be found. It was discovered in the form of the heavy receipts that came in, or could be made to come in, from the income tax. This revenue, it fell out, was collected from a comparatively small fraction of the total population, most of whom lived in the Northeast. But there was no gainsaying the fact that the earnings from which the income tax was paid were drawn from all over the nation. Coupled with the demand for better educational facilities and better transportation in the larger, poorer, and less densely populated states of the West and the South was the belief that in some fashion the government should attempt to redistribute among all the states the heavy earnings that were being piled up in the industrial areas of the Northeast. Southern and western votes on behalf of such a policy were easily accumulated, and the South and the West controlled the Democratic Party.

"Dollar-matching"

The new type of federal grants in aid of education began in 1914 with the passage of the Smith-Lever Act, which provided that the United States should match, dollar for dollar, the contributions of such states as chose to co-operate in a program of agricultural extension. The supervision of this work was left to the Department of Agriculture, working through the land-grant colleges. This measure was followed in 1917 by the Smith-Hughes Act, which appropriated funds, again on a dollar-matching basis, for education in commercial, industrial, and domestic-science subjects in schools of less than college grade. A board of vocational education, created by the act, was given the right to pass on the merits of the projects for which the various states proposed to use their allotments. The impetus which these acts gave to agricultural and vocational education, supplemented by the work of the Bureau of Education, the Children's Bureau, and other federal agencies, was felt in a steadily mounting number of the nation's high schools. Talk began in

[1] W. S. Holt, *The Federal Farm Loan Bureau* (1924).

educational circles of the need for a federal Department of Education with a seat in the cabinet, but opponents of the idea argued that federal control over the educational policies of the states must not be carried too far.[1]

The Federal Highways Act of 1916 carried the dollar-matching principle into the field of road-building. The automobile, which was at first

Federal Highways Act condemned because it tore up the roads, soon led to a demand for better roads that completely overtaxed the resources of the states. It was only natural in such an emergency to turn to the federal government for aid, and Democrats who could remember well Jackson's war on the Bank soon demonstrated that they had quite forgotten his Maysville veto. Aid was needed for a Lincoln Highway, just marked out from coast to coast, for a Dixie Highway from Lakes to Gulf, and for a half a hundred other projects. Yielding to the general pressure, Congress appropriated five million dollars the first year for distribution among the states. Size, population, and existing mail routes were all to be taken into consideration in determining the amounts allotted to each. Moreover, every dollar contributed by the federal government must be matched by a dollar from the state which received it, and federal control must be accepted in all such dollar-matching expenditures. When Congress made this first appropriation it knew little of the cost of road-building, but it soon found out a great deal. Nor could the process it had begun be ended until a complete set of federal highways, connecting every important center with every other, had been built.

Viewing the manifold activities into which under Democratic auspices the national government had plunged, historically minded individuals could not fail to note the contrasts between Jeffersonian and

Wilsonian vs. Jeffersonian democracy Wilsonian democracy. The Jeffersonian ideal, so Jefferson himself had said, was "a wise and frugal government which shall restrain men from injuring one another, shall leave them otherwise free to regulate their own pursuits of industry and improvement, and shall not take from labor the bread it has earned. This is the sum of good government." However the Wilsonian ideal might be described, it could hardly be reconciled with the dictum, "the less government the better." With Hamiltonian thoroughness the professed disciples of Jefferson had devised a great national banking system that so far forgot states' rights as to divide the United States into twelve districts instead of forty-eight; in their attempts to "restrain men from

---

[1] On the origin and expansion of federal activities, see W. L. Wanlass, *The United States Department of Agriculture* (1920); J. A. H. Keith and W. C. Bagley, *The Nation and the Schools* (1920); W. S. Holt, *The Bureau of Public Roads* (1923).

injuring one another," they had left industry only a closely circumscribed area in which to regulate its own pursuits; in protecting the rights of labor they had limited the freedom of individuals to a degree that Jefferson could scarcely have imagined; and in taking thought for the public welfare they had assumed for government paternalistic privileges far more sweeping than any he had fought. Fortunately historical consistency is often better honored in the breach than in the observance. It is no discredit to Wilson that in a new age he reversed the tenets of the founder of his party. States' rights and *laissez faire* in an era of rapidly expanding national organization would have been anachronisms. Only through a policy of enlightened nationalism could the Democrats of Wilson's time hope to find the "new freedom" which their leader extolled.[1]

---

[1] Excellent general accounts which include this period are D. L. Dumond, *America in Our Times: 1896–1946* (1947); Harvey Wish, *Contemporary America: The National Scene Since 1900* (1945); F. R. Dulles, *Twentieth Century America* (1945); O. T. Barck, Jr., and N. M. Blake, *Since 1900* (1947).

Special studies of particular value are George E. Mowry, *Theodore Roosevelt and the Progressive Movement* (1946); Gordon C. O'Gara, *Theodore Roosevelt and the Rise of the Modern Navy* (1943); R. H. Heindel, *The American Impact on Great Britain, 1898–1914* (1940); Louis Adamic, *A Nation of Nations* (1945); C. C. Tansill, *Canadian-American Relations, 1875–1911* (1943).

Biographic studies for this period are exceptionally numerous: Catherine Drinker Bowen, *Yankee from Olympus: Justice Holmes and his Family* (1944); Sister Marie Caroline Klinkhamer, *Edward Douglas White, Chief Justice of the United States* (1943); Eric F. Goldman, *Charles J. Bonaparte, Patrician Reformer* (1943); W. D. Puleston, *Mahan: The Life and Work of Captain Alfred Thayer Mahan, U.S.N.* (1939); Elmer Ellis, *Mr. Dooley's America: A Life of Finley Peter Dunne* (1941); H. D. Cater, *Henry Adams and his Friends* (1947); J. W. Barrett, *Joseph Pulitzer and his "World"* (1941). Matthew Josephson, *The President Makers: The Culture of Politics and Leadership in an Age of Enlightenment, 1896–1919* (1940), is primarily biographic.

33

Wilson's Foreign Policy

IT WAS APPARENT that Wilson in taking over the Presidency had little expectation of becoming a diplomat. His administration was organized with a view to domestic reform, a policy which extended even to his choice of Secretary of State, and neither in his inaugural address nor in his first message to Congress did he so much as mention foreign affairs. He was aware of impending difficulties between the United States and Mexico, but there is no evidence to show that this prospect caused him much concern. The imminence of a general war in Europe was as completely hidden from him as from other Americans.

Beginning in 1910, Mexico was in the throes of revolution. The old President, Porfirio Diaz, who for more than a third of a century had ruled **Mexico** as a military dictator, had at last been confronted with a revolt beyond his ability to suppress. From the point of view of outside investors Diaz had been a good ruler. By generous concessions he had encouraged foreign capital to develop the rich resources of his country, its railroads, mines, oil fields, public utilities, rubber and coffee plantations, and ranches. By 1912, so President Taft believed, American investments in Mexico had reached a total of not less than a billion dollars, while other huge sums came from European nations, particularly Great Britain, Germany, and France. Naturally such heavy investments did not come unaccompanied, and the number of foreign agents resident in Mexico was very great — at least forty thousand from the United States alone. Under Diaz order was strictly kept, and foreigners had no more reason to be afraid than if they had remained at home.[1]

Discontent with the Diaz régime was slow to develop, for the Mexican masses were ignorant and inarticulate, and Diaz had the guns. Diaz's policies, however, were as burdensome on Mexicans as they were helpful to foreigners. Political liberty was unknown in the republic, and active

[1] Carleton Beals, *Porfirio Diaz, Dictator of Mexico* (1932), presents the essential facts in excellent form. Interesting sidelights on the Mexican situation are contained in Edith O'Shaughnessy, *Intimate Pages of Mexican History* (1920).

opposition to the President amounted to flirtation with sudden death. Nevertheless, as Diaz grew old his power began to wane, and some even of those who had long supported him joined forces with Francisco Madero, a sincere liberal, who in November, 1910, had raised the banner of revolt in northern Mexico. In less than six months Diaz was forced to resign and flee the country, whereupon Madero triumphantly assumed the Presidency. But Madero's devotion to constitutional principles annoyed those who wished merely for a younger Diaz, and in February, 1913, by a typically Latin-American *coup d'état*, Madero was arrested and murdered, and Victoriano Huerta, the man most responsible for the crime, took over the reins of authority.

This was the situation that confronted Wilson when he took office. Deeply shocked by Huerta's behavior, the American President at once announced that he could show "no sympathy with those who seek to seize the power of government to advance their own personal interests or ambitions." Wilson's refusal to recog- **The fall of Huerta** nize Huerta as the President of Mexico left that country in an uproar, with counter-revolutionists active in nearly every section. When John Lind of Minnesota, whom Wilson sent on a special mission to treat with the various warring factions, failed to secure either the elimination of Huerta or the union of the forces opposing him, Wilson merely committed the American government to the policy of "watchful waiting," hoping that eventually Huerta would fall. Unfortunately, however, Huerta's régime was viewed with favor by most European nations, and with their encouragement and recognition it lasted on. Finally Wilson, fearful that munitions from a German ship were about to be landed for Huerta at Vera Cruz, ordered the navy to occupy that port, and on April 22, 1914, with considerable loss of life, the order was carried into effect. Three months later, Huerta gave up, and his leading opponent, Venustiano Carranza, took his place.

With Carranza posing as a "constitutionalist" and the rightful successor of Madero, the United States was able to withdraw from Mexico, and resume full diplomatic relations with the Mexican govern- **Carranza** ment. Arms that Carranza was permitted to purchase in the United States helped the new President to restore order, much to the disgust of other revolutionary factions to whom American manufacturers were forbidden to sell. Carranza's chief opponent, Francisco Villa, vented his rage at the United States for this affront by twice crossing the international border in 1916, and murdering American citizens upon American soil. With the consent of Carranza an American military expedition under the command of General John J. Pershing advanced into Mexico in search of Villa, but it failed to catch him, and was presently withdrawn at Carranza's insistence.

With a semblance of order restored, Carranza proclaimed a new constitution in 1917 which was both anti-foreign and anti-clerical. It proposed to break up the great landed estates for distribution among the people and made many other provisions for the welfare of the working classes; it asserted that the nation had an imprescriptible title to the oil and mineral deposits within its borders; it limited land-ownership and concessionary rights to Mexicans; it ended the union of church and state, declared church edifices national property, and secularized the administration of all educational and benevolent institutions. From this time forward the relations between the United States and Mexico hinged upon the effectiveness with which the anti-foreign provisions of the Constitution of 1917 were enforced. Some Mexican Presidents, such as Obregon, who succeeded Carranza in 1923, treated American investors with considerable generosity, whereas others, such as Calles, whose ascendancy lasted for ten years beginning in 1923, were hard to handle. Wilson's policy toward Mexico was much criticized, but in spite of much insistence on military intervention, it at least stopped short of actual war, and it probably saved the Mexicans from another reactionary régime such as they had suffered from with Diaz.[1]

Constitution of 1917

Keeping out of war with Mexico became a matter of secondary importance for Americans after the outbreak of the World War in the late summer of 1914. To say that such a development was a shock to the American people is a gross understatement. They could hardly believe the news they read. For years, in spite of the great earnestness with which they pursued the cause of world peace, they had taken it for granted that a general European war was impossible. The risks involved in such a conflict for all participants were too appalling. The international ramifications of capital formed too intricate a pattern; one great nation could not attack another without attacking itself. Little nations might fight each other, or a large nation might chastise a small one, but that the greatest and most enlightened nations of the world should fly at one another's throats seemed totally incredible.

War in Europe

Faced by the horrendous fact, the American public, mainly through newspapers, went to school again and brushed up on its European history. Europe, it appeared, had depended for years on a "balance of power" to keep the peace. On the one side were Germany, Austria, and Italy, whose agreements as to military co-operation dated back to the days of Bismarck; on the other were Great Britain, France, and Russia, ancient enemies whom

The balance-of-power system

---

[1] Satisfactory discussions of American policy toward Mexico are given in J. F. Rippy, *The United States and Mexico* (new edition, 1931); J. M. Callahan, *American Foreign Policy in Mexican Relations* (1932); G. M. Stephenson, *John Lind of Minnesota* (1935); Harold Nicolson, *Dwight Morrow* (1935).

the rise of modern Germany had driven together. France and Russia had been allies since 1891, but the *entente* that bound Great Britain to France dated no farther back than 1904, while the agreement between Great Britain and Russia came as late as 1907. Each set of partners made every effort to line up the lesser nations of Europe on its side. Some, like Switzerland, Belgium, the Netherlands, and the Scandinavian countries, maintained a rigid aloofness, but others more or less unofficially chose sides. The Triple Alliance, as the combination led by Germany was generally called, could count with some certainty on the support of Bulgaria and Turkey, while the Triple Entente, led by Great Britain, was on friendly terms with Spain and Portugal, and hoped for support from some of the Balkan nations.[1]

Imperial rivalry, Americans learned, was another part of the picture. England, France, and Russia had old established empires to which they had added liberally in the last quarter of the nineteenth century. Germany, too, wanted a "place in the sun," but she had entered the competition too late to obtain the share of spoils to which she felt herself, as a great nation, entitled. She had a few colonies, but they were definitely second-rate. The Triple Entente, she believed, was created only to draw a "ring of iron" about her that would prevent the legitimate fulfillment of her desires. Imperial rivalry went further, however, than the mere acquisition of colonies. In the development of backward nations lay an equally inviting field. Rivalry for concessions in China, in Persia, in Morocco, in Turkey, in the Balkans, everywhere that money could be invested and profits taken, was acute, with sometimes one nation ahead and sometimes another.

Imperial rivalry

In no region was the atmosphere more tense than in the Balkans and the Near East. Here, in addition to the ever-present activities of the British and the Germans, the Austrians, the Italians, and the Russians all claimed special interests based on proximity, while the Russian government, as a cloak for its ambition to secure free access to the Mediterranean, essayed the additional rôle of protector to Greek Orthodox Christians wherever they might be found. In 1908 Austria had annexed Bosnia and Herzegovina, two Serbian provinces handed her for administration in 1878, after the Russo-Turkish War;[2] in 1911 Italy had fought a war with Turkey to justify her conquest of Tripoli; and in 1912–13 two wars had been fought among the little Balkan

The Balkans

---

[1] Two of the best works (not entirely in agreement) on the background of the World War are S. B. Fay, *The Origins of the World War* (2 vols., 1928), and B. E. Schmitt, *The Coming of the War* (2 vols., 1930).

[2] Russia had protested, but had been compelled to withdraw her objection when warned that an attack upon Austria-Hungary would lead to a war with Germany also. She promised Serbia, however, that she would not yield in such a fashion again.

countries themselves, as a result of which both Turkey and Bulgaria had lost much territory to Greece, Serbia, and Rumania. America did not know it, but for months before the war broke out the Balkan situation had European diplomats all on edge.

Another factor in the situation was the exaggerated nationalism that the nineteenth century had bequeated to the twentieth. Anthropolo-

Nationalism
gists were able to prove conclusively that most European nations, certainly all the great powers, were peopled by mongrel breeds, with no faintest title to racial purity, but nationalism owed more to a common language and history than to race. Each nation prided itself upon its cultural heritage, perverted its history to make its glories seem greater, and aroused the patriotism of its people to the highest possible pitch. It became, therefore, a matter of national pride to draw within the boundaries of any given nation all who spoke its language or shared its culture. France looked forward to the time when Alsace-Lorraine, taken from her by Germany in 1871, should be again a part of France, Italy dreamed of drawing *Italia irredenta* within her borders; nearly every Balkan nation claimed a part of every other; subject nations like the Poles and the Czechs longed to be free. Austria-Hungary, a polyglot of nationalities, was every neighbor's envy.

All this was bad enough, but the dangers of the situation were compounded again and again by the rampant militarism and navalism that affected every European nation. Universal military training had long been a policy of all the great powers of Europe except Great Britain, and most of the lesser ones. Huge standing armies made every nation an armed camp, with preparedness a national watchword. The insular character of the British Isles saved Great Britain from the necessity of keeping pace in land armament with her rivals on the Continent, but she prided herself upon her navy, which she meant to keep overwhelmingly stronger than any other. Germany's challenge to British supremacy on the high seas — German naval officers toasted "the day" when they would meet the British navy — not only aroused Great Britain to new building, but also led her to abandon her position of "splendid isolation," and to seek allies. On this account she had ended her ages-old rivalries with France and Russia, had made an alliance with Japan, and had sought with great earnestness to win the friendship of the United States.

House's "great adventure"
In Europe the danger that war might break out at any moment was fully realized by the well-informed, and a few Americans understood the situation. Among them was Colonel House, the intimate adviser of the President, who in the spring of 1914 undertook what he called "the great adventure," a

trip to Europe to promote the reduction of land and naval armament. House visited the Kaiser and talked with him for half an hour, established close connections with Sir Edward Grey and others in England, and had a try at Paris only to be frustrated there by the customary cabinet crisis. Everywhere he found "militarism run stark mad," but the British told him they were ready to talk reduction, and he so reported to the Kaiser. On June 28, 1914, shortly before he sailed for the United States, he learned that the heir to the Austrian throne, the Archduke Franz Ferdinand, and his wife had been assassinated at Sarajevo, in the province of Bosnia, but neither House nor his English hosts appeared to realize that this somewhat commonplace Balkan incident would lead to war. But war came nevertheless by the time House reached home. His "great adventure" was undertaken too late.[1]

The incidents which led actually to the outbreak of war seemed trifling to Americans. The assassination of the Austrian heir-apparent, it appeared, was the work of some superpatriotic young Bosnian Serbs who disliked the Archduke's plan for making the "dual monarchy" of Austria and Hungary into a "triple monarchy" which would extend to the Slavs in the empire a right *Immediate causes of the war* of participation comparable to that enjoyed by the Austrians and the Magyars. Should such a plan succeed, the creation of a greater Serbia might be long delayed, and it was with this thought in mind that the fatal shots were fired. Naturally the Austrian government took a serious view of the situation, the more so because it claimed, probably with good reason, that the Serbian government had guilty knowledge of the plot and had made no effort to prevent its execution. On the assumption that Serbian officials were in reality responsible for what had happened, the Austrian government decided upon punitive measures against its diminutive neighbor, and on July 5 obtained the German Kaiser's permission to go ahead. On July 23 an Austrian ultimatum was delivered to Serbia, which was purposely made so strong as to prevent complete acceptance, and when the Serbian reply proved "evasive" Austria began to mobilize for war.

The ramifications of the European network of alliances now came quickly into play. Russia, in her rôle of protector to all Greek-Orthodox nations, professed to fear that Austria's real intention was annexation rather than punishment, and supported Serbia's plea that the affair should be settled by the Hague Tribunal. Some such settlement was also strongly urged by Great Britain, France, and Italy, but Austria re-

---

[1] Charles Seymour, editor, *The Intimate Papers of Colonel House* (4 vols., 1926–28), provide a running commentary upon all the principal undertakings of the Wilson administration.

mained obdurate, while Germany, although bending every effort to localize the affair, refused to abandon her ally. On July 28, Austria declared war on Serbia, and on the following day Russia began mobilization. At this point the German Kaiser telegraphed frantically to his kinsman, the Czar, to use his influence for peace, and the Czar ordered that mobilization should be confined strictly to the Austrian frontier. But the Russian military leaders easily persuaded the Czar to reverse himself, and on July 30 he gave the command for general mobilization. Thereupon the German government delivered an ultimatum to Russia, requiring the cessation of mobilization within twelve hours. When this demand fell on deaf ears, Germany on August 1 declared war.

France was the ally of Russia, and Germany now demanded to know in eighteen hours what France intended to do. Bound by her treaty with Russia, and ready to have a try at getting back Alsace-Lorraine, France replied that she would consult her own interests. Thereupon, on August 3, Germany declared war upon France and began at once to move troops toward the Belgian frontier. The German plan of campaign was to avoid the heavily fortified Franco-German frontier, demand passage through Belgium, and by speedy action outflank and destroy the French army before the anticipated Russian invasion of eastern Germany could do any vital damage — a plan that failed, for the Belgians resisted valiantly and the French re-formed their lines and eventually held the invaders at bay. Because the Belgians resisted, Germany, although bound by treaty to protect Belgian neutrality, declared war on Belgium. England, meantime, had been debating her obligations to France, which might mean less than aid in time of war, but the attack on Belgium, whose neutrality she, too, was pledged to defend, decided her. On August 4 she declared war on Germany.

The breath-taking speed with which Europe thus plunged into the abyss of war left Americans aghast. The American course, however, was clear. Neutrality, since the days of George Washington, **American neutrality** had become an American tradition. The only exception to the rule had been the War of 1812, an unconfessed blunder that no one expected to see repeated. On August 4 the President issued the first of a series of proclamations of neutrality by means of which the American State Department struggled to keep abreast of the rapidly spreading war. Two weeks later he urged the American public to be "neutral in fact as well as in name during these days that are to try men's souls. We must be impartial in thought as well as in action." Wilson's neutral course and the frenzied efforts of the government to bring stranded American tourists back from Europe met with universal approval. This was Europe's war, not America's, and with the help of a sizable army of war correspondents the American public prepared to stand by and watch while the fire burned itself out.[1]

But neutrality in thought and deed soon proved to be easier preached than practiced. Popular sympathy from the very outbreak of the war ran heavily in favor of the "Allies," as the nations opposed to Germany and Austria were called, and against the Central Powers. Austria and Germany had issued the first declarations of war; they were apparently the aggressors. Germany was the one nation which seemed wholly prepared for war. Her violation of her treaty with Belgium, called by one German diplomat a "scrap of paper," was hard to forgive. The ruthless progress of German troops through Belgium and northern France produced a deep feeling of sympathy for the under-dogs in the fight. Also, a certain amount of cultural solidarity between the English-speaking peoples came steadily to the fore. Not only Great Britain but the whole British Empire, including Canada, the near neighbor of the United States, was fighting with the Allies. Thus the war was in no small part a contest between the civilization that stemmed from England on the one side, and the German *Kultur* on the other.

American sympathy did not all run with the Allies. The large German element in the American population, ably led by the German-language press, sympathized whole-heartedly with the Fatherland, and believed that the war was a British-led conspiracy to dismember and destroy Germany. Immigrants and the descendants of immigrants from the other Central Powers (eventually Turkey and Bulgaria joined Germany and Austria) tended also to be guided by sentiments imported from the Old World. The large American population of Irish descent was traditionally anti-British, and sometimes the hatred of Irish-Americans for England made them pro-German. In view of the strong minority sentiment these elements represented, neutrality seemed all the more essential as an American policy. Americans, it seemed, possessed a double loyalty; they were loyal to the United States, but they were loyal also to the country from which they or their ancestors had come.[2]

But there were problems of neutrality and a law of neutrality. Once, a century before, these problems and the American interpretation of the law which they involved had brought the United States into a European

---

[1] The best single volume on this period of American history is Paxson's *Pre-War Years*, already cited. It may be supplemented on the strictly diplomatic side by Charles Seymour, *American Diplomacy During the World War* (1934).

[2] This problem with respect to the Germans has been well studied in Carl Wittke, *German-Americans and the World War* (1936), and C. J. Child, *The German-Americans in Politics, 1914–1917* (1939).

war; although most Americans thought of the War of 1812 as a mere continuation of the American Revolution, and were utterly unaware of the lessons it taught. Nevertheless, the similarities between the conditions that existed before 1812 and after 1914 were striking. In both cases the British navy commanded the high seas; in both cases the war meant an abnormal demand for American goods and American shipping; in both cases American neutral rights were frequently violated by both sides; and in both cases, as matters turned out, the United States was eventually drawn into the war.

International law was at least as old as Hugo Grotius, whose book, *De jure belli ac pacis*, was published in 1625. Its rules had nothing more behind them than custom and the common consent of sovereign states. There was a law of peace that was rarely broken, and a law of war that was rarely kept. Invariably in time of war disputes broke out as to what the law really was, and how it should be construed. The rights of neutrals were particularly subject to debate. In general, Great Britain, who expected always to control the seas, was inclined to interpret neutral rights as narrowly as possible, whereas the United States whose policy was permanent neutrality and most other nations whose navies were inferior to the British exaggerated the privileges of neutrals all they could. Attempts to obtain agreement on the meaning of the rules or to amend them met with no success. Neither the code of land warfare adopted by the Second Hague Conference, nor the Declaration of London with respect to naval warfare, was fully ratified. Promptly on the outbreak of the war Wilson asked the belligerents to adhere to the Declaration of London, and the Central Powers agreed to do so if the Allies would bind themselves similarly. But the British feared the limitations on sea-power contained in the new rules and refused to accept them. The United States, therefore, in defending its neutrality had nothing better to depend upon than the jumbled mass of precedents and opinions that had accumulated from the time of Grotius on down. Many of these rules were utterly unrelated to the conditions of modern warfare, but obsolete as they were, they were the only rules that existed.[1]

It was immediately apparent that the British had no notion of allowing the vast amount of American goods and shipping that soon took to the seas to proceed about its business as if there had been no war. This trade represented not merely, or mostly, the ordinary exports of the

(margin note: International law and the war)

---

[1] Alice M. Morrissey, *The American Defense of Neutral Rights, 1914–1917* (1939), is an excellent study of the problems in international law presented by the war. It should be compared with Edwin Borchard and W. P. Lage, *Neutrality for the United States* (1937), which takes the ground that the United States was not wholly neutral. An older but still useful study is J. W. Garner, *International Law and the World War* (1920).

United States to Europe, but rather millions of dollars' worth of goods that were shipped purely in response to the wartime needs of the belligerents. The products of American farms and factories were earnestly coveted by both sides, and the United States, recovering from a business panic that the outbreak of war had precipitated, was eager to sell. All this was entirely satisfactory to the British, with the single important exception that they were determined to prevent anything of value to the Central Powers from reaching its destination. American goods might flow freely to the Allies, but not to their enemies. To accomplish their purpose the British had only to make use of their naval strength, but, unlike the Germans, they did what they could to reconcile wartime necessities with the existing rules of international law. For authority in dealing with neutral trade, they invoked three well-recognized belligerent rights: (1) the stoppage of trade in contraband goods, (2) the doctrine of continuous voyages, and (3) the blockade.

In each instance, however, British policy tread heavily on neutral toes. The British definition of contraband — that is, goods that might be of direct (absolute contraband) or indirect (conditional contraband) use to the enemy — was so generous as to include every commodity that the Central Powers might wish to import. This, the American State Department claimed, was going too far. Further, British ships inspected trade between the United States and such neutrals as bordered on Germany, or on any of her partners, to make sure that none of it was ultimately intended for the enemy. If that was deemed to be the case, the trip was regarded as one continuous voyage which might be interrupted anywhere in its progress. This, too, was protested, although in the American Civil War the United States had done practically the same thing to prevent British commodities from reaching the South. Finally, a Ministry of Blockade was set up, which took good care that all shipping found anywhere on the high seas was carefully scrutinized to prevent the Central Powers obtaining anything that the British did not wish them to have. Such a blockade, the United States maintained, was illegal. It was enforced at long distance; it was applied against neutral as well as against belligerent coasts; and it was unenforceable against the countries that bordered on the Baltic Sea, because there the German navy, not the British, was supreme. But the British, while admitting that their methods might be somewhat unusual, argued that they were living up to the spirit, if not the letter, of the law.

The list of protests lodged by the United States against Great Britain included also vigorous denunciations of the British practice of taking neutral ships to Allied ports to be searched. The old rules contemplated search on the high seas, but with modern shipping such a practice was difficult, and after submarine warfare began, extremely dangerous. Sometimes American ships were held up for months at Allied ports. The British practice of searching American mail, both to and from Europe, also drew fire. The British held that American mail pouches, even when consigned to neutral countries, often contained things of value intended for the enemy, and they proposed also to know what information was going into and coming out of Germany. Exports from the Central Powers were given as scant courtesy as imports, and for long periods American industry was shut off from supplies obtainable only from Germany, such as dyestuffs, drugs, and sugar-beet seeds.

The American case against the British for their violations of neutrality was fully and conscientiously stated by the American State Department, but that was all. Probably the original intent was to collect damages after the war for proved violations, much as had been done after the Civil War. In private most American officials agreed that what the British were doing they must do to win, and that a British victory was to the best interests of the United States. Furthermore, American shippers soon grew accustomed to the British regulations, and by conforming to them escaped difficulty. Seized cargoes were usually paid for, but as time went on few cargoes were sent that were in any danger of being seized. Allied demands alone were sufficient to absorb all the surplus goods the United States could produce; indeed, war orders soon turned what might otherwise have been a depression into a boom. Other neutrals, such as Denmark and Holland, also acquiesced in the British regulations. Since the British rules occasioned no loss of life and practically no loss of property, and since for every market closed at least two new ones were opened, the American public had little heart to object.

The close community of interests that thus developed between the United States and the Allies was an object of great concern to the Germans, who were seriously handicapped by their inability to trade with America, and scarcely less to many German sympathizers in the United States itself. Some of the latter, including Senator William J. Stone of Missouri, chairman of the Senate Committee on Foreign Relations, favored a complete embargo on the sale outside the national borders of military supplies, particularly ammunition, but the State Department maintained with unimpeachable logic that such trade was not a violation of neutrality. If Germany could not buy in the United States, it was the fault of the British navy, not of the American government. The German Foreign Office was frantic with rage. It not only lodged frequent and vehement protests against American acquiescence in British trade regulations, but it also encouraged the sabotage by German agents of such American industries as were aiding the Allies. For proved complicity in such plots the Austrian ambassador, Constantin Dumba, and several attachés of the German embassy, including Franz von Papen, were ordered to leave the United States.[1]

Germany's most effective means of retaliation against the pressure of Allied sea-power proved to be the submarine, a type of craft her engineers had brought to extraordinary efficiency. On February 4, 1915, in protest against the British stoppage of food shipments to Germany, the German government declared a "war zone" about the British Isles, and announced its intention to sink on sight every enemy merchantman within the area described. The United States was warned to keep American shipping out of the danger zone lest by mistake American ships and lives might be lost. Against this new type of warfare the American government lodged an immediate protest. Its illegality was obvious even to the German government, which defended it only on the ground of retaliation for allegedly illegal actions by the Allies, and the willingness of neutrals to acquiesce in them. The war-zone decree could not be defended as a blockade, for a blockade, to be binding on neutral nations, must effectively stop a major part of the shipping plying to and from the blockaded ports, whereas German submarines could not possibly hope to intercept more than an occasional ship. Visit and search by a submarine to ascertain the character of the ship and the nature of its cargo would be a virtual impossibility. Sinking on sight defied all the rules that required the attacking warship to provide for the safety of non-combatant passengers and crews. Reciting the evidence as to the illegality of the war-zone decree, Wilson's note of protest declared that the United States was "reluctant to believe" that the warfare contemplated would ever be carried into effect, and warned that in case American ships or lives were lost the German government would be held to a "strict accountability."

The threat to American neutrality posed by the submarine blockade led Wilson to dispatch Colonel House to Europe on a "quest for peace." House cherished the chimerical hope that he might persuade the British to give up their blockade and the Germans their submarine attacks on merchantmen — the very weapons by which the two leading contenders hoped to win the war. Naturally his "quest" was fruitless, and on May 7, 1915, the British passenger liner, *Lusitania*, on which he had sailed to Europe a few weeks before, was torpedoed without warning and sunk off the Irish coast on her way to England. More than eleven hundred persons lost their lives, including one hundred and twenty-four Americans. The sinking was a perfectly clear violation of neutral rights. Warning had not been given by a shot across the

Submarine warfare

The Lusitania

[1] Constantin Dumba, *Memoirs of a Diplomat* (1932).

ship's bow, or in any other manner prescribed by sea usage. The fact that an advertisement in a New York paper had warned passengers of what might happen if they sailed on the *Lusitania* proved merely that the act was premeditated; no known rule of international law provided for a newspaper warning, and the advertisement was generally regarded as a hoax. The fact that the *Lusitania* carried ammunition designed for Allied use was equally irrelevant. The Germans had a perfect right to capture and confiscate the ship, even to sink it, but according to the existing rules they must first find out by a search what its cargo contained, and make satisfactory provision for the safety of non-combatants.

American opinion on the *Lusitania* disaster was not entirely unanimous. The sinking was vigorously condemned, and frequently the old battle-cry, "Remember the *Maine*," was raised. Theodore Roosevelt, the most bitter of the anti-German leaders in the United States, described the attack on the *Lusitania* as an "act of piracy," and demanded immediate war. There were many who agreed with him, particularly along the Atlantic seaboard where the importance of keeping open the sealanes to Europe was the more keenly felt, but in the West and the South there was a tendency to ask why American citizens needed to venture into the danger zone. Should the American government not prevent such incidents in the future by prohibiting its nationals from sailing on belligerent merchant ships, or on ships carrying munitions? Bryan himself took this attitude, which Easterners called "provincial," and he would have been willing even to submit the *Lusitania* incident to arbitration. He signed the first note of protest that Wilson wrote, but the next one was too much for him, and he resigned from the cabinet rather than be party to a policy which in his judgment might easily lead to war. The same sentiment appeared in Congress, where only the vigorous intervention of the President prevented the passage of resolutions, sponsored in the House by McLemore of Texas and in the Senate by Gore of Oklahoma, forbidding American citizens to travel on belligerent merchantmen, except at their own peril.

The *Lusitania* incident led to a diplomatic correspondence between the United States and Germany that lasted all through the summer of 1915. Wilson's statement, made in a public address just

Germany backs down

before his first note was sent, "There is such a thing as a man being too proud to fight," seemed to betoken an attitude of weakness, but in three successive notes he argued the case with Germany, taking stronger ground each time. The submarine, he held, used as Germany was using it, was an illegal weapon, and any repetition of the *Lusitania* offense would be regarded as a "deliberately unfriendly" act. This was a threat of war, as the German ambassador to the United States, Count von Bernstorff, well knew, but the offense was repeated on August 19, when the *Arabic* was sunk with the loss of two American lives. Thereupon von Bernstorff, acting on his own initiative, promised the American State Department in writing that liners would not be sunk "without warning and without safety to the lives of non-combatants, provided that the liners do not try to escape or offer resistance." Eventually the German government agreed to back up Bernstorff's words with deeds. Wilson had scored a signal diplomatic triumph, but he had won his victory only by the threat of war. When, either by accident or intent, a few more sinkings occurred, Wilson in a spectacular appearance before Congress renewed his threat and forced from the German government a reiteration of its promises. German insistence that the United States should also force the Allies to give up their illegal practices, Wilson refused to consider as in any way pertinent to the problem. For nine months, whether because it feared the United States or because it had discovered a need for more submarines, the German government kept its promise.

In part, at least, to implement his threats, Wilson now put himself at the head of a strong demand for military preparedness that, in spite of much "pacifist" protest, was sweeping the country. On the very day that he dispatched his third *Lusitania* note he **Preparedness** authorized the Army and Navy Departments to draft plans for the strengthening of the national defenses, and in his annual message to Congress of December, 1915, he called emphatic attention to these proposals. Early in 1916 he toured the country to speak for preparedness, and on Flag Day, June 14, he led a preparedness parade down Pennsylvania Avenue. His determination to make the United States ready for war was strengthened by the failure of another House mission to Europe, this time in order to offer the Allies a "plan to compel peace." The idea was that Wilson, with Allied foreknowledge, should demand the cessation of hostilities and a conference of the belligerents to discuss peace terms. If the proposals of the Allies — to be agreed upon in consultation with the United States — were not accepted by Germany, then the United States would "probably" join the Allied war effort. Wilson's use of the word "probably," as an afterthought, no doubt wrecked the plan, and the war went on. It was Wilson's fear that if the war should continue the United States would be drawn into it that had led him to accept House's scheme in the first place; now with the failure of the plan the President was even more fearful of war and determined to be ready for it.

The battle of Jutland, fought May 31–June 1, 1916, gave Americans a rude jolt. In that engagement the German High-Seas Fleet boldly challenged the British Grand Fleet in the North Sea and inflicted such serious damage upon it as to serve warning that British command of the seas might soon be threatened. Already the Chicago *Tribune*, persistent champion of a foreign policy based on national self-interest, had warned its readers of the dire consequences to the United States in case the British fleet should be destroyed. "British naval supremacy," it pointed out editorially, "has been the stable factor in world diplomacy for so many years that all but diplomats are inclined to forget it." Americans were reminded that the Monroe Doctrine had been "largely built upon it" and that even the Oriental policies of the United States "had to look to it for sanction." If the British fleet were annihilated, every item of American foreign policy "would have to be scrutinized in the light of unknown conditions," and the nation's future might be gravely imperiled. To forestall such a calamity, many Americans, including apparently some of the makers of *Tribune* policy, were ready to form a definite alliance with Great Britain and enter the war.[1]

Opposition to preparedness in Congress now lost ground steadily, for even those who were unwilling to concede that the British navy was the first line of defense for the United States were not unaware of the dangers to America that might flow from German control of the seas. A National Defense Act which authorized the increase of the standing army to 175,000, and the National Guard to 450,000, became law early in June. Even more important was the Naval Appropriation Act, passed two months later, which provided for the immediate construction of four dreadnoughts and four battle cruisers. The total appropriation carried in this measure ran to $313,000,000, the largest sum Congress had ever voted at any one time for naval purposes. Three capital ships, the *Nevada*, the *Oklahoma*, and the *Pennsylvania*, had just been completed. As two further means of promoting the national defense, Congress created (1) a Council of National Defense, to consist of six Cabinet officers, and seven unpaid civilian experts, and (2) a United States Shipping Board, which might build, or otherwise acquire, and operate a fleet of merchantmen. The nation was preparing for war as it had never prepared for war before. And there were few who could ask seriously, "What war?"

The campaign and election of 1916 occurred during the months immediately following Wilson's diplomatic victory over Germany. That **Election of 1916** he would be a candidate to succeed himself in spite of the fact that the platform on which he was elected opposed a second term was universally taken for granted. Wilson was

[1] Chicago *Tribune*, March 14, 1916, and May 11, 1916. "Isolation, splendid or sordid, is not possible in our age. If the war has taught us nothing else, it has carried that lesson to the uttermost parts of the earth for those who will think." *Ibid.*, December 18, 1915.

the leader of his party. Even the defection of Bryan gave the President no cause for alarm, for by the time Bryan quit the cabinet Wilson had wholly eclipsed him. The congressional elections of 1914 had found most of the Progressives back in the Republican fold, but the Democrats emerged triumphant in a straight-out two-party contest. The reason for this, everyone knew, was Woodrow Wilson. When the Democratic Convention met in St. Louis June 14, it had nothing to do but to renominate both Wilson and his running-mate of four years before, Thomas R. Marshall of Indiana, by acclamation, and to record in its platform complete approval of every action the administration had taken.

In a shrewd effort to unite all forces opposed to Wilson, the Republicans turned for their candidate to Associate Justice Charles Evans Hughes of the United States Supreme Court. With the discretion permitted to justices, Hughes had not openly taken sides for or against Germany, for or against intervention in Mexico, for or against preparedness. Nor had he been involved in any way in the disastrous split of four years before. His background as governor of New York was satisfying to the Progressive wing of the party, and his decisions as associate justice had caused the conservatives no alarm. Hughes's availability was so obvious, that the Republicans, meeting at Chicago June 7, named him on the first ballot, although he had done nothing to advance his candidacy and had not even said that he would accept the nomination. All fell out as planned. Roosevelt, by declining a Progressive nomination and supporting Hughes, dealt a deathblow to the party he had founded. Pro-Germans who thought Wilson had been unfair to Germany, anti-Germans who condemned his soft treatment of wanton aggressors, pacifists who were for peace with everybody at whatever price, war advocates who demanded, sometimes in the same breath, intervention in both Mexico and Europe, all rallied to the Republican standard. The day Hughes resigned from the Supreme Court to accept the proffered nomination he might have been elected, for then all factions could have claimed him as their own.

As the campaign progressed, the President's chances improved. His followers proclaimed truthfully that he had "kept us out of war," forgetting, perhaps, that he had a threat out that might draw the nation in. Many Progressives who had supported Roosevelt in 1912 were ready to change their allegiance to Wilson, for under his dynamic leadership a spectacular and comprehensive program of domestic reform had been achieved. Wilson got the "breaks" of the campaign. When a "hyphenate" American, Jeremiah A. O'Leary, whose object was to induce Irish-Americans and German-Americans to vote the Republican ticket, sent a long telegram to Wilson denouncing him for unfairness to Germany, the President's reply was tart: "I would feel deeply mortified to have you or anybody like you vote for me. Since you have access to many disloyal Americans and I have not, I will ask you to convey this message to them."

Hughes, on the other hand, was obliged to conduct a campaign of carping criticism, while not being free to take sides on anything. He had only one stroke of luck. The four great railway broth-

The Adamson Act

erhoods chose the Labor Day immediately preceding the election as a desirable time to strike for recognition of the basic eight-hour day and time and a half for overtime. Such a strike in an age when there was virtually no such thing as transportation by trucks would have throttled business and seriously hampered the President's efforts to speed up preparedness. Faced by this emergency, Wilson asked Congress to prevent the strike by enacting into law the demands of the brotherhoods. Congress obeyed with the passage of the Adamson Act, which became a law on September 1. Here Hughes had ample ground for criticism, and he made the most of it, but when he was asked if he would favor the repeal of the law, he could only reply, "You can't repeal a surrender."

The night of election day it appeared certain that Hughes had won. He had carried the East almost solidly, including the State of New York.

Wilson's narrow victory

He had carried also every state in the Old Northwest except Ohio. But the returns from the South and the farther West told a different story. The solid South was conceded to the Democrats, but nothing of the kind was expected from such dependable Republican centers as Kansas and California. Nevertheless Wilson carried every state west of the Mississippi except Minnesota, Iowa, South Dakota, and Oregon, which he lost by slender margins. In the electoral college the vote stood 277 to 254, the closest division since 1876, but the popular vote gave Wilson a lead of 9,129,606 to 8,538,221. Again the Democrats captured both houses of Congress. Significantly the protest vote of nearly a million that had been cast for Eugene V. Debs, the Socialist candidate in 1912, dropped to 585,113 for Allen Benson, in 1916.[1]

Deeply impressed by the popularity of the slogan, "He kept us out of war," Wilson made another attempt shortly after the election to bring the war to an end. In a note released December 20,

Wilson's bid for peace

1916, he asked the fighting powers for "an avowal of their respective views" as to terms upon which the war might be concluded. Both sides, he observed, claimed to be fighting for "vir-

[1] The story of this campaign and much other information pertinent to an understanding of the period is in Mark Sullivan, *Our Times,* v, *Over Here, 1914-1918* (1933).

tually the same" things, the rights of small nations and security for themselves. Perhaps if they would state their war aims more precisely, the differences between them would not be too great for statesmanship to bridge. Anticipating Wilson's offer, and with the military situation running strongly in their favor, the German authorities had already let it be known on December 12 that they were willing to enter a peace conference. They thus made Wilson's call for a statement of war aims appear to be a reinforcement of their offer. The Allies indignantly rejected the idea of treating with a victorious Germany, but, although deeply offended that Wilson should have made a move for peace at a time when Germany was winning, they replied at length to his inquiry. Peace, they said, must carry with it the restitution of conquered territories, full reparations for damages done, and guaranties that nothing of the kind would happen again. The Germans, however, refused in any way to divulge their peace aims, reserving for themselves full freedom of action at the council table.

Reading these replies, it seemed to Wilson that there could be no hope of a lasting peace if either side were permitted to have its way. On January 22, 1917, in an address before the Senate he began to argue the case for a "peace without victory," hoping that eventually the warring nations would heed the wisdom of his words. Such a peace as the victor might impose upon the vanquished, he said, "would be accepted in humiliation, under duress, at an intolerable sacrifice, and would leave a sting, a resentment, a bitter memory upon which terms of peace would rest, not permanently, but only as upon quicksand. Only a peace between equals can last." He even outlined the terms of what he thought would constitute a just peace: equality of rights for small and great nations; universal recognition of the principle that governments derive their just powers from the consent of the governed; the right of every great people to have an outlet to the sea; the freedom of the seas "in law and in fact"; the limitation of armaments; and the avoidance by all nations of entangling alliances. Already he had made known his belief that there must be a league to enforce peace, and he told the Senate that if such a peace as he had outlined could be made the United States must do its part to maintain it.

These were brave words and true words, but before they were spoken the German government had already decided upon the policy which was to rob them of their effect. Convinced by the German admiralty that unrestricted submarine warfare would speedily **The submarine again** destroy enough shipping to isolate Great Britain and force her to sue for peace, the German government announced on January 31, 1917, that its submarines would sink on sight all ships found within specified war zones, whether neutral or belligerent. Its promise to the United States not to sink without warning and without making provision for the safety of non-combatants it withdrew on the ground that the United States had failed to stop the illegal practices of the Allies. Wilson had no choice now but to break off diplomatic relations with Germany, and this he promptly did.

For a time it seemed that the President was seeking a formula short of outright war to resolve the situation. Harking back to the undeclared naval war between France and the United States in 1798, he spoke of "armed neutrality," and asked Congress to grant him authority to provide American merchantmen with guns for their defense. A "little group of willful men," as the President called them, filibustered this measure to death, but the needed authority was found in an unrepealed law of 1797, and the merchantmen were armed. It was clear that if either the United States or Germany struck a blow there would be war. Wilson professed to believe that the Germans would never carry out their threats, but on March 18 German submarines sank three ships with loss of American lives. Thereupon Wilson called Congress into special session for April 2, and on the evening of that day read his call to arms. Everything else had been tried, he claimed, and now the only recourse was war. The President disclaimed any desire to fight against the German people, and distinguished carefully between them and their government. That government, however, had challenged the security of democracy throughout the world. The United States was glad to fight it, he said,

> for the ultimate peace of the world and for the liberation of its peoples, the German peoples included: for the rights of nations great and small and the privilege of men everywhere to choose their way of life and of obedience. The world must be made safe for democracy. Its peace must be planted upon the tested foundations of political liberty.

The response of Congress to the President's eloquent appeal was not unanimous, but it was overwhelming enough to be convincing. On April 4 the Senate passed the war resolution by a vote of 82 to 6, and on April 6 the House concurred by a vote of 373 to 50. Diplomatic relations with Austria-Hungary were promptly broken, but war was not declared until December 7. Against Germany's other allies, Turkey and Bulgaria, the United States issued no declarations of war. Claiming that the war against Germany was being fought on behalf of neutral rights generally, the United States urged other neutrals also to join in the crusade. As a result Cuba, Panama, Siam, Liberia, China, and Brazil entered the war on the Allied side, and several other nations broke off diplomatic relations. Long

Congress declares war

before, Japan and Portugal had joined in order to fulfill their alliances with Great Britain, while Italy by generous promises and Greece by threats had also been brought into the Allied camp. Thus the war became in fact as well as in name a World War.

It is extremely difficult to catalogue all the factors that worked together to draw the United States into the war. Undoubtedly the diplomatic impasse over submarine warfare did in fact precipitate hostilities, and he who says that the United States would have entered the war even if illegal sinkings had not been resumed says far more than he can prove. But undoubtedly there were *Why America fought* other considerations at work to influence the American people. British propaganda was not necessary to convince the United States that the Central Powers were the aggressors, and that the rape of Belgium was a crime. The bulk of the American people took sides in August, 1914, and never wavered in their loyalties throughout the entire period of neutrality. But the British did present their case with skill, and they persuaded many Americans that a German victory would mean the beginning of the end for civilization.[1]

There was also an economic side to the picture which it is difficult to state without overemphasis. Most Americans were only faintly aware of it, but the facts were clear. The United States in the fall of 1914 escaped a depression only by virtue of war orders. *Economic factors* These purchases were entirely legal, even when they were of contraband, and were so described by the American State Department. On loans to the Allies by American citizens to pay for war purchases, however, the State Department pursued a shifting course. At first it said that such loans were inconsistent with American neutrality, then it attempted to draw a distinction between loans and credits, but finally in August, 1915, it sanctioned both. By that time American prosperity was more closely bound up than ever with war orders, and without more loans there was the gravest danger that the orders would stop. With the spring of 1917 the Allies had too nearly exhausted their credit in the United States for comfort; already they owed American moneylenders over a billion dollars, and the limit for the sale of their securities had almost been reached. There was point to the argument of the American ambassador to Great Britain, Walter Hines Page, that direct loans from the United States were now necessary, both to avert a panic in the United States, and to save the Allied cause from collapse.

An indication of how completely American economy was geared to

[1] H. C. Peterson, *Propaganda for War* (1939), examines closely the effects of British propaganda in America. It should be compared with J. P. Jones and P. M. Hollister, *The German Secret Service in America* (1918), and H. D. Lasswell, *Propaganda Technique in the World War* (1927).

the war was given when the German submarine threat of January, 1917, precipitated a sudden stoppage of shipments from Atlantic ports. Thoroughly frightened by the German sinkings, neutral shipping refused to put to sea. Belligerent merchantmen continued to come and go, but they were utterly unable to handle the traffic that cluttered the docks and warehouses of the eastern seaboard, and tied up the railroads with unloaded freight as far west as Pittsburgh. Out of the transportation snarl a food and fuel shortage developed in some metropolitan areas; from the lower East Side in New York City, quite in the best revolutionary tradition, there was a march of angry women on the City Hall demanding food. Without American shipping to move American goods overseas, the United States faced economic collapse. And Great Britain faced the loss of the war.

In the spring of 1917 the Germans seemed to have victory within their grasp. German offensives, particularly in the East, had been overwhelmingly successful; Allied offensives were invariably followed by "strategic retreats." Nearly all of Belgium and a large share of northern France lay in German hands. The Russians had lost most of Poland, while Rumania was no sooner in the war on the Allied side than her army was defeated and her territory occupied. Much of Serbia had long since

---

WORLD WAR I

WOODROW WILSON (1856–1924), *twenty-eighth President of the United States, "kept us out of war" until 1917, but when neutrality became impossible, he led us in. He was a believer in world co-operation to prevent war, and with American support the League of Nations, for which he fought so hard, might have saved the peace of the world.*

HERBERT HOOVER (1874–   ), *thirty-first President of the United States, was introduced to the American public first, during the period of neutrality, as chairman of the Commission for the Relief of Belgium, and then, during the American phase of the war, as United States Food Administrator.*

General JOHN J. PERSHING (1860–   ) *commanded the American Expeditionary Force in Europe during the first World War and held the rank of "General of the Armies of the United States."* NEWTON D. BAKER (1871–1937), *of Ohio, was Wilson's Secretary of War.* BERNARD M. BARUCH (1870–   ) *was head of the powerful War Industries Board.*

HENRY CABOT LODGE (1850–1924), *senator from Massachusetts, was the man who, more than any other, was responsible for the defeat of the Treaty of Versailles in the United States Senate and the wrecking of the League of Nations. His belief that the United States could live in political isolation from the rest of the world was not borne out by the events of the second World War. (Photos of Wilson and Hoover from Underwood & Underwood; photo of Baker from Harris & Ewing.)*

PERSHING

WILSON

BAKER

LODGE

BARUCH

HOOVER

been overrun. With Austria, Bulgaria, and Turkey completely subservient to the German will, the long-dreamed-of *Mitteleuropa* had become a fact. Germany had lost her colonies, and she was beginning to suffer from the Allied blockade, but with the assistance of the submarine she had good reason to believe that her road to victory was clear. From its inception unrestricted submarine warfare took a terrific toll. For weeks one ship out of every four that left British ports failed to return. Neutral shipping tended more and more to stay out of the war-zone. Even if the British navy remained afloat, Great Britain could be starved into submission.

That the United States was ready to rally to the Allied cause whenever such action should be necessary to prevent a German triumph seems far clearer today than it did at the time. Perhaps the Americans would have been willing to accept the "peace without victory" that Wilson advocated, provided that it left British sea-power in command of the eastern Atlantic. Whether they were ready to admit it to themselves or not, Americans knew that they dare not take the risk of the exchange of a friendly power on the Atlantic for an unfriendly power. For a full century the American government had depended upon the friendly support of the British navy to guard the sea-lanes of the Atlantic. That navy alone had maintained the Monroe Doctrine when there was no American navy worthy of the name to

Fear of a German victory

THE NEW ARCHITECTURE

FRANK LLOYD WRIGHT (1869–   ), *whose residence, "Taliesin," at Spring Green, Wisconsin, is shown here, broke completely with tradition. Wright's house architecture, which emphasizes long, low horizontal lines and strongly projecting eaves, has been designated "prairie style." His numerous public buildings also exhibit much originality, and his ideas have influenced architectural developments both in the Old World and the New. (Photo from Hendrich-Blessing.)*

The Nebraska state capitol is distinguished from most other such buildings in that it abandons the traditional dome and portico of American governmental architecture in favor of the skyscraper, long regarded as the most efficient style for office buildings. The central tower of this capitol rises four hundred feet from a massive two-story base and provides ample space for offices, whereas the dome of most American capitols provides decoration only. The architect, BERTRAM GROSVENOR GOODHUE (1869–1924), throughout his later career turned away from classical forms and sought to make the buildings that he created harmonize with modern materials and the conditions of modern society. (Photo from Keystone.)

assume the task. Anglo-American accord had made possible the location of most of the new American navy in the Pacific, where the threat of Japanese aggression was all too plain. Germany had long been restive under the restraints of the Monroe Doctrine, and had cast jealous eyes upon Latin-America as a field for colonial expansion. If she drove the British navy from the Atlantic, what would be her next move? As if to provide an unequivocal answer to this question, intercepted dispatches that the British secret service had turned over to the American government revealed on March 1, 1917, that Alfred Zimmermann, the German Foreign Minister, had offered Mexico the states of Texas, New Mexico, and Arizona, together with liberal financial aid, if Mexico would join Germany, in the event of war between Germany and the United States. Further, the President of Mexico was to urge Japan to shift to the side of the Central Powers, presumably in return for what spoils Japan might desire at the expense of the United States. After the news of the "Zimmermann plot" reached the public, a speedy declaration of war on Germany was inevitable.

In explaining why war had to come, the Chicago *Tribune*, two days after Congress had acted, stated the case with admirable clarity:

> So long as it seemed certain that Great Britain would retain control of the sea, the United States found merely an emotional interest in the war, regarding it as merely a question of European maps and European power.... The new naval weapon, the submarine, is effective. Great Britain's destiny is in doubt.... It is possible ... that control of the seas would pass from the British.... It will comfort most Americans to know that the nation is doing what is needed for the guarding of the present and the guarantee of the future American republic.[1]

In reality, the United States went to war in 1917 less because of German violations of international law, or Allied indebtedness to American producers, or the subtlety of British propaganda than because of the threat to American national interests that would have been implicit in German supremacy in the Atlantic. As a recent observer points out:

> The United States took up arms in the last analysis because it seemed likely that without American intervention the scepter of the Atlantic would pass from the hands of English-speaking peoples into those of a stranger. Of England the Americans had no genuine fears; the stranger might provoke them into a far more terrible war — with perhaps the Continent and a subdued Britain behind him — to settle the ascendancy of the Atlantic Ocean, and, beyond that, this Western Hemisphere.[2]

[1] Quoted from Warren Jenkins, "The Foreign Policy of the Chicago *Tribune*, 1914–1917" (unpublished Ph.D. thesis, University of Wisconsin, 1942).

[2] Forrest Davis, *The Atlantic System: The Story of Anglo-American Control of the Seas* (1941), p. 245. By permission of Reynal and Hitchcock, Inc., publishers. A similar view is taken by Walter Lippmann, *U.S. Foreign Policy: Shield of the Republic* (1943).

Wilson's argument that "we entered the war as the disinterested champions of right" was a rationalization. The United States entered the war because she dared not do otherwise. But Wilson touched a 'magic chord when he said, "The world must be safe for democracy." With Russia in the throes of a democratic revolution a fair case could be made for the assertion that the war was a conflict between autocracies and democracies. With autocratic rulers free to build up military machines and to declare war at will, the peace-loving democracies were at a serious disadvantage. As long as autocracy was enthroned among the great nations of the world, a lasting peace could never be made. Thus the war became not only a war to make the world safe for democracy, but also a "war to end war." With these emotional overtones — afterthoughts though they may have been — ringing in their ears, the American people went to war in a mood of the highest idealism. They fought for the survival of democracy and for peace on earth.[1]

> *The "war to end war"*

[1] On problems of neutrality precipitated by the war, see R. G. Albion and J. B. Pope, *Sea Lanes in Wartime* (1942); and T. A. Bailey, *The Policy of the United States toward the Neutrals, 1917–1918* (1941). Two books with a strong anti-Wilson bias, but packed with information, are T. A. Bailey, *Woodrow Wilson and the Great Betrayal* (1945); and by the same author, *Woodrow Wilson and the Lost Peace* (1944). William Diamond, *The Economic Thought of Woodrow Wilson* (1943), is stimulating. Ray Stannard Baker, *American Chronicle: The Autobiography of Ray Stannard Baker* (1945), devotes much space to the Wilson era. Other useful books on Wilson and his times are A. M. Arnett, *Claude Kitchin and the Wilson War Policies* (1937); H. C. F. Bell, *Woodrow Wilson and the People* (1945); George Creel, *Rebel at Large: Recollections of Fifty Crowded Years* (1947).

34

The First World War

BEFORE the entrance of the United States into the war most Americans had taken it for granted that geographic conditions would limit American participation primarily to naval and financial aid. A succession of missions to Washington from the Allied governments soon proved that the Allies needed everything — money, ships, supplies, men — if the Central Powers were ever to be defeated. Nor could they wait. The United States must act quickly, and avoid mistakes.

Most of all the Allies needed men, and the plans of the General Staff for raising an army in leisurely fashion were immediately speeded up. Convinced that the principle of volunteering, upon which **The American army** both Great Britain and the United States had relied mainly in earlier wars, had been proved by England's recent experiences to be inadequate, the military leaders persuaded Congress to approve in May, 1917, a Selective Service Act. This measure required all men between the ages of twenty-one and thirty (later eighteen and forty-five) to register for military service. The registrants were then divided by local civilian boards into five classes, the first of which consisted of able-bodied, unmarried men, without dependents. The 2,810,-296 men actually selected for service during the war came from this group alone. An elaborate lottery system determined the order in which they were called. Not all of the American army, however, was raised by the draft. The combined strength of the regular army and the National Guard stood at about 750,000 men when the Selective Service Act went into operation, and from this pool of trained and partially trained men the military leaders drew heavily in creating the various units that composed the new National Army. By the end of the war the continuous transfer of individuals and units from one division to another had broken down fairly completely distinctions as to origin. For the training of the men thirty-two camps and cantonments, mainly located in the South, were hastily constructed.

Almost as difficult as the problem of obtaining the men was the problem of supplying the army with competent officers. For the higher ranks, officers of the regular army and the National Guard were promoted, but for the lower grades the army depended upon the graduates of hastily organized officers' training camps from which "ninety-day wonders" were soon being turned out in profusion. At first only volunteers of excellent promise were accepted for officer training, but later candidates selected on merit from among the drafted men were also given a chance to earn commissions. Political appointments, such as had disgraced the formation of the Civil War armies, both North and South, were deliberately avoided. This decision was a great disappointment to Theodore Roosevelt, who had aspired to emulate his performance in the Spanish-American War, and lead a division of volunteers to France. The war, he complained, was a "very exclusive war," and his hatred for Wilson, already burning brightly, flamed up anew after his rejection.

Officer training

The problem of financing the war would have been great had the United States had only her own expenditures to consider, but she had also to finance her Allies in considerable part. Economists urged a "pay-as-you-go" system, with taxation of wartime profits and earnings furnishing most of the revenue, but such a system was a practical impossibility. For one thing, money was needed immediately, and newly devised taxes would take months, or even years, to produce the needed funds. Congress therefore resorted to loans, as well as taxes. The first loan act, which became law on April 24, authorized the borrowing of five billion dollars, and subsequent credits were voted as needed. Five huge bond issues were floated, the first four known as "Liberty Loans," and the last, which was offered after the fighting had ended, as the "Victory Loan." The total amounts so subscribed reached $21,448,120,300, and drew upon the savings of over sixty-five million individuals. Each loan was accompanied by a great "drive," in which every conceivable device was used to induce both those who had the means and those who had not to subscribe. The bonds were issued in denominations as low as fifty and one hundred dollars, and the purchase of such a bond, on the installment plan if need be, was made almost a test of loyalty. "Four-minute men" harangued theater, church, and school audiences on the iniquities of the Germans and the necessity of the war. Individuals who were suspected of being "pro-German" were compelled to prove their patriotism by particularly generous contributions; if they did not, their houses might be decorated with yellow paint, or they might even be subjected to rough handling. Corporations with large payrolls put pressure upon their employees to subscribe. Thrift stamps and war-savings certificates were devised to

Financing the war

tap even the savings of the children. Unfortunately the securities marketed by the government were negotiable, and because the government
refused to buy them back ahead of dates set for maturity they depreciated materially in value. Speculators thus made excellent profits; worse
still, the bonds, unlike the non-transferable bonds issued during the
second World War, served to promote rather than to restrict inflation.
Prices rose rapidly, and without serious attempt on the part of the government to hold them down.[1] .

The income tax, with its surtax feature, offered an easy means of
expanding the national revenue. The Revenue Act of 1916 had already
doubled the normal income tax, but the War Revenue Act of 1917 doubled it again, bringing it to four per cent, and taxed incomes as low as a
thousand dollars. The graduated surtax and the tax on corporation
earnings were also raised, and a new graduated excess profits tax took
from twenty to sixty per cent of such business earnings as exceeded the
average for the years 1911–1913. The excise taxes on liquor and tobacco
were steeply increased, and a host of "nuisance taxes" introduced — on
railroad and sleeping-car tickets, on theater tickets and club dues, on
telephone and telegraph messages, and on numerous other "luxuries."
Postage rates went up, the ordinary letter rate from two to three cents.
These were the beginning, and still higher taxes were written into the
Revenue Acts of 1918 and 1919. Altogether the United States raised a
total of $11,280,000,000 from taxation, less than one-third the amount
spent or lent during the same period. The total expenditures from
April, 1917, to October, 1919, aggregated $35,413,000,000, of which
$9,406,000,000 was lent to the Allies.

The contribution of the American people to the cost of the war included also millions of dollars expended for private benevolence. Probably the Red Cross, with its emphasis on medical care and
hospitalization, was most appreciated by soldiers and public
alike. Its first drive for funds, held immediately after the
flotation of the First Liberty Loan, netted over $100,000,000, and subse-
quent drives brought in other huge sums. The Young Men's Christian
Association, the Knights of Columbus, the United Hebrew Charities,
and the Salvation Army also solicited contributions for wartime activities, and spent lavishly in their efforts to make life in the army camps
and overseas more bearable. Besides all this, women's organizations
knitted socks, prepared bandages, and provided numerous other items of
consequence to the soldier's comfort. Undoubtedly the benevolent

*Private
benevolence*

---

[1] J. H. Hollander, *War Borrowing* (1919); E. L. Bogart, *Direct and Indirect Costs of the
Great World War* (new edition, 1920); J. M. Clark, *The Costs of the World War to the
American People* (1931).

agencies did much to substitute harmless amusements for the traditional resort of the soldier to intoxication and immorality, and they sought also to bolster up army morale. The "Y" suffered much criticism, mainly because it accepted the task of vending such supplies as candy and cigarettes, instead of confining its efforts more exclusively to straight-out gifts.[1] Nearly all of the work supported by benevolence had to be done; if private agencies had not undertaken it, the government itself would have been obliged to do so. So valuable did this work seem that the government encouraged all drives for funds by benevolent societies while the war was on. Gifts to churches, colleges, hospitals, and endowment funds, whether directly concerned in the war or not, at least cultivated the important habit of giving.

In general the government itself took care of the dependents of soldiers, and made what provision it could to prevent the men who fought the war from becoming objects of charity in the future. By rigorous examinations it kept out of the service all those who might reasonably be expected to break under the physical and mental strain of war. Men who had families dependent on them for support were given deferred classification, which amounted in effect to exemption from the draft. The Bureau of War Risk Insurance, established originally in 1914 to write marine insurance, was enlarged in October, 1917, so as to permit it to assume for the military forces of the United States the obligations ordinarily associated with employers' liability. A soldier who had dependents was obliged to allot a part of his pay to his family, and to this sum the government, in accordance with a prescribed schedule, added more. If a soldier died in service, his widow received seventy-five dollars a month until remarriage. If he were disabled, he received compensation commensurate with the degree of his disability. If he were maimed in such a way as to need re-education, the government accepted the responsibility for that also, and charged the Federal Board for Vocational Education with the duty of providing the necessary training. And for all who would take it the government offered an insurance policy of from one to ten thousand dollars, at cost, the premiums to be deducted from the soldier's pay. By 1919 over four and a half million such policies had been written, representing an aggregate of thirty-eight billion dollars. The pay of the American private was thirty dollars a month, the highest in the world, and it was supposed that the insurance system adopted by the government would forestall the customary drive for pensions at the end of the war. This hope, as events proved, was vain.

The raising of huge armies, the flotation of unprecedentedly large

War risk insurance

[1] Katherine Mayo, *That Damn Y* (1920).

loans, and the ruthless expansion of taxation were tasks that in a democracy would have been impossible but for the support of a
thoroughly aroused public opinion. When war was declared
in 1917, it is reasonable to suppose that the action was approved by a majority of the people as well as by a majority
of Congress. But the popular majority was by no means so overwhelming as the vote in Congress indicated; indeed, many a congressman would
have voted the other way had he dared. Most of those who doubted the
wisdom of American entrance into the war were sympathetic with the
Allied cause and ripe for conversion, but a small minority, composed of
pro-Germans, Socialists, and pacifists, were bitterly opposed. Many of
them were in complete agreement with Senator La Follette, who in casting his vote against the war resolution maintained, "I say Germany has
been patient with us," or with Morris Hillquit, the Socialist, who asserted, "The country has been violently, needlessly, and criminally involved in war." It was essential, if the sacrifices necessary to win the
war were to be borne, that public opinion should support the government
with virtual unanimity. Partly with this end in view the President, on
April 14, 1917, designated the Secretaries of State, War, and Navy as a
Committee on Public Information, charged with the duty of publishing
the facts about the war. As the executive officer directly responsible for
carrying on the work he named George Creel, a well-known and energetic
journalist.[1]

Public opinion on the war

Creel's task was both to disseminate the news and to "sell" the war to
the people. He had no commission to act as censor; only in so far as
military men and the Allies were able to exercise control of
the news were the facts suppressed. But he could spread
and interpret what news there was, and that he meant to do.
Gathering about himself as able a group of journalists and historians as
he could find, and adding artists, actors, photographers, and linguists as
needed, he began to release a spectacular barrage of information and
·propaganda. Through the *Official Bulletin*, published daily beginning
May 10, 1917, he told what was going on with little attempt to distort,
and set an example in the treatment of war news that most of the newspapers of the country followed. But he never forgot that a part of his
mission was to convince all Americans, and if he could the whole wide
world besides, that the American case for war against Germany was unimpeachable. Through "Red, White, and Blue" books, compiled by its
historians, the C.P.I. told the public the things it needed to know: *How
the War Came to America; The War Message and the Facts Behind It; The*

The Creel Committee

---

[1] George Creel, *The War, the World, and Wilson* (1920), and *How We Advertised America*
(1920); J. R. Mock and Cedric Larson, *Words that Won the War* (1939); G. G. Bruntz,
Allied Propaganda and the Collapse of the German Empire in 1918 (1938).

President's Flag Day Speech; German War Practices; Why Working Men Support the War; The War Cyclopedia; Conquest and Kultur; The German War Code; The Government of Germany. Ready-made editorials were distributed by the million to overworked country editors, who ran them gratefully and believed what they said. Foreign-language newspapers were objects of special solicitude, and soon got the idea as to what they were expected to print. Speech-making material for the seventy-five thousand four-minute men and other orators was ladled out with a free hand; motion pictures taught similar lessons to those who lacked either the mind or the will to read; strikingly designed posters helped along the various "drives" by which the war was to be won. Unfortunately, talking pictures and the radio were not yet available; had they been the imagination palls at the thought of the uses the C.P.I. would have made of them.

The net effect of this propaganda was to convince Americans more deeply than ever that only by winning the war could the "world be made safe for democracy"; only by a "war to end war" could a lasting peace be achieved. The war became a holy crusade, and those who dared oppose it were given short shrift. It was in response to this opinion rather than because there

Restrictions on civil liberties

was any longer reason to fear the minority that the drastic Sedition Act of May 16, 1918, was added to the milder Espionage Act of June 15, 1917. Freedom of speech and of the press meant little in wartime, as the Supreme Court quickly explained. Said Mr. Justice Holmes, voicing a unanimous opinion: "When a nation is at war many things that might be said in time of peace are such a hindrance to its effort that their utterance will not be endured so long as men fight, and that no court could regard them as protected by any constitutional right." Long prison sentences were meted out to prominent critics of the war, including Eugene V. Debs, four times the Socialist candidate for President, and Victor L. Berger, Socialist congressman from Milwaukee. Berger's newspaper, the Milwaukee *Leader*, and the even more outspoken New York *Masses*, a Socialist monthly, lost their second-class mailing privileges. Hundreds of conscientious objectors were sent to jail.

Neither the political nor the economic organization of the United States was fitted to meet the emergencies of war, and drastic changes had to be effected in both.[1] Fortunately the defense measures of 1916 had provided for a planning board known as the Council of National Defense. The six members of this council were cabinet officers with an abundance of other work to do,

Council of National Defense

---

[1] W. F. Willoughby, *Government Organization in War Time and After* (1919), is a survey of the federal civil agencies created for the prosecution of the war.

but they were expected to follow the recommendations of an Advisory Commission of seven civilians, also provided for in the law. Headed by Daniel Willard, president of the Baltimore and Ohio Railroad, and assisted by as many "dollar-a-year" volunteers as it could use, the Advisory Commission soon became what Professor Paxson has aptly called a "civilian general staff." Largely through the plans it devised, the government of the United States was reorganized for wartime efficiency, while industry, agriculture, labor, and every other form of American economic life were forced to operate with the single-minded purpose of winning the war. Temporarily the United States ceased to be a democracy, and the freedom of the individual was sacrificed to the larger necessity of a military victory. New and powerful administrative agencies, responsible only to the President, told the people of the nation what they might and might not do, and what they had to do.

Before the war was over, six great wartime agencies had taken over the chief responsibility for adjusting American economic life to the necessities of the war. The oldest of these was the United

The wartime government

States Shipping Board, which had been created the year before the war broke out. Through its Emergency Fleet Corporation it struggled valiantly, and with considerable success, to build ships faster than the submarines could sink them. A second agency, the Food Administration, had as its responsibility the supply of food, both for soldiers and for non-combatants, overseas. As Food Administrator, Herbert Hoover preached the "gospel of the clean plate," persuaded the American people to accept "wheatless" and "meatless" days, and encouraged all who could to plant "war-gardens." More important still, Hoover's Grain Corporation set high prices for wheat that led to a remarkable expansion of the nation's wheat acreage, with a corresponding increase in production. A Fuel Administration dealt similarly with the pressing coal and oil problem; a Railroad Administration took over all the railroads of the country and operated them as if they were a single system; a War Trade Board licensed foreign trade and took care that American commodities did not reach the enemy; and a War Industries Board, most powerful of all, took full command of American production. Under Bernard Baruch as chairman, the W.I.B. told manufacturers at will what materials they could use, and what materials they must save. It could order them to undertake totally new endeavors. It could determine priorities, and so give or withhold both the raw materials and the transportation upon which every manufacturer depended. It could standardize products, and with the President's approval it could, and did, fix prices. Of great assistance in working out the orders of the War Industries Board was the War Finance Corporation, which operated with a half-billion dollar revolving fund granted by Congress, and such other sums as it could borrow, lent to business that needed encouragement, while restraining vigorously all non-essential demands for capital.[1]

Long before the war was won, the government of the United States was exercising powers that in ordinary times would have been deemed incompatible with democracy. The six great "war boards" — Shipping, Food, Fuel, Railroads, War Trade, and War Industries — owed responsibility for their acts to the President alone. Beginning in March, 1918, the heads of these boards met with him weekly as a kind of war cabinet. Such legislation as they required, Congress ordinarily felt obliged to supply. The most sweeping of these grants was contained in the Overman Act, signed May 20, 1918, by which the President, until six months after the war should end, was given free rein "to utilize, co-ordinate, or consolidate any executive or administrative commissions, bureaus, agencies, offices, or officers" at will; to create new agencies and abolish old ones, and to utilize funds voted for any purpose in whatever way he deemed that purpose best served. One critic of the bill suggested ironically an amendment: "If any power, constitutional or not, has been inadvertently omitted from this bill, it is hereby granted in full." Working closely together under the President, and assured of support by state councils of defense locally maintained, the war boards all but supplanted the ordinary civil authorities. The amount of grumbling that accompanied the resulting regimentation of American life was surprisingly small. The nation took pride in the fact that a democracy could make war efficiently, even if in the process it had to sacrifice many traditional liberties. The tyranny that existed, people well understood, was of their own creation, and could be destroyed when the war was over.

The support of organized labor for the war was greatly promoted by the earnest efforts of Samuel Gompers, one of the seven members of the Advisory Commission, whose insistence that the war must not be used to depreciate wages or labor standards became a governmental policy.[2] Indeed, the draft, which took many *Labor and the war* men out of the labor market, and the cessation of immigration, which cut off an historic source of supply, led to a labor scarcity that drove wages to unprecedented heights. By 1918 the average worker was earning nearly twice as much as in 1914, and even allowing for the mounting

---

[1] B. M. Baruch, *American Industry in the War: A Report of the War Industries Board* (1921). Benedict Crowell and R. F. Wilson, editors, *How America Went to War* (6 vols., 1921), is an account from official sources of the nation's various war activities, and is admirably complete. Two volumes are devoted to *The Armies of Industry*. See also Arthur Bullard, *Mobilizing America* (1917), and Frederick Palmer, *Newton D. Baker: America at War* (2 vols., 1931). The best single volume on American participation in the war is F. L. Paxson, *American Democracy and the World War*, ii, *America at War, 1917–1918* (1939).

[2] Samuel Gompers, *American Labor and the War* (1919).

costs of living he was fully twenty per cent better off than he had been
when hostilities began. High wages and steady employment meant also
prosperity for the labor unions, whose membership shot upward during
the war by no less than thirty-seven per cent. To facilitate the mobility
of labor the government greatly expanded the United States Employment Service of the Labor Department, and to fill labor shortage it
encouraged the use of women in industry. Labor disputes were kept at a
minimum. A War Labor Conference Board, created early in 1918, laid
down the rules that should govern the relationship of capital and labor,
and a National War Labor Board, under the co-chairmanship of William
Howard Taft and Frank P. Walsh, acted as a court of last resort in the
settlement of labor disputes. The formulation of labor policies in the
new war industries was handed over to a War Labor Policies Board of
which Felix Frankfurter became chairman.

Inevitably every American came to feel keenly the effects of the war.
The Federal Reserve System stood up admirably under the unexpected
burdens it had to shoulder, but the huge bond issues and expanding
business they supported made for cheap money and currency inflation.
In theory the gold standard was maintained, but gold did not circulate,
and dollars bought less and less. Salaried employees had greater difficulty than laborers in obtaining the wage increases necessary to meet the
rising cost of living, and some of them suffered acutely. Women not
only invaded industry, but they were also increasingly in evidence in
business and the professions. For the most part the educational system
of the country carried on as usual, although higher education was hard
hit by enlistments, and, after the service age was lowered from twenty-
one to eighteen, by the draft. In an effort to combine education and
military training the Students' Army Training Corps was established in
practically all the colleges during the fall of 1918. Young men of draft
age were allowed to continue their studies in uniform and at the expense
of the government, while learning the art of war from army officers. The
compensation paid the colleges by the government for the use of their
facilities saved many of them from financial collapse, but as an educational experiment the S.A.T.C. was a failure.[1] With many of the nation's physicians mobilized for war, the influenza epidemic of 1918 became a serious plague. The "flu," indeed, baffled medical science, and
took a heavy toll both in the cantonments and among civilians.

The "home front"   Undoubtedly the most unlovely feature of the "home
front" was the ugly intolerance bred by the war. Americans of foreign extraction suffered from it more acutely than
any others, especially when they had been "pro-German" in the period

[1] P. R. Kolbe, *The Colleges in War Time and After* (1919).

of neutrality. Most of the acts of intolerance were not the acts of the government, but of the people. The German language, which before the war had been more widely taught in America than any other foreign language, was all but eliminated from the public schools, and suffered from drastic restrictions in the colleges. Printing, preaching, teaching, even talking in the German language were treated as if criminal offenses, and were sometimes made so. Musicians of German origin, such as Frederick Stock and Fritz Kreisler, were publicly humiliated. Honorary degrees granted to Germans before the war were revoked by the universities that had granted them. All aliens and all citizens of recent alien origin were made to feel their inferiority to the so-called "native Americans." It was as Wilson himself had said on the eve of war: "Once lead this people into war and they'll forget there ever was such a thing as tolerance. To fight you must be brutal and ruthless, and the spirit of ruthless brutality will enter into every fiber of our national life, infecting Congress, the courts, the policemen on the beat." Conformity, as the President had foreseen, became the only true virtue, and the man who refused to conform had to pay a severe penalty. Perhaps the nation would never in any other mood have endured the sacrifices of war.

For actual combat duty the navy preceded the army to Europe by many months. Indeed, Rear-Admiral William S. Sims, who was chosen for overseas command, was in London before the United States entered the war, and by May 4 the first detachment of American destroyers had crossed the Atlantic. Ultimately three hundred warships, large and small, and seventy-five thousand officers and men were serving in the overseas detachments of the American navy. Their activities extended from the vicinity of the British Isles to the Mediterranean. No doubt these reinforcements were partly responsible for the fact that the experiment of Jutland was not repeated. The American naval forces made no effort to operate separately, but became to all intents and purposes a part of the British Grand Fleet. American ships were used, among other things, to enforce the very rules of blockade against which the United States as a neutral had protested so vigorously.[1]

The greatest single concern of the combined navies when the United States entered the war was the defeat of the submarine. This was eventually accomplished by a variety of means. American insistence had much to do with the laying of a mine barrage across the opening of the North Sea, between the Orkney Islands and the coast of Norway.

---

[1] W. S. Sims and B. J. Kendrick, *The Victory at Sea* (1920); Louis Guichard, *The Naval Blockade, 1914–1918* (1930); Elting E. Morison, *Admiral Sims and the Modern American Navy* (1942).

This, and a similar mine barrage across the Straits of Dover, seriously crippled submarine activities. Cruising destroyers, armed with improved means of detection, also hunted down the "U-boats," and sank them with depth-charges. By the end of the war about half the German submarine flotilla had been destroyed. American ships likewise played a leading rôle in convoying merchantmen and troop-ships through the danger zone, thereby cheating the submarines of their prey.

The frantic pleas of the Allies for American troops in France led the General Staff to revise its plans with respect to the training of the American can army. It was decided that troops would have to be sent overseas only partly trained and partly equipped. The rest of the work could be done over there. Mainly as an earnest of good intentions General John J. Pershing was ordered to France in May, 1917, as head of the American Expeditionary Forces, and next month the first of the American detachments began to arrive. The American plan called for more than the mere transporting of troops. Already the facilities of France and her allies were being taxed to the limit to support their own armies, and the American contingent must be a help, not a burden. Ten thousand tons of wheat reached France in advance of the troops it was supposed to sustain, and, to make way for the coming of further detachments of the A.E.F., harbors had to be dredged, docks constructed, debarkation depots created, railroads made over, freight-yards laid out, telegraph and telephone lines erected, hospitals, barracks, and warehouses put together. All this was done by American labor on the American plan, and for the most part with American materials, although American sawmills sometimes condescended to turn European logs into lumber. Over five million tons of supplies were sent abroad by the United States before the armistice was signed. As to man-power, the American records show that 2,079,880 men were transported overseas. Not all of these were fighting men, but from them Pershing netted forty-two combat divisions.

From the first General Pershing, who had himself written the orders under which he operated, insisted upon the creation of a separate American army. This did not please the Allies, who wished to use the American troops as replacements, to be brigaded with French or British units. But Pershing was convinced that three years of defensive fighting had unfitted the Allied armies for effective offensive tactics, and finally forced the Allied leaders to give in. The American army thus became a wholly independent unit, and in October, 1917, began to take over a quiet sector of the battle line. When in March, 1918, however, Russia made a separate peace and the Germans began a great *Friedensturm*, designed to end the war in the West, Pershing did not hesitate to lend troops to the

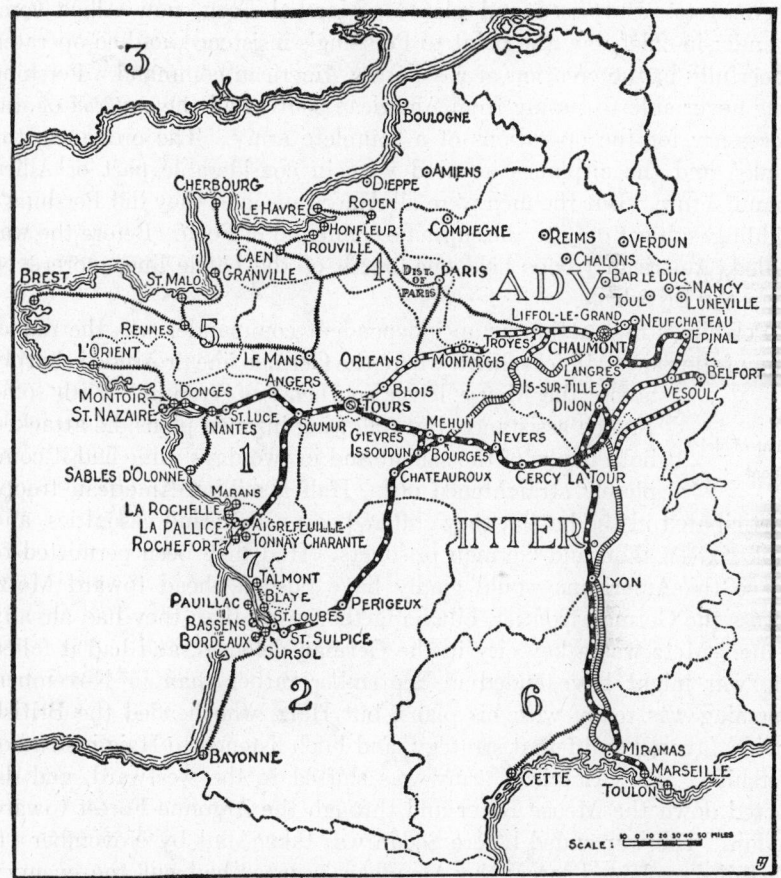

PRINCIPAL FRENCH PORTS AND RAILROADS
USED BY AMERICAN EXPEDITIONARY FORCES

⊕ GENERAL HEADQUARTERS   Ⓢ H.Q. SERVICES OF SUPPLY
⊘ PRINCIPAL PORTS   ⊕ SECONDARY PORTS   ⊙ IMPORTANT TOWNS
▬ MAIN LINES   ▬ SECOND LINES   ▬ THIRD LINES   ▬ OTHER LINES
Note: LARGE NUMBERS INDICATE SUBDIVISIONS OF THE BASE SECTION
INTER.•INTERMEDIATE SECTION   ADV.• ADVANCE SECTION

Map drawn from Pershing, *Final Report* (1919), Plate 8

hard-pressed French. In the summer fighting before Paris, especially at Château-Thierry early in June, the Americans gave a good account of themselves. Surprised and pleased, Marshal Foch, now Allied commander-in-chief, saw the point to Pershing's insistence, and co-operated cheerfully in the creation of a separate American command. Pershing was never able to supply from American sources all the *matériel* of war necessary for the operations of a complete army. The ordnance, the tanks, and the airplanes he used were in considerable part of Allied manufacture. But the men were all Americans, and they did Pershing's bidding, subject only to the supreme command of Foch. Before the war ended, American troops held one-fourth of the battle line, more even than the British.

Pershing's first action as an independent commander was the reduction of the Saint-Mihiel salient, where the German line protruded sharply across the Meuse River southeast of Verdun. With some
The Saint-Mihiel salient French assistance, but following his own plans, he attacked both flanks of the salient and in two days' time had it completely straightened out. Half a million American troops participated in the battle; they suffered seven thousand casualties, and took sixteen thousand German prisoners. Had they been permitted to do so the Americans would gladly have pushed ahead toward Metz, across the German frontier, but no farther away than they had already come. Metz was a key city in the German defenses, and had it fallen the war might have ended in September rather than in November. Pershing was ready with his plans, but Haig, who headed the British forces, favored a different strategy, and Foch listened to Haig instead of Pershing. The American army was shifted to the westward, and directed down the Meuse River and through the Argonne Forest toward Sedan. The war ended before Sedan was taken, but by November 11, Pershing explained later, the American troops "had cut the enemy's main line of communications, and nothing but surrender or an armistice could save his army from complete disaster." [1]

The advance of the American army in the Meuse–Argonne was only a part of the larger campaign by which Foch smashed his way to victory through the supposedly impregnable Hindenburg Line, be-
The Meuse-Argonne hind which the Germans had taken refuge. Three other major offensives, the Ypres–Lys, the Somme, and the Oise–Aisne, preceded and accompanied the American drive. With the Allied forces acting for once in complete co-ordination, an Allied drive was

---

[1] J. J. Pershing, *My Experiences in the World War* (2 vols., 1931), is straightforward and realistic, but far less charitable toward the general's civilian superiors than they were toward him.

begun north of Saloniki against Bulgaria, another against the Turks in Palestine, and a third against the Austrians in Italy. Everywhere the Allied arms were successful. Before the end of September, Bulgaria was out of the war; Turkey quit in October; Austria surrendered early in November; on November 11 Germany, too, with her armies everywhere in full retreat, gave up the fight.

American participation in the war was not wholly confined to the fighting in France. In July, 1918, an American regiment was sent to Italy, and in October two American divisions were lent to the French for use in Belgium. More debatable was the part played by American troops in Allied maneuvers against Bolshevist Russia. Without authority of a declaration of war against Russia, five thousand Americans fought with the Allies in the Archangel–Murmansk campaign that lasted from September, 1918, to May, 1919; while ten thousand Americans joined an Allied expedition to Vladivostok and eastern Siberia that lasted until January, 1920.[1]

The United States watched with tremendous interest the revolutionary experiment in Russia. As soon as possible after the overthrow of the Czar in March, 1917, an American mission headed by Elihu Root, former Secretary of State, and Hugh L. Scott, chief of staff of the United States Army, was sent to Petrograd to help the new government to a good start, and to encourage it in the continued prosecution of the war against Germany. But the wheel of revolution in Russia turned rapidly to the left, and before the end of the year Nicolai Lenin and Leon Trotsky, leaders of the most extreme advocates of Communism, the Bolshevists, had climbed to power with the assistance of German gold, and on the promise to the Russian people of peace. Late in December, 1917, at Brest-Litovsk, they agreed to close out the war on German terms.[2] Finland had declared its independence in July, 1917, and when the Treaty of Brest-Litovsk was finally signed in March, 1918, Poland, Lithuania, and the Ukraine were also separated from Russia, preparatory to leisurely German assimilation. It was clear from this peace that Germany at the moment, whatever her original intent, was engaged in a war of conquest. Should the fighting on the western front end in a German victory, it seemed reasonable to suppose that similar terms would be imposed upon the rest of the Allies. The defection of Russia thus was a tremendous help to Germany, and the repudiation by the Bolshevists of their foreign debts by no means improved the feelings of the Allies. Naturally they wished to bring to power in Russia

The Russian Revolution

---

[1] John Cudahy, *Archangel: The American War with Russia* (1924); W. S. Graves, *America's Siberian Adventure, 1918–1920* (1931).

[2] This was a preliminary agreement. The final treaty was signed three months later.

a government that would resume the war against Germany and agree to meet its financial obligations. The military activities on Russian soil, in which the United States participated, were parts of the ill-fated Allied projects for bringing about these results.

The military contribution that the United States made to the winning of the war was not inconsiderable.[1] An army of 3,500,000 men was raised, of whom 1,400,000 saw active service overseas. Had the hostilities lasted over into 1919, as the Allied plans anticipated, the American activities would have assumed a still more impressive character. As it was, the "Yanks" captured 44,000 prisoners, took 1400 guns, and brought down 755 enemy airplanes. The American contribution in the air was somewhat of a disappointment. In spite of the earnest activities of the Aircraft Production Board, and the creation of the new "Liberty engine," "the eyes of the army went aloft in foreign planes." But 11,000 aviators had been trained by the time of the armistice, and 4300 of them were in France. American casualties, considering the short period of time Pershing's troops were engaged, were heavy — heavier, probably, than in corresponding French and British units where the troops were better trained and the utmost effort was made to hold down losses in man-power. But the total number of deaths suffered by the American army from all causes reached only 125,000 and of these less than half were battle deaths. Compared with the 1,700,000 battle deaths suffered by the Russians, the 1,600,000 by the Germans, the 1,385,000 by the French, the 900,000 by the British, and the 800,000 by the Austrians, the American losses seemed inconsequential, but they were sustained during only about six months of actual fighting, while for the European belligerents the war lasted over four years. Excellent health precautions practically eliminated such filth diseases as dysentery and typhoid, from which so many American soldiers had died in previous wars, and skillful surgery and hospitalization returned five-sixths of those wounded to their regiments. The worst scourge came from the influenza, which took as heavy a toll among civilians as among soldiers.

America's contribution to victory

But it would be quite unfair to judge the part that the United States played in the war wholly from the military angle. The American troops came to Europe with a will to win, and their coming bolstered up enormously the morale of the war-wearied Allies. Confidence in victory was standard equipment for all Americans, and it was systematically whipped up at every training camp, both in the United States and in Europe. It was a singing war, with tunes and verses inspired by cocksureness. The men went to camp, embarked

The will to win

[1] L. P. Ayres, *The War with Germany* (1919), is a valuable statistical study.

and disembarked, marched and relaxed to "It's a long way to Tipperary," "Over There," and a dozen similar "hits." The American "doughboy" refused even to be depressed by the petty vexations of army life. He made fun of them in the stories passed along by word of mouth, and in the *Stars and Stripes*, a newspaper that the soldiers of the A.E.F. themselves edited in a style that combined the best and the worst of the college daily and the American sports page. Punctilious officers saw themselves as privates saw them in cartoons and comic strips drawn by professionals. The unlimited assurance with which the American army tackled its task impressed even the Germans.

There was much else for which the United States could claim credit. Pershing was quick to point out that the Allies needed above all else a unified command. "When one was attacking, the other was usually standing still." American insistence, together with the grave threat of German victory as a result of the *Friedensturm*, helped pave the way for the assumption of supreme command by Marshal Foch. The American genius for business organization led to another almost equally important reform — a unified system of supply.[1] The American idea was that all resources — shipping, food, munitions, and other supplies — should be pooled, and drawn upon as needed. To accomplish this end much inertia had to be overcome, but before the war was over a remarkable transformation had been wrought. For this change much credit was due to General Charles G. Dawes, Pershing's purchasing agent. Last, but not at all least came the ideal of a peace so even-handed in its justice toward all nations, great and small, victor and vanquished, that the causes of war would be forever abolished. Six thousand years of history proclaimed the illusiveness of such a hope, but the eloquent arguments of the American President made the hope itself a reality. Long before the entrance of the United States into the war, Wilson had been urging such a settlement, and before its close his preachments had gained an almost miraculous ascendancy over world opinion. What he stated in general terms every nation translated into the specific terms its national aspirations demanded. A "peace of justice" meant something quite different to each people, but in every case it meant something worth fighting for. And if this war should be indeed the war that would end all war, the goal was doubly worth the effort. Wilson's idealism became a two-edged sword. On the one hand it provided the Allies with a unified purpose in the war; on the other it tended to break down enemy morale. Why fight against a peace of justice?

> Unity of command and supply

[1] Johnson Hagood, *The Services of Supply: A Memoir of the Great War* (1927); C. G. Dawes, *A Journal of the Great War* (2 vols., 1921).

interest in a peace of justice had been stated clearly in his
...thout victory" speech of January, 1917. After the entrance
of the United States into the war, he modified his stand only
by insisting on a complete victory over the autocratic rulers
of the Central Powers, but for the *people* of Germany and of
her allies, as distinguished from their *governments*, he still adhered to
generous terms. When Pope Benedict XV urged a negotiated peace in
August, 1917, Wilson in reply drew this distinction clearly. The United
States, he said, wished neither punitive damages, nor the dismemberment of empires, nor the establishment of exclusive economic leagues
after the war, but the autocratic rulers must go. That his ideas com-
ported illy with the network of semi-secret treaties on the post-war
world that the Allies had agreed to among themselves, the President
must have known. These treaties planned a victor's peace rather than a
peace of justice, but Wilson seemed to believe that the popularity of his
views with the masses in all countries would bring the Allied governments eventually to his program. As a matter of fact, Lloyd George, the
British Prime Minister, while fully aware of his country's commitments,
echoed the President faithfully, although Clemenceau, the French Premier, admitted frankly, "My war aim is to conquer."

Wilson gave classic statement to his views in a speech delivered before
Congress in January, 1918. If the world were to become "a fit and safe
place to live in," the peace should embody these "Fourteen Points":

1. Open covenants of peace openly arrived at.
2. Freedom of navigation upon the seas, alike in peace and in war.
3. Equality of trade conditions among all nations consenting to the peace.
4. Guaranties that national armaments will be reduced.
5. The adjustment of colonial claims in the interests of the populations concerned.
6. The evacuation of all Russian territory.
7. Belgium must be evacuated and restored.
8. French territory should be freed and restored, and the wrong of Alsace–
   Lorraine should be righted.
9. Readjustment of Italian frontiers along clearly recognizable lines of
   nationality.
10. The peoples of Austria-Hungary should be accorded opportunity for
    autonomous development.
11. Rumania, Serbia, and Montenegro should be evacuated and restored,
    and Serbia secured in access to the sea.
12. The Turkish portions of the Ottoman Empire should be assured a secure
    sovereignty, but other nationalities under Turkish rule should have
    autonomy.

13. An independent Polish state with free and secure access to the sea.

14. A general association of nations for mutual guaranties of political independence and territorial integrity.

Wilson's program was not the product merely of his own thinking. In the main, it was suggested to him by the "Inquiry," a group of scholars drawn together by Colonel House to provide the American State Department with the specific data it would need at the peace conference. It was never formally accepted by the Allies as their own. Wilson spoke for himself and for the government he headed, but he could not speak officially for the nations he usually referred to as the "Associates" of the United States in the war.

The German government in repeated state papers showed that it had no interest whatever in the type of peace Wilson sought. Its real answer to the Fourteen Points was the Treaty of Brest-Litovsk with Russia in March, 1918. This treaty sheared off from **German aspirations** Russia over 300,000 square miles of territory, with a population of 56,000,000 people. It took away one-third of Russia's railway mileage, seventy-three per cent of her total iron output, eighty-nine per cent of her coal production, five thousand factories, mills, distilleries, and refineries. By a supplementary agreement signed in August, 1918, Germany exacted also an indemnity of six billion marks. There is no reason to suppose that the terms of this treaty were unpopular with the people of Germany. Probably the people, no less than the government, were ready for a peace of violence, similar to the Treaty of Brest-Litovsk, against the western nations. Wilson's Fourteen Points were described by one German writer as a "real symphony of a will to no peace." It was only in defeat that either the German government or the German people began to show an interest in a "just peace."

The German defeat, when it came, was thoroughgoing and complete in a strictly military sense. Later on the German people were persuaded to believe that they had laid down their arms in the hope of a just peace when they might have fought on indefinitely. **Defeat of Germany** But they were badly beaten, and their commanding officers knew it. Their allies had been knocked out, one by one. Their supposedly impregnable Hindenburg Line had cracked. Their submarine campaign had failed. Their services of supply were breaking down. The morale of their troops, in full retreat, was declining. Revolution, born less of Wilson's promises than of military disaster, was in the air. Ludendorff and Hindenburg informed the German Emperor in September that all was lost, and that peace must be made at once. Ludendorff had a nervous breakdown. It was the hopelessness of the military situation and the certainty of Allied victory that led the German government, like a drowning man grasping at a straw, to ask Wilson for an armistice on the basis of the Fourteen Points. It was the impending collapse of the military front, and not merely unrest at home, that forced Germany to sue for peace.[1]

The negotiations for an armistice were begun early in October, 1918, by a new German Chancellor, Prince Max of Baden, reputedly a liberal, who professed to Wilson that he spoke "in the name of the German government and the German people." Even so, the pre-armistice negotiations were long drawn out. Wilson's Fourteen Points were accepted by the Allied leaders only after elaborate interpretations and amendments, to all of which the Germans were obliged, because of the military situation, to consent. Among other things, Wilson's second point, the "freedom of the seas," was ruled out altogether at the insistence of the British, while with reference to invaded territories, it was expressly stipulated that full compensation must be made for all damage done "by land, by sea, and from the air." When the German envoys signed the armistice they knew, therefore, that they were obtaining substantially less than the Fourteen Points, but they knew also that failure to sign meant only the substitution of unconditional surrender for what was left of the Wilson program. Even so, the armistice was not actually signed until the German fleet at Kiel had mutinied rather than put to sea for a final test of strength, the Kaiser himself had been forced to abdicate, and leaders who owed no allegiance to the former "autocratic rulers" were in complete control. With the signing of the armistice, November 11, 1918, the war came to an end.

The military terms of the armistice revealed still further the extremity of the German collapse. No nation with the faintest hope of victory could have accepted them. The German army must retire to the left bank of the Rhine, surrendering huge stores of military supplies and railroad equipment; the bridgeheads at Cologne, Coblenz, and Mainz must be occupied by Allied troops; Allied prisoners of war and deported inhabitants of occupied territory must be returned without reciprocity; the German submarines and battle fleet must be taken to a neutral or Allied port for internment (the Germans took their ships to Scapa Flow as required, but ultimately scuttled them); and the predatory treaties of Brest-Litovsk and Bucharest, with Russia and Rumania respectively, must be cancelled. The

The armistice

Military terms of the armistice

---

[1] "The charge that Wilson purposely betrayed us over the Fourteen Points acquired greater prominence from the fact that a legend was fostered in Germany to the effect that we laid down our weapons in reliance on the Fourteen Points. This legend is a flat falsification of history, as everyone knows who then took any part in the negotiations. We had to lay down our arms because the Supreme Command insisted that we should do so in order to avoid a catastrophe, and then we invoked Wilson's help with an appeal to the Fourteen Points." *Memoirs of Count Bernstorff* (1936), p. 136.

Allies on their part were at liberty to requisition such German property as their armies of occupation might need, and to maintain the blockade of Germany that they had set up during the war. All this the German leaders knew and agreed to when they signed the armistice. Alone among the Allied commanders, General Pershing had opposed any armistice at all. He believed that only by a knockout blow delivered on German soil could the German people be made to realize the completeness of their defeat.

Wilson, meantime, had suffered a disastrous political setback at home. In the mid-term elections of 1918 the Republicans won the House of Representatives by a majority of twenty votes, and the Senate by a majority of one. Wilson himself had contrib- *Election of 1918* uted to the Democratic defeat by an appeal on October 25 for a Democratic majority in Congress through which alone, he maintained, he could hope to carry on his policies. The Republicans skillfully turned this statement into a charge that they had not supported the war, and undoubtedly gained many votes as a result. But the Wilson administration had already accumulated about all the enmity it could hope to carry; every European nation that participated in the war had already had at least one change of government since it began. Wilson's propaganda for an early peace and a just peace had small appeal for the "bitter-enders," who with Theodore Roosevelt at their head blamed the President for his delay in getting into the war, and made fun of his notewriting and idealism. But the fact that he had led the country into the war at all was equally offensive to the pacifists and the German-Americans. To critics of his war policy were added those who disliked the liberal legislation of his first administration, his surrender to labor in the Adamson Act, and his attitude toward Mexico. Most important of all, the Republican politicians after six long years of separation from the spoils of office were alert to every opening that would facilitate their return to power, and directed their campaign with skill.

The logical place for the making of the treaty of peace, as had so often been the case after previous wars, proved to be Paris. Unwisely, perhaps, Wilson chose to represent the United States in person at the Conference, and to take along with him a delegation that would in no way interfere with his wishes.[1] So many experts, however, some of whom had been active in Colonel House's "Inquiry," accompanied the official delegates, that a large liner, the *George Washington*, was required to transport them all to Europe. The President's party reached France December

[1] The other members of the American delegation were Robert Lansing, Secretary of State; Colonel House, the President's intimate friend; General Tasker H. Bliss, a military adviser; and Henry White, a Republican who had long since retired from active political life.

13, 1918, but the Paris Peace Conference did not actually convene until January 18, 1919. In the meantime Wilson paid official visits to Paris, London, and Rome, and inspected some of the battle-fields of the war. Everywhere he was received with the most whole-hearted enthusiasm on the part of the people, and with every show of hospitality on the part of the heads of the Allied governments, although many of them regretted the necessity of having to deal with him personally.

The Paris Peace Conference was an extraordinary gathering. All the Allies were represented, including such non-participating belligerents as

The Paris Peace Conference

China and Brazil, but the Germans for good reason were denied any voice whatever in the proceedings. It was clear that the problem of reconciling conflicting Allied opinions would be a serious enough task without the presence of a German delegation ready to take every advantage of Allied disagreements. The Conference, of course, was too large to carry on the actual negotiations, and met only for plenary sessions to confirm what had already been agreed upon behind the scenes. All matters of consequence were settled by the "Big Four," Clemenceau of France, Lloyd George of England, Orlando of Italy, and Wilson of the United States. Of this group, Wilson was still committed in principle to the Fourteen Points, although some of his points had been seriously modified in the pre-armistice negotiations. But Clemenceau, Lloyd George, and Orlando considered themselves bound primarily by the secret treaties which the Allies had negotiated with each other early in the war. These treaties promised France Alsace-Lorraine, the Saar Basin, and an independent government for the rest of German territory west of the Rhine. Great Britain was to receive most of the German colonies, and a free hand in Egypt, Persia, and Mesopotamia. Italy was assured her *Italia Irredenta* — the Trentino, the southern Tyrol, and control of the Adriatic. Rumania had been assigned Transylvania and other territorial acquisitions. Japan was to succeed Germany in Shantung and in the islands of the northern Pacific. Russia, whose withdrawal from the war had forfeited her claims, was to have been given Constantinople and the Dardanelles. To the Allies these terms signified a just and lasting peace, and they proposed to obtain them as nearly as they might.

Wilson had hoped that the influence of an aroused world opinion would enable him to persuade the Allies to forget their harsh terms, and

The Treaty of Versailles

to accept more literally his Fourteen Points program. In the end he won only a compromise. Compared with the infamous Treaty of Brest-Litovsk that Germany had forced upon Russia only the year before, the Treaty of Versailles was extremely moderate; but compared with what Wilson had hoped to get, it left much to be desired. When delegates from the new German republic agreed to this treaty on June 28, they surrendered Alsace-Lorraine to France; gave generous blocks of territory including a corridor to the sea along the Vistula to Poland; and ceded border rectifications to Belgium and Denmark. The German colonies were all taken away, and handed over to the Allied countries, not for outright annexation, to be sure, but under a League of Nations mandate system that in practice amounted to nearly the same thing. The Saar Basin, Germany's richest coal-mining area, was turned over to French exploitation for a period of fifteen years, during which time it was to be under the political control of an international commission; at the end of the stipulated period the people of the Saar might decide by plebiscite whether the region should be returned to Germany, continued under international control, or ceded to France. Reparations for the damages done by the German armies had been agreed to in the pre-armistice terms, but the Conference was unable to fix upon the amount due, and left this to be decided by a Reparations Commission after peace was restored.[1] In some ways harder for the Germans to bear than the reparations bill (most of which was never paid anyway) was the assertion in the treaty that their country and her allies were responsible "for causing all the loss and damage to which the Allied and Associated governments have been subjected as a consequence of the war." This "war-guilt" clause, they maintained, quite indefensibly placed full blame upon the Central Powers for the outbreak of war in 1914.

The Treaty of Versailles also provided for the complete disarmament of Germany. Her standing army was reduced to one hundred thousand men and conscription was abolished; frontier fortifications not in Allied hands were to be razed; the manufacture, importation, or exportation of war materials was virtually prohibited; and the German navy was reduced to insignificance. The treaty promised, however, that the Allies would themselves soon take steps toward disarmament, a promise that was only in part fulfilled. Nor did Germany remain long unarmed.

Harsh as these terms were, they did not satisfy Clemenceau, who conceded even this much only on condition that there be a separate alliance between Great Britain, the United States, and France to repel jointly any future attacks on France. Wilson consented to the alliance, but the Senate, as he should have

The League of Nations

[1] In May, 1921, the Commission set the German bill for damages at about thirty-three billion dollars, well beyond the ability of Germany to pay. In 1922, on the ground that Germany had defaulted in her payments, the French seized the Ruhr Valley coal fields. Finally, after several fruitless efforts to solve the problem by international agreement, Germany under Hitler openly repudiated her obligations, and the Allies were unwilling to fight about it. France relinquished the Ruhr in 1925. Ten years later, the Saar voted by an overwhelming majority for reunion with Germany.

foreseen, refused to accept so forthright a departure from the American tradition of non-intervention in European affairs. Wilson pinned his hope for future peace, however, less on the proposed alliance than upon the League of Nations, which by his persistent efforts the Allies were at length induced to include in the Treaty of Versailles. Through this organization, he hoped, many of the injustices of the treaty could be righted later on, when wartime fevers should have abated. The Covenant of the League described three principal agencies: (1) a permanent Secretariat with headquarters established presently at Geneva, Switzerland; (2) a Council of nine members (later enlarged), to consist of one representative from each of the great powers, France, Great Britain, Italy, Japan, and the United States, and four others to be chosen by the Assembly; (3) an Assembly in which every member nation was to have a representative and a vote. The members of the League agreed by the famous Article X "to respect and preserve as against external aggression the territorial integrity and existing political independence" of all other members, and to recognize the right of every member nation to bring problems that might disturb the peace to the attention of the Assembly or the Council. Peace was to be achieved primarily by arbitration or adjudication, and the establishment of a permanent court of international justice was contemplated; but disputes not so adjusted must be submitted for settlement either to the Council or to the Assembly. Against nations making illegal war the Council might impose drastic economic sanctions, and in case it deemed military measures necessary to check aggressors it might make appropriate recommendations to members of the League.[1]

The Treaty of Versailles was only one of many treaties that taken together may properly be called the Peace of Paris. Wilson's tenth point had expressly stated that he wished to see the place of Austria-Hungary among nations "safeguarded and assured," but the disintegration of that unhappy power had been so complete that its resurrection as one nation was beyond the realm of possibility. Each of the many national groups that composed the old Empire was now determined to be free, except, possibly, German-Austria, which would have preferred union with Germany. But the Treaty of Saint-Germain, signed September 10, 1919, warned the new "Republic of Austria" to "abstain from any act which might directly or indirectly or by any means whatever compromise her independence."

The Peace
of Paris

---

[1] R. S. Baker, *Woodrow Wilson and World Settlement* (3 vols., 1922), is friendly to Wilson, and invaluable for a study of the Peace Conference. It may be compared with David Lloyd George, *Memoirs of the Peace Conference* (2 vols., 1939). See also J. T. Shotwell, *At the Paris Peace Conference* (1937); and D. H. Miller, *The Drafting of the Covenant* (2 vols., 1928).

This action was taken partly in order to prevent Germany from being strengthened by the addition of so many Austrians, and partly to prevent the new state of Czechoslovakia from being nearly encircled by Germany. The Treaty of Trianon with Hungary was not signed until June 4, 1920. It cut down the domain of the old Magyar kingdom to an irreducible minimum. The Treaty of Neuilly with Bulgaria, signed November 27, 1919, trimmed off in similar fashion the borders of Germany's smallest ally, and the Treaty of Sèvres with Turkey, signed August 10, 1920, left little non-Turkish territory to the Turks.

Through these and numerous supplementary treaties the "Balkanization" of central Europe was completed. The states that had aided the Allies were rewarded by territorial gains; those that had supported the Central Powers were punished by territorial losses. Numerous new states appeared on the map of Europe: Finland, Estonia, Latvia, Lithuania, Poland, Czechoslovakia, Yugoslavia, Albania. Everywhere the problem of "minorities" threatened the permanence of peace, for boundary lines that would separate every nationality from every other simply could not be drawn. Even the victors were not wholly satisfied. During the Peace Conference Wilson had insisted that the Italians were not entitled to Fiume on the eastern coast of the Adriatic, and as a result the Italian delegation had left the Conference. Ultimately they came back, and by a *coup* Italy obtained the coveted port later on. But the Italians never forgave Wilson, although he consented to the inclusion within Italian borders of several hundred thousand Austrian Germans in the Trentino. This, like many another such decision, was condoned on the ground that it was necessary to provide the nation concerned with a defensible frontier. By the time these treaties were written, Wilson must have realized that in much of Europe "clearly recognizable lines of nationality" simply did not exist. Even less attainable was the hope seemingly cherished by each of these little states of achieving economic self-sufficiency.

The seeds of future wars were thus strewed plentifully about, but Wilson hoped that through the League of Nations their growth might be prevented. Unfortunately, he was soon to discover that on this innovation he was unable to win the support of his own government. All those forces that had worked to discredit him in the election of 1918 now made ready to destroy his latest handiwork, the Treaty of Versailles, and the League of Nations it established. The election had given the Senate to the Republicans by the narrowest possible margin, and Henry Cabot Lodge of Massachusetts, whose hatred for Wilson knew no bounds, had become chairman of the Senate Committee on Foreign Relations, to which the treaty must

The Senate and the treaty

be referred. Once, when Wilson had returned to Washington during the Peace Conference, Lodge and his followers had made their attitude clear, but Wilson felt sure that he could carry the people with him. It was his theory of government that the people, if thoroughly aroused, would and could force their rulers to heed the popular will. The Senate might prefer not to ratify the treaty, but in the end it would have to give in.

But Wilson overlooked the lengths to which his opponents were willing to go in their determination to discredit him. He was probably right in his assumption that the American people were for the time being ready to accept the treaty, including the plan for world co-operation implicit in the League of Nations Covenant. Indeed, only a few "bitter-enders," such as La Follette of Wisconsin, Reed of Missouri, and Johnson of California, were willing to go the whole length of outright rejection. The anti-Wilson forces pursued far shrewder tactics. Instead of voting to kill the treaty, they proposed to attach to it a series of reservations, or interpretations, most of which were directed against the League of Nations rather than the injustices of the treaty, and in reality meant comparatively little. But each reservation was well calculated to arouse the President's ire. If the opposition could make the reservations just strong enough to be sure that Wilson would reject them, and not so strong as to offend the public, they could not only insure the failure of the treaty, but could put the blame for its failure upon Wilson himself. The discrediting of the President and his following would thus be complete and devastating.

In the midst of the fight on the treaty, Wilson attempted to take his case to the people on an extensive speaking tour — had the radio then been available this hot summer trip, which completely sapped his vitality, would not have been necessary. Already badly shattered by an attack of influenza in Paris, and never robust, he broke down physically under the strain, and was obliged to return to Washington. There he suffered a paralytic stroke that for a time practically eliminated him as a factor in the government. The Senate did not hesitate to score a victory over its fallen foe. With fifteen reservations to outmatch by one Wilson's Fourteen Points, the majority stood ready to ratify, but the minority, staunchly loyal to Wilson, declined to accept the reservations, although it was well known that the leading European powers would have preferred ratification with the reservations to no ratification at all. Many votes were taken, and the treaty was twice before the Senate. On the final vote, March 20, 1920, the Senate was ready to accept the treaty by a vote of forty-nine to thirty-five, with the encumbering reservations attached. This was less than the necessary two-thirds, but a change of seven votes would

Wilson's collapse

have meant ratification.[1] Among those voting against the treaty were some of the President's closest adherents, Democratic regulars who were willing to accept the treaty precisely as it stood, but in no other form. Thus the treaty failed with an overwhelming majority of the Senate favoring its adoption, although some wanted it with reservations, and others only without reservations. Many observers believed that if Wilson had been well a compromise could have been reached, but others insisted that the reservations were designed to kill the treaty, and would have been made stronger had they been acceptable to the President. What would have transpired had Wilson followed the advice of House to resign the Presidency and leave the battle to Vice-President Marshall may only be surmised. By this time the friendship between the President and his former intimate had cooled, and House's letter was never answered. Himself a casualty of the war he had helped to make, Wilson could not yet understand the thoroughgoing nature of his defeat. From the news that filtered into his sick-room he continued to believe that the American people, who were now in reality drifting rapidly back into isolationism, were still with him. When Congress by joint resolution sought to declare the war with Germany at an end, he interposed his veto, charging that such a course would amount to an "ineffaceable stain upon the gallantry and honor of the United States." The election of 1920, he maintained, must be made a "solemn referendum" to decide whether the American people would accept or reject the obligations of the treaty and the League.

Looking backward from the vantage-point of a second World War, it would seem that the United States, by its half-hearted refusal to support the League of Nations, destroyed whatever chance there was to prevent another general war. Had the American nation shown itself willing to accept the responsibilities of world leadership, it is possible that the return to international anarchy which marked the next two decades might have been forestalled. Conceivably, also, the mistakes and the injustices of the treaty, of which there were many, might have been ironed out through instrumentalities provided for in the League. But when the richest and most powerful of all the nations refused to co-operate in any effective way for the maintenance of peace, the possibility of another world war became a certainty. During the fight on the League, Wilson had recorded his conviction that, in case his efforts failed, the war would have to be fought all over again. What might have happened can never be known, but a generation later the war that Wilson predicted came to pass.

---

[1] D. F. Fleming, *The United States and the League of Nations, 1918–1920* (1932), is the most comprehensive treatment of this subject. H. C. Lodge, *The Senate and the League of Nations* (1925), is bitterly hostile to the League, and to Wilson personally.

35

The Search for Normalcy

THE ELECTION of 1920 was hardly the "solemn referendum" for which
Wilson had hoped. It was rather a referendum on the Wilson administration as a whole, and ever since the election of 1918 the
prospect of a Republican victory had been growing. The
country was no longer in a reform mood; it resented having
had to fight a war; it was sick and tired of the long debate over the
Treaty of Versailles; it was eager for a return to what Senator Warren G.
Harding of Ohio described as "normalcy." The death of Theodore
Roosevelt in 1919 removed the logical Republican candidate from the
scene, and paved the way for the nomination of Harding, the choice of
the Republican leaders in the Senate. Harding's limited talents made it
seem certain that the charge of "executive usurpation" would never
need be brought against him. He was a reservationist during the fight
on the Treaty of Versailles, and always a dependable party regular.
For Vice-President the Republicans chose Calvin Coolidge of Massachusetts, whose national reputation was made when he called out the
state militia in 1919 to suppress a strike of the Boston police. To oppose
this ticket the Democrats nominated James M. Cox, Governor of Ohio,
for President, and Franklin D. Roosevelt, Wilson's Assistant Secretary
of the Navy, for Vice-President. On the issue of the League of Nations,
the Democratic platform stood earnestly by Wilson's record, and the
Democratic candidates stood on their platform. But the Republican
platform was vague on this issue, and the Republican candidates were
even vaguer. Such League advocates as Hughes, Root, and Taft were
able to maintain that the election of Harding would be the surest way to
get the United States into the League, while such irreconcilables as
Johnson of California and Borah of Idaho could declare with equal certainty that Harding would keep us out of the League. Exactly what the
public was thinking on this issue when it went to the polls would be
hard to state, but the returns as to candidates were decisive. Harding's
popular majority was nearly seven millions, and in the electoral college

Election of 1920

Courtesy of the Dallas News

HARDING'S PLATFORM ON THE LEAGUE

he received 404 votes to Cox's 127. He was assured, also, of a Congress that would be overwhelmingly Republican in both houses.

Warren Gamaliel Harding (1865–1923) had obtained most of his education as editor of the Marion, Ohio, *Daily Star*. He had drifted easily from journalism to politics, and had always associated himself with the most conservative wing of his party. It was Harding who had made the nominating speech for Taft against Roosevelt in the convention of 1912. He was defeated for the governorship of Ohio in 1910, but in 1914 won both nomination and election to the United

States Senate, his first important office. He was a genial good fellow, well liked by his neighbors, and thoroughly imbued with the common man's vanities and prejudices. He knew that he was no intellectual giant, but prided himself on his ability to "get along with" people, and took comfort in the thought that as President he could command the judgment of the "best minds" in the party. His most devoted political friend was Harry M. Daugherty, another Ohio machine politician, whose knowledge of the seamy side of politics was unexcelled. Daugherty's greatest ambition was realized when, as Harding's campaign manager, he piloted his candidate to victory at the Chicago Convention.[1]

In his appointments Harding showed a curious inability to distinguish between good and bad. Such selections as Charles Evans Hughes to be Secretary of State and Herbert Hoover to be Secretary of Commerce were above reproach, but they were matched by the appointment of Albert B. Fall of New Mexico, a notorious anti-conservationist, as Secretary of the Interior, and Harry M. Daugherty, whose legal talents were mediocre or less, as Attorney-General. For Secretary of the Treasury Harding finally decided upon Andrew W. Mellon of Pittsburgh, one of the two or three richest men in the United States, an understandable, but not wholly defensible, choice. Outside the Cabinet the President's lack of discrimination persisted. He made ex-President Taft Chief Justice of the Supreme Court when opportunity offered, a graceful and deserved compliment, but he turned over the newly organized Veterans' Bureau to a rogue named Charles R. Forbes who eventually landed in a federal prison. In general, the new President regarded political offices as the lawful spoils of victory, and to members of the unsavory "Ohio gang" that followed him to Washington went many choice plums.

There is no evidence that Harding had any other connection with the scandals that disgraced his administration than his bad judgment of men. One precious set of scandals revolved around the name of Daugherty, whose position as chief law-enforcement officer of the United States opened up infinite possibilities. A friend of Daugherty's, Thomas W. Miller, became Alien Property Custodian, with wide powers in restoring or retaining the possessions of aliens seized by the United States during the war. Miller's judgments were for sale; ultimately he was dismissed from office, and jailed on conviction of having taken a bribe. Daugherty's closest friend, next to Harding, was Jess Smith, who in a single case took fifty thousand dollars to arrange a settlement before Miller. Smith committed suicide. Daugherty's association with such characters naturally made him sus-

The Harding scandals

---

[1] The most complete study of the nomination of Harding is in Mark Sullivan, *Our Times*, VI. *The Twenties* (1935).

pect, but when finally he was brought to trial for having conspired to "defraud the United States," he was saved from conviction by a hung jury. Another focus of scandal, as already noted, was the Veterans' Bureau. Forbes, its chief, was not of Daugherty's choosing, but only a chance acquaintance to whom Harding had taken a liking. Forbes was soon making deals with contractors in the building of hospitals and the purchase and sale of supplies that meant great personal gains for himself, but heavy losses for the government. His closest adviser, Charles F. Cramer, committed suicide; Forbes resigned, but was eventually convicted of defrauding the government, and landed in a federal prison.

Most amazing of all the Harding scandals was the one associated with the name of Secretary Fall. As Secretary of the Interior, Fall professed to believe that certain oil lands, held as naval reserves by the Navy Department, should be in his custody, and he was able to persuade the Secretary of the Navy to agree to the transfer. Thereupon Fall, in return for a personal "loan" of a hundred thousand dollars, turned over the right to exploit the Teapot Dome reserve in Wyoming to the Sinclair oil interests, and for probably a much larger sum, the Elkhorn Hills reserve in California to the Doheny oil interests. Fall was ultimately exposed by a senatorial investigating committee headed by Senator Thomas J. Walsh of Montana, and in 1929 he was convicted of having taken a bribe, and sent to jail for a year. But the two multimillionaires to whom he had sold out, Harry F. Sinclair and Edward L. Doheny, won acquittals in the criminal cases lodged against them. In civil suits, however, their leases were annulled, by the United States Supreme Court, on the ground of "fraud and conspiracy" in the case of the Doheny lease, and "collusion and conspiracy" in the case of the Sinclair lease.[1]

Harding never knew the full truth about the scandals that disgraced his administration, but he knew enough by 1923 to make him sick at heart, and his acute distress at the misconduct of his friends may have had something to do with his physical collapse **Death of Harding** and death at San Francisco, August 2, 1923, on his way back from a trip to Alaska.

While the back-stage intrigues of the Harding administration were working themselves out, the spotlight was firmly fixed upon a precipitate retreat from the ideal of world co-operation that Wilson had urged upon the nation as its guide of conduct in foreign affairs. Those deluded

[1] Satisfactory accounts of the Harding scandals are contained in Mark Sullivan's *Our Times*, VI, and in F. L. Allen, *Only Yesterday* (1931), "an informal history of the nineteen-twenties." On the oil scandal see, also, M. E. Ravage, *The Story of Teapot Dome* (1924).

voters who had supposed that the best way to get the United States
into the League of Nations was to restore Republican rule
Peace with Germany soon learned that they had been misled, for Harding chose
to interpret his election as a mandate against American
participation in the League on any conditions whatever. The Treaty of
Versailles, therefore, could not be ratified, even with the reservations
which had once made it acceptable to Harding, for it contained the
Covenant of the League. This being the case, Congress resolved on
July 2, 1921, that the war with Germany was at an end, and negotiations
were opened for a separate treaty. The resulting document, signed
August 25, 1921, did not scruple to obtain for the United States all of
the advantages of the Treaty of Versailles, but it left to the other nations that had fought against Germany the enforcement of the terms
agreed upon. The United States had completed a full cycle, according
to one observer, "from isolation to leadership, and back again."

As if to break a little the fall from Wilsonian idealism to complete
national selfishness, Harding was persuaded to call an International
Conference on the Limitation of Armaments, to meet in
The Washington Conference Washington, Armistice Day, November 11, 1921. Every
possible device was employed to build up the Conference
as the Republican counterpart of the Wilsonian program.
It was persistently spoken of as the "Peace Conference," although it was
nothing of the kind.[1] The real purposes of the Conference were (1)
to end the unhealthy and expensive naval rivalry between Great Britain,
the United States, and Japan that had resulted from the building programs undertaken during the war; (2) to induce Great Britain to give
up her very real alliance with Japan in return for the mere hope of continued American friendship; and (3) to negotiate a settlement of Far
Eastern affairs that would check the aggressions of Japan in China.

The central figure of the Washington Conference was Secretary
Hughes, who at once presented a program of naval reduction so drastic
as to startle the Conference. Exhibiting a knowledge of detail that was
in itself amazing, he advocated that the naval strength of the great
powers should be fixed at stipulated ratios, that naval tonnage in excess
of specified maxima should be scrapped, and that no new ships should
be constructed for a period of ten years. In the end five powers, the
United States, the British Empire, Japan, France, and Italy, agreed to
limit their strength in capital ships to total tonnages that bore to each
other roughly the ratios of 5:5:3:1.7:1.7, respectively. Consent could
not be obtained, however, to extend this agreement to lesser craft.

---

[1] The atmosphere of the Conference is well captured in Mark Sullivan, *The Great Adventure at Washington* (1922). Certain behind-the-scenes activities, not often written about,
appear in H. O. Yardley, *The American Black Chamber* (1931).

But the limitations adopted at least resulted in tremendous budgetary savings for the nations concerned. In 1927, at the suggestion of President Coolidge, a conference met at Geneva to discuss the limitation of auxiliary ships, but failed to reach an agreement. In 1930 at London, a conference called by President Hoover fared somewhat better. Some limitations were imposed on the building of lesser craft, Japan was appeased by a more generous quota, and the naval holiday was extended to 1936. But Japan served notice in 1934 that after 1936 she would no longer be bound by any limitations, and after that date the race for naval supremacy was vigorously renewed.[1] An unforeseen, and perhaps unforeseeable, result of the disarmament program was to leave Japan relatively stronger in the Far East, and the United States and Great Britain relatively weaker. The extraordinary significance of this development was not fully realized until after the Japanese attack on Pearl Harbor.

The Washington Conference resulted in the drafting of two other noteworthy treaties, one signed by four powers, and the other by nine. The Four-Power Pact, agreed to by the United States, the British Empire, France, and Japan, paved the way for the **The Four-Power Pact** abrogation of the Anglo-Japanese Alliance, which had become distasteful to both Great Britain and the United States. The new pact proposed to preserve the peace in the Pacific by pledging the contracting powers mutually to respect one another's rights "in relation to their insular possessions and insular dominions in the region," and to refer to a joint conference such disputes as might cause trouble. The four powers also bound themselves to "communicate with one another fully and frankly" on the action to be taken in case their rights were "threatened by the aggressive action of any other power." Had the pact ever been taken seriously, as it was not, it might have constituted almost as decisive a departure from the American doctrine of isolation as if the United States had entered the League of Nations. Closely connected with it was Article XIX of the Treaty on Naval Limitation which bound the United States, the British Empire, and Japan to maintain the *status quo* with respect to "fortifications and naval bases in the Pacific."

The Nine-Power Treaty related to "principles and policies to be followed in matters concerning China," and was signed by the United States, Belgium, the British Empire, China, France, Italy, Japan, the Netherlands, and Portugal. The situation in the **The Nine-Power Pact** Far East had changed materially as a result of the World

---

[1] Useful accounts of the Conference are given in R. L. Buell, *The Washington Conference* (1922), and Yamato Ichihashi, *The Washington Conference and After* (1928).

War. In 1915 Japan had in effect repudiated the doctrine of the open door by presenting to China twenty-one notorious demands for special privileges, many of which China was forced to concede. In 1917, by the Lansing-Ishii Agreement, Japan once more gave lip-service to the open door, but won from the United States recognition "that territorial propinquity creates special relations between countries." At the Paris Peace Conference, Japan insisted on being awarded the German concessions in Shantung, although the Japanese delegates promised Wilson that Japan would eventually withdraw from the peninsula, which, at least in a military sense, she did. Japan was also given a mandate over the German island of Yap in the northern Pacific. The purpose of the Nine-Power Pact was to reconcile this situation, as nearly as possible, with the open door for world trade in China and the integrity of the Chinese Republic. In words the new treaty seemed to administer a strong rebuff to Japanese policy, for it pledged the signatory powers to respect Chinese sovereignty, to aid China in maintaining an effective government, to use their influence in favor of "equal opportunity for the commerce and industry of all nations" in China, and to "refrain from taking advantage of conditions in China to seek special rights." But Japan was soon violating all these pledges with impunity, and the treaty provided no means whereby an offending power could be restrained. Minor agreements not written into the Nine-Power Treaty adjusted the Shantung controversy, settled the status of the island of Yap, provided for the study of extraterritoriality in China, and dealt with several other problems of Far Eastern relations.[1]

The Washington Conference was not the only Republican effort to promote world peace. The idea of a permanent court of international justice had been advocated by the American delegation to the Second Hague Conference in 1907, and was far more closely identified with Republican than with Democratic policy. When, therefore, under Article XIV of the League of Nations Covenant, plans were drawn in 1922 for such a court, there seemed no good reason why a Republican administration should not give the new institution its blessing. Indeed, Elihu Root, respected elder statesman of the Republican Party, had assisted in drafting the World Court protocol, and John Bassett Moore, America's foremost authority on international law, was slated for a place on its bench of eleven (later fifteen) judges. The only difficulty in the way of American participation seemed to lie in the fact that the judges were to be chosen by the

The World Court

[1] On the Far Eastern situation, consult Eleanor Tupper and G. E. McReynolds, *Japan in American Public Opinion* (1937); F. R. Dulles, *Forty Years of American-Japanese Relations* (1937); and D. F. Fleming, *The United States and World Organization, 1920–1933* (1938).

Council and Assembly of the League of Nations, but it was proposed that for this purpose only the United States might have a voice in the proceedings. Certain that public opinion was "overwhelmingly in favor of participation," President Harding urged American adherence to the Court, only to be rebuffed by the Senate, in which the irreconcilables were able to prevent any action whatever being taken. Extreme isolationists professed to fear that adherence to the Court would be only the entering wedge to further involvement in world affairs, and the still-embittered critics of "Wilsonism" would have nothing to do with anything even remotely connected with the League.[1]

The search for "normalcy" in international relations, which took the form of a retreat to isolationism, was paralleled by an equally earnest endeavor on the part of the political leaders of the nation to turn back the clock as far as possible in domestic affairs. "Normalcy"
Even before Harding took office, the unusual wartime powers of the President had been withdrawn, the great war boards through which the economic life of the nation had been mobilized for action had been virtually scrapped, and the army itself had been sent home. These were but symbols. Thereafter for many years, in all matters that concerned the relationship of government and business, the efforts of those in authority were directed toward a restoration of the old American system of private enterprise, with a minimum of governmental interference.

Unhappily the return of peace was soon followed by a sharp business decline. A bad break in the stock market during October, 1919, served warning of evil days to come, and by the summer of 1920 the evidence of economic distress was everywhere apparent. Business depression
Undoubtedly the most important cause of the decline which then set in was the failure of Europe to continue its generous purchases of American goods. This was due in part to the unexpectedly rapid recovery of European agriculture, but there were other factors also. For months after the signing of the armistice the government of the United States continued the policy of lending to its associates in the war, but by 1920, confessing its inability to "assume the burdens of all the earth," it was making no new loans. Foreign exchange, influenced by the enormous debts owing the United States, dropped precipitately; in February, 1920, the English pound was worth only about three dollars, the French and Belgian francs only seven or eight cents each, and the

---

[1] M. O. Hudson, *The Permanent Court of International Justice and the Question of American Participation* (1925). Harding was not the last American President to advocate the adherence of the United States to the World Court. Coolidge, Hoover, and Roosevelt all urged the Senate to ratify its protocol, but they all failed to get results. In spite of non-participation by the United States, an American judge has always sat on the court. Moore was succeeded by Charles Evans Hughes in 1928; Hughes, by Frank B. Kellogg in 1930; Kellogg, by Manley O. Hudson in 1936.

German mark only two or three cents. European purchasers found it practically impossible to pay the prices demanded for American goods, the more so because of the high American tariff, raised still higher in 1921, which interfered seriously with their desire to exchange what they could produce for what they needed to buy. The American public itself added to the general distress by indulging in a "buyers' strike" against the abnormally high retail prices that were being charged. Aimed mainly at luxuries, the "strike" fell with particular force upon silk, which within a seven-month period fell from $18.40 a pound to $5.81. The resulting prostration of the silk industry in Japan lessened, in turn, the ability of the Japanese to buy American cotton.

The years 1920 and 1921 saw a general slackening in nearly every field of business. Retailers and wholesalers who had bought at high prices found their shelves stocked with goods that no one wished to buy. Manufacturers who had made heavy purchases of high-priced raw materials were confronted by wholesale cancellations of orders. Railroad earnings went down, and banks were forced to contract their loans. Stocks and bonds slumped disastrously, and speculators were particularly hard hit. A total of 8881 business failures, with liabilities of $295,121,805, occurred in 1920, and 19,652, involving $755,777,685, in 1921. With nearly three and a half million men out of work the country faced for the first time in many years a serious problem of unemployment.

The suffering in agriculture was even more acute than in industry. The European market upon which American farm prosperity had come to depend seemed irretrievably lost. Not only did European producers raise a greater percentage of the farm products their countries needed: European purchasers turned also to other sources of supply. Meat from the Argentine, wheat from Canada, Australia, and Russia, cotton from Egypt and India tended increasingly to supplant imports from the United States.[1] Even the American market failed the farmers, for the changed food habits of the people called for far less wheat and meat per capita than had been consumed earlier in the century. And yet the American farmer, equipped now with gasoline-driven tractors, could and did harvest larger crops than ever before. During the three years that followed the disastrous break of 1920, production levels in nine basic field crops maintained or surpassed the levels of the preceding three years. Naturally, the bottom dropped completely out of farm prices. With wheat at the lowest figure in twenty-five years, cotton at five cents a pound, and other farm commodities correspondingly deflated, statisticians could demonstrate at

Depression in agriculture

[1] E. G. Nourse, *American Agriculture and the European Market* (1924).

will that the cost of production for most farmers far exceeded the proceeds from sales. The dizzy boom in real-estate values that had accompanied the war and the first months of peace collapsed with a frightening crash.

Low prices, unpaid mortgages, and constant foreclosures conspired inevitably to drive the farmers together. During and immediately after the war the National Non-Partisan League of North Dakota, an organization designed to bring the entire resources of the state to the aid of the farmer, scored remarkable, although only temporary, successes. More permanent were such farm orders as the American Farm Bureau Federation, the American Society of Equity, the Farmers' Union, and the old Grange, which in these troubled times took on new life. Largely as a result of their endeavors, a bi-partisan "Farm Bloc" was formed in both houses of Congress to work together as a unit for whatever measures might benefit the farmers, and against anything that might injure them.

It was against this economic background of hard times that the Harding-Coolidge administration took form. Nearly every item of legislation, nearly every administrative policy, was devised with this situation in mind. The depression had to be broken and prosperity restored. Whatever the causal relationships, there can be no doubt that, at least with the exception of agriculture, the depression did wear itself out in a minimum of time, and that good times did return. The Republicans, as the party in power, took full credit for what had happened, and the public came to regard the name of Harding's successor, Calvin Coolidge (1872–1933), as synonymous with prosperity. Nominating conventions often choose their presidential candidate to represent one wing of his party, and the Vice-President another; this, indeed, was the intention of the manipulators who awarded the Republican nomination in 1920 to Harding. But the convention got out of hand and did as it pleased, with the result that the economic prejudices of the candidate for Vice-President corresponded precisely with those of the candidate for President. Throughout a long career of office-holding, Coolidge had done little to excite either opposition or approval. A Vermonter by birth, he attended Amherst College, studied law, and began to practice in 1897 at Northampton, Massachusetts. Always a dependable regular, he climbed aboard the political escalator in 1899 when he became a councilman; by 1901 he was city solicitor; by 1904 clerk of courts; by 1907 a member of the legislature; by 1910 mayor of Northampton; by 1912 a member of the state senate; by 1916 lieutenant-governor; and by 1919 governor. In these offices, and as President, Coolidge was conscientious in the discharge of his

Coolidge prosperity

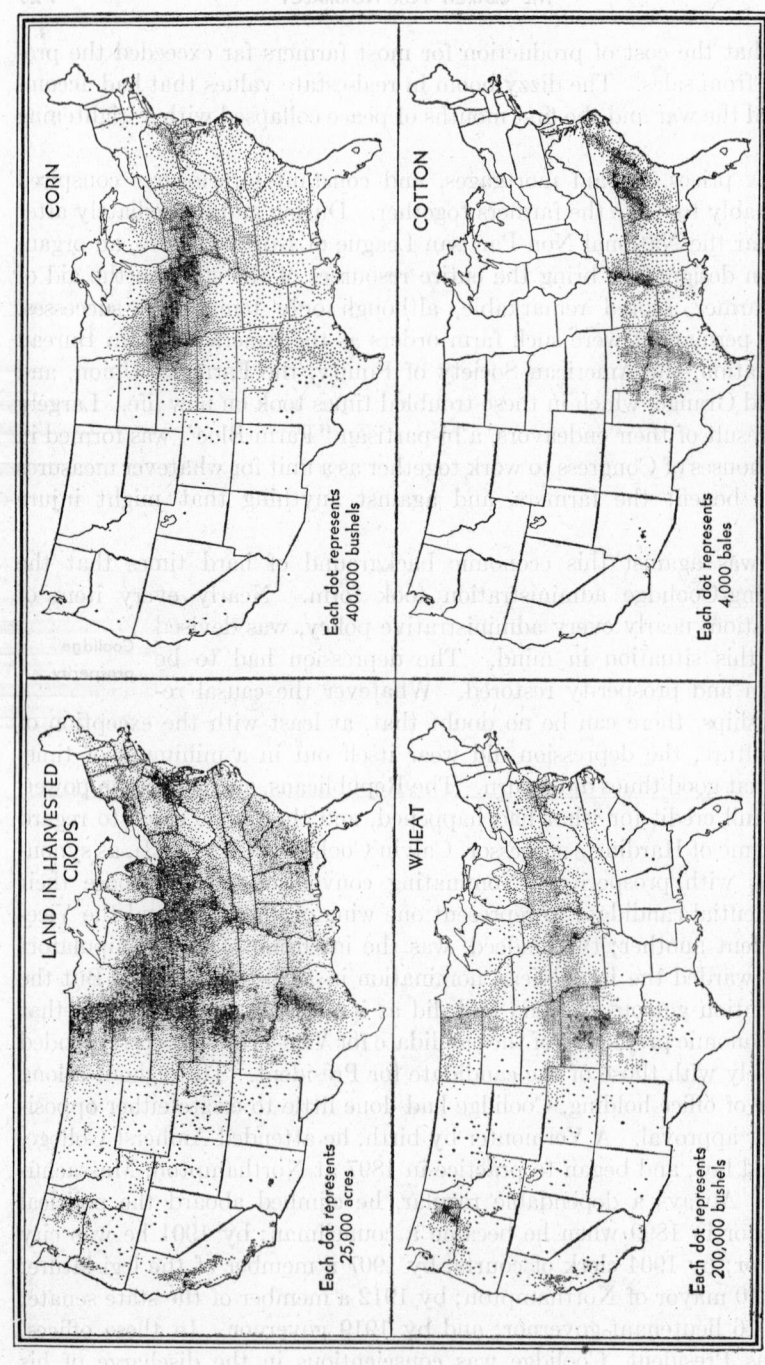

AGRICULTURAL PRODUCTION IN THE UNITED STATES, 1919

duties, abstemious of spoken words, utterly uninterested in trouble-making reforms. He accepted the Harding cabinet, including for a time even Daugherty (Fall had already resigned), made changes reluctantly and only under heavy pressure, and carried forward the work of the Harding administration without any perceptible change in direction.

The Harding-Coolidge formula for business recovery was never precisely stated in a political document, but it soon became fully apparent. First of all came economy in federal expenditures, a policy that under Harding was tolerated as a political necessity, but under Coolidge accurately reflected the presidential state of mind. In accordance with the terms of a Budget Act, passed in June, 1921, the President appointed a Director of the Budget, whose business it was to scrutinize all requests for congressional appropriations, to eliminate duplications, and to pare down excesses. Estimates so obtained were then submitted to Congress, where in each house a single Committee on Appropriations determined the final recommendations. Budget directors took their duties seriously, and the normal peace-time disbursements of the national government, if not actually reduced, were given little opportunity to expand. Considerable saving was accomplished by cutting down on the naval and military appropriations, but all such gains were seriously discounted by mounting bills for pensions and veterans' relief. Nevertheless, whereas expenditures due to war had absorbed ninety-four per cent of the national budget in 1920, they accounted for only eighty-six per cent in 1924. It is worth noting in this connection that throughout the early twenties state and local expenditures mounted even more rapidly than federal spending declined. It is difficult to believe, therefore, that there was the direct relationship between "Coolidge economy" and the return of prosperity that Republican politicians were wont to claim.

The recovery program — economy

As a matter of fact, after 1925 even federal expenditures began to mount. One reason for this was the passage in 1924, over President Coolidge's veto, of a Veterans' Bonus Bill, which granted "adjusted compensation" to veterans of the war. Such a measure had passed Congress two years earlier, but President Harding's veto had been sustained. Now, with the American Legion earnestly supporting the measure, it was voted to grant each veteran paid-up insurance to fall due twenty years later. The amount owing each soldier was computed on the basis of a dollar and a quarter for each day overseas, and a dollar for each day in service at home. While the grant was not made in cash, each veteran was permitted to borrow up to 22.5 per cent of the face value of his policy, and the ava-

The veterans' bonus

lanche of borrowings that set in materially increased the expenditures of the government.[1]

A second item in the recovery program was the reduction of taxes, particularly those that "penalized success" by robbing business of its "legitimate profits." Not content with the repeal of the excess-profits tax and the surtax reductions that Congress included in the Revenue Law of 1921, Secretary Mellon pressed insistently for further reductions:

Reduction of taxes

> High rates [he maintained] tend to destroy individual initiative and seriously impede the development of productive business. Taxpayers subject to the higher rates cannot afford for example to invest in American railroads or industries or embark on new enterprises in the face of taxes taking away 50 per cent or more of any return that may be realized. These taxpayers are withdrawing their capital from productive business and investing it instead in tax exempt securities and adopting other lawful methods of avoiding the realization of taxable income. The result is to stop business transactions that would normally go through and to discourage men of wealth from taking the risks incidental to developing and opening new businesses. Ways will always be found to avoid taxes so destructive in their nature and the only way to save the situation is to put taxes on a reasonable basis.

Mellon was unable to persuade Congress to reduce the maximum surtax as rapidly as he had hoped, but in the Revenue Act of 1924 the rate was brought down from fifty to forty per cent, and two years later to twenty per cent. Other reductions did away with most of the wartime excise taxes, radically reduced the normal income tax rates, modified the estate tax, and abolished the gift tax. In 1921 a man with a million-dollar income paid a federal tax of $663,000; by 1926, with the Mellon reductions in force, he paid less than $200,000. Unhappily a considerable proportion of the funds thus released for private use seems to have gone into highly speculative investments. Had the tax rates been permitted to remain at the wartime levels, it is reasonable to suppose that the liquidation of the national debt might have proceeded even more rapidly than it did, and that the speculative craze of the later twenties might have been avoided. As it was, Mellon was able to lower the obligations of the United States during the decade of the twenties from about twenty-four billion to about sixteen billion dollars.[2]

A third item in the Republican recovery program was the systematic

---

[1] Early in 1931, Congress voted over President Hoover's veto to permit veterans to borrow from the government as much as fifty per cent of the face value of their bonus certificates; and in 1936, over President Roosevelt's veto, it permitted them to collect the full face value, or as much of it as had not been previously obtained.

[2] Mellon's policies are critically examined in Harvey O'Connor, *Mellon's Millions* (1933), the extremely unfriendly "biography of a fortune."

elimination of the government from competition with private business.
The Transportation Act of 1920, although passed before
Wilson left office, was essentially a Republican measure, and **Government**
in full accord with the policies adopted during the Harding- **withdrawal**
Coolidge régime. Under its terms the railroads of the country **from business**
were handed back to their owners, with generous indemnification for such
damages as they had suffered during the period of governmental operation. The Jones Merchant Marine Act of 1920 dealt in similar spirit
with the shipping that the government had built or acquired for special
wartime service. A Merchant Fleet Corporation was created with
authority to operate the ships as long as necessary, to lay out new lanes
for American overseas commerce, and to turn over the ships and the
routes at minimum cost to private companies as fast as American purchasers could be found. The intent, never fully realized in fact, was to
get the government out of the shipping business. Possibly the most
striking case in point was the refusal of the administration to countenance
any plan for the effective governmental operation of the Muscle Shoals
power development in Alabama, begun during the World War to aid in
the production of nitrates. In a single stretch of thirty-seven miles the
Tennessee River falls one hundred and thirty-four feet. To make use
of this power the government planned a series of dams and two nitrate
plants. One of the nitrate plants was in operation by 1918, but the
great Wilson Dam was not completed until 1925, when the wartime
need for nitrates had long passed. To Senator Norris of Nebraska and
others who were undismayed by the prospect of a government-owned
business, the Muscle Shoals development seemed to offer an ideal opportunity for the production of cheap power, but Congress was persuaded
to offer the whole property for sale. The only bidder was Henry Ford,
whose terms involved so heavy a loss to the government that they could
not be accepted. A small trickle of power was leased to the Alabama
Power Company for distribution in the surrounding territory, but for the
most part the potentialities of this development remained unexploited
until the time of the New Deal.

The distaste of the administration for governmental interference in
business went far beyond these efforts to avoid competition with private
enterprise, and called also for a drastic reduction in the
amount of federal regulation. Legislation to accomplish **Restraints**
this end would have been difficult to obtain, but the same **on regulation**
purpose was achieved by indirect means. One by one the great regulatory bodies created by preceding administrations were packed with the
friends of the very businesses they were supposed to regulate. The
Interstate Commerce Commission was in effect handed over to the rail-

roads, the Federal Trade Commission to the trusts, and the Federal Reserve Board to the bankers. For good measure the Tariff Commission was delivered into the custody of the protectionists. In criticism of a series of such Coolidge appointments, Senator Norris had this to say:

> The effect of these appointments is to set the country back more than twenty-five years. It is an indirect but positive repeal of Congressional enactments, which no Administration, however powerful, would dare to bring about by any direct means. It is the nullification of federal law by a process of boring from within. If trusts, combinations, and big business are to run the government, why not permit them to do it directly rather than through this expensive machinery which was originally honestly established for the protection of the people of the country against monopoly and control?

Not content merely with removing in so far as possible all discouraging checks to private enterprise, the administration in a great variety of ways gave business direct and substantial aid. The most

Aids to business

traditional means of accomplishing this end was by protective tariffs, and these Congress promptly supplied through two measures, the Emergency Tariff Act of 1921, and the Fordney-McCumber Act of 1922. The new laws raised tariff rates to the highest levels yet known, and insured American producers as completely as might be against the threat of foreign competition. But government assistance to business went much further than the tariff. For the shipping industry and the new aircraft corporations the government provided generous subsidies. For individuals and companies with a taste for foreign investment, the State Department promised to lend a hand by denouncing bad foreign securities, and whether because of this, or in spite of it, American capital sped abroad in a seemingly endless stream. For the better promotion of foreign trade the Department of Commerce extensively and expensively reorganized its foreign service. For the benefit of domestic producers the Bureau of Standards offered elaborate facilities for testing, and recommended standard types in all sorts of manufactured articles from building-bricks to automobile tires. Secretary Hoover, as head of a commission to study waste in industry, brought in numerous suggestions bearing upon business efficiency. His work as head of the Department of Commerce was generally credited with having "elevated a relatively unimportant cabinet position to one of major rank." The *Detroit News* enthusiastically credited his activities with having ended the "threat to our prosperity."

The return of the Republicans to power was accompanied, also, by a drastic change in the attitude of the national government toward labor. Organized labor had been greatly strengthened by the war, which raised wages to unprecedented heights, steadied employment, and added to the unions many new, if somewhat undisciplined, members. The restraints imposed upon labor by the patriotic desire of all classes to win the war were removed by the return of peace, and the mounting cost of living gave rise to the charge that wages, high as they were, had not risen correspondingly. Furthermore, the long period of prosperity had unfitted labor psychologically to accept such readjustments as the restoration of peacetime conditions made inevitable. During the year 1919 strike after strike broke out, among the most notable being a general strike in Seattle that was calmed down only by the intervention of outside labor leaders, a strike in the steel industry that lasted for months before its failure was admitted, and a series of strikes among the coal miners and the textile workers.[1]

The disciplining of labor

The presence of many radicals among the strike leaders did much to give labor a black eye with the public, and to pave the way for an hysterical outburst against the "reds." The Department of Justice, both under Wilson's Attorney-General, A. Mitchell Palmer, and under Daugherty, waged vigorous war against the radicals, and sent many of them back to the lands from which they had come, or to jail.[2] Moreover, the federal courts, whose decisions on the legality of many labor policies remained of fundamental importance, showed a markedly conservative trend. To Harding in his brief term of office fell the selection of four members of the United States Supreme Court, and the men he chose, Taft, Sutherland, Butler, and Sanford, were all traditionalists of the old school. Less apparent, but hardly less important, was the careful attention given by Daugherty as Attorney-General to the records of all proposed appointees to the lower courts and to subordinate positions in the Department of Justice. Before he left office in 1924 he was thus able to make an indelible imprint upon the administration of justice in the United States. Characteristic of the stiffening attitude of the courts toward labor was the sweeping injunction he obtained when a strike of the railroad shopmen seriously disrupted interstate commerce. From Federal Judge J. H. Wilkerson of Chicago, a Harding appointee, Daugherty obtained a temporary injunction that forbade every conceivable type of strike activity. "Not merely violence but picketing of all sorts, strike meetings, statements to the public, the use of union funds to carry on the strike, and the use of any means of communication by the leaders to direct it," all fell under the ban of the court. The fact that

[1] V. W. Lanfear, *Business Fluctuations and the American Labor Movement, 1915–1922* (1924); Selig Perlman and Philip Taft, *History of Labor in the United States, 1896–1932* (Commons, *History of Labor in the United States*, IV, *Labor Movements*); Interchurch World Movement, *Report on the Steel Strike of 1919* (1920).

[2] Jane P. Clark, *Deportation of Aliens from the United States to Europe* (1931).

this injunction was sustained on appeal demonstrated the hollowness of the hope that the Clayton Anti-Trust Act had furnished an enduring "Magna Charta for Labor." [1]

With respect to agriculture, the Harding-Coolidge formula seemed to be to yield as little as possible to the agitators, mainly from the Middle West, who demanded farm relief. The Farm Bloc had little difficulty in obtaining as a part of the Emergency Tariff Act of 1921 increased duties on wheat to protect northwestern farmers against importation from Canada, and additional protection for such farm products as meat, wool, and sugar. But these duties, as every reputable economist knew, could not seriously affect the prices of commodities of which the United States had an "exportable surplus." The Farm Bloc was instrumental also in the passage of the Intermediate Credits Act of 1923, which created a system of banks designed to provide farmers with credits for periods not less than six months in length, nor more than three years. But remedies more radical than tariff protection and easier credits were consistently opposed. The McNary-Haugen Bill, an ingenious measure designed to raise the domestic price of certain farm crops by creating a governmental agency which could buy up and "dump" the surplus on foreign markets, was before Congress for several years beginning in 1924. Twice, in 1924 and in 1926, the bill was voted down, but in 1927 it passed both House and Senate, only to be vetoed by President Coolidge as "economically unsound." Another scheme for agricultural relief, the export debenture plan, proposed to place export bounties on specified agricultural commodities, the same to be paid by the United States in the form of debentures receivable for customs. On the presumption that these debentures would be purchased at a discount by importers, proponents of the plan argued that the bounty to the farmers would come directly out of the protective tariff. But this attempt, aimed no less than the McNary-Haugen Bill "to get the farmer up on stilts" along with the tariff-protected manufacturer, failed even to pass Congress. With little assistance from the government, agricultural organizations did what they could to restore prosperity to the farms by promoting co-operative marketing, but in spite of their best efforts the depression in agriculture continued.

Not exactly a part of the recovery program, but by no means unrelated to it, was the reversal of one of America's oldest and most cherished traditions — a hearty welcome to immigrants. Premonitions of the coming change were apparent in May, 1917, when Congress passed

Farm relief

---

[1] Felix Frankfurter and Nathan Greene, _The Labor Injunction_ (1930), is the leading authority on this subject, but see also E. E. Witte, _The Government in Labor Disputes_ (1932), and A. T. Mason, _Organized Labor and the Law_ (1925).

over Wilson's veto the same provision for a literacy test that he had defeated two years before. But the cessation of hostilities soon proved conclusively that something more drastic than a literacy test would be necessary if the distressed multitudes of Europe were to be prevented from seeking refuge in America. In the year ending June 30, 1921, over eight hundred thousand immigrants came to the United States, and in spite of the attempted restriction nearly two-thirds of them came from the countries of southern and eastern Europe. Confronted by this situation, Congress in 1921 passed an Emergency Immigration Act that assigned to each nation an immigrant quota consisting of not more than three per cent of the number of its nationals resident in the United States according to the census of 1910. Immigrants from other American nations were exempted from the quota system, but in 1922 an amendment required that all aliens resident in an American country must have lived there not less than five years before being freed from the quota restrictions.

Restrictions on immigration

The law of 1921 was meant merely as a temporary stopgap while the details of the new immigration policy were being worked out, and in 1924 Congress passed another immigration act. This time the quota was set at two per cent of the nationals resident in the United States in 1890, thereby reducing still further the numbers eligible for admission, particularly from southern and eastern Europe. The law also provided that after July 1, 1927, the number of quota immigrants was to be limited to one hundred and fifty thousand, while quotas were to be based upon "national origins," the same to be determined from a study of the census of 1920. The difficulty in determining the national origins of the American people completely baffled the committee of cabinet members (the Secretaries of State, Commerce, and Labor) charged with that duty, and not until 1929 were its half-hearted recommendations put into effect. Whatever their imperfections, the new quotas insured that an overwhelming proportion of the thin trickle of immigrants permitted to enter the United States originated in those countries that had first contributed to its settlement. Great Britain and northern Ireland, for example, were permitted to send 65,721 immigrants annually, while the Italian quota was only 5802. The special favors shown to citizens of other American nations led at first to a heavy immigration from Mexico, but immigration officials soon put a stop to this by refusing entrance to Mexican laborers on the ground that they were likely to become public charges. The census of 1930 revealed that the proportion of foreigners resident in the United States had indeed ceased to increase.[1]

---

[1] R. L. Garis, *Immigration Restriction* (1927); Manuel Gamio, *Mexican Immigration to the United States* (1930).

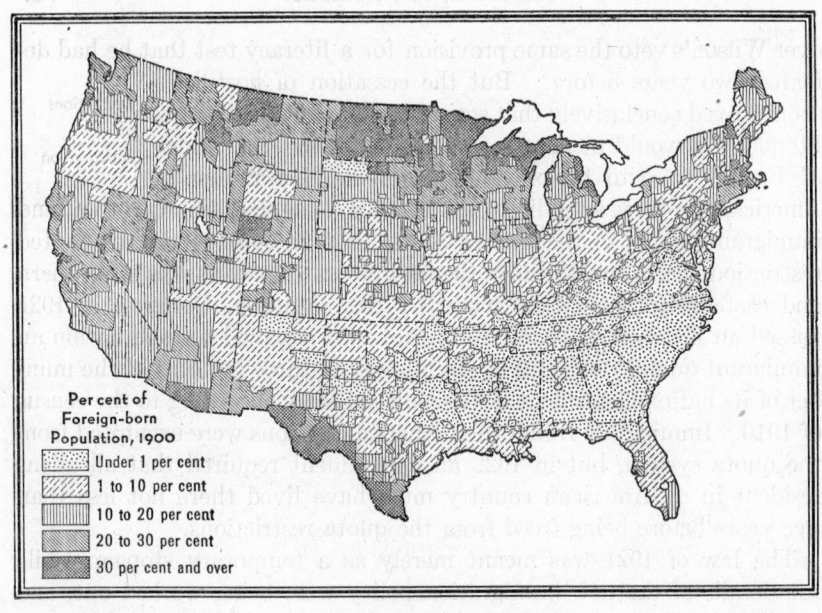

Per cent of
Foreign-born
Population, 1900

Under 1 per cent
1 to 10 per cent
10 to 20 per cent
20 to 30 per cent
30 per cent and over

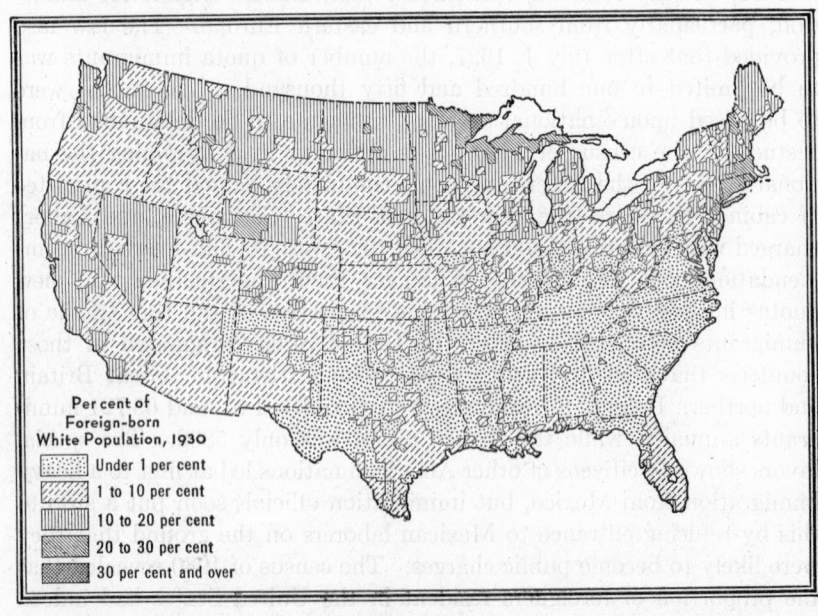

Per cent of
Foreign-born
White Population, 1930

Under 1 per cent
1 to 10 per cent
10 to 20 per cent
20 to 30 per cent
30 per cent and over

FOREIGN-BORN POPULATION IN THE UNITED STATES,
1900–1930

Whether because of the administration's policies, as their defenders claimed, or in spite of them, as a few critics contended, the recovery of business from the depression that had gripped the country when Harding was inaugurated was phenomenal. By the time Coolidge became President the tide had turned, and *Business recovery* when the campaign of 1924 had to be faced the Republicans could count on prosperity as their best talking point. Steady gains were reported in iron and steel, in the automobile industry, in the building trades, and among wholesalers and retailers. Dividends that had vanished during the depression were resumed by a large number of corporations in 1923 and 1924, while occasional stock dividends demonstrated still more conclusively that times had changed. Even the railroads began to increase their earnings, and all signs pointed to brightening economic skies.

Of fundamental consequence in the new business vitality was the rapid rise of the automobile industry, which was still in its infancy before the war, but during the twenties multiplied its output again and again. Between 1920 and 1925 the annual production of *The automobile industry* motor vehicles in the United States doubled, while the number of automobiles in actual use almost quadrupled. The growth of the automobile industry meant a corresponding prosperity for the manufacturers upon whom it depended for iron and steel, for fabrics, plate-glass, and tires; it brought into existence an unending number of new establishments for "sales and service"; it was the making of the oil industry, from oil well to filling station; it provided the wages and profits to promote a building boom that extended all the way from the humble dwelling-houses of the workers to the magnificent skyscrapers where the industrial leaders had their offices. The success of the automobile industry was made possible largely by the mass-production methods popularized by Henry Ford, and generally adopted. Ingenious machines fashioned standard parts and assembled them into cars with a maximum of speed and a minimum of human labor. The completed product was then offered to the public at a low price, on easy installments, with profits for manufacturer and dealer dependent primarily upon a large volume of business. Even the foreign market could sometimes be tapped, for the efficiency of mass production in American factories offset the lower wages paid abroad.

But automobiles were not the only products of the factory to be manufactured and sold in the Ford way. Phonographs and radios, household and office equipment, furnaces and plumbing, electrical supplies, and a thousand miscellaneous items were similarly *Installment buying* made available for the multitudes. American purchasers found themselves able to buy for a small payment down and for many

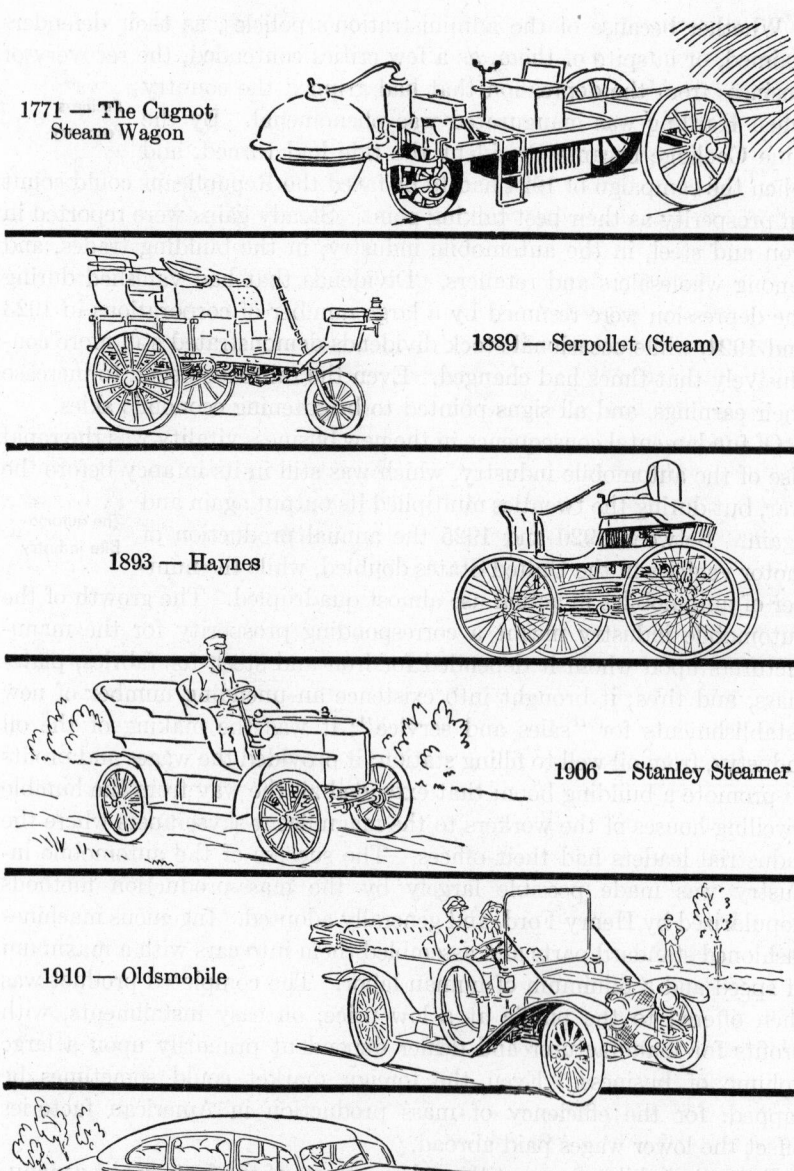

1771 — The Cugnot
Steam Wagon

1889 — Serpollet (Steam)

1893 — Haynes

1906 — Stanley Steamer

1910 — Oldsmobile

Modern Super-
Six Sedan

EVOLUTION OF THE AUTOMOBILE

similar payments in the months or years to come a host of luxuries that in an earlier age the ordinary citizen could never have hoped to own. Money was even left over for amusements, and "motion-picture palaces" provided low-priced theatricals not for just a few Americans but for all of them. Naturally this more abundant life came to be closely associated with Republican policies, for the Republicans were in power when it arrived, and they cheerfully admitted their responsibility for bringing it to pass.

With the all-powerful issue of prosperity working for them, the Republicans entered the campaign of 1924 with full confidence as to the outcome. Their nomination for President went naturally to Coolidge, whom the public had come to regard as a kind   Election of 1924 of personification of prosperity. For Vice-President the Republicans chose Charles G. Dawes, Harding's first Director of the Budget. The Democrats, seemingly determined to make certain of defeat, staged a long-drawn-out contest in their convention between William G. McAdoo, Wilson's Secretary of the Treasury and Railroad Administrator, and Alfred E. Smith, the idol of the New York City Democracy. The Ku Klux Klan, a nativist organization reminiscent of Know-Nothing days, had infected much of the South and West with its anti-Catholic, anti-immigrant, anti-Jewish, and anti-Negro prejudice, and because Smith was a loyal adherent of the Roman Catholic faith, Klan-conscious delegates refused to support him. Neither Smith nor McAdoo could win the necessary two-thirds majority then required for a Democratic nomination, and after more than one hundred ballots the convention turned to John W. Davis of West Virginia and New York, a brilliant but conservative lawyer whose connection with the firm of J. P. Morgan and Company completely disqualified him in the eyes of labor and the western liberals. To offset this blunder the convention made another. For Vice-President it chose Governor Charles W. Bryan of Nebraska, brother of William Jennings Bryan, a man who had nothing but his name to recommend him for the post, but whose name alone was sufficient to alienate the eastern conservatives. With such a ticket, nominated after such a fight, the Democrats had no slightest chance of winning the election. A Progressive ticket, supported by the discontented elements in organized labor, by discouraged farmers of the Middle West, and by most of the Socialists, was headed by Robert M. La Follette of Wisconsin, a "left-wing" Republican, with Burton K. Wheeler of Montana, a "left-wing" Democrat, for Vice-President.

The election was a Coolidge landslide. In the popular vote the Republican ticket won a plurality of more than seven million, and a majority of about two and a half million. The electoral college gave Coolidge

382 votes, Davis 136, and La Follette 13. All of the Davis vote came from the South and La Follette carried only his own state,

The Coolidge landslide Wisconsin. Congress was again safely Republican in both houses. A warning, however, that all was not as well as it seemed was contained in the fact that nearly five million voters had cast their ballots for La Follette.

In spite of the continuing devotion of most Americans to the doctrine of isolation, evidence that the United States must play a leading rôle in international affairs accumulated rapidly during the later

America and the world twenties. As a result of the war, the American nation had enormously expanded its industrial plant; it had discovered unsuspected possibilities by way of agricultural production; it had accumulated out of its profits huge sums for new investment. Moreover, if the high speed to which its economic machine had been geared were to be maintained, the country must import many materials which it could not produce, such as rubber, silk, nickel, and tin, and many others which it could produce only in limited quantities, such as sugar, wool, hides, and nitrates. What the United States really needed was a peaceful and friendly world generally committed to the open door. That American statesmen of the twenties failed to achieve this goal should have occasioned no surprise. They were faced at home by a determined devotion to political isolation and a deep-seated belief in the protective tariff system; they were faced abroad by the jealousies and hatreds engendered by the war and the peace, feelings compounded so far as they concerned the United States by the conviction that the American people had escaped most of the war's ravages, but had taken most of its profits.

Among the most perplexing of the problems before the American government during this period was the collection of the loans by which the United States had so largely financed the Allied cause after 1917, and the work of reconstruction after the war was over. To the American people these intergovernmental loans seemed no different from the loans of one individual to another, and their repayment was regarded as a matter of simple honesty. Europeans took a somewhat different view of the situation. The war, they argued, was a common endeavor, in which each nation had given all that it had to give. The United States had entered the conflict late, and its casualty list was short; why should it begrudge the dollars it had spent? Why should it not forgive its debtors, especially since American prosperity so far outstripped anything European nations could boast? Moreover, most of the money lent had been expended in the United States, and goods rather than gold had been sent abroad. Was it fair to ask European nations to pay back gold that they had never seen; indeed, half the world's supply of gold was already in the United States. Nor could European nations hope to build up large balances in America by the shipment of goods; the high American tariff forestalled that. To the war-heated imaginations of European critics "Uncle Sam" became "Uncle Shylock," and hostile feeling ran high.

Nevertheless, in 1922 Congress created a World War Foreign Debt Commission which opened negotiations with the various Allied nations, and ultimately succeeded in reaching refunding agreements with fifteen of them.[1] American policy called for settlements in accordance with ability to pay; hence the interest charges ranged from as low as four-tenths of one per cent in the case of Italy to the normal three and three-tenths per cent required of Great Britain and the more solvent states. The British settlement was effected as early as June, 1923, and the others during the next few years. Opposition to repayment reached its maximum in France, where the costly work of reparation threatened to bankrupt the government, but an agreement was signed in April, 1926, which set the interest rate at one and six-tenths per cent, and allowed a period of sixty-two years for payment. The grand total of all the funded debts was fixed at more than eleven and one-half billion dollars, with three-fourths of the amount owing by Great Britain (4.6 billions), France (4.02 billions), and Italy (2.04 billions). Repayments by December 31, 1930, amounted to about two and one-half billion dollars, of which more than seventy per cent came from Great Britain. Next year, following the Hoover moratorium, a few nations met their obligations, but thereafter payments from all nations except Finland virtually ceased.

Russia alone among the European nations that had borrowed from the United States refused to consider the funding of her debt. The Soviets, in keeping with their views on capitalism, repudiated all financial obligations incurred by preceding Russian governments, and denied the claims for indemnification lodged by foreigners whose property had been confiscated or destroyed during the revolutions of 1917. On this account, and also because of the persistent Communist propaganda carried on by Russian agents in the United States, the American government long refused to accord recognition to the Soviet government, although no attempt was made to prevent American firms from trading with Russia at their own risk.

Inevitably the problem of war debts became closely intertwined with the problem of German reparations. If Germany could meet her obli-

[1] A brief statement of the war debts problem is available in B. H. Williams, *Economic Foreign Policy of the United States* (1929). For fuller accounts consult National Industrial Conference Board, *The Inter-Ally Debts and the United States* (1925); H. G. Moulton and Leo Pasvolsky, *World War Debt Settlement* (1926); and *War Debts and World Prosperity* (1932).

gations to the Allies, then the Allies could make their payments to the
United States. Any connection between these two problems
Reparations was vigorously denied by the American government, but
its existence in fact if not in theory was abundantly clear. The difficulties experienced by Germany in paying the extortionate sums required
by the Reparations Commission in 1921 led to two efforts at readjustment, one in 1924, and another in 1929. It was significant that in each
case the commission of experts entrusted with the negotiations was
headed by an American, in the first instance by Charles G. Dawes, and
in the second by Owen D. Young. The Dawes Plan reduced the sums
required from Germany each year, arranged for a foreign loan to support the German monetary system, and required French withdrawal
from the Ruhr Valley, a district into which France had sent her troops
in 1922 because of German failure to meet reparations payments.
For four years, in large part by borrowing in the United States, Germany
was able to meet the new payments, but by 1928 she was again in
trouble. The Young Plan proposed another set of annuities to run for a
period of fifty-nine years, the capitalized value of which would amount
to only about ten billion dollars, approximately the sum due from the
Allies to the United States. Further, it stipulated that additional reductions might be made proportional to any readjustments in the inter-
Allied war debts; in other words, if the United States would reduce its
demands, the Allies would also reduce theirs. But the Young Plan, too,
overtaxed the resources of Germany, and after 1931 all reparation payments were discontinued. Altogether Germany had paid the Allies about
four and one-half billion dollars, more than half of which had been
borrowed from American investors.[1]

The search for a means to insure world peace went on insistently
throughout the period of Coolidge prosperity. Unfortunately the organizations most actively concerned with the problems were
The quest for in complete disagreement as to the best means to promote
peace the cause they held so dear. Peace-lovers of the Wilson
school kept up the fight for American entrance into the League as the
surest way to prevent the outbreak of war. They rejoiced when representatives of the United States, at first unofficially, but later on terms
of entire equality, sat in on the non-political discussions of League committees, such, for example, as the conference on the opium traffic. Ultimately, they asserted, the United States could no longer ignore the
obligations of membership. Others who still saw in the League nothing
more than a convenient instrument for enforcement of an unjust peace
urged that the United States should give its full support to the World

[1] Karl Bergmann, *History of Reparations* (1927).

Court. Still others, perhaps with greater faith than wisdom, believed that the peace could best be maintained by a simple declaration on the part of every nation that it would not resort to war. Chief leader of the third group, whose panacea was labeled the "outlawry of war," was Senator William E. Borah of Idaho. Most American politicians, including the President, were inclined to regard the "outlawry" scheme as impractical, and possibly contrary to the Constitution of the United States, which specifically gave Congress the right to declare war, but a pact signed by seven European nations at Locarno in 1925 seemed to indicate a certain willingness on their part to flirt with the idea. By that document Germany, Belgium, France, Great Britain, and Italy undertook mutually to guarantee the peace of western Europe, and Germany agreed to arbitrate her disputes with France, Belgium, Poland, and Czechoslovakia. Further, the signatory powers agreed not to attack each other, not to invade each other's territory, and not to resort to war against each other, except for purposes of defense or in response to their obligations under the League of Nations, to which, it was decided, Germany must be admitted.

Hailed as at least a partial renunciation of the "right to make war," the Pact of Locarno stimulated the "outlawry" advocates in the United States to renewed endeavors. The United States, they pointed out, stood now almost alone in its resistance to every plan for world peace. They were soon aided by Aristide Briand, Premier of France, who on April 6, 1927 — tenth anniversary of the entrance of the United States into the World War — urged a treaty between France and the United States similar to those agreed upon by the European nations at Locarno. What Briand really had in mind was to replace the Root Arbitration Treaty of 1908, which was due to expire in 1928, with a stronger one, but "outlawry" enthusiasts were quick to seize the opportunity he had given them. They persuaded the Secretary of State, Frank B. Kellogg of Minnesota, who had succeeded Hughes in 1925, to expand the scope of the negotiations. Replying to Briand, Kellogg said:

> It has occurred to me that the two governments, instead of contenting themselves with a bilateral declaration of the nature suggested by M. Briand, might make a more signal contribution to world peace by joining in an effort to obtain the adherence of all the principal Powers of the world to a declaration renouncing war as an instrument of national policy.

Kellogg's proposal resulted in prolonged negotiations which led finally to the signing at Paris, on August 27, 1928, of a general treaty along the lines he had proposed.[1] The representatives of fifteen nations, including Japan, Italy, and Germany,

The Kellogg-Briand Pact

[1] D. H. Miller, *The Peace Pact of Paris* (1928); J. T. Shotwell, *War as an Instrument of National Policy* (1929); David Bryn-Jones, *Frank B. Kellogg* (1937).

affixed their signatures to a document which contained the following clauses:

I. The High Contracting Parties solemnly declare in the names of their respective peoples that they condemn recourse to war for the solution of international controversies, and renounce it as an instrument of national policy in their relations with one another.

II. The High Contracting Parties agree that the settlement or solution of all disputes or conflicts of whatever nature or of whatever origin they may be, which may arise among them, shall never be sought except by pacific means.

Ultimately sixty-two nations gave their adherence to the Kellogg Pact; but the futility of all such declarations, unless buttressed by a firm desire to live up to them, was soon demonstrated by the attacks of Japan on China, Italy on Ethiopia, and Germany on Poland, Denmark, Norway, the Netherlands, Belgium, and Luxemburg. The pact may, indeed, have lulled into a sense of security nations that might otherwise have been better prepared for the assaults of their predatory neighbors. Nevertheless, European statesmen saw significance in the willingness of the United States to co-operate at last, however faintly, in the effort to maintain world peace, but the customary Senate reservations revealed the microscopic nature of the involvement. Although the Senate ratified the treaty with only one dissenting vote, it insisted that there could be no curtailment of America's right of self-defense, that no obligations had been assumed which were incompatible with the Monroe Doctrine, and that the United States was not bound to take action against states that broke the treaty. Kellogg did the best he could to make the pact to which he had given his name a success. He negotiated supplementary treaties of arbitration with such nations as would consent to them, and took particular pains to make arbitration compulsory between the United States and other American nations. But he must have known that without force behind it, the pact to which he had given his name would be a mere gesture of futility.

The election of 1928 gave the Republicans another vote of confidence. There was much talk of another nomination for Coolidge, but the **Election of 1928** President announced in 1927 that he did not "choose to run." As a result, the Republican choice fell upon Herbert Hoover, Coolidge's Secretary of Commerce, whose name was almost as closely connected with the current wave of prosperity as that of the President himself. The nomination of Hoover was far from satisfactory to the still unprosperous farmers of the Middle West, and to appease them Senator Charles Curtis of Kansas was named for Vice-President. The Democrats, with obvious reluctance, yielded to the pressure of the powerful Democratic city machines, and nominated Alfred E. Smith, with what comfort could be found for the rural South and West in the nomination of Senator Joseph T. Robinson of Arkansas for Vice-President. Smith was a Catholic, a "wet," and a Tammany man. Robinson was a "dry" from a state that had few Catholics and no large cities within its borders. But no one was deceived. The ticket of Smith and Robinson, despite its "one-hundred-per-cent American" names, represented primarily the descendants of recent immigrants who made up the bulk of the voting population in all the great cities of the East.

Hoover's triumphant victory at the polls in November was due primarily to four factors: (1) the belief which he assiduously cultivated that the continuance of Republican rule meant the continuance of prosperity; (2) the prejudice of rural America against the Tammany background of a corrupt machine based on immigrant votes from which Smith had risen; (3) the deepseated opposition of many American Protestants to the elevation of a Catholic to the Presidency; and (4) the determination of the evangelical churches to retain prohibition, which Smith denounced, but Hoover called a "noble experiment." "Hoover Democrats," voting the Republican ticket in large numbers, shattered the solid South; for the first time since reconstruction the Republicans carried Virginia, North Carolina, Tennessee, Florida, and Texas. Smith also lost his own state, New York, and every western and border state. The electoral vote stood 444 to 87, and the popular vote 21,392,190 to 15,016,443. Naturally the Hoover landslide carried with it overwhelming Republican majorities in Congress and in most of the states. The heavy protest vote that had been cast for La Follette four years before had dwindled to a mere quarter of a million votes for Norman Thomas, the Socialist candidate.[1]

Hoover's victory

---

[1] The best treatment of the Harding administration is F. L. Paxson, *Postwar Years: Normalcy, 1918–1923* (1948), but for a more popular account, see H. M. Robinson, *Fantastic Interim* (1943). On the naval situation, the best book is Harold and Margaret Sprout, *Toward a New Order of Sea Power: American Naval Policy and the World Scene, 1918–1922* (1940). On the peace movement, see R. J. Bartlett, *The League to Enforce Peace* (1944); and D. F. Fleming, *The United States and the World Court* (1945). K. C. MacKay, *The Progressive Movement of 1924* (1947), is an excellent monograph. Biographies: C. M. Fuess, *Calvin Coolidge, the Man from Vermont* (1940); W. A. White, *A Puritan in Babylon: The Story of Calvin Coolidge* (1938); J. E. Lawrence (ed.), *Fighting Liberal: The Autobiography of George W. Norris* (1945); A. T. Mason, *Brandeis: A Free Man's Life* (1946); Frank Graham, *Al Smith, American: An Informal Biography* (1945).

36

The New American Way

IT SEEMS PROBABLE that the automobile effected a greater change in the American way of life than ever proceeded from any other single cause.[1]

The automobile

The civilization of the nineteenth century remained to the end a "horse-and-buggy" affair; the civilization of the twentieth century was soon geared to the automobile. Starting from insignificance during the later nineties, the automobile industry by the time of the Great Depression outranked all others in importance, even steel. The new system of mass production at low cost which it introduced put motor transportation within the financial reach of nearly every American family; by 1929 twenty-six and one-half million motor cars of one kind or another were registered in the United States. The requirements of automobile travelers stimulated a movement for good roads, one significant result of which was to bring the city closer to the country, and the country to the city. With good roads available family vacations could be taken far from home, and every summer huge armies of tourists took to the road. Because the owner of an automobile might live a considerable distance from his work, suburban developments expanded as never before. Buses and trucks took over the short-haul traffic of streetcars and railroads. Hazards to life and health increased as traffic speeded up, and automobile accidents soon provided one of the commonest causes of death or injury. Crime was made easy, for the automobile assured law-breakers of a ready means of escape. Thousands of pleasure-bent children and youths at large on the roads increased the worries of parents, and drove the chaperon out of business. As a visiting senator from Hawaii complained, there were always "too many people in too many cars in too much of a hurry going in too many different directions to nowhere for nothing."

[1] The best study of American society during the twenties is P. W. Slosson, *The Great Crusade and After, 1914–1928* (1930). C. A. Beard and Mary R. Beard, *America in Mid-passage* (1939), which also features social history, begins where their *Rise of American Civilization* leaves off, and is followed by *The American Spirit* (1942). Much useful material is contained in the President's Research Committee on Social Trends, *Recent Social Trends in the United States* (2 vols., 1933).

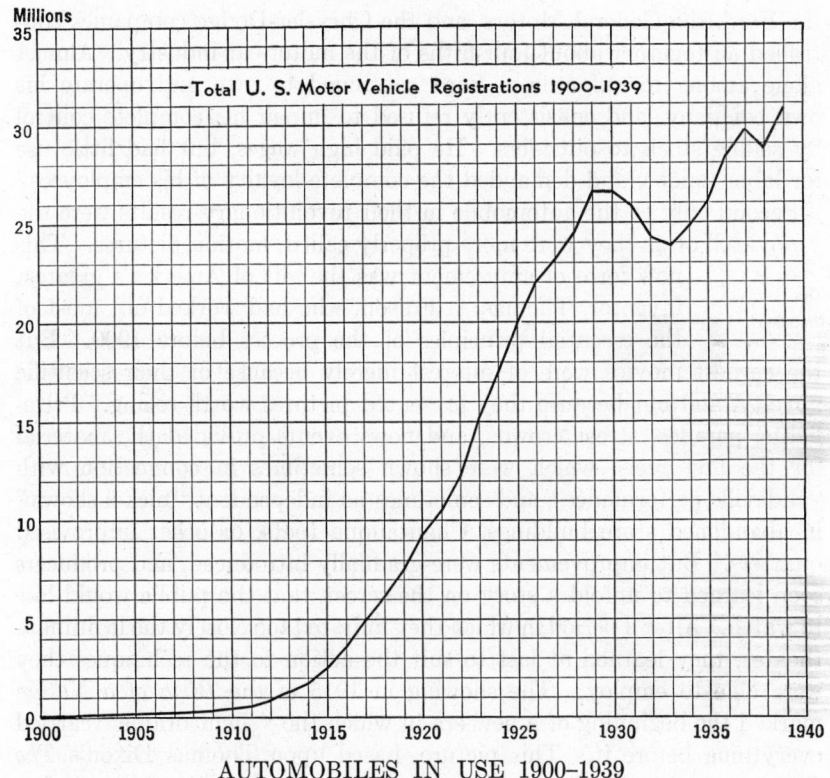

AUTOMOBILES IN USE 1900–1939

"The saga of the motor car" was intimately connected with the life-history of Henry Ford, whose dream of a good low-cost car was realized in an incredibly short time. Beginning at Detroit as early as 1893, Ford was making a fairly dependable car by the turn of the century, and by 1914 had produced a half-million of his famous "Model T." It was an unsightly car, designed for service and not for beauty, but it would run and it was cheap. Ford's methods of production were even more important than the car he built, for he used standardized, interchangeable parts, and by means of a "production line," along which each workman did his one assigned task and no other, he brought the process of manufacturing to a new level of efficiency. Other producers gave him competition, particularly the General Motors Corporation, which was established by William C. Durant as early as 1908. But for a long time Ford held the upper hand in the small-car field, and not until 1927 would he retool his plants in order to produce a better-looking car, the "Model A." Meantime, cars of every size and price had found their market, although three great companies, the Ford, the General Motors, and the Chrysler-Dodge companies controlled all together about four-fifths of the motor-car industry. Almost alone among manufacturers Ford continued to own and operate his own company, and consistently refused to impair his complete control by selling stock to outsiders. He paid high wages, but had little use for labor unions, and demanded the complete loyalty of his employees.[1]

Second only to the automobile in their revolutionary results were the "movies," or as they were more properly called, motion pictures. This new form of amusement was the gift of America's greatest inventor, Thomas A. Edison, who had worked out most of the essential principles of the process before 1900. But the earliest movies were of interest merely because of their scientific novelty, and not because they presented pictures worth seeing. Prize-fights, parades, street crowds, and news events provided the material for the first reels, which were shown sometimes in connection with vaudeville performances, and sometimes as independent "nickel shows" in abandoned store buildings, Chautauqua tents, or other improvised quarters. But improvements were gradually introduced, and producers soon learned to unfold a story on the screen that the public would like to watch. After a period in which they imitated too closely the legitimate theater, they learned at last to suit the action to the techniques they were able to employ. The showing in 1915 of the *Birth of a Nation* marked the beginning of a new era in which the "silent drama" carried everything before it. This picture, based upon Thomas Dixon's *The Clansman*, set forth effectively the agonies endured by the South during reconstruction. It was cheered by packed houses in North and South alike, and revealed clearly the profit possibilities of the new industry. With interest assured, elaborate motion-picture theaters appeared in every town and city, the price of admission was raised, and in southern California, where the sun shone dependably a good share of the year, the making of motion pictures became a major occupation. Film artists, such as Charlie Chaplin, Douglas Fairbanks, and Mary Pickford, were soon better known than politicians, and magazines devoted exclusively to the doings of the movie colony began to appear on most of the newsstands.

The movies had just succeeded in outgrowing their early crudities when the invention of talking pictures forced them to start all over again. In October, 1927, Al Jolson's success in *The Jazz Singer* proved that sound effects had come to stay, and within two years' time the movies had everywhere been converted into "talkies." The change eliminated scores of actors whose

The "movies"

Talking pictures

---

[1] Henry Ford, *My Life and Work* (1922); S. T. Bushnell, *The Truth About Henry Ford* (1922); H. L. Barber, *Story of the Automobile* (1917).

voices were unsuited to sound transmission, but it also served to open the profession to artists of the legitimate stage who had formerly regarded the screen performances with unconcealed contempt. Many competent artists passed back and forth freely from one medium to another, while successful plays on the legitimate stage were often reproduced in the movies. One of the best received of these was *The Barrets of Wimpole Street,* by Rudolph Bezier, in which the screen star, Norma Shearer, imitated closely the admirable acting of Katherine Cornell, America's greatest actress, on the legitimate stage. While many inferior pictures were made, the public tended more and more to become conscious of good acting, and to demand it as a matter of course. With the increasing perfection of sound instruments, musical plays grew rapidly in favor, paving the way for the successes of such singing artists as Jeanette MacDonald and Deanna Durbin. Walt Disney's *Silly Symphonies* introduced a new technique, the animated cartoon, which won many a well-earned laugh, and graduated eventually into the wholly admirable *Snow White and the Seven Dwarfs.* The invention of technicolor gave great vitality to the films that employed it, but was less generally used than had been anticipated. It attained a high degree of perfection in Margaret Mitchell's *Gone with the Wind,* starring Clark Gable and Vivien Leigh, which was produced in 1939. In general American pictures were preferred not only in the United States, but in many foreign countries also, but the popularity of such British films as *The Private Life of Henry VIII,* in which Charles Laughton played the title-rôle, showed that American producers could not safely ignore British competition.

The significance of the movies in American life was difficult to assess, but hard to overemphasize. Practically everyone, of high or low degree, attended the motion-picture shows with more or less regularity, and for the rising generation the lessons they taught were doubtless far more effective than the precepts of the schoolroom. The suggestions of the screen as to styles, manners, taste in furniture and art, and even morals, did not go unnoticed. It seems reasonable to suppose, for example, that there was some causal relationship between the popularity of the *Birth of a Nation* and the subsequent revival of the Ku Klux Klan. Pictures featuring the careers of criminals may also have accounted for numerous juvenile delinquencies, while such feminine fashions as the universal use of cosmetics probably owed at least as much to Hollywood as to Paris. Since the same movies were shown everywhere, they tended to emphasize strongly the national tendency toward uniformity. Probably the well-modulated voices and correct speaking of the film artists did far more than the high-school

Influence of the movies

teachers of English to make young Americans talk better and talk alike. Whether the morals of movie actors and actresses were above or below the average for the country as a whole would be difficult to prove, but the interest of stage stars in publicity, whatever the cost, made their doings generally known, and they may have had imitators. Censorship of pictures, sometimes effective but often of little consequence, was established in nearly every state, but producers learned mainly by trial and error what would be well received and what would not. As a kind of supreme arbiter in all matters of public relations, the picture industry chose Will H. Hays, who resigned as Postmaster-General under Harding to accept the assignment.[1]

Another new influence upon American life was furnished by the radio. Wireless telegraphy and telephony were known before the outbreak of the first World War, but during that struggle they proved to be of such tremendous military value that revolutionary improvements were made within a few years' time. After the war radio "fans," whose interest was primarily that of amateur scientists, bought millions of dollars' worth of equipment, and counted with joy the number of distant stations they could hear. By 1920 the manufacturers of radio supplies were beginning to furnish programs as a means of promoting the use of what they had to sell, and from this practice the institution of radio broadcasting developed. The pioneer station in this endeavor was KDKA of Pittsburgh, which among other things successfully broadcast the returns of the election of 1920. Soon many broadcasting stations, generously supported by advertisers, were competing for control of the air, and to prevent complete chaos Secretary Hoover maintained an informal system of licensing in the Commerce Department. When in 1926 the Attorney-General ruled that the Secretary of Commerce was exceeding his legal authority, the resulting confusion led Congress to establish next year a Federal Radio Commission of five members with the right to license broadcasting stations, and to determine the power, wave-lengths, and hours of operation to be allotted to each. Presently chains of stations, linked together at first as "stunts" but later because of the advantages observed, formed nation-wide networks over which the same program could be transmitted to every receiving set in the country. Steady improvements by what speedily became one of America's biggest businesses soon enabled listeners also to hear and enjoy broadcasts by short wave from abroad.[2]

Radio

[1] Alice M. Mitchell, *Children and Movies* (1929); H. B. Franklin, *Sound Motion Pictures* (1929); W. M. Seabury, *The Public and the Motion Picture Industry* (1926); Federal Council of the Churches of Christ in America, *The Public Relations of the Motion Picture Industry* (1931).

[2] Paul Schubert, *The Electric Word: The Rise of the Radio* (1928); Federal Council of the Churches of Christ in America, *Broadcasting and the Public* (1938).

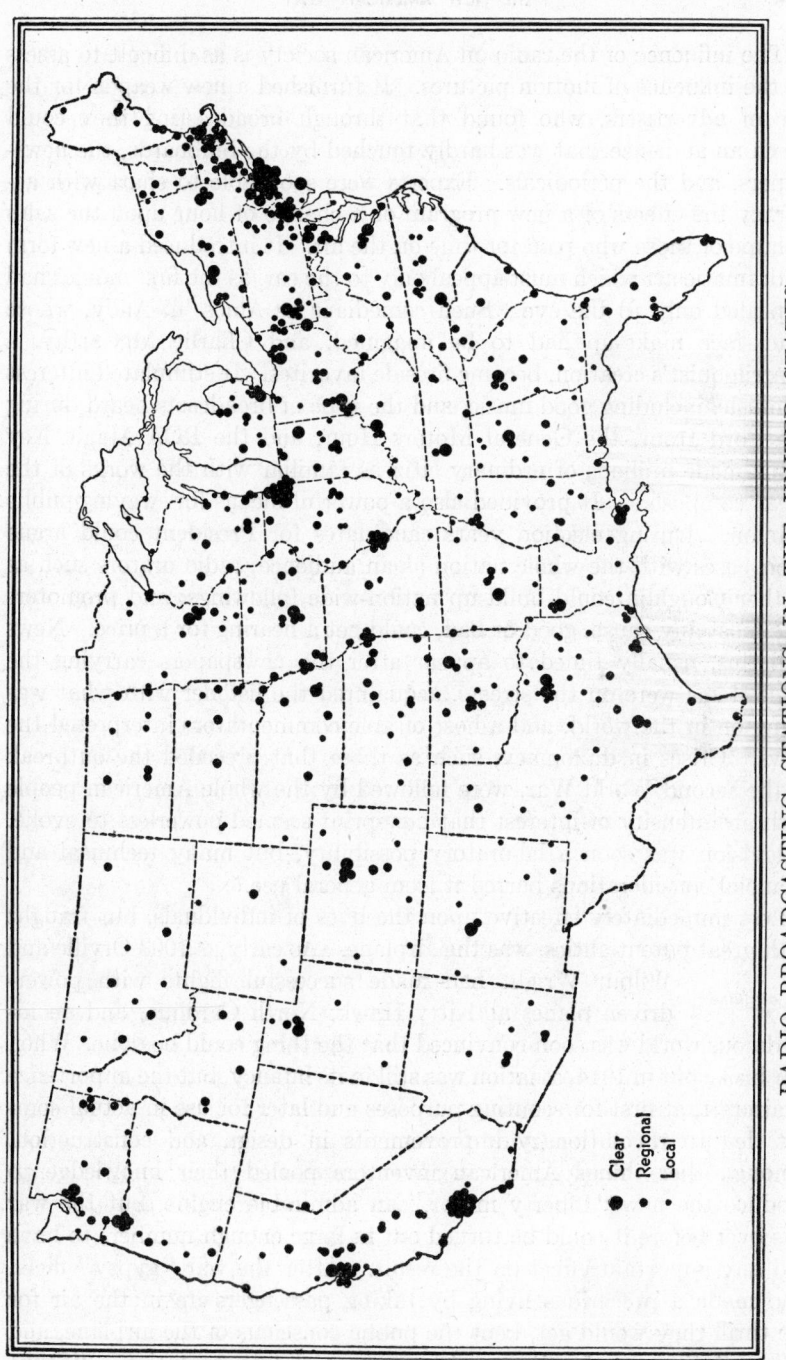

RADIO BROADCASTING STATIONS IN THE UNITED STATES

Clear ●
Regional ·
Local ·

The influence of the radio on American society is as difficult to assess as the influence of motion pictures. It furnished a new weapon for the use of advertisers, who found that through broadcasting they could reach an audience that was hardly touched by the billboards, the newspapers, and the periodicals. Experts were soon able to chart with accuracy the effects of a new program or a change of hour upon the sales volume of those who paid for time on the air. It introduced a new form of dramatic art which must appeal only to the ear, as the first movies had appealed only to the eye. Such comedians as Amos 'n' Andy, whose black-face make-up had to be imagined, and Charlie McCarthy, a ventriloquist's creation, became fireside favorites. It stimulated interest in music, including good music, and the type of broadcasts heard during the Ford Hour, the General Motors Hour, and the RCA Magic Key Hour made millions of ordinary citizens familiar with the works of the great composers. It provided also a powerful means for swaying public opinion. During election years candidates for President could argue their cases with the whole nation as an audience; radio orators such as Father Coughlin could build up nation-wide followings; and promoters of almost any cause, good or bad, could get a hearing for a price. News bulletins, usually timed to appear after the newspapers carrying the same items were on the streets, acquainted the listener with what was going on in the world, and a host of able commentators interpreted the news. Crises in diplomacy, such as those that preceded the outbreak of the second World War, were followed by the whole American people with an intensity of interest that newsprint seemed powerless to evoke. Television was soon a laboratory possibility, but many technical and financial considerations barred it from general use.

Less immediately effective upon the lives of individuals, but fraught with great potentialities, was the airplane. As early as 1903 Orville and Wilbur Wright had made successful flights with power-driven planes at Kitty Hawk, North Carolina, and an incredulous world was soon convinced that the thing could be done. When war broke out in 1914, aviation was still in its infancy, but the importance of aircraft, at first for scouting purposes and later for use in actual combat, led to revolutionary improvements in design and construction. Among other things American inventors pooled their knowledge to produce the new "Liberty motor," an admirable engine, but the war was over before it could be turned out in large enough numbers to have had any important effect on the result. After the war "gypsy" fliers, who made a precarious living by taking passengers up in the air for the thrill they would get, kept the public conscious of the airplane, and prepared the way for its use in commercial transportation. "Stunt

The airplane

1896 — Lilienthal Glider

1903 — Wright Brothers
(Glider)

1917 — Lawson Air Liner

1927 — Lindbergh
(Spirit of St. Louis)

1936 — Trans-Atlantic Liner

Batwing Plane

EVOLUTION OF THE AIRPLANE

fliers" also revealed its possibilities, particularly for long-distance flights. The Atlantic was crossed by way of the Azores as early as May, 1919; from Newfoundland to Ireland in June of the same year; and from Great Britain to New York by a British dirigible the following July. But the achievement that most caught the country's fancy was the solo flight of Charles A. Lindbergh, a youthful aviator who took off from Roosevelt Field, Long Island, on May 20, 1927, and thirty-three hours later landed successfully in the vicinity of Paris.[1] By order of President Coolidge Lindbergh was brought home on a warship, and rose immediately to the status of the nation's greatest hero. The fact that he was not the first to fly the Atlantic, and that two other Americans, Clarence D. Chamberlain and C. A. Lewis, flying from the same field on July 4 for Berlin, got within a hundred miles of their destination, in no wise diminished Lindbergh's fame. Later in the month Commander Richard E. Byrd at the head of a party of four also flew to Europe, and two army aviators reached Honolulu from California, while in June, 1931, Wiley Post flew around the world in less than eight days' time.

The development of commercial aviation in the United States did not begin in earnest until several years after the signing of the armistice, although the government early gave its assistance by air-mail contracts.[2] By 1924 a regular mail service had been established between New York and San Francisco, and four years later there were as many as forty-eight airways in the United States, covering twenty thousand miles, and serving three hundred and fifty-five cities. Most of these lines depended upon government mail contracts for their profits, and regarded the incidental carrying of passengers or freight as somewhat of a nuisance. When Hoover became President in 1929 his Postmaster-General, Walter Folger Brown, resolved to remedy this situation. The government subsidies were paid, he believed, not merely for carrying the mail, but also to encourage the development of a new and useful means of transportation which might incidentally serve the country well in time of war. Brown wrote new contracts, which, by abandoning the "per pound" basis for carrying the mail in favor of the "space-mile" principle, placed a premium on the building of larger planes. He also used his discretionary power in the awarding of contracts in such a way as to eliminate the small operators, whose ability to develop the industry was obviously less than that of the well-established and adequately financed lines.

Air mail (margin note)

---

[1] C. A. Lindbergh, "*We*" (1927), is the story of this flight. On the development of the airplane see Mark Sullivan, *Our Times*, II, and Faulkner, *Quest for Social Justice*.

[2] The slow progress of commercial aviation in the United States is evident from W. J. Davis, *The World's Wings* (1927). See also Henry Ladd Smith, *Airways* (1942).

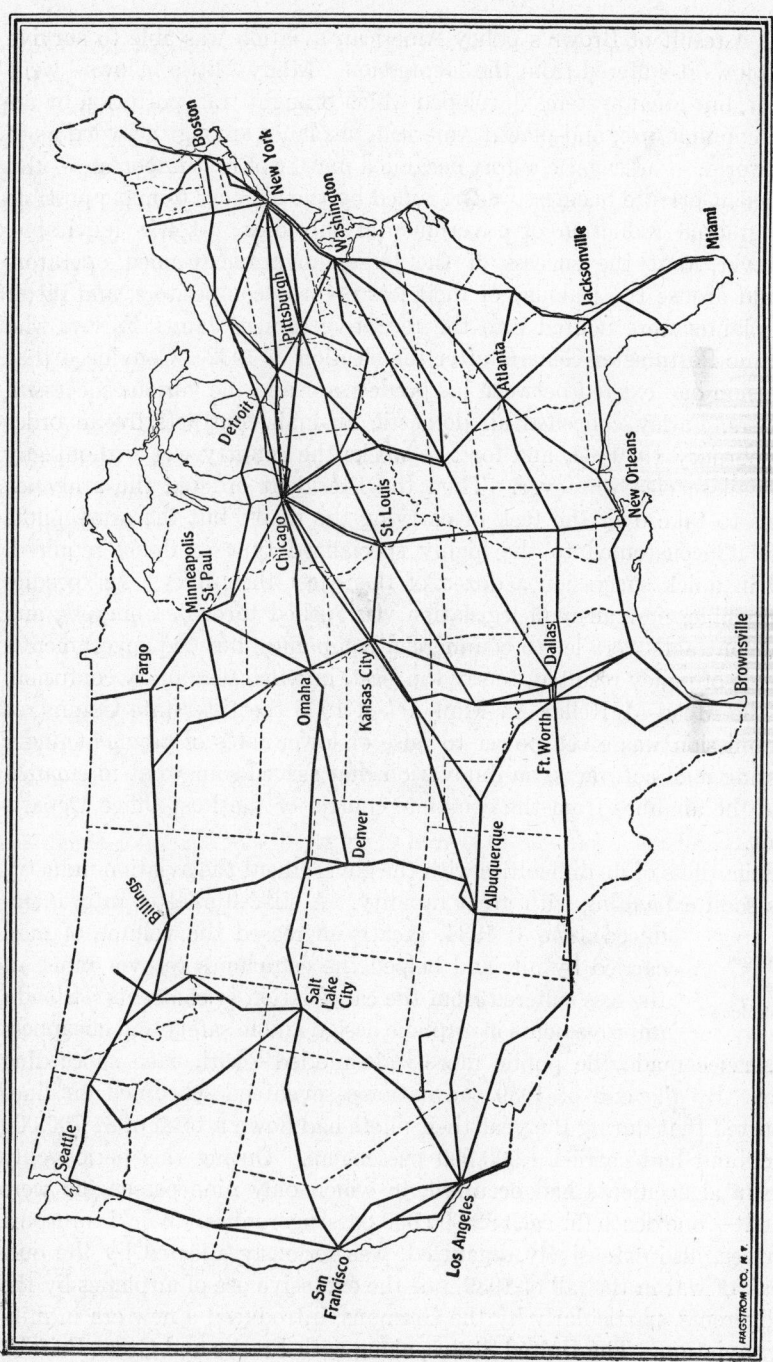

AMERICAN AIRWAYS

As a result of Brown's policy American aviation was able to survive the blows it suffered from the Depression. Many "little fellows" went under, but great systems developed which brought transportation by air into common use, and placed American airplanes among the wonders of the world. Passenger comfort became a matter of first importance, and sufficient private business was obtained by the air lines to make possible the gradual reduction of governmental subsidies. It was inevitable, however, that the success of the large, government-aided operators should arouse the jealousy of their less favored competitors, and bitter complaints were poured into the receptive ears of James Farley, who became Postmaster-General after the election of 1932. Convinced that collusion had existed between his predecessor and the various successful bidders, Farley cancelled all domestic air-mail contracts by an order of February 19, 1934, and for two weeks the country was without any air-mail service whatever. Then the President ordered the army air corps to take over the task of carrying the mails, but the army pilots were unaccustomed to the highly specialized type of flying required, and in quick succession a dozen of them lost their lives. As speedily as possible, new air-mail legislation was rushed through Congress, and new contracts were let to commercial companies, but the government's change of policy resulted, to say the least, in much temporary confusion. By the Mead-McKellar Air-Mail Act of 1935 the Interstate Commerce Commission was given power to raise or lower rates of payment under existing mail contracts, an innovation that served somewhat to emancipate the air lines from the complete control of the Post-Office Department.

Regardless of its difficulties with the government the aviation industry was soon expanding with great rapidity. A six-cents letter rate, introduced June 1, 1934, greatly increased the volume of mail carried by air, and helped the companies recover much of the loss suffered from the cancellation of contracts. Steady improvements in airplane design and in safety and cheapness of service made the public more "air-minded" with each succeeding year. By the end of 1939 the nation's seventeen scheduled air lines reported that during the year their pilots had flown a total of 81,700,000 miles and had carried 1,900,000 passengers. During this period only two fatal accidents had occurred, in which only nine passengers were killed — one death for each 82,000,000 passenger miles. World transport services, also extensively organized, was seriously affected by the outbreak of war in the fall of 1939, but the extensive use of airplanes by the belligerents, particularly by the Germans, introduced a new era in military aviation. The United States, along with France and Great Britain,

Passenger
travel
by airplane

came quickly to realize that the airplane as a weapon of war was indispensable. Thousands of orders, both from the American and from foreign governments, led to a period of more intense activity among the airplane builders of the United States than had ever been known before.

The automobile, the movies, the radio, and the airplane were but the more visible symbols of a highly mechanized age. The gadgets of science had invaded every phase of American life. The farmer no longer followed a plow, but drove a tractor. The most humble of physicians must surround himself with thousands of dollars' worth of expensive equipment. Alert industrialists expected to retool their plants at frequent intervals. School buildings must be elaborately provided with the machines necessary for vocational training. Ordinary citizens took a thousand things for granted that their ancestors would have regarded as miracles; central heating, running water, sanitary plumbing, gas for cooking, electric energy for lighting and a dozen other household purposes; direct telephone connections with the outside world. Thoughtful observers sometimes wondered about the effect of all these "improvements" upon the people who depended upon them. Was the resourcefulness of the individual being undermined? Was overreliance upon machines softening the fabric of American character? Whatever the answers, there were few to advocate that the new machines be scrapped, and the older and harder ways revived.[1]

To inheritors of the Puritan tradition there was much about the changing American scene that was alarming. Among most of the Protestant denominations church-going had declined precipitately. A few popular city preachers held their congregations, but in the country towns the competition of the automobile, the movies, the radio, and the golf links had proved impossible to meet. The younger generation made open sport of the old morality; styles in feminine apparel left little to the imagination; and flippancy in speech and manners became almost a national obsession. Fundamentalism was in full retreat. The action of several southern legislatures during the twenties in prohibiting the teaching of evolution was more in the nature of a confession of defeat than a call to action. William Jennings Bryan, by aiding the prosecution at Dayton, Tennessee, of a young man who had disobeyed the law,

[1] The literature of pessimism as applied to this period is painfully voluminous. Samples worth citing are J. T. Adams, *Our Business Civilization* (1929); Walter Lippmann, *A Preface to Morals* (1929); F. R. Kent, *Political Behavior* (1928); H. E. Stearns, editor, *Civilization in the United States: An Inquiry by Thirty Americans* (1922); M. A. Hallgren, *Seeds of Revolt* (1933). The nearest approach to a scientific study of the social scene is presented in R. S. and H. M. Lynd, *Middletown* (1929), and *Middletown in Transition* (1937).

was generally thought to have made himself and his cause ridiculous. But the greatest blow that the evangelical churches suffered was the failure of prohibition. Effectively organized through the Anti-Saloon League, the church people had won state after state to the temperance cause, and when the Eighteenth Amendment was adopted in January, 1919, they had rejoiced almost as immoderately as over the signing of the armistice. Less than fourteen years later they looked on with despair while the Twenty-First Amendment recalled the Eighteenth, and the "noble experiment" came to an end.[1]

The rock on which prohibition foundered was enforcement. It was one thing to outlaw the existing liquor traffic, but quite another to **Prohibition** prevent its replacement by illicit vendors of liquor who profited from breaking the law. The Eighteenth Amendment made no great change in the national appetite for strong drink, and a large minority of the population felt outraged that any such attack on personal liberty had been made. This was particularly true of the city populations in which the immigrant element constituted so important a part. Others who had never drunk before were impelled out of sheer perversity to do what the law forbade. Americans from colonial times on down had never felt obliged to obey a law that they did not like; indeed, many argued that the only way to defeat an obnoxious law was to prove that it could not be enforced. Thus a market for liquor still existed, and to supply it a whole new industry came into being. The ways of the "moonshiners," who since the days of the Whiskey Rebellion had hidden their stills in the mountains to avoid the payment of revenue, were extensively imitated; "rum-runners" brought a steady stream of cargoes from abroad to unpatrolled sections of the American coast; heavily laden smugglers crossed the border from Mexico and from Canada; chemical formulae, sometimes dependable and sometimes not, were used to "renovate" industrial liquor by the removal of denaturants; private citizens set up toy stills, manufactured "homebrew" and "bathtub gin," turned the pure unfermented juice of the grape into more or less palatable wine.

The Volstead Act, by which Congress (over Wilson's veto) defined intoxicating beverages as those containing as much as one-half of one per cent alcohol and created the machinery for enforcement, **Problems of enforcement** imposed upon federal officials an almost impossible task. "Bootleggers" had already gained valuable experience in the states where prohibition had preceded the Eighteenth Amendment.

[1] Charles Merz, *The Dry Decade* (1931), is a good popular account of prohibition. It may be compared with the Federal Council of the Churches of Christ in America, *The Prohibition Situation* (1925).

They knew how easily the problem of distribution could be solved by automobiles and trucks, and they were past-masters of the art of bribery and deception. Against these experts the Prohibition Bureau, which until 1927 was outside the civil service, mobilized a miscellaneous army of petty politicians and their friends. Furthermore, the entrance of the national government into the field of enforcement led the states to relax their efforts; wet states in many instances repealed the limitations they had once placed on liquor dealers, while dry states cheerfully resigned to federal agents the task of matching wits with the bootleggers. The United States Department of Justice found itself suddenly swamped with a type of business it had never known before, and prohibition cases clogged the federal courts. Thirty-five hundred civil cases and sixty-five thousand criminal cases were brought within a period of less than two years.

Soon the illicit liquor business was one of the nation's biggest and most profitable. Since it operated wholly outside the law, all restraints were eliminated, and competitors traded bloody blows. Backed by dependable gangs of thugs, the "big shots" The bootleggers fought furiously for the enormous profits of monopoly, and in each large city a well-recognized king of the underworld emerged, to whom, while his reign lasted, the whole business paid tribute. Deaths among the gangsters were numerous, but trials for these murders were rare and convictions still rarer. The gang leaders, successfully defended by highly paid criminal lawyers known as "mouthpieces," not only sneered openly at the prohibition agents, but systematically instituted one new "racket" after another. Gambling, prostitution, the trade in narcotics, and other illegal activities came naturally within the orbit of the "racketeers," but even the most legitimate of businesses were not immune. Restaurant keepers, cleaners and dyers, laundrymen, garage owners, anyone who took in cash might at a moment's notice be compelled to pay heavily for "protection" against these selfsame protectors. Failure to meet the racketeers' demands meant smashed windows, flattened tires, burned delivery trucks, bombed stores, and for the most obdurate sudden death. Labor unions were invaded for the chance to graft from membership dues, and in altogether too many instances city governments paid more attention to the demands of the racketeers than to the welfare of the citizens. Racketeering was at its worst in Chicago and New York, but few large cities escaped its ravages, and the whole nation paid tribute, directly or indirectly, to the gangsters.

With conditions fast becoming unbearable, a Law Enforcement Commission of eleven members was appointed by President Hoover in 1929 to conduct an investigation. Headed by George W. Wickersham, form-

erly Attorney-General under Taft, the commission took its duties seriously, but when it reported in 1931 it was still undecided.
The Wickersham Commission Its findings of fact seemed to recognize the hopelessness of adequate enforcement, but a majority of the commissioners recommended that the prohibition experiment be continued.[1] In the summer of 1932 President Hoover, in spite of the impending campaign, admitted that some changes in the existing system would have to be made, while the Democratic platform went the whole length of demanding repeal. Following the triumphant Democratic victory at the polls, Congress acted even before the new administration could take office. In February, 1933, the repeal amendment was submitted, and by the end of the year it was a part of the Constitution.

The end of prohibition, however, did not mean the end of racketeering, for by this time the gangsters were deeply entrenched in all sorts of rackets. One of the most amazing of these was the "snatch
Racketeering racket," which in May, 1932, claimed its most famous victim when the infant son of Charles A. Lindbergh was kidnaped for ransom by a lone operator, and killed. As the profits of bootlegging disappeared, criminals turned instead to kidnaping, bank burglaries, and other bold crimes, and in an alarming number of instances easily made good their escape. Finally Congress, by a series of "crime control" acts passed in the spring of 1934, faced squarely the responsibility of the federal government in bringing the situation under control. By the terms of these laws criminals who crossed state lines during the course of their exploits were made liable to drastic penalties (for kidnapers, death), and the Investigation Division of the Federal Department of Justice, headed by J. Edgar Hoover and known later as the Federal Bureau of Investigation, was given great freedom of action in enforcement. At the end of the year Hoover's agents had accounted by death for a dozen of the country's most notorious criminals, and had brought many others to justice. State officers, forced to compare results with the effective "G-men," also began to take their duties seriously. Early in 1935 the kidnaper of the Lindbergh baby was convicted and sentenced in New Jersey. That same year Thomas E. Dewey was made special prosecutor to conduct a drive against organized crime in New York, and achieved such conspicuous success that in 1937 he was given a popular mandate to continue the work as district attorney of New York County. When other evidence failed, racketeers were sometimes convicted for federal income-tax evasion. This had happened to "Scarface Al" Capone, the underworld ruler of Chicago, as far back as 1931, and his

---

[1] Report of the National Commission on Law Observance and Enforcement, Seventy-First Congress, third session, *House Document* no. 722 (serial 9361).

long imprisonment at Alcatraz, the escape-proof federal penitentiary located on an island in San Francisco Bay, served as a continual warning to would-be imitators. Toward the close of the decade there was reason to hope that at last the era of unrestrained lawlessness had approached its end.[1]

If young America embraced lawlessness, it was not because its education had been neglected. Compulsory school attendance up to sixteen or even eighteen years of age was required by law in most states, and was well enforced by public opinion. School buildings were elaborately equipped, not only with teaching paraphernalia, but also with auditoriums, gymnasiums, swimming pools, and such other facilities as might contribute to well-rounded lives on the part of the pupils. Bus service made possible the elimination of the weaker country schools, and the establishment, especially for the higher grades, of well-appointed consolidated systems. New principles of education, emanating chiefly from Teachers College, Columbia, revolutionized the methods of teaching, and emphasized the need of "education for life." The influence of John Dewey, who insisted that the chief end and aim of schooling should be the development of socially useful adults, permeated nearly every classroom.[2] Preparation for college played a diminishing rôle in high-school curriculums, where a host of young people who had no interest in nor aptitude for a college course must be kept occupied. Vocational education and manual training flourished as never before. For the most part primary and secondary education in the United States meant public education, although many private schools existed, particularly in the East. Toward the end of the twenties the annual bill for education in the United States approached three billion dollars.

Higher education flourished in spite of the indifference toward it exhibited in many of the lower schools. During that part of the twentieth century which preceded the outbreak of World War I the number of students enrolled in colleges and universities increased from about 114,000 to nearly a quarter of a million. The years of American participation in the war diminished somewhat the rate of acceleration, but after the war was over, the rise began again, and until 1929 continued at about the rate of an additional quarter of a

Educational trends

Colleges and universities

---

[1] M. A. Kavanagh, *The Criminal and his Allies* (1928), and R. W. Child, *Battling the Criminal* (1926), are somewhat sensational in character. R. B. Fosdick, *American Police Systems* (1920), and A. A. Bruce, *The Administration of Criminal Justice in Illinois* (1929), are more dependable. Of particular interest because of its author's position is J. Edgar Hoover, *Persons in Hiding* (1938).

[2] John Dewey, *The School and Society* (1899), and *Democracy and Education* (1916), state clearly the author's thesis that social utility should be the principal aim of education.

million every five years. Junior colleges were provided in many states so that the first two years of a college course could be obtained by great numbers of students without the necessity of leaving home. State teachers' colleges, designed to provide the proper "teacher training" for those whose duty it would be to put the new principles of education into effect, also multiplied amazingly. Graduate schools, with courses leading to the master's or the doctor's degree, appeared in all the larger universities, and the Ph.D. degree became almost as essential for the aspirant to a college instructorship as the teacher's certificate to the beginner in the public schools.[1]

In spite of their steady flow of customers the institutions of higher education in the United States were subjected to endless criticism. The elective system by which students were permitted to collect a hodge-podge of relatively unrelated courses toward a baccalaureate degree was denounced as warmly as in the days of President Eliot. To some observers the dominance of sports and society on college campuses constituted the principal shortcoming of higher education; others were disagreeably impressed by the ages-old tendency of youth to flirt with radical ideas. Probably most college students expected as a result of their educational endeavors to get a better job than would otherwise have been open to them. Many "bread-and-butter" courses aided them in this ambition, but wise employers recognized that a four years' residence in a stimulating environment was in itself a valuable experience. The advent of the Great Depression cut down materially on college and university enrollments, but not many institutions actually went under, and the students soon returned. It should be noted that college faculties were for the most part concerned not merely with instruction, but also with research. A large proportion of the discoveries in pure science, and a still larger proportion of the exploratory ventures in other fields, were the contributions of university professors. To a considerable extent on this account, most of the great foundations for philanthropy, such, for examples, as those established by Rockefeller and Carnegie, continued their interest in higher education.

Perhaps the most successful of the achievements that stemmed from the educational world lay in the realm of science and health. The diagnosis of deep-seated disease, and sometimes the cure also, **Scientific achievements** received an enormous impetus from the steady improvement in X-ray technique; the discoveries of bacteriologists sent such dread diseases as diphtheria into the discard along with ty-

[1] E. H. Wilkins, *The Changing College* (1927); R. L. Kelly, *Tendencies in College Administration* (1925); J. E. Kirkpatrick, *The American College and Its Rulers* (1926); R. C. Angell, *The Campus* (1928).

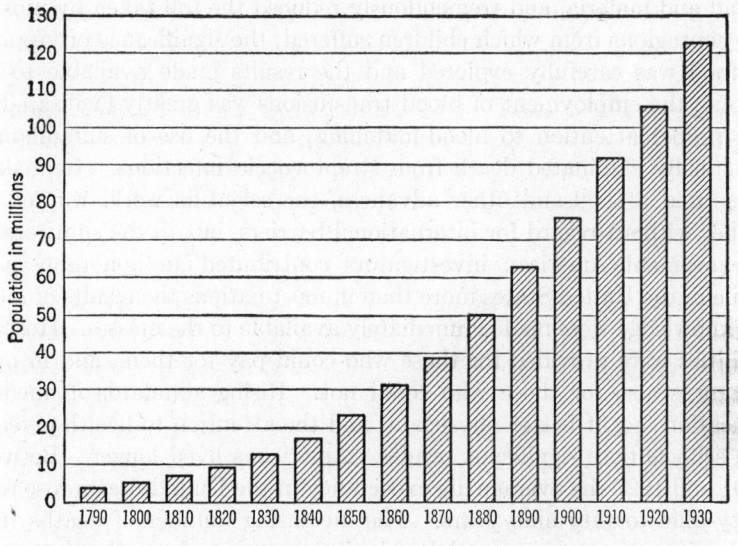

GROWTH OF POPULATION IN THE UNITED STATES

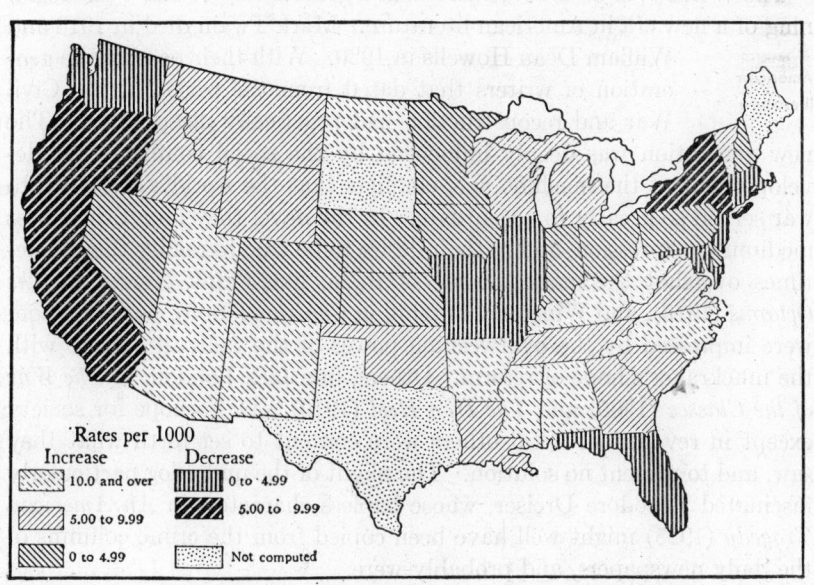

RATES OF NATURAL INCREASE IN
THE AMERICAN POPULATION

phoid and malaria, and tremendously reduced the toll taken by most of
the contagions from which children suffered; the significance of vitamins
in food was carefully explored and the results made available to the
public; the employment of blood transfusions was greatly facilitated by
the proper attention to blood-matching; and the use of sulfanilamide
practically eliminated death from streptococcic infections. In making
these and a thousand other advances, the scientific world worked together without regard for international barriers, but to the sum total of
advancement American investigators contributed an honorable part,
while in the United States more than in most nations the results of medical knowledge were made immediately available to the masses. Hospital
facilities were provided for those who could pay for them, and in most
instances also for those who could not. Rising standards in medical
education meant better physicians, and the attention to health given in
the schools bore significant results. Americans lived longer. Between
1901 and 1927 the average life expectancy in the United States rose from
forty-nine to fifty-nine years. The increasing number of deaths from
such diseases as cancer and heart ailments proved merely that more
people were living long enough to die from the afflictions of old age.[1]

The World War of 1914–18 served in a general way to mark the beginning of a new era in American literature. Mark Twain died in 1910 and

American literature

William Dean Howells in 1920. With their passing the generation of writers that dated from the period of the Civil
War and reconstruction had practically disappeared. The
new generation was deeply influenced by the social conflicts that developed out of the machine age, conflicts that the world's descent into
war served so greatly to accentuate. In the novel they found their best
medium of expression, and in their desire to be true to reality they sometimes overshot the mark. Some of them, like Frank Norris, in *The
Octopus* (1910), and Winston Churchill in *Coniston* (1906), both of whom
were impressed by the overweening power of the railroads, wrote with
the muckraker's hope of reform. Others, like Jack London, in *The War
of the Classes* (1905) and *The Iron Heel* (1910), saw no hope for society
except in revolution. Still others were content to set forth what they
saw, and to present no solution. The plight of the underdog particularly
fascinated Theodore Dreiser, whose hapless characters in *An American
Tragedy* (1925) might well have been copied from the crime columns of
the daily newspapers, and probably were.

The search for realism led to many re-examinations of the American

---

[1] Among the more popular books on scientific subjects are R. T. Young, *Biology in
America* (1922); Julius Stieglitz, *Chemistry in Medicine* (1928); L. I. Dublin, *Health and
Wealth* (1928).

past, none more fruitful than those pertaining to the frontier. Hamlin Garland's autobiographic *A Son of the Middle Border* (1917) recaptured much of the harshness of the pioneer environment, but only as an old man recounts experiences from which he emerged as a great success. Willa Cather in *O Pioneers* (1913) and *My Ántonia* (1918) strove also to strip away the glamour that had attached itself to the frontier, and in accomplishing her task displayed literary craftsmanship of a high order. James Boyd in *Drums* (1925) and *Long Hunt* (1930) did a similar, but less notably excellent, service for an earlier age. O. E. Rölvaag's *Giants in the Earth* (1927) told with stark realism the bitter struggle of the immigrant farmer against the bleak Northwest, while Mari Sandoz's *Old Jules* (1935) varied the scene to fit the conflict fought by another immigrant, the author's father, against the semi-arid, treeless plains. Ellen Glasgow, writing of the post-Civil-War South instead of the frontier, portrayed in a long series of volumes from the *Battle Ground* (1902) to *Vein of Iron* (1935) the decay of the old southern society, while Margaret Mitchell, exploiting in *Gone with the Wind* (1936) another phase of the same theme, revealed the soul-searing methods by which the New South was built.

Most American writers, however, preferred the theme of the present, and in dealing with the setting that lay about them none showed greater proficiency than Sinclair Lewis. Thoroughly out of patience with the selfish commercialism that was exhibited in every phase of American life, Lewis satirized the rundown country town in *Main Street* (1920), the growing city and its prosperous "realtors" in *Babbitt* (1922), the medical profession in *Arrowsmith* (1925), the evangelical clergy in *Elmer Gantry* (1927), and the American merchant princess in *Dodsworth* (1929). What Sinclair Lewis sought to do through fiction, Henry L. Mencken attempted in the field of criticism, first as a writer for the *Baltimore Sun*, but after 1924 as editor of an ultra-smart magazine *The American Mercury*, which for several years was the favorite diet of all who sought to appear sophisticated. Mencken's particular delight was to bait the prohibitionists, whose cant and sophistry he found it easy to expose. But neither Lewis nor Mencken was willing to approve an attack by revolution on the social system he criticized, and they soon lost caste with the radicals who had at first hailed them as prophets.

American verse of merit, for the first time since the days of Bryant and Whitman, was again being written. Most of it, too, was deeply critical of society. Edwin Arlington Robinson, whose *Collected Poems* (1921) won a Pulitzer prize, wrote chiefly of man's inability to deal effectively with the forces that beset him. Edgar

Lee Masters in his *Spoon River Anthology* (1915) recited with telling
irony the aimless life-histories of the people whose gravestones might be
seen in any village cemetery. Vachel Lindsay in *The Congo and Other
Poems* (1919) at once startled the literary world with his unusual verse
forms and turned attention toward the American Negro as a theme for
exploitation. Robert Frost in *North of Boston* (1914) and *New Hampshire* (1923) dealt sympathetically, but in utter realism, with the peculiarities of rural New Englanders. John G. Neihardt in *The Song of Hugh
Glass* (1915), *The Song of Three Friends* (1919), and *The Song of the Indian Wars* (1925) attempted with considerable success an epic of the
frontier. Stephen Vincent Benét in *John Brown's Body* (1928) and *A
Book of Americans* (1933) wrote good history in vivid verse. Carl Sandburg in *The People Yes* (1936) described in homespun language the drab
daily deeds of ordinary men, and dripped "corrosive sublimate" upon
"formalities, conventionalities, 'stuffed shirtfronts,' the high proprieties
of the high."[1]

The United States produced also a few good playwrights. Foremost
among them was Eugene O'Neill, whose long series of dramatic successes
included *Emperor Jones* (1921), *Desire Under the Elms*
(1924), *Marco Millions* (1924), *The Great God Brown* (1925),
Strange Interlude (1927), *Mourning Becomes Electra* (1931),
Ah, Wilderness (1932), and *Days Without End* (1933). O'Neill's plays
exploited complex psychological themes, and sometimes dwelt almost
morbidly upon the problems of sex. Of the many other less gifted but
extremely able American playwrights perhaps Maxwell Anderson and
Elmer Rice are most worthy of mention. Anderson in *What Price Glory*
(1924) brought home with tremendous effectiveness the grim realities of
war, including the artistic nature of military profanity, and in *Both Your
Houses* (1933) skillfully satirized the national capital in the throes of the
New Deal. Rice, in such plays as *On Trial* (1914), *For the Defense* (1919),
and *Counsellor-at-Law* (1931), dealt understandingly with legal complications, but rose to new heights in his *Judgment Day* (1934) which courageously faced the conflicting ideologies of the international scene. In
spite of strenuous competition from the movies the legitimate stage
maintained its hold upon New York and Chicago audiences, while many
of the more popular plays took to the road and were shown all over the
country. Stock companies generally succumbed, but amateur theatri-

*Plays and
playwrights*

---

[1] Beard and Beard, *America in Midpassage*, II, 680. On American poetry, see Amy
Lowell, *Tendencies in Modern American Poetry* (1917), and J. L. Lowes, *Convention and
Revolt in Poetry* (1919); on the novel, A. H. Quinn, *American Fiction* (1936), and F. L.
Pattee, *The New American Literature, 1890–1930* (1930). Granville Hicks, *The Great Tradi-
tion* (1933), is a left-wing view. On literature in general see W. P. Trent and others, *The
Cambridge History of American Literature* (3 vols., 1936), III.

cals, particularly those sponsored by the schools and colleges, flourished as never before.

American art, while far from barren in such fields as painting and sculpture, reached its highest peak in architecture. The possibilities of the skyscraper were not fully realized until designers gave Architecture up the attempt to embroider their buildings with irrelevant decorations, and began to emphasize vertical lines and related masses. In 1916 New York City furnished an unexpected boon to builders when it legislated the "set-back" into existence in order to insure that some daylight should reach the city streets. This furnished an opportunity to introduce variety into architectural designs that led to notable improvements, but the skyscraper was still not without its limitations. This became abundantly apparent when William F. Lamb's Empire State Building raised the New York skyline, perhaps for the last time, to a new altitude. Aside from the discovery that the building provided more office space than tenants could readily be induced to take, the physical difficulties involved in getting so many people into and out of so large a building, and back and forth from their homes to their work, indicated clearly the desirability of smaller buildings more widely dispersed. Public buildings offered another opportunity for significant architectural innovations. Outstanding among these was the state capitol at Lincoln, Nebraska, designed by Bertram Goodhue. Called by enthusiasts the most beautiful building in America, it broke the monotony of the Nebraska prairie with an imposing shaft which, unlike the customary dome, provided at the same time an abundance of well-lighted office space. Its decorations, generous with color and bold in design, told in well-thought-out symbolism the history of western civilization and its impact upon the Indian culture of the plains.

In domestic architecture many influences were at work, and much mere experimentation was in evidence. At once novel and practical were the designs of Frank Lloyd Wright whose house on the Wisconsin River, Taliesin, was extensively copied by himself and many mere imitators. But Wright's first principle was that a building must harmonize with its natural surroundings, and "be made to grow easily from its site." [1]

Of tremendous interest in revealing the trend away from traditionalism in architecture toward the new ideal of "functionalism" was the Century of Progress Exposition which opened in Chicago during the spring of 1933, just forty years after Chicago's Century earlier world's fair had first startled the nation. From an of Progress architectural point of view the two expositions could hardly Exposition have stood in greater contrast. Visitors of 1893 saw a dream of classical

[1] Frank Lloyd Wright, *An Autobiography* (1932).

beauty done in the purest white; visitors of 1933 saw huge, shapeless structures, painted with the boldest colors, and suggestive of nothing they had ever seen before. Only after night when the floodlights were loosed could the ordinary observer see a setting worthy of admiration. But the buildings, windowless and curiously shaped as they were, served well the purposes for which they were built, a lesson that was by no means lost on the millions who saw them. Soon "modernistic" structures appeared all over the nation as architects vied with one another in the effort to make an honest adjustment of their materials to the needs they were meant to serve. The location of the Exposition also taught a lesson. The land on which it stood was all "made land," dredged up from the bottom of Lake Michigan to provide a wide approach to the waterfront. After the fair was over the entire area was to be made into a city park, and still more dredged-up land was to facilitate the construction of an elaborate system of automobile highways bordering upon the lake. City planning had made much progress since 1893, and the example of Chicago in taking better advantage of its natural setting was followed by many other cities. The Fair, in spite of the hard times, was no less successful financially than its predecessor of forty years before, and was held over for the following year.

Six years later two other American cities, San Francisco and New York, held fairs. The setting for the Golden Gate Exposition was a four-hundred-acre man-made island in San Francisco Bay, and its purpose was to show how completely civilized western America and the Pacific Basin had become. The buildings essayed a blend of Mayan, Incan, Malayan, and other Pacific forms that registered a marked advance over the architectural innovations exhibited at Chicago. In New York the "World of Tomorrow" was the principal theme of the most elaborate fair ever staged in America. The exposition grounds occupied nearly two square miles of territory in Flushing Meadows, at the very heart of Greater New York, and the project involved an expenditure of over one hundred and fifty million dollars. The buildings showed that the search for architectural innovations had by no means ceased, but the garish colors and angular lines of the Century of Progress were much toned down. Both the Golden Gate Exposition and the World of Tomorrow were reopened the succeeding year, but in spite of large attendances neither was able to duplicate the financial success of the Century of Progress.

These three world's fairs, quite apart from the revolt they registered against architectural traditions, made significant contributions to American life. The millions who visited them came away with a better understanding of the intricate processes by which the scientific advancement

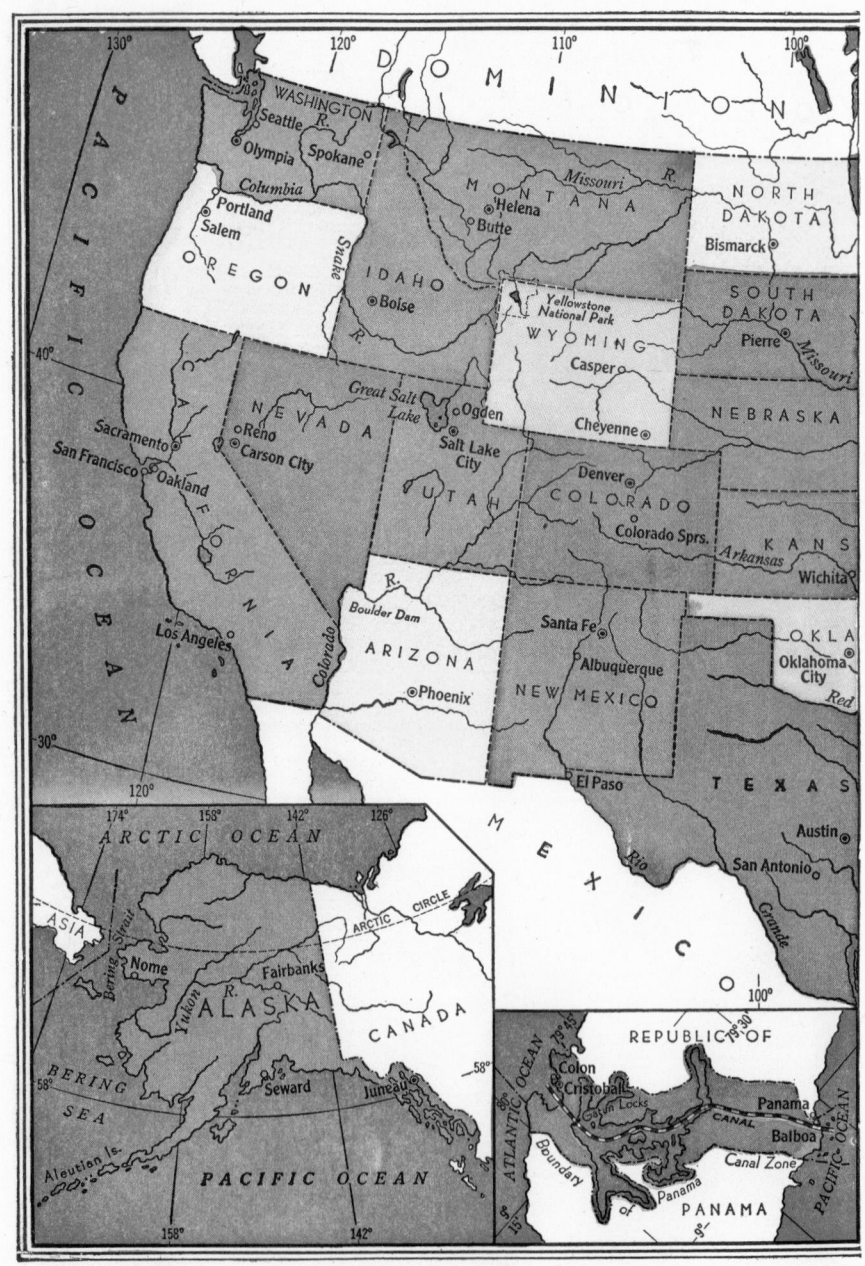

THE UNITED STATES IN 1940

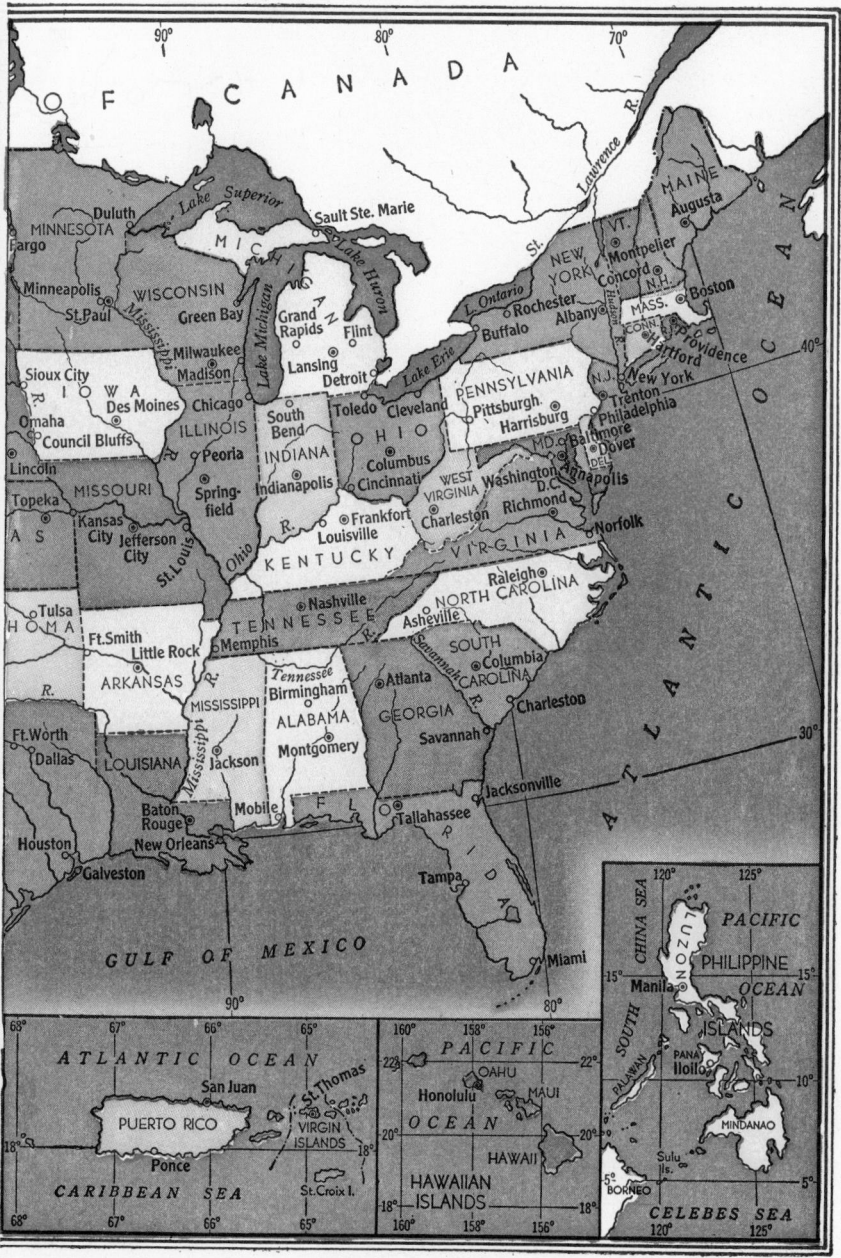

of their age had been attained, and with a conviction that the wonders of the future would far surpass anything they had yet seen. They learned much, too, about the rest of the world that schoolroom lessons in geography could never have taught them, and in consequence were better prepared for the era of international change so soon to burst upon them. And whether they traveled to the East or to the West or to both, by automobile or by streamlined train or by airplane, they could hardly fail to observe the limitless resources with which their country was blessed, and the anachronism of poverty and unemployment in a land so rich.[1]

[1] F. L. Allen, *Since Yesterday* (1940), is a worthy successor to *Only Yesterday*. D. W. Brogan, *The American Character* (1944), is the work of an observing Britisher. Walter Johnson, *William Allen White's America* (1947), covers both this period and the era that preceded it. John Gunther, *Inside U.S.A.* (1947), portrays journalistically the United States after the Second World War, but the number of similarities with the earlier period is surprisingly large. H. M. Jones, *Ideas in America* (1944), is thoughtful and provocative. R. H. Shryock, *American Medical Research Past and Present* (1948), fills a long-needed gap. Helen Clapesattle, *The Doctors Mayo* (1941), examines the record of a famous medical clinic. Angie Debo, *Prairie City: The Story of an American Community* (1944), is first-rate social history; and the same may be said of another book by the same author, *Tulsa: From Creek Town to Oil Capital* (1943). Bayrd Still, *Milwaukee* (1948), is another successful attempt at urban history. A. H. Quinn, *History of the American Drama from the Civil War to the Present Day* (1939), is a useful summary. Darrell Garwood, *Artist in Iowa: A Life of Grant Wood* (1944), shows the middlewestern contribution to painting. F. C. Kelly, *The Wright Brothers* (1943), does justice to the subject. Gunnar Myrdal, *An American Dilemma: The Negro Problem and Modern Democracy* (2 vols., 1944), is a work of extraordinary perspicacity.

37

The Great Depression

HERBERT HOOVER (1874–   ) was born at West Branch, Iowa, the son
of Quaker parents. Left an orphan at an early age, he worked his way
through college, and ultimately graduated in mining engineering at Leland Stanford University. In pursuit of his
specialty he saw much of the world — Mexico, Canada, Australia, India,
China, and Russia — and as a promoter he amassed a modest fortune.
Living in England at the outbreak of the World War, he was a natural
choice to head overseas relief work, and served as chairman, first of the
American Relief Commission, and later of the Commission for the Relief
of Belgium. In these offices, as Food Administrator during American
participation in the World War, and as Secretary of Commerce he had
demonstrated repeatedly his extraordinary ability as an administrator.
His life-history was the typical American success story; with variations
it could be made to fit the hopes of every normal American youth.

The Hoover administration was certain to encounter difficulties even
if it had been blessed with good times. The new President was fundamentally a business executive rather than a politician, and showed little
skill in appeasing the leaders of his party, many of whom were disgruntled at his success in "muscling in." His cabinet, headed by Henry
L. Stimson, formerly governor-general of the Philippines, was undistinguished, and added little to his political strength. Mellon was kept
on as Secretary of the Treasury less because Hoover wanted him, or so
many believed, than because of the esteem in which he was held by the
business interests of the country; all the others, including the Secretary
of State, were virtually unknown to the general public. Prohibition was
sure to be a nightmare, and farm relief a perpetual despair. Furthermore, tariff revision, the political reef upon which many preceding administrations had been wrecked, was imminent. During the campaign
Hoover in a weak moment had promised the farmers an increase in agricultural duties. He hoped to escape a general tariff revision, but a more
experienced politician would have foreseen that once tariff tampering
had begun, there would be little chance of limiting its scope.

Hoover was scarcely well seated in the presidential chair, however, when the Great Depression began, and his administration, like Cleveland's second, became indelibly associated in the public mind with hard times. Quite in the fashion of previous depressions, the Great Depression was preceded by a long period of speculation, this time mainly in the stocks and bonds of business corporations. The prosperity of the twenties was to a remarkable extent corporation prosperity. Few individuals owned great businesses; Henry Ford was an outstanding exception. Most "big businesses" were jointly owned by hundreds or thousands of stockholders, whose investments might vary from a hundred-dollar share to values running far into the millions. Throughout the prosperous twenties the multiplication of stocks went on with ever-increasing tempo, and into such investments multitudes of individuals placed their savings, great and small. The fact that American business was actually owned by millions of investors was regarded with satisfaction by President Hoover and others as proof of its essential democracy, but any careful examination of corporation statistics was apt to prove that a comparatively small number of investors owned the greater part of the stock. Moreover, the direction of a given industry lay inevitably with the few insiders who represented the largest holdings. In a sense the control of business was less democratic than ever before. With investments so widely diffused, the individual with a three per cent holding might be as powerful as the majority stockholder of an earlier age.

Background of the Great Depression

While many of those who purchased stocks were genuinely interested in obtaining sound investments, many others operated only as speculators, buying when prices were low, and selling when they rose. Most small purchasers bought "on margin," depositing only enough money with their brokers to cover the probable range of fluctuation. They were sure to encounter difficulties if their guesses went wrong. This speculative demand for stocks was to a great extent responsible for the generally high price-level to which securities rose during the later twenties. More frequently than not the actual earning power of a given stock was far too low to justify the prices at which it sold; valuations equal to twenty-five times the interest returns were by no means uncommon. Optimists refused to be alarmed at the situation, and insisted that the high prices paid for American securities were merely an evidence of the healthy condition of American enterprise. Investors had faith, and were willing to back it with their dollars, in the soundness of American business. Even the Federal Reserve Board, at least indirectly, supported the speculation, for it allowed loans to corporations ostensibly interested in programs of expansion, only to see the

Stock speculation

funds so obtained quickly passed along to the speculators. Between September, 1927, and September, 1929, borrowings for speculation on the New York Stock Exchange rose from three and one-third to eight and one-half billion dollars. Prices of stocks, in the language of one misguided observer, soared upward to "what looks like a permanently high plateau." An issue never known to pay a dividend climbed steadily from forty dollars to four hundred and fifty dollars a share.

In the midst of all this madness a few warning voices pointed out that the business cycle might not be as obsolete as many seemed to believe, and that a crisis was probably close at hand. Too much of the country's credit was being diverted into stock-exchange loans, and industry as a result of the easy money was being tempted to overexpand. Who was to buy all the goods that producers could make and sell? Already the building boom that had characterized the earlier twenties was on the decline, automobile sales were off, and oil production far exceeded the demand. But these wise protests were brushed aside by optimists in high places who counseled against selling America short, and assured investors that all was well. Two days before the market crashed, Charles E. Mitchell, president of the National City Bank of New York, asserted unequivocally: "I know of nothing fundamentally wrong with the stock market or with the underlying business and credit structures."

The stock-market collapse came in October, 1929, when English interest rates were raised to six and one-half per cent in order to bring home needed capital that had been attracted to the United States by the high speculative profits. As a result many European holdings were thrown on the market, and prices began to sag. Frightened at the prospect, and no longer able to borrow at will, American speculators also began to unload. On Thursday, October 24, 1929, 12,800,000 shares changed hands and until October 29, when the sales reached 16,410,030 shares, the frantic selling continued. During the month of October the value of stocks listed on the New York Stock Exchange declined from eighty-seven billion to fifty-five billion dollars, or about thirty-seven per cent. And this, it developed, was only the beginning. In spite of repeated assurances from high authorities, both in government and finance, that prosperity lay "just around the corner," no less than nine similar declines to "new low levels" were recorded within the next three years. By the first of March, 1933, the value of all stocks listed on the New York Stock Exchange was set at only nineteen billion dollars, less than one-fifth the inflated figures of October 1, 1929.

In spite of optimistic efforts to maintain that the stock-market collapse was purely a paper loss which would not seriously undermine the

Panic of 1929

fundamental soundness of American business, it was soon evident that a period of unparalleled depression had begun. Prices dropped sharply; foreign trade fell off; factories curtailed production, or in many cases closed their doors never to reopen them; real estate values (but not mortgages) declined; new construction, except on governmental works, practically ceased; banks went under; worst of all, wages were cut drastically and unemployment figures began to mount. By the end of 1930 about six or seven million workers were out of jobs; two years later the number had doubled. Nor was the United States alone in its distress. No longer able to secure American loans, foreign nations fell likewise into the abyss of depression; indeed, many of them, like Germany, had not far to fall. Once again the isolationist-minded people of the United States were to learn by experience that whatever seriously affected one great nation was bound to affect all.

Efforts to account for the plunge from prosperity to adversity soon demonstrated conclusively that no one factor alone, but only a great number of factors working together, could have produced such startling results. Economists were also able to reach substantial agreement as to the principal causes of the depression, although they were by no means in harmony as to the degree of responsibility to be assigned to each cause.[1] Among other disturbing influences they cited the following:

Causes of the depression

1. Agricultural overexpansion, both in the United States and elsewhere. American farmers produced more wheat, cotton, corn, livestock, and other commodities than they could sell at satisfactory prices, and to some extent the same condition existed in much of the rest of the world. Agricultural surpluses piled up at home and abroad with devastating effect on the price of each new crop. Farm purchases steadily declined, for the farmers had less and less with which to buy. Payments on the heavy mortgage burden assumed in more prosperous times still further curtailed the farmers' buying power, and drove many of them to tenancy.

Agricultural overexpansion

2. Industrial overexpansion. The American industrial plant had been overbuilt during the period of the boom, and could not be operated at maximum capacity. There were too many factories, and too much machinery. American industry was geared to produce far more than it could sell. Automobiles, for example, had been turned out in steadily increasing numbers during the

Industrial overexpansion

---

[1] The analysis of causes given in Brookings Institution, *The Recovery Problem in the United States* (1936), may be compared with the similar attempt in Hacker, *American Problems of Today*. See also W. Z. Ripley, *Main Street and Wall Street* (1927); W. B. Donham, *Business Adrift* (1931); Fred A. Shannon, *America's Economic Growth* (1940); and, for a popular account, G. V. Seldes, *The Years of the Locust: America, 1929–1932* (1933).

twenties to supply a new market. But the time came when every American family that could afford to own an automobile (and many who could not) had one or sometimes more than one. With twenty-six and one-half million motor cars in operation by 1929, the market for automobiles was confined largely to replacements. The same condition existed in the housing industry. Rapid building during the twenties had overexpanded the lumber industry and others concerned with the production of building materials. But the time came when all the people who could afford to build new houses had built them, and plants that had once flourished stood idle.

3. The increasing effectiveness of machines. Ingenious labor-saving devices made possible greater production with comparatively less labor. Fewer and fewer men produced more and more goods. "Technological unemployment" might not be permanent, but at least the men who were thrown out of work by the new machines had to seek other jobs, and they sometimes failed to find them. Thus the buying power of labor was diminished. The new machines might make more goods, but whose wages were to pay for them? Introduction of these labor-saving devices might well have been paralleled by increased wages, a shortening of the labor day and the labor week, and a diminishing use of women and children in industry. But only occasionally were such accompaniments recorded.

Labor-saving machines

4. Capital surpluses were too high; as a prominent banker, Frank D. Vanderlip, expressed it, "Capital kept too much and labor did not have enough to buy its share of things."[1] This was the more easily possible because of the monopolistic nature of much American business, which so greatly facilitated the control of prices. Throughout the boom years the tendency of business was to take too long profits, and to reinvest the capital thus accumulated in order to produce still more goods, which in return might produce still more profits. A wider distribution of earnings, particularly if paid out in the form of higher wages, might well have stimulated purchasing power and diminished the danger of ultimate collapse.

Capital surpluses

5. The overexpansion of credit, both for productive and consumptive purposes. Money was plentiful and cheap throughout the twenties, and the policy of the Federal Reserve Board was definitely to keep it so. It was too easy to borrow, whether for business expansion, for speculation, or for the satisfaction of personal desires. There was too much installment buying, and too much of the national income was diverted into interest payments. In keeping with

Overexpansion of credit

---

[1] Quoted by L. M. Hacker and B. B. Kendrick, *The United States Since 1865* (1932), p. 729.

the speculative spirit of the time, purchasers cheerfully mortgaged their futures to obtain goods that would often be consumed before they could be paid for.

6. International trade was out of balance. European nations, with their economies badly shattered by the war, had depended mainly on funds borrowed from American investors to pay for imports and to stabilize foreign exchange. The only way they might **Decline of** have repaid these obligations was by shipping goods to the **international trade** United States. But the Fordney-McCumber Act of 1922, followed by the Hawley-Smoot Act of 1930, definitely forestalled any such possibility. The debtor nations of Europe in self-defense were obliged to adopt high-tariff policies, and by various other expedients to stimulate whatever industries were necessary to cut down their reliance on foreign goods. During the years of 1922–27 the production of British-made automobiles, for example, was increased from forty-nine per cent of the domestic supply to eighty-six per cent. Thus the United States, blindly committed to the protective principles of an earlier age, stood to lose both its export business and a good share of the money by which this business had been sustained. Many manufacturers understood the situation, and did their best to prevent the adoption of tariffs that in the long run were certain to bring disaster, but most Americans were slow to recognize that international trade was a "two-way street," and were quite unprepared for the collapse that followed the withdrawal of American credits.

7. Political unrest throughout the world, particularly in Europe, Asia, and South America, added to the difficulties in the way of a sustained prosperity. The intergovernmental debts, whether **Political** funded or not, constituted a continuing threat both to trade **unrest** and to international good feelings. The reparations problem remained unsettled. Most countries were overburdened with governmental debts, and few national budgets were in balance. Agitation for independence was chronic in India, the designs of Japan toward China were abundantly clear, and warfare was imminent between Bolivia and Paraguay over the Chaco. Altogether the international skies seemed dark, and the prospects of a return to "normalcy" as far away as ever.

Hoover's program for the relief of agriculture actually was enacted into law well before the panic days of October, 1929, but the depression in agriculture was of long standing. The Agricultural Mar- **The FFB** keting Act, signed June 15, 1929, was designed to help agriculture help itself by means of voluntary co-operation. Proponents of the measure believed that, with appropriate federal encouragement, the farmers could work together through co-operatives in such a way as to apply in their businesses the same principles of orderly production and distribution that governed the activities of prudent manufacturers. They could thus find means to curtail production whenever necessary, to shift to different crops as demands changed, and to eliminate wasteful and expensive methods of marketing. The act created a Federal Farm Board of eight members, and provided it with a half-billion-dollar revolving fund from which it could lend to co-operatives, and to such stabilization corporations as it might set up for the purpose of buying, storing, and selling surpluses.[1]

The Federal Farm Board began operations at once, with Alexander Legge of the International Harvester Company as its chairman. In its efforts to stimulate the formation of co-operatives it was entirely successful, and loans for this purpose during the first year of its operation amounted to over $165,000,000. There is no reason to doubt that these activities contributed significantly to the orderly marketing of nearly every type of crop produced in the United States. Much sound advice was also distributed as to the curtailment of production in crops where the market was glutted, although other governmental agencies, particularly the Department of Agriculture and the agricultural colleges, considerably confused the situation by explaining to the farmers how more and more of the same commodities might be grown on less but better soil.

With respect to wheat and cotton it soon became apparent that something far more drastic than co-operative marketing was necessary if the rapid downward trend of prices was to be stopped. Accordingly, in 1930, a Grain Stabilization Corporation and a Cotton Stabilization Corporation were set up, each with authority to buy in the open market in order to raise prices. As long as governmental purchases continued, the effect on the price of wheat and cotton was good, but after a year or two the Stabilization Corporations found themselves in possession of vast stores of produce that they were unable to market. In June, 1931, the Grain Corporation, with an unmarketed and seemingly unmarketable supply of 257,000,000 bushels of wheat on its hands, ceased its purchases, and the next month the price of wheat dropped to fifty-seven cents. Meantime, the Cotton Corporation, after purchasing the carry-over from two successive seasons, had accumulated three and a quarter million bales of cotton in its warehouses, and was also forced to acknowledge defeat. In 1932 the price of cotton dropped to as low as five cents a pound. The following year the Federal Farm

Stabilization activities

---

[1] E. R. A. Seligman, *The Economics of Farm Relief* (1929); Bernhard Ostrolenk, *The Surplus Farmer* (1932); E. F. Dummeier and R. B. Heflebower, *Economics with Applications to Agriculture* (1934); E. G. Nourse and associates, *America's Capacity to Produce* (1934).

Board ended its brief career with total losses set at about $184,000,000. No doubt it also had much to its credit, but its tangible benefits were difficult to discover or assess.[1]

Meantime, Congress had plunged eagerly into the revision of the tariff that Hoover had promised. For months before the special session of Congress convened, the House Ways and Means Committee had been holding hearings, and on May 7, 1929, its chairman, Willis C. Hawley of Oregon, introduced a bill *The Hawley-Smoot Tariff* that did not far exceed the limited recommendations of the President. But a log-rolling generosity at once developed which resulted in the amendment of the original bill to suit the demands of practically every congressman with a constituency to conciliate. As it passed the House later in the month, the Hawley Bill was already a general revision of the tariff with a scale of duties far higher than those of the record-breaking Fordney-McCumber Act of 1922. The Senate Finance Committee, headed by Reed Smoot of Utah, altered the bill in detail, but not greatly in principle. When the Senate debate opened, insurgency developed, and for a time it seemed that a coalition of Democrats and independent Republicans might bring about some important readjustments. Unfortunately a succession of deals with individual members of the coalition weakened the opposition and made possible the retention of the extremely high rates. Some of the supposedly most intransigeant insurgents were induced to vote for increases that they would otherwise have opposed in order to obtain in return increases that pressure groups among their constituents earnestly desired. Such insurgents as could not be bought off tried to improve the measure by including within it the export debenture plan for the relief of agriculture, and a flexible schedule clause which would have given Congress rather than the President authority to act on changes recommended by the Tariff Commission; but ultimately, largely because of pressure from the President, both provisions were stricken out. The Hawley-Smoot Tariff, as it came from the conference committee, accepted in the main the higher rates proposed by either house, and raised the general level of protection by about seven per cent. In the Senate the final vote was 44 to 42. Five Democrats, from Louisiana (sugar), Florida (fruit), and Wyoming (wool), voted with the majority, while eleven Republicans and one Farmer-Laborite voted against it.

In spite of a rising volume of criticism directed against the measure, Hoover gave it his signature (June 17, 1930). It was not what he had

---

[1] The activities of the Hoover administration are covered intimately and defended in two difficult books, W. S. Myers and W. H. Newton, *The Hoover Administration: A Documented Narrative* (1936), and R. L. Wilbur and A. M. Hyde, *The Hoover Policies* (1937).

wished, and he did not disguise his disappointment; but neither did he heed the petition of more than a thousand American economists who explained cogently the pressing need for a presidential veto. According to this "round robin," which was signed by practically all the leading economists of the country, the Hawley-Smoot Tariff was certain (1) to raise prices for the American consumer; (2) to encourage wasteful and unnecessary concerns to remain in business; (3) to limit the exportation of American products, both from farm and factory, by restricting imports, (4) to yield no benefits to the farmers whose prices were fixed by what the exportable surplus would bring; and (5) to insure reprisals from foreign countries whose trade would be adversely affected. Probably all of these predictions came true, but on the last there was no room for doubt. While the bill was under consideration, protests against its passage were registered by trade associations in nearly every European country, and immediately after its passage reprisals set in. One of the first came from Canada, which promptly increased the rates on most of its important imports from the United States, and others came thick and fast. In 1932 Great Britain, whose devotion to free trade had long been slipping, veered completely over to the protective tariff policy. For the establishment of these higher trade barriers in the face of world-wide depression the United States bore a leading responsibility.[1]

There can be no doubt that Hoover was greatly shocked by the advent of the Great Depression. During the campaign of 1928 he had promised the electorate a "final triumph over poverty" if only the country were "given a chance to go forward with the policies of the last eight years." But instead of the promised prosperity, there was adversity on every hand. Faced by this situation, Hoover deemed it his duty as President to aid business in fighting its way back to recovery. For a time he directed his efforts mainly toward obtaining the voluntary co-operation of business and labor leaders in measures of self-help. At a series of conferences in Washington he talked against the curtailment of buying power that must inevitably follow the reduction of payrolls, and urged that "the first shock" of the depression "must fall on profits and not on wages." He insisted that wage scales ought not for the moment to be lowered at all, and that when reductions became unavoidable they should be made only in proportion as the cost of living went down. He hoped that expenditures for construction would not be curtailed, and succeeded in committing many industries to a policy of expansion in spite of the unsettled economic conditions. But "business as usual" soon proved to be a difficult formula for executives to maintain in the face of declining receipts and

Hoover fights the depression

[1] J. M. Jones, *Tariff Retaliation* (1934).

mounting inventories. Sometimes efforts were made to "spread the work" by lessening the number of hours per week permitted each individual, but in spite of good intentions wages did go down and unemployment figures began to mount.

As the economic skies continued to darken, Hoover began to inaugurate policies far more radical in character. Early in 1930 he asked and obtained from Congress huge sums to be used in the erection of public buildings, the improvement of rivers and harbors, and the building of federal roads. By these and similar expenditures, voted later, he sought earnestly to take up the slack of unemployment. Before he left office more than two and a quarter billion dollars had been appropriated for such purposes. For a long time, however, the President stood out against any more direct effort on the part of the national government to deal with the problem of unemployment. Direct relief, he maintained, was a function of the states, the municipalities, and voluntary organizations. But eventually he was obliged to admit that only the national government had the resources in taxes and credit necessary to meet the existing emergency. He therefore asked Congress for funds from which loans could be made to such states as were no longer able to finance their own relief expenditures, and in spite of the growing strain on the budget these appropriations were made. To administer these and other necessary loans, Hoover induced Congress to create a Reconstruction Finance Corporation, patterned somewhat after the War Finance Corporation of the Wilson administration. The RFC, with Charles G. Dawes of Chicago as its first president, lent freely not only to the states but also to banks, agricultural credit corporations, life insurance companies, and other financial organizations, and to the hard-pressed railroads. Many bankruptcies were thus forestalled or delayed. Loans actually disbursed before Hoover left office amounted to nearly two billion dollars. For the benefit of home-owners who were about to lose their property, Hoover encouraged the passage of the Home Loan Bank Act of July 22, 1932. Under its terms a series of Home Loan Banks were established to discount home mortgages, and thus to provide home-owners with a service similar to that rendered by the Federal Reserve Banks in the commercial field. The large appropriations necessary to carry these various measures into effect unbalanced the national budget by many billions of dollars long before the "New Deal" was inaugurated.[1]

Not all of the actions taken by the Hoover administration in its

[1] W. S. Myers, editor, *State Papers and Other Public Writings of Herbert Hoover* (2 vols., 1934), furnishes a complete documentary record of the Hoover administration. Also useful is T. G. Joslin, *Hoover — Off the Record* (1934).

efforts to deal with the depression were concerned with internal affairs.
When in March, 1931, France refused to permit Germany and Austria
to unite in a customs union, a train of events was set in motion which
led to the almost complete collapse of European finance. Until that
time the depression had remained primarily an American affair, but
from then on its world-wide character was abundantly apparent. The
finances of central Europe sank first, but eventually every European
nation was affected, including Great Britain, which in September, 1931,
was forced to abandon the gold standard. American investors in
foreign securities, particularly those of Germany, were hard hit, and
American trade with Europe was more drastically curtailed than ever
before.

Believing that the huge burden of intergovernmental debts constituted
one of the chief impediments to world trade, and therefore to world
recovery, Hoover in June, 1931, advocated a moratorium
for one year on both the principal and interest of all such
obligations. This action was deeply resented by France, who
wished to continue her collections from Germany, and it was far from
popular in the United States; but in due time it was accepted by the fifteen governments involved and went into effect. At the Lausanne Conference of 1932 the European powers attempted to solve the debt riddle
for all time by granting Germany a three-year moratorium on reparations, and by establishing a new low figure, $714,000,000, as the amount
to be paid. All this, however, was contingent upon the willingness of
the United States to cancel its war debts. Many American businessmen, believing that private debts from abroad could be more readily
collected if the public debt were out of the way, favored cancellation,
but neither Hoover nor his successor, Roosevelt, conceded this point.
Reparation payments were never resumed by Germany, and when the
moratorium ended in 1932 only six governments, Great Britain, Czechoslovakia, Italy, Finland, Latvia, and Lithuania, met their obligations
to the United States. The next year all these nations, except Finland,
made only small token payments, and after that no payments at all.
The attitude of Finland, which paid in full every year, even after its
territory was invaded by Russia in the winter of 1939–40, won much
acclaim in the United States, but the sums involved were small. In
1934 Congress passed the Johnson Act, which prohibited Americans
from purchasing the securities of any nation in default on its debt to the
United States. By this time the debts in fact, if not in law, had ceased
to be, and their restraining influence upon the course of international
trade could not have been great.

The effect of the depression upon the political fortunes of Herbert

Hoover and the party he represented was disastrous. The mid-term election of 1930, although held before there was any real comprehension of the seriousness of the economic situation, indicated clearly that the administration had lost the confidence of the country. As a result of the voting, the Senate was almost evenly divided between Republicans and Democrats, and the House was Democratic by a small margin. That the Republicans were due for a serious defeat in 1932 seemed clear, but the Republican convention had no choice but to stand on its record. Both Hoover and Curtis were renominated, and the Hoover policies were accorded unstinted praise. The Democrats, after a lively contest, emerged with Franklin D. Roosevelt, popular two-term governor of New York, as their candidate for President, and John Nance Garner, Speaker of the House during the preceding two years, as their candidate for Vice-President. During the campaign Roosevelt, in a series of carefully phrased speeches, called for a "New Deal" in government that aroused the greatest alarm in conservative circles, but the electorate liked the candidate's promises, and would probably have voted for him anyway. When the returns were in, it was apparent that Hoover had been as badly defeated by Roosevelt as four years before Smith had been defeated by Hoover. The electoral vote stood 472 to 59, and the popular vote, 22,809,638 to 15,758,901. Hoover carried only six states, Maine, New Hampshire, Vermont, Connecticut, Delaware, and Pennsylvania. Both houses of Congress were as overwhelmingly Democratic as they had been Republican four years before, and in the states the Democratic landslide carried into office many candidates who had regarded their names on the party ticket as either a courtesy or a joke. In general, the dissatisfied elements of society supported Roosevelt, but the existence of a small more radical minority was revealed by the vote of 884,781 for Norman Thomas, the Socialist candidate, and 102,991 for William Z. Foster, the Communist.[1] According to the Republican version, it was the prospect of Roosevelt's election, climaxed by the election itself, which gave the final blow to business confidence, and caused the very bottom to drop out of the depression.

The Twentieth Amendment to the Constitution, which was proclaimed in effect on February 6, 1933, was designed to do away with the "lame-duck" session of the defeated Congress, and to provide for an earlier date than March 4 for the inauguration. But the adoption of this Amendment came too late to save the Hoover administration the embarrassment of having to deal with a critical situation after it had been discredited at the

Election of 1932

[1] The Communist Party in the United States dated back to 1919, when an American section of the Third International was organized at Chicago. From the first it drew its inspiration from Russia. Known for a time as the Workers' Party, it operated covertly at first, but by 1924 was out in the open.

polls. Until March 4, 1933, Hoover was President, and the old Congress, not the one just elected, was in session.

In attempting to deal with this difficult situation, Hoover twice sought to enlist the co-operation of the President-elect, once with reference to the war-debts problem, and once in an effort to check the rapidly mounting number of bank failures. In each instance Roosevelt visited the White House, talked affably with the President, but refused to commit himself in advance as to the course his administration would take. He promised to discuss war debts and other economic problems with a representative of the British government soon after March 4, but he was wholly unwilling to join with Hoover in a statement that he would not countenance money inflation, an unbalanced budget, or the flotation of loans so heavy as to impair the credit of the government. In view of the later policies of the Roosevelt administration it is not surprising that the President-elect side-stepped this suggestion. As Hoover himself admitted, it would have meant the "abandonment of ninety per cent of the so-called New Deal." Congress, too, now more responsive to the wishes of Roosevelt than to the pleas of the President, turned down the latter's recommendations for reduced expenditures and new taxes to balance the budget, for a complete reorganization of the executive departments, and for such reforms in the nation's financial system as, he believed, would put an end to bank failures.

Hoover and Roosevelt

Whether it was fair or not to blame the banking crisis that had developed upon an administration that had not yet taken office, there could be no doubt as to the gravity of the situation. Unemployment was at its worst during the winter of 1932–33, with the number of men out of work estimated at anywhere from thirteen million to seventeen million. Production in one great industry after another dropped to almost negligible proportions. Fear that the financial structure of the country was endangered showed in the mounting totals of gold exported and of gold and currency hoarded; by the middle of February each item had grown to about fifteen million dollars a day. In Detroit, where the drastic curtailment of automobile production had created a peculiarly difficult situation, the banks held on grimly, but by Lincoln's Birthday they were near the breaking point. Loaded down with frozen assets and drained of their deposits by frightened customers, they escaped collapse only when the governor of the state on his own authority extended the holiday period by eight days, and then obtained from the legislature the right to prolong it if need be still further. With the Michigan banks suspended, the panic spread to one state after another, and nearly every state executive declared a long bank holiday. Meantime, President Hoover, unable to secure any co-operation from

The banking crisis

the President-elect, watched helplessly while the financial machinery of the nation came virtually to a standstill. When Roosevelt took office the zero hour had seemingly been reached.

In Franklin Delano Roosevelt (1882–1945) the nation had a President whose picturesque career rivaled that of his distant relative, Theodore Roosevelt. Born to a comfortable fortune, as the other Roosevelt had been also, he was a graduate of Groton and **Franklin D. Roosevelt** Harvard, had been frequently abroad, spoke French almost as fluently as English, and had acquired at least an elementary knowledge of the law. In 1905 he had married his sixth cousin, Eleanor Roosevelt, a favorite niece of the President's; and, like the other Roosevelts, they became the parents of a large and versatile family. Young Roosevelt, although a Democrat by birthright, never disguised his admiration for the President whose name he bore, and tended consciously or unconsciously to pattern after him. In 1910 he was a member of the New York legislature, and won the undying enmity of the Tammany machine by his fight against its candidate for the United States Senate, William F. Sheehan. Partly because his name was Roosevelt, and partly because he knew about ships, he became Assistant Secretary of the Navy under Woodrow Wilson, a post of great responsibility which he filled with ability during the World War. In 1920 he was the unsuccessful Democratic candidate for Vice-President, and after the campaign made preparations for a business career. The transformation of Roosevelt from a retired minor politician to a dynamic leader of men began when he was laid low in August, 1921, by an attack of infantile paralysis that left him hopelessly crippled in both legs. By an unsurpassed exhibition of will power he fought his way back to health and even learned to walk again, although not without need of firm support. Utterly unconquered in spirit, he read widely, corresponded with the leaders of the Democratic Party, and dedicated himself to its rebuilding along liberal lines. In 1928, in spite of the Hoover landslide, he was elected governor of New York, and two years later he was triumphantly re-elected. As governor he inaugurated few policies of note, but his ability to deal adroitly with all matters affecting human nature, his unfailing good humor, and his consuming interest in new ideas made him a marked man.[1]

Whatever unwillingness he might have shown to accept responsibility before he took office, the new President showed no such hesitation after March 4, 1933. His cabinet included none of the great names — Owen D. Young, Newton D. Baker, John W. **Roosevelt's "brain trust"** Davis, Alfred E. Smith, and the like — pressed upon him by

---

[1] Gerald W. Johnson, *Roosevelt: Dictator or Democrat* (1941), is a sympathetic study of Roosevelt's career and the underlying philosophy of the New Deal.

those who doubted his ability, and showed his evident determination to be his own master. All observers agreed that the little coterie of "bright young men" surrounding the President, called by the public the "brain trust," would have much more to do with the shaping of his policies than the somewhat nondescript cabinet he had constructed.[1] During his campaign he had relied heavily upon the assistance of this group, which included among others three Columbia University professors, Raymond Moley (public law), Rexford Guy Tugwell (economics), and Adolph A. Berle, Jr. (corporation law). From these advisers, scorned as theorists alike by "hard-headed" businessmen and "hard-boiled" politicians, he obtained many of the ideas he now proposed to translate into deeds.

There was no lack of presidential leadership in dealing with the banking crisis. The next day after the inauguration the President closed every bank in the country, and by the time he had assembled Congress in special session on March 9 he had ready for instant passage an Emergency Banking Act. Breaking all known records, the law received the Presi-

[1] The members of Roosevelt's original cabinet were: Cordell Hull, Secretary of State; William H. Woodin, Secretary of the Treasury (soon replaced by Henry Morganthau, Jr.); George H. Dern, Secretary of War; Claude A. Swanson, Secretary of the Navy; Harold L. Ickes, Secretary of the Interior; James A. Farley, Postmaster-General; H. S. Cummings, Attorney-General; Henry A. Wallace, Secretary of Agriculture; D. C. Roper, Secretary of Commerce; Frances Perkins, Secretary of Labor.

PROBLEMS OF THE DEPRESSION

Calling themselves the "Bonus Expeditionary Force," but called by the public the "Bonus Army," or the "B.E.F.," some fifteen thousand unemployed and needy veterans of the first World War descended upon Washington in the spring of 1932. They hoped to persuade Congress that the bonus certificates they had been voted in 1924 should be paid immediately, but in this they were disappointed. When Congress adjourned, a large proportion of the men accepted the government's offer of passage money home, but others stayed on, living in vacant Washington buildings or at "Bonus City" on Anacostia Island. Under orders from President Hoover, troops of the United States Army on July 28 expelled the veterans, some of whom were accompanied by their families, from their quarters and from the District. (Photo from Keystone.)

A quite different legacy of the war came from the western plains, where much grassland had been brought under cultivation during the war to provide the extra food needed. A series of unprecedentedly dry years during the nineteen-thirties left the top soil at the mercy of the high winds, which from 1933 on made a veritable "dustbowl" of certain portions of Kansas, Colorado, New Mexico, Oklahoma, and Texas. Certain parts of Wyoming, Nebraska, and the Dakotas suffered almost as much, and great dust clouds from the West appeared as far east as the Atlantic seaboard. A dust storm and its effects are shown in the pictures. (Photos from Keystone and the United States Department of Agriculture.)

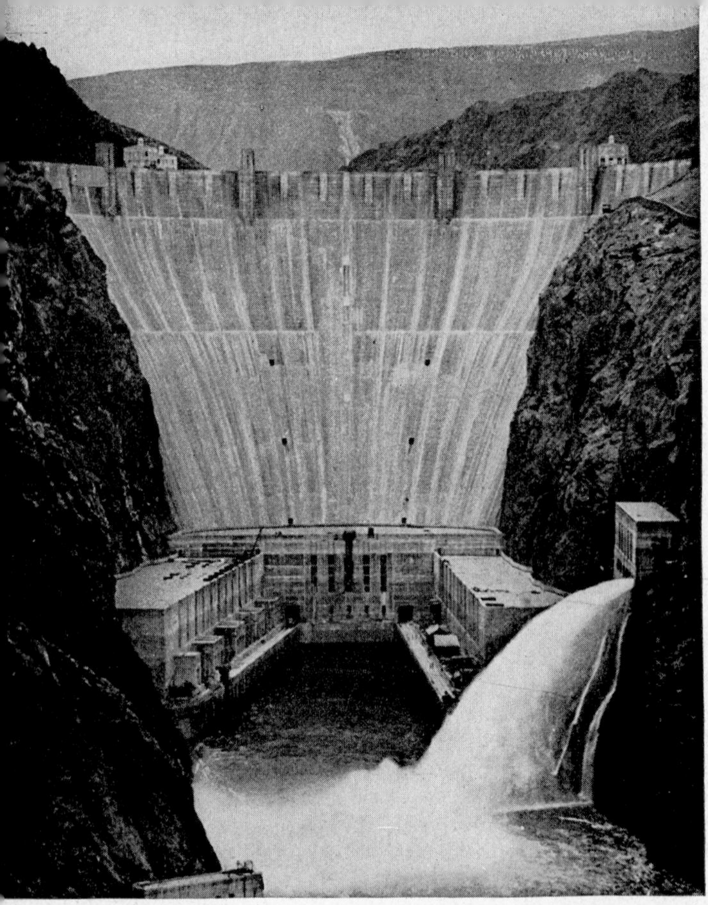

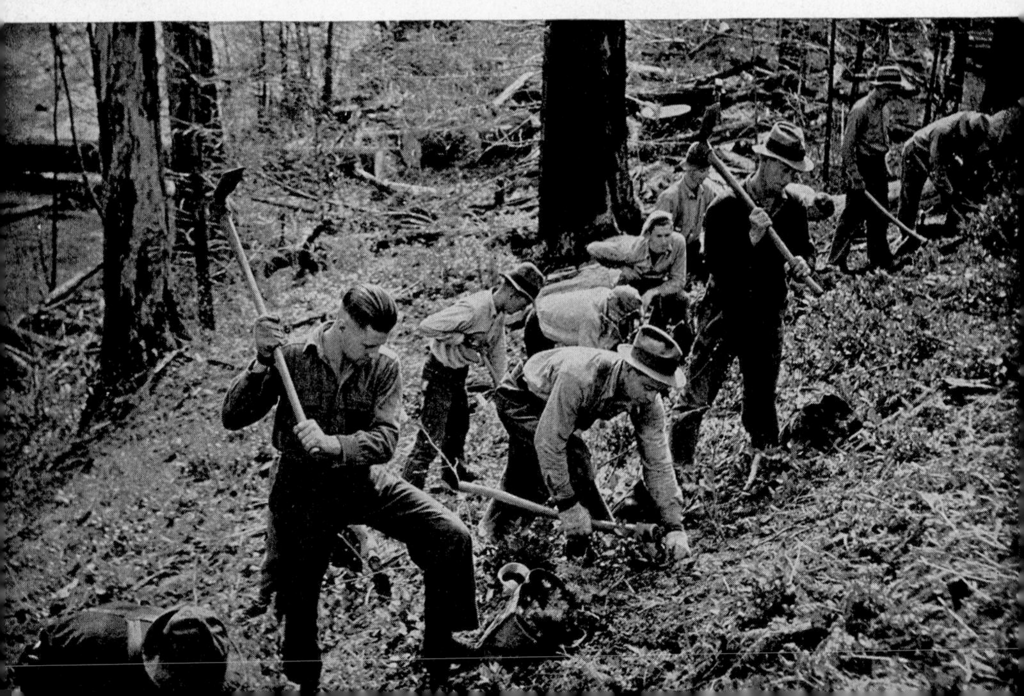

dent's signature before the day was over. This measure authorized the Secretary of the Treasury to call in all gold, whether in the shape of coin, bullion, or gold certificates; it provided for the examination and reopening of all banks deemed sound, and for a system of "conservators" to take charge of all others; and it authorized an extensive issue of emergency currency to be used if necessary in halting runs. By March 13, such banks as federal examiners found solvent began to reopen, and the government's guaranty of their stability proved sufficient to restore public confidence. Only fifteen million dollars' worth of the new emergency currency had to be used, and millions of dollars that the banks had paid out during the crisis to anxious depositors began to flow back. Some three thousand banks, scattered throughout the country, were either reopened under conservators or were not reopened at all, but there was no longer any reason to doubt the essential soundness of the banking structure, and business proceeded as usual.

During the next few weeks the President had occasion again and again to demonstrate his capacity for effective leadership. Relying as he must on the support of public opinion, he showed an unerring sense of the dramatic. Whether in a radio appeal to the nation or in a personally delivered message to Congress, he *Presidential leadership* never failed to time his pronouncements exactly and irresistibly right. He held frequent conferences with the representatives of the press, took

---

PRODUCTS OF THE THIRTIES

The Civilian Conservation Corps was established in March, 1933, and lasted until June, 1942, when its enrollees were discharged and its equipment turned over to the armed forces or to other agencies. During its lifetime the CCC was one of the most popular of the New Deal innovations. Its purpose was to conserve both "natural and human resources." Some three million youths participated in its activities, which were said to have advanced conservation in the United States by more than thirty years — a good start "in the direction of a balanced national resources budget." These men planting trees in a burnt-over forest region are typical of the CCC.

Boulder Dam is part of the Boulder Canyon Project initiated by the national government in 1928. It is located on the Colorado River between Arizona and Nevada and is over seven hundred feet in height. It impounds in a great artificial lake the surplus waters of the Colorado River and makes possible their use for irrigation and the generation of electrical energy. With only ten of its great generators installed, it had in 1942 a capacity of 952,300 kilowatts. Boulder Dam, for all its size, is only the third largest concrete dam in the United States, the largest being the Grand Coulee Dam in Washington, and the second largest, the Shasta Dam, part of the great Central Valley Project of California. (Photos from Galloway.)

them freely into his confidence, made them like him, and obtained through them a steady stream of favorable publicity. Like Theodore Roosevelt and Woodrow Wilson before him, he had no scruples as to the constitutional right of the Executive to direct the course of legislation. His energetic "brain-trusters," sometimes without much help from congressional committees, drafted the laws that Congress was called upon to pass. Whenever he could he used the same tactics on legislators that he used on newspapermen, but he was entirely capable of sterner measures. Farley, his patronage broker, kept books on every congressman, and it was an open secret that those who voted with the President could hope to have their recommendations for appointments honored, while those who voted against him could not. The President knew, too, that the best time to get his program through was while the country still regarded the steps taken as essential to meet an emergency, and while congressmen, with their hunger for patronage unappeased, were unwilling to interrupt the "honeymoon" period with which each new administration begins. To forestall long debates over bothersome details he frequently induced Congress to delegate much discretionary authority to the President himself, or to some executive officer. Thus many of the New Deal measures were passed in more or less skeleton form, with the details to be filled in later by the President and his advisers. Operating in this hasty fashion the special session of Congress enacted into law within a hundred days the principal policies of the New Deal.

The Emergency Banking Act foretold at the very outset the direction in which the New Deal was to go. With the whole financial system in a state of collapse, the President might have turned toward the left, with social revolution somewhat after the Russian pattern as his goal. Had he directed Congress to nationalize the banking system, a long step toward the state ownership and administration of all industry and finance would have been taken. He might also have turned to the right, toward what, in contrast with communism, was currently called fascism, and drew its inspiration from the exploits of Mussolini in Italy. His goal then would have been to preserve the private profit system at the expense, if need be, of democracy. But neither communism nor fascism had any deep rooting in America, and one seemed as likely as the other to develop into an irresponsible dictatorship. There is no evidence that Roosevelt considered either way. What he proposed was a middle course, more in line with American precedents. The business of the nation should be left in private hands, but controls should be set up by the government to prevent the ever-recurring booms and crises from which capitalism had suffered so long. Extreme individualism had already been limited by extensive governmental regulation; what Roose-

Direction of the New Deal

Copyright, 1935, Philadelphia Inquirer

"IT'S ALL PART OF A GREAT BIG PLAN"

velt had in mind was to extend regulation to the point where it would result in a planned economy. The powers of government would be amplified, but the rights of the individual would not be destroyed. In addition to this interest in permanent reform, the President was determined also to make more adequate provision for the relief of the unemployed, and to promote by every means at his disposal the restoration of a normal business prosperity.[1]

Very early in his administration the President was called upon to decide whether he could achieve these objectives and at the same time carry on a program of international co-operation. Apparently he at first thought that the two were not incompatible. He accepted, seemingly without reservation, the commitments of his predecessor with respect to American participation in the World Economic Conference to be held in London during the summer of 1933. He received cordially the British Prime Minister,

The London Economic Conference

---

[1] From its very inception the New Deal produced a host of interpreters and critics whose writings, for the most part, are best forgotten. Samples representing various points of view are as follows: C. A. Beard and G. H. E. Smith, *The Future Comes* (1934); E. K. Lindley, *The Roosevelt Revolution: First Phase* (1933); H. A. Wallace, *America Must Choose* (1934); William MacDonald, *The Menace of Recovery* (1934); Walter Lippmann, *The Method of Freedom* (1934); Norman Thomas, *After the New Deal, What?* (1936).

J. Ramsay McDonald, who visited Washington in April to discuss plans for the conference, and a little later he gave equally friendly audiences to the special emissaries of France, Italy, Germany, and Japan. He even showed some disposition to extend the scope of the conference to include the revision of war debts, and he appointed as head of the American delegation the Secretary of State, Cordell Hull, whose devotion to tariff reduction and the reopening of world trade amounted almost to a religion. The conference opened auspiciously on June 12, and in spite of much jockeying for position on the part of participants, its sessions seemed by no means destined to futility. Within two weeks Roosevelt proclaimed publicly his belief that its duty was to "establish order in place of the present chaos by a stabilization of currencies, by freeing the flow of world trade, and by international action to raise price-levels."

But for reasons not entirely clear the President soon changed his mind. Early in July he cut the ground completely from under Secretary Hull by renouncing any considerable interest in the stabilization of currencies, and by asserting his determination to seek recovery in America through the establishment of a "sound internal economic system." Whatever the motives that led the President to this decision, it was a fact that the program of legislation he had pushed through Congress was based on the assumption that the United States must "go it alone." For the moment international co-operation was to be side-tracked and economic isolation given a trial. Since American assistance was fundamental in the development of any world program, there was nothing left for the London Conference to do but to wind up its affairs and go home. To the surprise of most observers Secretary Hull resisted the temptation to resign from the cabinet, while Raymond Moley, the "brain-truster" who was credited with bringing about Roosevelt's change of front, soon lost favor with the President and returned to private life.[1]

[1] Broadus Mitchell, *Depression Decade* (1948), is a good attempt at economic history. Dixon Wecter, *The Age of the Great Depression, 1929–1941* (1948), is more on the social side. J. S. Davis, *On Agricultural Policy, 1926–1938* (1939), gives a good picture of the farmers' problems. The same subject is treated in more popular fashion in Arthur Moore, *The Farmer and the Rest of Us* (1945). J. A. Farley, *Jim Farley's Story: The Roosevelt Years* (1948), reflects Farley's unhappiness at having failed to achieve the Democratic nomination for President in 1940.

38

The New Deal

It was soon apparent that the New Deal had set itself the triple task of relief, recovery, and reform. The legislation of the "hundred days," hastily conceived as it was, all pointed toward one or more of these objectives. Inconsistencies were frequent; relief The three R's sometimes got in the way of recovery, and recovery in the way of reform. But occasionally, also, reform measures promoted recovery, and recovery almost always helped solve the problem of relief. Whatever their contradictions and interactions, the three goals remained constant, and they were never long forgotten. From time to time changes based on experience, or even on political expediency, appeared, but they were invariably defended as merely a better way of accomplishing what the New Deal had set out to do. Most of the New Deal measures cost money, and the Economy Act, signed by the President on March 20, 1933, was soon recognized as an empty gesture. Under its terms some savings were made, although only temporarily, in regular expenditures, particularly for pensions and the salaries of office-holders. But these slight savings were soon more than overbalanced by the extraordinary expenditures undertaken for relief, recovery, and reform.

In the matter of relief the New Deal amplified and extended what the Hoover administration had already begun. Through a Federal Emergency Relief Administration, created May 22, 1933, unreturnable contributions instead of RFC loans were made Relief —
FERA, CWA available to the states for relief purposes. The law permitted local authorities to provide either work relief or an outright dole, but since in practice the dole was far more economical than "made work," it was used unsparingly. By the end of 1934 about one-sixth of the population of the country was on relief. At the head of the FERA was Harry Hopkins, a professional social worker who had been in charge of relief activities in New York while Roosevelt was governor. Hopkins believed in work relief as preferable to the dole for psychological reasons, and under his urging the President established the Civil Works Administra-

tion in October, 1933, as a branch of the FERA. Through the CWA
an effort was made to provide emergency jobs for workers who might
otherwise have spent the winter on relief. The CWA actually gave the
first employment they had had for years to millions of men, but the
organization was so hastily devised that it became the happy hunting
ground of grafters, and partly on this account had to be discontinued the
following spring.

As year after year went by with no really significant falling-off in the
relief rolls, federal relief workers became convinced that the situation
they faced was no mere emergency, and must be dealt with
WPA
on a more or less permanent basis. In harmony with these
views, the new Relief Act of April 8, 1935, required the government to
provide "work relief, and to increase employment by providing useful
projects." For this purpose a total of nearly five billion dollars was appropriated on the understanding that federal relief officials would help
devise work projects, would prescribe rules for the selection of workers,
and would regulate the conditions of labor. During the summer of 1935
the FERA handed over to a new Works Progress Administration, established in July under the direction of the energetic Hopkins, the task of
providing work for all employables. The ideal which the WPA set for
itself was to provide the unemployed with the kind of work they were
best fitted to do. By this time the many trifling projects of the FERA
and the CWA had brought "made work" into ill-repute, and had even
provided it with a name, "boondoggling," but under WPA the nature of
the work projects undertaken steadily improved. For the unskilled
laborers, who constituted the great majority of the relief workers, jobs
were found in connection with such projects as the construction of country roads and city streets, the improvement of parks and playgrounds,
and the building of flood-control or irrigation dams. Carpenters, plas-
terers, masons, plumbers, and other skilled laborers were used to erect or
repair schoolhouses, libraries, city halls, courthouses, and other public
buildings. Even the "white-collar"classes were not neglected, and projects were devised to aid artists, writers, actors, musicians, architects,
and many others possessed of more or less professional abilities. Among
the projects undertaken were several of great interest to historians, such
as the surveys of historical records, and of national, state, and local
archives. There were indeed few aspects of American life that were not
in some way affected by the activities of the WPA. Supplementary to
its program was the work of the National Youth Administration through
which needy high-school and college students were enabled to earn small
sums for non-instructional assistance to their teachers, while equally
needy young people who were not in school were provided with useful

part-time jobs. NYA workers earned on an average more than fifteen dollars each per month.[1]

A relief project particularly dear to the President's heart was the Civilian Conservation Corps, created by law of March 31, 1933. The purpose of this organization was to establish conservation camps in every part of the country which would provide work for unmarried young men between the ages of eighteen and twenty-five. The CCC soon had more than a quarter of a million youths at work under army officers clearing forests, planting trees, improving roads, preventing floods, and performing other equally useful tasks. Enlistments were for one year. The men received a dollar a day each in addition to medical care and maintenance, but were required to allot twenty-five dollars a month to dependents or relatives. Thousands of young men who had roamed the city streets searching in vain for jobs, or with too frequent success for trouble, thus found something worthwhile to do. Most of them were immensely improved in health and morale as a result of their experience, and there was no dearth of volunteers. The CCC lasted on until well after the entrance of the United States into the second World War.

The CCC

Undoubtedly the original intent of the New Deal was to bring about a degree of business recovery that would provide normal employment for all who were capable of earning a living. To this end the RFC, which had been established during Hoover's administration, was continued, with the added function of lending to private industry as well as to financial institutions, railroads, and public agencies. All such loans were to be made on a strictly business basis, with the expectation of repayment. The easement of credit that the RFC provided was eagerly accepted by the business world, and its loans soon totaled many billions of dollars.

Recovery — RFC loans

To supplement its lending policy the government proposed to stimulate industry still further by a program of direct spending. This was to be accomplished mainly through a Public Works Administration, for the use of which the hundred days' session of Congress appropriated $3,300,000,000. It was supposed that the erection of public buildings and other such construction projects would provide much new business for the heavy industries in particular, and less directly for business in general. But the PWA developed slowly, partly because of the rigid honesty of its administrator, Secretary Harold

Public works — PWA

---

[1] Most of the literature provoked by the New Deal is both controversial and ephemeral, and in matters of opinion is not to be taken too seriously. With respect to unemployment and relief, the following may be found useful: Harry L. Hopkins, _Spending to Save; The Complete Story of Relief_ (1936); Nels Anderson, _The Right to Work_ (1938); Grace Adams, _Workers on Relief_ (1939). Congress voted in 1943 to discontinue the NYA.

L. Ickes, and partly because detailed plans for large projects took time to provide. Not until the business "recession" of 1937–38 did the PWA begin to come into its own. By that time the necessary plans had been worked out in abundance, and the PWA was able to give much immediate aid to industry. Before the year 1939 had ended, it had sponsored projects in all but three counties within the United States at an estimated cost of nearly six billion dollars. In many instances, however, the PWA bore only part of the expense, the rest being furnished by some local taxing agency.[1]

Quite the most ambitious of the New Deal efforts to restore prosperity was the National Recovery Administration, authorized June 16, 1933, under the terms of the National Industrial Recovery Act. The NRA was the principal New Deal effort to devise a planned economy. Its purpose was to facilitate the co-operation of all American employers in a gigantic scheme to shorten working hours, raise wages, and increase employment. Whatever anti-trust legislation barred the way to reasonable group understandings was swept aside. Just as the War Industries Board had promoted the smooth functioning of American business during the World War, so now the NRA was to enable industry to pull together in a joint battle against the depression. "Codes of fair competition" were to be devised by manufacturers, mine operators, common carriers, utility corporations, merchants, and every other type of business, according to which each group would standardize its behavior. The rights of employees "to organize and bargain collectively," to join unions of their own choosing, and to insist on conditions of employment approved by the President were carefully protected in Section 7 (a) of the Act, but labor and capital were expected to work together in a log-rolling rivalry to make NRA a success.

Under the energetic leadership of General Hugh S. Johnson, the NRA made a valiant effort to live up to the high hopes of those who sponsored it. A handsome emblem, the Blue Eagle, was devised for the use of businesses that agreed to follow NRA regulations, and for display by all householders who pledged themselves to buy only from Blue Eagle firms. For all businesses not organized under their own code authorities, the President issued a blanket code, which abolished child labor, fixed a thirty-five-hour week for ordinary labor and a forty-hour week in white-collar jobs, and established minimum wage scales of forty cents an hour for the former and from twelve to fifteen dollars a week for the latter. But difficulties in the enforcement of the NRA codes soon began to ap-

---

[1] H. L. Ickes, *Back to Work: The Story of PWA* (1935); A. D. Gayer, *Public Works in Prosperity and Depression* (1935); J. F. Isakoff, *The Public Works Administration* (1938).

pear that made the problems of prohibition pale into insignificance. "Chiselers" who made use of the Blue Eagle, but ignored the rules, put the honestly intentioned dealer at a serious disadvantage. Wartime methods of compulsion were lacking, and the hope that the code authorities set up by each business group could secure the obedience of all members proved illusive. A few important establishments, including the Ford Motor Company, refused entirely to co-operate. Finally Johnson, following a tempestuous outbreak against labor for its failure, as he saw it, to do its part, resigned in September, 1934, and the following May the United States Supreme Court found the law under which the NRA had been operating to be unconstitutional. The stand of the Court, that too much authority had been delegated by Congress to the President, and that the existing emergency gave Congress no authority that it would not have otherwise, greatly incensed the President, but he bowed to the Court's authority, and the whole NRA organization was rapidly dismantled.[1]

Efforts to salvage some of the gains attributed to NRA were not entirely lacking. At the insistence of the administration the Guffey-Snyder Act was passed in August, 1935, to promote the stabilization of conditions in the bituminous coal industry. NLRB But a five-to-four decision of the Supreme Court in May, 1936, invalidated the law, and returned the soft-coal business to its customary chaos. Another measure, the Wagner-Connery Labor Relations Act, was designed to soften the blow sustained by labor in the loss of Section 7(a). The new act stated that the policy of the United States was to protect the rights of laborers to organize and to bargain collectively with employers through representatives of their own choosing. A National Labor Relations Board of three members was authorized to halt unfair practices on the part of employers and to seek enforcement for its orders through the federal courts. The new NLRB successfully ran the gantlet of the Supreme Court, although the board's right to interfere where the process of manufacture was strictly local in character was sustained by a bare majority. In 1938 Congress took steps also toward the re-establishment throughout the country of minimum wages and maximum hours and the abolition of child labor. By the Wages and Hours Act it laid down rules that a wages and hours division of the Department of Labor was expected to enforce.

One result of the labor turmoil that characterized these years of change and experiment was the division of organized labor itself into two competing camps. The American Federation of Labor, led since

[1] H. S. Johnson, *The Blue Eagle from Egg to Earth* (1935); L. S. Lyon and others, *The National Recovery Administration* (1935); C. L. Dearing and others, *ABC of the NRA* (1934).

1924 by William Green, adhered consistently to the Gompers policy of
co-operating with capital as long as wages and working conditions remained satisfactory. With the capitalistic system as
such it refused to quarrel, provided only that labor obtained a

**The labor
split — CIO**

reasonable reward for the work it was called upon to do. Furthermore,
the A.F. of L. still set much store by the crafts union type of organization, and opposed with vigor all attempts to organize into one union all
the workers in a given industry, regardless of their skills or their lack of
skills. The Federation, so its critics complained, had thus lost touch
with the problems of the ordinary worker. After the destruction of the
NRA in 1935, John L. Lewis, militant head of the United Mine Workers,
took the lead in the formation of a Committee for Industrial Organization, the purpose of which was to promote the unionization of industries
as units, and not in accordance with specified trades or skills. In this
endeavor he was officially opposed by the A.F. of L., but, with the support
of his own and several other powerful unions, he sent organizers into
many of the great mass-production industries, such as automobiles,
steel, textiles, rubber, aluminum, plate-glass, and furniture. In most
instances the CIO plan of organization seemed to meet a long-felt need;
old unions took on new life, and new unions were founded as needed.
For co-operating with Lewis in this work ten unions were expelled in
1936 from the A.F. of L., and as a result the CIO assumed a permanent
character that its prime movers had not at first intended. Claiming to
represent a membership of nearly four million workers as against the
five million of the A.F. of L., the CIO changed its name in November,
1938, to the Congress of Industrial Organizations, adopted a constitution
after the A.F. of L. model, and elected Lewis as its first president.[1]

The methods by which the CIO had risen to such great importance
involved among other things the use of a weapon new to American labor
history, the "sit-down" strike. Workers instead of first
leaving the factories, and then picketing them to prevent
the employment of "scabs," simply retained in idleness the

**The
"sit-down"**

posts they ordinarily held, and forcibly resisted removal. This technique
was successfully employed in CIO strikes against two great automobile
companies, General Motors and the Chrysler Corporation. In both
instances, with the assistance of Governor Frank Murphy of Michigan,
agreements were finally reached to vacate the plants on condition that
the CIO union should be recognized as the bargaining agent for its
members, while later negotiations won other concessions. The United

[1] J. R. Walsh, *C.I.O., Industrial Unionism in Action* (1937); Benjamin Stolberg, *Story of
the CIO* (1938); Edward Levinson, *Labor on the March* (1938); Herbert Harris, *Labor's Civil
War* (1940).

States Steel Corporation, long the despair of labor leaders, did not await the coming conflict, but in March, 1937, accorded the CIO Steel Workers' Organizing Committee full bargaining authority for all its employees. Most of the other so-called "Big Steel" companies also capitulated, but "Little Steel," led by T. M. Girdler of the Republic Steel Corporation, fought back. Strikes that began in May, 1937, spread rapidly through Pennsylvania, Ohio, and Illinois, and were accompanied by much disorder. But the timely action of employers prevented "sit-down" strikes, and without this weapon the strikers lost. Moreover, the public had become thoroughly weary of labor conflict, and was disposed to blame the violence that accompanied CIO strikes on communist agitators. William Green, the A.F. of L. leader, complained bitterly that the CIO methods were discrediting the whole labor movement. Even when the police brutally shot down a number of picketers at the Republic Steel Works in South Chicago, there was little effective protest.

Parallel to the New Deal program for industry and labor was an equally comprehensive plan for the rehabilitation of agriculture. Striking out along what the President himself called "a new and untrod path," the Agricultural Adjustment Act of May 12, 1933, sought a remedy for the chronic overproduction that had for so long kept American farm prices down. Frankly recognizing that the foreign market could not be depended upon, the framers of the act proposed to restrict the American output, if need be, to what the United States alone could consume. By careful supervision of production, prices were to be brought back to the average levels of the five years preceding the World War. To accomplish these ends an Agricultural Adjustment Administration was set up with authority to buy and hold surpluses, and to contract with the producers of specified basic commodities for whatever co-operation might be needed to insure crop control. Since the farmers were to be paid generously for their co-operation, agriculture stood to receive a double subsidy, one by way of direct money payments on the basis of the contracts signed, and the other through higher prices for crops harvested. The cost involved in the crop-restriction program was to be met by a tax levied against the processors of farm produce, who in turn would pass the burden along to the consumers. The farmer, if this elaborate scheme of economic planning worked, would find himself at last on a parity with other economic groups. Basic commodities at first brought within the scope of the act were cotton, wheat, corn, hogs, rice, tobacco, and milk, but a year later the list was greatly lengthened.

Organized within the Department of Agriculture under the watchful eye of Secretary Wallace, the AAA experimented with crop-reduction programs, at first in cotton, wheat, corn, and hogs, then in numerous other farm products. As had been foreseen, benefit payments cut down production and brought up prices, although the prolonged drouth that set in throughout the western half of the Mississippi Valley probably affected the situation as much, or more, than the AAA. So complete was the drouth in some of the western states that many farmers had nothing to live on except the money they received from the government under their crop-reduction programs; furthermore, the windstorms that swept ceaselessly through the western "dustbowl" threatened to render much land permanently useless. Caustic criticism of the AAA program was of course inevitable. Crop reductions, at a time when drouth conditions threatened the country with actual shortages, was difficult to defend, and in many instances had to be modified. Farmers whose lifelong habits had been based upon growing more and more found it difficult to adjust themselves to an economy of growing less and less. They signed the contracts and accepted the benefit payments because they needed the money, but they resented the system. Processors complained bitterly at the heavy taxation forced upon them, and found themselves seriously handicapped in competing for markets outside the United States. Consumers paid steeply increased prices for nearly everything that came from the farm.[1]

In spite of these criticisms the country was hardly prepared for the drastic action of the United States Supreme Court which announced January 6, 1936, in a six-to-three decision, that the Agricultural Adjustment Act was unconstitutional. In an opinion read by Justice Roberts the Court held that there was nothing in the Constitution to justify federal control of agricultural production, and that, in attempting to deal with the strictly local business of farming, Congress had invaded a right reserved to the states. Since the processing taxes and benefit payments existed only as means to an illegal end, the Court held that they, too, were invalid. The implications of this decision worried the minority of the Court, which in a dissenting opinion read by Justice Stone warned the majority that "courts are not the only agency of government that must be assumed to have capacity to govern." Nor could agricultural economists quite understand how farming could be classified as a strictly local business when most farm prices, if unregulated, would depend upon nation-wide and even upon world-wide conditions.

The AAA
invalidated

In wrecking the AAA the Supreme Court did not destroy the entire New Deal structure for dealing with agriculture. A new Farm Credit Administration, established in March, 1933, had taken over every federal agency in the country that had anything to do

RA, FCA

[1] E. G. Nourse and others, *Three Years of the Agricultural Adjustment Administration* (1937); E. G. Nourse, *Marketing Agreements under the AAA* (1935).

with agricultural credits. By 1934 it was lending at the rate, on an average, of five million dollars a day. Much of this credit was used to refinance mortgages that might otherwise have been foreclosed, but loans for production and for marketing were also supplied. Frequently the new government loans were for less than the face of the old mortgage, but creditors gladly accepted the loss involved rather than take over the mortgaged property. Some loans were made also to buy back property that had been lost through foreclosure proceedings. As a further aid in dealing with the mortgage problem, the Frazier-Lemke Moratorium Act of 1935 delayed foreclosure proceedings for a three-year period, provided a court of law would give its approval, both to the propriety of the delay and to the adequacy of the rental to be paid. For the benefit of farmers who were still keeping up the unequal struggle against marginal or submarginal lands the Resettlement Administration was formed in April, 1935. Its chief purpose was to buy up and turn back to the government for forests, parks, and grazing permits land from which farmers could not ordinarily make a living, and then to "resettle" the dispossessed owners in "healthy rural communities." The RA was less successful than its proponents had hoped, and eventually, renamed the Farm Security Administration, it turned its attention chiefly to helping tenant-farmers become land-owners.

The hostility of the Supreme Court was sufficient to put an end to the NRA, which had begun to break down anyway, but the critical condition of agriculture required that some substitute be found immediately for the AAA. As a stopgap measure, designed mainly to save the situation until something better could be devised, Congress enacted in February, 1936, the Soil Conservation and Domestic Allotment Act. Instead of the control of production at which the AAA had aimed, the primary objective of the new act was to be soil conservation. The all-important payments to farmers were to be continued, but henceforth they were to be made in return for co-operation with the government in an elaborate program for the promotion of soil fertility, the prevention of erosion, and the more economic use of farm land. By placing restrictions on the planting of soil-depleting crops, some effort was made to hold down the production of such basic commodities as cotton, wheat, and corn, but by 1937 the cotton yield reached the startlingly high figure of 18,945,028 bales, while most other crops showed a wide margin over the nation's ability to consume. Furthermore, there was no longer a processing tax to meet the cost of the benefit payments, and the money had to come directly out of the Treasury.

Finally in 1938 Congress enacted a new Agricultural Adjustment Act as "the Nation's well-matured answer" to the needs of the American

farmer.   It retained the soil-conservation and benefit-payment features of the preceding program; it made provision in five
The new AAA   key crops, wheat, cotton, corn, tobacco, and rice, for the
limitation of acreage allotments in accordance with probable needs;
it authorized the making of storage loans as a means of holding agricultural surpluses off the market; and it sanctioned resort to marketing
quotas in emergencies, provided that two-thirds of the growers of the
commodity concerned recorded their approval in a referendum vote.
All this was a part of an elaborate effort to raise the income of farmers to
"parity," that is, to the same ratio with the incomes of other groups that
had existed in the five years prior to 1914; to make doubly sure of this
goal the sum of $212,000,000 was appropriated in 1939 for "parity pay-
ments" to help bridge the gap between current prices and "parity prices."
For the benefit of wheat-growers, a Federal Crop Insurance Corporation
was established in the Department of Agriculture from which guaranties
could be obtained to the amount of fifty or seventy-five per cent of
normal yields.   Payments of losses and premiums were to be made
either in wheat or in its cash equivalent.

Although participation in the AAA program was kept on a purely
voluntary basis, the generous subsidies offered were hard for farmers
to resist.   About five and a quarter million agricultural producers,
working through three thousand county conservation associations and
many more subordinate committees took part in the 1939 program.
Nearly three-fourths of the crop land of the nation was involved.   In
accordance with the wishes of Secretary Wallace, an "ever normal
granary" was promoted by loans on warehoused surpluses which
amounted approximately to nine cents per pound on cotton, sixty cents
per bushel on wheat, and fifty-seven cents per bushel on corn.   By this
device it was hoped that both producer and consumer would be protected against shortages and price fluctuations.   The marketing quota
provisions of the act were also promptly invoked to protect the prices
of cotton and of several types of tobacco, while nearly one hundred and
seventy thousand wheat-growers, some of them in drouth-threatened
areas where there was little prospect of a crop, took out federal crop
insurance.   The cost of all this to the government exceeded half a billion
dollars a year.[1]

The effect of the New Deal measures upon the social organization of
the deep South was far more revolutionary than had been foreseen.   Reductions in the cotton acreage meant that thousands of share-croppers
were left without land to work, while AAA benefit payments enabled

---

[1] H. I. Richards, *Cotton and the AAA* (1936).   Cotton and many other southern problems
are well discussed in Jonathan Daniels, *A Southerner Discovers the South* (1938).

landlords to purchase the machinery necessary to throw still other thousands off the land. Former sharecroppers dropped to the status of agricultural day laborers, with at best only seasonal employment, and with frequent to constant dependence on relief. Social changes in the South These conditions, greatly augmented in the southwestern dust bowl by the persistent drouths, raised up an army of wanderers who roamed the West in "jallopies," searching endlessly for employment. Far out into the Southwest, through New Mexico and Arizona to California, the blight of cotton-growing extended, and wherever it went the poverty-stricken cotton hand went with it. All over the South the need for diversified farming was as apparent as it was difficult to promote, while with "normalcy" forever fading into the future, the gains that industry was able to make over agriculture were slight.[1]

In many of the New Deal measures the reform motive stood out clearly. This was certainly the intent of the Beer Act, which was meant to break down as far as was constitutionally possible the effectiveness of the Prohibition Amendment. The rigid one-half of one per cent alcoholic content by which an intoxicating beverage had been previously defined, was changed to three and two-tenths by weight, a high enough percentage to pacify, if not entirely to satisfy, beer drinkers. As for the outright repeal of the Eighteenth Amendment, steps in that direction had been taken before the Roosevelt administration came to power. While Hoover was still President, Congress had submitted a Twenty-First Amendment to the Constitution, with the proviso that it should be ratified by special state conventions, instead of in the customary way by the action of state legislatures. Thus each state was able to vote directly on the question of repeal. It was soon apparent what the verdict would be, but not until December 6, 1933, did the Twenty-First Amendment become a part of the Constitution.

New Deal measures with reference to banking and currency were classified, also, by their sponsors as reforms. To supplement the Emergency Banking Act, passed during the first few days of the Roosevelt administration, the Glass-Steagall Act of FDIC 1933 created a Federal Deposit Insurance Corporation to guarantee small depositors against losses from bank failures; divorced commercial and investment banking; permitted national banks to establish branch banks in states that accorded that privilege to state banks; gave the Federal Reserve Board the right to place severe restrictions upon banks that lent too freely for speculative purposes; forbade loans from their own banks to the executive officers of Federal Reserve Banks; and expanded the Federal Reserve System to include industrial and savings banks. Two

[1] C. S. Johnson and others, *The Collapse of Cotton Tenancy* (1935).

years later, the old Federal Reserve Board was replaced by a Board of Governors of seven members appointed by the President, with widely expanded powers.

As to the money question, the President seemed determined to experiment with the idea of a managed currency which would have the same buying power at all times. To the dismay of many conserva-

Currency reform tives, he promptly took the United States off the gold standard and secured from Congress a Gold Repeal Resolution which invalidated the gold clauses employed in so many public and private contracts. Gold exports were forbidden; gold coin, gold bullion, and gold certificates were taken out of circulation; and a price fixed by the government was paid for all gold newly mined in the United States or offered for sale from abroad. Under authority of the Gold Reserve Act of January 30, 1934, the amount of gold in the standard dollar was reduced to 59.06 per cent of its former content. A few months later, under the terms of a new Silver Purchasing Act, the Treasury also began to purchase silver, ostensibly to increase the supply of silver in the national monetary stocks until it had reached a value equal to one-fourth the total amount. The effect of these measures upon the purchasing price of the dollar was far less marked than the President and his monetary advisers had anticipated, although the United States was soon in possession of most of the world's supply of gold and silver. As long as this treasure remained impounded, there seemed to be no grave threat of currency inflation, except by congressional issues of fiat money. Against this latter evil, however, the President took a firm and successful stand.[1]

Also included within the list of the Roosevelt reforms was an attempt to deal with the problems of speculative investments. A Federal Securi-

The SEC ties Act, signed on May 27, 1933, insisted that the vendors of securities must be made to tell the public the truth about what they had to sell, and imposed heavy penalties for the interstate circulation of fraudulent advertising, through the mails or otherwise. The next year another act established the Securities and Exchange Commission to take over from the Federal Trade Commission the administration of these regulations. While it was beyond the power of the SEC to guarantee the purchasers of securities against loss, it could and did compel the disclosure of such information as might enable investors to form intelligent opinions of their own. The SEC was authorized also to license stock exchanges, and to regulate their practices in such a way as to stimulate legitimate trading and to discourage mere gam-

---

[1] H. G. Moulton, *Financial Organization and the Economic System* (1938); W. R. Burgess, *Reserve Banks and the Money Market* (1936); A. D. Gayer, editor, *The Lessons of Monetary Experience* (1937).

bling. Efforts to obtain a "death sentence" for all public utility holding companies failed, but Congress gave the SEC authority to limit their operations "to a single integrated public-utility" system.[1]

On the time-honored question of tariff reform, the New Deal made excellent headway. Wisely refraining from the customary effort at direct revision downward, it left the Hawley-Smoot Tariff in force, but proposed through a series of reciprocal trade agreements to bring duties on imports down to more reasonable levels. By this means the inevitable log-rolling of congressmen to get aid for their constituents at all costs was avoided. A Trade Agreements Act, passed in June, 1934, authorized the President for a three-year period to negotiate agreements with other countries for the mutual lowering of tariff rates. Without so much as referring the matter back to Congress for its consent, he might lower the existing duties by as much as fifty per cent, provided only that the American free list be not disturbed, one way or the other. The exercise of this grant of authority, which was repeatedly renewed, fell to the Secretary of State, Cordell Hull, a lifelong devotee of the low-tariff principle. In five years' time he had concluded more than twenty agreements, including two with Great Britain and Canada that were particularly comprehensive. Perhaps three-fourths of the exports and imports of the United States were affected, and as a result of the improved trade relations thus made possible, good-will toward the United States mounted rapidly, especially among the nations of Latin America. In negotiating the agreements, Secretary Hull relied upon the advice of a committee of specialists, whose duty it was to make sure that for every American concession some foreign equivalent was obtained.[2]

The Hull Trade Agreements

Partly to promote recovery, but partly also with a view to reform, the New Deal instituted drastic changes in the control of transportation. The railroads in particular required attention, for the competition of automobiles, trucks, and pipe lines, with such inevitable loss of business as accompanied the depression, had brought them to the very brink of ruin. To assist in planning for their future, an Emergency Railroad Transportation Act was passed in June, 1933. This measure provided for a federal co-ordinator of transportation whose duty it was to eliminate wasteful competition, to co-ordinate train service, and to effect needed economies. As federal co-ordinator, the President appointed Joseph B. Eastman, a believer in government ownership who nevertheless exerted himself, successfully

Railroad co-ordination

[1] R. L. Weissman, *The New Wall Street* (1939), tells of the changes wrought by the new legislation.

[2] Hull's program is well set forth in H. J. Tasca, *Reciprocal Trade Policy of the United States* (1938).

as events proved, to make the existing system work. RFC loans were used freely to buy new railroad equipment, and to permit improvements in service. It was in this way that many of the roads obtained the funds necessary to experiment with streamlined, air-conditioned trains, drawn by Diesel-electric or steam-electric locomotives. Eastman's intelligent leadership had much to do with the fact that the railroads, on the entrance of the United States into the second World War, were able to deal with the emergency without being taken over by the government.

With respect to ocean-going means of transportation the New Deal frankly accepted the theory that a strong merchant marine was an essential part of the national defense. The Merchant Marine Act of 1936 declared: (1) that the United States should have shipping adequate to maintain its normal flow of water-borne commerce "at all times"; (2) that this shipping should be "capable of serving as a naval and military auxiliary in time of war"; (3) that it should be owned so far as possible by American citizens and operated under the American flag; (4) that it should be "composed of the best-equipped, safest, and most suitable types of vessels." The act supplanted the old Shipping Board and its subsidiary Merchant Fleet Corporation with a new Maritime Commission, one duty of which was to determine the ocean lanes in which American ships should ply, and another, to work out, in full co-operation with the Navy Department, a "long-range program for replacements and additions to the American merchant marine." So successful was the Maritime Commission with its endeavors that, when the second World War broke out, the total American tonnage was two-thirds as great as the British, and far in excess of any other. It was also vastly improved in serviceability.[1]

Social workers who knew well the faulty housing conditions from which many underprivileged Americans suffered were quick to urge governmental assistance for home-building as one of the best means of promoting both recovery and reform. Coupled with this problem, also, was the need of saving large numbers of home-owners from losing their property through mortgage foreclosures. To meet these needs government credit was for a time extended through the Home Owners' Loan Corporation, the purpose of which was to refinance home mortgages, and through Federal Savings and Loan Associations, locally established, which provided funds for new building. By June, 1936, when its lending ceased, the HOLC had acquired mortgages totaling three billion dollars and had helped at least a million home-owners. Another agency, the Federal Housing Administra-

The merchant marine

The housing problem

---

[1] National Industrial Conference Board, *The American Merchant Marine Problem* (1929); P. M. Zeis, *American Shipping Policy* (1938).

tion, established in 1934, undertook to insure home mortgages of which it approved up to eighty (later ninety) per cent of the appraised value of the property involved. This left to private capital the business of providing the money, but the FHA took most of the risk. The most ambitious of the efforts to deal with housing came with the establishment of the United States Housing Authority in 1937. The purpose of this agency was to aid local communities in remedying their "shortage of decent, safe, and sanitary dwellings for families of low income." As a result of USHA activities, nineteen low-rent apartment houses had been constructed by the end of 1939 in thirteen different cities, and loans of more than a half-billion dollars for the use of 155 communities had been approved.[1]

The conservation of hydroelectric power, and its use in the interest of the people as a whole rather than for the benefit of privately owned utility companies, was another reform dear to the hearts of most New Dealers. Here the Roosevelt administration The TVA was ready to go much farther than mere regulation, and to experiment with actual ownership and operation by the government. Effectively guided in all that concerned this subject by Senator George W. Norris of Nebraska, it singled out the Tennessee Valley for its first great project. This region, ramifying into seven different states — Tennessee, Kentucky, Alabama, Mississippi, Virginia, North Carolina, and Georgia — and embracing within its boundaries some forty thousand square miles, seemed to offer an ideal testing ground for the various New Deal theories on social and economic planning. It counted among its residents a high proportion of the underprivileged classes whose status cheap power was expected to benefit; and it possessed vast natural resources, most of which were either inadequately exploited or were being allowed to degenerate. Since the government had already spent huge sums upon the Muscle Shoals development, it was believed that here, if anywhere, results might speedily be obtained.

In May, 1933, Congress authorized the President to appoint a board of three directors, known as the Tennessee Valley Authority, into whose hands control of the mighty project was to be placed. The TVA was authorized to construct dams for the improvement of navigation and the control of floods; to develop new forms of fertilizer and to promote their use; to build and operate hydroelectric plants and to distribute the power they generated; and to take such other steps as it might see fit to promote the agricultural and industrial development of the region involved. The TVA was quickly organized, and with the Muscle

Shoals plant as a starting-point was soon able to supply cheap electric power to a limited area. With the help of PWA funds it pushed rapidly the construction of six new dams; the greatest of which, the Norris Dam, was completed in 1936. By 1940 TVA power was being generated at four dams, and was being used both to carry forward new construction and to provide cheap power for residential and commercial consumers. By June, 1939, according to TVA estimates, the Authority was serving about 180,000 customers, either directly or indirectly, and its acquisition later in the year of facilities belonging to the Tennessee Electric Power Company added perhaps 150,000 more.

The work undertaken by the TVA spread as time went on into a great variety of fields. It carried on an elaborate program for the control of water on the land, and the consequent checking of erosion; it produced great quantities of fertilizer, and tested its effectiveness in most of the states of the Union; it experimented with low-cost housing for the benefit of its employees; it promoted actively the use of the Tennessee River for commercial navigation; it extended the advantages of electricity to many farmers through a program of rural electrification; and it co-operated generously with local authorities in providing public health services, particularly with a view to checking the ravages of malaria and tuberculosis. These contributions to the general welfare were not invariably appreciated by the people they were meant to help, but the evidence seemed conclusive that the conditions of life in the Tennessee Valley had been enormously improved by the work of the TVA.[1] Other hydroelectric developments under the New Deal, such as the Grand Coulee and Bonneville Dams on the Columbia, Boulder Dam on the Colorado, and Fort Peck Dam on the upper Missouri, were not accompanied by the extensive program of social betterment promoted by the TVA, but they were all intended to provide whatever benefits to society might accrue from the existence of an unlimited flow of cheap power.

Varieties of TVA endeavor

Probably the most revolutionary of all the New Deal undertakings lay in the field of social security. By an act passed August 14, 1935, Congress established a Social Security Board, the business of which was to provide for or promote old-age annuities, unemployment insurance, and more adequate care for the needy, the dependent, and the disabled. The necessity of some such legislation seemed abundantly apparent. Medical efficiency and a better understanding of health requirements had promoted longevity, while employers tended more and more to keep down the average age of the men on their payrolls. Technological unemployment and business

Social security

[1] J. F. Carter, *The Future is Ours* (1939), is an optimistic view of the TVA development.

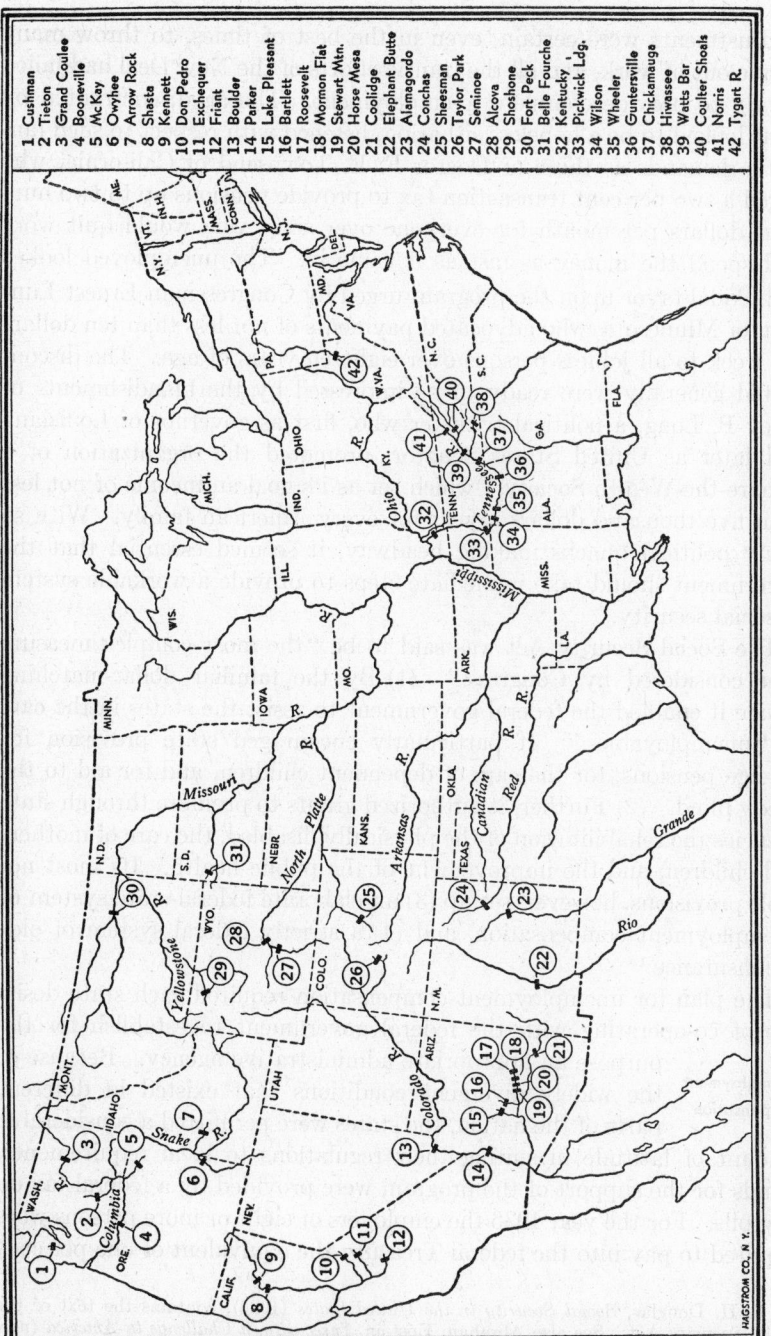

1 Cushman	22 Elephant Butte
2 Tieton	23 Alamagordo
3 Grand Coulee	24 Conchas
4 Booneville	25 Sheesman
5 McKay	26 Taylor Park
6 Owyhee	27 Seminoe
7 Arrow Rock	28 Alcova
8 Shasta	29 Shoshone
9 Kennett	30 Fort Peck
10 Don Pedro	31 Belle Fourche
11 Exchequer	32 Kentucky
12 Friant	33 Pickwick Ldg.
13 Boulder	34 Wilson
14 Parker	35 Wheeler
15 Lake Pleassant	36 Guntersville
16 Bartlett	37 Chickamauga
17 Roosevelt	38 Hiwassee
18 Mormon Flat	39 Watts Bar
19 Stewart Mtn.	40 Coulter Shoals
20 Horse Mesa	41 Norris
21 Coolidge	42 Tygart R.

IRRIGATION AND POWER DEVELOPMENT IN THE UNITED STATES

readjustments were certain, even in the best of times, to throw many people out of work, and all the frantic efforts of the New Deal had failed utterly to provide complete re-employment. The aged, confronted by what looked to be a hopeless situation, listened with respect to such fantastic demands as those of Doctor F. E. Townsend of California, who urged a two per cent transaction tax to provide pensions up to two hundred dollars per month for everyone over sixty who would quit work and spend the money as fast as it came in. The unemployed looked with equal favor upon the program urged by Congressman Ernest Lundeen of Minnesota, who advocated payments of not less than ten dollars per week to all jobless persons over eighteen years of age. The discontented generally were ready to be impressed by the blandishments of Huey P. Long, a political trickster who, first as governor of Louisiana and later as United States Senator, promoted the organization of a "Share-the-Wealth Society," which set as its goal an income of not less than five thousand dollars a year for every American family. With so many political quacks making headway, it seemed essential that the government should take immediate steps to provide a workable system of social security.

The Social Security Act was said to be "the most complex measure ever considered by Congress." (1) By the familiar dollar-matching device it enabled the federal government to assist the states in the care of "unemployables." It particularly encouraged state provision for old-age pensions, for the care of dependent children, and for aid to the needy blind. (2) Further, it authorized grants to promote through state agencies the rehabilitation of the physically disabled, the care of mothers and children, and the improvement of the public health. Its most notable provisions, however, set up (3) an elaborate federal-state system of unemployment compensation, and (4) a strictly federal system of old-age insurance.[1]

The plan for unemployment compensation required each state desirous of co-operating with the federal government to establish for the purpose an appropriate administrative agency. Because of Unemployment compensation the widely divergent conditions that existed in different parts of the nation, the states were permitted a considerable amount of latitude in suiting their regulations to local requirements. Funds for the support of the program were provided by a federal tax on payrolls. For the year 1936 the employers of eight or more persons were required to pay into the federal Treasury the equivalent of one per cent

---

[1] P. H. Douglas, *Social Security in the United States* (1936), contains the text of the Social Security Act. See also Abraham Epstein, *Insecurity, a Challenge to America* (new edition, 1938), and I. M. Rubinow, *The Quest for Security* (1934).

of the wages paid to all employees on their pay rolls as long as twenty weeks; the second year the tax was to be two per cent; thereafter, three per cent. Toward this tax, however, employers were permitted to credit all payments up to ninety per cent of the federal tax made toward the support of a federally approved state unemployment system. The cost of authorized state administration was met by federal grants, but all state unemployment funds had to be deposited in the United States Treasury for investment in federal obligations.

By the summer of 1937 every state in the Union, together with the District of Columbia, Alaska, and Hawaii, had complied with the requirements of the Social Security Act, and the next year the payment of benefits began. Although the law excluded from its operation all government employees, farm laborers, domestic servants, casual workers, and the employees of charitable organizations, probably half the working population of the country came under its protection. In 1939 the SSB took over the United States Employment Service, and thereafter attempted to co-ordinate job insurance with job placement. Anyone thrown out of work was required to register at his local employment office, which must try to help him find another job. If, after a specified waiting period, he remained unemployed, benefit payments were authorized. These payments, in practice, amounted to from five to fifteen dollars a week, and lasted on until the worker had either exhausted all his wage credits, or had reached the maximum period permitted by law, usually three or four months; provided, of course, that in the meantime he had failed to find another job.

The plan for old-age insurance included in the Social Security Act looked forward to the payment of monthly benefits to qualified workers in industry and commerce who retired from employment at the age of sixty-five. The same groups were excepted from its operation as were denied the advantages of unemploy-

Old-age insurance

ment compensation. Payments of from fifteen to eighty dollars a month, depending upon the total amount of wages earned by the beneficiary after 1936, were to begin on January 1, 1942, and were to continue until the time of death, with lump-sum settlements payable to the estates of those who died before reaching the age of sixty-five. Funds for the carrying-out of the program were to be obtained by an income tax on employees, deducted from their wages by employers, and an excise tax on payrolls. Equal sums were required of employers and employees, amounting in each case to one per cent of the worker's income in 1937, and rising gradually during the intervening years to three per cent in 1949. Amendments to the act added in 1939 changed the date of first payments to January 1, 1940, and expanded the system to include payments to the surviving dependents of deceased workers. By this time over forty-five million separate accounts had been opened, and in spite of the almost incredible amount of bookkeeping that the system entailed, the probabilities that it would function smoothly seemed good.

Naturally the extensive program of change that the New Deal had undertaken aroused the most intense opposition. The policy of spending as freely to defeat the depression as the nation would spend to defeat an enemy in time of war provoked critics to the direst prophecies. When Hoover took office the national debt had stood at more than seventeen billion dollars; when he left office, at nearly twenty-one billions. But the New Deal expenditures by 1940 had doubled the debt of 1933, and the forty-five-billion-dollar limit set by Congress during the first World War soon had to be raised. How long could the nation continue to spend so lavishly without danger of bankruptcy? To many observers the socialistic tendencies of the New Deal seemed even worse than the spending. With the government in complete control of nearly every aspect of the nation's economic life, what was to become of the "rugged individualism" of which Americans so long had boasted? More baldly stated, how could private business continue to make good profits in the face of crippling taxes, governmental regulation and competition, and an arrogance on the part of labor which the government had seemingly promoted? Roosevelt, as the personification of the New Deal, although highly esteemed by those who liked it, was intensely hated by those who did not. Himself a man of means, he was denounced bitterly as a "traitor to his class," who, in order to curry favor with the masses, stood ready to destroy his own kind. He was accused, too, of building up a powerful federal bureaucracy, the business of which was not only to man the various governmental agencies, but also to keep the Democratic Party in power.[1]

Whatever the reasons that lay back of the returns, early elections soon made clear the fact that the New Deal was not without astounding political vitality. In the state and congressional elections of 1934, the Democrats won again, as in 1932, by a landslide.

In the campaign of 1936 the Republicans were hard put to it even to find a presidential candidate, for by that time all the prominent members of their party had been disqualified by disastrous defeats. Their choice finally fell upon Governor Alfred M. Landon of Kansas, one of the very few Republican governors to escape the Democratic landslides. For Vice-President, the Republicans turned to a newspaper

Opposition to the New Deal

Election of 1936

[1] Among the many vigorous assaults on Roosevelt two of the most telling were J. P. Warburg, *Hell Bent for Election* (1935), and *Still Hell Bent* (1936). But Warburg finally supported Roosevelt for re-election. On the other side see J. P. Kennedy, *I'm for Roosevelt* (1936).

man, Colonel Frank Knox, owner and publisher of the Chicago *Daily News*. The Democrats, in full confidence of victory, renominated their ticket of 1932, and elected it by a third devastating landslide. Exactly in accordance with the predictions of James A. Farley, Democratic campaign manager, only two states, Maine and Vermont, voted for Landon. The electoral vote stood 523 for Roosevelt to 8 for Landon, and the popular vote 27,750,000 to 16,680,000. Not since James Monroe was re-elected in 1820 with but a single opposing electoral vote had an American election been so one-sided. In both houses of Congress the Democratic majorities became so large as to threaten dissension. In the House the Democrats won 328 seats out of 435, and in the Senate 77 out of 96.

Among the many post-election observations of analysts, one stood out pre-eminently. It was apparent that the "vertical" line of cleavage between the parties, so characteristic of nineteenth-century American politics, had given way to a "horizontal" division, which placed the more-favored economic groups in the Republican column and the less-favored elements in the Democratic. This was revealed with some clarity by the campaign contributions, which for the Republicans amounted to about nine million dollars, and for the Democrats to about five and one-half million dollars. The great trouble with such a contest, from the Republican point of view, was that the lower classes had the votes. Thousands of citizens whose only means of support had been the relief payments or the made work of New Deal agencies saw little reason to exchange such small favors for the "rugged individualism" promised by Republican campaign orators. Farmers whose antecedents were Republican were conscious of the fact that the benefit payments they received were quite as definitely Democratic. The country might be heading for disaster, as the Republicans claimed, but the personal prospects of a great host of voters seemed to hinge on Democratic success. All this, according to the Republican version, amounted to little less than wholesale bribery by the use of public funds. But for the Democrats it meant a dependable series of landslides.

Roosevelt's overwhelming victory in 1936 no doubt furnished in part the explanation for an attack on the Supreme Court that the President launched shortly after his second inauguration. Before the election he had not hesitated to express his irritation with decisions that were based upon precedents set in "horse-and-buggy days," but he had studiously refrained from attacking the Court during the campaign. Now, with sixty per cent of the nation's voters behind him, what might have been hazardous before seemed safe enough. That the Court majority was bitterly hostile to the New Deal seemed obvious. Out of nine important decisions involving New Deal measures, only twice did the government score victories, and in one of these, the law invalidating gold clauses in contracts, the majority was only five to four. Not a single member of the Court had been appointed by Roosevelt; only Andrew Johnson of all the Presidents since the Civil War had served so long without being privileged to choose at least one justice. Of the nine members of the Court, six were more than seventy years of age, and of these six, five were fairly consistently conservative. That some of these veterans were determined to retain their seats until Roosevelt was out of office seemed at least a reasonable inference. With a "second New Deal" in the making to replace the measures voided by the Supreme Court, the President decided on a course of action which, he believed, would prevent any similar disaster in the future.

There were two ways in which reform of the Court could be effected: (1) by an amendment to the Constitution, which might either require retirement at a given age or set limits to the doctrine of judicial review; (2) by a law of Congress to provide for an increase in the number of justices, thus permitting the President to "pack" the Supreme Court with new appointees of less conservative views. The President chose the latter alternative, probably because it seemed to permit of speedier action, but he coupled with it an ingenious provision for calling attention to the advanced age of some of the justices. The measure he urged on Congress would have set the age of seventy for the voluntary retirement of Supreme Court justices, and for each member of the Court who reached that age and failed to retire the President might appoint an additional justice until a maximum Court of fifteen members had been reached. The measure also provided for an extensive reorganization of the lower federal courts with a view to expediting business and increasing efficiency.

Probably the President was quite unprepared for the furor that his "court-packing" bill evoked. Many Democrats both in and out of Congress, professed to believe with the Republicans that the last safeguard of American liberty was endangered, and that what the President aspired to create was a dictatorship, pure and simple. In the Senate, where the administration forces chose to stage the initial contest, Burton K. Wheeler of Montana, an ardent New Dealer in every other respect, led the opposition with infinite resourcefulness. Wheeler held no brief for the Court as constituted, but whatever change was to be made, he held, should be made by constitutional amendment. In the end the President for the first time on a matter of major importance failed to carry Congress with him. Astutely led by Chief Justice Hughes, the Court itself took a major part in the proceedings; by a series of decisions favorable to the New Deal, it reminded older citizens of

Roosevelt attacks the Supreme Court

Mr. Dooley's famous observation, "The Supreme Court follows the illiction returns," and materially weakened the President's case. Probably also at Hughes's suggestion, Justice Willis Van Devanter, senior member of the Court in point of service and a pronounced conservative, announced his determination to take speedy advantage of the act which Congress passed March 1, 1937, granting full pay to retiring justices over seventy years of age. Finally, the sudden death of Senator Joseph Robinson, administration floor leader in charge of the Court bill, put an end to the President's hopes. Congress passed a bill which instituted some of the reforms Roosevelt had called for in the lower courts, but it left the Supreme Court intact.

Nevertheless the President soon got what he wanted most, a court less conservative in character, which would no longer stand in the way of New Deal objectives. Had he been less impatient, he might have obtained the same result with far less bitterness and party dissension. The fight well illustrated two outstanding features of the American constitutional system: (1) the difficulties involved whenever one department of the government attempts to dominate another; and (2) the inability of any department, including even the Supreme Court, to resist indefinitely the popular will.[1] Eventually Roosevelt appointed more justices to the United States Supreme Court than any other President since George Washington. The new members he selected were invariably ardent New Dealers, but he followed a Taft precedent in elevating to the Chief Justiceship a sitting member of the opposite political party. When Chief Justice Hughes, who owed his appointment to President Hoover, retired in 1941, Associate Justice Harlan F. Stone, a Coolidge appointee, was made Chief Justice. This was in a sense a fitting reward, for Stone, although a Republican in politics, had consistently stood with the minority of the Court in the days when the conservative majority seemed determined to emasculate the New Deal.

The new Supreme Court

The Supreme Court fight was barely ended when a downward trend in business, called by Democrats a recession and by Republicans a new depression, provided the administration with another major problem. The slump came unheralded, and caught New Dealers along with everyone else unawares. It was caused in no small part by the attempt of the national government beginning

The recession of 1937

---

[1] The powers exercised by the Supreme Court produced an immense amount of controversial literature. Among the many books worthy of note are Charles Warren, *Congress, the Constitution, and the Supreme Court* (1935); E. S. Corwin, *The Twilight of the Supreme Court* (1934), and *Court Over Constitution* (1938); Morris L. Ernst, *The Ultimate Power* (1937); Irving Brant, *Storm Over the Constitution* (1936); Walter Lippmann, *The Supreme Court, Independent or Controlled?* (1937).

in 1937 to curtail expenditures, a fact which supported the argument of Roosevelt's opponents that there had been no real recovery all along, but only a continuous process of pump-priming. New Dealers, on the other hand, charged that capital itself had gone on strike, and that business contraction in the interest of maintaining high price-levels was a principal cause of the trouble. Whatever the merit of these contentions, the administration moved rapidly to halt the decline. The Board of Governors of the Federal Reserve System promptly reversed the deflationary policy it had been pursuing since the summer of 1936, and the "second New Deal," at which Congress had balked while the Court battle went on, was promptly instituted. This included much additional pump-priming, particularly through the WPA, the PWA, the RFC, and the USHA; the creation of a new AAA, already described, for the revival of agriculture; and somewhat belatedly (1939) a wide grant of power to the President to reorganize the federal departments of government in the interest of greater efficiency. The conviction that methods of price control had been devised in monopolistic industries led also to an attempt to enforce the moribund anti-trust laws. Since the days of the ill-starred NRA these regulations had been more or less in abatement, but the President now chose Thurman W. Arnold of the Yale Law School to be Assistant Attorney-General, and charged him with the duty of making them live again.

The unpopularity of Roosevelt's fight on the Supreme Court, together with the bad effects of the "recession," left the New Deal vulnerable
Elections of 1938 politically for the first time, and the elections of 1938 accurately recorded the shifting of public opinion. Anti-Roosevelt Democrats took a greater part than formerly in party councils, and, in spite of a demand from the President that some of his severest critics in Congress be "purged," most of them were triumphantly renominated and re-elected. The election left both houses of Congress in Democratic hands, but Republican gains included seventy-nine seats in the House and eight in the Senate. Many states that had abandoned the Republican column in recent elections also returned to their former allegiance, electing Republican governors, or legislatures, or both. Noteworthy among these changes were Pennsylvania, Massachusetts, and Connecticut in the East, and Michigan, Wisconsin, and Minnesota in the West.[1]

---

[1] Two useful general studies of the New Deal are Basil Rauch, *The History of the New Deal, 1933–1938* (1944); and J. G. Frederick, *The New Deal: A People's Capitalism* (1944). Frances Perkins, *The Roosevelt I Knew* (1946), is excellent. Herbert Harris, *Labor's Civil War* (1940), tells the story of the CIO split. H. B. Hinton, *Cordell Hull: A Biography* (1942), is useful on diplomacy. It may be supplemented by J. M. Letiche, *Reciprocal Trade Agreements in World Economy* (1948). On the Supreme Court, see S. J. Konefsky, *Chief Justice Stone and the Supreme Court* (1945).

39

World Politics

DURING the two decades that followed the first World War Americans who had enthusiastically supported that struggle, in order "to make the world safe for democracy," suffered many disappointments. The failure of the United States to accept responsibility for anything that happened outside its borders was in itself disillusioning, and perhaps to some extent also a cause of the world's rapid descent into international discord. But quite as distressing was the discovery, as the years wore on, that democracy, both in Europe and in Asia, was on the wane; that dictatorships of such magnitude as modern times had never known before were being born; that the arbitrary will of autocrats to war, against which Wilson had hoped the League of Nations would insure the world, was present in an increasingly aggravated form. The League of Nations, in spite of American failure to participate in its counsels, was duly organized, but its weakness in the face of the appalling problems that confronted it soon became painfully apparent. What the League might have been had the United States chosen to be its leading member, the world can never know. But the strength it was able to muster, without American assistance, was insufficient to stem the tide that led to war.[1]

The first of the great European nations to undergo drastic revolutionary change was Russia. The Czar had abdicated in March, 1917, and had transferred his powers to a provisional government of liberal democrats, headed by Alexander Kerensky. But the real revolution began only in October, 1917, when the "Bolshevists," or extreme Communists, under the leadership of Nikolai Lenin and Leon Trotsky, undertook to establish their long-envisioned dictatorship of the proletariat. They made peace with Germany at the price of the infamous Treaty of Brest-Litovsk, and then fought off with incredible success numerous uprisings against their authority, both from within and without. By the end of 1922, they had formed a large por-

The Russian Revolution

[1] Two excellent compendiums of post-World War history are: W. C. Langsam, *The World Since 1914* (1948); and F. P. Chambers, C. P. Grant, and C. C. Bayley, *This Age of Conflict* (1943).

tion of the territory left to Russia into a Union of Soviet Socialist Republics, with the expectation that eventually non-Russian as well as Russian countries would wish to join up.[1]

The official guide of Bolshevist conduct was the *Communist Manifesto*, published in 1848 by Karl Marx and Friedrich Engels. In harmony with the Marxian ideal, the Bolshevist leaders sought to establish a classless society. The land and all large-scale industry was nationalized; only personal property was left in the hands of individuals. Such agencies of production as mines and factories were taken over by the state, and the government gradually assumed responsibility for the distribution of goods. Ideally there was only one employer, the government; and, while most labor was free, on occasion armies of "forced labor" were recruited for work in the forests or on the roads and railroads. Labor became the duty of every citizen; the "parasitic" classes of capitalist society who lived from past earnings or the earnings of others were to be no more. As the new order was set up, the old order was destroyed. The old bureaucracy, the professional classes, landowners, property-minded members of the upper and middle classes, whether great or small, were driven into exile or mercilessly liquidated. Slowly, but with inexorable certainty, the revolution penetrated even to the most remote country districts. "Collectivist" farms tended increasingly to replace the old peasant holdings, and well-to-do "kulaks" who resisted disappeared. The Russia that grew up was thus composed in large part of those who could be benefited by the new regime; the favored few who had prospered during the old regime had been eliminated.

In theory the Soviet system was extremely democratic, but practice and theory were sometimes unrelated. From the first thousands of local "soviets," or committees, each composed of workers or peasants, participated in governmental affairs, even selecting by indirect means a Congress of Soviets, supreme over all. Ultimately, under the enlightened Constitution of 1936, citizens of the "USSR," chose members to a Soviet of the Union according to electoral areas, on the basis of one deputy for each 300,000 of the population. But, since only the Communist party was tolerated, an inner circle of party leaders managed somehow to win practically all the higher offices. Party membership was rigorously restricted; in 1939 party members numbered only about a million and a half, all true and tested believers in the Marxian dogma, as interpreted by the leader of the Communist Party, originally Lenin, and some years after his death in 1924, Josef Stalin. The Soviet Union was thus ruled in fact, if not in name, by a

Communism (margin note)

The Soviet system (margin note)

---

[1] M. T. Florinsky, *Toward an Understanding of the U.S.S.R.* (1939).

small group of Communists, of whom Stalin was the chief. Whoever or whatever the state officials, all real authority was vested in the man, or the group, who could control the Communist Party.

The original Communist policy was that national revolution was only the prelude to world revolution. With this goal in mind, an organization known as the Third International,[1] or Comintern, was founded in 1919 by Lenin, with headquarters in Moscow. Theoretically, at least, the Comintern was not a part of the Russian government, but was wholly separate from it, a kind of supreme authority for Communists throughout the world. From this central agency revolutionary propaganda was dispensed, and to it professional revolutionaries operating outside Russia looked for guidance and support. But as time went on the Russian government showed more concern for internal national interests than for overthrowing the capitalist system elsewhere.[2] Particularly was this true after the accession of Stalin to power. Trotsky, a believer in immediate world revolution, was exiled, and three successive "five-year plans" were undertaken to make Russia self-sustaining, and able to defend herself in case of war. The Comintern continued to exist, but, since the Russian Communist Party had the largest number of dues-paying members, it reflected accurately the policies of the Russian government. Finally, in June, 1943, presumably at the suggestion of Stalin, the Comintern was abolished altogether.

Foreign as the Russian system was to the "American way of life," it was no more difficult for Americans to comprehend than the "Fascist" dictatorship in Italy that Benito Mussolini had set up in the years following 1922. Parliamentary government had never worked especially well in Italy, and in the face of Mussolini's rise in Italy the bewildering problems of the post-war era it threatened to break down altogether. Fear that in this event a Bolshevist revolution such as had overcome Russia might take place in Italy gave Mussolini his chance. His party, the Fascisti, although originally shot through with socialistic doctrines, had become "rightist" in character, and longed now for the opportunity to give Italy a strong government that could restrain the radicals and maintain order. Born to command, and with a personality almost irresistible to the Italian temperament, Mussolini had gathered into his following the sons of property-holders whose fear of socialism was only too well grounded, ex-veterans of the first World War who resented the aspersions cast on Italy's war record, and

---

[1] The First International was the work of Karl Marx and lasted from 1864 to 1876; the Second International was a Socialist organization that began in 1889, and was opposed by the Third International. A Fourth International was formed by the followers of Trotsky after his break with Stalin in 1929.

[2] Joseph E. Davies, *Mission to Moscow* (1941).

patriotic young bloods generally to whom his program of direct action against radicals strongly appealed. Organized Fascist bands, or "squadrists," called also "Black Shirts" from the garb they affected, paraded the streets in force, beat up the "reds," wrecked workers' clubs, and broke up strikes. By the summer of 1922 their strength was estimated at three hundred thousand.

It was well known that Mussolini was now prepared to seize authority, and late in October, 1922, his adherents began their famous "march on Rome." But to avert violence, the King made Mussolini Premier, and the Black Shirts went home without the bloody fighting they had expected. Thereafter parliamentary government in any normal sense did not last long. Non-Fascist members of the Cabinet were dropped, opposition parties were disbanded, and the whole government down to the most minor offices was thoroughly "fascistized." Personal liberty disappeared, the press was rigidly controlled, courts ruled as they knew they must. A Fascist militia, composed of the most dependable elements of the Black Shirts, gave the color of legality to "squadrist" attacks on individuals known to be critical of "Il Duce." Thus, Fascism

---

WORLD WAR II: AMERICAN FIGURES

HENRY A. WALLACE (1888–   ), *Vice-President, 1941–45, took a far more active part in governmental circles than is usual with vice-presidents. He failed of renomination, however, in 1944, and after the death of Roosevelt became one of the severest critics of the Truman Administration.*

HARRY L. HOPKINS (1890–1946) *was among President Roosevelt's closest personal friends and advisers. As chairman of the Munitions Assignments Board he made final decisions on the allocation of Lend-Lease materials. He was with Roosevelt at the fateful Yalta Conference.*

HAROLD L. ICKES (1874–   ) *was the handyman of the Roosevelt Administration much as McAdoo had been in Wilson's cabinet during the First World War. Ickes was, among other things, Petroleum Co-ordinator and Government Custodian of the Coal Mines.*

Most powerful official next to the President was JAMES F. BYRNES (*1879–   *), *formerly Associate Justice of the United States Supreme Court. As head of the Office of War Mobilization Byrnes was a kind of "assistant president." Later he became Secretary of State under Truman.*

The actual conduct of the war headed up for the Army in the Chief of Staff, General GEORGE C. MARSHALL (*1880–   *), *and for the Navy, in the Commander-in-Chief of the United States Fleet, Admiral* ERNEST J. KING (*1878–   *). *After the war ended Marshall was first sent on a diplomatic mission to China, then succeeded Byrnes as Secretary of State. (Photo of Wallace from Acme, of Hopkins from European, of Ickes courtesy of Reynal & Hitchcock, Inc., and of Byrnes from Harris & Ewing.)*

WALLACE

HOPKINS

MARSHALL

ICKES

KING

BYRNES

ROOSEVELT AND CHURCHILL

WILLKIE, GENERAL AND MADAME CHIANG KAI-SHE

STALIN

in Italy, like Communism in Russia, became a weapon through which the will of the dictator became supreme. The young Fascist who revised Descartes' *cogito, ergo sum,* to read, "I never think, therefore I am," had the spirit of Fascism in a nutshell.[1]

Fascist ideology set great store by the grandeur of ancient Rome. The party designation was derived from the word *fasces,* Latin designation for the bundle of rods surrounding a battle-axe that lictors once carried' as symbols of authority before kings, consuls, praetors, and emperors. What ancient Rome was, united and powerful, feared and respected, Fascist Italy aspired to become. Nationalism was exalted and stimulated by pride in the old Roman past. The Roman salute of the uplifted arm was revived, and every aspect of the Roman legend held in veneration. Fascism also idealized physical energy and force. It glorified all the warlike attributes, esteemed virility and efficiency, called for discipline and the will to conquer. Like ancient Rome, modern Italy must have the strength to expand its borders, and the right to boast of empire. Thickly spread over all Fascist activities was a heavy layer of theatricals and pageantry; Fascist pomposity and pretense always approached the very verge of the ridiculous. In political organization, Fascism experimented with the teachings of

Fascism

[1] H. W. Schneider, *Making the Fascist State* (1928).

WORLD WAR II: GLOBAL LEADERS

Early in the war the meetings of the two Axis leaders, Hitler and Mussolini, made headlines all over the world and presaged great events. Later on, the repeated conferences held by FRANKLIN D. ROOSEVELT *(1882–1945), thirty-second President of the United States, and* WINSTON CHURCHILL *(1874–   ), Prime Minister of Great Britain, made it clear that the initiative had passed from the Axis to the Allies. (Photo from Keystone.)*

Chief enigma among global leaders was JOSEF STALIN *(1879–   ), the Russian dictator. But Stalin's pledge that Russia had no desire to expand her territories, his willingness to make an alliance with Great Britain, and his dissolution of the Comintern were, probably mistakenly, regarded as gestures of good-will toward the rest of the world. (Photo from Acme.)*

CHIANG KAI-SHEK *(1886–   ), youngest of the Allied leaders, laid great emphasis upon the global character of the war. In calling insistently for world co-operation, he shared the views of* WENDELL L. WILLKIE *(1892–1944), defeated Republican candidate for the Presidency in 1940, who later became the emissary of President Roosevelt on two overseas missions, one to England in 1941, and one that took him around the world in 1942. (Photo from Paul Guillmette.)*

the national syndicalists, and in the "corporative state" claimed to have achieved a new governmental principle. Representation was based no longer upon political or geographic units, but upon organized economic interests, syndicates of employers as well as of employees. For the Fascists had no quarrel with capitalism; they meant to protect it, not to destroy it. And yet, the state must always be regarded as supreme; "nothing for the individual, all for Italy," was the motto of every believer. Only in this spirit could "the moral and material greatness of the Italian people" be achieved.[1]

Whatever may be said of its contradictory philosophic concepts, Fascism as personified in Mussolini did provide Italy with a government strong enough to govern. The Fascists despised democracy as outmoded, and too soft to confront the rigors of the twentieth century. Italian democracy had invited this criticism, but Mussolini's government was effective. The Duce soon had the national budget in balance, he launched public works that not only appealed to the national pride but helped also with the problem of unemployment, he stimulated both agricultural and industrial development, he put an end to labor strife, encouraged education, promoted foreign trade, developed natural resources, built up the army and navy, stimulated "air-mindedness," and to the everlasting joy of tourists "made the railroads run on time."

The third great dictatorship to make its appearance in Europe came in Germany. There the roots of democracy had never driven deep, and

Hitler's rise in Germany

the Weimar Republic, established at the close of the first World War, had the additional disadvantages to overcome of having agreed to the hated Treaty of Versailles, and of having permitted the nation to descend into a catastrophic currency inflation. Disgust with the new régime was evident in the elections of 1925, when the voters selected as President one of the outstanding heroes of the old Germany, Field Marshal Paul von Hindenburg. By this time the land was filled with revolutionaries, some of whom wished to follow the example of Communist Russia, while others favored rather the precepts of Fascist Italy. Noisiest among the latter was Adolf Hitler, an Austrian-born German with a talent for soapbox oratory, who was a member of the German Workers' Party, later renamed National Socialist. The "Nazis," as these agitators were called, adopted the Fascist salute, chose the swastika as their emblem, organized a black-shirted bodyguard for the Nazi leaders, sent forth brownshirted Storm Troopers to break up Communist meetings, made ready with small pretense at concealment to overthrow the existing democratic régime. A premature effort at revolution was made in 1923 at Munich.

[1] Herman Feiner, *Mussolini's Italy* (1935).

Its chief significance was the fact that it landed Hitler in jail, where he found time to write his dreams of a Nazi-dominated world into a book, *Mein Kampf*, thereafter the law and the gospel for all his followers.

Quite as hostile as the Nazis toward the democratic experiment in Germany was the army, organized after the war as the *Reichswehr* under General Hans von Seekt. This force, according to the Treaty of Versailles, was supposed to number only a hundred thousand men, but in actual fact it was probably much larger. Led by the ablest and most conservative elements in the old imperial army, the *Reichswehr* was quickly welded into a center of reactionary sentiment, where Social Democrats were unwelcome, even in the ranks, and where longing for the good old authoritarian days was outspokenly apparent. That the *Reichswehr* was intended as merely a nucleus around which to build a much larger army as soon as possible became clearer with each passing year. Its leaders tolerated, and perhaps even connived at, the training of numerous bands of irregular soldiery, "free corps" adventurers such as Hitler's, which in time of stress could be absorbed into the national military forces. As a result of this policy, Germany, far from being disarmed, as the Treaty of Versailles contemplated, had probably as many as two million men under arms by 1930, a formidable beginning for complete remilitarization. Army officers were sent to Russia for training in the new military techniques, airplane and submarine factories were located outside Germany's borders, and industrial plants designed to be transformed overnight into war plants were operated within Germany itself. To restore German faith in military leadership, the public was fed on the "stab-in-the-back" legend, according to which Germany had never really suffered military defeat, but had been forced to make peace because of disloyalty on the home front, disloyalty that was ascribed mainly to Social Democrats, Communists, and Jews.[1]

The ends sought by the Nazis and the army thus came to have much in common, and military leaders were able to view the rise of Hitler with considerable equanimity. To his support the Nazi spellbinder drew nearly all of the discontented elements of society for whom Communism had slight appeal — the white-collar workers, hard hit by the chronic hard times; small shopkeepers whose businesses were threatened by chain stores and trusts; discouraged peasants fearful of a Communist revolution; members of the professional classes who blamed Jewish competition for all their own shortcomings; unemployed intellectuals, particularly in and from the universities, for whom the existing economic system held little of promise; youth in search of adventure and a future; women intoxicated by the highly charged emotionalism of Hitler's appeal.

[1] Hans Ernest Fried, *The Guilt of the German Army* (1942).

All these, however, would hardly have been sufficient to install Hitler in power; it was the financial support of the great industrialists, who thought of the Nazis as a means of heading off the Communists, that insured the success of the movement.

As long as the Republic lasted, the Nazis were unable to command a majority of the Reichstag, but their growing strength was recognized by President Hindenburg in February, 1933, when he made Hitler his Chancellor. Within a few months the last vestige of democracy was wiped out, and the Nazification of the state was complete. Henceforth Hitler was the only "Führer," and a powerful secret police suppressed the slightest show of criticism. Germany, like Russia and Italy, had become a dictatorship. Just as Communism was what Stalin said it was, and Fascism was what Mussolini said it was, so now Naziism was what Hitler said it was. All three governments were totalitarian; in every instance the individual existed for the state, not the state for the individual.[1]

The Nazi ideology, like the Fascist, was less noted for common sense and consistency than for its wholesale appeal to the prejudices that Hitler found about him. The Nazis adopted in full the army
Naziism   theory that Germany had been betrayed in 1918, not defeated, and demanded the complete overthrow of the Versailles settlement. This was held to be Germany's due, not merely because of injustices in the treaty, but because Germans, as members of the master race, had superior rights. Raceism, more than anything else, was basic in the Nazi philosophy. The "Nordic," or "Aryan," races, among whom the Germans were held to be the only really pure strain, were born to command; all other races, Latin, Slav, Semite, Negro, Oriental, were born merely to take orders. Racial purity was supremely important, mixtures with "impure" blood an intolerable affront to the race. The Jewish race, of all races, was the most reprehensible. It was both parasitic and unassimilable, the source of most of the woes of the world. Acting on these principles, the most fiendish persecutions of the Jews were ordered by the Nazis on the slightest pretexts.

Blood-brother of raceism was German nationalism, for through the activities of the German nation the German race found expression. As nationalism was good, internationalism was the quintessence of evil. All organizations of an international nature were therefore suspect; Communism, which looked forward to world revolution, was the worst of all, but such international institutions as the Roman Catholic Church, the Masonic order, and the League of Nations came likewise under the ban. Furthermore, the German nation must have room to grow — *Lebensraum*. To fulfill its mission it must expand its borders to include

[1] F. L. Schuman, *The Nazi Dictatorship* (1936); William L. Shirer, *Berlin Diary* (1941).

the "heartland" of the European continent. Nazi-infected pseudo-scientists, calling their work geopolitics, drew ample boundaries for the greater, self-sufficient Germany that must come. To fill out these boundaries, and so accomplish the mission of the race, Hitler demanded an increase in the German birth rate — there should be two hundred and fifty million Germans instead of only eighty million. The German colonies, too, must be returned, and German mastery recognized throughout the world.

While the safety of democracy in Europe and America was being thus imperiled, news of alarming developments came also out of Asia. Although the government of Japan had been changed late in the nineteenth century to harmonize somewhat with Occidental practices, the theory of popular sovereignty had always been effectively excluded. The state was in a sense **The rise of Fascism in Japan** a theocracy, for the Emperor was worshiped as the Son of Heaven, and such privileges of government as were extended to the people were held to be merely gifts emanating from the divine will. In actual practice the Emperor was at the mercy of a small group of "elder statesmen" and privy councilors, whose advice he dare not reject. Following the form, if not the spirit, of the British constitution, a two-house Diet existed, the House of Peers and the House of Representatives, but the Cabinet was responsible to the Emperor rather than to the Diet, and a peculiarly independent status was assigned to the ministers of War and Navy. Invariably these men were selected from among the highest-ranking active officers of the branches concerned, and they were responsible for their acts, neither to the Diet nor to the Cabinet, but only to the Emperor himself.

During the first World War, Japan had enjoyed an unusual prosperity. Her military contribution to the defeat of the Central Powers had been comparatively slight, but she had profited greatly from the sale of war goods to the Allies, and from the use they made of her excellent fleet of merchantmen. After the war, American purchases of Japanese silk long staved off economic disaster, but the Great Depression cut down American buying power and seriously imperiled Japanese prosperity. This situation played directly into the hands of the nation's powerful military leaders, who had long maintained that Japan need only essay the rôle of conqueror to get whatever she needed. In taking such a stand, they had the support of a carefully nurtured mythology, according to which the Japanese people were a superior race, destined to rule the world. War would bring plunder, and was thus an end in itself, but the military leaders had much civilian support for the theory that Japanese expansion was an economic necessity.[1]

[1] Joseph G. Grew, *Ten Years in Japan* (1941), and *Report from Tokyo* (1942).

First on the calling list of the Japanese war lords was Manchuria.[1] This region, it was argued, if fully exploited by Japan, would provide the nation with the raw resources and the manufacturing outlet that it needed. Japanese bankers and industrialists were already entrenched in Manchuria, and they were eager for the security that conquest would bring them. After Manchuria there were other worlds to conquer — as much of the rest of China as might be needed to keep that still un-formed nation subject to the Japanese will, and, if the times broke aright, the white man's dominions in all eastern Asia and the Indies. Various terms were used to cloak the Japanese designs. For a time emphasis was laid on the similarity between Japanese ambitions in the Far East and the ambitions of the United States in the Americas. Japan wanted merely a "Monroe Doctrine for Asia." But the "New Order," or the "Co-Prosperity Sphere," that Japanese spokesmen soon began to talk about for eastern Asia exceeded the wildest dreams of American imperial-ists. What the Japanese leaders really wanted was to make their neigh-bors their slaves.[2]

The Manchurian "incident" of 1931 was the beginning of a procession of events that led directly toward the second World War. On the faint-

Manchukuo est pretexts, Japanese troops occupied large sections of Manchuria, organized it into the satellite state of Man-chukuo, and set a puppet Emperor, Henry Pu-yi, on its throne. Because this act of aggression constituted a direct violation of the Kellogg-Briand Peace Pact, the United States, through Secretary of State Henry L. Stimson, refused to recognize Manchukuo's government, but the Stimson policy had no effect on Japanese expansionists. When the British-dominated League of Nations voiced mild disapproval, Japan gave notice of her intent to withdraw from the League (March 27, 1933). Only the Chinese did anything really effective about the matter. Through a nation-wide boycott on Japanese goods, the Chinese people inflicted notable punishment upon Japanese industry. China, next to the United States, had been Japan's best customer, but in the months following the occupation of Manchuria sales of Japanese goods to China fell off by as much as two-thirds. Wholesale discriminations against Japanese busi-ness interests in China became also the order of the day.

Another result of the Japanese aggressions was to unite the faction-torn Chinese for self-defense. Even the deeply antagonistic National-

The Chinese "incident" ists under Chiang Kai-shek and the Communists under Chang Hsueh-liang found ways of co-operating, with Chiang Kai-shek as Generalissimo. When, therefore, the Japanese

---

[1] Owen Lattimore, *Manchuria, Cradle of Conflict* (1935).

[2] The background of the Far-Eastern situation is well set forth in H. S. Quigley and G. H. Blakeslee, *The Far East: An International Survey* (1939).

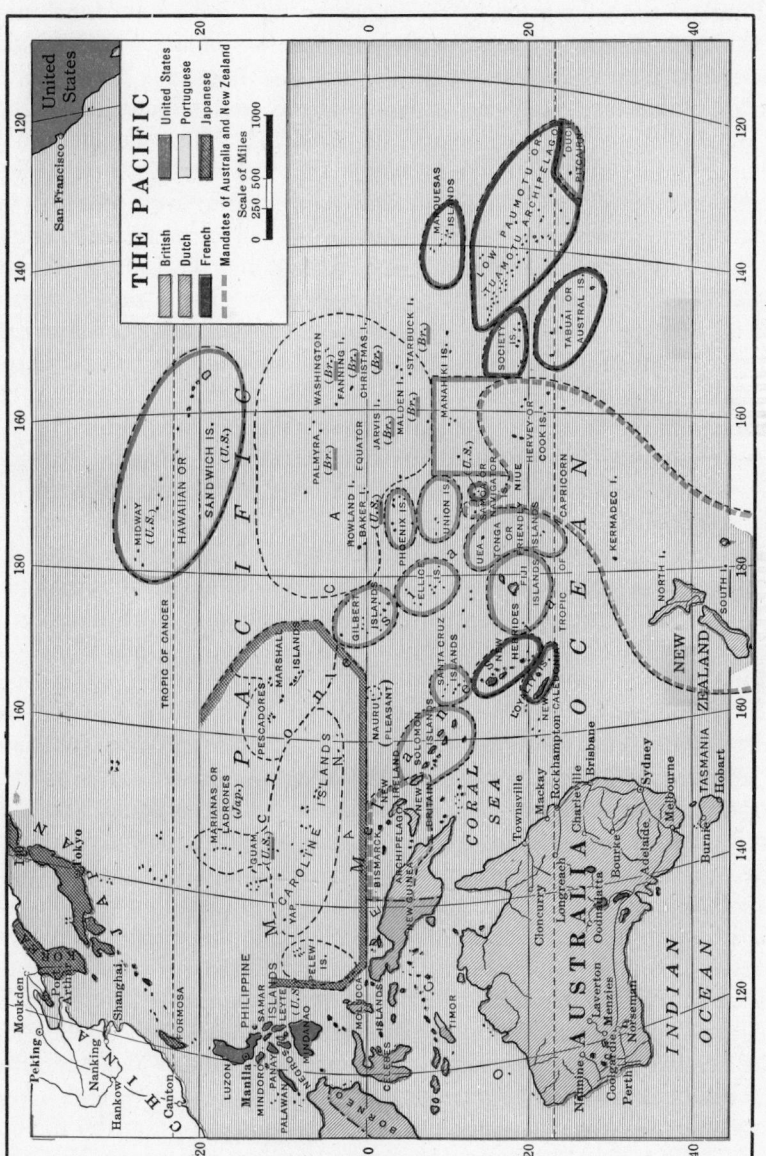

THE PACIFIC OCEAN

decided in 1937 to prosecute an undeclared war against China, their troops were confronted by organized opposition. But the Chinese were no match for the well-trained and well-supplied Japanese armies, who took territory almost at will, and eventually had under their control most of the Chinese seacoast and much of the adjacent interior. While the Japanese refused to admit that the China "incident" was a war, the League of Nations seemed to regard it as such, and after much delay recommended that the various member nations extend what aid they could to China. Over the Burma Road, which by 1938 American-trained engineers had completed with the use of Chinese coolie labor, China was able to import some useful war materials, and eventually both the British and the American governments extended credits to China. At all times the Japanese invaders were at pains to visit their wrath upon British and American residents and business interests in the military area. An incident of the war was the destruction on December 12, 1937, by Japanese bombers, of an American gunboat, the *Panay*. The act was deliberate and intended, but the American public was apathetic and the apologies of the Japanese government were accepted.[1]

Meantime, the "robber" nations of Europe were also on the march. In 1935, Mussolini began a war of conquest against Ethiopia, with the avowed intent of adding that backward African kingdom to his empire. This venture was so fraught with peril for the peace of Europe that for a time it seemed as if the League of Nations might employ effective economic "sanctions" to prevent it. If Italy could be kept from obtaining oil, it appeared that the war could not go on. But the League finally backed down. It applied sanctions, but not the oil sanctions that alone were well calculated to achieve results. Perhaps the reason for this weak attitude lay in the fact that the British navy, upon which the main brunt of enforcing the sanctions would have fallen, was inadequately prepared for war. Whatever the reasons, the League of Nations as a means of keeping the peace of the world became a farce from this time forward. Mussolini went ahead, practically unimpeded, with his plan of conquest, drove the Ethiopian monarch, Haile Selassie, into exile, and on May 9, 1936, announced that the Italian King had also assumed the title of Emperor.

Inflated with one victory, Mussolini soon sought another. When in 1936 a revolt broke out in Spain against the democratic government of the Spanish Republic, Mussolini sent his "legions" to the aid of the revolutionary leader, General Francisco Franco, whose Fascist tendencies were unmistakable. Aid for Franco came also from Germany, and a little help for the "Loyalists,"

Ethiopia

The Spanish Civil War

[1] Claude A. Buss, *War and Diplomacy in Eastern Asia* (1941).

as the government forces were called, came from Russia. The civil war in Spain was widely recognized as a dress rehearsal for the coming world war, but the democratic nations were unwilling to do anything effective for the hard-pressed Loyalists, who, after a bitter and bloody struggle, lost out. In General Franco, the new dictator of Spain, both Hitler and Mussolini recognized a kindred spirit and a potential ally.

Only those who wished to be deceived could believe that Hitler's rise to power in Germany would not still further unsettle the peace of Europe. The same year that Hitler became Chancellor —
Appeasement 1933 — Germany gave notice of her withdrawal from the League of Nations; two years later, after the plebiscite required by the Treaty of Versailles, she took back the Saar Basin; next year, in 1936, German troops reoccupied and remilitarized the Rhineland; two years after that, early in 1938, they occupied Austria, and added that formerly independent state to Hitler's "Third Reich." The portion of German *Lebensraum* next coveted by Hitler was Czechoslovakia, which Germany now almost completely surrounded, but the Führer chose at first to demand only the Sudetenland, a strip along the Czecho-German border mainly inhabited by Germans. To retain this region, which was essential to her defense, Czechoslovakia was ready to fight, but she was held back by nations she had thought were her friends, France and England. Among the people of the western democracies pacifism had become a passion; they simply would not have another war. Probably, therefore, their governments were quite in accord with public opinion when they proposed to keep Germany at peace by a policy of "appeasement." After extensive preliminary threats by Hitler and concessions by the western democracies, Prime Minister Chamberlain of Great Britain and Premier Daladier of France met with Hitler and Mussolini at Munich in September, 1938, to find a solution short of war. They found it by demanding that Czechoslovakia yield to Hitler's demands, and as a result German troops marched into the Sudetenland.[1] Then in March, 1939, Czecho-Slovakia itself, as the sadly mangled state was renamed, was occupied by Hitler, and most of its territory added to the Reich. Not to be outdone, Mussolini the very next month transported an army across the Adriatic and took possession of Albania. To diminutive Victor Emmanuel III went another title, King of Albania.

By this time a bond of friendship had been formed between Hitler and Mussolini, a bond that quite clearly was meant also to include Japan. The objection of all three nations to the spread of
Rome-Berlin Axis Communism found expression in the Anti-Comintern Pact signed between Germany and Japan in 1936, and adhered to

[1] John F. Kennedy, *Why England Slept* (1940).

by Italy in 1937. Then in May, 1939, immediately following the Czechoslovakian and Albanian incidents, Germany and Italy concluded also a ten-year military alliance — the "Rome-Berlin Axis." The agreement pledged that if either of the two powers should become involved in war, the other would come to its aid "with all its military forces, on land, sea, and in the air." Rumor had it that the next expansionist effort of the Axis Powers would be to acquire Tunisia for Italy.

What Mussolini had done in the Balkans, Great Britain and France were prepared to discount, but Hitler's extinction of Czechoslovakia, in complete disregard of his promise that the Sudetenland would be his final conquest, brought appeasement to an end. "If it is so easy to discover good reasons for ignoring assurances so solemnly and repeatedly given," said Chamberlain, "what reliance can be placed upon any other assurances that come from the same source?" That Hitler intended to press on with his program of expansion was clear to all. From Lithuania he demanded, and received, Memel. From Poland he demanded under threat of war consent to the restoration of the free city of Danzig to the Reich, and to the building of a strictly German highway and railroad across the Polish Corridor. Only a few years before, Hitler had signed a non-aggression pact with Poland, but by this time evidence of the worthlessness of his pledges was so overwhelming that these new demands occasioned little surprise. With British and French opinion now unwilling to support fur-

Roosevelt Hitler Mussolini

Courtesy of David Low

"WARMONGER"

ther appeasement, Prime Minister Chamberlain, with the full support of the French government as well as his own, promised the Polish government all possible aid in case the independence of Poland should be threatened. Similar guarantees were soon given Greece and Rumania, and an Anglo-Turkish pact provided for mutual assistance "in the event of aggression leading to war in the Mediterranean area." France, also, began to patch up her differences with Turkey over Syria, and even the United States showed concern. President Roosevelt, in a message of April 16, 1939, to the Axis dictators, asked them for assurance that they would not invade thirty named states. The recipients of the message treated it with ridicule, but they were unable to prove conclusively that their neighbors were not afraid of them.

Throughout these proceedings the great enigma had been Russia. That the signers of the Anti-Comintern Pact had anything but contempt for the Soviet system could hardly be doubted; they made it plain on every possible occasion that they intended to destroy it. But the western democracies had also had their suspicions of Russia; was not the Comintern as much dedicated to their destruction as to that of the Axis Powers? During the negotiations that preceded Munich, Russia had been deliberately slighted. In that conference, which decided the fate of Czechoslovakia, one of Russia's near neighbors, no Russian had been permitted a voice. Talk was rife that the western democracies were deliberately building up Nazi Germany as a counterweight to Soviet Russia, and that a war to the death between Germany and Russia was the real objective of British and French diplomacy. However this may have been, both Great Britain and France were by March, 1939, extremely eager for Russian collaboration, and a special British envoy was sent to Russia to negotiate an Anglo-Soviet pact. Throughout the summer of 1939, while Hitler breathed out more and more threatenings against Poland, these negotiations continued, but without results. Certain that nothing could drive such bitter enemies as Hitler and Stalin together, editorial writers and news commentators believed that the delay was over Russian insistence on a free hand in dealing with the Baltic countries, and speculated on just how much of what he wanted Stalin would be able to obtain. Then, to the amazement of the whole world, came the announcement that Russia and Germany had agreed late in August, first, to a commercial pact according to which German manufactured goods were to be exchanged for Russian raw materials, and then to a non-aggression pact which declared that each nation would respect the territory and sovereignty of the other. Thus reinforced, Hitler went ahead in a three weeks' blitzkrieg to conquer two-thirds of Poland, leaving the rest of that unhappy country to Russia.

The Russian-German accord

In response to the frantic demands of Poland, Great Britain and France, on September 3, declared war on Germany, but they were able to do nothing whatever to restrain the Nazi drive. Both nations mobilized fully; the British re-established the block- *The second World War* ade they had found so effective in the first World War, and the French manned their much-touted Maginot Line. But for more than half a year there was little real fighting, and the situation could be described with some propriety as a "phony war." During most of this period the spotlight was upon Russia rather than Germany, for Stalin took quick advantage of the opportunity presented him to seek a restoration of the old Russian frontiers along the Baltic. With only the slightest diplomatic preparation, his troops took over Latvia, Lithuania, and Estonia. His efforts to invade Finland, however, were met with stiff resistance, for the Finns were determined to retain their borders at all costs. From December, 1939, to March, 1940, the Russo-Finnish War went on, and the tenacity with which the Finns defended their borders against the vastly superior foe excited the amazement and admiration of the whole world. For her act of aggression Russia was expelled from the League of Nations, to which she had been admitted five years before, and war materials both from the Allied nations and from the Scandinavian countries were rushed in great quantity to the Finnish armies. Plans were even laid for the sending of an Allied expeditionary force to help the Finns, but before this could be done the Russians had begun to win, and the Finnish government made peace. By the terms agreed upon, the Finnish boundaries were "rectified," but the independence of Finland was left intact.

In April, 1940, the "phony war" in the West came to a sudden end. That month Hitler's armies overran Denmark and Norway, the former without resistance, and the latter in spite of all the help that Allied ships and Allied troops could give. In May *The fall of France* the Nazi blitzkrieg struck Belgium and Holland with devastating fury, and by the end of June it had brought, not them alone, but France also, to surrender. Two weeks before France confessed defeat, Mussolini forced an unwilling Italy into the war on Hitler's side, while such of the lesser nations of Europe as had not yet been conquered made every effort to curry favor with the victorious Third Reich. To most observers the invasion of England appeared imminent. The army that the British had landed on the Continent was able, almost by a miracle, to withdraw at Dunkirk, but it had lost practically all its equipment, and appeared to be easy prey for the conquering foe. Only the royal air and naval forces blocked the way. Fully mindful of this fact, the British navy took prompt action to keep as many French warships as possible out of Hitler's hands. The French squadron at Oran in North Africa was attacked by British units on July 3 and in large part destroyed, while a similar squadron at Alexandria was persuaded to remain immobilized.

In desperate but still defiant mood, the British nation and empire battened down to carry on the war alone. "I have nothing to offer," said the new Prime Minister, Winston Churchill, "but blood, toil, tears, and sweat." As if to help redeem this pledge the German *Luftwaffe* began an aerial bombardment of Britain in August, 1940, that destroyed large sections of London as well as many other British cities, and lasted on through the entire fall and winter. From fallen France, now ready to concede a German victory, there came few brave words or deeds. After the surrender to Germany, a government more subject to Hitler than to the will of the French people was set up at Vichy, with southeastern France and the overseas empire, theoretically at least, under its control. The Chief-of-State, aged Marshal Pétain, struggled with only slight success to maintain the fiction of French independence. As for the other conquered countries, most of them established exile governments in London, where also a faction of "Free French," under the leadership of General Charles de Gaulle, refused to recognize that the Vichy government really represented France.[1]

[1] On conditions in Nazi Germany, see W. E. Dodd, Jr., and Martha Dodd (eds.), *Ambassador Dodd's Diary* (1941). On the Stalin-Hitler deal, Raymond James Sontag and James Stuart Beddie (eds.), *Nazi-Soviet Relations, 1939–1941* (1948), reprints the pertinent documents from the archives of the German foreign office. Winston S. Churchill, *The Second World War*, vol. I, *The Gathering Storm* (1948), covers international relations from 1919 to 1940. For much of value on the American side of the picture, see H. L. Stimson, *On Active Service in Peace and War* (1948). On the Far East, T. A. Bisson, *American Policy in the Far East, 1931–1940* (1940), is excellent. For the earlier period, see also Dorothy Borg, *American Policy and the Chinese Revolution, 1925–1928* (1947).

Other good books on the coming of the war are: Walter Phelps Hall, *Iron Out of Calvary: A History of the Second World War* (1946); Francis T. Miller, *History of World War II* (1946); Floyd A. Cave and associates, *The Origins and Consequences of World War II* (1948); C. G. Haines and R. J. S. Hoffman, *The Origins and Background of the Second World War* (1943).

40

The Second World War

THE NEW DEAL that Roosevelt inaugurated in the United States at about the same time Hitler came to power in Germany was primarily concerned with domestic affairs. But that danger to the American continent existed from the aggressor nations of Europe and Asia was by no means overlooked. In part on this account the deep-seated interest in securing the friendship of Latin-America that had long characterized American foreign policy was continued and intensified under Roosevelt. Hoover as President-elect had made a "good-will tour" of eleven Latin-American republics, and as President had worked steadily toward the withdrawal of American troops from occupied areas. Roosevelt speedily let it be known that his policy toward Latin America was likewise to be that of the "good neighbor." He sent Secretary Hull to the seventh Pan-American Conference, held in Montevideo, and cordially approved the doctrine on which the Conference agreed, that "no state has the right to intervene in the internal or external affairs of another." Presently, in 1936, he journeyed seven thousand miles by sea to Buenos Aires in order to open a special Inter-American Conference for Peace, and told delegates that non-American states seeking "to commit acts of aggression against us will find a Hemisphere wholly prepared to consult together for our mutual safety and our mutual good."

A practical demonstration of how the "good neighbor policy" might be expected to operate was given in the case of Cuba, which dared at last to attempt the overthrow by revolution of its current dictator, Guerardo Machado. The depression which began in 1929 became particularly acute in Cuba after the passage in 1930 of the Hawley-Smoot Tariff, which increased the rates on sugar imported into the United States. Machado, a thoroughgoing tyrant who had maintained himself in office since 1924, should normally have been one of the first casualties of the depression and well deserved the honor. But American investors in Cuban securities liked him, for he consistently made the interest payments due on the huge sums that the Cuban government had borrowed in the United States.[1] Out of deference to their wishes the Hoover administration had so strongly supported Machado that the Cubans, fearing American intervention even more than they feared Machado's tyranny, dared not revolt. When Roosevelt became President, he let it be known that Machado could expect no further backing from the American government, and as a result the dictator was promptly driven from office. Unhappily, however, the government which succeeded him lasted only three weeks, when another revolution occurred. Undoubtedly American pressure was applied from this time forward to insure the establishment of an orderly and competent government in the island, but no American troops were landed, and American interests were watched over exclusively by recognized diplomatic agents. For the first time since the Spanish-American war a serious revolutionary outbreak in Cuba came to an end without the customary military intervention by the United States. Furthermore, on May 29, 1934, a treaty between the United States and Cuba formally released the latter from the terms of the Platt Amendment, which for a generation had rankled in Cuban breasts. That same year a reciprocal trade treaty materially reduced the tariff on Cuban exports to the United States and checked the decline of Cuban-American trade.

Other evidence that the "big stick" policy was really at an end accumulated rapidly. By an agreement reached in August, 1934, the financial receivership which the United States maintained in Haiti was greatly liberalized, and the last detachment of American marines was ordered to leave the republic. About the same time negotiations were begun with Panama to abolish the special privileges that that nation had been forced to accord the United States, and after a long delay this, too, was accomplished. Even the drastic action taken by Mexico in 1936, which ordered the expropriation of all foreign-owned oil property within Mexican borders, led only to relatively mild expostulations.[2]

The Roosevelt administration also made a systematic effort to draw Canada more closely into the fraternity of American nations. This was somewhat facilitated by the greater independence which Canada enjoyed, after the World War, within the British Empire, particularly by the fact that the United States and Canada had exchanged ministers since 1927 and were able to carry on their diplomatic relations directly instead of by way of London. Neither Hoover nor Roosevelt was able to obtain Senate ratification for the St. Law-

Canada

---

[1] Carleton Beals, *Crime of Cuba*, abundantly emphasizes the sins of American capital. See also H. F. Guggenheim, *The United States and Cuba* (1934).

[2] Nathaniel and Sylvia Weyl, *The Reconquest of Mexico: The Years of Lázaro Cárdenas* (1939), is wholly sympathetic with the Cárdenas program. On Panama see W. L. McCain, *The United States and the Republic of Panama* (1937).

rence Waterway Treaty, negotiated in 1932 to make possible a deep-sea channel from the Gulf of St. Lawrence to the Great Lakes, but Roosevelt, on a visit to Canada in 1938, reminded his hearers that the Monroe Doctrine applied as much to the territory north of the United States as to the territory south of it. "I give you assurance," he said, "that the people of the United States will not stand idly by if the domination of Canadian soil is threatened by any other empire." That Roosevelt meant precisely what he said became evident two years later when he conferred on measures of joint defense with Prime Minister Mackenzie King of Canada at Ogdensburg, New York. By this time Canada was at war with Germany and Italy, while the United States, at least in theory, was a neutral. Nevertheless, the heads of the two governments solemnly agreed that a Permanent Board on Defense should be set up, to consist of four or five members from each country, the business of which would be to "commence immediate studies relating to sea, land, and air ... defense of the north half of the Western Hemisphere." As head of the United States delegation, the President appointed Mayor Fiorello H. La Guardia of New York, a former Congressman who had distinguished himself as a member of the United States air service during the first World War. On both sides of the border this declaration was hailed as the practical equivalent of a military alliance.[1]

The rapid descent toward war in Europe led Roosevelt to renewed emphasis upon "continental solidarity" and "hemispheric defense." When the eighth Pan-American Conference met in Lima, December 10, 1938, the United States was acutely conscious of the inroads being made by German and Italian propaganda in Latin-American states, and sought to unite the twenty-one republics of the New World in a common defense against "aggressor nations." The agreement which Secretary Hull was able to obtain was not nearly as binding as the American government had hoped, but it affirmed that the peoples of America still had faith in "absolute adherence to the principles of international law," and that they would work together to defend the peace of the continent. When war actually broke out, delegates from the various American republics met at Panama, October 1, 1939, to consider a common policy of neutrality. After several days' deliberation they issued a declaration which asserted that the "waters adjacent to the American continent" must be "free from the commission of any hostile act by any non-American belligerent nation." Two months later an engagement between German and British naval units off the mouth of the River Plate demonstrated conclusively that

"Continental solidarity"

[1] J. M. Callahan, *American Foreign Policy in Canadian Relations* (1937).

something stronger than words would be required to keep the war far removed from American shores. In the spring of 1940 the assistance which Hitler's armies received from Nazi sympathizers in Norway, the Netherlands, Belgium, and France led to a new wave of excitement throughout the Americas. Was there a "fifth column" [1] in each American nation ready to betray it to some European invader? Fear that some such situation might indeed exist led many Latin-American governments to affirm more earnestly than ever before their desire to co-operate fully with the United States.

The occupation of the Dutch West Indies by the Allies after the defeat of the Netherlands brought no protest from the United States, but when France was compelled to sue for peace notice was promptly served on Germany that the United States under the terms of the Monroe Doctrine could permit no transfer of American colonies from one European nation to another. This contention was scornfully rejected by Germany, which insisted that the United States had no right to advance such an argument unless willing on its part to keep entirely aloof from European affairs. The surliness of the Nazi reply, coupled with the fact that after the French surrender British and French warships seemed to be on the verge of a clash in American waters, led the President to advocate that the Pan-American Conference scheduled to meet in Havana on July 20 should adopt a new rule for territorial readjustments in the American hemisphere. On behalf of the United States he formally renounced all territorial aspirations, and he urged that the twenty-one American republics should act together, each having equal voice, in determining what post-war rearrangements would be permitted in the New World. He suggested further that the system he favored for the Americas might well be applied in other continents also. Instead of Asia for the Japanese and Europe for the Germans, let each of the nations of Asia have an equal voice in Asiatic affairs, and each of the nations of Europe an equal voice in European affairs.

Neither Europe nor Asia was in position to heed the President's advice, but at the Havana Conference the patient diplomacy of Secretary Hull bore significant fruit. An Act of Havana was adopted
Act of Havana which forbade the transfer of any European colony to another non-American power, and stated that if any such transfer were attempted the colony in question would pass immediately under the joint control of the American states. To provide for the government of the colony a committee of twenty-one, to consist of one member for each

---

[1] This term was first used by General Mola, the commander of the Spanish insurgents, in his campaign against Madrid. Four columns, he announced, were marching on the city, and they would be joined by a secret "fifth column" from within the city itself.

American nation, might be summoned at will by any of the participating nations, and as an assurance against impotence this committee was to be considered fully constituted "from the date of the appointment of two-thirds of its members." Furthermore, actions might be taken with the approval of two-thirds of the members present, while a special emergency declaration gave the United States the support for the Monroe Doctrine from the other American nations that it long had craved:

> If the necessity for emergency action be deemed so urgent as to make it impossible to await action of the committee, any of the American republics, individually or jointly with others, shall have the right to act in a manner required for its defense or the defense of the continent.

In spite of these apparent successes, it was obvious that many obstacles blocked the way toward any real union of the Americas. Culturally the English-speaking peoples of North America were infinitely farther removed from the Latin-Americans than the latter were from the peoples of southwestern Europe. Economic interests tended also to bind Latin America to Europe rather than to the United States, for Europe could provide a market for Latin-American goods, whereas the United States already had too much of what the various Latin-American nations wished to sell. In respect to government, too, the same pattern persisted. Dictatorships were the rule rather than the exception in Latin America, and democracy was only a thin veneer. Even in the matter of geography "hemispheric solidarity" was far less significant than it sounded, for South America lay entirely to the east of North America, and much of it was closer to the Old World than to the United States. The one important bond of union that Roosevelt could count on was fear.

Roosevelt's insistence that the United States must take the lead in preparing for the defense of all the Americas found little opposition within the national boundaries, but many Americans, after reflecting on the results of the "war to end war" which they had entered in 1917, were convinced that the proper course of conduct for the United States was to maintain its neutrality, come what might. Undoubtedly this sentiment was greatly strengthened by the findings of a Senate committee, headed by Senator Gerald P. Nye of North Dakota, which in 1934 began to examine into the unsavory record of the munitions industries during and after the last war.[1] Extreme isolationists began to demand insistently that Congress enact neutrality laws so strict as to preclude all possibility of American involvement in case war again broke out in Europe.

Opposed to this point of view were the believers in "collective se-

[1] H. C. Engelbrecht and F. C. Hanighen, *Merchants of Death* (1934), is a popular exposé of the activities of the munitions-makers.

curity" who argued that the world had become too small for any nation
so large and influential as the United States to remain aloof
"Collective security" from what was going on. If war came it might easily engulf
the United States, regardless of any laws Congress might
pass, or of the will of the American people for peace. Even if the United
States failed to take part in a general war, it would still be intimately affected. Normal lines of trade would be broken up; the basis for a new
world depression more calamitous than any ever known before would be
laid; disease germs as destructive as those which in 1918 spread the
influenza to every nation, neutral or belligerent, would be unleashed; and
in a thousand other ways the United States would feel the impact of hostilities. The proper course, therefore, was to prevent war. Let the
United States join with peace-loving nations to curb aggressors and to
compel peace. Mere negative neutrality was not enough. War must be
prevented.

As early as 1933, when Hitler rose to power in Germany and began his
program of rearmament, Roosevelt made it clear that, whatever other
Americans might think, the President of the United States leaned
strongly in the direction of collective security. In an address to the
nations of the world issued May 16, 1933, the day before Hitler was to
make what was expected to be a warlike statement to the Reichstag,
Roosevelt urged the adoption of the MacDonald plan for the elimination of weapons designed primarily for aggressive warfare. "Modern
weapons of offense," he pointed out with admirable prescience, "are
vastly stronger than modern weapons of defense. Frontier forts,
trenches, wire entanglements, coast defenses — in a word, fixed fortifications — are no longer impregnable to the attack of war planes,
heavy mobile artillery, land battleships called tanks, and poison gas." If
the nations would agree not to possess or use these weapons, then the
"frontiers and independence of every nation" would become secure. A
few days later, Norman H. Davis, American representative at an international conference on disarmament, held in Geneva, told the delegates
that, provided only a satisfactory treaty could be arranged, the United
States would be willing to consult with the other nations in case of a
threat to peace. Further, should any disciplinary measures be undertaken against an aggressor nation, the United States "would refrain from
any action tending to defeat such collective effort," that is, from insisting
on its rights as a neutral. A good definition of an aggressor nation, Davis
suggested, was one "whose troops are found on alien soil in violation of
treaties." [1]

[1] The subsequent fate of such nations as Austria, Czechoslovakia, Poland, Finland,
Norway, Denmark, Belgium, and Holland led one observer to amend this definition as
follows: "An aggressor nation is a little nation that has something that a big nation wants."

The disarmament conference died a lingering death, and many Americans were relieved that Roosevelt was not obliged to live up to the pledges he had made.[1] The President nevertheless showed repeatedly that he had not changed his mind. His classic utterance on the subject, aimed apparently at Japan and Italy for their operations respectively in China and Ethiopia, came on October 5, 1937, during an address delivered in Chicago:

A quarantine of aggressors?

> It seems to be unfortunately true that the epidemic of world lawlessness is spreading. When an epidemic of physical disease starts to spread, the community approves and joins in a quarantine of the patients in order to protect the health of the community against the spread of the disease.... War is a contagion, whether it be declared or undeclared. It can engulf states and peoples remote from the original scene of hostilities. We are determined to keep out of war, yet we cannot insure ourselves against the disastrous effects of war and the dangers of involvement.... There must be positive endeavors to preserve peace. America hates war. America hopes for peace. Therefore, America actively engages in the search for peace.

The American search for peace did not stand in the way of active naval expansion, particularly after the breakdown of all plans for disarmament seemed assured. In January, 1938, the President asked Congress to appropriate a billion dollars for naval defense, and after some delay and debate Congress acquiesced. From the point of view of those who believed in collective security the navy was necessary if the United States was to have any influence in restraining "warmongers," while from the point of view of the isolationists it was necessary to defend American borders against a warmongering world.

Naval expansion

Probably the advocates of collective security were only a small minority in the United States, and Roosevelt found it expedient from time to time to tone down or disavow the sentiments he undoubtedly felt. In this instance Congress, rather than the President, represented the dominant public opinion. By a series of neutrality laws it attempted to legislate into oblivion all possible opportunities for the United States to be drawn into a non-American conflict. The first of these acts, passed in 1935 during the Italian attack on Ethiopia, required the President to impose an embargo upon the shipment of arms to belligerent nations, and authorized him to prohibit Americans from traveling upon the ships of belligerents. The second act, passed the following year, maintained these provisions, and added a prohibition against the flotation of loans in the United States by any non-American belligerent. The third act, more comprehensive than the

Neutrality legislation

[1] J. W. Wheeler-Bennett, *The Pipe-Dream of Peace: The Story of the Collapse of Disarmament* (1935).

rest, became law in May, 1937. It, too, included the preceding legislation on neutrality and imposed additional restrictions. American merchant ships might not carry munitions to belligerents nor arm themselves against attack. Certain discretionary powers were also bestowed upon the President. He might forbid American ships to transport commodities of any kind to a belligerent nation; he might require all shipments to be made on a strictly "cash-and-carry" basis; and he might exclude enemy warships, submarines, and armed merchantmen from the use of American ports. These acts went far toward eliminating all the various causes of conflict that had led the United States to enter the World War in 1917. By them notice was pointedly served upon European nations that the American people were no longer willing to defend the principles of neutrality for which they once had fought.

While the President found these laws somewhat unpalatable, he showed considerable facility in adapting them to his views on foreign policy. He recognized the existence of a state of war between Italy and Ethiopia, and declared the embargo on arms in force. This was advantageous to Ethiopia, which could not have purchased arms in America in any event, and an intended handicap to Italy, who might have done so. But since Japan had not declared war against China, he refused to recognize the hostilities in the Orient as war, presumably in order to enable the Chinese to continue their purchases of American munitions. In the case of Spain, where civil war existed, but with the Italians and Germans helping the insurgents and the Russians helping the Loyalists, he applied the embargo, much to the discomfiture of the Loyalists, who had the money with which to buy. The responsibility for this action, however, lay primarily with Congress, which by joint resolution of January 8, 1937, forbade the shipment of arms to Spain for the duration of the war.

Foreseeing clearly the trend of events in 1939, the President asked Congress to modify the Neutrality Act of 1937 by removing the mandatory feature of the embargo on arms to belligerents. It was the President's idea that the American government should be left free to follow traditional practice on this subject. Representative Rayburn, the administration leader in the House, stated one reason for the President's request when he asked, "Is there any immorality in our shipping arms to a little weak country so it can defend itself?" Secretary Hull, who also approved the change, took a larger view: "I profoundly believe that the first great step toward safeguarding this nation from being drawn into war is to use whatever influence it can, compatible with the traditional policy of our country of non-involvement, so as to make less likely the outbreak of a major war."

Roosevelt urges changes

No doubt the President believed that the cause of peace would be served if the European dictators knew in advance that their opponents would be able to buy arms in the United States. But Congress was recalcitrant, and late in July Senator Borah openly challenged the President's contention that the danger of war was very great. He, too, he claimed, had received advices from Europe, and in his opinion war was not as imminent as the President and his Secretary seemed to think. The President's efforts to amend the act came to nothing, but he was promised that neutrality legislation would be the first order of business at the next session of Congress.

When Germany on the following September 1 opened hostilities against Poland, the President was proved to be wholly right as to prophecy, and Senator Borah wholly wrong. Congress, convened in special session on September 21, was now persuaded to revise the Neutrality Act so as to permit the United States to sell arms, ammunition, and implements of war to such nations as were able to pay for them in cash and to carry them away in foreign-registered ships. But in thus ending the embargo on munitions, every effort was made to insure the United States against outright participation in the war. The prohibition on loans to belligerents was continued, American ships were barred from carrying passengers or materials to belligerent shores; and travel by American citizens on the vessels of belligerents was specifically forbidden. One result of the failure of the United States to defend its traditional rights as a neutral was that the minor neutral nations were left without a champion, and helpless before the superior might of their predatory neighbors. Hundreds of neutral ships went down as German submarine warfare assumed at once the unrestricted character that it had attained in the preceding war only after more than two years of fighting, and at the cost of American participation on the Allied side.

During the months of the "phony war" Americans generally believed that the struggle would, and should, end in a stalemate, with neither side the victor. The British navy was regarded as unbeatable, and whatever might happen to the continent of Europe, the Atlantic Ocean would still remain in friendly hands. But after the fall of France, confidence that the British could hold out indefinitely began to wane. Suppose Hitler succeeded in sinking the British navy, or, worse still, in capturing it. Would he then be content to rule in Europe and leave America alone? What would be his attitude toward Latin America? Heretofore British economic interests and American national policy had coincided in relation to the Americas. The Monroe Doctrine had been possible no more because American sea-power stood back of it than because the British, too, gave it tacit support. Would the United States eventually have to fight Hitler alone? And whether the war came to the New World or not, what would international relations be like with the democracy-hating dictatorships supreme in Europe, Asia, and Africa?

Nevertheless, a surprisingly large number of Americans were ready to take their chances on a Hitlerian victory. To them the consideration of first importance was that, come what might in Europe, the United States must keep out of the war. Since there was no danger whatever of American involvement on the German side, they concentrated their attacks on those who wished to show in any tangible way the partiality that most Americans felt for the beleaguered British. Chief among the advocates of an adamant "isolationism" were Senator Burton K. Wheeler, of Montana, who had broken with the Roosevelt administration over the Supreme Court issue; Colonel Charles A. Lindbergh, the aviator, whose father had suffered much persecution as an opponent of the first World War; William Randolph Hearst and his editorial writers for the Hearst newspapers; Colonel Robert R. McCormick, of the *Chicago Tribune*; the two La Follette brothers, of Wisconsin; Representative Hamilton Fish, of New York; and Senator Gerald P. Nye, of North Dakota. They were aided by a powerful and well-financed organization, attractively named the "America First Committee," which left no stone unturned to discredit all would-be "interventionists." Actually, very few Americans were prepared to advocate outright military intervention, but among those who were unable to look with complacency upon the final triumph of Hitler, all possible aid for the Allies "short of war" became an increasingly popular slogan. A "Committee to Defend America by Aiding the Allies" was headed for a time by the venerable William Allen White, of Kansas, but in general the "interventionists" lacked both the leaders and the funds to make their propaganda fully effective. They took comfort, however, in the fact that they had on their side the President of the United States. It was he who had persuaded Congress to permit the shipment of American-made munitions to the enemies of Germany and Italy; furthermore, he had deliberately turned back to the manufacturers as supposedly outmoded such military items as airplanes, knowing full well that they would promptly be shipped to the Allies.

Isolationists vs. interventionists

It is not surprising, considering the unparalleled situation they faced, that the American people began to look with critical eye at their defenses. Naval preparedness, they well knew, had long been regarded with considerable favor, but no attempt had been made to build up separate Atlantic and Pacific squadrons. The United States possessed a fleet approximately equal to the British navy, and

Preparedness

still, or so the American public fondly believed, somewhat superior to the Japanese. But American strategists had never faced the possibility of an attack in the Atlantic and Pacific at the same time. They had assumed always that the Panama Canal would enable American ships to shuttle back and forth as needed from one ocean to another, and they had counted, more or less subconsciously, upon the support of an invincible British fleet. Now, with Japan determined to push its "new order" to unpredictable lengths in the Pacific, and with the plainly visible threat of German domination in the Atlantic, the country awoke with a start from its pleasant dream of security. Even the Panama Canal was vulnerable, if only an enemy nation could obtain a near-by American base for aircraft operation.

The success of the German methods of land warfare had also to be taken into account. While the rest of the world had struggled ineffectively with the problems of peace, the German nation had prepared for war. Under the complete domination of the Nazi hierarchy its people had been disciplined and trained, both physically and psychologically, for the supreme effort that lay before them. Autocratic rulers had demanded and obtained perfect co-ordination of military might, on land, by sea, and in the air, regardless of all hamstringing traditions. German scientists had turned their remarkable talents to the improvement of the weapons of warfare found most useful in the last war, and had conducted a ceaseless search for new ways to strengthen the nation's fighting power. While other nations had failed miserably to solve their problems of unemployment, Germany had devoted herself so intensely to the quantity production of war machines as to produce a chronic labor shortage.

The various battles by which the Nazi victories were won proved the potency of the new weapons, and the hopeless inadequacy of the old. The United States was particularly lacking in the equipment necessary for mechanized warfare. If British and American sea-power should be overcome, the military invasion of North America was no more an impossibility than it had been during the American Revolution or the War of 1812. Indeed, Canada, the northern neighbor of the United States, was already at war, and Winston Churchill, the fighting British Prime Minister who had succeeded Chamberlain after the British *débâcle* in Norway, had promised, in case the British Isles were overcome, to move the British government to the "Empire beyond the seas," and from there to "carry on the struggle until, in God's good time, the New World, with all its power and might, steps forth to the rescue and liberation of the Old." Should Germany attempt to invade Canada, the Monroe Doctrine would auto-

Lessons from the Nazi victories

matically bring the United States into the war, and should a German invasion prove successful, the undefended border between the United States and its northern neighbor might not be the boon it had always seemed. To meet even a minor mechanized invasion, existing methods and weapons would be well-nigh helpless.

Under these circumstances it seemed clear to most Americans, "isolationists" and "interventionists" alike, that the least the United States

The defense program

could do was to arm to the teeth with all possible speed. But even this minimum necessity met vigorous opposition. Professional pacifists, among whom the most prominent were Socialists, Communists, and members of the liberal Protestant clergy, joined forces with other extreme advocates of neutrality to denounce preparedness as merely a prelude to war. Nevertheless, Congress early in June, 1940, appropriated by decisive majorities more than three billion dollars for the national defense, and made clear its intention of adding whatever other sums might be regarded as necessary. By the end of September, total appropriations for defense purposes had reached the astounding figure of thirteen billion dollars. To facilitate further large-scale borrowing, the national debt limit was raised to forty-nine billion dollars, the first, but not the last, such increase. Additional income and excise taxes were also voted, in defiance of the tradition that new taxes were not to be thought of in an election year.

Appropriating the money, however, was quite a different thing from actual rearmament. At best, according to the *Army and Navy Journal*, the United States would still be "a year and a half hence, far behind the fighting forces of the European nations." Plans had yet to be formulated for adjusting the nation's productive plant to the manufacture of the necessary tanks and other mechanized equipment, and for raising and training the essential man-power. To furnish political supervision over the activities of Army and Navy, the President broke precedents right and left by making Henry L. Stimson, formerly Secretary of State under Herbert Hoover, his Secretary of War, and Frank Knox, Republican Vice-Presidential candidate in 1936, his Secretary of the Navy. To put the nation on a war footing, so far as industry was concerned, he set up a National Defense Advisory Commission of seven members, headed by William S. Knudsen, president of the General Motors Corporation, and Edward R. Stettinius, Jr., chairman of the board of the United States Steel Corporation. When production bottlenecks and labor difficulties proved too difficult for the commission to handle, the President tried again, creating this time an Office of Production Management, with Knudsen as director-general, and Sidney Hillman as a representative of labor, associate director-general. Continuing complications were attributed by most critics to the President's unwillingness to place the whole problem of production under one-man control.

Unwilling to risk the delay involved in raising an army by volunteering, the President urged Congress to adopt a Selective Service Act comparable to the conscription measure of 1917. This plan met with the most determined opposition, but by the middle of September, 1940, preparedness leaders in Congress were able to score a complete victory. The new measure required all men between the ages of twenty-one and thirty-five inclusive to register for a year of military training, and on October 16 approximately seventeen million citizens presented themselves for the draft. From this number the Army planned to call into service during the first year about eight hundred thousand men, and to replace them with a similar number each succeeding year. Each class, at the end of its period of training, was to remain subject to recall for emergency service during a ten-year period. Congress might also at any time declare the nation in peril, and hold the men in training under arms indefinitely. As the nation's peril increased, the terms of the draft law were stiffened. The first class called had not yet completed its year of training when, on August 18, 1941, Congress authorized the President to hold all draftees in service for as much as eighteen months beyond the period for which they had been called originally. Four months later the requirement of registration was extended to include all men from eighteen to sixty-four years of age, with service liability limited to those from twenty to forty-five.[1] Meantime the National Guard, as the nation's second line of defense, had long since been called into service.

To President Roosevelt, and to a steadily increasing number of other Americans, it seemed clear that the defense of the United States should be further promoted by more effective measures "short of war" to help along the British war-effort. In line with this policy, when it became known that the British navy was perilously short of destroyers, whereas the United States was not, a strong demand set in for selling outmoded American destroyers to the British, just as previously military airplanes had been sold to the Allies. Although specific legislation seemed to bar the way to any such action, the President was advised by Attorney-General Jackson that his powers as Commander-in-Chief of the Army and Navy would permit him to exchange obsolete destroyers for such naval bases as he might deem essential to the defense of the United States. Accordingly, the

Measures "short of war"

---

[1] The decision to induct eighteen- and nineteen-year-old boys was reached reluctantly in November, 1942, after the United States had been at war for nearly a year. Thereafter volunteering, which had been encouraged before, was stopped, and not only the Army, but the Navy and the Marine Corps as well, were obliged to depend upon the draft for additional man-power.

President announced early in September that the United States had leased from the British government for a period of ninety-nine years eight bases, one each in Newfoundland, Bermuda, the Bahamas, Jamaica, St. Lucia, Trinidad, Antigua, and British Guiana. When these advanced positions were fully equipped, it was supposed that the Atlantic coast-line of the United States, as well as the Panama Canal, would be completely safeguarded against attack from the east. In return for this "dismemberment of the British Empire," as the Axis Powers chose to term the deal, fifty American destroyers were soon turned over to British crews. That the hard-pressed British, now fighting gamely against incessant attacks from the air as well as the constant threat of invasion by sea, could count on further aid from the United States when the need arose seemed evident.

With foreign relations at so critical a stage, and with the necessity of speeding up the national defense program so obvious, many observers regarded the necessity of holding a presidential election in **The presidential campaign** 1940 as almost a calamity. In nations such as Great Britain, where the parliamentary system of government was in operation, an election could be postponed, but in the United States the Constitution was inexorable on this point; the election had to be held. But, as events proved, this was no ordinary election. Shattering all precedents, the Democrats renominated Roosevelt for a third term, and chose Henry A. Wallace of Iowa, Secretary of Agriculture, as his running-mate. The Republicans, convinced that the leading contenders for their nomination lacked the popular appeal necessary to defeat the President, turned to an ex-Democrat and a businessman, Wendell L. Willkie of Indiana, with Senator Charles L. McNary of Oregon as vice-presidential candidate. Both conventions adopted platforms, the Democrats praising and the Republicans castigating the New Deal. But the platforms, as everyone knew, meant only what the candidates chose to make them mean. Roosevelt's record was not to be concealed, but where did Willkie stand on the issues of the day? Already he had made it clear that on many matters he saw eye to eye with the President, and as the campaign developed, it became evident that almost the only question at issue was whether Roosevelt or Willkie, limited, of course, by the parties they represented, would be the better fitted to carry on the New Deal policies, both foreign and domestic. Willkie made a splendid campaign, stressing that in a democracy no one man should be considered indispensable, but the voters preferred in the crisis to stand by the President. About fifty million voters went to the polls, the largest number in American history. Of these nearly fifty-five per cent voted for Roosevelt, who carried 38 states with 449 electoral votes, while Willkie carried only

10 states with 82 electoral votes. Both houses of Congress and a majority of the state governments remained safely Democratic.

The most obvious conclusion to be drawn from the election, one that foreign powers were quick to point out, was that Roosevelt's policy with reference to the European war had received the emphatic endorsement of the American people. Thus fortified, the *The Lend-Lease Act* President reasserted his determination to give all possible aid to Britain, and set "four freedoms" as the American goal for the post-war world — freedom of speech, freedom of religion, freedom from want, freedom from fear. He also submitted to Congress a plan whereby the government of the United States should lend, lease, or otherwise transfer to the nations resisting aggressors such military equipment as American factories were able to produce and the American government to acquire. This measure, which amounted almost to a declaration of partial war, was fought for weeks by the isolationists in and out of Congress, but it ultimately passed both houses by decisive, nonpartisan majorities, and on March 13, 1941, received the President's signature. Among other Republicans to give the Lend-Lease Act hearty support was Wendell Willkie, whose relations with the President had become almost cordial. When Willkie decided to pay a visit to England, he conferred first with Roosevelt, and took a letter from him to be delivered in person to Prime Minister Churchill.

Other actions that left no doubt as to exactly where the United States stood on the war were soon coming thick and fast. Huge appropriations were rushed through Congress for the purchase of lend-lease materials needed by the British. Axis, Danish, and French ships in American ports were seized, and crews deemed guilty of sabotaging their ships were arrested. An executive agreement, reached April 10, 1941, between Secretary of State Hull and the Danish minister to Washington (who had refused to co-operate with his Nazi-dominated government), gave the United States permission to make military use of the island of Greenland. Amidst steadily mounting tension, the President during the next few weeks turned over fifty sorely needed tankers to the British government, closed the Axis consulates in the United States and deported their personnel, and, following the sinking in the South Atlantic of an American merchantman, the *Robin Moor*, proclaimed a state of "unlimited national emergency." The last pretense of American neutrality had all but evaporated.

Meantime Hitler, after a winter of diplomatic preparation, made ready in the spring of 1941 to march his armies southward into the Balkans. Acting under irresistible pressure, Hungary, Rumania, and Bulgaria agreed to receive his troops and co-operate with his régime.

The government of Yugoslavia was like-minded, but the Yugoslav army revolted at the orders it was given, and staged a plucky but hopeless struggle against the invaders. Next the Greeks, whom Mussolini had been seeking in vain to conquer since the fall of 1940, were overwhelmed and the little British army sent to their aid from Egypt was expelled in tattered fragments. For a time the British held Crete, but by the first of June an airborne Nazi invasion had forced them back on Africa. There the British commander, General Sir Archibald Wavell, had recently pushed the Italians far to the westward along the coast of Libya, but whatever chance he might have had to expel them from Africa altogether he lost with the collapse of the ill-fated Greek venture. The hold of the British on the eastern Mediterranean seemed tenuous indeed. To anticipate a possible Nazi thrust through Turkey or Palestine toward the oil fields of Iraq and Iran, British and "Free French" forces, early in June, occupied Syria, but their chances of resisting a Nazi attack in force seemed slender indeed.

Then, to the amazement of all the world, Hitler on June 22, 1941, with Hungary, Rumania, and Finland as allies, attacked Russia. His explanation of this astounding reversal of policy was that Russia was about to attack him, but there is little or no evidence to support such a theory. On the contrary, ever since the Nazi-Communist pacts of 1939, Russia had sought desperately to avoid giving offense to Germany. The Russian dictator, Stalin, had, to be sure, kept his army mobilized, and as subsequent events proved he had made astonishing strides with preparedness. But he had encouraged Communists outside Russia to harass in every possible way the Allied war effort, and had seemed in all respects willing to play the rôle of non-belligerent assistant to Hitler. The new adherent to the anti-Nazi cause was received, however, with every show of cordiality. From Churchill came the prompt announcement: "Any man or state who fights against Naziism will have our aid. Any man or state who marches with Hitler is our foe." And from Roosevelt came the assurance that supplies would soon be flowing from the United States to Russia under the terms of the Lend-Lease Act. Non-Russian Communists also changed their tune with alacrity. In the United States they were transformed, overnight, from the bitterest of isolationists to the most belligerent of interventionists. To the surprise of most experts, the Russians offered sustained military resistance to the invading armies. The Germans and their allies took much territory, but the collapse that they had expected failed to materialize. In the winter of 1941–42, the Russian armies for several months even held the offensive, and regained some of the ground they had lost.

Hitler attacks Russia

Courtesy of David Low

"IT'S A LIE! WE'RE NOT RETREATING — JUST
ADVANCING BACKWARDS"

With Russia, a totalitarian nation, fighting on the Allied side, the
question of "war aims," so much discussed during the first World War,
attracted increasing attention, particularly in the United
States. In part to answer this question, and in part to give   **The Atlantic**
dramatic emphasis to the solidarity of Anglo-American   **Charter**
opinion, President Roosevelt and Prime Minister Churchill met at an
undisclosed point in the Atlantic, and on August 14, 1941, issued over
their joint signatures the so-called "Atlantic Charter." This document
disclaimed for Great Britain and the United States any desire for territorial, or other, aggrandizement, or for any territorial changes not in accord with the wishes of the people concerned. It asserted the right of all
peoples to choose the form of government under which they wished to
live, and promised to promote equal access for all states, "great or small,
victor or vanquished," to the raw materials of the world. Other objectives named were improved labor standards, economic advancement,
and social security, freedom from fear and want, the unhindered use of

the high seas, and the disarmament of aggressor nations as a step toward the abandonment of the use of force in international relations. In many ways the Atlantic Charter was reminiscent of Wilson's Fourteen Points, as it was no doubt meant to be, but it was couched in general terms, and lacked the specific statements of war aims that characterized the earlier document.

By this time the increasing tempo of submarine attacks had brought the "Battle of the Atlantic" to a crisis. Since a substantial number of the freighters being sunk carried lend-lease materials, many Americans demanded that the United States join with Great Britain in convoying merchant fleets overseas. A step in this direction had seemingly been taken when on July 7 the President had announced that units of the United States navy had arrived in Iceland to supplement, and ultimately to replace, the British forces already there. But Roosevelt seemed reluctant to start a "shooting war," and ordered merely that American ships and aircraft should "patrol" the western Atlantic in order to advise the British as to the whereabouts of Axis craft. The effectiveness of these patrols brought speedy Axis retaliation. Eight American freighters had already been sunk when, on September 4, 1941, the American destroyer *Greer* was attacked, but not hit, while trailing a German submarine. Thereupon the President ordered destroyers to shoot submarines "on sight." In mid-October another destroyer, the *Kearny*, was hit, and eleven of her crew were killed. That same month, the *Reuben James* was torpedoed and sunk, with the loss of seventy-six of her crew. After these attacks, Congress, by a measure signed November 17, authorized the arming of American merchant ships, and freed them from the remaining restrictions of the neutrality laws, which thus far had kept them outside "combat zones." Complete participation by the United States in the war seemed close at hand.

The final dénouement, however, was to come from another quarter. In the Far East the irreconcilable differences between the Japanese "new order" and the American "open door" had long been in evidence. Secretary Hull, throughout his administration, had refused to recognize the conquests of Japan in China, and on July 26, 1939, he had threatened economic action by notifying the Japanese government that the long-standing commercial treaty between Japan and the United States would be abrogated. This move was generally believed to anticipate an embargo on munitions shipments to Japan, but no such action was taken, and the conquest of China went on. In the summer of 1940, however, the United States forbade the export to any foreign country, without license, of essential war materials such as heavy scrap iron and petroleum, but by this time Japan was poised for action. From the

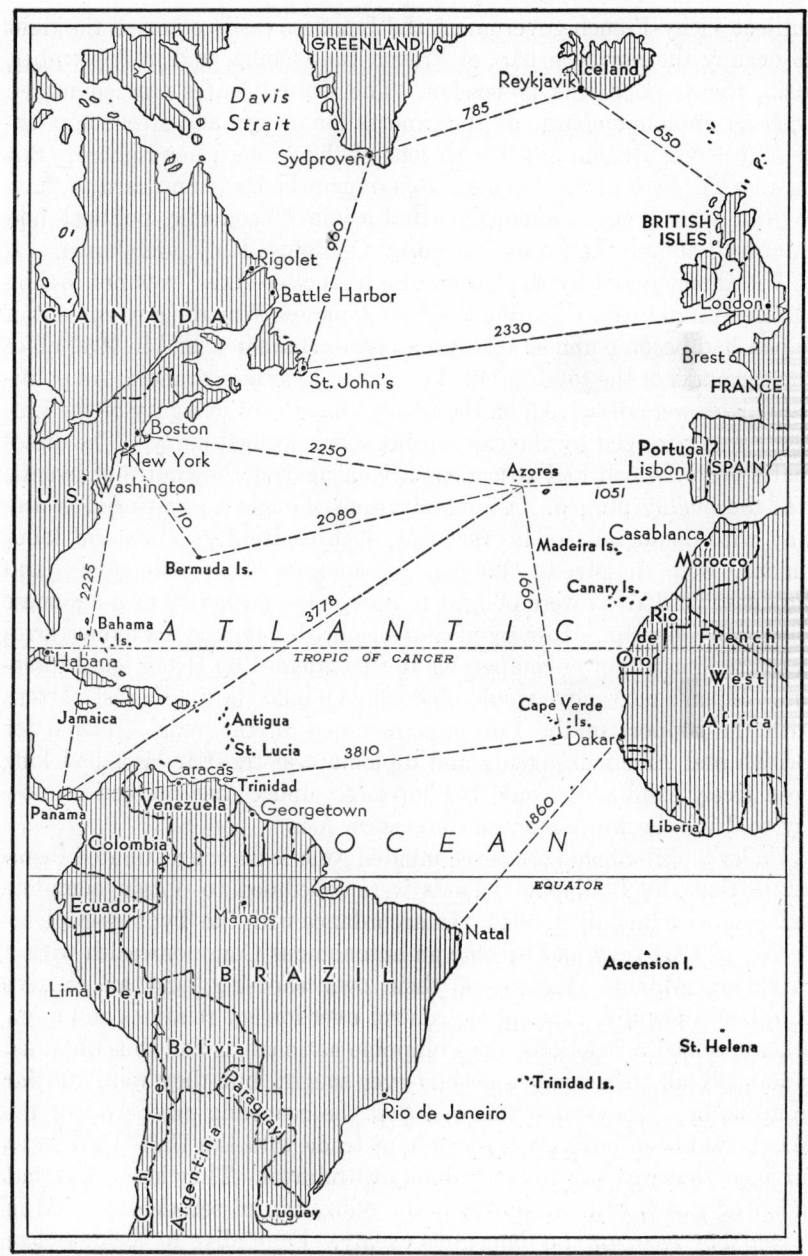

AIR LINE OR GREAT CIRCLE DISTANCES IN THE ATLANTIC

subject Vichy-French government the Japanese easily extorted the right to occupy the northern part of French Indo-China, and in September, 1940, their troops took possession. The United States now countered with a complete embargo on the exportation of iron and steel scrap, except to Great Britain and the nations of the western hemisphere. But against this action, the Japanese government had a trump card to play. Within a few hours it announced that a joint "economic, political, and military" alliance had been formed by Germany, Italy, and Japan.

The threat posed by the "Rome-Berlin-Tokyo Axis" was not lost on informed Americans. During the Sino-Japanese War the government of Japan had become unmistakably Fascist in character, and in 1940 all of the earmarks of the totalitarian state put in their appearance. All political parties were dissolved, on the theory that the sovereignty of the Emperor was infringed by the existence of even a single party. The diplomatic corps, which had struggled in vain against the course of events, was thoroughly purged. All organizations thought to be tinged in any way with democratic or liberal ideas, such as Rotary Clubs and labor unions, were dissolved. Foreign missionaries were sent home, and Japanese Christians were obliged to accept the authority of a Japanese Christian Church. Most significant of all, the Japanese Premier arrogated to himself power comparable to that wielded by Hitler and Mussolini. Japan's next move would obviously be made in the Fascist pattern with the support of the European members of the Axis. Hatred for British and American agents and diplomats in the Far East had long been freely exhibited; would the Japanese, under Axis protection, now try to drive the white man out of eastern Asia?

Under the circumstances peace-minded Americans congratulated themselves that the Philippine Islands were scheduled to obtain complete independence on July 4, 1946. In accordance with the Tydings-McDuffie Act of 1934 they had become an autonomous Commonwealth with a President, Manuel Quezon, of their own choosing, and an elective National Assembly. Except for control over foreign relations and a few other specified restrictions, the Philippine nationalists had thus obtained practically all the liberty they had ever sought, but they were still far from happy. They knew full well that the economic prosperity of the islands had been built upon freedom of trade with the United States, a privilege that was now to be gradually withdrawn. They knew also that independence would carry with it the obligation of self-defense, and in Japan they recognized a dangerous enemy. Fully alive to the Japanese threat, President Quezon in 1935 asked and obtained from President Roosevelt the services of Douglas MacArthur, retiring Chief-of-Staff of the United States Army, who first as military adviser to the Philippine government and then as Field Marshal in command of the Philippine army, made it his aim to create a native constabulary strong enough to hold any foreign invader at bay, pending the anticipated assistance of the United States navy.

Interest in the Atlantic theater blinded many Americans to the perilous situation in the Far East, but when Japan, in July, 1941, obtained permission from Vichy-France to occupy all of French Indo-China the American State Department knew full well that trouble was at hand. Japanese troops pouring into this area posed a grave threat, not only to the Philippine Islands, but also to the British and Dutch possessions in the Far East. In protest, therefore, the American government on July 24 froze all Japanese assets in the United States, an action which the Dutch and British governments quickly paralleled. During the protracted discussions which followed, the United States proposed a settlement based on the following principles: (1) respect for the territorial integrity and sovereignty of all nations; (2) non-interference in the internal affairs of other countries; (3) equality of commercial and other opportunities; and (4) non-disturbance of the *status quo* in the Pacific except by peaceful means. Finally, when these principles were spurned, the United States demanded assurance from the Japanese government that it intended to withdraw its troops from China and French Indo-China. A few weeks later, on November 15, a Japanese envoy, Saburo Kurusu, arrived ostentatiously by airplane in the United States with what purported to be new Japanese proposals. "We must all pull together for peace," Kurusu told American reporters.

But the Kurusu mission was only a blind, for the course Japan meant to follow had already been decided. On the early morning of December 7, while the peace conversations at Washington were still in progress, a Japanese carrier-borne air force of one hundred **Pearl Harbor** and five airplanes attacked the great American naval base at Pearl Harbor, in Hawaii. So complete was the surprise that most American aircraft were destroyed on the ground, leaving the American battle fleet at the mercy of the treacherous foe. Nineteen of the eighty-six American ships in the harbor were seriously hit, five great capital ships were either sunk or otherwise put out of action, and casualties to personnel reached 4575 killed, wounded, or missing. So complete was the catastrophe that the American government delayed an entire year before making public the full details. Had the Japanese brought with them troops to effect a landing, they might with ease have taken the whole of the Hawaiian Islands.

The day after Pearl Harbor was attacked, Congress, with only one dissenting vote, recognized the existence of a state of war between the

United States and Japan, while Japan issued its overdue declaration of war against the United States and the British Empire. When a few days later Germany and Italy, in conformity with their commitments to Japan, declared war against the United States, Congress, by a unanimous vote in both houses, responded with similar declarations against the Axis powers in Europe. Thus the total war that most Americans had hoped so earnestly to avoid became a fact at last. As in the First World War many other American nations were soon involved in the conflict. Some of them, notably Mexico and Brazil, went the whole length of declaring war, while others were content to show their "good-neighborliness" by measures "short of war." By July, 1943, only one American power, the Argentine, had failed to sever diplomatic relations with the Axis.

For many months the war in the Pacific went badly for the United Nations, as the Allies now began to call themselves. The attack on Pearl Harbor was followed immediately by attacks on the Philippine Islands, Wake Island, Guam, Hong Kong, British Malaya, and Thailand. The Thai government offered practically no resistance, Guam fell on December 11, Wake Island, December 24, and Hong Kong on Christmas Day. In the Philippines General MacArthur, whose forces during the last phases of the dispute with Japan had been somewhat augmented by troops from the United States, made a valiant stand on the Bataan peninsula and the island of Corregidor. But the assistance from the United States navy on which his campaign was predicated was not forthcoming, and in the end the Japanese won by sheer force of numbers. Bataan capitulated in April, and Corregidor in May. Well before the end came, General MacArthur, in response to an insistent demand from both the United States and Australia, left the Philippines by stealth to take command of the United Nations forces in Australia. Meantime Japanese troops overran Malaya, captured the great British base at Singapore, conquered Burma, and except for a few precarious footholds forced the United Nations completely out of the East Indies. With the Burma Road closed, aid to China decreased to next to nothing, and the Allies fell back upon India and Australia as bases of operation. To add to the general gloom, German submarines operating off the Atlantic coast-line and in the Caribbean sank hundreds of American freighters, and produced an acute gasoline and fuel-oil shortage along the Atlantic seaboard.

Stung to desperation by the unbroken procession of defeats, the people of the United States settled down with determination to create a war machine adequate to cope with their enemies. Early in 1942 a War Production Board headed by Donald M. Nelson, formerly an executive

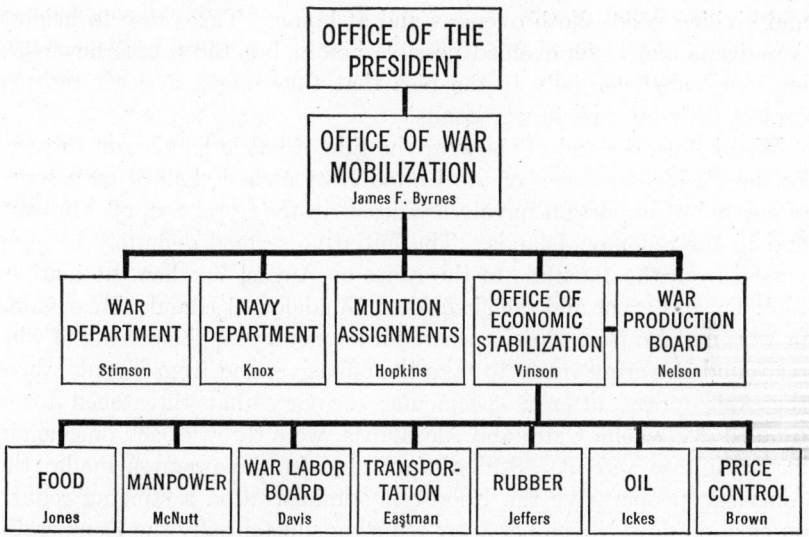

THE AMERICAN WAR GOVERNMENT

of Sears, Roebuck and Company, gave the country the one-man economic leadership that critics of the President had long demanded, while numerous other innovations, made as occasion demanded, gradually produced a war government not unlike the one developed in the first World War. Plans were laid to replace with home-manufactured synthetic products the nation's rubber supply, lost to the Japanese with the fall of Malaya and the East Indies. Low speed-limits for automobile traffic, as well as tire- and gasoline-rationing, were accepted as necessary evils. The army expanded its numbers with all possible speed, and before the year was over announced an ultimate goal of eight million men in uniform. American troops poured overseas, a million strong by the end of the year, to England and northern Ireland, to Australia and New Zealand, to East Africa and Egypt. A new highway was built through Canada to Alaska, and the tiny outposts seized by the Japanese in the Aleutians were subjected to constant air bombardment. Factories turned from the making of peace-time goods to build tanks, and supply other army needs; shipyards increased their capacity, and more than made good the losses sustained by both battle and merchant fleets. Labor, with but relatively few exceptions, forgot its internal conflicts, and carried on with only infrequent resort to strikes. Food conservation, including the rationing of many essential items, provided a steady flow of lend-lease foodstuffs abroad, while caring adequately for army

and civilian needs, both overseas and at home.   Taxes rose to heights
Americans had never deemed possible before, but the people nevertheless responded cordially to the plea that they invest at least ten per
cent of their incomes in war bonds.

Well before the end of the year the tide of battle had begun to turn.
In the Pacific the forces of the United Nations had chalked up a series
of costly but important naval victories — in the Coral Sea, off Midway,
and in the Solomon Islands. The initiative seemed definitely to have
passed from the Japanese to the Allies on August 7, when the marines
took Tulagi harbor and the air-field on Guadalcanal Island. Heartening
news came also from Russia, where for a second year the coming of winter found the army ready to take the offensive, and from Egypt, where
the Axis forces, after a spectacular recovery that threatened for a
time to overwhelm Cairo and Alexandria, were thrown back once again
in precipitate retreat. Still disappointed in the progress made, the
American people gave the Roosevelt administration a stinging rebuke
on election day, November 3, by reducing substantially the Democratic
majorities in both House and Senate, and by overthrowing Democratic
control in many of the states.

Four days later, but on November 8, North African time, came the
news that a huge Anglo-American armada had landed troops in French
Morocco and Algeria, with the avowed intention of occupy-
Invasion of North Africa ing the entire North African seacoast of the French Empire,
both Mediterranean and Atlantic. This daring operation
had been planned during a meeting of Churchill and Roosevelt in
Washington the preceding June, but the secret was well kept, and the
Axis Powers were seemingly taken completely by surprise. Without
serious loss five hundred transports, supported by three hundred and
fifty warships, brought the invasion forces to their destination. Thanks
to the fact that an Allied "fifth column" had carefully prepared the way
for the attack, General Dwight D. Eisenhower, in supreme command
of operations on land, got his troops ashore with a minimum of opposition.
Although Marshal Pétain's Vichy government, to which North Africa
professed to be loyal politically, ordered resistance, there was little
serious fighting except at Casablanca and Oran. By prearrangement,
General Henri Honoré Giraud, a high-ranking French officer who had
escaped to Vichy-France from imprisonment in Germany, appeared on
the scene in North Africa and counseled co-operation with the Allies.
Even more effective, however, was the unanticipated assistance of Admiral Jean François Darlan, Commander of the French navy, who happened at the time to be in Algeria on a visit to his son, recently stricken
with infantile paralysis. Not without difficulty, the Allied leaders

persuaded Darlan to cast his lot with them, and when it became evident that his word carried greater weight in North Africa than that of any other French official, he was promptly recognized by General Eisenhower as political chief of the entire region. At Darlan's insistence even French West Africa, with its important port of Dakar, came over to the Allied side, while Allied troops quickly penetrated eastward as far as Tunisia.

Both in the United States and in Great Britain, General Eisenhower's recognition of Darlan, a Vichyite and former collaborator with Hitler, was severely criticized, but this embarrassment was some- **Darlan and** what alleviated when, on December 24, 1942, Darlan was **Giraud** assassinated by a youthful French patriot. Thereupon General Giraud, in accordance with the original Allied plan, became French civil and military commander-in-chief in North Africa. This was by no means acceptable to the Free French leader in London, General de Gaulle, but in January, 1943, another Roosevelt-Churchill conference, held this time at Casablanca, was attended by both Giraud and de Gaulle, and some progress made toward their future collaboration. Eventually Giraud agreed to the elimination of many Vichyites from the North African governments, and to the direction of civilian affairs in these colonies by a council on which both he and de Gaulle had seats. As for the Vichy government in France, its subjection to German control now became more abject than ever. The southeastern half of France, which up to the time of the North-African invasion had not been occupied by German troops, was quickly taken over, and the remnant of the French fleet at Toulon was obliged to scuttle itself to escape capture by German land forces.

Obviously the Allied governments had hoped that their African conquests would extend to Tunisia before that colony could be occupied by the Axis, but in this they were disappointed because of bad weather, long lines of communication, and prompt antici- **Tunisia** pation of their action by the Axis authorities. During the early months of 1943, many German and Italian divisions under General Jürgen von Arnim were concentrated in Tunisia for a last-ditch fight, in which General Ervin Rommel's famous Africa Corps, still retreating from Egypt, was expected also to join. The final struggle came in May, 1943, when the British Eighth Army under General Sir Bernard Law Montgomery closed in from the east, and British, French, and American troops from the west. Von Arnim and Rommel were able to join forces, but they were nevertheless promptly and disastrously defeated. All of Tunisia, including the cities of Tunis and Bizerte, was occupied by the victorious Allied troops, who, during the final phases of the campaign,

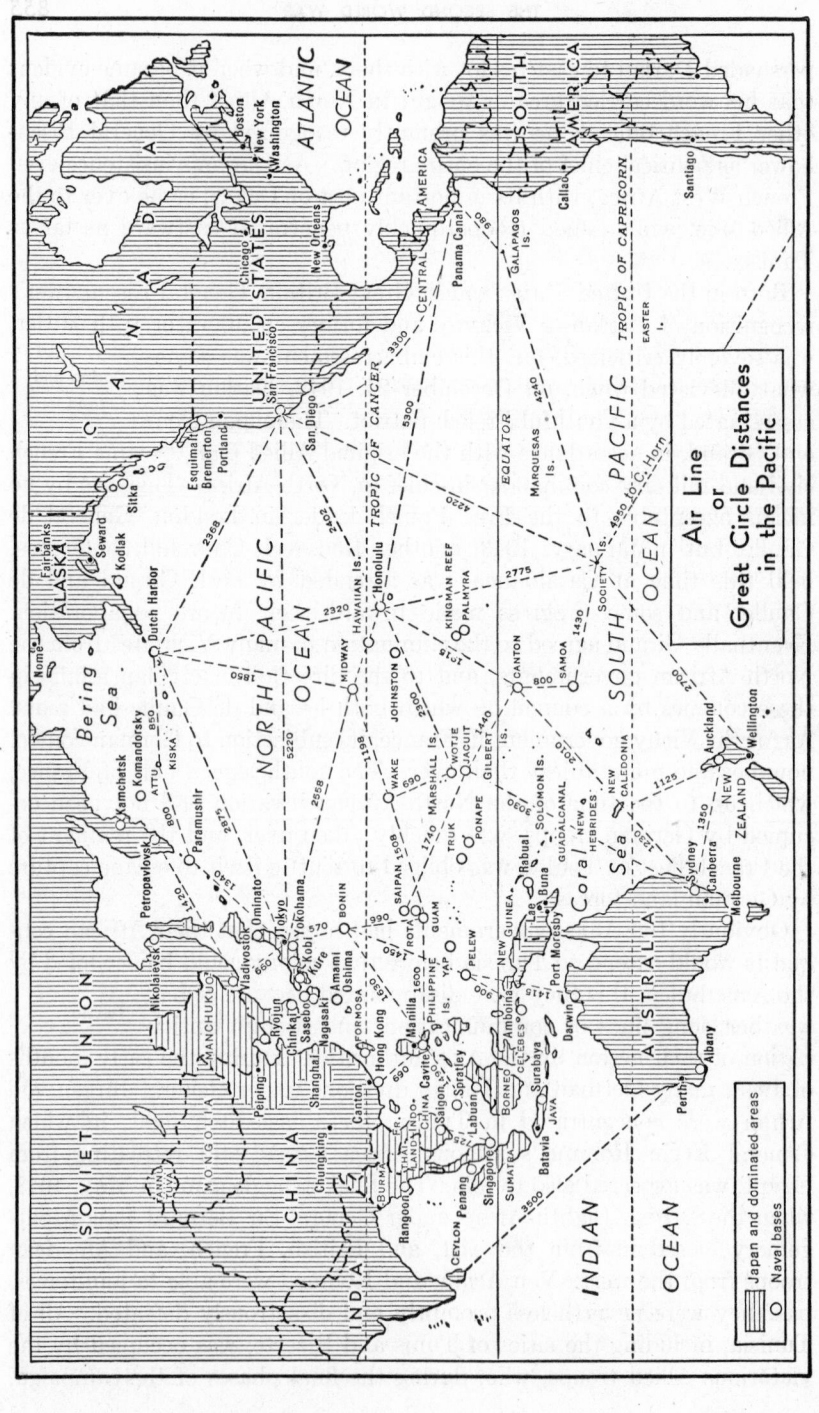

Air Line
or
Great Circle Distances
in the Pacific

took well over two hundred thousand prisoners, among them von Arnim himself. Before the final collapse, Rommel had left Africa for Europe, but practically all the Axis troops which he and von Arnim had commanded were either killed or captured.

The next great goal of Allied endeavor was Sicily, which Eisenhower's forces invaded on July 10, 1943, and conquered in less than six weeks. Before this task was completed, King Victor Emmanuel, assisted by elements in the Fascist Grand Council, forced **Italy** Mussolini out of power, and set up a new government under Marshal Pietro Badoglio as premier. Badoglio's aim was peace, but the Italian peninsula was invaded before he accepted Eisenhower's terms of unconditional surrender and turned over the entire Italian navy to the Allies. Stiff German resistance held the Allies back many months in Italy, but at length, on June 4, 1944, Rome was taken. Thereupon the King, although keeping his title, turned over his duties to his son, Humbert, and a new non-Fascist cabinet replaced the Badoglio government. The chief strategic purpose of the North African and Italian campaign was to clear the Mediterranean of enemy sea-power, and this end was fully accomplished. By the fall of 1944, with Italy recognized as a "co-belligerent," Allied arms had reached the valley of the Po.

The long-awaited "second front" was launched from England across the Channel to the coast of Normandy, June 6, 1944. To conduct this campaign Eisenhower and Montgomery were transferred from Italy. Despite great weather difficulties and the lack **The second front** of a harbor, the invasion was completely successful, and the reconquest of France began. On August 24–25, Paris was occupied by Allied troops amidst riotous demonstrations of joy by its inhabitants. To reinforce the Channel invaders, another expedition landed August 15 on the Mediterranean coast of France, and worked its way northward with extraordinary rapidity. When winter set in, nearly all of France and Belgium had been freed, part of the Netherlands had been cleared of enemy troops, and Allied armies were fighting on German soil. Somewhat tardily, the British and American governments recognized de Gaulle's "Free French" Committee as the provisional government of France. For Belgium and the Netherlands, governments-in-exile, long since functioning in England, had only to be transferred to the Continent.

In the air and on the seas the German situation grew steadily more desperate. The attempt of the *Luftwaffe* to bomb the British into submission had not only failed completely; it had brought devastating retaliation. While the Germans were able to make only "nuisance" raids over England, British bombers and American flying fortresses

attacked German, German-held, and Italian cities by night and day.
Harbor installations, airfields, war factories, railway yards, power
plants, bridges, and dams — every conceivable type of
construction that might aid the Axis war effort — were subjected to the most merciless bombing. After the Allied
landings on the French coast had been effected, a German secret weapon,
the robot bomb, did considerable destruction to the civilian population
of southern England, but it failed completely to halt the invasion. On
the high seas, where German submarines had long taken a discourag-
ingly high toll, new devices for detecting and destroying them diminished drastically their sinkings and all but eliminated them as a factor
in the war. Lend-lease supplies flowed in a steady stream to Russia,
while communications with the British Isles and the Mediterranean
approached peace-time conditions.

On the sea and in the air

Meantime on the eastern front the Germans had suffered equally
devastating reverses. Their second great drive into Russia, made in
1942, stalled completely at Stalingrad. Thereafter the
Russians took the offensive, and in one overwhelming display of strength after another drove the Germans from their
soil. By the fall of 1944 they had freed also three German satellite
states, Bulgaria, Rumania, and Finland, each of which, like Italy, joined
the Allies in the war against Germany. Much of Poland had also been
occupied, and Russian troops had invaded Hungary, Yugoslavia, Czechoslovakia, and East Prussia. By the end of the year, British troops were
far along with the re-conquest of Greece, and "Partisan" forces under
Marshal Tito in Yugoslavia were giving great aid in the liberation of
their country. The utter hopelessness of the German situation seemed
plain to all except the Nazi leaders.

The eastern front

Many optimists, including even General Eisenhower, had dreamed of
victory in 1944, but as winter set in, the Allied campaigns, both eastern
and western, slowed down to a halt. To make matters
worse, the Germans, under General Karl von Rundstedt,
launched on December 17 a terrific and utterly unanticipated counterattack in the Belgium-Luxembourg sector.
So spectacular were the initial German gains that for a time
it looked as if the important harbor of Antwerp, recently opened to
Allied shipping, would be cut off. But as the old year ended and the new
year began, the Allied command, mainly through the efforts of General
George S. Patton's Third American Army, brought the German drive to
a standstill, and regained the initiative. Before January was over, all
the ground lost by the Allies had been retaken, and the battle of Germany had begun in earnest.

The German counter-attack

The time had now come for the careful synchronization of Allied activities on the eastern and the western fronts. In the eastern theater, the Russians delayed their customary winter offensive until January 12, 1945. Then they struck out so forcefully with five huge armies that the German defenses were smashed all the way from the Baltic to the Carpathians. By the end of February, Russian troops, after clearing the Germans from most of Poland, and from much of Hungary and Czechoslovakia as well, stood on German soil only thirty-one miles from Berlin. In the west, Eisenhower had planned the destruction of the German armies facing him before they could retreat across the Rhine, and to a remarkable extent he was able to accomplish this feat. His principal attack was somewhat delayed by the von Rundstedt offensive, but the month of February saw him in full action, with his American, British, Canadian, and French troops fighting in admirable co-ordination. Before March was many days old, Allied troops had penetrated into nearly every stronghold of the famed Westwall, doing untold military damage, and taking prisoners by the hundreds of thousands. Many Germans succeeded in withdrawing across the Rhine, but on March 7, owing to the failure of the retreating forces to destroy a bridge at Remagen, they were followed by American soldiers in considerable numbers. The Remagen bridge soon collapsed, but from newly established bridgeheads Allied forces in great strength pushed forward through the very heart of the Reich. The "scorched-earth" policy that the Nazi leaders had ordered, together with the persistent bombing of German cities and the wholesale devastation incidental to military operations, left Germany a scene of incredible ruin.

By the last week of April the eastern and western invaders of Germany had met on the banks of the Elbe, and the end was in sight. Victorious Russian armies occupied Rumania, Bulgaria, Austria, and Hungary. The German armies that had long stalled the Allied advance in northern Italy began to crumble, then surrendered. Italian "partisans" caught and executed the hapless Mussolini, leaving his body and that of his mistress to the studied insults of a Milanese mob. The Russians fought their way street by street through the rubble of Berlin, and took possession of what was left of the stricken city. Hitler himself committed suicide, following a weird marriage ceremony in which he made his mistress his wife. Shortly after, Admiral Karl Doenitz, upon whom Hitler had directed that his mantle should fall, notified the Allies that Germany was ready to surrender, and on May 8, 1945, the Allied victory in Europe, "V–E Day," was officially proclaimed.

By this time Allied might had also made itself dominant in the Pacific.

There, in mid-November, 1942, the Japanese tried to oust the Americans from Guadalcanal, but failed, in large part because of naval defeats administered by American squadrons operating under the command of Admiral William F. Halsey. Japanese efforts to push across New Guinea to Port Moresby in order to strike at Australia were also frustrated. After that, the bitter fighting necessary to clear the way back to the Philippines could begin. By this time the American Navy had recovered from the losses sustained at Pearl Harbor, and with each succeeding month its strength increased enormously. Up in the cold and fog of the Aleutians, where since June, 1942, the Japanese had held two American islands, Kiska and Attu, the Americans struck at Attu, May 11, 1943, and before the end of the month had conquered the island. When Americans and Canadians landed on Kiska in August, they found that the Japanese had already departed. The next great effort of the American Navy was to drive the Japanese from the islands of the mid-Pacific. In November, 1943, marine and army forces successfully invaded several atolls in the Gilberts, among them Tarawa, where the fighting was particularly bloody. Kwajalein in the Marshalls was taken early in 1944.

It was now plain that the strategy of Admiral Chester W. Nimitz, commander-in-chief of the Pacific fleet, called for a direct advance across the Pacific to Asiatic waters. No effort was made to clear every island occupied by the Japanese, but important bases, together with air fields that could dominate wide stretches of ocean, were taken and strongly held. By June, 1944, the advance had reached Saipan in the Marianas, fifteen hundred miles from Tokyo and sixteen hundred miles from Manila. Frightened by the approaching danger, the Japanese sent carrier-based planes to attack the American ships off Saipan, but the attackers suffered heavily, while American planes in turn sought out the fleet from which the enemy planes had come and inflicted heavy damage upon it. The bloody but successful conquest of Saipan was followed in the next month by the occupation of Guam and Tinian, the former an American island held by the Japanese since the beginning of the war. Bomber attacks could now be made from these bases, as well as from China, upon Formosa and the Japanese homeland, and the exploit of the *Hornet*, which had sent its planes in April, 1942, to attack Tokyo, was repeated by land-based planes from Saipan, November 23, 1944. From this time on, the destruction of Japanese cities and industrial targets proceeded mercilessly.

In order to shorten the bombing range to Japan, two more islands were assaulted and taken by American land and naval forces early in 1945. The first, Iwo Jima, a tiny islet in the volcano group midway between

Guam and Tokyo, was only five miles long by three wide, but it provided the Japanese with three air fields and a radar station. Enemy intelligence was thus able to detect flights of Tokyo-bound American planes and to flash the news to the homeland of **Iwo Jima** their approach. So great was the nuisance value of this island that on February 19, after weeks of preparatory bombing, two divisions of marines, supported by a prodigious show of naval force, undertook its conquest. The fighting was terrific, for the Japanese had expected the attack, and had crowded the island with a maximum of men and armor. For a full month the battle lasted, and American casualties mounted to twenty thousand, but the coveted terrain was won.

The last major amphibious operation in the advance on Japan began on Easter Sunday, April 1, when Okinawa, largest island in the Ryukyus, situated only three hundred and seventy miles from Japan proper, was invaded. Fourteen hundred ships and upwards **Okinawa** of one hundred thousand American soldiers and marines participated in the action. At first, resistance was light, and the Americans got ashore easily, but in southern Okinawa, toward which the Japanese retreated the enemy staged a desperate and unexpectedly prolonged resistance. While the land engagement was in progress, a Japanese naval squadron sent perhaps five hundred planes to attack the American ships standing offshore, but most of the attackers were intercepted and shot down, while the Japanese naval units from which they operated were soon discovered and put out of action. During this engagement Japanese *Kamikaze*, specially trained pilots who deliberately sought to smash their bomb-laden planes into the American ships, first made their appearance in large numbers. Enough of them succeeded in their suicidal missions to inflict serious losses, both in ships and in personnel, upon the American fleet; but, despite this setback and persistent *Kamikaze* harassment thereafter, the battle of Okinawa went on to its inexorable end. By the middle of June, the Americans were in complete control of the island, and the doom of Japan was sealed. American bombers, operating, not only from convenient air fields, but also from the decks of a host of task-force carriers, now burned and blasted the Japanese islands at will.

Meantime, the campaign of MacArthur, who had promised to return from Australia to the Philippines, had made similarly notable strides. MacArthur's strategy, depending always on the careful co-ordination of land, sea, and air forces, was to bomb furiously **MacArthur's** and by-pass the principal Japanese bases, and by "leap- **return to the** frog" tactics to land at unexpected, and sometimes unde- **Philippines** fended, points along the route he must clear. By January, 1944, he had begun to advance in this fashion along the northern shores of New Guinea, and well before the end of the year he was ready to make the last long jump to the Philippines. On October 20, he landed in person with a large army of invasion on the island of Leyte, and began the reconquest he had promised. To defend MacArthur's movements, a heavy naval concentration under Admiral Halsey was obliged to fight one of the greatest sea-actions of history, for the Japanese at last decided that they must risk a major portion of their fleet. In the waters adjacent to Leyte, beginning on October 25, the Americans fought off the Japanese in a series of complicated and extensive actions so costly to the enemy as to reduce the Japanese Navy, the Americans claimed, to "fifth-rate" status.

After the battle of Leyte Gulf, organized resistance on Leyte and on the neighboring island of Samar disintegrated slowly but surely. By the end of the year, MacArthur had also landed troops on Mindoro Island, preparatory to his main attack, which he had reserved for Luzon. In January, 1945, with the aid of planes operating from Mindoro airfields, he put ashore a formidable force at Lingayen Gulf, and began the fateful march to Manila. Japanese resistance was light at first, but the approaches to the capital were stubbornly defended, and not until February 3 were American troops able to enter it. After that, the Japanese staged within the city a gruesomely effective last-ditch fight that lasted for weeks. Bitter fighting also continued elsewhere on Luzon, and the American reconquest of the island was hardly complete at the end of June, when it was officially announced by General MacArthur. Meantime Mindanao, the next largest of the Philippine Archipelago, as well as certain lesser islands, had been successfully invaded, and Japanese hopes were waning fast. Stiff fighting continued, however, in many of the islands until the end of the war.

While the war in the Pacific was thus being planned and fought, Allied forces were doing what little they could to hold the Japanese from further conquests on the mainland of Asia. The task

The Asiatic mainland

could hardly have been more difficult. With India as a base, some Allied aid to the Chinese was soon being flown in over the Himalayas, but it was never enough. Bad relations between the government of Chiang Kai-shek and the armed communist bands that controlled much of North China added to the turmoil from which that unhappy nation suffered. Meager American air forces, operating under General Joseph W. Stilwell, gave great aid to Chiang's armies, but in spite of their best efforts Japanese troops were able to penetrate into Chinese territory about as far as they cared to go.

Perhaps Stilwell scored his principal triumph in clearing the Japanese from northern Burma so that a new route from India to China, the Ledo Road, could be opened. Using American-trained Chinese troops, he was nearing the completion of this task when, in the fall of 1944, he was relieved of his command and recalled to the United States. Personal differences with Chiang Kai-shek over the training and disposition of Chinese troops were said to account for this strange action. Under Stilwell's successor, General David I. Sultan, American engineers went on with the construction of the road, and in January, 1945, the first motor caravan crossed it all the way from India to China. Allied successes farther to the south in Burma, under the leadership of Lord Louis Mountbatten, were also heartening, but in spite of the achievements in Burma the war ended with the Japanese still in control of their principal gains on the mainland of Asia.

Nevertheless, the Japanese will to continue the war had not much longer to go. Far-cruising American submarines, joining their successes to those of American surface forces, helped to drive the Japanese Navy and merchant marine almost completely **The** from the seas. In consequence, connections between the **atomic** home islands and the overexpanded "Co-Prosperity Sphere" **bomb** broke down. On occasion American task forces maneuvered close to the Japanese shore, and lobbed their shells into coastal installations. *Kamikaze* attacks became more numerous and daring, and they took a heavy toll of American lives and shipping, but the "softening-up process" preliminary to invasion went on. Early in August, the climax was reached with the dropping of an atomic bomb on Hiroshima, a military point of some importance that until then had escaped the activities of American airmen. Shortly thereafter, a similar bomb was dropped on Nagasaki. The results obtained were cataclysmic — a single bomb was as devastating to an enemy city as the concentrated action of a thousand ordinary bombers equipped with full loads of ordinary explosives. The development of the atomic bomb was the result of co-operative efforts by numerous American, British, and Canadian scientists, who, with the full backing of their governments, had pooled their talents in a successful effort to split the atom. The cost of their experiments to the American people alone probably reached two billion dollars, but the bomb that the scientists produced undoubtedly served to shorten the war materially. It served also to make the peoples of the world realize, fully perhaps for the first time, how totally catastrophic another World War would be.

For some months it had been known to the British and American chiefs of state that Russia intended eventually to enter the war against

Japan. With the end so nearly in sight, the Russian government found it inexpedient to delay longer, and on August 9, following a formal decla-

Japanese surrender

ration of war, issued the day before, Russian troops began to advance against light opposition into Manchuria. Faced by this new threat, and assured by the President of the United States that only surrender could save Japanese civilization from total annihilation by the further use of atomic bombs, the Japanese gave up. As early as August 10, the Japanese news agency, Domei, broadcast that Japan was willing to accept the terms of unconditional surrender, as defined by the Allies at Potsdam, Germany, the preceding month, provided only that Emperor Hirohito's sovereignty would not be questioned. The President of the United States, replying for the Allies, stated the willingness of the nations at war with Japan to retain the Emperor for the time being, on condition that he take orders from an Allied Supreme Commander, to be resident in Japan. This offer the Japanese government accepted, and by August 14 the world knew for sure that the war was over. Not for several days, however, did a Japanese delegation appear, as required, in Manila to arrange for the formal surrender, and not until September 1, when delegates from the principal Allies, with General MacArthur as their chief representative, received a delegation of Japanese officials aboard the battleship *Missouri* in Tokyo Bay, were the documents of surrender actually signed. Thereafter the occupation of Japan by American forces proceeded rapidly, and the American commander, General MacArthur, began to give orders to the Emperor of Japan. September 2, 1945, was officially designated V–J Day by the President, but by this time the chief celebrations were over.

Nearly a year before the end of the war, the people of the United States had been obliged to hold a presidential election. To many

Election of 1944

Americans the necessity of observing this constitutional requirement seemed even more unfortunate in 1944 than in 1940. The war was going well, and its successful prosecution had in most minds a long priority over domestic politics. But the Constitution still being what it was, the election had to be held, the first war-time election in the United States since 1864. Except for the existence of war, there is little reason to suppose that Roosevelt would, or could, have run for a fourth term, but the need of his continued leadership during the crisis was, for those who trusted him, a sufficient reason for continuing him as the Democratic candidate. He was nominated with little opposition by the Democratic convention, but the Democratic city bosses joined forces with the Southern conservatives to oust Henry A. Wallace, the idealistic New-Dealer, as Vice-Presidential candidate in favor of Senator Harry S. Truman, of Missouri, an inconspicuous regular whose chief service to his country had been made as head of a Senate Committee on the investigation of the national defense program. The Republicans had expected a hard-fought campaign for the nomination between Governor Dewey, of New York, and Wendell Willkie, with some third candidate, possibly Governor John W. Bricker, of Ohio, the probable nominee. But when, early in the campaign, Willkie was decisively defeated in the Wisconsin primary, he withdrew, and the nomination went to Dewey on the first ballot, with only one opposing vote. Before election time, Willkie died of a heart attack. For Vice-President the Convention turned enthusiastically to Bricker.

The campaign which followed, like the campaign which preceded it, was notable for the wide range of agreement between the two candidates. Both of them endorsed, in the main, the social legislation of the New Deal. Both urged some kind of international organization after the war for the maintenance of peace. Dewey even went so far as to approve the findings of the Dumbarton Oaks Conference at Washington, in which just before the campaign the leading Allies had drawn tentative plans for an organization to preserve peace — plans strongly reminiscent of Wilson's League of Nations. What the campaign lacked in issues, it made up in personalities. In a series of well-delivered speeches Dewey charged the President with failing to prepare the country for war, claimed that the administration was composed of tired, corrupt, and quarrelsome old men, pointed with concern at the support the Communists were giving Roosevelt, and urged insistently that it was time for a change. Roosevelt, in turn, capitalized on the willingness of the Republicans to accept so much of the New Deal program, noted the successes in the war that had been won under his leadership, questioned the devotion to international co-operation of the many pre-Pearl Harbor isolationists who supported Dewey, and implied that it was no time for a change.

For the fourth time Roosevelt won a decisive victory. The President led in thirty-six states with 432 electoral votes, while Dewey led in twelve states with only 99 electoral votes. The Democrats also retained their majority in the Senate, greatly improved it in the House, and won a majority of the governorships. The voting was closer, however, than these figures indicate. Roosevelt's popular majority, a little more than three million votes, was the slenderest given any successful candidate for the Presidency since Wilson's second election in 1916. Aside from registering the confidence of the majority in Roosevelt's military leadership, the election demonstrated clearly that the American people were far more ready than they had been twenty-five years earlier to accept for the United States an important rôle in international affairs. Isolationism might rise again, but for the moment that historic American policy seemed dead indeed. The discriminating defeat of numerous outstanding isolationists and ex-isolationists, such, for example, as Representative Fish, of New York, and Senator Nye, of North Dakota, made certain that the new Congress would be receptive to any plan of post-war co-operation that seemed to offer a reasonable hope of world peace.

During the campaign of 1944, the health of President Roosevelt had become a matter of considerable concern to the American public. From

Death of Roosevelt

photographs and moving pictures it was apparent that the cares of office had greatly aged the President. The lines on his face had deepened, he had lost weight, and he was noticeably less willing to exert himself to stand or walk. He suffered much from colds and bronchial infections, and was frequently obliged to take extended rests. So much was said on the subject that his personal physician publicly denied, almost too insistently, that the President was ill, while Roosevelt himself, in spite of an earlier promise not to "campaign in the usual partisan sense," took to the stump during the month of October, and gave a half-dozen full-length political speeches. He even braved a heavy downpour of rain to ride in an open car throughout a long campaign parade in New York City, and emerged seemingly none the worse for his experience. Apparently the country was convinced that he was capable of carrying on, or so the election returns seemed to show, but on April 12, 1945, he died suddenly at his winter home in Warm Springs, Georgia, of what his physicians called a massive cerebral hemorrhage.

Roosevelt was succeeded, of course, by Vice-President Harry S. Truman (1884–   ), whom the Democratic convention of 1944 had preferred to the far more prominent Wallace. As Roosevelt

Truman

was the perfect embodiment of the extraordinary American, so Truman, to an almost uncanny degree, was the typical ordinary American. He was a small-town product from Missouri, utterly undistinguished in appearance. He spoke with a flat Middle-Western accent, played the piano a little, belonged to the Lions' Club and the Baptist Church. He had never attended college, but had served acceptably as a National Guard officer in the First World War. He had worked on a farm in his youth, lost money keeping store, gone into politics because he needed a job. As a regular organization Democrat, he was not above accepting a county judgeship at the hands of "Boss" Pendergast, an unblushing corruptionist who controlled the destinies of the Democratic Party in Kansas City, and aspired to control the state.

In Missouri a county judge is an administrative officer, comparable to a county commissioner in many other states; Truman was neither a lawyer nor a "judge" in the usual sense. But he had under his control the expenditure of huge sums of money, particularly in the construction of highways and public buildings, and no faintest suspicion of dishonesty ever attached to any of his acts. At Pendergast's suggestion, he was nominated for the Senate in 1934, won as any other Democrat might have won that year, and in 1940 was renominated and re-elected. His emergence as a fearless and non-partisan senatorial investigator, one who was willing on occasion even to point out the shortcomings of the President, gave him much favorable publicity, but it was generally assumed that he had reached the zenith of his career. But when Wallace was passed by, Truman, partly because he was almost the only Middle-Westerner available, won the unexpected and unsolicited nomination that a few months later was to make him President.

The first great concern of the new President was to carry through to a successful conclusion the United Nations Conference on International Organization, already called by the United States, Great Britain, Russia, and China to meet in San Francisco, April 25, 1945. Roosevelt had earnestly promoted the holding of this conference before the war came to an end, and had promised to open it in person. Obviously, his hope was to utilize the habit of co-operation that had developed among the Allies in time of war as a foundation upon which to build a permanent world organization, designed to keep the peace in the future. He was eager, also, to avoid the complications that had embarrassed the similar efforts of Woodrow Wilson, when that President had sought in his day to create a League of Nations and to write a treaty of peace at the same time.

The unity of effort that the Allies, now commonly called the United Nations, had achieved in the war was truly remarkable. No longer could it be said, as during the First World War, that when one Ally advanced, the others were sure to be standing still. **Allied unity** Close co-ordination of policy, both in military and in diplomatic activities, was apparent on every hand. This fortunate development was due in considerable part to the frequent conferences held by heads of states, their foreign ministers, and their military advisers. As early as August, 1942, Prime Minister Churchill visited Stalin in Moscow, with the American Ambassador to Russia representing the United States. Stalin was then pressing hard for a second front in France, something he long failed to obtain, but this conference was only the beginning of a series. After the invasion of North Africa, Churchill and Roosevelt, as already noted, met at Casablanca, North Africa, in

January, 1943, to lay further plans. They conferred with de Gaulle and Giraud, and they had hoped that Stalin and Chiang Kai-shek would join them, but each of the latter two claimed that it was impossible for him to leave his own country at that time. Out of this conference came much undisclosed planning, and the announcement that only by "unconditional surrender" could the Axis nations obtain peace. At a conference of foreign ministers, held in Moscow during October, 1943, definite plans were laid for the second front in France, and for some kind of world organization to follow the war. Next came a conference of Churchill, Roosevelt, and Chiang Kai-shek in Cairo during mid-November, 1943, and immediately thereafter the first meeting of both Churchill and Roosevelt with Stalin, at Teheran. So complete were the plans worked out at the Cairo and Teheran meetings that more than a year elapsed before the conferees got together again. Then, early in January, 1945, the "Big Three," Churchill, Roosevelt, and Stalin, accompanied by large retinues of "top-drawer" military and governmental advisers, met at Yalta in the Crimea. The Yalta Conference not only reached agreements on the "timing, scope, and co-ordination of new and even more powerful blows" against Germany, but authorized also the call that brought the Conference of the United Nations to San Francisco the following April.

By this time much of the groundwork for the Conference had already been laid. Knowing full well that any plan of world co-operation, in order to succeed, must have the support of the four most powerful Allies — Great Britain, the United States, Russia, and China — representatives of those powers met at Dumbarton Oaks in Washington during the fall of 1944, and issued a set of tentative proposals. The Dumbarton Oaks plan foreshadowed a United Nations Charter, which would be similar in many respects to the Covenant of the League of Nations, but with conspicuous differences. The new plan contained nothing comparable to the famous "Article X" that had done so much to defeat the League of Nations for ratification by the United States Senate; it gave greater authority to the smaller Security Council (representing five great powers and six selected others) and less to the larger Assembly, thereby eliminating a principal cause for delay and indecisiveness in the actions of the League; it made more feasible the use of force against would-be aggressors, and put less trust in disarmament; it proposed as an integral part of the plan a Permanent Court of International Justice; and it presumed that the Charter, unlike the Covenant, would be entirely separate from any treaty of peace.

Invited to the Conference at San Francisco were all of the nations, now numbering upwards of fifty, that had joined in the hostilities against the Axis powers. At the Conference the smaller nations took an active and important part in the proceedings, and greatly influenced the results, although none of the fundamentals of the Dumbarton Oaks proposals was altered. Least palatable **The** to the small nations was the insistence by Russia, agreed **San** to by Churchill and Roosevelt at Yalta, that all of the five **Francisco** great powers (including France) must concur in important **Conference** decisions of the Security Council. This left each of the nations so favored free from any effective restraint on its military or diplomatic activities. Optimists could only hope that the rule of self-restraint would be stronger than the rule of law. Whatever the faults and virtues of the Charter, it was widely ratified, and in the United States Senate met only negligible opposition. The work of actual organization began in London during the winter of 1945–46.

In line with the general spirit of world co-operation exhibited at Dumbarton Oaks and San Francisco was a series of important international agreements already reached on a wide variety of subjects. At Bretton Woods in New Hampshire, a con- **Other** ference held in July, 1944, proposed an International Bank **conferences** for Reconstruction and Development, and a parallel organization to maintain stability in the exchange values of national currencies. Somewhat earlier, a United Nations Relief and Rehabilitation Administration (UNRRA), a Food and Agriculture Organization of the United Nations, and a Provisional International Civil Aviation Organization had been set up. Within the Americas a conference at Chapultepec, Mexico, did much to cement intracontinental solidarity. Much still remained to be done before these efforts could become truly effective, but the determination of the United Nations to act collectively in time of peace no less than in time of war seemed strong.

There was a good chance that world co-operation would succeed. That the United States and Great Britain, in spite of their inevitably numerous areas of conflict, would be able to compose their future differences short of war was generally taken for granted. They had only to maintain their one-hundred-and-thirty-year-old record of conciliation and arbitration. There was far greater concern over the relations of these and other nations with Russia, whose earlier policy of world revolution had so frightened all capitalistic countries. But Stalin's interest in co-operation seemed genuine, he had abolished the Comintern, he no longer warred on Christianity, he had great need of a prolonged era of peace during which Russia could develop her rich resources. If the three great Allies were ready to show the restraint necessary to keep the peace among themselves, it was evident that by acting together they could keep other nations at peace. Many observers professed to believe, also, that the lesser nations, as time went on, would achieve a steadily growing recognition in the councils of the United Nations.

Some of the more immediate problems of peace were settled by the "Big Three" in a meeting held at Potsdam near Berlin during the month of July, 1945. On this occasion President Truman **The** represented the United States, with his new Secretary of **Potsdam** State, James F. Byrnes, of South Carolina, taking an im-**Conference** portant part in the proceedings.[1] The British delegation was at first headed, as usual, by Churchill, but before the conference ended, the results of Britain's first general election since 1935 became known, and Churchill's place was taken by a new Prime Minister, Clement R. Attlee, leader of the Labor Party. Thus, when the Potsdam Conference ended, Stalin was the only member of the old war-time triumvirate to remain in power. The new "Big Three" laid down at Potsdam the political and economic principles that were to govern the treatment of Germany in the initial period of control. Supreme power was vested in an Allied Control Council, composed of American, British, Russian, and French generals. It had already been decided that the conquered Reich was to be divided into four zones of military occupation, one for each of the four nations mentioned, and Berlin, the capital, was to be similarly partitioned. From this conference came also the ultimatum to Japan, in conformity with which that nation surrendered.[2]

[1] Cordell Hull had retired on account of illness in November, 1944, and had been succeeded by Edward R. Stettinius, Jr., who as Secretary of State had headed the American delegation during the San Francisco Conference.

[2] Allan Nevins and L. M. Hacker, *The United States and Its Place in World Affairs, 1918–43* (1943), contains excellent chapters on the American wartime economy. Walter Johnson, *The Battle Against Isolation* (1944), is an excellent summary. Dwight D. Eisenhower, *Crusade in Europe* (1948), is both fascinating and informative. H. C. Butcher, *My Three Years with Eisenhower* (1946), gives the impressions of a staff officer. Walter Millis, *This is Pearl!* (1947), is a graphic account of how the war started in the Pacific. E. M. Zacharias, *Secret Mission: The Story of an Intelligence Officer* (1946), sheds further light on the Pacific theater. D. S. Ballantine, *U.S. Naval Logistics in World War II* (1947), is a concise and critical history. James A. Field, *The Japanese at Leyte Gulf* (1947), is an account of Japanese operations in the greatest sea-battle in all history. Clive Howard and Joe Whitley, *One Damned Island After Another* (1946), is as journalistic as its title. Herbert Millington, *American Diplomacy and the War of the Pacific* (1948), is a useful scholarly monograph.

41

From War to Peace

THE SOLIDARITY of the "home front" during the years of American participation in the Second World War was virtually unbroken. The Japanese attack on Pearl Harbor, followed as it was by declarations of war against the United States by both Germany and Italy, left little room for opposition to the war, **The home front** and even the isolationists accepted hostilities as a necessary evil. Few Americans of German or Italian descent were prepared to apologize for the behavior of Hitler or Mussolini, as the case might be, while the Japanese on the Pacific Coast and in Hawaii, for all the suspicion with which they were regarded, behaved themselves so well that not one of them was ever found guilty of an act of sabotage or espionage. Communists in the United States were violently anti-war and isolationist during nearly two years of American neutrality, but after Hitler's attack on Russia, the "party line" changed to the exact opposite. When the United States entered the war, American Communists gave their government consistent support. Some Socialists, led by Norman Thomas, a few of the evangelical clergy, particularly of the minor sects, and a comparatively small number of conscientious objectors furnished about all the opposition to the war there was. Under the circumstances, there was little persecution of non-conformists.[1]

The one notable blot on the American record of tolerance was the treatment of the Japanese in Hawaii and on the Pacific Coast. In the Hawaiian Islands between thirty and forty per cent of the population were of Japanese ancestry; hence it was not possible to remove them to the mainland, as was actually suggested, without completely disrupting the economic life of the Islands. But the political rights of Hawaiians, regardless of race, color, or nationality, were almost totally obliterated during the war. **Americans of Japanese ancestry**

[1] John Dos Passos, *State of the Nation* (1944), gives a good account of the United States in wartime.

Military law replaced civilian government, and army officers discharged the duties normally assigned to judges and police magistrates. Regulations that might have had a meaning right after Pearl Harbor were enforced with military ruthlessness long after the reasons for their adoption had disappeared. Only with the greatest difficulty did the Hawaiians regain their normal rights, and to guard against any repetition of unpleasantnesses associated with army rule they began immediately after the war an earnest movement for statehood. On the Pacific Coast, even in California where they were most numerous, the Japanese constituted only a tiny fraction of the total population, and their removal into the interior was a possibility. Under military orders, they were therefore herded together into "relocation camps" at a considerable distance from the Coast. Conditions in the camps were far from satisfactory, but in general the Japanese "evacuees" conducted themselves well. In spite of the wholesale discrimination against members of their race, many Americans of Japanese ancestry (AJA's), both from Hawaii and from the mainland, served in the Army of the United States during the war and made a superb record as loyal fighting men. After the war, the "relocation camps" were broken up, and their inmates were allowed to return to normal life. Most of the Japanese went back to their former homes, but a considerable number scattered throughout the country.[1]

Perhaps the American people inherited a lighter burden of intolerance from the Second than from the First World War, but the cost in dollars, lives, and social dislocations was much heavier. Expenditures for the Second World War reached about three hundred billion dollars, more than eight times as much as the nation spent on the First World War. The cost in lives was about 375,000, at least three times as many as in 1917–18, although far fewer in proportion to the amount of fighting done. The difference was due to better training before battle-action and greater medical efficiency. Population shifts due to the war brought many Negroes from the South to northern manufacturing centers, as in the First World War, but the major shift of population was from east to west. The Pacific Coast, especially the State of California, was the scene of many major war industries, and gained rapidly in population, both during and after the war. Cities everywhere, but particularly on the Pacific Coast, suffered from acute shortages in housing, water-supply, electric power, telephone service, and other similar necessities.

Cost of the War

---

[1] On the Japanese evacuation from the West Coast, see Dorothy Thomas, *The Spoilage* (1947). On Hawaii there are several excellent books: T. B. Clark, *Hawaii, the 49th State* (1947); S. D. Porteus, *And Blow Not the Trumpet: A Prelude to Peril* (1947); A. W. Lind, *Hawaii's Japanese* (1947). W. S. Tsuchida, *Wear It Proudly* (1947), is the war experience of an American Japanese.

The cost of the war in dollars, as was more or less inevitable, was met in large part by borrowing, although heavy taxation made it possible to finance about forty per cent of the war expenditures from current income. Income taxes took something from nearly everyone, and nearly everything from some. The flotation of loans followed practices well established during the First World War and during the Great Depression. The public was encouraged to invest in bonds at all times, by regular payroll deductions if necessary, but eight special "drives," with a tremendous fanfare of advertising appeal, sought to tap the nation's savings, particularly those of the small investor. Unlike the bonds of the First World War, which were transferable and were frequently sold at a discount by hard-pressed investors, the new series were non-transferable, and were redeemable by the government on demand. Thus purchasers who had over-bought, or who found that for any reason they could not hold their bonds, were spared the heavy losses that in the previous war had overtaken the buyers of "Liberty Bonds."

When the fighting finally ended the first concern of the American people was to "bring the boys home." This was not without its hazards, for the government had need of large forces for occupation purposes; further, the existence of a well-trained army and a **Demobilization** powerful navy would give the nation great diplomatic strength during the impending sparring among the Allies for a peace settlement. But public insistence was too strong to be denied, and the boys came home. Shortly after VE–Day a plan of demobilization was announced which discharged military personnel in accordance with an elaborate point system, based on such factors as length of service, length of time overseas, battle stars and decorations, and family responsibilities. By December, 1945, the military forces were disintegrating at the rate of over a million and a half a month, and by the next spring the time set for the expiration of the Selective Service Law, May 15, 1946, had to be extended for a year in order to keep military personnel at the minimum necessity. At the end of the year the Army numbered only 670,000 men, the Navy, 395,000, and the Marine Corps, 83,700. Under the "GI Bill of Rights," enacted in 1944, discharged veterans might receive unemployment compensation at the rate of $20 per week for as long as a year if necessary, a government loan of $2000 for the purpose of buying a home or starting up in business, and college education or "job-training" for up to four years, with generous allowances for tuition, books, and living expenses.

Next in importance to demobilization, as the public saw it, was "reconversion," meaning the restoration of the nation's business to its normal peacetime behavior. In anticipation of this drastic economic

change Congress in 1944 revised the Office of War Mobilization into an
Office of War Mobilization and Reconversion. Under able
**Recon-
version** leadership, the OWMR discharged its obligations with fair effectiveness. Wartime restrictions were loosened; the production of civilian goods started to climb; returning veterans and dislocated
war workers found new jobs; and profits, both in business and in agriculture, continued to be good. The chief difficulty lay in the bad relations
that developed between labor and management. Workers demanded
compensation in hourly rates for the loss of wages they had suffered
when extra pay for overtime, dependably present throughout the war,
was no longer available. Management, struggling with the problem of
wholesale cancellation of government contracts and the expense of re-
tooling and re-conditioning war plants, was unwilling to settle on terms
satisfactory to labor. Strike after strike, in the automobile industry, in
the steel plants, and in the coal mines, threatened to paralyze the economic life of the nation. Finally, when the railroad brotherhoods, late in
May, 1946, tied up the entire railroad system of the nation, the President
asked Congress for drastic anti-strike legislation and threatened to use
the Army to operate the roads if the strikers did not return to work. The
threat succeeded, and the railroad strike was called off, but the net result
of the epidemic of strikes was a wage increase of about seventeen or
eighteen per cent for most workers involved. Before the end of 1948, to
offset rapidly rising prices, a second and a third round of strikes or threatened strikes had brought a second and a third round of wage increases.

Higher wages, whether justifiably or otherwise, resulted in higher
prices, and pushed along the pronounced trend toward inflation that had
set in immediately after the war came to an end. Price con-
Inflation trols had been accepted as necessary evils as long as the war
had lasted; but with the fighting finished, the public echoed the impatience of businessmen for a return to "business as usual." Believers in
price controls argued that, if the great back-log of purchasing power
built up during the war should be turned loose, the resulting competition
for the limited amount of goods available would produce a violent inflation of prices. But the opponents of price controls, led by the National
Association of Manufacturers, held that if controls were taken off prices
might rise temporarily, but would decline eventually as the volume of
goods increased. Whatever the merits of the argument, the people were
tired of government restraints, and over the protest of President Truman
Congress emasculated the act under which the Office of Price Administration had operated. Finally, after frantic but ineffective efforts to
hold the line against higher prices on the few items on which Congress
still permitted price ceilings, the President announced by radio on Octo-

ber 14, 1946, that all controls, except on rents, would have to go. The effect was startling. By the end of the year the consumers' price index was 55.5 per cent higher than in August, 1939, and 31.7 per cent higher than in December, 1945. And prices had just begun to rise, for with each round of wage increases there came inevitably a round of price increases.

Undoubtedly, President Truman had an eye to the mid-term elections, to be held in November, 1946, when he succumbed to the popular pressure for an end to price controls. But the gesture did him no good. The Republicans won the Congressional elections by a landslide, 241 Republicans to 188 Democrats in the House, and 51 Republicans to 45 Democrats in the Senate. State and local elections showed a similarly strong Republican trend. Impatience with the chronic disagreements between a Democratic Congress and a Democratic President; irritation over the inflated prices, however much public pressure might have been responsible for them; labor unrest at the sternness with which the President had dealt with strikes; failure of the administration to deal effectively with the housing shortage; all these, together with a considerable amount of apathy that kept many Democratic voters from the polls, contributed to the Republican victory. On all sides it was generally conceded that the first presidential election after the Second World War, to be held in 1948, would result in a Republican victory, just as had happened after the First World War.

Elections of 1946

If a Democratic Congress and a Democratic President could not get along together, there was even less to hope for from a Democratic President and a Republican Congress. The Eightieth Congress was determined to make a record on economy and on tax reduction. The President could not restore appropriations that Congress had lopped off, however essential he might deem them, but he could, and did, veto a tax reduction bill. The continued high tax rates were far from popular, but at the end of the year the President was able to point with pride at the achievement of a balanced budget for the first time in a long period of years. Next year, however, he was unable to prevent substantial tax reductions, and the budget was unbalanced again. An even worse breach between the legislative and the executive branches of the government came with the passage of the Taft-Hartley Labor-Management Relations Act, which made substantial amendments to the Wagner-Connery Act of 1935. The new law included many provisions most unpalatable to organized labor. It permitted employers to sue unions for breach of contract and for damages due to jurisdictional strikes; it prohibited the closed shop, which forbade the hiring of any but union men; it required a sixty day "cooling off" period for strikes and lockouts that might disturb the national economy;

The Eightieth Congress

it forbade unions to contribute to political campaign funds; and it required union officials to swear that they were not Communists, or else the organizations they represented would be ineligible for such assistance as they might otherwise receive from the National Labor Relations Board. This measure, which labor found acutely distasteful, was vetoed by the President, but it was repassed by overwhelming majorities in each house, and became a law in spite of the President's opposition in June, 1947.

Meantime, in international affairs, the hope that the victorious Allies could work together successfully in the pursuit of peace had been all but blasted. As all the world knew, the key to the situation was in the hands of the Russian leaders. During the war they had seemingly renounced their policy of world revolution; but would this attitude carry over into the making and keeping of the peace, or would Stalin and his associates return to the original Bolshevik program of world revolution? President Roosevelt, in his time, knowing full well that Russian cooperation would be essential to world stability, had made every effort to win the confidence of the Russian leaders. He had accorded the most bountiful lend-lease aid to Russia; he had promoted in every possible way a spirit of friendliness between the American and the Russian peoples; and he had done his best, at the various international conferences, to make Stalin, the Russian leader, believe in American good-will and good-faith.[1]

Relations with Russia

The climax of Roosevelt's overtures to Russia came with the Yalta Conference of February, 1945. Roosevelt knew that any post-war world organization for keeping the peace must have Russian support to be effective. Hence, as part of the price necessary to win Stalin's cooperation, he acceded to the Russian demand that three of the Russian Soviet republics should be accorded membership in the United Nations. Also, as a gesture of conciliation, both to Russia and to the nationalistic tendencies of the United States Senate, he agreed to the principle of the great-power veto in all important acts of the Security Council. As to European boundary settlements, Roosevelt conceded to Russia the right to annex all of eastern Poland, and to Poland the right to make compensatory annexations at the expense of Germany. These things, the President believed, he could not have prevented if he had tried, and he secured from Russia in return what he hoped would be a valuable pledge, that the Polish government should be "reorganized on a broader democratic basis." He could not then have

The Yalta agreements

[1] John R. Deane, *The Strange Alliance: The Story of our Efforts at Wartime Cooperation with Russia* (1947), shows that American difficulties with Russia were not all post-war. John C. Campbell, *The United States in World Affairs, 1945–1947* (1947), is the best general survey of our post-war diplomacy.

known that this promise would be far more honored in the breach than in the observance. With regard to Yugoslavia Roosevelt made similar concessions, but Yugoslavia was already in the Russian orbit, and the President thought that he had obtained in return, as in the case of Poland, a chance for the creation of a democratic Yugoslavian government. On the Far East, Roosevelt's attitude was determined by his military advisers, who besought him to pay almost any price in order to obtain assurance that Russia would join in the war against Japan. The atomic bomb had not yet been proved, and the prospect of direct invasion of the Japanese homeland seemed grim indeed. Roosevelt therefore agreed to conditions that would make Russia dominant in Manchuria at the end of the war, and in addition promised the Soviets the southern half of Sakhalin, and the Kuril Islands. In return, Stalin promised again — he had said the same thing to Cordell Hull in 1943 — that "in two or three months after Germany has surrendered and the war in Europe has terminated the Soviet Union shall enter the war against Japan." [1]

The Yalta Conference also ratified a plan — which had been in process of development ever since Teheran — for the eventual dismemberment of Germany into four zones of military occupation, one each for the British, American, Russian, and French forces. Berlin, the capital, although located deep in the Russian zone, was to be an international area under joint four-power control. There is no reliable evidence to support the frequently-made assertion that Roosevelt, either at the time of Yalta or at any other time, conceded to Russian troops the honor of occupying Berlin in advance of the troops of other nations. The American advance was indeed halted when it might easily have reached Berlin far ahead of the Russians, but General Eisenhower took full responsibility for the decision, and justified it on military grounds. Military rather than political considerations seem also to account for the fact that American armies, which might have captured Prague, the Czechoslovakian capital, were stopped in their tracks, thus giving the Russians both the honor and the advantage of taking another capital city.

At the Potsdam Conference it had been agreed that peace treaties for Germany and Austria should not be undertaken until settlements had been reached on Italy, Finland, Hungary, Bulgaria, and Rumania. After much bickering, mainly because the Russians found endless fault with every proposition made by any of the western democracies, the task of drawing these treaties was turned over in each case to a council of the appropriate great-powers foreign ministers, while changes in the treaties so drafted might be sug-

Minor peace treaties

---

[1] Robert Emmet Sherwood, *Roosevelt and Hopkins; An Intimate History* (1948), has an illuminating chapter on the Yalta Conference.

gested by a general peace conference representing all the Allies, to be held in Paris, in May, 1946. It was during the course of these negotiations that President Truman and Secretary Byrnes at last came to realize that concessions to the Russians rarely, if ever, brought any concession in return. In dealing with Russia, there was no "give and take," it was all "give" and no "take." Moreover, Russian policy was seemingly designed to promote the indefinite prolongation of political and economic chaos in the countries concerned. Such conditions greatly facilitated the work of the Communist propagandists who, acting on orders from Moscow, were busily preparing the way in each country for Communist control of whatever governments the peace treaties might establish. Finally, in desperation, Secretary Byrnes and his advisers, with strong British and French backing, began to stand their ground against the Russians with such firmness that they were accused by Russian sympathizers of shifting to a "get-tough-with-Russia" attitude. Chief among their critics in the United States was Henry Wallace, who had become Secretary of Commerce in President Roosevelt's cabinet after the election of 1944, and had been retained by President Truman. In a speech delivered in New York on September 12, 1946, Wallace urged that the United States give Russia a free hand in eastern Europe and abandon its newly adopted attitude of "toughness." But President Truman, after some hesitation, dismissed Wallace from his cabinet and gave the Byrnes policy his full support.[1]

After almost interminable negotiations, the five treaties were at last officially signed in Paris on February 10, 1947. The war-making potential of all five former German satellites was reduced to insignificance, heavy reparations were assessed against them, and all except Bulgaria were obliged to make extensive territorial readjustments. Italy, once Germany's closest associate, ceded land to France, Greece, Albania, and Yugoslavia, and turned over the administration of her colonies to the four principal Allies. Even before the end of the war she had been forced to give back their freedom to her two conquered provinces, Ethiopia and Albania. In the final negotiations the city of Trieste, long a stumbling block to agreement, became also a free territory, with a governor to be chosen and paid by the Security Council of the United Nations. Among the Allied powers the principal gainer from these treaties was Yugoslavia, a nation in which the Communists under Marshal Tito had already achieved complete control. Yugoslavia's territorial holdings were greatly enhanced, her reparations bill topped the Allied list, and her right to arm remained unrestricted. In thus strengthening this strategically located satellite, the Russians had seemingly won a springboard for their expected jump to full control of the Mediterranean.

[1] James F. Byrnes, *Speaking Frankly* (1947), is a valuable memoir.

The restoration of peaceful relations with the minor enemy states had proved to be difficult, but with Germany and "liberated" Austria the task was to remain for years a total impossibility. In accordance with the Yalta decision, which was duly implemented at Potsdam, Germany was broken into four zones of military occupation, one for each of the "Big Four" powers, and the city of Berlin, although supposedly under joint four-power control, was similarly subdivided. The government of Germany as a whole was to be in the hands of an Allied Control Council composed of the four high commanding officers of the several zones. The conquered nation was to be administered as "a single economic unit," but all decisions of the Council had to be unanimous. Unfortunately, the western democracies neither asked nor received from Russia guarantees of uninterrupted access to Berlin, although the only way they could reach the city was through the Russian zone. This agreement was made at a time when it was assumed that Russian good-will was the only guarantee needed. A similar four-divisional plan was worked out for Austria, and for Austria's capital-city, Vienna. But there were important differences. Access to the Vienna region was possible from both the British and the American zones, while the Russians, in contrast with the trustful attitude of the western powers in the case of Berlin, obtained formal consent from the other powers to their maintenance of "communication lines" with Austria through both Hungary and Rumania. This gave the Russian government the opportunity to keep military forces not only in Austria but in the two neighboring states also, even after a treaty of peace with them had been signed and ratified.

The occupation of Austria proceeded with relatively minor difficulties, the chief of which were (1) Russian insistence that property seized on any pretext by the Nazis was now rightfully Russian property, and (2) consistent refusal to make progress toward the signing of a treaty of peace. Fortunately, the Austrians had been permitted to establish a provisional government, so that the whole responsibility for the government of the nation did not rest with the occupying powers. The occupation of Germany, in contrast, presented an interminable procession of virtually insoluble problems.[1] Germany in defeat was without a government, its cities and industries were in ruins, it was overrun with "displaced persons," and it was in no mood even to try to help itself. Almost miraculously, the Allied Control Council actually reached agreement on about fifty major measures, and as many minor directives, before the Russian policy of non-cooperation set in. The Allies also worked out a

Germany and Austria

---

[1] Julian Bach, *America's Germany: An Account of the Occupation* (1946); S. K. Padover, *Experiment in Germany: The Story of an American Intelligence Officer* (1946); Samuel Gardner Welles, *Profile of Europe* (1948).

ZONES OF OCCUPATION: GERMANY, AUSTRIA, BERLIN

plan for the trial of those Germans who were principally responsible for the war and were still alive. After ten months of hearings the international court constituted for the purpose sentenced eleven "war criminals" to be hanged, and eight others to long prison terms. Three of the defendants were freed, and one of the condemned, Göring, escaped execution by suicide. Later on, many less notable criminals were also brought to trial, and many convictions were obtained.[1]

As time wore on, it became evident that Russian policy with respect to Germany had shifted. At the time of the Potsdam Conference, all the great powers, Russia included, had wished to keep Germany decentralized, as the best available means of preventing the **"Bizonia"** revival of the nation's military might. All had agreed to **and** the removal of such industrial plants from Germany as **"Trizonia"** might serve a military end, and many such plants had been removed, particularly for shipment to Russia. But the Russians soon found that they could not use the booty effectively — sometimes they could not even put the dismantled plants together again. They therefore made up their minds that the best thing for them to do was to turn Germany into "a high-powered industrial state," with the capacity for production that the Russians themselves lacked, but with a political system that would insure German subordination to Russia. In short, what the Russians wanted was a centralized Germany under Communist control. For this project the western democracies naturally showed scant sympathy. Struggling against odds to keep their sections together economically, the British and Americans first consolidated their zones for administrative purposes into a "Bizonia," which the addition of the French zone presently made a "Trizonia." The break between East and West grew more marked with each succeeding month. Finally, in March, 1948, when the Russians refused all further participation in the Allied Control Council, almost the last vestige of governmental unity disappeared.

On the other side of the world, in eastern Asia, the road to peace was quite as long and tortuous as in Europe. In China the end of the war, instead of bringing peace, brought only a life-and-death con- **China** flict between the Nationalist government of Chiang Kai-shek (Kuomintang) and an increasingly powerful Communist faction which Russian backing had built up in Manchuria and northern China. In an effort to restore peace the government of the United States, in December, 1945, sent General George C. Marshall, then Chief of Staff of the United States Army, on a special mission to China to bring the warring factions together into one government.[2] But the Marshall mission,

---

[1] Sheldon Glueck, *The Nuremberg Trial and Aggressive War* (1946); R. H. Jackson, *The Case Against the Nazi War Criminals* (1946), and *The Nürnberg Case* (1947).

[2] F. R. Dulles, *China and America: The Story of their Relations since 1784* (1946), provides useful background.

in spite of the brief armistice it facilitated, failed utterly, and the war continued. On Marshall's recommendation, the United States adopted a "plague-on-both-your-houses" attitude toward the fighting factions. Unpalatable as the Communists were, they seemed hardly worse than the graft-ridden and hopelessly inefficient Nationalists. The United States withdrew most of its troops from China, cut down aid to Chiang's government to a thin trickle, and gave up all further efforts at mediation. As a result, the Communists went on from one triumph to another until by the spring of 1949 the Nationalist armies were in full rout, and Chiang himself had resigned and fled to Formosa.

In Korea, as in China, the pathway to peace encountered almost insuperable obstacles. At the Cairo Conference of 1943, Roosevelt, Churchill, and Chiang Kai-shek had pledged themselves to **Korea** establish an independent Korea, but at the end of the war the United States and Russia divided that unhappy nation between them at the thirty-eighth parallel for purposes of military occupation, the Russians taking the northern half of the country, and the Americans, the southern. The professed intent of the two occupying powers was the establishment of a native Korean government, but mutual distrust of each other's motives prevented any such development. Finally, during the summer of 1948, two Korean governments appeared, a Korean People's Republic in the northern zone, modeled on the Soviet pattern, and a Republic of Korea in the southern zone, based on a western-type democratic constitution. Here, as in so many other places, the tension between the United States and Soviet Russia was great, with an unstable peace at the mercy of the slightest incident.

In nearby Japan, American occupation had turned out somewhat better than had at first been expected.[1] The retention of the Emperor **Japan** and the speedy creation of a Japanese government reduced to a minimum the problems of the American occupation forces. Unlike the Germans, the Japanese people were docile and cooperative; MacArthur gave the orders, and the Japanese government carried them out. It was not long, however, before the other Allies, particularly Australia and Russia, demanded a greater voice in Japanese affairs. The result was an eleven-power Far Eastern Commission, with headquarters in Washington, to formulate policies for carrying out the Japanese terms of surrender, and to review directives sent to MacArthur, or issued by him. A somewhat similar Allied Council was established in Tokyo. But despite all this elaborate machinery, the Japanese occupation remained primarily an American affair. As in Germany, the war leaders were brought to trial, and eventually seven of them, including

---

[1] Mark Gayn, *Japan Diary* (1948), is an excellent journalistic account.

Hideki Tojo, the wartime premier, were sentenced to death and executed. In the economic sphere, efforts were made to break up large landed estates in the interest of a wider distribution of holdings, to dissolve the large industrial and banking corporations, to develop labor organizations after the western pattern, and to institute extensive educational reforms. But all these measures failed dismally to restore stable economic conditions in Japan, and far down into 1949 the very survival of the nation seemed to depend upon the steady importation of unpaid-for supplies from the United States. Efforts on the part of the United States to obtain a peace treaty with Japan were effectively blocked by Russian and Chinese opposition.

In the Philippine Islands the United States, in spite of the vastly changed conditions resulting from the war, undertook to deliver on its long-standing promise, under the Tydings-McDuffie Act, of independence on July 4, 1946. The Philippine President as **The Philippines** the war ended was Sergio Osmena, who as Vice-President had succeeded to the presidency in August, 1944, on the death of President Manuel Luiz Quezon, and it was to Osmena that General MacArthur surrendered full responsibility for Philippine civil administration in February, 1945. New elections, held in April, 1946, gave the Islands a new President, Manuel A. Roxas, a man far less inclined than Osmena to submit to American domination. With some reluctance, the Roxas government acquiesced in the terms of independence laid down by the United States. In military matters, the American government took pains to provide for the creation of an effective Philippine army, and for the retention by the United States of important military and naval bases. In economic matters, a Philippine Trade Act paved the way for the gradual institution of American tariffs on goods imported from the Philippines after an eight-year period of free trade on the quota basis. Congress also voted a total of $720,000,000 to compensate the Philippine government and the owners of private property in the Islands for the war damage they had suffered. These acts, however, failed to solve the pressing internal problems of the Philippine Republic. The old sugar-coconut-tobacco economy of the pre-war period, which had profited the landlord-merchant class a great deal, but the ordinary peasant very little, had been shattered by the war. Many of the peasants were loath to go back to it; and under the leadership of a left-wing organization known as the Hukbalahap they insisted, even to the point of open revolt, on radical agrarian reforms.[1]

---

[1] J. R. Hayden, *The Philippines Today* (1945); Manuel Luiz Quezon, *The Good Fight* (1946). President Roxas died April 15, 1948, and was succeeded by the Vice-President, Elpidio Quirino.

Although events in the rest of the Asiatic theater were seemingly of little consequence to the United States, the American people had begun to understand that anything which happened anywhere in the world might concern them eventually. They therefore viewed with more than passing interest post-war developments in the Asiatic empires of European nations. It was apparent that most of the colonial peoples had no intention whatever of going back to the old system of subservience to white dominion. They had seen the white man defeated and humiliated, and although they had little use for their Japanese conquerors, they had lost their awe and fear of the Europeans. What they wanted when the Japanese were driven out was self-rule, such as the United States unhesitatingly granted to the Philippines.

In recognizing this new spirit among colonial peoples, Great Britain was not far behind the United States. In India, the task was less one of getting the British out than of getting the Hindus and Moslems to agree on a plan of self-government. Finally, a divided India was agreed upon, with a Dominion of India dominated by Hindus and a Dominion of Pakistan dominated by Moslems. In Burma, where there was less internal friction, complete independence was granted. In Malaya, British control continued, but two new governmental units were set up, the Malayan Union, a federation of states that had previously been governed separately, and the colony of Singapore.

India, Burma, Malaya

Unfortunately the willingness of the United States and Great Britain to grant home rule to their dependencies was not fully shared by other European nations who had possessions in the Orient. In Indo-China the French at first recognized a locally constituted Viet Nam Republic, but differences developed that resulted in long continued warfare between French and native troops. In the populous Dutch East Indies the returning European overlords also met a determined Indonesian independence movement, and sharp fighting broke out. Efforts to work out a satisfactory agreement through the mediation of the United Nations seemed for a time to have achieved success, but late in 1948 warfare flared up anew.

Indo-China, Indonesia

The great significance that citizens of the United States had learned during the war to attach to events in Europe and Asia served in a way to detract from their interest in the other Americas. Before the war the "good neighbor" policy had seemed to be a matter of fundamental importance; after the war, whatever its importance, it was much less in the news. The Act of Chapultepec, adopted just before the San Francisco Conference, had asserted that aggression against any American nation by a non-American power was

Latin America

to be regarded by all as an attack on all. In other words, instead of a unilateral pledge by the United States to defend the Americas, as under the Monroe Doctrine, there was now an agreement among all the various American nations to accept joint responsibility for their common defenses.[1] But the most pressing diplomatic troubles of the American nations were in relation to each other, not in relation to the non-American world. For example, bitter feeling developed between the United States and Argentina. Economically the two nations were rivals, each with practically the same agricultural exports to sell; politically, the Argentine resented the leadership of the United States in the Americas, and sought to rally at least the South American republics around Argentine leadership. Bungling diplomacy, both in Washington and in Buenos Aires, magnified all differences, and the antagonism for the United States of the army colonel, Juan Domingo Perón, who became the Argentine dictator and president, was open and often-expressed. With Mexico, in contrast, the United States was on increasingly cordial terms. During 1947, as mutual gestures of good-will, President Truman visited Mexico City and President Miguel Alemán of Mexico visited Washington. It seemed clear that whatever remained of the old "good neighbor" policy was primarily designed to unite all American nations against the growing threat of Communism. By an Inter-American Military Cooperation Act of 1946, the President of the United States was permitted to extend military aid and advice to the other American nations, and in a sense to try to organize them for defense. Unfortunately, the United States made little effort to revive the economic life of Latin America, which the dislocations of war had left badly shattered.

For most Americans the chief hope of holding the world together lay in the United Nations.[2] The process of putting the San Francisco charter into effect began at London on January 10, 1946, when the General Assembly opened its first session. Among the most **The United Nations** important of the functions assigned to the Assembly was the selection of the six non-permanent members of the Security Council. The nations first selected for this honor were Egypt, Mexico, the Netherlands, Australia, Brazil, and Poland. The first session of the Security Council was held in London on January 18. On its recommendation, the Assembly chose Trigve Lie, a Norwegian Labor Party leader, as the first Secretary-General of the United Nations. Later meetings of the Security

---

[1] This same determination to act collectively against aggressors was written into the Treaty of Rio de Janeiro ratified by the United States Senate in December, 1947.

[2] Vera Micheles Dean, *The Four Cornerstones of Peace* (1946), deals with United Nations beginnings. Ruhl J. Bartlett (ed.), *The Record of American Diplomacy: Documents and Readings in the History of American Foreign Relations* (1947), includes valuable sections on wartime diplomacy and the United Nations.

Council were generally held in New York, first at Hunter College, and then at Lake Success, Long Island. After much argument, New York City was chosen as the permanent headquarters of the United Nations. Acceptance of an offer of $8,500,000 by John D. Rockefeller, Jr., for the purchase of a six-block tract along the East River determined that the new world organization would eventually have a skyscraper capital in the heart of the great American metropolis.

It soon became apparent that the Security Council, under existing regulations, could never become the effective instrument that at least some of the framers of the United Nations Charter had **The Russian** hoped. The chief difficulty lay in the provision which per-**vetoes** mitted each great power to veto any important action that might be proposed. When Roosevelt and Churchill agreed to this crippling provision they could hardly have foreseen the ruthlessness with which one nation, Russia, would exercise the veto power. During the first three years of the life of the United Nations, the Russian veto was interposed no less than thirty times. In practice, the Russian use of the veto power made the United Nations as ineffective after the second World War as the failure of the United States to ratify the Treaty of Versailles made the League of Nations ineffective after the first World War. In each instance the international organization continued in existence, but in each instance also its usefulness was almost fatally impaired.

In spite of the discouraging effect of the constant Russian vetoes, the United Nations was able to provide most of the machinery for world cooperation that had been contemplated by the San Fran-**UN** cisco Charter. This involved the creation of several im-**agencies** portant subordinate bodies. (1) The Economic and Social Council consisted of eighteen members elected by the Assembly. This Council in turn set up a wide variety of commissions through which to operate and to seek advice. It took over, also, comparable bodies from the now-defunct League of Nations, such as the Commission on Narcotic Drugs, and it gave the blessing of United Nations sponsorship to such previously created international bodies as the United Nations Educational, Scientific, and Cultural Organization (UNESCO). (2) A Trusteeship Council of twelve members had a somewhat ill-defined measure of authority over mandates and over territory detached from a defeated nation. "Strategic areas," however, such as the former Japanese mandates in the Pacific which were handed over to the United States for administration, were to be directly under the Security Council. (3) An International Court of Justice, with fifteen judges chosen by the Security Council in conjunction with the Assembly, was to hear such cases in dispute between nations as might be referred to it. (4) A Military Staff Committee, to be composed of the chiefs of staff of the five great powers — the United States, the United Kingdom, France, the U.S.S.R., and China — was to advise the Security Council on the means by which armed force might be used to carry out United Nations decisions. This Committee was rendered totally inoperative by Russian lack of cooperation. (5) A "Little Assembly," consisting of one representative from each member nation, although unauthorized by the United Nations Charter, was found desirable as a kind of substitute for the larger and more cumbersome Assembly, when the latter was not in session. The "Little Assembly" had no real authority, but its decisions, arrived at by a two-thirds vote, furnished a good cross-section of world opinion on controversial subjects. It was promptly boycotted by Russia and her satellites.

The record of the United Nations on the preservation of peace during its first three years of existence gave little room for optimism. Its first sessions were confronted by Iranian protests against the continued Russian military occupation of Iranian territory, **UN peace efforts** and perhaps the evidence that the overwhelming majority of the Security Council sympathized with Iran may have had something to do with the decision of the Soviet leaders to recall their troops. Charges made by the Ukraine that British troops in Greece threatened the peace of the Balkans were denied by the Greeks, who charged in turn that Albania, Bulgaria, and Yugoslavia were supporting Greek Communist insurgents in their attempt to overthrow the Greek government. A United Nations Commission investigated the situation, but a Russian veto prevented action being taken on its report, and the guerilla fighting continued. Efforts of the United Nations to intervene in the Dutch-Indonesian dispute, as noted, were inconclusive. Polish insistence that the United Nations take action against Franco's Spain, as a threat to world peace, resulted in a proposal that if the Spanish government did not mend its ways, the members of the United Nations should withdraw their representatives from Madrid. This mild action ran afoul of the usual Russian veto. Russian intransigence also prevented the Security Council from appointing a governor of Trieste, as provided for under the terms of the treaty with Italy. Thus Trieste remained under joint Anglo-American control, a persistent thorn-in-the-flesh to both Yugoslavia and Italy.

Infinitely perplexing, likewise, was the Arab-Jewish contest for the control of Palestine, which by 1947 reached the United Nations. Thousands of Jewish refugees had flocked into Palestine after the war, and had posed a serious problem for the British government, which held a man-

date over the "holy land" dating back to 1922. The influx of so many
Jews frightened and angered the local Arabs, who could count
Palestine
on the support of such neighboring Arabian states as Trans-
Jordan, Egypt, Iran, Iraq, and Saudi Arabia. Both Great Britain and
the United States, because of their need for Arabian oil, were reluctant
to offend the intensely anti-Jewish Arab kings, and British policy tended
generally to be pro-Arab, even to the setting of drastic limitations on the
number of Jews to be admitted to Palestine. But the large number of
Jewish voters in the United States, many of whom were "Zionists" and
as such strongly favored the establishment of a Jewish national state,
made a pro-Arab attitude on the part of the American government almost impossible. Efforts of the United States to promote the continuation of the British mandate, with more generous provision for the admission of Jewish refugees, pleased neither Arabs, Jews, nor British. Finally, with violence between Arabs and Jews on the increase, the British
government requested the Assembly of the United Nations to study the
problem. Thereupon, the Assembly in May, 1947, appointed a Special
Committee on Palestine, which three months later brought in an elaborate report favoring the partition of the country into three states, one
dominantly Arab and one dominantly Jewish, but with the City of
Jerusalem independent of both, and all three bound together in a single
economic union. This report, after prolonged debate, was adopted,
strangely enough with the United States and the Soviet Union both supporting it, but it failed to bring the contending factions any closer to
peace, and its intense unpopularity with the Arabs soon led the United
States virtually to repudiate it.

British action finally brought the situation to a head. Despairing of
its ability to restore peace, and unwilling to bear the continued expense
involved, the British government announced early in 1948
The new
state of
Israel
that it was withdrawing from Palestine. When in May, the
British High Commissioner actually took his departure, the
Jews proclaimed the independent state of Israel, as of midnight, May 14–15. The new state received immediate recognition by the
United States and the Soviet Union, but its Arab neighbors promptly
attacked it with what little military might they could muster. In the
fighting that followed, the Jews, in spite of their inferiority in numbers,
quite outmatched the Arabs, and made it clear that the Jewish state was
there to stay. The United Nations, faced with the necessity of trying to
do something to stop the fighting, at length decided through the General
Assembly to authorize the five great powers to send a mediator to Palestine. For this task the powers chose Count Bernadotte of Sweden, who
in June, 1948, achieved a truce, only to be assassinated by Jewish ex-

tremists who wished the war to continue until the new nation should dominate all Palestine. Despite this untoward incident and much irregular fighting, a settlement involving the establishment of a Jewish state was gradually worked out. Early in 1949 even the British government capitulated to the inevitable and accorded its recognition to Israel.

The seeming agreement between the United States and Russia over Palestine deceived no one. Long before this it had become apparent that these two great powers stood in deadly antagonism to each other. This antagonism was shown in a variety of ways, but perhaps most conclusively in the divergent attitudes of the two nations with reference to the control of atomic energy. Tests undertaken in July, 1946, by the United States Navy at Bikini Island demonstrated that a small number of bombs, strategically placed, could destroy a whole metropolitan area, while a considerable number could paralyze an entire nation.[1] A third world war might, with such weapons, mean the end of civilization. Mindful of this fact, the General Assembly of the United Nations had established, even before the Bikini tests, an Atomic Energy Commission to make recommendations for the international control of atomic energy. But a seemingly incurable difference of opinion developed between the American and the Russian points of view. The Americans called for the creation of an International Atomic Development Authority with full power to prevent the use of atomic energy for warlike ends anywhere in the world. This agency was to have unrestricted privileges of inspection in all nations, and its actions were not to be subject to the usual veto power of the United Nations. Over against this plan the Russians proposed merely an international agreement to abandon atomic warfare, with each nation to be fully trusted to enforce the agreement for itself. Furthermore, the veto power was to remain inviolate, and the United States was to proceed at once to destroy its stockpile of atomic bombs. And so no agreement could be reached. The United States was ready to give up its long lead in atomic development only to an international authority; the Russians, while ultimately willing to concede the necessity of some inspection, insisted on no impairment of national rights, and full freedom for each nation to use the veto power in any way it chose.

Although the United States was unable to accomplish anything in the way of international control of atomic energy, Congress laid careful plans for its control at home. A five-man commission was created, with exclusive authority over the development of atomic energy, and to head it the President chose David E. Lilienthal, for many years the efficient head of TVA. Under this commission American scientists went ahead to unlock

Atomic energy control

[1] David Bradley, *No Place to Hide* (1948), gives the results of the Bikini tests.

further the secrets of nuclear energy, and to make their findings useful for peaceful as well as for warlike purposes.

With the increasingly tense situation between Russia and the United States, the idea of "One World," which had seemed so sure of achievement during the war, became each month a dimmer hope.

One World, or two? Soviet dissolution of the Comintern in 1943 had been widely hailed as the end of the old Communist plan to promote world revolution, but in September, 1947, the hollowness of this hope was proved by the establishment of a Communist Information Bureau, or Cominform, the purpose of which obviously was to provide one leadership for Communist propaganda everywhere in the world. It was clear after the Warsaw Manifesto, which announced the new organization, that the old policy of world revolution had been resumed, and that the Russian leaders were bent on creating "One World," to be sure, but one Communist world.

Words were speedily matched with deeds. Wherever the Red Army controlled, either by direct occupation or by the heavy shadow it cast across an international border, free governments disappeared. By one means or another Communist minorities took over in Poland, Yugoslavia, Bulgaria, Hungary, and finally even Czechoslovakia. The Russian zones in Germany and Austria were separated from other zones of occupation by heavy Red Army patrols, and were stripped of their resources. From the Baltic to the Adriatic an "iron curtain" had descended, back of which the Soviet leaders could in safety and in secrecy consolidate their gains and lay plans for further expansion. In Italy and France they galvanized Communist minorities into action, preparatory to taking over those governments. In Turkey they served notice that directly or indirectly the Soviets must control the Dardanelles. In Greece they made every effort to promote a Communist revolution which would establish Russian influence on the shores of the Mediterranean.

It was this Greek situation which finally led the United States to take a positive stand against the Russian program of aggression. When the British government, in line with its general policy of re-

The Truman Doctrine trenchment, announced that it could no longer maintain a garrison in Greece, the United States determined that the time had come to make a stand. The government of Greece had little to recommend it, but it was anti-Communist, and at least subject to improvement. If the Communists came in, then down would come the "iron curtain," and the liberties of one more "liberated" country would disappear. Faced by this situation, President Truman, on March 12, 1947, sent a message to Congress calling for American aid both for Greece and for Turkey. The world was confronted with two ways of life, the

President pointed out, one based on majority rule, with generous guarantees for the freedom of the individual, and the other "based upon the will of a minority forcibly imposed upon the majority." The United States, the President declared, "must assist free peoples to work out their own destinies in their own way." To give strength to his words the President recommended that Congress vote $300,000,000 for aid to Greece and $100,000,000 for aid to Turkey. The Truman Doctrine, as this revolutionary demand came to be called, aroused much discussion in the United States. A small minority, headed by Henry Wallace, denounced it, while a few others regretted that the American nation had acted alone instead of through the United Nations. But the appropriations passed Congress substantially as the President requested, with Senator Vandenburg, a Republican, championing the President's cause. American foreign policy had by this time achieved a bi-partisan status, with a genuinely united front, except for Wallaceite and Communist opposition, against Russian "red imperialism." As further evidence of the non-party character of his policy, Truman in January, 1947, had appointed as Secretary of State, to succeed Secretary Byrnes whose health compelled him to resign, General George C. Marshall, a man who had never been in politics and had never expected to be.

Marshall soon supplemented the Truman Doctrine with what was sometimes called the "Marshall Plan," and sometimes the "European Recovery Plan." It seemed clear that American aid to one or two hard-pressed nations would never serve to turn back the Communist tide. Europe as a whole needed to be **The Marshall Plan** helped back to its normal economic life. If that could be done, the chief appeal of Communism would disappear. In an address delivered at Harvard University on June 5, 1947, Secretary Marshall called upon European nations first to get together to see what they could do to help themselves, and then to state in concrete terms what additional aid they would need from the United States. If they could demonstrate a determination to cooperate for their own good, and would give assurance that the aid they received would be used for the economic benefit of Europe as a whole, the United States would help pay the bill. The Marshall Plan was enthusiastically received throughout all western Europe, but Russia and her satellites, to whom it was also open, pointedly refused to have anything to do with it and branded it an instrument of American imperialism. One of the Russian satellites, Czechoslovakia, had at first signified its interest in the plan, but later, on the insistence of the Russian government, it was obliged to change its mind.

The European Recovery Plan (ERP) was by no means the first contribution of the United States toward the rehabilitation of the war-torn

world.   Lend-lease totals had recorded some $48,500,000,000 worth
of American assistance in return for reverse lend-lease worth
Background
of ERP $7,800,000,000, but in the post-war settlements the sums due
to the United States were reduced to millions rather than
billions.[1] Further, to take the place of lend-lease funds, to which the
British economy has been closely geared during the war, the United
States Congress, late in 1945, voted to lend the British government a
total of $4,400,000,000, with an interest charge of only two per cent, and
with repayments in fifty equal installments, beginning in 1951. American aid to recovery had also included substantial contributions to the
United Nations Relief and Rehabilitation Administration (UNRRA),
which was created in 1943 to bring relief to the victims of war in any area
under control of the United Nations. More than 72 per cent of the funds
expended by UNRRA came from the United States, and more than 90
per cent of the food and other supplies it distributed came from American firms and factories. UNRRA aid was distributed freely on both
sides of the iron curtain, but the American State Department soon became acutely dissatisfied with the way in which UNRRA supplies were
being used by such governments as Yugoslavia's "to feed their political
supporters and starve their political enemies." There were also charges
of graft and maladministration, notably with respect to China. Finally
the United States felt obliged to discontinue its support of UNRRA in
favor of direct relief "done by the United States unilaterally . . . and not
as a member of an international organization."

Thus in a sense the Marshall Plan grew out of American experience
with post-war relief. The problem that confronted the United States
was not how to avoid giving American aid, but rather how
ECA begins
work to avoid having American money and supplies used to build
up hostility to the nation that provided them. As a result
of the American overtures, sixteen nations of western Europe sent their
representatives to Paris in July, 1947, and reported, as the United States
had requested, what they could do to help themselves and what they
would need from the United States — a gigantic $19,330,000,000, to be
spread over a four-year period. Scaled down to $17,000,000,000, the
program thus devised was accepted in principle by the United States,
and in April, 1948, Congress voted $5,300,000,000 as the first annual ap-
propriation for ERP. To administer the program, an Economic Cooperation Administration (ECA) was set up, with Paul G. Hoffman, a Republican business executive from Indiana, as chief. The objects of ECA
were, first, to restore prosperity in western Europe to the point where
Communism would lose its appeal, and second, to speed the time when

---

[1] Russia steadfastly refused to negotiate a settlement.

the nations concerned would no longer need American aid and could look out for themselves.

Evidence that ERP had made a deep impression on European countries was not long in coming. The governments of France and Italy now made bold to eliminate all Communists from their cabinets, and despite the strikes and violence this entailed, stood their ground steadfastly. In Italy a free election, which the Communists felt sure they could win, showed 70 per cent of the electorate against the Communists, and only about 30 per cent in favor of their so-called "Popular Front." Progress toward economic unity in the low countries — Belgium, the Netherlands, and Luxembourg (Benelux) — was heartening, and the prospect of closer cooperation between these countries and their more powerful neighbors, Great Britain and France, seemed to indicate that the idea of economic unity was gaining ground. As American aid began to give visible proof that it was really promoting recovery, the North Atlantic nations that felt themselves in peril from Russian aggression began also to draw together in a military way. First Great Britain and France joined with the Benelux countries to create a **North Atlantic Treaty** regional system of collective defense, a course of action authorized by the United Nations charter. When the United States indicated its willingness to enter such an organization, negotiations began which ended on March 15, 1949, with the signing of the North Atlantic Treaty by twelve nations —: Belgium, Canada, Denmark, France, Great Britain, Iceland, Italy, Luxembourg, the Netherlands, Norway, Portugal, and the United States. According to this pact, "armed attack against one or more" of the member nations was to "be considered an attack against them all." Military aid from the United States to other member nations was confidently predicted.

But the Russians were by no means idle. The establishment of the Cominform in September, 1947, was apparently intended, at least in part, to offset the Truman Doctrine and the Marshall Plan. **Communist seizure of Czecho-slovakia** Then in February, 1948, with complete Russian support and connivance, the Communists seized power in Czechoslovakia, where until that time a middle-of-the-road multiparty government had been permitted to exist. Efforts were also made to discipline the Communist dictator of Yugoslavia, Marshal Tito, whom the Comintern in June, 1948, accused of deviation from the party line. But Tito, although fully cognizant of the hazards of his course, stood his ground and refused to be erased. Just what this Communist internal dissension meant, the western world was unable to fathom, but it was evident that the solidarity of the eastern bloc of nations in opposition to the West remained unshaken. This was registered clearly when an international conference on the control of the Danube River met in Belgrade on July 30, 1948. At every opportunity the seven Communist states of eastern Europe, including Yugoslavia, voted solidly against the three western powers — the United States, Great Britain, and France — to exclude all non-Danubian powers from a voice in the control of the river, and thus in effect to make Russia its mistress.

But the outstanding action taken by Russia to show her displeasure with the western world was with reference to Germany. When in the summer of 1948, despairing of ever reaching any further

The Berlin blockade

agreements on German affairs with the Russian authorities, the western occupation powers announced their intention of establishing a native German government for Trizonia, the intense displeasure of the Soviets was at once apparent. Russian policy called for a united Communist Germany, nothing less, with Berlin as its capital, and Russian promotion of discord and inefficiency in the four-power government had clearly been designed with that end in view. The three occupation authorities, as a step toward the union they contemplated, also issued a new currency to be used in common throughout western Germany and in the western-occupied portion of Berlin. On the pretext that this currency reform would "place Berlin's economy and her working population in an untenable situation which only can be solved by Berlin's close connection with the eastern part of Germany," the Soviet authorities laid down a blockade against the movement of supplies from the West into Berlin, whether by rail, highway, or canal. Since there were some two millions of people in the western-occupied section of the city whose lives might depend on the continued importation of food from the West, it seemed clear that the Soviet intent was to force the western powers out of Berlin by the threat of wholesale starvation. With the western powers eliminated, nothing further would stand in the way of Russian control of the entire capital city — an important step toward the goal of a united Communist Germany under Russian domination.

The answer of the western powers to this new Soviet approach could hardly have been anticipated by the Russians. The air lanes to Berlin were still open, and the western powers at once undertook to

The "air lift"

fly in the supplies necessary to feed the beleaguered Germans. Both British and American planes were used on the "air lift," which within a matter of days developed an amazing efficiency. New airfields were opened up, and soon coal to keep the people warm and even to keep the factories going was reaching Berlin by air. Hundreds of airplanes were brought from the United States to participate in the operation, and both British and American military pilots got a superb training, the possible significance of which the Russians could hardly have overlooked. Even dense fogs and winter weather failed to stop the steady movement of the all-essential cargoes across the Russian zone. General Lucius D. Clay, the United States Military Governor in Germany, stated clearly the American position with reference to Berlin when he said, "They can't drive us out by any action short of war." The Russians, however, did everything else they could think of. They withdrew their representative from the four-power Berlin city government, set up a separate police in their section of Berlin, excluded personnel of the lawful city government from the City Hall, which was within their area, and installed a German Communist of their own choosing as mayor. But in spite of all this, month after month, in good weather or bad, the air lift continued; furthermore, the western occupation authorities, not to be outdone by the Russians, clamped down a counter-blockade on trade between Trizonia and Soviet-dominated eastern Germany.

One of the most notable results of the air lift was the change in attitude on the part of the Germans toward the western Allies. Armies of occupation are rarely popular, nor do they often deserve to be, and German dislike for their conquerors, whether in the East or **Effect on** in the West, was intense. But the air lift did much to make **Germany** friends among the Germans for all who participated in it, particularly for the Americans who bore so large a proportion of the expense and furnished so many of the planes. With this assurance that they were not to be abandoned, the German leaders went promptly to work on the development of a constitution for the 45,000,000 Germans living in the western occupational zones. The chief requirements laid on them were (1) that the new constitution be democratic, (2) that it be based on the federal principle, and (3) that civil liberties be fully guaranteed. Nor need the new constitution be regarded as merely designed for that portion of Germany under western control. If and when the Russians should permit, there would be no bar on the states in eastern Germany joining in the support of the new government. In Berlin itself, although the failure of the air lift would mean dire retribution for all who had supported the western powers, the people in the city's western zones rallied strongly to the support of their deliverers. Eventually there emerged a divided city with two separate governments. In the Russian sector, as already noted, the Communists took over; but in the western zones, at a free election which the Russians had urged the people to boycott, well over eighty per cent of the voters came out to register their support of anti-Communist candidates.

Meantime the western powers had exerted themselves in every possible way to induce the Russian government to accept a compromise settlement. In August, 1948, their ministers in Moscow opened direct negotiations on the subject, and seemingly reached an agreement that in return for western concession of an exclusively Russian-controlled currency in Berlin, the embargo should be lifted. But in Berlin, due to the obduracy of the Russian representative, the implementation of this agreement broke down completely. Finally, in September, the western powers referred the whole matter to the Security Council of the United Nations, charging that it amounted to a threat to world peace. But here, too, every effort at agreement failed. During these proceedings, which were held in Paris, President Truman conceived the idea of sending a special mission to Moscow, headed by Chief Justice Frederick M. Vinson, but Secretary Marshall held that any such action would be an unwarranted snub for the Security Council, and the plan was abandoned. It was generally believed that the Russians, no less than the western powers, would be glad to find some face-saving way out of the situation, but the barriers were maintained for nearly a year. Finally, in the spring of 1949, the Russian leaders changed their tactics. Negotiations at Lake Success, New York, between a member of the Russian delegation to the United Nations, Yakov Malik, and a representative of the United States Department of State, Philip Jessup, showed that the Russians were now ready to lift their blockade if at the same time the western powers would end their counter-blockade, and agree to a meeting of the Council of Foreign Ministers to discuss the whole German question. Since the western powers had been ready to accept such a settlement all along, the deal was quickly closed. All blockades were lifted May 12, 1949, and the meeting of the Council of Foreign Ministers was set for May 23. Meantime, the West German constitutional convention had finished its work, and had submitted for approval of the eleven West German states its plan for a "Federal Republic of Germany." That the Russians hoped to forestall this development seemed clear, but neither the western powers nor the people of Trizonia seemed disposed to alter their course.

Efforts to deal with Russia

Tension over the Berlin situation and the air lift was heightened by the fact that 1948 was an election year in the United States. Would the two political parties split on the foreign issue? Could Russia count on dissension in the United States as her ally in the program of expansion she had cut out for herself? It was apparent from the beginning of the campaign that most of the leaders on both sides, Republicans no less than Democrats, were determined that the bi-partisan foreign policy to which they had subscribed must not be abandoned. So evident was this that Henry Wallace early announced his determination to head a third party movement in opposition to the "get-tough-with-Russia" program, which, he claimed, would eventually

Election of 1948

lead the two nations to war. In Wallace's opinion, the only correct procedure was to concede to Russia practically everything she wanted. He held, further, that on domestic affairs the Truman Administration had yielded to the conservatives, and he called for a revival of the New Deal philosophy of the first two Roosevelt administrations. He persuaded Senator Glen H. Taylor of Idaho to join his ticket as Vice-Presidential candidate, and with the enthusiastic cooperation of Communist and "fellow-traveler" leaders a so-called Progressive convention, held in Philadelphia late in the summer, ratified these two self-nominations. Russian sympathy for the Wallace movement was warmly and officially expressed, and the Russian leaders seemed to think that Wallace's candidacy would strike a responsive chord in American hearts.

Both Republicans and Democrats held their conventions in Philadelphia, also, the Republicans in June and the Democrats in July. The Republicans felt certain of victory, for they had won the mid-term elections of 1946, and they were sure that the Wallace candidacy would cut heavily into the Democratic **Republican confidence** vote. For a time it looked as if a strong public demand might force the Republicans to nominate General Dwight D. Eisenhower, but the popular war leader accepted instead the presidency of Columbia University and removed himself from consideration in no uncertain terms. This left Governor Thomas E. Dewey of New York, Senator Robert A. Taft of Ohio, and ex-Governor Harold E. Stassen of Minnesota as the principal candidates. Taft appealed strongly to the old-line conservatives, and Stassen to the younger, more liberal-minded element in the party. But Dewey took pains not to offend either side unduly, and lined up the votes. He was nominated on the second ballot, and at his suggestion the convention chose Governor Earl Warren of California as his running-mate. The Republican platform, while by no means ready to abandon all the social gains made during the Roosevelt era, urged that greater responsibility should be given to the states in such matters as housing, conservation, public health, and security for the aged. It favored also "minimum" governmental controls over business, and lauded the American free enterprise system as the "mainspring of material well-being and political freedom." On the moot labor problem, it pledged the party to protect "both workers and employers against coercion and exploitation." The conservatism of these pronouncements was thinly veiled, and reflected well the point of view of the Republican majority in the Eightieth Congress.

The Democrats had little hope of victory. Some of them were so certain of Truman's defeat that they imitated the Republicans in trying to induce Eisenhower to accept their nomination, with precisely the same

Dorman H. Smith for NEA Service, Inc.

."Look, No Hands!"

result.   The more disgruntled then tried to rally around Justice
William O. Douglas of the Supreme Court, but they could
Democratic   not persuade him to help them.   President Truman was thus
despair   practically unopposed when the convention met, and was
nominated without serious opposition.   The Convention experienced
· some difficulty in finding anyone of prominence willing to accept second
place on a ticket that seemed certain of defeat, but at length it chose
Senator Alben Barkley of Kentucky, the venerable leader of the Democratic minority in the Senate.   The chief excitement in the Democratic
convention came from a successful effort, led by Mayor Hubert Humphrey of Minneapolis, to write into the platform a plank calling on Congress to support the President "in guaranteeing these basic and fundamental rights: (1) The right of full and equal political participation, (2)
the right of equal opportunity of employment, (3) the right of security of
person, and (4) the right of equal treatment in the services and defense

of our nation." This action was resented deeply by many southern delegates whose states used the poll-tax and other devices, some legal and some extra-legal, to discriminate against the Negroes. But the platform as finally adopted carried the drastic civil rights plank. It also denounced unsparingly the record of the Eightieth Congress, called for the repeal of the Taft-Hartley Act, advocated an extension of social security benefits and an increase in the minimum wage from 40 cents an hour to 75 cents, urged more adequate federal legislation on housing, and promised strong federal support of farm prices.

On foreign policy the two platforms were in fundamental agreement. Both supported the United Nations warmly, while condemning the intemperate use of the veto by Russia. Both stood loyally by the foreign aid program, although the Republicans wished to be more generous to China than the Democrats had been. Both favored full recognition of the new Jewish state of Israel. Both accepted the policy of reciprocal trade agreements as a means of regulating the tariff. When Candidate Dewey criticized the Democratic platform for claiming that the Democrats had originated the bi-partisan foreign policy, President Truman countered by appointing Dewey's intimate friend and adviser, John Foster Dulles, as one of the United States representatives to the third session of the United Nations General Assembly, which was to open on September 24 in Paris. *Unity on foreign policy*

As the campaign got under way, all signs continued to point to the certainty of Republican victory. Republican chances were increased when the extreme states-rights faction of the Democratic Party, which had taken such offense at the civil rights plank in their party's platform, held a rump convention at Birmingham, Alabama, and nominated a separate States' Rights Democrat or "Dixiecrat" ticket, consisting of Governor J. Strom Thurmond of South Carolina for President and Governor Fielding Wright of Mississippi for Vice-President. It was apparent that this ticket would carry at least three or four states in the Lower South. All the various public opinion polls predicted with extreme confidence the election of Dewey. Sixty-five per cent of the newspapers of the country supported the Republican candidates. Dewey himself campaigned as if he were a sure winner, avoiding controversial issues, and scarcely recognizing the existence of an opposition. *The Dixiecrats*

Truman, on the other hand, conducted a vigorous campaign, almost unaided. He called a special session of the Republican-dominated Eightieth Congress to meet in July, right after the nominations, and asked it to put through legislation to halt rising prices, to meet the housing crisis, to protect civil rights, and *Truman's campaign*

THE DEMOCRATIC SWEEP

Democrats replacing Republicans:
❂ Governor
★ Senator
✓ Representative

■ Truman
▨ Dewey
▥ Thurmond

TIME Map by V. Puglisi, Courtesy of TIME, Copyright Time Inc., 1948

to take various other steps called for by both platforms. When it adjourned without acting on his suggestions, he toured the country condemning it for its failure to deliver on promises in the Republican platform and branding it the worst Congress the nation had ever had. As the campaign wore on, it became apparent that the crowds were coming to hear the President, but were not coming to hear Dewey. Wallace also lost ground as the President hammered home the gains that labor had won and might still expect to win from the Democrats, and pointed out the losses it had suffered, and would continue to suffer, if the Republicans won. But most observers discounted the results of the Truman campaign. People came out just to see a President, they said, and to hear his intemperate remarks. The Wallace vote might not be as heavy as expected, but it would be heavy enough to insure Dewey's victory.

The election results were probably the greatest political upset in all American history. With 49,363,798 voters coming to the polls, more than in any other election except that of 1940, the Republicans went down to a resounding defeat. Truman failed to capture a majority of all votes cast for President, but his share amounted to 49.5 per cent of the total to Dewey's 45.1 per cent, and 5.4 per cent for all others. The Wallace vote, due in considerable part to the consistency with which Wallace's speeches during the campaign followed the Communist party line, reached only a little

The Democrats win

over a million, less than 2.5 per cent.[1] In the electoral college, the vote stood Truman 303, Dewey 189, Thurmond 39, Wallace 0. One elector in Tennessee, although chosen on the Truman ticket, voted for Thurmond, otherwise Truman's vote would have been one more, and Thurmond's one less. In the Congressional and State elections the Democratic victory was even more decisive; indeed, 683,382 more voters cast their ballots for state, county, and local candidates than cast their votes for President. Since, in these elections, well over fifty per cent of the total number of voters cast Democratic rather than Republican ballots, both houses of Congress were overwhelmingly Democratic, and Democratic governors were chosen in most of the states.

Looking backward, it was easier to explain why Truman won than it had been, looking forward, to foresee his victory. The forces of labor had rallied to his standard, and had quietly but efficiently got out the labor vote. Middlewestern farmers in historically Republican states such as Iowa and Minnesota had voted Democratic because they feared that price supports for agricultural commodities might disappear under Republican rule. The housewives of the nation, harassed by inflationary prices on every purchase they made, remembered Truman's unsuccessful struggle to maintain price ceilings, and the assurances of conservative Republicans that if price ceilings were removed self-regulation would eventually bring prices down. Furthermore, many local Democratic candidates greatly appealed to the voters, and helped the national ticket along. In Minnesota, for example, the young and popular Mayor Humphrey easily defeated his Republican opponent in the race for Senator. In Illinois, Paul Douglas and Adlai E. Stevenson, candidates for Senator and Governor, respectively, and both dependable Democratic liberals, quite overwhelmed their old-guard Republican opponents. So it was to a great extent throughout the nation. As for the two presidential candidates, Dewey's best efforts failed to convince the voters that he was not cold and calculating, while Truman, for all his lack of dignity, at least proved himself to be thoroughly human and in touch with the common man. Most of all, the election showed that the American people were not yet ready to turn their backs on the New Deal. As Truman so effectively pointed out, that was exactly what the Eightieth Congress had tried to do, and what might have been expected from the Republicans if they had succeeded in winning both the executive and the legislative branches of the government. In a sense, as many observers pointed out, the election of 1948 was the fifth straight victory for Franklin D. Roosevelt.

[1] William B. Hesseltine, *The Rise and Fall of Third Parties in the United States from Anti-Masonry to Wallace* (1948).

In spite of the spectacular Democratic triumph, the "Fair Deal" program that Truman submitted to the Eighty-first Congress failed of complete acceptance. The President's efforts to establish equality of civil rights in the South by means of federal anti-poll tax and anti-lynching laws, and provisions to insure equal job rights for all, met death at the hands of a southern Democratic filibuster. The Republicans, aided by conservative Democrats, saved the Taft-Hartley Act from repeal. The President's ambitious and expensive plans for social security expansion, which included federal aid to schools, a public welfare department in the cabinet, and compulsory national health insurance, lost out. So also did his recommendation that means be found to raise four billion dollars in additional revenue in order to balance the budget, a proposition that the Republican minority insisted would, if carried out, seriously imperil the business life of the nation. The opponents of the President made much of the trend toward the "welfare state" they professed to see in the "Fair Deal."

The "Fair Deal"

Nevertheless the President found it possible to praise the Eighty-first Congress on its adjournment in October, 1949, for its "rather remarkable record of achievement." It had continued rent control to July, 1950, and had voted $2,734,000,000 for slum clearance and low-rent housing. It had balked at a new method of aiding agriculture by direct subsidies, submitted by Secretary of Agriculture Charles F. Brannan, but had agreed to maintain high farm price supports and to provide adequate storage facilities for surplus crops. It had also followed the President's recommendation that minimum wages be raised from forty to seventy-five cents per hour. But it was in the field of foreign affairs that it had given Truman his greatest victories. The Hull program of reciprocal trade treaties to lower customs duties was continued. The Marshall Plan for economic aid to Europe was maintained at the cost of $5,809,990,000 new appropriations. The North Atlantic Treaty was duly ratified, and, when it became known that Russia had mastered the secret of the atomic bomb, a total of $1,314,010,000 was appropriated to provide military assistance to the new allies of the United States. While Congress refused to go along with the President's recommendation of universal military training for all youths eighteen years of age, it did appropriate the unprecedented sum of over fifteen billion dollars for national peacetime defense. Investigations into an unfortunate quarrel within the newly-created Department of National Defense over the role of the Navy in future wars marred the closing weeks of the session, but, even so, when the first session of the Eighty-first Congress finally adjourned, it had served notice on any potential enemy that the United States was emphatically on guard.

Index

Abilene, Kans., cow-town, 505
Abolitionism, beginnings of, 288; leaders of, 295; organization of, 296; southern opposition to, 297; final triumph of, 408
Acadia, renamed Nova Scotia, 28
Adams, Charles Francis, Free-Soil candidate for Vice-President (1848), 316; minister to England, 401
Adams, Henry, on Chicago World's Fair, 582
Adams, John, defends British soldiers after Boston massacre, 81; portrait, opp. 83; peace commissioner, 98; mission to England, 111; Vice-President, 135; elected President, 142; sketch of, 143; makes peace with France, 146; defeated for re-election, 147; appoints Marshall Chief Justice, 148; midnight appointments, 155
Adams, John Quincy, peace commissioner, 179; library of, 193; negotiates treaty of 1819 with Spain, 206; helps formulate Monroe Doctrine, 209; portrait, opp. 210; candidate for President, 214; sketch of, 215; foreign policy of, 222; defeated for re-election, 225; member House of Representatives, 237; attacks on Van Buren, 251; on right of petition, 297
Adams, Samuel, revolutionary agitator, 81; portrait, opp. 83; opposes adoption of Constitution, 125
Adamson Act, terms of, 686
Addams, Jane, portrait, opp. 307; settlement worker, 596; supports Roosevelt (1912), 659
Agassiz, Louis J. R., zoologist, 265
Agricultural Adjustment Administration, established, 797; invalidated by Supreme Court, 798; the new AAA, 800
Agricultural Marketing Act (1929), terms of, 777
Agriculture, in early Virginia, 12; in the Carolinas, 23; the plantation area, 30; in New England, 36; the "bread colonies," 46; in New France, 67; rivalry with commerce, 117; affected by Hamilton's policies, 132; about 1800, 152; affected by Embargo Act, 167; sheep-raising, 184; cotton culture, 289; the cotton plantation, 290; the slavery system, 300; revolution in, 335; in North during Civil War, 388; southern tenant system, 418; agricultural education, 476; exhibits at Philadelphia Centennial, 487; in the "New South," 555; changed conditions of, 592; after first World War, 728; plans for farm relief, 736; overproduction, 775; Hoover's program of relief, 777; the AAA, 798; soil conservation, 799; the new AAA, 800
Aguinaldo, Emilio, Philippine insurgent, 608; brought back from exile by Dewey, 613
Aircraft Production Board, during first World War, 708
Airplanes, in first World War, 708; Wright brothers' experiments, 754; air mail, 756; passenger service, 758; in attack on England, 830; in Allied attacks on the continent, 857
Alabama, admitted as a state, 199; state banking in, 251; secession of, 360
Alabama, Confederate commerce destroyer, 377; *Alabama* claims, 442
Alaska, boundary of 1825, 305; purchased by United States, 404; gold discovery in, 612; highway to, 853
Alaskan Boundary Dispute, settled, 624
Albania, taken by Italy, 826
Albany Congress, discusses Franklin's plan of union, 70
Albany Regency, Democratic leaders in New York, 249
Alcott, Bronson, transcendentalist, 267
Aldrich, Nelson W., Republican protectionist leader, 653
Aldrich-Vreeland Act, banking reform, 641
Aleutian Islands, Japanese in, 858
Alexandria Conference, on navigation, 116
Algeciras Conference, American participation in, 630
Alien and Sedition Acts, passed, 144; lapse, 155
Allies, in first World War, 677
Allison, W. B., high-tariff advocate, 524
Alsace-Lorraine, French interest in, 676; returned to France, 715
Altgeld, John P., portrait, opp. 498; pardons anarchists, 548; during railway strikes of 1894, 571; ineligible for Presidency, 576
America First Committee, activities of, 840
American Anti-Slavery Society, launched, 296
American Expeditionary Forces (A.E.F.), in France, 704; at Saint-Mihiel and the Argonne, 706; in Russia, 707; losses of, 708
American Farm Bureau Federation, activities of, 729
American Federation of Labor, activities, 548; membership claims, 635; split in, 796
American Fur Company, operations of, 207
American Historical Association, founded, 584
American Legion, favors adjusted compensation for veterans, 731
American Party, unfriendly to immigrants, 339
American Peace Society, founded, 287
American Railway Union, supports Pullman strike, 571
American Relief Commission, headed by Hoover, 772
American Revolution, beginnings of, 76; conservative nature of, 100; socially considered, 103. *See also* Revolutionary War
American Society of Equity, activities of, 729
American System, proposed by Henry Clay, 218; lack of popular appeal, 225; favored by Anti-Masons, 241
American traits, as observed by foreigners, 186